FINANCIAL STATEMENT ANALYSIS

Theory, Application, and Interpretation

FINANCIAL STATEMENT ANALYSIS

Theory, Application, and Interpretation

Leopold A. Bernstein, Ph. D., C.P.A.
Professor of Accounting
Bernard M. Baruch College
The City University of New York

FIFTH EDITION

IRWIN

Homewood, IL 60430
Boston, MA 02116

Reprinted with permission from *CFA Examinations*. Association for Investment Management and Research, Charlottesville, Virginia.

Material from the Uniform CPA Examinations and Unofficial Answers, copyright © 1958, 1966, 1973, 1974, 1975, 1976, 1978, 1979, 1980, 1981, 1982, 1983, 1988, and 1989 by the American Institute of Certified Public Accountants is reprinted or adapted with permission.

Sponsoring editor: Jeff Shelstad
Editorial assistant: Branka Rnich
Marketing manager: Ron Bloecher
Project editor: Waivah Clement
Production manager: Bob Lange
Designer: Robyn Basquin
Art manager: Kim Meriwether
Compositor: Impressions, a division of Edwards Brothers, Inc.
Typeface: 10/12 Times Roman
Printer: R. R. Donnelley & Sons Company

Library of Congress Cataloging-in-Publication Data

Bernstein, Leopold A.
    Financial statement analysis : theory, application, and interpretation / Leopold A. Bernstein. — 5th ed.
        p.   cm.
    Includes bibliographical references and index.
    ISBN 0-256-10223-6
    1. Financial statements.   I. Title.
HF5681.B2B46   1993
657'.3—dc20   92–25686

Printed in the United States of America
1 2 3 4 5 6 7 8 9 0 DOC 9 8 7 6 5 4 3 2

In memory of
University Distinguished Professor
EMANUEL SAXE
Teacher, Colleague, Friend

THE IRWIN SERIES IN UNDERGRADUATE ACCOUNTING*

Hermanson, Edwards, and Maher
Accounting Principles
Fifth Edition

Hermanson, Plunkett, and Turner
Computerized Accounting with Peachtree Complete III

Hermanson, Strawser, and Strawser
Auditing Theory and Practice
Sixth Edition

Hopson, Spradling, and Meyer
Income Tax Fundamentals for 1992 Tax Returns, 1993 Edition

Hoyle
Advanced Accounting
Third Edition

Hutton and Dalton
Two 1992 Individual Tax Return Practice Problems

Hutton and Dalton
1992 Tax Return Practice Problems for Corporations, S Corporations, and Partnerships

Koerber
College Accounting

Larson and Miller
Fundamental Accounting Principles
Thirteenth Edition

Larson and Miller
Financial Accounting
Fifth Edition

Marshall
A Survey of Accounting: What the Numbers Mean
Second Edition

Miller and Redding
The FASB: The People, The Process, and the Politics
Second Edition

Mueller, Gernon, and Meek
Accounting: An International Perspective
Second Edition

Pratt and Kulsrud
Federal Taxation, 1993 Edition

Pratt and Kulsrud
Individual Taxation, 1993 Edition

Pratt, Burns, and Kulsrud
Corporate Partnership, Estate and Gift Taxation, 1993 Edition

Rayburn
Cost Accounting: Using a Cost Management Approach
Fifth Edition

Robertson
Auditing
Seventh Edition

Schroeder and Zlatkovich
Survey of Accounting

Short
Fundamentals of Financial Accounting
Seventh Edition

Smith and Wiggins
Readings and Problems in Accounting Information Systems

Whittington, Pany, Meigs, and Meigs
Principles of Auditing
Tenth Edition

Financial Statement Analysis: Theory, Application, and Interpretation, fifth edition, is also widely adopted for graduate-level courses. For a complete listing of Irwin graduate-level texts, consult your Irwin representative.

Preface

The major objective of this fifth edition, as was that of preceding editions, is to present a comprehensive and up-to-date treatment of the analysis of financial statements as an aid to decision making. While financial statement analysis serves many and varied purposes, its major usefulness is in making investing and lending decisions. Such decisions, and the actions to which they lead, are, of course, at the heart of the free market system.

Valid and competently assembled data may lead to good decisions. Incomplete or distorted data will usually lead to bad decisions. Investing and lending decisions require the application of thorough analysis to carefully evaluated data. They require, moreover, the ability to forecast— to foresee. Sound information is obtained by an *understanding* of the data from which it is derived as well as by the application of tools of analysis to aid in its extraction and evaluation. Foresight, which is essential to the assessment of opportunity and risk, is also rooted in understanding: understanding of the elements comprising the data and of the factors that can change them. The common denominator is understanding. Alfred North Whitehead assured us that foresight can be taught when he wrote: "Foresight depends upon understanding. In practical affairs it is a habit. But the habit of foreseeing is elicited by the habit of understanding. To a large extent, understanding can now be acquired by a conscious effort and it can be taught. Thus the training of foresight is by the medium of understanding."

Organization of This Work

The keynote of this work, thus, is understanding. It focuses on understanding the data that are analyzed as well as the methods by which they are analyzed and interpreted.

Part I is concerned with the relationship between the disciplines of financial analysis and accounting. First it examines the objectives of the users of financial statements. It then explores the objectives of accounting and the conventions accountants have adopted for their achievement. It concludes with an overview of analytical tools and techniques in common use.

Part II is devoted to an in-depth analysis of financial statements, and of the bases which underlie their preparation. A thorough understanding of the processes of income determination and of asset and liability measurement, as well as the distortions to which these may be subject, is an essential prerequisite to the intelligent analysis of financial data. These and other topics, such as the effects of price-level changes and the significance of the audit function, are examined here from the point of view of their implications to the user of financial statements. Analytical tools designed to shed light on the impact of alternative accounting methods are also emphasized.

Part III examines the processes and the methodology of financial statement analysis. The focus here is on the major objectives of users of financial statements and on the analytical tools and techniques applied by them in reaching significant conclusions and decisions. The analysis and evaluation of financial data are time-consuming and demanding tasks. Considering the importance of the decisions based thereon, however, and the magnitude of the resources that may be committed as a result, a painstaking job of analysis and evaluation is essential. Thorough analysis not only removes, to some degree, the great uncertainties inherent in investing and lending decisions, but also imparts to the decision maker a degree of confidence which is an essential precondition to timely and decisive action.

Since the ultimate decisions here must be quantified—that is, expressed, for example, in terms of the price of a stock or the amount of a loan—Part III emphasizes the need to link qualitative judgments to as many factors that lend themselves to quantification as is possible.

Major Users of This Work

This book should prove of value to all those who need a thorough understanding of the uses to which financial statements are put as well as to those who must know how to use them intelligently and effectively. This encompasses *accountants, security analysts, lending officers, credit analysts, investors, managers,* and all others who must make decisions on the basis of financial data. Teachers in this area should likewise benefit greatly from its use.

Accountants should benefit from this book in two major ways:

1. The primary justification of the accounting function is decision usefulness. By obtaining a full appreciation of the uses to which the end product of their work is put, accountants will be in a better position to improve upon it and to make it more responsive to the needs of users of financial statements.

2. Primarily because the analysis of financial statements demands a thorough understanding of how and on what bases financial statements are constructed, accountants have often been called upon to aid in their

analysis and interpretation. The study of the tools and techniques of financial statement analysis will open to the accountant important opportunities for the creative extension of his or her basic services into areas which are often as intellectually satisfying as they are financially rewarding.

Security analysts, lending officers, credit analysts, and investors, as well as others with financial responsibilities will find in this work a discussion of accounting concepts and measurements undertaken from their point of view as users of such data. The essential tools of the ingenious double-entry accounting system, such as the journal entry and the T-account, here are converted into primary useful tools for the analyst by means of which he or she can recapture the reality imbedded in published financial statements. Following this, in Part III, analysts will learn how knowledge of the accounting framework is integrated with the best tools and techniques available for the analysis and interpretation of financial statements.

Teachers of financial statement analysis will find that the organization and coverage of this work treats the subject matter of the field comprehensively and in depth and goes far beyond the superficial treatment often accorded to it. The constant link to published financial statements imparts a sense of reality that promotes interest, motivation, understanding, and learning. The book offers the instructor in this subject enough challenging material of substance to form the basis for courses in this area on both the undergraduate and the graduate levels of study. The instructor's manual provided with the book contains further specific suggestions on the organization of different course levels by chapter and subject matter.

THE FIFTH EDITION

This edition continues the emphasis on the knowledge and the skills required for the intelligent analysis of financial statements.

The first requirement clearly is the ability to read and understand a modern set of published financial statements and to comprehend the complex financial communications they contain. Part II, which covers the conceptual knowledge as well as analytical techniques needed for this task, has been completely updated. Practical illustrations which draw on comprehensive sets of financial statements have been expanded again. In order to provide a rich base upon which to draw for purposes of illustration and problem assignments, two full sets of financial statements are provided—one in Appendix 4B (to Chapter 4) and one in Appendix 23 (to Chapter 23). Extensive experience has shown that the use of published financial statements as principal teaching cases greatly heightens students' interest and participation while contributing to learning, to intellectual challenge, and to satisfaction.

The second major requirement is the ability to apply appropriate tools and techniques to the analysis and interpretation of financial statements. Here again numerous illustrations and problems refer to and draw on financial statements presented in Appendix 4B and Appendix 23.

Appendixes which follow the various chapters are designed to increase the flexibility of instructors in adding or deleting course material as well as varying its complexity. Generally, undergraduate courses will proceed from an assumption of a certain minimum background knowledge of accounting and then concentrate on the principal tools and techniques of financial statement analysis. Graduate courses should generally spend more time on an in-depth understanding of financial statements and communications as a step preceding the application of analytical tools and techniques. The instructor's manual contains additional suggestions for the organization of courses in financial statement analysis. As a further teaching aid, the reader is referred to *Cases in Financial Reporting and Analysis* by L. A. Bernstein and M. Maksy, also published by R. D. Irwin, and soon to be published in a revised edition.

Computer software options are available for use with this edition. For details please consult your local R. D. Irwin representative.

A major objective of this revision is to preserve and enhance those features of this work which have proved to be most valuable to its users and to update and improve that which experience indicates needs improvement. The valuable feedback provided by students, colleagues, CFA candidates, and other users of the previous editions have greatly aided in this task. Also of considerable help was my continuing experience in using these materials to teach graduate and undergraduate students, professional security analysts, bank loan officers, bond rating agency analysts, and others. Valuable feedback of other users ranged from those using this work in finance and investment courses or for purposes of CPA or CFA examination review, to those using it in the training of Chartered Life Underwriters and the teaching of Ph.D. candidates. Use of this work as a basis for expert testimony has also led to important improvements.

This revision reflects a comprehensive updating of all authoritative pronouncements on accounting and auditing standards and practices. Thus, relevant revised chapters reflect new authoritative pronouncements in areas such as financial instruments, off-balance-sheet obligations, postretirement benefits other than pensions, income taxes, cash flows, and auditing standards. Valuable suggestions of practicing financial analysts, credit analysts, and other users of financial data have also been incorporated.

Numerous useful comments and suggestions by fellow educators have resulted in many modifications which are motivated by pedagogical considerations. Many chapters have undergone considerable updating, refinement, and revision. Many modifications and new illustrations have been provided throughout, new problems have been added, and existing problem material has been revised, enhanced, and expanded. An important feature is the use of comprehensive annual reports and historical data time series as the basis of questions and problems for most chapters. Also included are a significant number of problems taken from past examinations given by the Institute of Chartered Financial Analysts and by the American Institute of Certified Public Accountants, whose permission to use these materials is hereby gratefully acknowledged.

An important feature of this work is the inclusion of many examples from practice. Many new examples have been added and older ones updated. In the cumulative chronicle of human experience, what is most recent is not necessarily the best. For this reason some older cases and citations have been retained because their more recent counterparts, if they exist, do not provide examples of equal quality.

The comprehensive and varied problem material has been thoroughly class tested.

ACKNOWLEDGMENTS

In performing the research for and the writing of this and the prior editions, I was fortunate to benefit from the encouragement, help, and suggestions of many colleagues, professional associates, and students. University Distinguished Professor Emeritus Emanuel Saxe, a teacher, an esteemed colleague, and friend to whom this book is affectionately dedicated, read the entire original manuscript as well as many revised parts of it and made numerous valuable suggestions. To me the thoroughness of his review served as a shining example of the kind of dedicated effort a professional approach to financial statement analysis demands.

Deserving special mention for extensive and especially valuable comments is my friend and coauthor on another work, Professor Calvin Engler, whose thoroughly professional review has provided many valuable comments. Also, my friend Professor Henry Jaenicke of Drexel University provided many valuable comments, especially on the chapter on the audit function.

Many other professionals have read portions of this work in its various editions. Professional debt or equity security analysts who have read portions of this work and made valuable suggestions include Gerald White of Grace & White, Inc.; Kenneth Alterman, Hyman C. Grossman, Richard Huff, and Robert J. Mebus of Standard & Poor's Corporation; Clyde Bartter, Portfolio Advisory Company; Michael A. Hyland, First Boston Corporation; David Norr, First Manhattan Corporation; Thornton L. O'Glove, the *Quality of Earnings Report*; Frances Stone, Merrill Lynch & Co., Inc.; Jack L. Treynor, of Treynor-Arbit Associates; Professor Jon A. Stroble, a skillful and outstanding trainer of bank loan officers from which association this book has benefited in many ways; and Dr. Neil Weiss of Jon Stroble & Associates, Ltd. William C. Norby, an outstanding and leading financial analyst, has read important portions of prior revisions and provided many insights as well as very valuable comments and suggestions.

Appreciation is also due to Fred Spindel, partner of Coopers & Lybrand; Robert Mednick, partner of Arthur Andersen; and Paul Rosenfield of the American Institute of Certified Public Accountants, for valuable comments on specific chapters.

My present and past colleagues at the City University of New York—Abraham J. Briloff, Martin Mellman, William T. Baxter, Douglas Carmichael, Peter M. Gutman, Peter Lloyd Davis, Hugo Nurnberg, Stanley C. W. Salvary, and Reed Storey—have read portions of this work and contributed valuable comments and suggestions; while Martin Benis, John Liapakis, Steven Lillien, William Ruland, and Harry Davis have contributed valuable comments as a result of class use of the book. Especially valuable assistance was provided by my friend and colleague Mostafa Maksy who has also coauthored a related case book.

Other colleagues in academe who provided valuable comments and suggestions include Robert N. Anthony, Harvard University; Hector R. Anton, New York University; Rashad Abdel-Khalik, University of Florida; Terry Arndt and John Gentis, Ball State University; Shyam Bhandari of Bradley University; Fred Bien and Vince Brenner, Louisiana State University, John S. Bildersee, New York University; Garry Bulmash, American University; Joseph Bylinski, University of North Carolina; Benny R. Copeland, North Texas State University; Maurice P. Corrigan, Teikyo Post University; Philip Chuey, Youngstown State University; Wallace N. Davidson III, North Texas State University; Eric S. Emory, Sacred Heart University; William P. Enderlein, Golden Gate University; Thomas J. Frecka, University of Notre Dame; Philip Gerdin, University of New Haven; Edwin Grossnickle, Western Michigan University; J. Larry Hagler, Mississippi State University; Yong-Ha Hyon, Temple University; Kenneth H. Johnson, Mississippi State University; Homer Kripke, New York University; Russ Langer, San Francisco State University; Burton T. Lefkowitz, C. W. Post College; Thomas Lopez, Pace University; Stephen Penman, University of California at Berkeley; Larry Prober, Ryder College; Jerrold Weiss, Lehman College; Richard F. Williams, Wright State University; Philip Wolitzer, Long Island University; Stephen Zeff, Rice University, and Christine V. Zavgren, Clarkson University.

Professor Terry L. Arndt performed a valuable problem review; and Ibrahim H. Qteishat provided valuable support with illustration and problem material. So did Kwok Lam and Cheuk L. Fu. Peggy Schubert thoughtfully reviewed and proofread critical chapters. Jean Greenbaum proofread and reviewed grammar.

Graduate assistants who provided valuable assistance include Tae-Whan Cho, Barbara Loveman, Anne Kaplan, Nashwa El Gallab, Amal El Sabbagh, Michael Chen, and Jayesh Goradia.

Outstanding typing service was performed by Mrs. Dorothy Conklin. Thanks are also due to project editor Waivah Clement for a job well done.

Finally, I wish to express appreciation to my wife Cynthia for valuable editorial help, to my daughter Debbie and to my son Jeffrey for earlier assistance with indexing, and to my late mother Jeanette, as well as to Cynthia, for their patience and understanding over the many years during which the successive editions of this work were being written and revised, and for having provided me with the inspiration that helped bring them to a successful completion.

Users of this work have, over the years, provided many valuable insights and comments. I continue to earnestly solicit comments, suggestions, and constructive criticism from interested educators, professional financial and credit analysts, accountants, and other users in the hope that I shall be able to continue the unending task of improving this book.

Leopold A. Bernstein

Contents

Developments. Problem Loans of Banks. Tangible Fixed Assets: *Asset Valuation, Wasting Assets, Method of Acquisition, Implications for Analysis.* Intangible Assets: *Identifiable Intangibles, Unidentifiable Intangibles, Amortization of Intangibles, Other Considerations Regarding the Accounting for Intangibles, Accounting for the Costs of Computer Software, Implication for Analysis.* Prepaid Expenses and Deferred Charges: *Prepaid Expenses and Deferred Charges Distinguished, Why Costs Are Deferred, Research and Development Costs, Other Types of Deferred Charges, Implications for Analysis.* Unrecorded Intangible or Contingent Assets. Questions.

Current Liabilities. Long-Term Liabilities. Extinguishment of Debt. Implications for Analysis: *Evaluation of Terms of Indebtedness.* Obligations under Leases: *Accounting by Lessees, Accounting by Lessors, Sales-Type Leases, Direct-Financing Leases, Operating Leases, Principal Disclosures, Leases Involving Real Estate, Sale-Leaseback, Leveraged Leases.* Accounting for Capital Leases: *Capital versus Operating Lease—the Effect on Income, Capital versus Operating Lease—the Effect on Cash, Implications for Analysis.* "Off-Balance-Sheet" Financing. Off-Balance-Sheet Obligations. Liabilities under the Pension Plans. Recognition of Additional Pension Liability. Implications for Analysis. Postretirement Benefits Other than Pensions. Implications for Analysis. Liabilities at the "Edge" of Equity. Deferred Credits (Income): *Deferred Taxes.* Implications for Analysis. Minority Interest. Reserves and Provisions. Accounting for Contingencies. Implications for Analysis. Commitments. Financial Instruments with Off-Balance-Sheet Risks. Contingent Liabilities. Implications for Analysis—Assessing Uncertainties. Questions.

The Distinction between Liability and Equity Instruments. Classification of Capital Stock: *Disclosure Regarding Capital Stock, Additional Capital, Treasury Stock.* Retained Earnings: *Dividends, Prior Period Adjustments, Appropriations of Retained Earnings, Restrictions on Retained Earnings.* Book Value per Share: *Significance of Book Value.* Implications for Analysis. Questions.

Intercorporate Investments: *Consolidated Financial Statements, The Equity Method, The Cost Method, Example of Difference in Income Recognition—Equity versus Cost Method, Intercorporate Investments—*

Less than Majority Ownership, Implications for Analysis. Implications for Analysis. Accounting for Business Combination: *Reasons for Mergers, Distortions in Accounting for Mergers, Accounting for Business Combinations: Two Methods.* Accounting for Business Combinations: *Pooling of Interests and Purchase Accounting Compared, Illustration of Accounting Mechanics: Purchase versus Pooling of Interest Accounting, Pooling Accounting, Purchase Accounting, Implications for Analysis.* Accounting for Goodwill—A Major Problem Area. Accounting for Foreign Operations: *Foreign Accounting Practices and Auditing Standards, Translation of Foreign Currencies, Evolution of the Accounting for Foreign Exchange Translation, Major Provisions of SFAS 52, Illustration of the Translation Procedure, Additional Information.* Analysis of Translation Gain or Loss: *Disclosure Requirements, Accounting for Investment by Parent Company, Accounting on Sale of Subsidiary, Remeasurement under the Temporal Method.* Implications for Analysis. Questions.

A Simple Illustration, A Variety of Concepts of Income. The Accrual of Revenue: *Conditions for Revenue Recognition, Uncertainty as to Collection of Receivables, Revenue Recognition When Right of Return Exists, Accounting for Franchise Fee Revenue, Product Financing Arrangements, Transfers of Receivables with Recourse, Timing of Revenue Recognition, Contract Accounting, Finance Company Accounting, When Should the Recording of Interest Income Be Discontinued, Accounting for Lease Income, "Sales" to Leasing Subsidiaries, Additional Examples of Income Recognition Problems, Income of Subsidiaries and Affiliates, Implications for Analysis.* Cost and Expense Accrual: *Depreciation and Depletion, Factors Influencing the Rate of Depreciation, Implication for Analysis.* Analytical Measures of Plant Age. Misconceptions Regarding the Nature of Depreciation. Questions.

Pension Costs and Other Supplementary Employee Benefits: *Pension Costs, Basic Concepts of Pension Accounting.* Employer's Pension Benefit Obligation. Elements of Periodic Pension Expense: *Expected Return on Plan Assets.* Amortization of Unrecognized Pension Costs. Amortization of Prior Service cost: *Amortization of Net Gains or Losses, Amortization of Unrecognized Transition Costs.* Computation of Net Periodic Pension Cost: *Pension Liabilities.* Required Footnote Disclosure. Overfunded Pension Plans. Accounting for Curtailments and Settlements of Defined Benefit Pension Plans and Termination Benefits: *Implications for Analysis.* Accounting for Other Postretirement Employee Benefits (OPEB). Implications for Analysis. Other

Supplementary Employee Benefits: *Implications for Analysis.* Research, Exploration, and Development Outlays: *Types of Research and Development, The Accounting Problem, FASB Statement 2, Implications for Analysis, Accounting for the Costs of Computer Software, Exploration and Development in Extractive Industries, Implications for Analysis.* Goodwill: *Implications for Analysis.* Other Intangible Asset Write-Offs. Interest Costs: *Interest Capitalization, Implications for Analysis.* Income Taxes: *Statement of Financial Accounting Standards, Accounting for Income Taxes, Permanent Income Tax Differences, Temporary Differences, Treatment of Tax Loss Carrybacks and Carryforwards, Disclosure Requirements, Implications for Analysis, Analytical Significance of Disclosure Requirements.* Extraordinary Gains and Losses: *Crosscurrents of Theory—the Case of Debt Retirements, Discontinued Operations, Implications for Analysis.* Accounting Changes: *Change in Accounting Principle, Change in Accounting Estimate, Change in Reporting Entity, Correction of an Error, Materiality, Historical Summaries of Financial Information, Implications for Analysis.* The Income Statement—Implications for Analysis, an Overview. Questions.

Major Provisions of *APB Opinion 15: Simple Capital Structure, Computation of Weighted Average of Common Shares Outstanding.* Complex Capital Structure: *Primary Earnings per Share, Options and Warrants, The Treasury Stock Method, Fully Diluted Earnings per Share.* Illustration of the Computation of Primary and Fully Diluted Earnings per Share. Examples of EPS Computations When Business Combinations Occur: *Pooling of Interests, Purchase.* Restatement of Prior Period Earnings per Share: *Illustration of Prior Period EPS Restatement, Requirements for Additional Disclosures in Conjunction with the Presentation of Earnings per Share Data.* Implications for Analysis: *Statement Accounting for Changes in Earnings per Share.* Questions.

The Significance of Cash Flows. What Is Cash Flow? Objectives of This Chapter. Evolution of the Accounting for Funds and Cash Flows. *SFAS 95 "Statement of Cash Flows": Basis of Preparation, Classification Requirements, Expanded Balance Sheet Diagram, Changes within the Noncash B Group, Simple Illustration of Preparation of Statement of Cash Flows, Illustration of T-Account Technique.* Determining Net Cash Flow From Operations: *T-Accounts.* Reconstruction of Transactions: *The Debits and Credits Are to T-Accounts and Are Needed to Construct the SCF, Fixed Assets, Accumulated Depreciation, Bonds Payable, Deferred Income Taxes, Capital Stock and Paid-In Capital,*

"Reviewed" Financial Statements. The SEC's Important Role. Implications for Analysis: *Implications Inherent in the Audit Process, Audit Risk and Its Implications.* Implications Stemming from the Standards that Govern the Auditor's Opinion. The Audit Function as Perceived by the Auditor: *Qualification, Disclaimers, and Adverse Opinions.* Questions.

PART III
FINANCIAL STATEMENT ANALYSIS—THE MAIN AREAS OF EMPHASIS
535

Significance of Short-Term Liquidity. Working Capital: *Current Assets, Current Liabilities, Other Problem Areas in the Definition of Current Assets and Liabilities, Working Capital as a Measure of Liquidity.* Current Ratio: *Limitations of the Current Ratio, Implications of Current Ratio Limitations, The Current Ratio as a Valid Tool of Analysis, Measures That Supplement the Current Ratio, Measures of Accounts Receivable Liquidity.* Average Accounts Receivable Turnover Ratio: *Collection Period for Accounts Receivable, Evaluation.* Measures of Inventory Turnover: *Inventory Turnover Ratio, Days to Sell Inventory, The Effect of Alternative Methods of Inventory Management, Prepaid Expenses.* Current Liabilities: *Differences in the "Nature" of Current Liabilities, Days Purchases in Accounts Payable Ratio.* Interpretation of the Current Ratio: *Examination of Trend, Interpretation of Changes over Time, Possibilities of Manipulation, The Use of "Rules of Thumb" Standards, The Net Trade Cycle, Valid Working Capital Standards, The Importance of Sales, Common-Size Analysis of Current Assets Composition, The Liquidity Index.* Acid-Test Ratio. Other Measures of Short-Term Liquidity: *Cash Flow Related Measures.* The Concept of Financial Flexibility. Management's Discussion and Analysis (MD&A): *Projecting Changes in Conditions or Policies.* Questions.

Overview of Cash Flow Patterns. Short-Term Cash Forecasts: *Importance of Sales Estimates, Pro Forma Financial Statements as an Aid to Forecasting, Techniques of Short-Term Cash Forecasting, Differences between Short-Term and Long-Term Forecasts.* Electronic Spreadsheet Programs. Analysis of Statements of Cash Flows. Illustration of the Analysis of Statements of Cash Flows. Evaluation of the Statement of Cash Flows. Projection of Statements of Cash Flows. Illustration of the Projection of Statements of Cash Flows: *The Impact of Adversity, Published Financial Forecasts, The Cash Flow Adequacy Ratio, Cash Reinvestment Ratio.* Conclusion. Questions.

Use of ROI: *As Indicator of Managerial Effectiveness, A Measure of Enterprise Ability to Earn a Satisfactory ROI, A Method of Projecting Earnings, Internal Decision and Control Tool.* Basic Elements of ROI: *Defining the Investment Base, Book versus Market Values in the Investment Base, Difference between Investor's Cost and Enterprise Investment Base, Averaging the Investment Base, Relating Income to the Investment Base.* Adjusting the Components of the ROI Formula: *Analysis and Interpretation of ROI.* Analysis of Asset Utilization: *Evaluation of Individual Turnover Ratios, Use of Averages, Other Factors to Be Considered in Return on Asset Evaluation, Return on Shareholders' Equity.* Analysis of Return on Common Stockholders' Equity (ROCSE). Illustration of Analysis of Return on Total Assets and on Equity: *Expanded Disaggregation of ROCSE, Equity Growth Rate, Sustainable Growth Rate, Analysis of Financial Leverage Effects.* Return on Equity versus Return on Shareholder Investment. Questions.

The Significance of Income Statement Analysis. The Major Objectives of Income Analysis: *What Is the Relevant Net Income of the Enterprise?* Analysis of Components of the Income Statement: *Accounting Standards Used and Their Implication, Tools of Income Statement Analysis.* The Analysis of Sales and Revenues: *Major Sources of Revenue.* Financial Reporting by Diversified Enterprises: *Reasons for the Need for Data by Significant Enterprise Segments, Disclosure of "Line of Business" Data, Income Statement Data, Balance Sheet Data, Research Studies, Statement of Financial Accounting Standards 14, SEC Reporting Requirements, Implications for Analysis.* Stability and Trend of Revenues. Management's Discussion and Analysis of Financial Condition and Results of Operations. Implications for Analysis. Methods of Revenue Recognition and Measurement. Questions.

Analysis of Cost of Sales. Gross Profit: *Factors in the Analysis of Gross Profit.* Analysis of Changes in Gross Margin. Example of Analysis of Change in Gross Margin: *Interpretation of Changes in Gross Margin.* Break-Even Analysis: *Concepts underlying Break-Even Analysis, Equation Approach, Graphic Presentation, Contribution Margin Approach, Pocket Calculator Problem—Additional Considerations, Break-Even Technique—Problem Areas and Limitations, Analytical Implications of Break-Even Analysis, The Significance of the Variable-Cost Percentage, The Significance of the Fixed-Cost Level, The Importance of the Contribution Margin.* Analysis of the Relationship between Sales, Accounts Receivable, and Inventories. Additional Considerations in the Analysis

Part I

FINANCIAL STATEMENT ANALYSIS AND THE ACCOUNTING FRAMEWORK

Chapter 1

OBJECTIVES OF FINANCIAL STATEMENT ANALYSIS

THE NATURE OF FINANCIAL ANALYSIS

The process of financial statement analysis consists of the application of analytical tools and techniques to financial statements and data in order to derive from them measurements and relationships that are significant and useful for decision making. Thus, financial statement analysis first and foremost serves the essential function of converting *data,* of which in this age of the computer there are a bewildering quantity and variety, into useful information, which is always in scarce supply.[1]

The processes of financial analysis can be described in various ways, depending on the objectives to be attained. Thus, financial analysis can be used as a preliminary *screening* tool in the selection of investments or merger candidates. It can be used as a *forecasting* tool of future financial conditions and results. It may be used as a process of *diagnosis* of managerial, operating, or other problem areas. It can serve as a tool in the *evaluation* of management. Above all, financial analysis reduces reliance on pure hunches, guesses, and intuition, and this reduces and narrows the inevitable areas of uncertainty that attend all decision-making processes. Financial analysis does not lessen the need for judgment but rather establishes a sound and systematic basis for its rational application.

APPROACHES TO THE SUBJECT

There are a number of possible approaches to a discussion of the tools and techniques of financial analysis. One way, popularly employed in books on the subject, is to describe the analysis of specific financial statements, such as balance sheets, without a concurrent emphasis of objectives to be attained. The approach employed here will be to examine the

---

[1] Walter B. Wriston put it this way: "The incessant production of new data ... creates a paradox; information, the thing that eliminates uncertainty, now increases everybody's feeling of insecurity because of the failure to convert data into knowledge." See Walter B. Wriston, "The World according to Walter," *Harvard Business Review,* January–February 1986, p. 65.

process of financial statement analysis with emphasis on the major objectives (see Chapter 4, "Building Blocks of Financial Statement Analysis") that they are designed to achieve. In order to do this, we turn first to an examination of the information needs and the specific analytical objectives of the most important categories of users of financial data, namely:

Credit grantors.

Equity investors.

Management.

Acquisition and merger analysts.

Auditors.

Other interested groups.

Objectives of Credit Grantors

Credit grantors are lenders of funds to an enterprise. Funds are lent in many forms and for a variety of purposes.

Trade creditors usually extend very short-term credit. They ship goods or provide services and expect payment within the customary period that forms the terms of trade in their industry. Most trade credit ranges from 30 to 60 days, with cash discounts occasionally allowed for specified earlier payment. The trade creditor does not usually receive interest for an extension of credit. The trade creditor's reward takes the form of the business transacted and the possible profit that flows from it.

An enterprise receives other short-term and longer-term credit or loans from a variety of sources. Short-term credit is often provided by various sources, mainly by banks or by sale of commercial paper. Longer-term credit is provided by banks in the form of term loans and by financial institutions, such as insurance companies, through their purchase of bonds or notes or through private placements. Companies also obtain longer-term funds through the public sale of notes or bonds in the securities markets. Leasing and conditional sales are other forms of long-term financing. The sale of convertible, and generally subordinated, bonds combines the borrowing of money with the added feature of an option to the lender to exchange his or her claim for an equity interest should the lender find it profitable to do so. Similarly, the issuance of preferred stock, which is senior to the common equity but junior to debt, combines the fixed reward features of a loan with the absence of definite principal repayment requirements that characterize equity securities.

One outstanding characteristic of all pure credit extension relationships is the fixed nature of the rewards accruing to the credit grantor. Thus, should the enterprise prosper, the credit grantor will still be limited to his or her contractually fixed rate of interest, or to the profit on the goods supplied. However, should the enterprise incur losses or meet other adversities, the credit grantor's principal may be placed in jeopardy. This uneven nature of the lender's risk-reward ratio has a major effect on the lender's point of view and on the manner in which he or she analyzes the possibilities of credit extension.

The difference in the point of view of the lenders as compared to that of the equity investor results in differences in the way they analyze future prospects and in the objectives they seek. The equity investor looks for reward primarily to future prospects of earnings and to changes in those earnings. The credit grantor, on the other hand, is concerned primarily with specific security provisions of his or her loan, such as the fair market value of assets pledged; and for repayment of principal and interest, the credit grantor looks to the existence of resources and the projections of future flows of funds (The term *funds* refers to cash and to assets very readily convertible to cash, such as cash equivalents) and the reliability and stability of such flows. Equity investors, as a result of the theoretically unlimited nature of their rewards, may be receptive to highly abstract descriptions of "concepts," potentials, and future probabilities. Lenders, on the other hand, require a more definite link between the projections of the future and the resources already at hand as well as the demonstrated ability to achieve operating results. Whereas equity investors look to the rewards of earnings growth, creditors are more concerned with how low earnings will shrink during recessionary periods. Credit grantors generally are more conservative in their outlook and approach and rely on financial statement analysis to an even greater extent than do equity investors, for it serves to reassure them regarding the borrower's demonstrated ability to control the flow of cash and to maintain a sound financial condition under a variety of economic and operating circumstances. The more speculative the loan, the more similar are the lender's analytical approaches to those of the equity investor.

The techniques of financial statement analysis used by lenders as well as the criteria of evaluation used by them vary with the term, the security, and the purpose of the loan.

In the case of short-term credit extension, the credit grantor is concerned primarily with the current financial condition, the liquidity of the current assets, and the rate of their turnover. These considerations are covered in Chapter 16.

The evaluation of longer-term loans, which includes the valuation of bonds, requires a far more detailed and forward-looking inquiry and analysis. Such an analysis includes projections of cash flows and fund flows and the evaluation of the longer-term earning power of the enterprise as the ultimate source of assurance of an enterprise's ability to meet the fixed charges arising from its debt as well as from its other commitments under a variety of economic conditions. This subject is examined in Chapter 18.

Since the profitability of an enterprise is a major element in the lender's security, the analysis of profitability is an important criterion to the credit grantor. Profit is viewed as the primary source for interest payments and as a desirable source of principal repayment.

Credit analysis, whether long term or short term, is concerned with capital structure because it has a bearing on risk and on the creditor's margin of safety. The relationship of equity capital to debt is an indicator of the adequacy of equity capital and of the cushion against loss that it provides. This relationship also reflects on the attitude of management toward risk and influences the income coverage of fixed charges.

Lenders, and bankers among them, generally look at asset values in the context of published financial statements, that is, in the context of the going-concern assumption. Clearly, the assumption of liquidation could often lead to realizable values of assets that would generally be lower than those stated on a going-concern basis. For this reason, bankers tend to attach very conservative values to fixed and other assets, and to make allowance for all possible future contingencies.

Objectives of Equity Investors

The equity interest in an enterprise is the supplier of its basic risk capital. The capital is exposed to all the risks of ownership and provides a cushion or shield for the preferred and loan capital that is senior to it. Since the equity interest is entitled to distributions only after the claims of senior securities have been met, it is referred to as the *residual* interest. In the course of normal operations as a going concern, this residual interest may receive distributions (dividends) after the prior claims of senior security holders for bond interest and/or preferred dividends have been satisfied. In liquidation, it has a claim to what remains *after* the prior claims of creditors and preferred stockholders have been met. Thus, when an enterprise prospers, the equity owners stand to reap all the gains above the fixed amount of senior capital contributors' claims and, conversely, the equity owners will be the first ones to absorb losses should the enterprise flounder.

From the above it is clear that the information needs of equity investors are among the most demanding and comprehensive of all users of financial data. Their interests in an enterprise, of which they own a share, are the broadest because their interest is affected by all aspects and phases of operations, profitability, financial condition, and capital structure.

Common Stock Valuation   The valuation of common stock is a complex procedure involving, in addition to financial statement analysis, an assessment of such factors as the general state of the economy, industry position, competitive stance, and the quality of management. Since the

most thorough and sophisticated analysis and evaluation of equity securities, for the purpose of deciding whether to buy, sell, or hold, is
performed by professional security analysts, their point of view will be
examined here.

A common stockholder, having no legal claim to a definite dividend
or to a capital distribution, looks for three principal rewards from his or
her holdings: current dividends, special distributions such as rights, and
a market value of the security at a given time in the future that will,
hopefully, result in a capital gain. The most important determinant of
both dividends and market values is earnings. Current earnings, which
are the basic source of dividends and the accumulation of undistributed
earnings, as well as the earnings record, current and prospective, are major
elements in the determination of the market price of the common stock.

Approaches to Common Stock Valuation   The basis of most modern
stock valuation techniques and models is present value theory. This approach, first set forth in detail by John B. Williams,[2] maintains that the
present value of a share of stock is equal to the sum of all dividends
expected to be received from it, discounted to the present at an appropriate rate of interest. The difficulty here, of course, as in all other approaches based on this theory, is the estimation of such future distributions.[3] What is clear, however, is that all expected distributions, be
they of a current dividend or of a liquidation residual nature, are based
largely on earnings and the earning power of assets.

Security valuation models used by security analysts bear out the proposition that earnings, and particularly estimated future earnings, are the
most important determinant of the value of common shares.[4]

---

[2] *The Theory of Investment Value* (Cambridge, Mass.: Harvard University Press, 1938).

[3] The importance of expected distributions is largely responsible for the focus on cash
flows. However, so far, most valuation models have not concerned themselves with the
purchasing power equivalent of such cash flows, a consideration that looms large in times
of significant price-level changes. Thus, a security represents a contingent claim not only
because of the uncertain outcome of future events but also (including here a "riskless"
bond) because of an uncertain command over future goods and services. For a further
discussion of these issues, see Chapter 14.

[4] While earnings are unquestionably a most important factor they are by no means the
only factor. At times other considerations may predominate in the creation or determination
of values. For example:

a. There is value to a controlling interest in a company. While such value is not
available to true minority investors it is available to those who through operating
control can avail themselves of compensation arrangements and other executive
perquisites.

b. Value can be derived by rearranging ownership interests in an entity. It can be
rearranged in such a way that favorable tax treatments result (e.g., from write-ups of
assets for depreciation purposes; or from the replacement of equity with debt).
Thus the income stream going to the government is diminished and that going to
owners and creditors is increased.

Graham, Dodd, and Cottle emphasized the importance of earnings as follows:

> The standard method of valuation of individual enterprises consists of capitalizing the expected future earnings and/or dividends at an appropriate rate of return. The average earnings will be estimated for a period running ordinarily between five and ten years.[5]

Most common stock valuation models incorporate earnings growth and earnings payout ratios as factors of prime importance.

The normal procedure in dynamic models is to state the price of a stock as the present value of a growing stream of dividends with each component of this stream discounted at the rate k. One of the best-known dynamic stock valuation models presented in recent years is that by Gordon and Shapiro. Assume that $E(t)$ are the earnings of an enterprise at time t, b is the dividend payout ratio, k is the market discount rate (the cost of capital), and g is the projected annual growth rate in earnings. The valuation formula for the company's justified market price V (intrinsic value) is:

$$V = \frac{bE(t)}{k - g}$$

The above formula reduces long and awkward statements to more manageable but nevertheless mathematically equivalent terms. It states in effect that the market value V is equal to the current dividend discounted at a rate $k - g$; that is,

$$V = \frac{\text{Current dividend rate}}{\text{Discount rate} - \text{Growth rate}}$$

The elegance and the simplicity of the above formula should not obscure the fact that the most critical element in this or similar approaches to equity valuation is the valid quantification of the variables or inputs themselves. The more conventional approach by practitioners in the field of security analysis is to value a security by multiplying its earnings, which are really a surrogate for present and future dividends, by a *price-earnings ratio*[6] that is usually an imprecise expression of their assessment of external economic factors as well as of the growth prospects, financial

---

[5] *Security Analysis* (New York: McGraw-Hill, 1962), p. 435. This volume is the successor to the seminal work in this area, Benjamin Graham and David L. Dodd, *Security Analysis* (New York: McGraw-Hill, 1934).

[6] Expressed in terms of the foregoing Gordon-Shapiro formula, the price-earnings ratio (P/E) can be stated as follows:

$$\text{P/E} = \frac{b}{k - g}$$

Thus, for example, if the dividend payout ratio *(b)* changes, so would the P/E ratio.

strengths, capital structure, and other risk factors associated with the enterprise.

The similarity of the present value models of common stock valuation to the conventional method of bond valuation is quite obvious. In the case of bonds, the value, or proper purchase price, is calculated by discounting each coupon and the ultimate principal repayment to present value at a discount rate equal to the desired yield. In the case of growth stock valuations, the expected dividend corresponds to the bond coupon and the assumed market price of the stock at the model target date corresponds to the repayment of bond principal at maturity date.

The similarity of the bond and stock valuation models under these theories has led Molodovsky and others to construct stock valuation tables that can be used in a fashion similar to the use of bond tables.[7] The formula used by them for the value *(V)* of a stock is:

$$V = D_0 + \frac{D_1}{1 + k} + \frac{D_2}{(1 + k)^2} + \dots + \frac{D_n}{(1 + k)^n} + \dots$$

where:

D_0 is the dividend initially.

D_n is the dividend in the *n*th year.

k is the discount rate, or the desired rate of return.

The model does not include a residual market value of the stock (similar to bond principal to be repaid) because it assumes dividend projections taken out to infinity. With regard to the latter, the authors assure us that because the discount factor becomes so large in the distant future, these increments to value become negligible. It is easy to bring the model closer in form to a bond model by assuming a specified sales price (realization of principal) at a specified date, but that price will itself depend on the application of the foregoing formula.

While we can readily understand why the stock valuation model builders have been attracted by the logic as well as the mathematical elegance of the bond valuation model, we must recognize the important differences that exist between the inputs required by the bond model as opposed to those required by the stock model. The focus on these differences is all the more important since the basic purpose of our discussion in this chapter is to relate the scope and the techniques of financial statement analysis to the purposes that they are designed to serve—in this instance, the valuation of equity securities.

In the case of bond valuation, the bond coupon is known and so is the amount of principal to be repaid at the maturity of the bond. Thus, as we saw in the section dealing with the objectives of credit grantors,

---

[7] N. Molodovsky, C. May, and S. Chottiner, "Common Stock Valuation—Principles, Tables, and Application," *Financial Analysts Journal,* March–April 1965.

the major questions to be considered are the *availability* of funds for the payment of interest and the repayment of principal. While the assessment of the probabilities of such availability of funds does involve the totality of enterprise prospects, the process of estimation is nevertheless less complex than the one involved in arriving at the proper parameters for the stock valuation model.

There is a basic and important difference in the certainty of results that can be expected from an analysis of debt instruments (such as bonds) and those that can be expected from the analysis of equity securities. In the case of debt instruments, the results of the analysis depend almost entirely on a valid assessment of the borrower's ability to make timely payments of interest and principal. The relationship between analysis and the results achieved are far more complex in the case of equity securities. Thus, no matter how "right" the analyst is in assumptions and forecasts, a major part of the reward of that analysis, that is, future capital values, depends on the perceptions of others. That is, on buyers agreeing with the analyst's conclusions and seeing things his or her way. No such dependence on validation by the marketplace exists in the case of results to be achieved from the analysis of debt instruments.

This difference, as well as the enormous complexities to which the analysis and evaluation of equity securities are subject, is in large part behind the skepticism with which many practicing security analysts treat those who attempt to compress the market reality into neat, streamlined, and elegant mathematical formulations.

Data Required for Stock Valuation   Let us now consider the data that are required in order to quantify the factors present in most of the stock valuation models discussed above.

The expected dividend stream in the future is dependent on earnings and dividend payout policy. The latter depends on the company's financial condition, capital structure, and its need for funds both in the present and in the future.

The projection of future earnings (see Chapter 22) is always a complex process subject to varying degrees of uncertainty. The reported earnings must be evaluated and adjusted and, in turn, form the basis for projection. Unlike the bond coupon, which remains constant, the further into the future that earnings are projected, the more conjectural the estimates become.

The size of the discount factor that may properly be used in computing the present value of a future stream of dividends and residual interests depends to a significant extent on the risk involved. The risk reflects such factors as the stability of the industry, the past variability in earnings, and the leverage inherent in its capital structure.

No stock valuation formula has yet been devised and published that has proved to be an accurate forecaster of security market values under all conditions. Perhaps the factors that bear on the determination of security values are too numerous and too complex for inclusion in a workable formula, and possibly not all such factors can be adequately measured, particularly because of the simplifying assumptions that are introduced in many such models.

Whatever method of stock valuation is used by the security analyst, be it either a simple short-term projection of earnings to be capitalized at a predetermined rate or a complex and sophisticated formula involving elegant mathematical techniques, the results can never reach a higher level of accuracy or be more reliable than the inputs used in such calculations. The reliability and the validity of these inputs, be they earnings projections, expected payout ratios, or various risk factors such as those inherent in capital structure, depend on the quality of the financial statement analysis performed.

The above view was best expressed by Douglas A. Hayes:

> Although the concept that investment results are likely to be heavily related to corporate performance in a long-term sense is generally accepted, some recent contributions to the field have alleged that the implementation methodology should be completely revolutionized. For example . . . a text of financial analysis alleges . . . that a critical investigation of the past financial statements to reveal potential problems of consistency and comparability of reported income and balance sheet data can be largely discarded because accounting and disclosure standards have improved to the point where the underlying data require no critical review. Moreover, they allege that financial risk factors no longer require appraisal because of the greatly improved stability features of the economy; in lieu thereof, they suggest elegant mathematical techniques to develop the theoretical effects of assumed patterns of various management decisions and economic data on security values.
>
> However, the empirical evidence would suggest that these allegations are seriously in error.[8]

In short, while the goal of the analyst may be to go forward *from* the figures, a thorough financial analysis requires that he also go *behind* the figures.[9] No present or prospective developments in the field of accountancy justify the assumption that this can be significantly changed in the near future (see also discussion at end of Chapter 3 and examples throughout the text).

---

[8] "The Dimensions of Analysis: A Critical Review," *Financial Analysts Journal,* September–October 1966.

[9] Author's note: Women have been analysts and auditors for years, and their numbers are growing. However, in this book, masculine pronouns are often being used for succinctness and are intended to refer to both males and females.

DEVELOPMENTS IN INVESTMENT THEORY

The methods and approaches of practicing security analysts have come under repeated challenge by their academic counterparts who have developed a number of theories designed to provide insight into the overall investment process.

Portfolio Theory

A pioneering contribution was that of Markowitz, who addressed the problem of portfolio construction given analysts' estimates of possible future returns from securities.[10] He demonstrated that both risk and return must be considered, provided a formal framework for quantifying both, and showed how the relationship among security risks and returns could be taken into account in portfolio construction.

He begins with the observation that the future return on a security can be estimated, and he equates risk with the variance of the distribution of returns. Markowitz demonstrated that under certain assumptions there is a linear relationship between risk and return. Using these variables, he provided a framework for deciding how much of each security to hold in constructing a portfolio. The two-dimensional risk-return approach offers the investor the ability to choose in the trade-off between risk and return. Markowitz's work is based on the assumption that rational investors will resist increases in risk without commensurate increases in expected returns. By proper diversification, one can lower risk while preserving returns.

Evaluation of Risk and Return

The relationship between the risk that must be accepted and the return that may be expected is central to all modern investing and lending decisions. It may seem obvious that the greater the perceived degree of risk of an investment or of a loan, the greater is the required rate of return to compensate for such risk.

Categories of Risk

Risk is commonly associated with the uncertainty surrounding the outcome of future events. While many investors and lenders make subjective evaluations of risk, academicians have developed statistical measures of risk that belong to the overall concept known as beta coefficient theory.

---

[10] H. Markowitz, "Portfolio Selection," *Journal of Finance,* March 1952, pp. 77–91. In 1990, Dr. Markowitz along with W. Sharpe and M. Miller shared the Nobel Prize in economics.

Under this theory, the total risk associated with an investment is composed of two elements:

1. *Systematic risk,* which is that portion of total risk attributable to the movement of the market as a whole.
2. *Unsystematic risk,* which is the residual risk that is unique to a specific security.

In the application of the theory, a quantitative expression of systematic risk (known as beta)[11] equal to one is attributed to the volatility of the market as a whole. The higher a security's beta, the greater will be its expected return. Treasury bills have a beta of zero because they are essentially riskless; that is, they do not fluctuate with the market. A stock having a beta of 1.20 could rise or fall 20 percent faster than the market, while one having a beta of 0.90 would on average register market value changes 10 percent less in amplitude than those of the market as a whole. Thus, high beta stocks can expect high returns in a "bull market" and also larger than average declines during a "bear market."

Since by definition, unsystematic risk[12] is the *residual risk* that is unexplained by market movements, no unsystematic risk exists for the market as a whole and almost none exists in a highly diversified portfolio of stocks. Consequently, as portfolios become larger and more diversified, their unsystematic risk will approach zero.

Adherents to this theory hold that the market will not reward those exposing themselves to unsystematic risk that can be removed by proper diversification. They believe that the implication of the theory for common stock investors is to diversify, and if they expect the market to rise, to increase the beta of their portfolios and vice versa. Some experimental studies have indicated that between 30 and 50 percent of an individual stock's price is due to market (systematic) risk and that such influence reaches 85 to 90 percent in a well-diversified portfolio of 30 or more stocks.[13]

It follows that the portfolio manager who does not wish to rely only on market action for returns or who cannot forecast overall market action

---

[11] Beta indexes are computed by use of regression analysis to relate the historical price movements of a stock to the movements of a general market price index such as the S&P 500 stock index. Alas, because of the ever-changing environment, capital structure, and operations of an enterprise, beta coefficients have exhibited a high degree of instability over time.

[12] A measure of unsystematic risk is alpha, which measures a stock's expected rate of return when the expected market rate of return is zero. Many academicians maintain that the expected alpha for a well-diversified portfolio is zero because the specific business circumstances that give rise to positive and negative alphas tend to cancel out in a portfolio of stocks. Practicing security analysts strive, however, to construct portfolios having positive alphas. In essence, alpha is derived from virtues in a stock that are not recognized by the market, thus resulting in returns above what beta would suggest.

[13] J. B. Cohen, E. D. Zinbarg, and A. Zeikel, *Investment Analysis and Portfolio Management,* 5th ed. (Homewoood, Ill.: Richard D. Irwin, 1987).

should seek nondiversification, that is, exposure to the amount of unsystematic risk required for achieving the desired rate of return. Such a strategy would emphasize the analysis of individual securities, as discussed in this work, as opposed to overall portfolio risk balancing. Thus, reaping the rewards of exposure to nonsystematic risk is dependent on an ability to identify undervalued securities and on the proper assessment of their risk. (See discussion of efficient market hypothesis later in this chapter.)

Components of Unsystematic Risk

Those who want to obtain their rewards from exposure to unsystematic or nonmarket risk through the rigorous analysis of individual securities must focus on the various components of such risk. While those components are undoubtedly interrelated and subject to the influence of such elements of systematic risk as overall political, economic, and social factors, they can nevertheless be usefully classified as follows:

Economic risk reflects risks of the overall economic environment in which the enterprise operates including general economic risk (fluctuations in business activity), capital market risk (including changes in interest rates), and purchasing power risk—some aspects of which are discussed in Chapter 14.

Business risk is concerned with the ever-present uncertainty regarding a business enterprise's ability to earn a satisfactory return on its investments as well as with the multitude of cost and revenue factors that enter into the determination of such a return. It includes the factors of competition, product mix, and management ability (see Chapters 19–22).

Financial risk is basically concerned with capital structure and with the ability of an enterprise to meet fixed and senior charges and claims. These factors of short-term liquidity and long-term solvency are discussed in detail in Chapters 16, 17, and 18.

For a discussion of the concept of *accounting risk,* see Chapter 3.

Those who assume, as do beta theorists, that all investors are averse to risk and that they seek to diversify away the specific or unsystematic risks[14] of a security thus exposing themselves only to market risk, must also realize that the historical betas for individual securities have proven quite unstable over time and that consequently such betas seem to be poor predictors of future betas for the same security. Thus, while overall concepts and theories are easier to apply to stock aggregates than to the evaluation of individual stocks, they are at the same time far less reliable and accurate instruments for the achievement of investment results.

---

[14] What is often overlooked is that those who seek to diversify away unsystematic risk are also diversifying out a great deal of the rewards that equity investing holds for more aggressive investors.

Another, and perhaps even more troublesome, question is the assumption of beta theorists that past volatility alone is an acceptable measure of risk without reference to the current price of a security. Is a security that sells significantly *above* its value, as determined by some method of fundamental analysis, no more risky than a security of equal volatility (beta) that sells significantly *below* such fundamentally determined value? We know that paying an excessive price for a stable quality security can amount to as rank a speculation as investing in the most unseasoned of speculative securities.

While market theorists have not yet addressed the above troublesome question, they have addressed the problem of how securities are valued by the market.

The Relationship between Accounting and Market Measures of Risk

A study conducted by Professors W. Beaver, P. Kettler, and M. Scholes[15] found that accounting measures of risk, such as dividend payout ratios, capitalization ratios, coverage, and asset growth are reflected in market price risk measures such as beta. They also concluded that "a strategy of selecting and ranking portfolios according to accounting risk measures is essentially equivalent to the strategy of ranking these same portfolios according to market-determined risk measures."

Robert G. Bowman[16] illustrated a theoretical relationship between systematic risk and the firm's leverage and other accounting risk measures.

Barr Rosenberg[17] has pioneered the use of "fundamental betas" (i.e., those which are basically a function of a company's changing fundamentals such as earnings, financial structure, growth rates, etc). The important implication here is that the same economic (accounting expressed) determinants that cause a stock to be risky also cause it to have a high systematic risk (e.g., beta).

The Capital Asset Pricing Model

Sharpe[18] and Lintner[19] have extended portfolio theory to a capital asset pricing model (CAPM) that is intended to explain how prices of assets

---

[15] "The Association between Market Determined and Accounting Determined Risk Measures," *Accounting Review,* October 1970.

[16] "The Theoretical Relationship between Systematic Risk and Financial (Accounting) Variables," *Journal of Finance,* June 1979.

[17] B. Rosenberg and J. Guy, "Prediction of Beta from Investment Fundamentals," *Financial Analysts Journal,* July-August, 1976.

[18] W. F. Sharpe, "Capital Asset Prices: A Theory of Market Equilibrium under Conditions of Risk," *Journal of Finance,* September 1964, pp. 425–42.

[19] J. Lintner, "The Valuation of Risky Assets and the Selection of Risky Investments in Stock Portfolios and Capital Budgets," *Review of Economics and Statistics,* February 1965, pp. 13–37.

are determined in such a way as to provide greater return for greater risk. This model is based on the assumption that investors desire to hold securities in portfolios that are efficient in the sense that they provide a maximum return for *a given level* of risk. Moreover, the model was derived under the following simplifying assumptions:

1. That there exists a riskless security.
2. That investors are able to borrow or lend unlimited amounts at the riskless rate.
3. That all investors have identical investment horizons and act on the basis of identical expectations and predictions.

Based on these assumptions, it can be shown that when capital markets are in a state of equilibrium, the expected return on an individual security, $E(\tilde{R}_i)$, is related to its systematic risk β_i in the following linear form:

$$E(\tilde{R}_i) = E(\tilde{R}_0) + [E(\tilde{R}_M) - E(\tilde{R}_0)]\beta_i$$

The above formulation states in essence that under conditions of equilibrium, a security's expected return equals the expected return of a riskless security, $E(\tilde{R}_0)$, plus a premium for risk taking. This risk premium consists of a constant, $[E(\tilde{R}_M) - E(\tilde{R}_0)]$, which is the difference between the return expected by the market and the return on a riskless security (such as a short-term government bond) multiplied by the systematic risk of the security β_i (its beta) as discussed earlier.

The CAPM thus indicates that the expected return on any particular capital asset consists of two components: (1) the return on a riskless security and (2) a premium for the riskiness of the particular asset computed as outlined above. Thus, under the CAPM, each security has an expected return that is related to its risk. This risk is measured by the security's systematic movements with the overall market, and it cannot be eliminated by portfolio diversification. A major implication here is that only the bearing of systematic (i.e., beta) risk is rewarded by the market, whereas the holding of unsystematic risk that could be eliminated through diversification would earn no additional return.

It remains for us to consider a related hypothesis that attempts to describe a different property of security prices, that is, the efficient market hypothesis.

The Efficient Market Hypothesis

Efficient market hypothesis (EMH) deals with the reaction of market prices to financial and other data. The EMH has its origins in the random walk hypothesis that basically states that at any given point in time the size and direction of the next price change is random relative to what is known about an investment at that given time. A derivative of this hypothesis is what is known as the *weak form* of the EMH, which states that current prices reflect fully the information implied by historical price time series. In its *semistrong form,* the EMH holds that prices fully reflect all publicly available information.[20] Moreover, in its *strong form,* the theory asserts that prices reflect *all* information including that which is considered "inside information."

The EMH, in all its terms, has undergone extensive empirical testing with much of the evidence apparently supportive of the weak and semi-strong forms of the theory. Lorie and Hamilton,[21] for example, present three studies in support of the semistrong form of the hypothesis indicating that:

1. Stock splits do not assure unusual profit for investors.
2. Secondary offerings depress the market price of a stock because such offerings imply that knowledgeable people are selling.
3. Unusual earnings increases are anticipated in the price of the stock before the company's earnings for the year are reported.[22]

None of these findings would, incidentally, clash with the intuition of experienced analysts or seasoned market participants.

Research supportive of the EMH by accounting scholars on the effect of accounting changes on security prices has found that changes from accelerated to straight-line depreciation for accounting purposes only had no significant effect on stock prices.[23] Another study found that the stock market ignored the effects on income of changes in accounting procedures such as those relating to inventories, depreciation, revenue recognition, and so forth.[24]

Implications for Financial Statement Analysis

The EMH is almost completely dependent on the assumption that competent and well-informed analysts, using tools of analysis such as those described in this book, will constantly strive to evaluate and act upon

---

[20] For one good discussion of this hypothesis, see E. F. Fama, "Efficient Capital Markets: A Review of Theory and Empirical Work," *Journal of Finance,* May 1970, pp. 383–417.

[21] J. H. Lorie and M. T. Hamilton, *The Stock Market: Theories and Evidence* (Homewood, Ill.: Richard D. Irwin, 1973).

[22] See, for example, R. Ball and P. Brown, "An Empirical Evaluation of Accounting Numbers," *Journal of Accounting Research,* Autumn 1968, pp. 159–78; and W. Beaver, "The Informational Content of Annual Earnings Announcements," *Empirical Research in Accounting: Selected Studies,* 1968, University of Chicago, Graduate School of Business 1969, pp. 48–53.

[23] T. R. Archibald, "Stock Market Reaction to the Depreciation Switch-Back," *The Accounting Review,* January 1972, pp. 22–30.

[24] R. Kaplan and R. Roll, "Accounting Changes and Stock Prices," *The Financial Analysts Journal,* January-February 1973, pp. 48–53; also R. Ball, "Changes in Accounting Techniques and Stock Prices," *Empirical Research in Accounting: Selected Studies,* 1972 (Chicago: Institute of Professional Accounting, Graduate School of Business, University of Chicago, 1974), pp. 1–38.

the ever-changing stream of new information entering the marketplace. And yet the theory's proponents claim that since all that is known is already instantly reflected in market prices, any attempt to gain consistently an advantage by rigorous financial statement analysis is not possible. As H. Lorie and M. T. Hamilton put it, "The most general implication of the efficient market hypothesis is that most security analysis is logically incomplete and valueless."[25]

This position presents an unexplained and unresolved paradox. The thousands of intelligent analysts are assumed to be capable enough to keep our security market efficient through their efforts, but they are not intelligent enough to realize that their efforts can yield no individual advantage. Moreover, should they suddenly realize that their efforts are unrewarded, the market would cease to be efficient.

There are a number of factors that may explain this paradox. Foremost among them is the fact that the entire EMH is built on evidence based on an evaluation of *aggregate*[26] rather than individual investor behavior. The focusing on macro or aggregate behavior results not only in the highlighting of average performance and results but also ignores and masks the results achieved by individual ability, hard work, and ingenuity, as well as by superior timing in acting on information as it becomes available.[27]

Few would doubt that important information travels fast. After all, enough is at stake to make it travel fast. Nor is it surprising that the securities markets are rapid processors of information. In fact, using the same type of deductive reasoning as used by the efficient market proponents, we could conclude that the speed and the hardworking efficiency of the market must be evidence that the market participants who make it happen are motivated by substantial rewards.

The reasoning behind the EMH's alleged implication for the usefulness of security analysis fails to recognize the essential difference between information and its proper interpretation. Even if all the information available on a security at a given point in time is impounded in its price, that price may not reflect *value*. It may be under- or overvalued depending on the degree to which an incorrect interpretation or evaluation of the

---

[25] Lorie and Hamilton, *The Stock Market,* p. 100.

[26] R. J. Chambers put it most effectively: "It is very difficult to escape the conclusion that the whole enterprise of aggregate market analysis with the object of resolving questions about the quality of accounting information is misguided. Men have never advanced their finite knowledge of any subject by attention only to what occurs in the aggregate or on average." "Stock Market Prices and Accounting Research," *Abacus,* June 1974, pp. 39–54.

[27] Evidence about superior investment performance by *individuals* is not a matter of public record and is consequently not readily available. But evidence of superior investment performance by portfolio managers is available, one example being *Forbes* magazine's annual "Honor Roll" of consistent long-term superior investment results by investment companies in both up and down markets. Such decidedly superior performance over the long term cannot be dismissed as a statistical quirk.

available information has been made by those whose actions determine the market price at a given time. Market efficiency depends not only on availability of information but also on its correct interpretation.

The work of financial statement analysis is complex and demanding. The spectrum of users of financial statements varies all the way from the institutional analyst who concentrates on only a few companies in one industry to the unsophisticated chaser of rumors. All act on financial information but surely not with the same insights and competence.[28]

The competent evaluation of "new information" entering the marketplace requires the possession of a prior fund of knowledge, of an information mosaic into which the new information can be fitted, as part of a link in a chain of analytical information, before it can be evaluated and interpreted. Only a few have the ability and are prepared to expend the efforts and resources needed to produce such information mosaics, and it is only natural that they would reap the rewards by being able to act both competently and confidently on the new information received. This advantage in timing is all-important in the marketplace. Thus the movement of new information and its correct interpretation flows from the well-informed and -prepared segments of the market to less-informed and slower-absorbing segments. That explains the *gradual* pattern rather than the immediate discounting of new information.

The vast resources that must be brought to bear on the competent analysis of equity securities have caused some segments of the securities markets to be more efficient than others. Thus, the market for shares of the largest companies is more efficient because many more analysts follow such securities and find it worthwhile to do so compared to those who follow small and lesser-known companies. Advocates of the EMH commit the common error of sweeping generalizations. In his 1988 annual report to the shareholders of Berkshire Hathaway, chairman and famed investor Warren Buffet expressed amazement that the EMH is embraced not only by academicians but also by many investment professionals. This, Buffet maintains, is because by observing correctly that the market was *frequently* efficient, they went on to conclude incorrectly that it is *always* efficient. As Buffet puts it "the difference between these propositions is night and day."

Buffet cites personal experience to refute the validity of EMH. The continuous 63-year experience of Graham Newman Corporation, Buffet Partnership, and Berkshire Hathaway resulted in unleveraged annual returns of 20 percent whereas over the same period the general market delivered returns of just under 10 percent. Recent evidence, calling into question the validity of EMH, continues to accumulate. The October

---

[28] B. Graham declared: "I deny emphatically that because the market has all the information it needs to establish a correct price, the prices it actually registers are in fact correct," in "C. D. Ellis, Ben Graham: Ideas as Momentos," *Financial Analysts Journal,* July-August 1982, p. 47.

1987 single-day sharp drop in stock prices (of 23 percent) raises the serious question of whether the opening as well as the closing prices of that day could have possibly represented efficiently priced market levels. The 1988 RJR Nabisco takeover contest offers another puzzling question to adherents of market efficiency. How can a company priced at $55 per share in the auction market be worth $75 per share to the management team and $109 per share to the winning buyout group?

The function and purpose of the analysis of equity securities is construed much too narrowly by those who judge its usefulness in an efficient market.[29] While the search for overvalued and undervalued securities is an important function of security analysis, the importance of risk assessment and loss avoidance, in the total framework of investment decision making, cannot be overemphasized. Thus, the prevention of serious investment errors is at least as important a factor in overall investment success as is the discovery of undervalued securities. Yet, our review of the CAPM and of beta theory earlier in this discussion tends to explain why this important function of analysis is neglected by adherents to these macro models of the security markets. For to some it is a basic premise of these theories that the analysis of unsystematic risk is not worthwhile because that kind of risk taking is not rewarded by the market. They maintain that such risks should be diversified away and that the portfolio manager should look only to systematic or market risk for rewards.[30]

Our basic premise here is that investment results are achieved through the careful study and analysis of *individual* enterprises rather than by an exclusive focus on market aggregates. Our approach in this area is to emphasize the value of fundamental investment analysis not only as a means of keeping our securities markets efficient and our capital markets rational and strong but also as the means by which those investors who, having obtained information, are willing and able to apply knowledge, effort, and ingenuity to its analysis.[31] For those investors, the fruits of fundamental analysis and research, long before being converted to a "public good," will provide adequate rewards. These rewards will not be discernible, however, in the performance of investors aggregated to comprise major market segments, such as mutual funds. Instead, they will remain as individual as the efforts needed to bring them about.

---

[29] For a more comprehensive discussion of these issues, see the author's article "In Defense of Fundamental Investment Analysis," *Financial Analysts Journal,* January-February 1975, pp. 57–61.

[30] An investment practice, based on the efficient market adherents' disenchantment with investment results, is the index fund. An index portfolio is merely designed to copy the composition of a market index to such an extent that it will replicate its market performance. This approach represents a mechanical substitute for analysis and judgment, and may not satisfy its adherents over the longer term.

[31] The value of such analysis for other purposes, such as credit evaluation, is not even at issue here.

The role of financial statement analysis in the professional decision-making process leading to the buying, selling, or holding of equity securities has always been the subject of controversy and debate. In times of high speculative market activity, fundamental factors inevitably give way in relative importance to the psychological or technical ones in the overall security appraisal and "valuation" process. The fact that these fundamental factors, based as they are on a concrete analysis of measurable elements, can lead to sounder decisions and to the avoidance of serious judgmental errors will not always prevent their abandonment in favor of the snap decisions that occur in times of speculative frenzy. Nevertheless, the ultimate return of more sober times after periods of speculation and the inevitable corrections of speculative excesses recurringly bring along with them a rediscovery of the virtues of thorough financial analysis as a sound and necessary procedure. In the aftermath of the 1969–70 bear market, David L. Babson urged such a return by stating:

> What we all should do now is to roll up our sleeves and go back to doing what we are paid for—to follow company and industry trends closely, to really dissect balance sheets and to dig into accounting practices—and maybe some future Jim Lings, Delbert Colemans and Cortes Randells won't make monkeys out of many of the prestigious firms in our industry again.[32]

The collapse in security values in the early 1970s was, of course, not the first such occurrence that was preceded by a widespread and reckless disregard for fundamentals. It is noteworthy that each generation of analysts has to relearn the lessons so heavily paid for by its predecessors. A. P. Richardson, in an editorial on "The 1929 Stock Market Collapse" published in the *Journal of Accountancy* of December 1929, emphasized this recurring phenomenon of the flight from facts and reason into the world of fancy and wishful thinking:

> The astounding feature of the decline and fall of the stock market in late October and early November was not the fact of descent itself, but the altogether unreasoning consternation which the public in and out of Wall Street displayed. There was nothing at all in the course of events which distinguished the break from its many predecessors. Month after month, even year after year, market prices of securities had climbed to even dizzier heights. Now and then a Jeremiah uttered warning and lament, but the people gave no heed. They thought and consequently dealt in far futures. What a company might earn when the next generation would come to maturity was made the measure of the current value of its stock. In many cases companies whose operations had never yet produced a penny of profit were selected, fortuitously or under artificial stimulation,

---

[32] "The Stock Market's Collapse and Constructive Aftermath," *The Commercial and Financial Chronicle,* June 4, 1970.

as a sort of Golconda of the next voyage; and otherwise sane men and women eagerly bought rights of ownership in adventures whose safe return was on the knees of the sea gods. It was not considered enough to look ahead to what was visible. The unseen was the chief commodity. Good stocks, bad stocks and stocks neither good nor bad but wholly of the future rose with almost equal facility, until at last they were sold at prices which seemed to be entirely uninfluenced by the rates of dividend or even by the earnings of the issuing companies. Government bonds and other "gilt-edged" securities were sold at prices nearer the actual interest yield than were the prices of highly speculative stocks to the dividend return or even to the net earnings, past or soon expected, of the companies concerned. Anything was possible when vision was so blurred by success.

The bull market that started in the early 1980s proved again that financial history repeats itself because we ignore the lessons of the past. Or, as Professor J. K. Galbraith put it, all that is required for genius on Wall Street is a rising market and a short memory. Thus, as long as the motivating forces behind the buying and selling of securities are measurable fundamental factors affecting the security-issuing enterprises, financial statement analysis has an important part in the investment decision process. However, once the dynamics of speculation take over, rational considerations begin to be relegated to a minor role. As the euphoria of rising prices takes hold, the speculative component in the price structure grows larger and larger. It is no longer a question of whether this speculative component, which has no basis in rational analysis, will be deflated but only when. The October 1987 stock market crash proved again that when equity yields reach historic lows and price-earnings ratios climb to unreasonable heights, the deflation of the speculative component can occur suddenly and with dramatic speed. Since it is created by nothing measurable or subject to value analysis, it can be deflated by a mere change in sentiment. Thus the speculative component is not subject to analysis by means of the approaches described in this work.

Financial statement analysis, while certainly not providing answers to all the problems of security analysis, at least keeps the decision maker in touch with the underlying realities of the enterprise that is investigated. It imposes the discipline of comparing the results already attained with the wide-ranging promises made for the future. As a very minimum, it represents a safeguard against the repetition of the grievous mistakes of judgment recurringly made by investors in time of speculative euphoria.

We have, in this section, examined the needs for information by equity investors. Not all such information can be obtained by means of financial statement analysis nor is the information so obtainable always the most critical in the determination of security values. However, it should by now be clear to the reader that any rational and systematic approach to the valuation of common stocks must involve the use of quantified data that are mostly the end product of financial statement analysis, evaluation, and interpretation.

Objectives of Management

Management's interest in an enterprise's financial condition, profitability, and progress is pervasive and all-encompassing. Management has a number of methods, tools, and techniques available to it in monitoring and keeping up with the ever-changing condition of the enterprise. Financial data analysis is one important type of such methods.

Financial data analysis can be undertaken by management on a continuous basis because it has unlimited access to internal accounting and other records. Such analysis encompasses changes in ratios, trends, and other significant relationships. Ratio, change, and trend analysis is based on an intelligent, alert, and systematic surveillance of significant relationships in a business situation and the timely detection and interpretation of problem areas by an analysis of changes taking place.

Management's primary objective in utilizing the tools of analysis described in this book is to exercise control over and to view the enterprise in the way important outsiders, such as creditors and investors, view it.

Ratio change and trend analysis make use of the numerous and inevitable relationships and interrelationships among the variables occurring in any business situation. Constant surveillance over the size and amplitude of change in these interrelationships provides valuable clues to important changes in underlying financial and operating conditions. Recognition of such changes and timely action to check adverse trends is the essence of control.

Management derives a number of important advantages from a systematic monitoring of financial data and the basic relationships that they display:

1. There is recognition that no event in a business situation is isolated and that it represents a cause or the effect of a chain of which it is but a link. This approach aims at discovering whether a given event or relationship is the cause or the effect of an underlying situation.
2. There is a recognition that one should not act on an isolated event, but rather by an examination of related changes, one should determine the basic causes of the event. Thus, an event cannot be judged as positive or negative until it has been properly related to other factors that have a bearing on it.
3. Such monitoring prevents management from getting submerged in a maze of facts and figures that in the typical business situation consist of a great variety of factors of varying sizes, velocities of change, and degrees of impact. Instead, it organizes the data and relates them to a pattern of prior experience and external standards.
4. Such monitoring calls for prompt and effective action as the situation unfolds, rather than for "*post mortem*" analyses of causes and effects.

Objectives of Acquisition and Merger Analysts

The valuation of an enterprise in its entirety, for the purpose of purchasing a going concern or for the purpose of assessing the merger of two or more enterprises, represents an attempt to determine economic values, the relative worth of the merging entities, and the relative bargaining strengths and weaknesses of the parties involved. Financial statement analysis is a valuable technique in the determination of economic value and in an assessment of the financial and operating compatibility of potential merger candidates.

The objectives of the acquisition and merger analyst are in many respects similar to those of the equity investor except that the analysis of the acquisition of an entire enterprise must go further and stress the valuation of assets, including intangible assets such as goodwill, and liabilities included in the acquisition or merger plan.

Objectives of Auditors

The end product of the financial audit is an expression of opinion on the fairness of presentation of financial statements setting forth the financial conditions and the results of operations of an enterprise. One of the basic objectives of the audit process is to obtain the greatest possible degree of assurance about the absence of errors and irregularities, intentional or otherwise, that if undetected could materially affect the fairness of presentation of financial summarizations or their conformity with generally accepted accounting principles (GAAP).

Financial statement analysis and ratio change and trend analysis represent an important group of audit tools that can significantly supplement other audit techniques such as procedural and validation tests.[33] This is so because errors and irregularities, whatever their source, can, if significant, affect the various financial operating and structural relationships; and the detection and analysis of such changes can lead to the detection of errors and irregularities. Moreover, the process of financial analysis requires of the auditor, and imparts to him, the kind of understanding and grasp of the audited enterprise that indicates the most relevant type of supportive evidence required in his audit work.

The application of financial statement analysis as part of the audit program is best undertaken at the very beginning of the audit because such analysis will often reveal the areas of greatest change and vulnerability, areas to which the auditor will want to direct a major part of his attention. At the end of the audit, these tools represent an overall check on the reasonableness of the financial statements taken as a whole.[34]

---

[33] In 1978, the accounting profession formally recognized the importance of analytical audit approaches through issuance of *Statement of Auditing Standards No. 23,* "Analytical Review Procedures."

[34] For a more detailed discussion of this subject, see Leopold A. Bernstein, "Analytical Auditing," in *Handbook for Auditors,* ed. James A. Cashin (New York: McGraw-Hill, 1986).

Objectives of Other Interested Groups

Financial statement analysis can serve the needs of many other user groups. Thus, the Internal Revenue Service can apply tools and techniques of financial statement analysis to the audit of tax returns and the checking of the reasonableness of reported amounts.[35] Various governmental regulatory agencies can use such techniques in the exercise of their supervisory and rate-determination functions.

Labor unions can use the techniques of financial statement analysis to evaluate the financial statements of enterprises with which they engage in collective bargaining. Lawyers can employ these techniques in the furtherance of their investigative and legal work, while economic researchers will find them of great usefulness in their work.

Similarly, customers can use such approaches to determine the profitability (staying power) of their suppliers, the returns they earn on capital, and other factors of consequence to them.

DESIGN OF THIS BOOK

The *first* part of this book (Chapters 1 through 4) examines the objectives of financial statement analysis and the objectives of financial accounting, as well as the relationship of one to the other. Chapter 4 provides an early overview of some of the major tools and techniques used in the analysis of financial statements.

The *second* part deals with the accounting model with particular emphasis on the implications that the variety of accounting standards and procedures have on financial statement analysis. Also examined are tools and techniques that can be used by the analyst to reconstruct, from the highly summarized financial statements and related disclosures, the transactions and events that represent the underlying reality of the enterprise.

The *third* part examines in depth the major areas of concern in the analysis of financial statements, the analytical adjustments to be applied, and the major tools and techniques in use. Chapter 23 concludes with an example of a comprehensive analysis of financial statements.

CONCLUSION

This chapter has examined the points of view and the objectives of a variety of important users of financial statements. These various objectives determine what aspects of financial statement analysis are relevant

---

[35] Among the areas that can be analyzed are questions such as whether (1) the income reported is enough to support exemptions or expenses claimed, (2) the profit margin reported is out of line with that normal for that type of business, (3) the return reported is less than that which can be earned by banking the money, and (4) the changes in net worth support the amounts of reported income.

to the decision-making process of a particular user. In the chapters that follow, we shall first examine the relationship between financial statement analysis and the accounting framework as well as the tools and techniques of financial statement analysis in general. This will be followed in Part III by an examination of the major missions or objectives of financial analysis and the means by which they can be realized.

QUESTIONS

1. Describe some of the analytical uses to which financial statement analysis can be put.
2. Why are the information needs of equity investors among the most demanding of all users of financial statements?
3. Why is the measurement and evaluation of earning power the key element in the valuation of equity securities?
4. What is the essential difference between a bond valuation model based on the present value of future inflows and a stock valuation model based on the same principles?
5. Differentiate between systematic risk and unsystematic risk and discuss the various components of the latter.
6. Discuss the capital asset pricing model (CAPM) and explain how it deals with the problem of securities valuation by the market.
7. Explain how the efficient market hypothesis (EMH) deals with the reaction of market prices to financial and other data.
8. Explain the concept of the trade-off between risk and return as well as its significance to portfolio construction.
9. Discuss the implications that the CAPM and the EMH present for financial statement analysis.
10. Why is the reliability and the validity of any method of stock valuation, no matter how complete and sophisticated, dependent on the prior performance of a quality analysis of financial statements?
11. Identify clearly three separate factors which have a significant influence on a stock's price-earnings ratio. (CFA)
12. What are the differences in point of view between lenders and equity investors? How do these differences express themselves in the way these two groups analyze financial statements and in the objectives that they seek?
13. a. Outline the principal risks inherent in a preferred stock as an investment instrument, relative to a bond or other credit obligation of the same company.
    b. Discuss the various influences of U.S. (or Canadian) income taxation trends on the inherent risks and yields of preferred stocks.
    c. What terms can be included in a preferred stock issue to compensate for its subordination to debt and its relationship to common stock? (CFA)
14. What uses can the management of an enterprise make of financial statement analysis?
15. Of what use can financial statement analysis be to the audit of an enterprise?

Chapter 2

FINANCIAL STATEMENT ANALYSIS AND ACCOUNTING

THE FUNCTION OF FINANCIAL STATEMENT ANALYSIS

Financial statement analysis is the judgmental process that aims to evaluate the current and past financial positions and the results of operations of an enterprise, with the primary objective of determining the best possible estimates and predictions about future conditions and performance.

As was discussed in Chapter 1, financial statement analysis may be undertaken for many purposes. The security analyst is interested in future earnings estimates and in financial strength as an important element in the valuation of securities. The credit analyst wants to determine future funds flows and the resulting financial condition as a means of assessing the risks inherent in a particular credit extension. Present owners of securities analyze current financial statements to decide on whether to hold, enlarge, or sell their positions. Merger and acquisition analysts study and analyze financial statements as an essential part of their decision-making processes leading to recommendations regarding the merger and acquisition of business enterprises. These are examples of situations involving outsiders—external analysts—trying to reach conclusions principally on the basis of published financial data.

Internal financial analysts, on the other hand, utilize an even larger and more detailed financial database to assess, for internal management and control purposes, the current financial condition and results of an enterprise.

Two Major Foundations

The discipline of financial statement analysis rests on two major foundations of knowledge:

The *first* foundation involves a thorough understanding of the accounting model as well as the language, the meaning, the significance, and the limitations of financial communications, as most commonly reflected in published statements.

27

A prerequisite to effective decision making is to "get the facts." The facts about an enterprise's financial condition and results of operations are rarely available in plain English. They are first assembled and subsequently summarized and reported in a special-purpose language—the language of accounting. We are also dealing here with a complex measurement system that must be understood. Thus, the first essential step in "getting the facts" is to understand this language and to translate the meaning of "the facts" from that special-purpose language.

A thorough understanding of financial statements is the condition precedent to the valid and intelligent computation and use of tools of analysis. In many cases, the amounts as shown on the financial statements cannot be used without adjustments. Moreover, some of the amounts that need to be included in the computation of ratios and relationships are found in or must be computed from data provided in footnotes or elsewhere.

The *second* foundation, which inevitably builds on the first, consists of the mastery of the tools of financial analysis by means of which the most significant financial and operating factors and relationships can be identified and analyzed for purposes of reaching informed conclusions.

THE RAW MATERIAL OF ANALYSIS

The analytical processes that underlie the conclusions of security analysts, credit analysts, and other external analysts, as well as internal analysts, make use of a vast array of facts, information, and data—economic, social, political, and other. However, the most important quantitative data utilized by these analysts are the financial data that are the output of an enterprise's accounting system. Presented for external use, principally in the form of formal financial statements, these data are among the most important quantified elements in the entire mix of inputs utilized by the decision maker. Since financial accounting data are the product of a whole range of conventions, measurements, and judgments, their apparent precision and exactness can be misleading. Such data cannot be intelligently used in financial analysis without a thorough understanding of the accounting framework of which they are the end product, as well as of the conventions that govern the measurement of resources, liabilities, equities, and operating results of an enterprise. This book examines the accounting framework that underlies financial accounting data as well as the tools of analysis that have been found useful in the analysis and interpretation of such data.

IMPORTANCE OF ACCOUNTING DATA

Decision-making processes, such as those relating to the choice of equity investments or the extension of credit, require a great variety of data processing, a wide range of reliability, and relevance to the decision at hand. The information used includes data on general economic conditions and on industry trends, as well as data on intangibles such as the character and motivation of the management group. Financial statements and other data emanating from the accounting process represent measurable indexes of performance already achieved and of financial conditions presently prevailing.

In any given decision situation, the relative importance of unquantifiable intangibles, as against quantified actual experience reflected in financial statements, will, of course, vary. Nevertheless, in most cases, no intelligent, well-grounded decision can be made without an analysis of the quantifiable data found in financial accounting reports.

In the realm of data available for meaningful analysis, financial statements are important because they are objective in that they portray actual events that already happened; they are concrete in that they can be quantified; and being quantifiable they can, perhaps most importantly, be measured. This attribute of measurability endows financial statement data with another important characteristic: since they are expressed in the common denominator of money, this enables us to add and combine the data, to relate them to other data, and to otherwise manipulate them arithmetically. The above attributes contribute to the great importance of financial accounting data, both historical or projected, to the decision-making process.

The Indispensability of Accounting Statements

As this book will discuss and illustrate, financial accounting as the social science it is, is subject to many shortcomings, imperfections, and limitations. It is also an evolving discipline subject to continuous change and attempted improvement, based mostly on experience.

Some users of accounting data, particularly those from other disciplines, become at times so impatient with these shortcomings, imperfections, and limitations as to suggest that some substitute be used instead. There is no such substitute. Double-entry bookkeeping, an ingenious recording and accounting system spawned in the Middle Ages[1] and perfected ever since into the modern discipline of accounting, is and remains the only viable system for the systematic recording, classification, and summarization of myriads of business activities. The only realistic hope for improvement lies in the improvement of this time-tested system rather than in its substitution by some other method which, while possessing theoretical elegance, cannot be implemented in practice.

It is thus incumbent on anyone who desires to analyze intelligently the financial position and the results of operations of an enterprise, to

---

[1] By Luca Pacioli in *Summa de Arithmetica* published in Venice in 1494.

study the accounting framework, its terminology, and its conventions, as well as the imperfections and limitations to which it is subject.

While the improvement of accounting statements and presentations is a continuing process, these statements cannot be improved to the point where users will be able to utilize them without a need for a prior rigorous study and mastery of the intricacies of the accounting framework.

LIMITATIONS OF ACCOUNTING DATA

Recognition of the importance of financial accounting data should be tempered by a realization of the limitations to which they are subject. The following sections discuss some of the more important limitations.

Monetary Expression

The first and most obvious limitation is that financial statements can only present information that lends itself to quantification in terms of the monetary unit; some significant facts about the enterprise do not lend themselves to such measurement. For example, the financial statements, as such, contain very little direct information about the character, motivation, experience, or age of the human resources. They do not contain, except in terms of aggregate final results, information about the quality of the research and development effort or the breadth of the marketing organization. Nor can we expect to find in the financial statements any detailed information on product lines, machinery efficiency, or advance planning. Equally absent will be information on organization structure and on such behavioral problems as the fact that the marketing manager is not on speaking terms with the controller, or that the entire success of the enterprise hinges on the talents of a single person. Nevertheless, without a uniform unit of measurement, financial statements, as we know them, would not be possible.

Simplifications and Rigidities Inherent in the Accounting Framework

The portrayal by means of accounting statements of highly complex and diverse economic activities involves the need for simplification, summarization, and the use of judgments and estimates.

The simplification process is necessary in order to classify the great variety of economic events into a manageable number of categories. Inevitably, this simplification can be achieved only at the expense of clarity and detail, which, in some instances, may be useful to the user of financial data.

The need to keep the size of and detail in the financial statements within reasonable bounds, as well as cost versus benefit considerations, requires a high degree of summarization of economic events both in the initial recording of these events in the accounting records and subsequently in the preparation of the financial statements. Inevitably, in the process of such summarization, financial statements lose, perhaps more often than they should, comprehensiveness of description and clarity. This process does represent, in effect, the translation of events of the real world into numerical abstractions.

The simplifications and the rigidities inherent in the accounting framework, as well as the high degree of summarization present in the financial statements, make it imperative that the analyst be able to analyze and to reconstruct the events and the business transactions that they reflect. Indeed, it is an essential skill of the analyst to be able to recover from the financial presentations the realities imbedded in them and to recognize that which cannot be recovered, and thus have a basis for asking meaningful questions of those able to provide additional information.

Use of Individual Judgment

The use of individual judgment in the preparation of financial statements is inevitable. The limitation to be recognized here is the resulting variety in the quality and reliability of financial statement presentations. Financial statements may not be of uniform quality and reliability because of differences in the character and the quality of judgments exercised by accountants in their preparation. Moreover, financial statements are general-purpose presentations; the extent of detail reflected therein is determined by the accounting profession's current view of the "average reader's" requirements and expectations. Such envisioned requirements do not necessarily coincide with those of a user with a specific purpose in mind.

Interim Nature and the Need for Estimation

A further limitation of financial statements stems from the need to report for relatively short periods of the total life span of an enterprise. To be useful, accounting information must be timely; and therefore determinations of financial condition and results of operations must be made frequently. But such frequency of reporting, particularly on the results of operations, requires a great deal of estimation; and the greater the degree of such estimation required, the greater the amount of uncertainty that is inevitably introduced into the financial statements. Examples of estimates are:

- Amount and timing of cash collections on receivables.

- Future sales price and sales volume of inventory items.
- Life and salvage value of fixed assets.
- Future warranty claims.
- Percentage completion and costs to complete for long-term contracts.
- Tax expense.
- Loss reserves.

It is important to clarify the connection between the length of a period reported on and the degree of accounting uncertainty introduced. Many business transactions and operations require a long period of time for final completion and determination of results. For example, fixed assets are acquired for a long period of usefulness. The longer such period of use, the more tentative must be the estimates of their ultimate useful life span. Similarly, the value, if any, of investments in mining or exploration venturing may not become apparent until many accounting periods after the one in which they are incurred. Long-term contracts are another example in which the greater the length of time involved, the more tentative the estimation process must be.

Cost Balances

As will be seen in Chapter 3, it still is a basic convention of accounting in the United States that accounting determinations be subject to objective ascertainment.[2] Since the cost of an asset arrived at by arm's-length bargaining may generally be objectively determined by inspection, it is claimed that the cost figure enjoys an objectivity surpassing any subsequent unrealized appraisal of value. Primarily for this reason, accounting adheres, with few exceptions, to the cost concept. The price we pay for this objectivity in accounting adds up to yet another important limitation upon the usefulness of accounting statements. Cost balances do not, in most cases, represent current market values. Yet the users of financial statements usually look for an assessment of value, and to them, historical-cost balances are of very limited usefulness. Moreover, the analyst must be aware of valuation bases other than cost that are used in financial statements.

Unstable Monetary Unit

The first accounting limitation that we discussed above identified accounting expressions as being limited to those that could be expressed

---

[2] There is slow movement in this country and more determined movement abroad toward some forms of current value accounting. These moves are prompted particularly by a desire to give recognition to the effects of inflation on accounting determinations. That the accounting profession here has moved from mandatory to voluntary price-level disclosures does not bode well for early progress in this area (see also Chapter 14).

in monetary terms. The advantage of the monetary expression is, of course, that it provides a common denominator and enables us to add up the cost aggregates of such diverse assets as, say, shares of stock, tons of lead, and store furniture.

Over the years, however, the value of money in terms of general purchasing power has undergone significant fluctuations and generally has had a pronounced downward trend. The monetary unit has not retained its quality as a "standard of value," and, consequently, adding up the money cost of goods purchased in year 1 with those bought in year 8 may result in serious distortions.

The accounting profession has recognized that "the assumption that fluctuations in the value of money can be ignored is unrealistic" and, as discussed in Chapter 14, *Statement of Financial Accounting Standards (SFAS) 33* required certain large companies to issue supplementary statements that reflect the effect of price-level changes on conventional financial statements. However, *SFAS 89* which made such disclosures elective, rather than mandatory, has greatly diluted these initiatives. Moreover, no framework for relating the supplementary statements to the primary ones has yet evolved, and thus, present-day financial statements remain subject to serious limitations.

THE RELATIVE IMPORTANCE OF FINANCIAL STATEMENT ANALYSIS IN THE TOTAL DECISION EFFORT

The analysis of financial statements and data is an indispensable component of most lending, investing, and other related decisions. It is, however, important to understand that its relative importance in the total decision context can vary significantly.

In the lending decision, the lender looks mainly to the enterprise for his or her rewards, which come in the form of interest and principal repayment. We are not concerned with interim changes in interest rates that depend on factors outside the scope of our discussion here. Since almost all the rewards (returns) that the lender expects come directly from the enterprise, financial statement analysis is a relatively large and important part of the total decision process. It is, in fact, the most important element in the entire decision set with which the lending officer or bond investor is concerned.[3]

While there may be wide agreement on what is included in a given decision set and what the relative importance of the various parts are, there will always be exceptions and differences of opinion. Consider the

---

[3] A decision set consists of the totality of all factors that enter into the making of a decision. The lending decision set includes many other important factors such as management ability and integrity, industry, as well as broad economic conditions.

following response[4] by D. C. Platten, chairman of Chemical Bank, to the question of whether banks have endangered themselves by lending hundreds of billions to slow or nonpaying foreign countries. "I have never worried that the international banking system would collapse as a result of the current problems. It's too unacceptable to allow that to happen. Everybody has too much at stake and all will have a role to play, including Congress, foreign governments, the International Monetary Fund, and commercial banks. In some manner, shape or form, it will be worked out. I don't consider that to be Pollyanna, I consider it to be pragmatic."

It is obvious that Platten's lending decision set contains elements that loom larger than does the analysis of the debtor's financial statements as a basis for judging ability to pay. In retrospect, his reliance on "other factors" to bail him out of bad credit decisions appears to be unwarranted. Most banks do regard the ability to understand and analyze financial statements as one of the most critical skills to be possessed by the lending officer.

The role that financial statement analysis plays in the equity investing decision is quite different. One important reason for this is that the equity investor looks for his reward to two different sources: dividends and capital appreciation.

Dividends depend in the long run directly on profitability, growth, and liquidity—elements that lend themselves to evaluation by means of an analysis of the financial statements of the paying enterprise. But dividends, which come from and are subject to enterprise discretion, are only one part, and often the smaller element, of the total sought-for reward (return). In fact, many growing and successful enterprises pay minimal or no dividends.

The other, and often major portion, of the expected rewards comes not from the company directly but rather from other investors who, it is expected, will be willing, at some future time, to pay more for the equity investment than did our decision-making investor. While the willingness of investors to pay higher prices for an equity security depends importantly on earnings power and earnings growth, it often depends even more on the psychology of the marketplace, on its valuation of earnings retained, as well as on factors such as the rates of return available from other investments.

Thus, the investor's decision set must include considerations of market psychology and confidence that are factors of great importance not subject to analysis by use of the enterprise's financial statements. Consequently, investors in many successful and growing companies often do not obtain the expected returns when the marketplace, in its collective wisdom, refuses to capitalize the earnings they bought at prior higher multiples.

---

[4] As quoted in *Forbes,* October 24, 1983, p. 10.

For these reasons, the relationship between the rates of return realized by the enterprise and those that the investor in it actually realizes in the marketplace is far from direct. This is often puzzling to those who do not fully appreciate the great importance of the marketplace as the final validator of equity values. Equity security markets are both logical and psychological, and the relative importance of these two factors is ever-changing. Since the analysis of financial statements relates to the logical processes, the relative importance of financial statement analysis in the equity investing decision set varies with circumstances and the time on the market clock. Its importance is relatively greater when market valuations are low than when these valuations are determined by general market euphoria. Its relative importance is always greater when it is directed to the assessment of risk and to the detection of areas of vulnerability or of potential problems. The value of financial statement analysis in defensive investing and in the avoidance of loss is far clearer and direct than is its value in the detection of investment opportunity. See also the discussion in Chapter 19 regarding the lack of a significant correlation between rewards to shareholders (owners) and company performance as it is presently measured.

Having explored the relationship of financial statement analysis to the decision-making process and to the accounting framework on which it relies, we turn next to a more comprehensive consideration of the accounting process.

THE FUNCTION OF ACCOUNTING

Accounting is concerned with the quantitative expression of economic phenomena. As a discipline, it evolved from a need for a framework for recording, classifying, and communicating economic data. In the basic form existing today, it reflects the constant change and modification that it has undergone since its inception, in response to changing social and economic needs.

One of the best and most succinct definitions of the functions of accounting is found in *Accounting Research Study (ARS) 1,* entitled "The Basic Postulate of Accounting," which had as its aim the identification of the postulates or conventions of the discipline. According to this study, the function of accounting is:

1. To measure the resources held by specific entities.
2. To reflect the claims against and the interests in those entities.
3. To measure the changes in those resources, claims, and interests.
4. To assign the changes to a specifiable period of time.
5. To express the foregoing in terms of money as a common denominator.[5]

---

[5] Maurice Moonitz, "The Basic Postulate of Accounting," *Accounting Research Study No. 1* (New York: American Institute of Certified Public Accountants, 1961).

The function and purposes of accounting are accomplished at two levels. One is the recording function which is that part of the discipline that governs the mechanics of recording and summarizing the multitude of transactions and economic events that occur in an enterprise and that can be quantified in terms of money. The other level, a more complex one and more subject to individual judgment and opinion, governs the methods, procedures, and principles by which accounting data are measured and presented. This chapter will concern itself with an examination of the recording level of the accounting discipline, while subsequent chapters will take up the conventions and principles that govern accounting measurements and their presentation.

The Recording Function

The recording function in accounting is governed by the principle of double-entry bookkeeping, an ingenious system of accounting that has stood the test of time since its description by an Italian mathematician in 1494.

The study of the theory of double-entry bookkeeping is an integral part of the study of accountancy. Users of accounting statements will find that a general understanding of the double-entry system will aid them significantly in the analysis of financial statements as well as in the reconstruction of business transactions.

The basic concept of the double-entry system is based on the duality of every business transaction. For example, if a business borrows $1,000, it acquires an asset (cash), and counterbalancing this is a claim against the enterprise (a liability) in an equal amount. Regardless of how many transactions an enterprise engages in, this duality and balance prevails at all times and provides the advantages of order, consistency, and control.

Continuing with a more generalized example, when an entity acquires an asset the counterbalancing effect results in one or a number of the following:

1. The incurrence of a liability.
2. The enlargement of the ownership's claim (capital funds).
3. The disposal of another asset.

Similarly, a liability is extinguished by:

1. The disposal of an asset, or
2. The enlargement of the ownership claim, or
3. Incurrence of another liability.

At all times, the assets of an enterprise equal the outsider's claims against these assets (i.e., liabilities) and the equity of the ownership (i.e., capital). Thus, the basic equation prevailing under the double-entry system is:

$$\text{Assets} = \text{Liabilities} + \text{Capital}$$

An expense or a cost incurred in the operations of the enterprise is accompanied by one, or a combination of, the following:

1. Reduction of assets.
2. Increase in liabilities.
3. Increase in the ownership's claim.

Conversely, revenue received by the enterprise—

1. Increases assets, or
2. Decreases liabilities, or
3. Decreases the ownership's claim or affects a combination of the above.

Under the double-entry system, all transactions are recorded and classified and then summarized under appropriate account designations. Financial statements are formal, condensed presentations of the data derived from these accounts.

One of the best ways of visualizing the basic system of record-keeping and the principal interrelationships within it is by means of a diagram that portrays the major classes of accounts as well as the typical relationships among them.

Exhibit 2–1 is a graphic portrayal of the accounting cycle. A careful study of the illustration and the main movements reflected therein will enable the reader to follow the principal basic financial relationships and flows within a manufacturing enterprise. For the sake of clarity, infrequent or unusual flows and relationships have not been included.

The arrows connecting the principal asset, liability, capital, income, cost, and expense accounts indicate the direction of the usual flows. They do not, of course, indicate the relative size of the flows, which vary considerably from business to business and from one set of circumstances to another. The reader will notice that no account is dead-ended; that is, there are flows in and out of all accounts. This simply emphasizes the dynamic aspects of business and the accounting system that portrays its financial flows. As management invests, buys, makes, incurs costs, and sells, the quantity of money represented in each account is changing while the system as a whole remains in balance, its debit accounts (generally assets, costs, and expenses) always equaling its credit accounts (generally capital, liabilities, and income).

The flows into and out of each account shown in Exhibit 2–1 can be clearly traced in the diagram, and the chapters that follow—on the measurement of assets, liabilities, capital, and income—should increase and

Exhibit 2–1   The accounting cycle

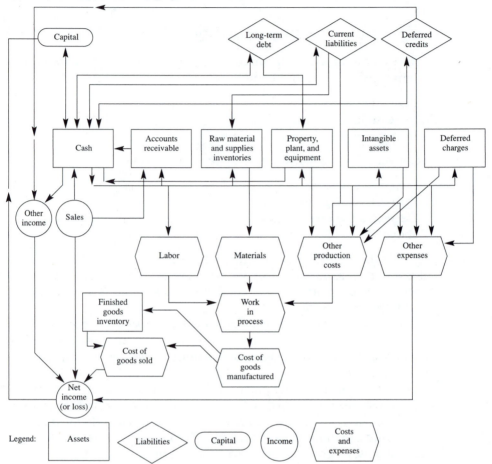

sharpen the reader's understanding of these flows as well as the principles governing their measurement.

The flows shown in the diagram of Exhibit 2–1, while always expressed in dollars, can be in many forms, such as cash, costs, and so forth. Thus, for example, if we trace the inflows and outflows affecting the Property, Plant, and Equipment account in Exhibit 2–1, we can learn a great deal about the interrelationships among the various accounts. The reader can, of course, focus in similar fashion on any account or constellation of accounts. Exhibit 2–2 presents those accounts appearing in the accounting cycle diagram (Exhibit 2–1) that relate to the Property, Plant, and Equipment account and the flows into and out of it.

Three distinct phases can be discerned here:

1. The accounting for the acquisition and disposition of property, plant, and equipment (PPE).

Exhibit 2-2   Typical flows to and from the Property, Plant, and Equipment account

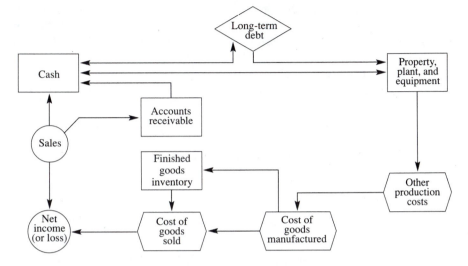

2. The accounting for the use of PPE (depreciation).
3. Accounting for the recovery, out of revenue, of amounts invested in PPE.

Acquisition and Disposition of PPE   The acquisition of PPE can be made by payment of cash or the incurrence of debt or both. Hence, the arrows in Exhibit 2-2 point to a flow from cash and/or long-term debt. Ultimately, the debt is paid back by cash, and this accounts for the flow from cash toward long-term debt. The flow from PPE to cash represents instances where PPE is sold for cash at any stage of its use. In all cases, the flows are equal; for example, an increase in PPE will result in an equal decrease in cash or a commensurate increase in long-term debt.

Use of PPE   PPE is acquired mostly for productive use. Consequently, its cost is allocated by means of the depreciation process (see Chapter 11) to "cost of goods manufactured." The flows shown in Exhibit 2-2 are from PPE to the Other Production Costs account from where they are charged to the Costs of Goods Manufactured account. The cost of goods manufactured that are sold is charged to the Cost of Goods Sold account, which, in turn, flows into the Net Income (or Profit and Loss) account, where all costs and revenues of the period are accumulated. The unsold goods manufactured remain in the Finished Goods Inventory, which is an asset account to be carried over to the next period. Ultimately, when the finished goods are sold, they find their way into the Costs of Goods Sold account.

Recovery of Cost of PPE   To complete the cycle, we observe in Exhibit 2–2 that the sales of finished goods, which normally are made at amounts designed to recover all costs and earn a profit, generate sales that are either for cash or result in claims, such as accounts receivable, which are subsequently collected in cash. It is through these sales that the outlay for PPE is ultimately recovered by the enterprise.

This completes our tracing of the Exhibit 2–2 subcycle of the accounting system where cash was used to buy PPE and was finally collected from the sale of the products in whose production the PPE was used. Examination of Exhibit 2–1 will reveal the existence of numerous other subcycles that make up the integrated whole.

Financial Statements

The accounting system that we examined above continually collects, summarizes, and updates data on assets, liabilities, capital, revenues, costs, and expenses. Periodically, it is necessary to take stock in order to ascertain the financial condition and the results of operations of the enterprise. This is done by presenting in summary form the details contained in the accounts. Based on the accounts included in the diagram of the accounting cycle (Exhibit 2–1), we can illustrate the composition of two major financial statements as follows:

Balance Sheet (statement of financial condition)   Exhibit 2–3 shows all assets, liabilities, and capital accounts extracted from Exhibit 2–1 and presented in conventional balance sheet format. This presentation reveals a number of basic relationships worth noting. On the left side are all the assets and unexpired costs in which the resources of the enterprise are invested at a specific point in time. On the right side of the statement are the sources from which these invested funds were financed, that is, the liabilities and the equity (capital) accounts. Since the *current liabilities* represent a short-term claim against the enterprise, the balance sheet shows the *current assets* generally available to meet these claims, principally cash, accounts receivable, and inventories. The difference between current assets and current liabilities is the working capital.

Income Statement (results of operations)   The second major financial statement differs in some important respects from the balance sheet. The income statement format shown in Exhibit 2–4 does not show the account balances as of a certain date, as is the case with the balance sheet, but rather shows the cumulative activity in the revenue, cost, and expense accounts for the period reported open. This is a report on the dynamic aspects of the enterprise—its results of operations. The final net income

Exhibit 2–3   Statement of financial condition (balance sheet)

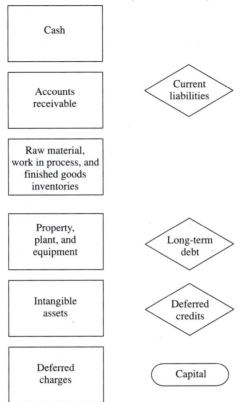

(or loss) is added to or deducted from capital through the Retained Earnings account. Thus, the net results of operations are incorporated in the balance sheet through their inclusion in the capital accounts.

Statement of Cash Flows   This third major financial statement is designed to provide information about the cash receipts and cash payments during a period. As will be seen from our discussion in Chapter 13, this statement is of major importance and interest to the financial analyst.

Ingenious as the recording framework of accounting is, it represents only the mechanical aspects of the discipline. Controlling the method of recording of assets, liabilities, and capital, as well as the size and the timing of cost and revenue flows, is an elaborate and pervasive set of standards. These standards in turn reflect the application of the basic objectives and conventions of accountancy. Since this body of conventions and standards determines the methodology involved in the basic measurements in financial statements, as well as their form and the degree

Exhibit 2–4   Income statement

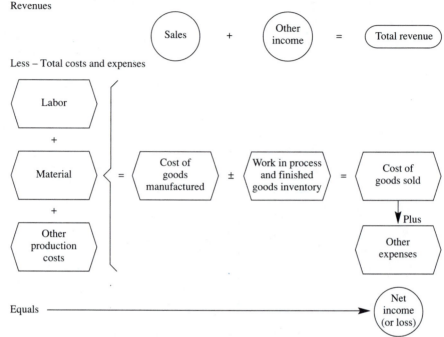

Revenues

of disclosure therein, the intelligent analysis of these statements requires a thorough familiarity with, and an understanding of, these conventions and standards.

QUESTIONS

1. What is financial statement analysis?
2. Describe the major foundations of the financial statement analysis discipline.
3. Why are financial statements important to the decision-making process in financial analysis?
4. List some of the more important limitations to which accounting data are subject.
5. What are some of the simplifications and the rigidities inherent in the accounting framework?
6. Discuss the relative importance of financial statement analysis in the total decision effort.
7. Define briefly the function of accounting.
8. The functions and purposes of accounting are accomplished at two levels; describe them.
9. What is the basic equation prevailing under the double-entry system of bookkeeping?

Chapter 3

ACCOUNTING OBJECTIVES, CONVENTIONS, AND STANDARDS—THEIR IMPLICATIONS FOR ANALYSIS

THE OBJECTIVES OF ACCOUNTING

While accountants have enjoyed some degree of success in agreeing upon the proper accounting in specific areas of practice, agreement on the basic bedrock objectives of accounting has, so far, eluded them. Not that there is a lack of broad generalizations on the subject—one firm suggested "fairness" as such a basic underlying tenet—but there is no broad consensus on objectives in a way that would help accountants settle their differences of opinion by referring to them. Accounting is, after all, not an exact science. It is rather a social science—its concepts, rooted in the value system of the society in which it operates, are socially determined and socially expressed. Consequently, broad agreement on *useful* generalizations regarding its basic objectives may be as hard to achieve in the future as it was in the past. The fact that the setting of accounting standards is basically a political process involving many parties at interest makes such agreement all the more difficult to attain.

In 1973, The Objectives of Financial Statements Study Group (Trueblood Committee) reported its conclusions in the "Objectives of Financial Statements." After agreeing with the generally held conclusion[1] that "the basic objective of financial statements is to provide information useful for making economic decisions," the Study Group listed, among others, the following two significant objectives:

> An objective of financial statements is to provide information useful to investors and creditors for predicting, comparing, and evaluating potential cash flows to them in terms of amount, timing, and related uncertainty.

---

[1] The Financial Accounting Standards Board (FASB) reports that only *37 percent* of respondents to its *First Discussion Memorandum* on the Conceptual Framework of Accounting could agree even with this basic conclusion. This provides an insight into the magnitude of the problem of reaching agreement on even the most basic accounting objectives.

> An objective of financial statements is to provide users with information for predicting, comparing, and evaluating enterprise earning power.

These objectives established a definite link between accounting and the basic decision functions that it serves, that is, the investing and lending processes. The Study Group recognized, however, that the objectives it enunciated can be attained only in stages and over time.

THE FASB CONCEPTUAL FRAMEWORK

In the mid-1970s, the Financial Accounting Standards Board (FASB) embarked on its Conceptual Framework (CF) project whose purpose it described as the establishment of a coherent system of interrelated objectives and concepts that are expected to lead to consistent financial accounting and reporting. These concepts are expected to guide the selection of events to be accounted for, the measurement of those events, as well as the means of their summarization and their communication to interested users.

It is expected that the CF should enable investors, creditors, and others to obtain increased understanding of and confidence in financial reporting. A CF centered on objectives can help narrow the range of acceptable accounting methods as well as promote increased comparability of financial information.

The FASB believes that without conceptual underpinnings, measures provided by accounting and financial reporting are essentially matters of judgment and personal opinion. Thus, the more precise definitions provided by the CF are expected to narrow subjectivity, circumscribe the areas for applying judgments, as well as provide a frame of reference for those judgments.

ORGANIZATION OF THE CONCEPTUAL FRAMEWORK (CF)

To implement the development of the CF, the FASB established a program to issue *Statements of Financial Accounting Concepts (SFACs)*. The purpose of *SFACs* is to set forth fundamentals on which financial accounting and reporting standards should be based, and these should serve the Board in developing standards of financial accounting and reporting.[2]

To date, the FASB has issued six *SFACs*. In *SFAC 1* (1978), "Objectives of Financial Reporting by Business Enterprises," the Board establishes

---

[2] Unlike *Statements of Financial Accounting Standards* (SFASs), *SFACs* do not establish generally accepted accounting principles (GAAP) and therefore are not intended to invoke Rule 203 of the Code of Professional Ethics of the AICPA, which deals with adherence to professional pronouncements.

the objectives of general-purpose external financial reporting by business enterprises. In most respects, *SFAC 1* does not diverge from the above-mentioned Trueblood Report.[3] The *Statement* in essence states that financial reporting can best serve investors and creditors to predict the amount, timing, and uncertainty of future cash flows *to them* by facilitating the prediction of the amount, timing, and uncertainty of future cash flows *to the business entity*. Moreover, financial reporting should provide information about the economic resources of an enterprise, the claims to those resources, and the effects of transactions, events, and circumstances that change its resources and claims to those resources.

A primary focus of financial reporting is information about earnings and its components. Financial reporting is also expected to provide information about an enterprise's financial performance during a period and about how management has discharged its stewardship responsibility to owners.[4]

SFAC 2 (1980), "Qualitative Characteristics of Accounting Information," is designed to examine the characteristics of accounting information that make it useful. These characteristics are viewed as a hierarchy of qualities (see Exhibit 3–1) among which usefulness for decision making is first in importance.

The hierarchy of accounting qualities separates user-specific qualities (e.g., understandability) from qualities inherent in the information. Information cannot be useful to decision makers unless it is understood by them regardless of how relevant it may otherwise be.

Relevance and *reliability* are two primary qualities that make accounting information useful for decision making. Information is relevant if it has the capacity to confirm or change a decision maker's expectations.

If information is received by a user too late to have an effect on a decision, it cannot have an impact on that decision. Hence, *timeliness* is an important aspect of relevance. So are *predictive value,* that is, value as an input into a predictive process, as well as *feedback value,* which is a characteristic of information that helps to confirm and to correct earlier predictions.

Information is *reliable* if it can be verified by agreement among a number of independent observers and if it represents what it purports to represent; that is, it has *representational faithfulness.* Reliability also implies completeness and *neutrality* of information.[5]

---

[3] Unlike the Trueblood Report, *SFAC 1* does not focus on forecasts or on accounting for social goals.

[4] While stewardship responsibilities are still mentioned, the shift in focus from stewardship accounting to user-oriented accounting is unmistakable. In earlier times, owners dissatisfied with the quality of stewardship moved to change managers. Modern investors, however, are more likely to change investments and thus need information on alternatives available to them.

[5] David Salomons in "The Politicization of Accounting," *Journal of Accountancy,* November 1978 stated: "Information cannot be neutral—it cannot therefore be reliable—if it

Exhibit 3–1 A hierarchy of accounting qualities

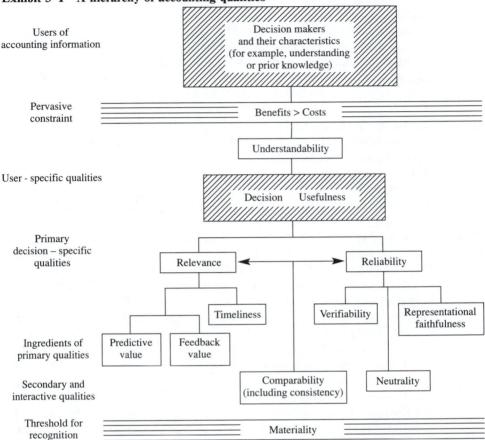

Source: FASB, *Statement of Financial Accounting Concepts No. 2,* "Qualitative Characteristics of Accounting Information" (Stamford, Conn., 1980).

Comparability, which includes consistency, interacts with relevance and reliability to contribute to the usefulness of information. Comparison is one of the most basic tools of analysis for decision making. Almost all

is selected or presented for the purpose of producing some chosen effect on human behavior. It is the quality of neutrality which makes a map reliable; and the essential nature of accounting, I believe it is cartographic. Accounting is financial map-making. The better the map, the more completely it represents the complex phenomena that are being mapped."

Oscar S. Gellein has provided us with an excellent and graphic description of neutrality: "Financial reporting is more like a barometer than a rainmaker. The barometer produces a reading for someone else to use in assessing the prospects of storm or clemency. The barometer has an impact if it causes someone to buy an umbrella, or not to buy an umbrella, or if someone invokes the power on high to prevent a storm, or sends a rainmaker up to seed the clouds. The barometer is useful to those with adverse interests if it describes what it purports to show and measures that accurately—that is, if it is neutral. But suppose those who designed the barometer decided that the public interest would be served better if evaluations and alternative-choice judgments involve comparisons of one sort or another. Thus, the ability to compare sets of accounting data of the same enterprise over time, or those of one enterprise with that of another, is very important to the decision-making process.

Overriding all these qualitative characteristics are *pervasive qualities* such as cost and benefits and materiality.

Information is costly to gather, process, interpret, and use. As with other services, information should be supplied only if its benefits exceed its costs.

Materiality is defined as "the magnitude of an omission or misstatement of accounting information that, in the light of surrounding circumstances, makes it possible that the judgment of a reasonable person relying on the information would be changed or influenced by the omission or misstatement."

In accounting, the concept of materiality assumes special significance because by its nature accounting information is not comprehended easily by the reader. The introduction therein of redundancy can make the task of its absorption and analysis even more difficult. Hence, to keep the information from being misleading, trivia should be kept out of it.

If the issue were simply one of omitting trivia, where there is general agreement on what trivia are, materiality would not be the problem area it is. At its root, the problem of materiality rests on the claim by users that some preparers of financial statements and their auditors use the concept to avoid disclosing that which they do not wish disclosed. It is this aspect that makes this concept significant to users of accounting data who must realize that accountants do omit, reclassify, or ignore data and information on the basis of what they consider to be their materiality, but that there are, as of now, no set criteria that guide either the accountant or the user of information to distinguish between what is material and what is not.

This state of affairs has resulted in action on a number of fronts. Some professional pronouncements (such as those on earnings per share and intercorporate investments) contain quantitative materiality benchmarks, and some recent Securities and Exchange Commission (SEC) pronouncements also specify materiality boundaries. Moreover, the FASB has issued a voluminous *Discussion Memorandum* on the subject on which it accepted comments through early 1976. The subject is supposed to be considered as part of the overall conceptual framework, but so far has not been so considered.

---

forebodings of storm were minimized and, accordingly, a bias toward clemency was built into the calibrations of the barometer. Surely, it is reasoned, an improved expectation of sunshine would be for the public good. The difficulty is that some would get wet because they did not have umbrellas, others would beseech for rain not knowing that it was on its way, clouds would be seeded needlessly, and worst of all, some persons would not duck into storm cellars or batten down the hatches soon enough to protect against imminent storm. And so it is with financial reporting."

SFAC 3 (1980), "Elements of Financial Statements of Business Enterprises," defines the following 10 elements of financial statements of business enterprises:

1. *Assets* are probable future economic benefits obtained or controlled by a particular entity as a result of past transactions or events.
   - An asset has three essential characteristics:
     - It embodies a probable future benefit that involves a capacity, singly or in combination with other assets, to contribute directly or indirectly to future net cash inflows.
     - The enterprise can obtain the benefit and control others' access to it.
       - Legal enforceability of a claim to the benefit is not a prerequisite for a benefit to qualify as an asset if its receipt by the enterprise is otherwise probable.
     - The transaction or other event giving rise to the enterprise's right to or control of the benefit has already occurred.
   - Once acquired, an asset continues as an asset of the enterprise until the enterprise collects it, transfers it to another entity, or uses it, or some other event or circumstance destroys the future benefit or removes the enterprise's ability to obtain it.
   - Valuation accounts that reduce or increase the carrying amount of an asset are sometimes found in financial statements; these are part of the related assets and are neither assets in their own right nor liabilities.

2. *Liabilities* are probable future sacrifices of economic benefits arising from present obligations of a particular entity to transfer assets or provide services to other entities in the future as a result of past transactions or events.
   - A liability has three essential characteristics:
     - It embodies a present duty or responsibility to one or more other entities that entails settlement by probable future transfer or use of assets at a specified or determinable date, on occurrence of a specified event, or on demand.
     - The duty or responsibility obligates a particular enterprise, leaving it little or no discretion to avoid the future sacrifice.
       - The existence of a legally enforceable claim is not a prerequisite for an obligation to qualify as a liability if the future payment of cash or other transfer of assets to settle the obligation is otherwise probable.
     - The transaction or other event obligating the enterprise has already happened.
   - Once incurred, a liability continues as a liability of the enterprise until the enterprise settles it, or another event or circumstance discharges it or removes the enterprise's responsibility to settle it.

3. *Equity* is the residual interest in the assets of an entity that remains after deducting its liabilities.
   - In a business enterprise, the equity is the ownership interest (owners' equity).

4. *Investment by owners* are increases in net assets of a particular enterprise resulting from transfers to it from other entities of something valuable to obtain or increase equity (ownership interests).
   - That which is received includes most commonly assets, but may also include services or satisfaction or conversion of liabilities of the enterprise.
   - Investments by owners increase equity (ownership interests).

5. *Distributions to owners* are decreases in net assets of a particular enterprise resulting from transferring assets, rendering services, or incurring liabilities by the enterprise to owners.
   - Distributions to owners decrease equity (owners' interest).
     - When dividends are declared, the enterprise incurs a liability to transfer assets to owners in the future, resulting in equity being reduced and liabilities increased.
     - Reacquisition by an entity of its own equity securities by transferring assets or incurring liabilities to owners is a distribution to owners.

6. *Comprehensive income* is the change in equity (net assets) of an enterprise during a period from transactions and other events and circumstances from nonowner sources. It includes all changes in equity during a period except those resulting from investment by owners and distributions to owners.
   - Over the life of a business enterprise, its comprehensive income equals the net of its cash receipts and cash outlays (excluding cash investments by owners and cash distributions to owners).
   - Comprehensive income results from:
     - Exchange transactions and other transfers between the enterprise and other entities that are not its owners.
     - The enterprise's productive efforts.
     - Price changes, casualties, and other effects of interaction between the enterprise and its economic, legal, social, political, and physical environment.
   - Comprehensive income, as defined, is a return on financial capital as distinguished from a return on physical capital.
     - The major difference between the two capital maintenance concepts is that "holding gains and losses" are included in return on capital under the financial capital concept, but these are called capital maintenance adjustments under the physical capital concept and are included directly in equity and are not included in return on capital (see also Chapter 14).
     - The term *earnings* has not been used because it may be used to designate a different concept that is a component part of (narrower or less than) comprehensive income, and earnings, when defined, may be a return on physical capital or may be a return on financial capital.
   - The Board has not as yet chosen between the financial and physical capital maintenance concepts for deciding the meaning and appropriate display of "earnings."

- Capital maintenance concepts are the subject of another project.
- Comprehensive income comprises two related but distinguishable types of components:
  - ○ Revenues, expenses, gains, and losses.
  - ○ Intermediate components or measures that result from combining revenues, expenses, gains, and losses (in effect, subtotals); examples are gross margin, contribution margin, income from continuing operations (pretax and after tax), and operating income.

7. *Revenues* are inflows or other enhancements of assets of an entity or settlements of its liabilities (or a combination of both) during a period of delivering or producing goods, rendering services, or other activities that constitute the entity's ongoing major or central operations.
   - Revenues represent actual or expected cash inflows (or the equivalent) that have occurred or will eventuate as a result of the enterprise's ongoing major or central operations during the period.

8. *Expenses* are outflows or other using up of assets or incurrences of liabilities (or a combination of both) during a period of delivering or producing goods, rendering services, or carrying out other activities that constitute the enterprise's ongoing major or central operations.
   - Expenses represent actual or expected cash outflows (or the equivalent) that have occurred or will eventuate as a result of the enterprise's ongoing major or central operations during the period.

9. *Gains* are increases in equity (net assets) from peripheral or incidental transactions of an entity and from all other transactions and other events and circumstances affecting the entity during a period except those that result from revenues or investments by owners.

10. *Losses* are decreases in equity (net assets) from peripheral or incidental transactions of an entity and from all other transactions and other events and circumstances affecting the entity during a period except those that result from expenses or distributions to owners.

SFAC 3 also defines or describes certain other concepts that underlie the 10 elements listed above:

Items that qualify under the definitions of elements of financial statements and that meet the criteria for recognition and measurement are accounted for and included in financial statements by the use of accrual accounting procedures. Accrual accounting and related concepts include the following processes:
- Accrual accounting attempts to recognize noncash events and circumstances as they occur; specifically, accrual is the accounting process of recognizing assets, liabilities, and components of comprehensive income for amounts expected to be received or paid, usually in cash, in the future.
- Deferral is the accounting system process of recognizing a liability from a current cash receipt or an asset resulting from a current cash payment, with deferred recognition of components of comprehensive income.

- Allocation is the accounting process of reducing a liability recorded as a result of a cash receipt by recognizing revenues or reducing an asset recorded as a result of a cash payment recognizing expenses or cost production payment.
- Realization is the process of converting noncash resources and rights into money and is most precisely used in accounting and financial reporting to refer to sales of assets for cash or claims to cash. The related terms, realized and unrealized, therefore, identify revenues or gains or losses on assets sold and unsold, respectively.
- Recognition is the process of formally recording or incorporating an item in the financial statements of an entity. Thus, an asset, liability, revenue, expense, gain, or loss may be recognized (recorded) or unrecognized (unrecorded). "Realization" and "recognition" are not used as synonyms, as they sometimes are in accounting and financial literature.

The Board emphasizes that the definitions in this *Statement* neither require nor presage upheavals in present practice, although they may in time lead to some evolutionary changes in practice or in the ways certain items are viewed.

The Board expects most assets and liabilities in present practice to continue to qualify as assets or liabilities under the definitions in this *Statement.*

SFAC 4 deals with objectives of financial reporting by nonbusiness organizations and is outside the scope of this work.

SFAC 5 (1984) "Recognition and Measurement in Financial Statements of Business Enterprises" basically endorses present practices while allowing for gradual, evolutionary change.

The *Statement* emphasizes that a full set of financial statements should show:

a. Financial position at the end of the period.
b. Earnings for the period.
c. Comprehensive income for the period.
d. Cash flows during the period.
e. Investments by and distributions to owners during the period.

A significant change here is the distinction between what the Board refers to as *earnings* and what it terms *comprehensive income.* Earnings is equivalent to net income as currently reported, except that it does not include the cumulative effect of accounting changes. Comprehensive income is the sum of earnings, cumulative effect adjustments, and certain other changes in net assets such as due to decline in the value of marketable equity securities charged to shareholders' equity under *SFAS 12* and foreign currency translation adjustments under *SFAS 52.*

The basic approach to the recognition issue is the identification of the information that financial statements should show. According to the

Board, the primary financial statements consist of elements—assets, liabilities, revenues, and expenses. To be included in the financial statements, the recognition of an item is required when all of the following four criteria are met:

1. The item must meet the definition of an element of financial statements as defined by *SFAC 3*.
2. The item is reliably measurable.
3. The item is relevant, that is, the information about it is capable of making a difference in user decisions.
4. The information about the item is reliable; that is, it is representationally faithful, verifiable, and neutral.

This *Statement* did not resolve the major measurement dilemma of current value versus historical cost. Several measurement attributes are used in present practice, and the Board expects the use of different attributes to continue. However, the Board gives itself an option to pursue more extensive use of current values, stating that: "Information based on current prices should be recognized if it is sufficiently relevant and reliable to justify the costs involved and more relevant than alternative information."

SFAC 6 (1985) had modified *SFAC 3* so as to make it applicable to nonbusiness organizations as well.

IMPLICATIONS FOR ANALYSIS

The CF project represents an earnest attempt by the FASB to establish a logical and coherent framework of interrelated objectives and concepts that are intended to enhance the conceptual foundations of accounting standards and to promote confidence in and acceptance of these standards.

The analyst must understand that contrary to what some would have us believe, accounting is *not* a science (concerned as science is with natural laws and predictions based on them) but rather a service activity[6] that in order to be useful to society draws for its execution and improvement on related fields of science and, particularly, social science.

Being rooted in the social system of which it is part, accounting, whose issues affect different parties at interest in different ways, is always subject

---

[6] K. S. Peasnell, in "Statement of Accounting Theory and Theory Acceptance: A Review Article," *Accounting and Business Research,* Summer 1978, pp. 220–21, stated it as follows: "Accounting is not a science; it is a service activity. Accounting therefore should be equated not with the sciences, but with fields like medicine, technology, and law of which the principal raison d'etre is an external social need. Sure, service professions make use of scientific (i.e., empirical) knowledge—they often contribute to it—but their principal concern is with doing a particular job of work, fulfilling a social need."

to political processes.[7] Thus, the setting of accounting concepts and standards is in itself a political process.[8]

As one astute observer put it, "Too often, accounting theory is invoked more as a tactic to buttress one's preconceived notions rather than as a genuine arbiter of contending views."[9] This problem was exemplified in the debate surrounding the replacement of *SFAS 8* by *SFAS 52* in which Board members for and against the change referred to identical portions of the CF as support for their respective positions.

Analysts should be understanding of the accounting profession's efforts in its attempts to establish a sound CF and should be supportive of its goals, which are, ultimately, in the analysts' best interests. At the same time, analysts must be aware of the fact that previous attempts at establishing conceptual frameworks have not yielded universally accepted concepts or "truths"—universal in the sense that men would settle differences of opinion by referring to them.[10] In its preamble to the exposure draft of *SFAC 5* the Board admitted that the statement "would not produce instant, indisputable answers to questions about whether a particular event should be recognized and when, and what amount best measures it." Thus, those who have pinned high hopes on *SFAC 5* may have their doubts about the value of the CF reinforced. The Board took the cautious position that the "establishment of objectives and identification of fundamental concepts will not directly solve financial accounting and reporting problems. Rather objectives give direction, and concepts are tools for solving problems. Therefore different people can obtain different directions and the use of tools is up to the user.

According to FASB Chairman Kirk, *SFAC 5* represents the "end of the trail" for the CF. The Board seems to have come to the conclusion that change in accounting will continue as an evolutionary process and will *not* come as the result of the CF. Since up to now accounting change has always come about as the result of an evolutionary process, the question arises of whether this entire exercise of establishing a CF has been worthwhile. If *SFAC 5,* on which most hopes were pinned, merely describes

---

[7] For example, in the United States, the investor is the primary focus of financial reporting. In other countries, the focus may be on different constituencies (e.g., creditors or labor) that have vital and legitimate interests in financial reporting.

[8] R. C. Watts and J. L. Zimmerman in "Towards a Positive Theory of the Determination of Accounting Standards," *The Accounting Review,* January 1978, demonstrate that accounting theories have been utilized in large measure to support a particular group's lobbying positions on existing or proposed standards.

[9] S. Zeff in R. Sterling, ed., *Institutional Issues in Public Accounting* (Lawrence, Kan.: Scholars Book Co., 1974), p. 177.

[10] Such views were expressed by this author on earlier attempts at establishing conceptual frameworks in "Whither Accounting Research?" *Journal of Accountancy,* December 1965. A pessimistic assessment of the potential value and effect of the FASB's statement of objectives and definitions is reached by Professors N. Dopuch and S. Sunder in an excellent analysis: "FASB's Statement on Objectives and Elements of Financial Accounting: A Review," *The Accounting Review,* January 1980.

and endorses present accounting practices, what is its contribution? Substantial questions regarding the nature of earnings and of comprehensive income and the differences between them were left unanswered. Similarly the resolution of questions relating to accounting for changing prices (inflation), the recognition of executory contracts, and a host of other problem areas were left on the knees of future evolving conditions.

The CF has had some positive results. It has contributed to a good debate on the objectives of accounting and identified the major users of financial statements. It also identified the qualitative characteristics of accounting information and the qualities which make it useful. Moreover, it defined elements of financial statements, such as assets, liabilities, owners' equity, revenues, expenses, gains, losses, and comprehensive income. It has resulted in some better and more thought-through terminology and superior definitions of accounting-related concepts. It may even contribute to a higher degree of internal consistency in promulgated standards. But it has disappointed those who thought that a group of people in Connecticut was going to come up with a solid framework for resolving today's as well as tomorrow's vexing problems of accounting. By stating its reliance on gradual change and evolution, the Board has admitted that it cannot meet the great expectations many placed in it. From the point of view of users and analysts of financial statements, this admission is a healthy development which will give them a more realistic view of what can and cannot be accomplished in financial reporting standard setting.

Change in accounting has come mostly as a process by which the standard setters of the time addressed the problems which demanded prompt solutions. The motivations for diligent effort and for compromise were at hand and so solutions were found. And so it will probably continue in the future. The resolution of these problems will always be influenced by the cries and protestations of those most affected by them.

To many observers, including the author, this will not come as a surprise. For one, social sciences, such as accounting is, do not have codified conceptual frameworks. There are none for law, economics, or finance. Moreover, Board members who have experienced firsthand how difficult it is to settle even more limited problems of practice, such as those of foreign operations, pensions, or taxes, realize that to settle great issues of accounting in advance is beyond them. The limited areas which have been addressed so far have required a great many compromises and adjustments to contemporary conditions and forces. The CF remains a shining theoretical ideal—worthy of trial but, in large part, unattainable.

Analysts must realize that agreement on accounting objectives or standards is often obtained by couching such statements in language that is vague enough so as to allow room for various interest groups to adopt their own interpretations of their operational meaning. It follows that in using the accountant's product, analysts must continue to be alert to the fact that in practice considerations of self-interest can govern accounting presentations just as much as can logic and rational objectives.

ACCOUNTING PRINCIPLES OR STANDARDS

Accounting principles are the rules and operative guides of accounting. These rules, which are now more accurately viewed as standards, determine such matters as how assets are measured, when liabilities are incurred, when income is recognized as earned, and when expenses and losses accrue. Thus, to the user of accounting data and statements, an understanding of these rules is essential. No intelligent and valid analysis of financial statements can be undertaken without ascertaining as fully as possible which accounting principles were used in the preparation of such statements and how they were applied.

How Accounting Standards Are Established

Accounting principles have been long in developing and are subject to continuous innovation, modification, and change. Thus, the principle of depreciation accounting, under which the cost of a productive fixed asset is allocated to revenue over the useful life of such asset, is well established today, but it was not fully accepted as recently as the turn of the century. The tremendous growth of leasing after World War II has moved the accounting profession to reconsider the accounting for leases and change it significantly. Over the years, accounting principles have changed in response to developments in, and the needs of, the business community and its requirements and expectations.

It is now generally accepted that the primary responsibility for the fair presentation of financial statements rests with the reporting management of an enterprise. However, the responsibility for the development of accounting standards, which govern this reporting, has been borne primarily by the organized accounting profession and by the Securities and Exchange Commission (SEC) and, to a lesser extent, by the American Accounting Association (AAA) and the New York Stock Exchange (NYSE).

The Role of the Accounting Profession   The reasons for the accounting profession's assumption of early leadership in the development of accounting principles are not hard to find. One of the profession's major and unique functions is that of attesting to the fairness of presentation of financial statements. Yet, the term *fairness of presentation* requires a frame of reference by which it may be judged. Generally accepted accounting principles (GAAP) are intended to provide such a frame of reference, and the accounting profession is presumed to have both the independence and the technical capability required for their development. In pursuing the development of GAAP, the profession was not only performing a vital public service but was also catering to its own vital interests.

The earliest effort of the profession was a "Memorandum on Balance Sheet Audits" prepared by the American Institute of Certified Public Accountants (AICPA) at the request of the Federal Trade Commission. It was published in 1917 in the *Federal Reserve Bulletin* under the title "Uniform Accounting." A revision of this compendium of approved methods of preparing financial statements was prepared by the AICPA and published in 1929 by the Federal Reserve Board under the title "Verification of Financial Statements."

The winds of social and economic change that blew fast and furious starting with the 1929 financial collapse have exerted a strong and decisive influence on the pace of accounting change. While no knowledgeable source would place the major blame for the economic debacle at the door of poor accounting and inadequate reporting, there was, nevertheless, a general recognition of the fact that improvements in accounting principles and in disclosure were long overdue. The profession found a willing partner favoring change in the NYSE whose reputation was, to say the least, tarnished by the debacle that began in 1929. Propelled by strong and renewed incentives to lift the financial accountability of companies listed with it to higher standards, the NYSE cooperated with a committee of the AICPA to spell them out. The result of a two-year correspondence between the AICPA Committee and the Committee on Stock List of the NYSE was published in 1934. It embodied a number of basic principles of accounting to be followed by listed companies—clarification on the limitations of financial statements and agreement with regard to the wording of the auditor's opinion. This was the first recorded instance where the phrase "accepted accounting principles" (later changed to "generally accepted accounting principles") was used.

With the establishment of a research department, the AICPA undertook in 1938 to put the effort of developing accounting principles on a permanent basis. To this end, a Committee on Accounting Procedure was established whose purpose was to reduce the areas of difference in accounting and to narrow the choices available in the area of alternative accounting principles.

The Committee on Accounting Procedure at first endeavored to prepare a comprehensive statement on accounting principles but abandoned this goal for the more attainable one of dealing with individual areas of controversy and difficulty. During its tenure, the committee considered a great many accounting problems and issued pronouncements in the form of 51 *Accounting Research Bulletins (ARBs)*. Issued with the approval of at least two thirds of committee members, the authority of the

ARBs, except in cases in which formal adoption by the Institute membership has been asked and secured, rested upon the general acceptability of opinions so reached.

By 1959, criticism from outside as well as from within the accounting profession led to the replacement of the Committee on Accounting Procedure by the Accounting Principles Board (APB). This body, vested with greater authority and supported by an enlarged research staff, was charged with narrowing the areas of differences in accounting principles and in promoting the written expression of what generally accepted accounting principles are. The APB, which was replaced by the Financial Accounting Standards Board (FASB) in 1973, issued 31 *Opinions,* some of which have improved the theory and the practice of significant areas (such as the area of pension accounting), some of which may have improved the theory but had an inadequate impact on practice (such as in the area of leasing), and some of which confused the areas of theory and practice (such as the areas of earnings per share).

It is clear that in many cases the APB has attempted to change a principle adopted by its predecessor committee, not because the theory behind it was inherently deficient but rather because it had been ignored or abused in practice. The adoption of a new theory does not, however, remedy the original deficiency, which was a lack of voluntary observance of the old one by members of the profession. It does not, moreover, assure observance of the new theory introduced in place of the old one. The crux of the matter, especially as concerns the user of financial data, is, in short, that he must not only understand the theory behind the accounting principles promulgated by the accounting profession but he must also know:

1. To what extent the spirit as well as the letter of these principles is observed in practice.
2. What degree of latitude of implementation these principles, by their very nature, permit.

Generally, in determining the accounting standards applicable to a given situation, the auditor will first turn to official pronouncements of the FASB, which also incorporate pronouncements of its predecessors that are still in force, FASB Interpretations, specialized sources such as AICPA Industry Guides and AICPA Interpretation and, as applicable, to official pronouncements of the SEC, such as their regulations pertaining to disclosure in financial statements, the *Accounting Series Release (ASRs),* now codified as *Financial Reporting Releases (FRRs), Staff Accounting Bulletins (SABs),* or administrative rulings.

In the absence of any authoritative pronouncement in the first category, the auditor will turn to books and articles written by eminent and well-known authors. He may also review published financial statements with a view to finding authority and precedent for various principles.

It appears that under the AICPA's directives, which required disclosure of departures from the pronouncements of the FASB and predecessors, the auditor will, for all practical purposes, have to follow the accounting principles laid down or adopted by the FASB. Use of alternative principles also enjoying authoritative support will shift the burden of their defense onto the auditor.

A departure from promulgated principles is, however, far from easy to identify. The criteria of many pronouncements and opinions are often so vague and broad and so much subject to a wide range of interpretation that at present definite departures from such pronouncements would be difficult to identify unequivocally. Consequently, the practical effect of the requirement to disclose departures from professional *Opinions* is more apparent than real.

Disclosure of Accounting Policies   In recognition of the fact that information about the accounting policies adopted and followed by both profit-oriented and not-for-profit entities is essential to users of financial statements, the APB issued *Opinion 22,* "Disclosure of Accounting Policies."

The *Opinion* requires disclosure of accounting policies either in a summary or a footnote that is an integral part of the financial statements. The disclosure would identify and describe accounting principles followed and the methods of applying those principles that materially affect the determination of financial position, changes in financial position, or results of operations. Emphasis should be placed on describing principles and methods where a selection had been made from existing acceptable alternatives and where unusual, innovative, or industry-oriented principles and methods had been followed. In addition, the *Opinion* provides examples, not necessarily all-inclusive, of the other types of disclosures that would be common.

The *Financial Accounting Standards Board* (FASB), composed of seven full-time paid members, began to function as the accounting standards-setting body of the accounting profession in 1973. Board members are appointed by a group of trustees which in addition to AICPA members include representatives from private industry, security analysts, and others.

In spite of expected criticism from many quarters, the FASB represents a very significant improvement over its predecessors. Before issuing a Financial Accounting Standard on a subject, the Board issues, in most cases, a *discussion memorandum* that is exposed for public comment. Written comments can be filed with the Board, and oral comments can be voiced at public hearings that generally precede the issuance of an Exposure Draft of a *Statement of Financial Accounting Standards (SFAS).* After further exposure and comment, a final *SFAS* is usually issued. Interpretations of previously issued pronouncements are also issued from time to time.

Another significant improvement in procedure is the inclusion in most *SFASs* of careful and elaborate explanations of the rationale of the Board for the statements it issues, explanations of how comments to the Board were dealt with, as well as examples of actual applications.

The Financial Accounting Foundation (the FASB's parent body) adopted a number of structural changes in the FASB's operations, including greater participation by financial statement users in the rule-making process.

The Influence of the Securities and Exchange Commission   The SEC, which is an independent quasi-judicial agency of the U.S. government, administers, *inter alia,* the Securities Act of 1933 and the Securities Exchange Act of 1934.

The primary purpose of the 1933 act is to ensure that there be given to a potential investor in a security being offered for public sale all the material facts relating to the security that are needed in order to decide whether to buy it. Such facts are disclosed in a registration statement, which must be filed with the SEC and which must contain specified information.

The function of the SEC as regards a registration statement filed with it under the 1933 act is to examine it to see that a full and accurate disclosure is made of all pertinent information relating to the company's business, its securities, its financial position and earnings, and the underwriting arrangements relating to the particular security that is being marketed. The SEC can require such changes to be made in the original registration statements as are necessary to achieve this objective. Until the SEC approves the statement, amended as necessary, it can prevent the registration statement from becoming effective and the securities from being sold. The SEC is not, however, concerned with the merits of any security registered with it.

Since its inception, the SEC has encouraged the development and improvement of accounting and auditing practice. That encouragement has, in practice, taken on a number of forms. The Commission has issued specific rules and regulations concerning the preparation of financial statements that have to be filed with it and the degree of detail that they should contain. The Commission's prosecution of numerous accounting and auditing infractions of its rules has resulted in a form of "case law" that provides important clues and precedents in the area of accounting principles and auditing procedure. Some of the most important decisions on accounting and auditing, as well as other important pronouncements on these subjects, are incorporated in *Accounting Series Releases (ASRs)* which numbered 307 when the Commission codified them in 1982 into *Financial Reporting Release (FRR)* No. 1 and for enforcement-related releases into *Accounting and Auditing Enforcement Releases (AAERs).* Less formal *Staff Accounting Bulletins (SABs)* are also issued.

While many of the aforementioned sources on the SEC's position on accounting and auditing matters deal with specific instances and applications, the Commission has recognized the impossibility of issuing rules to cover all possible situations. Thus, an important part of the SEC's influence on matters of accounting takes the form of conferences between companies and their accountants and the SEC staff and the numerous unpublished rulings and guidelines that are a result thereof.

The importance of the SEC position can be understood best in the light of the statutory authority vested in it. It has the ability to enforce adherence to its rules over an ever-increasing number of companies that have come under its jurisdiction.

In over 60 years of its existence, the SEC has grown in competence and experience. It has wide regulatory authority over accounting and has the ability to enforce it. Moreover, it has assembled a fine and most experienced pool of accounting talent. It seems to have understood the great difficulties and complexities involved in finding universally valid and acceptable accounting principles. As a result, it has recognized the superiority of a system of widely diffused research efforts to mere promulgation by central edict. The SEC has recognized that the requirement for certification of financial statements to be filed with the Commission has placed a heavy responsibility upon the accounting profession and has encouraged it to exercise leadership in accounting and auditing matters. At the same time the Commission has not hesitated to criticize and prod, to take exception to accounting presentations, and to discipline members of the profession when circumstances warranted. In short, the Commission has so far exemplified not a rigid and arbitrary exercise of governmental authority but the sparing use of this authority in a helpful way.

The SEC approach toward accounting practice is, in large measure, determined by current public attitudes toward, and confidence in, financial reporting and to some extent by the personality and the temperament of its chief accountant. These have changed over the years and so we have seen from time to time the application of novel approaches to the enforcement of auditing standards. Thus, in recent years, audit firms were forced to consent to quality reviews of their practice by committees of peers, and the FASB was confronted with a flood of new SEC requirements in areas it considered as being under its jurisdiction. Moreover, the SEC has become increasingly aggressive in modifying FASB standards as, for example, by its modification of the effective date of *SFAS 13* on leases, and its intervention in price-level accounting and in oil and gas accounting.

In 1973, the SEC reiterated in *FRR* No. 1, Section 101,[11] its policy of "looking to the private sector for leadership in establishing and improving

---

[11] In 1982, the *ASRs* were codified into *Financial Reporting Release (FRR)* No. 1 and will be referred to by section number.

accounting principles and standards." It officially recognizes FASB *statements* as authoritative.

The constructive influence that the SEC has been exercising over the development of accounting principles should, however, not mislead the financial analyst into believing that the financial statements included in documents filed with the Commission are more reliable than others from the point of view of the accounting used in their preparation. They are unfortunately not much more reliable because they rarely reflect a higher-than-average level of the "state of the art" and also because the staff of the SEC is far too limited in number and in capabilities to enable it to review thoroughly all the documents submitted to it.

The Influence of Other Organizations   Two other bodies whose influence on the formation of accounting principles must be considered are the American Accounting Association (AAA) and the Stock Exchanges, particularly the New York Stock Exchange (NYSE).

The AAA has a membership composed primarily of accounting educators. Being one step removed from the practice of the profession, they have a more detached point of view and, by the very nature of their calling, a more scholarly and theoretical one. The AAA has long considered the inconsistencies in accounting theory as calling for a broad effort to establish an integrated framework of accounting theory. To this they have contributed significantly with a series of monographs (starting in 1937) and with statements on accounting principles and theory, the first one published in 1936 and the most recent in 1977. While the AAA statements on accounting theory have been influential in shaping accounting thought, they have no official standing in the accounting profession on which they are in no way binding.

Committees of the AAA have made significant contributions to deliberations on accounting standards. However, the great contributions which independent academicians are capable of, have, so far, not materialized. Thus, most academic research has, regrettably, avoided the issues of contemporary financial reporting and the concurrent problems and abuses of practice with which this work deals.

The role of the NYSE in the formulation of accounting theory has never been an active one. As already shown, the Exchange had in the early 1930s taken an interest in financial reporting and in correspondence with the AICPA has promoted the setting down of accounting and auditing standards.

Like the SEC, the NYSE has the ability to enforce adherence to standards. The basic instrument by which the Exchange secures compliance to its standards is the listing agreement. This agreement defines, among other things, the minimum accounting disclosure required in the financial statements of the listed company.

One important way in which the New York and American Stock Exchanges have lent support to the efforts of the AICPA in the area of accounting improvements is by urging listed companies to comply with specific professional pronouncements.

Improvements in Accounting Principles—Implications for Financial Analysis

Substantial progress has been made by professional bodies and by the SEC in their endeavor to narrow the range of acceptable alternatives in accounting principles, to increase the amount of meaningful disclosure, and to improve the overall level of financial accounting. This progress notwithstanding, the serious user of published financial reports knows that the room for further necessary improvements is great indeed and that much remains to be done in these areas.

It would be naive and unrealistic to hope that the time is anywhere near when the financial analyst will no longer need to concern himself with the accounting principles that underlie the financial statements that he uses and "go forward from the figures" with his analysis rather than spending time and energy to first "go behind those figures." The critical examination, analysis, and evaluation of the accounting behind the financial statements is, and will, remain an important part of the totality of the analyst's task. Among the more important reasons for this conclusion are the following:

1. The vital interest of management in the results of operations and the financial position that it reports has in the past, and will continue in the future, to exert a strong influence on the manner in which it accounts for and presents these results. While the attesting auditor may, over the years, have increased the ability and the resolve to withstand management pressure, at the present time the evidence of practice indicates that both his ability and his willingness to do so are limited. In addition to problems related to professional and financial independence, there are problems inherent in the accounting conventions and principles themselves:

a. There is the difference between theory and practice. Rarely are accounting theory pronouncements so well and so comprehensively spelled out as to prevent practice from deviating from their spirit and intent.[12] Moreover, most accounting principles apply only to factors that are considered "material," and yet, so far the profession has failed to provide guidelines and a working definition of what is

---

[12] For an informative analysis of abuses in financial reporting, see A. J. Briloff, *Unaccountable Accounting* (New York: Harper & Row, 1972); and by the same author, *More Debits than Credits* (New York: Harper & Row, 1976), and *The Truth about Corporate Accounting* (New York: Harper & Row, 1981). Subsequent articles by this author, particularly in *Barron's,* as well as examples throughout this text document the persistence as well as the pervasiveness of financial reporting problems.

to be considered "material." (See also discussion earlier in this chapter.)

b. A number of important areas of accounting theory, such as, for example, business combinations and product cost accounting and allocations, are not adequately covered by professional pronouncements. This contributes to even greater leeway and variety of practice.

c. New industries, changing business practices, and the ingenuity of "financial architects" result in an inevitable lag of accounting theory behind accounting practice. In general, accounting theory is developed to cope with existing problems rather than to anticipate new and emerging ones such as those recently found in the real estate development, franchising, savings and loan, and scientific development industries.

2. Progress toward the development of uniform and fair accounting principles has been and continues to be hampered by powerful interest groups. These exert pressure to have their interests represented in the formulation of accounting requirements that affect reporting practices in their particular industries. Recent examples of such lobbying are the efforts of bankers, of the insurance industry, the extractive industries, and the real estate industry to have their reporting interests reflected in the formulation of accounting principles.

A particularly ominous development was the intervention of congressional legislation in the establishment of accounting principles.[13] Also, in its apparent desire to allow reflection of the maximum improvement in corporate reported earnings from the investment tax credit, Congress has stated that no taxpayer shall be required to use any particular method of accounting for the investment credit in reports subject to the jurisdiction of any federal agency. This legislation thwarted the second attempt by the APB to develop a single uniform method of accounting for the investment credit. While the Tax Reform Act of 1986 has rendered this a moot point, the precedent of legislative intervention has been established.

A few more recent examples should be mentioned where accounting policy was dictated not by the requirements of full disclosure and fair presentation but by a desire to avoid certain perceived unfavorable economic consequences:

a. The problems of U.S. banks with loans extended to less developed countries (LDC) are well known. Approaches dealing with this problem have focused on methods of accounting that would soften

---

[13] That legislation, in 1975, obligated the SEC to prescribe accounting practices for the oil and gas industry in the United States. This specialized accounting topic was in recent years the subject of policy declarations and reversal by both the SEC and the FASB (see Chapter 11).

the impact of inevitable loan write-offs. Bankers and regulators charged with insuring the integrity of the banking system and its insured deposits considered various proposals to spread the loan write-off losses over a number of years instead of accounting for them, as is proper, in the year in which they were identified. There were even suggestions that U.S. banks not be required to write off debts to LDC on the grounds that doing so would be bad for the earnings of U.S. banks and would plunge the global financial system into disarray. Only slowly and grudgingly, after seeing the quoted market for LDC loans develop at mere fractions of par, did some bankers, led by Citicorp, start to provide partially for these loan losses. The size of such loan loss provisions, however, were related more to the bank's ability or willingness to record such losses than to the size of actual economic losses incurred.

b. The problems of the nation's savings and loan (S&L) industry and the related bailout at taxpayer expense resulted from the blunders and the dishonesty of many participants. However, unsound accounting motivated by a desire to postpone recognition of losses and insolvency played a disturbingly important role here. One area of ostrich accounting related to an unwillingness to recognize the decline in value of mortgages receivable when interest rates soared. Timely recognition of such losses would have resulted in earlier remedial action and avoidance of much larger losses. Another area of abuse consisted of "regulatory assistance" offered by regulators to healthy S&Ls in order to induce them to absorb failing savings units. That assistance took the form of in effect allowing the acquiring units to debase the acquisition accounting by allowing accumulated deficits to be accounted for as goodwill which could be written off over an extended period of time.

c. When the Auditing Standards Division of the AICPA proposed that an industry practice under which costs associated with growing crops were expensed be changed to the inventorying of these costs, the Hawaii sugar and pineapple industry rose up against the proposal. The fear was that the proposed accounting, which would have improved income reporting, would also lead to a loss of special tax treatments. The industry prevailed. When on January 4, 1984, the AICPA issued its final draft on "Accounting by Agricultural Producers and Agricultural Cooperatives" it stated in part "This statement also does not apply to growers of timber, pineapple and sugarcane grown in tropical regions. . . ."

d. In 1986 the SEC, responding to pressures of small independent oil producers, decided against a staff recommendation that the agency consider abolishing the full cost accounting method under which drilling costs, even those resulting in dry holes, can be capitalized.

The decision was based on the conclusion that the harm to struggling producers would outweigh any benefits to investors from the more realistic accounting.

e. That the influence of economic consequences on accounting policy is a worldwide phenomenon is illustrated in an article on government-imposed accounting in Sweden.[14] To help rescue Uddeholm, a leading manufacturer of steel and forest products, the Swedish government extended a substantial loan to the company. However, since accounting for this transaction as a loan, which it was, would not have improved Uddeholm's financial condition sufficiently, the Swedish Parliament forced by means of legislation an accounting for this transaction *as if* it were a subsidy. Thus, the proper accounting was defeated by legislative fiat.

3. Even if progress toward the establishment of sound and uniform principles of accounting were to proceed at a much more rapid pace than can now be envisaged, the analyst cannot safely abdicate the job of scrutinizing and evaluating the accounting assumptions and principles that underlie the financial statements that he analyzes. As a prerequisite to a thorough and intelligent analysis, a firm understanding of the data being analyzed is needed. Experience has shown that improvements in accounting principles are accompanied by a significant increase in the complexity of accounting data and determinations. Financial analysis bears on decisions of such importance that under no circumstances can the analyst place undue reliance on the data with which he works without examining it and adjusting it to conform it to his own objectives.

4. Regardless of how well covered by sound and accepted theory accounting procedures may be, the analyst must realize that much of the data presented in financial statements is of the "soft" variety. This is true in spite of the appearance of precision conveyed by neatly balanced presentations. "Soft" information is information based on subjective evaluation, on heavy reliance on forecasts of future conditions, and on assumptions regarding the integrity, competence, intent, or motives of managements that are generally expressed by means of unquantifiable adjectives. Such information must always be evaluated as part of a complete analysis.

5. Finally, a firm overall understanding of the accounting model is of fundamental importance to the analyst. Thus, at present the basic orientation of financial statements is toward the income statement with balance sheet amounts representing mostly residuals rather than amounts derived from a valuation process. Income statements are, for example,

---

[14] S. A. Zeff and S. Johansson, "The Curious Accounting Treatment of the Swedish Government Loan to Uddeholm," *The Accounting Review,* April 1984.

not based on current cash flows but are designed instead to measure long-run average net cash flows at a *current or assumed level of activity.* These orientations have significant implications for those who make decisions on the basis of financial communications.

THE PERVASIVE HUMAN FACTOR

As we observed earlier in this chapter, accounting is a social science, and consequently no assessment of the value or the reliability of accounting concepts or standards or of the financial statements that are based on them can be complete without a consideration of the pervasive influence of human nature on them.[15]

While formally the objective of accounting is to supply information useful for making economic decisions, we must recognize that in fact many interested parties engaged in the accounting function have more specific (and more narrow or selfish) objectives in mind. For example:

- Management, individual executives,[16] or owners of an enterprise may want accounting presentations to help them with individual and specific objectives such as:

  a. Obtaining credit in order to ensure the survival of an enterprise in financial difficulties.

  b. The ability to sell securities in the open market in order to ensure survival, growth, the preservation of jobs, or similar objectives.

  c. To enhance the compensation of executives or employees or to reflect favorably on their operating performance or their egos.[17]

---

[15] In a summary of his book "On the Accuracy of Economic Observations" prominent economist Oskar Morgenstern discusses (in *Fortune* of October 1963) the differences in the nature of measurements in natural sciences and social or economic sciences:

"People gathering statistics all too often face a deliberate attempt to hide information. In other words, economic and social statistics are frequently based on evasive answers and even deliberate lies. Lies arise principally from fear of tax authorities, from dislike of government interference, or from the desire to mislead competitors. Nothing of this sort stands in the path of the physical scientists. Nature may hold back information, is always difficult to understand, but it is believed that she does not lie deliberately. Einstein has aptly expressed this fact by saying: *"Raffiniert ist der Herr Gott, aber boshaft ist er nicht."* ("The Lord God is sophisticated, but not malicious.")

[16] Harvard Business School Professor W. S. Krasker (in *HBS Bulletin,* December 1983, p. 70) observed: "Both owners and managers want the firm to succeed but conflicts arise because the manager's stake in the firm is much larger than that of the shareholder, whose interests are presumably diversified." Shareholders may want to accept risks but to the manager the loss of his job may be an unacceptable risk.

[17] Peter F. Drucker (in *Managing in Turbulent Times* [New York: Harper & Row, 1980], p. 12) observed: "The U.S. tax system greatly favors stock options and bonuses tied to reported earnings, making it very much to the executives' self-interest to report inflated earnings. But in countries where stock options or bonuses of this kind are unknown, such as Japan, executives resist just as strenuously attempts to any adjustment of their reported figures for inflation. The major reason is surely vanity: executives like to take credit for record earnings even when they know that the figures are mere delusion.

> *d.* To help management fend off hostile takeover attempts.[18]
>
> *e.* To help managers to enrich themselves at the expense of owners.[19]
>
> *f.* To enhance the wealth of present owners of the enterprise.[20]

- Governments may want accounting to promote objectives such as helping to control inflation, enhance labor peace, foster economic growth, aid in antitrust enforcement, enlarge tax revenues, or help industries in distress.[21] (See also discussion in preceding section.)

- Public accountants may want accounting to increase the market for their services, help maintain positive relations with important clients, as well as help those clients attain their own objectives.

Examples of the use of accounting for the attainment of such, often more narrow, objectives abound in practice and are illustrated throughout this book. For example, Chapter 6 refers to Datapoint Corporation's reversal of questionable sales booked in an attempt to improve operating results. Chapter 22 discusses the H. J. Heinz case of income smoothing

---

[18] Bendix Corporation's 1982 takeover attempt of Martin Marietta Corporation and the latter's countermeasures finally involving two other suitors, presents a graphic illustration, in a related field, that the objectives of managers may not coincide with those of the owners that they are supposed to represent. Commented one observer of this wasteful use of corporate assets, "You don't see these things in closely held companies when the president is spending his own money."

More recent examples of manager disregard of shareholders' interests are "golden parachute" arrangements under which executives are granted very generous compensation when a company is taken over; also the "greenmail" phenomenon, a takeover defense crafted by managements to buy out corporate raiders at a premium price, another name for corporate blackmail paid by managers fearful of losing their jobs and perquisites.

[19] The management-led buyouts, culminating in the late 1980s in bidding wars such as that for R. J. R. Nabisco, provides a most graphic example of how far some managers will go in acting in their own interest and to the detriment of shareholders. *Barbarians at the Gate*, by B. Burrough and J. Helyar, Harper & Row (1990), provides a dramatic account of such an attempt and of its failure. Another example which symbolizes the disregard by entrenched managers of shareholder interest is the action in 1989 of Time, Inc. managers in going to court to deny shareholders the chance to accept a $200 per share offer from Paramount Corporation; deciding instead to merge with Warner Corporation, the managers caused shareholders to lose more than half of the value of the Paramount offer.

[20] Possible irregularities here range from attempts by owners to use their privileged position of inside knowledge to outright fraud and deception. Thus, the SEC prevailed in charging the principal stockholder and associates of Crazy Eddie, Inc. with a scheme to overstate the company's income by tens of millions of dollars by exaggerating inventory and falsely reducing liabilities to suppliers. As a result, Crazy Eddie officials reaped millions in illegal stock profits and in 1990 a federal judge ordered the principal stockholder to pay $73 million.

[21] An example of attempted tampering with accounting by a governmental agency with the motivation of "helping out" an industry in financial difficulty is the 1982 proposal by the Federal Deposit Insurance Corporation to permit savings banks to defer and amortize all gains and losses on disposition of financial assets acquired prior to January 1, 1983. What was intended was the deferral of losses so that nonregulatory users of financial statements would be led to believe that the savings banks have not incurred the losses which they in fact did incur. When being questioned regarding the propriety of his state's fiscal policies and accounting maneuvers designed to obscure them, Governor Mario Cuomo of New York, known for his ethical stands on many issues, responded by saying that he did not run for office in order to win an accounting award.

by "second tier" executives and the J. W. T. Group case in which fictitious assets and revenues were created by divisional executives who desired to look good by meeting increasing performance goals. Moreover, Chapter 11 refers to Itel Corporation's philosophy of "programmed" earnings as a means of promoting the corporate image of growth. Chapter 10 refers to the Yale Express case of substantial underaccruals of costs and of auditor carelessness in detecting them. Finally, Chapter 15 describes the huge and protracted Equity Funding fraud that involved management greed and deception and (luckily as an infrequent exception) auditor collusion in management's deception for purposes of achieving its own accounting "goals."

Now, as we all know, these narrow interests are not, nor should they be, the objectives of accounting. The FASB, a body independent of all parties at interest, including the accounting profession, is in fact society's representative charged with the unwritten mission of ensuring that, at least in theory, the objectives of accounting coincide with those of society at large.

Human nature being what it is,[22] analysts must be ever aware that those with strong personal interests at stake will continue to try to bend the theory so that the practice favors their own more narrow interests. Society's most powerful countermeasures include institutions such as the SEC, the courts, as well as the organized auditing profession. While significant progress has been made in improving the overall integrity and reliability of financial reporting in this country, the analyst must be aware that individual exceptions have occurred, are occurring, and are likely to recur in the future.

The Concept of Accounting Risk

The reader and user of accounting determinations must recognize a variety of risks. There is first the all-pervading risk associated with profit-seeking business enterprises: the risk of losses, of adversities, contingencies, and so forth. There is also the risk associated with reliance on audited financial statements on which we will elaborate in Chapter 15.

The user of financial statements prepared "in accordance with generally accepted accounting principles" must recognize yet another type of risk, best termed *accounting risk*.[23] This risk results from the human nature factor discussed in the preceding section as well as from the imprecision inherent in the basic accounting process. It is also due to the

---

[22] Soichero Honda, founder of Honda Motor Company, expressed it as follows: "God seems to give humans good things, and proportionately, the same degree of bad things to go with it. We humans must develop means to eliminate those bad aspects."

[23] This risk is greatest in companies with a strong stock market orientation whose managements need to produce earnings growth and companies in dire need for borrowed funds where accounting methods are regarded by managements as means of achieving reported results.

existence of alternative accounting principles, the loose criteria that define them, and the consequent instances of loose standards of practice. This lack of assurance about the standards used or the method and rigor of their application may lead to a wide variety of results and hence to a great degree of uncertainty. In this concept of accounting risk, we may also include the degree of conservatism of accounting principles in the use or the lack of it. As we shall see in the following chapters, assumptions play an important role in accounting determinations; and such assumptions may be conservative or cautious, or they may be optimistic, daring, or too anticipative of favorable outcomes of things subject to normal doubt. Thus, the degree of conservatism found in the accounting principles in use will determine the magnitude of the setback that may result from assumptions that time shows to be overly optimistic. This aspect of analysis will be explored further in Chapter 22.

QUESTIONS

 1. What is the basic purpose of financial accounting?
 2. What is the purpose of the FASB's conceptual framework?
 3. What are the salient features of *SFAC 1?*
 4. What is *SFAC 2* concerned with? What are the characteristics that make accounting information useful? Discuss.
 5. Discuss the "pervasive qualities" mentioned by *SFAC 2.*
 6. Discuss the elements of financial statements identified by *SFAC 3.*
 7. *SFAC 5* specifies that a full set of financial statements should include certain components. What are they?
 8. Which criteria are specified by *SFAC 5* for an item to be included in the financial statements?
 9. What are some implications for analysis resulting from the conceptual framework project?
10. What are accounting standards?
11. How are accounting standards established?
12. Does the FASB represent a significant improvement over its predecessors? Why?
13. Trace briefly the accounting profession's endeavors to promulgate accounting principles.
14. Can the user of financial statements rely on the use of "generally accepted accounting principles (GAAP)" to produce reliable financial presentations? Of what implication to financial analysis is the rate of progress of improvement in accounting principles and practice?
15. Accounting concepts and standards and the financial statements that are based on them are subject to the pervasive influence of human nature. Discuss.

Chapter 4

TOOLS AND TECHNIQUES OF FINANCIAL STATEMENT ANALYSIS–AN OVERVIEW

Basic Approaches to Financial Statement Analysis

In the first chapter, we examined the various objectives of financial statement analysis as viewed from the point of view of specific user groups. In the performance of an analysis, such objectives can, in turn, be translated into a number of specific questions to which the decision maker needs an answer. Thus, for example, the equity investor may want to know:

1. What has the company's operating performance been over the longer term and over the recent past? What does this record hold for future earnings prospects?
2. Has the company's earnings record been one of growth, stability, or decline? Does it display significant variability?
3. What is the company's current financial condition? What factors are likely to affect it in the near future?
4. What is the company's capital structure? What risks and rewards does it hold for the investor?
5. How does this company compare on the above counts with other companies in its industry?

The banker who is approached with a short-term loan request may look to the financial statements for answers to questions such as the following:

1. What are the underlying reasons for the company's needs for funds? Are these needs truly short term, and if so, will they be self-liquidating?
2. From what sources is the company likely to get funds for the payment of interest and the repayment of principal?
3. How has management handled its needs for short-term and long-term funds in the past? What does this portend for the future?

An important first step in any decision-making process is to identify the most significant, pertinent, and critical questions that have a bearing on the decision. Financial statement analysis does not, of course, provide answers to all such questions. However, each of the questions exemplified above can, to a significant extent, be answered by such analysis.

RECONSTRUCTION OF BUSINESS ACTIVITIES AND TRANSACTIONS

Basic to the analyst's work is the ability to reconstruct the business transactions that are summarized in the financial statements. One can visualize this important skill as the ability to replicate the accountant's work but in reverse order. The flow of the accountant's work is as follows:

◄───────────────────── FLOW OF ACCOUNTANT'S WORK ─────────────────────►

| Perception of the reality behind business transactions | GAAP–The framework of accounting for these transactions | Express the transaction in the form of journal entries | Accumulate transactions in T-accounts | Summarize and classify in the form of financial statements |

◄───────────────────── FLOW OF ANALYST'S WORK ─────────────────────

The accountant's effort and skill is first directed to understanding the reality of the transactions or events to be recorded. Next, there must be brought to bear the knowledge of the accounting framework—the generally accepted accounting principles (GAAP) that govern the recording of the transaction, its expression in the form of a journal entry, and its accumulation in accounts. No matter what form data recording and accumulation takes in this electronic age, the basic concepts of the journal entry and the T-account prevail. These, as we shall see, are particularly useful in analytical work. Finally, continuing to be guided by accepted standards of the accounting framework, the accountant summarizes all accounts of a period in the format of financial statements.

The flow of the analyst's work is basically in reverse order. Moreover, while the accountant's work is basically oriented to events of the past, that of the analyst is focused on future developments. The analyst starts with the financial statements made available by the enterprise. The basic task is to recapture, as far as possible, the reality that is imbedded and summarized in these financial statements—the degree to which this is done being dependent on the particular analytical objectives at hand. This analytical process requires that the analyst visualize the journal entries made and that he or she reconstruct, in summary fashion, all or selected accounts in the financial statements. It also requires an understanding of the reality underlying such business transactions as well as a knowledge of the *accounting standards* employed in recording it properly within the accounting framework.

By these means, the analyst will be able to understand the changes in specific balance sheet items, trace the effect of a given transaction or specific accounts, and answer questions such as the following:

- What was the reason for the increase or the decrease in the investment in X Company?
- What effect did the debt refunding have on working capital or on cash?
- How much long-term debt was repaid this year?
- What was the effect of income taxes on the financial statements and how much tax was actually paid this year?

The reconstruction of business transactions (i.e., significant economic events) requires a knowledge of accounting, that is, the ability to visualize how a particular transaction is recorded and what kind of activities or events will increase or decrease a specific account. It also requires the ability to read carefully, understand, and interpret financial statements and related footnotes. Thus, the knowledge of what information can be found in financial statements, where it is to be found, and how to reconstruct transactions, including the making of reasonable assumptions, are important skills in the analysis of financial statements.

Financial statement analysis depends on a knowledge of related disciplines, such as accounting, economics, and finance, as well as on skills of analysis such as derivation and inference. It involves a degree of detective work based on marshaling all known facts while using the limited and incomplete data that are available. As the creator of Sherlock Holmes put it: "After you have eliminated the impossible, whatever remains, however improbable, must be the truth." Thus, in reconstructing transactions, the analyst will work with known information before attempting to deduce unknown facts. The degree of accuracy that can be expected in such reconstructions and the resulting analysis cannot be expected to be nor need it approach the degree of accuracy required in the accounting and recording function.

Throughout this book the T-account will be used as an important analytical tool. The emphasis is not on bookkeeping mechanics but rather on the use of T-account analysis in the reconstruction and understanding of transactions. Thus, while the emphasis is on analysis rather than on accounting or bookkeeping technique, the analyst must recognize that we use the accounting function as a most useful analytical technique. The use of T-account analysis depends on the analyst's ability to visualize transactions in the form of journal entries which are in turn summarized in T-accounts.

ILLUSTRATION 1.   The analyst of the financial statements of the Campbell Soup Company (also referred to as Campbell, see Appendix 4B) needs to determine the amount of cash collected from customers during the fiscal year 1991 (also referred to as 1991). In this simple example the analyst will reconstruct the accounts receivable account. For ease of reference, boldface numbers in squares refer to those found in the financial statements of Campbell.

The analyst finds the Accounts Receivable account on the balance sheet (item **33**) and knows that the reconstruction of this account is the key to a determination of the cash collected from customers in fiscal 1991. Also needed is a knowledge of the typical entries that can be expected in the Accounts Receivable account.

The first step is to set up the accounts receivable T-account with opening and closing balances (details are in Note 13):

Accounts Receivable (Net)

148A Bal	534.1	
Net sales **13**	6204.1	6276.5—collections-to balance
148A Bal	461.7	

The second step is to determine the aggregate debits to this account. Note that the analyst, working with financial statements which represent summarizations, can only work with aggregates rather than the multitude of detailed entries which comprise them. Knowing that the debits represent the counterpart of sales **13** we debit accounts receivable with total sales of $6,204.1 (all in millions). We know that not all sales are for cash, but to arrive at cash collections from customers it does not matter whether the charges are cash sales or credit sales. The amount needed to balance the accounts receivable account, that is, $6276.5, represents the best estimate of approximate cash collections from customers. In fact, we know that this amount is overstated because it includes credits to customers for cash discounts and bad debts. However, in order to reconstruct the Allowance for Bad Debts account we would need at least the amount of the bad debt expense charged to income during the year—a detail not provided in the financial statements. These amounts are, however, small in relation to total collections so that the estimated collections are not off by much.

When there is inadequate information, the analyst may have to combine accounts and transactions and consider them together. Having pinpointed what type of information is lacking, the analyst can develop informed questions for management in order to obtain the desired information that was not disclosed in the financial statements.

The analyst must also know what information is not generally available in financial statements so that he or she may attempt to secure it. In addition to information such as commitments, lines of credit, and order backlogs, the analyst will also generally not find the details of changes in many important accounts. Thus, for example, a Notes Payable account or a Loan to Officers account may show little or no change in year-end balances but may, in fact, have had significant interim balances that were liquidated during the year.

The analysis and reconstruction of business transactions is an important analytical procedure and will be illustrated throughout this book. Some illustrations will be based on the financial statements of Campbell Soup Company, (Appendix 4B), and others on the financial statements of Quaker Oats Company (Appendix to Chapter 23, referred to as Appendix 23).

IMPORTANCE OF THE STATEMENT OF CASH FLOWS

The analytical steps involved in the reconstruction of business transactions often involve use of the statement of cash flows (SCF). For this and other reasons, this statement is of key importance to the analyst. Consequently, the placement of a chapter dealing with this statement in this book involves difficult choices. It would be advantageous to consider this subject as early as possible. On the other hand, a thorough and detailed consideration of the statement can be undertaken only *after* a consideration of all elements of the financial statements. For this reason, it is recommended that at this point Chapter 13 be read in a cursory fashion. Later, after Chapters 5 to 11 have been studied, Chapter 13 can be delved into much more thoroughly.

ADDITIONAL ANALYTICAL FUNCTIONS

The following are some additional analytical processes in widespread use:

Direct Measurements   Some factors and relationships can be measured directly. For example, the relationship between the debt and the equity of an entity is a direct measurement. Both the amount of debt and that of equity can be measured in absolute terms (i.e., in dollars) and their relationship computed therefrom.

Indirect Evidence   Financial statement analysis can provide indirect evidence bearing on important questions. Thus, the analysis of past statements of cash flows can offer evidence as to the financial habits of a management team. Moreover, the analysis of operating statements will yield evidence regarding management's ability to cope with fluctuations in the level of the firm's business activity. While such indirect evidence and evaluation are often not precise or quantifiable, the data derived therefrom nevertheless possess importance because the effects of almost all managerial decisions, or the lack of them, are reflected in the entity's financial statements.

Predictive Functions   Almost all decision questions are oriented toward the future. Thus, an important measure of the usefulness of financial statement analysis tools and techniques is their ability to assist in the prediction of expected future conditions and results.

Comparison   This is a very important analytical process. It is based on the elementary proposition that in financial analysis no number standing by itself can be meaningful, and that it gains meaning only when related to some other comparable quantity. By means of comparison, financial analysis is useful in performing important evaluative, as well as attention-directing and control, functions. Thus, it focuses on exceptions and variations, and saves the analyst the need to evaluate the normal and the expected. Moreover, by means of comparison, selection among alternative choices is accomplished.

Comparison may be performed by using:

1. A company's own experience over the years (i.e., internally derived data);
2. External data, such as comparisons with individual companies or industry composites; or
3. Compiled yardsticks, including standards, budgets, and forecasts.

Historical company data can usually be readily obtained and most readily adjusted for inconsistencies.

Uses of External Data   Useful comparison may also be made with external data. The advantages of external data are: (1) they are normally objective and independent; (2) they are derived from similar operations, thus performing the function of a standard of comparison; and (3) if current, they reflect events occurring during an identical period having as a consequence similar business and economic conditions in common.

External information must, however, be used with great care and discrimination. Knowledge of the basis and method of compilation, the period covered, and the source of the information will facilitate a decision of whether the information is at all comparable. At times, sufficient detail may be available to adjust data so as to render them comparable. In any event, a decision on a proper standard of comparison must be made by choosing from those available. Differences between situations compared must be noted. Such differences may be in accounting practices or specific company policies. It must also be borne in mind that the past is seldom an unqualified guide to the future.

SOURCES OF INFORMATION

For basic data on an enterprise and for comparative data of comparable entities in its industry, published financial statements provide the best and most readily available source.

Appendix 4A to this chapter presents a listing of sources of information on financial and operating ratios of various industries as well as sample presentations from these sources. These data, while representing valuable sources for comparison, must be used with care and with as complete a knowledge of the basis of their compilation as is possible to obtain. A realistic and sometimes superior alternative for the analyst is to use as a basis of comparison the financial statements of one or more comparable companies in the same industry. In this way, one can usually have a better command over, and comprehension of, the data entering into the comparison base.

Annual reports to shareholders contain an ever-expanding amount of information required by either GAAP or by specific SEC requirements.[1]

In addition, company filings with the SEC, such as Registration Statements[2] pursuant to the Securities Act of 1933, supplemental and periodic reports which are required to be filed (such as Forms 8-K, 10-K, 10-Q, 14-K, and 16-K), or proxy statements contain a wealth of information of interest to the analyst.

Additional information may be available and may require an extra effort to obtain. Some companies offer financial analysts and others additional financial and operating data which can be obtained on request (e.g., by postcard included in the annual report). Information required to be filed with federal or state regulatory agencies (e.g., insurance, banking) is usually publicly available. Such differential disclosure is made available to those who seek it out.

Some information is not generally available but can be obtained by those able to exert a degree of influence. Thus, bond rating agencies are generally provided with financial and operating details that go beyond those found in published financial statements. Major lenders and investors may also have access to more detailed information. This is also true of potential lenders and investors.

THE TOTAL INFORMATION SET

In Chapter 2, we discussed the relative importance of financial statement analysis to the total decision effort. The total information set on which

---

[1] For example, Rule 14c-3 of the Securities Exchange Act of 1934 specifies that annual reports furnished to stockholders in connection with the annual meeting of stockholders include, among others, the following financial information: (1) audited financial statements—balance sheets as of the two most recent fiscal years, and statements of income and changes in financial position (now cash flows) for each of the three most recent fiscal years; (2) selected quarterly financial data for each quarterly period within the two most recent fiscal years; (3) summary of selected financial data for last five years; (4) management's discussion and analysis of financial condition and results of operations; (5) market price of company's common stock for each quarterly period within the two most recent fiscal years; and (6) segment information.

[2] SEC Regulation S-X, which specifies the form and content of financial statements filed with the Commission, contains numerous requirements for specific disclosures.

the decision maker draws includes financial as well as other types of information, and the relative importance of each varies from decision to decision. Exhibit 4–1 presents the composition of this information set (or spectrum).

THE PRINCIPAL TOOLS OF ANALYSIS

In the analysis of financial statements, the analyst has available a variety of tools from which he can choose those best suited to his specific purpose. The following principal tools of analysis will be discussed in this chapter:

1. Comparative financial statements.
   a. Year-to-year changes.
2. Index-number trend series.
3. Common-size financial statements.
   a. Structural analysis.
4. Ratio analysis.
5. Specialized analyses.
   a. Cash forecasts.
   b. Analysis of changes in cash flows.
   c. Statement of variation in gross margin.
   d. Break-even analysis.

The application of these tools as well as other aspects of analysis will be illustrated throughout by means of the financial statements of Campbell Soup Company presented in Appendix 4B and those of Quaker Oats Co. in the Appendix to Chapter 23. Further examples of tabulations of analytical measures can be found in Chapter 23 and throughout the text.

Comparative Financial Statements

The comparison of financial statements is accomplished by setting up balance sheets, income statements, or statements of cash flows (SCF), side by side, and reviewing the changes that have occurred in individual categories therein from year to year and over the years.

The most important factor revealed by comparative financial statements is *trend.* The comparison of financial statements over a number of years will also reveal the direction, velocity, and the amplitude of trend. Further analysis can be undertaken to compare the trends in related items. For example, a year-to-year increase in sales of 10 percent accompanied by an increase in freight-out costs of 20 percent requires an investigation and explanation of the reasons for the difference. Similarly, an increase of accounts receivable of 15 percent during the same period would also warrant an investigation into the reasons for the difference in the rate of increase of sales as against that of receivables.

Exhibit 4–1 Information set (or spectrum)

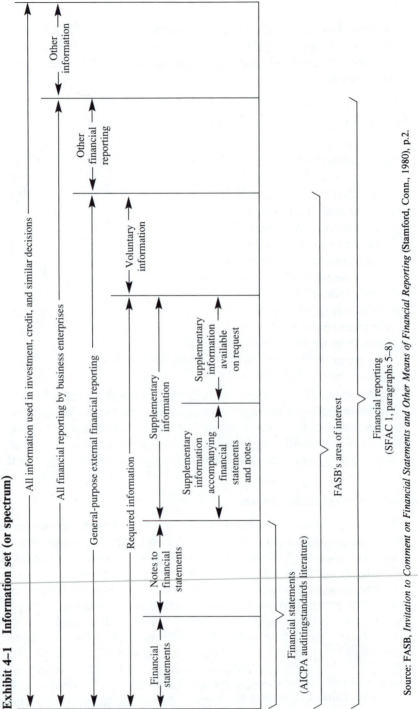

Source: FASB, *Invitation to Comment on Financial Statements and Other Means of Financial Reporting* (Stamford, Conn., 1980), p.2.

Year-to-Year Change   A comparison of financial statements over two to three years can be undertaken by computing the *year-to-year change* in absolute amounts and in terms of percentage changes. Longer-term comparisons are best undertaken by means of *index-number trend series.*

Year-to-year comparisons of financial statements are illustrated in Appendix 4B. When a two- or three-year comparison is attempted, such presentations are manageable and can be understood by the reader. They have the advantage of presenting changes in terms of absolute dollar amounts as well as in percentages. Both have to be considered because the dollar size of the different bases on which percentage changes are computed may yield large percentage changes that are out of proportion to their real significance. For example, in the same financial statements, a 50 percent change from a base figure of $1,000 is far less significant than the same percentage change from a base of $100,000. Thus, reference to the dollar amounts involved is always necessary in order to retain the proper perspective and to reach valid conclusions regarding the relative significance of the changes disclosed by this type of analysis.

The computation of year-to-year changes is a simple matter. However, a few clarifying rules should be borne in mind. When a negative amount appears in the base year and a positive amount in the following year, or vice versa, no percentage change can be meaningfully computed. When an item has a value in a base year and none in the following period, the decrease is 100 percent. Where there is no figure for the base year, no percentage change can be computed. The following summary will illustrate this:

Item	Year 1	Year 2	*Change increase (decrease)* Amount	Percent
Net income (loss)	$(4,500)	$ 1,500	$ 6,000	—
Tax expense	2,000	(1,000)	(3,000)	—
Notes payable	—	8,000	8,000	—
Notes receivable	10,000	—	(10,000)	(100)

Comparative financial statements can also be presented in such a way that the cumulative total for the period for each item under study and the average for that period are shown.

The value of comparing yearly amounts with an average covering a number of years is that unusual factors in any one year are highlighted. Averages smooth out erratic or unusual fluctuations in data.

Index-Number Trend Series

When a comparison of financial statements covering more than three years is undertaken, the year-to-year method of comparison may become too cumbersome. The best way to effect such longer-term trend comparisons is by means of index numbers. Such a comparative statement for Campbell Soup Company is illustrated in Chapter 23.

The computation of a series of index numbers requires the choice of a base year that will, for all items, have an index amount of 100. Since such a base year represents a frame of reference for all comparisons, it is best to choose a year that, in a business conditions sense, is as typical or normal as possible. If the earliest year in the series compared cannot fulfill this function, another year is chosen. In our example of the Campbell comparative statements, the year 1986 was chosen.

As is the case with the computation of year-to-year percentage changes, certain changes, such as those from negative to positive amounts, cannot be expressed by means of index numbers. All index numbers are computed by reference to the base year.

ILLUSTRATION 2.   Assume that in the base year at 12/31/20xA, there is a cash balance of $12,000. Based on an index number of 100 for 20xA, if the cash balance in the following year (at 12/31/20xB) is $18,000, then the index number will be

$$\frac{\$18,000}{\$12,000} \times 100 = 150$$

On 12/31/20xC the cash balance is $9,000, the index will stand at 75 arrived at as follows:

$$\frac{\$9,000}{\$12,000} \times 100 = \left(\frac{\text{Balance in current year}}{\text{Balance in base year}} \times 100 \right)$$

It should be noted that when using index numbers, percentage changes cannot be read off directly except by reference to the base year. Thus, the change of the cash balance between 20xA and 20xB is 50 percent (index 150 − index 100), and this can be read off directly from the index numbers. The change from 20xB to 20xC, however, is not 75 percent (150 − 75), as a direct comparison may suggest, but rather 50 percent (i.e., $9,000/$18,000), which involves computing the 20xB to 20xC change by reference to the amount at 20xB. The percentage change can, however, be computed by use of the index numbers only, for example, 75/150 = 0.5, or a change of 50 percent.

In planning an index-number trend comparison, it is not necessary to include in it all the items in the financial statements. Only the most significant items need be included in such a comparison.

Care should be exercised in the use of index-number trend comparisons because such comparisons have weaknesses as well as strengths. Thus, in trying to assess changes in the current financial condition, the analyst may use to advantage comparative statements of cash flows. On the other hand, the index-number trend comparison is very well suited to a comparison of the changes in the *composition* of working capital items over the years.

The interpretation of percentage changes as well as those of index-number trend series must be made with a full awareness of the effect that the inconsistent application of accounting principles over the years can have on such comparisons. Thus, where possible, such inconsistencies must be adjusted. In addition, the longer the period covered by the comparison, the more distortive are the effects of price-level changes on such comparisons likely to be, and the analyst must be aware of such effects (see Chapter 14).

One important value of trend analysis is that it can convey to the analyst a better understanding of management's philosophies, policies, and motivations, conscious or otherwise, that have brought about the changes revealed over the years. The more diverse the economic environments covering the periods compared are, the better a picture can be obtained by the analyst of the ways in which the enterprise has weathered its adversities and taken advantage of its opportunities.

Common-Size Financial Statements

In the analysis of financial statements, it is often instructive to find out the proportion that a single item represents of a total group or subgroup. In a balance sheet, the assets as well as the liabilities and capital are each expressed as 100 percent, and each item in these categories is expressed as a percentage of the respective totals. Similarly, in the income statement, net sales are set at 100 percent and every other item in the statement is expressed as a percent of net sales. Since the totals always add up to 100 percent, this community of size has resulted in these statements being referred to as "common size." Similarly, following the eye as it reviews the common-size statement, this analysis is referred to as "vertical" for the same reason that the trend analysis is often referred to as "horizontal" analysis.

Selected common-size statements of Campbell are presented in Chapter 23.

Structural Analysis   The analysis of common-size financial statements may best be described as an analysis of the internal structure of the financial statements. In the analysis of a balance sheet, this structural analysis focuses on two major aspects:

1. What are the sources of capital of the enterprise, that is, what is the distribution of equities as between current liabilities, long-term liabilities, and equity capital?

2. Given the amount of capital from all sources, what is the distribution of assets (current, fixed, and other) in which it is invested? Stated differently, what is the mix of assets with which the enterprise has chosen to conduct its operations?

The common-size balance sheet analysis can, of course, be carried further and extended to an examination of what proportion of a subgroup, rather than the total, an item is. Thus, in assessing the liquidity of current assets, it may be of interest to know not only what proportion of total assets is invested in inventories but also what proportion of current assets is represented by this asset.

In the case of the income statement, common-size statement analysis is a very useful tool transcending perhaps in importance the analysis of the balance sheet by such means. This is so because the income statement lends itself very well to an analysis whereby each item in it is related to a central quantum, that is, sales. With some exceptions, the level of each expense item is affected to some extent by the level of sales, and thus it is instructive to know what proportion of the sales dollar is absorbed by the various costs and expenses incurred by the enterprise. There are exceptions, of course. For example, income taxes are not related to sales but rather to pretax income.

Comparisons of common-size statements of a single enterprise over the years are valuable in that they show the changing proportions of components within groups of assets, liabilities, costs, and other financial statement categories. However, care must be exercised in interpreting such changes and the trend that they disclose. For example, the table below shows the amount of patents and total assets of an enterprise over three years:

	Year 3	Year 2	Year 1
Patents	$ 50,000	$ 50,000	$ 50,000
Total assets	$1,000,000	$750,000	$500,000
Patents as a percentage of			
total assets	5%	6.67%	10%

While the amount of patents remained unchanged, the increase in total assets made this item a progressively smaller proportion of total assets. Since this proportion can change with either a change in the absolute amount of the item or a change in the total of the group of which it is a part, the interpretation of a common-size statement comparison requires an examination of the actual figures and the basis on which they are computed.

Common-size statements are very well suited to intercompany comparison because the financial statements of a variety of companies can be recast into the uniform common-size format regardless of the size of individual accounts. While common-size statements do not reflect the relative sizes of the individual companies that are compared, the problem of actual comparability between them is a matter to be resolved by the analyst's judgment.

Comparison of the common-size statements of companies within an industry or with common-size composite statistics of that industry can alert the analyst's attention to variations in account structure or distribution, the reasons for which should be explored and understood. A comparison of selected common-size statement items of the Campbell Soup Company with similar industry statistics will be found in Chapter 23.

Ratio Analysis

Ratios are among the best known and most widely used tools of financial analysis. At the same time, their function is often misunderstood, and consequently their significance may easily be overrated.

A ratio expresses the mathematical relationship between one quantity and another. The ratio of 200 to 100 is expressed as 2:1, or as 2. While the computation of a ratio involves a simple arithmetical operation, its interpretation is a far more complex matter.

To begin with, to be significant, the ratio must express a relationship that has significance. Thus, there is a clear, direct, and understandable relationship between the sales price of an item, on one hand, and its cost, on the other. As a result, the ratio of cost of goods sold to sales is a significant one. On the other hand, there is no a priori or understandable relationship between freight costs incurred and the marketable securities held by an enterprise; and hence, a ratio of one to the other must be deemed to be of no significance.

Ratios are tools of analysis that in most cases provide the analyst with clues and symptoms of underlying conditions. Ratios, properly interpreted, can also point the way to areas requiring further investigation and inquiry. The analysis of a ratio can disclose relationships as well as bases of comparison that reveal conditions and trends that cannot be detected by an inspection of the individual components of the ratio.

Since ratios, like other tools of analysis, are future oriented, the analyst must be able to adjust the factors present in a relationship to their probable shape and size in the future. He must also understand the factors that will influence such ratios in the future. Thus, in the final analysis, the usefulness of ratios is wholly dependent on their intelligent and skillful interpretation. This is, by far, the most difficult aspect of ratio analysis. Let us, by way of example, consider the interpretation of a ratio derived from an area outside that of the business world: In comparing the ratio of gas consumption to mileage driven, A claims to have a superior performance, that is, 28 mpg compared to B's 20 mpg. Assuming that they drove identical cars, the following are factors that affect gas consumption and that will have to be considered before one can properly interpret the ratios and judge whose performance is better:

1. Weight of load driven.
2. Type of terrain (flat versus hilly).
3. City or country driving.
4. Kind of gasoline used.
5. Speed at which cars were driven.

Numerous as the factors that influence gas consumption are, the evaluation of the gas consumption ratio is, nevertheless, a simpler process than the evaluation of most ratios derived from business variables. The reason for this is that the interrelationships of business variables and the factors that affect them are multifaceted and very complex.

Factors Affecting Ratios

In addition to the internal operating conditions that affect the ratios of an enterprise, the analyst must be aware of the factors, such as general business conditions, industry position, management policies, as well as accounting principles, that can affect them. As far as the latter are concerned, the discussion of accounting principles in Part II of this book points up their influence on the measurements on which ratios are based. Weaknesses in the accounting model impact the validity of ratios as well. Thus, historical costs are often far less relevant than current market values.

Before ratios, or similar measures such as trend indexes or percentage relationships, are computed, the analyst must make sure that the figures entering into their computation are valid and consistent. For example, when inventories are valued on the LIFO basis (see Chapter 5), under conditions of increasing prices, the current ratio may be understated because LIFO basis inventories may be significantly understated in terms of current value. Similarly, some pension liabilities may be unrecorded and disclosed in footnotes only (see Chapter 7). Some analysts may wish to recognize these liabilities when computing the debt-to-equity ratio of an enterprise. Care must also be taken to recognize that when such adjustments are made in one ratio, consistency may also require that they be made in other ratios as well. Thus, the omission of the pension liability also means that pension expenses have been understated. As a result, the net income amount used in the computation of certain ratios may require adjustment.

The validity of ratios depends also on the validity of the numbers entering into their computation. Thus, when a company's internal controls are such that the accounting system cannot be relied upon to produce reliable figures, the ratios based on such figures are, of course, also unreliable. It is widely believed that such was the situation in the case of W. T. Grant Company in the years immediately preceding the giant retailer's bankruptcy. (See also discussion in Chapter 13.)

Interpretation of Ratios

Ratios should always be interpreted with great care since factors affecting the numerator may correlate with those affecting the denominator. Thus, for example, it is possible to improve the ratio of operating expenses to sales by reducing costs that act to stimulate sales. If the cost reduction consequently results in a loss of sales or share of market, such a seeming improvement in profitability may, in fact, have an overall detrimental effect on the future prospects of the enterprise and must be interpreted accordingly.

It should also be recognized that many ratios have important variables in common with other ratios, thus tending to make them vary and be influenced by the same factors. Consequently, there is no need to use all available ratios in order to diagnose a given condition.

Ratios, like most other relationships in financial analysis, are not significant in themselves and can be interpreted only by comparison with (1) past ratios of the same enterprise, or (2) some predetermined standard, or (3) ratios of other companies in the industry. The range of a ratio over time is also significant as is the trend of a given ratio over time.

MARKET MEASURES

Analysts and investors use a variety of measures to evaluate the price and yield behavior of securities. The *price-earnings ratio* measures the multiple at which the market is capitalizing the earnings per share of a company at any given time. The *earnings yield* is the inverse of the price-earnings ratio and represents the income-producing power of a share of common stock at the current price. The *dividend yield* is the cash return accruing to an investor on a share of stock based on the current dividend rate and current price. Thus, part of the earned yield may be distributed as dividends and the balance retained in the business. The *dividend payout ratio* measures the proportion of earnings that is currently paid out as common stock dividends.

COMPARABILITY OF FINANCIAL DATA

The task of comparing data of enterprises in a given industry presents the analyst with a number of challenges.

Data of companies in a given industry may be limited or unavailable. This may be due to reasons such as lack of disclosure of segmental data (see also Chapter 20), or to companies being privately held and thus not providing public disclosure. Other obstacles to comparability are discussed below.

Differing Reporting Periods   While many companies use the calendar year-end, others use a variety of different year-ends for reporting purposes.

The adjustments required in order to allow for different year-ends among companies included in comparisons depend on the size of the year-end time gap and on other factors.

If the year-end time difference does not exceed three months, adjustments will generally not be required. If the year-end time difference exceeds three months, then quarterly reports (see also Chapter 21) may be used to make data comparable so that a valid financial statement analysis can be performed. By adding up four quarters, year-ends can be adjusted to end, for example, in March, June, September, or December. The need to adjust for year-end time differences and the degree of such adjustments also depends on whether extraordinary events, such as strikes or severe property damage, will distort the results of a given quarter. In addition, the effects of seasonal and cyclical influences on the comparability of time periods will need to be carefully evaluated.

Differences on the Application of Accounting Principles   As will be seen in discussion throughout this book, the use of alternative accounting principles or methods can render the data of companies noncomparable. Such lack of comparability must be corrected by the analyst by means of data adjustments before a valid financial statement analysis can be performed. The table below gives *examples* of alternative accounting principles and the chapters where their effect on financial statements are discussed.

Alternative accounting principles	*Discussed in chapter*
Depreciation method	
Straight line, declining balance, sum-of-the years'- digits	6, 11
Inventory valuation	
Acquisition cost, standard cost, lower of cost or market	5
Inventory cost flow assumption	
First in–first out (FIFO), last in–first out (LIFO), weighted average	5
Leases	
Operating and capital leases	7
Corporate acquisitions	
Purchase, pooling of interests	9

Investments in securities	
Cost, lower of cost or market, equity	5, 6, 9
Foreign currency translation	
All current, temporal method	9
Income recognition	
Percentage of completion, completed contract	10

SEC *Staff Accounting Bulletin No. 74* requires disclosure about the potential impact of accounting standards that have been promulgated but not yet adopted by the company.

Restatement and Reclassification of Financial Statements

A number of circumstances require that financial statements be restated:

1. The merger of entities under the pooling method of accounting requires that prior years be restated as if the entities had been merged from inception (see Chapter 9). As a practical matter only the financial statements presented at the time the merger is reported will be presented in restated form.
2. Discontinuances or disposals of a segment of a business require that revenues and expenses of the disposed units as well as losses expected on disposal be classified in the income statement under "discontinued operations." Similarly, the net assets of business expected to be discontinued are shown as a single category on the balance sheet (see Chapter 11). Financial statements presented at the time the discontinuances are reported must be restated accordingly.
3. Certain accounting principles changes (e.g., changes in inventory cost flow assumptions or changes in income recognition on long-term contracts) require that the prior years of financial statements presented at the time the change is reported be restated to reflect the newly adopted accounting method (see Chapter 11).

Since analysis is forward-looking, financial analysts will want to use the restated data in most cases. Inevitably difficulties will arise because the restated period may be shorter than the time period under analysis. Generally, companies present balance sheets for two years and income statements and statements of cash flow for three years. These are the periods for which restated financial statements are likely to be available although restatements for longer periods may be found in SEC filings such as registration statements. Financial analysts will have to utilize restated as well as originally reported financial statements in the most creative manner possible.

Finally, we must recognize that there can exist account classification differences between financial statements used in comparisons. Some classification differences are easier to adjust for than are others. If, for example, one company includes depreciation expense in cost of goods sold while another shows this expense as a separate item, adjustments to put analytical measures (such as ratios) on a comparable basis can be readily made.

ILLUSTRATION OF RATIO COMPUTATIONS

A great many ratios can be developed from the multitude of items included in an enterprise's financial statements. Some ratios have general application in financial analysis, while others have specific uses in certain circumstances or in specific industries. Listed below in Exhibit 4–2 are some of the more significant ratios that have general applicability to most business situations. They are grouped by major objectives of financial analysis, and the data used to illustrate their computation are taken from the financial statements of Campbell Soup Company (see Appendix 4B).

Each of the above five major areas of objectives of financial statement analysis will be examined in Part III of this book; and therein the computation, use, and interpretation of the ratios listed under each category as well as other ratios will be examined in detail and thoroughly discussed.

TESTING THE UNDERSTANDING OF RELATIONSHIPS

The following is an example of an exercise designed to test the reader's understanding of various intra- and interstatement ratios and relationships.

ILLUSTRATION 3.   Given the following information, we are to complete the balance sheet below:

Cash
Accounts receivable
Inventory .... $ 50
Building
Land
Current liabilities
Common stock
Retained earnings 100

Assets − Liabilities = $600.
Stockholders' equity = 3 × debt.
The carrying amount of land is two thirds of that of the building.
Acid-test ratio = 1.25.
Ending inventory turnover is 15.
Gross profit is 44 percent of the cost of goods sold.
There are 20 days' sales in accounts receivable.

(text continues on page 94)

Exhibit 4–2 Illustration of major categories of ratios

Major categories of ratios	*Method of computation (dollars in millions)*	*Campbell Soup ratio for 1991*

Short-term liquidity ratios:

Current ratio ....

$$\frac{\text{Current assets}}{\text{Current liabilities}} = \frac{1518.5 \ \boxed{36}^{(a)}}{1278. \ \boxed{45}} = \qquad 1.19$$

Acid test ratio ....

$$\frac{\text{Cash} + \text{Cash equivalents} + \text{Receivables}}{\text{Current liabilities}} = \frac{178.9 \ \boxed{31} + 12.8 \ \boxed{32} + 527.4 \ \boxed{33}}{1278.0 \ \boxed{45}} = \qquad 0.56$$

Days' sales in receivables (collection period) ....

$$\frac{\text{Accounts receivable*}}{\text{Credit sales} \div 360} = \frac{527.4 \ \boxed{33}}{6204.1 \ \boxed{13} \div 360} = \qquad 31 \text{ days}$$

*Year-end in this case

Inventory turnover ....

$$\frac{\text{Cost of goods sold}}{\text{Average inventory during period}} = \frac{4095.4 \ \boxed{14}}{706.7 + 819.8 \ \boxed{34} \div 2} = \qquad 5.37$$

Capital structure and long-term solvency ratios:

Total debt to total capital(b) ....

$$\frac{\text{Current liabilities} + \text{Long-term liabilities}}{\text{Equity capital*} + \text{Total liabilities}}$$
$$= \frac{2355.6 \ \boxed{45} + \boxed{46} + \boxed{47} - 23.5 \ \boxed{178}}{1793.4 \ \boxed{54} + 2355.6 \ \boxed{45} + \boxed{46} + \boxed{47}} = \qquad 0.56$$

Long-term debt to equity capital ....

$$\frac{\text{Long-term liabilities}}{\text{Equity capital*}} = \frac{1077.6 \ \boxed{46} + \boxed{47} - 23.5 \ \boxed{178}}{1793.4 \ \boxed{54} + 23.5 \ \boxed{178}} = \qquad 0.58$$

Times interest earned(b) ....

$$\frac{\text{Income before interest and taxes}}{\text{Interest}} = \frac{667.4 \ \boxed{26} + 116.2 \ \boxed{100}}{136.9 \ \boxed{98}} = \qquad 5.72$$

*Including minority interest.

Exhibit 4–2 Continued

Major categories of ratios	Method of computation (dollars in millions)	Campbell Soup ratio for 1991
Return-on-investment ratios:		
Return on total assets	$\dfrac{\text{Net income + Interest expense (1 – Tax rate)}^{(c)}\text{ + Minority interest income}}{\text{Average total assets}}$ $= \dfrac{401.5\ \boxed{28} + 116.2\ \boxed{100}\ (1 - 0.34) + 7.2\ \boxed{25}}{(4149.0 + 4115.6)\ \boxed{39A} \div 2} =$	11.75%
Return on equity capital	$\dfrac{\text{Net income}}{\text{Average equity capital}} = \dfrac{401.5\ \boxed{28}}{(1793.4 + 1691.8)\ \boxed{54} \div 2} =$	23.04%
Operating performance ratios:		
Gross margin ratio	$\dfrac{\text{Gross profit (margin)}}{\text{Sales}} = \dfrac{6204.1\ \boxed{13} - 4095.5\ \boxed{14}}{6204.1\ \boxed{13}} =$	33.99%
Operating profits to sales	$\dfrac{\text{Operating profit}}{\text{Sales}}$ $= \dfrac{6204.1\ \boxed{13} - 5415.6\ \boxed{14} - \boxed{15} - \boxed{16} - \boxed{17} + \boxed{19} - \boxed{20} - \boxed{21}}{6204.1\ \boxed{13}} =$	12.71%
Pretax income to sales	$\dfrac{\text{Pretax income}}{\text{Sales}} = \dfrac{667.4\ \boxed{26}}{6204.1\ \boxed{13}} =$	10.76%
Net income to sales	$\dfrac{\text{Net income}}{\text{Sales}} = \dfrac{401.5\ \boxed{28}}{6204.1\ \boxed{13}} =$	6.47%

Asset-utilization ratios:

Sales to cash . . . . $\dfrac{\text{Sales}}{\text{Cash}} = \dfrac{6204.1\ \boxed{13}}{178.9\ \boxed{31} + 12.8\ \boxed{32}} =$ 32.36

Sales to accounts receivable . . . $\dfrac{\text{Sales}}{\text{Accounts receivable}} = \dfrac{6204.1\ \boxed{13}}{527.4\ \boxed{33}} =$ 11.76

Sales to inventories . . . . $\dfrac{\text{Sales}}{\text{Inventories}} = \dfrac{6204.1\ \boxed{13}}{706.7\ \boxed{34}} =$ 8.78

Sales to working capital . . . . $\dfrac{\text{Sales}}{\text{Working capital}} = \dfrac{6204.1\ \boxed{13}}{1518.5\ \boxed{36} - 1278.0\ \boxed{45}} =$ 25.80

Sales to fixed assets . . . . $\dfrac{\text{Sales}}{\text{Fixed assets}} = \dfrac{6204.1\ \boxed{13}}{1790.4\ \boxed{37}} =$ 3.47

Sales to total assets . . . . $\dfrac{\text{Sales}}{\text{Total assets}} = \dfrac{6204.1\ \boxed{13}}{4149\ \boxed{39A}} =$ 1.50

*Interest income

Exhibit 4–2 Continued

Major categories of ratios	Method of computation (dollars in millions)	Campbell Soup ratio for 1991
Market measures:		
Price-earnings ratio	$\dfrac{\text{Market price}}{\text{Earnings per share}} = \dfrac{(84.88 + 72.38) \div 2^{(d)}}{3.16 \boxed{29}} =$	24.88
Earnings yield	$\dfrac{\text{Earnings per share}}{\text{Market price}} = \dfrac{3.16 \boxed{29}}{(84.88 + 72.38) \boxed{184} \div 2} =$	4.02%
Dividend yield	$\dfrac{\text{Dividends per share}}{\text{Market price per share}} = \dfrac{1.12 \boxed{89}}{(84.88 + 72.38) \boxed{184} \div 2} =$	1.42%
Dividend payout ratio	$\dfrac{\text{Dividends per share}}{\text{Earnings per share}} = \dfrac{1.12 \boxed{89}}{3.16 \boxed{29}} =$	35.44%

[a] Key references are to financial statements of Campbell Soup Company.

[b] These are simpler versions of more elaborate ratios discussed in Chapter 18.

[c] Using the marginal (corporate) tax rate.

[d] Average of high and low price for last quarter $\boxed{184}$.

The determination of the balance sheet that follows is based on the steps described below:

Cash	$190	Current liabilities	$200
Accounts receivable	60	Common stock	500
Inventory	50	Retained earnings	100
Buildings..............	300		$800
Land	200		
	$800		

STEP 1:

Assets–Liabilities	=	$600
Stockholders' equity	=	600
Retained earnings	=	100 (as given)
Common stock	=	500

STEP 2:

Equity = 3 × debt

3 × current liabilities (which are the total debt) =	$600
Add current liabilities	200
So total assets equal	$800

STEP 3:

Acid test = 1.25

$$\frac{\text{Cash + Accounts receivable}}{\$200} = 1.25$$

Hence,

   Cash + Accounts receivable = $250

STEP 4:

Inventory + Buildings + Land = $550 [i.e., Total assets − (Cash + A/R)]
        Buildings + Land = $500 (since inventory is given at $50)
Land = ⅔ of building; thus, if x = carrying amount of building
   x + ⅔ x = $500 x = $300 (building)

      Land = $500 − $300 = $200

STEP 5:

$$\frac{\text{Cost of goods sold (CGS)}}{\text{Inventory}} = \text{Inventory turnover;} \quad \frac{\text{CGS}}{\$50} = 15$$

Cost of goods sold = $750   Gross profit, 44% of $750 = $330

STEP 6:

Cost of goods sold + Gross profit ($750 + $330) = Sales = $1,080

Amount of sales per day $\dfrac{\$1,080}{360}$ = $3

Accounts receivable = 20 days sales = 20 × $3 = $60
Cash = $250 − Accounts receivable ($60) = $190

Specialized Tools of Analysis

In addition to the multipurpose tools of financial statement analysis that we discussed above, such as trend indexes, common-size statements, and ratios, the analyst has at his or her disposal a variety of special-purpose tools. These tools focus on specific financial statements or segments of such statements, or they can address themselves specifically to the operating conditions of a particular industry, for example, occupancy-capacity analysis in the hotel, hospital, or airline industries. These special-purpose tools of analysis include cash forecasts, analyses of cash flows, statements of variation in gross margin, and break-even analyses.

BUILDING BLOCKS OF FINANCIAL STATEMENT ANALYSIS

Whatever approach to financial statement analysis the analyst takes and whatever methods are used, he or she will always have to examine one or more of the important aspects of an enterprise's financial condition and results of its operations. All such aspects, with perhaps the exception of the most specialized ones, can be found in one of the following six categories:

1. Short-term liquidity.
2. Funds flow.
3. Capital structure and long-term solvency.
4. Return on investment.
5. Operating performance.
6. Assets utilization.

Each of the above categories and the tools used in measuring them will be discussed in greater depth in Part III of this book. In this way, the financial analysis required by any conceivable set of objectives may be structured by examining any or all of the above areas in any sequence and with any degree of relative emphasis called for by circumstances. Thus, these six areas of inquiry and investigation can be considered as building blocks of financial statement analysis.

COMPUTER-ASSISTED FINANCIAL ANALYSIS

The major emphasis throughout this book is on the application of thoughtful and logical analysis upon carefully evaluated and verified data. Financial statement analysis does, however, involve a significant amount of work of a computational nature as well as numerous logical steps that can be preplanned and programmed. It is in these areas that the financial analyst can utilize computers to great advantage.

The modern electronic computer has a remarkable facility for performing complex computations with great speed. Moreover, it can perform these computations, comparisons, and other logical steps for long periods of time without exhaustion and once properly programmed will do them without error. In today's environment, when business complexity has outstripped our ability to grasp it and when our ability to generate information has outrun our ability to utilize it, the computer can render vital assistance.

The intelligent use of the computer's formidable capabilities in financial analysis depends, however, on thorough understanding of the limitations to which this powerful tool is subject. Thus, the computer lacks the ability to make intuitive judgments or to gain insights, capabilities that are essential to a competent and imaginative financial analysis.[3]

There is nothing that the computer can do that a competent analyst armed with a calculator cannot do. On the other hand, the speed and the capabilities of modern computers are such that to accomplish what they can do would require so many hours of work as to render most such efforts uneconomical or infeasible. Computers have thus effectively automated some of the statistical and analytical steps that were previously done manually.

With the exception of databases which provide a full on-line presentation of financial reports, the stored databases on which computer-assisted security analysis often relies do not include all the information that, as discussed in Part II of this book, is needed to adjust accounting data in order to render it comparable or in order to make it conform to the analyst's specific needs. This is particularly true for the following reasons:

1. The data banks generally lack information on accounting policies and principles employed by a given enterprise. This information is essential to an interpretation of the data and to its comparison to other data.
2. Footnotes and other explanatory or restrictive information usually found in individual enterprise reports containing the financial statements are also generally not available in any meaningful detail.
3. Lack of retroactive adjustments because the necessary data are often not available. Such adjustments are not made even if audited data are subsequently found to be wrong or misleading.
4. Errors and omissions may occur when large masses of financial data are processed on a uniform basis for purposes of inclusion in the database. In addition, data may be classified inconsistently across firms.
5. The aggregation of dissimilar or noncomparable data results in a

---

[3] To date, developments in the area of artificial intelligence do not require us to qualify this statement significantly.

loss of vital distinctions and thus reduces its meaning and its value for analysis.

Given an understanding of the capabilities as well as the limitations to which the computer is subject, the following are the more significant uses that can be made of this important tool in the broad area of financial analysis.

1. Data Storage, Retrieval, and Computational Ability

A machine-accessible comprehensive database is essential to the use of the computer in most phases of security and credit analysis. The ability of the computer to store vast amounts of data and to afford access to them is one of its important capabilities. Another is the ability to sift these data, to manipulate them mathematically, and to select from among them in accordance with set criteria, as well as to constantly update and modify them. Moreover, the ability of computers to perform computations (of ratios, etc.) is almost unlimited.

A large commercially available database comprising financial information on thousands of corporations covering 20 or more years is available from COMPUSTAT, a service of Standard & Poor's Corporation. Another important database is that provided by Value Line. Many other specialized databases and time-sharing services are available from various sources and those include the AICPA time-sharing program library. See, however, comments in the preceding section on the limitations on the use of such databases in financial statement analysis.

2. Screening Large Masses of Data

The computer can be used to screen for specified criteria as a means of selecting investment opportunities and for other purposes. A variation of these techniques consists of "filtering" data in accordance with a set of preselected criteria (e.g., certain sales levels, returns, growth rates, financial characteristics, etc.)

3. A Research Tool

The computer can be used as a research tool for uncovering characteristics of and relationships between data on companies, industries, market behavior, and the economy.

4. Specialized Financial Analyses

The computer can be an input tool for financial analysis in credit extension and security analysis.

A. Financial analysis in credit extension.[4]
1. Storage of facts for comparison and decision making.
2. Projection of enterprise cash requirements under a variety of assumptions.
3. Projection of financial statements under a variety of assumptions showing the impact of changes on key variables. Known as *sensitivity analysis,* this technique allows the user to explore the effect of systematically changing a given variable repeatedly by a predetermined amount.
4. The introduction of probabilistic inputs. The data can be inserted as probability distributions, either normally shaped or skewed, or random probability distributions, otherwise known as Monte Carlo trials.

B. Security analysis.
1. Calculations based on past data.
2. Trend computations.
   a. Simple
   b. Regression analysis.
3. Predictive models.
4. Projections and forecasts.
5. Sensitivity analysis.
6. Complex probabilistic analysis.

Given an understanding of the capabilities of the modern electronic computer, both mainframe and PC, as well as the limitations to which it is subject, the financial analyst will find in it an important tool that promises to grow in importance as new applications to which it can be put are perfected.

ANALYTICAL REVIEW OF ACCOUNTING PRINCIPLES—PURPOSES AND FOCUS

In the chapters that follow, we shall present a review of accounting standards used in the preparation of financial statements. The purpose of this review is to examine the variety of standards that can be applied to similar transactions and circumstances, as well as the latitude that is possible in the interpretation and application of these standards in practice. Thus, the focus is on an understanding of accounting standards as well as on an appreciation of the impact that the application of these standards can

---

[4] Software for so-called expert systems has been developed through interviews with senior loan officers and is designed to capture both objective and subjective factors they use in lending decisions. Beyond number crunching they are programmed to make judgments about many important factors entering the lending decision.

have on the reported financial condition and results of operations of an enterprise. Such possible impact must be appreciated and understood before any intelligent analysis can be undertaken or any useful and meaningful comparison is made.

Example of Importance of Accounting Assumptions, Standards, and Determinations: Illustration of a Simple Investment Decision

The importance of standards and assumptions in accounting determinations can perhaps be best illustrated and understood within the framework of a very simple example of a business situation. Let us assume that the owner of an apartment building has found an interested buyer. How should the price be set? How should the buyer gain confidence in the soundness and profitability of such investment at a given price?

The first question is the method to be followed in arriving at a fair value of the building. While many approaches are possible, such as comparable current values, reproduction costs, and so forth, let us settle here on the most widely accepted method for the valuation of income-producing properties as well as other investments: the capitalization of earnings. If earning power is the major consideration, then the focus must be on the income statement. The prospective buyer is given the following income statement:

184 EAGLE STREET APARTMENT HOUSE
Income Statement
For the Year Ending December 31, Year 9

Revenue:		
Rental revenue		$46,000
Garage rentals		2,440
Other income from washer and dryer concession . .		300
Total revenue		48,740
Expenses:		
Real estate taxes	$4,900	
Mortgage interest	2,100	
Electricity and gas	840	
Water	720	
Superintendent's salary	1,600	
Insurance	680	
Repairs and maintenance	2,400	13,240
Income before depreciation		35,500
Depreciation		9,000
Net income*		$26,500

*Income taxes are excluded from consideration here because they depend on the owner's tax status.

The first questions the prospective buyer will want to ask about the foregoing income statement are these:

1. Can I rely on the fairness of presentation of the income statement?
2. What adjustments have to be made so as to obtain a net income figure that can be used with confidence in arriving at a proper purchase price?

In our society, the most common way of gaining assurance about the fairness of presentation of financial statements is to rely on the opinion of an independent certified public accountant. This professional is assumed to perform a skillful audit and to satisfy himself that the financial statements do accurately portray the results of operations and the financial position, in accordance with principles that are generally accepted as proper and useful in the particular context in which they are applied. Such an auditor is also presumed to understand that someone like our prospective buyer will rely on his or her opinion in reaching a decision on whether to buy and at what price. In Chapter 15, we will explore in more detail the function of the auditor and what his opinion means to the user of financial statements.

Our prospective buyer's second question is far more complex. The auditor's opinion relates to the income statement as representing fairly the net income for the year ended December 31, year 9. That in no way means that this is *the* relevant figure to use in arriving at a valuation of the apartment building. Nor would an auditor ever claim that his opinion is directed at the relevance of financial statement figures to any particular decision. Let us then examine what information our buyer will need and what assumptions will have to be made in order to arrive at a figure of net income that can be used in setting the value of the apartment building.

Rental Income   Does the $46,000 figure represent 100 percent occupancy during the year? If so, should an allowance be made for possible vacancies? What are rental trends in the area? What would rents be in five years? In 10 years? Are demand factors for apartments in the area going to stay stable, improve, or deteriorate? The aim, of course, is to come nearest to that figure of yearly rental income that approximates a level that, on the average, can be expected to prevail over the foreseeable future. Prior years' data will be useful in judging this.

Real Estate Taxes   Here the trend of taxes over the years is an important factor. That in turn depends on the character of the taxing community and revenue and expense trends within it.

Mortgage Interest   This expense is relevant to the buyer only if he or she assumes the existing mortgage. Otherwise the interest cost that will be incurred as a result of new financing will have to substituted.

Utilities   These expenses must be scrutinized with a view to ascertaining whether they are at a representative level of what can be expected to prevail.

Superintendent's Salary   Is the pay adequate to secure acceptable services? Can the services of superintendent be retained?

Insurance   Are all foreseeable risks insured for? Is the coverage adequate?

Repairs and Maintenance   These expenses must be examined over a number of years in order to determine an average or representative level. Is the level of expenses such that it affords proper maintenance of the property or is the expense account "starved" so as to show a higher net income?

Depreciation   This figure is not likely to be relevant to the buyer's decision unless his cost approximates that of the seller. If the cost to the buyer differs, then depreciation will have to be computed on that cost using a proper method of depreciation over the useful life of the building, so as to recover the buyer's original cost.

The buyer must also ascertain whether any expenses that he will be properly expected to incur are omitted from the above income statement. Additional considerations concern the method of financing this acquisition and other costs related thereto.

It should be understood that most of the above questions will have to be asked and properly answered even if the auditor issues an unqualified opinion on the financial statements. Thus, for example, while generally accepted accounting principles (GAAP) require that insurance expense include accruals for the full year, they are not concerned with the adequacy of insurance coverage or of the maintenance policy, or the superintendent's pay, or with expected, as opposed to actual, revenues or expense levels.

If one views the many complex questions and problems that arise in the attempt to analyze this very simple income statement for decision-making purposes, one can begin to grasp the complexities involved in the analysis of the financial statements of a sizable, modern business enterprise.

It is clear that essential to an intelligent analysis of such statements is an appreciation of what financial statements do portray as well as what they do not or cannot portray. As we have seen, there are items that properly belong in such statements and there are items that, because of an inability to quantify them or to determine them objectively, cannot be included.

Those items that properly belong in the financial statements should be presented therein in accordance with principles of accounting that enjoy general acceptance. The wide variety of standards that are "acceptable" as well as the even greater variety in the ways in which they can be applied in practice make it imperative that the user of financial statements be fully aware of these possibilities and their implications. The following chapters will explore this important area.

The example of the apartment house buyer illustrates the obvious fact that despite their limitations, financial statements and presentations are indispensable to the decision-making process. While the potential buyer could not use the income statement without obtaining more information and making further assumptions and adjustments, he or she would not have had any basis for his decision without it. Had he not received one, he would have had to make one up without utilization of the objectivity and the benefit of the experience of actual transactions over a period of time. Thus, in most cases, the interpretation of historical financial statements represents the essential first step in the decision-making process.

APPENDIX 4A

SOURCES OF INFORMATION ON FINANCIAL AND OPERATING RATIOS

A good way to achieve familiarity with the wide variety of published financial and operating ratios available is to classify them by the type of source that collects or compiles them. The specific sources given under each category are intended to exemplify the type of material available. These are by no means complete lists:

Professional and Commercial Organizations

Dun & Bradstreet, Inc., Business Economics Division, New York, N.Y.
  Industry Norms and Key Business Ratios.
  Key Business Ratios. Important operating and financial ratios in 190 lines.
  Selected operating expense figures for many retailing, wholesaling, manufacturing lines, as well as for contract construction; service/transportation/communication; finance/insurance/real estate; agriculture/forestry/fishing; mining.
  Cost-of-Doing Business Series. Typical operating ratios for 185 lines of business, showing national averages. They represent a percentage of business receipts reported by a representative sample of the total of all federal tax returns. (Published irregularly.)
Moody's Investor Service, New York, N.Y.
  Moody's Manuals contain financial and operating ratios on individual companies covered.

Nelson's Directory of Investment Research, Port Chester, N.Y.: W.R. Nelson & Co./Nelson Publications, annual.

Robert Morris Associates. *Annual Statement Studies.*

Financial and operating ratios for about 300 lines of business—manufacturers, wholesalers, retailers, services, and contractors—based on information obtained from member banks of RMA. Data is broken down by company size.

Standard & Poor's Corporation

Industry Surveys in two parts: (1) Basic Analysis and (2) Current Analysis contains many industry and individual company ratios.

Analysts Handbook. "Composite corporate per share data—by industries," for over 90 industries. Statistics and percentages cover 13 components, including sales, operating profits, depreciation, earnings dividends, and the like.

Industry Surveys. Basic data on 36 important industries, with financial comparisons of the leading companies in each industry. Includes a "Basic Analysis" for each, revised annually. A "Current Analysis" is published quarterly for each industry. A monthly "Trends and Projections" includes tables of economic and industry indicators.

Almanac of Business and Industrial Financial Ratios by Leo Troy. Prentice Hall, Englewood Cliffs, N.J.

A compilation of corporate performance ratios (operating and financial). The significance of these ratios is explained. All industries are covered in the study, each industry is subdivided by asset size.

Value Line Investment Survey, New York: Value Line Publishing, Inc. weekly updating

The Federal Government

Small Business Administration

Publications containing industry statistics (published sporadically—may not be up to date):

Small Marketers Aid.

Small Business Management Series.

Business Service Bulletins.

U.S. Department of Commerce

Census of Business—Wholesale Trade—Summary Statistics. Monthly Wholesale Trade Report. Ratio of operating expenses to sales.

Department of the Treasury

Statistics of Income, Corporation Income Tax Returns. Operating statistics based on income tax returns.

Federal Trade Commission—Securities and Exchange Commission.

Quarterly Financial Report for Manufacturing, Mining and Trade Corporations. Contains operating ratios and balance sheet ratios as well as the balance sheet in ratio format.

U.S. Internal Revenue Service

Source Book: Statistics of Income: Corporation Income Tax Returns. Washington, D.C. Annual. "Balance sheet, income statement, tax and investment credit items by major and minor industries, broken down by size of total assets."

Statistics of Income: Corporation Income Tax Returns. Washington, D.C.: U.S. Government Printing Office. Annual. Balance sheet and income statement statistics from a sample of corporate returns. Includes tables by major industry, by asset size, and so on. Includes historical summaries.

Sources of Specific Industry Ratios

Many retail and wholesale trade associations compile and publish periodic ratio statistics. Very few manufacturing associations compile ratios they make available to the public; and so for most manufacturing industries one must rely on general sources or on annual reports of specific entities.

American Meat Institute. *Annual Financial Review of the Meat Packing Industry.* Washington, D.C. Includes operating ratios.
Bank Operating Statistics. Federal Deposit Insurance Corporation. Annual.
  Institute of Real Estate Management. Experience Exchange Committee. *A Statistical Compilation and Analysis of Actual (year) Income and Expenses Experienced in Apartment, Condominium and Cooperative Building Operation.* Annual.
Discount Merchandiser. *The True Look of the Discount Industry.* June issue each year. Includes operating ratios.
National Electrical Contractors Association. *Operation Overhead.* Annual.
National Farm & Power Equipment Dealers Association. *Cost of Doing Business Study.* Annual.
National Retail Hardware Association. *Lumber/Building Material Financial Report.* Indianapolis. Annual.
Journal of Commercial Bank Lending. "Analysis of Year End Composite Ratios of Installment Sales Finance and Small Loan Companies."
National Association of Music Merchants. *Merchandising and Operating Statistics.* New York. Annual.
National Decorating Products Association. *NDPA'S Annual Cost of Doing Business Survey.* St. Louis. Taken from *Decorating Retailer,* e.g., September 1980 issue.
National Office Products Association. *NOPA Dealers Operating Results.* Alexandria, Va. Annual.
Restaurant Industry Operations Report for the United States. Washington, D.C.: National Restaurant Association. Annual.

Computerized Databases

ABI/Inform. [On-line database and CD-ROM.] Ann Arbor, MI: University Microfilms International. Weekly [on-line], monthly [CD-ROM].
Corporate Information Research Reports (CIRR). [Microfiche collection, on-line database, and CD-ROM database.] East Chester, NY: J.A. Micropublishing, monthly.
Compact Disclosure. [CD-ROM database.] Bethesda, MD: Disclosure Incorporated, monthly.

Compustat. [Computer tape files and CD-ROM database.] New York: Standard & Poor's Compustat Services, Inc., weekly.

Lotus OneSource. [CD-ROM database.] Cambridge, MA: Lotus Development Corporation, monthly.

APPENDIX 4B

This appendix contains the financial statements of Campbell Soup Company contained in its 1991 annual report. These financial statements, along with financial summaries contained in Appendix 23, form the basis for illustrations[5] throughout the text as well as the basis of a comprehensive analysis of the financial statements of the company contained in Chapter 23.

Chapter 23 contains a description of the company's business. For ease of reference the most important captions in Campbell Soup's financial statements, and selected Form 10-K schedules, have been identified by key numbers.

_____

[5] In order to draw on a richer database, the text also contains illustrations based on similarly keyed-in captions contained in the 1991 financial statements of Quaker Oats Co. found in Appendix 23.

SUPPLEMENTAL SCHEDULE OF SALES AND EARNINGS   **Campbell Soup Company**
                                                              Annual Report 1991

(million dollars)

	1991		1990		1989	
	Sales	**Earnings**	Sales	Earnings	Sales	Earnings
1 **CONTRIBUTIONS BY DIVISION:**						
Campbell North America						
Campbell U.S.A.	**$3,911.8**	**$632.7**	$3,932.7	$370.8	$3,666.9	$242.3
Campbell Canada	**352.0**	**35.3**	384.0	25.6	313.4	23.8
	4,263.8	**668.0**	4,316.7	396.4	3,980.3	266.1
Campbell Biscuit and Bakery						
Pepperidge Farm	**569.0**	**73.6**	582.0	57.0	548.4	53.6
International Biscuit	**219.4**	**17.6**	195.3	8.9	178.0	11.7
	788.4	**91.2**	777.3	65.9	726.4	65.3
Campbell International	**1,222.9**	**39.4**	1,189.8	(168.6)	1,030.3	(117.8)
Interdivision	**(71.0)**		(78.0)		(64.9)	
TOTAL SALES	**$6,204.1**		$6,205.8		$5,672.1	
TOTAL OPERATING EARNINGS		**798.6**		293.7		213.6
Unallocated corporate expenses		**(41.1)**		(16.5)		(31.3)
Interest, net		**(90.2)**		(94.0)		(55.8)
Foreign currency translation adjustments		**.1**		(3.8)		(20.0)
Taxes on earnings		**(265.9)**		(175.0)		(93.4)
NET EARNINGS		**$401.5**		$4.4		$13.1
NET EARNINGS PER SHARE		**$3.16**		$.03		$.10

Contributions by division in 1990 include the effects of divestitures, restructuring and unusual charges of $339.1 million as follows:
Campbell U.S.A. $121.8 million, Campbell Canada $6.6 million, Pepperidge Farm $11.0 million, International Biscuit $14.3 million,
and Campbell International $185.4 million. Contributions by division in 1989 include the effects of restructuring and unusual
charges of $343.0 million as follows: Campbell U.S.A. $183.1 million, Campbell Canada $6.0 million, Pepperidge Farm $7.1 million,
International Biscuit $9.5 million, and Campbell International $137.3 million.

**MANAGEMENT'S DISCUSSION AND ANALYSIS OF
RESULTS OF OPERATIONS AND FINANCIAL CONDITION**
. . . .

[2] **RESULTS OF OPERATIONS**

Overview

Campbell had record net earnings in 1991 of $401.5 million, or $3.16 per share, compared to net earnings of $4.4 million, or 3 cents per share, in 1990. Excluding 1990's divestiture and restructuring charges, earnings per share increased 34% in 1991. In 1991, the Company sold five non-strategic businesses, sold or closed several manufacturing plants, and discontinued certain unprofitable product lines. Net sales of $6.2 billion in 1991 were even with 1990. Sales were up 4% excluding businesses that were divested and product lines that were discontinued in 1991.

In 1990, the Company incurred charges for divestitures and restructuring of $2.33 per share, reducing net earnings to 3 cents per share. In 1989, restructuring charges of $2.02 per share reduced earnings to 10 cents per share. Excluding these charges from both years, earnings per share rose 11% in 1990. Sales increased 9%. In 1990, the Company's domestic divisions had strong earnings performances, excluding the divestiture and restructuring charges, but the International Division's performance was disappointing principally due to the poor performance of United Kingdom frozen food and Italian biscuit operations. The Italian biscuit operations were divested in 1991.

The divestiture and restructuring programs were designed to strengthen the Company's core businesses and improve long-term profitability. The 1990 divestiture program involved the sale of several low-return or non-strategic businesses. The 1990 restructuring charges provided for the elimination of underperforming assets and unnecessary facilities and included a write-off of goodwill. The restructuring charges in 1989 involved plant consolidations, work force reductions, and goodwill write-offs.

1991 Compared to 1990

[3] RESULTS BY DIVISION

CAMPBELL NORTH AMERICA—Operating earnings of Campbell North America, the Company's largest division, were $668.0 million in 1991 compared to $396.4 million in 1990 after restructuring charges of $128.4 million. Operating earnings increased 27% in 1991 over 1990, excluding the restructuring charges from 1990. All of the division's core businesses had very strong

earnings growth. Continued benefits of restructuring drove significant improvements in operating margins.

Sales were $4.26 billion in 1991. Excluding divested businesses and discontinued product lines, sales increased 2% with overall volume down 2%. Soup volume was off 1.5% as a result of reduced year-end trade promotional activities. Significant volume increases were achieved in the cooking soup, ramen noodle and family-size soup categories and "Healthy Request" soup. Exceptionally strong volume performances were turned in by "Swanson" frozen dinners, "Franco-American" gravies and "Prego" spaghetti sauces with positive volume results for "LeMenu Healthy" entrees, Food Service frozen soups and entrees, and Casera Foods in Puerto Rico.

CAMPBELL BISCUIT AND BAKERY—Operating earnings of the Biscuit and Bakery division, which includes Pepperidge Farm in the United States, Delacre in Europe and an equity interest in Arnotts Limited in Australia, were $91.2 million in 1991 compared with $65.9 million in 1990 after restructuring charges of $25.3 million. Operating earnings were flat in 1991, excluding the restructuring charges from 1990. Sales increased 1%, however, volume declined 3%.

Pepperidge Farm operating earnings in 1991 increased despite a drop in sales, which reflects the adverse effect of the recession on premium cookies. Several new varieties of "Hearty Slices" bread performed well. Delacre, benefitting from new management and integration into the worldwide biscuit and bakery organization, turned in significant improvements in 1991 sales and operating earnings. Arnotts' performance in 1991 was disappointing and included restructuring charges. Its restructuring program should have a positive impact on fiscal 1992 results. The 1991 comparison with 1990 was also adversely impacted by gains of $4.0 million realized in 1990 on the sales of businesses by Arnotts.

CAMPBELL INTERNATIONAL—Operating earnings of the International division were $39.4 million in 1991 compared to an operating loss of $168.6 million in 1990 after restructuring charges of $185.4 million.

In 1991, Campbell International achieved a significant turnaround. Operating earnings for the year more than doubled above the pre-restructuring results of the prior year. There were margin improvements throughout the system. Europe led the division's positive results. A key component was the United Kingdom's move from a loss position to profitability, driven by the benefits of restructuring and product line reconfiguration. European Food and Confectionery units turned in another year of solid earnings growth. Mexican operations, strengthened by a new management team, also turned around from a loss to a profit position. Sales were $1.22 billion in 1991, an increase of 6%, excluding divested businesses and discontinued product lines, and the effects of foreign currency rates. Volume was approximately the same as in 1990.

☐4☐   STATEMENTS OF EARNINGS

Sales in 1991 were even with 1990. Excluding divested businesses and unprofitable product lines discontinued during 1991, sales increased 4% while volume declined approximately 2%. The decline in volume was caused by reduced year-end trade promotional activities and the adverse effect of the recession on certain premium products.

Gross margins improved 2.6 percentage points to 34.0% in 1991 from 31.4% in 1990. All divisions improved due to the significant benefits from restructuring and the divestitures and product-pruning activities. Productivity improvements worldwide and declining commodity prices also contributed to the higher margins.

Marketing and selling expenses, as a percentage of net sales, were 15.4% in 1991 compared to 15.8% in 1990. The decrease in 1991 is due to more focused marketing efforts and controlled new product introductions. For each of the prior 10 fiscal years, these expenses had increased significantly. Advertising was down 11% in 1991. Management expects advertising expenditures to increase in 1992 in order to drive volume growth of core products and to support the introduction of new products.

Administrative expenses, as a percentage of net sales, were 4.9% in 1991 compared to 4.7% in 1990. The increase in 1991 results principally from annual executive incentive plan accruals due to outstanding financial performance and foreign currency rates.

Interest expense increased in 1991 due to timing of fourth quarter borrowings in order to obtain favorable long-term interest rates. Interest income was also higher in 1991 as the proceeds from these borrowings were invested temporarily until needed. Interest expense, net of interest income, decreased from $94.0 million in 1990 to $90.2 million in 1991 as the increased cash flow from operations exceeded cash used for share repurchases and acquisitions.

Foreign exchange losses declined principally due to reduced effects of currency devaluations in Argentina.

Other expense was $26.2 million in 1991 compared to $14.7 million in 1990. The increase results principally from accruals for long-term incentive compensation plans reflecting changes in Campbell's stock price.

As discussed in the "Overview" section above, 1990 results include divestiture, restructuring, and unusual charges of $339.1 million ($301.6 million or $2.33 per share after taxes).

Equity in earnings of affiliates declined in 1991 principally due to the disappointing performance at Arnotts and to a $4.0 million gain on sales of businesses realized by Arnotts in 1990.

1990 Compared to 1989

☐5☐

RESULTS BY DIVISION

CAMPBELL NORTH AMERICA—In 1990, Campbell North America had operating earnings of $396.4 million after restructuring charges of $128.4 million. In 1989, the division had operating earnings of $266.1 million, after restructuring charges of $189.1 million. Excluding restructuring charges from both 1990 and 1989, operating earnings increased 15% in 1990, led by strong performances by the soup, grocery, "Mrs. Paul's" frozen seafood, and Canadian sectors. The olives business performed poorly in 1990.

Sales increased 8% in 1990 to $4.32 billion on a 3% increase in volume. There were solid volume increases in ready-to-serve soups, "Great Starts" frozen breakfasts, and "Prego" spaghetti sauces. Overall soup volume was up 1%. "Mrs. Paul's" regained the number one share position in frozen prepared seafood.

CAMPBELL BISCUIT AND BAKERY—In 1990, Campbell Biscuit and Bakery had operating earnings of $65.9 million after restructuring charges of $25.3 million. In 1989, the division's operating earnings were $65.3 million after restructuring charges of $16.6 million. Excluding restructuring charges from both 1990 and 1989, operating earnings of the division increased 11% in 1990. The increase in operating earnings was driven by Pepperidge Farm's biscuit and bakery units along with Arnotts' gain on sales of businesses. Pepperidge Farm's frozen unit and Delacre performed poorly. Sales increased 7% to $777.3 million. Volume increased 1%, with Pepperidge Farm's biscuit, bakery and food service units and Delacre the main contributors to the growth.

**MANAGEMENT'S DISCUSSION AND ANALYSIS OF
RESULTS OF OPERATIONS AND FINANCIAL CONDITION**
. . . .

CAMPBELL INTERNATIONAL — In 1990, Campbell International had an operating loss of $168.6 million after restructuring charges of $185.4 million. In 1989, the division sustained an operating loss of $117.8 million after restructuring charges of $137.3 million. Excluding restructuring charges from both 1990 and 1989, operating earnings declined 14% in 1990, as strong performances in the European Food and Confectionery and Argentine operations were more than offset by poor performances in the United Kingdom frozen food and Italian biscuit operations. Sales in 1990 were $1.19 billion, an increase of 15%. Volume was up 14% of which 11% came from acquisitions.

6   STATEMENTS OF EARNINGS

'In 1990 sales increased 9% on a 5% increase in volume, about half of which came from established businesses.

Gross margins improved by 1.9 percentage points to 31.4% in 1990 from 29.5% in 1989. All divisions had improved margins in 1990, with Campbell North America operations posting substantial improvements.

Marketing and selling expenses, as a percentage of net sales, were 15.8% in 1990 compared to 14.4% in 1989. The 1990 increase was due to heavy marketing expenditures by Campbell U.S.A. at both the national and regional levels.

Administrative expenses, as a percentage of net sales, were 4.7% in 1990 compared to 4.4% in 1989. The increase in 1990 was driven by some unusual one-time expenditures, employee benefits, the weakening dollar and acquisitions.

Interest expense increased in 1990 due to higher debt levels resulting from funding of acquisitions, higher inventory levels during the year, purchases of Campbell's stock for the treasury and restructuring program expenditures. Interest income declined in 1990 because of a shift from local currency to lower-yielding dollar denominated temporary investments in Latin America to minimize foreign exchange losses.

Foreign exchange losses resulted principally from currency devaluations in Argentina. There was a large devaluation in Argentina in 1989. Also, 1990 losses were lower due to the shift in temporary investments described in the previous paragraph.

Other expense was $14.7 million in 1990 compared to $32.4 million in 1989. This decline results principally from reduced accruals for long-term incentive compensation plans reflecting changes in Campbell's stock price.

As discussed in the "Overview" section above, results include divestiture, restructuring and unusual charges of $339.1 million ($301.6 million or $2.33 per share after taxes) in 1990 and $343.0 million ($260.8 million or $2.02 per share after taxes) in 1989.

Equity in earnings of affiliates increased in 1990 principally due to a $4.0 million gain on sales of businesses realized by Arnotts in 1990.

7

Income Taxes

The effective income tax rate was 39.8% in 1991, 97.5% in 1990 and 87.7% in 1989. The principal reason for the high tax rates in 1990 and 1989 is that certain of the divestiture, restructuring and unusual charges are not tax deductible. Excluding the effect of these charges, the rate would be 41.0% in 1990 and 38.9% in 1989. The variances in all years are principally due to the level of certain foreign losses for which no tax benefit is currently available.

8

Inflation

The Company attempts to mitigate the effects of inflation on sales and earnings by appropriately increasing selling prices and aggressively pursuing an ongoing cost improvement effort which includes capital investments in more efficient plants and equipment. Also, the divestiture and restructuring programs enacted in 1989 and 1990 have made the Company a more cost-effective producer, as previously discussed with reference to cost of products sold.

9

Recent Developments

In December 1990, the Financial Accounting Standards Board issued Statement of Financial Accounting Standards No. 106, "Employer's Accounting for Post-retirement Benefits Other Than Pensions," which requires employers to account for retiree health obligations on an accrual basis beginning with the Company's 1994 fiscal year. For a discussion of its impact on the Company, see Note 8 to the Consolidated Financial Statements.

10

LIQUIDITY AND CAPITAL RESOURCES

The Consolidated Statements of Cash Flows and Balance Sheets demonstrate the Company's continued superior financial strength.

Campbell Soup Company

. . . .

☐11☐ **Statements of Cash Flows**

OPERATING ACTIVITIES—Cash provided by operations was $805.2 million in 1991, an 80% increase from ☐12☐ $448.4 million in 1990. This increased cash flow was driven by the Company's record earnings level and reduced working capital resulting from improved asset management and the restructuring program.

INVESTING ACTIVITIES—The majority of the Company's investing activities involve the purchase of new plant assets to maintain modern manufacturing processes and increase productivity. Capital expenditures for plant assets amounted to $371.1 million in 1991, including $10.0 million of capital lease activity, down slightly from 1990. The Company expects capital expenditures in 1992 to be about $400 million.

Another key investing activity of the Company is acquisitions. The total cost of acquisitions in 1991 was $180.1 million, most of which was spent to acquire the publicly-held shares of the Company's 71% owned subsidiary, Campbell Soup Company Ltd in Canada. This will allow Campbell North America to more efficiently integrate its U.S. and Canadian operations to provide Campbell with competitive advantage in North America.

One of the Company's strategies has been to prune low-return assets and businesses from its portfolio. In 1991 the Company realized over $110 million in cash from these activities, with $67.4 million coming from sales of businesses and $43.2 million realized from asset sales.

Also, during 1991 the Company made contributions to its pension plans substantially in excess of the amounts expensed. This was the principal reason for the increase in other assets.

FINANCING ACTIVITIES—During 1991, the Company issued debt in the public markets for a total of $400 million: $100 million of 9% Notes due 1998, $100 million of Medium-Term Notes due 2001 at interest rates from 8.58% to 8.75%, and $200 million of 8.875% Debentures due 2021. The proceeds were used to reduce short-term debt by $227 million, pay off long-term debt maturing in 1991 of $129.9 million, and to fund the purchase of the minority interest of Campbell Canada.

During 1991, the Company repurchased approximately 3.4 million shares of its capital stock at a cost of $175.6 million. Cash received from the issuance of approximately 1.1 million treasury shares pursuant to the stock option and long-term incentive plans amounted to $47.7 million in 1991.

Dividends of $137.5 million represent the dividends paid in 1991. Dividends declared in 1991 were $142.2 million or $1.12 per share, an increase of 14% over 1990.

Balance Sheets

Total borrowings at the end of fiscal 1991 were $1.055 billion compared to $1.008 billion at the end of 1990. Even after the effects of the borrowing and treasury stock activity previously discussed, total debt as a percentage of total capitalization was 33.7%—the same as a year ago. The Company has ample sources of funds. It has access to the commercial paper markets with the highest rating. The Company's long-term debt is rated double A by the major rating agencies. It has filed a shelf registration with the Securities and Exchange Commission for the issuance from time to time of up to $100 million of debt securities. Also, the Company has unused lines of credit of approximately $635 million.

Debt-related activity is discussed in the Statements of Cash Flows section above. In addition to that, the debt balances on the Balance Sheets were affected by current maturities of long-term debt and by the classification of commercial paper to be refinanced as long-term debt in 1990.

Aggressive management of working capital and the effect of divested businesses are evidenced by a $235.5 million decrease in current assets exclusive of changes in cash and temporary investments. Receivables are down $97.1 million and inventories declined $113.1 million from 1990. Accounts payable are down $42.8 million because of the reduced inventory levels and divestitures. Accrued liabilities and accrued income taxes declined $61.9 million as increases due to higher earnings levels and the timing of certain payments were offset by payments and charges resulting from the divestitures and restructuring programs.

Plant assets increased $72.7 million due to capital expenditures of $371.1 million offset by the annual provision for depreciation of $194.5 million, asset sales and divestitures. Intangible assets increased $52.1 million as the acquisitions resulted in $132.3 million of additional goodwill. Amortization and divestitures accounted for the remainder of the change. Other assets increased principally as the result of the pension contribution.

Other liabilities decreased $14.9 million as the reduction of minority interest resulting from the purchase of the publicly-held shares of Campbell Canada and changes in foreign currency rates on other liabilities offset the annual deferred tax provision.

CONSOLIDATED STATEMENTS OF EARNINGS   Campbell Soup Company

(millions)

		1991	1990	1989
13	**NET SALES**	**$6,204.1**	$6,205.8	$5,672.1
	Costs and expenses			
14	Cost of products sold	**4,095.5**	4,258.2	4,001.6
15	Marketing and selling expenses	**956.2**	980.5	818.8
16	Administrative expenses	**306.7**	290.7	252.1
17	Research and development expenses	**56.3**	53.7	47.7
18	Interest expense (Note 3)	**116.2**	111.6	94.1
19	Interest income	**(26.0)**	(17.6)	(38.3)
20	Foreign exchange losses, net (Note 4)	**.8**	3.3	19.3
21	Other expense (Note 5)	**26.2**	14.7	32.4
22	Divestitures, restructuring and unusual charges (Note 6)	**—**	339.1	343.0
22A	Total costs and expenses	**5,531.9**	6,034.2	5,570.7
23	Earnings before equity in earnings of affiliates and minority interests	**672.2**	171.6	101.4
24	Equity in earnings of affiliates	**2.4**	13.5	10.4
25	Minority interests	**(7.2)**	(5.7)	(5.3)
26	Earnings before taxes	**667.4**	179.4	106.5
27	Taxes on earnings (Note 9)	**265.9**	175.0	93.4
28	**NET EARNINGS**	**$ 401.5**	$ 4.4	$ 13.1
29	**NET EARNINGS PER SHARE (NOTE 22)**	**$3.16**	$.03	$.10
30	Weighted average shares outstanding	**127.0**	129.6	129.3

The accompanying Summary of Significant Accounting Policies and Notes on pages 26 to 33 are an integral part of the financial statements.

CONSOLIDATED BALANCE SHEETS   Campbell Soup Company

(million dollars)

	July 28, 1991	July 29, 1990
CURRENT ASSETS		
[31] Cash and cash equivalents (Note 12)	$ 178.9	$ 80.7
[32] Other temporary investments, at cost which approximates market	12.8	22.5
[33] Accounts receivable (Note 13)	527.4	624.5
[34] Inventories (Note 14)	706.7	819.8
[35] Prepaid expenses (Note 15)	92.7	118.0
[36] Total current assets	1,518.5	1,665.5
[37] **PLANT ASSETS, NET OF DEPRECIATION (NOTE 16)**	1,790.4	1,717.7
[38] **INTANGIBLE ASSETS, NET OF AMORTIZATION (NOTE 17)**	435.5	383.4
[39] **OTHER ASSETS (NOTE 18)**	404.6	349.0
Total assets	$4,149.0	$4,115.6
CURRENT LIABILITIES		
[40] Notes payable (Note 19)	$ 282.2	$ 202.3
[41] Payable to suppliers and others	482.4	525.2
[42] Accrued liabilities (Note 20)	408.7	491.9
[43] Dividend payable	37.0	32.3
[44] Accrued income taxes	67.7	46.4
[45] Total current liabilities	1,278.0	1,298.1
[46] **LONG-TERM DEBT (NOTE 19)**	772.6	805.8
[47] **OTHER LIABILITIES, PRINCIPALLY DEFERRED INCOME TAXES (NOTE 21)**	305.0	319.9
SHAREOWNERS' EQUITY (NOTE 22)		
[48] Preferred stock; authorized 40,000,000 shares; none issued	—	—
[49] Capital stock, $.15 par value; authorized 140,000,000 shares; issued 135,622,676 shares	20.3	20.3
[50] Capital surplus	107.3	61.9
[51] Earnings retained in the business	1,912.6	1,653.3
[52] Capital stock in treasury, 8,618,911 shares in 1991 and 6,353,697 shares in 1990, at cost	(270.4)	(107.2)
[53] Cumulative translation adjustments (Note 4)	23.6	63.5
[54] Total shareowners' equity	1,793.4	1,691.8
[55] Total liabilities and shareowners' equity	$4,149.0	$4,115.6

The accompanying Summary of Significant Accounting Policies and Notes on pages 26 to 33 are an integral part of the financial statements.

CONSOLIDATED STATEMENTS OF CASH FLOWS Campbell Soup Company

(million dollars)

		1991	1990	1989
	CASH FLOWS FROM OPERATING ACTIVITIES:			
56	Net earnings	$401.5	$ 4.4	$ 13.1
	To reconcile net earnings to net cash provided by operating activities:			
57	Depreciation and amortization	208.6	200.9	192.3
58	Divestitures and restructuring provisions		339.1	343.0
59	Deferred taxes	35.5	3.9	(67.8)
60	Other, net	63.2	18.6	37.3
61	(Increase) decrease in accounts receivable	17.1	(60.4)	(46.8)
62	(Increase) decrease in inventories	48.7	10.7	(113.2)
63	Net change in other current assets and liabilities	30.6	(68.8)	(.6)
64	Net cash provided by operating activities	805.2	448.4	357.3
	CASH FLOWS FROM INVESTING ACTIVITIES:			
65	Purchases of plant assets	(361.1)	(387.6)	(284.1)
66	Sales of plant assets	43.2	34.9	39.8
67	Businesses acquired	(180.1)	(41.6)	(135.8)
68	Sales of businesses	67.4	21.7	4.9
69	Increase in other assets	(57.8)	(18.6)	(107.0)
70	Net change in other temporary investments	9.7	3.7	9.0
71	Net cash used in investing activities	(478.7)	(387.5)	(473.2)
	CASH FLOWS FROM FINANCING ACTIVITIES:			
72	Long-term borrowings	402.8	12.6	126.5
73	Repayments of long-term borrowings	(129.9)	(22.5)	(53.6)
74	Increase (decrease) in borrowings with less than three month maturities	(137.9)	(2.7)	108.2
75	Other short-term borrowings	117.3	153.7	227.1
76	Repayments of other short-term borrowings	(206.4)	(89.8)	(192.3)
77	Dividends paid	(137.5)	(124.3)	(86.7)
78	Treasury stock purchases	(175.6)	(41.1)	(8.1)
79	Treasury stock issued	47.7	12.4	18.5
80	Other, net	(.1)	(.1)	23.5
81	Net cash provided by (used in) financing activities	(219.6)	(101.8)	163.1
82	Effect of exchange rate changes on cash	(8.7)	.7	(12.1)
83	**NET INCREASE (DECREASE) IN CASH AND CASH EQUIVALENTS**	98.2	(40.2)	35.1
84	Cash and cash equivalents at beginning of year	80.7	120.9	85.8
85	**CASH AND CASH EQUIVALENTS AT END OF YEAR**	$178.9	$ 80.7	$120.9

The accompanying Summary of Significant Accounting Policies and Notes on pages 26 to 33 are an integral part of the financial statements.
Prior years have been reclassified to conform to the 1991 presentation.

CONSOLIDATED STATEMENTS OF SHAREOWNERS' EQUITY   Campbell Soup Company

(million dollars)

	Preferred stock	Capital stock	Capital surplus	Earnings retained in the business	Capital stock in treasury	Cumulative translation adjustments	Total Shareowners' Equity
86 Balance at July 31, 1988	—	$20.3	$ 42.3	$1,879.1	$ (75.2)	$28.5	$1,895.0
Net earnings				13.1			13.1
Cash dividends							
($.90 per share)				(116.4)			(116.4)
Treasury stock purchased					(8.1)		(8.1)
Treasury stock issued under							
Management incentive and							
Stock option plans			8.5		12.6		21.1
Translation adjustments						(26.4)	(26.4)
87 Balance at July 30, 1989	—	20.3	50.8	1,775.8	(70.7)	2.1	1,778.3
Net earnings				4.4			4.4
Cash dividends							
($.98 per share)				(126.9)			(126.9)
Treasury stock purchased					(41.1)		(41.1)
Treasury stock issued under							
Management incentive and							
Stock option plans			11.1		4.6		15.7
Translation adjustments						61.4	61.4
Balance at July 29, 1990	—	20.3	61.9	1,653.3	(107.2)	63.5	1,691.8
88 *Net earnings*				*401.5*			*401.5*
89 *Cash dividends*							
($1.12 per share)				*(142.2)*			*(142.2)*
90 *Treasury stock purchased*					*(175.6)*		*(175.6)*
91 *Treasury stock issued under*							
Management incentive and							
Stock option plans			*45.4*		*12.4*		*57.8*
92 *Translation adjustments*						*(29.9)*	*(29.9)*
93 *Sale of foreign operations*						*(10.0)*	*(10.0)*
94 *Balance at July 28, 1991*	—	*$20.3*	*$107.3*	*$1,912.6*	*$(270.4)*	*$23.6*	*$1,793.4*

95 **CHANGES IN NUMBER OF SHARES**

(thousands of shares)

	Issued	Out- standing	In Treasury
Balance at July 31, 1988	135,622.7	129,038.6	6,584.1
Treasury stock purchased		(250.6)	250.6
Treasury stock issued under Management incentive and Stock option plans		790.6	(790.6)
Balance at July 30, 1989	135,622.7	129,578.6	6,044.1
Treasury stock purchased		(833.0)	833.0
Treasury stock issued under Management incentive and Stock option plans		523.4	(523.4)
Balance at July 29,1990	135,622.7	129,269.0	6,353.7
Treasury stock purchased		*(3,395.4)*	*3,395.4*
Treasury stock issued under Management incentive and Stock option plans		*1,130.2*	*(1,130.2)*
Balance at July 28, 1991	*135,622.7*	*127,003.8*	*8,618.9*

The accompanying Summary of Significant Accounting Policies and Notes on pages 26 to 33 are an integral part of the financial statements.

NOTES TO CONSOLIDATED FINANCIAL STATEMENTS
. . . .

(million dollars)

96 ❶ **SUMMARY OF SIGNIFICANT ACCOUNTING POLICIES**

CONSOLIDATION—The consolidated financial statements include the accounts of the Company and its majority-owned subsidiaries. Significant intercompany transactions are eliminated in consolidation. Investments in affiliates owned 20% or more are accounted for by the equity method.

INVENTORIES—Substantially all domestic inventories are priced at the lower of cost or market, with cost determined by the last-in, first-out (LIFO) method. Other inventories are priced at the lower of average cost or market.

INTANGIBLES—The excess of cost of investments over net assets of purchased companies is amortized on a straight-line basis over periods not exceeding forty years.

PLANT ASSETS—Alterations and major overhauls which substantially extend the lives of properties or materially increase their capacity are capitalized. The amounts for property disposals are removed from plant asset and accumulated depreciation accounts and any resultant gain or loss is included in earnings. Ordinary repairs and maintenance are charged to operating costs.

DEPRECIATION—Depreciation provided in costs and expenses is on the straight-line method. The United States, Canadian and certain other foreign companies use accelerated methods of depreciation for income tax purposes.

PENSION PLANS—Pension costs are accrued over employees' careers based on plan benefit formulas.

CASH AND CASH EQUIVALENTS—All highly liquid debt instruments purchased with a maturity of three months or less are classified as Cash Equivalents.

FINANCIAL INSTRUMENTS—In managing interest rate exposure, the Company at times enters into interest rate swap agreements. When interest rates change, the difference to be paid or received is accrued and recognized as interest expense over the life of the agreement. In order to hedge foreign currency exposures on firm commitments, the Company at times enters into forward foreign exchange contracts. Gains and losses resulting from these instruments are recognized in the same period as the underlying hedged transaction. The Company also at times enters into foreign currency swap agreements which are effective as hedges of net investments in foreign subsidiaries. Realized and unrealized gains and losses on these currency swaps are recognized in the Cumulative Translation Adjustments account in Shareowners' Equity.

97 ❷ **GEOGRAPHIC AREA INFORMATION**

The Company is predominantly engaged in the prepared convenience foods industry. The following presents information about operations in different geographic areas:

	1991	1990	1989
Net sales			
United States	$4,495.6	$4,527.2	$4,233.4
Europe	1,149.1	1,101.4	983.7
Other foreign countries	656.0	673.6	542.9
Adjustments and eliminations	(96.6)	(96.4)	(87.9)
Consolidated	$6,204.1	$6,205.8	$5,672.1
Earnings (loss) before taxes			
United States	$ 694.8	$ 427.8	$ 294.5
Europe	48.8	(178.7)	(21.3)
Other foreign countries	55.0	44.6	(59.6)
	798.6	293.7	213.6
Unallocated corporate expenses	(41.1)	(16.5)	(31.3)
Interest, net	(90.2)	(94.0)	(55.8)
Foreign currency translation adjustments	.1	(3.8)	(20.0)
Consolidated	$ 667.4	$ 179.4	$ 106.5
Identifiable assets			
United States	$2,693.4	$2,535.0	$2,460.5
Europe	711.3	942.2	886.9
Other foreign countries	744.3	638.4	584.7
Consolidated	$4,149.0	$4,115.6	$3,932.1

Transfers between geographic areas are recorded at cost plus markup or at market. Identifiable assets are all assets identified with operations in each geographic area.
. . . .

❸ **INTEREST EXPENSE**

	1991	1990	1989
98 Interest expense	$136.9	$121.9	$97.6
99 Less interest expense capitalized	20.7	10.3	3.5
100	$116.2	$111.6	$94.1

Campbell Soup Company

(million dollars)

101 ④ FOREIGN CURRENCY TRANSLATION

Fluctuations in foreign exchange rates resulted in decreases in net earnings of $.3 in 1991, $3.2 in 1990 and $19.1 in 1989.

The balances in the Cumulative translation adjustments account are the following:

	1991	1990	1989
Europe	$ 5.6	$43.2	$(3.5)
Canada	3.8	3.6	(2.5)
Australia	13.4	16.1	7.3
Other	.8	.6	.8
	$23.6	$63.5	$ 2.1

⑤ OTHER EXPENSE

Included in other expense are the following:

		1991	1990	1989
102	Stock price related incentive programs	$15.4	$ (.1)	$17.4
103	Amortization of intangible and other assets	14.1	16.8	16.4
104	Other, net	(3.3)	(2.0)	(1.4)
		$26.2	$14.7	$32.4

105 ⑥ DIVESTITURES, RESTRUCTURING AND UNUSUAL CHARGES

In 1990, charges for divestiture and restructuring programs, designed to strengthen the Company's core businesses and improve long-term profitability, reduced operating earnings by $339.1; $301.6 after taxes, or $2.33 per share. The divestiture program involves the sale of several low-return or non-strategic businesses. The restructuring charges provide for the elimination of underperforming assets and unnecessary facilities and include a charge of $113 to write off goodwill in the United Kingdom.

In 1989, charges for a worldwide restructuring program reduced operating earnings by $343.0; $260.8 after taxes, or $2.02 per share. The restructuring program involved plant consolidations, work force reductions, and goodwill write-offs.

106 ⑦ ACQUISITIONS

Prior to July 1991, the Company owned approximately 71% of the capital stock of Campbell Soup Company Ltd ("Campbell Canada"), which processes, packages and distributes a wide range of prepared foods exclusively in Canada under many of the Company's brand names. The financial position and results of operations of Campbell Canada are consolidated with those of the Company. In July 1991, the Company acquired the remaining shares (29%) of Campbell Canada which it did not already own at a cost of $159.7. In addition, the Company made one other acquisition at a cost of $20.4. The total cost of 1991 acquisitions of $180.1 was allocated as follows:

107

Working capital	$ 5.1
Fixed assets	4.7
Intangibles, principally goodwill	132.3
Other assets	1.5
Elimination of minority interest	36.5
	$180.1

During 1990, the Company made several small acquisitions at a cost of $43.1 which was allocated as follows:

108

Working capital	$ 7.8
Fixed assets	24.7
Intangibles, principally goodwill	18.5
Long-term liabilities and other	(7.9)
	$43.1

During 1989, the Company made several acquisitions at a cost of $137.9, including a soup and pickle manufacturing business in Canada. The cost of the acquisitions was allocated as follows:

109

Working capital	$ 39.9
Fixed assets	34.6
Intangibles, principally goodwill	65.5
Long-term liabilities and other	(2.1)
	$137.9

These acquisitions were accounted for as purchase transactions, and operations of the acquired companies are included in the financial statements from the dates the acquisitions were recorded. Proforma results of

---

NOTES TO CONSOLIDATED FINANCIAL STATEMENTS

· ·

(million dollars)

operations have not been presented as they would not vary materially from the reported amounts and would not be indicative of results anticipated following acquisition due to significant changes made to acquired companies' operations.

· ·

[110] ❽ PENSION PLANS AND RETIREMENT BENEFITS

PENSION PLANS—Substantially all of the employees of the Company and its domestic and Canadian subsidiaries are covered by noncontributory defined benefit pension plans. Plan benefits are generally based on years of service and employees' compensation during the last years of employment. Benefits are paid from funds previously provided to trustees and insurance companies or are paid directly by the Company or its subsidiaries. Actuarial assumptions and plan provisions are reviewed regularly by the Company and its independent actuaries to ensure that plan assets will be adequate to provide pension and survivor benefits. Plan assets consist primarily of shares of or units in common stock, fixed income, real estate and money market funds.

Pension expense included the following:

For Domestic and Canadian trusteed plans:	1991	1990	1989
[111] Service cost-benefits earned during the year	$ 22.1	$ 19.3	$17.2
[112] Interest cost on projected benefit obligation	69.0	63.3	58.8
[113] Actual return on plan assets	(73.4)	(27.1)	(113.8)
[114] Net amortization and deferral	6.3	(38.2)	57.8
	24.0	17.3	20.0
[115] Other pension expense	7.4	6.4	6.8
[116] Consolidated pension expense	$ 31.4	$ 23.7	$26.8

Principal actuarial assumptions used in the United States were:

	1991	1990	1989
Measurement of projected benefit obligation—			
[117] Discount rate	8.75%	9.00%	9.00%
[118] Long-term rate of compensation increase	5.75%	5.50%	5.00%
[119] Long-term rate of return on plan assets	9.00%	9.00%	9.00%

The funded status of the plans was as follows:

[120]	July 28, 1991	July 29, 1990
Actuarial present value of benefit obligations:		
Vested	$(679.6)	$(624.4)
Non-vested	(34.8)	(35.0)
Accumulated benefit obligation	(714.4)	(659.4)
Effect of projected future salary increases	(113.3)	(101.0)
Projected benefit obligation	(827.7)	(760.4)
Plan assets at market value	857.7	773.9
Plan assets in excess of projected benefit obligation	30.0	13.5
Unrecognized net loss	122.9	86.3
Unrecognized prior service cost	54.9	55.9
Unrecognized net assets at transition	(35.3)	(39.5)
Prepaid pension expense	$ 172.5	$ 116.2

Pension coverage for employees of the Company's foreign subsidiaries, other than Canada, and other supplemental pension benefits of the Company are provided to the extent determined appropriate through their respective plans. Obligations under such plans are systematically provided for by depositing funds with trusts or under insurance contracts. The assets and obligations of these plans are not material.

SAVINGS PLANS—The Company sponsors employee savings plans which cover substantially all domestic employees. After one year of continuous service the Company matches 50% of employee contributions up to five percent of compensation within certain limits. In fiscal 1992 the Company will increase its contribution by up to 20% if certain earnings' goals are achieved. Amounts charged to costs and expenses were $10.0 in 1991, $10.6 in 1990, and $10.7 in 1989.

(million dollars)

RETIREE BENEFITS—The Company and its domestic subsidiaries provide certain health care and life insurance benefits to substantially all retired employees and their dependents. The cost of these retiree health and life insurance benefits are expensed as claims are paid and amounted to $15.3 in 1991, $12.6 in 1990 and $11.0 in 1989. Substantially all retirees of foreign subsidiaries are provided health care benefits by government sponsored plans. The cost of life insurance provided to retirees of certain foreign subsidiaries is not significant.

In December 1990, the Financial Accounting Standards Board issued Statement of Financial Accounting Standards No. 106, "Employer's Accounting for Post-retirement Benefits Other Than Pensions," which will require the Company to account for retiree health obligations on an accrual basis beginning with the 1994 fiscal year. The Company is in the process of studying the effects of this complex new accounting standard. The standard permits an employer to recognize the effect of the initial liability either immediately or to amortize it over a period of up to 20 years. The Company has not yet decided which option to select. Management expects that the adoption of this standard will increase annual expense, but the amount has not yet been determined.

. . . .

121 ⑨ **TAXES ON EARNINGS**

The provision for income taxes consists of the following:

	1991	1990	1989
Currently payable			
122 Federal	$185.8	$132.4	$118.8
123 State	23.4	20.8	20.9
124 Foreign	21.2	17.9	21.5
124A	230.4	171.1	161.2
Deferred			
125 Federal	21.9	1.2	(49.3)
126 State	7.5	2.6	(8.0)
127 Foreign	6.1	.1	(10.5)
127A	35.5	3.9	(67.8)
127B	$265.9	$175.0	$ 93.4

The deferred income taxes result from temporary differences between financial statement earnings and taxable earnings as follows:

	1991	1990	1989
128 Depreciation	$ 5.9	$ 18.6	$ 11.9
129 Pensions	13.6	11.7	8.3
130 Prefunded employee benefits	(3.3)	(4.8)	(3.4)
131 Accruals not currently deductible for tax purposes	(11.4)	(5.8)	(5.3)
132 Divestitures, restructuring and unusual charges	29.3	(11.1)	(78.2)
133 Other	1.4	(4.7)	(1.1)
	$35.5	$ 3.9	$(67.8)

The following is a reconciliation of effective income tax rates with the statutory Federal income tax rate:

	1991	1990	1989
134 Statutory Federal income tax rate	34.0%	34.0%	34.0%
135 State income taxes (net of Federal tax benefit)	3.0	3.7	3.6
136 Nondeductible divestitures, restructuring and unusual charges		56.5	48.7
137 Nondeductible amortization of intangibles	.6	.9	1.1
138 Foreign earnings not taxed or taxed at other than statutory Federal rate	(.3)	1.2	.2
139 Other	2.5	1.2	.1
140 Effective income tax rate	39.8%	97.5%	87.7%

The provision for income taxes was reduced by $3.2 in 1991, $5.2 in 1990 and $3.5 in 1989 due to the utilization of loss carryforwards by certain foreign subsidiaries.

Certain foreign subsidiaries of the Company have tax loss carryforwards of approximately $103.4 ($77.4 for financial purposes), of which $10.5 relate to periods prior to acquisition of the subsidiaries by the Company. Of these carryforwards, $54.8 expire through 1996 and $48.6 may be carried forward indefinitely. The current statutory tax rates in these foreign countries range from 20% to 51%.

NOTES TO CONSOLIDATED FINANCIAL STATEMENTS

(million dollars)

Income taxes have not been accrued on undistributed earnings of foreign subsidiaries of $219.7 which are invested in operating assets and are not expected to be remitted. If remitted, tax credits are available to substantially reduce any resultant additional taxes.

The following are earnings before taxes of United States and foreign companies.

	1991	1990	1989
[141] United States	$570.9	$277.0	$201.5
[142] Foreign	96.5	(97.6)	(95.0)
	$667.4	$179.4	$106.5

[143] **⑩ LEASES**

Rent expense was $59.7 in 1991, $62.4 in 1990 and $60.2 in 1989 and generally relates to leases of machinery and equipment. Future minimum lease payments under operating leases are $71.9.

⑪ SUPPLEMENTARY STATEMENTS OF EARNINGS INFORMATION

	1991	1990	1989
[144] Maintenance and repairs	$173.9	$180.6	$173.9
[145] Advertising	$195.4	$220.4	$212.9

[146] **⑫ CASH AND CASH EQUIVALENTS**

Cash and Cash Equivalents includes cash equivalents of $140.7 at July 28, 1991 and $44.1 at July 29, 1990.

⑬ ACCOUNTS RECEIVABLE

	1991	1990
[147] Customers	$478.0	$554.0
[148] Allowances for cash discounts and bad debts	(16.3)	(19.9)
	461.7	534.1
[148A] Other	65.7	90.4
[150]	$527.4	$624.5

⑭ INVENTORIES

	1991	1990
[151] Raw materials, containers and supplies	$342.3	$384.4
[152] Finished products	454.0	520.0
	796.3	904.4
[153] Less-Adjustments of inventories to LIFO basis	89.6	84.6
	$706.7	$819.8

Liquidation of LIFO inventory quantities had no significant effect on net earnings in 1991, 1990 or 1989. Inventories for which the LIFO method of determining cost is used represented approximately 70% of consolidated inventories in 1991 and 64% in 1990.

⑮ PREPAID EXPENSES

	1991	1990
[154] Pensions	$19.8	$ 22.3
[155] Deferred taxes	36.6	37.7
[156] Prefunded employee benefits	1.2	13.9
[157] Other	35.1	44.1
	$92.7	$118.0

⑯ PLANT ASSETS

	1991	1990
[158] Land	$ 56.3	$ 63.8
[159] Buildings	758.7	746.5
[160] Machinery and equipment	1,779.3	1,657.6
[161] Projects in progress	327.6	267.0
[161A]	2,921.9	2,734.9
[162] Accumulated depreciation	(1,131.5)	(1,017.2)
	$1,790.4	$1,717.7

Depreciation provided in costs and expenses was $194.5 in 1991, $184.1 in 1990 and $175.9 in 1989. Approximately $158.2 of capital expenditures is required to complete projects in progress at July 28, 1991.

Campbell Soup Company

(million dollars)

⑰ INTANGIBLE ASSETS

	1991	1990
163 Cost of investments in excess of net assets of purchased companies (goodwill)	$347.8	$281.1
164 Other intangibles	129.8	134.0
	477.6	415.1
165 Accumulated amortization	(42.1)	(31.7)
	$435.5	$383.4

⑱ OTHER ASSETS

	1991	1990
166 Investment in affiliates	$155.8	$169.4
167 Noncurrent prepaid pension expense	152.7	93.9
168 Other noncurrent investments	44.2	52.0
169 Other	51.9	33.7
169A	$404.6	$349.0

Investment in affiliates consists principally of the Company's ownership of 33% of the outstanding capital stock of Arnotts Limited, an Australian biscuit manufacturer. This investment is being accounted for by the equity method. Included in this investment is goodwill of $28.3 which is being amortized over 40 years. At July 28, 1991, the market value of the investment based on quoted market prices was $213.8. The Company's equity in the earnings of Arnotts Limited was $1.5 in 1991, $13.0 in 1990 and $8.7 in 1989. The 1990 amount includes a $4.0 gain realized by Arnotts on the sales of businesses. Dividends received were $8.2 in 1991, $7.4 in 1990 and $6.6 in 1989. The Company's equity in the undistributed earnings of Arnotts was $15.4 at July 28, 1991 and $22.1 at July 29, 1990.

170 ⑲ NOTES PAYABLE AND LONG-TERM DEBT

Notes payable consists of the following:

	1991	1990
Commercial paper	$ 24.7	$191.8
8.25% Notes due 1991		100.3
13.99% Notes due 1992	182.0*	
Banks	23.6	91.1
Other	51.9	69.4
Amounts reclassified to long-term debt		(250.3)
	$282.2	$202.3

Present value of $200.0 zero coupon notes, net of unamortized discount of $18.0.

At July 29, 1990, $150 of outstanding commercial paper and $100.3 of currently maturing notes were reclassified to long-term debt and were refinanced in 1991.

Information on notes payable follows:

171	1991	1990	1989
Maximum amount payable at end of any monthly accounting period during the year	$603.3	$518.7	$347.1
Approximate average amount outstanding during the year	$332.5	$429.7	$273.5
Weighted average interest rate at year-end	10.1%	10.7%	12.1%
Approximate weighted average interest rate during the year	9.8%	10.8%	10.6%

The amount of unused lines of credit at July 28, 1991 approximates $635. The lines of credit are unconditional and generally cover loans for a period of a year at prime commercial interest rates.

NOTES TO CONSOLIDATED FINANCIAL STATEMENTS

(million dollars)

Long-term debt consists of the following:

[172]

Fiscal year maturities	1991	1990
13.99% Notes due 1992	$	$159.7***
9.125% Notes due 1994	100.6	100.9
10.5% Notes due 1996*	100.0	100.0
7.5% Notes due 1998*	99.6	99.5
9.0% Notes due 1998	99.8	
8.58%-8.75% Medium-Term Notes due 2001**	100.0	
8.875% Debentures due 2021	199.6	
Other Notes due 1992-2004 (interest 4.7%-14.4%)	58.2	82.5
Notes payable, reclassified		250.3
Capital lease obligations	14.8	12.9
	$772.6	$805.8

*Redeemable in 1993.

**$50 redeemable in 1998.

***Present value of $200.0 zero coupon notes, net of unamortized discount of $40.3.

[173] Future minimum lease payments under capital leases are $28.0 and the present value of such payments, after deducting implicit interest of $6.5, is $21.5 of which $6.7 is included in current liabilities.

Principal amounts of long-term debt mature as follows: 1992-$227.7 (in current liabilities); 1993-$118.9; 1994 $17.8; 1995-$15.9; 1996-$108.3 and beyond-$511.7.

The Company has filed a shelf registration statement with the Securities and Exchange Commission for the issuance from time to time of up to $300 of debt securities, of which $100 remains unissued.

Information on financial instruments follows:

At July 28, 1991, the Company had an interest rate swap agreement with financial institutions having a notional principal amount of $100, which is intended to reduce the impact of changes in interest rates on floating rate commercial paper. In addition, at July 28, 1991, the Company had two swap agreements with financial institutions which covered both interest rates and foreign currencies. These agreements have a total notional principal amount of $103, and are intended to reduce exposure to higher foreign interest rates and to hedge the Company's net investments in the United Kingdom and Australia. The Company is exposed to credit loss in the event of nonperformance by the other parties to the interest rate swap agreements; however, the Company does not anticipate nonperformance by the counterparties.

At July 28, 1991, the Company had contracts to purchase approximately $109 in foreign currency. The contracts are mostly for European currencies and have maturities through 1992.

20 ACCRUED LIABILITIES

	1991	1990
[174] Divestiture and restructuring charges	$ 88.4	$238.8
[175] Other	320.3	253.1
	$408.7	$491.9

21 OTHER LIABILITIES

	1991	1990
[176] Deferred income taxes	$258.5	$235.1
[177] Other liabilities	23.0	28.5
[178] Minority interests	23.5	56.3
	$305.0	$319.9

Campbell Soup Company

(million dollars)

[179] **22 SHAREOWNERS' EQUITY**

The Company has authorized 140 million shares of Capital Stock of $.15 par value and 40 million shares of Preferred Stock, issuable in one or more classes, with or without par as may be authorized by the Board of Directors. No Preferred Stock has been issued.

The following summarizes the activity in option shares under the Company's employee stock option plans:

(thousands of shares)	1991	1990	1989
Beginning of year	4,301.1	3,767.9	3,257.0
Granted under the 1984 long-term incentive plan at average price of $63.64 in 1991; $47.27 in 1990; $30.37 in 1989	2,136.3	1,196.0	1,495.5
Exercised at average price of $29.82 in 1991; $24.78 in 1990; $20.65 in 1989 in form of:			
Stock appreciation rights	(14.9)	(110.2)	(137.3)
Shares	(1,063.7)	(367.2)	(615.1)
Terminated	(216.9)	(185.4)	(232.2)
End of year	5,141.9	4,301.1	3,767.9
Exercisable at end of year	2,897.0	2,654.4	2,104.1
Shares under option-price per share:			
Range of prices: Low	$14.68	$ 6.98	$ 6.98
High	$83.31	$57.61	$34.31
Average	$46.73	$33.63	$28.21

In addition to options granted under the 1984 long-term incentive plan, 233,200 restricted shares of capital stock were granted to certain key management employees in 1991; 168,850 in 1990; and 162,000 in 1989.

There are 4,229,111 shares available for grant under the long-term incentive plan.

Net earnings per share are based on the weighted average shares outstanding during the applicable periods. The potential dilution from the exercise of stock options is not material.

23 STATEMENTS OF CASH FLOWS

	1991	1990	1989
[180] Interest paid, net of amounts capitalized	$101.3	$116.3	$ 88.9
[181] Interest received	$ 27.9	$ 17.1	$ 35.5
[182] Income taxes paid	$199.3	$152.8	$168.6
[183] Capital lease obligations incurred	$ 10.0	$ 9.7	$ 18.0

[184] **24 QUARTERLY DATA (unaudited)**

	1991			
	First	Second	Third	Fourth
Net sales	$1,594.3	$1,770.9	$1,490.8	$1,348.1
Cost of products sold	1,082.7	1,152.6	981.6	878.6
Net earnings	105.1	135.3	76.4	84.7
Per share				
Net earnings	.82	1.07	.60	.67
Dividends	.25	.29	.29	.29
Market price				
High	54.00	60.38	87.13	84.88
Low	43.75	48.50	58.75	72.38

	1990			
	First	Second	Third	Fourth
Net sales	$1,523.5	$1,722.5	$1,519.6	$1,440.2
Cost of products sold	1,057.2	1,173.0	1,049.3	978.7
Net earnings (loss)	83.0	105.2	54.6	(238.4)
Per share				
Net earnings (loss)	.64	.81	.42	(1.84)
Dividends	.23	.25	.25	.25
Market price				
High	58.50	59.63	54.13	62.00
Low	42.13	42.50	45.00	50.13

The fourth quarter of 1990 includes divestitures, restructuring and unusual charges of $301.6 after taxes, or $2.33 per share.

ELEVEN YEAR REVIEW—CONSOLIDATED

(millions except per share amounts)

Fiscal Year	1991	1990	1989
SUMMARY OF OPERATIONS		*(a)*	*(b)*
Net sales	$6,204.1	$6,205.8	$5,672.1
Earnings before taxes	667.4	179.4	106.5
Earnings before cumulative effect of accounting change	401.5	4.4	13.1
Net earnings	401.5	4.4	13.1
Percent of sales	6.5%	.1%	.2%
Return on average shareowners' equity	23.0%	.3%	.7%
FINANCIAL POSITION			
Working capital	$ 240.5	$ 367.4	$ 369.4
Plant assets—net	1,790.4	1,717.7	1,540.6
Total assets	4,149.0	4,115.6	3,932.1
Long-term debt	772.6	805.8	629.2
Shareowners' equity	1,793.4	1,691.8	1,778.3
PER SHARE DATA			
Earnings before cumulative effect of accounting change	$ 3.16	$ .03	$ .10
Net earnings	3.16	.03	.10
Dividends declared	1.12	.98	.90
Shareowners' equity	14.12	13.09	13.76
OTHER STATISTICS			
Salaries, wages, pensions, etc.	$1,401.0	$1,422.5	$1,333.9
Capital expenditures	371.1	397.3	302.0
Number of shareowners (in thousands)	37.7	43.0	43.7
Weighted average shares outstanding	127.0	129.6	129.3

(a) 1990 includes pre-tax divestiture and restructuring charges of $339.1 million; $301.6 million or $2.33 per share after taxes.
(b) 1989 includes pre-tax restructuring charges of $343.0 million; $260.8 million or $2.02 per share after taxes.
(c) 1988 includes pre-tax restructuring charges of $49.3 million; $29.4 million or 23 cents per share after taxes. 1988 also includes
*   cumulative effect of change in accounting for income taxes of $32.5 million or 25 cents per share.*
(d) Includes employees under the Employee Stock Ownership Plan terminated in 1987.

Campbell Soup Company

1988	1987	1986	1985	1984	1983	1982	1981
(c)							
$4,868.9	$4,490.4	$4,286.8	$3,916.6	$3,636.9	$3,292.4	$2,955.6	$2,797.7
388.6	417.9	387.2	333.7	332.4	306.0	276.9	244.4
241.6	247.3	223.2	197.8	191.2	165.0	149.6	129.7
274.1	247.3	223.2	197.8	191.2	165.0	149.6	129.7
5.6%	5.5%	5.2%	5.1%	5.3%	5.0%	5.1%	4.6%
15.1%	15.1%	15.3%	15.0%	15.9%	15.0%	14.6%	13.2%
$ 499.6	$ 744.1	$ 708.7	$ 579.4	$ 541.5	$ 478.9	$ 434.6	$ 368.2
1,508.9	1,349.0	1,168.1	1,027.5	970.9	889.1	815.4	755.1
3,609.6	3,097.4	2,762.8	2,437.5	2,210.1	1,991.5	1,865.5	1,722.9
525.8	380.2	362.3	297.1	283.0	267.5	236.2	150.6
1,895.0	1,736.1	1,538.9	1,382.5	1,259.9	1,149.4	1,055.8	1,000.5
$ 1.87	$ 1.90	$ 1.72	$ 1.53	$ 1.48	$ 1.28	$ 1.16	$ 1.00
2.12	1.90	1.72	1.53	1.48	1.28	1.16	1.00
.81	.71	.65	.61	.57	.54	.53	.51
14.69	13.35	11.86	10.69	9.76	8.92	8.19	7.72
$1,222.9	$1,137.3	$1,061.0	$ 950.1	$ 889.5	$ 755.1	$ 700.9	$ 680.9
261.9	328.0	251.3	212.9	183.1	154.1	147.6	135.4
43.0	41.0	50.9(d)	49.5(d)	49.4(d)	40.1	39.7	41.6
129.4	129.9	129.5	129.1	129.0	129.0	129.0	129.6

186   **Form 10K**

Schedule V
CAMPBELL SOUP COMPANY AND CONSOLIDATED SUBSIDIARIES
Property, Plant, and Equipment at Cost
(million dollars)

	Land	Buildings	Machinery and equipment	Projects in progress	Total
Balance at July 31, 1988 ..	$53.2	$735.5	$1,624.4	$126.6	$2,539.7
Additions	2.8	47.6	216.4	35.2	302.0
Acquired assets*	4.8	13.6	22.6	—	41.0
Retirements and sales	(4.5)	(88.4)	(238.3)	—	(331.2)
Translation adjustments ..	(.5)	(2.5)	(5.9)	.4	(8.5)
Balance at July 30, 1989 ..	55.8	705.8	1,619.2	162.2	2,543.0
Additions	3.2	69.2	219.6	105.3	397.3
Acquired assets*	3.8	14.1	6.8	—	24.7
Retirements and sales	(2.8)	(64.0)	(222.9)	(1.1)	(290.8)
Translation adjustments ..	3.8	21.4	34.9	.6	60.7
Balance at July 29, 1990 ..	63.8	746.5	1,657.6	267.0	2,734.9
Additions	1.5	70.2	239.5	59.9	371.1
Acquired assets*	.5	3.3	.9	—	4.7
Retirements and sales	(7.5)	(49.3)	(99.9)	—	(156.7)
Rate variance	(2.0)	(12.0)	(18.8)	.7	(32.1)
Balance at July 28, 1991 ..	$56.3	$758.7	$1,779.3	$327.6	$2,921.9

*See "Acquisitions" in Notes to Consolidated Financial Statements.

187

Form 10K

Schedule VI
CAMPBELL SOUP COMPANY AND CONSOLIDATED SUBSIDIARIES
Accumulated Depreciation and Amortization of Property, Plant, and Equipment
(million dollars)

	Buildings	Machinery and Equipment	Total
Balance at July 31, 1988	$285.4	$745.4	$1,030.8
Additions charged to income	31.5	144.4	175.9
Retirements and sales	(57.8)	(143.5)	(201.3)
Translation adjustments	(.8)	(2.2)	(3.0)
Balance at July 30, 1989	258.3	744.1	1,002.4
Additions charged to income	34.2	149.9	184.1
Retirements and sales	(32.5)	(154.7)	(187.2)
Translation adjustments	5.2	12.7	17.9
Balance at July 29, 1990	265.2	752.0	1,017.2
Additions charged to income	35.3	159.2	194.5
Retirements and sales	(17.4)	(52.1)	(69.5)
Translation adjustments	(2.8)	(7.9)	(10.7)
Balance at July 28, 1991	$280.3	$851.2	$1,131.5

QUESTIONS

1. Compare the flow of the analyst's work in reconstructing business transactions to that of the accountant's work. How does such reconstruction of accounts contribute to the analysis of financial statements?
2. As a potential investor in a common stock, what information would you seek? How do you get such information?
3. The president of your client company approached you, the financial officer of a local bank, for a substantial loan. What could you do?
4. What, in broad categories, are some of the approaches utilized by the financial analyst in diagnosing the financial health of a business?
5. How useful is a comparative financial analysis? How do you make useful comparison?
6. What are some of the precautions required of a financial analyst in his comparative analytical work?
7. Give four broad categories of analysis tools.
8. Is the trend of the past a good predictor of the future? Give reasons for your argument.
9. Which is the better indicator of significant change—the absolute amount of change or the change in percentage? Why?
10. What conditions would prevent the computation of a valid percentage change? Give an example.

11. What are some of the criteria to be used in picking out a base year in an index number comparative analysis?
12. What information can be obtained from trend analysis?
13. What is a common-size financial statement? How do you prepare one?
14. What does a common-size financial statement tell about an enterprise?
15. Do all ratios have significance? Explain.
16. What are some of the limitations of ratio analysis?
17. Give five ratios that can be prepared by use of balance sheet figures only.
18. Give five ratios that can be prepared by use of income statement data only.
19. Give seven ratios that require data from both the balance sheet and the income statement.
20. Give four examples of special-purpose analytical tools commonly utilized by the financial analyst.
21. What are the steps generally taken by the financial analyst in his work? What do these steps achieve?
22. Identify and explain two significant limitations associated with ratio analysis of financial statements. (CFA)
23. A number of circumstances require the restatement of financial statements. Which are they?
24. What are some of the principal uses of computers in investment analysis? (CFA)
25. What are the most important limitations or disadvantages to the application of computers to security analysis? (CFA)

Part II

FINANCIAL STATEMENTS—THE RAW MATERIAL OF ANALYSIS

Chapter 5

ANALYSIS OF
CURRENT ASSETS

In considering the variety of standards that govern accounting transactions, determinations, and financial presentations, we shall be primarily concerned here with an examination of their significance to the intelligent user and analyst of financial statements. In this chapter, we shall deal with the principles that underlie the measurement and presentation of current assets.

CASH

Cash is considered the most liquid of assets. In fact, it represents the starting point, as well as the finish line, of what is known as the accounting cycle. This cycle encompasses the purchase and manufacture of goods and services as well as their sale and the collection of the proceeds. The realization of a transaction is measured by sale and later by the ultimate conversion of the consideration received into cash. Excepting fixed commitments to the satisfaction of which cash must be applied, cash represents that point in the accounting cycle at which management has the maximum discretion with regard to the deployment and use of the resources.

By the very nature of its inherent liquidity, cash does not present serious valuation problems even though this characteristic requires special precautions against theft and defalcation. Care should be taken in the classification of cash items when restrictions have been placed on its disposition. For example, in the case of a segregation for plant expansion or for some other type of specific restriction, the cash balance involved should be separately shown. It may not, of course, be properly includable among current assets, which heading denotes liquidity and availability for the payment of current obligations. Cash set aside for "debt service" or "maintenance" under bond indenture is usually segregated on the balance sheet.

Accountants do not regard compensating balances maintained under a loan agreement as a restriction on cash because banks would generally

129

honor checks drawn against such a balance. However, in accordance with guidelines promulgated by SEC *Financial Reporting Release (FRR),* No. 1 Section 203, compensating balances must be segregated on the balance sheet if they are legally restricted. Otherwise such balances must be disclosed in notes to the financial statements.

Compensating balances constitute that part of a demand deposit that is maintained to support existing borrowing arrangements and to assure future credit availability. Even though informal, such arrangements have considerable practical significance. Thus, in assessing the current ratio, the analyst must consider the repercussions that may follow from the breaking of a tacit agreement with the bank. This may involve the loss of a credit source, and thus have an effect on a company's liquidity and its future access to funds. Vulnerability in this area can be measured by computing the ratio of restricted cash to total cash.

Ordinarily, in reporting the cash balance, companies deduct checks issued but not yet paid by the bank (e.g., the float). Analysts should be aware of the practice of a few companies of including the float in the cash balance and including outstanding checks in accounts payable.

ILLUSTRATION 1.   Dominion Resources Inc., in its 1990 annual report, shows on its balance sheet a cash balance of $58.8 million. On the liability side, however, Dominion shows "Cash due to banks" of $59.7 million. The latter amount represents checks which the company issued but which, at year-end, were not presented for payment. This presentation of the substantial "float" is rare but in accordance with FASB rules which forbid companies from lumping together money they are owed by their bank (an asset) and money they owe their bank (a liability) unless the right of offset exists. In the Statement of Cash Flows, however, Dominion reconciles to a negative cash balance of $900,000—a lack of conformity with the balance sheet presentations which rules governing this statement forbid.

ILLUSTRATION 2.   Waste Management Co. has no cash balance in its balance sheet and carries an investment in marketable securities. In its statement of Cash Flows the company, year after year, reconciles to a zero cash balance.

Blockbuster Entertainment shows a 12/31/1988 cash balance of $9 million. Management's Discussion and Analysis reveals that the entire amount was borrowed. There is no rule prohibiting a company from window-dressing its cash balance in this manner.

MARKETABLE SECURITIES

Marketable securities represent in most instances temporary repositories of excess cash. Alternatively, they may represent funds awaiting investment in plant and equipment, and so on. They are usually shown among current assets. However, marketable securities that are temporary investments of cash designated for special purposes such as plant expansion or the meeting of requirements under sinking fund provisions should be shown among long-term investments.

Certain marketable equity securities carried as current assets must now be accounted for in accordance with *SFAS 12* entitled "Accounting for Certain Marketable Securities." The following are some of the salient provisions of this *Statement,* some of which apply also to marketable securities carried as noncurrent assets or carried in unclassified balance sheets and which are discussed under the appropriate heading in Chapter 6:

An equity security encompasses any instrument representing ownership shares or the right to acquire or dispose of ownership shares in an enterprise. This definition specifically excludes convertible bonds, treasury stock, and redeemable preferred stock.

The *Statement* basically requires that marketable equity securities held by enterprises in industries that do not have specialized accounting practices (e.g., investment companies, security brokers and dealers, stock life insurance companies, and fire and casualty insurance companies) shall be stated at the lower of cost or market.

For those securities classified as current assets by the enterprise, market value changes recognized in applying the lower-of-cost-or-market rule are to be included in the determination of net income. This will be accomplished by use of a "valuation allowance" that will generally represent the net unrealized loss in the portfolio. Marketable securities classified as current are treated as one portfolio, and those shown as noncurrent are considered a separate portfolio.

The lower-of-cost-or-market approach is based on the aggregate value of the portfolio of marketable equity securities rather than on the values of individual securities. A parent must group its securities with those of its consolidated subsidiaries (other than those in industries with specialized accounting practices) for the current and noncurrent classification.

Companies in certain industries where specialized accounting practices are applied for marketable securities generally are not required to change their reporting practices for gains or losses on marketable securities. However, those that carry their marketable equity securities on the basis of cost would be required to change to the lower of cost or market for those securities, except that they could adopt the market basis of accounting where that basis is an accepted alternative.

When a subsidiary follows accepted accounting practices that differ from those of the parent company, those practices must be retained in the consolidated financial statements in which the subsidiaries are included. However, when the parent company does include realized gains and losses in net income, the accounting by the subsidiary must be adjusted in consolidation to conform to that of the parent company.

If there is a change in classification of a marketable security between current or noncurrent or vice versa, the security must be transferred at the lower of cost or market at the date of transfer. If the market value is less than cost, it becomes the new cost basis, and the write-down must be charged to income as if it were a realized loss.

The following disclosures are required:

1. Aggregate cost and market value of the separate portfolios as of the balance sheet date, with identification as to which is the carrying amount.
2. Gross unrealized gains or losses related to market value over cost or cost over market value for all marketable equity securities in the portfolio.
3. Net realized gain or loss included in income determination, the basis on which cost was determined and the change in the valuation allowance that has been included in the equity section of the balance sheet during the period and, when a classified balance sheet is presented, the amount of such change included in the determination of net income.

Post balance sheet changes in market prices or realized gains and losses shall not be cause for adjusting the financial statements, although the effect of significant post balance sheet realized and unrealized gains and losses should be disclosed.

An exception to the general practice of valuing marketable securities at cost can be found in the stock brokerage industry where traditional thinking of necessity gave way to operating realities and needs. In this industry, it was agreed that it was appropriate to carry marketable securities, including those held as investments, at market quotations and that it was also appropriate in this industry to carry securities that are not readily marketable at fair values.

The Annual Report of Merrill Lynch states:

> Securities inventory is valued at market with the resulting net unrealized gains and losses reflected in earnings of the current period.

"Specialized" industries, such as insurance, that have evolved their own methods of dealing with marketable securities are similarly unaffected by *SFAS 12*.

Implications for Analysis

While *SFAS 12* has, in general, improved the accounting for "certain" marketable securities, there remain many gaps and inconsistencies in that accounting of which the analyst must be aware.

The definition of equity securities in the *Statement* is somewhat arbitrary and inconsistent. Often convertible bonds derive all or most of their value from their conversion feature (as has, indeed, been recognized by *APB Opinion 15,* "Earnings per Share") and are much more akin to equity securities than to debt instruments. Thus, the exclusion of these securities from the equity classification is not logical. Nor, for that matter, is there a sound reason for excluding from the valuation process debt securities and marketable mortgages that can fluctuate in value significantly either due to interest rate changes or to changes in credit standing. The continued carrying at cost and above market of debt obligations of issuers in default is particularly unwarranted.

SFAS 12 does not define when marketable securities should be carried as current and when as noncurrent, thus introducing a degree of arbitrariness in the decisions of how change in the market value of such securities should be accounted for. It is by no means self-evident that the manner of classifying securities in the balance sheet should determine whether changes in their value are reflected in income or not. While the *Statement* requires the transfer of a marketable security from one category to the next at the lower of cost or market, category switching could still allow a company some leeway in the determination of future results.

While the *Statement* does not address the question of how "cost" is determined, the analyst must be aware that a number of methods of determining the "cost" of marketable securities exists (e.g., specific identification, average, first-in, first-out) and that they can affect reported results.

It should be noted that under this *Statement,* the valuation concept accorded to marketable securities is analogous to that of accounts receivable valuation, and inconsistent with the concept of valuation applied to inventories—where once they are written down, subsequent write-ups are not allowed. The *Statement* also introduces an inconsistent treatment of anticipating gains, whereby it is acceptable to anticipate gains except when that would result in a valuation higher than original cost.

The aggregation of unrealized gains and losses can have an inconsistent effect on income recognition as is demonstrated by the following examples:

	End of year 1	
	Cost	*Market*
Security A	$10	$15
Security B	20	30
Security C	10	5
Security D	40	10
	$80	$60

Example 1   According to the *Statement,* a valuation allowance of $20 would be provided in year 1. If security D were sold in year 2 (assuming no change in market prices), an additional loss of $10 would be recorded (actual loss of $30 less elimination of $20 allowance). Thus, the $30 loss will have been recognized over two years rather than one.

Example 2   If security C is sold for a realized loss of $5, in year 2 (assuming no change in other market prices) the loss would be completely offset by a decrease in the allowance for unrealized losses and there would be no impact on net income.

Example 3   Assume that at the end of year 2, the portfolio of marketable securities is as follows:

	End of year 2	
	Cost	*Market*
Security A	$10	$20
Security B	20	30
Security C	10	25
	$40	$75

Any security or combination of securities can now drop a total of $35 in value before any loss will be recognized. Thus, security B could drop to $5 and security A to $10 (with C remaining unchanged) without any need for recognition of the loss. This is so because as long as the aggregate market value of the portfolio remains above cost, no individual gains or losses are recorded.

Additional considerations and analytical implications that relate to the accounting for marketable securities not carried as current assets will be considered in Chapter 6.

The current market value of investments is always relevant to an assessment of management performance. The argument that unrealized gains are only "paper profits" that could melt away before the investments are actually sold or otherwise disposed of does not recognize the fact that management makes the decision to hold or sell. Thus, a reduction in unrealized appreciation of an investment is as much a loss as would be a similar size loss on inventories or on equipment that became prematurely obsolete.

The analyst should treat with suspicion the amortization of bond discount (i.e., write-up of bond by crediting income) of an issue that from all available evidence sells at a discount because of doubt as to the ultimate collectibility of the principal amount.

The analyst, aware of accounting principles governing the presentation of investments, must pay particular attention to their valuation. On the one hand, they can be grossly undervalued on the balance sheet because of the convention prohibiting their write-up to market value no matter how obvious and soundly based such value may be.

On the other hand, the analyst must be alert to impairment of market value which because of loose standards in practice may not be fully reflected on the financial statements. If separately disclosed, the income generated by an investment may, at times, provide a clue to its fair value.

While the recognition of profits in nonequity securities must, according to present theory, await realization (i.e., in most cases sale), losses must be taken when they are deemed to be permanent in nature. However, the criteria for determining when a loss is "permanent" in nature are indefinite and allow for much leeway. With hope springing eternal, such write-downs occur in practice only when the evidence of loss in value is overwhelming. Since proper disclosure requires that the market value of securities be indicated, the alert analyst will be on the lookout for this information so that he can exercise his own judgment regarding the proper value to assign to these securities for the purpose of his analysis.

RECEIVABLES

Receivables are amounts due arising generally from the sale of goods or services. They may also represent accrued amounts due, such as rents, interest, and so forth. Notes receivable represent a more formal evidence of indebtedness due, but this characteristic does not make them more readily collectible than accounts receivable. Generally speaking, notes receivable are more easily negotiable and pledged for loans than are accounts receivable and, consequently, are considered the more liquid of the two. As a practical matter, this is, however, a superficial distinction.

Receivables classified as current assets should be reasonably expected to be realized or collected within a year or within the normal operating cycle of a business. *The normal operating cycle* is a concept that is important in the classification of items as current or noncurrent. The operating cycle generally encompasses the full circle of time from the commitment of cash for purchases until the collection of receivables resulting from the sale of goods or services. Exhibit 5–1 illustrates the concept.

ILLUSTRATION 3.   Great Lakes Dredge & Dock Company's Annual Report contains the following note: "Certain contracts entered into by the Company vary up to five years in length. For these contracts the Company classifies its contracting assets and liabilities as current."

If the normal collection interval of receivables is longer than a year (e.g., longer-term installment receivables), then their inclusion as current assets is proper provided the collection interval is normal and expected

Exhibit 5–1   Operating cycle

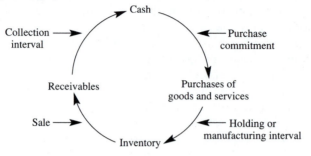

for the type of business the enterprise is engaged in. Because of their nature, certain types of receivables require separate disclosure. Examples are receivables from affiliated companies, officers, or employees.

Certain types of receivables are established without formal billing of the debtor. Thus, costs accumulated under a cost-plus-fixed-fee contract or some other types of government contracts are recorded as receivables as they accumulate.[1] Similarly, claims for tax refunds from the government are usually classified as receivables if no substantial question of technical compliance is involved.

To the financial analyst, the valuation of receivables is important from two main points of view:

1. The realization value of the assets.
2. The impact on income.

These two aspects are, of course, interrelated. It is a fact supported by experience that not all receivables will be collected nor will they all necessarily be collected in their entirety.

While a judgment about the collectibility of any one account can be made at any appropriate time, the collectibility of receivables as a group is best estimated on the basis of past experience with due allowance for current conditions. The "accounting risk" here is that the past experience may not be an adequate measure of future loss or that current developments may not have been fully taken into account. The resulting loss can be substantial and will affect both the current asset position as well as the net income for the period under review.

ILLUSTRATION 4.   While Brunswick is an older case, it still represents such a good and relevant example that it has been retained here. In 1963, Brunswick Corporation

---

[1] SEC *FRR No. 1* Section 206 requires disclosure of amounts relating to long-term contracts included in receivables applicable to items billed but not paid under retainage provisions, items not yet billed or billable, and items representing claims subject to uncertainty as to their ultimate realization. Amounts expected to be collected after one year must also be disclosed.

made a "special provision for possible losses on receivables" of $15 million *after* taxes. The assumption was that factors that became clear in 1963 were not "visible" or obvious to the auditor at the end of 1962 when a substantial amount of the receivables provided for was outstanding. Management explained the write-off as follows:

"Delinquencies in bowling installment payments, primarily related to some of the large chain accounts, *continued* at an unsatisfactory level. Nonchain accounts, which comprise about 80 percent of installment receivables, are generally better paying accounts.

"In the last quarter of 1963, average bowling lineage per establishment fell short of the relatively low lineage of the comparable period of 1962, resulting in an aggravation of collection problems on certain accounts. The bowling business may have felt the competition of outdoor activities associated with the unseasonably warm weather during the latter part of 1963. Some improvement in bowling lineage was noted in the early months of 1964 which tends to confirm this view. However, the fact that collections were lower in late 1963 contributed to management's decision to increase reserves. After the additional provision of $15 million, total reserves for possible future losses on all receivables amounted to $66 million, including $30 million *transferred from deferred income taxes.*" [Author's emphasis.]

While it may be impossible to define the precise moment when the collection of a receivable is doubtful enough to require provision, the question may be properly asked whether the analyst could not, in 1962, have made an independent judgment on the adequacy of the bad debt provision in the light of developments in the bowling industry with which he should have been thoroughly familiar. It should be noted that Brunswick's earnings peaked out in early 1962.

Another aspect of receivable valuation relates to long-term receivables that are noninterest bearing or that bear unrealistically low rates of interest.

APB Opinion 21, "Interest on Receivables and Payables"

Objective   The primary objective of this *Opinion* is to refine the manner of applying existing accounting principles when the face amount of a note (as defined below) does not reasonably represent the present value of the consideration given or received in an exchange.

The *Opinion* covers receivables and payables that represent contractual rights to receive or pay money on fixed or determinable dates. These are collectively referred to as "notes."

The *Opinion* does not apply to trade receivables and payables due within one year, progress payments, deposits, retainages, customary activities of lending institutions, notes that bear interest at rates prescribed by governmental agencies, or intercompany transactions.

Significant Provisions   A note may be issued for cash or for property, goods, or services.

When issued for cash, a note is presumed to have a present value at issuance measured by the cash proceeds exchanged, unless other rights or privileges (stated or unstated) are included (such as the issuance of a noninterest-bearing loan to a supplier who, in turn, charges less than the prevailing market price for products purchased by the lender under a contractual agreement).

When issued in a noncash transaction, the stated face amount of the note is generally presumed to represent the fair value of the consideration exchanged unless:

1. Interest is not stated,
2. The stated interest rate is unreasonable, or
3. The stated face amount of the note is materially different from the current sales price for the same or similar items or from the market value of the note at the date of the transaction.

When the stated face amount of the note does not represent the fair value of the consideration exchanged, the present value of the note must be established, taking into consideration:

1. The fair value of the consideration exchanged,
2. The market value of the note, or
3. The present value of all future payments.

The imputed rate of interest used for valuation purposes will normally be at least equal to the rate at which the debtor can obtain financing of a similar nature from other sources at the date of the transaction and may be influenced by:

1. An approximation of the prevailing market rates for the sources of credit that would provide a market for sale or assignment of the note;
2. The prime or higher rate for notes that are discounted with banks, giving due weight to the credit standing of the maker;
3. Published market rates for similar quality bonds;
4. Current rates for debentures with substantially identical terms and risks that are traded in open markets; or
5. The current rate charged by investors for first or second mortgage loans on similar property.

The difference between the present value and the face amount of the note should be treated as discount or premium and amortized as interest expense or income over the life of the note in such a way as to result in a constant rate of interest when applied to the amount outstanding at the beginning of any period (interest method).

The discount or premium should be reported in the balance sheet as a direct deduction from or addition to the face amount of the note.

Example of Application of Imputation of Interest   The XYZ Corporation issued a noninterest-bearing note (face amount $5,180) to Toro Machinery Company for purchase of machinery on August 17, year 1. The face amount of the note is to be paid on July 31, year 8. It is felt that for a similar type note an interest rate of 8 percent is applicable.

Toro Machinery Company will record as sales and as the receivable from XYZ, $3,032, representing the present value of $5,180 to be received on July 31, year 8. Over the intervening periods, Toro Machinery will pick up as interest income the increases in the present value of the receivable from XYZ. If we assume that Toro's fiscal year-end is September 30, the pattern of interest income pickup on a yearly basis and the carrying amounts of the receivable will be as follows:

Year	Month-end	Face amount	Imputed interest income	Unamortized discount	Discounted value of receivable (rounded)
1	8	$5,180.00	—	$2,147.54	$3,032.00
1	9	5,180.00	$ 29.65	2,117.89	3,062.00
2	9	5,180.00	245.69	1,872.20	3,307.00
3	9	5,180.00	264.62	1,607.58	3,572.00
4	9	5,180.00	285.79	1,321.79	3,858.00
5	9	5,180.00	308.66	1,013.13	4,166.00
6	9	5,180.00	333.35	679.78	4,500.00
7	9	5,180.00	360.02	319.76	4,860.00
8	7	—	319.76	—	—
Total			$2,147.54		

Implications for Analysis

The two most important questions facing the financial analyst with respect to receivables are:

1. Is the receivable genuine, due, and enforceable?
2. Has the probability of collection been properly assessed?

While the unqualified opinion of an independent auditor should lend assurance with regard to an affirmative answer to these questions, the financial analyst must recognize the possibility of an error of judgment as well as the lack of it.

1. The description of the receivables or the notes to the financial statement will usually not contain sufficient clues to permit an informed judgment as to whether a receivable is genuine, due, and enforceable. Consequently, a knowledge of industry practices and supplementary sources of information must be used for additional assurance.

In some industries, such as the phonograph record, toy, or bakery business, customers enjoy a substantial right of merchandise return, and allowance must be made for this.

ILLUSTRATION 5.   Here is another older case which is nevertheless fresh in the sense of remaining most relevant. This is the case of Topper Corporation, a manufacturer and marketer of toys. It is quite instructive and should serve as a significant lesson and warning to financial analysts about the dangers inherent in the evaluation of accounts receivable.

In mid-1970, Topper issued a prospectus for the public sale of common stock. The 1970 calendar-year financial statements indicated sales of $64 million, and a terse footnote related to the accounts receivable of $31 million at December 31, 1970, stated that "approximately $14 million of sales made in December 1970 carried extended credit terms of five to eight months. The comparable amount for the prior year was $2 million."

While the credit terms granted under the December sales program were by no means unusual or excessively extended, this "casual" footnote proved in retrospect to be an extraordinarily important piece of information for the analysts. For not only did the company, in its desire to report higher sales and earnings as a means to obtaining loans, grant its customers extended credit terms, free storage, and substantial discounts, it also granted them substantial rights of merchandise return and exchange to the point where the risk of ownership did in effect not pass from Topper to its customers.

The auditors, who gave Topper a clean opinion for 1970, claimed that they first learned about letters giving Topper's customers the right of merchandise return only in early 1972 and a full year later withdrew their opinion on the 1970 financial statements.

In May 1972, Topper incurred huge write-downs of receivables and inventory, and a year later Topper was adjudged bankrupt. Losses to shareholders and to some large pension funds that extended credit on the basis of information contained in the 1971 prospectus were very substantial.

The analyst must be ever alert to the possibility that either "loose" agreements with customers by suppliers anxious to sell or swiftly changing demand conditions can seriously impair the collectibility of accounts receivable.

ILLUSTRATION 6.   Dayco Corporation announced that it incurred an after-tax write-off of $11.7 million because a foreign agent placed invalid orders. The company had to write off $20 million in accounts receivable, inventories, and prepaid expenses.

The following note to the financial statements appearing in the annual report of the O. M. Scott & Sons Company exemplifies the type of disclosure that does shed additional light on the contingencies to which receivables are subject:

> *Accounts receivable:* Accounts receivable are stated net after allowances for returns, allowances, and doubtful accounts of $472,000.
> Accounts receivable include approximately $4,785,000 for shipments made under a deferred payment plan whereby title to the merchandise is

transferred to the dealer when shipped; however, the Company retains
a security interest in such merchandise until sold by the dealer. Payment
to the Company is due from the dealer as the merchandise is sold at
retail. The amount of receivables of this type shall at no time exceed $11
million under terms of the loan and security agreement.

In some instances, a receivable may not represent a true sale but rather
a merchandise or service advance; these receivables cannot be considered
in the same light as regular receivables.

A sale of receivables with recourse does not effectively transfer the risk
of ownership of the receivables. The analyst must be alert to accounting
treatments that consider the risk as having passed to the buyer and that
mention such sales as creating merely contingent liabilities for the seller.

Some companies sell portions of their receivables to financial institutions, sometimes captive, finance subsidiaries. Since the risk of carrying
the receivable is still with the company until the ultimate customer pays,
the analyst can make the following *analytical* adjustment to reflect this:

Receivables .... $ of receivables sold
Short-Term Debt .... $ of receivables sold

2. Most provisions for uncollectible accounts are based on past experience, although they should also make allowance for current and
emerging industry conditions. In actual practice, the accountant is likely
to attach more importance to the former than to the latter. The analyst
must bear in mind that while a formula approach to the calculation of
the provision for bad debts is convenient and practical for the accountant,
it represents a type of mechanical judgment that can easily overlook
changing or emerging conditions. The analyst must use his or her own
judgment and knowledge of industry conditions to assess the adequacy
of the provision for uncollectible accounts (see example of the Brunswick
Corporation above).

Unfortunately, information that would be helpful in assessing the general level of collection risks in the receivables is not usually found in
published financial statements. Such information can, of course, be
sought from other sources or from the company directly. Examples of
such information are:

1. What is the customer concentration? What percentage of total
   receivables is due from one or a few major customers? Would failure
   of any one customer have a material impact on the company's
   financial condition?
2. What is the age pattern of the receivables?
3. What proportion of notes receivable represent renewals of old
   notes?
4. Have allowances been made for trade discounts, returns, or other
   credits to which customers are entitled?

The financial analyst, in assessing the current financial position and a company's ability to meet its obligations currently, as expressed by such measures as the current ratio (discussed in Chapter 16), must recognize the full import of those accounting conventions that relate to the classification of receivables as "current." Thus, the operating cycle theory allows the inclusion of installment receivables that may not be fully collectible for years. In balancing these against current obligations, allowance for these differences in timing should be made.

DISCLOSURES ABOUT FAIR VALUE OF FINANCIAL INSTRUMENTS

As part of its overall consideration of financial instruments, the FASB issued *SFAs 107* (1991) on disclosures about the fair value of financial instruments. It requires that

"An entity shall disclose, either in the body of the financial statements or in the accompanying notes, the fair value of financial instruments for which it is practicable to estimate that value. An entity also shall disclose the method(s) and significant assumptions used to estimate the fair value of financial instruments."

For trade receivables and payables, no disclosure is required when carrying amount approximates fair value.

A further discussion of this standard and related standards of the financial instruments project (such as *SFAS 105*) will be found in the next chapter.

INVENTORIES

With the possible exception of some service organizations, in most businesses inventories represent assets of great importance. From the point of view of the analyst of financial statements, inventories are significant for two main reasons:

1. They represent a significant, major component of the assets devoted to the conduct of the business.
2. They enter importantly in the determination of net income.

Asset Valuation

Inventories are goods that are acquired for resale or that enter into goods produced for resale. In nonmanufacturing enterprises, such as retail establishments, purchased merchandise requires little or no additional work before resale. In manufacturing organizations, we classify three main types of inventories according to their stage of completion in the production process:

1. Raw materials.
2. Goods in process.
3. Finished goods.

The importance attached to methods of inventory valuation and the controversies surrounding them is due primarily to the fact that they enter into the determination of the cost of goods sold and thus into the determination of net income. It is easy to understand why this is so. All material or goods purchased by an enterprise for resale are either sold or carried in inventory for use and sale at some future time. Thus, excluding material written off as worthless or missing, whatever is not on hand in the ending inventory must have been disposed of and, therefore, be part of the cost of goods sold and vice versa.

A most important factor to be recognized about accounting principles that govern the valuation of inventories is that they are primarily aimed at obtaining the best matching of cost and revenues. As a result of this orientation toward the income statement, the resulting, or residual, balance sheet inventory figure may be rendered inaccurate or even meaningless. This, as we shall see, can often be the case.

The basic principle of inventory valuation is that it be valued at "the lower of cost or market." This simple phrase belies the complexities and the variety of alternatives to which it is subject. This variety can, in turn, lead to significantly different figures of periodic income all "in accordance with generally accepted accounting principles."

What Is Cost?   The complexities of cost determination are caused by a diversity of assumptions and of practice in two main areas:

1. What is includable cost?
2. What assumptions do we make about the flow of inventory costs through an enterprise?

What Is Includable Cost?   Let us start with a simple example. An office supply store buys a desk for resale. The invoice cost of the desk is obviously the basic cost. To that may properly be added the cost of freight-in as well as the costs of assembling the desk if that is the form in which it is kept in inventory. If the desk was imported, duty and other direct costs of clearing the desk through customs may properly be added. Suppose the president and others expend a great deal of time and effort in purchasing the desks. Should any part of the cost of their time be allocated to it, that is, inventoried if the desk is unsold at year-end? Here the answer is not so clear. Accounting principles would sanction allocation of such costs to inventories, but they would also sanction the current expensing of such costs. This will, of course, make a difference in the reported results for the year. Should expenses incurred in selling desks be added to their cost? Here there is more unanimity of view that such costs do not belong in inventory.

In spite of its importance, the matter of what costs are included in inventory or, conversely, excluded therefrom, is only rarely discussed or disclosed in published financial statements. The following example of disclosure by Chrysler Corporation represents an unusual inventory costing practice by a subsidiary:

> In accordance with industry practice (Program Accounting), Gulfstream Aerospace Corporation's inventoried costs relating to aircraft programs are stated at actual production costs, including factory overhead and tooling costs reduced by costs attributed to units delivered based on the estimated average gross profit margins of all units expected to be produced. Revisions in the gross profits recognized are made on a prospective basis as the need for such changes becomes evident.

Campbell Soup Company (see Appendix 4B) describes its inventory accounting policy (item 96) and the composition of inventory (item 14).

It is important to understand the difference between the current expensing of a cost and its inclusion in inventory. The current expensing of a cost converts it into what is known as a period cost, that is, a cost deemed to expire during the fiscal period in which it is incurred, rather than its continuance by virtue of its conversion into an asset. Conversely, a cost that is inventoried is a product cost and does not become a charge against current income and remains, instead, as an asset to be charged against future operations that are presumed to benefit from it. It can be readily seen that a decision to inventory a cost rather than expense it *shifts* a charge to income from the present to the future.

Cost Accounting

The foregoing desk inventory example was relatively simple because the inventory problem was that of a retailer. If we consider the cost problem of the desk manufacturer, additional complexities are introduced.

In producing the desk from its basic components, the manufacturer will incur three main types of cost:

1. Raw materials going into the desk.
2. Labor to produce and assemble the desk.
3. Indirect expenses such as wear and tear of machinery, auxiliary supplies, heat, light and power, various factory occupancy costs, supervisory costs, etc.

While the first two categories of expense may present some problems of classification, it is in the third group that we will find the greatest variety of treatments and the most problems. This category is also known as indirect expenses or overhead costs.

Overhead Costs   While it may be reasonably feasible to maintain control over the direct material and direct labor costs that go into the making of a desk, it is not practicable, if not impossible, to trace the specific overhead costs to the desk. This requires *allocation* of an entire pool of costs to the many products (e.g., desks, chairs, shelves, bookcases, etc.) that the manufacturer produces. This allocation requires a number of assumptions and decisions such as:

1. What items should be includable in overhead costs?
2. Over how many units (e.g., desks) do we allocate the overhead costs?

Includable Costs in Overhead   When we examine the costs that the retailer could include in the "cost per desk," we see that certain costs were generally accepted as includable while others were not clearly includable. In the area of manufacturing overheads, differences between theory and practice are even more prevalent because of the far greater variety of expenses involved and because of the wide variety of acceptable methods or because of practice that is not subject to meaningful restraints. In the matter of includable expenses, consider, for example, the following questions:

a. Should costs of testing new designs and materials of a desk be charged to inventories? If so, on what basis and over how many units?
b. Should general and administrative costs be included in inventory?

As of now there may be general acceptance of a number of ways in which to answer these questions. But there is by no means a single answer that is accepted more than all others.

Assumptions of Activity   The allocation of overhead costs to all the desks, chairs, and other items produced must, of course, be done on a rational basis designed to get the best approximation of actual cost. However, this is far from an easy matter. The greatest difficulty stems from the fact that a good part of overhead represents "fixed costs," that is, costs that do not vary with production but vary mostly with the passage of time. Examples are rent payments and the factory manager's salary. Thus, assuming for a moment that only desks are produced, if the fixed costs are $100,000 and 10,000 desks are produced, each desk will absorb $10 of fixed costs. However, if only 5,000 desks are produced, each desk will have to absorb $20 of fixed costs. Clearly, then, the level of activity itself is an important determinant of unit cost. In other words, wide fluctuations in output can result in wide fluctuations in unit cost.

Since the allocation of overhead depends also on an accurate estimate of total overhead costs that will be incurred during the period, variations between estimated and actual costs can also result in overabsorbed or underabsorbed overhead.

In order to allocate fixed costs over output, an assumption must be made at the outset of the fiscal period as to how many units (desks) the company expects to produce, and that in turn will determine over how many units the overhead costs will be allocated. This procedure entails estimates of sales and related production. To the extent that the actual production differs from estimated production, the overhead will be either overabsorbed or underabsorbed. That means that production and inventory are charged with more than total overhead costs or with an insufficient amount of overhead costs.

A cost system that charges cost of goods sold and inventories with predetermined estimated costs is called a *standard cost* system. Variations between the estimates or standards and actual costs are called cost accounting variances. Generally speaking, when an inventory is described as being valued at standard cost, that should mean that variances are insignificant or have been allocated or otherwise adjusted; in other words, standard costs would approximate actual costs. Under generally accepted accounting standards, it is not permissible to carry inventories at only direct costs with the current expensing of all fixed overheads.

The next area of inventory cost determination that we will examine relates to assumptions regarding the *flow* of goods and their costs. While the methods used in this connection (LIFO, FIFO, average cost) are the most controversial methods associated with inventory accounting, it should be clear from the foregoing discussion that the problems of cost accounting and overhead allocations may produce even more variation in reported results than can the assumptions about cost flows.

Inventory Cost Flows

In order to keep the discussion simple, let us return to our example of the office furniture retailer and assume that in the fiscal year ended December 31, year 2, the inventory record of desks showed the following details:

Inventory on January 1, Year 2	100 desks @ $40	$ 4,000
First purchase in Year 2	200 desks @ $50	10,000
Second purchase in Year 2	100 desks @ $50	5,000
Third purchase in Year 2	200 desks @ $60	12,000
Total available for sale	600 desks	$31,000

Assuming that 50 desks are in inventory as at December 31, year 2, how should they be valued?

There are a number of methods, all enjoying the "generally accepted" label, of which the three most common are discussed in the sections that follow.

First-In, First-Out (FIFO)   This method assumes what is probably the most common and justified assumption about the flow of goods in a business, that is, that those units bought first are sold (or used) first. This conforms also to the best inventory management practice. Under this method, the 50 desks will be valued at $60 each, the unit cost of the last purchase, or $3,000. The resulting cost of goods sold is $28,000 ($31,000 representing the cost of all goods available for sale less $3,000 the value assigned to the ending inventory) based on the formula:

$$\underbrace{\frac{\text{Beginning}}{\text{inventory}} + \text{Purchases}}_{\text{Goods available for sale}} - \frac{\text{Ending}}{\text{inventory}} = \frac{\text{Cost of goods}}{\text{sold}}$$

Last-In, First-Out (LIFO)   The assumption that the earliest purchases are the ones in inventory has been likened to the pile "flow" of inventory. If an inventory consists of a pile of salt or coal, then the last quantity bought is likely to be the first removed and sold. But this concern with a parallel to physical movement of inventories misses the real intention in inventory valuation. That relates primarily to an assumption about the flow of *costs* rather than of physical units, and the flow of costs is chosen not because it parallels the physical goods movement but rather because it achieves certain objectives of inventory valuation. The major objective of the LIFO method is to charge cost of goods sold with the most recent costs incurred. Quite obviously where the price level remains stable, the results under either the FIFO or the LIFO method will be much the same; but under a changing price level, as the advancing one in our example, the results in the use of these methods will differ significantly. The use of the LIFO method has increased greatly due to its acceptance for tax purposes. Our tax law stipulates that its use for tax purposes makes mandatory its adoption for financial reporting, although some *reporting* requirements were relaxed.

The basic aim of LIFO accounting is to obtain a better matching of current revenues with current costs in times of inflation. As will be seen in the discussion of the effects of price-level changes, this objective is not always achieved. Nevertheless, in *FRR* No. 1 Section 205, the SEC exhorts preparers of financial reports to make sure that LIFO accounting is justified, based on the LIFO *accounting* concept of matching current costs with current revenues.

In our example, the inventory of 50 desks under the LIFO method will be valued at $40 each, or $2,000. The cost of goods sold is $29,000 ($31,000 − $2,000). The inventory figure of $2,000 on the balance sheet will be one third below current market (or at least one third below the latest cost), but the income statement will be more realistically presented in terms of matching current costs with current revenues.

Average Cost   The average-cost method smoothes out cost fluctuation by using a weighted-average cost in valuing inventories and in pricing out the cost of goods sold. While the weighted-average cost of goods sold will depend on the timing of sales, we can, in this example, consider the average cost of all purchases during the year and the opening inventory. On that basis, the average price per desk is $51.67 ($31,000 ÷ 600), and the 50 desks will be valued at $2,583.50. The cost of goods sold would be $28,416.50 ($31,000 − $2,583.50).

To summarize, under the three methods, the following results are obtained:

	FIFO	*LIFO*	*Average*
Ending inventory	$ 3,000.00	$ 2,000.00	$ 2,583.50
Cost of goods sold	28,000.00	29,000.00	28,416.50

Assuming that the sales of desks for the period amounted to $35,000, the gross profit under each method would be as follows:

	FIFO	*LIFO*	*Average*
Sales	$35,000.00	$35,000.00	$35,000.00
Cost of goods sold	28,000.00	29,000.00	28,416.50
Gross profit	$ 7,000.00	$ 6,000.00	$ 6,583.50

It is clear that the choice of method (i.e., the assumption about cost flows) can make a significant difference in the determination of cost of goods sold and the valuation of inventories. Generally, the FIFO method provides a "good" inventory figure because it reflects the latest costs. The LIFO method, on the other hand, produces a better matching of costs and revenues. In times of changing prices, both virtues cannot be achieved simultaneously under the historical-cost method.

A method of inventory valuation in use especially for interim statement results is the gross profit method. This method derives the inventory figure by estimating the cost of goods sold on the basis of a normal gross profit ratio experienced in practice. This method is accurate only if the gross profit ratio has in fact not changed and if there are no unusual inventory shortages or spoilage.

The retail method of inventory estimation is an extension of the gross profit method. It uses sophisticated techniques that involve physical inventory taking, priced first at retail, and the reduction of this inventory to cost by means of gross profit ratios.

LIFO and Changing Price Levels

Inflation usually sparks the business community's interest in the LIFO method. The rationale advanced for the flight to LIFO is that this method adjusts the financial statements for inflation. In fact, it merely postpones the recognition of the effects of inflation, although such postponement can be long term if prices continue to rise and the LIFO inventory base is not liquidated. The major reason for the method's popularity is, of course, the long-term postponement of taxes under such conditions, which is a very real and tangible benefit.

A good way to understand the concept of inventory profits as well as the effect of changing price levels is to trace the operating results recorded under different inventory methods. The following examples and analysis are designed to accomplish this.

ILLUSTRATION 7.   The effects of price-level changes on reported earnings under different inventory costing methods.

Following are inventory purchase costs and selling prices for quarterly periods starting with the fourth quarter of year 2. It is assumed that prices rise steadily in the first, second, and third quarter of year 3, that they level off in the fourth quarter, and decline in the first quarter of year 4. It is also assumed—for simplicity's sake— that the company's markup on cost is given as a constant $200 and that the company holds three units in inventory at all times and buys and sells one unit each quarter.

	4th Q year 2	1st Q year 3	2nd Q year 3	3rd Q year 3	4th Q year 3	1st Q year 4
Selling price	$1,300	$1,400	$1,500	$1,600	$1,600	$1,500
Inventory purchase cost	1,100	1,200	1,300	1,400	1,400	1,300

The following tables show the results under the three inventory costing methods, FIFO, LIFO, and weighted average. The tables show cost of inventory on hand at the start of each quarter and also the gross profit recorded under the three methods.

Table 1   FIFO inventories on hand

	Purchased						Balance sheet amount of inventory
Start of	*4th Q Year 2*	*1st Q Year 3*	*2nd Q Year 3*	*3rd Q Year 3*	*4th Q Year 3*	*1st Q Year 4*	*inventory*
2d Q Year 3 ..	$1,100	$1,200	$1,300				= $3,600
3d Q Year 3 ..		1,200	1,300	$1,400			= 3,900
4th Q Year 3 ..			1,300	1,400	$1,400		= 4,100
1st Q Year 4 ..				1,400	1,400	$1,300	= 4,100

Table 2   FIFO gross profit recorded

	2nd Q Year 3	3rd Q Year 3	4th Q Year 3	1st Q Year 4
Sales	$1,500	$1,600	$1,600	$1,500
Cost	1,100	1,200	1,300	1,400
(Purchased)	*(4th Q-x2)*	*(1st Q-x3)*	*(2d Q-x3)*	*(3d Q-x3)*
Gross profit	$ 400	$ 400	$ 300	$ 100

Table 3   LIFO inventories on hand

		Purchased						*Balance sheet amount of inventory*
Start of	*4th Q Year 2*	*1st Q Year 3*	*2nd Q Year 3*	*3rd Q Year 3*	*4th Q Year 3*	*1st Q Year 4*		
2d Q Year 3 . .	$1,100	$1,200	$1,300				=	$3,600
3d Q Year 3 . .	1,100	1,200		$1,400			=	3,700
4th Q Year 3 . .	1,100	1,200			1,400		=	3,700
1st Q Year 4 . .	1,100	1,200				$1,300	=	3,600

Table 4   LIFO gross profit recorded

	2nd Q Year 3	3rd Q Year 3	4th Q Year 3	1st Q Year 4
Sales	$1,500	$1,600	$1,600	$1,500
Cost	1,300	1,400	1,400	1,300
(Purchased)	*(2d Q-x3)*	*(3d Q-x3)*	*(4th Q-x3)*	*(1st Q-x4)*
Gross profit	$ 200	$ 200	$ 200	$ 200

Table 5   Average-cost inventories on hand

	Opening average cost[a]	Purchased						*Balance sheet amount of inventory*
		4th Q Year 2	*1st Q Year 3*	*2nd Q Year 3*	*3rd Q Year 3*	*4th Q Year 3*	*1st Q Year 4*	
2d Q Year 3 . .	—	$1,100	$1,200	$1,300				= $3,600
3d Q Year 3 . .	$2,400[b]				$1,400			= 3,800
4th Q Year 3 . .	2,533.3[c]					$1,400		= 3,933.3
1st Q Year 4 . .	2,622.2[d]						$1,300	= 3,922.2

[a] Balance sheet value of inventory − Average cost of goods sold (B/S value ÷ 3).
[b] $3,600 − ($3,600 ÷ 3) = $3,600 − $1,200 = $2,400.
[c] $3,800 − ($3,800 ÷ 3) = $3,800 − $1,266.7 = $2,533.3.
[d] $3,933.3 − (3,933.3 ÷ 3) = $3,933.3 − $1,311.1 = $2,622.2.

Table 6   Average-cost gross profits recorded

	2nd Q year 3	3rd Q year 3	4th Q year 3	1st Q year 4
Sales	$1,500	$1,600	$1,600	$1,500
Cost (average)	1,200	1,266.7	1,311.1	1,307.4*
Gross profit	$ 300	$ 333.3	$ 288.9	$ 192.6

* Balance sheet value of inventory ÷ 3 = $3,922.2 ÷ 3 = $1,307.4.

Analysis.   *Under FIFO,* we note that the oldest cost in inventory at the start of the second quarter of year 3, $1,100, is the first to be sold in that quarter. Compared with a sale price of $1,500, this produces a gross profit of $400.

This $400 is really composed of two elements. There is the normal $200 markup on cost and an additional $200 resulting from the matching of an older, lower inventory cost with a current selling price. This $200 is referred to as the "inflation profit."

As long as the inflation rate remains unchanged, reported profits will include both the normal markup of $200 and the inflation profit of $200. In the third quarter of year 3, as the inflation continues, the gross profit remains at $400.

However, in the fourth quarter of year 3, the price level remains unchanged from the third quarter. Following the established pattern, a higher priced FIFO inventory cost layer flows into cost of goods sold, but with the steady price level, the sales price does not rise and this results in a drop of 25 percent in gross profit to $300. In the first quarter of year 4, there is a drop in price level, and both cost of new purchases and the sales price move down $100. The FIFO inventory system, however, continues as usual to place the oldest unit (the item purchased for $1,400 in the third quarter of year 3) into cost of goods sold to be matched against the reduced sale price of $1,500 with the gross profit dropping to $100.

Here, then, is the vulnerability of FIFO. Inventory costs flow into cost of goods sold after a delay equal to the inventory turnover period. In periods of continuing inflation, this matching produces a continuous inflation of profit. When the rate of inflation declines, revenues should immediately reflect the change; costs will not. For the length of one inventory turnover period, costs will continue to reflect the earlier rate of inflation and will constantly increase. *Thus, any reduction in the rate of inflation will affect the profits of FIFO companies adversely.*

Under LIFO, we note that the gross profits reported are the same for all quarters and they equal the normal markup of $200. This is so because under the LIFO system, the most recent purchase is the first deemed to be sold. Thus, LIFO cost is close to current cost, and the effects of inflation—both as the prices rise and as they fall—are largely eliminated from the income statement. Note, however, that in the real world, the correspondence between current cost and LIFO cost may not be quite as exact as in this illustration. However, there will rarely be any significant difference, unless there is a reduction in inventory *quantities.*

Thus, the LIFO inventory method will provide at least a temporary correction for the distorting effects of changing inflation rates, if purchases and sales are both made frequently and continually. In most cases, the price level at the time of the "last-in" purchase should be about the same as the price level at time of sale.

However, when purchases and sales are not closely linked, such as is the case with companies making seasonal purchases, the LIFO correction will not work. In this case, a time lag exists between purchase and sale. Reported income will tend to behave as if the company is on FIFO, even though it uses LIFO.

Under the average cost, we note that gross profits do vary with the price level, but not with as wide swings as under FIFO. This results because the time length of the time lag—in matching older costs with current revenues—is shorter under average cost than under FIFO, but longer than under LIFO. Thus, the inflation accounting problems of companies using average cost will be similar to those using FIFO, but the effects will be more moderate.

Inventory Valuation at "Market"

The inventory at cost must be compared with inventory at market and the lower of the two used.[2]

"Market value" is defined as current replacement cost except that market shall not be higher than net realizable value nor should it be less than net realizable value reduced by the normal profit margin.

The upper limit of market value in effect considers the costs associated with sale or other disposition costs. The lower limit means that if the inventory is written down from cost to market, it be written down to a figure that will ensure the realization of a "normal" gross profit on its sale in a subsequent period.

Inventories Under Long-Term Contracts

The accumulation of costs under long-term contracts, reduced by progress billings, are in the nature of inventories. Two methods of accounting are acceptable here, but it is intended that their use should be dictated by surrounding circumstances (see also Chapter 10).

1. Where estimates of the final outcome or results of the contracts are difficult or impossible to make and are too speculative to be reliable, the *completed-contract* method should be used. Under this method, all costs of the contract, including related general and administrative costs, are accumulated and carried as assets (inventories) until completion of the contract when final net profit or loss is determined.

2. Where estimates of cost and related incomes at each stage of completion of the contract can be made, the *percentage-of-completion* method of long-term contract accounting should be used. Under

---

[2] The use of the lower of cost or market for LIFO inventories, while not permitted for tax purposes, can be used in the financial statements and would not violate the Internal Revenue Code requirement that if the tax return is on LIFO, reports to outsiders must also be on this basis. Some modifications in the "LIFO conformity rule" have occurred in recent years.

this method, the estimated proportionate profit earned up to any particular point in time may be credited to income and correspondingly included in accumulated costs (inventories).

Under either method, losses that are ascertainable at any point in time should be recognized and accounted for when first determined.

SEC *FRR No. 1* Section 206 requires separate disclosure of inventoried costs related to long-term contracts, methods of determining cost, methods of determining market, and description of method by which amounts are removed from inventory.

Classification of Inventories

Generally, inventories are classified as current assets. Indeed, they represent in most cases a very important part of the current asset group, although, ordinarily, they are considered less liquid than cash or receivables.

Under the "normal operating cycle" concept, inventories that would be kept beyond a year because of the requirements typical of an industry would nevertheless be classified as current. Thus, inventories in the tobacco industry or the liquor industry, which go through prolonged aging cycles, are nevertheless classified as current.

Inventories in excess of current requirements should not be classified as current.

ILLUSTRATION 8.   Chrysler Corporation had the following footnote:

> In accordance with industry practice, the entire service parts inventory has been included in current assets, although in many instances parts are carried for estimated requirements during the serviceable lives of products sold and are, therefore, not expected to be sold within one year. Adequate provision has been made for obsolescence of service parts.

IMPLICATIONS FOR ANALYSIS

It is obvious that to the extent to which alternative choices of accounting standards, and the methods of their application, proliferate, the wider is management's flexibility in reporting results and in presenting the enterprise's financial condition. In the area of inventory accounting, where the impact of differing methods on income can be substantial, this flexibility is all the more likely to be availed of by management.

The auditor's opinion should provide assurance that certain minimum standards were upheld in the exercise of discretion with which such principles are applied. However, in some areas of inventory accounting, the permitted leeway is so considerable that management can exercise a great deal of discretion in its choices. Thus, as a minimum, the financial analyst must understand what these choices are, and they must be judged in the light of conditions that apply to each specific situation.

With regard to inventories, the financial analyst will expect information and assurance as to the following:

1. Is the inventory physically in existence and is it fairly valued?
2. Has the accounting for inventories been consistent?
3. Can the effect of the different accounting methods used be measured?

Audit procedures designed to give assurance about the physical existence of inventories have been improving over the years and have been especially tightened up since the 1938 SEC hearings in the matter of McKesson & Robbins, Inc. In this case, large-scale fraud that resulted in a substantial overstatement of inventories was not uncovered by the audit primarily because no attempt was made by the auditors to establish physical contact with the inventories. The SEC stated:

> In our opinion, the time has come when auditors must, as part of their
> examination whenever reasonable and practicable, make physical contact
> with the inventory and assume reasonable responsibility therefore as
> had already become the practice in many cases before the present hearings.
> By this we do not mean that auditors should be, or by making such tests
> become, the guarantors of inventories any more than of any of the other
> items in the financial statements but we do mean that they should make
> all reasonable tests and inquiries, and not merely those limited to the
> books, in order to state their professional opinion, as auditors, as to the
> truthfulness of that item in the same way as they do for the other items in
> the statements.

The accounting profession responded by adopting the requirement that auditors observe the taking of physical inventories whenever it was reasonable and practicable to do so. This requirement, as well as the refinement of audit techniques, has brought about great improvements in the reliability of inventory audits. Nevertheless, a variety of cases involving inventory accounting abuses still arise. Cenco, Inc., was almost driven to insolvency because of a systematic inventory inflation scheme carried on over a number of years in a major division. These irregularities of about $25 million forced Cenco's auditors to settle for damages of $3.5 million.

In the early 1980s Saxon Industries, in order to continue borrowing from banks and possibly for other reasons, overstated inventories of its copier division by about $50 million. Management took honest inventory counts to determine the true conditions and subsequently inflated the counts to meet predetermined profit reporting goals. When the scheme collapsed the company filed for bankruptcy.

In 1984 the SEC charged Staufer Chemical Company with (1) improperly structuring inventory layers so as to cause artificial LIFO liquidations, (2) improperly recognizing inventory profits resulting from intracompany product transfers, and (3) causing sales to be recognized prematurely by extraordinary incentives to distributors to stock up on chemicals in excess of their real sales needs. These actions resulted in Staufer's earnings being overstated by 25 percent.

Given the substantial number of companies which use the LIFO inventory method and the room for manipulation which that method makes possible, it is surprising that more authoritative guidelines have not been issued. In late 1984 the AICPA's standards division published and sent to the FASB an Issues Paper that identified more than 50 unresolved financial accounting and reporting issues relating to LIFO. The FASB has decided not to add this project to its agenda.

In early 1985 the SEC issued *Staff Accounting Bulletin No. 58* which endorsed the AICPA paper as representing a summary of existing acceptable LIFO accounting practices and recommended that companies and their auditors use it as a guidance. In fact it warns that companies, if challenged, will have to justify to the SEC departures from the paper. While the paper provides no definitive guidance on establishing LIFO pools (i.e., layers), it does state that there should be valid business reasons for the number and composition of such pools. It is unacceptable to establish pools with the principal objective of facilitating inventory liquidations (which, in effect, decrease cost of goods sold artificially).

The fair statement of inventories is, of course, dependent not merely on a proper accounting for physical quantities but also on their proper pricing and summarization.

The analyst must be alert to the types of cost that are included in inventory. For example, under Internal Revenue Regulations, marketing, sales, advertising and distribution expenses, interest costs, past service pension costs, and general and administrative costs pertaining to overall, rather than only to manufacturing activities, must be excluded from the overhead included in inventory under a full-absorption cost system. A reading of footnotes can reveal unusual accounting policies regarding the carrying costs of inventory. Thus, for example, in accounting for the cost of inventories in its aircraft division Chrysler Corp. built some hope about future profit margins into current costs:

> The estimated number of aircraft to be produced from the date of acquisition under the combined Gulfstream III/IV program is 308. At year-end, 13 aircraft had been delivered under the program and the backlog included 3 Gulfstream III and 84 Gulfstream IV orders. The Gulfstream III/IV inventoried costs at year-end ($301.2 million) together with the additional estimated costs to complete the 87 orders exceeded the expected aggregate cost of sales of these aircraft by approximately $198.9 million.

Chrysler anticipates that profit margins to be realized on delivery of aircraft against both existing unfilled orders and additional anticipated orders will be sufficient to absorb the inventoried costs.

While under the going-concern convention accountants are not concerned with the sale of inventories other than in the normal course of business, the analyst, and especially the credit analyst concerned with current values, may be interested in the composition of inventories. Thus, raw material may be much more readily salable than work in process since once raw material is converted into parts of certain specifications, it rapidly loses its value in case it then has to be liquidated.

The composition of total inventory between raw materials, work-in-process, and finished goods can hold important analytical clues[3] as to future production plans or as to the existence of a divergence between actual as against expected sales. Thus, a decline in raw materials against an increase in work-in-process and finished goods may indicate a production slowdown, while an *inventory divergence* in the opposite direction may indicate actual or expected increases in orders booked. Chapter 21 contains further discussion and illustration of the application of these analytical tools.

The level of inventories (and of accounts receivable to which they are related) over time and in relation to sales can hold important analytical clues regarding inventory quality and the effect on it of such factors as demand, returns, and so on.

ILLUSTRATION 9.   Toro Company thought that snow throwers were a perfect complement to its lawnmower business, particularly when heavy snowfalls occurred two years in a row. The company tooled up and produced snowblowers as if snow were a growth business and as if snow fell as reliably as grass grows. When, in the third year, winter proved to be a snowless season both the company and its dealers were loaded up with inventory that did not move. To compound the difficulty, dealers were so financially pressed that they were unable to finance needed lawnmower inventories for the summer season. It took years before Toro was able to work its way out of this disastrous experience.

ILLUSTRATION 10.   Because of poor product quality Regina Company experienced an unusually high rate of vacuum cleaner returns. Early analytical symptoms of these problems were an almost doubling of finished goods inventories and receivables concurrent with much slower sales increases. When the news of these problems became public knowledge it was too late for investors and creditors. The company admitted that past results were materially incorrect and withdrew its financial statements.

Accepted reporting standards (which are part of generally accepted auditing standards) require that changes in the application of accounting

---

[3] Credit for the development of these analytical tools belongs to Thornton L. O'Glove of Reporting Research Corporation.

principles be noted and the impact of the change reported. Thus, in audited financial statements, the analyst will expect to be alerted to changes in principles of inventory accounting, such as, for example, from LIFO to FIFO. However, the analyst must be aware of the fact that whereas changes in accounting principles call for disclosure, other changes affecting comparability do not necessarily call for disclosure in the auditor's report.

Of the various inventory methods in use, LIFO is the most complex and in addition has not only bookkeeping implications for management but behavioral ones as well. Thus, for example, in the case of LIFO, the year-end inventory level makes a definite difference in results, and management must plan and act accordingly.

The analyst must realize that the LIFO method of inventory accounting is not unitary but has rather many variations that can produce different results. It can be applied to all inventory components or to only a few.[4] It can be applied to material costs while other inventory methods are used for labor and overhead costs. Footnotes that merely disclose the variety of methods in use without giving breakdowns of respective inventory amounts have limited analytical value.

The LIFO method permits income manipulation (refer also to earlier illustrations) and analysts must be ever alert to this possibility. For example, changing purchasing policy at the end of the year can affect reported results. This is not possible under FIFO.

ILLUSTRATION 11.   The following purchases occurred in year 1:

> January to June . . . . . .   7,000 widgets at $1 per unit
> July to November . . . .   5,000 widgets at $1.20 per unit
> December . . . .   2,000 widgets at $1.30 per unit

The ending inventory consisted of 1,000 units. Under LIFO these would be reported at a cost of $1 per widget. Now, assume the enterprise had purchased 3,000 widgets in December—an additional 1,000. The additional purchase would have cost $1,300, but the additional ending inventory would have been only $1,000, thus decreasing profits by $300. Under different conditions, the act of buying more widgets could have increased profits.

When a reduction in the LIFO inventory quantities (base) takes place, old LIFO costs are matched with current revenues, thus resulting in increased profit margins. This is also known as LIFO liquidation.

ILLUSTRATION 12.   Assume that the widget company shows the results below for year 2:

Sales (2,000 @ $1.375)		$2,750
Cost of sales:		
Beginning LIFO inventory (1,000 @ $1) . . .	$1,000	
Purchases (2,000 @ $1.10)	2,200	
Ending LIFO inventory (1,000 @ $1)	(1,000)	2,200
Gross profit		$ 550
Gross profit percentage		20%

---

[4] Some meat packers, for example, have used LIFO for pork but not for beef and lamb.

Assume that in year 3 the company continues the policy of marking up widgets by 25 percent and that purchase and selling prices increase by 10 percent. However, a strike during the year prevents replacement of widget inventory, and this part of the LIFO base is liquidated. As can be seen below, this will increase profit margins as follows:

Sales (2,000 @ $1.5125)		$3,025
Cost of sales:		
Beginning LIFO inventory (1,000 @ $1) ...	$1,000	
Purchases (1,500 @ $1.21)	1,815	
Ending LIFO inventory (500 @ $1)	(500)	2,315
Gross Profit		$ 710
Gross profit percentage		23.5%

In the same fashion, managements can by deliberate action manipulate profit levels by dipping into LIFO inventory pools. Analysts must watch for disclosure of LIFO liquidations. The following is the disclosure by Federal Mogul Corporation:

> Inventory quantities were reduced resulting in liquidations of certain LIFO inventory layers, which increased net earnings by $11,701,000 ($0.52 per share), $3,682,000 ($0.16 per share) and $1,038,000 ($0.04 per share) in 1990, 1989, and 1988, respectively.

While spotting an undisclosed LIFO inventory chargeout is not always easy, a crude check that the analyst can apply is to see whether the dollar value of the LIFO inventory has declined on a year-to-year basis. Moreover, information about such changes can also be found in the "Management's Discussion and Analysis of Financial Condition and Results of Operations" section of published financial reports.

The analyst must be particularly wary about the reliability of quarterly results published by companies using LIFO. By definition of the tax laws, LIFO is an *annual* calculation. Thus, at interim periods, the preparation of quarterly statements requires forecasts of costs of inventory items purchased or produced as well as projections of future changes in inventory quantities and mix within the entire year. These estimates are bound to be subjective and thus subject to managerial manipulation. Chapter 22 contains a more extensive discussion of problems associated with interim reports.

ANALYTICAL RESTATEMENT OF LIFO INVENTORIES TO FIFO

As is clear from the discussion above and the example that will follow, the LIFO inventory method understates inventories significantly in times of rising price levels thus understating a company's debt-paying ability (as measured, for example, by the current ratio). It overstates inventory turnover and in addition contains the means of income manipulation. An analytical technique available to the analyst is to adjust LIFO statements to the approximate pro forma situation that would exist had they been prepared on a FIFO basis. This is possible when the current cost of LIFO inventories is disclosed, a disclosure now generally available.

ILLUSTRATION 13.   To illustrate the restatement of financial statements from a LIFO to a FIFO basis, we will use data from the financial statements of Campbell Soup Co. (see Appendix 4B).

   The inventory note 153 tells us that inventories are net of adjustments to reduce inventories to the LIFO basis (referred to by some as the LIFO reserves) of (all amounts in millions) $89.6 in 1991 and $84.6 in 1990. Thus, to restate the 1991 *balance sheet* to the FIFO basis requires an entry as follows:

Inventories (A)	89.6	
Deferred Tax Payable (B)		30.5
Retained Earnings (C)		59.1

(A) Inventories increased to approximately current replacement cost. (A slow turnover can result in inventories at FIFO not being stated at the most current cost.)

(B) Since inventories are increased, a provision for taxes payable in the future on this increase must be made—here at a tax rate of 34 percent (per item 134). The reason for the tax deferral is that the pro forma balance sheet entry reflects an accounting method that differs from that used on the tax return (see also Chapter 11).

(C) Higher ending inventories mean lower cost of goods sold and a corresponding increase in cumulative net income to date that in the balance sheet flows into retained earnings (net of tax).

   In order to calculate the effect on 1991 income of a restatement of inventories to FIFO, we must know the adjustment not only to the ending inventories but also to the beginning inventories as well. A good way to visualize this is by means of the following tabulation:

Computation of cost of goods sold

	1990 (in thousands)		
	Under LIFO	Difference	Under FIFO
Beginning inventory ...	819.8[a]	84.6[b]	904.4
+ Purchases (P)[c]	P	—	P
− Ending inventory	(706.7)[d]	(89.6)[b]	(796.3)
= Cost of goods sold	P + 113.1	−5.0 [d]	P + 108.1

[a] As reported per balance sheet 34 or Note on Inventory 153A.
[b] Per Note 153 on Inventory.
[c] Since purchases are the same under either the LIFO or FIFO basis, the amount of purchases need not be inserted to arrive at the effect on cost of goods sold or net income. If desired, the amount of purchases for 1991 can be computed as follows:
$4095.5 (CGS per income statement) + $706.7 (ending inventory)
            − $819.8 (beginning inventory) = $3982.4

(d) The effect of the restatement to FIFO is to decrease CGS by $5.0. The resulting effect on net income is an increase by $5.0 (1 − 0.34), or $3.3, under a 34 percent tax rate assumption. Thus the effect of the restatement to the FIFO basis on 1991 income is to increase it by $3.3. It should be noted that under conditions of rising prices, LIFO net income is usually lower than FIFO net income. However, the net effect of the restatement in any given year depends on the combined effect of the change in beginning and ending inventories and other factors such as liquidation of LIFO inventory layers.

The adjustment of the 1990 balance sheet to the FIFO basis will require the following adjusting entry:

Inventory(d) 84.6
    Deferred Tax Payable(e) 28.76
    Retained Earnings(f) 55.84

(d) Per item ([153A]).
(e) At 34 percent tax rate.
(f) Residual.

The earlier calculated effect of restatement to FIFO on the 1991 income of $3.3 can now be reconciled with the credits to retained earnings in the foregoing two journal entries restating the 1991 and 1990 balance sheet inventories to the FIFO basis. Thus,

$$\frac{1990 \text{ credit to}}{\text{Retained earnings}} - \frac{1991 \text{ credit to}}{\text{Retained earnings}} = \frac{\text{Increase in}}{1991 \text{ net income}}$$
$$\$55.84^* \qquad\qquad \$59.14^* \qquad\qquad \$3.3^\dagger$$

* Per above journal entries.
† See preceding computation.

The above illustration exemplifies the general methodology of the analytical restatement of LIFO-based statements to FIFO.

Analytical Adjustment Required if the LIFO Method Is Preferred

When the financial statements are already prepared using the LIFO inventory method, and that is the method preferred by the analyst, the income statement requires no adjustment because the cost of goods sold already reflects current cost. The adjustment of LIFO inventories to FIFO has been illustrated above and may also approximate current cost.[5]

Under the historical-cost model, it is characteristic of the LIFO method that it introduces current costs *only* into the income statement while leaving inventories on the balance sheet at older, often understated costs. This can render meaningless measures such as the current ratio or the inventory turnover ratio. To correct for this and to establish current costs for inventories on the balance sheet, the analyst can make the following pro forma analytical entry to adjust Campbell Soup's 1991 balance sheet:

---

[5] Under *SFAS* 89 large companies now disclose the current cost of inventories only on a voluntary basis (see also Chapter 14.)

Inventory 89.6
    Deferred Tax Payable 30.46
    Revaluation Surplus 59.14

See the Illustration above for an explanation of the derivation of these amounts.

It should be noted that the above is strictly an *analytical* adjustment because under present generally accepted accounting standards in the United States, the establishment of a Revaluation Surplus account in the primary financial statements, as part of shareholder's equity, is not sanctioned.

As noted in the discussion earlier in this section, under the LIFO method, a reduction in inventories that are not replaced by year-end may result in the costing out of lower-cost inventory layers, a result also known as LIFO liquidation. Analytically, the amount of the LIFO liquidation gain, which is usually disclosed along with the tax effect, can be considered separately as an unusual nonrecurring item by removing it from the cost of goods sold amount in a recast income statement (see Chapter 22).

OTHER ANALYTICAL CONSIDERATIONS

Analysts, such as lending officers or investors with clout, who have access to managements can ask additional questions about LIFO inventories as follows:

1. How are LIFO inventories calculated—on an item-by-item basis or by use of dollar value pools (in which different items are grouped)?
2. Was income affected by changes in inventory pools and if so by how much? Was it affected by year-end purchasing decisions?
3. Did the company record extra expenses or losses in order to offset income arising from the involuntary liquidation of LIFO inventories?
4. What assumptions concerning LIFO inventories underlie the quarterly reported results?

The "lower-of-cost-or-market" principle of inventory accounting has additional implications for the analyst. In times of rising prices it tends to undervalue inventories regardless of the cost method used. This in turn will depress the current ratio below its real level since the other current assets (as well as the current liabilities) are not valued on a consistent basis with the methods used in valuing inventories. Under *SFAS 89* certain companies can now disclose on a voluntary basis the current cost of inventories (see Chapter 14).

It is a fact that most published reports contain insufficient information to allow the analyst to convert inventories accounted for under one method to a figure reflecting a different method of inventory accounting.

Most analysts would want such information in order to be able to better compare the financial statements of companies that use different inventory accounting methods.

To illustrate the effect that the use of a variety of inventory methods can have on reported net income or financial ratios, let us examine the case of a retailer who deals in only one product. We assume here no opening inventory, operating expenses of $5 million, and 2 million shares outstanding. The following purchases are made during the year:

	Units	Per unit	
January	100,000	$10	$ 1,000,000
March	300,000	11	3,300,000
June	600,000	12	7,200,000
October	300,000	14	4,200,000
December	500,000	15	7,500,000
Total	1,800,000		$23,200,000

Ending inventory at December 31 was 800,000 units. Assets, excluding inventories, amounted to $75 million, of which $50 million were current. Current liabilities amounted to $25 million, and long-term liabilities came to $10 million.

The tabulation which follows shows the net income arrived at by applying the FIFO, LIFO, and average-cost method, respectively. Sales are at $25 per unit, and taxes are ignored.

Computation of net income

	FIFO method	LIFO method	Average costs
Sales:			
1 million units @ $25	$25,000,000	$25,000,000	$25,000,000
Cost of sales:			
Beginning inventory	—	—	—
Purchases	23,200,000	23,200,000	23,200,000
Cost of goods available for sale ...	23,200,000	23,200,000	23,200,000
Less: Ending inventory	11,700,000	9,100,000	10,312,000
Cost of sales	11,500,000	14,100,000	12,888,000
Gross profit	13,500,000	10,900,000	12,112,000
Operating expenses	5,000,000	5,000,000	5,000,000
Net income	$ 8,500,000	$ 5,900,000	$ 7,112,000
Net income per share	$4.25	$2.95	$3.56

The FIFO inventory computation was based upon 500,000 units at $15 and 300,000 at $14 which yields a total of $11,700,000. The LIFO inventory cost was obtained following the assumption that the units purchased last were the first sold. Therefore, the 800,000 units are priced as 100,000 units at $10, 300,000 units at $11, and 400,000 units at $12, totaling $9,100,000. The average cost was obtained by dividing $23,200,000 by 1,800,000 units purchased, yielding an average unit price of $12.89. The $12.89 unit price multiplied by 800,000 ending inventory units gives a total inventory cost of $10,312,000.

The table below shows the effect of the three inventory methods on a number of selected ratios:

	FIFO method	LIFO method	Average costs
Current ratio	2.47 : 1	2.36 : 1	2.41 : 1
Debt-to-equity ratio	1 : 5.17	1 : 4.91	1 : 5.03
Inventory turnover	2 : 1	3 : 1	2.5 : 1
Return on total assets	9.8%	7.0%	8.3%
Gross margin	54%	44%	49%
Net profit as percent of sales ...	34%	24%	29%

As the above discussion and examples clearly show, the analysis of financial statements where inventories are important requires that the analyst bring to bear a full understanding of inventory accounting methods and their impact on results.

QUESTIONS

1. Under presently accepted but changing practice, compensating balances under a bank loan agreement are considered as unrestricted cash and are classified as current assets.
   a. From the point of view of the analyst of financial statements, is this a useful classification?
   b. Give reasons for your conclusion and state how you would evaluate such balances.
2. a. What are some salient provisions of *SFAS 12?*
   b. What are the disclosures required by *SFAS 12?*
3. What are some of the gaps and inconsistencies in *SFAS 12* of which the analyst must be aware?
4. a. What is meant by the "operating cycle"?
   b. What is the significance of the operating cycle concept to the classification of current versus noncurrent items in the balance sheet?
   c. Is this concept useful to those concerned with measuring the current

debt-paying ability of an enterprise and the liquidity of its working capital components?

d. Give the effect of the operating cycle concept on the classification of selected current assets in the following industries:

(1) Tobacco.

(2) Liquor.

(3) Retailing.

5. a. What are the financial analyst's primary concerns when it comes to the evaluation of accounts receivable?

b. What information, not usually found in published financial statements, should the analyst obtain in order to assess the overall risk of noncollectibility of the receivables?

6. Why do financial analysts generally attach such great importance to inventories?

7. Comment on the effect that the variety of accounting methods for determining the cost of inventories have on the determination of an enterprise income. As to the inclusion of which costs in inventories, is there considerable variation in practice? Give examples of three types of such cost elements.

8. Of what significance is the *level* of activity on the unit cost of goods produced by a manufacturer? The allocation of overhead costs requires the making of certain assumptions. Explain and illustrate by means of an example.

9. What is the major objective of LIFO inventory accounting? What are the effects of this method on the measurement of income and of inventories, particularly from the point of view of the user of the financial statements?

10. Comment on the disclosure with respect to inventory valuation methods which is practiced today. In what way is such disclosure useful to the analyst? What type of disclosure is relatively useful to the reader?

11. Accountants generally follow the lower-of-cost-or-market basis of inventory valuations.

a. Define *cost* as applied to the valuation of inventories.

b. Define *market* as applied to the valuation of inventories.

c. Why are inventories valued at the lower of cost or market? Discuss.

d. List the arguments against the use of the lower-of-cost-or-market method of valuing inventories. (AICPA)

12. Compare and contrast effects of the LIFO and FIFO inventory cost methods on earnings during a period of inflation. (CFA)

13. Discuss the ways and conditions under which the FIFO and LIFO inventory costing methods produce different inventory valuations. Do not discuss procedures for computing inventory cost.

14. What are some of the important questions about LIFO inventories that lending officers and investors with clout can ask?

Chapter 6

ANALYSIS OF
NONCURRENT ASSETS

In this chapter, we conclude our examination of the measurement of assets by a discussion of the analysis of noncurrent assets.

LONG-TERM INVESTMENTS

Long-term investments are usually investments in assets such as debt instruments, equity securities, real estate, mineral deposits, or joint ventures acquired with longer-term objectives in mind. Such objectives may include the ultimate acquisition of control or affiliation with other companies, investment in suppliers, securing of assured sources of supply, and so forth.

Marketable Securities

The accounting for investments in common stock of certain sizes is discussed below. With the exception of (1) convertible bonds, (2) preferred shares with a stated redemption value, and (3) nonequity securities, marketable equity securities classified as noncurrent assets or shown in balance sheets of enterprises that issue unclassified balance sheets (e.g., finance or real estate companies), are now accounted for in accordance with the provision of *SFAS 12,* the salient points of which are covered in the "Marketable Securities" section of Chapter 5.

The following provisions of *SFAS 12* apply to the equity securities not classified as current:

Market value changes are to be reflected directly in the equity section of the balance sheet and are not to enter the determination of net income except where the change is other than temporary. Marketable equity securities held by enterprises that issue unclassified balance sheets are to be regarded as noncurrent.

For those marketable equity securities not classified as current assets (including marketable securities in unclassified balance sheets), a

165

determination must be made as to whether a decline in market value as of the balance sheet date for each individual security is other than temporary. If the decline is other than temporary, the cost basis is to be written down, as a realized loss, to a new cost basis. The new cost basis is not to be changed for subsequent recoveries in market value.

Accumulated changes in the valuation allowance of noncurrent marketable securities shall be included in the equity section of the balance sheet and presented separately.

The valuation allowance, which may be called "net unrealized loss on noncurrent marketable equity securities," can be reduced for subsequent recoveries in market value, but at no time should the aggregate of marketable securities be carried on the balance sheet at an amount in excess of original cost.

SEC *Staff Accounting Bulletin 59* (1985) discussed how to (*a*) interpret the phrase "other than temporary" in *SFAS 12*, when making a determination about a decline in market value below cost and (*b*) determine the amount of a write-down.

The staff believes that "other than temporary" should not be interpreted to mean "permanent impairment." The following are some examples of factors that by themselves or in combination indicate that a decline is other than temporary and that a write-down of carrying value is required:

The length of time and the extent to which the market value has been less than cost.

The financial condition and near-term prospects of the issuer, including specific events that may influence the operations of the issuer such as changes in technology or discontinuance of a segment of the business.

The intent and ability of the holder to retain its investment in the issuer for a period sufficient to allow for any anticipated recovery in market value.

According to the bulletin, when management determines that a write-down should be accounted for as a realized loss, the carrying value of the investment should be written down to reflect realizable value. The particular facts and circumstances of each case dictate the amount of realized loss to be recognized.

MOVES TOWARD REALISM IN ACCOUNTING FOR DEBT SECURITIES

Under prodding by the SEC the AICPA's standard-setting committee has been reconsidering the accounting for note and bond investments by financial institutions such as banks, savings associations, insurance companies, and finance companies.

When a financial institution acquires debt securities it classifies them to a "short-term trading" account or to an "investment account." Trading securities must be carried at current market values and changes in these values affect periodic earnings. By contrast, "investment" securities can be kept at historical cost on the theory that they will be held to maturity and redeemed at par. In practice financial institutions classified most of their debt securities in the investment category in order to insulate income from changes in valuation even though they were trading such securities quite actively. Moreover, financial institutions can selectively sell securities which appreciated, thus benefiting income, while retaining those which lost market value.

Under an AICPA proposal a financial institution can classify debt securities as investments *only* if they (a) have the financial ability and (b) the intention to hold them long enough to recover their book value. Otherwise such securities must be classified to a trading account and carried at market value or a "held for sale" account and carried at lower of cost or market.

Concerned that such accounting will introduce volatility into their income determination, financial institutions have opposed these proposals and predicted dire economic consequences such as a reluctance to invest in longer-term debt.

In 1990 the AICPA issued *Statement of Position 70–11* providing guidance of disclosures required by financial institutions about debt securities held as assets. The information required to be disclosed includes accounting policies, amortized cost, estimated market values by category and by maturity dates and information on gross realized and unrealized gains and losses.

SFAS 105 (1990) establishes requirements for all entities to disclose information about (a) significant concentrations of credit risk from financial instruments and (b) financial instruments with an off-balance sheet risk of accounting loss. The term "financial instrument" is broadly defined to include trade and other receivables, bank deposits as well as instruments such as options and forward contracts.

Disclosures about Fair Value of Financial Instruments, (*SFAS 107*)

As noted in the previous chapter, the FASB issued *SFAS 107* which requires all entities to disclose the fair value of financial instruments in the body of the financial statements or in the accompanying notes.

A financial instrument is defined as cash, evidence of an ownership interest in an entity, or a contract that both:

- Imposes on one entity a contractual obligation to deliver cash or another financial instrument to a second entity, or to exchange other financial instruments on potentially unfavorable terms with the second entity

- Conveys to that second entity a contractual right to receive cash or another financial instrument from the first entity, or to exchange other financial instruments on potentially favorable terms with the first entity.

The *Statement* requires disclosures about the fair value of all financial instruments, whether recognized or not recognized in the balance sheet, for which it is practicable to estimate that value. An entity should also disclose the methods and significant assumptions used to estimate the fair value of financial instruments.

Quoted market prices, if available, are the best evidence of fair value. If quoted market prices are not available, management's best estimate of fair value may be based on the quoted market price of a financial instrument with similar characteristics or on valuation techniques (e.g., present value of estimated future cash flows, option pricing models, or matrix pricing models). Reasons why it is not practicable to estimate fair value must be given when needed.

Investments in Common Stock

Investments in common stock representing less than 20 percent of the equity securities of the investee must be accounted for in accordance with *SFAS 12* as detailed above and in the preceding chapter.

Companies 20-Percent to 50-Percent Owned   *APB Opinion 18* concluded that even a position of less than 50 percent of the voting stock may give the investor the ability to exercise significant influence over the operating and financial policies of the investee. When such an ability to exercise influence is evident, the investment should be accounted for under the equity method. Basically, this means at cost plus the equity in the undistributed earnings or losses of the investee since acquisition, with the addition of certain other adjustments. The mechanics of the equity method are discussed in Chapter 9.

Evidence of the investor's ability to exercise significant influence over operating and financial policies of the investee may be indicated in several ways, such as management representation and participation; but in the interest of uniformity of application, the APB concluded that in the absence of evidence to the contrary, an investment (direct or indirect) of 20 percent or more in the voting stock of an investee should lead to the presumption of an ability to exercise significant influence over the investee.[1] Conversely, an investment in less than 20 percent of the voting stock of the investee leads to the presumption of a lack of such influence unless the ability to influence can be demonstrated.

It should be noted that while the eligibility to use the equity method is based on the percentage of voting stock outstanding, which may include, for example, convertible preferred stock, the percentage of earnings that may be picked up under the equity method depends on ownership of *common stock* only.

ILLUSTRATION 1.   Company A owns 15 percent of the common stock of Company B. By virtue of additional holdings of convertible preferred stock, the total percentage of voting power held is 20 percent. While the total holdings entitle Company A to account for its investment in Company B at equity, it can pick up only 15 percent of Company B residual income because that is the percentage of ownership of *common* stock that it holds.

The above principle of picking up income under the equity method is not consistent with the concept of "common stock equivalents" used in the computation of earnings per share (see Chapter 12). The effect of possible conversions and so on must, however, be disclosed.

Corporate Joint Ventures   Joint ventures represent investments by two or more entities in an enterprise with the objective of sharing sources of supply, the development of markets, or other types of risk and reward. A common form of joint venture is a 50–50 percent sharing of ownership, although other divisions of interest are also found. An investment in a *corporate* joint venture should, according to *APB Opinion 18,* be accounted for by the equity method. An investment in a joint venture not evidenced by common stock ownership may presumably be accounted for at cost.

Overview of How Investments in Common Stock Are Accounted for
Exhibit 6–1 presents a summary indicating how investments in common stock of different sizes are accounted for under *APB Opinion 18* and other pronouncements governing the principles of consolidation accounting.

Recent Development   In mid-1992 the FASB tentatively agreed to a compromise proposal that will require companies to value more of their investments at market value. These proposals will continue the recent

---

[1] *SFAS Interpretation 35* finds the following factors as weighing against a finding of "significant influence": the company files a lawsuit against the investor or complains to a government agency; the investor tries and fails to become a member of the board of directors; the investor agrees to refrain from increasing its holding; the company is operated by a small group that ignores the investor's wishes and the investor tries and fails to obtain more financial information from the company.

Exhibit 6–1 Summary of accounting treatments by investor for investments in common stock

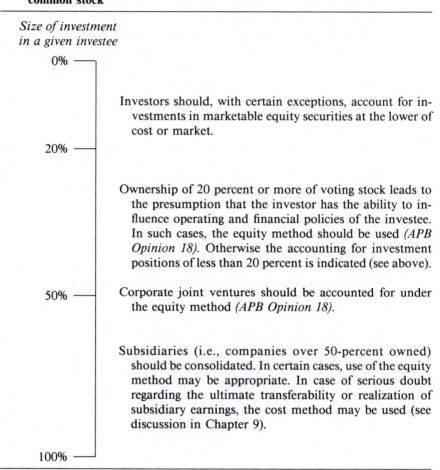

Size of investment in a given investee

0% ——

Investors should, with certain exceptions, account for investments in marketable equity securities at the lower of cost or market.

20% ——

Ownership of 20 percent or more of voting stock leads to the presumption that the investor has the ability to influence operating and financial policies of the investee. In such cases, the equity method should be used *(APB Opinion 18)*. Otherwise the accounting for investment positions of less than 20 percent is indicated (see above).

50% ——

Corporate joint ventures should be accounted for under the equity method *(APB Opinion 18)*.

Subsidiaries (i.e., companies over 50-percent owned) should be consolidated. In certain cases, use of the equity method may be appropriate. In case of serious doubt regarding the ultimate transferability or realization of subsidiary earnings, the cost method may be used (see discussion in Chapter 9).

100% ——

trend, undesirable from the analyst's point of view, of reflecting changes in market value (primarily losses) in the equity section of the balance sheet but *not* on the income statement.

Implications for Analysis

The analyst, aware of accounting principles governing the presentation of investments, must pay particular attention to their valuation. On the one hand, they can be grossly undervalued on the balance sheet because of the convention prohibiting their write-up to market value (except in certain industries), no matter how obvious and soundly based such value may be.

On the other hand, the analyst must be alert to impairment of market value that, because of loose standards in practice, may not be fully reflected on the financial statements. If separately disclosed, the income generated by an investment may, at times, provide a clue to its fair value.

In Chapter 5, we considered some of the overall flaws and inconsistencies in the accounting for marketable securities brought on by *SFAS 12*. Following are some further considerations that the analyst must be aware of in accounting for marketable securities not carried as current assets.

SFAS 12 does require the write-down of marketable securities classified as noncurrent to market with a charge to income in cases where the change in value is deemed to be other than temporary. However, there is no agreement as to what constitutes "temporary" in this context. While the accounting profession has issued some guidelines of how to audit the carrying amounts of marketable securities (*Journal of Accountancy,* April 1975, p. 69), they by no means ensure logical and consistent procedures in this regard. Thus, practice will in all probability reflect arbitrary determinations that will make the carrying of marketable securities by one company not comparable to that of another. The effect of SEC *Staff Accounting Bulletin 59* on practice, discussed previously, is not clear. It is possible that it will remove some flagrant abuses in practice and cause the write-down of equity securities whose values had obviously shrunk below cost.

It is possible to view *SFAS 107,* which requires *disclosure* of fair values of financial instruments, as a watershed position and the beginning of a departure from the historical cost accounting model in the United States. However, there is a difference between *disclosure* and the recording of fair value, the latter affecting actual reported financial position and the measurement of income.

Nevertheless, such disclosures allow analysts to better assess the short-term liquidity and long-term solvency of entities. Moreover, the effect of changing values of financial instruments on income can be assessed and adjusted for.

The analyst must also bear in mind that equity securities of companies in which the enterprise has a 20 percent or larger interest, and in some instances an even smaller interest than 20 percent, need not be adjusted to market but must instead be carried at equity that may at times be significantly below, and at other times above, market. Thus, with regard to such relatively substantial blocks of securities, the values at which they are carried on the balance sheet may be substantially in excess of their realizable value.

The creation of a new category in the equity section of the balance sheet where the "net unrealized loss on noncurrent marketable securities" is lodged must be regarded as a somewhat regressive step. One of the achievements of *APB Opinion 9* was the elimination, except in cases of prior year adjustments, of direct charges of losses to equity accounts. *SFAS 12* brings us back, even if under different circumstances, to an area we were glad to leave in 1966.[2]

The accounting for investments in substantial blocks of *common stock* has undergone significant improvement. The carrying of investments representing control of 20 percent or over at equity is an improvement over prior practice. While the equity method is more realistic than cost, it must be borne in mind that it is not the equivalent of fair market value that, depending on circumstances, may be significantly larger or lower than the carrying amount at equity.

The analyst must remember that the assumption that an investment in 20 percent or more of the voting securities of an investee results in significant influence over that investee is an arbitrary one that had to be made in the interest of accounting uniformity.[3] If such influence is indeed absent, then there may be some question regarding the investor's ability to realize the amount stated at equity. The marketplace does not necessarily pay close attention to book values, and "equity" is book value. An improvement brought about by *APB Opinion 18* is the requirement that, where available, the market value of investments in common stock (other than in subsidiaries) be disclosed.

APB Opinion 18 states that "a loss in value of an investment which is other than a temporary decline should be recognized the same as a loss in value of other long-term assets." This leaves a great deal to judgment and interpretation, and in the past this approach has resulted in companies being very slow to recognize losses in their investments. Since the *Opinion* does not consider a decline in market value to be conclusive evidence of such a loss, the analyst must be alert to detect situations where hope rather than reason supports the carrying amount of an investment. It must be recognized that the equity method reflects only current operating losses rather than the capital losses that occur when the earning power of an investment deteriorates or disappears.

The accounting for other long-term investments (such as regular or convertible bonds) is presently not helpful to the analyst since historical cost is in most cases not relevant to decisions affecting the evaluation of profitability or of managerial performance. Moreover, the analyst must be alert to the overvaluation of longer-term investments under the still persisting theory of lack of "permanent" impairment in value. Managements, as is well known, often take a very optimistic view of the final workout of their investments that have temporarily fallen in market value.

---

[2] See also Chapter 9 for similar provisions of *SFAS 52,* and Chapter 7 dealing with the accounting for pension liabilities.

[3] As an example of an exception to this rule, Curtiss-Wright carried its 14 percent investment in Kennecot Copper at equity.

ILLUSTRATION 2.   Centran, a bankholding company, which reported a profit of $9.5 million for the year, did not include in its computation losses of over $120 million in its bond portfolio that was carried at cost, and far above market. This is acceptable accounting that seems to have fooled even its own management and directors who *increased* the dividend payout. When a *hoped-for* decline in interest rates failed to materialize, the subsequent quarters' reported results began to portray the company's operating realities.

ACCOUNTING BY DEBTORS AND CREDITORS FOR TROUBLED DEBT RESTRUCTURINGS

SFAS 15 specifies the accounting in situations where a creditor for economic or legal reasons related to a debtor's financial difficulties grants a concession to the debtor.

The statement divides troubled debt restructurings into two broad categories: (1) those in which the debtor transfers receivables, real estate, or other assets to the creditor or issues its stock or otherwise grants an equity interest to the creditor to satisfy the creditor's claim; and (2) those in which the debt is continued but the terms are modified to defer or reduce cash payments the debtor is required to make to the creditor.

In cases falling under the first category, both debtor and creditor are required to account for the fair value of assets transferred and equity interests granted in a troubled debt restructuring. The statement requires debtors to recognize a gain and creditors a loss for a difference between those fair values and the recorded amount of the debt satisfied. Debtors must also recognize a gain or loss on assets transferred if their fair values differ from their recorded amounts.

The statement specifies that both debtor and creditor must account prospectively for the effects of modifications of terms of continuing debt as reduced interest expense or interest income for periods between the restructuring and maturity and should record no gain or loss at the time of restructuring. The one exception occurs when the total future cash payments specified by the new terms of the debt are less than the recorded amount of the debt at the time of restructuring. In that case, the debtor records a gain and the creditor records a loss to the extent of the differences.

Troubled debt restructurings that involve partial settlement by transfer of assets or grant of equity interests, as well as modification of terms of the debt remaining outstanding after the restructuring, are accounted for by combining the accounting for the two broad categories.

Implications for Analysis

SFAS 15 raises serious questions for financial analysts regarding the realism and the validity of the accounting recommended therein.

The existing framework of accounting for most receivables and payables, governed by *APB Opinions 21* and *26,* is based on the present value, at inception, of the cash flows embodied in them. *SFAS 15,* in stressing form over substance, considers a modification of terms of debt to result in loss to the creditor (and gain to the debtor) only when the total future cash payments specified by the new terms of the debt (without regard to present value considerations) are less than the recorded amount of the debt. Thus, as shown in the following example, under *SFAS 15,* a loan that has been carried at $10,000,000 before a modification of terms will be carried as an asset of an identical amount after modification, even though its present value is 43 percent less.

	Before modification	*After modification*
Loan maturity	3 years	10 years
Effective interest rate	10%	3%
Total interest over life of loan	$ 3,000,000	$ 3,000,000
Principal amount of loan	10,000,000	10,000,000
Total cash receipts	13,000,000	13,000,000
Present value of total cash flow at market rate of interest (10%)	$10,000,000	$ 5,703,000

It is hard to understand how such disregard of reality can result in financial presentations that are useful to the analyst. In evaluating the carrying amounts of restructured loans, analysts, and particularly bank analysts, must be careful to question closely the basis of the computation.

When it was first issued, the Federal Deposit Insurance Corporation (FDIC) opposed the use of *SFAS 15* by banks. However, in 1986 its chairman was reported ready to abandon this opposition in order to give relief to troubled farm and energy lenders. When faced by a move in Congress by senators of farm and energy states to *legislate* permission for banks to defer loan losses outright for as long as 10 years, the FDIC decided that *SFAS 15* was a less radical departure from sound accounting. This illustration of the influence of power and politics on the accounting process can be compared to other such examples given in Chapter 3.

RECENT DEVELOPMENTS

As part of its financial instruments project, the FASB is now considering a statement on "Accounting By Creditors for Impairment of a Loan." It has been tentatively concluded that this proposed Statement on loan impairment will change the net carrying amount of loans whose terms have been modified in troubled debt restructuring. Also supported is an approach for amending *SFAS 15* to specifically identify this change.

PROBLEM LOANS OF BANKS

Banks, while subject to regulatory restraints, are generally reluctant to provide realistically for losses in their loan portfolios. One important motivation is that realistic provisions for bad and nonperforming loans can erode the equity capital base of banks which is thin in relation to substantial investments in loans. Nonperforming loans are those on which interest payments are not being received currently or which are seriously in arrears. Some banks lend funds to debtors with which to pay interest or otherwise disregard the fact that these debtors do not earn currently such interest (e.g., on real estate loans) and that such a situation cannot continue indefinitely. Consequently analysts must be particularly careful and cautious when evaluating bank loan loss provisions.

ILLUSTRATION 3.   The value of the huge real estate loans made by banks in the 1980s has been seriously compromised by overbuilding and by resulting vacancies, particularly in commercial real estate. For example, when the loans were made the real estate developer's vacancy rate of 5% and $25 per square foot rents were accepted and built into the pro forma projections supporting the loan requests. However, market realities soon revealed that such projections were far too optimistic and that lower rents and higher vacancy rates eroded the developer's ability to service the loans.

ILLUSTRATION 4.   An interesting case is presented by the valuation of foreign loans (particularly to developing countries) carried on the books of banks. The problems which banks with such loan portfolios have in collecting even interest, let alone principal repayments due, are widely known and publicized. Evidence of the impairment of value of such loans became available in the form of market rates at mere fractions of par. Concurrently, insurance rates against risks in these loans commanded hefty premiums. And yet, starting in the late 1980s banks only grudgingly began to face up to foreign loan losses. Often the loan loss provisions they established were related more to their willingness to accept charges to their reported income than to the impairment in the value of their foreign loan portfolios.

TANGIBLE FIXED ASSETS

Assets that have an expected useful life of over a year and are used in operations and not acquired for sale in the ordinary course of business comprise this category. Property, plant, and equipment is the most important asset group included in it. They consist of those tangible assets used by business enterprises for the purpose of producing and distributing their goods and services.

Asset Valuation

Currently, the only permissible basis of accounting for fixed assets in this country is historical cost. Historical cost means the amount of dollars paid for the asset at the date of acquisition plus any other costs properly includable, such as freight, installation, setup costs, and so forth.

The primary reasons advanced for retention of the historical-cost basis are that it is conservative in that it does not anticipate replacement costs; it is the amount for which management is accountable; and, above all, it is the best objectively determinable cost available. Moreover, after many years of acceptance as the basis at which fixed assets are stated, historical costs are recognized as not representing value but rather original costs that have not yet been charged to operations. Some even question the usefulness of costs based on some concept of current value that would change from year to year.

To the analyst of financial statements, the concept of fixed assets at (historical) cost is not a complicated one. The distinction between a current expenditure and an outlay that results in an asset that will be allocated to future operations is a well-established one that depends primarily on the purpose of the outlay, the expected life of the asset, and, for internal accounting expediency, on the amount involved. Accounting principles in this area, if consistently applied, do not lend themselves to serious distortion. Such, of course, is not the case with the determination of depreciation, which is another matter to be discussed later.

One type of expense, sometimes included in the cost of fixed assets and which is subject to some debate, is interest cost during construction. This represents the cost of funds tied up while the property is being constructed by the company and before it becomes productively utilized. This cost of funds committed to construction becomes part of the cost of the plant and equipment and is allocated to future operations along with all other costs. The inclusion of this cost in the cost of fixed assets was customary for public utilities and some other companies until in 1979 *SFAS 34* required the capitalization of interest and defined the circumstances under which this is to be done (see also Chapter 11).

An area of some variety of practice relates to costs to be included in fixed assets constructed in a company's own facilities. While most direct costs are includable without question, one problem area is the allocation of variable overhead and particularly fixed overhead cost to such assets. Where idle capacity has been utilized to construct capital assets, the inclusion of fixed overhead may be debatable. However, if usable production was forgone to build such assets, there is full justification for the inclusion of all proportionate overhead in the cost of the fixed assets.

One serious problem that confronts the analyst of financial statements that include fixed assets stated at historical cost is that these long-lived assets are not expressed in terms of a stable measuring unit. The accumulation of costs of assets purchased in different years represents the aggregation of units of differing purchasing power. Since depreciation—that is, the currently expired portion of the cost of these assets—is based on this original cost, the distortion is carried into the income statement. Thus, repeatedly the case has been made for adjusting original cost for changes in the price level—not as an attempt to arrive at some kind of current market value but rather to adjust the original cost for changes in the purchasing power of the dollar. Others have argued for computing depreciation on the basis of the current replacement cost of the fixed assets. Under either model, it is argued, such more realistic measures will not only result in more valid income statements and in a proper distinction between income and "real" capital but will also present a fairer measure of how responsibly management has dealt with invested capital in terms of the purchasing power or the physical capital that has been entrusted to it.

The above discussion has pointed out the possible distortions to which historical-cost accounting for long-lived assets may be subject. *SFAS 33,* as amended, makes optional current-cost supplementary disclosures for certain companies. Further discussion of this broad subject will be found in Chapter 14 dealing with the problem of accounting under changing price levels.

The Property, Plant, and Equipment account is assumed to include assets in active or productive use. If such assets are temporarily idle, disclosure of this fact will usually be made in notes or comments in order to explain the resulting excess cost and lower profit margins.

The SEC in *FRR No. 1,* section 209 points out the need for disclosure of significant idle facilities and changes in current year idle facilities that have a material impact on results of operations.

Should a substantial segment of assets be idle for a longer period of time and without definite prospects of use, they should no longer be included in the property, plant, and equipment designation where their inclusion would distort such relationships as that of sales to plant or the return on fixed assets. Instead, they should be segregated from other assets pending their reactivation, sale, or other disposition. Such idle assets represent not only an investment on which no return is earned, but they often involve expenses of upkeep and maintenance.

Kaiser Aluminum & Chemical Corporation had the following footnote in an annual report:

> Idle facilities include the corporation's Chalmette, Louisiana, aluminum smelter which is temporarily closed because of high energy costs and generally poor market conditions for primary aluminum. The corporation wrote down its Baton Rouge, Louisiana, alumina refinery which had been included in idle facilities last year. Currently, production of alumina at Alumina Partners of Jamaica (ALPART) was temporarily suspended due to the continuing adverse economic conditions impacting the aluminum industry . . .

Management believes that market conditions will improve and that operating costs of the idle facilities can be reduced sufficiently to permit economic operation of these facilities in the future. The corporation's policy is to continue normal depreciation for temporarily closed facilities.

While the write-up of assets to current market or appraised values is not an accepted accounting procedure in the United States, the convention of conservatism requires that a permanent impairment of value and/ or loss of utility of fixed assets be reflected in the accounts by a write-down. This is needed not only to reflect a loss of value and utility but also in order to relieve future periods of charges that the usefulness and productivity of the assets can no longer support and justify. Thus, for example, Amerada Hess Corporation revealed the following asset write-downs in an annual report:

> 2. *Special Charge*
> The Corporation recorded a special charge to earnings of $536,692,000 ($432,742,000 after income taxes, or $5.12 per share). The special charge consists of a $146,768,000 write-down in the book value of certain ocean-going tankers and a $389,924,000 provision for marine transportation costs in excess of market rates.

Mistakes and errors of judgment are part of the realities of business life. The critical issue for the analyst is to become aware of an economic loss as soon as possible after it has been incurred. Presently, the lack of definitive standards enables companies to defer the disclosure of the economic loss of facilities beyond the point where it became apparent to managements. When the inevitable write-off occurs it distorts reported results. There is always the assumption that the market forgives past mistakes. The economic loss is, however, always real.

ILLUSTRATION 5.   Some projects fail even before they become operative. Thus, Caterpillar Co. wrote off $212 million mostly due to the uneconomical nature of an unfinished parts center. Philip Morris, having overestimated U.S. beer consumption, incurred a $280 million pretax loss in the write-down of a newly completed brewery which was promptly mothballed.

ILLUSTRATION 6.   Other business operations fail after a period of unsuccessful results or after political or economic conditions undermine the viability of operations. Thus in 1988 Pillsbury Co. recorded a $113 million loss in the sale or shutdown of several money-losing restaurant operations. In 1986 Squibb Corporation declared its South American and Asian pharmaceutical operations permanently impaired due to adverse political and economic conditions. This action resulted in a $68 million writedown.

In *SFAS 19* (1977) the FASB acknowledged explicitly that "The question of whether to write down the carrying amount of productive assets to an amount expected to be recoverable for future use of those assets is unsettled under present generally accepted accounting principles. This is a pervasive issue that the board has not addressed."

In the mid-1980s the Emerging Issues Task Force of the FASB discussed the issue and concluded that write-downs are permissible under current practice; assets should not be written down below a break-even point based on undiscounted future cash flows; and assets that have been written down should not be written up for a subsequent recovery in value. Moreover, the SEC informally stated its position that no asset should be carried above its recoverable value and that companies should consider the carrying amount of operating assets for possible loss in economic value.

Considering these recent developments, the FASB may add this topic to its agenda. Among the questions the Board will need to answer are:

When has an impairment occurred: when there is a substantial decline in estimated future gross profit; when projected cash flows are less than the carrying amount; when a long-term net loss is forecast?

Should analysis of an economic impairment consider only the operating asset, the segment to which the asset belongs, or the whole company?

What is the definition of "permanent" as it relates to economic impairment?

How should the amount of the write-down be calculated? Should the amount be discounted?

How should a permanent impairment be reported? Should it be merely disclosed, or should a loss be recognized?

The subject of depreciation, an important cost factor in most companies, is complex and subject to controversy. Its importance to the analyst cannot be overrated. It will be considered in Chapter 10 dealing with income determination.

Wasting Assets

A category of assets that requires separate consideration is natural resources. With the exception of resources such as timber, which can be replenished by planned cutting and reseeding, most of such assets once exhausted cannot be used and lose most of their value. Examples of such resources are oil, gas, coal, iron ore, and sulfur.

Generally accepted accounting principles (GAAP) require that such assets be stated at original cost plus costs of discovery, exploration, and development. That means that the very significant value increment that occurs following the discovery of natural resources is not given immediate accounting recognition. It shows up through the income stream when and as the resource is exploited, or when it is sold.

The total cost of a wasting asset is generally allocated over the total units of estimated reserves available. This allocation process is known as depletion. Some companies in the mining field do not charge depletion to the income statement primarily because they believe the related assets to be grossly understated in terms of current and potential value. The subject of depletion will be discussed in Chapter 11, where the accounting for oil exploration is also discussed.

Method of Acquisition

Generally speaking, the method of acquiring assets or the use of assets should have no bearing on the basis on which they are carried in the accounting records. One method of acquisition that deserves separate mention, however, is leasing. Where leasing is short term, where it covers a period shorter than the asset's useful life, and where no property rights are acquired, no asset accounting is called for. The practice of acquiring assets by means of leases that are in essence a financing method of purchases has grown and proliferated. Such leases should be accounted for as purchases, thus calling for the setting up of an asset at an amount equal to the present value of future rental payments, and this is essentially required by *SFAS 13*. Since the outstanding characteristic of this transaction is the *method* of financing, this topic will be considered in Chapter 7 which is devoted to the measurement of liabilities.

Implications for Analysis

In measuring property, plant, and equipment and in presenting it in conventional financial statements, accountants are concerned with a number of the objectives and conventions discussed in Chapter 3. They are concerned with the objectivity of original cost and the conservatism implicit therein, and with an accounting for the number of dollars originally invested in such assets. Judging from the resulting figures, they are quite clearly not overly concerned with the objectives of those who analyze financial statements. They are content to proclaim that "a balance sheet does not purport to reflect and could not usefully reflect the value of the enterprise." Not that the accountant is necessarily unmindful of the interests of those who use his statements; it is rather that his overwhelming concern lies in the real or imagined problems of his own art.

Only by sheer coincidence, or in the specialized case of industries such as utilities, can historical costs be useful to analysts. They are not relevant to questions of current replacement or of future needs. They are not directly comparable to similar data in other companies' reports. They do not enable us to measure the opportunity cost of disposal and alternative use of funds, nor do they provide a valid yardstick against which to measure return. Moreover, in times of changing price levels, they represent an odd conglomeration of a variety of purchasing power disbursements.

It may be claimed that the value of assets is derived from their ability to earn a return and that consequently the key to their value lies in the income statement. While this is true in a significant number of cases, it does not provide the only avenue to an evaluation of an asset's worth. Thus, the earning of a return on an investment is dependent on managerial skill, and assets have a value tied to their capacity to produce. But in recognizing the importance of net income in the assessment of an asset's worth, the analyst must be aware of the problem which the method of depreciation has on the determination of net income. This aspect of the valuation of fixed assets and its effect on income is discussed fully in Chapter 10 on the analysis of income.

Analysts must be aware that the issue of the write-down of obsolete and uneconomic plant is far from settled. In recent years write-offs have become more common. Diamond Shamrock Company revised the discounted cash flow value of its oil and gas properties with a $600 million write-down. Standard Oil wrote off $200 million in gas and oil reserves for similar reasons.

Reductions in estimated useful lives of assets represents a quicker write-off to operations. IMC Fertilizer Group reported:

> In 1990, the Company reduced the estimated useful lives of its New Wales uranium plant assets because of the uncertainty whether sales contracts, covering most of the production, will be renewed when they expire in 1992, and whether the market price of uranium oxide will be favorable enough to warrant continued operation of the plant beyond that date. As a result, 1990 depreciation expense increased $4.3 million because of this change.

In the public utility area the question of valuation arises for assets the value of which has been impaired because of reasons such as plant cost overruns and an unwillingness of regulatory bodies to allow the recovery of such costs from customers through utility rates. As part of a realistic assessment of the value of operating assets affected by deregulation, American Telephone & Telegraph Co. took a $7.3 billion pretax write-down of its network facilities and telephone equipment.

Supplementary data on the current cost of fixed assets and on depreciation computed on this basis are now provided, on a voluntary basis, by very few companies pursuant to the requirements of *SFAS 33* as amended (see Chapter 14). In using such data, the analyst must be aware that they are not audited and that the method of their derivation can vary significantly from company to company.

INTANGIBLE ASSETS

Intangible assets represent rights to future benefits. One distinguishing characteristic of these assets, which is not, however, unique to them, is that they have no physical existence and depend on such expected future benefits for most of their value. In many cases, the value of these benefits is inextricably tied to the continuity of the enterprise.

Some important categories of intangibles are:

1. Goodwill.
2. Patents, copyrights, and trademarks.
3. Leases, leaseholds, and leasehold improvements.
4. Exploration rights and cost of development of natural resources.
5. Formulas, processes, and designs (e.g., software).
6. Licenses, franchises, memberships, and customer lists.

The basic rule in accounting for purchased intangibles is that they be carried at cost. If property other than cash is given in exchange for the intangible, it must be recorded at the fair market value of the consideration given. If liabilities are assumed, the intangible is valued by taking into consideration the present value of the future obligations.

There are some paradoxes in the valuation of intangibles that should be understood by the analyst. If a company spends material and labor in the construction of a "tangible" asset, such as a machine, these costs are capitalized and recorded as an asset that is depreciated over its estimated useful life. On the other hand, a company that spends a great amount of resources advertising a product or training a sales force to sell and service it, which, as we shall see, is a process of creating internally developed "goodwill," cannot usually capitalize such costs even though they may be as, or more, beneficial to the company's future operations than is the "tangible" machine. The reason for this inconsistency in accounting for the two assets is steeped in such basic accounting conventions (discussed in Chapter 3) as conservatism, which casts greater doubt on the future realization of unidentifiable intangible costs (such as advertising or training which create "goodwill") than costs sunk into tangible "hard" and visible goods.

APB Opinion 17 distinguishes between identifiable and unidentifiable intangible assets.

Identifiable Intangibles

Identifiable intangibles can be separately identified and given reasonably descriptive names such as patents, trademarks, franchises, and the like. Identifiable intangibles can be developed internally, acquired singly, or as part of a group of assets. In either case, they should be recorded at cost and amortized over their useful lives. Write-down or complete write-off at date of acquisition is not permitted.

Unidentifiable Intangibles

Unidentifiable intangibles can be developed internally or purchased from others. They cannot, however, be acquired singly but form part of a group of assets or part of an entire enterprise. The excess of cost of an acquired company over the sum total of identifiable net assets is the most common unidentifiable intangible asset. *APB Opinion 17* refers to this unidentifiable mass of assets as "goodwill," and this is actually a residual amount in an acquisition after the amount of tangible and identifiable intangibles have been determined. It represents an expansion of the goodwill concept from what has obtained before this *Opinion* was issued.

The costs of developing, maintaining, or restoring intangibles that are unidentifiable, have indeterminate lives, or are inherent in a continuing enterprise should be expensed as incurred. By contrast, such intangible assets that are purchased must be carried at cost and amortized over their useful lives and cannot be written down or written off at date of acquisition.

Amortization of Intangibles

Both types of intangibles, those identifiable as well as those unidentifiable, are believed to have limited useful lives and must be amortized accordingly. Depending on the type of intangible asset, its useful life may be limited by such factors as legal, contractual, or regulatory provisions; demand and competition; life expectancies of employees; and economic factors.

The cost of each intangible should be amortized over its individual useful life, taking into account all factors that determine its length. The period of amortization cannot, however, exceed 40 years. Goodwill arising before 1970 (when *APB Opinion 17* was promulgated) need not be amortized.

Other Considerations Regarding the Accounting for Intangibles

Goodwill is often a sizable asset. Since it can be recorded only on acquisition from a third party, it can be recorded only upon the purchase of an on-going business enterprise. The description of what is being paid for varies greatly, and the variety of views add to the confusion surrounding this subject. Some refer to the ability to attract and keep satisfied customers, while others point to qualities inherent in an enterprise that is well organized and is efficient in production, service, and sales. This distinction can also be seen in the difference that obviously exists between a business that is just starting and one that is successful and well established in its industry and that has spent a great deal on training and research to get there. Thus, what is obviously being paid for here is earning power, and since any given amount of invested capital should expect a minimum return adjusted for risk, most accountants agree that goodwill is associated with a level of earnings over and above that minimum. These are otherwise referred to as "super-earnings." Thus, goodwill implies exceptional profitability, and that should normally be evident when goodwill is being purchased, except in those cases where there is obvious mismanagement and the potential is evident and waits to be tapped by good management.

Dun & Bradstreet Corporation describes its goodwill and other intangible accounting policy as follows:

> *Other Assets.* Computer software ($86,332,000) and data files ($25,656,000), certain other intangibles ($99,118,000), and goodwill ($288,322,000) are being amortized, using principally the straight-line method, over 5 to 15 years, 12 to 40 years and 40 years, respectively. Remaining intangibles, including other intangibles of $5,979,000 and goodwill of $11,022,000 which arose from acquisitions initiated prior to October 31, 1970, are considered to have continuing value and are not being amortized.

Campbell Soup Company (see Appendix 4B) spells out its goodwill amortization policy in item 96 .

When a business is being acquired, the book values, that is, the amounts at which its net assets are carried in accordance with accounting principles discussed in this book, are quite obviously not relevant in arriving at a purchase price, if only because they represent unamortized cost balances rather than values. Thus, the first requirement in purchase accounting is that the amount paid for the entity as a whole be allocated to all identifiable assets in accordance with their fair market values. If an excess remains after such allocation is made, it may be ascribed to the intangible "goodwill." If the fair market value of assets acquired exceeds the purchase price, a "bargain purchase credit" results, and it can, after adjustments, be amortized to income over a reasonable number of years. A detailed examination of the accounting for business combinations will be found in Chapter 9.

Most other intangible assets have a useful life that is limited by law, regulation, or agreement. Thus, *patents* are rights conveyed by government authority to the inventor, granting the exclusive right to the invention for a term of years. Registered copyrights and trademarks also convey exclusive rights for specified periods of time. The cost of these assets should be written off against the revenues they help create over the maximum period coinciding with their legal life or over the minimum period of their estimated economic life.

The cost of franchises, licenses, or other such benefits must be written off over the period during which they are deemed to be economically productive. The cost of leaseholds and leasehold improvements are benefits of occupancy that are contractually limited. Thus, their cost must be amortized over the period of the lease contract.

As is true with all assets, accounting principles require that if it is evident that an intangible has lost all or most of its value or utility, it should be written down to its net realizable value measured by either future estimated utility or selling price, whichever is more appropriate in the circumstances.

Accounting for the Costs of Computer Software

SFAS 86 (1985), "Accounting for the Costs of Computer Software to Be Sold, Leased, or Otherwise Marketed," establishes criteria for capitalization of the costs to develop internally or purchase a computer software product. These products include computer software used as an integral part of a product (e.g., machine tools or diagnostic equipment) or a service (e.g., the activities of a service bureau).

The *Statement* distinguishes between software development activities that are research and development, where the costs must be expensed, and production activities, where costs are to be capitalized. It uses the term *technological feasibility* to describe the point when capitalization should begin.

Companies use different product development methods, so the *Statement* says technological feasibility can be demonstrated in two ways. If a company's development methodology includes preparing a detail program design, which is like a blueprint that can be used by programmers for coding, it must be completed to establish technological feasibility. If a detail program design is not prepared, a working model must be completed before costs are to be capitalized.

Companies that purchase or develop computer software as an integral part of a product or process will have to establish the software's technological feasibility and complete all R&D activities for the other components of the product or process before any computer software production costs can be capitalized.

Amortization of capitalized costs should be based on estimated future revenues, but should not be less than a straight-line amortization amount.

Implication for Analysis

Because of their very nature, intangibles have often been treated with suspicion by financial analysts. In fact, many analysts associate "intangibility" with riskiness. Quite obviously, caution and clear understanding of the nature of these assets is required in the evaluation of their worth to the enterprise. However, since these assets may, in many instances, be the most valuable asset an enterprise owns and since they can be undervalued as well as, as is often the case, carried at inflated amounts, it is inadvisable to remove them from all consideration in financial analysis.

Goodwill is a case in point. Having understood the accounting conventions governing the recording of goodwill, the analyst realizes that only purchased goodwill can be found among the recorded assets and that more "goodwill" may exist off the balance sheet than on it.

Another key point here is that if there is value in goodwill it must be reflected in earnings. True, if a mismanaged situation with great potential was purchased, the profits may not become visible immediately; but if there is value to goodwill, then such an asset should give rise to superior earnings within a reasonably short time after acquisition. If those earnings are not in evidence, it is a fair assumption that the investment in goodwill is of no value regardless of whether it is or is not found on the balance sheet. Goodwill represents an advantage that must evidence itself in superior earnings or else it does not exist. However, the write-off of goodwill, as was reported by Inter City Gas Corporation is relatively rare:

> Pursuant to this reorganization and as a result of the losses incurred by KeepRite in the past two years, the Company has re-assessed its investment in KeepRite Inc. As a result of this re-assessment, it has been determined that the value of the underlying assets in KeepRite have been impaired by an amount of $4,697,000. Accordingly, the Company has written off goodwill of $4,697,000 as an extraordinary charge against income.

Campbell Soup reported in 1990 that its substantial restructuring expenses included the write-off of goodwill.

Another important factor of which the analyst must be aware is that in practice, the accounting for goodwill is far from faithful to the theory. Due to the beneficial effect that an absence of write-off of assets has on the results of operations, particularly since goodwill amortization is *not* deductible for tax purposes, goodwill and other intangibles may not be written off as speedily as a realistic assessment of their useful life may require. While the overall limitation of 40 years on the assumed useful life of intangibles is arbitrary and may, in some instances, result in excessive amortization, it is safe to assume that in most cases the bias will be in the direction of too slow a rate of amortization. The analyst must be alert to this possibility.

Regardless of the amount of outlays incurred in the acquisition or in the internal development of an intangible, the rule applicable to the carrying amount of any asset is that it be carried at an amount not in excess of realizable value in terms of sales price or future utility. That, at least, is the intention and the theory. But, as in most other categories of accounting theory, actual implementation in practice is another matter, and the analyst must be prepared to form his or her own judgment on the amounts at which intangible assets are carried. The analyst must also bear in mind that goodwill recorded as a result of business combinations initiated before November 1, 1970, does not have to be amortized at all and that at the cutoff date there were billions of dollars of unamortized goodwill on corporate balance sheets in this country. Only in extreme and rare situations will the auditors qualify their opinion with respect to the continuing value of unamortized goodwill.

The analyst must also be alert to the consideration with which the enterprise has parted in the acquisition of goodwill, for this may affect the amount of the intangible recorded. Payments in promoter stock should be thoroughly scrutinized. Also of concern to the analyst is the rate at which goodwill is amortized. The 40-year maximum, after all, is a long period exceeding a generation. The assumption of useful life should be realistic and should reflect the proper allocation of costs to revenues. A lump-sum write-off of an intangible may bring the asset down to its proper realizable value but by no means does it make up for the implicit overstatement of earnings of preceding years.

Further discussion about the nature and the analytical implications of goodwill are found in Chapter 9.

PREPAID EXPENSES AND DEFERRED CHARGES

Prepaid Expenses and Deferred Charges Distinguished

Prepaid expenses represent advance payments for services yet to be received. Examples are advance payments for rent or prepaid insurance on a longer-term policy. Small supplies of stationery or stamps are often included in prepaid expenses. Prepaid expenses are generally classified among current assets because the services due that they represent would otherwise require the use of current resources during the following operating cycle. For reasons of expediency and lack of materiality, services due beyond one year are usually included among prepaid expenses classified as current.

Unlike prepaid expenses that represent advance payments for services yet to be received, *deferred charges* represent charges already incurred that are deferred to the future either because they are expected to benefit future revenues or because they represent a proper allocation of costs to future operations.

Over the years, the complexities of business operations as well as custom have sanctioned an ever-increasing number and types of deferred charges.

Why Costs Are Deferred

The basic theory behind the deferral of expenses and costs is relatively simple. If a cost incurred in one period is going to benefit a future period or periods by a contribution to revenues or reduction in costs, then such a cost should be deferred to such future period. The basic accounting convention involved here is that of matching costs and revenues. Thus, if an enterprise incurs substantial start-up costs in placing into operation new, better, or more efficient facilities, it may defer such costs and charge (amortize) them to the periods that are expected to benefit from them.

Research and Development Costs

Under FASB *SFAS 2,* almost all research and development (R&D) costs are required to be charged to expense when incurred. That requirement applies to a tangible or intangible asset that is purchased for use in a single R&D project, although a purchased asset that has alternative future uses should be capitalized and amortized as such.[4]

Some public utility regulatory commissions require the deferral and amortization of significant R&D expenditures, and where they affect the rate-making process, they can be accounted for in this manner.

The costs of R&D activities conducted for others under a contractual arrangement, including indirect costs that are specifically reimbursable, can be treated as work in progress or receivables under contracts and are not covered by the expensing requirement. A further discussion of the implications of the accounting for R&D outlays will be found in Chapter 11.

Other Types of Deferred Charges

Another category of deferred charges that borders on a deferral of costs of dubious future benefit is that of moving expenses and, to a lesser degree, start-up costs. Thus, Willcox & Gibbs, Inc., had the following note in its annual report:

> The Company has deferred approximately $782,000 related to moving expenses and start-up costs associated with new facilities placed into operation. It is the Company's intention to amortize these costs over a five-year period.

Neptune International describes the deferral of start-up costs as follows:

> *Other assets.* The Corporation has incurred costs prior to attaining normal levels of production in connection with the start-up of two new manufacturing facilities and the start-up of a new foundry. These costs are being amortized over three-year periods.

---

[4] The fair value of the R&D of an acquired enterprise must be determined and a suitable allocation of the purchase price made so that those costs that will not be used in R&D activities can be capitalized—those that will be used in such activities must be written off.

As indicated before, the variety of deferred costs has been growing because of new complexities in both technology and in business practice. Since deferred charges represent future intangible benefits, they are sometimes very close in nature to intangible assets. Regardless of terminology, the following list should give the reader an indication of the variety of deferred charges now found in financial statements:

1. Business development, expansion, merger, and relocation costs.
   a. Preoperating expenses, initial start-up costs, and tooling costs.
   b. Initial operating losses or preoperating expenses of subsidiaries.
   c. Moving, plant rearrangement, and reinstallation costs.
   d. Merger or acquisition expenses.
   e. Purchased customer accounts.
   f. Noncompete agreements.
2. Deferred expenses.
   a. Advertising and promotional expenses.
   b. Imputed interest.
   c. Selling, general, and administrative expenses.
   d. Pension plan costs.
   e. Property and other taxes.
   f. Rental and leasing costs.
   g. Vacation pay.
   h. Seasonal growing and packing expenses.
3. Intangible costs.
   a. Intangible drilling and development costs.
   b. Contracts, films, copyright materials, art rights, etc.
   c. Costs of computer software.
4. Debt issue expenses.
5. Future income tax benefits.
6. Organization costs.
7. Advance royalties.

While we are here focusing on the validity of the assets represented by deferred charges, we must always bear in mind that each of these assets has "another side of the coin," that is, the deferral of a cost that would otherwise have been charged to results from operations. The impact of this aspect will be more fully discussed in Chapter 11, which is devoted to principles of income measurement.

Implications for Analysis

While prepaid expenses are usually neither of the size nor the significance sufficient to be of real concern to the analyst, deferred charges can be both sizable and significant and, hence, can present real challenges in understanding and interpretation.

Certain types of deferred charges, such as start-up costs or debt issue expenses, can be easily understood and defended on the basis of accounting theory. Moreover, the period of their amortization is clearly dictated by the circumstances that gave rise to them. Deferred charges, such as organization costs, on the other hand, while clearly designated to benefit an organization in the future, cannot be amortized on a logical or obvious basis. Thus, while an indefinite life may be inferred from the going-concern or continuity convention of accounting, organization costs are nevertheless usually amortized over an arbitrarily determined period of time.

However, the validity of deferring many other charges, such as moving costs, promotional costs, or initial operating losses of, say, loan offices, is subject to many imponderables and estimates. Similarly, the period over which they should properly be amortized is often subject to serious doubt. The analyst must be alert to the situation where the deferred charge is not really an asset representing a future benefit but is rather a deferred loss that is being carried forward for no better reason than the desire of management not to burden current operating results. While the auditor's opinion or mention of such assets can be helpful to the analyst, he or she must be prepared to evaluate on his own the evidence and information regarding such deferrals. In any event, deferred charges represent mostly assets that are incapable of satisfying claims of creditors. The other and perhaps even more significant implication that deferred charges carry is their effect on proper income determination, and this aspect will be examined in Chapter 11, which is devoted to this subject.

The analyst must, in general, treat with suspicion the propensity of managements to defer into the future the costs and problems of today. For example, following severe price increases of fuel some electric utilities refused to face reality and deferred the absorption of these costs to future periods in the hope that these would be recouped through subsequent rate increases. This practice is symptomatic of the illusory accounting of which some companies are capable. The following is an additional illustration:

ILLUSTRATION 7.   Throughout the 1970s, Lockheed Corporation stuck with its unprofitable TriStar Jetliner program. Management's repeated forecasts about future favorable developments and new orders proved time and again to be overoptimistic. Management deferred "initial planning and tooling and unrecovered production start-up costs," and in 1975 adopted a policy of amortizing these deferred charges over a period planned at that time to end in 1985.[5] By the 1980 year-end, these deferred

---

[5] Deferrals are also made under the so-called program method in which each plane is assigned an estimated average cost (over the entire program period). Early in the program, actual costs exceed the estimated average costs and the excess is deferred on the assumption that when benefits from the learning curve are realized, subsequent actual costs will be below estimated costs thus permitting the absorption of previously deferred costs.

TriStar costs amounted to $281 million. Finally in 1981, the company had to abandon the program, recognize the inevitable, and write off the deferred charges that had overstated operating results over so many years. Inventory write-downs added substantially to the overall losses on this program.

UNRECORDED INTANGIBLE OR CONTINGENT ASSETS

A discussion of principles of asset measurement would not be complete without an examination of that category of assets that under GAAP would not be recorded in a statement of financial condition.

One category of assets that are not recordable has already been mentioned in the discussion of goodwill. In this case, if the intangible is internally developed rather than purchased from an outside party, it cannot normally be capitalized and results instead in a charge to current operations. Thus, to the extent that a valuable asset has been created, one that can be either sold or which generates superior earning power, the income charged with the expense of its development has been understated. This the analyst must realize and, if significant, take into consideration.

ILLUSTRATION 8.   Examples of valuable assets which are unrecorded in published financial statements abound in practice. Because of the emphasis in accounting on tangible assets, such as brick, steel, and mortar, valuable intangible assets, such as of the service or "idea" industries go unreported. TV programs carried at amortized cost but which continue to bring in millions of dollars in licensing fees are one example. Successful drugs which take years to develop but whose costs are currently written off are another. Other familiar examples include long-developed trade names, such as Coca Cola, McDonalds, Polaroid, and Xerox. The real value of intangibles ultimately depends on the earnings they produce.

A contingent asset is disclosed by Allegheny Ludlum Industries, Inc., as follows:

> A Federal District Court in Houston, Texas, following a jury trial completed earlier, entered judgment of approximately $18,900,000 in favor of Chemetron Corporation, a wholly-owned subsidiary of Allegheny, against Marathon Manufacturing Corporation and two individual defendants in a suit brought for securities law violations. That judgment has been appealed by the defendants and, since the outcome cannot be predicted at this time, no portion of the judgment has been reflected in the accompanying financial statements.

The Securities and Exchange Commission has encouraged companies to discuss in the required "Management's Discussion and Analysis" section not only the risks facing an enterprise but also positive aspects of a company that the members don't make clear. Analysts should, consequently, expect to find some discussion of unrecorded or understated assets in this discussion section.

QUESTIONS

1. What are the provisions of *SFAS 12* that apply to the equity securities not classified as current assets?
2. What accounting principles govern the valuation and presentation of long-term investments? Distinguish between the accounting for investments in the common stock of an investee of *(a)* less than 20 percent of the shares outstanding and *(b)* 20 percent or more of the shares outstanding.
3. *a.* Evaluate the accounting for investments in between 20 percent to 50 percent of the common stock of an investee from the point of view of an analyst of the financial statements.
   b. When are losses in long-term investments recognized? Evaluate the accounting that governs the recognition of such losses.
4. What are some of the flaws and inconsistencies of *SFAS 12*, with regard to accounting for marketable securities not carried as current assets, of which the analyst must be aware?
5. What are the requirements of *SFAS 107?*
6. How should idle plant and equipment be presented in the balance sheet? Explain the reasons for the presentation you describe.
7. The income of an enterprise from the exploration of wasting assets often bears no logical relation to the amount at which such investment is shown on the balance sheet.
   a. Why is this so?
   b. Under what circumstances would a more logical relationship be more likely to exist?
8. From the point of view of the user of financial statements, what are the objections to the use of original cost as the basis of carrying fixed assets?
9. *a.* What are the basic principles governing the valuation of intangible assets?
   b. Distinguish between the accounting for internally developed versus purchased intangibles.
   c. Of what significance is the distinction between (1) identifiable intangibles and (2) unidentifiable intangibles?
   d. What principles and guidelines underlie the amortization of intangible assets?
10. What are the implications for analysis of the accounting for goodwill?
11. List five categories of deferred charges and describe the rationale that is usually given for this deferral.
12. *a.* Give examples of two or more types of assets that are not recorded on the balance sheet.
    b. How should such assets be evaluated by the analyst?

Chapter 7

ANALYSIS OF LIABILITIES

Liabilities are obligations to pay money, render future services, or convey specified assets. They are claims against the company's present and future assets and resources. Such claims are usually senior to those of the ownership as evidenced by equity securities. This discussion will be broadly construed to include current liabilities, long-term liabilities, capital leases, and deferred credits which, as shall be seen, can vary significantly from conventional liabilities. Also discussed will be securities which straddle the boundary that separates liabilities from equity capital.

CURRENT LIABILITIES

Current liabilities are usually obligations for goods and services acquired, taxes owed, and any other accruals of expenses. They include deposits received, advance payments, trade acceptances, notes payable, short-term bank loans, as well as the current portion of long-term debt.

To be properly classified as current, a liability should require the use of current resources (assets) or the incurrence of another current liability for its discharge. As in the case of current assets, the period over which such liabilities are expected to be retired is one year or, for operating liabilities, the current operating cycle, whichever is longer.

As a general principle, the offsetting of assets against liabilities is permissible only where such a right specifically exists. Thus, the availability of cash for the payment of a liability does not justify the offset of one against the other. In practice, the only instances where offset is permissible is where government securities specifically designated as acceptable for the payment of taxes are acquired for that purpose.

The SEC in *Financial Reporting Releases (FRR) No. 1,* section 203, has significantly expanded the disclosure requirements in SEC filings (not necessarily in annual reports) regarding the terms of short-term debt:

1. Footnote disclosure of compensating balance arrangements including those not reduced to writing.

2. Balance sheet segregation of *(a)* legally restricted compensating balances and *(b)* unrestricted compensating balances relating to long-term borrowing arrangements if the compensating balance can be computed at a fixed amount at the balance sheet date.
3. Disclosure of short-term bank and commercial paper borrowings:
   a. Commercial paper borrowings separately stated in the balance sheet.
   b. Average interest rate and terms separately stated for short-term bank and commercial paper borrowings at the balance sheet date.
   c. Average interest rate, average outstanding borrowings, and maximum month-end outstanding borrowings for short-term bank debt and commercial paper combined for the period.
4. Disclosure of amounts and terms of unused lines of credit for short-term borrowing arrangements (with amounts supporting commercial paper separately stated) and of unused commitments for long-term financing arrangements.

SFAS 6 (1975) superseded some provisions of the above by establishing criteria for the balance sheet classification of short-term obligations that are expected to be refinanced.

Certain short-term obligations such as trade accounts payable and normal accrued liabilities always should be classified as current and included in a total of current liabilities of a company balance sheet. Other short-term obligations also should be classified as current liabilities unless the company intends to refinance them on a long-term basis and can demonstrate its ability to do so. Short-term obligations are those scheduled to mature in less than a year.

Refinancing on a long-term basis is defined to mean either replacing the short-term obligation with a long-term obligation or with equity securities; or renewing, extending, or replacing it with other short-term obligations for an uninterrupted period extending beyond one year from the balance sheet date.

Ability to refinance on a long-term basis should be demonstrated either (1) by actually having issued a long-term obligation or equity securities to replace the short-term obligation after the date of the company's balance sheet but before it is released, or (2) by having entered into an agreement with a bank or other source of capital that clearly permits the company to refinance the short-term obligation when it becomes due. Financing agreements that are cancelable for violation of a provision that can be evaluated differently by the parties to the agreement (such as "a material adverse change" or "failure to maintain satisfactory operations") do not meet this condition.[1] Also, an "operative" violation of the agreement should not have occurred.

---

[1] The FASB has proposed that where a company violates an objective provision (e.g., maintenance of specified amount of working capital) of a long-term debt agreement, the debt should be classified as a current liability unless a waiver in writing is obtained.

SFAS 78 (1983), "Classification of Obligations that Are Callable by the Creditor," requires current classification for obligations that are or will be due on demand within one year of the balance sheet date.

If a company violates a long-term debt covenant, such as a minimum level of working capital, *SFAS 78* specifies that the loan could continue to be classified as long term if one of the following conditions is met:

> The lender either waives or loses the right to demand repayment for more than a year from the balance sheet date. For example, a lender might lose the right to demand repayment if a violation existing at the balance sheet date is subsequently cured and the debt is no longer callable at the time the financial statements are issued.
>
> The obligation will not become callable because it is probable that a violation existing at the balance sheet date will be cured within a specified grace period. In such cases, the attendant circumstances should be disclosed.

The *Statement* does not apply to subjective covenants (for example, "if the lender deems itself insecure"). The FASB believes such clauses are adequately dealt with in an earlier *Technical Bulletin,* which says they would not by themselves trigger a current liability.

Long-term debt may have to be classified as current when certain covenants are in default. For example, BMC Industries made the following disclosure:

> The third quarter loss, which included the $46,300 provision for loss on disposal of discontinued operations, placed the Company in default of net worth covenants under both its revolving credit and subordinated debt agreements. Because the defaults triggered a technical acceleration of the Company's senior (revolving credit) debt and allow the subordinated lenders to accelerate, the related debt has been classified as current at December 31. The Company intends to eliminate defaults under its debt agreements by restructuring the agreements through the use of proceeds from divestitures. Until the Company is able to reduce its debt through divestitures and achieve a related restructuring of its debt agreements, it will remain in default of, and subject to the lenders' rights of acceleration under, those agreements.

LONG-TERM LIABILITIES

Long-term liabilities may either represent term loans by financial institutions such as banks, insurance companies, and so on or more formal issuance of bonds, debentures, or notes. They represent obligations payable beyond the period of one year or beyond that encompassed by the operating cycle. Debt obligations may assume many and varied forms, and their full assessment and measurement requires disclosure of all significant conditions and covenants attached to them. Such information should include the interest rate, maturities, conversion privileges, call features, subordination provisions, and restrictions under the indenture. In addition, disclosure of collateral pledged (with indication of book and possible market values), sinking fund provisions subordination, revolving credit provisions, and sinking fund commitments should be disclosed. Any defaults in adherence to loan provisions, including defaults of interest and principal repayments, must also be disclosed.

Since the exact interest rate that will prevail in the bond market at the time of issuance of bonds can never be predetermined, bonds are sold in excess of par, or at a premium, or below par, that is, at a discount. The premium or discount represents in effect an adjustment of the effective interest rate. The premium received is amortized over the life of the issue, thus reducing the coupon rate of interest to the effective interest rate incurred. Conversely, the discount allowed is similarly amortized, thus increasing the effective interest rate paid by the borrower.

A variety of incentives are offered in order to promote the sale of bonds and to reduce the interest rates that would otherwise be required. They may take the form of convertibility features, attachments of warrants to purchase the issuer's common stock, or even warrants to purchase the stock of another company. It requires no great persuasion to understand that to the extent that these incentives are valuable they carry a cost to the issuing company. Whether the cost represents dilution of the equity or a fixed price call on an investment, these costs should be recognized. Although slow in doing so, accountants have recognized such costs and given expression to them as follows:

1. In the case of convertible features—through their effect on the computation of earnings per share (see Chapter 12).
2. In the case of warrants—by assigning a discount factor at the time of debt issuance which charge is amortized to income. In addition, the dilutive effects of warrants are given recognition in earnings per share (EPS) computations (see also Chapter 12).

Generally, the prohibitions against offsetting of assets against liabilities apply to the offsetting of debt against related assets. However, if a real estate company buys property subject to a mortgage that it does not assume, it may properly deduct the amount of the mortgage from the asset, thus showing it net.

When debt is not interest bearing, it is appropriate to show it at the present value of the amount that will be payable in the future discounted at the rate at which the company would otherwise borrow money. This not only shows debt as a proper amount, comparable to other interest-bearing debt obligations, but it also provides for the computation of the interest charge that reflects the use of these funds. Moreover, if the debt is the result of the acquisition of an asset, this treatment ensures that its cost is not overstated through the overstatement of the amount of debt incurred.

Reference to the discussion on the imputation of interest in the "Receivables" section of Chapter 5 will show that under the provisions of *APB Opinion 21,* noninterest-bearing obligations, or those bearing unreasonable rates of interest, must, under certain conditions, be shown at an amount that reflects the imputation of a reasonable discount rate.

Under *SFAS 84* (1985) "Induced Conversions of Convertible Debt," companies must recognize an expense equal to the fair value of any conversion incentive paid to the holders of its convertible debt. A company may offer holders of its convertible debt an incentive to exercise their rights promptly to convert the debt to equity securities. Such an offer has sometimes been referred to as a convertible debt "sweetener." Under *SFAS 84* a company is required to recognize only the conversion incentive as an expense, and it should not be reported as an extraordinary item.

Valuable disclosure, from the analyst's point of view, is the yearly loan payment requirement for a significant number of future years.

SFAS 47 requires footnote disclosure of commitments under unconditional purchase obligations that provide financing to suppliers. It also requires disclosure of future payments on long-term borrowings and redeemable stock. Among required disclosures are:

For purchase obligations not recognized on purchaser's balance sheet:
1. Description and term of obligation.
2. Total fixed and determinable obligation. If determinable, also show these amounts for each of the next five years.
3. Description of any variable obligation.
4. Amounts purchased under obligation for each period covered by an income statement.

For purchase obligations recognized on purchaser's balance sheet payments for each of the next five years.

For long-term borrowings and redeemable stock:
1. Maturities and sinking fund requirements for each of the next five years.
2. Redemption requirements for each of the next five years.

An example of disclosure of short- and long-term debt can be found in Items 170, 172, and 173 of the financial statements of Campbell Soup Company (Appendix 4B).

EXTINGUISHMENT OF DEBT

SFAS 76 (1983), "Extinguishment of Debt," provides guidance as to when debt should be considered to be extinguished for financial reporting purposes. The *Statement* amends *APB Opinion 26* to make it apply to all extinguishments of debt, whether early or not, other than those currently exempted from its scope, such as debt conversions and troubled-debt restructurings (see Chapter 6).

The *Statement* provides that debt (excluding variable interest or convertible debt) is to be considered extinguished if the debtor is relieved of primary liability for the debt by the creditor, and it is probable that the debtor will not be required to make future payments as guarantor of the debt. In addition, even though the creditor does not relieve the debtor of its primary obligation, debt is to be considered extinguished if the debtor irrevocably places cash or other essentially risk-free monetary assets in a trust solely for satisfying that debt, and the possibility that the debtor will be required to make further payments is remote.

The monetary assets placed in the trust are to be denominated in the currency in which the debt is payable. For debt denominated in U.S. dollars, essentially risk-free monetary assets are limited to:

Direct obligations of the U.S. government

Obligations guaranteed by the U.S. government

Certain securities backed by U.S. government obligations as collateral under an arrangement by which the interest and principal payments on the collateral generally flow immediately through to the holder of the security.

In addition, the monetary assets held by the trust must provide cash flows (from interest and maturity of those assets) that approximately coincide, as to timing and amount, with the scheduled interest and principal payments on the debt that is being extinguished.

Under this technique, known as in-substance defeasance, the difference between the face value of debt and the cost of securities used to extinguish the debt is taken into income.

The SEC, which had imposed a moratorium on debt defeasance accounting pending a pronouncement by the FASB on the proper accounting, removed the moratorium and in *FRR 15* specified that, in addition to the *SFAS 76* requirements, registrants should be sure that:

The trustee is independent.

The trust assets are risk free as to the timing of principal and interest payments. (The SEC believes that generally only direct obligations of the U.S. government will qualify as risk-free assets.)

The trust is designed so that neither the corporation nor its creditors or others can gain access to the assets.

IMPLICATIONS FOR ANALYSIS

Liabilities are prior claims against a company's assets and resources; and the analyst needs assurance that they are fully stated with proper descriptions as to their amount, due dates, and the conditions, encumbrances, and limitations to which they subject the company.

The means by which auditors satisfy themselves that all liabilities have been properly recorded are such procedures as direct confirmation, scrutiny of board of director meeting minutes, the reading of contracts and agreements, and inquiry of those who may have knowledge of company obligations and liabilities. Since the nature of double-entry bookkeeping requires that for every asset, resource, or cost, a counterbalancing obligation or investment be booked, the areas subject to considerable difficulty are those relating to commitments and contingent liabilities because they do not involve the commensurate recording of assets or costs. Here, the analyst must rely on the information that is provided in the notes to financial statements and in the general management commentary found in the text of the annual report and elsewhere. The analyst can also check the accuracy and reasonableness of debt disclosures by reconciling them to the company's required disclosure of the amounts of interest expensed and paid in cash. Any significant unexplained difference will require analysis and/or management explanations.

The analyst must be aware of the possibility that understatement of liabilities can occur, and when it does, income will most likely be adversely affected. Thus, for example, the SEC found that Ampex Corporation did not disclose that it was obligated to pay royalty guarantees to record companies totaling in excess of $80 million, that it did not disclose that it was selling substantial amounts of prerecorded tapes that were improperly accounted for as "degaussed" or erased tapes to avoid payment of royalty fees, and that it understated by several millions of dollars the allowances for doubtful accounts receivable and provisions for losses arising from royalty contracts and overstated income due to inadequate credit allowances for returned tapes.

If short-term bank debt is included in the current liability section, it may mean that the company does not plan to refinance or the company cannot get a refinancing agreement with a lender that meets the requirements of *SFAS 6*. The analyst should attempt to determine the reason for the current liability classification of bank debt since an inability to secure a satisfactory refinancing agreement could indicate the company has problems beyond those revealed in its financial statements.

The analyst should realize that some companies are constantly on the lookout for ways to reduce the amount of liabilities in their financial statements. Moreover, liabilities may be misclassified or inadequately described.

With regard to in-substance defeasance of debt, the analyst must bear in mind that, since government bonds are usually of higher quality than corporate debt, the use of this technique may be costly to shareholders because of the premium paid for risk-free debt. Also, this technique is attractive only when market rates of interest are substantially above the coupon rates of debt to be extinguished.

Evaluation of Terms of Indebtedness

The disclosure of the terms and conditions of regular recorded indebtedness and liabilities is another area deserving the analyst's careful attention. Here, the analyst must examine critically the description of debt, its terms, conditions, and encumbrances with a view to satisfying himself or herself as to the term's feasibility and completeness. Important in the evaluation of a liability's total impact are such features as:

1. The terms of the debt.
2. Restrictions on deployment of resources and freedom of action.
3. Ability to engage in further financing.
4. Requirements such as those relating to maintenance of ratios of working capital, debt to equity, and so forth.
5. Dilutive conversion features to which the debt is subject.
6. Prohibitions of certain disbursements, such as dividends.

Minimum disclosure requirements as to debt provisions vary somewhat, but auditors are bound by reporting standards to disclose any breaches in loan provisions that may restrict a company's freedom of action or set it on the road to insolvency. Thus, the analyst should be alert to any explanations or qualifications in the notes or in the auditor's opinion. For example, American Shipbuilding Company made the following disclosures in its 1988 annual report:

> The credit agreement was amended during fiscal 1988, converting the facility from a revolving credit arrangement to a demand note. Under the amended agreement, the Company is required to satisfy specified financial conditions and is also required to liquidate its indebtedness to specified maximum limits. At September 30, 1988, the Company had satisfied all these requirements except for the working capital covenant. Subsequent to that date, the Company has not maintained its compliance as to maximum indebtedness. In addition, the tangible net worth requirement was not met by the Company as of November 8, 1988. The Company has given notices to the agent bank of its failure to satisfy these requirements.
>
> In addition to the restrictions described above, this credit facility places restrictions on the Company's ability to acquire or dispose of assets, make certain investments, enter into leases and pay dividends. At September 30, 1988 the credit agreement disallowed the payment of dividends.

Naturally, an analyst would like to be able to foresee developments such as those described in the American Shipbuilding situation. One of the most effective ways of doing this is by means of financial analysis that compares the terms of debt with the margin of safety by which existing compliance exceeds the minimum requirements under those terms.

OBLIGATIONS UNDER LEASES

Leasing, as a means of acquiring assets and the services and use of assets, has been known for a long time, but in recent decades its use has grown considerably. Our consideration of lease obligations at this point is due to their similarity to debt. Lease terms usually obligate entities to make a series of payments over a future period of time, and it is well known that in many cases such payments may contain, among others, elements of interest and principal amortization. The debate over which features of a lease agreement clinch it as a purchase (i.e., as a financing method) and which characteristics cause it to retain the nature of a rental contract has been going on for a long time.

When the accounting profession first recognized the problem of accounting for leases it recommended in *ARB 38* that long-term leases be disclosed. It was reasoned that if a lease arrangement was in substance an installment purchase of property, it should be reflected as an asset and as a liability of the lessee. The spirit and intent of this pronouncement were largely ignored in practice.

As the attraction of leasing as a means of "off-balance-sheet financing" grew, so did the clamor for a more realistic accounting. While *Accounting Research Study (ARS) 4,* published by the AICPA in 1962, concluded that leases that give rise to property rights be so reported in the financial statements, the *APB Opinion* that followed (5 of 1964) focused principally on the creation of a material equity in the property as a determining criterion requiring capitalization. This concept as well as the "soft" criteria that accompanied this *Opinion* were no match to the countervailing forces against capitalization that were motivated by considerations of the most favorable financial structure presentation and income pattern determination. Thus, only relatively few of the most obvious financing leases were capitalized in the financial statements in accordance with the provisions of *APB Opinion 5.*

In its last *Opinion* (*31* of 1973), the outgoing APB called merely for improved lease disclosure. In an apparent reaction to slow progress, the SEC issued in the same year *ASR 147,* which called for footnote *disclosures* that went beyond those specified in *APB Opinion 31.* These included disclosure of details on the present value of financing leases, as defined, and of the impact on net income of the capitalization of such leases.

It was, however, not until 1976 that a real tightening up of the accounting for leases occurred with the issuance of the more rigorous *SFAS 13* that superseded most prior pronouncements. The provisions of the *Statement* derive from the view that a lease that transfers substantially all of the benefits and risks incident to the ownership of property should be accounted for as the acquisition of an asset and the incurrence of an obligation by the lessee and as a sale or financing by the lessor. All other leases should be accounted for as operating leases. The *Statement* does not apply to leases relating to rights to explore natural resources or to licensing agreements. In 1977, the SEC moved to conform its lease accounting requirements to those of *SFAS 13*.

Accounting by Lessees

In the case of the lessee, the *Statement* requires that a lease be classified and accounted for as a capital lease (shown as an asset and an obligation on the balance sheet) if at the inception of the lease it meets *one* of four criteria: (1) the lease transfers ownership of the property to the lessee by the end of the lease term, (2) the lease contains an option to purchase the property at a bargain price, (3) the lease term is equal to 75 percent or more of the estimated economic life of the property, or (4) the present value[2] of the rentals and other minimum lease payments at the beginning of the lease term equal 90 percent of the fair value of the leased property less any related investment tax credit retained by the lessor. If the lease does not meet any of those criteria, it is to be classified and accounted for as an operating lease.

With regard to the last two of the above four criteria, if the beginning of the lease term falls within the last 25 percent of the total estimated economic life of the leased property, neither the 75 percent of economic life criterion nor the 90 percent recovery criterion is to be applied for purposes of classifying the lease. As a consequence, such leases will be classified as operating leases.

The lessee shall record a capital lease as an asset and an obligation at an amount equal to the present value of minimum lease payments[3] during

---

[2] A lessor shall compute the present value of the minimum lease payments using the interest rate implicit in the lease. A lessee shall compute the present value of the minimum lease payments using its incremental borrowing rate unless *(a)* it knows the lessor's computation of the implicit rate and *(b)* the implicit rate computed by the lessor is less than the lessee's incremental borrowing rate. If both of those conditions are met, the lessee shall use the implicit rate. The incremental borrowing rate is defined as the rate that at the inception of the lease, the lessee would have incurred to borrow the funds necessary to buy the leased asset on a secured loan basis with repayment terms similar to the payment schedule called for in the lease.

[3] These include the following: *(a)* minimum rental payments, *(b)* any guarantee by the lessee of the residual value at the expiration of the lease term, *(c)* any payment the lessee must make upon failure to renew or extend the lease at its expiration, and *(d)* the payment called for by a bargain purchase price.

the lease term, excluding executory costs (if determinable) such as insurance, maintenance, and taxes to be paid by the lessor together with any profit thereon. However, the amount so determined should not exceed the fair value of the leased property at the inception of the lease. If executory costs are not determinable from the provisions of the lease, an estimate of the amount shall be made.

Amortization, in a manner consistent with the lessee's normal depreciation policy, is called for over the term of the lease except where the lease transfers title or contains a bargain purchase option; in the latter cases, amortization should follow the estimated economic life.

In accounting for an operating lease, the lessee will charge rentals to expense as they become payable except when rentals do not become payable on a straight-line basis, in which case they should be expensed on such a basis or on any other systematic or rational basis that reflects the time pattern of benefits derived from the leased property.

Accounting by Lessors

In the case of the lessor, except for leveraged leases, if a lease meets any one of the preceding four criteria plus two additional criteria, it is to be classified and accounted for as a sales-type lease (if manufacturing or dealer profit is involved) or as a direct-financing lease. The additional criteria are: (1) collectibility of the minimum lease payments is reasonably predictable, and (2) no important uncertainties surround the amount of unreimbursable costs yet to be incurred by the lessor under the lease. A lease not meeting those tests is to be classified and accounted for as an operating lease.

Sales-Type Leases

1. The minimum lease payments plus the unguaranteed residual value accruing to the benefit of the lessor shall be recorded as the *gross investment* in the lease.
2. The difference between gross investment and the sum of the present values of its two components shall be recorded as unearned income. The net investment equals gross investment less unearned income. Unearned income shall be amortized to income over the lease term so as to produce a constant periodic rate of return on the net investment in the lease. Contingent rentals shall be credited to income when they become receivable.
3. At the termination of the existing lease term of a lease being renewed, the net investment in the lease shall be adjusted to the fair value of the leased property to the lessor at that date, and the difference, if any, recognized as gain or loss. (The same procedure applies to direct-financing leases—see below.)

4. The present value of the minimum lease payments discounted at the interest rate implicit in the lease shall be recorded as the *sales price.* The cost, or carrying amount, if different, of the leased property, plus any initial direct costs (of negotiating and consummating the lease) less the present value of the unguaranteed residual value shall be charged against income in the same period.

5. The estimated residual value shall be periodically reviewed. If it is determined to be excessive, the accounting for the transaction shall be revised using the changed estimate. The resulting reduction in net investment shall be recognized as a loss in the period in which the estimate is changed. No upward adjustment of the estimated residual value shall be made. (A similar provision applies to direct-financing leases.)

Direct-Financing Leases

1. The minimum lease payments (net of executory costs) plus the unguaranteed residual value plus the initial direct costs shall be recorded as the *gross investment.*

2. The difference between the gross investment and the cost, or carrying amount, if different, of the leased property, shall be recorded as *unearned income. Net investment* equals gross investment less unearned income. The unearned income shall be amortized to income over the lease term. The initial direct costs shall be amortized in the same portion as the unearned income. Contingent rentals shall be credited to income when they become receivable.

Operating Leases

The lessor will include property accounted for as an operating lease in the balance sheet and will depreciate it in accordance with his normal depreciation policy. Rent should be taken into income over the lease term as it becomes a receivable, except that if it departs from a straight-line basis, income should be recognized on such basis or on some other systematic or rational basis. Initial cost should be deferred and allocated over the lease term.

Principal Disclosures

The principal items of information required to be disclosed by lessees are (1) future minimum lease payments, separately for capital leases and operating leases, in total and for each of the five succeeding years; and (2) rental expense for each period for which an income statement is presented. Information required to be disclosed by lessors includes (1) future minimum lease payments to be received, separately for sales-type and direct-financing leases and for operating leases; and (2) the other components of the investment in sales-type and direct-financing leases— estimated residual values and unearned income.

Leases Involving Real Estate

These can involve (1) land only, (2) land and buildings, (3) equipment as well as real estate, or (4) only part of a building or building complex.

Generally, the above discussed accounting procedures will apply here with the following exceptions:

a. Where land only is involved, the lessee should account for it as a capital lease if either criterion (1) or (2) on page 202 is met. Land is not usually amortized.

b. In a lease involving both land and building(s), if the capitalization criteria applicable to land (see above) are met, the lease will retain the capital lease classification and the lessor will account for it as a single unit. The lessee will have to capitalize the land and buildings separately, the allocation between the two being in proportion to their respective fair values at the inception of the lease.

c. If the capitalization criteria applicable to land are not met, and at the inception of the lease the fair value of the land is less than 25 percent of total fair value of the leased property, both lessor and lessee shall consider the property as a single unit. The estimated economic life of the building is to be attributed to the whole unit. In this case, if either criteria (3) or (4) (see page 202) is met, the lessee should capitalize the land and building as a single unit and amortize it.

d. If the conditions in *(c)* above prevail *but* the fair value of land is 25 percent or more of the total fair value of the leased property, both the lessee and the lessor should consider the land and the building *separately* for purposes of applying capitalization criteria (3) and (4) (see page 202). If either of the criteria is met by the building element of the lease, it should be accounted for as a capital lease by the lessee and amortized. The land element of the lease is to be accounted for as an operating lease. If the building element meets neither capitalization criteria, both land and buildings should be accounted for as a single operating lease.

e. Equipment that is part of a real estate lease should be considered separately, and the minimum lease payments applicable to it should be estimated by whatever means are appropriate in the circumstances.

f. Leases of certain facilities such as airport, bus terminal, or port facilities from governmental units or authorities are to be classified as *operating leases.*

Sale-Leaseback

When the lease meets the criteria for treatment as a capital lease, any gain on the sale should be deferred and amortized over the lease term in proportion to the amortization of the leased asset. When a capital lease is not present, any gain should be recognized at the time of the sale if the fair rental for the lease term is equal to or greater than the rental called for by the lease. If the lease rental exceeds the fair rental, any gain on the sale should be reduced by the amount of such excess.

When the leaseback is for only a portion of the property sold, an assessment should be made as to whether the leaseback of the portion of property sold at a profit represents a continued involvement in the property sufficient to require deferral of all or part of the profit on the sale.

SFAS 98 (1988) clarifies *SFAS 13* in that it concludes that a sale-leaseback involving real estate (including real estate with equipment), should be accounted for as a sale only if the transaction qualifies as a sale under *SFAS 66* "Accounting for Sales of Real Estate." That statement requires among others, that before a profit or loss is recognized on sales of real estate, the receivables from the sale are collectible and that the seller have no significant remaining obligations to fulfill (see also Chapter 10).

Leveraged Leases

Leveraged leasing, in which a lessor borrows heavily in order to finance a leasing transaction with a small, or even negative, equity in the leased property, is a highly specialized topic.

Basically, the accounting method prescribed for use by lessors for leveraged leases, as they are defined in the statement, is called the separate phases method. This method recognizes the separate investment phases of a leveraged lease in which the lessor's net investment declines during the early years of the lease and rises during the later years. In the case of lessees, leveraged leases are to be classified and accounted for in the same manner as nonleveraged leases.

ACCOUNTING FOR CAPITAL LEASES

ILLUSTRATION 1

I. Lease terms and assumptions

A. Lessor acquires equipment to be leased for $10,000

B. Fair value of the leased property at inception of the lease, January 1, Year 1 . . . . $10,000

C. Estimated economic life of the leased property . . . . 8 years

D. The lease has a fixed noncancelable term of five years with a rental of $2,400 payable at the end of each year. The lessee guarantees the residual value at the end of the five-year lease term in the amount of $2,000. The lessee is to receive any excess of the sales price of property over the guaranteed amount at the end of the lease term. The lessee pays executory costs.

E. The rentals specified are determined to be fair, and the guarantees of residual value are expected to approximate realizable value. No investment tax credit is available.

II. Additional information

A. The lessee depreciates its owned equipment on a straight-line basis.

B. The lessee's incremental borrowing rate is 10 percent per year.

C. At the end of the lease term, the equipment is sold for $2,100.

1. *Determination of minimum lease payments*

   Minimum lease payments for both the lessee and the lessor are computed as follows:

   Minimum rental payments over the lease term
   = ($2,400 × 5 years) $12,000
   Lessee guarantee of the residual value at the
   end of the lease term 2,000
   Total minimum lease payments $14,000

2. *Determination of lessor's rate of interest implicit in the lease*

   This is the rate that equates the recovery of the fair value of the property at the inception of the lease ($10,000) with the present value of both the minimum lease payments ($2,400 × 5) plus the lessee's guarantee of the residual value at the end of the lease ($2,000). This rate can be arrived at on a trial and error basis. At 10 percent, the two discounted amounts add up to $10,340; at 11 percent, to $10,057; while at 12 percent, they equal $9,786. Through interpolation, we arrive at an implicit interest rate of 11.21 percent.

3. *Classification of the lease*

   The *lessee* will classify this as a capital lease because the present value of the minimum lease payments at $10,340 (using its incremental borrowing rate of 10 percent) exceeds 90 percent of the fair value of the property at the inception of the lease ($10,000). The lessee will use its incremental borrowing rate (10 percent) in discounting because it is less than the implicit interest rate in the lease. The *lessor* will classify the lease as a direct-financing lease because the present value of the minimum lease payments using the implicit rate of 11.21 percent ($10,000) exceeds 90 percent of the fair value of the property, cost and fair value of the amount are equal at inception of lease, and all other conditions of capitalization have been met.

III. Accounting on the lessee's books

January 1, Year 1:

Leased property under Capital Leases	10,000	
Obligations under Capital Leases		10,000*

To record the capital lease at the fair value of
the property.

* Obligation due within one year will be classified as current.

December 31, Year 1:

Obligations under Capital Leases	1,279	
Interest Expense	1,121[a]	
Cash		2,400

To record first-year rental payments.

[a] Obligation balance outstanding × Implicit interest rate = $10,000 × 11.21% = $1,121.

Depreciation Expense	1,600[b]	
Accumulated Depreciation of Leased Property		
under Capital Leases		1,600

To record first-year depreciation.

$$\text{(b)} \quad \frac{\text{Cost-residual value}}{\text{Term of lease}} = \frac{\$10,000 - \$2,000}{5} = \$1,600.$$

December 31, Year 5 (selected journal entry):

Cash	100	
Obligations under Capital Leases	2,000	
Accumulated Depreciation, Leased Property		
under Capital Leases	8,000	
Leased Property under Capital Leases		10,000
Gain on Disposition of Leased Property ...		100

To record liquidation of obligations under capital leases and receipt of cash
in excess of guaranteed residual value.

IV. Accounting on the lessor's books

January 1, Year 1:

Equipment	10,000	
Cash		10,000

To record purchase of equipment for purpose of
financing lease.

Minimum Lease Payments Receivable	14,000	
Equipment		10,000
Unearned Income		4,000

To record investment in direct-financing lease.

December 31, Year 1:

Unearned Income	1,121[c]	
Earned Income		1,121

To recognize the portion of unearned income
that is earned during first year of investment.

[c] Net investment × Implicit interest rate = 10,000
× 11.21% = $\underline{\$1,121}$

```
Cash . . . . . . . . . . . . . . . . . . . . . . . . . . . . . . . . . . . . . .    2,400
          Minimum Lease Payments Receivable . . . . .                    2,400
          To record receipt of first year's rental.
```

December 31, Year 5 (selected journal entry):

```
Cash . . . . . . . . . . . . . . . . . . . . . . . . . . . . . . . . . . . . . .    2,000
          Minimum Lease Payments Receivable . . . . .                    2,000
          To record the receipt of the lessee's guarantee.
```

Capital versus Operating Lease—the Effect on Income

As can be seen from the tabulation that follows, the interest expense pattern of the capital lease follows that of a fixed payment mortgage with interest expense decreasing over time as the principal balance decreases. The attraction of operating-lease accounting to the lessee is also clear because under the capitalization procedure expenses incident to the lease, that is, interest plus depreciation ($1,121 + $1,600), exceed the rental expense by $321. In later years, this excess reverses, as over the lease period total expense under either method is equal, but the pattern of expense recognition is an important consideration to many enterprises, and the higher beginning charge under capitalization is viewed as a distinct disadvantage of that method.

The tabulation also indicates the pattern of finance income recognition by the lessor that is proportional to the investment at risk.

	Rental	Interest: income (lessor) expense (lessee)	Principal: receipts (lessor) payment (lessee)	Balance of obligations
Year 0	—	—	—	$10,000
Year 1	$ 2,400	$1,121	$1,279	8,721
Year 2	2,400	977*	1,423	7,298
Year 3	2,400	818	1,582	5,716
Year 4	2,400	641	1,759	3,957
Year 5	2,400	443	1,957	2,200
Total	$12,000	$4,000	$8,000	$ 2,000

* Year 2 interest is balance of obligation ($8,721) × 11.21%.

Capital versus Operating Lease—the Effect on Cash

It should be noted that as far as the flow of cash is concerned, there is only one reality, that is, the yearly outflow of the $2,400 rental.

Under capital-lease accounting, "cash from operations" is reduced yearly by declining interest charges (i.e., $1,121, $977 . . .), while the payment of lease obligations represents a financing use of cash that increases yearly (i.e., $1,279, $1,423 . . .). The two always equal the rental payment of $2,400. The amortization (depreciation) of the property right of $1,600 annually has no effect on cash because it is a noncash-using expense.

Example of disclosure

Campbell Soup Co. (see Appendix 4B) discloses lease obligations in item ⟦173⟧.

Implications for Analysis

Leasing as a means of financing is an area deserving the analyst's particular scrutiny. The major objective here is to make sure that accounting form is not permitted to mask the economic substance of debt[4] and its effect on capital structure, as well as exposure to fixed charges and the effects of leverage.

It is quite obvious that many long-term leases have all or most of the earmarks of debt. They create an obligation for payments under an agreement that is not cancelable. This represents a commitment to fixed payments that is what a debt obligation amounts to. The adverse effects of debt are also present in the case of a lease, that is, an inability to pay may result in insolvency. The fact that statutory limitations on lease obligations in case of bankruptcy limit the obligation to pay rent for one or a number of years is not a mitigating factor of substance because the process of financial analysis is usually designed to evaluate the probability of insolvency and the attendant adverse effects on asset values and credit standing, rather than an evaluation of the amount and standing of the obligations after insolvency proceedings have been started. The importance of the leased property to company operations is also a factor, since it may be so vital as to preclude the company's abandonment of the lease in reorganization proceedings.

It is very difficult, if not impossible, to compare the financial position of companies that use different methods of financing, including installment purchase in the form of a lease, for the financing of different assets. This is also true of comparisons of income, since when accounted as an operating lease, rentals are usually less than interest expense and depreciation expenses in the early stages of ownership in the form of a lease.

SFAS 13 and amendments represent a major step in the direction of providing the analyst with the information required for the proper reflection of leases in the financial statements and the evaluation of their

---

[4] Under Section 502(7) of the Bankruptcy Act of 1978, the damages allowable to the landlord of a debtor are limited to the greater of (I) one year or (II) 15 percent of the remaining portion of the lease not to exceed three years after the date of filing or surrender, whichever is earlier.

impact on the financial position and results of operations of an enterprise. The criteria as well as the disclosure requirements embodied in this *Statement* are comprehensive and explicit. Nevertheless, the analyst, mindful of the historical tendencies and developments in areas of accounting that are affected by strong special interests, should be ever alert to the possibility that managements, aided by the seemingly inexhaustible ingenuity of their accountants, lawyers, and other financial advisers, will often attempt to devise ways to circumvent this *Statement.* Accounting standards may, in time, be changed to meet these challenges, and so it is the interim period that presents the time of greatest risk exposure for the analyst. Many interpretations of *SFAS 13* have been issued since the original promulgation of this standard. While, under the standards which preceded *SFAS 13,* only relatively few leases were capitalized, the new rules require the capitalization of most leases where there is an effective transfer of substantially all of the benefits and risks of ownership from lessor to lessee.

A research report[5] published by the FASB in 1981 concluded that it has not become more expensive for lessee companies to raise money or obtain waivers of restrictive covenants as a result of the issuance of *SFAS 13*. Nevertheless, a majority of respondents to an extensive mail survey indicated that new lease contracts were drafted to avoid capitalization, many indicated an increase in buying or constructing of assets instead of leasing them, and almost half of users and auditors surveyed indicated that existing lease contracts were renegotiated to avoid capitalization. In addition, the study revealed that more than 40 percent of the trained analysts surveyed considered a company that did not capitalize a lease as being more profitable than its identical counterpart that did capitalize. Thus, the need for a more informed approach to the reading of financial statements by analysts is ever-present.

The provisions of *SFAS 13* that entail assumptions of fair values, selling prices, salvage or residual values, implicit rates of interest, and incremental borrowing rates are not so tight as to preclude substantive changes in accounting through manipulations of these relatively "soft" factors. Thus, the analyst must be alert and vigilant when analyzing the impact of leases on financial statements.

"OFF-BALANCE-SHEET" FINANCING

In addition to leases, there are other "off-balance-sheet" financing methods that range from the simple to the highly complex. Moreover, this is an ever-changing field where as one standard is brought out to limit their

---

[5] A. Rashad Abdel-Khalik, "The Economic Effects on Leases of FASB Statement No. 13, Accounting for Leases."

use, new and innovative methods are devised to take their place. Thus, the analyst must be always on the lookout for methods by which debt is kept off the balance sheet.

Property, plant, and equipment can be financed by having an outside party acquire the facilities while the company agrees to do enough business with the facility to provide funds sufficient to service the debt. Examples of these kinds of arrangements are through-put agreements, in which the company agrees to run a specified amount of goods through a processing facility, or "take-or-pay" arrangements in which the company guarantees to pay for a specified quantity of goods whether needed or not. A variation of these arrangements involves the creation of separate entities for ownership and the financing of the facilities less than 51 percent owned (such as joint ventures or limited partnerships) that are carried as an investment at equity and not consolidated with the company's financial statements and are, thus, excluded from its liabilities.

ILLUSTRATION 2.   Avis-Rent-A-Car set up a trust to borrow money in order to finance the purchase of automobiles which were, in turn, leased to Avis for its rental fleet. Because the trust was separate from Avis and its parent, the debt of about $400 million was kept off their balance sheets. R. D. Walter, principal accounting officer of the parent, was quoted as saying: "One of the big advantages of off-balance-sheet financing is that it permits us to make other borrowings from banks for operating capital that we could not otherwise obtain." Hertz and National Car Rental, the competitors of Avis, bought rather than leased their rental cars.

ILLUSTRATION 3.   Oil companies resort to less than 50-percent-owned joint ventures as vehicles used to raise money to build and operate pipelines. While the debt service is the ultimate responsibility of the oil company, it simply states in footnotes that it may have to advance funds to help the pipeline joint venture meet its debt obligations if sufficient crude oil needed to generate the necessary funds is not shipped.

In recent years, companies have been financing inventory without reporting on their balance sheets the inventory or the related liability. These are generally product financing arrangements in which an enterprise sells and agrees to repurchase inventory with the repurchase price equal to the original sales price plus carrying and financing costs or other similar transactions such as a guarantee of resale prices to third parties.

SFAS 49 specifies criteria for determining when an arrangement involving the sale of inventory is in substance a financing arrangement that should be accounted for as a borrowing, with excess repurchase costs treated as financing or holding costs.

Seagram Company provides an example of an inventory financing agreement:

> The Company entered into a five-year contract whereunder it agreed to purchase Scotch whiskey from a subsidiary of a British bank. The amount of the commitment is $28,279,000.

Another means of financing is to sell accounts receivable either with or without recourse. *SFAS 77* (1983) "Reporting by Transferors for Transfers of Receivables with Recourse" allows companies which sell their receivables with a guarantee (i.e., retaining some risk of loss) to book them as a sale rather than as a loan if they meet three criteria:

1. That the seller surrenders control of future economic benefits embodied in the receivables. (Control is absent if seller retains a subsequent repurchase option.)
2. That the buyer can estimate his obligation (e.g., bad debt losses, collection costs, discounts, etc.).
3. That the buyer cannot require the seller to repurchase except pursuant to recourse provisions.

If any one of the above three conditions is not met, the transfer of the receivables is considered as a loan with the receivables pledged as security for such loan.

SFAS 105 (1990) specifies additional disclosures which are required when receivables are transferred with recourse.

OFF-BALANCE-SHEET OBLIGATIONS

Companies have devised and are constantly devising new ways to reduce debts and obligations and to remove them to off-balance-sheet status. Auto makers and other major capital goods manufacturers can sell their receivables as backing for debt sold to the public. This "securitization" of loans removes such receivables, or mortgage loans in the case of savings and loan associations, or credit card receivables in the case of banks, and converts them into debt held by the public backed by such receivables assets. This enables companies to convert assets to cash more quickly, and to remove financing obligations which arise from assets created by expanding business activities. Companies need to report as liabilities only the usually small fraction of the receivables they guarantee.

While the above described strategies and their disclosures may conform to current accounting standards, new strategies are constantly being tried. Analysts must be careful to analyze the full measure of debts and obligations to which the entity under analysis is exposed.

LIABILITIES UNDER THE PENSION PLANS

Like the accounting for most obligations, that for pensions also has a dual aspect. Their impact on results of operations will be considered in Chapter 11, while the liability aspect will be discussed here.

SFAS 87 (1985), the relevant provisions of which are also examined in Chapter 11, introduced revised concepts of pension obligations:

The *accumulated benefit obligation* is an estimate of the employer's obligation for pensions based on current and past compensation levels. No assumption regarding future compensation levels is included and for pension plans, such as flat benefit plans or those with nonpay-related formulas, the accumulated benefit obligation accurately measures the entire or final obligation.

The *projected benefit obligation* takes into consideration the effect of future salary increases as is necessary in order to determine the full obligations in pension plans such as those based on career-average pay or final pay.

Contrary to the position taken by the superceded *APB Opinion 8,* which recognized essentially no obligation in excess of amounts accrued as the pension expense, *SFAS 87* recognizes an additional minimum liability. Since, as will be seen, this additional liability is based on the accumulated rather than on the projected benefit obligation, it represents a compromise position between the full-fledged recognition of pension liabilities and their much less adequate recognition before *SFAS 87.*

RECOGNITION OF ADDITIONAL PENSION LIABILITY

SFAS 87 specifies that an additional balance sheet liability for pensions must be recognized if the accumulated benefit obligation exceeds the fair value of plan assets. Thus, an unfunded benefit obligation is recognized. The amount of the liability is increased by any debit balance in a prepaid pension cost account so that the minimum liability amount is actually shown on the balance sheet. Conversely, the amount of the liability is decreased by any credit balance in the accrued pension cost account because that amount is taken into account in showing the total minimum liability. For reporting purposes the additional pension liability is combined with the accrued or prepaid pension cost account.

The following tabulation illustrates the determination of the additional liability amount under different circumstances:

	Case 1	Case 2	Case 3	Case 4
	(in thousands)			
Accumulated benefit obligation	$1,000	$1,000	$1,000	$1,000
Less: Fair value of plan assets	700	700	700	1,400
Unfunded (overfunded) accumulated benefit obligation	$ 300	$ 300	$ 300	$ (400)
Accrued pension cost (CR)	—		(200)	*
Prepaid pension cost (DR)	—	100		
Additional minimum pension liability	$ 300	$ 400	$ 100	–0–

* Balance not relevant because of overfunding.

Even though an additional liability will be recognized by a company with an underfunded plan, an asset would *not* be recognized if the company maintains a plan with assets in excess of accumulated benefits. Underfunding in one pension plan cannot be offset by overfunding in another plan.

The recognition of the minimum pension liability in part remedies the fact that the unrecognized (i.e., unamortized) prior service cost, losses, and transition amounts already represent the postponement (delay) in pension liability recognition.

The recording of the additional minimum pension liability as a credit to an appropriately designated liability account requires an offsetting debit which will be to an intangible asset, representing, in the Board's opinion, a future economic benefit in the form of employee goodwill. However, if the intangible asset exceeds the amount of the company's unrecognized prior service cost, a different accounting is required. In this case this yet unrecognized net cost must be recognized in that the debit is charged to a separate component of *equity* net of any tax benefits that result from considering such losses as timing differences for tax accounting purposes. Thus, depending on circumstances, as described above, the entry to record an additional minimum liability may create both an intangible pension asset and a contra shareholders' equity account.

To illustrate, assume that in the preceding tabulation in Case 1 the company had an unrecognized prior service cost of $180,000. The entry to record the additional minimum liability would be as follows:

Intangible Pension Asset[a] 180,000
Stockholders' Equity—Unrealized
Pension Cost[b]   120,000
   Pension Liability   300,000

[a] Amount not to exceed unrecognized prior service cost.
[b] A contra account to stockholder's equity.

In the absence of unrecognized prior service cost, the entire debit for the liability would be to Stockholder's Equity.

Each year a new determination of the additional minimum pension liability (if any) is made and the liability account is adjusted accordingly.

IMPLICATIONS FOR ANALYSIS

From the point of view of a fuller recognition of pension liabilities, *SFAS 87* represents a decided improvement over the preceding pension accounting standards. Nevertheless, the compromises that had to be made within the FASB to secure adoption of *SFAS 87* as well as the concessions which were made to a very critical corporate constituency have resulted in a standard that falls short of recognizing the full liabilities which pension obligations entail. Thus, while *SFAS 87* does recognize that if the fair value of pension assets falls short of the accumulated pension benefit obligation a liability exists, it does not take into consideration for this purpose the projected benefit obligation. The latter recognizes an estimate for future pay increases and when pension plans base their benefits on future pay formulas (as many do) any liability computation that fails to factor these in understates the pension obligations. There is also a lack of symmetry of treatment here. While the effects of inflation are ignored when future pay increases are disregarded, the interest rate used to discount these obligations to present value does factor in inflationary expectations. This reinforces the downward bias in the pension liability determination process. Clearly then the difference between the projected benefit obligation and the fair value of pension plan assets is a better measure of pension liabilities than the one adopted by the FASB. And yet, it does not measure the full economic obligation for pensions which is the present value of amounts expected to be paid to employees based on total years of service (past and present) *and* expected future salaries. The latter, in effect, tie the company's obligation for pensions to price-level changes, a risky obligation indeed.

The intangible asset that is created when many of the pension liabilities are booked is of doubtful economic significance and thus its recognition as an asset blunts the effect of the liability on a company's debt to equity ratio.

SFAS 87 has a number of built-in inconsistencies. While the projected benefit obligation is disregarded in the computation of pension liabilities to be booked (see preceding discussion), it is taken into account in the computation of the periodic pension service cost. In addition, while underfunded plans will lead to liability recognition, overfunded plans cannot result in assets.

The analyst must recognize that the liability for pensions will be computed and evaluated yearly and, unlike the case with most other liabilities, can and will fluctuate in size from period to period. Thus, strong equity markets may diminish it or make it disappear altogether. Conversely, weak markets can increase it or make one appear where none existed before.[6] Volatility in this area is clearly also the result of the new pension liability determination rules. These rules attempt to measure pension obligations and the assets available to meet them as of any given moment in time. Since the factors which affect these are ever-changing, it is inevitable that the size of unfunded pension obligations will always be subject to change. Thus the volatility is induced, as it should be, by outside factors and market conditions.

---

[6] When interest rates decline pension assets rise, but pension liabilities rise simultaneously even faster. That is because the long-term pension promises cost more to fund in current dollars. The opposite situation prevails when interest rates rise. This leads some companies to try and manage the match between assets and liabilities so as to reduce the disparities between them.

Managements, often with the help of their auditors, try by means of various devices to diminish volatility, because of the enterprise risk which it implies. Analysts, on the other hand, do welcome accounting that portrays reality as it is and which consequently measures risk realistically.

Finally, a useful way to view the accounting for pensions is to consider the enterprise liability for pensions as an obligation which is not completely discharged by the act of placing the amounts charged to pension expense in the hands of an independent trustee. The assets in the pension fund are rather collateral or back-up for that obligation which can change due to many factors including the potentially significant one of inflation.

A development in 1991 reinforces this view of pension obligations. The Department of Labor filed suit against Maxxam, Inc., of Houston and Magnetex, Inc., of Los Angeles, who financed payments to retirees with annuities bought from an insurer whose financial problems later left it unable to meet all its obligations. These suits reinforce the ultimate obligation which companies bear towards their retirees.

POSTRETIREMENT BENEFITS OTHER THAN PENSIONS

In addition to promises for pensions, as discussed above, companies promise other benefits to their employees, such as health benefits and life insurance. However, unlike the accounting for pensions which has been required for many years and has also been mandated by ERISA legislation, company recognition of obligations for these other postretirement benefits has ranged from inadequate to nonexistent. Thus, prior to the promulgation of *SFAS 106* (1990) covering the accounting for Other Postretirement Employee Benefits (OPEB), IBM, for example, followed a policy of "terminal accrual" by providing for the liability for OPEB only when an employee retired while not accruing any costs for active employees. Most companies, however, provided little or no accrual of the liability for OPEB which they either considered immaterial or simply refused to consider. Instead they charged outlays for actual costs paid for retirees on a pay-as-you-go basis. Issuance of *SFAS 106* followed years of controversy and discussions during which the enormous size of the unrecorded liabilities for OPEB became increasingly recognized.

As in the case of pensions, the liability aspect of this subject will be discussed in this chapter while the cost aspect will be discussed in Chapter 11, dealing with the analysis of the income statement.

Because of the similarity of the OPEB to pensions, *FASB 106* has drawn heavily on the pension accounting model of *SFAS 87* (see above and Chapter 11). There are, however, significant differences.

One such difference relates to the accounting for the unfunded OPEB obligation. When a company adopts *SFAS 106* (effectively by or before calendar year 1993 for public companies and companies with more than

500 participants) the unfunded OPEB obligation *at the date of adoption,* also referred to as the "transition obligation," can be recognized as either (1) a cumulative effect of an accounting change (included as a charge to income) *or* (2) over future periods as a component of the annual OPEB expense (see Chapter 11) over a period not to exceed 20 years. Thus, if a company elects to amortize its transition obligation over future years, then, unlike under pension accounting, it will not be required to recognize immediately a minimum liability on the balance sheet for the unfunded OPEB obligation attributable to present retirees and active employees that are eligible to receive benefits.

The other major difference from pension accounting relates to *funding.* Because there are no legal requirements for OPEB benefits, similar to ERISA requirements for pensions, and also because funding OPEB benefits does not enjoy the favorable tax treatment accorded to the funding of pension plans, few companies have funded their OPEB liabilities or are likely to do so in the near future. Thus, what we have here are sizable unrecorded, as well as increasing amounts of recorded, OPEB liabilities which are *unfunded* and are consequently backed by assets on the companies' balance sheets rather than assets in the hands of independent trustees.

It will be instructive to summarize here the components of (1) the Accrued OPEB Cost which is a liability on the balance sheets and (2) the Unrecognized OPEB Obligation which remains unrecorded until it will be recognized (generally on a straight-line basis over 20 years or less). *The Accrued OPEB Cost consists of:*

I. *The net annual OPEB cost (see Chapter 11 for fuller discussion of elements) is comprised of:*
    Service cost.
    Interest cost.
    Actual return on plan assets (if any) (cost reduction).
    Amortization of unrecognized prior service cost.
    Amortization of actuarial gains or losses (cost increase or reduction).
    Amortization of transition obligation (if not recognized initially as cumulative effect of accounting change).

II. *Benefit Payments* (which is the cash basis OPEB expense).

less

The Unrecognized OPEB Obligation consists of:

I. The Unrecognized Transition Obligation which was measured on the date of adoption of *SFAS 106* and which the company elected to amortize rather than charge to income immediately, *LESS* sum of yearly amortization to net annual OPEB cost— to date.

II.   Unamortized net Gain or Loss (unrecognized on balance sheet).

III. Unamortized Prior Service Cost (unrecognized on balance sheet).

Exhibit 11–1 (Chapter 11) reconciles the relationship between OPEB-related accounts, including costs, accruals, the Accumulated Postretirement Benefit Obligation (APBO) and the unrecognized liabilities, technically accounted for as deferred charges (i.e., offsets) to the APBO which, in its gross amount, includes both recognized and unrecognized obligations.

Required Disclosures

Under *SFAS 106* the required disclosures include:

- Description of the plan.
- Net periodic postretirement benefit cost and its components.
- Reconciliation of funded status of the plan with amounts reported in balance sheet.
- Assumed health-care-cost trend rate used to measure covered benefit costs for the next year. Also, a description of the direction and pattern of change in the assumed trend rates thereafter.
- Weighted-average discount rate, rate of compensation, and expected long-term rate of return used to measure the APBO.
- The effect on various amounts reported of a 1 percent increase in the health-care-cost trend rate.
- Amounts and types of employer securities held.

SFAS 106 amends *APB Opinion 12* to require that companies recognize fully the present value of an individual's deferred compensation by the date the employee is fully eligible to receive benefits.

In item [120] Campbell Soup Company (Appendix 4B) discloses the possible effects of adopting *SFAS 106*.

IMPLICATIONS FOR ANALYSIS

Companies have been making promises of OPEB to various degrees for a long time. Since most have not recorded the obligations implicit in these promises, unrecorded liabilities which have been estimated to run in the hundreds of billions of dollars have accumulated and are growing. Contributing to the pressure to take steps and begin to account for these mounting obligations were the following:

- A recognition that because of inflation in medical costs, increasing life expectancies, early retirement programs, and decreasing Medicare reimbursements these liabilities were large and growing.

- A recognition that the promises were real and that the courts have limited management's ability to reduce or revoke the promised benefits.

To the analyst promulgation of *SFAS 106* means that companies will now have to *begin* to recognize liabilities which hitherto had to be estimated without benefit of mandated disclosures.

Companies like IBM, General Mills, LTV, and Abbott Labs, which have elected to take a one-time charge to income and show the liability for OPEB on the books, will now present a more realistic, albeit more leveraged, capital structure. Companies which, for various reasons, elect thus to face the issue head on will, because of decreased equity and diminished future income charges, show increases in their returns on equity.

Companies electing to amortize their unrecognized transition obligations over as many as 20 years will continue to have substantial unrecorded liabilities. Most companies are likely to keep the liabilities for OPEB *unfunded.*

Analysts must be aware of the fact that whether liabilities are booked or not, they are subject to difficulties of measurement which generally exceed those of other estimates concerned with financial reporting. The reason for the higher degree of uncertainty is the subjectivity involved in estimating the cost of providing benefits for 20 or 30 years in the future in terms of costs which are presently escalating at rates far exceeding those of general price level inflation. In addition, the estimation process is made more difficult by assumptions regarding intensity of services, medical service delivery methods, and impact of technological advances in the health care industry. Thus, the health-care-cost trend rate used by a company must be carefully evaluated.

The fact that the cost flow effects resulting from the implementation of *SFAS 106* are minor is no cause for complacency. These are real obligations which will require increasing cash outflows to satisfy. Many factors will affect the rate of cash demands on the company, important among which is the ratio of active employees (producing for the company) to retired employees which, as they age, may lay increasing claims on the company's resources.

While *SFAS 106* will cause the gradual booking of at least some of the liabilities for OPEB, the analyst will have to use the enhanced disclosures now available in order to compute the best estimate of the obligations to which the company under analysis is subject.

LIABILITIES AT THE "EDGE" OF EQUITY

The analyst must be alert to the existence of equity securities (typically preferred stock) that because of mandatory redemption provisions are more akin to debt than they are to equity. Whatever their name, these securities impose upon the issuing companies obligations to lay out funds at specified dates, which is precisely a burden that a true equity security is not supposed to impose. Such preferred issues exist, for example, at Lockheed Corporation and Koppers Company, Inc., and are referred to in Tenneco Inc.'s 1990 annual report as follows:

> The aggregate maturities applicable to preferred stock issues outstanding at December 31, 1990, are none for the year 1991, $10 million for 1992, and $23 million for each of the years 1993, 1994 and 1995.

In *FRR No. 1,* section 211, the SEC concluded that redeemable preferred stocks are significantly different from conventional equity capital and that they should not be included in the general caption of stockholders' equity or combined in a total with nonredeemable equity securities. The release also requires disclosure of redemption terms and five-year maturity data.

SFAS 47, "Disclosure of Long-Term Obligations" requires disclosure of redemption requirements of redeemable capital stock for each of the five years following the date of the latest balance sheet.

In *SFAS 76* (1983), "Extinguishment of Debt," the FASB intentionally chose to exclude preferred stock with mandatory redemption features from the *Statement* scope because it had not yet resolved the question of whether such preferred stock should be accounted for as debt or equity.

Private companies, that is, those not subject to SEC requirements, continue to show redeemable preferred stock as part of equity. The analyst should, however, treat them as what they are, an obligation to lay out cash at a future date.

DEFERRED CREDITS (INCOME)

An ever-increasing variety of items and descriptions is included in this group of accounts. In many cases, these items are akin to liabilities; in others, they represent deferred income yet to be earned, while in a number of cases, they serve as income-smoothing devices. The confusion confronting the analyst is compounded by a lack of agreement among accountants as to the exact nature of these items or the proper manner of their presentation. Thus, regardless of category or presentation, the key to their analysis lies in an understanding of the circumstances and the financial transactions that brought them about.

At one end of this group's spectrum, we find those items that have the characteristics of liabilities. Here, we may find included such items as advances or billings on uncompleted contracts, unearned royalties and deposits, and customer service prepayments. Quite clearly, the outstanding characteristic of these items is their liability aspects, even though, as in the case of advances of royalties, they may, after certain conditions are fulfilled, find their way into the company's income stream. Advances on uncompleted contracts represent primarily methods of financing the work in process while deposits of rent received represent, as do customer service prepayments, security for performance of an agreement. Even though found sometimes among "deferred credits," such items are more properly classified as liabilities, or current liabilities if due within the company's operating cycle.

Next, we consider deferred income items that represent income or revenue received in advance and that will be earned over future periods through the passage of time, the performance of services, or the delivery of goods. Examples of deferred income items are magazine subscription income, representing the receipts by magazine publishers of advance payment for long-term subscriptions, and unearned rental income, which represents receipt of advance payment for rent. Other examples are unearned finance charges, deferred profit on installment sales, deferred gain on sales-and-leaseback arrangements, and unrealized profit on lay-away sales.

It should be noted that this category includes a liability for future performance as well as a possible profit component in such income items received but not yet earned as, for example, subscription income, the future earning of which is dependent on the delivery of magazines. It also includes unearned finance charges that have already been deducted but that are allocated to the future on the assumption that they are earned with the mere passage of time. Still further along the "earned" scale are profits on installment sales that are deferred, not because they have not been earned but rather because the collection of the receivable resulting from such sales is going to occur over a period of time in the future. The preferred accounting treatment is not to defer such gains on installment sales but rather to give expression to any doubts about future collectibility of receivables by establishing a provision for doubtful accounts for that purpose.

Further on the other extreme of the deferred credit spectrum are so-called bargain purchase credits that arise in cases where the fair value of certain assets of an acquired company exceeds the consideration given. (Purchase accounting, which is governed by *APB Opinion 16,* is discussed in Chapter 9.) In such cases, the resulting credit is amortized to income over what is usually an arbitrarily determined number of years. What we have here is a benefit derived from what is presumably an advantageous acquisition. This benefit is deferred and taken up in income over a number of years not necessarily because it has not been realized, but because of a desire to spread out, or smooth its effect, over a number of years.

One of the most complicated and controversial, as well as most substantial, of deferred credits is deferred income taxes.

Deferred Taxes

Tax allocation, which is the accounting process giving rise to deferred tax credits (or debits in reverse circumstances), is primarily a device for matching the applicable tax expense with corresponding pretax income. A more comprehensive analysis of this accounting technique and its implications will be undertaken in Chapter 11 on the measurement of income. Here, we will examine primarily the nature of the deferred credit to which it gives rise.

For purposes of understanding how this deferred tax credit arises, let us consider the example of the depreciation deducted under circumstances where a company may elect an accelerated-depreciation method for tax purposes while using the straight-line method for book purposes. Since more depreciation is deducted for tax purposes in the early years, two things are evident: (1) there is a tax deferral in the early years and (2) it will have to be made up in the later years since in no event can depreciation for tax purposes exceed the total original cost. Thus, in theory, the tax savings are temporary; and under tax allocation, these savings are not used to reduce the tax expense but are rather accumulated as a deferred tax liability.

In practice, as a study by the firm of Price Waterhouse and Company (as well as other studies) shows, this "deferred tax liability" is rarely paid in full.[7] The reason for this is that most companies keep expanding their plant, with inflation swelling the nominal dollar amounts further, so that every year there is new accelerated depreciation on new facilities to balance—and usually outweigh—the reduced depreciation on facilities that got the accelerated treatment earlier.[8]

The accounting profession has adopted the concept of comprehensive tax allocation and now regards deferred taxes as a liability.

Now that we have covered the entire spectrum of that family of accounts designated as deferred credits, we can clearly see that each must be examined and understood on its own merits if its significance to the analyst it to be properly assessed.

IMPLICATIONS FOR ANALYSIS

The key to the proper analysis of deferred credits is a clear understanding of what has brought them about. In the discussion concerning the accounting principles involved, we have pointed out that they encompass a wide variety of dissimilar items.

---

[7] It is interesting to note that in Britain, deferred tax accounting is now used only on a partial basis.

[8] Enterprises whose plant is shrinking are generally not likely to remain profitable for very long. Under such circumstances, they will not pay income taxes in any event.

Those items that represent prepayments on services yet to be performed or goods yet to be delivered must be regarded as temporary sources of funds. In fact, often advances on contracts yet to be executed serve exactly the purpose of affording temporary financing to the supplier.

Deferred revenues may be viewed by the analyst as items that are on their way to the income stream of a company. What should not be lost sight of is the fact that many such items do not represent pure income elements as may be the case with interest or deferred installment sale profit that are deemed to be earned by the mere passage of time without the incurrence of additional expense. Thus, deferred subscription income represents the amount received in advance for magazines yet to be delivered. In spite of the fact that the earning of such subscription revenue will require paper, printing, editorial, and postage expense, such costs are usually not provided for when the revenue is deferred. Thus, while such items do represent temporary sources of funds, they are not sources of net profit and may, in fact, ultimately result in a net loss.

Certain deferred income items are clearly created, not for the purposes of fair presentation of financial positions but rather for purposes of income smoothing or equalization. Thus, the "bargain purchase credit" discussed earlier has as its main purpose and justification the smoothing of income over a period of years and must be regarded as such. Similarly the ratable taking up of installment sales profit is designed to provide for the contingency of possible noncollection of the sales price.

Perhaps the most confusing deferred credit to many analysts is the deferred tax credit. Because of its size, it is, by far, the most important item in this category. Its location in the twilight zone between liabilities and equity indicates that it is neither, but that in itself does not shed light on its true nature.

The reason that the deferred tax credit is not a liability is that it lacks some of the more important characteristics of debt. The government has no present claim for taxes nor is there a timetable for repayment. While the deferred tax account represents the loss of future deductibility of assets for tax purposes, the drawing down of this account to reduce tax expenses depends on future developments, such as asset acquisition and depreciation policies that are not predictable with certainty.

This kind of uncertainty attests to the fact that the deferred tax credit is also not in the nature of equity capital because it represents a tax benefit in the nature of a postponement of taxes rather than a savings of taxes.

The most meaningful thing that can be said about this account from the point of view of financial analysis is that it represents an often important source of cash derived from the postponement of taxes and that the duration of the overall postponement depends on factors such as the future growth or stability of the company's depreciable assets pool. It is the assessment of such factors and their future likelihood that will be helpful to the analysis of the deferred tax account.

The analyst who concludes that all or part of the deferred income taxes should be eliminated would make the following analytical adjusting entry:

Deferred Income Taxes (current and noncurrent credits) X
  Deferred Income Taxes (current and noncurrent debits) ..   Y
  Retained Earnings ....   Z

Elimination of the annual provision for deferred taxes can be effected by the following adjusting entry:

Deferred Income Taxes X
  Income Tax Expense   X

In some cases, the debits and credits of the above entry may be reversed.

MINORITY INTEREST

Found among liabilities, and sometimes in the equity section, but not really representing an immediate claim on company resources, are the minority interests in consolidated entities. These represent the proportionate interest of minority stockholders in a majority-owned subsidiary that is consolidated. Since all the net assets (i.e., assets less liabilities) of the subsidiary are included in the consolidated statements, the minority's portion is shown on the credit, or financing, side of the consolidated balance sheet. (See Chapter 9.) Chapter 18 includes a discussion of the analytical treatment accorded to minority interests.

RESERVES AND PROVISIONS

Another group of accounts, found between long-term liabilities and the stockholders' equity section, is that of reserves and provisions. These accounts are often lumped together or even found among current liabilities or as deductions from related asset accounts; consequently, it is most useful to classify them broadly so as to facilitate an understanding of their true nature.

The first category is most correctly described as comprising provisions for liabilities and obligations that have a high probability of occurrence, but which are in dispute or are uncertain in amount. As is the case with many financial statement descriptions, neither the title nor the location in the financial statement can be relied upon as a rule of thumb guide to the nature of an account. Thus, the best key to analysis is a thorough understanding of the business and financial transactions that give rise to the account. The following are representative items in this group: provisions for product guarantees, service guarantees, and warranties, which are established in recognition of the fact that these undertakings involve future costs that are certain to arise though presently impossible to measure exactly and whose timing is uncertain. Consequently, the provision is established by a charge to income at the time products covered by guarantees are sold, in an amount estimated on the basis of experience or on the basis of any other reliable factor.

Another type of obligation that must be provided for on the best basis available is the liability for unredeemed trading stamps issued. To the company issuing the trading stamps, there is no doubt about the liability to redeem the stamps for merchandise. The only uncertainty concerns the number of stamps that will be presented for redemption.

An important group of future costs that must be provided for is that of employee compensation. These, in turn, give rise to provisions for vacation pay, deferred compensation, incentive compensation, supplemental unemployment benefits, bonus plans, welfare plans, and severance pay.

Finally, the category of estimated liabilities includes provisions for claims arising out of pending or existing litigation.

The second category comprises reserves for expenses and losses, which by experience or estimate are very likely to occur in the future and which should properly be provided for by current charges to operations.

One group within this category comprises reserves for operating costs such as maintenance, repairs, painting, or furnace relining. Thus, for example, since furnace relining jobs may be expected to be required at regularly recurring intervals, they are provided for ratably by charges to operations in order to avoid charging the entire cost to the year in which the actual relining takes place.

Another group comprises provisions for future losses stemming from decisions or actions already taken. Included in this group are reserves for relocation, replacement, modernization, and discontinued operations.

ACCOUNTING FOR CONTINGENCIES

SFAS 5 sets definitive criteria for the accrual and disclosure of loss contingencies.

A loss contingency is defined in the *Statement* as an existing condition, situation, or set of circumstances involving uncertainty as to possible loss that will be resolved when one or more future events occur or fail to occur. Examples provided of loss contingencies are litigation, threat of expropriation, collectibility of receivables, claims arising from product warranties or product defects, self-insured risks, and possible catastrophe losses of property and casualty insurance companies.

The *Statement* specifies two conditions, both of which must be met before a provision for a loss contingency should be charged to income.

First, it must be probable that an asset had been impaired or a liability incurred at the date of a company's financial statements. Implicit in that condition is that it must be probable that a future event or events will occur confirming the fact of the loss. The second condition is that the amount of loss can be reasonably estimated. The effect of applying these criteria is that a loss will be accrued only when it is reasonably estimable and relates to the current or a prior period.

In the Board's opinion, losses from uncollectible receivables and obligations related to product warranties and product defects would normally meet the conditions for accrual at the time a sale is made. On the other hand, accrual for loss or damage of a company's property and loss from injury to others, damage to the property of others, and business interruption—sometimes referred to as self-insurance risks—would not be appropriate until the actual event of loss has taken place. Catastrophe losses of property and casualty insurance companies and reinsurance companies would not be accruable until the catastrophe has occurred. According to the *Statement,* catastrophe losses do not meet the conditions for accrual because predictions of losses over relatively short periods of time are subject to substantial deviations. Accruals for losses from such matters as expropriation, litigation, claims, and assessments would depend on the facts in each case.

The *Statement* permits appropriations of retained earnings for specified risks provided these are kept in the equity section of the balance sheet and are not used to relieve the income statement of actual losses (see also Chapter 8).

The *Statement* requires that if no accrual is made for a loss contingency because one or both of the conditions for accrual are not met, disclosure of the contingency shall be made when there is at least a reasonable possibility that a loss may have been incurred. The disclosure shall indicate the nature of the contingency and shall give an estimate of the possible loss or range of loss, or state that such an estimate cannot be made.

IMPLICATIONS FOR ANALYSIS

Provisions, such as for service guarantees and warranties, represent, in effect, revenue received for services yet to be performed. Of importance to the analyst is the adequacy of the provision that is often established on the basis of prior experience or, absent that, on the basis of other estimates. Concern with adequacy of amount is a prime factor in the analysis of all other reserves, whatever their purpose. Reserves and provisions appearing above the equity section should almost invariably be created by means of charges to income. They are designed to assign charges to the income statement based on when they are incurred rather then when they are paid.

Analysts must always be aware of the possibility that some liabilities are either not recognized or are underprovided for.

ILLUSTRATION 4.   One example of such liabilities are unredeemed frequent flyer mileage credits entitling airline passengers to billions of miles of free travel. Frequent flyer programs which assure customer loyalty and have other marketing benefits are not cost free. Yet, so far, airlines have resisted providing realistically for these obligations and a two-year effort by the American Institute of CPAs to formulate accounting guidelines for their recognition ended in a decision to drop further consideration of this project.

Reserves for future losses represent a category of accounts that require particular scrutiny. While conservatism in accounting calls for recognition of losses as they can be determined or clearly foreseen, companies tend, particularly in loss years, to overprovide for losses yet to be incurred such as on disposal of assets, relocation, or plant closings. Overprovision does, of course, shift expected future losses to a present period that already shows adverse results. (A more extended discussion of such practices will be found in Chapter 11.) The problem with such reserves is that once established there is no further accounting for the expenses and losses that are charged against them. Only in certain financial statements required to be filed with the SEC (such as Form 10-K) are details of changes in reserves required, and even here there is no requirement for detailed disclosure of the nature of the changes. Normally, no information is given, and the analyst must adopt a critical attitude toward the establishment of such reserves and the means of their disposition.

Reserves have traditionally been a popular management device for earnings manipulation and smoothing. Overprovision of loss reserves were recorded in years when results of operations were richer than management wanted to report, or when they were so poor that the creation of a cushion for the future did not matter to reported results which were already adverse.

SFAS 5 has gone a long way toward removing or at least reducing this management option. The much stricter criteria that must now be met means that greater earnings volatility will be experienced by companies subject to foreign risks, casualty insurers, self-insurers, and companies in certain industries such as oil (e.g., risks affecting offshore rigs and tankers).

The *Statement* also recognized that "accounting reserves" do not protect against risk, have no "cash flow" significance, and do not provide an alternative to insurance.

The analyst cannot, however, safely assume that overprovisions or, for that matter, underprovisions for losses are a thing of the past. Analysts should always attempt to obtain the full details of reserves by category and amount. Under the Internal Revenue Code, only a few categories of anticipated losses are specifically tax deductible. Thus, one method by which the analyst can detect undisclosed provisions for future expenses or losses is by an analysis of deferred taxes. The book expense not currently allowable for tax purposes should have its effect on the deferred (prepaid) tax account.

ILLUSTRATION 5.   Cigna Corporation, a large property and casualty insurer, provides a good example of how tenuous the reserve estimation process can be in what is admittedly an industry where surprises can and do happen.

    At the end of 1983 Cigna, according to the company, could look back on 10 years of very stable patterns of claims. (Insurance reserves are designed to provide for such claims.) During 1984, however, the incidence and severity of claims suddenly worsened. The company considered this an aberration and did not increase reserves for future losses. Only an intensive year-end review in 1985 revealed enormous miscalculations. In early 1986 the company announced a charge to income of $1.2 billion (!) in order to bring 1985 year-end insurance reserves to required levels. In 1985 as well as in prior years the auditor's opinion was unqualified. And yet, it is obvious that the net income of many prior years was seriously misstated.

It is interesting to note that the disclosure requirements of *SFAS 5* with respect to contingency losses charged to income appear weaker than those concerning unbooked amounts. The analyst needs as much disclosure as possible because it is important to assess the adequacy of provisions for future losses, particularly in such areas as claims and litigation where existing guidelines and standards are far from clear or rigorous.

A study by Professor Robert D. Fesler[9] found that of 126 law suits lost by publicly traded companies almost 36 percent were not even disclosed in years preceding the loss. Among the conclusions reached by the study author were that companies are reluctant to disclose pending litigation and that wide reporting diversity will continue. The implication for analysis is that the possibility of a lack of disclosure of significant loss contingencies cannot be ruled out.

COMMITMENTS

Commitments are claims that may occur upon the future performance under a contract. They are not given expression in accounting records, since the mere signing of an executory contract or the issuance of a purchase order does not result in a completed transaction.

Examples of commitments are long-term noncancelable contracts to purchase goods or services at specified prices or purchase contracts for

---

[9] Reported in the *Journal of Accountancy,* July 1990, p. 15

fixed assets that call for payments during construction. In a sense, a lease agreement is also regarded by some as a form of commitment.

Commitments call for disclosure of all the factors surrounding the obligation, including amount, conditions, timing, and other facts of importance.

For example, Intermec Company revealed the following commitment in its annual report:

> In March 1990, the Company signed a patent license agreement with its former principal supplier of hand-held laser scanning devices. This agreement provides that the Company may manufacture and sell certain laser scanning products of its own design and that the Company pay minimum royalties and purchase minimum quantities of other products from that supplier.

Professor Yuji Ijirr[10] has defined "firm commitments" as those whose performance cannot be avoided without incurring severe penalty and recommends their recording as assets and liabilities.

FINANCIAL INSTRUMENTS WITH OFF-BALANCE-SHEET RISKS

New and innovative financial instruments have been created in recent years primarily due to factors such as deregulation, foreign exchange and interest rate volatility, and tax law changes.

The FASB added a project on financial instruments to its agenda in 1986. As an interim measure, pending completion of the recognition and measurement phases of the financial instruments project, the Board issued *SFAS 105* (1990), "Disclosure of Information about Financial Instruments with Off-Balance-Sheet Risk and Financial Instruments with Concentrations of Credit Risk." This accounting standard establishes requirements for all entities to disclose information principally about financial instruments with off-balance-sheet risk of accounting loss.

All entities will be required to disclose the following information about financial instruments with off-balance-sheet risk of accounting loss:

- The face, contract, or notional principal amount.
- The nature and terms of the instruments and a discussion of their credit and market risk, cash requirements, and related accounting policies.
- The accounting loss the entity would incur if any party to the financial instruments failed completely to perform according to the terms

---

[10] FASB, "Recognition of Contractual Rights and Obligations" (Stamford, Conn., 1981).

of the contract, and the collateral or other security, if any, for the amount due proved to be of no value to the entity.

• The entity's policy for requiring collateral or other security on financial instruments it accepts, and a description of collateral on instruments presently held.

Information about significant concentrations of credit risk from an individual counterparty or groups of counterparties for all financial instruments is also required.

Examples of financial instruments with off-balance-sheet risk include outstanding loan commitments written, standby and commercial letters of credit written, financial guarantees written, options written, recourse obligations or receivables sold, and similar obligations.

SFAS 105 specifies disclosure requirements only for credit risk and market risk.

CONTINGENT LIABILITIES

Business enterprise is subject to constant and all-pervading uncertainty. It is assumed that the informed reader of the financial statements is aware of this. However, certain events may point to specific probabilities and contingencies in the future and should be disclosed as such. *Accounting Research Bulletin (ARB) 50* states that "in accounting, a contingency is an existing condition, situation, or set of circumstances, involving a considerable degree of uncertainty, which may, through a related future event, result in the acquisition or loss of an asset, or the incurrence or avoidance of a liability, usually with the concurrence of gain or loss."

The basic nature of a contingency is its dependence on a future development or intervening factor or decision by an outside factor. Usually the contingency is uncertain as to probability of occurrence, timing, and amount. The financial statements must disclose the degree of probability of occurrence and, if possible, the best estimate of financial impact.

Examples of contingent liabilities are those that could arise from litigation, from guarantees of performance, from agreements and contracts, such as purchase or repurchase agreements, and from tax assessments or renegotiation claims.

Wells Fargo & Co. makes the following disclosure:

Commitments and Contingent Liabilities
In the normal course of business, there are various commitments outstanding and contingent liabilities that are properly not reflected in the accompanying financial statements. Losses, if any, resulting from these commitments are not anticipated to be material. The approximate amounts of such commitments are summarized below:

	In millions
Standby letters of credit	$ 2,400
Commercial and similar letters of credit ...	400
Commitments to extend credit[1]	17,300
Commitments to purchase futures and forward contracts	5,000
Commitments to purchase foreign and U.S. currencies	1,500

[1] Excludes credit card and other revolving credit loans.

Standby letters of credit include approximately $400 million of participations purchased and are net of approximately $300 million of participations sold. Standby letters of credit are issued to cover performance obligations, including those which back financial instruments (financial guarantees).

In 1990 the New York Times Company reported the following as contingent liabilities:

There are various libel and other legal actions that have arisen in the ordinary course of business and are now pending against the Company. Such actions are usually for amounts greatly in excess of the payments, if any, that may be required to be made. It is the opinion of management after reviewing such actions with counsel that the ultimate liability which might result from such actions would not have a material adverse effect on the consolidated financial statements.

FASB *Interpretation 34* requires that indirect guarantees of indebtedness (such as to advance funds or to cover fixed charges of another entity) be disclosed as contingencies.

The SEC staff has expressed its views regarding accounting for and disclosure of guarantees of debts of others.

Staff Accounting Bulletin No. 60 (1986) states that when aggregate amounts of loan guarantees are material to consolidated equity or when there is a material effect on results of operations before income taxes and realized gains or losses on investments, the guarantor should:

Recognize any fee income over the guarantee period.

Disclose the guarantee by footnote, if material.

Perform an ongoing assessment of the probability of loss.

Recognize direct costs associated with the guarantee in a manner relative to the fee income.

The bulletin also points out the disclosures that should be made with respect to debt guarantees, which include, among others:

Description of the obligation guaranteed and the degree of risk involved.

Amount of exposure with respect to guaranteed debts of others and how the participation of others in the guarantees was treated in determining that exposure.

Whether any reserves for losses have been provided by charges against income.

The SEC has encouraged—but not required—companies to provide forward-looking information about possible future events. The Commission has been reviewing the content of Management's Discussion and Analysis (MD & A) sections of filings with it in order to make them more informative and useful (see also Chapter 20).

IMPLICATIONS FOR ANALYSIS— ASSESSING UNCERTAINTIES

Due to the uncertainties involved, the descriptions of commitments and especially of contingent liabilities in footnotes are often vague and indeterminate. In effect, that means that the burden of assessing the possible impact of the contingencies as well as the probabilities of their occurrence is passed on to the reader. The analyst should always determine whether the auditors feel that a contingency is serious enough and material enough to call for elaboration in their report. The auditor report in the 1990 financial statements of Harsco Corporation contained the following:

> As discussed in Note 10 to the consolidated financial statements, the Company is subject to the Government exercising an additional option under a certain contract. If the Government exercises this option, additional losses could be incurred by the Company. Also, the Company has filed or is in the process of filing various claims against the Government relating to certain contracts. The ultimate outcome of these matters cannot presently be determined. Accordingly, no provision for such potential additional losses or recognition of possible recovery from such claims (other than relating to the Federal Excise Tax and related claims) has been reflected in the accompanying financial statements.

In this case the analyst is facing a situation in which the auditors express their inability to form a judgment on the outcome of certain events.

Care must be exercised in accepting management's opinions on potential liabilities. In 1981 Manville Corporation stated that it had substantial defenses to legal actions against it and in 1982 it declared bankruptcy because of asbestos-related law suits.

The analyst must be alert to *potential* liabilities. Managements may be reluctant to divulge "unasserted claims" and so may their lawyers. In some cases, they may at the time be unknown even to the potential plaintiffs. However, as the case of Westinghouse Electric's uranium supply contracts commitment has shown, potential liabilities have a way of becoming actual liabilities.

The area of potential liabilities that overhang companies is constantly changing and evolving. If the past is a guide, auditors usually react to, rather than foresee, areas of potential danger. By the time new rules are written it is usually too late for the investor or lender whom the analyst represents. In recent years companies have obligated themselves to substantive payments to executives known as "golden parachutes" in the event control of the company changes hands. Yet very little is revealed, let alone provided for, in company financial statements for these potential fund drains.

Banks present a particularly good current example where enormous exposure to loss has been largely ignored or confined to obscure footnotes. One such area is that of losses on foreign loans (which we alluded to before) and where all the signs pointing to impairments of assets are present but where banks and their auditors continue to look the other way.

Another area is that of off-balance-sheet commitments of many banks. They represent such diverse commitments as standby letters of credit, municipal bond and commercial paper guarantees, currency swaps, and foreign exchange contracts. Unlike loans, these commitments represent promises that banks are betting (or hoping?) they will not have to keep. And also unlike loans, these do not show up on the balance sheet, with the result that financial analysis may not fully identify the enormous risks to which banks are in reality exposed.

There are, however, positive developments which hold the promise to be helpful to analysts. One such development are the disclosure requirements of *SFAS 105* discussed above as "Financial Instruments with Off-Balance-Sheet Risks." Completion of the FASB's project on financial instruments promises to result in additional useful disclosures.

While utilizing all the information available, the analyst must bring his own critical evaluation to bear on the assessment of all the contingencies to which the company may be subject. This process must draw not only on available disclosure and information but also on an understanding of industry conditions and practices.

QUESTIONS

1. What are the major disclosure requirements in SEC *FRR No. 1*, section 203, regarding the terms of short-term debt?
2. What are the conditions required by *SFAS 6* that will demonstrate the ability of a company to refinance its short-term debt on a long-term basis?
3. How do bond discounts and premiums usually arise? How are they accounted for?

4. Both the conversion feature of debt as well as warrants attached to debt instruments aim at increasing the attractiveness of debt securities and at lowering their interest cost. Describe how the costs of these two similar features are accounted for.
5. Describe the nature of *SFAS 47* and its major disclosure requirements.
6. What are the major provisions of *SFAS 76* regarding extinguishment of debt?
7. What should the analyst be aware of if a company includes short-term bank debt in its current liabilities?
8. How does the analyst of financial statements evaluate an enterprise's liabilities—both present and contingent?
9. *a.* What are the criteria, stipulated by *SFAS 13,* for classifying leases by the lessee?
    b. Provide a summary of accounting for leases by lessee according to *SFAS 13.*
10. *a.* What are the different classifications of leases—according to *SFAS 13*—by lessors? What are the criteria for classifying each type?
    b. What are the accounting procedures for leases by lessors according to *SFAS 13?*
11. What are the provisions of *SFAS 13* concerning leases involving real estate?
12. What are the principal disclosures required by lessees and lessors according to *SFAS 13?*
13. What are the implications of *SFAS 13* for the financial analyst?
14. Companies use various financing methods to avoid reporting debt on the balance sheet. What are some of these methods?
15. Under *SFAS 77* what criteria must a company meet before a transfer of receivables with a guarantee can be booked as a sale rather than as a loan?
16. Under *SFAS 87* on pensions, what is:
    a. The accumulated benefit obligation?
    b. The projected benefit obligation?
17. *FASB 106,* dealing with the accounting for other postretirement employee benefits, has drawn on the accounting model of *SFAS 87,* with some important differences. What are these differences?
18. What are the required disclosures under *SFAS 106?*
19. What types of equity securities are akin to debt? Discuss.
20. Distinguish between different kinds of deferred credits appearing on a balance sheet. How should those be analyzed?
21. Describe the nature of deferred tax credits. How should the analyst interpret this account?
22. Into what types should reserves and provisions be subdivided for purposes of financial statement analysis?
23. Why must the analyst be particularly alert to the accounting for reserves for future costs and losses?
24. *SFAS 105* established disclosure requirements about financial instruments with off-balance-sheet risk of accounting loss. What are they?
25. *a.* What is a loss contingency? Give some examples.
    b. What two conditions (as specified by *SFAS 5*) must be met before a provision for a loss contingency can be charged to income?

Chapter 8

ANALYSIS OF STOCKHOLDERS' EQUITY

The stockholders' equity section of the balance sheet represents the investment of the ownership in the net assets of a business entity. While the claims of the ownership are junior to those in the current and long-term liability sections of the balance sheet, they represent, on the other hand, residual claims to all assets, once the claims of creditors have been satisfied. Thus, while being exposed to the maximum risk associated with the enterprise, the ownership is entitled to all the residual rewards that are associated with it.

The accounting for the equity section as well as the presentation, classification, and footnote disclosure associated therewith have certain basic objectives, the most important among which are:

1. To classify and distinguish the major sources of capital contributed to the entity.
2. To set forth the rights and priorities of the various classes of stockholders and the manner in which they rank in partial or final liquidation.
3. To set forth the legal restrictions to which the distribution of capital funds may be subject for whatever reason.
4. To disclose the contractual, legal, managerial, or financial restrictions to which the distribution of current or retained earnings may be subject.
5. To disclose the terms and provisions of convertible securities, of stock options, and of other arrangements involving the future issuance of stock, contingent and otherwise.

THE DISTINCTION BETWEEN LIABILITY AND EQUITY INSTRUMENTS

In 1990 the FASB had issued a DISCUSSION MEMORANDUM entitled "Distinguishing between Liability and Equity Instruments and Accounting for Instruments with Characteristics of Both." The purpose of this study, which is part of the Board's major agenda project on financial instruments and off-balance-sheet financing, is to provide a basis for considering the issues involved in *distinguishing between liability and equity instruments,* and accounting for financial instruments that have characteristics of both liabilities and equity.

The following are some of the issues discussed in the memorandum:

- Is a financial instrument, such as mandatorily redeemable preferred stock or a put option written on an issuer's common stock, that obligates an enterprise to redeem or repurchase its own stock for a specified or determinable amount (that is, to deliver assets to owners), a liability or equity instrument?

- Is a financial instrument, such as a stock purchase warrant or an employee stock option, that obligates an enterprise to issue its own stock for a specified or determinable amount, a liability or equity instrument?

- Is a right to issue or repurchase an enterprise's own stock for a specified or determinable amount an asset or a part of equity?

- Should a third "capital" element be added to handle instruments that combine certain features of liabilities and equity? If so, how should that element be defined?

CLASSIFICATION OF CAPITAL STOCK

There are two basic kinds of capital stock—preferred and common. There are a number of different varieties within each category, and these, too, have basic differences worth noting.

The preferred stock is usually preferred in liquidation and preferred as to dividends. It may be entitled to par value in liquidation or it may be entitled to a premium. On the other hand, its rights to dividends are generally fixed, although they may be cumulative, which means that preferred shareholders are entitled to arrearages of dividends before the common stockholders may receive any dividends. The preferred features, as well as the fixed nature of the dividend, give the preferred stock some of the earmarks of debt with the important difference that preferred stockholders are not generally entitled to demand redemption of their shares. Nevertheless, there are preferred-stock issues that have set redemption dates and that may require sinking funds to be established for that purpose. These are more akin to debt than to equity and are discussed in Chapter 7.

Characteristics of preferred stock that may make them more akin to common stock are dividend participation rights, voting rights, and rights of conversion into common stock.

Within the preferred stock classes we may find a variety of orders of priority and preference relating to dividends and liquidation rights.

The common stock is the basic ownership equity of a company, having no preference but reaping all residual rewards as well as being subject to all losses. Occasionally, there is more than one class of common stock. In such cases, the distinctions between one class and the other express themselves in dividend, voting, or other rights.

The preferred stock generally has a par value that may or may not be the amount at which it was originally issued. Common stock may have a par value, and if not, it is usually assigned a stated value. The par value of the common stock is a matter of legal requirements and has no substantive significance for analytical purposes.

Disclosure Regarding Capital Stock

Proper disclosure requires that an analysis and explanation of changes in the number of shares of capital stock be given in the financial statements or in the notes related thereto. Such changes may be due to a variety of reasons including the following:

1. *Increases in capital stock outstanding:*
   a. Sale of stock.
   b. Conversion of debentures or preferred stock.
   c. Issuance pursuant to stock dividends or stock splits.
   d. Issuance of stock in acquisitions or mergers.
   e. Issuance of stock pursuant to stock options granted or warrants exercised.
2. *Decreases in capital stock outstanding:*
   a. Purchase and retirement of stock.
   b. Purchase of treasury stock.
   c. Reverse stock splits.

Another important aspect of disclosure with regard to the various classes of capital stock is the various options held by others which, when exercised, would cause the number of shares outstanding to be increased. Such options include:

1. Conversion rights of debenture or preferred stock into common.
2. Warrants outstanding for a specified period entitling the holder to exchange them for stock under specified conditions.
3. Stock options under supplementary compensation and bonus plans that call for the issuance of capital stock over a period of time at prices fixed in advance, such as qualified stock option plans and "employee stock purchase plans."
4. Commitments to issue capital stock, such as under merger agreements that call for additional consideration contingent on the happening of an event such as the reaching of certain earning levels by the acquired company, and so on.

The importance of such disclosures lies in the need to alert all interested parties to the potential increase in the number of shares outstanding. The degree of the resultant dilution in earnings and book value per share depends, of course, on such factors as the amount to be paid in per share and other rights given up when conversions of securities are effected.

Many years ago, the accounting profession had almost completely ignored the effect that potential dilution has on such basic valuation yardsticks as earnings per share (EPS) and, to a lesser extent, book value per share. Alerted at last by the use of ever more complex securities, the profession has recognized that dilution represents a very real cost to a company, a cost that had been given little if any formal recognition in financial statements. The impact of dilution on EPS will be examined in Chapter 12. Problems in the computation of book value are examined at the end of this chapter.

Disclosure must be made of a variety of terms to which preferred stock may be subject, including:

1. *Dividend rights,* including participating and cumulative features.
2. *Liquidation rights.* In *APB Opinion 10* the board stated:

> Companies at times issue preferred (or other senior) stock which has a preference in involuntary liquidation considerably in excess of the par or stated value of the shares. The relationship between this preference in liquidation and the par or stated value of the shares may be of major significance to the users of the financial statements of those companies and the Board believes it highly desirable that it be prominently disclosed. Accordingly, the Board recommends that in these cases, the liquidation preference of the stock be disclosed in the equity section of the balance sheet in the aggregate, either parenthetically or "in short" rather than on a per share basis or by disclosure in notes.

Such disclosure is particularly important since the discrepancy between the par and liquidation value of preferred stock can be very significant as is the case, for example, in General Aniline & Film Corporation where at one point in time the par value was $3.9 million as against a liquidation value of $85.7 million!

3. *Redemption rights. SFAS 47* requires disclosure of mandatory redemption requirements of redeemable preferred stock. In *FRR* No. 1, section 211, the SEC requires separate balance sheet presentation of such shares. Because such shares have the characteristics of liabilities, they are considered in Chapter 7.
4. *Voting rights,* which may change with conditions such as arrearages in dividends.
5. *Conversion rights.*
6. *Sinking fund provisions,* which are not too common.
7. *Call provisions,* which usually protect the preferred stockholder against premature redemption. Call premiums often decrease over time.

In addition to a description of terms, disclosure must be made of any conditions affecting the relative standing of the various classes of stock such as, for example, dividend arrearages on preferred stock, which must generally be paid before the common stock can receive any distribution at all.

Additional Capital

Amounts paid in for capital stock are usually divided into two parts. One part is assigned to the par or stated value of capital shares, and the rest is shown in the capital surplus section. The term *surplus* is actually falling into disuse so that the additional capital section contains accounts having such descriptive titles as Capital in Excess of Par or Stated Value, Additional Capital, Additional Paid-in Capital, and Paid-In Capital. No matter what the title, these accounts signify the amounts paid in for capital stock in excess of par or stated value.

The additional accounts in the "capital" group do not result only from amounts paid in excess of par but include also charges or credits from a variety of other capital transactions, examples of which are:

1. Gains or losses from sale of treasury stock.
2. Capital changes arising from business combinations.
3. Capital donations, usually shown separately as donated capital.
4. Capital stock expenses, merger expenses, and other costs of a capital nature.
5. Capitalization of retained earnings by means of stock dividends.

Informative financial statements must contain a reconciliation of all capital surplus accounts so as to explain the changes which have occurred therein.

Treasury Stock

Treasury stock is stock that has once been issued and was outstanding and that has been subsequently reacquired by the company. Treasury stock is generally carried at cost, and the most common method of presentation is to deduct such cost from the total equity section. Some companies that reserve their own treasury stock for such purposes as profit sharing, contingent compensation, deferred compensation, or other compensation plans, or for purposes of acquisitions of other companies do sometimes present such stock among assets which, while not a very logical procedure, is nevertheless acceptable.

RETAINED EARNINGS

While the capital stock and capital surplus accounts show primarily the capital contribution by various classes of stock, the Retained Earnings account represents generally the accumulation of undistributed earnings since inception. Conversely, a deficit account represents the accumulated net losses of the corporation.

Although some states permit distributions to shareholders from capital surplus accounts, such distributions represent, in effect, capital distributions. Thus, the Retained Earnings account is the prime source of dividend distributions to shareholders, and amounts distributed by charge to other accounts do not, strictly speaking, deserve the label *dividend.*

Dividends

The most common form of dividend is the cash dividend that, once declared, becomes a liability of the company. Another form of dividend is the dividend in kind, such as dividends in goods (e.g., cases of liquor) or dividends in the stock of another corporation. Such dividends should be valued at the fair market value of the assets distributed.

Yet another form of dividend is the stock dividend that, in effect, represents the permanent capitalization of company earnings. As evidence of such a shift from retained earnings to the permanent capital accounts, shareholders receive additional shares. GAAP require that the stock dividends be valued at the fair market value of the shares to be issued as determined at the date of declaration. This principle is designed to put a realistic limit to the number of shares that can be issued as stock dividends. A stock distribution exceeding 20–25 percent is not to be accounted as a stock dividend and should instead be accounted for as a stock split. The latter represents, in essence, the subdivision of the net corporate pie into smaller shares.

Prior Period Adjustments

SFAS 16 requires that, except for corrections of errors in the financial statements of a prior period and adjustments that result from realization of income tax benefits of preacquisition operating loss carry-forwards of purchased subsidiaries, all items of profit and loss recognized during a period, including accruals of estimated losses from loss contingencies, be included in the determination of net income for that period. The *Statement* permits limited restatements in interim periods of an enterprise's current fiscal year.

In addition to dividends and prior year adjustments, changes in retained earnings may include adjustments due to business combinations and other capital adjustments such as premiums on redemption of preferred stock losses on sales of treasury stock, and so forth.

Appropriations of Retained Earnings

By managerial action, or in compliance with legal requirements, retained earnings are often appropriated or reserved.

Appropriated retained earnings, also known as reserves, established by managerial action include reserves for general contingencies, plant expansion, self-insurance, and other business contingencies. The basic idea here is to preserve a specific amount of capital that is available for absorption of possible losses or is frozen to provide permanent funds, such as for expansion. Thus, such appropriations should never be used to relieve the income statement of charges that are properly chargeable against it. After having served their purpose, such appropriations should be restored to unappropriated retained earnings.

Appropriations of retained earnings in an amount equal to the cost of treasury stock purchased is an example of appropriations established under the legal requirements of certain states. Such appropriations are restored to retained earnings after the treasury stock is sold, retired, or otherwise disposed of.

Restrictions on Retained Earnings

An important aspect of disclosure relating to retained earnings involves restrictions imposed on its distribution as dividends. This is, obviously, information of importance to potential investors and others. Examples of such restrictions which stem from debt indentures are:

The Leslie Fay Companies:

On December 29, 1990, under the most restrictive of these agreements, approximately $33,000,000 was available for distribution of earnings to stockholders. Presently, the Company has no plans to declare any dividends.

Allied Van Lines:

Restrictive loan covenants. The various loans include restrictive covenants which provide as follows: That the Company must maintain consolidated tangible net worth of $28,000,000 plus 50 percent of cumulative net income commencing from period January 1, 1985; current assets not less than 115 percent of current liabilities at all times and 120 percent at year-end; long-term debt not more than 35 percent of consolidated tangible net worth; income available for fixed charges not less than 125 percent of fixed charges; guarantees of loans made to or leases entered into by agents or owner-operators cannot exceed $3,500,000; the Company must maintain consolidated net working capital of not less than $6,000,000; and the sum of cash flow (principally working capital provided from operations) plus current notes receivable must be at least 130 percent of current maturities of long-term debt.

BOOK VALUE PER SHARE

The term *book value* is conventional terminology referring to net asset value, that is, total assets reduced by the senior claims against them. Thus, the book value of the common stock equity is equal to the total assets less liabilities and claims of securities senior to the common stock, such as preferred stock, mostly at amounts at which they are carried on the financial statements but also unbooked claims of the senior securities. A simple way of computing book value is to add up the common stock equity accounts and reduce the total by any senior claims not reflected in the financial statements such as preferred stock dividend arrearages, liquidation premiums, or other asset preferences to which the preferred shares are entitled.

Book value is almost always presented on a per share basis (the significance of this figure will be considered later in the chapter). Once the underlying principles of computation are understood, the calculation of book value is relatively simple.

ILLUSTRATION 1.   The following is the equity section of the Zero Corporation for periods ended in years 4 and 5:

	Year 5	*Year 4*
Preferred stock, 7% cumulative, par value $100 (authorized 4,000,000 shares; outstanding 3,602,811 shares)	$ 360,281,100	$ 360,281,100
Common stock (authorized 90,000,000 shares; outstanding 54,138,137 shares at December 31, year 5, and 54,129,987 shares at December 31, year 4)	3,264,581,527	3,122,464,738
Par value $16⅔ per share . . . . $ 902,302,283		
Income reinvested in business 2,362,279,244		
Total	3,624,862,627	3,482,745,838

The preferred shares are nonparticipating but are callable at 105. Dividends for 19×5 are in arrears.

Required:

Calculate the book value per share of both the common and preferred stock as of December 31, year 5.

Computations

	Preferred	+	Common	=	Total
Preferred stock* (@ $100) ..	$360,281,100				$ 360,281,100
Dividends in arrears (7%) ..	25,219,677				25,219,677
Common stock			$ 902,302,283		902,302,283
Retained earnings (net of amount attributed to dividend in arrears)			2,337,059,567		2,337,059,567
Total	385,500,777		3,239,361,850		$3,624,862,627
Divided by number of shares outstanding	3,602,811		54,138,137		
Book value per share	$107.00		$59.84		

* The call premium does not normally enter into the computation of book value per share because the call provision is at the option of company.

ILLUSTRATION 2.   The following is the stockholders' equity section of the balance sheet of the XYZ Company on June 30, year 1:

Preferred stock—authorized 200,000 shares, issued and outstanding 100,000 shares, par value $100; 6% cumulative, nonparticipating	$10,000,000
Common stock—authorized 375,000 shares, issued and outstanding 200,000 shares, par value $100	20,000,000
Capital contributed in excess of par value	5,000,000
Retained earnings (deficit)	(7,000,000)
Total stockholders' equity	$28,000,000

The preferred shares have a liquidation value of $105 and are callable at $110. No dividends have been declared or paid by the company for either the preferred or common shares for two years. Assume that the preferred stock has a preference on assets in liquidation.

Required:

Compute the book value (equity) per share of all classes of stock as of June 30, year 1.

Computations

	Preferred	*Common*
Par value	$10,500,000	$20,000,000
Dividends in arrears	1,200,000	
Net deficit (all applicable to common stock) .		(3,700,000)
Total	11,700,000	16,300,000
Divided by number of shares outstanding . . .	100,000	200,000
Book value (equity) per share	$117.00	$81.50

Explanations:
1. Liquidation value for preferred shares ($105) is used; call value does not enter into the computation of book value per share.
2. Preferred shares are entitled to two years' dividends (12% of $10,000,000 = $1,200,000).
3. Preference of assets for preferred shares means that the deficit is wholly applicable to the common.
4. Computation of net deficit:

Retained earnings (deficit)	$(7,000,000)
Paid-in capital	5,000,000
Dividends in arrears	(1,200,000)
Preferred liquidation premium . .	(500,000)
Net deficit	$(3,700,000)

As can be seen from the above illustrations, the major adjustments in book value per share computations arise from rights and priorities of securities that are senior to the common. In most cases, these are premiums and liquidation priority rights of a variety of classes of preferred stock.

Care must be taken to determine the liquidation value of preferred stock. Some companies have preferred stock issues outstanding that give the right to very substantial liquidation premiums that are far above the par value of such shares. The effect of such liquidation premiums on the book value of the common and other junior equities can be substantial.

ILLUSTRATION 3. In a listing application (A-25189) of Glen Alden Corporation appear the following details of book value computation:

Equity per share:
   Equity per share of Glen Alden, Warner, and the Surviving Corporation, based on the initial redemption values of the preferred stocks and on the consolidated balance sheets of Glen Alden and Warner at December 31 and August 27, respectively, and the pro forma combined balance sheet follows:

Initial redemption per share values	Preferred stocks	Glen Alden December 31,	Warner, August 27,	Pro forma surviving corporation
$ 52.50	Senior stock	$52.50		$ 52.50
$107.00	Class B senior stock			$100.70
$110.00	Preferred stock	$88.89		None
$ 90.00	Class C stock	$72.73		None
None	Common stock	None	$19.51	None

Based on the pro forma combined balance sheet, there would be no book value attributable to the preferred stock, class C stock, and common stock of the Surviving Corporation when the equity applicable to the senior stock and the class B senior stock is considered at aggregate initial redemption value. The aggregate initial redemption value of the senior stock and class B senior stock exceeds total pro forma stockholders' equity by approximately $141,816,000.

The pro forma initial redemption and liquidation prices of the preferred stocks in the aggregate ($343,821,848) exceed their stated values by $296,179,211, and such excess exceeds the aggregate amount of common stock and surplus by approximately $141,816,000. Upon liquidation, the senior stock is first in order of preference followed by the class B senior stock. The preferred stock and class C stock are junior to the class B senior stock, but rank on a parity with each other. There are no restrictions upon surplus arising out of such excess.

As the above example shows, the liquidation premium of the senior stocks is of such magnitude as to wipe out the entire residual book value of the junior preferred and common stock issues.

The accounting profession has, in *APB Opinion 10,* recognized the problem posed by preference rights in involuntary liquidation that are substantially in excess of stated par values. Thus, the *Opinion* recommends that the aggregate liquidation preference be prominently disclosed in the equity section of the balance sheet. The *Opinion* also calls for disclosure of call prices and dividend arrearages.

Judging by actual practice, the rules involving "common stock equivalents" that govern the computation of earnings per share (EPS) (see Chapter 12) do not seem to apply to the computation of book value per share. Nevertheless, a case can be made for extending the EPS rules to book value computations. The merger movement has given rise to increasingly complex securities, and there is not much justification for ignoring these in book value computations.

ILLUSTRATION 4.   Company A has the following simplified balance sheet:

Assets less current liabilities ... $1,000,000
Convertible debentures   100,000
Net assets .... $ 900,000
Common shares   100,000

The debentures are convertible into 20,000 shares of common stock.

The company also has warrants outstanding entitling the holder to buy 10,000 shares at $6 per share. Stock options to buy 10,000 shares at an average price of $8 per share are also outstanding.

The conventional method of book value calculations would yield a book value per share of $9 (net assets/common shares = $900,000/100,000).

Giving effect to possible conversions, the book value computation will look as follows:

Net assets (as above) .... $ 900,000
Add convertible debentures 100,000
Proceeds from exercise of warrants (10,000 × $6) 60,000
Proceeds from exercise of stock options (10,000 × $8) .   80,000
Adjusted net asset value $1,140,000

Common shares outstanding 100,000
Add:
   Conversion of debentures 20,000
   Exercise of warrants 10,000
   Exercise of options   10,000
Adjusted number of common shares 140,000
Book value per share ($1,140,000/140,000) $8.14

Clearly, the effect of conversions of debentures, options, and so forth, on book value depends on the conversion terms. If stock is converted at prices below conventional book value per share, the effect is, as in the above example, dilutive. Conversely, if the conversion is at prices above conventional book value, the effect will be antidilutive. Applying the conservative principles that have been devised by the accounting profession for the computation of EPS (see Chapter 12), antidilutive effects (i.e., those which enhance book value per share) would not be allowed to enter the computations.

Significance of Book Value

Once an important variable in investment decision making, book value has gradually dwindled in importance. The basic reason for this is that investment analysis generally emphasizes earning power and not asset size. Thus, the value of a company's securities is based primarily on the earning capacity of its asset base rather than on its size.

There are, of course, exceptions to this generalization, and they account for the continued use of the book value per share statistic:

1. Book value, properly adjusted, is often used in an assessment of merger terms.
2. Due to the fact that the rate base of public utilities often approximates its book value, this measure is important in this industry.
3. The analysis of companies that have mostly liquid assets such as those in the finance, investment, insurance, and banking fields, rightfully affords greater than usual importance to book values.
4. The analyst of high-grade bonds and preferred stock usually attaches considerable importance to asset coverage in addition to earning capacity.

There are, of course, other factors that make net assets a measure of some importance in financial analysis. A company's earnings growth is sooner or later dependent on growth in assets and, consequently, on a choice of how to finance them. A large asset base has, depending on its composition, a certain potential of profitable utilization.

The accounting considerations that enter into computation of book value should be thoroughly understood by any user of this statistic:

1. The carrying values of assets, particularly long-lived assets such as plant and equipment, long-term investments, and some inventories, is usually at cost and may differ significantly from current market values.[1] Moreover, such carrying values will, as was seen in the preceding chapters, vary according to the accounting principles selected. Thus, for instance, in times of rising prices, the carrying value of inventories under the LIFO method of inventory accounting will be lower than under the FIFO method.
2. Intangible assets of great value may not be reflected in book value nor are contingent liabilities, which may have a high probability of occurrence, usually so reflected.

The decline in the use of book value may be due to a lack of usefulness of this measure. It is, undoubtedly, also due to the very crude approaches taken in its reporting and application. Thus, for example, the blanket exclusion from book value of goodwill, patents, franchises, and other intangibles cannot make up for the lack of the analysis required to adopt this measure to the particular objective it is designed to meet. Either book value is computed on a "current value" basis or on a cost basis. In the

---

[1] The voluntary disclosure requirements of *SFAS 89* of the current cost of certain assets of specified companies (see Chapter 14) may be helpful in arriving at more realistic book value figures.

latter case, the arbitrary exclusion of intangible assets makes no sense. If, for example, book value is to be used in comparing the relative value of two companies engaged in merger negotiations, adjustments, such as the following, may be required so that an intelligent comparison can be made:

1. The carrying value of assets should be adjusted to current market values.
2. Differences in the application of accounting principles should be adjusted for.
3. Unrecorded intangibles should be given recognition.
4. Contingent liabilities should be assessed and given appropriate recognition.
5. Accounting and other errors should be adjusted on the books of both companies.

Other adjustments may also be called for. Thus, if the preferred stock has the characteristics of debt, it may be appropriate to capitalize it at the prevailing interest rate, thus reflecting the benefit or disadvantage of it to the company.

The emphasis of earning power has, as was discussed above, resulted in a de-emphasis of asset size. Sterile or unproductive assets are worse than worthless. They are often a drag on earnings because they require a minimum of upkeep and management expenses. Like any other analytical tools, book value is a measure that can be useful for certain purposes provided it is used with discrimination and understanding.

IMPLICATIONS FOR ANALYSIS

The accounting principles that apply to the equity section do not have a marked effect on income determination and, as a consequence, do not hold many pitfalls for the analyst. From an analytical point of view, the most significant information here relates to the composition of the capital accounts and to the restrictions to which they may be subject. It is important that the analyst know how to reconstruct and to explain changes in the capital accounts.

The composition of the equity capital is important because of provisions affecting the residual rights of the common equity. Such provisions include dividend participation rights, conversion rights, and the great variety of options and conditions that are characteristic of the complex securities frequently issued under merger agreements, most of which tend to dilute the common equity.

An analysis of restrictions imposed on the distribution of retained earnings by loan or other agreements will usually shed light on a company's freedom of action in such areas as dividend distributions or required levels of working capital. Such restrictions also shed light on the company's bargaining strength and standing in credit markets. Moreover, a careful reading of restrictive covenants will enable the analyst to assess how far a company is from being in default of these provisions.

QUESTIONS

1. What are the objectives of the classifications and the footnote disclosure associated with the equity section of the corporate balance sheet? Of what significance are such disclosures to readers of financial statements?
2. What features of a preferred stock issue make it akin to debt? What features make it more like common stock?
3. Why is it important from the point of view of the analyst of financial statements that the liquidation value of preferred stock, if different from par or stated value, be clearly disclosed?
4. Presidential Realty Corporation reported as follows on distributions paid on common stock:
   "The cash distributions on common stock were charged to paid-in surplus because the parent company has accumulated no earnings (other than its equity in undistributed earnings of certain subsidiaries) since its formation."
   a. Are these cash distributions dividends?
   b. Why do you suppose did this realty company make such distributions?
5. Why does the proper accounting for stock dividends require that the fair market value, rather than the par value, of the shares distributed be charged against retained earnings?
6. What items of gain or loss may be treated as prior period adjustments?
7. Some companies present "minority interests in subsidiary companies" between the long-term debt and the equity sections of the consolidated balance sheet; others present them as part of equity capital.
   a. What is a "minority interest"?
   b. Where on the consolidated balance sheet does it belong? What different points of view do these differing presentations represent?
8. What is book value per share? How is it computed? What is its significance? (CFA)
9. Why has the use of the book value per share declined in relative importance over the past decades? What valid uses of book value are still made today?
10. What are some of the accounting considerations that enter into the computation of book value and about which the analyst should be aware?
11. What adjustments may be necessary to render the book value per share measure comparable as between two enterprises?

Chapter 9

INTERCORPORATE INVESTMENTS, BUSINESS COMBINATIONS, AND FOREIGN OPERATIONS

In this chapter, we shall examine the analytical implications of a number of specialized topics in accounting, most of which straddle the areas of asset, liability, and income measurements and are thus discussed best in their entirety and in a separate and distinct fashion.

INTERCORPORATE INVESTMENTS

When one corporation owns all or a majority of the voting equity securities of another corporation, a parent-subsidiary relationship is said to exist. The reasons why one company may form or buy control of another entity are many and include sources of supply, enlargement of market coverage, entrance into new lines of business, taxes, reduction of risk because of limited liability, and the requirements of government regulation.

There are three basic methods by which a parent company can account for its ownership in a subsidiary. These are:

1. Consolidated financial statements.
2. Equity method.
3. Cost method.

We shall examine these hereunder in this order, which is the order of their preference from an accounting theory standpoint. This order of preference coincides also with that from the point of view of the financial analyst since, as we will see from the discussion that follows, the methods differ significantly in the amount of information they provide the analyst about the financial condition and results of operations of the combined parent-subsidiary entity.

Consolidated Financial Statements

On the parent company's financial statements, the ownership of stock in a subsidiary is evidenced by an investment account. From a legal point of view, the parent company owns the stock of its subsidiary; it does not own the subsidiary's assets nor is it normally responsible for the subsidiary's debts, although it frequently guarantees them. Consolidated financial statements disregard the legality of this situation in favor of its business substance and reflect the economic reality of a business entity under centralized control. There is a presumption that, in most cases, consolidated financial statements are more meaningful than separate financial statements and that they are required for fair presentation of financial conditions and results of operations.

Basic Technique of Consolidation   Consolidated financial statements combine the assets, liabilities, revenues, and expenses of subsidiaries with the corresponding items in the financial statements of the parent company. To the extent that the parent does not own 100 percent of a subsidiary's equity securities, the minority interest of outsiders is recognized in the consolidation. Intercompany items are eliminated in order to avoid double counting and the premature recognition of income.

ILLUSTRATION 1.   Exhibit 9–1 presents the simplified balance sheet of Company P (the parent) at the time of its acquisition of Company S (the subsidiary). The assets and liabilities included in the balance sheet of Company S are already stated at their fair market values at the time of acquisition. Company P paid $78,000 for 90 percent of Company S's common stock. Accounts receivable of Company P include $4,000 owed it by Company S.

The adjustments in the worksheet that combine the two companies are as follows:

a. The investment at acquisition is eliminated against 90 percent of the equity (capital stock plus retained earnings) of Company S. The remaining 10 percent of Company S's equity belongs to outside stockholders and is shown as "minority interest" in the consolidated balance sheet. The amount of $6,000 that Company P paid in excess of the fair value of 90 percent of the tangible net assets of Company S is carried as "goodwill" in the consolidated balance sheet. The method of determination of goodwill will be discussed later in this chapter under "Purchase accounting."

b. The accounts receivable of Company P and the corresponding payable of Company S are eliminated in consolidation.

Under the consolidation method, the income statement of Company S will be combined with that of Company P, and the 10 percent share of the minority interest in the net income or loss of Company S for the period will be deducted from the consolidated income (or loss) and added to the minority's interest in order to show the consolidated net results of operations of the group.

Exhibit 9–1

COMPANY P AND COMPANY S
Consolidated Balance Sheet Worksheet
Date of Acquisition

	Company P	Company S	Adjustments and eliminations Dr. (Cr.)	Minority interest	Con-soli-dated
Assets					
Cash	16,000	11,000			27,000
Accounts receivable	32,000	19,000	*(b)* (4,000)		47,000
Inventories	42,000	18,000			60,000
Fixed assets	64,000	42,000			106,000
Investment in Company S:					
Fair value at acquisition	72,000	—	*(a)* (72,000)		—
Excess of cost over fair value (goodwill)	6,000	—			6,000
Total assets	232,000	90,000			246,000
Liabilities and Equity					
Accounts payable	12,000	10,000	*(b)* 4,000		18,000
Capital stock:					
Company P	120,000				120,000
Company S		50,000	*(a)* 45,000	5,000	
Retained earnings:					
Company P	100,000				100,000
Company S		30,000	*(a)* 27,000	3,000	
Minority interest					8,000
Total liabilities and equity	232,000	90,000			246,000

In consolidating the income statement of subsidiary Company S with parent Company P, intercompany profits on sales of inventories that remain within the consolidated group at year-end and intercompany profits on other assets, such as fixed assets, must be eliminated. This is so because the equity interest in the earnings of a consolidated entity relate to earnings with parties *outside* the group. Transactions among members within the group result in the profit being considered as unrealized.

Principles Governing Consolidation Policy   There is a general presumption that consolidated statements are more meaningful than separate parent and subsidiary statements. Consequently, consolidation is the preferred method of presenting the financial statements of a parent and its subsidiaries. There are, however, a number of reasons why a subsidiary should not be consolidated. They are:

1. *Incomplete or temporary control.* In general, in order to consolidate a subsidiary, a parent should have ownership or effective management control over the subsidiary. Thus, ownership of over 50 percent of the voting stock is generally required for consolidation, and consolidation is inappropriate where the control is temporary, where control does not rest with the majority owner, or where the subsidiary will be disposed of or control is expected to be lost in the near future.

2. *Uncertainty as to income.* Where there is reason for serious doubt whether an increase in equity in a subsidiary has really accrued to the parent, consolidation is not appropriate. Such doubt can occur particularly in the case of foreign subsidiaries when there are restrictions on the conversion of foreign currencies or on the remittance of foreign earnings.

SFAS 94 (1987) requires consolidation of a majority-owned subsidiary even if it has nonhomogeneous operations, a large minority interest, or a foreign location. The standard requires that summarized information about the assets, liabilities, and results of operations (or separate statements) of previously unconsolidated majority-owned subsidiaries continue to be provided after those subsidiaries are consolidated.

The Need to Consolidate Leasing Subsidiaries   *APB Opinion 18* and *SFAS 13* reaffirm the requirement that subsidiaries whose principal business activity consists of leasing property or facilities to their parents or other affiliates be consolidated with such parents. The reason for this requirement is the significance of the assets and liabilities of such subsidiaries to the consolidated financial position of the entire group.

The Equity Method

The equity method should be used in consolidated financial statements for investments in common stock of all unconsolidated subsidiaries (foreign or domestic) where for reasons, such as those discussed above, consolidation is not appropriate. Under *APB Opinion 18,* the equity method is not a valid substitute for consolidation and should not be used to justify exclusion of a subsidiary when consolidation is otherwise appropriate.

The difference between consolidation and the equity method lies in the details reported in the financial statements. Under the equity method, the parent's investment in the subsidiary and the parent's share of the subsidiary results are presented in its financial statements as one-line items and this has resulted in the equity method being also referred to as "one-line consolidation."

As we saw in the discussion of the accounting for intercorporate investments in Chapter 6, the equity method of accounting should, generally, be used for investments in common stock that represent interests 20 percent or over in the voting stock of a company's equity securities, and it may be appropriate in some cases even for investments representing an interest of less than 20 percent.

Recognizing the wide application of the equity method to investments in subsidiaries, to investments in corporate joint ventures, as well as to investments in less than majority-owned investees, *APB Opinion 18* listed a number of procedures that should be followed in applying this method:

1. Intercompany profits and losses should be eliminated until realized by the investor or investee as if a subsidiary, corporate joint venture, or investee company were consolidated.
2. A difference between the cost of an investment and the amount of underlying equity in net assets of an investee should be accounted for as if the investee were a consolidated subsidiary. (*APB Opinion 17* requires amortization of goodwill over a term not exceeding 40 years.)
3. The investment(s) in common stock should be shown in the balance sheet of an investor as a single amount, and the investor's share of earnings or losses of an investee(s) should ordinarily be shown in the income statement as a single amount except for the extraordinary items and prior period adjustments that should be separately classified in the income statement of the investor.
4. A transaction of an investee of a capital nature that affects the investor's share of stockholders' equity of the investee should be accounted for as if the investee were a consolidated subsidiary.
5. Sales of stock of an investee by an investor should be accounted for as gains or losses equal to the difference at the time of sale between selling price and carrying amount of the stock sold.
6. If financial statements of an investee are not sufficiently timely for an investor to apply the equity method currently, the investor ordinarily should record its share of the earnings or losses of an investee from the most recent available financial statements. A lag in reporting should be consistent from period to period.
7. A loss in value of an investment that is other than a temporary decline should be recognized the same as a loss in value of other long-term assets. Evidence of a loss in value might include inability to recover the carrying amount of investment, decline in market value, and so on. All relevant factors must be evaluated.
8. The investor ordinarily should discontinue applying the equity method when the investment (and net advances) is reduced to zero and should not provide for additional losses unless the investor has guaranteed obligations of the investee or is otherwise committed to provide further financial support for the investee. If the

investee subsequently reports net income, the investor should resume applying the equity method only after its share of that net income equals the share of net losses not recognized during the period the equity method was suspended.

9. When an investee has outstanding cumulative preferred stock, an investor should compute its share of earnings (losses) after deducting the investee's preferred dividends, whether or not such dividends are declared.

10. The carrying amount of an investment in common stock of an investee that qualifies for the equity method of accounting as described above may differ from the underlying equity in net assets of the investee. The difference should affect the determination of the amount of the investor's share of earnings or losses of an investee as if the investee were a consolidated subsidiary. However, if the investor is unable to relate the difference to specific accounts of the investee, the difference should be considered to be goodwill and amortized over a period not to exceed 40 years, in accordance with *APB Opinion 17.*

SEC Position on Consolidated Financial Statements   In 1986 the SEC clarified its rules dealing with the presentation of consolidated financial statements by amendments to Regulation S-X. The amendments emphasize the need to consider substance over form in determining appropriate consolidation policy. The amended rule also eliminates wording that suggests an absolute prohibition from consolidating "any subsidiary which is not majority owned."

While not changing current generally accepted accounting principles, the regulations specifically address the possible need to consolidate a less than majority-owned subsidiary and the possible need to employ the equity method or a valuation allowance to achieve a fair presentation. The amended rules also require disclosure of the consolidation policies followed, including any departures from the normal practice of consolidating majority-owned subsidiaries and not consolidating entities that are less than majority owned.

The Cost Method

Under the prevailing system of accrual accounting, the cost method is the method least preferred among the three alternative ways of presenting investments in subsidiaries. Under this method, the investment in a subsidiary is recorded at cost and income is recognized only as it is received in the form of dividend distributions. A permanent impairment in the value of the investment, due to losses or other causes, should be recognized by a write-down of the investment.

The use of the cost method is now restricted to cases where there is considerable doubt that the equity in the earnings of a subsidiary is effectively accruing to the benefit of the parent. Such cases include foreign subsidiaries that operate under conditions of exchange restrictions, controls, or other uncertainties of a type that casts doubt on the parent's ability to achieve an ultimate realization of these earnings.

Example of Difference in Income Recognition— Equity versus Cost Method

On January 1, year 1, Company P acquired 80 percent of Company S for $900,000. The net assets of Company S at date of acquisition were $1,000,000.

During year 1, Company S earned $100,000 and paid $40,000 in dividends, while in year 2 it lost $20,000 and paid a dividend of $30,000. Exhibit 9–2 contrasts the accounting by Company P for the investment in Company S and the income derived from it under (1) the cost method and (2) the equity method.

The disparity in the amount of income reported by the parent under the two methods is readily apparent. Under the cost method, the income pickup bears no relationship to actual results achieved during the period but is, instead, dependent on the amount of dividend distributions, a factor over which the parent has control.

The amount at which the investment is carried on the books of the parent company also varies considerably among these two methods. Under the cost method, the investment account remains unchanged (except in the case of losses that lead to a permanent impairment in value), while under the equity method the investment account reflects the parent company's equity in the underlying net assets of the subsidiary. Goodwill should, however, be amortized also under the cost method.[1]

Intercorporate Investments—Less than Majority Ownership

Investments by one company in less than the majority of the voting security of another enterprise and investments in joint ventures are discussed in Chapter 6.

Implications for Analysis

From the analyst's point of view, the financial reporting of intercorporate investments has undergone consistent improvement. This improvement

---

[1] The goodwill element can, of course, also be present in an investment account of an unconsolidated subsidiary.

Exhibit 9–2 Cost and equity methods of accounting for investment in subsidiary

	Cost method		Equity method	
	Invest-ment	Income (loss)	Invest-ment	Income (loss)
Cost acquisition	$900,000		$900,000	
Earnings for year 1			80,000	$ 80,000[a]
Amortization of goodwill			(2,500)	(2,500)[b]
Dividends—year 1		$32,000[c]	(32,000)	
Earnings pickup— year 1		$32,000		$ 77,500
Loss for year 2			(16,000)	$(16,000)[d]
Amortization of goodwill			(2,500)	(2,500)[b]
Dividends—year 2		$24,000[e]	(24,000)	
Earnings (loss) pickup—year 2		$24,000		$(18,500)
Investment at December 31, year 2 ..	$900,000		$903,000	

[a] 80% equity in earnings of $100,000.

[b] Cost of 80% interest in Company S	$900,000
80% of net assets ($1,000,000—assumed to represent fair market value)..	800,000
Excess of cost over net assets (goodwill)	100,000
Yearly amortization (40-year basis)	$ 2,500

[c] 80% of $40,000.
[d] 80% of $20,000.
[e] 80% of $30,000.

is due in large measure to the sharp restrictions that are now placed on the use of the cost method of accounting.

Under the cost method, dividends remitted, rather than income earned, are the basis on which a parent company recognizes the earnings accruing from an investment in a subsidiary. The obvious disadvantage of the cost method is that the cost basis does not reflect the results of operations of the subsidiary and lends itself to income manipulation. Thus, dividends included in the parent company's income may be unrelated to the subsidiary's earnings, and losses of the subsidiary may go unreported for a number of periods. The trend in earnings can be completely distorted by use of the cost method.

The requirement of *SFAS 94* that nonhomogeneous majority-owned subsidiaries be consolidated is a plus from the analyst's point of view. It will, however, increase the complexity of consolidated financial statements. See the discussion of the limitations of consolidated financial statements below. The summarized information required by *SFAS 94* will aid the analysis of such statements.

The consolidation of previously unconsolidated nonhomogeneous subsidiaries, such as finance subsidiaries, is generally expected to increase debt to equity ratios, decrease asset turnover ratios, decrease profit margins, increase interest expense, and decrease the fixed-charge coverage ratios.

Validity of Taking Up Earnings   Consolidation and the equity method are based on the assumption that a dollar earned by a subsidiary is equal to a dollar's worth of parent company earnings. Even disregarding the possible tax liability that the parent company may incur on the remittance of earnings by the subsidiary, this dollar-for-dollar equivalence in earnings cannot be taken for granted. The following are some possible reasons for this:

1. The subsidiary may be under the supervision of a regulatory authority that can intervene in dividend policy.
2. The subsidiary may operate in a foreign country where there exist restrictions on the remittance of earnings abroad and/or where the value of the currency can deteriorate rapidly. Furthermore, changes in political climate may result in hampering the subsidiary's operations.
3. Dividend restrictions in loan agreements may become effective.
4. The presence of a stable or powerful minority interest may reduce the parent's discretion in setting dividend and other policy.

While considerations such as the above should govern the independent accountant's decision on whether or not to use the cost method, the analyst should, as a check on that judgment, form his or her own opinion in each given situation on whether a dollar earned by a subsidiary can indeed be considered the equivalent of a dollar earned by the parent company.

There are other problems in the analysis of consolidated financial statements or investments in subsidiaries carried at equity that the financial analyst must consider carefully.

Provision for Taxes on Undistributed Earnings of Subsidiaries   Under the prevailing accounting for income taxes—the inclusion of undistributed earnings of a subsidiary in the pretax accounting income of a parent company, either through consolidation or accounting for the investment by the equity method, may or may not require a concurrent provision for taxes depending on the actions and intent of the parent company.

Under this accounting, it is presumed that all undistributed earnings will be transferred to the parent and that a provision for taxes should be made by assuming that the unremitted earnings were distributed to the parent in the current period and that the tax provision is based on a computation benefiting from all the tax-planning alternatives to which the company may be entitled.

The foregoing presumption can be overcome if persuasive evidence exists that the subsidiary has or will invest the undistributed earnings permanently or that the earnings will be remitted in a tax-free liquidation. In *SFAS 109* the Board decided to continue this accounting even though it considers such accounting inconsistent with the objectives of the statement.

The analyst should be aware that the decision of whether taxes on undistributed earnings should or should not be provided is, in effect, left largely to management. However, the amount of earnings on which no income taxes were provided by the parent must be disclosed.

In contrast, ownership in an investee (20 percent to 50 percent owned) calls for provision of taxes on equity in earnings because a presumption of an ability to reinvest earnings is not assumed to exist.

Debt Shown in Consolidated Financial Statements   Liabilities shown in the consolidated financial statements do not operate as a lien upon a common pool of assets. The creditors, be they secured or unsecured, have recourse in the event of default only to assets owned by the individual corporation that incurred this liability. If, on the other hand, a parent company guarantees a specific liability of a subsidiary, then the creditor would, of course, have the guarantee as additional security.

The consolidated balance sheet obscures rather than clarifies the margin of safety enjoyed by specific creditors. To gain full comprehension of the financial position of each part of the consolidated group, the analyst needs also to examine the individual financial statements of each subsidiary. Legal constraints are not always effective limits to liability. Thus, American Express made good on obligations of a warehousing subsidiary not because it was legally obliged to do so but because of concern for its own financial reputation.

Additional Limitations of Consolidated Financial Statements   Consolidated financial statements generally represent the most meaningful presentation of the financial condition and the results of operations of a group. However, they do have limitations in addition to those discussed above:

1. The financial statements of the individual companies in the group may not be prepared on a comparable basis. Accounting principles applied and valuation bases and amortization rates used may differ, thus destroying homogeneity and the validity of ratios, trends, and

relationships. Year-end dates of individual members of a group can vary by as much as 90 days.

2. Consolidated financial statements do not show the restrictions on the use of cash of individual companies. Nor do they show intercompany cash flows or the restrictions placed on such flows, thus obscuring the relationship between the liquidity of assets and the liabilities that they may be available to meet.

3. Companies in relatively poor financial condition may be combined with sound companies, thus obscuring information necessary for analysis. The assets of one member of the consolidated group may not be used to pay the liabilities of another.

4. The extent of intercompany transactions is unknown unless *consolidating* financial statements are presented. The latter generally reveal the adjustments involved in the consolidation process.

5. Unless specifically disclosed, the amount of the consolidated Retained Earnings account actually available for payment of dividends may be difficult to establish.

6. The composition of the minority interest, for example, as between common and preferred, cannot be determined because the minority interest is generally shown as a combined amount in the consolidated balance sheet.

7. The provisions of *SFAS 94*, requiring the consolidation of finance and insurance subsidiaries, may pose as many new problems of analysis for the analyst as the standard intended to solve. In addition to considerations mentioned above, it must be realized that the aggregation of dissimilar enterprises can distort many ratios and relationships. For example, the current assets of finance subsidiaries may not be available to satisfy the current liabilities of the parent. Assets and liabilities of separate entities are neither fungible nor readily exchangeable. Additionally, consolidated financial statements obscure the priority of claims of various creditors.

IMPLICATIONS FOR ANALYSIS

Consolidation is not a universally accepted accounting concept. In fact, it has only recently been accepted in Japan and was slow in being accepted in many countries in Europe. It has, however, been a generally accepted accounting concept in the United States, and the presentation of consolidated financial statements with adequate disclosures is a helpful presentation from the point of view of the financial analyst.

It must be noted, however, that the consolidation process obscures as well as it reveals. Thus it can obscure restrictions on transfers of resources among members of a consolidated group. For example, the stockholders of ITT Corporation cannot access the assets of the consolidated Hartford

Insurance Group without permission from the relevant regulatory authority which must protect the interests of policyholders. The same type of restriction may, in effect, prevail where the subsidiary has a significant outside minority which is hostile to the parent management.

The consolidation process can also obscure the financial difficulties of individual members of the consolidated group.

Analysts must recognize that a consolidated reporting entity is not a single enterprise. It is rather a group of companies united by common control.

Analysts must also be aware that the exclusion from consolidation of an entity which should be consolidated can result in substantially misleading results.

ILLUSTRATION 2.   Digilog Inc., formed DBS International in 1981 to market its new line of microcomputers. Digilog searched for a method of penetrating the domestic market without having to include in its financials expected losses of such operations. To this end it obtained approval from its auditors that it need not consolidate DBS if it capitalized it by taking in return notes convertible into 90 percent of common stock. It also ultimately extended $2.5 million in credits to DBS. In 1984 the SEC brought charges stemming from accounting irregularities against Digilog and its auditors. The SEC also forced Digilog to restate its financial statements by consolidating DBS since its inception. Thus, the reported pretax income of Digilog of $10,591 for 1981 and $2,382,441 for 1982 became a pretax loss of $449,000 for 1981 and a pretax income of only $1,183,000 for 1982. The restatements were, of course, little consolation to investors and others who had relied on the published inflated results of those years.

ACCOUNTING FOR BUSINESS COMBINATIONS

The combination of business entities by merger or acquisition is not a new phenomenon on the business scene. What is a relatively more recent development is the utilization of the merger technique as an instrument for the creation of "glamour" or of an image of growth, and as a means of increasing reported earnings.

Reasons for Mergers

There are, of course, many legitimate reasons for *external* business expansion, that is, expansion by means of business combinations under which two or more entities are brought under common control. These reasons include: (1) acquisition of sources of new materials, productive facilities, production know-how, marketing organizations, and established shares of a market; (2) the acquisition of financial resources; (3) the acquisition of competent management; (4) savings of time in entering new markets; and (5) achieving economies of scale and acquiring tax advantages such as those relating to tax-loss carryovers.

Consistent with our discussion at the end of Chapter 3, in which the importance of understanding and of factoring in human nature in our analytical considerations is discussed, we must recognize additional reasons for mergers, some of which may be more psychological than logical. Only an appreciation of such reasons or rationale can explain some of the exorbitant prices which some managements are willing to pay for companies they desire to acquire. Such reasons may relate to increasing the size rather than the profitability of the organization with a view to garnering advantages such as prestige, added compensation, and commensurately larger managerial perquisites. Often the accounting chosen to record such acquisitions can also be better understood in the light of such considerations and motivations.

Distortions in Accounting for Mergers

In addition to the above legitimate reasons for entering into business combinations, financial "architects" and operators have utilized merger techniques and loose merger accounting to serve up to a stock market obsessed with "earnings growth" a picture of growth that is, in large part, illusory.

The means by which such illusions of earnings growth are achieved are many. Briefly, some are as follows:

1. In the past a great variety of convertible securities were issued without any recognition being given to their future potential dilutive effects on the common stockholder's equity. This phenomenon reached such heights of abuse that it was finally remedied by the issuance of *APB Opinion 15*. Chapter 12 contains a more extended discussion of this subject.

2. The merger of growing companies that have earned a high price-earnings ratio in the marketplace with companies of lesser growth prospects was achieved by payment in high price-earnings ratio stock. This contributed to further earnings per share growth, thus reinforcing and even increasing the acquiring company's high price-earnings ratio. However, in many cases, the market failed to take into account the lower quality of the *acquired* earnings. This is mostly a transitory problem inherent in the market evaluation mechanism and is not readily subject to remedy by external factors.

3. The utilization of loose accounting rules governing merger accounting can create the illusion of earnings growth where, in fact, there is none. This is to be distinguished from the genuine economies and advantages that can accrue from business combinations. This problem area will be discussed below in our consideration of alternative accounting methods for business combinations.

Accounting for Business Combinations: Two Methods

Prior to World War II, the accounting for business combinations was governed by the legal form that the combination assumed and that resulted in a majority of acquisitions by one company of another being treated as purchases. To businessmen, the one immediate disadvantage of purchase accounting was the creation of "goodwill" as an asset representing the excess of cost of acquisition over the amounts at which the acquired company's net assets were recorded on the acquiring company's books. Not only is goodwill a nontax-deductible item which results in a reduction of earnings, but it is also an asset that bankers and other lenders consider of dubious value.

Pooling of Interests   For this and other reasons, the search for an alternative method of accounting for business combinations led to the pooling of interests method. The rationale behind this method is that instead of an acquisition of one company by another, a pooling of interests reflects the merging of two stockholder groups that share in future risks and opportunities. It is as if the method reflects the combining of two or more streams, previously running separately and now brought together. The history of the common stream is the sum of the histories of its components.

This accounting convention, which gained wide acceptance in the post-1945 period, is based on the following assumptions about the two corporations combining—

1. That they would exchange voting securities; essentially, ownership would be continuing.
2. That the two corporations would be roughly comparable in size.
3. That management personnel would continue with the merged corporation.

The great attraction of the pooling method along with the vague criteria that were promulgated to govern its accounting led to a significant deterioration in actual practice. The criterion of relative size eroded, all manner of equity securities became acceptable, various means of circumventing the continuity of ownership provisions were devised, and where it was clearly impossible to justify the use of a full pooling, a part-pooling part-purchase method was devised. In short, we had here a classic illustration of the operation of Gresham's law in accounting.

With the growth in these abuses, the chorus of criticism grew, and this resulted in a call by many for the abolition of pooling of interests accounting. Instead, members of the APB compromised and issued *Opinion 16* which, as we shall see, established stricter and more specific conditions for use of this method of accounting in the future.

Purchase Accounting   In the permissive atmosphere of the 1960s, accounting under the "purchase" convention also deteriorated in relation to its original intent. Abuses occurred in two major areas:

1. Assets and liabilities of purchased entities were not revalued at fair value before being included in the accounts of the acquiring company.
2. The resulting "goodwill" represented merely the excess of amounts paid over the carrying amounts of assets and liabilities assumed without even the pretense that such assets and liabilities were fairly valued. This resulting "goodwill" was very rarely amortized. It thus became a repository for all kinds of costs incurred in acquiring the company, costs that were thus kept out of present and future income statements. The curt note found in the Gould, Inc., prospectus dated February 17, 1970, was characteristic of this kind of treatment: "The cost of acquired businesses in excess of recorded net assets at dates of acquisition are considered to be attributable to intangible assets which will not be amortized."

While in theory a purchase is in substance quite a different business combination from a pooling of interests, by the late 1960s, the accounting for them became *in effect* quite similar. Under the pooling method, the understatement of assets took the form of carrying forward the merged company's assets at book value, while under the "polluted purchase"[2] method, the assets were similarly understated and the excess of cost over these understated assets was merely carried as a nondescript composite intangible that was rarely amortized. Thus, under either method, substantial costs were kept out of the income statement.

In theory the distinction between pooling and purchase is quite clear. Under a purchase one company acquires one or more other companies. The acquirer continues while the acquired disappears. The history of the combined enterprise is that of the acquirer. The acquisition is accounted for in the same way as is the acquisition of any other asset.

ACCOUNTING FOR BUSINESS COMBINATIONS

In an attempt to improve the accounting for business combinations, the APB issued in 1970 *Opinions 16* and *17*. However, in late 1976, the FASB issued a voluminous *Discussion Memorandum* on the subject which was designed to lead to public hearings in 1977 and to a reconsideration of

---

[2] This term was coined by Professor Abraham J. Briloff who has done more than anyone else to expose the abuses under both pooling and purchase accounting. Starting in 1967, his incisive and analytical articles, appearing mostly in the *Financial Analysts Journal* and *Barron's,* contributed greatly to a wider understanding of the distortions for which this type of accounting was responsible.

the entire subject. In 1982, the reconsideration of the subject was postponed pending completion of the Board's "conceptual framework."

We shall first consider the accounting required under these two *Opinions.* Following this consideration, we shall consider the implications that the present accounting holds for the analyst.

Pooling of Interests and Purchase Accounting Compared

Pooling of interests accounting is based on the assumption that the combination is a uniting of ownership interests achieved by means of an exchange of equity securities. Under this method, the former ownership interests continue and the recorded assets and liabilities of the constituents are carried forward to the combined entity at their recorded amounts. Since this is a combining of interests, income of the combined corporation includes income of the constituents for the entire fiscal period in which the combination occurs. Prior periods are also restated to show the combined companies as merged since their respective inceptions.

The purchase method of accounting views the business combination as the acquisition of one entity by another. The acquiring entity records the acquired assets, including goodwill, and liabilities at its cost which is based on fair values at date of acquisition. The acquiring entity picks up the income of the acquired entity, based on its cost, only from date of acquisition.

APB Opinion 16 concluded that if a business combination meets the 12 specific criteria enumerated in it, the combination must be accounted for as a pooling of interests. Otherwise, the combination must be accounted for as a purchase.

Conditions for the Pooling of Interests Method   There are 12 conditions that must be met under the provision of *APB Opinion 16* before a business combination may be accounted for as a pooling of interests. These can be grouped under three main categories:

   I. Attributes of the combining companies.
  II. Manner of combining interests.
 III. Absence of planned transactions.

   I. Attributes of the combining companies.
      A. Each of the combining companies should be autonomous and not have operated as a subsidiary or division of another company within two years before the plan of combination is initiated. An exception to this condition concerns the divestiture of assets that was ordered by a governmental or judicial body. A subsidiary that is divested under an order, or a new company that acquires assets disposed of under such an order, is considered autonomous for this condition.

B. Each of the combining companies must be independent of each other. That means that no combining company or group of combining companies can hold as an intercompany investment more than 10 percent of the outstanding voting common stock of any other combining company. To illustrate the 10 percent requirement, let's assume that Company A plans to issue its voting common stock to acquire the voting common stock of Companies B and C. If Companies A and B each own 7 percent of Company C's outstanding common stock, A can pool with B, but the combined entity cannot subsequently pool with C since more than 10 percent of Company C's outstanding stock would have been held by the other combining companies.

II. Manner of combining interests.

C. The combination should be effected in a single transaction or should be completed in accordance with a specific plan within one year after the plan is initiated. The *Opinion* provides an exception to this one-year rule when the delay is beyond the control of the combining companies because of proceedings of a governmental authority or pending litigation.

D. The combination should involve the issuance of voting common stock only in exchange for substantially all of the voting common stock interest of the company being combined. "Substantially all" in this context means at least 90 percent of the voting common stock interest of the company being combined. Thus, the issuer may purchase for cash or other nonvoting common stock consideration up to 10 percent of the voting common shares of the company to be pooled. Such a cash outlay may be necessary to eliminate fractional shares or to pay dissenting stockholders. The rationale of this criterion is that substantially all of the voting common stock interest in each party to a pooling should be carried forward as a voting common stock interest in the issuer in the pooling. The payment of cash, debt, or an equity instrument that does not satisfy this test destroys the most fundamental basis of a pooling. If the company being combined has securities other than voting stock, such securities may be exchanged for common stock of the issuing corporation or may be exchanged for substantially identical securities of the issuing corporation.

E. None of the combining companies should change the equity interest of their voting common stock in contemplation of effecting the combination. This restriction applies during the period from two years preceding the date the plan is initiated through the date the plan is consummated. Changes in the equity interest of the voting common stock that may violate this condition include distributions to shareholders, additional issuance or exchange of securities, and the retirement of securities. The purpose of this rule is to disallow changes in equity interests prior to a combination because such changes indicate a sale rather than a combining and sharing of risks.

F. Each combining company may reacquire shares of voting common stock only for purposes other than business combinations, and no company may reacquire more than a normal number of shares between the date the plan of combination is initiated and consummated.

G. The ratio of the interest of an individual common stockholder to those of other common shareholders in a combining company should remain the same as a result of the exchange of stock to effect the combination. This condition ensures that no common stockholder is denied his potential share of a voting common stock interest in a combined corporation.

H. The stockholders of the resulting combined corporation cannot be deprived of, nor restricted in, their ability to exercise their voting rights on common stock of the combined corporation. For example, establishing a voting trust to hold some of the shares issued in the combination disqualifies the combination as a pooling of interests.

I. The combination must be resolved at the date the plan is consummated, and there must be no contingent arrangements for the issuance of additional securities or other consideration. All consideration to be given to effect the combination of the companies must be determinable as of the date the plan of combination is consummated. The only exception to this would be a provision to adjust the exchange ratio as a result of a subsequent settlement of a contingency such as an existing lawsuit.

III. Absence of planned transactions.

J. The combined corporation should not agree directly or indirectly to retire or reacquire any of the common stock issued to effect the combination.

K. The combined corporation cannot enter into other financial arrangements for the benefit of the former stockholders of a combining company, such as a guarantee of loans secured by stock issued in the combination. This financial arrangement may require the payment of cash in the future that would negate the exchange of equity securities, and thus the combination would not qualify for pooling of interests treatment.

L. The combined corporation may not intend to dispose of a significant part of the assets of the combining companies within two years after the combination. Some disposal of assets may be effected within the two-year period provided the disposals would have been in the ordinary course of business of the formerly separate companies or if the disposals were to eliminate duplicate facilities or excess capacity.

If a combining company remains a subsidiary of the issuing corporation after the combination is consummated, the combination could still be accounted for as a pooling of interests, as long as all the conditions for a pooling are met. Any business combination that meets all of the above conditions *must* be accounted for under the pooling of interests method.

Application of the Purchase Method   As we have seen in the foregoing discussion, under purchase accounting the business combination is viewed as the acquisition of one entity by another.

Problem of Valuation of the Consideration   One of the major problems in accounting for a purchase is to determine the total cost of an acquired entity. The same accounting principles apply whether determining the cost of assets acquired individually, in a group, or in a business combination. It is the nature of the transaction that determines which accounting principles apply in arriving at the total cost of assets acquired.

There usually is no problem in determining the total cost of assets acquired for cash, since the amount of cash disbursed is the total cost of the acquired assets. The difficulty is, however, in the proper allocation of the total cost to the individual assets acquired.

If assets are acquired by incurring liabilities, total cost of the assets is the present value of the amounts to be paid in the future. The present value of a debt security is the fair value of the liability. If the debt security has been issued at an interest rate that is substantially above or below the present effective rate for a similar security, the appropriate amount of premium or discount should be recorded. In some cases, the characteristics of a preferred stock may be so similar to a debt security that it should be valued in the same manner.

If assets are acquired in exchange for stock, the general rule for determining the total cost of the assets acquired would be that it is the fair value of the stock given or the fair value of the assets received, whichever is more clearly evident.

The fair value of securities traded in the market is normally more clearly evident than is the fair value of the acquired company. Quoted market price should serve as a guide in determining total cost of an acquired company after considering market fluctuations, the quantities traded, issue costs, and so forth.

If the quoted market price is not a reliable indicator of the value of stock issued, the fair value of the assets received, including goodwill, must still be determined, even though this valuation is difficult.

In these cases, the best means of estimation should be used, including a detailed review of the negotiations leading up to the purchase and the use of independent appraisals.

Contingent Additional Consideration   The amount of any additional contingent consideration payable in accordance with the purchase agreement is usually recorded when the contingency is resolved and the consideration is to be issued or becomes issuable. Two of the most common types of contingencies are based on either earnings or security prices.

The following guides to the accounting for such contingent additional consideration are contained in *APB Opinion 16:*

1. A contingent issuance of additional consideration should be disclosed but should not be recorded as a liability or shown as outstanding securities unless the outcome of the contingency is determinable beyond a reasonable doubt.
2. A contingent issuance of additional consideration based on future earnings should be recorded as an additional cost of the acquisition when the contingency is resolved. In this case the total amount of consideration representing cost is not determinable at the date of acquisition.
3. A contingent issuance of additional consideration which is based on future security prices should be considered as an adjustment of the amount originally recorded for the securities at the date of acquisition.

Allocation of Total Cost   Once the total cost of an acquired entity is determined, it is then necessary to allocate this total cost to the individual assets received. All identifiable assets acquired and liabilities assumed in a business combination should be assigned a portion of the total cost, normally equal to their fair value at date of acquisition. The excess of the total cost over the amounts assigned to identifiable assets acquired, less liabilities assumed, should be recorded as goodwill. Such goodwill must be amortized over a period not to exceed 40 years.

It may be possible in some cases that the market or appraisal values of identifiable assets acquired, less liabilities assumed, exceeds the cost of the acquired company. In those cases, the values otherwise assignable to noncurrent assets acquired (except long-term investments in marketable securities) should be reduced by a proportionate part of the excess. Negative goodwill should not be recorded unless the value assigned to such long-term assets is first reduced to zero. If such allocation results in an excess of net assets over cost, the excess should be classified as a deferred credit and should be amortized systematically to income over the period estimated to be benefited but not in excess of 40 years.

Guidelines for Valuation of Assets and Liabilities   APB Opinion 16 established general guides for assigning amounts to individual assets and liabilities assumed, except goodwill, as follows:

1. Marketable securities should be recorded at current net realizable values.

2. Receivables should be recorded at the present values of amounts to be received, determined at appropriate current interest rates, less allowances for uncollectibility and collection costs, if necessary.
3. Inventories:
   a. Finished goods should be recorded at selling prices less cost of disposal and reasonable profit allowance,
   b. Work-in-process inventories should be stated at estimated selling prices of finished goods less the sum of the costs to complete, costs of disposal, and a reasonable profit allowance for the completing and selling effort of the acquired corporation.
   c. Raw materials should be recorded at current replacement costs.
4. Plant and equipment to be used in the business should be stated at current replacement costs for similar capacity unless the expected future use of the assets indicates a lower value to the acquirer. Replacement cost may be determined directly if a used asset market exists for the assets acquired. Otherwise, replacement cost should be approximated from replacement cost new, less estimated accumulated depreciation.
5. Identifiable intangible assets should be valued at appraised values.
6. Other assets, such as land, natural resources, and nonmarketable securities, should be recorded at appraised values.
7. Accounts and notes payable, long-term debt, and other claims payable should be stated at present values of amounts to be paid, determined at appropriate current interest rates.

An acquiring corporation should not record as a separate asset goodwill previously recorded by an acquired company, and it should not record deferred income taxes previously recorded by an acquired company. Amounts assigned to identifiable assets and liabilities should recognize that their value may be less, if part or all of the assigned value is not deductible for income taxes. However, the acquiring corporation should not record deferred tax accounts for the tax effect of these differences at the date of acquisition.

Treatment of Goodwill   *APB Opinion 17* provides that for the intangible assets acquired in a business combination, the method of allocating the total cost of the acquired company depends on whether or not the asset is identifiable, such as a patent, or unidentifiable, such as goodwill. The cost of an identifiable intangible asset should be based on the fair value of the asset. The cost of an unidentifiable intangible asset is measured by the difference between total cost and the amount assigned to other assets acquired and liabilities assumed.

The cost of an intangible asset should not be written off in the period of acquisition but instead should be amortized based on the estimated life of that specific asset; the period of amortization, however, should not exceed 40 years. The straight-line method of amortization should be used unless the company can demonstrate that another systematic method is more appropriate. The method and period of amortization should be disclosed in the financial statements.

Pro Forma Supplementary Disclosure   Under the purchase method, notes to the financial statements of the acquiring corporation for the period in which a business combination occurs should include as supplemental information the following results of operations on a pro forma basis:

1. Combined results of operations for the current period as though the companies had combined at the beginning of the period unless the acquisition was at or near the beginning of the period.
2. If comparative financial statements are presented, combined results of operations for the immediately preceding period should be reported as though the companies had combined at the beginning of that period.

This supplemental pro forma information should, as a minimum, show revenue, income before extraordinary items, net income, and earnings per share (EPS).

Illustration of Accounting Mechanics: Purchase versus Pooling of Interest Accounting

Company Buy has agreed to acquire Company Sell in a transaction under which it will issue 1,200,000 of $1 par value common shares for all the common shares of Company Sell. The transaction qualifies as a pooling of interests, and consequently the fair market value of Sell's assets and liabilities at date of the merger do not enter into the accounting for it. Exhibit 9–3 presents in columnar fashion the balance sheets of Company Buy and Company Sell as well as the adjustments needed to effect the combination under pooling of interests accounting.

Pooling Accounting

Briefly, the pooling method requires taking up Sell's assets and liabilities at recorded amounts and carrying forward the equity account balances, subject to adjustments required by differences in the par values of the securities exchanged.

Since the amount of the par value of the common stock of Company Buy ($1,200,000) is smaller than the amount of the par value of the stock of Company Sell, which is exchanged ($1,285,000), the difference is credited to Additional Paid-In Capital. In a pooling where the reverse to the above situation prevails, additional par value is taken out first of the existing paid-in capital accounts of the constituents and, if insufficient, from retained earnings. The balance in the retained earnings accounts is carried forward.

Exhibit 9–3   Merger of Company Sell into Company Buy

Summary of Pro Forma Condensed Combining Balance Sheet
(in thousands)

	Company Buy	Company Sell	Combining adjustments Debit	Combining adjustments Credit	Combined
Assets	$157,934	$28,013	—	—	$185,947
Liabilities	$ 42,591	$11,218	—	—	$ 53,809
Stockholders' equity:					
Company Buy:					
Preferred stock	810	—	—	—	810
Common stock	7,572	—	—	$1,200	8,772
Company Sell:					
Common stock	—	1,285	$1,285	—	—
Additional paid-in					
capital	31,146	137	—	85	31,368
Retained earnings	75,815	15,373	—	—	91,188
Total stockholders'					
equity	115,343	16,795	1,285	1,285	132,138
	$157,934	$28,013	$1,285	$1,285	$185,947

The entry on Company Buy's books of the pooling with Company Sell will be as follows (in thousands of dollars):

	Debit	Credit
Assets	28,013	
Liabilities.................................		11,218
Common Stock		1,200
Additional Paid-In Capital ($137 + $85).........		222
Retained Earnings		15,373

To record the issuance of 1,200,000 shares of $1 par value common stock for the merged net assets of Sell and to credit to Retained Earnings the balance of retained earnings of Sell at date of acquisition.

Exhibit 9–3 reflected the pooling as a "statutory merger," that is, the assets and liabilities of the two companies were combined and Company Sell ceased its separate existence. If we assume that Company Sell was to continue as a wholly owned subsidiary of Company Buy, the pooling would be recorded as shown in Exhibit 9–4.

The accounting entries made on the parent company's books are as follows (in thousands of dollars):

Exhibit 9–4   Merger of Company Buy and Company Sell (Company Sell remains as a fully owned subsidiary of Company Buy)

Summary of Pro Forma Condensed Balance Sheet
(in thousands)

	Company Buy	Parent company only		
		Adjustments		
	Before pooling	Debit	Credit	After pooling
Assets	$157,934	—	—	$157,934
Investment in Sell		$16,795	—	16,795
	$157,934	16,795	—	$174,729
Liabilities	$ 42,591	—	—	$ 42,591
Stockholders' equity:				
Company Buy:				
Preferred stock	810	—	—	810
Common stock	7,572	—	$ 1,200	8,772
Company Sell: Common stock ..	—	—	—	—
Additional paid-in capital	31,146	—	222	31,368
Retained earnings	75,815	—	—	75,815
Retained earnings from pooled company	—	—	15,373	15,373
Total stockholders' equity ...	115,343	—	16,795	132,138
	$157,934	—	$16,795	$174,729

	Debit	Credit
Investment in Company Sell	16,795	
Common Stock		1,200
Additional Paid-In Capital		222
Retained Earnings from Pooled Company		15,373

To record the issuance of 1,200,000 shares of $1 par value common stock for the common stock of Sell and to credit to Retained Earnings the balance of retained earnings of Sell at date of acquisition.

The investment in Company Sell will continue to be carried on an equity basis by Company Buy, the parent. In consolidation, the investment account in Company Sell will be eliminated against subsidiary Company Sell's common stock, additional paid-in capital, and the parent company's retained earnings from the pooled company, all in accordance with normal consolidation procedure.

Purchase Accounting

Let us now assume that instead of acquiring Company Sell in an exchange of common stock, Company Buy acquires Company Sell for $25,000,000 in cash. Since this acquisition must be accounted for as a purchase, it is necessary to determine the fair values of Company Sell's assets and liabilities. The following tabulation compares Company Sell's recorded asset and liability amounts with indicated fair values at date of acquisition (in thousands):

	Amounts on Company Sell books	Fair values determined at date of acquisition
Assets	$28,013	$34,000
Liabilities	11,218	13,000
Net assets	$16,795	21,000
Cost to Company Buy	—	25,000
Amount assigned to goodwill	—	4,000

Assets and liabilities are valued in accordance with the valuation principles outlined in *APB Opinion 16*. The excess of purchase price over the fair value of net assets acquired assigned to goodwill must be amortized over its useful life not to exceed 40 years.

Exhibit 9–5 presents the consolidated balance sheet of Company Buy right after the purchase of Company Sell so as to enable a contrast with the balance sheet obtained right after the pooling accounting presented in Exhibit 9–3.

A cash acquisition is, of course, not the only method requiring purchase accounting. As described earlier, under a great number of conditions involving an acquisition for stock, purchase accounting would be required.

The following difference between the pooling and the purchase accounting should be noted. In the purchase—

1. The assets and liabilities are recorded at fair value. Goodwill is recognized. These will result in higher charges to income reflecting the higher net asset values acquired.
2. The total stockholder equity remains unchanged. There has been an exchange of resources, that is, Company Sell's net assets of $25,000,000 for Company Buy's cash.

Exhibit 9–5 Purchase of Company Sell by Company Buy

Summary of Pro Forma Condensed Balance Sheet Consolidated
(in thousands)

	Company Buy	Company Sell (at fair values on date of acquisition)	Combining and consolidating adjustments		After purchase
			Debit	Credit	
Assets					
Assets (exclusive of goodwill)	$157,934	$34,000		$25,000	$166,934
Goodwill			$ 4,000		4,000
Total assets	$157,934	$34,000	4,000	25,000	$170,934
Liabilities and Stockholders' Equity					
Liabilities	$ 42,591	$13,000			$ 55,591
Stockholders' equity:					
Company Buy:					
Preferred stock	810				810
Common stock	7,572				7,572
Additional paid-in capital	31,146				31,146
Retained earnings	75,815				75,815
Net assets at fair value of Company Sell		21,000	21,000		
Total stockholders' equity	115,343	21,000	21,000	—	115,343
Total liabilities and stockholders' equity	$157,934	$34,000	$25,000	$25,000	$170,934

3. Company Buy will record the acquisition on its books as follows:

Investment in Company Sell...............	25,000,000	
Cash		25,000,000

Campbell Soup Co. (see Appendix 4B), discloses business acquisitions in item 106 including details of purchase and pooling transactions.

Implications for Analysis

An examination of the revised guidelines and principles governing the accounting for mergers and acquisitions reveals a serious attempt by the accounting profession to improve the accounting in this area and to prevent some of the glaring distortions and abuses of the past, as they perceived them, from recurring.

The rules that govern the accounting for pooling of interests and for purchases are the result of a lengthy process of compromise; another important objective was the elimination of *specific* abuses of practice. The analyst must recognize this as well as the fact that the rationale that accountants use in distinguishing pooling of interests from purchases combinations is not necessarily relevant to an attempt to measure and analyze the economic consequences of business combinations.

Thus, in determining the implications that the accounting rules for business combinations hold for the analyst of financial statements, we must examine the impact that these rules have on the realistic portrayal of the results of mergers and acquisitions.

Pooling versus Purchase Accounting   Before we examine the effect of pooling accounting on the financial statements of a combined entity, let us summarize the main arguments that have been advanced in defense of this method.

1. If cash is given as consideration in a business acquisition, the acquirer parts with a resource. But if a company's own unissued stock is given in exchange, no resource is given; instead, the equity is increased.
2. In exchange of common stock, the "seller" is getting back a part of itself as well as part of the buyer. Since it does not part with ownership in its own company, there is no valid basis for establishing new values.
3. In a combination of equals, which results from an exchange of stock, it is hard to determine who acquired whom.

It is not at all clear that cash is a resource while unissued stock is not. After all, if stock is an acceptable consideration to a seller, it should also command a price on the market. Some regard the ability to issue stock as equivalent to "a license to print money." The valuation of noncash consideration is a problem that accountants have to face frequently. Moreover, if a combination fails as a pooling on any one of the technical conditions enumerated in *APB Opinion 16,* a valuation of the stock issued will become necessary in order to account for the combination as a purchase.

There is some validity to the second argument above, but in most business combinations the relative size of the pooled-in company to the surviving entity is small indeed.

The third argument is rarely relevant today because the size test of poolings has been abandoned and consequently a large company can acquire a very small enterprise and still account for the combination as a pooling.

Aside from the above considerations, from the point of view of the analyst it is the results of pooling accounting that really matter. These can be best illustrated by means of a simplified example.

Assume that Company B, which wants to acquire Company S, earns $1,000 of net income and has 500 shares outstanding. Company S's condensed balance sheet is as follows:

Fixed assets*	$ 400	Liabilities	$ 200
Other assets	600	Capital accounts	800
	$1,000		$1,000
* Current value	600		

Company S has a net income of $200 after deduction of $20 for depreciation (10 percent of $400 in fixed assets less 50 percent tax effect).

Let us now consider the operating results of Company B one year after the acquisition of Company S for a price of $1,400 paid in (1) cash or (2) stock. Let us assume that the earnings of both companies remain unchanged and that the $1,400 purchase price (of Company S) is arrived at as follows:

Fixed assets (current value)	$ 600
Other assets	600
Goodwill	400
	1,600
Less liabilities assumed	200
Purchase consideration	$1,400

Payment in Cash   If the purchase price were in cash, the combined company's income statement would be accounted for on a purchase basis as follows:

Income of B			$1,000
Income of S (before depreciation)		$220	
Depreciation (10% of $600)	$30*		
Goodwill amortization (2½% of 400†) ...	10	40	180
Net income of the combined enterprise			$1,180

* After-tax effect.
† Assuming amortization over 40 years, no tax deduction.

Payment in Stock   If, however, the purchase price was in stock, under the pooling method of accounting the income statement of the enterprise would be as follows:

Income of B	$1,000
Income of S	200
Net income of the combined enterprise ..	$1,200

The difference in the net income is due to the inclusion, under the pooling method, of fixed assets at $400, the original cost on the books of Company S, and the complete omission of the goodwill that Company B paid in the acquisition of Company S.

Whether the reported income of the combined company is $1,200 or $1,180 depends in this case on how the purchase price was paid. Moreover, if the purchase price is paid in common stock and *any* of the other 11 conditions of a pooling are not met, the acquisition would have to be accounted for as a purchase and the reported income would be $1,180 instead of $1,200.

This, then, is the basic difference between pooling and purchase accounting. The nonrecording or suppression of asset values for which the acquiring company paid generally results in an understatement of assets and an overstatement of income. This is the primary reason why earnings that are the result of pooling combinations are viewed as being overstated in comparison with similar earnings resulting from purchase accounting.

As an astute financial analyst put it, "Dow Chemical with a market value of near $6 billion, offered stock worth $419 million for General Crude. The basis of accounting in a pooling will remain book value of General Crude which is about $82 million. Suppose instead International Paper had been successful and offered $419 in cash in a purchase. Then the new basis of General Crude's assets could have been $419 million. It seems that form prevails over substance in permitting pooling."[3]

APB Opinion 16 has done nothing to remove this problem which is inherent in the pooling of interests method. It has removed some of the abuses of the original criteria of the pooling of interests concept such as part pooling-part purchase, issuance of complex securities other than common stock in a pooling, retroactive pooling, and contingent additional consideration. But these features, while enabling the application of pooling accounting to many mergers, are not in themselves responsible for the suppression of asset values. This suppression is *inherent* in the pooling of interests concept, and all that *APB Opinion 16* achieved in this regard is to limit significantly the application of the concept by making it more difficult for companies to meet the criteria of a pooling. But once these criteria are met, many of the old problems and distortions remain.

ILLUSTRATION 3.   Two examples taken from a study* by Professors A. J. Briloff and C. Engler highlight some significant effects of the pooling method of accounting (in millions), shown in the following table (page 280):

---

[3] D. Norr, *Accounting Theory Illustrated* (New York: First Manhattan Co., 1974), p. 4.

Name of acquiring and pooled company (year of acquisition)	Market value of shares issued in acquisition	Book value of acquired company	Unrecorded value of assets
Pepsico, Inc., and Taco Bell (1978)	$ 139	$ 36	$ 103
General Electric Company and Utah International, Inc. (1976)	2,130	640	1,490†

* "Accountancy and the Merger Movement: A Symbiotic Relationship," *The Journal of Corporation Law,* Fall 1979.
† In 1983 General Electric sold Utah International's Australian division for $2.4 billion. Substantial amounts of these unrecorded assets were destined to surface as gains in GE's income statement. Indeed, in 1985 incident to GE's acquisition of RCA, a company spokesman reportedly bragged that GE "made $1 billion" on the Utah sale. The magic allowed by pooling accounting!

Clearly then, had these acquisitions been recorded on the purchase basis of accounting, the acquiring companies' books would have had to reflect substantially higher values for the assets they acquired with the result, among others, that the return on investment, operating performance, and other measures, such as liquidity, would have been significantly affected.

Let us now summarize the most important features of pooling of interests accounting which, from the point of view of the analyst, differentiate it from purchase accounting:

1. Assets acquired are carried at "book value" rather than at the current fair values reflected in the consideration given. To the extent that "goodwill" is paid for, the amount is not shown on the acquiring company's balance sheet.
2. The understatement of assets leads to an understatement of capital employed by the enterprise.
3. The understatement of assets such as inventory, property, plant, and equipment, as well as goodwill and other intangibles, will lead to an understatement of expenses such as cost of goods sold, depreciation, and amortization of goodwill and intangibles. In turn, this will lead to an overstatement of income.
4. The understatement of assets can lead not only to an understatement of expenses but can also result in an overstatement of gains realized on their disposition. Thus, the acquiring corporation can claim as part of its results of operations gains on the sale of assets that at the time of their acquisition were carried forward at unrealistically low amounts, amounts that are actually far below the amount that in the negotiations preceding the merger was the agreed fair values of these assets. In these cases, income is overstated and

management performance is overrated. What we have here is clearly a recovery of cost that is reported as a profit.

5. Both the understatement of invested capital and the overstatement of income will lead to an overstatement of the return on investment.
6. The retained earnings of the acquired enterprise can be carried forward to the surviving company.
7. The income statements and the balance sheets of the combined enterprise are restated for all periods presented. Under purchase accounting, they are combined only since the date of acquisition, although pro forma statements showing preacquisition combined results are also furnished.

ILLUSTRATION 4.   This restatement of all prior periods can lead to a type of double counting similar in effect to an acquiror of a pooled company reporting gains on the sale of undervalued acquired (pooled) assets.

Blockbuster Entertainment (BV) has enhanced its earnings by means of acquisitions accounted for as poolings. That, in turn, increased the value of the stock it used to consummate additional poolings. In 1989, BV acquired its largest franchisee, Video Superstore, for stock. In the past, sales of video tapes by Blockbuster to Video Superstore contributed greatly to BV's profits. When Video Superstore was pooled, the revenues and profits related to the intercompany video tape sales were eliminated in comparative statements. With prior sales and profits reported at lower levels, BV's growth curve appeared all the more impressive.

A crude way of adjusting for omitted values in a pooling is to determine the difference between carrying amounts and the fair or market value of assets acquired. This difference can then be amortized against reported income on some reasonable basis in order to arrive at results that would be comparable to those achieved under purchase accounting.

Purchase Accounting   Since purchase accounting is designed to recognize the acquisition values on which the buyer and seller of a business entity bargained, it is a more meaningful method of accounting from the analyst's point of view. Purchase accounting is more relevant to the analyst's needs because he or she is interested in values that were exchanged in a business combination rather than in amounts that represent original costs to the seller.

As we have noted earlier in this chapter, the abuses in purchase accounting that preceded the issuance of *APB Opinions 16* and *17* centered on attempts by acquiring companies to suppress the fair values of net assets acquired and paid for and to transplant the values paid for to a nondescript intangible asset account that was not amortized.

Push-Down Accounting   *APB Opinion 16* determined that the acquired assets and assumed liabilities of an acquired company should be included in the consolidated financial statements of the purchaser at their fair values. A controversial question remains as to how these assets and liabilities should be presented in the acquired company's separate financial statements (if that company survives as a separate entity).

The SEC, in *Staff Accounting Bulletin 54* (1983), decided that purchase transactions that result in an entity becoming substantially wholly owned (as defined in Reg. S-X) establish a new basis of accounting for the purchased assets and liabilities. Thus, if Company A acquires substantially all of the common stock of Company B in one or a series of purchase transactions, Company B's financial statements must reflect the new basis of accounting arising from its acquisition by Company A.

When the form of ownership is within the control of the parent, the basis of accounting for purchased assets and liabilities should be the same regardless of whether the entity continues to exist or is merged into the parent's operations. Therefore, Company A's cost of acquiring Company B should be "pushed down," that is, used to establish a new accounting basis, in Company B's separate financial statements.

The staff recognizes that the existence of outstanding public debt, preferred stock, or a significant minority interest in a subsidiary might impact the parent's ability to control the form of ownership. Although encouraging its use, the staff generally does not insist on the application of pushdown accounting in these circumstances.

The Theory and the Practice   While *APB Opinions 16* and *17* have directly and forthrightly addressed themselves to the problem and have as their primary objective the elimination of these abuses, the analyst must not confuse theory with practice. It must be realized that the objectives of many merger- and acquisition-minded managements with respect to the accounting for these business combinations were in the past and are now likely to remain—

1. To reduce as much as possible the impact on present and future income of charges arising from assets acquired in the purchase.
2. To increase the post-acquisition income by understating assets acquired or by overproviding for future costs and contingencies.

Remaining Room for Distortions   While *APB Opinion 16* contains specific provisions on the valuation of assets and liabilities, room for abuses and loose interpretations remains. In addition to the leeway that inevitably exists when broad rules of valuation and appraisal are applied, the analyst must also be alert to understatements of assets and overstatement of liabilities that result from provisions for future costs and losses.

ILLUSTRATION 5.   The acquisition by Gulf United of Southwestern Drug Company as analyzed by Professor C. Engler[4] points up some opportunities for income management in purchase accounting.

---

[4] Paper presented at the Annual Meeting of the American Accounting Association in Chicago, Illinois, on August 7, 1981.

Originally, pro forma financial statements indicated that the approximately 1 million shares of Southwestern to be exchanged and purchased for cash were to be valued at $16 million (or $16 per share), and this would have resulted in a bargain purchase of Southwestern Drug that could not be explained by its financial statements or justified by its recent earnings history. In a supplement to its prospectus, Gulf United indeed increased the per share valuation to a more realistic $22.50 (when Gulf United's stock was trading at $23.50). However, a review of the final accounting by Gulf United of its acquisition of Southwestern revealed that only 116,000 shares of Southwestern that were purchased for cash were recorded at $22.50 per share while the balance of 900,000 shares exchanged on a one-for-one basis were valued at only $16 per share. The result of this accounting was that Southwestern's equipment was reduced to zero value and negative goodwill was booked that was to increase Gulf United's income for the following 20 years. So eager was Gulf United to use the purchase method for this acquisition that it made its ability to use this method of accounting a contractual condition for consummating the acquisition.

Thus, in assessing the effect of a business combination accounted for as a purchase, the analyst must evaluate in detail the disclosures found regarding the process of valuation applied by the acquiring company. On the basis of such information, he or she must reach conclusions regarding the fairness of presentation of the acquired company's assets and liabilities. *Particular* attention must be paid to the possible overprovision for future costs and losses.

Acquisitions for Equity Securities   When an acquisition accounted for as a purchase is effected for stock or other equity securities, the analyst must be alert to the valuation of the net assets acquired in the combination. In periods of high market price levels, purchase accounting may tend to introduce inflated values when net assets, and particularly the intangible assets, of acquired companies are valued on the basis of market prices of the stock issued and where such inflated prices are not otherwise adjusted for. Such values, while determined on the basis of temporarily inflated stock prices, remain on a company's balance sheet and affect its operating results on a long-term basis.

Provision for Costs Incident to a Purchase   The analyst should be aware that acquiring companies using purchase accounting find it to their advantage to provide (and overprovide) for costs, such as plant closing, excess employee costs, and termination benefits which then become part of the cost of the purchase. Thus if a liability or provision for such costs is established, the goodwill account is correspondingly increased. While the costs provided for insulate the income statement over the short term of charges which it would otherwise have to absorb, the goodwill amortization generally affects income only over a longer period of time.[5]

---

[5] In *SAB 42A* the SEC states that 25 years is the maximum goodwill amortization period for business combinations of financial institutions initiated after 1982. There are other examples, where a shorter amortization period is prescribed.

The FASB is moving to restrict the setting up of various liabilities as part of purchase accounting but the analyst must be aware of and on the lookout for such income management practices. In this, as in many other cases, practice can depart considerably from theory and from the basic intent of promulgated standards. In no area is the potential impact greater than in the accounting for goodwill.

ACCOUNTING FOR GOODWILL—A MAJOR PROBLEM AREA

In theory, the excess of the purchase price over the fair market value of identifiable assets acquired is assumed to represent payment for super earnings which are generated by brand names or other evidences of a superior market position developed over the years. Not only does such a superior market position have to be maintained but such a market standing is subject to change by a myriad of economic and environmental forces. With effort and the constant expenditure of resources, such superior market position can be maintained but will usually not last forever. Thus, goodwill cannot be assumed to be permanent or indestructible. Moreover, the present value of super earnings diminishes as we discount them back from years far into the future. The accounting compromise reached after much discussion in the United States,[6] and which called for amortization of the cost of goodwill over a maximum of 40 years, or a generation, represents a very generous assumption about the longevity of this asset.

The excess earnings acquired are expected to show up in the acquiring entity's income statement over as many as 40 years, although the time period can be considerably shorter. Fair and accurate accounting thus requires that the cost of these acquired excess earnings be allocated to (amortized against) those earnings as they enter the new entity's earnings stream.

In practice, the area of accounting for goodwill is subject to substantial abuse because of the method of measuring its cost, that is, by defining it as a mere arithmetic residual, the difference between price paid and the fair market value of net assets acquired.

ILLUSTRATION 6.   Alexander & Alexander (AA) bought the British insurance broker Alexander Howden Group (AHG). It paid $300 million for the acquisition which included $120 million in assets with the balance being charged to goodwill. When, subsequently, AA discovered that $40 million of AHG's assets were missing, they simply increased

---

[6] In Britain where business is relieved of the need to account for the cost of goodwill, businessmen have found a related disadvantage. Massive goodwill write-offs, which are sanctioned, deplete the stated equity capital thus raising the debt-equity ratio and weakening other measures of financial health. Some managements attempt to solve this problem by proceeding to write up brand names and other intangibles in order to restore the depleted equity base. Shades of the pre-SEC "roaring twenties" when asset write-up abuses were common?

goodwill by a like amount. Only pressure from the SEC forced AA to take this as a $40 million charge to earnings instead.

The SEC has recently begun to insist that companies relate the amortization period of goodwill to the nature of the business acquired. Thus high-tech acquisitions require 5- to 7-year amortization and banks 15 to 20 years. The International Accounting Standards Committee limits the goodwill amortization period to no more than 20 years.

The mechanical way in which the amount assigned to goodwill is arrived at gives rise to a major uncertainty (i.e., what, besides superior earning power, is included in the residual labeled "goodwill"?). Thus, payments which are the result of errors in judgment, of heated bidding contests, or of carelessness with owner or creditor resources all get swept into the nondescript mass called goodwill. Such payments can even include substantial finder's fees, legal, and investment banker fees as well as interim financing costs.

Astute investor Warren E. Buffett, chairman of Berkshire Hathaway Inc., recognized this mechanical approach to the booking of goodwill when he wrote to his shareholders: "When an overexcited management purchases a business at a silly price . . . the silliness ends up in the goodwill account. Considering the lack of managerial discipline that created the account, under the circumstances it might better be labeled no-will."

The crux of the issue is: Does the goodwill account represent superior or excess earning power which was bought and from which the purchaser will benefit continuously over the period of its amortization or does it just represent a residual which is there and which is to be written off over the longest possible period of time? The analyst must realize that in all too many cases it merely represents the latter.

ILLUSTRATION 7.   In 1979 United Technologies (UT) purchased semiconductor maker Mostek Corp. for $345 million, of which $234 million represented goodwill.[7] Obviously, only the expectation of substantial profits, if not superprofits, would justify the payment of such a substantial premium. Instead of profits, Mostek continued its loss history (it lost $19 million in 1978 and $11 million in the preacquisition months of 1979). In 1985 UT wrote off $75 million in inventories of the semiconductor division. And yet, amortization of the goodwill continued at the slow 25-year pace apparently unrelated to the nonexistent value of this account.

When companies finally do write off goodwill in the face of substantial losses by purchased subsidiaries, the timing of the write-off betrays a motivation that differs from that of a prompt recognition of loss in value. Thus:

ILLUSTRATION 8.   Bangor Punta Corp. (BP) acquired Piper Aircraft for a payment that included a substantial amount for goodwill. As it turned out the payment was for

---

[7] As described by Professor A. J. Briloff in *Barron's* of July 22, 1985.

superlosses rather than superprofits. In fiscal 1982 when BP earned $3.1 million on a consolidated basis, Piper lost $22.4 million. Only when faced with an operating loss of $38.5 million by Piper and an overall consolidated loss for fiscal 1983 did BP decide to write off the Piper goodwill of $54.7 million. This appears to have been done on the basis of the "big bath" theory under which the recognition of losses is delayed until their impact is diminished by the fact that the company will report a loss in any event. At such time the write-off is beneficial since it relieves future income of expense charges. (For a further discussion of this topic, see Chapter 22.)

The basic dilemma facing the analyst in this area can be better understood if we contrast realistic operational definitions of goodwill from the point of view of the accountant and that of the quite different point of view of the analyst:

Accountant's Definition   The excess of cost over fair market value of assets acquired in a purchase transaction, also known as goodwill, is a differential arrived at mechanically. No attempt is made or is expected to identify components of this asset or the economic values that should be assigned to them. Whatever it is that has been paid for and cannot be separately identified is included in the amount assigned to goodwill. Presently, no realistic responsibility exists in practice to evaluate at each reporting period's end whether such recorded amounts in fact represent economic value. The requirement to amortize goodwill over a reasonable number of years, not exceeding 40, means in effect that in many cases management's wishes to use the longest period allowable will prevail. (See, however, the SEC's intervention described above.)

Financial Analyst's Definition   The nondescript asset "goodwill" can range greatly in both meaning and value. The accounting process that led to its recording provides few, if any, clues to its economic worth. It can represent solid value such as the purchase of widely accepted brand names which required many years of costly development and promotion. It can, at the other extreme, represent overpayments for assets due to unrealistic expectations, undisciplined zeal, or lack of sound judgment and proper analysis. There are, of course, a whole range of possibilities in between. The evaluation of the carrying amount and the amortization policy of the goodwill asset requires careful analysis of the market position and the superior earning power, if any, of the operations acquired. Goodwill represents a nonpermanent advantage that must evidence itself in current superior earning power or else it does not exist.

The process by which billions of goodwill are placed on corporate balance sheets is well illustrated by the much publicized battle for control of RJR Nabisco (RJRN):

ILLUSTRATION 9.   Just before the bidding battle for RJRN started, the market (dominated by astute financial institutions which held 40 percent of the stock) valued the company at about $12 billion. When a group, led by RJRN's CEO, started the bidding it offered $17 billion for the company. Let us designate the amount of the excess of that offer over the fair value of RJRN's tangible net assets (or goodwill) as X, an amount already larger by $5 billion than that assigned to it by the market. Ultimately, RJRN was sold for $25 billion which included X + $8 billion of goodwill. Undoubtedly swept into this account were very significant costs of financing, professional and investment banking talent, and other expenses involved in this costly bidding war. Does this huge asset then happen to represent the present value of future excess earning power? And, if not, what does it represent?

The problem of "goodwill" continues to be a serious one. Many billions of dollars of goodwill are found on the balance sheets of U.S. corporations. In some companies it represents a substantial part of net worth or even exceeds the total capital. Undoubtedly, some payments for "superior earning power" are warranted. But the analyst must be aware that in many cases the asset "goodwill" represents nothing more than the mechanical application of accounting rules which give no consideration to value received in return.

The analyst must also realize that the goodwill found on corporate books represents only that part of a company's intangible earning power (due to market position, brand names, or other proprietary advantages) which has been *purchased*. Self-developed goodwill cannot be booked as an asset.

ILLUSTRATION 10.   The acquisition of General Foods Corp. (GF) by Philip Morris Inc. (PM), for $5.8 billion involved about $2.8 billion as payment for goodwill. Quite possibly, GF's brand names justify this premium. On PM's balance sheet the goodwill account represented 78 percent of net worth but does *not* include the considerable value of PM's own brand names.

ACCOUNTING FOR FOREIGN OPERATIONS

When the user of financial statements attempts to analyze an entity that has investments and operations in a foreign country,[8] he or she must add to the problems that are discussed throughout this book those that are peculiar to foreign operations. These subdivide, broadly speaking, into two major categories:

1. Problems related to differences in accounting standards and practices that are peculiar to the foreign country in which the operations are conducted.[9]
2. Problems that arise from the translation of foreign assets, liabilities, equities, and results of operations into the U.S. dollar.

---

[8] *SFAS 14* now requires information about foreign operations and export sales (see also Chapter 20).

[9] Foreign companies raising capital in the United States or listed on U.S. stock exchanges must conform substantially to U.S. GAAP in filing registration statements.

Foreign Accounting Practices and Auditing Standards

Accounting practices can vary significantly among countries. There are a variety of reasons for this including a lack of agreement on objectives of financial statements, the requirements of national company laws, the influence of tax laws, and differences in the strength and the development patterns of local professional bodies.

In recent years, serious attempts have begun to bring more conformity into international accounting practices. The most ambitious program for the establishment of international accounting standards was the establishment in 1973 of the International Accounting Standards Committee (IASC) by the professional institutes of nine countries. Its objective is to "formulate and publish in the public interest, basic standards to be observed in the presentation of audited accounts and financial statements and to promote their worldwide acceptance and observance." The IASC has published a number of standards covering a variety of areas such as accounting for changing prices, for income taxes, for contingencies, for pensions, and other topics.

These are modest, yet important, beginnings, and much remains to be done if the significant differences between the accounting practices of various countries are to be narrowed.

Differences in Auditing Standards   In the area of auditing, which is discussed in Chapter 15 and is concerned with the function of attesting to the reliability of financial statements, a wide variety of standards exist in international practice. In some countries, such as the United Kingdom and Canada, for example, the auditing profession is strong and well regarded, while in others its standing may be weak and, consequently, the reliability of financial statements may be subject to considerable doubt. Nevertheless, an auditing firm of international repute can enhance the credibility of a company's financial statements regardless of the location of the company's home base. Thus, the analyst must assess the reliability of the financial statements that are used on the basis of the individual circumstances surrounding their preparation and attestation.

Peculiarities of Foreign Accounting Practices   One of the central theses of this text is that no intelligent analysis of financial statements is possible without a thorough understanding of the assumptions and of the standards on the basis of which such statements were prepared. It follows that in the case of foreign companies, the analyst must at least obtain a working familiarity with such assumptions and principles.

Accounting practices can vary significantly from country to country and there are many reasons for such variations.

One important category of reasons for such variations relate to how the objectives of financial accounting are viewed in various countries.

Accounting is a social science and its objectives are socially determined and socially expressed. For this reason alone, harmonization of international accounting practices remains difficult and elusive. For example, in the United States we prepare financial statements primarily with the interests of equity holders in mind. In other countries, such as Britain, the interests of creditors are the main focus, while in still others, such as France, the interests of taxing authorities take precedence. In some countries, such as Switzerland and Germany, the emphasis is on extreme conservatism where reserves, some secret in nature, are used to understate assets and income or to overstate liabilities. It is obvious that not all countries share the same view of the function of accounting as a discipline devoted to the communication of economic data.

While the differences in accounting practice between those obtaining in the United States and those in other countries vary significantly from country to country, they can be substantial. The following are merely indicative of the nature and extent of such differences. Thus, in some countries—

1. Inventory reserves and other secret reserves may be sanctioned.
2. Excessive depreciation may be recorded.
3. Because of substantial price-level changes, restatements of property accounts may be effected based on coefficients established by, and frequently revised by, the local government.
4. "Legal reserves" amounting to a fixed percentage of net income may be established.
5. Tax allocation may not be practiced.
6. Stock dividends may be recorded only on the basis of the par value of the stock issued.
7. Pooling of interests accounting may not be sanctioned.
8. Consolidation of parent and subsidiary financial statements may not be required.
9. The recognition of pension liabilities can vary widely.
10. General provisions (reserves) and subsequent reversals of such reserves may be used to shift income between periods.
11. It may not be acceptable to capitalize lease obligations.
12. Certain assets may be omitted from the financial statements.
13. No significance may be attached to consistency of application of accounting policies, and no disclosure of changes therein may be required.

A recitation of the differences in accounting as practiced in the United States and in other countries is beyond the scope of this book. The analyst must consult up-to-date sources of information that are relevant to the proper understanding and analysis of financial statements.[10]

---

[10] See, for example, the most recent survey by Price Waterhouse such as "A survey in 46 countries" or "International Accounting Standards and Guidelines," Deloitte & Touche.

In consolidating their foreign subsidiaries, U.S.-based multinational companies will usually conform their subsidiaries' accounting to the principles generally accepted in this country.

Translation of Foreign Currencies

In the discussion of intercorporate investments earlier in this chapter, it was emphasized that the consolidation of majority-owned subsidiaries is now a generally accepted procedure, and the reasons for nonconsolidation are few and well defined. With respect to subsidiaries of U.S.-based multinational companies, the most common reason for nonconsolidation would be substantial uncertainty regarding the ultimate realization or transferability of foreign earnings.

In addition to the above provisions, *APB Opinion 18* requires a parent company to recognize in its financial statements the equity in earnings or losses of (1) unconsolidated foreign subsidiaries; (2) corporate joint ventures; and (3) other companies, less than 50 percent owned, over which the investor company exerts a significant influence.

The consolidation of, as well as equity accounting for, foreign subsidiaries and affiliates requires that their financial statements be translated into U.S. dollar equivalents. This is, of course, necessary before the accounts of such foreign subsidiaries or affiliates can be combined with those of the U.S.-based company.

Evolution of the Accounting for Foreign Exchange Translation

Chapter 12 of *ARB 43* as modified by paragraph 18 of *APB Opinion 6* was the basic authoritative pronouncement on the subject before the FASB undertook to reconsider it. Chapter 12 of *ARB 43* called for the use of the *current-noncurrent* method of translation, that is, the translation of current assets and liabilities at current rates and the translation of noncurrent assets and liabilities at historical rates.

The pronouncement contained some exceptions to the current-noncurrent rule; and in 1965, paragraph 18 of *APB Opinion 6* sanctioned further changes such as the translation of all payables and receivables at the current rate. This, in effect, was a move to permit another method of translation known as the *monetary-nonmonetary method.* Under this method, monetary assets and liabilities are translated at the current rate while nonmonetary assets and liabilities are translated at applicable historical rates. Assets and liabilities are regarded as monetary if they are expressed in terms of a fixed number of foreign currency units, for example, cash, receivables, liabilities expressed in the foreign currency; all other assets and liabilities are regarded as nonmonetary.

Two other methods of foreign currency translation were also advanced during protracted discussions that preceded and continued during the FASB's consideration of the subject.[11]

The *current rate method* provides for the translation of all assets and liabilities at the current rate.

Under the *temporal method,* cash, receivables, and payables, as well as assets and liabilities carried at present or future prices, are translated at current rates while assets and liabilities carried at past prices (historical costs) are translated at applicable historical rates.

In 1975, the FASB adopted *SFAS 8* which basically follows the temporal method of translation.

Since its issuance, *SFAS 8* has been one of the most controversial of all the standards promulgated by the FASB. In response to repeated criticism of this standard, the Board decided in 1979 to reconsider this *Statement* and in 1981 issued *SFAS 52.*

SFAS No. 52, "Foreign Currency Translation," emphasizes a "local" perspective whereby a foreign entity and its economic relationships are treated as a separate business unit. The financial statements of this unit are prepared in the currency of the unit's economic environment. This is in contrast to the philosophy of *SFAS No. 8,* which is based on the parent company perspective. This perspective, which is consistent with the temporal method, requires that all transactions be measured as though they were made in U.S. dollars.

The major objectives of *SFAS No. 52* are (1) to provide information that is generally compatible with the expected economic effects of a change in exchange rates on an enterprise's cash flows and equity and (2) to reflect in consolidated statements the financial results and relationships as measured in the primary currency of the economic environment in which the entity operates—referred to as its **functional currency.**[12] The standard places reliance on management's judgment in determining what the functional currency of a foreign subsidiary is.

As to the first objective, *SFAS 52* recognizes that changes in exchange rates need not have a real effect on the operations of the foreign subsidiary.

The second objective recognizes that entities in foreign countries operate in their own economic environment which may be quite different from that prevailing in the United States. The translation process should

---

[11] In fact, nine distinct methods of foreign currency translations are illustrated in the FASB's *Financial Statement Model on Accounting for Foreign Currency Translation* (Stamford, Conn., 1974).

[12] For an entity with operations that are relatively self-contained and integrated within a country, the functional currency will generally be the currency of that country. However, for example, if the foreign operations are a direct component or extension of a parent company's operations, then the parent's currency would be the functional currency. In this case, the translation principles of *SFAS 8* would generally hold, including the requirement for current inclusion in income of all translation gains and losses. Under *SFAS 52,* all deferred income taxes are to be translated at current exchange rates.

not change financial relationships, such as the current ratio, inventory turnover, or debt-equity ratios, which are expressions of the financial statements expressed in local currency.

The functional currency approach does not translate foreign operations as though they were originally conducted in the parent company currency (e.g., dollars). Instead, the functional currency approach reflects and retains the relationships prevailing in the economic environment in which the foreign entity operates.

A major feature of the functional currency approach is the current rate translation method. A foreign entity's assets, liabilities, and operations exist basically in the economic environment of its functional currency. Its costs are incurred in its functional currency, and its revenues are produced in its functional currency. Use of a current exchange rate retains those historical costs and other measurements but restates them in terms of the reporting currency, thereby preserving the relationships established in the entity's economic environment. Accordingly, use of the current exchange rate reflects in the consolidated financial statements the inherent relationships appearing in the functional currency financial statements.

The functional currency approach entails:

a. Identifying the functional currency of the entity's economic environment.
b. Measuring all elements of the financial statements in the functional currency.
c. Using the current exchange rate for translation from the functional currency to the reporting currency, if they are different.
d. Distinguishing the economic impact of changes in exchange rates on a net investment from the impact of such changes on individual assets and liabilities that are receivable or payable in currencies other than the functional currency.

In adopting the functional currency approach, the Board had the following overall objectives of foreign currency translation in mind:

a. To provide information that is generally compatible with the expected economic effects of a rate change on an enterprise's cash flows and equity.
b. To present the consolidated financial statements of an enterprise in conformity with U.S. GAAP.
c. To reflect in consolidated financial statements the financial results and relationships of the individual consolidated entities as measured in their functional currencies.

Another major change in the Board's approach is to report the adjustment resulting from translation of foreign financial statements not as a gain or loss in the income of the period but as a separate accumulation as part of equity that, in accordance with FASB *SFAC 3,* can be viewed as part of "comprehensive income."[13] This must be clearly distinguished from gains or losses on foreign currency *transactions* which, with specific exceptions,[14] must be currently included in *income*. These include gains and losses on settled as well as *unsettled* transactions, such as may occur when, for example, a U.S. company takes out a 20-year debt denominated in Swiss francs.

A change in the exchange rate between the U.S. dollar and the other currency produces a change in the U.S. dollar equivalent of the net investment, although there is no change in the net assets of the other entity measured in its functional currency. A strengthening of the foreign currency against the dollar enhances the U.S. dollar equivalent; a weakening reduces the U.S. dollar equivalent. Accordingly, the translation adjustment reflects an economic effect of exchange rate changes. However, that change in the U.S. dollar equivalent of the net investment is an unrealized enhancement or reduction, having no effect on the functional currency net cash flows generated by the foreign entity that may be currently reinvested or distributed to the parent. It is for this reason that the translation adjustment is reported separately from the determination of net income.

Major Provisions of *SFAS* 52:

Based on the objectives and the considerations outlined above, the following are the major provisions of *SFAS 52:*

1. The translation process requires that the functional currency of the entity be identified first. Ordinarily it will be the currency of the country in which the entity is located or the U.S. dollar. All financial statement elements of the foreign entity must then be measured in terms of the functional currency in conformity with U.S. GAAP.

2. Translation from the functional currency into the reporting currency, if they are different, is to be at the *current* exchange rate[15] except that revenues and expenses are to be translated at the *average* exchange rates prevailing during the period.[16] The functional currency translation approach generally considers the effect of exchange

---

[13] See Chapter 3 for a definition of *comprehensive income*.

[14] These exceptions are:

a. Gains and losses attributable to a foreign currency transaction that is designated as, and is effective as, an economic hedge of a net investment in a foreign entity.

b. Gains or losses attributable to intercompany foreign currency transactions that are of a long-term investment nature when the entities to the transaction are consolidated, combined, or accounted for by the equity method in the reporting enterprise's financial statements.

[15] Usually the year-end rate that can be used for purposes of dividend remittances.

[16] A foreign entity's revenues, expenses, gains, and losses should be translated in a manner that produces amounts approximately as if the underlying elements had been translated on the dates they were recognized (sometimes referred to as the weighted-average exchange

rate changes to be on the net investment in a foreign entity rather than on its individual assets and liabilities.

3. Translation adjustments are not to be included in net income but are to be disclosed and accumulated as a separate component of stockholders' equity until such time that the net investment in the foreign entity is sold or completely or substantially liquidated. To the extent that the sale or liquidation represents realization, the relevant amounts should be removed from the separate equity component and included as a gain or loss in the determination of the net income of the period during which the sale or liquidation occurs.

4. Exchange gains and losses attributable to intercompany foreign currency transactions and balances that are of a trading nature are to be included in income, while those that are of a long-term financing or capital nature for which settlement is not contemplated in the foreseeable future are to be reported in the separate component of shareholders' equity where adjustments arising from the translation of foreign currency financial statements are accumulated.

Using the current rate method to translate the nonmonetary assets of foreign subsidiaries located in highly inflationary economies can produce distorted results. The Board concluded that if a foreign entity's functional currency has been affected by cumulative inflation of 100 percent or more over a three-year period, it is to be considered not stable enough to serve as a functional currency, and consequently, the financial statements of the entity shall be remeasured into the reporting (i.e., parent) currency. This remeasurement process, in effect, results in translation by the temporal method (i.e., the method of *SFAS 8*). Under *SFAS 52*, when the functional currency of a foreign subsidiary is that of the parent company (e.g., the dollar in the case of U.S. parents), translation will follow the principles of *SFAS 8*, except that the translation of deferred taxes is to be at the current rate of exchange. *SFAS 52* stipulates that preceding any translation, the foreign currency financial statements be prepared in conformity with U.S. generally accepted accounting principles.

Illustration of the Translation Procedure

Britco, a wholly owned British subsidiary of Dollarco, was incorporated several years ago when the exchange rate was £1 = U.S.$1.10. No capital stock changes have occurred since then. The trial balance of Britco at December 31, year 6, expressed in £ units is shown on the next page.

---

rate). This also applies to accounting allocations (e.g., depreciation, cost of sales, and amortization of deferred revenues and expenses) and requires translation at the current exchange rates applicable to the dates those allocations are included in revenues and expenses (i.e., not the rates on the dates the related items originated). In most cases, the average exchange rate prevailing during the year would be used.

Additional Information

1. The above trial balance has been adjusted to conform with U.S. generally accepted accounting principles. The pound is the functional currency of Britco.
2. The balance of the Cumulative Foreign Exchange translation adjustment account at December 31, year 5 was $30,000 (credit).
3. The dollar balance of retained earnings at December 31, year 5 was $60,000.
4. Exchange rates were as follows: January 1, year 6   £1 = $1.20
   December 31, year 6 £1 = $1.40
   Average for year 6   £1 = $1.30
5. All accounts receivable and payable and long-term debt amounts are denominated in the local currency.

Cash	£ 100,000
Accounts receivable	300,000
Inventories, at cost	500,000
Prepaid expenses	25,000
Property, plant, and equipment (net)	1,000,000
Long-term note receivable	75,000
	£2,000,000
Accounts payable	£ 500,000
Current portion of long-term debt	100,000
Long-term debt	900,000
Capital stock	300,000
Retained earnings, January 1, year 6	50,000
Sales	5,000,000
Cost of sales	(4,000,000)
Depreciation	(300,000)
Other expenses	(550,000)
	£2,000,000

6. Sales, purchases, and all operating expenses are assumed to have occurred evenly throughout the year. Therefore the application of the average exchange rate will produce results as if each individual month's revenues and expenses were translated using the rate in effect during each month. It is appropriate here to convert the cost of goods sold by use of the average rate.
7. Income tax consequences, if any, relating to this account are to be ignored[17] in this illustration.

---

[17] Generally interperiod tax allocation is required in accordance with *SFAS 109* if taxable exchange gains or tax-deductible exchange losses resulting from an entity's foreign currency transactions are included in net income in a different period for financial statement purposes than for tax purposes.

BRIT CO
Translation Working Paper
Year Ended December 31, year 6

	£	Exchange rate	Translation code or explanation	U.S. dollars
Balance Sheet				
Cash	100,000	1.4	C	140,000
Accounts receivable	300,000	1.4	C	420,000
Inventories, at cost	500,000	1.4	C	700,000
Prepaid expenses	25,000	1.4	C	35,000
Property, plant, and equipment (net)	1,000,000	1.4	C	1,400,000
Long-term note receivable	75,000	1.4	C	105,000
Total assets	2,000,000			2,800,000
Accounts payable	500,000	1.4	C	700,000
Current portion of long-term debt ..	100,000	1.4	C	140,000
Long-term debt	900,000	1.4	C	1,260,000
Total liabilities	1,500,000			2,100,000
Capital stock	300,000	1.1	H	330,000
Retained earnings:				
Balance, 1/1/year 6	50,000		B	60,000
Current year net income	150,000		F	195,000
Balance, 12/31/year 6	200,000			255,000
Cumulative foreign exchange translation adjustment Balance, 1/1/year 6			B	30,000
Current year translation adjustment			G	85,000
Balance, 12/31/year 6				115,000
Total stockholders' equity	500,000			700,000
Total liabilities and equity ..	2,000,000			2,800,000
Income Statement				
Sales	5,000,000	1.3	A	6,500,000
Cost of sales	(4,000,000)	1.3	A	(5,200,000)
Depreciation	(300,000)	1.3	A	(390,000)
Other expenses	(550,000)	1.3	A	(715,000)
Net income	150,000			195,000

Translation code or explanation:
C = current rate.
H = historical rate.
A = average rate.
B = balance in U.S. dollars at the beginning of the period.
F = per income statement.
G = amount needed to balance the financial statements.

In the solution which follows, the translation is done in balance sheet and income statement (versus the trial balance) format so as to highlight the FASB's treatment of classifying translation adjustments as a separate component of stockholders' equity.

A review of the translation working paper of Britco reveals the following noteworthy elements:

1. All items in the simplified income statement are converted at the average rate of exchange prevailing during the year.
2. All assets and liabilities are translated at the current rate of exchange. The capital stock account is translated at the historical rate. If all of a foreign entity's assets and liabilities are measured in its functional currency and are translated at the current exchange rate, the net accounting effect of a change in the exchange rate is the effect on the net assets of the entity. Such an accounting result is compatible with the broad concept of economic hedging on which the net investment view is based. No gains or losses arise from hedged assets and liabilities, and the dollar equivalent of the un-hedged net investment increases or decreases when the functional currency strengthens or weakens.
3. It will be noted that after the translated net income for year 6 of $195,000 is added to the retained earnings section of the balance sheet, a translation adjustment of $85,000 must be inserted in order to balance the balance sheet. When this current year translation adjustment (credit) of $85,000 is added to the $30,000 opening credit balance of the Cumulative Foreign Exchange Translation Adjustment account, the resulting ending balance for this account is a credit of $115,000. This will be the opening balance of this equity account as of January 1, year 7.
4. In this particular example the Cumulative Foreign Exchange Translation Adjustment account was affected only by the translation adjustment that was required in order to balance the translated balance sheet. In different circumstances this account could also be debited or credited for:
   a. Gains and losses attributable to a foreign currency transaction that is designated as, and is effective as, an economic hedge of a net investment in a foreign entity.
   b. Gains or losses attributable to intercompany foreign currency transactions and balances that are of a long-term financing or capital nature when the entities to the transaction are consolidated, combined, or accounted for by the equity method in the reporting entity's financial statements.

ANALYSIS OF TRANSLATION GAIN OR LOSS

Use of the current rate translation method resulted in a balancing figure of $85,000 needed to balance the translated balance sheet. This resulted, in the above Britco example, in a translation gain of $85,000 which was added to the Cumulative Foreign Exchange Translation Adjustment account in the equity section. This $85,000 gain which was derived indirectly can also be computed directly.

Accounts that are translated at historical rates are not affected by exchange rate changes because they are always assigned the dollar amount which prevailed at their origination. Thus, exchange gains or losses arise from the translation of assets or liabilities at the current rate. Since only the equity accounts are translated at historical rates, the net assets that are translated at current rates are exposed to the risk of changes in exchange rates. If the dollar strengthens against the foreign exchange the dollar value of the foreign net assets declines, thus producing exchange losses. Conversely, if the dollar weakens against the foreign currency, the dollar value of the foreign net assets increases. This produces exchange gains as was the case of Britco in year 6.

To derive the net exchange gain for year 6 of Britco directly we start with the beginning net asset position of £350,000 (i.e., capital stock of £300,000 + Retained earnings of £50,000). We multiply that opening balance of net assets by the change in the exchange rates between the beginning and end of year—here a strengthening of $0.20 ($1.40–$1.20) per pound. Since net assets increased in year 6 this balance was exposed to the change in exchange rates for the full year and resulted in a gain of $70,000 on this part of the net asset position.

The *change* in net assets during the year must be multiplied by the difference between the year-end rate (here $1.40) and the rate prevailing at the date or dates when the cause of change occurred. We know that in the case of Britco the only cause of the change was due to net income earned. Income and expense items are translated at the average exchange rate (here $1.30) and thus the increase in net assets is multiplied by the difference between the year-end rate and the average rate ($1.40–$1.30), i.e., $0.10.

Thus, the computation of the translation gain is arrived at as follows:

Translation gain on beginning net assets:	
£350,000 × ($1.40–$1.20)	$70,000
Translation gain on increase in net assets during year 6:	
£150,000 × ($1.40–$1.30)	15,000
Total	$85,000

It should be noted that when the cause of the change in net assets during the year is due to reasons additional to those related to operations, they have to be identified and the rate of exchange at which they have been translated must be determined as well. They then will enter the computation of translation gain or loss as was illustrated above.

Disclosure Requirements

SFAS 52 requires disclosure of the aggregate transaction gain or loss included in net income for the period as well as presentation of an analysis of the changes during the period in the separate component of equity for cumulative translation adjustments.

In *FRR 6,* the SEC notes its concern regarding the adequacy of financial statement disclosure about the effects of translating foreign operations. The Release suggests that management's discussion and analysis should provide more information to supplement what's in the financial statements, such as:

> Information about how rate changes affect reported operating results—for example, the depressing effect of weakening foreign currencies on reported sales.
>
> Identification of functional currencies used for significant foreign operations, and the extent of exchange rate risk involved.
>
> Availability of cash flows from foreign operations to meet the company's overall needs.

In an interpretative release (1982) the SEC suggested disclosures of foreign currency translation effects such as the following:

- A display of net investments by major functional currency.
- The functional currencies used to measure significant foreign operations.
- The degree of exposure to exchange rate risks.
- The company's intracompany financing practices.
- The nature of the translation component of equity.
- An analysis of the translation component of equity by functional currency or geographical area.

Accounting for Investment by Parent Company

When the investment in the foreign subsidiary is accounted for by the parent company on the equity method, the parent will have to pick up its share[18] of the translation adjustment. Thus, in the case and our illustration Dollarco will, for year 6, make the following entries (figures in U.S. dollars):

Investment in Britco	195,000	
Equity in Earnings of Subsidiary		195,000
To pick up equity in earnings of Britco.		
Investment in Britco	85,000	
Translation Adjustment		85,000
To pick up the current year translation adjustment.		

Accounting on Sale of Subsidiary

Continuing with the example in our illustration, should Dollarco sell its investment in Britco on January 1, year 7, then, *in addition* to recording

---

[18] Thus, if a parent owns only 80 percent of a subsidiary, it will pick up 80 percent of the translation adjustment.

a gain or loss on the difference between the proceeds of the sale and the carrying (book) value of the investment, Dollarco will close out the Cumulative Foreign Exchange Translation Adjustment account with a credit balance of $115,000 into income as part of this completed and realized sales transaction.

Remeasurement under the Temporal Method

As discussed earlier, the temporal method should be used to remeasure the foreign entity's financial statements into its functional currency if its books were not kept in that currency or if the subsidiary is located in a highly inflationary economy. If, after remeasurement, the foreign entity's functional currency is not the parent's reporting currency (i.e., the dollar) the remeasured statements must then be translated into the reporting currency using the current rate method described above.

In some cases a foreign entity's functional currency differs from its local currency because its functional currency is the parent company's reporting currency. In these cases, once the remeasurement has been accomplished, no further currency translation is necessary.

The remeasurement of foreign currency financial statements into the currency deemed to be the functional currency by means of the temporal method is essentially[19] equivalent to translation under the superseded *SFAS 8*. Foreign exchange gains and losses resulting from the remeasurement are included in *income.*

SFAS 52 states that the remeasurement process shall produce the same result as if the entity's books of record had been maintained in the functional currency. This objective is achieved by remeasuring the following accounts using *historical exchange rates.*

Marketable securities carried at cost:
    Equity securities;
    Debt securities not intended to be held until maturity;

Inventories carried at cost;

Prepaid expenses such as insurance, advertising, and rent;

Property, plant, and equipment;

Accumulated depreciation on property, plant, and equipment;

Patents, trademarks, licenses, and formulas;

Goodwill;

Other tangible assets;

Deferred charges and credits, except deferred income taxes and life
    insurance policy acquisition costs;

---

[19] The principal difference between the *SFAS 8* process and that mandated by *SFAS 52* is that deferred taxes are remeasured at current rates.

Deferred income;

Common stock;

Preferred stock carried at issuance price.

All equity-related accounts and transactions, retained earnings, and paid-in capital are also remeasured using historical exchange rates. Dividends are remeasured using the rate prevailing at the date they were declared.

The remeasurement of the following revenue and expense items, for example, which are related to nonmonetary items will also be based on historical rates:

Cost of good sold;

Depreciation of property, plant, and equipment;

Amortization of intangible items such as goodwill, patents, licenses, etc.;

Amortization of deferred charges or credits except deferred income taxes and life insurance policy acquisition costs.

All other accounts are to be remeasured by use of the *current rate.*

IMPLICATIONS FOR ANALYSIS

The fact that *SFAS 8* was one of the most controversial statements issued by the Board, as well as the fact that its replacement, *SFAS 52,* was issued by the narrow margin of 4 to 3, attests to the difficult and complex nature of the accounting for foreign exchange translation. In order for the analyst to be able to evaluate that accounting as well as to forecast the effect of currency rate changes on the results that it produces, he or she must have a thorough understanding of both the philosophy underlying this accounting standard as well as the mechanics which flow from it.

The temporal method of translation under *SFAS 8* was the method most faithful to and consistent with the historical cost accounting model in present use. Under this method, and under the focus on the dollar that it embraced, nonmonetary items such as property, plant, and equipment and inventories are stated at the translated dollar amounts at date of acquisition. Similarly depreciation and cost of goods sold are reflected on the basis of such historical-dollar costs.

Since fluctuations in exchange rates did not affect the carrying amounts of these nonmonetary assets, it is clear that the real exposure to balance sheet translation gains and losses was measured by the excess of *monetary* assets over *monetary* liabilities (which were translated at *current* rates), or vice versa. Thus, under the temporal method if a foreign subsidiary has an excess of monetary liabilities over monetary assets (i.e., heavy debt), then if:

As against local currency	Balance sheet translation effect is a—
Dollar strengthens	Gain
Dollar weakens	Loss

Conversely, if the foreign subsidiary has an excess of monetary assets over monetary liabilities (e.g., substantial equity capital), then if:

As against local currency	Balance sheet translation effect is a—
Dollar strengthens	Loss
Dollar weakens	Gain

It is clear that the impact of balance sheet translation under *SFAS 8* depended on circumstances, but the real complaint was that all these unpredictable gains and losses were included immediately in income thus resulting in earning volatility. As can be expected, company criticism was not as vocal when the translation process resulted in gains as when it resulted in losses. For that reason, not all companies were or are opposed to the methodology of *SFAS 8*.

SFAS 52 changed the accounting significantly except in two circumstances when the methodology of *SFAS 8* (i.e., the temporal method of translation) must continue to be employed:

1. When by virtue of its nature the foreign operation is merely an extension of the parent and consequently the dollar is its functional currency.
2. When hyperinflation (as defined) would cause the translation of nonmonetary assets at the current rate to result in unrealistically low carrying values. In such cases, in effect, the foreign currency has lost its usefulness as a measure of performance and a more stable unit (i.e., the dollar) is used.

SFAS 52 introduced two radical departures. By moving away from the temporal method to the current exchange rate basis, it, in effect, selectively introduced current value accounting into this one area. Moreover, in allowing gains and losses to bypass the income statement, it reintroduced, in somewhat modified form, the long-discredited "charge to surplus" approach (see Chapter 11). That, in effect, removed from current operations the effects of the risk of operating in a foreign environment along with the risks of changes in exchange rates.

While unquestionably insulating income from balance sheet *translation* gains and losses, as opposed to transaction gains and losses and income statement translation effects, *SFAS 52* introduced a translation exposure that differs from that of *SFAS 8*.

While under *SFAS 8* the translation exposure was measured by the excess of monetary assets over monetary liabilities (or vice versa), under *SFAS 52, all* balance sheet items, except the net equity, are translated at the current rate, and thus, the exposure is measured by the size of the net equity or net investment. This can be illustrated as follows:

ILLUSTRATION 9. Assume that Swissco, a subsidiary of Amerco, started operations on January 1, year 1, with a balance sheet in Swiss Francs (SF) as follows:

	SF		*SF*
Cash	100	Accounts payable ..	90
Receivables	120	Capital stock	360
Inventory	90		
Fixed assets	140		
	450		450

The income statement for the year ending December 31, year 1, was:

	SF
Sales	3,000
Cost of sales (including depreciation of SF 20) .	(1,600)
Other expenses	(800)
Net income	600

The year-end balance sheet was as follows:

	SF		*SF*
Cash	420	Accounts payable ..	180
Receivables	330	Capital stock	360
Inventories	270	Retained earnings ..	600
Fixed assets (net) ..	120		
	1,140		1,140

For ease of computation, the above changes were kept simple and we assume the following exchange rates:

January 1, year 1 ..... $1 = SF 2
December 31, year 1 .. $1 = SF 3
Year 1 average .... $1 = SF 2.50

The opening and closing balance sheets would be translated into dollars as follows:

	January 1, year 1			December 31, year 1		
	SF	Conversion	$	SF	Conversion	$
Cash	100	÷2	50	420	÷3	140
Receivables	120	÷2	60	330	÷3	110
Inventory	90	÷2	45	270	÷3	90
Fixed assets	140	÷2	70	120	÷3	40
	450		225	1,140		380
Accounts payable	90	÷2	45	180	÷3	60
Capital stock	360	÷2	180	360	÷2	180
Retained earnings				600	*	240
Translation adjustment ..						(100)
	450		225	1,140		380

* Per income statement—since *each* individual income statement item is translated at the average rate, net income in dollars is SF 600 ÷ 2.50 = $240.

The translation adjustment account (which is part of equity) can be independently calculated as follows:

		$
Total equity (which equals net assets):		
In SF at December 31, year 1	SF 960	
Converted into dollars at year-end rate ÷ 3		$ 320
Less:		
Capital stock at December 31, year 1 per	$180	
converted balance sheet (in dollars)		
Retained earnings balance at December 31, year 1	240	420
per converted balance sheet (in dollars)		
Translation adjustment—loss		$(100)

A number of analytical insights can be derived from this illustration:

1. The translation adjustment (in this case, a loss of $100 for Year 1) is a function of the net investment in Swissco at end of year 1 (SF 960) times the change in the exchange rates. Since the exchange rate had declined from SF 2 to the dollar for the capital stock and from SF 2.50 to the dollar for retained earnings to the year-end rate of SF 3 to the dollar, the SF investment expressed in dollars has suffered a loss of $100. That makes sense—when you have an investment expressed in a foreign currency and that currency weakens in relation to the dollar then the value of your investment, in terms of dollars, declines. The reverse is, of course, also true.

2. While under *SFAS 52*, net income is not affected by *balance sheet* translation, the equity capital is. That will affect the debt to equity ratio (the level of which may be specified by certain debt covenants) and book value per share of the translated balance sheet but not of the foreign currency balance sheet. Since the entire equity capital is the measure of exposure to balance sheet translation gain or loss, that exposure may be even more substantial than that under *SFAS 8* particularly with regard to a subsidiary financed with low debt and high equity. The analyst can estimate the translation adjustment impact by multiplying year-end equity by the estimated change in the period-to-period rate of exchange.

3. The effect of a change in exchange rates on the translation of the income statement is another matter. If for simplicity we assume that in year 2 Swissco will have exactly the same net income but that the SF has weakened further to SF 3.50 (average for year) to the dollar, then the translated net income will total SF 600 ÷ 3.50 = $171, or a decline of $69 from the year 1 level of $240. This loss will, of course, be reflected in the translated income statement.

Conversely, should the SF strengthen to SF 2 to the dollar (average for year), the translated net income will total SF 600 ÷ 2 = $300, or a gain of $60 from the year 1 level of $240. Here again this is a gain that will be reflected in net income since the income earned in SF is worth more dollars. Note that under *SFAS 52*, translated reported earnings will vary directly with changes in exchange rates and that this makes estimation by the analyst of the "income statement translation effect" easier. Estimation of earnings under *SFAS 8* was more difficult.

The analyst must also be aware that in addition to the above, income will also include the results of completed foreign exchange transactions. Also, any gain or loss on the translation of a current payable by the subsidiary to parent (which is not of a long-term capital nature) will pass through consolidated net income.

A substantial drop in the dollar relative to many important currencies has, under the provisions of *SFAS 52*, the effect of increasing the reported income of consolidated foreign subsidiaries. It also has the result of increasing stockholders' equity, in some cases, by relatively substantial amounts. That, however, in turn, reduces such measures as the return on equity (see Chapter 19). Under such conditions criticism of *SFAS 52* is not likely to be heard. Should the dollar make a substantial turnabout and recover, the results under *SFAS 52* will be the opposite and the chorus of criticism is certain to rise to a higher level.

The analyst must bear in mind that it is basically a management decision to determine whether the functional currency is the local currency or the dollar.

ILLUSTRATION 10. In the mid-1980s the managements of Unocal, Occidental Petroleum, and Texaco designated the dollar as the functional currency of most of their foreign operations. On the other hand, their competitors Mobil Oil, Exxon, and Amoco designated the local currencies of their foreign businesses as the functional currencies.

Thus, should dollar weakness continue, companies may, by designating the dollar as the functional currency, choose the temporal translation method which may afford them better reported results. Conversely, a strengthening dollar may, in most cases, make it more advantageous to use the "all current" translation method of *SFAS 52*.

While *SFAS 52* results in smaller fluctuations in income relative to fluctuations in exchange rates, it does result in much more substantial changes in the stockholders' equity because of the changes in the Cumulative Translation Adjustment (CTA) account. For companies with a large equity base these changes may not be significant but for companies with a weaker equity base such changes, which diminish the equity, can have a serious effect on the debt to equity ratios and may affect debt covenants as well. As we have seen, the exposure to changes in the CTA account depends on the degree of exposure of foreign subsidiary net assets to changes in exchange rates. Companies can, of course, act to reduce their exposure by reducing the net assets of their foreign subsidiaries. This can, for example, be achieved by withdrawing foreign investment in the form of dividends or by substituting foreign debt for equity.

An increasing debit balance in the CTA account is usually symptomatic of a failure to manage properly the foreign exchange exposure. That can result from many causes including investments denominated in chronically weak currencies.

QUESTIONS

1. What significant information may be disclosed by inspection of individual parent company and subsidiary statements that is not found in the consolidated statements? (CFA)
2. "A parent company is not responsible for the liabilities of its subsidiaries nor does it own the assets of the subsidiaries. Therefore, consolidated financial statements distort legal realities." Evaluate this statement from the financial analyst's viewpoint.
3. Which of the following cases would require consolidated financial statements?
   a. The parent company has a two-fifths ownership of the subsidiary.
   b. The parent company has temporary but absolute control over the subsidiary.
   c. The parent company has a controlling interest in the subsidiary but plans to dispose of it.
   d. Control of the subsidiary is to be relinquished in the near future as a result of a minority shareholder's derivative suit.
   e. A conglomerate parent company has a majority interest in diversified subsidiaries.

> *f.* The parent company has a 100 percent interest in a foreign subsidiary in a country where the conversion of currencies and the transfer of funds is severely restricted by the governmental authorities.
>
> *g.* The parent company has a 100 percent interest in a subsidiary whose principal business is the leasing of properties to the parent company and its affiliates.

4. Why is the cost method of accounting for investments in subsidiaries regarded as the least desirable?

5. Give some examples of situations in which the use of the cost method, rather than the equity method, is more appropriate.

6. What are some of the important limitations to which consolidated financial statements are subject?

7. The following note appeared in the financial statements of the Best Company for the period ending December 31, Year 1:

> "*Event subsequent to December 31, Year 1:* In January Year 2, the Company acquired Good Products, Inc., and its affiliates by the issuance of 48,063 shares of common stock. Net assets of the combined companies amounted to $1,016,198, and net income for Year 1 approximated $150,000. To the extent that the acquired companies earn in excess of $1,000,000 over the next five years, the Company will be required to issue additional shares not exceeding 151,500, limited, however, to a market value of $2,000,000."

> *a.* Is the disclosure necessary and adequate?
>
> *b.* If the Good Products, Inc., was acquired in December Year 1, at what price should the Best Company have recorded the acquisition, assuming the Best Company's shares are traded at $22 on that day?
>
> *c.* On what is the additional consideration contingent?
>
> *d.* If the contingency materializes to the maximum limit, how should Best Company record the investment?

8. How would you determine the valuation of assets acquired in a purchase in the following cases?
   a. Assets acquired by incurring liabilities.
   b. Assets acquired in exchange of common stock.

9. Assuming the total cost of a purchased entity is appropriately determined, how should the total cost be allocated to the following assets?
   a. Goodwill.
   b. Negative goodwill (bargain purchase).
   c. Marketable securities.
   d. Receivables.
   e. Finished goods.
   f. Work-in-process.
   g. Raw materials.
   h. Plant and equipment.
   i. Land and mineral reserves.
   j. Payables.
   k. Goodwill recorded in the book of the acquired company.

10. One of the arguments for pooling of interests is that in pooling no resource is given in exchange for the acquisition: since the acquiring company

gives its unissued stock, the acquisition cannot be regarded as purchase. Do you agree?

11. Company A uses the pooling of interests method to account for the acquisition of Company B, the market value of whose net assets is much higher than their book value. What will be the effect of the pooling of interests method on Company A's income statement? On its balance sheet? What significance does *APB Opinion 16* have on such effects?

12. How is "goodwill" treated in an acquisition accounted for as a pooling of interests?

13. If assets are understated as a result of a pooling of interests, what effect(s) would the understatement have on the following items?
    a. Capital account.
    b. Various expenses.
    c. Disposition of assets acquired.

14. Is there any way an analyst can adjust the income statement under the pooling of interests method so that it can be comparable to a purchase method income statement?

15. From the analyst's point of view, which method of accounting for a business combination is preferable and why?

16. When an acquisition accounted for as a purchase is effected for stock or other equity securities, what should the analyst be alerted to?

17. When the balance sheet shows a substantial amount of goodwill, to what should the analyst be alert?

18. A current accounting controversy concerns the widespread use of pooling in mergers. Opponents of the use of pooling believe that the surviving company often uses pooling (rather than purchase) to hide the "true" effects of the merger. What may be "hidden," and how is the analysis of a company's securities affected by pooling practices? (CFA)

19. Company X has engaged in an aggressive program of acquiring other companies through exchange of common stock.
    a. Explain briefly how an acquisition program might contribute to the rate of growth in earnings per share of Company X.
    b. Explain briefly how the income statements of prior years might be adjusted to reflect the potential future earnings trend of the combined companies. (CFA)

20. What are some factors that could change management's original estimates of the useful life of intangible assets?

21. What are some significant problem areas in accounting for foreign operations?

22. When a consolidated financial statement includes foreign operations, to what must the financial analyst be particularly alert?

23. What are the major objectives of *SFAS 52?*

24. What are the major provisions of *SFAS 52?*

25. Discuss the major changes that were introduced by *SFAS 52* on translation of foreign currency.

26. Under what circumstances must the temporal method of translation of foreign currency be employed?

27. What are the implications for analysis resulting from *SFAS 52?*

Chapter 10

ANALYSIS OF THE
INCOME STATEMENT—I

The income statement portrays the net results of operations of an enterprise. Since results are what enterprises are supposed to achieve and since their value is, in large measure, determined by the size and quality of these results, it follows quite logically that the analyst attaches great importance to the income statement.

This chapter and the one that follows will examine the principles that underlie the preparation and presentation of the income statement. The analysis and interpretation of this important financial statement are discussed in Chapters 20, 21, and 22. Such analysis can be undertaken intelligently only after the principles outlined in these chapters are fully understood.

What is income? An examination of this subject will reveal that significant differences of opinion exist among thoughtful and competent accountants, economists, and financial analysts on what income is and on how the net income of an enterprise for a given period should be measured.

A Simple Illustration

Take, for example, the very simple case of a business unit that has only $1,000 in cash, with which it buys at the beginning of the year a bond priced at par and carrying a 6 percent coupon. While we may readily agree that the gross income is $60 (the interest), the determination of net income depends, among other factors, on the value of the bond at year-end. Thus, if the market price at year-end is $950, the $50 loss would be recognized by the economist while the accountant may or may not recognize it, depending on a judgment of whether there has been a permanent impairment in the value of the bond and, also, on whether the loss must be recognized if it is the present intention of the enterprise to hold it to a not too distant maturity date. The economist would claim that it is not right to recognize the income of $60 without the offsetting shrinkage in capital in the amount of $50. The essence of this argument is that the enterprise was not as well off at the end of the period as it was at the beginning if the $60 is all recognized as income and so distributed.

If, instead, the bond had a market quotation at year-end of $1,100, then some economists would consider the $100 accretion as a gain to be added to the $60 in interest earned. This most accountants would not do because the gain is not realized and the market value of the bond could fluctuate in either direction before it is finally sold. Other theoreticians would not rely on the current market price of the bond but, taking the going interest rate into account, would value the bond at the present value of future interest receipts ($60 a year) plus the present value of the bond principal at maturity discounted at the appropriate rate and would use such value in the determination of net income for the period. There again, accountants have, so far, shied away from such approaches mostly because the variables that make up the bond value can change very frequently before final realization through sale or redemption of the bond. They consider such realization as the necessary objective evidence needed to warrant recording of the gain.

Price-level changes complicate matters even further, and their effects are considered in Chapter 14.

If such a simple income-producing asset as a bond, which involves no complexities on the expense side, can give rise to so many possible interpretations of what the amount of the net income it produced is, obviously the determination of the amount of net income of a full-fledged business enterprise is far more complex. It is in this light that one can, at least, understand, even if not fully agree with, the principles of income determination that accountants have established over the years.

A Variety of Concepts of Income

Going from our simple specific example to generalizations, we see that the economist's concept of income is the amount that could be consumed or distributed by an entity during a period and still leave it as "well-off" at the end of the period as it was at the beginning.

It is in the area of measuring the degree of "well-offness" of an enterprise that the gap between the economist's view and that of the accountant is widest. The economist maintains that capital value can be measured by the present value of future net receipts. But such receipts are based on highly subjective and constantly shifting estimates of future probabilities applying to both the *size* of the net receipts and the discount factors to be applied to them. The degree of uncertainty present here dwarfs that involved in estimating, for example, the future useful life of plant and equipment or the probability of debt collection, which are estimates of a kind that accountants now make. Thus, while the economist, cognizant of the uncertainty pervading all of business life, is impatient with the accountant's great concern for objectivity, verifiability, and conservatism, the latter believes that the very utility of his professional service to the community is dependent upon his upholding these qualities and characteristics.

Because of the divergencies in viewpoint such as those discussed above, the differences in the concepts of income of economists and accountants have not been appreciably narrowed. This is, in large measure, also due to difficulties that a practicing profession found in implementing in practice the theoretical concepts of economic thought.

One way in which income can be measured is by comparing the capital balances at the beginning and end of a period.[1] Since capital is the excess of assets over liabilities, the problem of income determination is thus inseparable from the problem of asset and liability measurement. While, as we have seen, the economist focuses on a comparison of capital balances at successive points in time, in modern accounting, the income determination process centers around the relating of current costs and revenues within a specific span of time. To the analyst who is interested in using the income statement as a means of predicting future streams of income and expense, this is a much more useful approach, because he or she is very much interested in all the elements that make up the final net income figure.

The process of income determination thus involves two basic steps: (1) identification of the revenues properly attributable to the period reported upon and (2) relating of the corresponding costs with the revenues of this period either through direct association with the cost of the products sold therein or by assignment as expenses properly applicable as costs of the period.

THE ACCRUAL OF REVENUE

SFAC 3 defines revenues as "inflows or other enhancements of assets of an entity or settlements of its liabilities" resulting from the entity's "ongoing major or central operations" (par. 63). The *Statement* defines gains as increases in an entity's net assets resulting from all other transactions and events affecting the entity (par. 67).

For every profit-seeking enterprise, the first step in the process of profit or loss recognition is the accrual of revenue. Thus, the very important question that arises is when, or at what point, in the entire sequence of revenue-earning activities in which an enterprise is engaged, is it proper to recognize revenue as earned? The improper accrual of revenue can have one of two undesirable effects:

---

[1] FASB *SFAC 3*, "Comprehensive Income," best fits this concept of measurement and is defined as the overall return on financial capital (i.e., the change in net assets other than from transactions with owners).

1. Revenue may be recorded prematurely or belatedly, that is, it may be assigned to the wrong fiscal period.
2. Revenue may be recorded before there is a reasonable certainty that it will actually be realized. This in turn can lead to reporting of gain derived from such revenue in one period and the cancellation or reversal of such profit, with a resultant loss, in a subsequent period. The effect of this is to overstate net income in one period and to understate it in a subsequent period.

Conditions for Revenue Recognition

These two effects are, of course, highly undesirable and misleading; and in order to minimize such possibilities, accountants have adopted strict and conservative rules regarding the recognition of revenues.[2] The following criteria exemplify the rules that have been established to prevent the premature anticipation of revenues. Thus, recognition is deemed to take place only after the following conditions have been met:

1. The earning activities undertaken to create revenue have been substantially completed, for example, no significant effort is necessary to complete the transaction.
2. In case of sale, the risk of ownership has been effectively passed on to the buyer.
3. The revenue, as well as the associated expenses, can be measured or estimated with substantial accuracy.
4. The revenue recognized should normally result in an increase in cash, receivables, or marketable securities, under certain conditions in an increase in inventories or other assets, or a decrease in a liability.
5. The business transactions giving rise to the income should be at arm's length with independent parties (i.e., not with controlled parties).
6. The transaction should not be subject to revocation, for example, carrying the right of return of merchandise sold.

While the above criteria may appear to be pretty straightforward, they are, in fact, subject to a number of exceptions and have, in practice, been interpreted in a variety of ways. The best way to understand these variations is to examine the application of these concepts in a variety of circumstances.

---

[2] For an excellent summary of rules as well as the rationale behind them, see H. R. Jaenicke, *Survey of Present Practices in Recognizing Revenues, Expenses, Gains, and Losses* (Stamford, Conn.: FASB, 1981).

Uncertainty as to Collection of Receivables

In normal circumstances, doubts about the collectibility of receivables resulting from a sale should be reflected in a provision for doubtful accounts. *APB Opinion 10* affirms this when it states that "profit is deemed to be realized when a sale in the ordinary course of business is effected, unless the circumstances are such that the collection of the sales price is not reasonably assured." At what point the collection of a receivable is no longer reasonably assured is, of course, a matter of judgment based on all the surrounding circumstances. Moreover, such judgment may be conservative or it may be based on liberal or optimistic assumptions.

Installment Sales   Installment sales normally result in a receivable that is collectible over a period of many months or even many years. Time is an important dimension in the assessment of risk, for the more distant the time of the collection of the proceeds of the sale, the more uncertain the final collection of the receivable. Conceivably, then, the length of time of collection is an important factor in assessing the probability of ultimate collection. Except in situations where the doubt about the collection of installment receivables is such as to make a reasonable estimate impossible, profit on installment sales is properly recognized at the time of sales.

Cost Recovery Method   When an entity has no reasonable basis for estimating the degree of collectibility of receivables, it may use the cost recovery method under which no profit is recognized until the cost of the item sold has been recovered from actual collections.

Real Estate Accounting   The sale of real estate is often characterized by payment terms stretching over long time periods. A long-delayed collection period increases uncertainty, and thus the recognition of profit on such sales is dependent on an ability to assess the probability of collection of the full sales price.

SFAS 66, "Accounting for Sales of Real Estate," stipulates that for retail land sales, the full accrual method can be used only if the real estate seller's receivables from land sales are collectible and if the seller does not have any significant remaining construction or development obligations. In cases where these conditions are not met, the sales are to be reported under the percentage-of-completion or the installment method of accounting.

For sales of real estate other than retail land sales, *SFAS 66* requires the sale to be consummated, the buyer's down payment and commitment for continuing investment in the property sold to be adequate, and the seller not to have a substantial continuing involvement with the property after the sale.

SFAS 67, "Accounting for Costs and Initial Rental Operations of Real Estate Projects," stipulates that when a rental project is being developed, the project changes from nonoperating to operating when it is substantially completed and held available for occupancy—that is, a completion of tenant improvements, but no later than one year from the cessation of major construction activities. From that time, only development and construction costs should be capitalized, and all capitalized costs should begin to be amortized. Costs that should be capitalized and those that should not are also identified.

Revenue Recognition When Right of Return Exists

SFAS 48, "Revenue Recognition When Right of Return Exists," specifies that revenue from sales transactions in which the buyer has a right to return the product should be recognized at the time of sale only if *all* of the following conditions are met:

- At the date of sale, the price is substantially fixed or determinable.
- The buyer has paid the seller, or is obligated to pay the seller (not contingent on resale of the product).
- In the event of theft or physical damage to the product, the buyer's obligation to the seller would not be changed.
- The buyer acquiring the product for resale has economic substance apart from that provided by the seller.
- The seller does not have significant obligations for future performance to directly bring about resale of the product.
- Product returns can be reasonably estimated.

If these conditions are not met, revenue recognition is postponed; if they are met, sales revenue and cost of sales should be reduced to reflect estimated returns and expected costs or losses should be accrued.

The *Statement* does not apply to accounting for revenue in service industries if part or all of the service revenue may be returned under cancellation privileges granted to the buyer, transactions involving real estate or leases, or sales transactions in which a customer may return defective goods, such as under warranty provisions.

Right of return problems vary from industry to industry. In the newspaper or perishable foods industry, returns follow sales relatively quickly. On the other hand, in book or record publishing, returns may occur after a longer period.

Warner Communications, Inc., made the following disclosure:

> In accordance with industry practice, records, tapes, magazines and books are usually sold to customers with the right to return unsold items.

Revenues from these and other sales represent gross sales less a provision for future returns. It is WCI's general policy to value returned goods included in inventory at estimated realizable value but not in excess of cost.

The ability to estimate future returns is an important consideration. Items that would appear to impair ability to reasonably predict returns include:

Susceptibility to significant external factors, such as technological obsolescence or swings in market demand.

Long return privilege periods.

Absence of appropriate historical return experience.

Accounting for Franchise Fee Revenue

SFAS 45, "Accounting for Franchise Fee Revenue," establishes accounting and reporting standards for franchisors. It requires that franchise fee revenue from individual and area franchise sales be recognized only when all material services or conditions relating to the sale have been substantially performed or satisfied by the franchisor. This *Statement* also establishes accounting standards for continuing franchise fees, continuing product sales, agency sales, repossessed franchises, franchising costs, commingled revenue, and relationships between a franchisor and a franchisee.
Church Fried Chicken makes the following disclosure:

> **Application, License, and Royalty Fees.** All fees from licensed operations are included in revenue as earned. Management accelerated the revenue recognition for application fees from the time the site was approved or construction begun to the time cash is received. Management believes this method will more accurately relate the income recognition to performance of the related service.
>
> License fees are earned when the related store opens. Unearned license fees which have been collected are included in current liabilities. Royalty fees are based on licensee revenues and are recognized in the period the related revenues are earned.

Product Financing Arrangements

Unlike the two *SFAS*s discussed above, which deal with the *timing* of revenue recognition, *SFAS 49,* "Accounting for Product Financing Arrangements," is concerned with the issue of whether revenue has been earned.

A product financing arrangement is an agreement involving the transfer or sponsored acquisition of inventory which, although it sometimes resembles a sale of inventory, is in substance a means of financing inventory. For example, if a company transfers inventory to another company in an apparent sale, and in a related transaction agrees to repurchase the inventory at a later date, the arrangement may be a product financing arrangement rather than a sale and subsequent purchase of inventory.

In essence, if the party bearing the risks and rewards of ownership transfers inventory to a purchaser, and in a related transaction agrees to repurchase the product at a specified price, or guarantees some specified resale price for sales of the product to outside parties, the arrangement is a product financing arrangement and should be accounted as such (see also Chapter 7).

Transfers of Receivables with Recourse

Another important revenue recognition issue is the question of the circumstances under which transfers of receivables with recourse are to be accounted for as sales rather than borrowing transactions.

SFAS 77 (1983) specifies that a transfer of receivables with recourse would be reported as a sale, and gain or loss would be recognized if all of the following conditions are met:

1. The transferor surrenders control of the future economic benefits of the receivables.
2. The transferor's recourse obligation can be reasonably estimated.
3. The transferee cannot require the transferor to repurchase the receivables, except under the recourse provisions.

Otherwise, the proceeds from the transfer would be reported as a liability. A transfer to a wholly owned finance subsidiary would not prohibit recognition as a sale.

Timing of Revenue Recognition

A major problem area in revenue recognition is the matter of *timing*. It is a basic principle of accounting that gains accrue only at the time of sale and that gains may not be anticipated by reflecting assets at their current sales prices. There are some exceptions to the rule, primarily in the case of smaller agricultural producers who, facing difficult cost determination problems, often use "the farm price method" (in which revenue is measured by the current market price less estimated costs of disposition) to value inventory. This method in essence recognizes revenue when production is complete. For example, Seaboard Corporation states "Grain inventories are valued at market after adjustment of open purchases and sales contracts to market." A variation of this method is the recording of a farmer's "sale" to a cooperative as the basis for revenue recognition. This practice is often of doubtful validity because the cooperative is not sufficiently independent for the "sale" to constitute an effective transfer of risk.

In the area of service revenues, Symbol Technologies, Inc. disclosed the following accounting in 1990:

> g. *Deferred Service Revenues* Field service maintenance agreements are sold for certain of the Company's products. When such revenues are received prior to providing repair and maintenance service, they are deferred and recognized over the term of the related agreements.

Another area of *seeming* exception to the principle that gains accrue only at the time of sale is contract accounting where, in effect, the contract to sell normally precedes production or construction and where profit may, under certain conditions, be taken up in proportion to activity.

Contract Accounting

The basis of recording income on short-term construction or production contracts poses no special problems. Profit is ordinarily recognized when the end product is completed and has been accepted by the owner.

Long-term construction contracts, be they for buildings, battleships, or complex machinery, present a more difficult accounting problem. Here the construction cycle may extend over a number of accounting periods while substantial costs accumulate, financed in part by progress billings. Two generally accepted methods of accounting are in use:[3]

1. The *percentage-of completion* method is preferred when estimates of costs to complete and estimates of progress toward completion of the contract can be made with reasonable dependability. A common basis of profit estimation is to record that part of the estimated total profit that corresponds to the ratio that costs incurred to date bear to expected total costs.[4] Other methods of estimation of completion can be based on units completed, on qualified engineering estimates, or on units delivered.
2. The *completed-contract* method of accounting is preferable where the conditions inherent in the contracts present risks and uncertainties that result in an inability to make reasonable estimates of costs and completion time. Problems under this method concern the point at which completion of the contract is deemed to have occurred as well as the kind of expenses to be deferred. Thus, some companies defer all costs to the completion date, including general

---

[3] ACSEC's *Statement of Position No. 81–1,* "Accounting for Performance of Construction-Type and Certain Production-Type Contracts," emphasizes that these two methods should not be used as acceptable alternatives for the same circumstances.

[4] Under this method the current year contract revenues equals

$$\left[\frac{\text{Total costs incurred to date}}{\text{Estimated total costs}} \times \frac{\text{Contract}}{\text{price}}\right] \text{less} \left[\begin{array}{c}\text{Contract revenue recognized} \\ \text{in prior years}\end{array}\right]$$

and administrative overhead, while others consider such costs as period costs to be expensed as they are incurred.

Under either of the two contract accounting methods, losses, present or anticipated, must be fully provided for in the period in which the loss first becomes apparent.

Parker Haunifin Corp. disclosed the following accounting in 1990:

> *Long-Term Contracts*—The Company enters into long-term contracts for the production of products. For financial statement purposes, sales are recorded as deliveries are made (units of delivery method of percentage-of-completion). Unbilled costs on these contracts are included in inventory. Progress payments are netted against the inventory balances. Provisions for estimated losses on uncompleted contracts are made in the period in which such losses are determined.

Finance Company Accounting

Generally, the accrual of interest is a function of time. The income on a bond or a loan to others depends on principal outstanding, time elapsed, and rate.

Finance companies, such as in the consumer or sales finance fields, make loans under which a finance charge is added on to the face amount, also referred to as discount.

A number of alternative methods of taking up this discount exist. Thus, if the face of the note is $2,400 and the cash advanced is $2,160, the $240 unearned finance charge can be taken up over, say, 12 months, in a number of ways:

1. Under the *straight-line method,* one twelfth or $20 would be taken up each month as an installment is collected.
2. Under the *sum-of-the-months' -digits* method, larger amounts of income are recognized in the early part of the loan contract than in its latter period. In the case of a 12-month loan, the sum of the digits is 78. In the first month of the contract, 12/78th of the finance charge ($36.92) is taken into income; and in the last month, 1/78th ($3.14) is taken up. Under this method, the interest earned bears a closer relationship to funds out at risk than it does under the straight-line method. That is also true of other methods that take up income in proportion to the decreasing balance of the loan outstanding.
3. A variation of either of the above methods involves taking into income, immediately on granting of the loan, an amount, also called acquisition factor, which is designed to offset the initial loan acquisition expenses incurred by the company. The balance of the unearned finance charge is then taken into income by means of one of alternative methods.

When Should the Recording of Interest Income Be Discontinued

An AICPA *Statement of Position* on "Accounting Practices of Real Estate Investment Trusts" states that the recognition of interest revenue should be discontinued when it is not reasonable to expect that it will be received. The following conditions should be regarded as establishing such a presumption:

1. Payments of principal or interest are past due.
2. The borrower is in default under the terms of the loan agreement.
3. Foreclosure proceedings have been or are expected to be initiated.
4. The creditworthiness of the borrower is in doubt because of pending or actual bankruptcy proceedings, the filing of liens against his assets, and so on.
5. Cost overruns and/or delays in construction cast doubt on the economic viability of the project.
6. The loan has been renegotiated.

Accounting for Lease Income

Another special branch of revenue accounting is found in the case of companies leasing property to others. Their methods of revenue recognition are discussed in Chapter 7.

"Sales" to Leasing Subsidiaries

Before revenue under a sale can be considered as realized, there must be a genuine transfer of risk from seller to buyer. An interesting example of the importance of this principle is provided by the furor caused by the attempt by Memorex Corporation to treat as an immediate sale the transfer of equipment to the company's unconsolidated leasing subsidiary.

The basic flaw in the proposed accounting was (1) that the subsidiary had not been capitalized by the infusion of third-party capital and could, as a consequence, not pay Memorex for the equipment; and (2) that Memorex had agreed to protect the subsidiary against losses. In short, these conditions clearly demonstrated that there was no transfer of the risk of ownership from Memorex to third parties, and consequently there was no genuine sale. Thus, the company had to agree to treat the transfer of the leased equipment as a lease rather than as an outright sale.

Additional Examples of Income Recognition Problems

Additional examples of problems regarding the timing of revenue recognition can be found in a number of industries.

Thus, Dow Jones & Company reports as follows on the accounting for unearned subscriptions that are carried as current liabilities:

> *Subscription revenue* is recorded as earned, pro rata on a monthly basis, over the life of the subscriptions. Costs in connection with the procurement of subscriptions are charged to expense as incurred.

In the liquor industry, Schenley Industries, Inc., reported on a timing aspect of income recognition as follows:

> The company sells certain whiskey in barrels in bond under agreements which provide for future bottling. In prior years, profits on such transactions were reflected as of the date of sale. The present company policy is to treat such profits as deferred income until the whiskey is bottled and shipped.

Income of Subsidiaries and Affiliates

When a company owns a part or the whole of another entity, the interest of the company in the subsidiary's income may be accounted for in a number of ways (see also Chapter 9).

1. Consolidated financial statements may be prepared, thus including the subsidiary's results in the consolidated income statement while excluding any minority interest in that income or loss. It is generally recognized that such financial statements do in most cases represent the most meaningful presentation of the financial position and the results of operations of the consolidated entity.

2. If a subsidiary is not consolidated, two methods of reporting the parent company's investment in it are possible:

a. The cost method under which only dividends received are recorded as income by the parent. Because the latter has the power to control the amount and timing of dividend declarations by the subsidiary, the dividends may not reflect the actual earnings performance of the subsidiary and thus may lead to income distortion or manipulation.

Because of the above-mentioned possible distortions, *APB Opinion 18* now requires that if consolidation is not appropriate, for whatever reason, the investments in subsidiaries be carried "at equity."

Exceptions may nevertheless be warranted:

ILLUSTRATION 1. Chevron Corp. Reports as follows:

> The company's 36.6 percent interest in UNC Resources, Inc. (UNC), carried at $82, which approximated its market value, is accounted for on the cost basis because of restrictions imposed on Chevron's ability to influence UNC.

b. The equity method takes up the parent company's proportionate part of a subsidiary's profits and losses, thus reflecting best the parent company's share of the subsidiary's results. The equity method is, thus, appropriate in all cases except those where there are serious limitations or restrictions on remittance of dividends, or where control is likely to be temporary, or where it is not adequate.

When the parent company and its subsidiary are consolidated or when the parent picks up the equity in the earnings of the subsidiary, intercompany sales and profits must be eliminated from the consolidated statements and intercompany profits must be eliminated from the amounts the parent picks up as equity in the subsidiary's earnings.

Jointly Owned Companies   Frequently, two or more corporations join in forming a new entity which, in effect, represents a joint venture in which each owns a partial interest and has a voice in management. *APB Opinion 18* concluded that the equity method reflects best the underlying nature of investments in such ventures and calls for accounting for the investment at equity, thus recording a proportionate share of the results as they are earned. This method should be used regardless of the percentage of ownership, provided the corporate joint venture is operated by a small group of businesses for their mutual benefit and encompasses a pooling of resources and a sharing of risks and rewards as well as participation in the overall management of the investee.

Implications for Analysis

The income statement, presenting as it does the results achieved by an enterprise and the return achieved on invested capital, is of great importance to the analyst in the valuation of an enterprise. For this reason and for such reasons as pride, pressure to achieve results, compensation based on income, and the value of stock options, management is greatly interested in the results it reports. Consequently, the analyst can expect managements to choose those accounting principles and procedures that come closest to achieving their purposes.

The objectives of income reporting that management is desirous of achieving do not always result in the fairest or most proper measurement of results, and consequently the analyst must be ever alert to management's propensities as well as the choices available to it.

THE DATAPOINT CORPORATION CASE.   In 1982, it was discovered that Datapoint Corporation would have to reverse a significant amount of sales that hard-pressed sales representatives booked by asking customers to order millions of dollars of computer equipment months in advance with payment to be made much later. On this basis, Datapoint recorded sales as revenue even though in many cases the equipment had not even been manufactured. It was reported that these sales representatives were under corporate pressure to achieve unreasonable or unattainable goals. In 1984 the company consented to an order barring it from future violations of the Securities Exchange Act and SEC rules.

For additional cases, see the "Revenue Smoothing and Revenue Distortion" section of Chapter 22.

Since the recording of revenue is the first step in the process of income recognition and on which the recognition of any and all profit depends, also referred to as the "critical event" in revenue recognition, the analyst should be particularly inquisitive about the accounting methods chosen so as to ascertain whether they reflect economic reality. Thus, for example, if a manufacturer records profits on sale to the dealer, the analyst must inquire about dealer inventories because the real earning activity consists in selling to the ultimate consumer. Similarly, when a membership fee to a golf club is recorded at the time a contract is signed, the analyst must determine whether the crucial earning activity consists of selling memberships or in delivering the services of the golf club.

Managements' propensities and strong motivations to tamper with the revenue recognition process has resulted in many pronouncements on the subject of income recognition by the accounting profession, the FASB, and the SEC. In spite of these the analyst must remain alert to a great variety of "creative" accounting approaches designed to circumvent the spirit, if not the letter, of these pronouncements.

ILLUSTRATION 2.   Prime Motor Inns has earned a major portion of its income, not from core operations, but rather from hotel sales, construction fees, and interest. However, in booking such nonrecurring earnings, Prime has stretched recognition criteria by accepting notes and receivables of doubtful value and by guaranteeing to the buyers of their hotels, and their bankers, certain levels of future income. While profits are booked, the contingent liabilities connected with these are barely provided for.

Another technique of booking profits and not providing for related contingencies is to extend loans in return for substantial fees. While such "consulting fees" are recorded as profit, the poor quality of the loans is not immediately provided for.

Aware of such revenue recognition problems the SEC, in *SAB 81* (1989), stated that the Staff believes there often exist significant uncertainties about the seller's ability to realize noncash proceeds received in transactions in which the purchaser is a thinly capitalized, highly leveraged entity, particularly when its assets consist principally of those purchased from the seller. Such uncertainties raise doubt as to whether immediate gain recognition is appropriate. Factors that may lead to question the recognition of gain include:

- Situations in which the assets or operations sold have historically not produced cash flows from operations that will be sufficient to fund future debt service and full dividend requirements on a current basis.

- The lack of any substantial amount of equity capital in the purchasing entity other than that provided by the registrant.

- The existence of contingent liabilities of the registrant, such as debt guarantees or agreements that require the registrant to infuse cash into the purchasing entity under certain circumstances.

Even where the company receives solely cash proceeds, the recognition of any gain would be impacted by the existence of any guarantees or other agreements that may require the company to infuse cash into the purchasing entity, particularly when the first two factors listed above exist.

If immediate recognition is not appropriate under the circumstances, the deferred gain should not be recognized until such time as cash flows from operating activities are sufficient to fund debt service and dividend requirements (on a full accrual basis) or the company's investment in the purchasing entity has been or could be readily converted to cash (e.g., active trading market develops in the purchasing entity's securities and the company is not restricted from selling such securities, the company sells the securities received on a nonrecourse basis, etc.) and the company has no further obligations under any debt guarantees or other agreements that would require it to make additional investments in the purchasing entity.

The amount of any deferred gain (including deferral of interest or dividend income on securities received) should be disclosed on the face of the balance sheet as a deduction from the related asset account (i.e., investment in the purchasing entity). The notes to the financial statements should include a complete description of the transaction, including the existence of any commitments and contingencies, the terms of the securities received, and the accounting treatment of amounts due thereon.

In a related area SEC *SAB 82* (1989) prohibits the accounting as a sale of a transfer by a financial institution of nonperforming assets to a new entity. In order to be accounted as a sale all risks and rewards of ownership must be effectively transferred to such new entity.

Problem of Collectibility   One element that casts doubt on the recording of revenue is *uncertainty about the collectibility* of the resulting receivable. We have examined the special problems relating to installment sales, real estate sales, and franchise sales. Problems of collection exist, however, in the case of all sales, and the analyst must be alert to them. Sales with right of return can often turn out not to be sales at all, and the analyst should be alert to these.

Let us conclude the consideration of the collection problem by an example from the bowling equipment manufacturing industry. The early 1960s witnessed a bowling boom that was attended by the building of a large number of bowling alleys that competed for a limited amount of business in restricted territories. The two major manufacturers of bowling equipment sold it to inexperienced and poorly financed operators against notes and receivables, mostly secured by the equipment itself. The full profit on this equipment was immediately taken up while the provision for bad debts concurrently established underestimated by a wide mark the special risks involved. Brunswick Corporation wrote off very substantial amounts of accounts receivable in 1963, while American Machine & Foundry made similarly substantial write-offs of receivables only five years later. Long before the write-offs were announced, the alert analyst could have taken his cue from the deteriorating business conditions in the bowling industry. There was, however, little in the financial statements of the bowling manufacturers to forewarn of the losses yet to come.

Timing of Revenue   The emphasis on transactions rather than performance has resulted often in the anticipation of earnings ahead of completion of the earnings process. The analyst must be alert to the problems related to the *timing of revenue recognition.* We have examined the accounting concept of realization and the reasons for the accountant's great preoccupation with objective and verifiable evidence in this area. While the justification for this position is the subject of much debate both within and outside the accounting profession, it behooves the analyst to understand the implications of present accounting in this area on his or her work.

The present rules of realization generally do not allow for recognition of profit in advance of sale. Thus, increases in market value of property such as land, equipment, or securities, the accretion of values in growing timber, or the increase in the value of inventories are not recognized in the accounts (see also, Chapter 14). As a consequence, income will not be recorded before sale, and the timing of sales is, in turn, a matter that lies importantly within the discretion of management. That, in turn, gives management a certain degree of discretion in the timing of profit recognition.

ILLUSTRATION 3.   Thousand Trails, a membership campground operator, recorded as revenue membership fees when a new member signed up even though these were nearly 90 percent financed and many cancelled within days of signing up. When this practice became public knowledge the price of the company's stock declined sharply.

FASB *Technical Bulletin 90–1* (1990) establishes the accounting for revenue and costs from separately priced warranty or product maintenance contracts. It requires that revenue from these types of contracts be deferred and recognized in income on a straight-line basis over the contract period except in those circumstances in which sufficient historical guidance indicates that the costs of performing services under the contract are incurred on other than a straight-line basis.

Another issue of providing for costs related to the earning of revenues is that of unredeemed frequent flier credits issued by airlines. While some industry experts estimate the unprovided for potential costs to be in the billions, airlines have been providing for the much smaller incremental cost of simply putting a passenger in an otherwise empty seat. A proposal to have airlines defer a portion of their revenues from each ticket sold in order to create a "liability reserve" has encountered strong industry resistance.

Contract Accounting   In the area of contract accounting, the analyst should recognize that the use of the completed-contract method is justified only in cases where reasonable estimates of costs and the degree of completion are not possible. In fact, from the statement user's point of view it is a poor method because results can be unpredictable and very erratic.

The percentage-of-completion method of accounting is, however, not free of problems and pitfalls. The analyst usually has no basis on which to check on the judgments of management, the internal cost allocations, or the degree of actual completion of the contracts. This can be seen from the following examples:

ILLUSTRATION 4.   Stirling Homex, a company that built modular houses, had strong incentives to show earnings growth because it was a "glamour company" and needed financing as well. Invoking percentage-of-completion contract accounting principles, it recognized the earnings process as completed when housing modules were "manufactured and assigned to specific contracts." In fact, this method was nothing but an earning-by-producing process, and the spurious "sales" had to be reversed— a process which triggered loan defaults and ultimately led to bankruptcy.

ILLUSTRATION 5.   The case of Four Seasons Nursing Centers, a company which ended in failure, presents a particularly vivid example of the dangers and the pitfalls of percentage-of-completion contract accounting *in actual application.* When, during their audit, the auditors, for whatever reasons, found physical engineering estimates of job completion to be unacceptable, the company was forced to base the degree of contract completion on the percentage that the costs incurred to date bore to total estimated costs. The company, which was at the time on the "glamour treadmill" of Wall Street with strong incentives to produce increasing earnings, proceeded to supply the auditors with cost invoices that later proved fictitious or inapplicable to the situation at hand.[5] These formed the basis for a higher percentage of completion with the resultant increased profit pickup. That was the road to the company's ultimate collapse.

Cost incurrence is at best a convenient rather than a precise method of estimating the degree of contract completion. Auditors are supposed to satisfy themselves that the cost-incurred method is a reliable substitute for more precise methods such as engineering estimates, and so on.

---

[5] ACSEC's *Statement of Position No. 81–1* now specifies that materials bought for a contract but not yet used be treated as inventory rather than as a cost.

In addition to the basic choice of method, the matter of which costs are to be considered contract costs and which period costs remains, to a significant degree, an area of management discretion.

Other Problem Areas of Revenue Recognition   In finance company accounting, the analyst must be aware of the variety of methods, as outlined earlier in this chapter, available in the recognition of income as well as the option of taking into income of amounts designed to offset loans acquisition costs at the inception of loan agreements.

Other alternative methods of taking up revenue, as in the case of lessors, must be fully understood by the analyst before he attempts an evaluation of a company's earnings or a comparison among companies in the same industry.

Concept of Materiality in Income Determination   The analyst must be aware of the fact that the concept of materiality remains undefined in accounting and is consequently subject to abuse and uncertainty. It is all too often employed by auditors in defense of the omission of disclosure when their clients are adamant in their resistance to certain disclosures. The analyst must also realize that the accountant's concept of materiality is presently a very narrow one indeed. It does not attempt to take into account the future implications of an emerging situation. All too often, what looks like a small problem area may be the beginning of a serious future problem. Recent examples of this were provided by Celanese Corporation, which lost heavily from what was initially a relatively small foreign venture, and American Express Company, which had to make good the losses of its relatively insignificant warehousing subsidiary when large-scale defalcations in the famous "salad oil swindle" were discovered. The FASB had the entire subject under study, but has not given serious consideration to this subject for years.

COST AND EXPENSE ACCRUAL

SFAC 3 defines expenses as "outflows or other using up of assets or incurrence of liabilities" resulting from the entity's "ongoing major or central operations" (par. 65). It also defines losses as decreases in an entity's net assets resulting from all other transactions and events affecting the entity (par. 68).

Costs and expenses are resources and service potentials consumed, spent, or lost in the pursuit or production of revenues. The major problems of accounting for costs concern the measurement (size) of costs and the timing of their allocation to production time periods.

A basic objective of income accounting is to relate costs to the revenues recognized during a period. This is far from easy to do. There are many kinds of costs, and they behave in a variety of ways. Some costs can be specifically identified with a given item of revenue. At the other end of the spectrum are costs that bear no identifiable relationship to specific elements of revenue at all and can be identified only with the time period during which they are incurred. This variation in behavior of costs has given rise to certain useful classifications that are helpful in understanding the matching and allocation problems.

Variable costs are those that vary in direct proportion to activity, whether the latter is measured by means of sales, production, or other gauges of activity. Thus, for example, in the manufacture of electric cable, the consumption of copper wire may be said to vary in direct proportion to the sales volume of wire. The higher the cable sales figure, the higher the copper wire cost. In practice, many costs contain both fixed and variable elements and are usually referred to as semivariable costs.

Fixed costs are those that remain relatively constant over a considerable range of activity. Rent, property taxes, and insurance are examples of fixed costs. No category of cost can remain fixed indefinitely. For example, after reaching a certain level of activity, an enterprise will have to rent additional space, thus bringing the rent expense to a new and higher level.

Costs can be classified in many additional ways depending on the purpose. Focusing on the problem of matching costs with revenues, we have *product costs* that attach to a specified good or service from which revenue is derived. Costs that cannot be identified with a product or service are called *period costs* because they can be identified only with the period in which they occur. We have already touched on this distinction of costs in our examination of inventory and related costs of goods sold accounting in Chapter 5. The allocation of costs to products sold and particularly manufactured products gives rise to a distinction among three major classes of cost:

1. *Direct product costs* represent charges that can be identified specifically with a product. Thus, for example, in a retailing business it is the cost of the item sold as well as the direct freight and other acquisition cost incurred in obtaining it. In a manufacturing enterprise, it represents the specific or direct cost of material and labor entering the production of the item. Direct product costs generally vary in amount in direct proportion to revenues, a characteristic that results in their being classified as variable costs. Direct product costs are among the easiest costs to match with specific revenue flows.

2. The cost of materials acquired for resale or manufacture should logically include in addition to invoice costs such additional costs as receiving, inspecting, purchasing, and storing. In reality, most enterprises find it impractical to allocate such costs or costs such as

indirect labor directly to specific products. Consequently, such *indirect costs* are allocated to products on some reasonable basis. Most fixed costs, such as depreciation or supervision, are treated as indirect overhead costs and are allocated to products or services on bases that attempt to reflect consumption or benefits derived.

3. *Joint product costs* are costs that cannot be identified with any of a number of products that they jointly benefit as for example is the case in the meat-processing industry. Such costs are usually allocated on some reasonable basis which may include that based on the selling prices of end products, relative sales volume, or net realizable value.

Having outlined some basic aspects of cost behavior and the methods of cost allocation that have been devised in response to it, we shall now proceed to examine the accounting problems that are encountered in the measurement and allocation of major categories of costs and expenses. Generally, a cost is a measure of service potential or utility that may be utilized in one accounting period or another. Those costs that relate to the revenue of future periods may be viewed as deferred costs and are shown as assets on the balance sheet. Major examples of such assets are inventories; property, plant, and equipment; intangibles; and deferred charges. The accounting problems of inventories are examined in Chapter 5. Property, plant, and equipment gives rise to allocations of costs in the form of depreciation and depletion, and they will be considered in this chapter. The allocation and amortization of intangibles and deferred charges have been examined in the chapter on asset measurement, and the income measurement aspects of these costs will be further considered in this chapter.

Generally, expenses are costs that are immediately chargeable to income. Most period costs become current expenses; and some categories of expense, such as selling and administrative,[6] are not usually deferred to the future. The measurement of costs and expenses is complicated whenever a significant lapse of time occurs between the time of payment for or incurrence of the cost and the time of its utilization in the earning of revenues. The longer such lapse of time, the more complicated and speculative such allocations and measurements become.

Let us now consider some important categories of costs and the principles governing their allocation to revenue.

---

[6] The controversy surrounding the growing deferrals of marketing costs by SafeCard Services, Inc., (reaching about $25 million early in 1981) highlights the unsettled status of the proper accounting for these costs. In an article in *Barron's* of 7/6/1981 entitled "Lost and Found," Professor A.J. Briloff took issue with the escalating deferrals of marketing costs, maintaining that the deferrals were based on excessively optimistic expectations about future contract renewals and resulting revenues. Those trying to rebuff his arguments pointed primarily to *present* cash flow patterns and to high discounted present value of those optimistic future expectations.

Depreciation and Depletion

The cost of assets that are in productive use, or otherwise income producing, must be allocated or assigned to the time periods that comprise their useful life. It is a basic principle of income determination that income that benefits from the use of long-lived assets must bear a proportionate share of their cost. Thus, the net cost of the long-lived assets should, at the end of their useful lives, have been charged to operations.

Depreciation is the process whereby the cost of property, plant, and equipment is allocated over its useful life. The purpose of depreciation is to recover from operations, by means of this allocation, the original cost of the asset. Consequently, if operations are not profitable, the depreciation becomes an unrecovered cost, that is, a loss. This is as true of depreciation as it is of any other cost that cannot be recovered because of inadequate revenues. The depreciation process in itself is not designed to provide funds for the replacement of an asset. That objective can only be achieved by means of a financial policy that accumulates funds for a specific purpose to be available at a given time.

The above principles of depreciation accounting are now so firmly established that there are no significant differences of opinion about them. Nevertheless, depreciation remains an expense item that is the subject of confusion and controversy among users of financial statements. The controversy and confusion stems from the methods and the assumptions on the basis of which the cost of assets is allocated to operations over their useful lives.

Factors Influencing the Rate of Depreciation

1. Useful Life   Almost all assets are subject to physical deterioration. A major exception is land that is consequently not subject to depreciation. While the "indestructible powers of the earth" have an unlimited life span, this quality does not ensure a similar resistance to loss of economic value. Such loss is, however, not provided for by means of depreciation but is instead recognized as and when it occurs. The exhaustion of natural resources lodged in or above the earth is recognized by means of depletion accounting, which will be discussed later.

Useful lives of assets can vary greatly. *Depreciation Guidelines and Rules,* published by the Internal Revenue Service, list the useful lives of assets and are based in part on policies influenced by economic and fiscal considerations. The accounting assumption as to the useful lives of assets should be based on economic and engineering studies, on experience, and on any other available information about an asset's physical and economic properties.

Physical deterioration is one important factor that limits the useful life of an asset. The frequency and quality of maintenance has a bearing on it. Maintenance can extend the useful life but cannot, of course, prolong it indefinitely.

Another limiting factor is obsolescence. Obsolescence is the impairment of the useful life of an asset due to progress or changes in technology, consumption patterns, and similar economic forces. Ordinary obsolescence occurs when technological improvements make an asset inefficient or uneconomical before its physical life is fully exhausted. Extraordinary obsolescence occurs when inventions of a revolutionary nature are developed or radical shifts in demand take place. Electronic data processing equipment and propeller-driven aircraft were subject to rapid obsolescence. The development of Xerography brought about extraordinary obsolescence in equipment using alternative methods of reproduction.

The integrity of the depreciation charge, and with it that of income determination, is dependent on a reasonably accurate estimate of useful life. That estimate should be determined solely by projections relating to physical life and economic usefulness and should not be influenced by management's desires with regard to the timing of income reporting.

2. Methods of Allocation   Once the useful life of an asset has been determined, the amount of the periodic depreciation cost depends on the method used to allocate the asset's cost over its useful life. As will be seen hereunder, that cost can vary significantly, depending on which method is chosen from the array of acceptable alternatives available:

Straight-Line Method   This method of depreciation assigns the cost of the asset over its useful life on the basis of equal periodic charges. Thus, in Table 10–1, we can see how an asset that cost $110,000, has an estimated useful life of 10 years, and an estimated salvage value of $10,000 at the end of that period, is depreciated. Every one of the 10 years is charged with an allocation of one tenth of the asset's cost less the estimated salvage value.

The basic rationale of the straight-line depreciation method is that the process of physical deterioration occurs uniformly over time. This is a

Table 10–1 Straight-line method of depreciation

Year	Depreciation	Accumulated depreciation	Undepreciated asset balance
			$110,000
1	$10,000	$ 10,000	100,000
2	10,000	20,000	90,000
⋮			
9	10,000	90,000	20,000
10	10,000	100,000	10,000

more valid assumption with regard to fixed structures than with regard to, say, machinery where utilization or running time is a more important factor. Moreover, the other element of depreciation, that is, obsolescence, does not necessarily occur at a uniform rate over time. However, in the absence of concrete information on the probable rate of actual depreciation in the future, the straight-line method has the advantage of simplicity. This faculty, perhaps more than any other, accounts for the method's popularity and widespread adoption in practice.

There are other theoretical flaws in the straight-line depreciation method. If the service value of an asset is to be charged evenly over its useful life, then the loss of productivity and the increased maintenance costs should not be ignored. Under the straight-line method, however, the depreciation charges in the first years is the same as in the last years when the asset can be expected to be less efficient and to require higher cost of repairs and maintenance.

Another objection to the straight-line method, one which is of particular interest to the financial analyst, is that it results in a distortion in the rate of return on capital by introducing a built-in increase in this return over the years. Assuming that the asset depreciated in Table 10–1 is a heavy crane that yields a uniform return of $20,000 per year *before* depreciation, we can see that the return on investment will be as follows:

Year	Book value	Income before depreciation	Depreciation	Net income	Return on book value
1	$110,000	$20,000	$10,000	$10,000	9.1%
2	100,000	20,000	10,000	10,000	10.0
3	90,000	20,000	10,000	10,000	11.1
10	10,000	20,000	10,000	10,000	100.0

Increasing maintenance costs may render the constant "income before depreciation" assumption a bit too high but will not negate the overall effect of a constantly increasing return on investment. Obviously, this increasing return on the investment in an aging asset is not an entirely realistic portrayal of the economic realities of investments. Under accelerated methods of depreciation, this kind of distortion in the return on book value of the asset can be even more marked.

Decreasing-Charge Method   The decreasing-charge method of depreciation, also known as declining-balance or accelerated depreciation, is a method whereby charges for depreciation decrease over the useful life of an asset.

The strongest support for this method arose from its approval by the Internal Revenue Code in 1954. Its value for tax purposes is obvious and relatively simple to understand. The earlier an asset is written off for tax purposes, the larger amount of tax deferred to the future and the more funds are available for current operations.

Arguments in favor of the decreasing-charge method of depreciation are that over the years an asset declines in operating efficiency and service value and that lower depreciation charges would offset the higher repair and maintenance costs that come with the older age of assets. Moreover, it is claimed that to compensate for the increasing uncertainty regarding the incidence of obsolescence in the future, the earlier years should bear a larger depreciation charge.

There are two principal methods of computing the decreasing charge to depreciation. One, the declining-balance method, applies a constant percentage to the declining asset balance. Given the salvage value (S), the original cost (C), and the number of periods over which the asset is to be depreciated (N), the rate (percentage) to be applied to the asset can be found by the following formula:

$$\text{Rate (\%)} = 1 - \sqrt[N]{\frac{S}{C}}$$

In practice, an approximation of the proper rate of declining-charge depreciation is to take it at twice the straight-line rate. Thus, an asset with an assumed 10-year useful life would be depreciated at a declining-balance rate of 20 percent. This is referred to as the double-declining-balance method.

The other method, involving simpler computations, is known as the sum-of-the-years'-digits method. Thus, the cost of an asset to be depreciated over a five-year period is written off by applying a fraction whose denominator is the sum-of-the-years' digits $(1 + 2 + 3 + 4 + 5)$, that is, 15 and whose numerator is the remaining life from the beginning of the period, that is, $5/15$ in the first year and $1/15$ in the last year of assumed useful life.

Table 10–2 illustrates the depreciation of an asset having a cost of $110,000, a salvage value of $10,000, and an assumed useful life of 10 years under the double-declining-balance method and the sum-of-the-years'-digits method. Since under the first method an asset can never be depreciated to a zero balance, salvage value is not deducted before applying the yearly rate (20 percent) to the original cost.

The main theoretical justification for the decreasing-charge method is that charges for depreciation should decrease over time so as to compensate for (1) increasing repair and maintenance charges, (2) decreasing revenues and operating efficiency, and, in addition, to give recognition to the uncertainty of revenues in the later years of assumed useful life.

Other Methods of Depreciation   A method of depreciation found in some industries, such as steel and heavy machinery, relates depreciation

Table 10–2   Accelerated Depreciation Methods

	Depreciation		Cumulative amount	
Year	Double declining	Sum-of-the-years' digits	Double declining	Sum-of-the-years' digits
1	$22,000	$18,182	$22,000	$ 18,182
2	17,600	16,364	39,600	34,546
3	14,080	14,545	53,680	49,091
4	11,264	12,727	64,944	61,818
5	9,011	10,909	73,955	72,727
6	7,209	9,091	81,164	81,818
7	5,767	7,273	86,931	89,091
8	4,614	5,455	91,545	94,546
9	3,691	3,636	95,236	98,182
10	2,953	1,818	98,189	100,000

charges to activity or intensity of use. Thus, if a machine is assumed to have a useful life of 10,000 running hours, then the depreciation charge will vary with number of hours of running time rather than the lapse of time. In order to retain its validity, it is particularly important that the initial assumption about useful life in terms of utilization be periodically reviewed in order to check its validity under changing conditions.

ILLUSTRATION 6.   Bethlehem Steel Corporation presented the following description of its depreciation policy:

> *Depreciation*—Depreciation is based upon the estimated useful lives of each asset group, which for most steel producing assets is 18 years. Steel and most raw materials producing assets are depreciated on a straight-line basis adjusted by an activity factor. This factor is based on the ratio of production and shipments for the current year to the average production and shipments for the five preceding years at each operating location. Annual depreciation after adjustment for this activity factor is not less than 75 percent nor more than 125 percent of straight-line depreciation.
>
> The costs of blast furnace linings are depreciated on a unit-of-production basis. All other assets are depreciated on a straight-line basis.

Another method of depreciation once advocated by some utilities but not now in general use is the compound interest method of depreciation. This method views an investment in property as the present value of anticipated earnings. Thus, the depreciation charge is the amount that, invested yearly at a capital cost rate, will equal the cost of the asset, less any salvage value, at the end of its useful life. The addition of this interest factor causes this method to result in systematically increasing depreciation over the years. One advantage claimed for it is that it will result in a more uniform rate of return on investment than is the case with other methods.

Depletion   Depletion is the process by means of which the cost of natural resources is allocated on the basis of the rate of extraction and production. The essential difference between depreciation and depletion is that the former represents an allocation of the cost of a productive asset over time, and the latter represents the exploitation of valuable resources such as coal deposits, oil pools, or stands of timber. Thus, in the case of depletion, the proportionate allocation of cost is entirely dependent on production; that is, no production, no depletion.

The computation of depletion is easy to understand. If the cost of an ore body containing an estimated 10,000,000 recoverable tons is $5,000,000, then the depletion rate per ton of ore mined is $0.50. A yearly production of 100,000 tons would result in a depletion charge of $50,000 and a cost balance in the asset account at the end of the year of $4,950,000. The analyst must be aware of the fact that here, as in the case of depreciation, a simple concept may nevertheless result in a multitude of complications. One is the reliability of the estimate of recoverable resources, and it should be periodically adjusted to reflect experience and new information. Another is the definition of "cost," particularly in the case of a property still in process of development. Also, in the case of oil fields, for example, the depletion expense will vary with the definition of what constitutes an "oil field," since the depletion computation may not be based on individual wells but rather on entire fields. The depletion expense can vary with the definition of the boundaries of the field.

The argument, sometimes advanced, that the discovery value of a natural resource deposit is so great in relation to its cost that no depletion need be allowed for, is not a valid one nor is the argument that depletion should be ignored because of the very tenuous nature of the estimate of reserves.

Implication for Analysis

From the point of view of the analyst, a very important dimension of cost and expense accounting is their proper accrual—that means that the income of a given period has been charged with all expenses properly assignable to it. Accountants refer to the procedure that ensures this as expense cutoff, that is, properly cutting off at the point where expenses for a period end and those of the following period begin.

ILLUSTRATION 7.   Yale Express acquired Republic Carloading and Distributing Company (twice its own size) in a merger that resulted in substantial operating problems that contributed to the ultimate downfall of the combined enterprise. Yale (a short-haul trucker) used a fast cutoff method, that is, it assumed (generally with validity) that most of its unpaid bills reached it shortly after its freight was trucked. Thus, it assumed that all bills due arrived within 20 days of year-end. Trouble arose when Yale extended this method of accrual to Republic where freight-handling bills came in months after performance of its service. This led to a substantial underaccrual of costs, and by the time this was discovered it led to the restatement of net income of $1 million to a loss of almost $2 million. In the resulting litigation, facts emerged that pointed to both auditor carelessness as well as management collusion to withhold all facts.

Most companies utilize long-lived productive assets in their operations, and whenever this is the case, depreciation tends to become a significant cost of operations. If we add to this the fact, as we have seen in the foregoing discussion, that many subjective assumptions enter into the determination of the depreciable basis and of useful lives of assets, and that alternative methods of depreciation coexist and that these factors can result in widely differing depreciation charges, all "in accordance with generally accepted accounting principles," it is obvious that the financial analyst needs a thorough understanding of all the factors entering into the depreciation computation before he or she can assess a reported earnings figure or attempt to compare it with that reported by another company.[7]

Revisions of useful lives of fixed assets based on studies of actual experience over the years can lead to more accurate estimates and better depreciation accounting. Analysts must, however, approach such revisions with critical skepticism for often these are devices used to shift and smooth income and to relieve future operations of depreciation charges properly assignable to them.

ILLUSTRATION 8.   In its 1987 annual report General Motors reported that:

> In the third quarter of 1987, the corporation revised the estimated service lives of its plants and equipment and special tools retroactive to January 1, 1987. These revisions, which were based on 1987 studies of actual useful lives and periods of use, recognized current estimates of service lives of the assets and had the effect of reducing 1987 depreciation and amortization charges by $1,236.6 million or $2.55 per share of $1-2/3 par value common stock.

This was a significant revision. If these were presumably such careful studies of useful lives of plant and equipment then it must have come as a surprise to many analysts to learn that in 1990 GM took a $2.1 billion charge to cover cost of closing several plants, including plants which will not be actually closed for a number of years. Analysts were left to wonder whether it was possibly a "clearing of the decks" operation instituted by a newly elected chairman who explained this as "a major element in GM's long-term strategic plan to improve the competitiveness and profitability of its North American operations." Whether this action improves competitiveness remains to be seen. However, charging expense

---

[7] For a discussion of possible variations in practice, see AICPA, "Accounting for Depreciable Assets," *Accounting Research Monograph No. 1* (New York, 1975).

currently for the cost of $2.1 billion of plant that would otherwise have to be depreciated as a future cost will certainly reduce expense in future accounting periods, and improve reported profits in future periods by a like amount. See also the discussion of income smoothing in Chapter 22.

The information on depreciation methods presently available in corporate reports varies, and generally speaking, more is available in documents filed with the SEC than is available in annual reports. Thus, typically the more detailed information will contain the method or methods of depreciation in use as well as the range of useful lives assumptions that are applied to various categories of assets. Two things are obvious to the intelligent reader of information. One is that it is practically useless for purposes of deriving any conclusion from it. After all, what can one conclude from a statement that talks about this or that method being used without a quantitative specification of the extent of its use and the assets to which it applies. The second is that this information is supplied because it is required and not because of the supplying company's conviction about its usefulness.

Giving the ranges of useful lives or depreciation rates looks more informative than it is. It actually contributes very little to the basic objectives of the analyst, that is, the ability to predict future depreciation charges or the ability to compare the depreciation charges of a number of companies in the same industry.

The typical information supplied appears something like this:

> The estimated useful lives vary but generally fall within the following ranges: buildings and special-purpose structures . . . 10 to 25 years; leasehold improvements . . . estimated useful life or remaining term of lease, whichever is shorter; machinery and equipment . . . 3 to 5 years; special-purpose equipment . . . expensed or over the life of the initial related contract. Tooling costs are expensed as incurred.

There is usually no identification of the relationship between the depreciation rates disclosed and the size of the asset pool to which such rates apply. Moreover, there is normally no identification between the rate used and the depreciation method applied; that is, which rates are used in conjunction with straight-line methods of depreciation and which with accelerated methods.

There are, of course, additional complications. While the straight-line method of depreciation enables the analyst to approximate future depreciation charges with some degree of accuracy, accelerated methods of depreciation make this task much more difficult unless the analyst is able to obtain from the company additional data not now disclosed in public reports.

Another problem area in depreciation accounting arises from differences in the methods used for book purposes and those used for tax purposes. Three possibilities exist here:

1. The use of straight-line depreciation methods for both book and tax purposes.
2. The use of straight-line depreciation for book purposes and accelerated methods for tax purposes. The favorable tax effect that results from the higher depreciation for tax purposes compared to that for book purposes is offset by the use of interperiod tax allocation that will be discussed in the next chapter. The advantage to the reporting company is the postponement of tax payments, that is, the cost-free use of funds.
3. The use of accelerated methods for both book and tax purposes. This method gives a higher depreciation charge than does method 1 in early years, and for an expanding company, even in subsequent years.

Unfortunately, the amount of disclosure about the impact of these differing methods is not always adequate. The best type of disclosure is the one that gives the amount of depreciation that would have been charged under a number of alternatives, such as, for example, what the difference in depreciation would have been under an accelerated method as opposed to a straight-line method. If a company gives the amount of deferred taxes that arose from accelerated depreciation for tax purposes, the analyst can get the approximate amount of extra depreciation due to acceleration by dividing the deferred tax amount by the current tax rate. See the information yielded by expanded requirements of the composition of deferred taxes, discussed in the next chapter.

ANALYTICAL MEASURES OF PLANT AGE

There are a number of measures relating to plant age that are useful in comparing depreciation policies over time as well as for intercompany comparisons.

The average total life span of plant and equipment can be approximated as follows:

$$\frac{\text{Gross plant and equipment}}{\text{Current year depreciation expense}}$$

For Campbell Soup Company (see Appendix 4B), for 1991 this can be computed as follows:

$$\frac{\$2538.0^{(a)}}{\$194.5^{(b)}} = 13.05 \text{ years}$$

[a] Item [159] buildings ($758.7) plus machinery and equipment ($1779.3) [160].
[b] From Form 10-K, item [187].

The average age of plant and equipment can be computed as follows:

$$\frac{\text{Accumulated depreciation (reserve)}}{\text{Current year depreciation expense}}$$

For Campbell Soup Company it is computed as follows for 1991:

$$\frac{\$1131.5 \; \boxed{162}}{\$194.5 \; \boxed{187}} = 5.82 \text{ years}$$

The average remaining life of plant and equipment is computed as follows:

$$\frac{\text{Net depreciated plant and equipment}}{\text{Current year depreciation expense}}$$

Again, for Campbell Soup, it is computed as follows for 1991:

$$\frac{\$2538.0 - \$1131.5}{\$194.5} = 7.23 \text{ years}$$

Amounts per computations above

As can be seen from the computations above, and as is logical:

$$\frac{\text{Average total}}{\text{life span}} = \text{Average age} + \text{Average remaining life}$$

or

$$13.05 \text{ years} = 5.82 \text{ years} + 7.23 \text{ years}$$

The above ratios are helpful in assessing an enterprise's depreciation policies and assumptions over time. The ratios can be computed on a historical-cost basis as well as on a current-cost basis.

When these ratios are used as bases of comparison with other companies in the same industry, care must be exercised because depreciation expense will vary according to the method of depreciation used as well as the assumptions of useful life and salvage values. The average age of plant and equipment can be used in the evaluation of a number of factors including profit margins and financing requirements.

Thus, capital-intensive companies with relatively old facilities may have profit margins that do not reflect the higher costs of replacing the aging plant. Similarly, the capital structure of such companies may not yet reflect the financing necessary for the replacement of the aging plant.

MISCONCEPTIONS REGARDING THE NATURE OF DEPRECIATION

Analysts who have despaired of making meaning out of depreciation information have tended to ignore it altogether by looking at income before depreciation in comparing company results. As will be more thoroughly discussed in the chapter on cash flows, depreciation is an expense that derives from cash spent in the past and thus does not require the current outlay of cash. For this reason, income before depreciation has also been called cash flow, an oversimplification because it omits other factors affecting cash flow from operations. This is, at best, a limited and superficial concept since it involves only selected inflows without considering a company's commitment to such outflows as plant replacement, investments, or dividends.

Another and even more dangerous misconception that derives from the cash flow concept, and against which the analyst must guard, is that depreciation is a kind of bookkeeping expense somehow different from such expenses as labor or material and that it can be ignored or at least accorded less importance than is accorded to other expenses.

One reason for this thinking is the cash outlay aspect already mentioned above. This represents, of course, entirely fallacious thinking. The purchase of a machine with a useful life of, say, five years is, in effect, a prepayment for five years of services. Let us assume that the machine is a bottle-filling machine and that its task can be performed normally by a worker working eight hours a day. If, as is not common but quite feasible, we contract with the worker for his services for a five-year period and pay him for it in advance, we would obviously have to spread this payment over the five years of his work. Thus, at the end of the first year, one fifth of the payment would be an expense and the remaining four-fifths prepayment would represent an asset in the form of a claim for future services. It requires little elaboration to see the essential similarity between the labor contract and the machine. In year 2 of the labor contract, no cash is spent, but can there be any doubt about the validity of the bottle-filling labor cost? The depreciation of the machine is a cost of an essentially identical nature.

Another reason for doubts about the genuine nature of depreciation expense is related to doubts about the loss of value of the asset subject to depreciation. On further examination, we can break these doubts into two major categories:

1. Doubts about the rate of loss in utility of productive equipment.
2. Doubts about loss in market value of assets such as real estate.

1. When we see one airline depreciating a jet plane over 8 years and another airline spreading the depreciation of an identical aircraft over, say, 12 years, we realize that depreciation rates are matters of opinion. What is not a matter of opinion is that the effect on income of such differing assumptions can be significant and can distort comparisons. Thus, the effect must be assessed by the analyst as best as he or she can in the light of industry practice as well as the apparent reasonableness of the useful life assumption. While there may be some guidelines about

useful lives of assets for tax purposes, there are practically none for financial accounting purposes. Auditors are not specialists in the longevity or useful life of equipment, and they will challenge management's estimates only when they are way out of line with industry practice or recorded experience. Where recorded experience is nonexistent, as in the case of a new industry such as computer leasing, the auditor's willingness to question management's estimate is further reduced. All this leaves a great deal of room for interpretation and income manipulation. While it does nothing to render depreciation as less of a genuine expense than any other, it does raise questions about the proper allocation of a productive asset's cost over time. Moreover, as between two estimates of useful life on similar equipment in an industry, there is obviously more risk to the longer life assumption than to the shorter.

The rate of write-off is another aspect of depreciation the analyst must be alert to. When the tax laws first permitted a variety of accelerations in the computation of depreciation, many companies adopted the method for both book and tax purposes. Later, however, a number of companies, such as those in the steel and paper industries, wanted to soften the impact of depreciation on reported income and switched back to the straight-line method while retaining accelerated methods for tax purposes. Such switching back and forth can usually not be said to be made in the interest of better reporting. Thus, though mostly unjustified and contributing to a discontinuity in comparability, it is nevertheless accepted by the accounting profession whose limited self-imposed responsibility is to highlight the change and report its effect in the year in which it occurs. This practice along with the leeway allowed in setting useful lives has contributed in good measure to the skepticism regarding the measurement of depreciation expenses. *APB Opinion 20,* "Accounting Changes," which is more fully considered in the next chapter, is designed to remedy this obvious reporting deficiency by insisting that changes be made only in the direction of "preferable" accounting principles. Since the concept of "preferable" in relation to accounting principles remains undefined, the analyst must retain a vigilant and critical attitude toward this area of accounting practice.[8]

2. In the case of assets such as real estate, the problem of depreciation is somewhat different. For one thing, constant maintenance can prolong its useful life considerably more than can maintenance of, say, machinery or automobiles. Moreover, those who look at loss of market value as a true index of depreciation claim that in times of rising price levels buildings gain rather than lose in value.

These are, however, not arguments against depreciation as such but rather questions of useful economic life and the proper time period over

---

[8] See, however, Chapter 15 for a discussion of new SEC requirements that the auditor take a position on the preferability of a switch in accounting methods.

which an asset's cost should be written off. There is not more justification to a depreciation rate that is excessive than there is to one that is insufficient. Possibly, those companies that depreciate buildings at a rate exceeding their physical and economic decline do so in order to justify the rates they use for tax purposes. This procedure does not, however, result in proper income determination and must be understood as such by the analyst.

Rising real estate values are, of course, no reason to discontinue providing for depreciation. The adequacy of depreciation is dependent on many factors, both physical and economic. The process of depreciation can be retarded but never abolished or reversed. The following note to the financial statements of Louis Lesser Enterprises, Inc., covering a period of generally rising prices, makes this clear:

> As a result of the general decline in certain aspects of the real estate industry, accentuated by conditions in the money market and continuing vacancy factors in certain of the Company's rental properties, management is of the opinion that the full cost of certain properties and investments in and advances to companies not majority owned will not be recovered in the normal course of operations or through sale. Accordingly, the carrying values of such properties and investments and advances have been reduced to the amount of expected recovery.

The losses above provided for exceeded $4 million in a year when the company's total revenues were only about $6 million. In retrospect, it is clear that management and its auditors underestimated the process of depreciation and value erosion of the company's income-producing properties. The values of such properties depend more on their income-generating capacity under a variety of economic conditions than on physical characteristics and maintenance levels.

As the above case illustrates, it is not prudent to rely on temporary economic conditions or market quotations to redress overoptimism that results in the willful underestimation of depreciation. After all, the depreciation concept encompasses a number of factors such as physical life, economic usefulness, and technological and economic factors which affect obsolescence. The difficulties of such real estate operators as Zeckendorf, Kratter, and Glickman attest to the fact that real estate values move in a two-way street.

Changing price levels also introduce many complexities to the depreciation problem. Particularly in industries that are based on holdings of real estate, the argument is often advanced that rising prices (due in great measure to the decline in the purchasing power of money) obviate or reduce the need for depreciation charges. These arguments confuse the problems resulting from price-level changes, which affect all accounts rather than only the fixed assets, with the function of depreciation that is designed to allocate the cost of an asset over its useful life. Price-level changes in themselves do not, of course, prolong the useful life of an asset. The problem of price-level changes must be dealt with fully and apart from that of depreciation. Price-level problems will be examined in Chapter 14.

The analyst should realize that the variety of depreciation methods in use will cause not only problems of comparisons with other companies but internal measurement problems as well. This is particularly true with regard to the rate of return earned on the carrying value (book value) of an asset subject to different methods of depreciation. As the following example shows, only the "annuity" method of depreciation provides a level return on investment over the useful life of an asset. This method is, however, rarely found in practice.

ILLUSTRATION 9.   Assume that a machine costing $300,000 and having a useful life of five years with no salvage value generates a yearly income before taxes of $100,000. According to the annuity method of depreciation, the cost of depreciable assets is the present value of an anticipated stream of future services, determined at some rate of discount. In our illustration, the assumed rate of discount is 19.86 percent. The following are the rates of return realized annually under *(a)* straight-line, *(b)* sum-of-the-years' digits, and *(c)* annuity depreciation methods (which is identical to the sinking fund depreciation method):

Year	Income before depreciation	Depreciation	Income after depreciation	Asset book value at beginning of year	Rate of return
a. Straight-line depreciation					
1	$100,000	$ 60,000	$ 40,000	$300,000	13.3%
2	100,000	60,000	40,000	240,000	16.7
3	100,000	60,000	40,000	180,000	22.2
4	100,000	60,000	40,000	120,000	33.3
5	100,000	60,000	40,000	60,000	66.7
	$500,000	$300,000	$200,000		
b. Accelerated depreciation (sum-of-years' digits)					
1	$100,000	$100,000	$—	$300,000	0.0%
2	100,000	80,000	20,000	200,000	10.0
3	100,000	60,000	40,000	120,000	33.3
4	100,000	40,000	60,000	60,000	100.0
5	100,000	20,000	80,000	20,000	400.0
	$500,000	$300,000	$200,000		
c. Annuity depreciation					
1	$100,000	$ 40,421	$ 59,579	$300,000	19.86%
2	100,000	48,450	51,550	259,579	19.86
3	100,000	58,076	41,924	211,129	19.86
4	100,000	69,612	30,388	153,053	19.86
5	100,000	83,441	16,559	83,441	19.86
	$500,000	$300,000	$200,000		

From the foregoing discussion it is clear that the accounting for depreciation, which is a very real and significant cost of operation, contains many pitfalls for the analyst. Moreover, the information frequently supplied in published reports is mostly useless from the point of view of meaningful analysis. Thus, the analyst has to approach the evaluation of this cost with an understanding of the factors discussed above and with an attitude of questioning independence. In assessing the depreciation provision, he or she may have to evaluate its adequacy by such measures as the ratio of depreciation expense to total asset cost as well as its relationship to other factors which affect its size.

QUESTIONS

1. Why does the financial analyst attach great importance to the analysis of the income statement?
2. What conditions should usually be met before revenue is considered realized?
3. What conditions should usually be present before a sale with "right of return" can be recognized as a sale and the resulting receivable can be recognized as an asset?
4. The ability to estimate future returns (when right of return exists) is an important consideration. What are some of the factors that might impair such ability to predict returns?
5. What is the main difference between *SFASs 48* and *45* and *SFAS 49?* How does *SFAS 49* define a product financing arrangement?
6. Distinguish between the two major methods used to account for revenue under long-term contracts.
7. According to the AICPA Statement of Position on "Accounting Practices of Real Estate Investment Trusts," the recognition of interest income should be discontinued when it is not reasonable to expect that it will be received. What are some of the conditions that would be regarded as establishing such a presumption?
8. How is income in a jointly owned company accounted for?
9. To what aspects of revenue recognition must the financial analyst be particularly alert?
10. Can the analyst place reliance on the auditor's judgment of what constitutes a "material" item in the income statement?
11. Distinguish between *(a)* variable, *(b)* semivariable, and *(c)* fixed costs.
12. Depreciation accounting leaves a lot to be desired; and no real progress, from the analyst's point of view, is imminent. Comment on the following observation:

    "The analyst of course cannot accept the depreciation figure unquestioningly. He must try to find out something about the age and efficiency of the plant. He can obtain some help by comparing depreciation, current and accrued, with gross plant, and by comparisons among similar companies. Obviously, he still cannot adjust earnings with the precision that the accountant needs to balance his books, but the security analyst doesn't need that much precision."

13. What are some of the analytical tools used in evaluating depreciation expense? Why are they helpful?
14. What means of adjusting for inconsistencies in depreciation methods are sometimes employed by analysts? Comment on their validity.
15. Which method of depreciation would result in a level return on asset book values? Why?

Chapter 11

ANALYSIS OF THE INCOME STATEMENT—II

This chapter continues and concludes the discussion of the analysis of the income statement that was begun in Chapter 10.

PENSION COSTS AND OTHER SUPPLEMENTARY EMPLOYEE BENEFITS

Pension Costs

Pensions are a major employee-benefit cost designed to contribute to security after retirement. Pension commitments by companies are formalized in a variety of ways by means of pension plans. As pensions grew in importance and in size as a significant cost of operations, so did the accounting for such costs become a matter of great significance.

Following 10 years of study and deliberations the FASB issued in 1985 *SFAS 87,* "Employers' Accounting for Pensions," which represents a major revision of the prior accounting for pensions. At the same time the Board issued *SFAS 88* dealing with "Employers' Accounting for Settlements and Curtailments of Defined Benefit Pension Plans and for Termination Benefits." Chapter 7 considers the liability aspects of pensions while this chapter considers issues involved in the determination of pension costs.

Basic Concepts of Pension Accounting

Pension plans are established in order to provide employees with retirement benefits. Pension expense attempts to measure the current cost of providing for these future promised benefits. This is an accrual concept which differs from the funding of these costs; that is, the transfer to a pension fund trustee of cash or other assets so as to provide the sources of cash for present and future pension payments.

Most employers have *defined benefit* pension plans which specify the amount of pension benefits to be provided. Under such plans the risk of pension fund performance is borne by the employer. A *defined contribution* pension plan specifies the contributions required of the employer while the amount of the employee's pension depends on the performance of the pension fund (i.e., a risk borne by the employee).

We are concerned here mostly with the accounting for defined benefit pension plans by employers. *SFAS 35* (1980), "Accounting and Reporting by Defined Benefit Plans," addresses the financial reporting of the funding agency which is not our concern here.

The pension plan defines the pension benefit accruing to each employee upon retirement. The amount of the benefit is determined by a formula which includes a variety of actuarial factors. These are based on estimates of variables such as retirement age, life expectancies, employee turnover rates, future salary levels, future returns on pension plan assets, and vesting provisions. *Vesting* refers to an employee's right to a pension benefit regardless of whether or not he or she remains in the company's employ.

Once the amount of the pension expense has been determined by reference to the plan provisions and the relevant actuarial assumptions, the funding of the expense becomes a fiscal decision which is, however, also influenced by legal and tax considerations. The tax law has minimum funding requirements to ensure the security of employees' retirement benefits. It also has expense deductibility limitations in the case of overfunded pension plans. Under the Employee Retirement Income Security Act (ERISA) minimum funding requirements were also established. The company can *fund* the expense fully by turning over an amount of cash equal to the expense to the plan trustee. It can *underfund* it by retaining a liability for accrued pension cost or it can *overfund* it by prepaying some future pension cost.

We can visualize better the process of funds accumulation for the purpose of paying a future pension by focusing on the provision of a pension for one employee who we shall name John Worker (J. W.). J. W. joins the plan at age 45 and is expected to retire at age 65. The plan specifies that J. W. will be entitled to a $20,000 annual pension and is expected to draw it for 15 years (i.e., he has a life expectancy of 80 years). It is assumed that the pension fund will earn 7 percent on its assets. From the retirement date onward (i.e., during the pension disbursing period) the fund is expected to earn 8 percent on its assets.

This process of accumulation and disbursement can be graphically portrayed as illustrated on the page which follows.

Under this simple example which assumes that all the expectations will be realized, the employer will make the following yearly entry:

Pension Expense 4,176
    Cash (to Pension Trustee) 4,176

| Yearly* payments into fund required to accumulate to $171,190 in 20 years when $i = 7\%$ | Fund required on J. Worker's retirement (i.e., present value of 15 yearly* payments of $20,000 where $i = 8\%$) | Benefits of $20,000 per year* to be paid for 15 years when fund is expected to earn 8% |

Yearly payment = $4,176

$171,190

*Yearly, rather than monthly, payments assumed for simplicity. The yearly payment is $4,176.

The pension trustee (with whose accounting we are not concerned here) will book the receipts during the accumulation period thus:

```
Cash  ........................................  4,176
    Pension Liability  ...........................         4,176
```

as well as the returns on the investment of these funds.

During the distribution period the pension trustee will continue to record income on these funds and will discharge the pension obligation on a yearly basis as follows:

```
Pension Liability  .............................  20,000
    Cash ......................................         20,000
```

In actuality the accounting by the employer is far more complex because assumptions made in the present rarely are fully realized in the future. In large measure the provisions of *SFAS 87* deal with how to account for the ever-changing disparities between expectations and realizations.

Although a pension plan benefits at any given moment in time a *group* of employees which represents a composite of all the assumptions, we will, for the sake of clarity and simplicity, continue to focus, as far as possible, on the case of John Worker.

EMPLOYER'S PENSION BENEFIT OBLIGATION

Let us start with the obligation (i.e., liability) the employer enters into when the pension is promised to J. W. *SFAS 87* defines three different pension benefit obligations:

1. *Projected benefit obligation* is the estimate (generally made, along with all other estimates, by an actuary) of the employer's obligation to J. W. based on assumptions regarding his *future* compensation level. Recall that our example was based on a fixed $20,000 yearly pension. If, however, J. W.'s pension depends, say, on his average salary level during his last five years of service, then the *projected* benefit obligation must make an assumption about such future salary levels.

2. *Accumulated benefit obligation,* on the other hand, is based on an estimate of the employer's obligation based on *current and past* compensation levels. Thus, no assumptions about future compensation levels are included here. It could amount to the employer's current obligation if the plan were discontinued presently; that is, as of the measurement date. Under our original example where J. W.'s pension is not based on future compensation, the accumulated benefit obligation and the projected benefit obligation are equal.

3. *A vested benefit obligation* is the employer's obligation for a pension which is not contingent on the beneficiary remaining an employee. Thus, if J. W.'s pension plan stipulated that his rights do not vest until he worked for five years then during those first five years of the accumulation period the benefit obligation would not be vested.

With respect to a pension plan the following tabulation, in hypothetical amounts, presents the relationship between the various elements of the actuarial present value of benefit obligations:

Vested benefits	$10,000
Benefits not vested	3,000
Accumulated benefit obligation . .	13,000
Effect of future estimated compensation levels	2,000
Projected benefit obligation	$15,000

Accounting and reporting requirements make it necessary that all three pension benefit obligations be known at each measurement date.

ELEMENTS OF PERIODIC PENSION EXPENSE

Continuing with our simplified example of the pension of J. W. we will now consider the elements which make up the employer's periodic pension cost.[1]

The service cost for each period is the actuarial present value of the pension benefit earned by J. W. (or a group of employees) based on the pension benefit formula. If the pension formula is as simple as was stated in the example above (and it can be much more complex), then the service cost for year one for J. W. will be $4,176.

The interest cost component of the periodic pension expense must be recognized because the projected benefit obligation carried over from the

---

[1] The term *cost* recognizes that some portions of the pension cost are not *expensed* during a period and find their way into assets such as inventory and self-constructed assets.

preceding year must earn the assumed rate of interest if the future expected value (i.e., $171,190 in the illustration) is to be realized.

The interest cost component of the periodic pension cost is computed by multiplying the projected benefit obligation as of the end of the prior year by the discount rate (7 percent in our example). Thus, for example, in year 2 the interest added to pension cost will be the projected benefit obligation at end of year 1 of $4,176 times 7 percent or $292. Under *SFAS 87* the discount rate is based on the current price of settling the employer's obligation. For many employers this rate can be determined by using the discount rates published by the Pension Benefit Guarantee Corporation.

Expected Return on Plan Assets

With the pension cost *increased* by the return to be earned on assets at the assumed rate, *SFAS 87* specifies that the cost be *reduced* by the expected return on plan assets.

The reason pension costs are reduced by the *expected* (rather than actual) return on plan assets is that use of the actual return would subject pension costs to the fluctuations of the financial markets; that is, annual pension costs would be too volatile. Thus, the gains or losses which represent the difference between expected and actual returns are to be deferred and amortized in order to reduce this volatility. The treatment of deferred gains and losses will be discussed below.

In order to disclose the actual return on assets in the cost computation, the expected return on plan assets is shown as in the tabulation below. For clarity of illustration hypothetical amounts of pension cost components are also shown:

Periodic pension expense:		
Service cost		$1,000
Interest cost		200
Expected return on plan assets:		
Actual return on plan assets	($180)	
Add—Unrecognized (deferred) loss		
on plan assets	(10)	(190)
Amortization of various cost elements		
(as discussed in pages that follow)		
Unrecognized prior service cost		20
Unrecognized loss (gain)		(10)
Unrecognized transition cost		30
Total periodic pension cost		$1,050

In the above presentation the expected return on plan assets is shown as the difference between actual return on plan assets and the deferred gain or loss. In this way the actual return on plan assets is disclosed and linked to the computation.

The actual return on plan assets consists of investment income plus realized or unrealized appreciation or depreciation of plan assets during the year. It can be positive or negative. Plan assets used in operations (as opposed to investments) are valued at cost less depreciation.

Deferred gain or loss on plan assets is the current period's unrecognized gain or loss on plan assets and is computed as follows:

> Actual return on plan assets (as discussed above)
> *minus*   Expected return on plan assets
> *equals*   Deferred gain or loss on plan assets

The *expected* return on plan assets for a period is computed by multiplying the expected long-term rate of return on plan assets by the market-related value of plan assets at the beginning of the period. The market-related value of plan assets is either the fair value or a calculated value that recognizes changes in fair value in a systematic manner over five years. The long-term rate of return on plan assets is estimated by the pension trustee.

As will be discussed later, the deferred gain or loss on plan assets will be amortized over an appropriate period of time and included in the periodic pension cost.

AMORTIZATION OF UNRECOGNIZED PENSION COSTS

In addition to the three components of periodic pension cost outlined above (i.e., service cost, interest cost, and expected return on plan assets), there are other components of cost based on unrecognized pension costs which relate to unrecognized pension liabilities (or assets). The principle of delayed recognition is not new to pension accounting. The Board has reiterated its support for deferrals and delayed recognition as a departure from accrual accounting which is justified by a need to avoid too great a change from past practice. The following are major elements of recognition of delayed costs in pension expense:

Amortization of Prior Service Cost

Prior service cost can arise from the granting of retroactive pension benefits at the initiation of a pension plan or by plan amendments. Referring to the example of John Worker, his pension benefits may be increased after his admission to the pension plan or retroactive benefits may be granted at the inception of the plan.

SFAS 87 does not require immediate recognition of the cost of retroactive benefits granted. This cost does, however, increase the projected

benefit obligation and is recognized as expense gradually over the remaining careers of existing employees in the plan. The deferred recognition allows the cost of granting retroactive benefits to be matched
against the future economic benefits that the employer is expected to
realize from the granting of such benefits. The amortization can be based
on the future service period of qualified employees or it can be applied
on a straight-line basis.

Amortization of Net Gains or Losses

Gains and losses result from the inevitable differences which arise between *actual* results achieved and the *estimates* of results on which pension costs are based. These differences come from:

a. The difference between the actual and the expected return on plan
   assets as already discussed above.
b. Changes in the projected benefit obligation due to changes in assumptions. (These are computed by the actuary and reflect changes
   in factors such as compensation rates, turnover, mortality assumptions, retirement estimates, and discount rates.)

SFAS 87 specifies a minimum and a systematic method of amortization
of net unrecognized gains and losses. A "corridor" approach shields actuarial gains and losses falling within a corridor from required amortization; the corridor is the greater of 10 percent of the market-related asset
value or 10 percent of the projected benefit obligation at the beginning
of the year.

Amortization of Unrecognized Transition Costs

On adopting *SFAS 87* the employer will obtain the following:

1. The projected benefit obligation (from the actuary).
2. The fair value of plan assets (from the trustee).
3. Any previously recognized unfunded or prepaid pension cost (from
   company records).

The difference between (1) and the sum of (2) and (3) above is designated as the unrecognized transition cost or gain. The recognition of
this transition cost or gain (mostly cost) is amortized on a straight-line
basis over the average remaining service period of qualified employees.

COMPUTATION OF NET PERIODIC PENSION COST

To summarize the above discussion the amount of net periodic pension
cost for a period is the sum of the following six components:

a. Service cost.

b. Interest cost.

c. Expected return on plan assets (reduction).

d. Amortization of unrecognized prior service cost, if any.

e. Amortization of net gains or losses, if material.

f. Amortization of the unrecognized net obligation (and loss or cost) or unrecognized net asset (and gain) existing at the date of initial application of *SFAS 87*.

Pension Liabilities

The disclosure of pension liabilities and the recognition of additional obligations was discussed in Chapter 7.

REQUIRED FOOTNOTE DISCLOSURE

SFAS 87 calls for a significant expansion of the pension footnote in the employer's annual report. Included in the required disclosures are the following:

1. A description of the plan including employee groups covered, type of benefit formula, funding policy, and types of assets held.
2. The amount of net periodic pension cost for the period. Service cost, interest cost, and the actual return on assets are to be shown separately. Various amortization charges (e.g., unrecognized prior service costs, gains and losses) can be netted and disclosed as a single amount.
3. A schedule reconciling the funded status of the plan with amounts shown in the employer's financial statements.
4. Assumptions—the weighted-average assumed discount rate and rate of compensation increase (if applicable) used to measure the projected benefit obligation and the weighted-average expected long-term rate of return on plan assets.

OVERFUNDED PENSION PLANS

When the market value of the assets in the pension fund exceeds the projected benefit obligation the pension fund is overfunded. There are various reasons for overfunding including excessive contributions, possibly to accumulate funds tax free, or better than expected investment and/or actuarial performance. Potential company raiders sometimes view overfunded pension plans as sources of funds which can help finance their acquisitions.

Among the implications of overfunded pension plans are:

a. That the overfunding is due to favorable investment performance that may not continue and may even reverse. Consequently no change in expense accrual or funding policy is indicated.

b. That contributions to the pension fund can be discontinued or reduced until such time as pension assets equal the projected benefits obligation. Such a reduction has income as well as cash flow implications.

c. That excess assets can be withdrawn by the company with the recaptured amounts being subject to income taxes. Because pension funding has been used as a tax shelter, reversion excise taxes have also been imposed. Such actions have cash flow implications.

Clearly, companies with overfunded pension plans have greater flexibility than do companies without such plans. They can reduce or eliminate pension contributions in the short run or consider modifying the plan so as to recapture excessive assets. These are analytical considerations which deserve attention.

Excess pension fund assets, while subject to possible recapture, cannot be shown as company assets on its balance sheet.

ACCOUNTING FOR CURTAILMENTS AND SETTLEMENTS OF DEFINED BENEFIT PENSION PLANS AND TERMINATION BENEFITS

SFAS 88 dealing with this specialized subject was developed in response to an increase in the number of companies terminating pension plans with assets in excess of accumulated benefits. Such excess assets can be recaptured by companies for general corporate use. *SFAS 88* specifies how the gain from recapturing excess pension assets is to be computed and when it is to be recognized. The statement also specifies (1) how companies should account for decreases in their pension obligations that would arise from employees' future services and (2) how companies should account for special termination events currently covered by *SFAS 74*.

Implications for Analysis

The FASB has striven for and, with *SFAS 87*, has achieved improvements in the accounting for pensions. It has removed the wide freedom of choice of actuarial methods previously available and has settled on basically a single method—the projected unit credit method. This should, even given the considerable remaining managerial flexibility, lead to greater comparability. Moreover, the arbitrary amortization periods permitted hitherto have been replaced with more company-specific amortization schedules.

In spite of these improvements a great deal of management discretion and flexibility remains in the determination of pension costs. These costs will be fluctuating and volatile. If the volatility reflects changing economic conditions, then the accounting for pensions will achieve its proper objective. There will, however, also be volatility and change induced by management choice. The analyst, in evaluating pension expense, must bear in mind these two types of volatility and must, as far as possible, distinguish between them.

The expected return on pension plan assets is an important factor affecting pension costs. There is flexibility and room for maneuver here. For example, interest rate assumptions which have been in the area of 7 to 8 percent can now be increased by using the higher market-related settlement rates. This settlement rate can be used regardless of the plan's actual investment holdings. Hitherto high-yield investments were held in order to justify a high discount rate. This need no longer be done. Managements may, however, if they wish, keep the expected rate of return on plan assets and the discount rate equal, as was often done previously.

Management also retains flexibility in its choice of assumptions regarding inflation, not only through choice of the discount rate, but also through choice of an expected rate of inflation for future compensation levels.

In general, when long-term interest rates (on which settlement rates are based) increase, pension service costs will decrease and vice versa.

Smoothing of results is achieved by valuing pension assets on a market-related basis rather than on a market basis, with up to five-year averaging of values permitted.

Pension cost levels are also smoothed by the deferral of a variety of cost elements (e.g., prior service cost, unrecognized losses, and so on) which represent in essence a sanction to remove a burden from current pension costs and defer them into the future.

For many companies the fresh start allowed by *SFAS 87* will create credit transition components (due to overfunded plans) which will be amortized so as to lower pension costs over many years to come. Thus, the new rules allow the benefits of overfunding to benefit earnings much sooner than under the old rules.

The intangible asset entered into the balance sheet through the recording of a pension liability presents the analyst with an interesting problem of interpretation. It is basically devoid of economic value and should not be included in computations such as, for example, book value. FASB member Sprouse objected to this treatment on the grounds that it is inconsistent with the Conceptual Framework. How, he asked, can a loss in assets (i.e., pension assets) result in the creation of an intangible asset? Conversely, how can a gain in (pension) assets justify a reduction in the intangible asset?

ACCOUNTING FOR OTHER POSTRETIREMENT EMPLOYEE BENEFITS (OPEB)

The liability aspects as well as other related provisions of *SFAS 106,* dealing with the accounting for Postretirement Benefits other than Pensions, have been discussed in Chapter 7. In this chapter we are concerned with the cost aspects of these significant benefits.

Prior to promulgation of *SFAS 106,* most companies provided for OPEB costs on a pay-as-you-go basis (i.e., expensing only actual cash outlays incurred). Some companies accrued the liability for these costs to employees as they retired, a procedure referred to as terminal funding.

SFAS 106 adopted the full accrual method of *SFAS 87* on pension accounting which was discussed in the preceding section. While there are some differences between the OPEB mandated accounting and that for pensions, three fundamental aspects of pension accounting are retained.

- *Net cost reporting:* The consequences of events and transactions affecting the OPEB plans are reported as a single amount. That amount includes at least three components: (1) the present value of the *accrued* cost of deferred compensation promised by OPEB in exchange for employee service, (2) the interest cost accruing from the passage of time until these benefits are paid, and (3) the returns from the investment in plan assets. These returns will not reduce the cost of many OPEB plans because, as discussed in Chapter 7, most are presently not funded.
- *Delayed recognition:* Certain changes in OPEB obligations, including those arising as a result of a plan initiation or amendment, and certain changes in the value of plan assets set aside to meet that · obligation are recognized systematically over future periods rather than as they occur. These measures are designed to insulate current costs from fluctuations in values and other factors.
- *Offsetting:* Plan assets restricted for the payment of OPEB benefits offset the Accumulated Postretirement Benefit Obligation (APBO) in determining amounts recognized in the employer's statement of financial position.

The following tabulation summarizes the main elements of the *Net Annual OPEB Cost* of a plan:

A. Service cost   These are the costs of promises of postretirement benefits. The total actuarially determined costs of providing the future benefits—referred to as the Expected Postretirement Benefit Obligation (EPBO) are to be recognized over the employee service period (i.e., the date the employee is fully eligible to receive benefits—even if that date precedes the expected retirement date). The FASB mandated a single attribution method, the "benefits/years of service" approach to allocate, generally on a straight-line basis, the EPBO to each year in the service period. The portion of the EPBO that has been "earned" by employee services on a given date is the Accumulated Postretirement Benefit Obligation (APBO).

B. **Interest cost**   This reflects the imputed growth in the APBO during the period using the assumed discount rate. Interest compounds because the APBO is recognized on a present value basis.

C. **Amortization of gains and losses**   Gains and losses arise when actual experience of the plan differs from initial estimates or if the expected return on assets, if any, differs from the actual return. Because such gains and losses can fluctuate significantly they are deferred. However, if the cumulative net amount of previously unrecognized gain or losses exceeds 10 percent of the APBO, that excess portion must be amortized into income over the average remaining service period.

D. **Amortization of unrecognized prior service cost from plan amendments**   Plan amendments that change benefits and that are attributed to employee service rendered prior to the date of the amendment give rise to prior service costs. These costs are recognized on a prospective basis by assigning equal amounts to the remaining future service periods.

E. **Amortization of unrecognized transition obligation**   On the date *SFAS 106* is initially adopted, an unfunded OPEB obligation, referred to as the *Transition Obligation,* is identified and is measured as the difference between the APBO and plan assets (if any) *minus* any OPEB liabilities that have been previously booked.

   If the company does not recognize immediately the transition obligation by a charge to income (as a cumulative effect of an accounting change) it can amortize this obligation over the remaining employee service period or over an optional period of 20 years.

F. **Actual return on plan assets**   If all or part of the plan is funded, the actual return on plan assets reduces the Net Annual OPEB Cost.

Exhibit 11–1 summarizes, by use of hypothetical amounts, the interrelationship between the OPEB cost, liability, and other balance sheet accounts.

A careful study of Exhibit 11–1 will reveal to those interested in the technical accounting aspect of OPEB obligations, the interrelationship

Exhibit 11–1 Interrelationship between OPEB related accounts (dollars in thousands)

	Accumulated postretirement benefit obligation (APBO)	Unrecognized[a] Transition obligation	Unrecognized[a] Prior service cost	Unrecognized[a] Net (gain) or loss[b]	Accrued OPEB cost[c]	Net annual OPEB cost
Balance—on adoption of SFAS 106—or beginning	$(20,000)	$20,000				
Activity in period						
Service cost	(1,600)					$1,600
Interest cost	(2,200)					2,200
Liability gain or loss	(200)			$200		
Plan amendments	3,000		$3,000			
Amortization of						
Unrecognized prior service costs			(200)			200
Unrecognized transition obligation		(1,000)[d]				1,000
Net annual OPEB cost					(5,000)	$5,000
Benefit payments	1,600				1,600[e]	
Balance at year-end	$25,400	$19,000	$2,800	$200	$3,400	

Note: In this illustration plan is not funded.
[a] The unrecognized liabilities represent unbooked deferred charges which offset the APBO.
[b] Net gains and losses on assumptions or plan experience deemed to be below level requiring amortization.
[c] This is the balance sheet liability for OPEB costs.
[d] Here the transition is amortized over 20 years.
[e] Benefit payments represent a discharge of plan obligation—they represent also the cash basis, OPEB outlay.

between all related accounts, those both on and off the financial statements.

From a technical accounting point of view, when on adoption of *SFAS 106* a company decides to defer and amortize its Unrecognized Transition Obligation ($20,000) over 20 years, it may record it as follows:

Deferred Charge	20,000	
Transition Obligation		20,000

When amortization of 1/20th of the Transition Obligation is recorded, the following is the hypothetical accounting entry:

APEB expense....................................	1,000	
Deferred charge		1,000

At year-end what is shown as part of the Accumulated Postretirement Benefit Obligation (APBO) is—

Transition Obligation	20,000
Minus Unamortized Deferred Charge	19,000
Transition Obligation now shown as liability	1,000

The Transition Obligation recognized in the balance sheet will grow yearly by the amount with which OPEB expense is debited and the unrecorded Deferred Charge is credited.

The APBO can be reconciled to the Accrued OPEB cost as shown on Exhibit 11–1:

APBO at year-end		$25,400
Less—Unrecognized obligations – Deferrals representing deferred charges which are offset against APBO for balance sheet purposes:		
Unrecognized:		
Transition obligation	$19,000	
Prior service cost	2,800	
Net (gain) or loss	200	$22,000
Net liability – Accrued OPEB cost		$ 3,400

IMPLICATIONS FOR ANALYSIS

While *SFAS 106* has provided a start and a framework for recognizing OPEB costs and liabilities, the analyst, armed with an understanding of this framework, must carefully evaluate the recorded as well as the unrecorded amounts.

The mandated accrual accounting requires an estimate of *future* OPEB costs. While the estimation process is similar to that of estimating pension costs it is more difficult and more subjective. *First,* data about current costs are harder to obtain. Pension benefits involve either fixed dollar amounts or defined dollar amounts based on pay levels. Health benefits, by contrast, are estimates not easily computed by actuarial formulas. Many factors enter into such estimates, including deductibles, age, marital status, and number of dependents. *Second,* more assumptions than those governing pension calculations are needed. In addition to retirement dates, life expectancies, turnover, and discount rates there is a need for estimates of the medical costs trend rate, Medicare reimbursements, and so forth.

Analysts should realize that in some industries OPEB costs will bypass the income statement. Thus, utilities may record such expenses as receivables to be recovered in the future from rate increases. Thus, Pinnacle West explains this as follows:

> Accordingly, this statement should not have a significant impact on Pinnacle West's financial position or results of operations . . . [since] management expects that most of the increased benefits expense will either be recovered currently through APS rates or that a regulatory asset will be recorded to reflect amounts to be recovered through rates in the future as the costs are paid.

Defense contractors may elect to pass on OPEB costs to the government with the result that such costs may be inventoried or deferred. Martin Marietta, which concludes that adoption of *SFAS 106* is not expected to have a material effect on earnings, explains this as follows:

> . . . reported annual cost (under *SFAS 106*) is expected to be significantly greater than current claims-paid-method outlays . . . [A]n accrual method also is allowable under U.S. Government Cost Accounting Standards, and hence, [Martin Marietta has] elected to use accrual accounting in pricing work to be performed in 1993 and thereafter.

OTHER SUPPLEMENTARY EMPLOYEE BENEFITS

Social pressures, competition, and the scarcity of executive talent have led to the proliferation of employee benefits that are supplementary to wages and salaries. Some fringe benefits, such as vacation pay, bonuses, current profit sharing, and paid health or life insurance are clearly identifiable with the period in which they are earned or granted and thus do not pose problems of accounting recognition and accrual.

Other supplementary compensation plans, because of the tentative or contingent nature of their benefits, have not been accorded full or timely accounting recognition, but some accounting pronouncements have resulted in improvements in this area.

SFAS 43, "Accounting for Compensated Absences," requires employers to accrue the costs of compensated absences on a current basis when all of the following conditions are met:

a. The employer's obligation relating to an employee's rights to receive compensation for future absences is attributable to that employee's services already rendered.
b. The obligation relates to rights that vest or accumulate.
c. Payment of the compensation is probable.
d. The amount can be reasonably estimated.

Such absences include vacation, holidays, illness, or other personal activities for which it is expected that an employee will be paid. Not included are severance or termination pay, postretirement benefits, deferred compensation, stock or stock options issued to employees, other long-term fringe benefits (e.g., group insurance, long-term disability pay), or absences due to an employee's illness.

Deferred compensation contracts are usually awarded to executives with whom the company wants to develop lasting ties and who are interested in deferring income to their postretirement and lower tax bracket years. Generally, provisions in such contracts that specify an employee's undertaking not to compete or that specify his or her availability for consulting services are not significant enough to justify deferring the current recognition of such costs. Thus, *APB Opinion 12* requires that at least the present value of deferred compensation to be paid in the future "be accrued in a systematic and rational manner over the period of active employment from the time the contract is entered into, unless it is evident that future services expected to be received by the employer are commensurate with the payments or a portion of the payments to be made." Similar accruals are called for in cases of contracts that guarantee minimum payments to the employee or his/her beneficiaries in case of death.

A company can offer an executive *stock appreciation rights* (SAR) on a given number of shares of stock identified for this purpose. SAR awards are based upon the increase in market value of a company's stock since date of grant, which may be awarded in either cash, stock, or a combination of both. Under such plans, the company records compensation cost at the end of each period. The amount is computed as the difference between the award market price of the shares and their grant date option price. The accounting also provides a methodology for apportioning the expense over the service period. Changes in the quoted market price from period to period should be reflected as an adjustment to compensation expense.

In the case of *junior stock plans,* executives buy shares of a special class of stock at a fair market value (determined by independent appraisal) which is much less than that of the company's common stock because of reduced voting, dividend, and liquidation rights. At some future date, this junior stock can be exchanged for regular common if certain performance goals (e.g., sales or earnings increases) are met.

SFAS Interpretation 38 provides that junior stock awards should be accounted for similarly to stock appreciation rights. Compensation expense is measured by the difference between the amount the company receives for the junior stock and the market price of common stock on the date conversion is certain. Under the *Interpretation,* companies should start recognizing expense when it becomes probable that performance targets will be met and the junior stock will be converted to regular common. Periodic charges to income are based on end-of-period common stock prices and are subject to change until the final amount is set at the date conversion is certain.

The analyst should be aware that a great variety of stock-based compensation plans have been spawned by companies, some of which are covered by current accounting standards and others which are not yet envisaged by them. In this, like in other quickly changing areas, practice leads theory. As the example below indicates, under these plans earnings may be impacted by charges for compensation based on stock price benchmarks and they may be affected negatively as well as positively by changes in the market price of a company's stock.

ILLUSTRATION 1.   In its financial statement Trasonics discloses a share options plan as follows:

> Under the performance share option plans, the Company records a charge to earnings and a credit to additional paid-in capital for shares potentially earned, based on earnings performance levels achieved, to the extent the fair market value of such shares exceeds the option price at fiscal year-end. Upon exercise, the investment in the treasury share account is credited with the cost of the treasury shares issued and additional paid-in capital is adjusted to reflect the balance of the option price.

Stock options are incentive compensation devices under which an executive receives the right to buy a number of shares at a certain price over a number of years subject to conditions designed to identify him with the employer's interests.

Executive stock options fit into two broad categories: incentive and nonqualified. Incentive or tax-favored (qualified) options are not taxed until the stock is sold by the executive. They must be granted at fair market value and the stock must be held for two years from the date of the grant and one year from the date they are exercised. The difference between the exercise price and the selling price is generally taxed as ordinary income.

Nonqualified stock options do not have the tax benefits of their qualified counterparts. They are sometimes granted at a discount from fair market value and executives are taxed at the time of exercise on the difference between the exercise price and the stock's fair market value. In this case, the company benefits from a tax deduction equal to the amount of income recognized by the executive.

The usual rationale advanced in defense of stock options is that business will be run better by managers who are important share owners. Options allow executives to build an estate and offer significant tax advantages.

In theory, the accounting for stock options defines the compensation to be recognized as the excess of the fair value of the optioned shares, at the dates the options are granted, over the option price. In practice, since the spread, if any, between the market price and the option price at the date of grant is negligible, the compensation inherent in stock options is generally not recorded on the basis of lack of materiality.

APB Opinion 25, "Accounting for Stock Issued to Employees," specifies that when stock options are granted, the excess of the market price of the stock over the option price should be accounted for as compensation over the periods benefited. In this computation, the discounting of market value to allow for restrictions placed on the use or disposition of the stock by the employee is not permitted.

Quaker Oats Company (appendix to Chapter 23) has elaborate deferred compensation plans described in item 150 which include an Employee Stock Ownership Plan (ESOP). Item 151 describes the company's Employee Stock Option and Award Plans.

Implications for Analysis

The accounting for stock appreciation rights and the related accounting for junior stock plans has now become more realistic. While under the latter an executive incurs more financial risk than under the former, both are in effect compensation plans under which the company parts with economic resources.

It is clear that the analyst has to study the provisions of incentive stock plans carefully in order to assess their potential impact on income. Since the impact on income of some of these plans depends on the price levels of the company's stock, such an evaluation is far from easy. The great variety of stock plans could also cause potential dilution of earnings per share in ways not yet envisaged by relevant professional standards.

In the case of stock options, the executive is receiving a similar benefit yet the impact on the company's earnings is quite different. The accounting problem regarding stock options is serious. Basically there is a failure to reflect in operating costs compensation granted to employees. No serious student of accounting and finance can deny the real cost to a company and its shareholders, of selling its shares at prices below what it could get on the open market. The justification of the lack of accounting for the cost of stock options is a sort of "coin-clipping" operation whereby the small annual dilution of stockholder equity is overlooked without an assessment of its more significant cumulative effect.

The plain fact is that the compensation inherent in stock options is unrecorded under present GAAP. The improvements brought about by *APB Opinion 25* are more apparent than real. This *Opinion* continues the accounting profession's long-standing reluctance to face up to the fact that an option to buy a share of stock for a number of months or years at the current market price is a valuable privilege. The prices at which call options as well as longer-term warrants sell in the marketplace is adequate testimony to this.

In 1972, the United States Pay Board faced the problem of valuing stock options and decided that their value is equivalent to 25 percent of the fair market value of the stock at the date of grant plus the excess of fair market value of the shares over the option price at the time of grant (Regulation 201.76). This rule is somewhat arbitrary in that it may fail to take into account restrictions to which a stock option is subject or the length of its duration. Nevertheless, it proves that stock options can be valued, and this valuation is a far more realistic approach than that adopted by the accounting profession in this matter. Financial analysts may well use the Pay Board's valuation rule as a rough guide whenever they want to estimate the unbooked compensation inherent in stock option plans.

One saving feature in the stock option accounting problem is a development brought about through "the back door" by *APB Opinion 15,* "Earnings per Share." Under this *Opinion,* stock options that have a dilutive effect on earnings per share (EPS) must enter into the computation of that figure, thus showing in this statistic some of the effect which is missing in the reported "net income" figure. The computation and evaluation of EPS is discussed in Chapter 12.

The FASB is now reevaluating the accounting for stock options.

RESEARCH, EXPLORATION, AND DEVELOPMENT OUTLAYS

Research, exploration, and development efforts are undertaken by business enterprises for a variety of reasons, all aiming at either short-term improvements or longer-term profit and improved market position. Some research efforts are directed toward maintaining existing product markets, while others aim at the development of new products and processes.

Types of Research and Development

One type of research is *basic* or *pure research,* that is, directed toward the discovery of new facts, natural laws, or phenomena without regard to the immediate commercial application to which the results may be put. Benefits from such research programs are very uncertain, but if successful, they may be among the most rewarding of all.

Unlike pure research, *applied research* is directed toward more specific goals such as product improvement or the perfection and improvement of processes or techniques of production.

Exploration is the search for natural resources of all kinds. Exploration is always an "applied" kind of activity in that it has a definite and known objective.

Development begins where research and exploration end. It is the activity devoted to bringing the fruits of research or the resources discovered by exploration to a commercially useful and marketable stage. Thus, development may involve efforts to exploit a new product invention or it may involve the exploitation of an oil well, a mineral deposit, or a tract of timber.

Research and development (R&D) may be one part of many activities of an ongoing enterprise, or it may be virtually the sole activity of an enterprise in its formative stages.

Definition of Research and Development Activities

Research activities are aimed at discovery of new knowledge for the development of a new product or process or in bringing about a significant improvement to an existing product or process.

Development activities translate the research findings into a plan or design for a new product or process or a significant improvement to an existing product or process.

R&D specifically excludes routine or periodic alterations to ongoing operations and market research and testing activities.

The Accounting Problem

The problem of accounting for R&D costs is difficult and defies easy solutions. There are a number of reasons for this, among which the most important are:

1. The great uncertainty of ultimate results that pervades most research efforts. Generally, the outcome of a research project is more uncertain than that of an immediately productive operation.
2. In most cases, there is a significant lapse of time between the initiation of a research project and the determination of its ultimate success or failure. This time lapse, in effect, is another dimension of uncertainty.
3. Often the results of research are intangible in form, a fact that contributes to the difficulty of evaluation.

It is this all-pervading uncertainty of ultimate results that causes the difficulty in accounting for R&D costs rather than the absence of logical reasoning or a lack of clear objectives of accounting. Such objectives are clear and well known:

1. Costs should be related to the revenues with which they are associated.
2. Costs should not be deferred unless there is a reasonably warranted expectation that they will be recovered out of future revenues or will benefit future operations.

FASB *Statement 2*

After a great deal of discussion and deliberation, the FASB has arrived in its *SFAS 2* at a rather simple solution to the complex problem of accounting for R&D costs: They should be charged to expense when incurred.

SFAS 2 has expanded considerably the definition of what is to be included in R&D costs. It maintains that only a very small percentage of R&D projects are successful (recognizing the difficulty in defining what constitutes a successful project) and that even if the rate of success could be predicted with reasonable accuracy, it still would be difficult to forecast the period of future benefit.

The Board concluded, therefore, that subject to exceptions indicated below, all R&D costs should be charged to expense as incurred.

Accounting for Research and Development Costs

The majority of expenditures incurred in R&D activities as defined above constitutes the costs of that activity and should be charged to expense when incurred.

Costs of materials, equipment, and facilities that have alternative future uses (in R&D projects or otherwise) should be capitalized as tangible assets.

Intangibles purchased from others for R&D use that have alternative future uses should also be capitalized.

Elements of costs that should be identified with R&D activities are:

a. Costs of materials, equipment, and facilities that are acquired or constructed for a particular R&D project and purchased intangibles, that have no alternative future uses (in R&D projects or otherwise).
b. Costs of materials consumed in R&D activities, the depreciation of equipment or facilities, and the amortization of intangible assets used in research and development activities that have alternative future uses.
c. Salaries and other related costs of personnel engaged in R&D activities.

d. Costs of services performed by others.

e. A reasonable allocation of indirect costs. General and administrative costs that are not clearly related to R&D activities should be excluded.

Disclosure Requirements

For each income statement presented, the total R&D costs charged to expense shall be disclosed.

Government-regulated companies that defer R&D costs in accordance with the addendum to *SFAS 2* must make certain additional disclosures.

While it is difficult to estimate the future benefits from R&D outlays, it is even more difficult and speculative to estimate the future benefits to be derived from costs of training programs, product promotions, and advertising. Consequently, deferral of such costs is very difficult to justify.

Implications for Analysis

The evaluation of R&D outlays presents a serious problem in the analysis of financial statements. Often the size of these outlays is such that they must be taken into account in any analysis of current income and of future prospects.

The FASB's simplistic solution to the accounting for R&D outlays has been described as "really a way of avoiding responsibility" and as arriving at "too easy a solution to an extremely difficult problem."[2] Professors Bierman and Dukes, in questioning the basic reasoning that led the FASB to arrive at the expensing solution, maintain that it is "incorrect to conclude that, because it has been difficult to observe a significant correlation between expenditures and subsequent benefits, future benefits are not generated by research and development expenditures." The professors conclude that "from the point of view of accounting theory, the expenditures for R&D, which are made in the expectation of benefiting future periods, should not be written off against the revenues of the present period. Justification for such practice must be found elsewhere, if it is to be found."

Professor B. Lev[3] maintains that the arbitrariness of some accounting rules, such as for R&D outlays, adversely affects the usefulness of reported earnings. Thus, when a firm makes a large R&D outlay the effect is a

---

[2] Harold Bierman Jr. and Ronald E. Dukes, "Accounting for Research and Development Costs," *Journal of Accountancy,* April 1975.

[3] Baruch Lev. "On the Usefulness of Earnings and Earnings Research: Lessons and Directions from Two Decades of Empirical Research." *Journal of Accounting Research* 27 (Supplemental 1989), pp. 153–92.

decline in reported earnings at the same time that the market may revalue upward the price of the stock.

The analyst should realize that while *SFAS 2* assures that there will be no overstated R&D deferrals on the balance sheet, it does so at the expense of any reasonable attempt to match the expenditure of the resources against the revenues that it helps produce. Thus, this new accounting is safe rather than more useful; it overlooks the history of productivity of many ongoing research efforts as opposed to the uncertainty involved in one-shot research projects.

It is possible that the FASB's pragmatic solution that requires the current expensing of practically all R&D outlays will help accountants achieve a uniformity of approach in this area and at the same time avoid the difficult choices and judgments that a policy of capitalization and deferral imposes. It is doubtful that such a policy of, in effect, nonaccounting for R&D costs along with the very limited disclosure requirements it requires will really serve the needs and interests of serious analysts of financial statements.

Granting the difficulty of measuring and estimating the future benefits to be derived from R&D outlays, it is nonetheless reasonable to assume that managements enter into such projects with firm expectations of returns on these investments. Moreover, in many cases, they have specific expectations about such potential returns that the realization or non-realization of which can be monitored and estimated as a research project progresses. In the past, a policy of deferral of R&D costs afforded managements and their independent accountants, who normally judge uncertainties and estimate results in most of their work, an opportunity to carry to the reader their estimate of the future potential promise of such outlays at a given point in time. Under the new rules, all R&D is treated as if it has no future value, and the analyst will no longer have the benefit of the estimates of those in the best position to offer them.

Recognizing the limitations of such accounting, the Institute of Chartered Accountants of Scotland took the position that pure and applied research are akin to maintenance expenses essential to preserving a company's business and its competitive position and should consequently be written off as incurred. However, expenditures for new and improved products that are made with a reasonable expectation of specific commercial success may, if they satisfy stringent criteria established for their evaluation, be carried forward and amortized over the period that they are expected to benefit.

SFAS 2 requires only disclosure of total R&D outlays charged to expense in a given period. In order to form an opinion on the quality and the future potential value of research outlays, the analyst needs to know, of course, a great deal more than the totals of periodic R&D outlays. Information is needed on the types of research performed, the outlays by category, as well as the technical feasibility, commercial viability, and future potential of each project assessed and reevaluated anew at the time of each periodic report. He or she also needs information on a company's success-failure experience in its several areas of research activity to date. Of course, present disclosure requirements will not give the analyst such information, and apparently, except in cases of voluntary disclosures, only an investor or lender with the necessary influence will be able to obtain such information.

In general, one can assume that the outright expensing of all R&D outlays will result in more conservative balance sheets and fewer painful surprises stemming from the wholesale write-offs of previously capitalized R&D outlays. However, the analyst must realize that along with a lack of knowledge about future potential, he or she will—unless the analyst probes widely and deeply—also be unaware of the potential disasters that can befall an enterprise tempted or forced to sink ever greater amounts of funds in R&D projects whose promise was great but whose failure is nevertheless inevitable.

Accounting for the Costs of Computer Software

The development of computer software is a specialized activity and the accounting for it did not fit in with the requirements of *SFAS 2*. The development of software to be marketed is an ongoing activity leading directly to future revenues. At some point in the development cycle, costs need to be deferred and matched against future revenues.

SFAS 86 (1985), "Accounting for the Costs of Computer Software to be Sold, Leased, or Otherwise Marketed," identifies a point referred to as technological feasibility where the costs can be capitalized and matched against future revenues. Up to the point where technological feasibility is established all costs are to be expensed as being in the nature of research and development. Costs incurred *after* this point and until the product is ready for general release to customers are to be capitalized as an intangible asset. Additional costs to actually produce software from the masters and package it for distribution are inventoriable and should be charged against revenue as the product is sold.

Exploration and Development in Extractive Industries

The search for new deposits of natural resources is the function of a very important industry segment encompassing the oil, natural gas, metals, coal, and nonmetallic minerals industries. While the unique accounting problems of these industries deserve separate consideration, no new accounting principles are involved here but rather the application of such principles and concepts to special circumstances. Thus, while the search for and development of natural resources is characterized by exposure to high degrees of risk, so is, as we have seen, the search for new knowledge, new processes, and new products. Risk involves uncertainty; and within a framework of periodic income determinations, uncertainty always presents very serious problems of income and expense determination.

In extractive industries, under the historical-cost model, the major problems lie on the cost and expense side. Essentially, the problem is one of whether exploration and development costs that may reasonably be expected to be recovered out of the future lifting of the natural resources should be charged in the period incurred or should be capitalized and amortized over expected future recovery and production.

While many companies charge off all exploration costs currently, some charge off only a portion and capitalize another portion. A few companies capitalize almost all development costs and amortize them over future periods.

The accounting profession has recognized that the divergent practices create a need for reforms in this area. As a first step, *Accounting Research Study (ARS) 11,* "Financial Reporting in the Extractive Industries," makes the following recommendations, among others:

> Expenditures for prospecting costs, indirect acquisition costs and most carrying costs should be charged to expense when incurred as part of the current cost of exploration.
>
> Direct acquisition costs of unproved properties should be capitalized and the estimated loss portion should be amortized to expense on a systematic and rational basis as part of the current cost of exploration.
>
> Unsuccessful exploration and development expenditures should be charged to operations even though incurred on property units where commercially recoverable reserves exist.

When the Committee on Extractive Industries of the APB rendered its final report with the purpose of providing the FASB with a summary of the committee's research in accounting for the oil and gas industry it stated:

> Throughout the committee's deliberations it became increasingly clear that there exists in practice two basic concepts or philosophies regarding accounting in the oil and gas industry; namely, full-cost accounting and successful efforts accounting. The basic concept of the full-cost method is that all costs, productive and nonproductive, incurred in the search for oil and gas reserves should be capitalized and amortized to income as the total oil and gas reserves are produced and sold. The basic concept of the successful efforts method is that all costs which of themselves do not result directly in the discovery of oil and gas reserves have no future benefit in terms of future revenues and should be expensed as incurred. It was equally clear that the application of the two concepts in practice varies to such an extent that there are in fact numerous different methods of accounting.

In recent years, the standard-setting process for oil and gas producing companies was marked by disagreements, indecision, and changes in direction.

SFAS 19 prescribed the "successful efforts" method of cost accounting for all oil and gas producing companies. That is, all exploration costs except the costs of drilling exploratory wells are capitalized as "construction in progress" when incurred, to be expensed later if the well is unsuccessful or to be reclassified as an amortizable asset if proved oil or gas reserves are discovered.

The SEC disagreed with *SFAS 19* and focused instead on Reserve Recognition Accounting (RRA—a current value accounting method), while allowing either successful efforts or full-cost accounting in the interim. That led the FASB to issue *SFAS 25* which suspended the effective date of *SFAS 19* for requiring successful efforts accounting, in effect allowing the existing alternative to continue.

In early 1981, the SEC abandoned its attempt to substitute RRA for the two historical accounting methods and returned jurisdiction on the issue to the FASB with the request that it develop supplementary disclosures, including value-based disclosures.

SFAS 69, "Disclosures about Oil and Gas Producing Activities," supersedes the disclosure requirements of previous board statements in this area and requires that the following supplementary information be disclosed by publicly owned oil and gas producers:

- Proved oil and gas reserve quantities.
- Capitalized costs relating to oil and gas producing activities.
- Costs incurred in acquisition, exploration, and development activities.
- Results of operations for oil and gas producing activities.
- Standardized measures of discounted future net cash flows related to proved reserves.

Both publicly traded and other companies will continue to be required to disclose the method of accounting for costs incurred in oil and gas producing activities and the manner of disposing of related capitalized costs.

The statement also allows companies to use historical-cost/constant-dollar measures in presenting current cost information about oil and gas mineral interests.

The SEC has adopted final rules requiring compliance with *SFAS 69* with minor modifications.

Disclosure is, however, one thing and accounting is another.

The accounting profession has been unable to prevail in imposing the more realistic successful efforts accounting method. However in sanctioning the use of the full-cost accounting method the SEC provided that under this method costs could be capitalized only up to a ceiling. That ceiling is determined by the present value of company reserves. Capitalized costs exceeding the ceiling would have to be written off. When falling oil prices in 1986 began to lower those ceilings alarmingly, the oil companies affected, with support of the SEC staff, attempted to persuade the Commission to suspend or modify the rules. Fortunately for accounting integrity the Commission rejected these attempts—the Chairman saying that "the rules are not stretchable at a time of stress."

Implications for Analysis

With regard to exploration and development costs in the extractive industries, the analyst faces at present the problem of a variety of acceptable methods of treating such costs. This variety in turn hampers the comparison of results among companies in the same industry.

In the aftermath of the SEC's espousal and subsequent abandonment of RRA, it will take additional time for the accounting in this industry to be brought to some degree of standardization. The two methods in current use, and the many variations within these methods, can yield significantly differing results, and the analyst must be aware of this. An earlier survey found that a large majority of financial analysts favor successful efforts accounting over the full-cost method because it improves matching of costs with related revenues and is more consistent with the accounting model in present use.[4] This method does, in fact, require that a direct relationship be established between costs incurred and specific oil and gas reserves discovered before such costs are identified as assets. The full-cost method, on the other hand, allows companies to label dry holes as assets.

GOODWILL

Finally, in a consideration of intangible costs, we should add here to the discussion of goodwill that was begun in Chapter 6 and continued in Chapter 9.

Goodwill is usually the measure of value assigned to a rate of earnings above the ordinary. It is, in some respects, similar to the premium paid for a bond because its coupon rate exceeds the going interest rate. The size and the timing of those excess earnings is, however, uncertain to a much higher degree. Thus, the real problem with the accounting for purchased goodwill is that of measuring its expiration. There is no need to write off against earnings an asset whose value does not expire. Land is a prominent example of such an asset. However, the superior earning

---

[4] A. Naggar, "Oil and Gas Accounting: Where Wall Street Stands," *Journal of Accountancy,* September 1978.

power of an enterprise is not indestructible or everlasting. It must, in fact, be nurtured and renewed and changes, such as in management style or philosophy, can diminish its value in short order.

Being simply the residual amount in the computation of the cost of a purchase goodwill can, at times, be the major part of the consideration paid for a going business. Thus, Standard & Poor's Corporation reported as follows:

> Standard & Poor's purchased all the stock of Trendline Corp. and O.T.C. Publications, Inc., for a price of approximately $2,425,000, which exceeded the net tangible assets of the acquired companies by $2,154,061. That amount was charged to goodwill.

As can be seen in the more comprehensive discussion of the subject in Chapters 6 and 9, *APB Opinion 17* requires that the excess paid over fair market value of net assets acquired in a purchase, that is, goodwill, be amortized to income over a period not to exceed 40 years.

Implications for Analysis

One of the most common solutions applied by analysts to the complex problems of the analysis of goodwill is to simply ignore it. That is, they ignore the asset shown on the balance sheet. And yet by ignoring goodwill, analysts ignore investments of very substantial resources in what may often be a company's most important asset.

Ignoring the impact of goodwill on reported periodic income is, of course, also no solution to the analysis of this complex cost. Thus, even considering the limited amount of information available to the analyst, it is far better that he or she understand the effects of accounting practices in this area on reported income rather than dismiss them altogether.

Goodwill is measured by the excess of cost over the *fair market value* of tangible net assets acquired in a transaction accounted for as a purchase. It is the excess of the purchase price over the fair value of all the tangible assets acquired, arrived at by carefully ascertaining the value of such assets. That is the theory of it. At least up to 1970 when *APB Opinion 17* took effect, companies have failed to assign the full fair market value to tangible assets acquired and have, instead, preferred to relegate as much of the purchase price as possible to an account bearing the rather literally descriptive, but meaningless, title of "excess of cost over book value of assets acquired." The reasons for this tendency are simple to understand. Costs assigned to such assets as inventories, plant and equipment, patents, or future tax benefits must all ultimately be charged to income. Goodwill, prior to *APB Opinion 17,* had to be amortized only when its value was impaired or was expiring, and such a judgment was difficult to prove let alone to audit or second-guess. Thus, many companies have included much of the cost of acquisition over the book value on the *seller's* books in the "excess of cost . . ." account and thereafter proceeded to claim that the amount is not amortized because its value to the enterprise is undiminished. We may add here that since the amortization of goodwill is not a tax-deductible expense, its deduction for financial reporting purposes has a magnified adverse impact that managements desire to avoid. The change in accounting requirements toward mandatory amortization will change the effects of the aforementioned practices over time. Financial analysts should, however, be aware of the large stagnant "pools" of goodwill that will remain on the books of many corporations. American Medical International, Inc., reports this as follows:

> Goodwill acquired prior to November 1, 1970, was $10,000,000 and is not being amortized since, in management's opinion, there has been no diminution in the value of these purchased businesses. Similar costs relating to subsequent acquisitions are being amortized on a straight-line basis over 40 years.

The financial analyst must be alert to the makeup and the method of valuation of the Goodwill account as well as to the method of its ultimate disposition. One way of disposing of the Goodwill account, frequently chosen by management, is to write it off at a time when it would have the least serious impact on the market's judgment of the company's earnings, for example, a time of loss or reduced earnings. Goodwill should be written off when the superior earning power originally justifying its existence is no longer present. Dow Jones & Company did this as follows:

> As a result of *Book Digest Magazine's* continuing losses, management concluded that there had been a substantial reduction in the value of the magazine's net assets. Accordingly . . . Excess of Cost over Net Assets of Businesses Acquired was reduced by $9,400,000.

Under normal circumstances, goodwill is not indestructible but is rather an asset with a limited useful life. Whatever the advantages of location, of market dominance and competitive stance, of sales skill or product acceptance, or other benefits are, they cannot be unaffected by the passing of time and by changes in the business environment. Thus, the amortization of goodwill gives recognition to the expiration of a resource in which capital has been invested, a process which is similar to the depreciation of fixed assets. The analyst must recognize that a 40-year amortization period, while adhering to the minimum accounting requirement, which represents a compromise position, may not be realistic in terms of the time expiration of economic values. Thus, he or she must assess the propriety of the amortization period by reference to such evidence of continuing value as the profitability of units for which the goodwill consideration was originally paid.

OTHER INTANGIBLE ASSET WRITE-OFFS

The Motor Carrier Act of 1980 which deregulated interstate trucking eliminated the value of exclusive franchises of truckers. This was dealt with by *SFAS 44* as explained by Purolator, Inc.:

> Enactment of the Motor Carrier Act of 1980 and recent actions of the Interstate Commerce Commission and various states which regulate the motor carrier industry simplified entry by new carriers and eliminated many route, territory and commodity restrictions for existing carriers. As a result, the Financial Accounting Standards Board issued Statement No. 44 requiring the write-off in 1980 of costs assigned to operating rights which resulted in an extraordinary charge of $12,363,000.

INTEREST COSTS

The interest cost to an entity is the nominal rate paid including, in the case of bonds, the amortization of bond discount or premium. A complication arises when companies issue convertible debt or debt with warrants, thus achieving a nominal debt coupon cost that is below the cost of similar debt not enjoying these added features.

After trial pronouncements on the subject and much controversy, *APB Opinion 14* has concluded that in the case of *convertible debt,* the inseparability of the debt and equity features is such that no portion of the proceeds from the issuance should be accounted for as attributable to the conversion feature.

In the case of debt issued with stock warrants attached, the proceeds of the debt attributable to the value of the warrants should be accounted for as paid-in capital. The corresponding charge is to a debt discount account that must be amortized over the life of the debt issue, thus increasing the effective interest cost.

Interest Capitalization

Interest, being an expense that accrues with the lapse of time, was generally considered a period cost except in the case of public utilities and industries such as real estate. Over the years, the practice of interest capitalization spread, and the resulting uneven practice led the SEC to impose a moratorium on new switches to capitalization of interest pending a resolution of this entire matter by the FASB.

The FASB acted by issuing *SFAS 34,* "Capitalization of Interest Cost," which requires capitalization of interest cost as part of the historical cost of "assets that are constructed or otherwise produced for an enterprise's own use (including assets constructed or produced for the enterprise by others for which deposits or progress payments have been made)." Inventory items that are routinely manufactured or produced in large quantities on a repetitive basis do not qualify for interest capitalization.

The objectives of interest capitalization according to the FASB are (1) to measure more accurately the acquisition cost of an asset and (2) to amortize that acquisition cost against revenues generated by the asset.

The amount of interest to be capitalized is based on the entity's actual borrowings and interest payments. The rate to be used for capitalization may be ascertained in this order: (1) the rate of specific borrowings associated with the assets; and (2) if borrowings are not specific for the asset, or the cost of the asset exceeds specific borrowings therefor, a weighted average of rates applicable to other appropriate borrowings may be used. Alternatively, a company may use a weighted average of rates of all appropriate borrowings regardless of specific borrowings incurred to finance the asset. Interest capitalization may not exceed total interest costs for any period, nor is imputing interest cost to equity funds permitted. A company without debt will have no interest to capitalize.

The capitalization period begins when three conditions are present: expenditures for the asset have been made by the entity, work on the asset is in progress, and interest cost is being incurred. Interest capitalization ceases when the asset is ready for its intended use.

SFAS 34 requires disclosure of: (1) for an accounting period in which no interest cost is capitalized, the amount of interest charged to expense during the period; and (2) for an accounting period in which interest is capitalized, the total amount of interest incurred during the period, and the amount that has been capitalized.

The New York Times Company reported interest capitalization as follows:

> In connection with various construction projects, interest of approximately $19,118,000, $30,806,000 and $17,393,000 was capitalized as property, plant and equipment for 1990, 1989 and 1988, respectively.

Implications for Analysis

Financial analysts should realize that in spite of the position taken in *APB Opinion 14,* there are many who disagree with the *Opinion's* position on convertible debt. The dissenters, which included members of the APB, contend that by ignoring the value of the conversion privilege and instead using as a sole measure of interest cost the coupon rate of interest, the *Opinion* specifies an accounting treatment that ignores the true interest cost to the corporation.

It should be noted, however, that *APB Opinion 15,* "Earnings per Share," by requiring in specified circumstances the inclusion in the computation of earnings per share (EPS) of the number of shares issuable in the event of conversion of convertible debt, in effect creates a charge additional to the coupon interest cost by way of diluting the reported EPS figure.

The capitalization of interest is a controversial subject. The concept passed the FASB by only a four to three margin. The Financial Analysts Federation's position was that interest is basically a period cost.

The analyst must realize that many of the definitions and criteria in *SFAS 34* are loose enough to lead to significant variations in their application. Materiality thresholds also lead to significant variations. Moreover, the criteria for capitalization are arbitrary with, for example, some inventories qualifying while others do not.

Generally, capitalized interest is included in the cost of fixed assets and enters periodic expense via the depreciation and amortization process. In order to assess the impact of the capitalization of interest on the net income of a period, the analyst needs to know the amount of capitalized interest that is currently charged to income via the depreciation and amortization process. This amount is also needed in order to compute correctly the fixed-charge coverage ratio (see Chapter 18). Unfortunately *SFAS 34* does not require disclosure of these amounts so that the analyst will often not be able to obtain it from published financial statements. One possible source may be Schedule VI of SEC Form 10-K.

Changes in the interest rate at which a company borrows money is of significance to the analyst. Thus, an increase in the borrowing rate of interest which is not explained by a market increase in interest rates would indicate that the credit rating of the company has deteriorated.

INCOME TAXES

Income taxes are a very substantial cost of doing business. In many cases, they amount to a substantial portion of a corporation's pre-tax income. It follows that the accounting for income taxes is an important matter that should be clearly understood. This discussion is not primarily concerned with matters of tax law but rather with the accounting standards that govern the proper computation of the periodic tax expense. *SFAS 109* is the accounting profession's authoritative pronouncement on this subject. The SEC has additional requirements.

Statement of Financial Accounting Standards 109—
Accounting for Income Taxes

This statement, issued in 1991, superseded *SFAS 96* which was was controversial and widely opposed. *SFAS 109* establishes financial accounting and reporting standards for the effects of income taxes that result from an enterprise's activities during the current and preceding years and requires an asset and liability approach.

SFAS 109 requires that deferred taxes should be determined separately for each tax-paying component (an individual entity or group of entities that is consolidated for tax purposes) in each tax jurisdiction. The determination includes the following procedures:

- Identify the types and amounts of existing temporary differences and the nature and amount of each type of operating loss and tax credit carryforward, plus the remaining length of the carryforward period.
- Measure the total deferred tax liability for taxable temporary differences, using the applicable tax rate.
- Measure the total deferred tax asset for deductible temporary differences and operating loss carryforwards, using the applicable tax rate.
- Measure deferred tax assets for each type of tax credit carryforward.
- Reduce deferred tax assets by a valuation allowance if, based on the weight of available evidence, it is more likely than not (a likelihood of more than 50 percent) that some portion or all of the deferred tax assets will not be realized. The valuation allowance should be sufficient to reduce the deferred tax asset to the amount that is more likely than not to be realized.

Deferred tax assets and liabilities should be adjusted for the effect of a change in tax laws or rates. The effect should be included in income from continuing operations for the period that includes the enactment date.

The statement continues the exception to the application of these basic principles by retention of *APB Opinion 23,* one principal provision of which allows a parent company not to recognize a liability for deferred taxes which would arise because of a subsidiary's unremitted earnings.

The concepts of *permanent* income tax differences (a term not used in the statement) and that of *temporary* tax difference are discussed below.

Permanent Income Tax Differences

The current provision for taxes is governed by any number of tax regulations that may apply in a given situation. Regulations such as those concerning the depletion allowance or credits allowed by law can reduce the effective tax rate of a corporation below statutory levels. Proper disclosure requires that information be given regarding the reasons for deviations from normal tax incidence.

The net income computed on the basis of GAAP (also known as book income) is often not identical to the taxable income computed on the entity's tax return. This is because of two types of differences: permanent differences, which are discussed here, and temporary differences, which are covered in the section that follows.

Permanent differences result from provisions of the tax law under which:

	Examples
A. Certain items may be nontaxable.	Income on tax-exempt obligations; proceeds of life insurance on officer.
B. Certain deductions are not allowed.	Amortization of goodwill; penalties for filing certain returns; fines; officer life insurance premiums.
C. Special deductions have been granted.	Dividend exclusion on dividends from unconsolidated subsidiaries and on dividends received from other domestic corporations.

In addition, the effective tax rate paid by a corporation on its income will vary from the statutory rate (e.g., 34 percent) because:

D. The basis of carrying property for accounting purposes may differ from that for tax purposes as a result of reorganizations, business combinations, etc.
E. Nonqualified as well as qualified stock option plans may result in tax-book differences.
F. Certain industries, such as savings and loan associations, shipping lines, and insurance companies, enjoy special tax privileges.
G. Up to $100,000 of corporate income is taxed at lower rates.
H. Certain credits may apply—(e.g., research and development credits, foreign tax credits).
I. Foreign income is taxed at different rates.
J. State and local income taxes, net of federal tax benefit, are included in total tax expense.
K. Tax loss carryforward benefits apply.

What makes these differences and factors permanent is the fact that they do not have any future repercussions on a company's taxable income. Thus, as we shall see, they must be taken into account when reconciling a company's actual (effective) tax rate to the statutory rate of, say, 34 percent.

Temporary Differences

Financial accounting, which is governed by considerations of fair presentation of financial position and results of operations, does not share in all respects the principles that govern the computation of taxable income, the latter being governed by economic or revenue-raising objectives. Consequently, there are a great many cases of differences between tax and "book" accounting.

Unlike permanent differences, these are known as temporary differences because they are expected to affect taxable income at some future time; that is, they are expected to reverse.

ILLUSTRATION 2.   For financial accounting purposes, a company depreciates a $1,000 asset over 10 years on a straight-line basis. To conserve its cash, the company elects for tax purposes to use the double-declining-balance method of depreciation. In the first year, the book depreciation is $100 while the tax depreciation is $200. In later years, the book depreciation will exceed the tax depreciation because under either method the total depreciation cannot exceed $1,000. Thus, the difference is temporary.

There are a variety of temporary differences between tax and financial accounting. They subdivide into four categories as follows:

1. Revenue or gain is deferred for tax-reporting purposes but is recognized in the current period for financial reporting purposes.
    a. The installment method is used for tax purposes; the accrual method is used for financial reporting purposes.
    b. The completed-contract method is used for tax purposes; the percentage-of-completion method is used for financial reporting purposes.
2. Expenses deducted for tax purposes in the current period exceed expenses deducted for financial reporting purposes.
    a. Accelerated depreciation is taken for tax purposes; straight-line depreciation is used for financial reporting purposes.
    b. Land reclamation and similar costs are deducted for tax purposes; capitalization and amortization are utilized for financial reporting purposes.
3. Revenue or gain is recognized for tax purposes in the current period, but all or part of the amount is deferred for financial reporting purposes.
    a. Rent income or other income received in advance is recognized for tax purposes.
    b. Unearned finance charges and other deferred credits are recognized for tax purposes but are taken into income over a number of years for financial reporting purposes.
4. Expenses deducted for financial reporting purposes in the current period exceed expenses deducted for tax purposes.
    a. Estimated expenses (repair and maintenance, warranty servicing costs, and vacation wages) are accrued for financial reporting purposes but not deducted for tax purposes.

b. Estimated refunds due the government for price redetermination and renegotiation are accrued for financial reporting purposes.

These four categories may be summarized as follows:

Category of transaction	Reported on		Initial income tax journal entries	
	Income statement	*Tax return*	*Income tax expense*	*Balance sheet deferred tax accounts**
1. Revenue or gain	Earlier	Later	Debit	Credit
2. Expenses	Later	Earlier	Debit	Credit
3. Revenue or gain	Later	Earlier	Credit	Debit
4. Expenses	Earlier	Later	Credit	Debit

* These may reverse later. Some reversals may occur in the normal course of business, while some may occur due to a switch in policy, e.g., deferred installment profits reverse when receivables are sold to a bank and deferred tax must be paid; or tax deferrals due to accelerated depreciation reverse because the company switches from owning assets to leasing them.

While all four categories are found in practice, the desirable temporary differences that companies that owe income taxes strive to have are those that result in initial credits to the balance sheet deferred tax account— thus resulting in a postponement of taxes. Categories 3 and 4 are undesirable in that they result in the prepayment of taxes.

In a classified statement of financial position, an enterprise should separate deferred tax liabilities and assets into a current amount and a noncurrent amount. Deferred tax liabilities and assets should be classified as current or noncurrent based on the classification of the related asset or liability for financial reporting. A deferred tax liability or asset that is not related to an asset or liability for financial reporting, including deferred tax assets related to carryforwards, should be classified according to the expected reversal date of the temporary difference. When a valuation allowance, which measures the likelihood of realizing deferred tax assets, is used, it should be allocated between current and noncurrent deferred tax assets on a pro rata basis.

The basic problem with these temporary differences, from the accounting point of view, is that there will be differences between the income before tax shown in the income statement and the taxable income shown in the tax return. Thus, if the actual tax paid is considered as the period expense, it will not match the pre-tax income shown in the income statement. This would violate the basic accounting principle that there should be a matching of income and related costs and expenses. Interperiod tax allocation is designed to assure that in any one period, income shown in the financial statements is charged with the tax applicable to it regardless of how such income is reported for tax purposes. Thus the basic objective of recognizing the tax consequences of an event in the same year that the event is recognized in the financial statements will be realized.

ILLUSTRATION 3.   Application of the principle of tax allocation:

A retailer sells air conditioners on the installment basis. On January 1, year 1, he sells a unit for $720 payable at the rate of $20 a month for 36 months. For purposes of this illustration, we ignore finance charges and assume a gross profit to the retailer of 20 percent and a tax rate of 50 percent.

In accordance with proper accrual accounting, the retailer will recognize in the year of sale (year 1) a gross profit of $144 (20 percent of $720). For tax purposes, he can recognize profit based on actual cash collections as follows:

	Cash collection	Taxable gross profit (20%)	Actual tax payable
Year 1	$240	$ 48	$24
Year 2	240	48	24
Year 3	240	48	24
Total ...	$720	$144	$72

In the absence of tax allocation, the results shown by the retailer on this transaction would be as follows:

	Pre-tax profit	Tax payable	Profit (loss)
Year 1	$144	$24	$120
Year 2	—	24	(24)
Year 3	—	24	(24)
Total ...	$144	$72	$ 72

The flaws in this presentation are readily apparent. The book profit of year 1 does not bear its proper share of tax, thus resulting in a profit overstatement of $48, which distortion is carried over to year 2 and year 3, whose profits will be understated by $24 each because they will bear a tax in the absence of the revenues that give rise to it. Moreover, this kind of accounting would appear to suggest that in year 1, our retailer is more profitable than his competitor who may have sold the air conditioner for cash ($720), realized a gross profit of $144, and paid a tax of $72, thus realizing an after-tax profit of $72 (versus $120 on the installment sale).

Tax allocation is designed to remedy the above distortions by means of a deferred tax account, which results in the matching of tax with the corresponding revenue as follows:

	Pre-tax profit	Taxes Actually payable	Taxes Deferred	Taxes Total	After-tax profit	Deferred tax account
Year 1 ...	$144	$24	$ 48	$72	$72	$48
Year 2 ...	—	24	(24)	—	—	24
Year 3 ...	—	24	(24)	—	—	—

SFAS 109 has adopted the position that the deferred tax account (e.g., the $48 in year 1) is a liability (or an asset) and it can be adjusted for the effect of enacted changes in tax laws or rates in the period of enactment.

As will be seen in Chapter 13, the provision for deferred taxes does not require cash, and the tax credit arising from the reversal of deferred taxes is not a source of cash.

The above installment sale example is a simplification of a complex process. While the tax deferral pertaining to the *specific* air conditioner is, as shown in the example, completely extinguished at the end of the third year, the aggregate tax deferral account will usually not behave this way. Thus, if another air conditioner is sold in year 2, the aggregate deferred tax account will stay the same; and if a growing number of air conditioners are sold, the deferred tax account will also grow. In the case of tax-book differences attributed to depreciation, where the assets are long lived, the deferred tax account may grow over the years or at least stabilize. A study by Price Waterhouse & Company of 100 major corporations concluded that the bulk of the deferred tax accounts were not likely to be "paid off" or drawn down.

Another form of tax allocation concerns the distribution of the tax effect within the various segments of the income statement. The basic principle here is that each major category should be shown net of its tax effect. Thus, for example, an extraordinary item should be shown net of its appropriate tax effect so that the tax related to operating results is properly stated. This is known as *intra*period allocation. Other examples of tax effects which must be disclosed include discontinued operations, cumulative effects of accounting changes, and prior period adjustments.

Treatment of Tax Loss Carrybacks and Carryforwards

Generally a corporation incurring an operating loss may carry such loss *back;* and if it cannot be fully utilized in the preceding 3 years, it may be carried *forward* for 15 years.[5] The status of a tax loss *carryback* is usually simple to determine: either it is available or it is not. The value of a tax loss *carryforward* depends on a company's ability to earn taxable income in the future, and that, in most cases, is not a certainty.

An asset can be recognized for the amount of taxes paid in prior years that is refundable by carryback of an operating loss or unused tax credit of the current year. An operating loss or tax credit carryforward can be recognized as a reduction of a deferred tax liability for temporary differences that will result in taxable amounts during the operating loss carryforward period.

The tax benefit of an operating loss or tax credit carryforward that cannot be recognized as a reduction of a deferred tax liability can be booked as a deferred tax asset and must be reduced by a valuation allowance if, based on the weight of available evidence, it is more likely than not that some portion or all of the deferred tax assets will not be realized.

For example, in the year of a loss when both a Net Operating Loss (NOL) carryback and carryforward are available the following entry will apply:

```
Income Tax Refund Receivable . . . . . . . . . . . . . . . . . . . . .   xxx
Future Benefit from NOL Carryforward . . . . . . . . . . . . . .   xxx
        Income Tax Benefit from NOL Carryback  . . . . . . . .          xxx
        Income Tax Benefit from NOL Carryforward . . . . . .          xxx
```

ILLUSTRATION 4.   Accounting for tax loss carrybacks and carryforwards.
The Erratic Corporation had taxes and income (loss) as follows (for simplicity assume a 50 percent tax rate throughout):

Tax return data (in thousands)

	Year 1	Year 2	Year 3	Year 4	Year 5	Year 6	Year 7
Taxable income (loss)	$120	$80	$160	$100	$(600)	$100	$220
Tax loss carryback[a]		80	160	100			
Tax loss carryforward[b] . . .						100	160
Refund of prior year taxes (carryback)[c]					(170)		
Carryforward benefits (which reduce current year taxes)[d]						50	80

[a] Taxable income of preceding three years—here $340, which is all usable being less than the year 5 loss of $600.

[b] Having used up $340 of the $600 loss in carrybacks, the tax loss carryforward available at the end of year 5 stood at $260 ($600–$340) and can be carried forward to reduce taxes of the following 15 years.

[c] The tax refund amounts to 50 percent of $340 (i.e., $80 + $160 + 100). Regardless of tax rate prevailing at any given time, only taxes actually paid are recoverable.

[d] In year 6, $100 in tax loss carryforwards are used up resulting in a $50 tax benefit. In year 7, the remaining $160 tax loss carryforward is used up which results in a $80 tax benefit.

---

[5] As an alternative, a taxpayer can elect to forgo the carryback and carry the entire loss forward for up to 15 years.

Income statement presentation (in thousands)

	Year 1	Year 2	Year 3	Year 4	Year 5	Year 6	Year 7
Income (loss) before taxes (assumed were same as taxable income)	$120	80	$160	$100	$(600)	$100	$220
Less: Tax expense	60	40	80	50		50[e]	110[f]
Tax refund[g] NOL Carryback					(170)		
Tax benefit NOL Carryforward					(130)[h]		
Net income (loss)	60	40	80	50	(300)	50	110

[e] Credit is to asset "Future Benefit from NOL Carryforward."
[f] 80 (110–30) of this is credited to "Future Benefit" asset accounts, the balance of $30 results in taxes payable.
[g] For three years to year 4—50 percent of income.
[h] The resulting asset subject to a valuation allowance (50% of 600 less 170), if needed.

Tax reductions resulting from tax loss carryforwards will show up as part of the reconciliation of the tax expense to that which would have resulted from applying domestic federal statutory rates to pre-tax income from continuing operations. Analysts will reach conclusions regarding future effective tax rates on the basis of an analysis of this reconciliation.

Disclosure Requirements

The components of the net deferred tax liability or asset recognized in an enterprise's statement of financial position should be disclosed as follows:

- The total of all deferred tax liabilities
- The total of all deferred tax assets
- The total valuation allowance recognized for deferred tax assets.

Additional disclosures are significant components of income tax expense attributable to continuing operations for each year presented which include:

a. Current tax expense or benefit
b. Deferred tax expense or benefit (exclusive of the effects of other components listed below)
c. Investment tax credits
d. Government grants (to the extent recognized as a reduction of income tax expense)
e. The benefits of operating loss carryforwards
f. Tax expense that results from allocating certain tax benefits either

directly to contributed capital or to reduce goodwill or other noncurrent intangible assets of an acquired entity

g. Adjustments of a deferred tax liability or asset for enacted changes in tax laws or rates or a change in the tax status of the enterprise

h. Adjustments of the beginning-of-the-year balance of a valuation allowance because of a change in circumstances that causes a change in judgment about the realizability of the related deferred tax asset in future years.

Also to be disclosed is a reconciliation between the effective income tax rate and the statutory federal income tax rate. In addition, the amounts and expiration dates of operating loss and tax credit carryforwards for tax purposes shall be disclosed.

Implications for Analysis

Taxes are almost always substantial expense items, and the analyst must be sure that he or she understands the relationship between pre-tax income and the income tax expense.

The analyst should note that the procedures applied to loss carryforwards differ from those applied to carrybacks. The tax loss carryback results in a tax refund in the loss year and is recognized as such. A loss carryforward is recognized and results in a deferred-tax asset. It must be reduced by a valuation allowance to the extent that "it is more likely than not" that some portion or all will not be realized by reduction of taxes payable on taxable income during the carryforward period.

In spite of all the heated arguments surrounding tax allocation, this accounting principle makes an important contribution to proper tax accrual and, hence, income reporting. It separates tax strategy from the reporting of results of operations, thus removing one possibility of management determining the size of results by means of bookkeeping techniques alone.

Another good argument for tax allocation, from an analytical point of view, is the fact that assets whose future tax deductibility is reduced cannot be worth as much as those that have a higher tax deductibility. Thus, for example, if two companies depreciate an identical asset costing $100,000 under different tax methods of depreciation that result in a first-year depreciation of $10,000 and $20,000, respectively, then it is obvious that at the end of that year, one company has an asset that it can still depreciate for tax purposes to the tune of $90,000 while the other can depreciate it only to the extent of $80,000. Obviously the two assets are not equally valuable, and the tax deferral adjustment recognizes this fact.

One of the flaws remaining in tax allocation procedures is that no recognition is given to the fact that the present value of a future obligation, or loss of benefits, should be discounted rather than shown at par as today's tax deferred accounts actually are. This was a question that was debated within the APB, but the Board decided to postpone a decision on this matter.

In its comprehensive review of accounting for income taxes which led to *SFAS 109,* the FASB considered the issue of whether the deferred tax liability should be presented on a present value or discounted basis. The Board decided not to address this problem at the time because of the complex conceptual and implementation issues involved.

While issues involved in discounting are complex they did not prevent the FASB from dealing with discounting in such important areas of accounting as leases and pensions.

The failure of the accounting profession to face the issue of discounting squarely should cause the analyst to be even more aware of the serious objections many in industry continue to have to the tax deferral concept in general and to the relentless buildup of deferred tax liabilities which, while reducing income, do not represent a legal obligation to an outsider.

The Board bowed to pressure from its constituencies when it retained the provisions of *APB Opinion 23* which allowed parent companies to avoid providing deferred taxes on unremitted earnings of subsidiaries.

An error sometimes committed by analysts is to assume that deferred tax accounting acts as a complete offset to differences between tax and financial accounting methods. Actually, if we assume that the accelerated depreciation method used for tax purposes is more realistic than the straight-line method used in reporting income, then the effect of deferred taxes is to remove only approximately one third of the overstatement of income that results from the use, for book purposes, of the slower depreciation method.

Analytical Significance of Disclosure Requirements

The SEC disclosure requirements (*FRR* No. 1, section 204) and the integrated disclosure system amendments provide the analyst with significant income tax information. *SFAS 109* has now adopted most of these disclosure requirements.

The requirements for an explanation of why the effective tax expense percentage differs from the current statutory rate (e.g., 34 percent), if it does, gives the analyst important means to judge whether the present tax benefits or extra costs that an enterprise enjoys or fears, can be expected to continue in the future. This judgment can improve predictions of cash flow and earnings. Thus, such benefits as the Research and Development Credit, DISCS, foreign tax shelter (e.g., Puerto Rico), depletion allowances, and capital gains treatment depend on legislative sanction and are always subject to change, repeal, or expiration. Other differences, such as those arising from foreign tax differentials and tax loss carryforwards, depend on conditions that must be carefully monitored. Some tax benefits may or may not remain part of the tax laws. Thus, the long-standing and substantial benefit of the Investment Tax Credit was repealed in 1986. Other benefits depend on the company's ability to take advantage of them (e.g., capital expenditures) in order to earn investment tax credits when these are available.

The continuation of accounting-related differentials, such as those relating to the use of the equity method income pickup or the amortization of goodwill, can be evaluated by the analysis of underlying transactions. In the same way that a low effective tax rate will lead the analyst to investigate the likelihood of the recurrence of tax benefits, so will a higher than normal tax rate be reason for further inquiry. Thus, for example, a higher than normal effective tax rate may be due to subsidiary losses that for one reason or another the company may not be able to offset on the tax return.

New information can also be obtained by an analysis of the effective tax rate reconciliation. Thus, for example, if the analysis indicates that tax-free interest reduced taxes by $144,000, one can determine the amount of tax-free income by dividing $144,000 by 0.34 (the statutory tax rate) which equals $423,530.

A reconciliation of the tax rate of Campbell Soup (see Appendix B in Chapter 4), can be found in item $\boxed{134}$.

The analysis of components of the deferred income tax expense can lead to significant analytical insights. The analyst may through this medium find out about the capitalization of costs, the early recognition of revenues, or about other book accounting methods of which he would otherwise not have been aware. Campbell Soup's analysis of the principal items giving rise to deferred income taxes is found in items $\boxed{128}$ to $\boxed{133}$.

Information about expected "substantial" future reductions in deferred income taxes, which do, of course, spell higher tax expense cash outlays, is valuable for the liquidity implications that it carries. Whenever a deferred tax credit "reverses," the book-tax *expense* is reduced by the amount of the reversal but the *actual* tax bill is higher than the net expense appearing in the income statement. The implication is a cash drain.

In its 1980 amendments, the SEC unfortunately deleted the requirement for disclosing expected future outlays for income taxes. The SEC encourages use of this type of information, where appropriate, in the liquidity section of "management's discussion and analysis."

EXTRAORDINARY GAINS AND LOSSES

Most items of revenue and cost discussed so far in this chapter are of the ordinary operating and recurring variety. Thus, it can be assumed that their inclusion in the income statement results in a figure that is a fair reflection of the period's operating results. Such reported results are a very important element in the valuation of securities, in the evaluation of managements, and in many other respects; and they are used as indicators of a company's earning power (see Chapter 22). Consequently, ever since the income statement became the important financial statement it is today, the treatment of unusual and extraordinary gains and losses and prior period adjustments has been a major problem area of income measurement and reporting.

Extraordinary items are distinguished by their unusual nature *and* by the infrequency of their occurrence. Examples of extraordinary items include substantial uninsured losses from a major casualty (such as an earthquake) or a loss from an expropriation.

Items affecting results of prior years are now limited by *SFAS 16* to correction of errors in prior period financial statements and to adjustments resulting from realization of income tax benefits of preacquisition operating loss carryforwards of purchased subsidiaries.

There are two main schools of thought on how to handle extraordinary gains and losses. One is the "all-inclusive" concept, which gives recognition in determining net income to all items affecting the change in equity interests during the period except dividend payments and capital transactions. The other is the so-called current-operating-performance concept. This concept would exclude from net income any items that, if included, would impair the significance of the net income as a measure of current earning power. Under this latter concept, prior to 1966, actual income reporting practice had deteriorated to such an extent that a complete reversal in philosophy and approach became necessary.[6] The change came in stages, first with *APB Opinion 9* (1966) and in 1973 with *APB Opinion 30* which restricted still further the use of the extraordinary category by requiring that in order to qualify for this designation an item be *both* unusual in nature and infrequent of occurrence. It defined these terms thus:

a. *Unusual nature*—the underlying event or transaction should possess a high degree of abnormality and be of a type clearly unrelated to, or only incidentally related to, the ordinary and typical activities of the entity, taking into account the environment in which the entity operates.

b. *Infrequency of occurrence*—the underlying event or transaction should be of a type that would not reasonably be expected to recur in the foreseeable future, taking into account the environment in which the entity operates.

---

[6] For a comprehensive discussion of all aspects of this issue, see Leopold A. Bernstein, *Accounting for Extraordinary Gains and Losses* (New York: Ronald Press, 1967).

APB Opinion 30 held that certain gains and losses should not be reported as extraordinary items because they are usual in nature and may be expected to recur as a consequence of customary and continuing business activity. Examples include:

1. Write-down or write-off of receivables, inventories, equipment leased to others, deferred R&D costs, or other intangible assets.
2. Gains or losses on disposal of a segment of a business.
3. Other gains or losses from sale or abandonment of property, plant, or equipment used in the business.
4. Effects of a strike, including those against competitors and major suppliers.
5. Adjustment of accruals on long-term contracts.

The *Opinion* also calls for the separate disclosure in income before extraordinary items of unusual *or* nonrecurring events or transactions that are material but that do not meet both conditions for classification as extraordinary.

Crosscurrents of Theory—The Case of Debt Retirements

When the APB considered in 1972 the question of gains and losses on debt retirement, its desire to limit further the items qualifying for the "extraordinary" label led it to the conclusion that these should be shown as ordinary items of gain and loss. Gains and losses on debt retirement arise when, due to changes in interest rates and/or credit standing, a debt can be satisfied by repurchase in the open market or otherwise at an amount below (gain) or above (loss) par.

Thus when, in 1974, soaring interest rates reduced the price of older, low coupon bonds, companies rushed to exchange high coupon bonds of lower aggregate par values for outstanding low coupon bonds. The resulting "profits" were substantial, as was the case of General Host which included in ordinary income $16 million of such gains which in turn represented 9 percent of net income.

Cases such as that of General Host prompted the SEC to induce the FASB to issue *SFAS 4* (1975) which requires material debt retirements of all kinds, except for sinking fund purchases, to be separately disclosed as extraordinary items. Material sinking fund gains and losses must, however, be aggregated and separately identified in the income statement.

These shifting theories reflect an ambivalence (i.e., a desire to do away with the label "extraordinary," on the one hand, and on the other, an attempt to counter the ever-present propensity of some managements to augment income with a variety of "profits").

Discontinued Operations

APB Opinion 30 also deals with the accounting for and the presentation of discontinued operations and the disposal of a segment of a business.

These are not extraordinary items but should be presented separately as in the model of the lower part of an income statement as shown below.

The analyst will recognize that in the estimation of *future* earning power, results from discontinued operations should be omitted. The losses on disposal must be treated analytically in a way similar to that accorded to extraordinary items, that is, while not entering the computation of the results of a single year, they must be included in the longer-term earnings record of the enterprise.

Implications for Analysis

To the intelligent analyst, the single most desirable characteristic in the income statement is that of adequate disclosure. Most analyses of the income statement, except possibly for evaluation of the quality of management, are predictive in nature. Analysts rely on factors whose stability of relationship and recurrence facilitate the extrapolation and forecasting function. Similarly, adjustments must be made for the erratic, sporadic, and nonrecurring elements of reported income. For all this, the analyst needs, above all, sufficient information about the nature of all the material elements entering the determination of the results of operations of a period. He needs such information presented in adequate detail so as to enable him to form an opinion as to its impact on his conclusions and projections, and he needs it presented without bias so that he can use it with confidence. This, then, is the reason for the need for the largest possible measure of fair and adequate disclosure.

Model of lower part of an income statement

Income from continuing operations before income taxes		$xxx
Provision for income taxes		xxx
Income from continuing operations		xxx
Discontinued operations (described in a note):		
Income (loss) from discontinued operations (less applicable		
income taxes of $xxx)[a]	$xxx	
Loss on disposal of discontinued operations including		
provision of $xxx for operating losses during phaseout		
period (less applicable income taxes of $xxx)[b]	xxx	xxx
Extraordinary item less income taxes of $xxx		xxx
Cumulative effect on prior years of change in accounting		
principle (less tax effect of $xxx)		xxx
Net income		$xxx

[a] Includes operating losses to date of commitment to formal disposition of a segment, i.e., a separately identifiable entity—physically, operationally, and financially.

[b] Includes estimated operating losses from date of decision to discontinue to expected disposal date. (Expected net gains on disposals can be recorded only *when realized.*)

While there is need for full details of all normal operating elements of revenue and expense, the need for information regarding the nature of extraordinary gains and losses is even more essential. This is true because of the material nature of such items as well as the need to form judgments and conclusions regarding how they should be treated in an assessment of the overall results of operations and what probability of recurrence should be assigned to them. It is this special nature of extraordinary items that has caused so much debate and controversy within the accounting profession as to their treatment.

The financial analyst should realize that one important aspect of that controversy is of no real concern to him or her. This aspect focuses on the one figure of net income that many superficial users of financial data rely upon almost to the exclusion of all other factors. In such a context, the matter of whether an extraordinary item is or is not included in the determination of net income is of great importance. To the analyst who most carefully analyzes all elements of the income statement, the exact positioning of the extraordinary item within the income statement is not of great import. He or she is much more concerned with the adequate description of the extraordinary item as well as the circumstances that gave rise to it, so that he or she can classify it properly in the context of long run as well as short-term analysis.

APB Opinion 9 represented the start of a reversal of attitude on the part of the accounting profession with regard to its responsibilities toward income reporting. Apparently discouraged by the abuses that resulted under the former approach, the profession has all but abandoned its professed intention to arrive at a meaningful or reliable measure of current operating performance. Instead, in order to insulate itself from the pressures of managements, the profession decided that with the exception of "rare" prior year adjustments, *all* items of income and expense shall be included in the determination of a "net income" figure which thus assumed a new and altogether different meaning.[7]

While one may wonder whether those who rely on the sole "net income" statistic will be helped by this new approach, the analyst must clearly understand the implications that the reporting under *APB Opinion 30* and *SFAS 16* holds for him.

To begin with, the analyst should not assume that the accountant's designation of an item as "extraordinary" even under the stricter criteria set forth by *Opinion 30* renders it automatically excludable from the measure of periodic operating results. The best that can be expected here is that under the requirements of the *Opinion,* full disclosure will be made

---

[7] *SFAS 52* departed from this "all inclusive" approach by allowing translation gains and losses to be accumulated in the equity section of the balance sheet. *SFAS 12* on marketable equity securities and *SFAS 87* on pensions are other examples of a departure from the all inclusive income approach. These items are part of "comprehensive income" a new and broader concept. (See also Chapters 3, 6, 7, 9, and 11.)

of all *material* credits and charges in the income statement regardless of their designation. However, despite the fact that "materiality" is an important criterion in determining whether an item is "extraordinary" or not, the profession has, so far, not developed a meaningful standard that would guide it in distinguishing between items which are material and those which are not. Consequently, practice enjoys an undue amount of flexibility in this area.

An extraordinary item is now defined as being nonrecurring and outside an enterprise's normal operations. It is, sometimes, the result of an unexpected or unpredictable occurrence. However, this concept of normalcy is one that must not be taken too seriously. Business is always subject to contingencies and to the unexpected. This is the very essence of business risk.[8] Moreover, variability is a fact of business life; and in spite of management's desire for stable growth trends, business results do not come in neat uniform installments. Thus, the "bunching up" of positive and negative factors that often causes items to become extraordinary should not lead to the conclusion that since they require adjustment of any one year's result, they should be disregarded in an evaluation of an entity's long-term average performance.

Extraordinary items should never be completely disregarded. They often bear the mark of the particular type of risks to which an enterprise is subject. While they may not recur yearly, the fact of their occurrence attests to the possibility of their recurrence. In their final impact on a business entity, they are not different from operating items. After all, a loss from a flash flood affects the entity's wealth every bit as much as does an equal loss on the sale of merchandise below cost. Moreover, the cumulative importance of extraordinary items can be considerable.

The analyst should always be aware of management's reporting propensities and the fact that often it is in its power to decide both the size and the *timing* of gains and losses. Thus, management can decide when to sell an asset, when to discontinue a product line, or when, subject to the limiting provisions of *SFAS* 5 discussed in Chapter 7, to provide for a future loss; and often the timing of such decisions is affected by the probable impact on reported results. Since materiality is a consideration in the determination of whether an item is "extraordinary" or not, losses that are small and considered "operating" can be permitted to accumulate to the point where they are large enough to be labeled extraordinary. In assessing extraordinary items, the analyst should be aware of the possibility that both their size and their timing can be "managed."

There is a tendency for extraordinary items to bunch up in such a way that gains are offset by losses. Companies' motivations for making this happen are easy to understand—the practice helps smooth the earnings curve. For example Macmillan, Inc. presented the following:

---

[8] See Chapter 1 for a discussion of unsystematic risk.

Extraordinary items

The extraordinary items recorded are as follows:

(a) Gain on termination of pension plan	$8,200
(b) Settlement of litigation	(3,500)
(c) Discontinuance of South African encyclopedia operation	(3,400)
Net gain before income taxes	1,300
Income taxes	600
Net gain after income taxes	$ 700

Eaton Corp. discloses the following:

Unusual and Extraordinary Items

During the third quarter of 1990, the Company settled a portion of its obligation under several of its domestic pension plans through the purchase of annuity contracts by the pension funds. As a result, income from continuing operations included a settlement gain of $26 million, before income taxes of $9 million. Also included in income from continuing operations for the third quarter of 1990 was a provision of $24 million, before income tax credits of $9 million, for the estimated costs of closing several manufacturing plants.

The propensity of management to offset items of gains with provisions for present and future losses is not difficult to understand. The practice accomplishes two objectives: (1) it removes from the income stream an unusual profit boost that an earnings-trend conscious company may find difficult to match in the following year, and (2) it provides a discretionary "cushion" against which future losses and expenses can be charged so as to improve the earnings trend, or it provides for losses that up to now the company did not find expedient to provide for. Thus, the timing of income and loss recognition can be "managed."

In *FRR No. 1,* section 305, the SEC reminds companies that full and timely disclosure of material charges or credits to income is expected irrespective of the absence of a requirement in a specific form.

Chapter 22 contains additional discussion of the analytical significance of extraordinary and other unusual items. What must be emphasized here is that regardless of the good intentions of those who promulgate official accounting policies, the analyst can never assume that the intent and spirit of these pronouncements will be implemented in practice. Instead, we must pay close attention to actual practice. For example, the author has documented the abuses of practice that have occurred after the promulgation of *APB Opinion 9.*[9] In spite of a considerable tightening

---

[9] See "Reserves for Future Costs and Losses—Threat to the Integrity of the Income Statement," *Financial Analysts Journal,* January-February 1970, pp. 45–48; and "Reporting the Results of Operations—A Reassessment of *APB Opinion 9,*" *Journal of Accountancy,* July 1970, pp. 57–61.

up of the rules, opportunities for violating their spirit or their letter still exist and will occur.

The above discussions make clear the necessity for financial analysts to adopt an independent and critical attitude toward items in the income statement, be they classified as unusual, extraordinary, or in any other fashion. Only on the basis of a full understanding of the nature of such items can a conclusion be reached regarding their impact on the earnings performance of a business entity.

ACCOUNTING CHANGES

In an attempt to reduce the unwarranted switching by management from one accepted method of accounting to another, *APB Opinion 20* states that:

> in the preparation of financial statements there *is a presumption that an accounting principle once adopted should not be changed in accounting for events and transactions of a similar type.* Consistent use of accounting principles from one accounting period to another enhances the utility of financial statements to users by facilitating analysis and understanding of comparative accounting data.
>
> *   *   *   *   *
>
> The presumption that an entity should not change an accounting principle *may be overcome* only if the enterprise justifies the use of an alternative acceptable accounting principle on the basis that *it is preferable.*[10] (Emphasis supplied.)

The Board distinguishes in this *Opinion* among three types of accounting changes, that is, a change in (1) an accounting principle, (2) an accounting estimate, and (3) the reporting entity.

Change in Accounting Principle

As a general rule (see exceptions below), the cumulative effect of the change (net of taxes) on the amount of retained earnings at the beginning of the period in which the change is made should be included in net income and shown in the statement of income between "extraordinary items" and "net income." This is the so-called catchup adjustment. Previously issued financial statements should *not* be adjusted.

A change in the method of allocating the cost of long-lived assets to various accounting periods, if adopted only for newly acquired assets, does not result in the catchup adjustment described above.

---

[10] In *FRR No. 1,* section 304, the SEC introduced the requirement that when an accounting change is made: "a letter from the registrant's independent accountants shall be filed as an exhibit indicating whether or not the change is to an alternative principle which in his judgment is *preferable* under the circumstances." (Emphasis added.)

Under this general rule, the following disclosures are called for:

1. Nature of, and justification for, adopting the change.
2. Effect of the new principle on income before extraordinary items and net income for the period of change, including related earnings per share data.
3. Pro forma effects of retroactive application of the accounting change on income before extraordinary items and the net income (and related earnings per share data) should be shown on the face of the income statement for all periods presented.

When pro forma effects are not determinable, disclosure must be made as to why such effects are not shown.

There are three specific exceptions to the general rule that previously issued financial statements not be restated. In the case of the following accounting changes, previously issued statements should be restated:

1. Change *from* LIFO to another inventory pricing method.
2. Change in accounting method for long-term construction type contracts.
3. Change *to* or *from* the "full cost" method used in extractive industries.

These exceptions were included presumably because these adjustments normally result in large credits to income. The FASB has extended the exceptions to include changes resulting from the adoption of accounting standards required in *SFASs 2, 5, 8, 9,* and *52*.

ILLUSTRATION 5.   The Changing Company's year 5 annual report states: "Effective as of January 1, year 4, the Company adopted the last-in, first-out (LIFO) method of determining inventory cost. . . . LIFO inventories at December 31, year 4, and year 5 were $58,970,000 and $55,723,000, respectively. Under the average-cost method of accounting, hitherto in use, inventories would have been $14,580,000 and $19,311,000 higher than those reported at December 31, year 4, and year 5, respectively."

The effect of the *change* from average cost to LIFO cost is as follows (in thousands):

		Debit (credit)		
		Year 5	Year 4	Year 3
On income statement:				
1.	△ Cost of sales	$ 4,731	$ 14,580	
2.	△ Tax expense..................	(1,609)	(4,957)	
3.	△ Net income (net decrease)	3,122	9,623	
On retained earnings statement:				
4.	△ Beginning balance	9,623	–0–	
5.	△ Net income	3,122	9,623	
6.	△ Ending balance	12,745	9,623	
On balance sheet:				
7.	△ Inventories	$(19,311)	$(14,580)	–0–
8.	△ Taxes payable—current	6,566	4,957	
9.	△ Retained earnings	12,745	9,623	

1. The effect on the cost of sales is calculated as the difference in the inventory change. Thus, in year 5, the inventory *reduction* was higher at year-end than at the beginning, resulting in an increase in cost of goods sold of $4,731 ($19,311–$14,580). Similarly, in year 4 the change in ending inventory to a reduction of $14,580 (when comparing average cost to LIFO) resulted in a corresponding increase in cost of goods sold because opening inventory was unchanged.
2. Since inventories were reduced (credited) under the new method, tax expense will also be reduced (debited) by 34 percent of the amount of the inventory reduction. (Lower ending inventories, compared to the beginning of the period, result in higher costs and in lower profits.)
3. Sum of (1) and (2).
4. The change in beginning retained earnings is the result of the change in net income from the prior year. Since the company switched to LIFO on January 1, year 4, there was no change in net income from the prior year. Thus, zero effect is shown for year 4.
5. Change in net income of current year shown in (3) above.
6. Sum of (4) and (5).
7. The change in inventories is given in the annual report.
8. The reduction in inventories is accompanied by a reduction in taxes payable (i.e., a reduced cash drain) here calculated at 34 percent of ending inventories.
9. Agrees with (6) above.

Change in Accounting Estimate

Periodic income determination requires the estimation of future events such as inventory obsolescence, useful lives of property, warranty costs, or uncollectible receivables. These are known as accounting estimates.

The following provisions in *APB Opinion 20* apply to changes in accounting estimates:

1. Retroactive restatement is prohibited.
2. The change should be accounted for in the period of change and, if applicable, future periods.
3. A change in accounting estimate that is recognized by a change in accounting principle should be reported as a change in estimate.
4. Disclosure is required of the effect on income before extraordinary items and net income (including related earnings per share data) of the current period when a change in estimate affects future periods as well.

Change in Reporting Entity

A change in the reporting entity can occur in the following ways:

1. Initial presentation of consolidated financial statements.
2. Changing the consolidation policy with respect to specific subsidiaries.
3. A pooling of interests.

APB Opinion 20 calls for restatement of all periods presented in the financial statements and for disclosure of the nature of the change and the reasons therefore.

Correction of an Error

Errors in financial statements can arise from mistakes in arithmetic, mistakes in the application of accounting principles, or even the use of an unacceptable accounting principle.

APB Opinion 20 does not consider the correction of an error as being in the nature of an accounting change. Consequently, the correction of an error should be treated as a prior period adjustment, and disclosure should include:

1. The nature of the error.
2. The effect on previously reported income before extraordinary items and net income (and related earnings per share data).

Materiality

The materiality of an accounting change for reporting and disclosure purposes should be considered in relation to current income on the following bases:

1. Each change separately.
2. The combined effect of all changes.

3. The effect of a change on the trend of earnings.
4. The effect of a change on future periods.

The APB, in what appears to be a reaction to the increasing dissatisfaction of financial statement users with the failure of the profession to promulgate criteria for judging materiality, has narrowed its interpretation of this concept as applied to *Opinion 20*. Particularly noteworthy is the recognition by the Board of the importance that the analyst and other users of financial statements accord to earnings *trends*.

Historical Summaries of Financial Information

APB Opinion 20 also applies to historical summaries of financial information that customarily appear in published financial statements or elsewhere. However, since these summaries are not normally covered by the auditor's opinion and their presentation is not mandatory, companies can avoid the need for restatement by merely shortening the period that they cover or by omitting them altogether.

Implications for Analysis

The requirement that changes in accounting principles be undertaken only when the change is in the direction of preferable accounting is significant. Much depends on the judgment that independent accountants will use in deciding when a change is in the direction of preferable accounting and when it is not.

Similarly, the SEC's controversial rule on preferability is a favorable development from the analyst's point of view. To reduce an accountant's propensity for liberal interpretation of this rule, the Commission stated that it would expect accounting firms to be consistent between clients when making their preferability judgments.

The inclusion of the catchup adjustment, which results from accounting changes, in the determination of the net income of the period in which the change takes place strengthens the need to deemphasize the net income of any one year and to focus instead on the average earnings achieved over a number of years.

The analyst will often need to assess the effect on the financial statements of the use of different accounting principles or estimates. That may occur because the analyst may want to adjust the financial statements to reflect a different accounting principle for analytical purposes, or in order to compare financial statements of companies using different accounting policies, or because he or she may want to estimate the effect on the various components of the current or past financial statements of such a change. Alternatively, the analyst may want to estimate the effect of such changes on past financial statements where restatements have not been provided.

The best technique of analysis in this case, as in so many others, is first to establish what journal entries are required by each alternative and then to compare these.

THE INCOME STATEMENT—IMPLICATIONS FOR ANALYSIS, AN OVERVIEW

The position of importance and predominance assumed by the income statement is due to a number of factors. For one, this financial statement presents the dynamic aspects of an enterprise, the results of its operations, and the quality of its performance. Moreover, it is the basis on which extrapolations and projections of future performance are built. The income statement's importance is emphasized by the accounting process that favors it and focuses on it, often to the neglect of the balance sheet. The attempt to increase the significance of the income statement has often resulted in distortions in the balance sheet. Thus, for example, the use of the LIFO method of inventory accounting in times of rising price levels introduces current costs into the income statement but undermines the significance of the balance sheet where inventories are carried at unrealistically low amounts. The balance sheet is cast mostly in a supporting role, containing residual balances of assets and deferred credits that will ultimately become costs and revenues, the investments and working funds necessary to conduct operations, and the various sources of funds such as the liability and capital accounts.

As we have seen throughout this and the preceding chapters, the accounting rules governing the determination and measurement of periodic income are far from uniform, and much leeway exists in their selection, interpretation, and application. It may be useful to conclude this discussion with an overview of the possibilities that exist in the distortion of reported income.

If we accept the proposition that there is such a thing as "true" or "real" income, that is, income that could be determined when all the facts are known and all the uncertainties are resolved, then obviously most reported income must deviate somewhat from this ideal figure. We can never be sure about the useful life of an asset until it has actually come to an end; we cannot be certain about the ultimate profitability of a contract until it is fulfilled, nor can we be certain about the revenue received from a transaction until the sales price is actually collected. There is nothing one can do about these uncertainties except to estimate their ultimate disposition on the basis of the best information and judgment available. Periodic income reporting requires that we not wait for final disposition of uncertainties but that we estimate them as best we can. Such a system is subject to many errors: errors of estimation, errors of omission, and errors of commission. The better and the more conscientious a company's management and the better its internal controls, the less likely that such errors will substantially distort reported results.

The more serious and frequent cases of income distortion arise when managements set out to "manage" reported results. In such cases, instead of portraying economic results as they are, they are presented as nearly as possible as management wants them presented.

Thus, for example, *Forbes,*[11] in writing on the earnings reporting practices of Itel Corporation, a major equipment marketing and leasing company, had this to say:

> Itel's hard sell is aimed at its shareholders, too. Since the debacle of the early Seventies, the company's earnings-per-share curve has been rising steadily and magnificently, from $1.28 in 1974 to $3.86 in 1978—a fact which, former Itel officials say, is a big deal with Redfield. "Programmed earnings are a part of his philosophy," says a former Itel executive. By this he means that where there is a discretion as to when to take a profit, Itel will advance or retard the profit-taking in the interest of a smooth earnings curve. For example, management has great discretion as to when to cash in on residual values of leased equipment. If earnings are falling short of projections, Itel can simply cash in on some residuals. This practice is common in a corporate environment where security analysts award high P/Es on the basis of smooth upward earnings curves, and Redfield is sophisticated enough to play this corporate game with the best of managements.

We have seen that such distortions can be accomplished by means of the timing of transactions, the choice from a variety of generally accepted principles, the introduction of conservative or, alternatively, very optimistic estimates, and the arbitrary choice of methods by which elements of income and expenses are presented or their nature is disclosed. (See also the discussion on the evaluation of earnings quality in Chapter 22.)

Generally, an enterprise wishing to benefit current income at the expense of the future will engage in one or a number of practices such as the following:

1. It will choose inventory methods that allow for maximum inventory carrying values and minimum current charges to cost of goods or services sold.
2. It will choose depreciation methods and useful lives of property that will result in minimum current charges as depreciation expense.
3. It will defer all manner of costs to the future such as, for example:
   a. Preoperating, moving, rearrangement, and start-up costs.
   b. Marketing costs.
   Such costs would be carried as deferred charges or included with the costs of other assets such as property, plant, and equipment.

---

[11] May 28, 1979, p. 40.

4. It will amortize assets and defer costs over the longest possible period.

   Such assets include:

   a. Goodwill.

   b. Leasehold improvements.

   c. Patents and copyrights.

5. It will select the assumptions leading to the lowest possible pension and other employment compensation cost accruals.

6. It will inventory rather than expense administrative costs, taxes, etc.

7. It will choose the most accelerated methods of income recognition such as in the areas of leasing, franchising, real estate sales, and contracting.[12]

Enterprises that wish to "manage" the size of reported income can still regulate to some extent the flow of income and expense by means of reserves for future costs and losses.

Exhibit 11–2 illustrates the possible impact on reported income of some of the alternative accounting principles available to managements.

The financial analyst, while welcoming improvements in the scope and quality of financial statements as well as in their integrity and reliability, must nevertheless be ever alert to the innumerable possibilities and avenues available for the distortion of reported results.

QUESTIONS

1. Distinguish between a defined benefit pension plan and a defined contribution pension plan.

2. *SFAS 87* defines three different pension benefit obligations. Please describe them.

3. List the required pension plan disclosures mandated by *SFAS 87.*

4. What are some implications of overfunded pension plans?

5. Which fundamental aspects of pension accounting were retained by the accounting for other Postretirement Employee Benefits (OPEB)?

6. Why is the estimation process for OPEB costs more difficult than that for pension costs?

7. How is compensation granted by means of stock options measured? Does *APB Opinion 25* call for a realistic recognition of the compensation cost inherent in stock options granted?

8. *a.* Discuss the accounting standards that govern R&D costs as stipulated by *SFAS 2.*

---

[12] The profession is, of course, continuously working on restricting the free choices available in the selection of accounting alternatives. Thus, in the "Introduction and Background Information" section of *SFAS 56,* we find the statement that "The percentage-of-completion and completed-contract methods are not intended to be free choice alternatives for the same circumstances. . . ."

Exhibit 11-2   Example of the effect of the variety of accounting principles on reported income

RIVAL MANUFACTURING COMPANY
Consolidated Statement of Income
For Year Ended 20xx

	Method A	Method B
Net sales	$ 365,800,000	$ 365,800,000
Cost of goods sold (1) (2) (3) (4) (5)	(276,976,200)	(274,350,000)
	88,823,800	91,450,000
Selling, general, and administrative expenses (5) (6)	(51,926,000)	(42,700,000)
	36,897,800	48,750,000
Other income (expenses):		
Interest expenses	(3,085,000)	(3,095,000)
Net income—subsidiaries	1,538,000	1,460,000
Amortization of goodwill (7)	(390,000)	(170,000)
Miscellaneous expenses	(269,000)	(229,000)
Income before taxes	34,691,800	46,716,000
Taxes:		
Income taxes—deferred	(556,000)	(850,000)
Income taxes—current	(13,906,500)	(18,639,500)
Net income	$ 20,229,300	$ 27,226,500
Earnings per share	$6.98	$9.39

Explanations:
  (1) Inventories
        A uses last-in, first-out
        B uses first-in, first-out
            Difference—$1,780,000
  (2) Administrative costs:
        A includes some administrative costs as period costs
        B includes some administrative costs as inventory costs
            Difference—$88,000
  (3) Depreciation:
        A uses sum-of-the-years'-digits method
        B uses straight-line method
            Difference—$384,200
  (4) Useful lives of assets:
        A uses conservative assumption—8 years (average)
        B uses liberal assumption—14 years (average)
            Difference—$346,000
  (5) Pension costs:
        A uses realistic assumptions regarding rates of return on assets and future
            inflation
        B uses less realistic assumptions regarding rates of return on assets and future
            inflation
            Difference—$78,000
  (6) Executive compensations:
        A compensates executives with cash bonuses
        B compensates executives with stock options
            Difference—$840,000
  (7) Goodwill from acquisition:
        A amortizes over 10 years
        B amortizes over 40 years
            Difference—$220,00

Note: the above is not a complete list of differences.

    b. What are the disclosure requirements as stipulated by the same statement?

9. What information does the financial analyst need regarding R&D outlays, especially in light of the limited disclosure requirements stipulated by *SFAS 2?*

10. To what aspects of the valuation and the amortization of goodwill must the analyst be alert?

11. Contrast the computation of total interest costs of a bond issue with warrants attached with that of an issue of convertible debt.

12. *a.* What is the main provision of *SFAS 34* and what are its objectives?
    b. How is the amount to be capitalized computed and how is the rate to be used ascertained?
    c. What restrictions to capitalization are imposed by *SFAS 34* and when does the capitalization period begin?

13. The net income computed on the basis of book income will often differ from taxable income due to permanent differences. What are permanent differences and how do they arise?

14. What factors will cause the effective tax rate to differ from the statutory rate?

15. What are the main requirements of *SFAS 109,* "Accounting for Income Taxes"?

16. List four circumstances giving rise to book-tax temporary differences.

17. What are the disclosure requirements of *SFAS 109?*

18. Name one flaw to which tax allocation procedures are still subject.

19. How has the accounting profession defined an extraordinary item? Give three examples of such items.

20. What conditions are necessary before an item qualifies as a prior period adjustment?

21. In the never-ending debate on the proper treatment of extraordinary items, what should be the financial analyst's main interest?

22. Describe some of the abuses in the area of extraordinary item reporting that are found in practice and that have not been dealt with by recent pronouncements on this subject.

23. Why do some companies try to offset items of gains with provisions for present and future losses?

24. Why is it impossible to arrive at an absolutely "precise" measure of periodic net income?

25. What are some of the types of methods by means of which income can be distorted?

26. For each of the items below (1–3), explain:
    a. Two acceptable accounting methods for corporate reporting purposes.
    b. How each of these two acceptable accounting methods will affect the earnings of the current period.
    (1) Depreciation.
    (2) Inventory.
    (3) Installment sales. (CFA)

27. What are the objectives of *APB Opinion 20?* It distinguishes among four types of accounting changes. Which are they?

Chapter 12

EARNINGS PER SHARE— COMPUTATION AND EVALUATION

The determination of the earnings level of an enterprise that is relevant to the purposes of the analyst is a complex analytical process. This earnings figure can be converted into an earnings per share (EPS) amount that is useful in the evaluation of the price of the common stock, in the evaluation of dividend coverage and dividend paying ability, as well as for other purposes. The analyst must, consequently, have a thorough understanding of the principles that govern the computation of EPS.

The intelligent analyst will never overemphasize the importance of, or place exclusive reliance on, any one figure, be it the widely used and popular EPS figure or any other statistic. In using the EPS figure, he or she should always be alert to the composition of the "net income" figure used in its computation.

In the mid-1960s, when a wave of mergers brought with it the widespread use of convertible securities as financing devices, the attention of analysts and of accountants turned also to the denominator of the EPS computation, that is, the number of shares of common stock by which the earnings should be divided. It became obvious that the prior practice of considering only the common shares actually outstanding, without a consideration of the future potential dilution that is inherent in convertible securities, had often led to an overstatement of EPS.

The managements of merger-minded companies had discovered that it was possible to buy the earnings of a company by compensating its owners with low-yield convertible securities that in effect represented a deferred equity interest. Since the acquired earnings were immediately included in the combined income of the merged enterprise while the dilutive effect of the issuance of convertible securities was ignored, an illusory increase in EPS was thus achieved. Such growth in EPS increased the value of the securities, thus enabling the merger-minded company to carry this value-enhancing process even further by using its attractive securities to effect business combination at increasingly advantageous terms to its existing stockholders.

ILLUSTRATION 1.   Merging Company A, which pays no dividend and whose stock sells at $35, issued to merged Company B, which is earning $3 per share, $1 convertible preferred, on a share-for-share basis that allows for conversion into Company A's common at $40 per share. Because of the dividend advantage, there is no prospect of an early conversion of the convertible preferred into common. Thus, prior to *APB Opinion 15,* Company A realized "instant earnings" by getting a $3 per share earnings boost in return for a $1 preferred dividend requirement. It is obvious that the $1 convertible preferred derives most of its value from the conversion feature rather than from its meager dividend provision.

MAJOR PROVISIONS OF *APB OPINION 15*

APB Opinion 15 put an end to this unrealistic disregard of the potential dilutive effect of securities convertible into common stock. The *Opinion* looks to the substance of a securities issue rather than merely to its legalistic form.

Simple Capital Structure

If a corporation has a simple capital structure that consists only of common stock and nonconvertible senior securities and does not include potentially dilutive securities, then most of the provisions of the *Opinion* do not apply. In that case, a single presentation of EPS is called for and is computed as follows:

$$\frac{\text{Net income less claims of senior equity securities}}{\begin{array}{c}\text{Weighted-average number of common shares outstanding during}\\ \text{the period after adjustments for stock splits and dividends (including}\\ \text{those effected after balance sheet date but before completion of}\\ \text{financial statements)}\end{array}}$$

In the above computation, dividends of cumulative senior equity securities, whether earned or not, should be deducted from net income or added to net loss.

Computation of Weighted Average of Common Shares Outstanding

The theoretically correct weighted-average number of shares is the sum of shares outstanding each day, divided by the number of days in the period. Less precise averaging methods, such as on a monthly or quarterly basis, where there is little change in the number of shares outstanding, is also permissible.

In the Computation
1. Reacquired shares should be excluded from date of acquisition.

2. Shares sold or issued in a purchase of assets should be included from date of issuance.
3. Previously reported EPS data should be adjusted retroactively for changes in outstanding shares resulting from stock splits or stock dividends.

Example of computation or weighted-average number of shares outstanding

Year 1	Transactions in common stock	Number of shares
January 1	Outstanding	1,200
February 2	Stock options exercised	200
April 15	Issued at 5% stock dividend	70
August 16	Issued in pooling of interests . . .	400
September 2	Sale for cash	300
October 18	Repurchase of treasury shares . .	(100)
		2,070

Computation of weighted-average number of shares

		Shares outstanding		Product:
		Number	Days	Share—days
Date of change:				
January 1		1,200		
Retroactive adjustment:				
For stock dividend (5%)		60		
Issued in pooling		400		
January 1—adjusted		1,660	32	53,120
February 2—stock option	200			
+5% stock dividend	10	210		
		1,870	212	396,440
September 2—sale for cash . . .		300		
		2,170	46	99,820
October 18—repurchase		(100)		
		2,070	75	155,250
			365	704,630

$$\text{Year 1 weighted-average number of shares } \frac{704,630}{365} = 1,930 \text{ shares}$$

As can be seen in the illustrations above, shares issued in a pooling of interests are included in the computation of EPS as of the beginning of all periods presented. This is so because under the pooling of interests concept, the merged companies are assumed to have been combined since their respective inceptions. In the case of purchases, the EPS reflect new shares issued only from date of acquisition.

Stock dividends are also adjusted retroactively, thus applying to the computation of the entire year. Issuances of stock (as a result of stock options or sale) as well as repurchases of stock all involve changes in entity resources and thus enter the computation only from the date of the transaction.

The term *earnings per common share* should be used without qualifying language only when the company has in fact a simple capital structure and no agreements exist for contingent issuances of common stock. A company can also make such presentation of EPS if the total dilution from dilutive securities or other provisions does not exceed 3 percent (i.e., if the adjusted net income divided into total shares that include dilutive securities results in an EPS number not lower than 97 percent of that arrived at without considering such dilutive securities).

COMPLEX CAPITAL STRUCTURE

A company is deemed to have a complex capital structure if it has outstanding potentially dilutive securities such as convertible securities, options, warrants, or other stock issue agreements.

By dilution is meant a reduction in EPS (or increase in net loss per share) resulting from the assumption that convertible securities have been converted into common stock, or that options and warrants have been exercised, or that shares have been issued in compliance with certain contracts.

A company having a complex capital structure has to give a dual presentation of EPS if the aggregate dilutive effect of convertible and other securities is more than 3 percent. Such dual presentation is to be effected with equal prominence on the income statement and show (1) primary EPS and (2) fully diluted EPS.

Primary Earnings per Share

Primary EPS is the amount of earnings attributable to each share of common stock outstanding plus dilutive common stock equivalents.

Definition of Common Stock Equivalents (CSE)   The concept of CSE is basic to the approach adopted in *APB Opinion 15*. It denotes a security that derives the major portion of its value from its common stock characteristics or conversion privileges. Thus, a CSE is a security that because of its terms or the circumstances under which it was issued is deemed to be in substance equivalent to common stock. The following are examples of CSE.

1. *Convertible debt and convertible preferred stocks* are CSE only if at the time of issuance they have an effective yield[1] of less than 66⅔ percent of the then average Aa corporate bond yield.[2] If a convertible security is issued that is a CSE and that same security was previously issued when it was not a CSE at time of issuance, the earlier issued shares or debt should be considered a CSE *from the date of issuance of the later shares or debt.* Prior periods EPS should not be restated. Similarly, any subsequent issuance of shares or debt with the same terms as previously issued shares or debt classified as a CSE should be classified as a CSE at its time of issuance even though the later issue of shares or debt would not be a CSE under the yield test at the later date of issue. This requirement can be overcome by a change in a term or condition having economic significance that is expected to affect prices in the securities market.
2. *Stock options and warrants (including stock purchase contracts)* are always to be considered as CSE.
3. *Participating securities and two-class common stocks* are CSE if their participation features enable their holders to share in the earnings potential of the issuing corporation, on substantially the same basis as common stock, even though the securities may not give the holder the right to exchange his shares for common stock.
4. *Contingent shares*—if shares are to be issued in the future upon the mere passage of time, they should be considered as outstanding for purposes of computing EPS. If additional shares of stock are issuable for little or no consideration upon the satisfaction of certain conditions, they should be considered as outstanding when the conditions are met.
5. *Securities of subsidiaries* may be considered common stock equivalents and conversion or exercise assumed for computing consolidated or parent company EPS when—
   a. *As to the subsidiary.*
      (1) Certain of the subsidiary's securities are CSE in relation to its own common stock.
      (2) Other of the subsidiary's convertible securities, although not CSE in relation to its own common stock, would enter into the computation of its fully diluted earnings per share.

---

[1] As modified by *SFAS 85,* the effective yield test is expected to reflect more accurately economic substance of zero and low-coupon convertible securities which have little or no annual cash yield.

[2] Modified by *SFAS 55,* which also stated that if the convertible securities are sold outside the United States, the most comparable long-term yield in the foreign country should be used for this test.

b. *As to the parent.*
   (1) The subsidiary's securities are convertible into the parent company's common stock.
   (2) The subsidiary issues options and warrants to purchase the parent company's common stock.

Computation of Primary EPS   If CSE with a dilutive effect are present, then primary EPS should be based on the weighted-average number of shares of common stock and CSE. The computation is also based on the assumption that convertible securities that are CSE were converted at the beginning of the period (or at time of issuance, if later), and that requires adding back to net income any deductions for interest or dividends, net of tax effect, related to such securities, a procedure known as the "if converted" method.

It can be summarized as follows:

Numerator	*Denominator*
Net income for the period.	Average shares outstanding.
(Less preferred dividends applicable to preferred stock not considered as CSE).	Add—number of common shares into which convertible preferred shares and convertible bonds (which are deemed to be CSE) are convertible adjusted for proportion of time outstanding.
Add back tax adjusted interest on convertible bonds considered as CSE.	

Options and Warrants

Options and warrants are instruments that entitle the holder to buy a given amount (or fraction) of common shares at a given price for a specified period of time (usually shorter in the case of options than in the case of warrants). The computation of the dilutive effects of options and warrants, which are always considered as CSE, must, in turn, recognize the benefits accruing from the cash, or "boot," which the converter of these instruments into common must pay to the issuing company. This has given rise to the *treasury stock* method.

The Treasury Stock Method

The *treasury stock* method recognizes the use of proceeds that would be obtained upon exercise of options and warrants in computing EPS. It assumes that any proceeds would be used to purchase common stock at current market prices. For options and warrants, the treasury stock method of computing the dilution to be reflected in EPS should be used (except for two exceptions to be explained). Under the treasury stock method:

1. EPS data are computed as if the options and warrants were exercised at the beginning of the period (or at time of issuance, if later) and as if the funds obtained thereby were used to purchase common stock at the average market price during the period.
2. But the assumption of exercise is not reflected in EPS data until the market price of the common stock obtainable has been in excess of the exercise price for substantially all of three consecutive months ending with the last month of the period to which EPS relate.[3]

Example of Treasury Stock Method

Assumptions:
  1,000,000 common shares outstanding (no change during year)
    $80 average market price for the common stock for the year
    100,000 warrants outstanding exercisable at $48

Computation:
  Shares
  100,000   shares issuable on exercise of warrants (proceeds $4,800,000)
  (60,000) shares acquirable with $4,800,000 proceeds (at $80 per share)
    40,000   CSE
  1,000,000   common shares
  1,040,000   shares used for computing primary EPS

First Exception to Treasury Stock Method   Warrants or debt indentures may permit or require certain uses of funds with exercise of warrants.
    Examples:

1. Debt is permitted or required to be tendered toward exercise price.
2. Proceeds of exercise are required to retire debt.
3. Convertible securities require cash payments upon conversion.

In these cases, an "if converted" method, which assumes conversion on exercise at the beginning of the period, should be applied as if retirement or conversion of the securities had occurred and as if the excess proceeds, if any, had been applied to the purchase of common stock under the treasury stock method.

---

[3] The following will yield the number of incremental shares that will result from applying the treasury stock method to options or warrants *(Y)*;

$$Y = \frac{M - E}{M} (N)$$

where M is the market price per share, E is the exercise price of option or warrant per common share, and N is the total number of shares obtainable on exercise.

Second Exception to Treasury Stock Method   If the number of shares of common stock obtainable upon exercise of outstanding options and warrants in the aggregate exceeds 20 percent of the number of common shares outstanding at the end of the period for which the computation is being made, the treasury stock method should be modified. In these circumstances, all the options and warrants should be assumed to have been exercised and the aggregate proceeds therefrom to have been applied in two steps:

1. As if the funds obtained were first applied to the repurchase of outstanding common shares at the average market price during the period (treasury stock method) but not to exceed 20 percent of the outstanding shares; and then
2. As if the balance of the funds were applied first to reduce any short-term or long-term borrowings and any remaining funds were invested in U.S. government securities or commercial paper, with appropriate recognition of any income tax effect.

The results of steps 1 and 2 of the computation (whether dilutive or antidilutive) should be aggregated, and if the net effect is dilutive, it should enter into the EPS computation.

Example of Second Exception of Treasury Stock Method

	Case 1	Case 2
Assumptions:		
Net income for year	$ 4,000,000	$ 3,000,000
Common shares outstanding (no change during year)	3,000,000	3,000,000
Options and warrants outstanding to purchase equivalent shares	1,000,000	1,000,000
20% limitation on assumed repurchase	600,000	600,000
Exercise price per share	$15	$15
Average market value per common share to be used	$20	$14*
Interest rate on borrowings	6%	6%
Computations:		
Application of assumed proceeds ($15 × 1,000,000 shares) toward repurchase of outstanding common shares at applicable market value (600,000 × $20) and (600,000 × $14)	$12,000,000	$ 8,400,000
Reduction of debt	3,000,000	6,600,000
	15,000,000	15,000,000

Adjustment of net income:		
Actual net income	4,000,000	3,000,000
Interest reduction on debt (6%) less 50% tax		
effect	90,000	198,000
Adjusted net income (A)	$ 4,090,000	$ 3,198,000
Adjustment of shares outstanding:		
Actual number outstanding	3,000,000	3,000,000
Net additional shares issuable (1,000,000 −		
600,000)	400,000	400,000
Adjusted shares outstanding (B)	3,400,000	3,400,000
Primary EPS:		
Before adjustment	$1.33	$1.00
After adjustment (A ÷ B)	1.20	0.94

* The three consecutive months test has previously been met.

Provisions concerning Antidilution   Antidilution is an increase in EPS resulting from the assumption that convertible securities have been converted or that options and warrants have been exercised or other shares have been issued upon the fulfillment of certain conditions. For example, although stock options and warrants (and their equivalents) and stock purchase contracts should always be considered CSE, they should not enter into EPS calculations until the average market price of the common stock exceeds the exercise price of the option or warrant for preferably three consecutive months before the reporting period.

Computations of primary EPS should not give effect to CSE or other contingent issuance for any period in which their inclusion would have the effect of increasing the EPS amount or decreasing the loss per share amount otherwise computed.

Fully Diluted Earnings per Share

Definition of Fully Diluted EPS   Fully diluted EPS is designed to show the maximum potential dilution of current EPS on a prospective basis. Fully diluted EPS is the amount of current EPS reflecting the maximum dilution that would have resulted from conversions of all convertible securities whether they are CSEs or not, as long as they are dilutive. Fully diluted EPS are also intended to reflect dilution resulting from exercises and other contingent issuances that individually would have decreased EPS and in the aggregate would have had a dilutive effect. All such issuances are assumed to have taken place at the beginning of the period (or at the time the event or contingency arose, if later).

When Required   Fully diluted EPS data are required for each period presented if shares of common stock (1) were issued during the period on conversions, exercise, and so on; or (2) were contingently issuable at the close of any period presented and if primary EPS for such period would have been affected (dilutively or incrementally) had such actual issuances taken place at the beginning of the period or would have been reduced had such contingent issuances taken place at the beginning of the period.

Computation of Fully Diluted EPS   The computation should be based on the assumption that all such issued and issuable shares were outstanding from the beginning of the period (or from the time the contingency arose, if after the beginning of the period). Interest charges applicable to convertible securities and nondiscretionary adjustments that would have been made to items based on net income or income before taxes—such as profit-sharing expense, certain royalties, and investment credit—or preferred dividends applicable to the convertible securities should be taken into account in determining the balance of income applicable to common stock.

Use Ending Market Price for Treasury Stock Method   The treasury stock method (along with the two exceptions) should be used to compute fully diluted EPS if dilution results from outstanding options and warrants; however, in order to reflect maximum potential dilution, the market price at the close of the period reported upon should be used to determine the number of shares that would be assumed to be repurchased (under the treasury stock method) if such market price is higher than the average price used in computing primary EPS.

Example of Computation of Fully Diluted EPS   Assume that there are 1,000,000 shares of class A preferred stock and 1,500,000 shares of class B preferred stock outstanding, both issues convertible into common on a share-for-share basis. Two million shares of common are outstanding. Class A preferred is a CSE with a $1.80 dividend; class B is a nonCSE preferred with a $1 dividend. Net income before either preferred dividend was $7,300,000.

Computation

	Shares	*Net income*	*EPS*
Net income		$ 7,300,000	
Shares outstanding	2,000,000		
$1.80 preferred dividend		(1,800,000)	
$1.00 preferred dividend		(1,500,000)	
($2 per share)	2,000,000	4,000,000	
Assume conversion of CSE class A			
preferred	1,000,000	1,800,000	
	3,000,000	5,800,000	
Primary EPS			$1.93
Assume conversion of nonCSE class B			
preferred	1,500,000	1,500,000	
	4,500,000	$ 7,300,000	
Fully diluted EPS (beginning with primary			
EPS).............................			$1.62

Since the intention in presenting fully diluted EPS is to show the *maximum* dilution possible, an alternative computation is possible in this case that would yield a lower figure of fully diluted EPS. This computation has as a starting point the outstanding common shares and income after preferred dividends rather than the primary EPS.

Computation

	Shares	*Net income*	*EPS*
Shares outstanding and income after			
dividends........................	2,000,000	$4,000,000	
Assume conversion of nonCSE class B			
preferred	1,500,000	1,500,000	
	3,500,000	$5,500,000	
Fully diluted EPS—beginning with			
outstanding shares and income after			
preferred dividends			$1.57

The reason why the alternative computation yields a lower fully diluted EPS is that while the $1.80 preferred issue is dilutive for purposes of computing primary EPS, it is antidilutive for purposes of computing the fully diluted EPS.

Provisions regarding Antidilution   As with primary EPS, no antidilution should be recognized. Consequently, computations should exclude those securities whose conversion, exercise, or other contingent issuance would have the effect of increasing the EPS amount or decreasing the loss per share amount for each period. Therefore, fully diluted EPS should be $1.57 rather than the $1.62 shown in the preceding computation.

ILLUSTRATION OF THE COMPUTATION OF PRIMARY AND FULLY DILUTED EARNINGS PER SHARE

The Complex Corporation had the following changes in its capital structure during year 6:

	Number of shares
Common stock:	
Balance on January 1	500,000
April 1—issued in conversion of preferred stock	200,000
July 1—sold for cash	100,000
Balance on December 31	800,000

Preferred stock:
$10 par 8 percent, each convertible into two common shares, issued in year 3 at $12 per share when the average Aa corporate bond yield was 7½ percent (dividend requirement on outstanding shares is $80,000)

Outstanding, January 1, year 6	175,000
Converted on April 1, year 6 (into 200,000 common)	100,000
Outstanding since April 1, year 6 (and year-end)	75,000

Subordinated debentures:
$800,000 of 4 percent debentures issued at par in year 4 when the average Aa corporate bond yield was 9 percent. The debentures are convertible into 12,000 shares of common and are all outstanding.

Warrants:
100,000 warrants issued in year 4, each to purchase one common share at $80 per share until December 31, year 9. So far none have been exercised.

Additional information:
Market prices of common for year 6 were as follows:

	Average for quarter	End of quarter
First quarter	$78	$79
Second quarter	80	85
Third quarter	90	89
Fourth quarter	88	86
Preferred dividends paid in year 6:		
First quarter		$ 35,000
Second quarter		15,000
Third quarter		15,000
Fourth quarter		15,000
Income before extraordinary item in year 6		1,200,000
Extraordinary item—condemnation gain (net of tax effect)		300,000
Income tax rate		50%

The following are the steps in the computation of primary and fully diluted EPS of the Complex Corporation for year 6:

Primary earnings per share

Step 1: Computation of weighted-average number of common shares outstanding in year 6:

	Shares outstanding	No. of months	Product
January 1	500,000	3	1,500,000
April 1	700,000	3	2,100,000
July 1	800,000	6	4,800,000
		12	8,400,000

$$\text{Weighted average: } \frac{8,400,000}{12} = 700,000 \text{ shares}$$

Step 2: Identification of common stock equivalents (CSE):

Security	(A) Effective yield at issuance	(B) Two thirds of average Aa corporate bond rate at date of issuance	Classification and elaboration
8% convertible preferred	$\dfrac{\$0.80}{\$12} = 6.67\%$	⅔ of 7½% = 5%	Not a CSE because (A) exceeds (B)
4% subordinated debentures	4% (issued at par)	⅔ of 9% = 6%	A CSE because (B) exceeds (A)
Warrants	—	—	Warrants are always considered as CSE

Step 3: Computation of primary EPS:

	Shares	Earnings
Income before extraordinary item		$1,200,000
Dividends requirements of outstanding preferred stock (as also paid in year 6)		80,000
Income available for common shares		1,120,000
Weighted average of common shares outstanding (see computation)	700,000	
Assumed conversion of 4% subordinated debentures . .	12,000	

Add back to income interest:
  4% of $800,000 = $32,000
  Less tax effect at 50% <u>16,000</u>   16,000

Effect of assumed exercise of warrants:
  1st quarter Assumed exercise of warrants should
  ⎡ not be reflected until market price
  ⎢ of common has been in excess of
  2d quarter ⎨ exercise price for substantially all of
  ⎢ three consecutive months (a *one-time*
  ⎣ test).
  3d quarter In this quarter above condition was
          fulfilled.
          Total shares issuable on exercise 100,000
          $\dfrac{\text{Proceeds}}{\text{Average price for quarter}} = \dfrac{\$8,000,000}{\$90}$ 88,889
          Incremental shares for quarter   <u>11,111</u>

4th quarter Total shares available for exercise 100,000

$$\frac{\text{Proceeds}}{\text{Average price for quarter}} = \frac{\$8,000,000}{\$88} \quad 90,909$$

Incremental shares for quarter 9,091

Total incremental shares for all quarters 20,202

20,202 divided by 4 5,050

Totals 717,050 $1,136,000

Primary EPS—before extraordinary item	$\dfrac{\$1,136,000}{717,050}$ =	$1.58
Extraordinary item	$\dfrac{\$300,000}{717,050}$ =	0.42
Net income per share	$\dfrac{\$1,436,000}{717,050}$ =	$2.00

Step 4: Computation of fully diluted EPS:

	Shares	Earnings
Income before extraordinary item		$1,200,000
Weighted average of common shares (as above)	700,000	
Add: Assumed conversion of 4% debentures[a]		
Assumed conversion of 8% convertible preferred (175,000 × 2)	350,000	
Less: Converted preferred already included in 700,000 weighted-average 200,000 × ¾ year ..	150,000	200,000[b] —
Warrants: Assumed exercise:		
Total shares available for exercise	100,000	
$\dfrac{\text{Proceeds}}{\text{Year-end market price}} = \dfrac{100{,}000 \times \$80^{(c)}}{\$86^{(d)}} = \ldots\ldots$	93,023	
Incremental shares	6,977	
	906,977	$1,200,000

[a] These debentures are excluded from this computation because they are antidilutive (i.e., they result in an EPS increment of $1.33). Interest requirement is $32,000 (4 percent of 800,000) less 50% tax = $16,000. $16,000 ÷ 12,000 (shares) = $1.33. Thus, the inclusion of the debentures in the computation would *increase* EPS.

[b] *Alternative proof:*

	Months	Product
175,000 pfd × 2 outstanding 1st Q 350,000	3	1,050,000
75,000 pfd × 2 outstanding 3rd Q 150,000	9	1,350,000
		2,400,000 ÷ 12 = 200,000

[c] Note that a computation using individual quarters would have resulted in *fewer* incremental shares.

[d] Compared to average price for year of $84.50.

Fully diluted EPS:

Income before extraordinary item: $\dfrac{\$1,200,000}{906,977} = \$1.32$

Extraordinary item: $\dfrac{\$300,000}{906,977} = \underline{0.33}$

Net Income: $\dfrac{\$1,500,000}{906,977} = \underline{\underline{\$1.65}}$

EXAMPLES OF EPS COMPUTATIONS WHEN BUSINESS COMBINATIONS OCCUR

Pooling of Interests

Assumptions: On July 1, year 2, Company A and Company B merged to form Company C. The transaction was accounted for as a *pooling of interests.*

	Company A	Company B
Net income January 1 to June 30, year 2	$100,000	$150,000
Outstanding shares of common stock at June 30, year 2 ...	20,000	8,000
Shares sold to public April 1, year 2	10,000	

	Company C
Net income July 1 to December 31, year 2	$325,000
Common shares issued for acquisition of:	
Company A	200,000
Company B	400,000
Computation:	
Net income ($100,000 + $150,000 + $325,000)	575,000
Average shares outstanding during year, using equivalent shares for pooled companies:	
Company A:	
100,000[a] × 3 months 300,000	
200,000[b] × 3 months 600,000	
Company B:	
400,000 × 6 2,400,000	
Company C:	
600,000 × 6 .... <u>3,600,000</u>	
6,900,000	
Weighted-average (6,900,000 ÷ 12) ... 575,000	

Net income per weighted-average number of shares of common stock outstanding during the year (equivalent shares used for pooled companies) $1.00

[a] 10,000 × 10 (exchange ratio).
[b] 20,000 × 10 (exchange ratio).

Purchase

Assumptions: Company X has outstanding at December 31, year 2, 120,000 shares of common stock. During the year (October 1), Company X issued 30,000 shares of its own common stock for another company. This transaction was accounted for as purchase. Net income for year 2 was $292,500.

Computation:

9 months × 90,000 shares outstanding	810,000
3 months × 120,000 shares outstanding	360,000
	1,170,000

$$\text{Average shares } \frac{1,170,000}{12} = 97,500$$

Net income per weighted-average number of shares of common

$$\text{stock outstanding during the year } \frac{\$292,500}{97,500} = \$3.$$

RESTATEMENT OF PRIOR PERIOD EARNINGS PER SHARE

Whenever comparative EPS figures are presented for a number of years, these must be restated to reflect changes in the number of common shares outstanding due to stock dividends, stock splits (and reverse stock splits), issuance of shares in an acquisition accounted under the pooling of interests method, and prior period adjustments of net income. On the other hand, issues of stock for cash or in an acquisition or the repurchase of stock do not require adjustment because the earnings generated are deemed to be affected by the new resources acquired or relinquished in exchange for the shares.

Illustration of Prior Period EPS Restatement

The following are the reported EPS of Stock Splitters, Inc. for the respective fiscal years shown:

	Year 9	Year 8	Year 7	Year 6	Year 5	Year 4
EPS	$5	$5	$9	$6	$3	$4

The following changes in capitalization took place at the beginning of each of the years shown:

Year 5 . . . .   100% stock dividend paid
Year 6 . . . .   500,000 shares of common stock
                 issued for cash
Year 7 . . . .   200,000 shares of common stock
                 issued on conversion of bonds
Year 8 . . . .   3-for-1 stock split
Year 9 . . . .   50% stock dividend paid

The table adjusting the reported EPS figures for the above changes follows. Note that since the change of the 50 percent stock dividend, for example, occurred in year 9, it has already been allowed for in that year's EPS computation. All prior years, however, must be adjusted for that dividend by multiplying reported EPS figures by a factor of 100/150.

		Reported EPS	Adjustments	Adjusted EPS
50% stock dividend accounted for:	Year 9	$5.00	None	$5.00
3-for-1 stock split accounted for:	Year 8	5.00	(100/150)	3.33
	Year 7	9.00	(100/300)(100/150)	2.00
	Year 6	6.00	(100/300)(100/150)	1.33
100% stock dividend accounted for:	Year 5	3.00	(100/300)(100/150)	0.67
	Year 4	4.00	(100/200)(100/300)(100/150)	0.44

Requirements for Additional Disclosures in Conjunction with the Presentation of Earnings per Share Data

Complex capital structures require additional disclosures either on the balance sheet or in notes. Financial statements should include a description sufficient to explain the pertinent rights and privileges of the various securities outstanding.

With regard to EPS data, disclosure is required for—

1. The bases upon which both primary and fully diluted EPS are calculated, identifying the securities entering into computations.
2. All assumptions and any resulting adjustments used in computations.
3. The number of shares issued upon conversion, exercise, and so on, during at least the most recent year.

Supplementary EPS data should be disclosed (preferably in a note) if—

1. Conversions during the period would have affected primary EPS (either dilutive *or* incremental effect) if they had taken place at the beginning of the period, or
2. Similar conversions occur after the close of the period but before completion of the financial report.

This supplementary information should show what primary EPS would have been if such conversions had taken place at the *beginning* of the period or date of issuance of security if within the period.

It should be understood that the designation of securities as CSE is done solely for the purpose of determining primary EPS. No changes from practices in the accounting for such securities or in their presentation within the financial statements are required.

IMPLICATIONS FOR ANALYSIS

APB Opinion 15 has been criticized, particularly by accountants, because it covers areas outside the realm of accountancy, relies on pro forma presentations that are influenced in large measure by market fluctuations, and because it deals with areas properly belonging to financial analysis.

Whatever the merit of these criticisms, and they do have merit, the financial analyst must welcome this initiative by the accounting profession. It does provide specific and workable guidelines for a meaningful recognition of the dilutive effects, present and prospective, of securities that are the equivalents of common stock. The elements entering the consistent computation of primary EPS and fully diluted EPS are so many and varied and require so many internal data that it is best that the accounting profession has assumed the responsibility for their computation rather than choosing the alternative of disclosing the information and leaving it to outsiders to make their own computations. The financial analyst must, however, have a thorough understanding of the bases on which EPS are computed.

APB Opinion 15 has a number of flaws and inconsistencies that the analyst must consider in his interpretations of EPS data:

1. There is a basic inconsistency in treating certain securities as the equivalent of common stock for purposes of computing EPS while not considering them as part of the stockholders' equity in the balance sheet. Consequently, the analyst will have difficulty in interrelating reported EPS with the debt-leverage position pertaining to the same earnings.
2. There are a number of arbitrary benchmarks in the *Opinion,* such as the 20 percent treasury stock repurchase assumption limitation and the 66⅔ percent of the average Aa corporate bond rate test.

3. Generally EPS are considered to be a factor influencing stock prices. The *Opinion* considers options and warrants to be CSE at all times, and whether they are dilutive or not depends on the price of the common stock. Thus, we can get a circular effect in that the reporting of EPS may influence the market price, which, in turn, influences EPS. Also, under these rules earnings may depend on market prices of the stock rather than only on economic factors within the enterprise.

   Under these rules, the projection of future EPS requires not only the projection of earnings levels but also the projection of future market prices.

4. Since the determination of whether a security is a CSE or not is made only at the time of issuance, it is quite possible that a security that was not originally a CSE is later so recognized in the marketplace. Nevertheless, the status of the security in the computation of EPS cannot be changed to recognize the new reality.

Despite these limitations, primary EPS and fully diluted EPS computed under the provisions of *APB Opinion 15* are more valid measurements of EPS than those which were obtained under the rules which were previously in effect.

In analyzing the factors that cause changes in the EPS figure, the analyst must focus on changes in earnings as well as changes in the number of shares outstanding. Regarding the latter, the analyst will now find details in "management's discussion and analysis" section required by the SEC (see Chapter 20). In *Staff Accounting Bulletin 29,* the SEC staff concluded that an increase in EPS resulting from an improvement in earnings with an unchanged number of shares outstanding has significantly different implications from an increase in per share earnings achieved by a reduction of the company's capital base.

Regardless of the reasons for and method of a company's purchase of its own equity securities, the transaction can have a material effect on reported earnings and EPS amounts. In such cases, the following explanations should be made:

- The effect of the transaction on the trend of reported earnings;
- Any increased leveraging resulting from the transaction, such as a higher debt to total capitalization ratio;
- The effect of the transaction on the trend of reported earnings per share amounts.

Also, any material issuer equity purchase transaction that occurs toward the end of the reporting period and does not significantly affect current EPS (because of the use of a weighted average) should be explained when such a transaction may have a significant effect on future reported results.

Statement Accounting for Changes in Earnings per Share

When analyzing or projecting EPS, the analyst can focus on changes in income on a per share basis. Table 12–1 presents an analysis of the changes in the EPS of a large chemical company for Year 4.

This published analysis is noteworthy particularly because it contains details such as those pertaining to changes due to sales volume and selling prices, which are normally available only to those with access to internal management records. This information, whenever available, can be of significant help to the analyst in the evaluation and prediction of earnings and EPS.

Table 12–1   Analysis of changes in earnings per share

			EPS
Year 3 earnings			$2.77
Additional earnings resulting from:			
Higher sales volume		$1.20	
Manufacturing cost savings		0.37	
Lower raw material prices		0.06	
		1.63	
Reductions in earnings caused by:			
Lower selling prices	$ 0.25		
Higher selling, administrative research,			
development, and other expenses	0.49	0.74	
Increase in operating results			0.89
			3.66
Nonoperating items:			
Lower income taxes, due primarily to difference in			
tax rate		$0.12	
Higher tax credits		0.12	
Other income and charges—net		0.03	
Unusual write-offs:			
Obsolescence	(0.06)		
Self-insurance reserve	(0.07)		
Other	0.03	(0.10)	
Effect on earnings of shares issued during			
the year		(0.11)	0.06
Year 4 earnings			$3.72
Increase in EPS.............................			$0.95

QUESTIONS

    1. Why is a thorough understanding of the principles governing the computation of EPS important to the financial analyst?

2. What developments caused the accounting profession to issue an *Opinion* on the computation of EPS?

3. Discuss uses of EPS and reasons or objectives of the method of reporting EPS under *APB Opinion 15.*

4. What is the purpose in presenting fully diluted EPS?

5. How do cumulative dividends on preferred stock affect the computation EPS for a company with a loss?

6. What is the two-class method and when is it used?

7. At the end of the year a company has a simple capital structure consisting only of common stock, as all its preferred stock was converted into common shares during the year. Is a computation of fully diluted EPS required?

8. If a warrant is not exercisable until seven years after the end of the period presented, should it be excluded from the computation of fully diluted EPS?

9. Under *APB Opinion 15* how should dividends per share be presented?

10. How does the payment of dividends on preferred stock affect the computation of EPS?

11. When and why would the following securities be considered CSE:
   a. Convertible debentures?
   b. Shares issuable in the future upon satisfaction of certain conditions?

12. EPS can affect market prices. Can market prices affect EPS?

13. Can CSE enter into the determination of EPS in one period and not in another?

14. What is meant by the term *antidilution?* Give an example of this condition.

15. How do we include stock options and warrants as CSE? What is the treasury stock method?

16. Is the treasury stock method always used? Which are the exceptions?

17. What are supplementary EPS? How are they disclosed?

18. *APB Opinion 15* has a number of flaws and inconsistencies that the analyst must consider in the interpretation of EPS data. Discuss these.

19. In estimating the value of common stock, the amount of EPS is considered to be a very important element in the determination of such value.
   a. Explain why EPS are important in the valuation of common stock.
   b. Are EPS equally important in valuing a preferred stock? Why or why not? (CFA)

Chapter 13

STATEMENTS OF CASH FLOWS

THE SIGNIFICANCE OF CASH FLOWS

Cash is universally acknowledged to be the most liquid of assets, one that affords an enterprise the greatest degree of liquidity and flexibility of choice. It is thus not surprising that cash represents the beginning as well as the end of the operating cycle. The profit-directed activities of an enterprise (e.g., operations) require that cash be converted into a variety of assets (e.g., inventories of all kinds), which in turn are converted into receivables as part of the sales process. Operating results are finally and definitively realized when the collection process returns the cash stream to the entity so that a new cycle, expected to have profitable potential at the time, can begin.

Analysts of financial statements and other users have long recognized that the increasing intricacy of the accrual accounting system masks cash flows from operations and widens their divergence from reported net income. Not only do they point to net operating cash inflows as ultimate validators of profitability, they also emphasize that it is cash, and not *net income,* that must be used to repay loans, to replace and expand the stock of plant and equipment in use, and to pay dividends.

The valid measurement of an enterprise's cash inflows and outflows from various sources, be they of an operating, financing, or investing nature, is, thus, an important analytical tool in the assessment of short-term liquidity, long-term solvency, and operating performance.

While fragmentary information on sources and uses of cash can be obtained from comparative balance sheets and income statements, a comprehensive picture of this important area of activity can be gained only from a statement of cash flows (SCF). This fact accounts for the growing importance and use of this statement that can provide information on such questions as:

1. What was the cash generated by or used in operations?
2. What utilization was made of cash provided by operations?
3. What was the source of cash invested in new plant and equipment?

4. What use was made of cash derived from a new bond issue or the sale of common stock?
5. How was it possible to continue the regular dividend in the face of an operating loss?
6. How was the debt repayment achieved, or what was the source of cash used to redeem the preferred stock?
7. How was the increase in investments financed?
8. Why, despite record profits, is the cash position lower than last year?

WHAT IS CASH FLOW?

Few analytical terms are more widely used and, at the same time, more poorly understood than the term *cash flow.*

Standing alone and unqualified, the term *cash flow* is, in its literal sense, meaningless. A company can experience cash *inflows* (i.e., cash receipts) and it can experience cash *outflows* (i.e., cash disbursements). Moreover, these cash inflows or outflows can relate to a variety of activities (e.g., the profit-directed activities) which we will refer to as *operations,* or to *financing* activities or to *investing* activities. We can also identify the difference between the inflows and outflows of cash for each of these activities as well as for all activities of the enterprise combined. These differences then can best be referred to as net inflows or net outflows of cash. Thus a net inflow of cash will reconcile to an *increase* in the cash balance for the period while a net outflow will correspond to a *decrease* of the cash balance during the period. To avoid confusion it is best to describe specifically what type of cash flow is referred to. Is it, for any given period, the net change in the cash balance, or the difference between the cash inflows and outflows related to operations, or some other specified type of cash flow? Most, but by no means all, writers when referring to cash flow mean cash generated by operations. The problem, from an analyst's point of view, is that the computation of this figure is often simplistic, incorrect, or misleading. Moreover, erroneous concepts of cash flow from operations are often used by those with specific objectives of persuasion in mind.

OBJECTIVES OF THIS CHAPTER

Credit analysts, equity analysts, and other analysts use cash flow analysis as an important analytical tool. As we shall see, the Statement of Cash Flows (SCF) is key to the reconstruction of many transactions, which is an important analytical process and skill.

The analysis of the SCF requires a thorough understanding of the basis on which the statement is prepared as well as the method of its preparation. Thus, we shall first focus on an understanding of this important accounting process.

Next we shall focus on the analytical uses to which the statement can be put as well as on the implications which the use of the statement has for the analysis of financial statements.

EVOLUTION OF THE ACCOUNTING FOR FUNDS AND CASH FLOWS

Accountants have long recognized the need to explain changes in funds, however defined, from period to period. However, it was only in 1971 that *APB Opinion 19,* "Reporting Changes in Financial Position" required that a statement of changes in financial position be presented as a basic financial statement and that it explain changes in either working capital or cash.

Analysts and other sophisticated users of financial statements have recognized that the most useful focus is on the change in *cash* rather than on any other measure of liquid funds. Since financial statements are prepared on an accrual basis and many important analytical objectives focus on an entity's ability to meet cash obligations, such as for interest, principal repayment, capital outlays, and dividends, the analyst needs to know the cash consequences of the entity's operating, financing, and investing activities.

While accountants have recognized these needs, they have been slow in recognizing cash as *the* preferred definition of funds. This reluctance can be traced in part, to an emphasis on accrual accounting as the best method of determining income and to the apparent contradiction between cash flow and accrual accounting. In fact no such contradiction exists because these two methods of measurement, as will be seen, measure different things.

In 1976, the Financial Accounting Standards Board (FASB) began a major project to formulate a *conceptual framework* of accounting and reporting. As part of its work on the conceptual framework, the FASB issued a *Discussion Memorandum* in December 1980, "Reporting Funds Flow, Liquidity and Financial Flexibility," which discussed funds flow reporting issues. The major issues discussed were the concepts of funds which should be adopted for the funds flow statement and the form of presentation of funds flow information. Feedback received by the FASB in connection with the conceptual framework project indicated an overall consensus among users of financial statements that a cash flow statement would be more useful than any other funds flow statement.

In December 1983, as part of its study on recognition and measurement concepts, the Board issued an *Exposure Draft,* "Recognition and Measurement in Financial Statements of Business Enterprises," which discussed the role of the cash flow statement. This exposure draft led to the issuance of Statement of *Financial Accounting Concepts 5* (1984) which states that a *full* set of financial statements for a reporting period should, among others, show "Cash flows during the period."

SFAS 95 "STATEMENT OF CASH FLOWS"

SFAS 95 (1987) "Statement of Cash Flows" (SCF) requires that a business enterprise that provides a set of financial statements that reports both financial position and results of operations must also provide a statement of cash flows for each period for which results of operations are provided.

Basis of Preparation

In order to focus on changes in cash, let us visualize two highly condensed balance sheets that are divided into sections disclosing (1) cash and (2) all other balance sheet accounts:

DR (CR)	Year-end 1	Year-end 2
Cash (and cash equivalents)	$ 3,000	$ 5,000
Other balance sheet accounts:		
Current assets (other than cash)	$ 9,000	$11,000
Noncurrent assets	6,000	8,000
Current liabilities	(8,000)	(10,000)
Long-term liabilities	(3,000)	(5,000)
Equity accounts	(7,000)	(9,000)
Net	$(3,000)	$ (5,000)

While the above is certainly not a conventional form of balance sheet presentation, it provides a useful framework for understanding the interaction between cash and all other balance sheet accounts. Thus we can readily observe that the net change in cash from year-end 1 to year-end 2 (a debit change of $2,000) is matched exactly by the $2,000 change in other balance sheet accounts between these two year-ends of $2,000 (an increase in net credits). This is, of course, true because assets must always equal liabilities plus capital; and consequently a change in one sector of the balance sheet must be matched by an equal change in the remaining accounts.

This relationship between cash and the other balance sheet accounts provides a useful means for understanding the basis underlying the preparation of the SCF. Visualizing the two sections of the balance sheet in the diagram below,

| Cash (A) | Cash Marketable securities | |
| Other balance sheet accounts (B) | Other current assets Fixed assets Other assets | Current liabilities Long-term liabilities Deferred credits Equity accounts |

we can generalize the interrelationships between cash and the other balance sheet accounts as follows:

1. Net changes in cash (Group A above) can be explained in terms of net changes in all other balance sheet accounts (Group B above). Thus the SCF will contain only items that affect *both* Groups A and B.
2. Internal changes within the "Other Balance Sheet Accounts" section do not affect cash. However, *SFAS 95* does require that all significant financing and investing activities be disclosed. Thus, noncash transactions which include the conversion of debt to equity, the acquisition of assets through the issuance of debt, and exchanges of assets or liabilities, should be disclosed in a *separate* schedule of noncash investing and financing activities.
3. Internal changes in cash (Group A) need not be reported. Thus, if a company, as part of its cash management activities, invests its excess cash in short-term highly liquid investments—cash equivalents—such as commercial paper, Treasury bills, or money market funds, such investments or sales for cash need not be reported in the SCF.

Classification Requirements

SFAS 95 requires that the SCF classify cash receipts and payments by operating, financing, and investing activities.

Operating activities encompass all the earning-related activities of the enterprise. Thus they encompass, in addition to all the income and expense items found in the income statement, all the net inflows and outflows of cash that operations impose on the enterprise as a result of activities, such as the extension of credit to customers, investment in inventories, and obtaining credit from suppliers. Thus, operating activities relate to all items in the statement of income (with minor exceptions) as well as to balance sheet items that relate to operations—mostly working capital accounts such as accounts receivable, inventories, prepayments, accounts payable, and accruals.

SFAS 95 also specifies that operating activities include all transactions and events that are not of an investing or financing nature, for example, amounts received to settle a lawsuit.

Financing activities include obtaining resources from owners and providing them with a return of or a return on (i.e., dividends) their investment. They also include obtaining resources from creditors and repaying the amounts borrowed or otherwise settling the obligations.

Investing activities include acquiring and selling or otherwise disposing of securities which are not cash equivalents, and productive assets that are expected to generate revenues over the long term. They also include lending money and collecting on those loans.

The SCF shall report the effect of exchange rate changes on cash balances held in foreign currencies as a separate part of the reconciliation of cash during the period.

Except for specialized cases, such as quick turnover items, investing and financing cash inflows and outflows shall be reported separately in an SCF. For example, proceeds of borrowing shall be reported separately from repayments: asset acquisitions separately from asset dispositions.

SFAS 104 (1989) amends *SFAS 95* to permit banks, saving institutions, and credit unions to report in a statement of cash flows certain net cash receipts and cash payments. Investing and financing activities that do not involve cash shall be reported separately in related disclosures either in narrative or in summarized form.

Expanded Balance Sheet Diagram

Because of the need to classify items in the SCF and in order to focus better on effects of account changes, we present a more detailed version of the preceding balance sheet diagram:

Balance Sheet

Group A	Cash and cash equivalents

	Current
Accounts receivable*	Accounts payable*
Inventories*	Accrued liabilities*
Prepayments*	Notes payable to banks
Receivable from officers	Current portion—long-term debt
	Dividends payable

Group B	*Noncurrent*
Investments	Long-term debt
Fixed assets	Deferred tax liabilities
Other assets	Equity accounts
	(including retained earnings)

* Related to operations (also referred to as *operating working capital* items).

Changes in cash involve interaction of the cash account with any item or items in Group B. In the examples which follow, the account affected and the activity classification are indicated:

Cash sale (credit to retained earnings via income) (Operations)

Collection of accounts receivable (Operations)

Cash payment for insurance policy (charge to retained earnings via income or to prepaid expenses) (Operations)

Cash payment of interest (income) (Operations)

Payment of accounts payable (Operations)

Collection of noncurrent receivable related to operations (Operations)

Payment for fixed assets (Investing)

Sale of investment (Investing)

Repayment of loans (Financing)

Payment of dividends (Financing)

Changes within the Noncash B Group

As we have already indicated, changes *within* this group do not affect cash flows. However, their impact on the presentation of the SCF must be thoroughly understood. It is useful to classify them as follows:

1. Internal changes related to operations:
   a. Changes affecting operating working capital, for example:
      Purchase of inventory on credit.

Sale of merchandise on credit.

Liability for electricity accrued.

These transactions become part of the net change in operating working capital items for the period. *Only* those net changes which interact with the cash account enter into the computation of cash provided by operations.

b. Changes reflecting items of income or expense which do not affect cash, for example:

Depreciation and amortization expense.

Provision for deferred tax expense.

Equity in earnings of affiliated companies.

These expenses or income items, rather than affecting cash, affect noncash accounts such as accumulated depreciation, intangible assets, or investments in affiliated companies. These income and expense items represent adjustments to net income when that figure is converted from the accrual basis to the cash basis of accounting.

2. Internal changes reflecting significant investing or financing activities, for example:

Conversion of debt to equity.

Purchase of asset for long-term debt (e.g., a mortgage).

Acquisition of a subsidiary partially for debt or equity.

These internal changes in Group B, while not affecting cash, must be disclosed in a separate schedule to the SCF detailing noncash investing or financing activities.

3. Internal changes reflecting events not sufficiently significant to require separate reporting, for example:

Stock dividends and stock splits.

Write-off of fully depreciated assets.

Dividends declared and not paid.

Long-term debt becomes current.

Let us now advance our understanding of the preparation of the SCF by focusing on a simple illustration.

Simple Illustration of Preparation of Statement of Cash Flows

To illustrate the preparation of a Statement of Cash Flows (SCF), the condensed comparative balance sheets as at two consecutive year-ends (shown in Exhibit 13–1) will be utilized. These balance sheets are condensed here for convenience of illustration. The preparation of the SCF requires details about account changes and supplementary data. These details are revealed in the discussion below of the individual effects on cash or noncash transactions:

1. The $20 decrease in cash is the change which the SCF sets out to explain. It is explained by the changes in all other balance sheet accounts.
2. The decrease in accounts receivable is a positive (cash inflow) adjustment to income in arriving at cash flow operations and will be elaborated upon later. It means that cash collections exceeded accrual basis sales.
3. The increase in inventories is a negative (cash outflow) adjustment to income because cash outlays for inventory exceeded purchases included in cost of sales.
4. The T-account below summarizes the change in the fixed asset account:

Fixed Assets

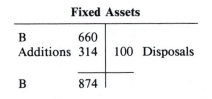

B	660		
Additions	314	100	Disposals
B	874		

Both the additions and the disposals are part of investing activities. While each event is shown separately in the SCF, in Exhibit 13–1 they net out to $214 ($314 − $100).

5. The T-account below summarizes the change in the accumulated depreciation account:

Accumulated Depreciation

		200	B
Accumulated Depreciation on assets disposed	20	64	Depreciation for period
		244	B

As we discussed above, depreciation ($64) is a noncash expense and represents an internal change in Group B—a debit to income (retained earnings) and a credit to accumulated depreciation. It is, thus, added back to income in arriving at cash from operations. The $20 in accumulated depreciation relates to the $100 (original cost) of fixed assets disposed. The assets were sold at book value (i.e., $100 − $20 = $80). The $20 of accumulated depreciation adjusts the $100 amount included in the investing activity (see line 4).

6. The decline of $50 in intangible assets represents amortization. Since amortization is a noncash expense similar to depreciation it is added back to income in the operating activity column.

Exhibit 13–1

WIDGET CORPORATION
Condensed Balance Sheets
(in thousands)

| | December 31 | | Changes during Year 2* | | | |
	Year 1	Year 2	Operating activity	Investing activity	Financing activity	Noncash transactions
1. Cash	$ 120	$ 100				
2. Accounts receivable	200	145	55			
3. Inventories	150	175	(25)			
4. Fixed assets	660	874		(214)		
5. Accumulated depreciation	(200)	(244)	64	(20)		
6. Intangible assets	150	100	50			
Total assets	$1,080	$1,150				
7. Accounts payable	150	130	(20)			
8. Long-term debt	420	400			(10)	(10)
9. Capital stock and paid-in capital	250	300			40	10
10. Retained earnings	260	320	180		(120)	
Total liabilities and equity	$1,080	$1,150				
Totals			$304	$(234)	$ (90)	$ 0

*Items in parentheses reflect *decreases* in cash or noncash resources.

435

7. The decrease in accounts payable is a negative (cash outflow) adjustment to income, because amounts due to suppliers for preceding periods were paid in cash.
8. The decrease of $20 in long-term debt represents $10 in repayment (classified as financing outflow) and $10 reduction due to conversion of debt into equity (classified as a noncash transaction).
9. The increase of $50 in capital stock represents sale of stock of $40 (a financing inflow) and $10 in stock issued by conversion of debt (a noncash transaction).
10. The change in retained earnings is summarized in the T-account below:

Retained Earnings

		260	B
Dividends paid 120		180	Net income
		320	B

The net income of $180 is the figure which, after adjustments, becomes the source of cash from operations of $304.
The dividend of $120 is a financing cash outflow.

In summarized fashion the change in cash can now be explained as follows:

Net cash flow from operations	304
Cash flows for investing activities	(234)
Cash flows for financing activities	(90)
Decrease in cash	20

Exhibit 13–2 presents these results in a formal and more detailed Statement of Cash Flows.

In the simple illustration of Widget Corporation we constructed the SCF directly from the comparative balance sheets and information given. Where financial statements of more detail and complexity are involved, a more structured and systematic method of preparation is needed. In the sections that follow we will illustrate the T-account technique for the systematic preparation of an SCF. We shall also discuss and elaborate upon the computation of Cash Flow from Operations (CFO).

Illustration of T-Account Technique

The simple illustration above indicated some of the more common steps involved in the preparation of the SCF. These, and others found in more complex examples, are:

Exhibit 13–2

WIDGET CORPORATION
Statement of Cash Flows
For the Year Ended December 31, Year 2
(in thousands)

Net cash flow from operating activities:

Net income $180

Add (deduct) adjustments to cash basis:

Depreciation	64	
Amortization of intangibles	50	
Decrease in accounts receivables	55	
Increase in inventory	(25)	
Decrease in accounts payable	(20)	
Net cash flow from operating activities		$304

Cash flows from investing activities:

Purchase of fixed assets	(314)	
Sale of fixed assets	80	
Net cash used in investing activities		(234)

Cash flows from financing activities: ....

Sale of capital stock	40	
Payment of dividends	(120)	
Repayment of long-term debt	(10)	
Net cash used in financing activities		(90)

Net increase (decrease) in cash .... $ (20)

Schedule of noncash financing and investing activities:*

Common stock issued in conversion of long-term debt .... $ 10

* May also be presented in a footnote

Note: Amounts paid for interest and income taxes must also be disclosed.

1. An analysis of net changes based on further detail and information provided.
2. The reversal or elimination of transactions internal to noncash accounts (Group B).
3. Regrouping and reconstruction of transactions in the noncash group that affect, and hence explain, the changes in cash.

The methods used to implement these adjustments vary from elaborate multicolumn worksheets to highly summarized adjustments that are performed mentally. One of the most direct and most flexible methods utilizes the reconstruction of summarized T-accounts. This method, developed by Professor W. J. Vatter, and which, as we shall see, is most suited to analytical work, will be illustrated here.

The basic objective of the T-account method is to reconstruct in *summary fashion* by means of T-accounts for all balance sheet accounts, the transactions reflected in them during the reporting period. If the reconstructed transaction reveals that it was a source or use of cash, it is posted to the summary cash T-account. If the transaction has no effect on cash, and is not of a significant investing or financing nature, it is reversed among the applicable noncash T-accounts.

Exhibits 13–3 and 13–4 present the comparative balance sheet and the income statement of the Vatter Company.

The following additional information is available:

1. On March 1, year 2, the company bought for cash of $510,000 a business concern with fixed assets having a value of $450,000, with current assets (no cash)[1] equal to current liabilities, and the excess of $60,000 being considered as the cost of goodwill acquired.
2. Old machinery was sold for $18,000; it originally cost $36,000, and $20,000 of depreciation had been accumulated to date of sale.

Exhibit 13–3

VATTER COMPANY
Comparative Balance Sheet
As of December 31
(in thousands)

	Year 1	Year 2	Increase (decrease)
Assets			
Current assets:			
Cash	$ 240	$ 120	$ (120)
Receivables	360	450	90
Inventories	750	1,053	303
Total current assets	1,350	1,623	273
Fixed assets	4,500	6,438	1,938
Accumulated depreciation	(1,500)	(1,740)	(240)
Investment in affiliate	1,000	1,050	50
Goodwill	950	980	30
Total assets	$6,300	$8,351	$2,051
Liabilities and Capital			
Accounts payable	$ 360	$ 590	$ 230
Bonds payable	300	700	400
Deferred income taxes	240	260	20
Capital stock	2,400	3,200	800
Additional paid-in capital	900	1,300	400
Retained earnings	2,100	2,301	201
Total liabilities and capital	$6,300	$8,351	$2,051

---

[1] If cash is acquired it is deducted from the amount of cash spent in the acquisition.

Exhibit 13–4

VATTER COMPANY
Income Statement
December 31, 20x2
(in thousands)

Sales		$19,950
Cost of goods sold (includes $360 of depreciation)		11,101
Gross profit		8,849
General selling and administrative expenses	$7,000	
Amortization of goodwill	30	7,030
		1,819
Equity in earnings of unconsolidated affiliate*		50
Gain on sale of fixed assets		2
Income before taxes		1,871
Income taxes:		
Current	900	
Deferred	20	920
Net income		$ 951

* No dividends received

3. In April, the company acquired $100,000 in fixed assets by issuing bonds with $100,000 par value.
4. In June, the company received $1,000,000 in cash for a new issue of capital stock with a par value of $600,000. $200,000 of convertible bonds were converted into capital stock, par value $200,000. Long-term bonds were also sold for $500,000 (at par).
5. Fully depreciated assets of $100,000 were written off.
6. Dividends paid amounted to $750,000.
7. General selling and administrative expenses included $50,000 of interest paid.
8. There were no liabilities for income taxes at beginning or end of year 2.

Based on the financial statements and the additional data above an SCF will be prepared using the following steps:

1. A T-account is set up for each noncash account appearing in the comparative balance sheet. The opening and closing balance of the account is posted to the T-account as follows:

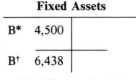

Fixed Assets

B*	4,500	
B†	6,438	

* Signifies opening balance.
† Signifies closing balance.

2. A Cash T-account, divided into four sections: Operations, Investing Activities, Financing Activities, and Noncash Transactions, as illustrated in the comprehensive example that follows, is also opened.
3. Based on information supplied and inferences drawn from the changes in the noncash accounts, the balance in the T-account is reconstructed by:
   a. Debiting or crediting items of income or loss, as well as items converting them to the cash basis, to the Operations section.
   b. Debiting or crediting all remaining items to the other three sections to which they relate.
4. When the process is completed the Cash T-account will contain the detail necessary for the preparation of the SCF.

DETERMINING NET CASH FLOW FROM OPERATIONS

Let us first examine the concepts and the method of determining the Cash from Operations (CFO) amount. The items of Vatter Company's income statement (Exhibit 13–4) relate to cash, operating working capital, or to other balance sheet accounts, generally as shown in the table on page 441.

Items such as sales, cost of goods sold, general selling and administrative expenses, and current income taxes (1) generate or require cash or (2) their receipt or payment is delayed taking the form of receivables, assets, or payables which form part of the operating working capital of companies. This includes current deferred income taxes. Other accounts which relate to operations, such as noncurrent receivables, also belong to this group. They all are considered as relating to operations and thus affect the conversion of income from the accrual basis to the cash basis.

The other items do not affect cash and thus must be added back to, or deducted from, net income in order to arrive at cash from operations. Thus, depreciation interacts with the accumulated depreciation account, amortization with the intangibles account, the equity in earnings with the investment in affiliates account, and deferred tax expense with deferred tax liability accounts.

In addition to the above, the following are further examples of items that may appear in the income statement and that have no effect on cash:

		Operating working capital				
	Cash	Accounts receivable	Inventories	Prepayments	Accounts payable and accruals	Other noncash accounts
Sales	X	X				
Cost of goods sold	X		X		X	
Depreciation						X
General selling and administrative expenses	X			X	X	
Amortization of goodwill						X
Equity in earnings of unconsolidated affiliate						X
Gain on sale of fixed assets						X
Income taxes—current	X				X	
Income taxes—deferred				X	X	X

Income statement item	*Related to the following noncash balance sheet item*
Amortization of bond premium	Unamortized bond premium
Amortization of bond discount	Unamortized bond discount
Warranty expenses	Estimated liability for warranty costs (noncurrent)
Amortization of leasehold improvements	Leasehold improvements
Subscription income	Deferred subscription income (noncurrent portion)
Minority interest in income (loss)	Minority interest

This concept can also be summarized as follows:

Income statement item	*Related to contra account*	*Effect on cash from operations*
Dr. expense or loss	Cr. to cash	Use of cash
	Cr. to noncash account	Add back—not using cash
Cr. income, or gain, or expense	Dr. to cash	Source of cash
	Dr. to noncash account	Deduct—not providing cash

The gain on sale of fixed assets deserves separate consideration. It is removed from income not because it did not bring in cash but rather because the total cash received on the sale (including the gain) is classified as part of investing activities. Thus, if the gain on sale of the fixed assets is not removed from income the total proceeds from the sale of the fixed assets ($18,000) will be found in two places (1) recovery of book value of fixed assets of $16,000 ($36,000 − $20,000) and (2) gain on sale in net income.

Considering operations as encompassing broadly the *earning related activities* of the enterprise, it is clear that changes in operating working capital accounts, as described above, would affect operations so defined. This is so because the focus is not only on income and expense items but also on the inflows and outflows of cash that operations impose on the enterprise; for example, extension of credit to customers, investment in inventories, and, conversely, obtaining credit from suppliers.

Let us take the change in accounts receivable as an example. They increased by $90,000 during year 2, and that means that on a net basis, the sales figure for the year is $90,000 higher than the collections of cash from sales. This can also be shown by a reconstruction of the *aggregate* entries in the Accounts Receivable account for year 2.

Accounts Receivable (in thousands of dollars)

	B	360		
Sales		19,950	19,860	Cash collections*
	B	450		

* In this simplified example we did not consider whether the accounts receivable were net of an allowance for bad debts or whether the company practices the direct write-off method of accounting for bad debts. In the latter case the $19,860 cash collections are overstated by the amount of accounts receivable written off because the credit to accounts receivable resulting from the write-off does produce cash. If an allowance for bad debts is used and the receivable is shown *net*, then the $19,860 cash collection figure is overstated by the amount of bad debt provision expense for the period (as will be discussed in a later section of this chapter).

SFAS 95 requires that changes in operations-related accounts, such as accounts receivable, be shown in the SCF adjusted for noncash entries such as the write-off of accounts receivable. Similarly, an increase in accounts receivable due to an acquisition must be adjusted to remove such increase from the computation of cash from operations and reclassified as an investing outlay of cash (part of the acquisition of a company).

Using a similar line of analytical reasoning, we can see that changes in the following operating working capital accounts would have effects as follows:

Account	*Change:* *Dr. (debit)* *Cr. (credit)*	*Effect on operations*
Accounts Receivable	Increase (Dr.)	Sales not collected in cash.
	Decrease (Cr.)	Collections exceed sales for the period, i.e., some prior period receivables collected.
Inventories	Increase (Dr.)	Cash purchases exceed cost of goods sold.
	Decrease (Cr.)	Some of the cost of goods sold represents a reduction in inventories, i.e., cash purchases are less than cost of goods sold.
Prepaid Expenses	Increase (Dr.)	Cash paid for expenses that are to be charged to future periods. Thus cash spent exceeds expenses in income statement.
	Decrease (Cr.)	Some expenses in the income statement were paid for in prior years and consequently did not require a current cash outlay.
Trade Accounts or Notes Payable	Increase (Cr.)	Some purchases were not yet paid for in cash.
	Decrease (Dr.)	Cash payments to suppliers exceed purchases for the period.

Exhibit 13–5

THE VATTER COMPANY
Statement of Cash Flows
For the Year Ended December 31, Year 2
(in thousands)

Cash flows from operating activities:		
Net income	$ 951	
Add (deduct) adjustments to cash basis:		
Depreciation	360	
Amortization of goodwill	30	
Deferred income taxes	20	
Gain on sale of equipment	(2)	
Equity in earnings of affiliate	(5)	
Increase in receivables	(90)	
Increase in inventories	(303)	
Increase in accounts payable	230	
Net cash flow from operating activities		$1,146
Cash flows from investing activities:		
Purchase of fixed assets	(1,974)	
Purchase of goodwill	(60)	
Sale of fixed assets	18	
Net cash used by investing activities		(2,016)
Cash flows from financing activities:		
Net proceeds from sale of bonds	500	
Sale of capital stock	1,000	
Payment of dividends	(750)	
Net cash provided by financing activities		750
Net decrease in cash		$ (120)
Supplemental disclosure of cash flow information		
Interest paid during year		$ 50
Income taxes paid during the year		900
Schedule of noncash investing and financing		
activities:		
Bonds issued to acquire fixed assets		$ 100
Stock issued in conversion of bonds		$ 200

A study of the preceding chart reveals that the use of the debit and credit designation for changes in the current accounts is a useful check on the effects of changes on sources and uses of cash. Thus, a *credit* change *adds* to cash from operations while a *debit* change *reduces* cash from operations.

Note that the listed "effects on operations" involve the basic assumption that only *operating* items flow through the current accounts (e.g., that receivables do not include amounts receivable for sales of fixed assets and that accounts payable do not include amounts due for purchases of long-lived assets). This is a crucial and inevitable assumption that will in most cases be *substantially* (but not entirely) correct. The analyst must be aware, however, that in some cases additional information from management may be required to clarify substantial exceptions to this assumption.

Also note that some current accounts do not relate to operations and must be classified by type of activity to which they do relate. For example:

Account	Type of activity
Loans Receivable (e.g., from officers)	Investing
Current portion of Long-Term Debt	Financing
Notes Payable to Bank	Financing
Dividends Payable	Financing

In our illustration of Vatter Company, we do not happen to have such nonoperating current accounts.

To summarize, we can distinguish among three categories of adjustments which convert accrual basis net income to CFO:

I. Expenses, losses, revenues, and gains which do not use or generate cash, that is, those involving noncash accounts (except those in II below).

II. Net changes in noncash accounts (mostly[2] in the operating working capital group) which relate to operations. These adjustments modify the accrual-based revenue and expense items included in income.

III. Gains or losses (such as on sales of assets) which are transferred to other sections of the SCF so as to show there the entire cash proceeds of the sale.

The T-accounts, explanation of transactions, and the SCF of Vatter Company (Exhibit 13–5) follow:

T-Accounts (in thousands)

Cash

B	240	

---

[2] An example of a nonworking capital account in this category is a long-term receivable resulting from sales in the ordinary course of business.

Operations

Depreciation expense	(g)	360	2	(b)	Gain on sale of fixed assets
Deferred income taxes	(k)	20	50	(p)	Equity in earnings of
Net income	(m)	951			affiliate
Goodwill amortization	(o)	30	90	(q)	Increase in receivables
Increase in accounts payable	(s)	230	303	(r)	Increase in inventories

Investing Activities

Sale of fixed assets	(b)	18	450	(a)	Acquisition of fixed assets
			60	(a)	Acquisition of goodwill
			1,524	(f)	Acquisition of fixed assets

Financing Activities

Bonds sold	(h)	500	750	(n)	Dividends paid
Sale of stock	(l)	1,000			

Noncash Transactions

Bonds issued to acquire fixed assets	(d)	100	100	(c)	Fixed assets acquired with bonds
Stock issued in conversion	(j)	200	200	(i)	Bond conversion to stock
	B	120			

Receivables

B	360	
(q)	90	
B	450	

Inventories			Accounts Payable		
B	750			360	B
(r)	303			230	(s)
B	1,053			590	B

Fixed Assets

B	4,500		
(a)	450	36	(b)
(c)	100	100	(e)
(f)	1,524		
B	6,438		

Accumulated Depreciation

		1,500	B
(b)	20	360	(g)
(e)	100		
		1,740	B

Investment in Affiliate

B	1,000
(p)	50
B	1,050

Goodwill

B	950		
(a)	60	30(o)	
B	980		

Bonds Payable

		300	B
(i)	200	100	(d)
		500	(h)
		700	B

Deferred Income Taxes

	240	B
	20	(k)
	260	B

Capital Stock

	2,400	B
	200	(j)
	600	(l)
	3,200	B

Paid-in Capital

	900	B
	400	(l)
	1,300	B

Retained Earnings

		2,100	B
(n)	750	951	(m)
		2,301	B

RECONSTRUCTION OF TRANSACTIONS

The Debits and Credits Are to T-Accounts and Are Needed to Construct the SCF

Fixed Assets

(a) The acquisition of the business concern is reconstructed as follows:

Fixed assets	450,000	
Goodwill	60,000	
Cash—Investing		510,000

In the Statement of Cash Flows the acquisition is treated as an investing activity. It represents the acquisition of productive assets that are expected to generate revenue over a long period of time. In this case, for the sake of simplicity, we assume that current assets acquired (no cash) equal current liabilities acquired. However, in more realistic circumstances increases in operating working capital items due to the acquisition will need to be eliminated so that only changes in operating working capital items due to operations will be included in adjustments to convert net income to CFO. Working capital items (e.g., receivables, inventory payables) acquired will be removed from adjustments to arrive at CFO and considered part of cash outlay for acquisitions (investing activity).

(b) The transaction for the sale of equipment is as follows:

Cash—Investing	18,000	
Accumulated Depreciation	20,000	
Fixed Assets		36,000
Cash—Operations (gain on sale)		2,000

The entire proceeds of $18,000 are debited to "Cash from investing activities." In the Statement of Cash Flows, the sale of property, plant, and equipment represents an investing activity.

"Cash from operations" is credited in order to remove the gain on the sale of equipment from net income. This gain must be removed from net income so as to link it up with the recovery of book value of $16,000 and show the entire proceeds as part of cash from investing activities.

SFAS 95 requires that all significant investing and financing activities be disclosed whether or not cash is directly affected. Therefore the following entries are necessary to account for the acquisition of fixed assets through the issuance of debt:

(*c*) Fixed Assets 100,000
      Noncash Transactions   100,000

(*d*) Noncash Transactions................. 100,000
      Bonds Payable   100,000

The write-off of depreciated assets does not affect cash, nor does it represent an important investing or financing activity. Therefore, it does not have to be reflected in the statement of cash flows. The transaction is reconstructed as follows:

(*e*) Accumulated Depreciation 100,000
      Fixed Assets   100,000

All known transactions have been posted to the Fixed Assets account. In order to arrive at the ending balance it is necessary to debit the account by $1,524,000. The most probable assumption is that fixed assets for this amount were acquired.

(*f*) Fixed Assets 1,524,000
      Cash—Investing   1,524,000

Accumulated Depreciation

In order to balance the Accumulated Depreciation account a credit of $360,000 is needed. This amount represents the depreciation expense found on the income statement.

(*g*) Cash—Operations 360,000
      Accumulated Depreciation   360,000

Depreciation expense is added back to income because it is an expense not using cash.

Bonds Payable

The issuance of bonds is considered a financing activity in a Statement of Cash Flows. The entry for the issuance of bonds is as follows:

(*h*) Cash—Financing 500,000
      Bonds Payable   500,000

The conversion of bonds into common stock does not affect cash.

However, as a significant financing activity it must be disclosed in a separate schedule of the SCF.

(*i*) Bonds Payable   200,000
        Noncash Transaction   200,000

(*j*) Noncash Transaction   200,000
        Capital Stock   200,000

Deferred Income Taxes

The charge for deferred income taxes does not require the use of cash. It is an add back to net income as an expense not requiring cash.

(*k*) Cash—Operations   20,000
        Deferred Income Taxes   20,000

Capital Stock and Paid-In Capital

The sale of stock is considered a financing activity in a Statement of Cash Flows. The entry for the sale of stock is as follows:

(*l*) Cash—Financing   1,000,000
        Capital Stock   600,000
        Paid-in Capital   400,000

Retained Earnings

Net income of $951,000 is the starting number which is adjusted for items needed to convert it to a cash basis.

(*m*) Cash—Operations   951,000
        Retained Earnings   951,000

Cash dividends paid to stockholders are treated as a financing activity in the Statement of Cash Flows. Cash dividends paid amounted to $750,000:

(*n*) Retained Earnings   750,000
        Cash—Financing   750,000

Goodwill Amortization

The income statement shows $30,000 of goodwill amortization. Since this charge to income does not require cash, it should be added back to net income:

(*o*) Cash—Operations 30,000

   Goodwill 30,000

Investment in Affiliate

Equity in earnings of unconsolidated affiliate (none were distributed as dividends) is a source of income which does not affect cash. Thus, it must be removed from net income:

(*p*) Investment in Affiliate 50,000

   Cash—Operations 50,000

Accounts Receivable

The change in accounts receivables should be reflected in arriving at "cash flows from operating activities" in order to convert income from an accrual basis to a cash basis. An increase in accounts receivables indicates that some sales were not collected in cash. In this case, the $90,000 increase reduces CFO by an adjustment to income:

(*q*) Accounts Receivable 90,000

   Cash—Operations 90,000

Inventories

The change in inventories affects "cash flows from operating activities." An increase in inventories indicates that purchases exceeded the cash outlays reflected in cost of goods sold. Thus, an adjustment reducing CFO is called for.

(*r*) Inventories 303,000

   Cash—Operations 303,000

Accounts Payable

The change in accounts payable should also be reflected in arriving at "cash flows from operating activities." An increase in accounts payable indicates that some purchases have not yet been paid for in cash. Thus, expenses exceed cash outlays requiring an adjustment which increases cash from operations.

(*s*) Cash—Operations 230,000

   Accounts Payable 230,000

Now that all the transactions have been reconstructed, a comprehensive Statement of Cash Flows can be developed from the cash T-account.

The adjustments to convert Vatter Company's net income to the cash basis can also be explained as shown on page 452.

Item	Amount (000s)	Explanation
Net income, accrual basis	$ 951	Starting point of conversion
Add (deduct) adjustments to cash basis:		
Depreciation	360	Add back because expense involves no cash outflow.
Amortization of goodwill	30	Add back because expense involves no cash outflow.
Deferred income taxes	20	Add back because expense involves no cash outflow.
Equity in earnings of affiliate	(50)	Deduct because revenue item does not result in cash inflow.
Gain on sale of equipment	(2)	Remove gain (because it is nonoperating) so that total cash inflow can be shown as cash from investing activities.
Increase in receivables	(90)	Deduct because cash flow from sales is *less* than accrual sales revenue.
Increase in inventories	(303)	Deduct because cash outflow for inventory *exceeds* accrual basis inventory cost included in cost of goods sold.
Increase in accounts payable	230	Add because cash outflows for purchases (included in cost of goods sold) is *less* than accrual purchase cost.
CFO (Exhibit 13–5)	$1,146	

DETERMINING CASH FROM OPERATIONS—TWO METHODS

In Exhibit 13–5 the amount of Cash from Operations (CFO) of Vatter Company was obtained indirectly.

Indirect Method   Under this method net income is adjusted for non-cash items required to convert it to CFO. The advantage of this method is that it is a reconciliation which discloses the differences between net income and CFO. Some analysts estimate future cash flows by first estimating future income levels and then adjusting these for leads and lags between income and CFO; that is, for the noncash adjustments referred to above. Primarily for this reason the Financial Analysts Federation came out in favor of the indirect method.

Direct or Inflow-Outflow Method   This method lists the gross cash receipts and disbursements related to operations. Most respondents to the Exposure Draft which preceded *SFAS 95,* and especially credit analysts among them, prefer this method because this presentation discloses the total amounts of cash which flowed into the enterprise and out of the enterprise due to operations. This gives analysts a better measure of the size of cash inflows and outflows over which management had some degree of discretion. The risks to which lenders are exposed relate more to fluctuations in CFO than to fluctuations in net income. Thus, information on the amounts of operating cash receipts and payments is important in assessing the nature of those fluctuations.

These important analytical considerations at first convinced the Board to require the direct method of computing CFO but, influenced by arguments of providers of information who claimed that this method would impose excessive implementation costs, the Board decided to encourage use of the direct method and to permit use of the indirect method.

When enterprises report under the direct method they must provide a reconciliation of net income to CFO in a separate schedule. They must also, at a minimum, report on the following cash receipts and payments:

a. Cash collected from customers, including lessees, licensees, and the like.
b. Interest and dividends received.
c. Other operating cash receipts, if any.
d. Cash paid to employees and other suppliers of goods or services, including suppliers of insurance, advertising, and the like.
e. Interest paid.
f. Income taxes paid.
g. Other operating cash payments, if any.

Enterprises are encouraged to provide further details of operating receipts and payments but they must disclose, under either method, the amount of interest paid (net of amounts capitalized) and income taxes paid.

Implications for Analysis

SFAS 95 encourages the use of the direct (inflow-outflow) method of presenting cash flow from operations but does not require it.

Based on the facts that very few companies have so far used the direct method of presentation and that preparers lobbied[3] the FASB in order to have them reverse the direct method requirement, analysts most likely

---

[3] A review of letters of comment to the FASB on the subject of cash flow indicates an unwillingness on the part of many preparers to provide data on operating cash inflows and outflows. Many claim that such data are not readily available, that is, that they are too expensive to produce.

Indirect format	
Net income as reported	951
Remove—gain on sale of PPE	(2)
Add—Depreciation	360
Amortization	30
Deferred taxes	20
Deduct equity in earnings of affiliates	(50)
Add (deduct) changes in	
Receivables	(90)
Inventories	(303)
Payables	230
CFO	1,146

Inflow-outflow format	
Total revenues (19,950 + 50 + 2)	20,002
Remove gain on sale	(2)
Less equity in earnings of affiliates	(50)
Less increase in receivables cash inflows	(90)
	19,860
Total expenses (11,101 + 7,030 + 920)	19,051
Less—Depreciation	(360)
Amortization	(30)
Deferred taxes	(20)
Add increase in inventories	303
Less increase in payables	(230)
	18,714
CFO	1,146

must be prepared to convert on their own the CFO presentations from the indirect to the inflow-outflow or direct method.

The accuracy of the conversion depends, as will be seen from the discussion which follows, on adjustments which use data available only from internal accounting records. However, in most cases the method of conversion described in the section which follows, as well as in Appendix A to Chapter 13, will be sufficiently accurate for most analytical purposes.

CONVERSION FROM THE INDIRECT TO THE INFLOW-OUTFLOW PRESENTATION

An analyst working with published financial statements can convert a CFO presentation from the indirect format to the inflow-outflow format. The conversion from the indirect format to the inflow-outflow format can be visualized in the diagram on page 454 (the amounts used are those of the Vatter Company illustration).

Note that we always start by disaggregating (grossing up) the net income figure (here $951) into total revenues ($20,002) and total charges and expenses ($19,051). After that, the conversion adjustments are applied to the relevant category of revenue or expense.

Based on this approach the inflow-outflow presentation of Vatter Company's CFO is shown in Exhibit 13-6. Please note that the equity in earnings of affiliates (a noncash revenue item) and the gain from sale of equipment (transferred to investing activities) are omitted from this exhibit.

Relating Adjustments to Individual Income and Expense Items

The CFO statement (inflow-outflow format) can sometimes be improved by relating adjustments to the revenue and expense category to which they apply. Analytical objectives or requirements may also make it desirable that adjustments be related to the relevant revenue or expense category.

In some cases such relating is obvious. For example, the change in receivables, when used to adjust sales, will approximate the amount of cash collections from customers. Similarly, the amount of cash outflow for taxes may be determined as follows:

Tax expense:	
Add (deduct)	(Increase) decrease in deferred tax credits
	Increase (decrease) in deferred tax debits
	(Increase) decrease in taxes payable
	Increase (decrease) in tax refunds receivable
Equals	Cash outflow for taxes

Exhibit 13–6

VATTER COMPANY
Cash Flow from Operations
For Year Ended December 31, Year 2
(in thousands)

Sales	$19,950	
Less increase in receivables	90	
Cash collections		$19,860
Cash outflows:		
Cost of goods sold	11,101	
Less depreciation	360	
	10,741	
Add: Increase in inventories	303	
	11,044	
General, selling and administrative expenses (7,030–30)	7,000	
Less: Increase in accounts payable	(230)	17,814
Income taxes—current (920–20)		900
Total cash outflows		18,714
Cash from operations (CFO)		$ 1,146

Since *SFAS 95* requires that income taxes and interest paid be disclosed, the analyst should have these amounts available without need for further computation.

In many cases, relating adjustments cannot be accurately accomplished. For example, the total depreciation expense may relate not only to cost of goods sold, but also to general selling and administrative expenses. Similarly, payables, accruals, and prepayments may relate to more than one expense category. Thus, analytical presentation will depend on need, data availability, and the degree of accuracy required. The more detailed the categories of operating cash receipts and payments needed, the more detailed is the information needed to determine their amount.

Required Adjustments

SFAS 95 provides that if enterprises choose not to present the CFO component of the SCF in the direct, or inflow-outflow format, they must determine the *same* amount of CFO by the indirect or reconciliation method. To do this properly, the preparer needs sufficiently detailed information; that is, information generally available only from internal records. Thus, the analyst is entitled to assume that the items disclosed by the entity which reconcile income to cash from operations (CFO) reflect adjustments based on such detailed information.

So that the analyst has at all times a thorough understanding of the pertinent financial data, it is important that these required adjustments are well understood.

In order for operating cash receipts and payments to be accurate, receivables and payables that relate to operations must be segregated from those that relate to investing and financing activities. In addition, the effects of all noncash entries to accounts receivable and payable, inventories, and balance sheet accounts used in the calculation must be eliminated.

ILLUSTRATION 1.   In the example of Vatter Company previously given the receivable is shown net of the allowance for doubtful accounts. Also, because the amount of bad debt expense and the write-off of doubtful accounts are not disclosed, the amount we determined as collections from customers (as follows) is not entirely correct:

Receivables

B	360		
Sales	19,950	19,860	Collections (plug)
B	450		

Thus collections of $19,860 are overstated because noncash entries to the account were not considered.

If, however, we know that the opening and closing balances of the Allowance for Doubtful Accounts account are $20 and $25, respectively (generally disclosed), and that selling expenses include a provision for bad debts of $40 (only rarely disclosed), we can reconstruct the accounts and determine collections more accurately as follows:

	Receivables				**Allowance for Doubtful Accounts**		
B	380					20	B
		35	(b)	(b)	35	40	(a)
Sales	19,950	19,820	Collections (plug)				
B	475					25	B

(a) Bad debt expense—given.
(b) Bad debts written off—derived (plug).

Note that unadjusted collections of 19,860 are overstated by the amount of the bad debt expense.

Another example of a noncash entry exists when an entity includes depreciation costs in inventories. If, under the indirect method of computing CFO, the preparer does not adjust for these cost inclusions, the related increase in inventories is considered a cash outflow which it, in fact, is not.

Another important set of adjustments are needed when the entity purchases another company and consolidates its various assets and liabilities (full details including those of all operations-related accounts are seldom disclosed).

ILLUSTRATION 2.   *Assume* that Vatter Company purchased Company X in year 2 and that included were inventories of $500. If we do not know this we assume that the entire year-to-year increase in inventories of $303 relates to operations and this amount, as we saw in Exhibit 13–5, was used to reduce CFO.

However, with the acquisition information in hand, the adjusting entry changes to the following (focusing here only inventory):

Inventory   303
Cash-Operations   197
    Cash-Investing   500

Thus, the 197 *decrease* in inventory becomes an adjustment which *increases* CFO while the $500 cash outlay becomes part of the total amount paid for Company X included in investing activities.

The effect of a lack of adjustments does not affect *net* cash flows but does affect their proper classification among categories of activity.

Compromises with Reality

In *SFAS 95* the Board concedes that a "more comprehensive and presumably more useful approach would be to use the direct method in the Statement of Cash Flows and to provide a reconciliation of net income and net cash flow from operating activities in a separate schedule—thereby reaping the benefit of both methods while maintaining the focus of the Statement of Cash Flows in cash receipts and payments." And yet, the Board decided to encourage but not to require the direct method. As partial compensation to users the Board requires disclosure of interest and taxes paid as well as separate disclosure of changes in inventories, receivables, and payables.

Many other compromises with needs of analysts and other users are evident:

1. For unspecified reasons, *SFAS 95* does not require separate disclosure of cash flows pertaining to extraordinary items or discontinued operations.
2. In the interest of simplicity and in order to minimize the number of adjustments to net income:
    a. Interest and dividends received and interest paid are classified as operating cash flows, whereas some analysts consider interest paid as a financing outflow and interest and dividends received as cash inflows from investing activities.

   b. All income taxes are classified as operating cash flows even though such classification can distort the three major activity categories if significant tax benefits or costs arise from investing and/or financing activities.

   c. Similarly, the removal of pre-tax (rather than after-tax) gains or losses on sale of plant or investments from the operating activities category will distort this category as well as the investing activity category by the amount of related tax left as part of total tax expense in the operating activity category.

RECASTING THE SCF TO ANALYTICALLY DESIRABLE FORMATS

The analyst who prefers the analytically more significant inflow-outflow presentation will need to convert to it from the indirect presentation by using the methodology described above. Appendix A to Chapter 13 presents a worksheet which organizes and facilitates the conversion process. This appendix also presents the format of an analytically useful form of the SCF, so that a SCF presented in any other format can be converted into this more useful format.

DIFFERENT STATEMENTS—DIFFERENT OBJECTIVES

In the Vatter Company illustration, we have considered two statements (or portions of statements) that dealt with operations:

Income statement

Cash from operations (CFO)

There seems to be endless confusion, particularly among users of financial statements, about the concept of "operations" and about the different aspects of operations that these two statements are designed to portray.

A good way in which we can focus on the differences between these statements and on the different objectives they are designed to serve is to consider them side by side. Exhibit 13–7 presents this for the Vatter Company.

The function of the *income statement* is to measure the *profitability* of the enterprise for a given period. This is presently done by relating, as well as is possible, expenses and revenues. While no other statement measures profitability as well as the income statement, it does not show the *timing* of cash flows and the effect of operations on liquidity and solvency. This information is presented in the Statement of Cash Flows and its subset CFO which represents a different aspect of the same reality.

Exhibit 13–7

THE VATTER COMPANY
Comparison of Two Bases of Reporting

	Income statement	Operating cash receipts and disbursements (CFO)	
Sales	19,950	$19,860†	Collections from customers
Equity in earnings of unconsolidated subsidiary	50	—	
Gain on sale of fixed assets	2	—‡	
	20,002	19,860	Total collections
Cost of goods sold*	10,741	10,814§	Payments to suppliers and labor
Depreciation	360	—	
General selling and administrative expenses	7,000	7,000	Payments for expenses
Amortization of goodwill	30	—	
Income taxes: Current	900	900	Payments for taxes
deferred	20	—	
	19,051	18,714	Total disbursements
Net income	$ 951		
Cash from operations		$ 1,146	

* Exclusive of depreciation.
† $19,950 (sales)—$90 (increase in receivables).
‡ Omitted because it is linked up with proceeds from sale assets.
§ $10,741 (cost of goods sold) + $303 (increase in inventories)—$230 (increase in payables)
Note that the linkage of accounts payable to cost of goods sold is arbitrary because some may relate to other expense categories. However no further breakdown is possible.

Cash from Operations (CFO) encompasses the broader concept of operations of the two measures. Here we encompass all earning-related activities of the enterprise. As the earlier discussion made clear, here we are not concerned only with costs and revenues but also with the cash demands of these activities, such as investments in customer receivables and in inventories as well as the financing provided by suppliers of goods and services. This can be clearly seen from Exhibit 13–7, where we arrive at operating cash receipts and disbursements by adjusting the items comprising the income statement by changes in operating assets and liabilities.

The CFO focuses on the liquidity aspect of operations and is *not* a measure of profitability because it does not include important items of cost such as the use of long-lived assets in operations or revenue items such as the noncash equity in the earnings of nonconsolidated subsidiaries or affiliates.

Further Analytical Considerations

It must be borne in mind that a *net* figure, as such, be it net income, or CFO, is of very limited analytical value. Whether the purpose of the analyst is the evaluation of past performance or the prediction of future performance or conditions, the key to such analytical procedures is information about the *components* of such net measures.

As the discussion in Chapter 22 shows, the analyst, in the evaluation of operating performance and in the determination of present or future earning power, focuses not on net income but rather on the components that make up that number.

CFO, as a measure of performance, is less subject to distortion than is the net income figure. This is so because the accrual system, which produces the income number, relies on accruals, deferrals, allocations, and valuations, all of which involve higher degrees of subjectivity than what enters into the determination of CFO. For this reason, analysts prefer to relate CFO to reported net income as a check on the quality of that income. Some analysts believe that the higher the ratio of CFO to net income the higher the quality of that income. Put another way, a company with a high measure of net income and low cash flow may be using income recognition or expense accrual criteria which are suspect.

CFO can serve as a check on net income but *not* as a substitute for it. CFO has a financing rather than profit-measurement focus and is consequently particularly well suited to the evaluation and the projections of short-term liquidity and longer-term solvency.

The CFO concepts are subject to the limitation that they *exclude,* by definition, those elements of revenue and expense that do not currently affect cash. That, as we saw, means that they exclude from consideration such important costs as those associated with the operating use of long-lived assets. No comprehensive, longer-term analysis of operations and profitability should, of course, be undertaken without a consideration of all elements of costs and expenses.

Accounting is a complex measurement system governed by many conventions and specialized definitions. The special-purpose statements examined here, the income statement and that which measures CFO, have been developed to fill specialized needs by the use of specific and sometimes narrow perspectives.

The income statement properly uses accrual accounting so that all revenues earned and all costs and expenses incurred are given full recognition. CFO is alternatively concerned with which revenues have been received in cash and which costs and expenses have been paid for. It is never a question of which statement is superior to the other—only a matter of what we desire to measure. The valid analytical use of these statements requires that the analyst bear firmly in mind these specialized definitions as well as their inherent limitations.

CASH FLOW—CONFUSION IN TERMINOLOGY

The term *cash flow* was probably first coined by financial analysts. They recognized, long before accountants were ready to admit, that the accrual system of income measurement permits the introduction of a variety of alternative accounting treatments and possible distortions. Thus, the crude concept of cash flow, that is, net income plus the best-known non-cash expense (depreciation), was invented in order to bypass such possible distortions and to bring income measurement closer to the discipline of actual cash flows. This cash flow measure, a popular surrogate for cash from operations (CFO)[4] is crude because, as we have learned earlier in this chapter, it falls far short of even approximating, in most cases, the correct measure of CFO. It stayed crude because the people who developed and used it lacked the will or the accounting sophistications to improve it.

A valid analytical use that can be made of this crude measure of cash flow is when security analysts compare the earnings of companies *before* depreciation. In such cases the term *income before depreciation* (which, to be entirely correct, should be tax adjusted) is much better and accurate than the term *cash flow.* Such comparisons are made to eliminate differences that can arise from the variety of depreciation methods in use and the loose standards that govern assumptions of the useful lives of assets.

ILLUSTRATION 3.   The following example points up the distortions in net income comparisons that can occur due to the use of different depreciation methods. The use of different useful-life assumptions for the same kind of fixed assets can, of course, introduce additional distortions.

Assume that two companies (A and B) each invest $50,000 in a machine that generates $45,000 per year cash from operations before provision for depreciation. Thus, for the five-year assumed useful life of the machine, the results are as follows:

	Five-year period
Cash provided by operations	
($45,000 × 5 years)	$225,000
Cost of the machine	50,000
Income from operations of the machine	175,000
Average yearly net income	$ 35,000

However, the same $175,000 income over five years can be reported quite differently by using straight-line or sum-of-the-years'-digits depreciation. Thus (ignoring taxes), we have:

---

[4] It remains to be seen whether the correctly computed Cash from Operations figure, now more widely available because of *SFAS 95,* will drive the cruder measures out of circulation.

Year	Income before depreciation*	Company A: Straight-line depreciation		Company B: Sum-of-the-years'-digits depreciation	
		Depreciation	Net income	Depreciation	Net income
1	$ 45,000	$10,000	$ 35,000	$16,667	$ 28,333
2	45,000	10,000	35,000	13,334	31,666
3	45,000	10,000	35,000	10,000	35,000
4	45,000	10,000	35,000	6,667	38,333
5	45,000	10,000	35,000	3,332	41,668
Total	$225,000	$50,000	$175,000	$50,000	$175,000

* Popularly termed *cash flow.*

As the above example shows, the predepreciation "cash flow" of the two companies is identical, correctly indicating identical earning power. However the after-depreciation income, while identical for the entire five-year period, can be quite different on a year-to-year basis, depending on the depreciation method in use.

The use of *cash flow,* or, more properly labeled, *income before depreciation,* is thus a valid analytical tool so long as the user knows specifically what its significance is and what its limitations are.

The limitations of the cash flow concept are primarily due to the widespread confusion of the term's meaning and to its misuse.

One source of confusion stems from the incorrect computation of the crude measure of cash flow as noted above. The figure is simply not what it is represented to be.

Another and even more serious confusion arises from the assertion of some, and particularly those managements that are dissatisfied by the level of their reported net income, that cash flow is a measure of performance superior to or more valid than net income.[5] This is like saying that depreciation, or other costs not involving the use of cash, are not genuine expenses. This misconception is also discussed in Chapter 11. Only net income can be properly regarded as a measure of performance and can be validly related to the equity investment as an indicator of operating performance. If we add back depreciation to net income and compute the resulting return on investment, we are, in effect, confusing the return *on* investment with an element of return *of* investment in fixed assets. Moreover, it should also be borne in mind that not only is depreciation a valid cost but that in times of inflation the depreciation funds

---

[5] In *FRR No. 1* Sec. 202, the SEC concluded that certain approaches to cash flow reporting may be misleading to investors. Per share data other than that relating to net income, net assets, and dividends should be avoided in reporting financial results. *SFAS 95* prohibits the reporting of cash flow per share.

recovered from sales may not be sufficient to replace the equipment because the charges are based on the lower historical costs (see also Chapter 14).

ILLUSTRATION 4.   Coca-Cola Enterprises Inc. marketed a large initial share offering, not on the basis of traditional measures such as price earnings ratios (which would have been close to 100), but on the basis of "operating cash flow" (i.e., earnings *before* taxes, depreciation, interest, and amortization of goodwill). The latter far exceeded net income which was depressed because of heavy noncash charges.

  Warren Buffett, the successful value-based investor, when asked why the cash flow number is so often invoked, reportedly responded: "We believe those numbers are frequently used by marketers of businesses and securities in attempts to justify the unjustifiable (and thereby to sell what should be the unsalable)."

An essential fact to be understood is that aside from certain miscellaneous sources of income, the *basic* source of cash from operations in any enterprise is sales to customers. It is out of sales that all expenses are borne and a profit, if any, is earned. If the sales price is sufficient to cover *all* costs, that is, those requiring and those not requiring cash, then the process of sales will recover the depreciation costs in addition to other costs. If the sales price is not sufficiently high to cover total costs, depreciation will not be recovered or will not be fully recovered. Thus, the importance of revenues as *the* source of cash from operations should never be lost sight of.

The above discussion clearly points out that the financial analyst must approach the SCF as well as such concepts as "cash flow" and depreciation with understanding and with independence of viewpoint so as to avoid being trapped by the numerous cliches and useless generalizations which are all too often employed even by those who should know better.

IMPLICATIONS FOR ANALYSIS

The balance sheet portrays the variety of assets held by an entity at a given moment in time and the manner in which those assets are financed. The income statement portrays the results of operations for a specific fiscal period. Income results in increases of a variety of kinds of assets, some cash, some current, and some noncurrent. Expenses result in the consumption of different kinds of assets (or the incurrence of liabilities)—some cash, some of a current, and some of a noncurrent nature. Thus, net income cannot be equated with an increment in cash. It is quite conceivable that a very profitable enterprise may find it difficult to meet its current obligations and to lack cash for further expansion. The very fact that a business is successful in expanding sales may bring along with it a worsening of liquidity and the tying up of its cash in assets that cannot be liquidated in time to meet maturing obligations.

Clear thinking and analysis demands that we separate issues of operating performance and profitability from those concerned with the financing of the enterprise. Both are vital; they are interconnected; but they are not identical, and confusing the two can lead to fuzzy analysis.

The SCF sheds light on the effects of earning activities on cash resources, and on what assets were acquired and how they were financed. It can highlight more clearly the distinction between net income and cash provided by operations.

The ability of an enterprise to generate cash from operations on a consistent basis is an important indicator of financial health. No business can survive over the long term without generating cash from its operations. However, the interpretation of CFO figures and trends must be made with care and with a full understanding of all surrounding circumstances.

Prosperous as well as failing entities may find themselves unable to generate cash from operations at any given time—but for different reasons. The entity caught in the "prosperity squeeze" of having to invest its cash in receivables and inventories in order to meet ever-increasing customer demand will often find that its profitability will facilitate financing by equity as well as by debt. That same profitability should ultimately turn CFO into a positive figure. The unsuccessful firm, on the other hand, will find its cash drained by slowdowns in receivable and inventory turnovers, by operating losses, or by a combination of these factors. These conditions usually contain the seeds of further losses and cash drains and may also lead to the drying up of trade credit. In such cases, a lack of CFO has different implications. Even if the unsuccessful firm manages to borrow, the costs of borrowing will only magnify the ultimate drains of its cash. Thus, profitability is a key consideration, and while it does not insure CFO in the short run, it is essential to a healthy financial condition in the long run.

The unsuccessful or financially pressed firm can increase its CFO by reducing accounts receivable and inventories, but usually this is done at the expense of services to customers, which may lower future profitability.

Changes in operating working capital items must be interpreted in the light of attending circumstances. An increase in receivables may mean expanding consumer demand for enterprise products or it may mean an inability to collect amounts due in a timely fashion. Similarly, an increase in inventories (and particularly of the raw material component) may mean preparations for an increase in production in response to consumer demand. It may also mean, particularly if the finished goods component of inventories is increasing, an inability to sell (i.e., that anticipated demand has not materialized).

As the above discussion suggests, the evaluation and the interpretation of CFO must be done with great care and with a consideration of all surrounding circumstances.

Inflationary conditions add to the financial burdens and challenges of enterprises. Most significant among these are the needs to replace plant and equipment at costs far exceeding the related provision for depreciation, added investments in inventories and receivables, and a dividend distribution policy that is based on a profits calculus that does not provide fully for current costs of resources used up in operations (see also Chapter 14).

It is true to say that in times of inflation, a company's managerial decisions are not necessarily made on the basis of its published historical-cost statements. The analyst, however, looks to the SCF for information on the fund effects, in *current* dollars, of how managements have actually coped under such conditions. This leads to a focus on how much cash the management had available after deducting from CFO capital expenditures and dividends.

The Concept of Free Cash Flow

A valuable analytical derivative of the SCF is the computation of *free cash flow*. As with any other analytical measure, analysts must pay careful attention to components of the computation. Here, as in the case of "cash flow" measures (see discussion below) ulterior motives may sometimes affect the validity of the computation.

One of the analytically most useful computations of free cash flow is as follows:

Start with Cash from Operations (CFO)

Deduct   Capital expenditures required to maintain productive capacity used up in the production of income

Dividends (on preferred stock and maintenance of desired payout on common stock)

Equals   Free Cash Flow (FCF)

If a company has a FCF that means that this is the amount available for corporate purposes after provisions for financing outlays and expenditures to maintain productive capacity at current levels.[6] Internal growth and financial flexibility depend on an adequate amount of FCF.

Note that the amount of capital expenditures needed to maintain productive capacity at current levels is generally not disclosed by companies.[7] It is included in total capital expenditures which may also include outlays for expansion of productive capacity. Breaking down capital expenditures

---

[6] See also discussion of this concept in A. C. Sondhi, G. H. Sorter, and G. I. White in "Transactional Analysis," *Financial Analysts Journal,* September-October 1987.

[7] One known exception is Celanese Corp.

between these two components is difficult. The repeal of mandatory inflation disclosures (*SFAS 89*) made this task even more difficult. The FASB considered this issue and in *SFAS 95* decided not to require classification of investment expenditures into maintenance and expansion categories.

Other Analytical Uses

The SCF is also of great value to the analyst who wants to project operating results on the basis of productive capacity acquired and planned to be acquired, and who wants to assess a company's future capacity to expand, its capital needs, and the sources from which they may be met. The statement is, thus, an essential bridge between the income statement and the balance sheet.

The SCF probably owes its inception to a desire to learn about the inflows and outflows of liquid resources through a business. However, the SCF can provide more than information on the changes in cash and their effect on a company's ability to meet current obligations. To the financial analyst, the statement provides important clues to matters such as:

1. Feasibility of financing capital expenditures and possible sources of such financing.
2. Sources of cash to finance an expansion in the volume of business.
3. Dependence of the enterprise on external sources of financing, for example, borrowing or new equity.
4. Future dividend policies.
5. Ability to meet future debt service requirements.
6. Financial flexibility, that is, the firm's ability to generate sufficient cash so as to respond to unanticipated needs and opportunities.
7. An insight into the financial habits of management and resulting indications of future policies.
8. Indications regarding the quality of earnings.

Regarding the last-mentioned use, the SCF is useful for identifying misleading or erroneous operating results. Analysts are aware that cash flows are not as easy to manipulate as are accrual-based bookkeeping entries. In the income statement true operating results may be masked for a time through the use of devices such as premature revenue recognition or unwarranted cost deferrals. A further discussion of earnings quality will be found in Chapter 22.

The SCF as a summary of overall investment and financing activities of an enterprise is, of course, far more reliable and credible evidence of a company's actions and intentions than are the statements and speeches of its management.

The analyst must be careful to examine the form in which the SCF is presented. Some transactions are definitely related such as, for example, the purchase of certain assets and the issuance of debt. The analyst must, however, be careful not to impute relationships among items merely on the basis of their presentation lest misleading conclusions are reached.

The significance of a change in liquidity, whether positive or negative, cannot be judged by means of the statement of cash flows alone. It must, of course, be related to other variables in a company's financial structure and operating results. Thus, for example, an increase of cash may have been gained by selling off various assets whose earning power will be missed in the future; or the increase may have been financed by means of incurrence of debt which is subject to high costs and/or onerous repayment terms.

RESEARCH INTO THE USEFULNESS OF CASH FLOW NUMBERS

Over the years there has been a growing interest in information concerning funds flows and, in particular, cash flows. A study prepared for the Financial Accounting Foundation[8] focused on what key users are looking for in financial reports. It found "an important shift away from the traditional importance given to income measurement." Two thirds of those interviewed identified funds flows (a broader concept than cash flows) as highly important to users of financial reports.

Backer and Gosman[9] found that information about funds flows is important in credit analysis. The ratio of funds flows to total debt was found to be of great importance to the analysis of creditworthiness for intermediate-term bank loans and for long-term bonds.

Beaver,[10] in a study of the usefulness of financial information for the prediction of business failure, found that the ratio of funds flow to debt was one of the most reliable predictors.

In their research into investment-decision practices, Hawkins and Campbell[11] found that funds flows analysis was used to examine the ability of a company to finance capital expenditures and dividends from internal sources. They also found that the relationship between cash flows and earnings was used in the assessment of the quality of those earnings.

---

[8] Louis Harris and Associates, Inc., *A Study of the Attitudes Toward and an Assessment of the Financial Accounting Standards Board* (Stamford, Conn.: Financial Accounting Foundation, 1980).

[9] M. Backer and M. L. Gosman, *Financial Reporting and Business Liquidity* (New York: National Association of Accountants, 1978).

[10] W. H. Beaver, "Alternative Accounting Measures as Predictors of Failure," *The Accounting Review,* January 1968.

[11] D. F. Hawkins and W. J. Campbell, *Equity Valuation: Models, Analysis and Implications* (New York: Financial Executives Research Foundation, 1978).

Thus they found that the funds statement has become the key financial statement for many institutional researchers and investors.

A number of academic studies[12] have been undertaken with the objective of testing, on a statistical basis, whether CFO numbers can predict insolvency. The basic test in such studies is whether the behavior of CFO numbers, per se, prior to the insolvency or bankruptcy event, has predictive value.

Although these studies are serious and commendable efforts, the problem with them and with the conclusions derived from them is that, as the discussion in this chapter brought out, in actual analysis for any serious purpose, we do not use such numbers per se but use them only in conjunction with an examination of the detailed factors which comprise them as well as all the surrounding and attending circumstances.

Broad statistical studies do not focus on the components of CFO nor do they, nor can they, capture or incorporate the varied and ever-changing attending circumstances which every serious analysis must consider. Moreover, because of the complexities which attend the computation as well as the analytical adjustments of CFO numbers, the computer-stored databases on which such studies rely are easily contaminated by inaccuracies and inconsistencies in the data.

APPENDIX 13A

WORKSHEETS TO CONVERT DATA TO CASH FROM OPERATIONS (INFLOW-OUTFLOW FORMAT) AND TO THE ANALYTICAL STATEMENT OF CASH FLOWS

Worksheet to Convert Data to CFO (Inflow-Outflow Format)

As was discussed earlier in the chapter, the analyst may want to convert a company's indirect presentation of CFO to the analytically more significant inflow-outflow format.[13] Form A is a worksheet designed to facilitate this process. The sources for data for this worksheet are generally

---

[12] See, for example, C. J. Casey and N. J. Bartczak, "Cash Flow—It's Not the Bottom Line," *Harvard Business Review,* July-August 1984, and letters to the editor in subsequent issues. This study concluded that the CFO number has little predictive value. In "Predicting Bankruptcy: If Cash Flows Not the Bottom Line, What is?," *Financial Analysts Journal,* September-October 1985, J. A. Gentry, P. Newbold, and D. T. Whitford reach an opposite conclusion. J. M. Gallon and R. L. Wigeland in "Early Warning Signs of Bankruptcy Using Cash Flow Analysis," *The Journal of Commercial Bank Lending,* December 1988, identify cash flow variables which capture significant differences between bankrupt and nonbankrupt firms as many as five years prior to bankruptcy.

[13] Research by T. P. Klammer and S. A. Reed, "Operating Cash Flow Formats: Does Format Influence Decisions?," *Journal of Accounting and Public Policy,* 217–35 (1990) concludes that analysts and loan officers presented with an indirect format produced different loan decisions than did those presented with the direct approach. Their perception was affected by arrangement of the cash flows. The direct method of displaying cash flows from operating activities reduced errors and enhanced the user's ability to understand and apply information.

the SCF, the income statement, and relevant footnotes to the financial statements. In cases of inadequate disclosure, changes in balance sheet accounts and reconstruction of transactions (see Appendix B of this chapter) may also be necessary. The footnotes to the worksheet elaborate on items to be included, their source as well as reconciliation to key items in the financial statements.

Many items which are taken from published financial statements to the inflow-outflow worksheet should, because of the requirements of *SFAS 95,* be more accurate and relevant than was the case heretofore. That is so because the *SFAS 95* presentation requires companies to use information, available only from internal records, in order to effect adjustments such as for noncash entries and for acquisitions of assets and liabilities related to operations (see also discussion in this chapter).

In other areas, *SFAS 95* is not as helpful to the analyst. For the evaluation of current cash flows and to facilitate the forecasting of future cash flows from operations, analysts need to know the cash effects of extraordinary items and of discontinued operations. Unfortunately the Statement is explicit in not requiring such disclosures. Thus, information on such cash effects can be inserted on these worksheets only on the basis of voluntary disclosures by managements or as a result of inquiries from them.

Worksheet to Convert Data to an Analytical Statement of Cash Flows

Conceptually, the Statement of Cash Flows required by *SFAS 95* represents, from the viewpoint of the analyst, an important improvement on its predecessors. Its analytical value and significance depends, however, on how well the letter and the spirit of this standard is implemented in actual practice.

Some Statements of Cash Flows will be presented in a format and with a degree of detailed disclosures that will meet the needs of financial analysts. The analyst must however be prepared to modify and recast any published statements that do not meet his or her needs.

Form B is designed to facilitate the recasting of any statement of cash flows, or of funds however defined, into an analytically useful SCF. The process involves inserting *all* amounts found in the statement to be recast into the analytical statement of cash flows which conforms generally to the requirements of *SFAS 95*.

IMPROVING AND ADJUSTING THE SCF FORMAT

In some cases, the analyst may need to examine the format of the SCF in order to determine whether the explanations of changes in balance sheet accounts in the statement are adequate to serve his or her purposes. To the extent that such explanations appear not to be adequate, the analyst should reconstruct all or selected accounts in order to determine the extent of missing information that needs to be obtained or taken into account. Only a complete reconstruction will assure that all aspects of transactions listed in the SCF have been considered, but such a step is not always required. Appendix B illustrates such a reconstruction of transactions.

Information that is gleaned from such a reconstruction or from a further analysis of disclosures should be presented in footnotes to the cash statement so that the reader can fully understand the details as well as the limitations of the statement.

EXAMPLE 1.   When operations are discontinued during a period, their effect on operations is often given only in net or aggregate form (e.g., if pro forma net income or loss and sales are provided total expenses can be derived). Because the related changes in operating current assets and liabilities are usually not disclosed, discontinued operations can generally not be segregated from continuing operations.

The analyst must also consider whether income statement or SCF items need to be adjusted or rearranged to make them responsive to the analyst's need or assumptions. As is illustrated in the example that follows, such adjustments are made by adding an "adjustments" column to the analytical statement of cash flows.

The following are additional examples of such adjustments.

EXAMPLE 2.   The operating-nonoperating distinction is merely one of definition or convenience. Thus, we consider an outlay for long-lived productive assets as nonoperating simply because their costs do not enter the income statement in the year of acquisition. The same is true of the acquisition of a patent that is amortized rather than immediately expensed or motion-picture films that are amortized as costs over a number of fiscal periods. The analyst must decide what a useful definition of operations is in any given situation. Thus, he or she will choose to consider changes in noncurrent receivables as relating to operations to the extent that they arose from the sale of operating assets such as inventories. Such information is often not found in published financial statements but *SFAS 95* requires that managements do take it into account when preparing an SCF.

EXAMPLE 3.   When a company sells its receivables to a financial institution with recourse, the risk of ownership of these receivables remains with that company. Consequently, the analyst may choose not to consider the reduction in receivables occurring because of such sales as equivalent to collections from customers, but rather as short-term borrowing. Analytically this is accomplished by reducing cash receipts from operations and increasing short-term borrowing. (A financing source of cash.)

EXAMPLE 4.   When a business is purchased during a period, information on operating working capital items acquired is often available only in the aggregate. Thus, part of the change in receivables, inventories, or payables may be due to the acquisition and should not be used to adjust sales and cost of sales which affect operating

FORM A
Worksheet to Compute Cash Flow from Operations (CFO)
Inflow—Outflow Presentation
For: _____

Year Ended _____

(in thousands)

		Year	
	20____	*20____*	*20____*
Operating cash receipts and disbursements:			
Cash receipts from operations:			
Net sales or revenues[a] *1	$	$	$
Other revenue and income (see also lines 22 and 25) *2			
(I) D in current receivables 3			
(I) D in noncurrent receivables[b] 4			
Other adjustments[c] 5			
= Cash collections 6			
Cash disbursements for operations:			
Total expenses (include interest and taxes)[a] . *7			
Less: Expenses and losses not using cash:			
– Depreciation and amortization 8			
– Noncurrent deferred income taxes, etc. ... 9			
– Other _____ 10			
– Other _____ 11			
– Other _____ 12			
Changes in current assets and liabilities related to operations:			
I (D) in inventories 13			
I (D) in prepaid expense 14			
(I) D in accounts payable 15			
(I) D in taxes payable 16			
(I) D in accruals 17			
I or D other _____ 18			
I or D other _____ 19			
I or D in noncurrent accounts[b] 20			
= Cash disbursements for operations[d] 21			

Dividends received:

Equity in income of unconsolidated affiliates *22 _____ _____ _____

  – Undistributed equity in income of affiliates 23 _____ _____ _____

  = Dividends from unconsolidated affiliates .. 24 ══════ ══════ ══════

Other cash receipts (disbursements)[e] ....*25 ══════ ══════ ══════

Describe _____[a] .... 25 _____ _____ _____

_____[b] .... 25 _____ _____ _____

Cash flow from operations[f] .... 26 ══════ ══════ ══════

---

* These five lines must equal reported net income per income statement.

[a] Including adjustments (grossing up) of revenue and expense of discontinued operations disclosed in footnote(s). Describe computation. Include other required adjustments and describe fully.

[b] Which have been determined to relate to operations—describe in footnotes.

[c] Such as removal of gains included above—describe in footnotes.

[d] Which include (from supplemental disclosures):

  Cash paid for interest (net of amount capitalized) .... $_____ _____ _____

  Cash paid for income taxes .... $_____ _____ _____

[e] These include extraordinary items, discontinued operations and any other item not included above. The amount in line 25 is *after* adjustment to cash basis while the * refers to item(s) included in income *before* such adjustment. (Present details in footnotes.)

[f] Reconcile to amount reported by company. If not reported, reconcile to change in cash for period along with investing and financing activities.

Footnote all amounts which are composites or which are not self-evident. Indicate all sources for figures.

FORM B
Analytical Statement of Cash Flows*
For: _____
Year Ended _____
(in thousands)

		Year		
		_20 _____	_20 _____	_20 _____
Cash flow from operations:				
Income before extraordinary items	1	$ _____	$ _____	$ _____
Add (deduct) adjustments to cash basis:				
Depreciation and amortization	2	_____	_____	_____
Deferred income taxes	3	_____	_____	_____
Equity in income of investees	4	_____	_____	_____
.... [a]	5	_____	_____	_____
.... [a]	6	_____	_____	_____
(I) D in receivables	7	_____	_____	_____
(I) D in inventories	8	_____	_____	_____
(I) D in prepaid expenses	9	_____	_____	_____
I (D) in accounts payable	10	_____	_____	_____
I (D) in accruals	11	_____	_____	_____
I (D) in taxes payable	12	_____	_____	_____
I or D in other current operating accounts[a]	13	_____	_____	_____
I or D in noncurrent accounts relating to operations[a]	14	_____	_____	_____
Extraordinary items net of noncash items[b]	15	_____	_____	_____
Discontinued operations net of noncash items[b]	16	_____	_____	_____
Cash from operations[c]	17	_____	_____	_____
Cash flows from investing activities:				
Additions to properties	18	_____	_____	_____
Additions to investments (advances)	19	_____	_____	_____
Additions to other assets	20	_____	_____	_____
Cost of acquisition—net of cash	21	_____	_____	_____
Disposals of properties	22	_____	_____	_____
Decreases in other assets[a]	23	_____	_____	_____
Other[a]	24	_____	_____	_____
Total sources (uses)	25	_____	_____	_____

Cash flows from financing activities:

Net I (D) in short-term debt . . . . 26 _____ _____ _____

I (D) in long-term debt . . . . 27 _____ _____ _____

I (D) of common and preferred stock[a] . . . . . . 28 _____ _____ _____

Dividends paid . . . . 29 _____ _____ _____

Other[a] . . . . 30 _____ _____ _____

      Total sources (uses) . . . . 31 _____ _____ _____

Effect of exchange rate changes on cash: . . . . . . 32 _____ _____ _____

Net increase (decrease) in cash and   33 _____ _____ _____
equivalents . . . . _____ _____ _____

Schedule of noncash activities[a]:

. . . . 34 _____ _____ _____

. . . . 35 _____ _____ _____

. . . . 36 _____ _____ _____

* Use all figures from company's Statement of Cash Flows (or other funds statement).

[a] Provide full details in statement or in separate footnotes.

[b] This information is not required by *SFAS 95*. Provide details if this information is disclosed or can otherwise be obtained or reconstructed.

[c] To convert to the inflow-outflow format use Form A.

cash flows for the period. *SFAS 95* requires that operating cash flows be adjusted for assets or liabilities acquired in a purchase of a business. However, if the analyst determines that such adjustments have not been made, he or she must footnote the analytical SCF accordingly.

The following is a simplified example of the adjustments which the acquiring company must make in preparing an SCF in accordance with *SFAS 95:*

Entry for purchase of Company X (in $000)

Cash	20	
Accounts Receivable	200	
Inventories	300	
Other assets (including goodwill)	600	
Payables		120
Other liabilities		400
Cash		600

In preparing the SCF an investing outlay of cash of $580 ($600 − $20) will be shown and the gross changes in operating working capital items will be adjusted as follows:

Accounts receivable	reduced by $200
Inventories	reduced by $300
Payables	reduced by $120

After adjustment of all other assets and liabilities, the total will equal the $580 investment in Company X. In this way, for example, the increase in accounts receivable of $200 will not be attributed to uncollected sales (i.e., operations) but rather to part of the investing cash outflow.

ILLUSTRATION OF THE RECASTING AND ADJUSTING PROCESS

We will now illustrate the recasting of Campbell Soup Company's published SCF into the analytically more useful formats shown in Forms A and B above. We will also make the following adjustment:

> For purposes of this illustration *only* we assume that Campbell disposed of a division in 1991 which had revenues of $1.2 million and an after-tax loss of $100,000. This after-tax loss is included in expenses. In the adjustment we substitute for the after-tax loss of $100,000; revenues of $1.2 million and expenses of $1.3 million minus the loss of $100,000 already included.

Exhibit 13A–1 shows the recasting process by means of Form A and Exhibit 13A–2 presents the recasting process by means of Form B. Campbell acquired the balance of "Campbell Canada" in 1991. In computing

FORM A

Worksheet to Compute Cash Flow from Operations (CFO)

Inflow–Outflow Presentation

For: Campbell Soup Company

Year Ended July 28, 1991

(in millions)

		1991 Reported	Adjustments	1991 Revised	Year 19___	19___	19___
Operating cash receipts and disbursements:							
Cash receipts from operations:							
Net sales	*1	$ 6204.1	$ 1.2[(d)]	$ 6202.9	$	$	$
Other revenue and income[(e)]	*2						
(I) D in current receivables	3	17.1		17.1			
(I) D in noncurrent receivables	4						
Other adjustments	5						
= Cash collections	6	6221.2	1.2	6220.0			
Cash disbursements for operations:							
Total expenses (include interest and taxes)[(a)(e)]	*7	5805.0	(1.2)[(d)]	5803.8			
Less: Expenses and losses not using cash:							
– Depreciation and amortization	8	(208.6)		(208.6)			
– Noncurrent deferred income taxes, etc.	9	(35.5)		(35.5)			
– Other, Net[(c)]	10	(57.4)		(57.4)			
– Other	11						
– Other	12						

Changes in current assets and liabilities related to operations:

I (D) in inventories	13	(48.7)		(48.7)
I (D) in prepaid expense	14			
(I) D in accounts payable	15			
(I) D in taxes payable	16			
(I) D in accruals, payrolls, etc.	17			
	18			—
I or D other current assets & liab.	19	(30.6)		(30.6)
I or D in noncurrent accounts	20			
= Cash disbursements for operations	21	5424.2	(1.2)	5423.0

Dividends received:

Equity in income of unconsolidated affiliates	*22	2.4	2.4
Distribution in excess of income of affiliate 169A	23	5.8	5.8
= Dividends from unconsolidated affiliates 169A	24	8.2	8.2
Other cash receipts (disbursements)	*25		
Describe _____ (a)	25		
_____ (b)	25		
Cash flow from operations (b)	26	805.2	805.2

* These five lines must equal reported net income per income statement.

(a) Total expenses 22A + taxes on earnings 27 + minority interests 25 (5531.9 + 265.9 + 7.2)

(b) As reported

(c) 60 − (Line 24 − Line 22) ⇒ 63.2 − (8.2 − 2.4) = $57.4. Dividends received from Armotts Ltd 169A $8.2 exceeds Equity in Earnings of affiliates 24 of $2.4. This difference is removed from other, net 60 of $63.2 and included on line 23.

(d) To record revenues of discontinued operations and expenses of discontinued operations of $1.3mil minus loss from discontinued operations of $.1mil.

(e) It is also acceptable to remove interest income of $26 from total expenses and include it on line 2.

Exhibit 13A–2

FORM B
Analytical Statement of Cash Flows*
For: Campbell Soup Company
Year Ended July 28, 1991
(in millions)

		1991 As reported	Adjustments[b]	1991 Revised	19___	19___	19___
Cash flow from operations:							
[56] Income before extraordinary items	1	$ 401.5	$	$	$	$	$
Add (deduct) adjustments to cash basis:							
[57] Depreciation and amortization	2	208.6					
[59] Deferred income taxes	3	35.5					
Equity in income of investees	4						
[60] Other—net	5	63.2					
Decrease in Dividend Payable	6						
[61] (I) D in receivables	7	17.1					
[62] (I) D in inventories	8	48.7					
(I) D in prepaid expenses	9						
I (D) in accounts payable	10						
I (D) in accruals, payrolls, etc.	11						
I (D) in taxes payable	12						
[63] I or D in other current operating accounts	13	30.6					
I or D in noncurrent accounts relating to operations[a]	14						
Extraordinary items net of noncash items[a]	15						
Discontinued operations net of noncash items[a]	16						
Cash from operations	17	805.2					

Cash flows from investing activities:

|63| Additions to properties .... 18 | (361.1) |
Additions to investments (advances) ... 19 |
69	Additions to other assets 20	(57.8)
67	Cost of acquisition—net of cash 21	(180.1)
66	Disposals of properties 22	43.2
68	Decreases in other assets[a] 23	67.4
70	Other[a]—Net change in temp.
investments 24	9.7
Total sources (uses) .... 25 | (478.7) |

Cash flows from financing activities:

|74| + |75| – |76| Net I (D) in short-term debt .... 26 | (227.0) |
|72| – |73| I (D) in long-term debt
($402.8 – 129.9) .... 27 | 272.9 |
|78| – |79| I (D) of common and preferred stock—
Treasury Stock (net)[a] ($175.6 –
47.7) .... 28 | (127.9) |
|77| Dividends paid .... 29 | (137.5) |
|80| Other net[a] .... 30 | (0.1) |
Total sources (uses) .... 31 | (219.6) |

|82| Effect of exchange rate changes on cash: .. 32 | (8.7) |

|83| Net increase (decrease) in cash and
equivalents .... 33 | 98.2 |

Schedule of noncash activities[a]:

.... 34
.... 35
.... 36

* Use all figures from company's statements of cash flows.
[a] Provide full details in statement or in separate footnotes.
[b] No adjustments required in this case.

480

CFO the company, to conform with the requirements of *SFAS 95,* probably adjusted operating assets and liabilities for amounts included in the acquisition (see entry (4) of analysis of unexplained differences on page 488).

APPENDIX 13B

ANALYTICAL RECONSTRUCTION OF ALL TRANSACTIONS

As was indicated in Appendix A, a reconstruction, in the aggregate, of all transactions for a period can determine whether the SCF satisfactorily explains all the changes in the balance sheet accounts, can provide additional information that is helpful in understanding the SCF, and generally can provide analytically useful insights into the aggregate transactions of a period and the relationships among them.

In the process of reconstruction, light is shed on those summary transactions which management, for whatever reason, has chosen not to disclose and to combine in categories usually designated as "Other-net." In addition to immaterial items and nonsignificant noncash transactions, various adjustments, such as those relating to acquisitions and disposals, will result in unexplained differences in the reconstruction. While such undisclosed adjustments can relieve the SCF of unimportant detail (such as stock dividends or the write-off of fully depreciated assets) they can also hide significant transactions (such as new investments) about which the analyst needs to know. This process also provides a check on management's classification and descriptions of items in the SCF.

The process of *reconstruction* is basically the reverse of the process of preparing the SCF as outlined in Chapter 13. The steps of reconstruction are as follows:

1. Establish T-accounts for all noncash accounts and one master T-account for cash with subdivisions for (1) Operations, (2) Investing Activities, (3) Financing Activities, and (4) Noncash Transactions.
2. Insert opening and closing balances in all accounts. Check to see that when added up, the debits and credits of all accounts are in balance.
3. Use *all* the items in the SCF as well as additional information found in other financial statements, in footnotes, and elsewhere to reconstruct all the T-accounts.
4. Items which cannot be posted to specific T-accounts, as well as amounts needed to balance T-accounts, are posted to an Unexplained Differences account which must balance. (If it does not, an error in posting or arithmetic has been made.) Based on all available information, these unexplained differences are analyzed and explained as best as is possible.

Exhibit 13B–1

CAMPBELL SOUP COMPANY
Reconstruction of T-Accounts
For the Year Ended July 28, 1991

Cash and Equivalents

Beg.	80.7

Operations

56	Net income	401.5
57	Depreciation & amortization	208.6
59	Deferred taxes	35.5
60	Other, net	63.2
61	Decrease in account receivables	17.1
62	Decrease in inventories	48.7
63	Net change in other current assets and liabilities	30.6

Investing, Financing,* and Other

66	Sales of plant assets	43.2	361.1	65	Purchase of plant assets
68	Sales of business	67.4	180.1	67	Business acquired
70	Net change in other temporary investments	9.7	57.8	69	Increase in other assets
72	Long-term borrowings	402.8	129.9	73	Repayments of long-term borrowings
75	Other-short-term borrowings	117.3	137.9	74	Decrease in borrowings with less than 3 month borrowings
79	Treasury stock issued	47.7	206.4	76	Repayments of other short-terms borrowings
			137.5	77	Dividends paid
			175.6	78	Treasury stocks purchases
			0.1	80	Other, net
			8.7	82	Exchange rate effect to cash

Ending	178.9

* These two categories, as well as the noncash category may be shown separately.

Temporary Investments				Accounts Receivables			
Beg.	22.5	9.7	70	Beg.	624.5	17.1	61
						80.0	A
Ending	12.8			Ending	527.4		

Inventories

Beg.	819.8	48.7	[62]
		64.4	[B]
Ending	706.7		

Prepaid Expenses

Beg.	118.0	25.3	[C]
Ending	92.7		

Plant Assets—Net

[161A] [65]	Beg. 2,734.9	174.1	[D]
	361.1		
[161A]	End. 2,921.9		

Accumulated Depreciation

[E]		80.2	1,017.2	Beg. [162]
			194.5	[57]
			1,131.5	End. [162]

Intangible Assets—Net

Beg.	383.4	14.1	[57]
[F]	66.2		
Ending	435.5		

Other Assets

Beg.	349.0	2.2	[G]
[69]	57.8		
Ending	404.6		

Notes Payable

[74]	137.9	202.3	Beg.
[76]	206.4	117.3	[75]
		306.9	[H]
		282.2	Ending

Payable to Suppliers & Others

[I]	42.8	525.2	Beg.
		482.4	Ending

Accrued Liabilities

[J]	83.2	491.9	Beg.
		408.7	Ending

Dividends Payable

	32.3	Beg.
	4.7	[K]
	37.0	Ending

Accrued Income Taxes

	46.4	Beg.
	21.3	[L]
	67.7	Ending

Long-Term Debt

[73]	129.9	805.8	Beg.
[M]	306.1	402.8	[72]
		772.6	Ending

Deferred Income Taxes

N	12.1	235.1	Beg. 176
		35.5	59
		258.5	End. 176

Other Liabilities

O	5.5	28.5	Beg. 177
		23.0	End. 177

Minority Interest

P	32.8	56.3	Beg. 178
		23.5	End. 178

Common Stock

	20.3	Beg.
	20.3	Ending

Capital Surplus

	61.9	Beg.
	45.4	Q
	107.3	Ending

Retained Earnings

77	137.5	1,653.3	Beg.
R	4.7	401.5	56
		1,912.6	Ending

Treasury Stocks

Beg.	107.2	47.7	79
78	175.6		
S	35.3		
Ending	270.4		

Cumulative Translation Adj.

T	39.9	63.5	Beg.
		23.6	Ending

Unexplained Differences

67	Business acquired	180.1	63.2	60	Other, net
80	Other, net	0.1	30.6	63	Net change in other current assets and liabilities
82	Exchange rate effect on cash	8.7	43.2	66	Sales of plant assets
A	Account receivables	80.0	67.4	68	Sales of business
B	Inventories	64.4	80.2	E	Accumulated depreciation
C	Prepaid expenses	25.3	66.2	F	Intangible assets
D	Plant assets—net	174.1	42.8	I	Payable to suppliers and others
G	Other assets	2.2			
H	Notes payable	306.9	83.2	J	Accrued liabilities
K	Dividend payable	4.7	306.1	M	Long-term debt
L	Accrued income taxes	21.3	12.1	N	Deferred income taxes
Q	Capital surplus	45.4	5.5	O	Other liabilities
			32.8	P	Minority interest
			4.7	R	Retained earnings
			35.3	S	Treasury stock
			39.9	T	Cumulative translation adj.
		913.2	913.2		

Exhibit 13B–1 presents the reconstruction of the T-accounts of Campbell Soup Co. for 1991 (see Appendix B to Chapter 4). Note that *all* items in the SCF are listed in the cash T-account. In order not to omit any items from consideration, the best way of doing this systematically is to list the items in the exact order in which they appear in the SCF. Placing the corresponding debits or credits in the related T-accounts requires a basic knowledge of accounting as well as use of all available information found within the financial report.

As the posting journal entries indicate, most items can readily be posted to the appropriate account or accounts. However, a number of items cannot be posted to a logical contra T-account and must consequently be posted to an Unexplained Differences T-account which is best analyzed after all unexplained items have been posted to it.

After the posting process is completed, we review all T-accounts in order to determine whether in each of them the posted items explain fully the change from the opening to the closing balance. In some T-accounts unexplained debit or credits are needed (plugged) in order to reconcile the account. These are posted on the opposite side (debit or credit) of the Unexplained Differences account and keyed in with letters (A, B, C, etc.) for ease of reference and checking.

To summarize, the items posted to the Unexplained Differences Account (U.D. A/C) include the following categories:

  I. Items whose description in the SCF is inadequate to enable a posting to a related T-account. For example, "Other, net" (items 60 and 80) or items such as "Effect of exchange rate changes on cash." 82.

 II. Items which are part of complex transactions such as "Businesses acquired" 67, "Sales of businesses" 68, or "Net change in other current assets and liabilities" 63 which represent an aggregation of assets and liabilities which relate to operations.

III. Items needed to balance all T-accounts after all items from the statement of cash flows have been posted. These are items identified as (A) (B) (C). . . . and so on.

Since the plugged amounts in the individual accounts must equal the unexplained items already posted to the Unexplained Differences account the account must balance.

The posting of all above-described items to the U.D. A/C facilitates their analysis as will be exemplified below.

The following journal entries are used here to explain in detail the posting of each item in Campbell's SCF to the related T-accounts.

56	Cash—Operations	401.5	
	Retained Earnings		401.5
57	Cash—Operations	208.6	
	Accumulated Depreciation 187		194.5
	Intangible Assets—Net		14.1

59	Cash—Operations	35.5	
	Deferred income taxes		35.5
60	Cash—Operations	63.2	
	Unexplained Differences		63.2

We know this amount to be composed of a
number of items. We transfer it to the
unexplained T-account. After all items are
posted we will be in a better position to
assign its amount to the proper accounts.

61	Cash—Operations	17.1	
	Account Receivables		17.1
62	Cash—Operations	48.7	
	Inventories		48.7
63	Cash—Operations	30.6	
	Unexplained Differences		30.6

This amount is also composed of a number
of items related to current assets and
liabilities. Therefore, we post it to the
unexplained T-account.

65	Plant Assets—Net	361.1	
	Cash—Investing		361.1
66	Cash—Investing	43.2	
	Unexplained Differences		43.2

Since we do not know the book value for
assets sold, we transfer this amount to
unexplained T-account.

67	Unexplained Differences	180.1	
	Cash—Investing		180.1

This amount represents business acquired
which relates to a number of different
accounts. The best way is to post it to the
unexplained T-account.

68	Cash—Investing	67.4	
	Unexplained Differences		67.4

We do not have enough information on the
sales of business. Hence, we transfer this
amount to the unexplained T-account.

69	Other Assets	57.8	
	Cash—Investing		57.8
70	Cash—Investing	9.7	
	Temporary Investments		9.7
72	Cash—Financing	402.8	
	Long-term Debt		402.8

| 73 | Long-term Debt .... | 129.9 | |
| | Cash—Financing .... | | 129.9 |

| 74 | Notes Payable .... | 137.9 | |
| | Cash—Financing .... | | 137.9 |

| 75 | Cash—Financing .... | 117.3 | |
| | Notes Payable .... | | 117.3 |

| 76 | Notes Payable .... | 206.4 | |
| | Cash—Financing .... | | 206.4 |

| 77 | Retained Earnings .... | 137.5 | |
| | Cash—Financing .... | | 137.5 |

| 78 | Treasury Stocks .... | 175.6 | |
| | Cash—Financing .... | | 175.6 |

| 79 | Cash—Financing .... | 47.7 | |
| | Treasury Stocks .... | | 47.7 |

| 80 | Unexplained Differences .... | 0.1 | |
| | Cash—Financing .... | | 0.1 |

Again, we post it to unexplained T-account because we do not know to which accounts this amount is related.

| 82 | Unexplained Differences .... | 8.7 | |
| | Cash—Financing .... | | 8.7 |

We do not know to what specific accounts these translation adjustments relate, so they are posted to unexplained T-account.

CAMPBELL SOUP COMPANY
Analysis of Unexplained Differences
For Year Ended July 28, 1991

Ref.
Items

⟨**1**⟩

| R | Retained Earnings .... | 4.7 | |
| K | Dividend Payable .... | | 4.7 |

Non-cash entry

⟨**2**⟩

| M | Long-term Debt .... | 306.1 | |
| H | Notes Payable .... | | 306.9 |

Transfer from long-term debt to current, unexplained = 0.8

⟨ 3 ⟩

	Cash (or receivables)	22.5	
S	Treasury Stock	35.3	
Q	Remaining Capital Surplus		45.4
	Treasury stock issued—Management Incentive and Stock Option Plan—see data in 91 —unexplained TS transactions.		12.4

⟨ 4 ⟩

63	Net change in other current asset and liabilities (related to operations)	30.6	
I	Payable to suppliers and others	42.8	
J	Accrued Liabilities	83.2	
A	Accounts Receivable		80.0
B	Inventories		64.4
C	Prepaid Expenses		25.3
L	Accrued Income Taxes		21.3
	Unexplained*	34.4	

* Difference is composed of adjustments to those accounts due to acquisitions and dispositions.

⟨ 5 ⟩

66	Sales of Plant Assets—Cash	43.2	
68	Sales of Business—Cash	67.4	
E	Accumulated Depreciation	80.2	
N	Deferred Income Taxes	12.1	
P	Minority Interest	32.8	
T	Translation Adjustments		?
D	Plant Assets		174.1
	Incomplete entry relating to asset and business disposition		

⟨ 6 ⟩

F	Intangible Assets	66.2	
T	Translation Adjustments	?	
67	Business Acquired—Cash		180.1
	Asset and Liabilities Acquired	?	?
	(part of unexplained entry ⟨4⟩) Incomplete entry relating to business and assets acquired		

FURTHER ANALYTICAL IMPLICATIONS

The analysis of all transactions of Campbell has provided us with insights into many undisclosed and unexplained items. It can also provide a basis for informed questions to management about these items.

Going from the specific example of Campbell to generalizations about this type of analysis it must be emphasized that unexplained changes are *net* in nature. That is, they can be the result of a number of significant debit and credit transactions which may net out to a relatively small amount. Moreover, such transactions can have informational value about a company's activities (e.g., new or additional investments, losses, etc.) which can go far beyond the significance of the amounts involved. The analyst can identify the composition of such items up to a certain point. Beyond that, however, he or she must, when necessary, use this information as the basis for further inquiries of management or as a basis for further analytical steps.

QUESTIONS

1. What type of information can the user of financial statements obtain from the SCF?
2. Trace the evolution of accounting for funds and cash flows.
3. Describe the three major activities into which the SCF is classified.
4. Describe the three categories of adjustments which convert net income to CFO.
5. Describe the two methods of determining CFO.
6. Contrast the function of the income statement with that of CFO.
7. What is meant by the term *cash flow?* Why is this term subject to confusion and misrepresentation?
8. Discuss the analytical significance of the SCF and the considerations which enter into the interpretation of the cash from operations measure.
9. Describe the computation of free cash flow. What is the significance of this measure?
10. List some clues which the SCF can provide to the financial analyst.
11. What is the objective of the analytical reconstruction of all transactions?

Chapter 14

Effects of Price Changes on Financial Statements

The comparability over time of accounting measurements expressed in dollars can be fully valid only if the general purchasing power of the dollar remains unchanged. This has only rarely been the case; indeed, the value of the dollar in terms of purchasing power has changed over any length of time. In recent experience, such change has invariably been a decline in purchasing power (i.e., inflation).

In times of inflation, the monetary unit becomes increasingly distorted as a measure of the actual or physical dimensions of business activities. The distortive effect of general price-level changes on accounting measurements has long been recognized by leaders of industry and finance as well as by economists and accountants.[1] However, as long as the annual rate of inflation was moderate, accountants, as those best situated to move toward change, elected to rely on education and disclosure rather than on a restatement of the financial statements as the means of conveying such effects to the general reader.

In times of more severe inflation, there is always clamor for a more formalized and systematic approach designed to allow for the distortions arising from changes in the price level. There are businessmen who feel that recovery of depreciation based on original cost is not sufficient to provide for replacement of assets used up in production. They are, of course, except under certain imposed circumstances, not bound to historical-cost depreciation in setting their prices, and thus their arguments are often directed toward the goal of having the tax authorities accept price-level adjusted depreciation in computing taxable income. This quest has, so far, not borne fruit.

RESEARCH AND PROFESSIONAL PRONOUNCEMENTS

In the early 1960s, the accounting profession recognized that it could no longer ignore the effect of continuing inflation on financial statements.

---

[1] We must distinguish between specific price changes and general price-level changes affecting the purchasing power of the currency. For example, price changes in goods and services reflecting changes in quality do not affect the general purchasing power of the currency.

Accordingly, it commissioned a research study which was published in 1963 as *Accounting Research Study (ARS) 6,* "Reporting the Financial Effects of Price-Level Changes."

Following a period of further significant inflation, the APB issued, in June 1969, its *Statement 3* entitled "Financial Statements Restated for General Price-Level Changes." This advisory pronouncement for the first time spelled out specific steps to be followed in the preparation of general price-level restated financial statements.

After public exposure and discussion, the FASB issued in 1974 an exposure draft of a *Statement* that would have required the inclusion with conventional financial statements, of certain specified financial information stated in terms of units of general purchasing power patterned after the concepts embodied in *APB Statement 3.* However, in 1976 the SEC took the initiative and required larger registrants to disclose the current replacement cost of inventories, depreciable and amortizable assets used in operations, cost of sales, and the provision for depreciation and amortization.

The SEC requirements were primarily designed to move from a debating phase to some actual experimentation with supplementary disclosure. The FASB, aware that it had the primary responsibility to come up with a satisfactory reporting framework, undertook field tests in order to experiment with various reporting approaches. After considerable debate and continuing disagreements, the FASB chose in 1979 an experimental approach that was embodied in *SFAS 33,* "Financial Reporting and Changing Prices."

SFAS 33   *SFAS 33,* "Financial Reporting and Changing Prices," was a five-year experiment that required about 1,300 large U.S. corporations to report the effects of general inflation and other price changes using two inflation accounting models: historical cost/constant dollar and current cost.

SFAS 82   As the result of its continuing evaluation of the inflation accounting experiment, the FASB decided to issue in 1984 *SFAS 82* in which the Board decided to eliminate the historical cost/constant dollar disclosure requirements because it believed that requiring two different methods of reporting the effects of changing prices detracts from the usefulness of the information.

SFAS 89   In 1986, the FASB effectively suspended the inflation accounting experiment by issuing *SFAS 89* on "Financial Reporting and Changing Prices." This statement superseded *SFAS 33* in that it makes voluntary the supplementary disclosure of current cost/constant dollar information.

In an appendix *SFAS 89* gives guidance on measurement and presentation of supplementary information on effects of changing prices for those who elect to give it. In effect it represents a standby model of reporting the effects of price changes available for current or future use.

IMPLICATIONS FOR ANALYSIS

By making the reporting of the effects of changing prices voluntary, *SFAS 89* has basically sanctioned, at least for now, the demise of such reporting. Not surprisingly, a review of published financial statements reveals almost no companies that have chosen to report such data voluntarily.

The Board arrived at the decision to issue *SFAS 89* by a 4 to 3 vote. Substantial forces were at work to bring this about. Research indicated that published *SFAS 33* data were not widely used. A great majority of respondents to the exposure draft preceding *SFAS 89* favored elimination of the requirements for supplementary disclosure. Companies did not like the work entailed nor did they like the results they had to report. For example, in 1982 American Telephone and Telegraph reported conventional earnings of $7 billion and current cost earnings of only $1.4 billion. Exxon's conventional earnings of $4.2 billion became a loss when converted to the current cost basis.

The double-digit inflation rate prevailing at the time *SFAS 33* was adopted has subsided. After five years of declining inflation even the SEC, an earlier champion of such disclosures, withdrew its support of *SFAS 33*. In England, the accounting profession has, for the time being, essentially given up on accounting for inflation.

All these forces can be readily discerned and understood, but where does this leave financial statement analysts and their need for information in this critical area?

Inflation is more of a political problem than an economic one. Politicians are firmly against inflation but largely in favor of policies which produce it. Thus, if the past is a guide, inflation is here to stay. It is low as this is written, but it can heat up again. In any event, its cumulative effect is substantial, and so is the distortion it causes in conventional historical-cost accounts. It leads to illusory reported profits, masks the erosion of capital, and invalidates many analytical measures. The plant built in 1980 with money borrowed in 1978 on land bought in 1965 and using raw materials purchased in 1993 is included in results expressed in 1993 dollars. Profits tend to be overstated because depreciation and other costs are understated. Balance sheets understate the value of many assets and owners do not know whether the purchasing power of their capital is being maintained.

While there are many flaws in the methods devised to measure profits and the maintenance of physical or financial capital under such conditions, it is better to try to build on and perfect the tools with which we have some years of experience than to abandon their approximate results for the "precision" found in wrong historical-cost measures.

A number of respondents to the FASB exposure draft that preceded *SFAS 89* claimed that mandatory disclosure requirements became unnecessary because users have developed their own methods of adjusting financial information for changing prices. This view is not well-founded. If such analytical adjustments were difficult to make by use of mandated company-generated supplementary information, then it would be all the more difficult to make meaningful adjustments without such disclosures.

In conclusion, the elimination of supplementary disclosures about the effects of price-level changes has diminished the sources of reliable information available to financial analysts.

OBJECTIVES OF THIS CHAPTER

While an important source of company-generated data on the effects of price-level changes on financial statements has now been effectively removed, analysts need to understand the nature of the problem and the basic approaches taken toward their solution. Some companies may still provide such information and foreign financial statements may reflect adjustments made necessary by their more serious levels of inflation. Therefore, this chapter will provide a general, rather than detailed, overview of methods of adjusting for the effects of changing prices.

ACCOUNTING AND REPORTING ALTERNATIVES

For hundreds of years, accounting has evolved around the concept of historical costs and measurements in terms of money, whatever the purchasing power of that money was. In spite of their complexity, accounting presentations enjoyed a degree of acceptance and were understood by informed users. The accelerating erosion of the value of the currency has caused financial statements based on that framework to become less relevant to users of financial statements. Thus started the search for either new models of accounting or for supplementary disclosures that would make financial statements more relevant and useful in light of these conditions.

TWO SCHOOLS OF THOUGHT

Let us examine the problem of accounting when prices change by using a simplified example that ignores taxes. A fuel dealer needs an inventory of 100,000 gallons of oil in order to conduct business. The present inventory of fuel was bought on January 1, 20x1, at $1 per gallon when the general price-level index (GPI) stood at 100. On March 1, 20x1, the dealer sold 10,000 gallons for $2 per gallon, at which time the oil would cost $1.50 per gallon to replace and the GPI was 110.

On an average basis, our conventional accounting model would show a profit of $10,000 on the sale (sales of $20,000 minus cost of sales $10,000), and most observers would agree that this accounting does not fully reflect reality. But there is disagreement on how to account for this transaction.

The Financial Capital Maintenance Concept

While most observers agree that income is earned only after a provision is made to keep capital intact, there is disagreement on the nature of that capital. Those who claim that investors are concerned with maintaining the general purchasing power of their invested capital adhere to the financial capital concept. Under this concept, the $10,000 cost of 10,000 gallons of oil on January 1, 20x1, is equivalent to $11,000 ($10,000 × 110/100) in constant dollars on March 1, 20x1. That is, since the *general* price level increased by 10 percent, it would take, on average, 10 percent more dollars or $11,000 to buy the same goods and services that cost $10,000 on January 1, 20x1. Since the receipts for the sale of oil are in March 1, 20x1, dollars, we must measure the cost in the same, or constant, dollars (i.e., $11,000). Under this concept, a charge of $11,000 as cost of oil sold will recover the financial capital invested in the 10,000 gallons sold and will result in a profit of $9,000 (i.e., sales of $20,000 less cost of $11,000). This accounting for profit is designed to prevent the distribution of the purchasing power residing in the financial capital of the enterprise.

The Physical Capital Maintenance Concept

Adherents to this concept claim that an enterprise cannot be said to earn income unless it has first provided for the maintenance of existing operating capability. In terms of our example, this means that the cost of sales of the 10,000 gallons of oil is computed as $15,000 (10,000 gallons × $1.50 current cost at time of sale) and that the profit is $5,000 ($20,000 − $15,000 cost). Any distribution of profit in excess of $5,000 would prevent the fuel dealer from fully replenishing the 10,000 gallons of oil sold and thus from carrying the 100,000-gallon inventory of oil needed to conduct business.

TWO ACCOUNTING MODELS

The two schools of thought about the nature of capital as well as other considerations have given rise to two main models of accounting:

Constant-dollar (or general price-level) accounting (CDA) is advocated by those who want to deal with the effects of the decline in the purchasing power of the currency and who prefer the financial concept of capital.

Current-cost accounting (CCA) is advocated by those who want to focus on changes in specific prices affecting a firm's operations and who are concerned with the maintenance of the physical capital of the enterprise.

While constant-dollar accounting focuses on the *measuring unit,* current-cost accounting focuses on the *attribute being measured.* Consequently, though they are often discussed as alternative methods, they cannot truly be so regarded. Constant-dollar accounting retains the historical accounting model but changes the unit of measurement to a constant dollar. Current-cost accounting changes the historical accounting model because, it is felt, it does not deal satisfactorily with the problem of price changes.

Reflecting its inability to decide which model is better in dealing with financial reporting and price changes, the FASB, in *SFAS 33,* included both in its experimental approach. As we saw above, the FASB subsequently decided to eliminate the constant-dollar accounting disclosure requirements in favor of disclosure under only the current-cost accounting model. For this reason we will discuss the latter first although both models are useful to an understanding of the issues of accounting for price changes.

FOUR REPORTING FRAMEWORKS

In our subsequent discussions, we refer to four reporting frameworks as follows:

*Historical cost/nominal dollars (HC/ND)—*the framework under which the conventional primary financial statements are now prepared.

*Historical cost/constant dollars (HC/CD)—*financial statements restated for general price-level changes and expressed in a constant dollar of a given date.

*Current cost/nominal dollars (CC/ND)—*financial statements restated for specific price changes.

*Current cost/constant dollars (CC/CD)—*financial statements restated for both specific and general price-level changes.

CURRENT COST ACCOUNTING (CCA)

Current cost accounting (CCA), which in our present discussion uses the current cost/nominal dollar (CC/ND) framework, is advocated by those who believe that the more useful way to account for price changes is to depart from the historical-cost model. They argue that historical costs, even when restated for general price-level changes, are not fully relevant to decision making. Business enterprises are directly affected by *specific* price changes of the specific goods and services that they use rather than by general price-level changes. Consequently, specific price changes are the ones that are more useful to use in preparing financial statements.

There are a number of concepts of current cost (CC), but here we shall use the concept originally adopted by *SFAS 33,* which focuses on the current cost of replacing the service potential of specific existing assets[2] of a firm.

RESTATEMENT APPROACH

Assets such as cash, or accounts receivable, as well as current liabilities, are usually stated at their cash equivalent value. The CC of investments can often be obtained from market quotations, while the CC of inventories and of plant and equipment can be obtained from price lists, standard manufacturing cost computations, or by use of specific price indexes. Debt may have to be adjusted to reflect current market rates of interest if they differ from those prevailing at the time the debt was issued.

Revenues as well as most expenses (except cost of goods sold, and depreciation) are likely to be stated at approximate current cost. Cost of goods sold must be restated to the current cost of goods at times of sale based on sources such as price lists or invoice prices. The computation of CC depreciation is subject to controversy, but the *SFAS 33* requirement is to measure as expense the CC of the service potential used up, even when value changes in the remaining asset offset this expense.

Though some hold that the income tax provision should be based on pre-tax CC income, *SFAS 33* requires that it be recorded on the basis of pre-tax historical-cost income.

The concept of current cost income can be understood best through the following simple illustration:

ILLUSTRATION 1.   A holds for sale 10 widgets that were purchased at a cost of $20 each, constituting a starting capital of $200. In a given week, three widgets are sold for $30 each and the inventory is replenished at a price of $25 each. As shown in

---

[2] Other concepts of asset valuation include the current price at which assets could be sold (also known as net realizable value or exit value) and the present value of future cash flows, which equals the discounted net cash flows expected to be generated from an asset.

Chapter 5, conventional accounting can provide three different profit figures for this transaction, that is, $30 under FIFO, $26.50 under average cost, and $15 under the LIFO assumption with the latter most closely approximating (but not necessarily equaling, as it does here by coincidence) current cost.

CCA departs from both historical cost and the concept of realization. Under the assumption that the units sold had a cost equal to the units that replaced[3] them, the operating profit of $15 is arrived at by deducting the current cost of sales $75 (3 × $25) from sales $90 (3 × $30), and this profit is represented by cash that can indeed be distributed without affecting the business's ability to carry its normal inventory of 10 widgets, that is, 10 × $25 = $250. It is in fact, a basic principle of CCA that no profit should be reported as earned until the replacement of inventory (or of productive capacity) has been provided for. In addition, the increment in the current cost of the original seven widgets still in inventory $35 (7 × $5) is recognized as an unrealized holding gain. There is also a cost saving[4] or realized holding gain of $15 by having bought the three widgets that were sold at a cost of $20 each instead of the $25 current cost. Adding the $50 total holding gain to operating profit of $15, we get a net income of $65 (assuming no other expenses), and this separate classification of results is one of the advantages of CCA. A's CCC balance sheet is now as follows:

Cash	$ 15	Owner's equity at beginning		$200
Inventory (10 × $25)	250	Operating profit .... Holding gains:		15
		Realized	$15	
		Unrealized	35	50
	$265			$265

The income statement could have these captions:

Sales (3 × $30)	$90.00
Cost of sales (3 × $25)	75.00
Sustainable income*	15.00
Realized holding gains	15.00
Realized income† (equals conventional net income)	30.00
Unrealized holding gains	35.00
Net income	$65.00

* Income that would enable entity to sustain present level of operations were price changes to stop.

† Sustainable income plus realized holding gains (income realized in transactions with outsiders).

These concepts and terms were introduced by S. Davidson and R. L. Weil in "Inflation Accounting," *Financial Analysts Journal,* March–April 1976, pp. 57–66.

---

[3] Just as under historical-cost accounting we assume the flow of inventory, under current cost, we conveniently assume that sales occur on inventory purchase dates.

[4] This term paper appears in Edwards and Bell, *The Theory and Measurement of Business Income* (Berkeley: University of California Press, 1961), a seminal work in this area.

The illustration reflects two additional matters. One is that, unlike CDA (discussed below), CCA, in comparison with historical cost, changes only the *timing* but not the amount of the total profit recognized. Thus, when the 10 widgets are finally sold, the profit under both historical and CCA bases will be identical, but the timing will not be, because under CCA we recognize both current costs and holding gains. The other is that some accountants believe that unrealized holding gains do not belong in income and should instead bypass it and be shown directly in stockholders' equity.

CONSTANT DOLLAR ACCOUNTING (CDA)

A basic problem with HC/ND financial statements as presently prepared is that they include dollar amounts that represent a variety of purchasing power units. Thus, because of the decline in the purchasing power of the dollar, $100,000 spent on a plant in 1978 represents a far greater sacrifice in purchasing power than does $100,000 spent on a plant bought in 1993. Yet HC/ND financial statements do not recognize that difference and would, in fact, add up the dollar costs of the two assets even though they are not expressed in terms of a common unit of measure.

The basic purpose of financial statements restated for general price-level changes (HC/CD financial statements) is to present all elements of the financial statements in terms of units of the same general purchasing power restated by means of a general price-level index. General price-level financial statements differ from historical-dollar financial statements only in the unit of measure used in them. Consequently, they do not depart from the historical-cost principle. Moreover, they are subject to the same accounting standards as are used in the preparation of HC/ND financial statements with the exception that gains or losses in the purchasing power of the dollar are recognized in HC/CD statements.

A general price-level index measures the price behavior of a group or "basket" of representative items. While there are a number of indexes that measure general purchasing power, we will use here a widely used index selected for *SFAS 33* (i.e., the Consumer Price Index for All Urban Consumers [CPI-U]).

The restatement of financial statements by the HC/CD basis requires a distinction between monetary and nonmonetary items.

Monetary items represent claims to fixed numbers of dollars such as cash, accounts and notes receivable, and investments in bonds, or those representing obligations to pay fixed numbers of dollars such as accounts and notes payable and bonds payable. *SFAS 33* classifies deferred taxes as monetary.

Conversely, *nonmonetary items* are those that represent claims other than to a fixed number of dollars, such as inventory, property, plant, and equipment, common stock, and equity accounts such as capital stock and retained earnings. If an item does not qualify as monetary, it is non-monetary, as for example, prepaid expenses, which represent claims to future services.

RESTATEMENT APPROACH

Monetary items, representing the general purchasing power of dollars at any given point in time, require no restatement. Because monetary items represent a claim or an obligation of a fixed number of dollars rather than a given amount of purchasing power, they give rise to purchasing power gains and losses. Therefore, holding monetary assets in times of inflation results in a *loss* of purchasing power, while owing monetary liabilities results in a gain of purchasing power. Because nonmonetary items do not represent a fixed number of dollars, they must be restated. Thus, if a piece of land is bought on January 1, 20x2, for $10,000, when the index was 100, it will be converted (restated) to December 31, 20x2, dollars (when the index is 120) by multiplying the January 1, 20x2, cost of $10,000 by a conversion factor expressed as:

$$\frac{\text{Index at measurement date}}{\text{Index at date of acquisition}} : \frac{120}{100}, \text{ or } \$12,000$$

The $12,000 expresses the 10,000 January 1, 20x2, dollar acquisition in terms of December 31, 20x2, dollars. Put another way, when the inflation rate is 20 percent, it takes 20 percent more dollars to have the same amount of general purchasing power as is residing in this piece of land.

ILLUSTRATION 2.   On January 1, 19x3, when the index was 100, Fred Inactive had assets and equities as follows. No transactions took place until December 31, 19x3, when the index was 110.

The loss on monetary assets (e.g., cash, receivables) is computed by taking what these assets would have been stated as had they maintained their purchasing power, that is, $1,000 × 110/100 = $1,100 and comparing it with their actual purchasing power on December 31, 20x3, that is, $1,000. Similarly, the monetary liabilities (e.g., payables, short- and long-term debt) cause a gain because, had the purchasing power inherent in the obligation been maintained, it would have amounted to $2,000 × 110/100 or $2,200 on December 31, 20x3, while, in fact, it is only $2,000 on that date. The net monetary gain is added to capital as part of retained earnings. The restatement of the nonmonetary items completes the conversion and remeasures all items in terms of December 31, 20x3, dollars.

	January 1, 20x3, dollars	Restatement ratio	Purchasing power gain (loss)	On December 31, 20x3, c$*
Monetary assets	$1,000	None—but holding results in	(100)	$1,000
Inventories	2,000	110/100		2,200
Land	4,000	110/100		4,400
	$7,000			$7,600
Liabilities (monetary) .	$2,000	None—but owing results in	200	$2,000
Capital	5,000	110/100	___	5,500
Net general purchasing power gain		. . . .	100	100
	$7,000			$7,600

* c$ signifies constant dollar of a particular date.

The simplified discussion above is intended to acquaint the reader with the general concepts underlying these two methods of accounting for price changes. Having listed earlier four reporting frameworks we conclude with an example of the accounting for a single transaction.

Illustration of Accounting for a Transaction Using Four Reporting Frameworks

Assume that Edwards, Inc., acquired a truck on January 1, 20x1, for $4,000 when the relevant consumer price index (CPI) was 120. On June 30, 20x8, when the truck was sold for $2,200, the accumulated depreciation on the truck was $3,000, the CPI stood at 198, and the CC of the truck was $2,100. Exhibit 14–1 presents the computation of the gain on sale of the truck under four reporting frameworks, assuming that the transaction is reported as of December 31, 20x8, when the CPI stood at 203.

Column 1 presents the conventional HC/ND computation of gain on sale of the truck. Column 2 measures this transaction in terms of December 31, 20x8, dollars. Column 3 accounts for the transaction on a CC/ND basis and separates the gain on sale of equipment based on current cost on date of sale from the holding gain which occurred between the date of acquisition and the date of sale. Column 4 expresses both the gain on sale and the holding gain in terms of dollars of December 31, 20x8, purchasing power.

Exhibit 14–1   Calculation of gain on sale of truck under four reporting frameworks

	(1) HC/ND	(2) HC/CD	(3) CC/ND	(4) CC/CD
Selling price:				
Nominal price	$2,200		$2,200	
CD price = $2,200 × $\frac{203 \text{ (year-end)}}{198 \text{ (time of sale)}}$		$2,256		$2,256
Less adjusted cost:				
HC/ND ($4,000[a] − $3,000[b])	1,000			
HC/CD $1,000[d] × $\frac{203 \text{ (year-end)}}{120 \text{ (acquisition)}}$		1,692		
CC/ND (given)			2,100	
CC/CD $2,100 × $\frac{203}{198}$				2,153
Gain on sale (before realized holding gain)	1,200	564	100	103
Plus realized holding gain:				
CC/ND $2,100[c] − 1,000[d]			1,100	
CC/CD $\left(\$2,100^{[c]} \times \frac{203}{198} \right) - \left(\$1,000^{[d]} \times \frac{203}{120} \right)$				461
Total gain	$1,200	$ 564	$1,200	$ 564

[a] Original cost.
[b] Accumulated depreciation on date of sale.
[c] CC on data of sale.
[d] Net book value on date of sale (HC/ND).

IMPLICATIONS FOR ANALYSIS

As can be seen from a study of this work, the accounting framework is a measurement system of considerable complexity. If we superimpose on it the problem of an unstable measurement unit (money), this complexity is compounded to a considerable degree. And yet, the greater the rate of price-level changes, the more necessary it becomes for the analyst to comprehend the factors that affect changes in financial statements and the manner in which such changes occur in real terms.

Price changes have many causes including changes in technology, product quality, or circumstances. Thus, even without changes in the purchasing power of money, accounting for historical costs only would not be fully relevant. However, the unquestionably major problem is purchasing power changes, or specifically, *inflation.*

Earlier in the chapter we examined two major schools of thought on how accounting should deal with and reflect the effect of price changes. It is clear that the concerns that *both* constant dollar accounting (CDA) and current cost accounting (CCA) address, and the objectives that they seek, have considerable validity.

ANALYTICAL CONSIDERATIONS IN THE USE OF
CURRENT COST ACCOUNTING

CCA overcomes the criticism that businesses experience specific price changes rather than general inflation. Under CCA, profits are reported only when the sales price exceeds the current cost of the item sold. Thus, physical capital maintenance is at the heart of this system. The excess of CC over HC is considered as holding gains. While both realized and unrealized holding gains are often considered part of net income, their exact treatment is controversial. Because profit determination under CCA more closely parallels management decision processes, it provides a more consistent basis for the evaluation of management's actions and performance. As the rate of inflation increases, the separation of operating income from holding gains becomes more important in terms of capital maintenance.

Distributable earnings measured on the basis of CCA provide a sound basis for the evaluation of dividend policy.[5]

CC balance sheets present a more realistic indication of the current economic value of assets and liabilities than do either HC/ND or HC/CD balance sheets. Lower CC earnings in conjunction with higher CC equity generally reduces the return on equity. However, the inclusion of unrealized holding gains in income will generally result in returns on equity exceeding those calculated on a HC basis.

A CCA system is a form of current value accounting. Opponents of CCA worry that it will lead to income recognition on a pre-realization basis. That is not necessarily so because while unrealized holding gains can be considered as income, they can also be considered as capital maintenance adjustments.

A CCA system will be most effective in reflecting the effect of price changes on nonmonetary items; however, it will not deal with the erosion in value of monetary assets or the declining economic significance of liabilities.

Not surprisingly, the greatest strengths of CDA are most often cited as the weaknesses of CCA and vice versa. Thus, CCA in ND fails to recognize that the unit of measure used to calculate CC is not uniform. Therefore, comparability is impaired when CC amounts of one period are compared with those of another. Moreover, CCA fails to recognize the effects of inflation on monetary items in the form of monetary gains and losses.

---

[5] The study reported on by W. C. Norby in *Financial Analysts Journal* of November–December 1986, revealed that dividends in 1980 exceeded earnings on a CC basis, thus resulting in a disinvestment rate of 2.4 percent.

ANALYTICAL CONSIDERATIONS IN THE USE OF CONSTANT DOLLAR ACCOUNTING

There are a few basic facts about the effect of price-level changes on the conventional financial statements that must be thoroughly understood. One is that money, whether expressed in dollars or any other currency, is worth only what it will buy. Thus, if the price level changes, the value of money changes along with it; and hence a dollar received or spent in one period may not be comparable with that received or spent in another period, the distortion being in proportion to the cumulative change in the general price level. It is part of the "money illusion" to consider a dollar a dollar and to forget the obvious fact that the 1983 dollar represents a much smaller unit of general purchasing power than did, say, the 1965 dollar.

In times of changing prices, the income statement, to single out one of the important measures of corporate performance, is composed of at least two distinct elements: (1) results of business activities expressed in terms of units of equal purchasing power and (2) changes resulting from price-level changes. An intelligent assessment and analysis of these results require a separation and an understanding of these two disparate effects.

ILLUSTRATION 3.   In times of significant inflation, a small-loan company whose assets are mostly monetary must charge a rate of interest that will compensate it not only for the use of its funds but also for the loss of purchasing power of the funds lent. Thus, the proper interpretation of its interest income, which by conventional standards may seem unduly large, must include recognition of the offsetting general price level loss incurred on monetary assets.

A major objective of financial statements expressed in CD is thus to present them in terms of uniform units of purchasing power rather than in terms of units of money that distort interperiod and intercompany comparisons.

GENERAL VERSUS SPECIFIC PRICE CHANGES

A major objection to CDA is that it focuses on *general* price-level changes rather than on changes in the prices of the *specific* goods and services in which a given enterprise deals. Thus, for example, when prices of petroleum products skyrocketed, adjustment by a general price-level index failed by far to reflect the price increase in these specific commodities. Conversely, prices of small calculators or of semiconductors experienced cost and price declines in recent years, and the restatement by a general price index of financial statements of companies in this field may lead to a distortion of real effects and trends.

Opponents of CDA object also to the abstract nature of the unit of measure. They claim that business is transacted with money, not with bundles of purchasing power. Moreover, they claim that statements expressed in CD are not useful in the prediction of cash flows, which is a central function of financial analysis.

Monetary Gains and Losses

A highly controversial product of CDA are monetary gains and losses. In theory, monetary losses represent the loss of holding on to items representing claims to a depreciating currency. Conversely, monetary gains represent the reduced economic significance of repayments of obligations in depreciating currency. Carried to an extreme, the example of the debtor in the Germany of 1923 can be cited. His obligation dwindled to nothing when the purchasing power of the mark virtually disappeared.

One reason these gains and losses are poorly understood is that they produce no parallel cash inflows or outflows. Moreover, there is no identifiable change in accounts as a result of a change in the purchasing power of assets and liabilities. These gains and losses are basically arrived at by means of a retrospective calculation.

A further objection is that the advantage of borrowing differs from company to company depending on how profitably the assets acquired with debt are employed. Moreover, the largest monetary gains are likely to be shown by highly leveraged companies which may be near insolvency. Thus, the need for concurrent funds flow analysis is critical.

Any evaluation of purchasing power gains and losses requires an understanding of their relation to interest expense. The interest rate charged by lenders and agreed to by borrowers reflects their expectations of future inflation. Both recognize that the higher the expected inflation the higher the nominal interest rate must be to compensate the lender for being paid back in progressively "cheaper" dollars. Thus, the borrower's interest expense should be offset by the purchasing power gains recorded on the monetary liabilities.

ILLUSTRATION 4.   In its commentary on information reflecting the effects of inflation, McDonald's Corporation stated that "the effect of inflation on property and equipment is inseparable from its effect on debt used to finance such assets. The purchasing power gain on the debt is an economic benefit to the company since, with inflation, the debt is paid back in cheaper dollars. Accordingly, we believe that this gain should be viewed as an adjustment to interest and therefore have included it in arriving at constant dollar net income." Interestingly, in its comprehensively restated HC/CD financial statements, the company shows interest expense as c$95 million and at the same time credits income with c$146 million in "purchasing power gains on net amounts owed." As a result, reported HC/CD net income is considerably higher than its HC/ND counterpart.

Effects of Inflation

Inflation acts as a tax on cash balances. It is, in fact, a far more devastating tax than anything enacted formally by a legislature. It causes losses on monetary assets, gains on monetary liabilities, and significant changes in the values (expressed in terms of money) of other assets as well as changes in funds flows, the demand for funds, and in the uncertainties and risks affecting with differing impacts business enterprises of various kinds. In the words of Professor John Lintner, ". . . higher inflation rates would increase a firm's relative dependence on external funds *even if* there were no phantom inventory profits, and depreciation could be charged on replacement costs and there were no added needs due to backups of unsold inventories, increased sales on credit, or delays in collections or credit losses, and so on. Any adverse change in any of these conditions of course merely compounds the adverse effects of increased inflation rates."[6]

The effect of price-level changes on an entity's financial statements depends on both the rate of price-level changes and the composition of assets, liabilities, and equities. Empirical studies have shown that inflation can cause very significant changes in reported operating and financial results.[7]

The composition of assets, liabilities, and equities is an important determinant of the effect of price-level changes on an entity and on its financial statements.

The following are some useful generalizations regarding such effects in times of significant inflation.

1. The larger the proportion of depreciable assets and the higher their age, the more unrestated income tends to be overstated. Thus, the income of capital-intensive companies tends to be affected more than that of others by price-level restatements. Accelerated depreciation reduces this effect.
2. The rate of inventory turnover has a bearing on price-level effects. The slower the inventory turnover, the more operating income tends to be overstated, unless the LIFO method is used.
3. The mix of assets and liabilities as between monetary and nonmonetary is important. A net investment in monetary assets will, in times of rising price levels, lead to purchasing power losses, and, conversely, purchasing power gains will result from a net monetary liability position.

---

[6] John Lintner, "Inflation and Security Returns," *The Journal of Finance,* May 1975, pp. 273–74.

[7] W. C. Norby reported in the *Financial Analysts Journal* of November–December 1981 that a study of *SFAS 33* disclosures for 1979 and 1980 showed that the "inflation adjustments reduced aggregate earnings from continuing operations by 60 percent on a current-cost basis and by 53 percent on a constant-dollar basis."

4. The methods of financing also have an important bearing on results. The larger the amount of debt, at fixed and favorable rates relative to the inflation rate, and the longer its maturities, the better is the protection against purchasing power losses or the better is the exposure to purchasing power gains.

Effects of Price-Level Changes on Specific Industries and Companies

Not all industries are affected equally by price level restatements. Thus, for example, because most of their assets are in monetary items, in industries such as banking, finance, and some insurance companies, current cost or replacement value accounting will produce results similar to those produced by the conventional accounting model.

Companies which are well adapted to an inflationary environment are those which can increase prices easily without fear of loss of market share and those which can accommodate larger dollar volume increases with only modest additional investment of capital. On the other extreme are laggards in profitability which, under inflationary conditions, develop insatiable needs for additional capital. Not only are the needs for added capital dictated by rapid expansion in receivables, inventories, and other operating assets, but they are also fed by a desire to improve return on equity by increasing leverage (see Chapter 19).

MOVES TO REQUIRE MARKET VALUE DATA

While concerns about the impact of inflation on U.S. financial statements are presently dormant, the savings and loan crisis has highlighted the need for information on the current value of assets and liabilities. In 1991 the FASB issued *SFAS 107* "Disclosures About Fair Value of Financial Instruments." This statement requires that firms disclose information about the fair value of their financial instruments, both assets and liabilities on- and off-balance sheet. This first step within the FASB's financial instruments project may possibly represent an initial departure from the historical-cost model.

QUESTIONS

1. Trace briefly the evolution of research and professional pronouncements on the subject of "accounting for the effect of price-level changes" preceding issuance of *SFAS 33*.
2. Summarize the essential objectives of accounting standards regarding price-level reporting starting with *SFAS 33* to the present.

3. What are the analytical implications of the issuance of *SFAS 89*?
4. Differentiate between the financial capital maintenance concept and the physical capital maintenance concept. You may use an example to illustrate the difference between the two.
5. Differentiate among the four reporting frameworks discussed in the chapter.
6. Differentiate between monetary and nonmonetary items.
7. Why are monetary gains and losses so poorly understood?
8. List some useful generalizations regarding the effects of price-level changes on an entity and its financial statements in times of significant inflation.

Chapter 15

THE AUDITOR'S OPINION—
MEANING AND SIGNIFICANCE

An entity's financial statements are the representations of its management. Management bears a primary responsibility for the fairness of presentation and the degree of informative disclosure in the financial statements it issues to interested parties, such as present and potential owners, creditors, and others. It has, however, become generally accepted that there is a need for an independent check on management's financial reporting.

The profession that serves society's need in this respect by performing the attest function is the public accounting profession. It may be readily observed that the more developed a country's economy and the more diverse, free, and mobile its capital and money markets, the stronger and the more important its public accounting profession is likely to be. Surely, the United States experience supports this conclusion, for the public accounting profession here is perhaps the world's largest and most vital.

Some states recognize and license "Public Accountants" and "Licensed Accountants," and the requirements for practice under these titles vary from strict to feeble. However, there is another title that has the most consistent significance—that of "Certified Public Accountant." It can be acquired only by those who have passed the CPA examination, a rigorous series of tests that are uniform in all states and that are graded centrally under the auspices of the American Institute of Certified Public Accountants (AICPA). While no profession can ensure uniformity of quality among its members, the successful completion of these examinations does ensure that the candidate has demonstrated a sufficiently acceptable knowledge of accounting and auditing principles and practices.

Since the CPAs represent by far the most important segment of public accounting practice in the United States, our consideration of the auditor's opinion will be confined to that issued by the CPA and governed by the various pronouncements issued by their professional association, the AICPA.

Author's Note: Women have been analysts and auditors for years, and their numbers are growing. In this book masculine pronouns are often used for succinctness and are intended to refer to both males and females.

In spite of the many real and imagined shortcomings of the auditor's work, and, as this book illustrates, there are many of both varieties, the auditor's function is of critical importance to the financial analyst. While improvements are needed in many areas of the auditor's work, his or her attestation to the fair presentation of the financial statements greatly increases their reliability to the analyst as well as the degree and quality of disclosure provided in them.

As in many areas of endeavor, so in the analysis of financial statements, partial or incomplete knowledge can be more damaging than a complete lack of it. This truth applies to the analyst's understanding and knowledge of the auditor's work and the significance of his opinion.

WHAT THE ANALYST NEEDS TO KNOW

In relying on the auditor's opinion, which covers the financial statements subject to review, the analyst must—

1. Learn as much as possible about the auditor upon whom reliance is placed.
2. Understand fully what the auditor's opinion means and the message it is designed to convey to the user.
3. Appreciate the limitations to which the opinion is subject, as well as the implications that such limitations hold for the analysis of financial statements covered by the opinion.

Knowing the Auditor

The possession by the auditor of the CPA certificate does assure the analyst of a reasonable qualification for practice as an auditor. However, as is the case in other professions, differences in ability, competence, and qualifications can be considerable.

The relationship between the auditor and those who rely on his opinion differs markedly from that existing in other professional relationships. While the auditor has both an obligation and a concurrent responsibility to users of his opinion, he is in most cases neither appointed nor compensated by them. He must look mostly to management for both recommendation for his appointment and the determination of his fee. When management's desires with respect to financial reporting are in conflict with the best interests of the outside users of financial statements, the auditor's integrity and independence are put to a stern test. Thus, one criterion of the auditor's reliability is his reputation for integrity and independence in the community at large and among respected members of the financial community. Whatever else the auditor must have, and his qualifications and skill must be considerable, without these attributes nothing else counts for very much. The reputation of an auditor for competence and for knowledge of his work can be established in a variety of ways. The auditor's professional credentials, including the length, breadth, and quality of his experience, are one element; his membership and standing in state and national accounting associations another; and his participation in professional organizations yet another factor to be assessed by the analyst. An auditing firm's activities and past performance are usually well known in the community in which it operates.

Finally, the analyst from his own experience is often able to form a judgment about the auditor's reputation for quality work. Since there exists considerable leeway in adherence to audit standards and in the application of accounting principles, an audit firm's "track record" of actual level of performances in these critical areas provides a firsthand guide to its reliability and integrity. The analyst would do well to note instances in which a CPA firm (1) has accepted the least desirable acceptable accounting principle among the available alternatives, (2) has equivocated unnecessarily in its opinion, or (3) was found wanting in adherence to auditing standards.

Good sources of information on the reputation and the capabilities of an audit firm include local bankers, investment bankers, attorneys, and particularly numerous findings and orders concerning auditor performance issued by the SEC.

The Auditor's Opinion

The auditor's opinion is the culmination of a lengthy and complicated process of auditing and investigation. It is here, and only here, that the auditor reports on the nature of his work and on the degree of responsibility he assumes. While his influence may be indirectly felt throughout the financial statements by the presentation, description, and footnote disclosure that he may have suggested or insisted upon, the opinion, and the opinion alone, remains his exclusive domain. Thus, the opinion and the references to the financial statements which it contains should always be carefully read. To ignore the auditor's opinion, or to assume that it does not mean what it says, or that it means more than it says, is unwarranted.

The auditor's responsibility to outsiders whom he does not know and who rely on his representations is considerable, and his exposure to liability arising therefrom is growing. Thus, the obligations that the standards of his profession impose on him, while extensive, are at the same time defined and limited. Consequently, no analyst is justified in assuming that the association of the auditor's name with the financial statements goes beyond what the auditor's opinion says, or is a form of insurance on which the analyst can rely to bail him out of bad decisions.

The accounting profession has increasingly had to cope with an "expectations gap," a gap between the responsibility it wants to assume as reflected by professional standards and the responsibility the public thinks is assumed by the auditor in his attesting opinion. In general terms that responsibility was clearly stated by Chief Justice Burger in a unanimous decision of the U.S. Supreme Court in March 1984:

> ... By certifying the public reports that collectively depict a corporation's financial status, the independent auditor assumes a *public* responsibility transcending any employment relationship with the client. The independent public accountant performing his special function owes ultimate allegiance to the corporation's creditors and stockholders, as well as to the investing public. The "public watchdog" function demands that the accountant maintain total independence from the client at all times and requires complete fidelity to the public trust.
>
> It is not enough that financial statements *be* accurate; the public must also *perceive* them as being accurate. Public faith in the reliability of a corporation's financial statements depends upon the public perception of the outside auditor as an independent professional ... if investors were to view the auditor as an advocate for the corporate client, the value of the audit function itself might well be lost.

The court's definition of the independent auditor's public responsibility laid down the general expectations the public is entitled to have with regard to his opinion, but the application of this doctrine to specific cases remains difficult and controversial. For example, does the financial failure of an enterprise shortly after an unqualified opinion has been rendered mean that the auditors fell short in their reporting responsibility? The answer to that question is complex and depends on many attending circumstances, all weighed by a public that believes the auditor's report (opinion) is in the nature of a guarantee of accuracy.

AUDITOR'S REPORT

To narrow the gap between the responsibility auditors intend to assume and the responsibility the public believes them to assume, the Auditing Standards Board (ASB) has revised language for the audit report. The language is intended to be less technical and to more explicitly address the responsibility the auditor assumes, the procedures which he performs, and the assurance which he provides. To this end the report:

1. States that the financial statements were *audited,* which is hoped will be a more descriptive term than the word *examined* used previously.
2. States specifically that the financial statements are the responsibility of *management* and that the auditor's responsibility is to express

        an opinion on the financial statements, thus giving readers a clearer notice of the responsibilities assumed by each party.

3. States in the scope paragraph that the audit was conducted in accordance with generally accepted auditing standards and as such is designed to obtain reasonable assurance that the financial statements are free of *material misstatement.*
4. States that the steps the auditor takes to achieve *reasonable* assurance that the financial statements are free of material misstatement include *(a)* examining on a *test basis* evidence that supports the amounts and disclosures in the financial statements, *(b)* assessing the accounting principles used and estimates made by management, and *(c)* evaluating the overall financial statement presentations.
5. Indicates that the financial statements present fairly in all material respects the financial position, results of operations, and cash flows of the company for the period reported upon.

The Scope of the Audit

The introductory and scope paragraphs of the auditor's report set forth the financial statements examined, the period of time that they cover, and the scope of the audit to which they and the underlying records have been subjected.

The standard terminology refers to an audit made in accordance with "generally accepted auditing standards" (GAAS). This is "shorthand" for a very comprehensive meaning that is elaborated upon in the profession's literature and particularly in *Statements on Auditing Standards* and subsequent codifications. These auditing standards are broad generalizations classified under three headings: (1) general standards, (2) standards of fieldwork, and (3) standards of reporting.

General standards define the personal qualities required of the independent CPA. They are:

1. The examination is to be performed by a person or persons having adequate technical training and proficiency as an auditor.
2. In all matters relating to the assignment an independence in mental attitude is to be maintained by the auditor or auditors.
3. Due professional care is to be exercised in the performance of the examination and the preparation of the report.

Standards of fieldwork embrace the actual execution of the audit and cover the planning of the work, the evaluation of the client's system of internal control, and the quality and sufficiency of the audit evidence obtained. *SAS 1* enumerates them as follows:

1. The work is to be adequately planned and assistants, if any, are to be properly supervised.
2. There is to be a proper study and evaluation of the existing internal

control as a basis for reliance thereon and for the determination of the resultant extent of the tests to which auditing procedures are to be restricted.

3. Sufficient competent evidential matter is to be obtained through inspection, observation, inquiries, and confirmations to afford a reasonable basis for an opinion regarding the financial statements under examination.

Reporting standards govern the preparation and presentation of the auditor's report. They are intended to ensure that the auditor's position is clearly and unequivocally stated and that the degree of responsibility he assumes is made clear to the reader. These standards are:

1. The report shall state whether the financial statements are presented in accordance with generally accepted accounting principles.
2. The report shall identify those circumstances in which such principles have not been consistently observed in the current period in relation to the preceding period.
3. Informative disclosures in the financial statements are to be regarded as reasonably adequate unless otherwise stated in the report.
4. The report shall either contain an expression of opinion regarding the financial statements, taken as a whole, or an assertion to the effect that an opinion cannot be expressed. When an overall opinion cannot be expressed, the reasons therefore should be stated. In all cases where an auditor's name is associated with financial statements, the report should contain a clear-cut indication of the character of the auditor's examination, if any, and the degree of responsibility he is taking.

Audit standards are the yardsticks by which the quality of audit procedures are measured.

Auditing Procedures   The scope section describes auditing procedures as were considered necessary in the circumstances.

These encompass the wide sweep of auditing theory brought to bear on the particular examination, as well as the professional discretion the auditor uses in the performance of his work.

The subject of auditing is, of course, a discipline in itself requiring for successful mastery a period of study and practical application. Thus, while we obviously cannot go with any degree of detail into what constitutes the process of auditing, it behooves all who use its end product to have a basic understanding of the process by which the auditor obtains assurance about the fair presentation of the financial statements as to which he expresses an opinion.

A basic objective of the financial audit is the detection of errors and irregularities, which if undetected would materially affect the fairness of presentation of financial summarizations or their conformity with GAAP. Errors are distinguished from irregularities in the latter result from *intentional* misconduct.

To be economically feasible and justifiable, auditing can aim only at a reasonable level of assurance in this respect about the data under review. This means that under a testing system, assurance can never be complete, and that the final audit conclusions are subject to this inherent probability of error.

The Importance of Internal Control or Control Structure   After ascertaining, by means of investigation and inquiry, what management's plan and design for a system of internal control is, if any, the auditor proceeds to test the system in order to ascertain whether it is in existence and is, in fact, being implemented as intended. This testing is called compliance testing or Control-Risk-Assessment Procedures.

If after application of compliance testing, the control structure is found to be well conceived and in proper operation, the amount of testing to which income statement items or individual assets and liabilities will be subjected can be significantly reduced. The latter type of testing, which is called substantive testing, or Tests of Financial Statement Balances, will have to be increased significantly if compliance testing reveals the control structure to be deficient or not operational.

This method of evaluating the system and then performing additional sample tests on the basis of this evaluation does, of course, leave room for a great deal of professional discretion, for "corner-cutting," and for a variety of qualities of judgment. Hence, this method is subject to the risk of failure. However, an examination conducted in accordance with GAAS should be designed to detect material misstatements that affect the financial statements.

From the above discussion it should be clear that reliance on an audit must be based on an understanding of the nature of the audit process and the limitations to which it is subject.

The Opinion Section

The auditor's opinion deals with:

1. The fairness of presentation of the financial statements.
2. Their conformity with GAAP. (These two points are interrelated as many believe GAAP include a requirement for the disclosure needed to ensure that the financial statements are not misleading.)
3. Disclosure when a material change in accounting principle(s) has occurred.

"Fair Presentation"

One of the great debates among auditors and between auditors and society in general, particularly in the courts, concerns the meaning of the phrase "present fairly" which is found in the auditor's report. Most auditors maintain that financial statements are fairly presented when they conform to GAAP and that "fairness" is meaningful only when measured against some established standard such as GAAP.

Yet, clearly, in quite a number of cases reaching the courts, financial statements that, according to expert testimony were prepared in accordance with GAAP, were nevertheless found to be misleading in an overall sense. This became particularly apparent in the landmark *Continental Vending* case where the lack of disclosure of certain highly dubious transactions was defended as not being, at that time, required by GAAP. In refusing to instruct the jury that conformity with GAAP was a complete defense to the charge of fraud, the trial judge maintained that the critical question was whether Continental's financial statements, taken as a whole, "fairly presented" its financial picture. He found that while conformity with GAAP might be very persuasive evidence of an auditor's good faith, it was not necessarily conclusive evidence.

The auditors, in an attempt to respond to a clear divergence between their and society's views of what is meant by "present fairly," issued a statement maintaining that "fairness" must be applied within the framework of GAAP, and that "fair presentation" within that framework requires that—

a. The accounting principles selected and applied must have general acceptance.[1]
b. The accounting principles must be appropriate in the circumstances.
c. The financial statements must be "informative of matters that may affect their use, understanding, and interpretation."
d. The information must be presented and summarized "in a reasonable manner, that is, neither too detailed nor too condensed."
e. The financial statements must reflect "the underlying events and transactions" in a way that states the results within "a range of acceptable limits that are reasonable and practicable."

As part of the accounting profession's periodic attempts at self-examination and assessment, especially in the face of congressional and public scrutiny and criticism, an AICPA-appointed Commission on Auditor's Responsibilities issued its "Report, Conclusions, and Recommendations" in 1978. Only a few of the Commission's recommendations were adopted.

In 1987 the Report of the National Commission on Fraudulent Financial Reporting (the Treadway Commission) included recommendations on the audit report. The ASB in issuing its *Statement on Auditing Standards (SAS)* on "Reports on Audited Financial Statements" was guided by many of these pressures, ideas, and recommendations.

---

[1] *SAS 69* (1992) "The Meaning of Present Fairly in Conformity with Generally Accepted Accounting Principles in the Independent Auditor's Report" details a hierarchy of Generally Accepted Accounting Principles.

Modification of the Opinion

The standard short-form report may contain a "clean opinion"; that is, the auditor had no qualifications to record as to any of the criteria enumerated above. Any modifications of substance in the language of the auditor's opinion paragraph is, technically speaking, considered to be a qualification, a disclaimer, or an adverse opinion. Not all modifications are, of course, of equal significance to the user. Some deviations in language are explanatory in character reflecting matters that the auditor wishes to emphasize and may not affect the auditor's opinion significantly. References to the work of other auditors is not regarded as a qualification but rather an indication of divided responsibility for the financial statements. Other explanatory comments may not carry over to affect the auditor's opinion and, at times, one may wonder why mention of them is necessary. On the other hand, certain qualifications or disclaimers are so significant as to cast doubt on the reliability of the financial statements or their usefulness for decision-making purposes.

Let us then examine the major categories of the auditor's explanatory language, qualifications and disclaimers, the occasions on which they are properly used, and the significance which they hold to the user of financial statements.

CIRCUMSTANCES GIVING RISE TO EXPLANATORY LANGUAGE, QUALIFICATIONS, DISCLAIMERS, OR ADVERSE OPINIONS

There are four main categories of conditions that require explanatory language, qualifications, adverse opinions, or a disclaimer of opinion:

1. Limitations in the scope of the auditor's examination affected by *(a)* conditions that preclude the application of auditing procedures considered necessary in the circumstances or *(b)* restrictions imposed by the client.
2. The financial statements do not present fairly the financial position and/or results of operations because *(a)* they fail to conform with GAAP or *(b)* they do not contain adequate disclosure.
3. There exist uncertainties about the future resolution of material matters, the effect of which cannot presently be estimated or the outcome of which cannot reasonably be determined. This includes concerns regarding the enterprise's ability to continue in existence.
4. Inconsistent application of GAAP.

Before we consider the variety of conditions that call for qualified opinions, let us examine the major types of qualifications that the auditor may express.

QUALIFICATIONS—"EXCEPT FOR"

These qualifications express an opinion on the financial statements except for repercussions stemming from conditions that must be disclosed. They may arise from limitations in the scope of the audit which, because of circumstances beyond the auditor's control or because of restrictions imposed by the audited company, result in a failure to obtain reasonably objective and verifiable evidence in support of events which have taken place. They may arise from a lack of conformity of the financial statements to GAAP.

When there are uncertainties about future events that cannot be resolved or the effect of which cannot be estimated or reasonably provided for at the time the opinion is rendered, such as one due to operating losses or serious financial weakness that calls into question the fundamental assumption that an entity can continue to operate as a going concern, a separate paragraph should refer the reader to the note to the financial statements that provides data about the uncertainty. In cases of pervasive uncertainty that cannot be adequately measured, an auditor may, but is not required to, issue a disclaimer of opinion rather than merely call the reader's attention to the uncertainty.

ADVERSE OPINIONS

An adverse opinion should be rendered in cases when the financial statements are not prepared in accordance with GAAP, and this has a significant effect on the fair presentation of those statements. An adverse opinion results generally from a situation in which the auditor has been unable to convince his client to amend the financial statements so that they reflect the auditor's estimate about the outcome of future events or so that they otherwise adhere to GAAP. The issuance of an adverse opinion must always be accompanied by a statement of the reasons for such an opinion.

DISCLAIMER OF OPINION

A disclaimer of opinion is a statement of inability to express an opinion. It must be rendered when, for whatever reason, insufficient competent evidential matter is available to the auditor to enable him to form an opinion on the financial statements. It can arise from limitations in the scope of the audit as well as from the existence of uncertainties, the ultimate impact of which cannot be estimated. Material departures from GAAP do not justify a disclaimer of opinion.

Adverse Opinions versus Disclaimers of Opinion

The difference between adverse opinions and disclaimers of opinion can be best understood in terms of the difference that exists between exceptions that affect the quality of the financial statements, on one hand, and those that express uncertainties affecting the auditor's opinion, on the other. Thus, a situation that may call for an "except for" opinion may at some point result in such a degree of pervasive or material disagreements with management that it will require an adverse opinion.

THE FORM OF THE REPORT

Whenever the auditor expresses a qualified opinion, he must disclose in a middle paragraph, or in a footnote that is referred to in that paragraph, the substantive reasons for the qualification. The explanatory paragraph should disclose the principal effects of the subject matter of the qualification on financial position, results of operations, and changes in cash flows, if reasonably determinable.

All qualifications must be referred to in the opinion paragraph, and a qualification due to scope or lack of sufficient evidential matter must be also referred to in the scope paragraph. Thus, a mere explanatory statement should not be referred to in either the scope or the opinion paragraphs.

Having covered the various types of opinions an auditor can express, let us now turn to the various conditions that call for qualifications in such opinions.

LIMITATIONS IN THE SCOPE OF THE AUDIT

A limitation in the scope of the auditor's examination, that is, an inability to perform certain audit steps that he considers necessary, will, if material, result in a qualification or disclaimer of his opinion.

Some limitations in the scope of the auditor's examination arise from an inability to perform certain audit steps because of conditions beyond the auditor's and the client's control, for example, an inability to observe the opening inventory where the audit appointment was not made until the close of the year. Other limitations may result from a client-imposed restriction on the auditor's work. Whatever the reason for an incomplete examination, the auditor must report the inadequacy of the examination and the conclusions that flow from such an inadequacy.

The accounting profession has given special status to procedures with respect to observation of inventories and the confirmation of accounts receivable. If these steps cannot be reasonably or practically performed, the auditor must, in order to issue an unqualified opinion, satisfy himself about the inventories and accounts receivable by alternative means. For ending inventory in the balance sheet there are no alternative procedures to making or observing some counts of inventory items.

FAILURE OF FINANCIAL STATEMENTS TO CONFORM TO GENERALLY ACCEPTED ACCOUNTING PRINCIPLES

The auditor brings to bear his expertise in the application of auditing techniques and procedures to satisfy himself about the existence, ownership, and validity of presentation of the assets, the liabilities, and net worth as well as the statement of results. As an expert accountant, the auditor judges the fairness of presentation of financial statements and their conformity with GAAP. The latter judgment is one of the most important functions of the auditor's opinion.

Fair presentation is, to an important extent, dependent on the degree of informative disclosure provided. This is consistent with GAAP, which requires adequate disclosure. *Opinions* of the APB and *Statements* of the FASB enjoy, by definition, authoritative support. If the accountant concurs in a company's use of an accounting principle which differs from that approved by an authoritative body but which he believes enjoys the support of other authoritative sources, he need not qualify his opinion, but he must disclose that the principle used differs from those approved by such authoritative body. This, of course, puts the onus on the auditor in justifying the departure from a principle which enjoys authoritative approval.

If, because of lack of adequate disclosure or the use of accounting principles that do not enjoy authoritative support, the auditor concludes that the financial statements are not fairly presented, he must qualify his opinion or render an adverse opinion. The decision of whether to make his opinion an "except for" type, which is a qualified opinion, or to render an adverse opinion, which states that the "financial statements do not present fairly . . ." hinges on the materiality of the effect of such a deficiency on the financial statements taken as a whole. The concept of materiality in accounting and auditing is, however, very vague and remains so far unquantified.

It is obvious that a qualification due to a lack of disclosure or a lack of adherence to GAAP is the result of the auditor's inability to persuade his client to modify the financial statements. Thus, an "except for" type of opinion is not proper, and an adverse opinion is called for together with a full description of the shortcomings in the financial statements as well as their total impact thereon.

The following are pertinent excerpts from an opinion qualified because of lack of adherence to GAAP:

As explained in Note A, the year 3 financial statements include interest expense that has not been capitalized as required by *SFAS 34*.

In our opinion, except that in year 3 interest expense has not been capitalized as described in the preceding paragraph . . .

FINANCIAL STATEMENTS SUBJECT TO UNRESOLVED KNOWN UNCERTAINTIES

In cases where uncertainties about the future cannot be resolved, or their effect cannot be estimated or reasonably provided for at the time of the issuance of the auditor's opinion, an unqualified opinion with a required explanatory paragraph is called for. Such uncertainties may relate to lawsuits, tax matters, or other contingencies, the outcome of which is dependent upon decisions of parties other than management. Or the uncertainties may relate to the recovery of the investment in certain assets through future operations, or through their disposition.

Hitherto, a material uncertainty may have resulted in an uncertainty qualification. Under the *SAS*, "Reports on Audited Financial Statements," the qualification is replaced by explanatory language that discloses the uncertainty.

The practical effect of explanatory language because of uncertainty is to state the auditor's inability to assess the impact of the contingency, or the likelihood of its occurrence, and to pass on to the reader the burden of its evaluation.

One variety of explanatory language relates to the question of whether the going-concern assumption in accounting (see Chapter 3) is justified. This question may arise when a company is incurring continued operating losses, deficits in the stockholders' equity, working capital insufficiencies, or defaults under loan agreements or litigation. In such cases, the auditor expresses his doubt about the propriety of applying practices implicit in the going-concern concept such as the valuation of fixed assets at cost.

The following is an example of the pertinent portion of an auditor report relating to uncertainties. The explanatory language follows the opinion paragraph:

> The accompanying financial statements have been prepared assuming that Company Y will continue as a going concern. As discussed in Note X to the financial statements, Company Y has suffered recurring losses from operations and has a net capital deficiency that raise substantial doubt about the entity's ability to continue as a going concern. Management's plans in regard to these matters are also described in Note X. The financial statements do not include any adjustments that might result from the outcome of this uncertainty.

Inconsistent Application of GAAP   When there has been a material change between periods in accounting principles or in the method of their application, the auditor should refer to the change in explanatory language which follows the opinion paragraph.

SPECIAL REPORTS

In certain cases the standard report of the auditor is not appropriate because of special circumstances or because of the limited scope of the examination that the auditor is requested to undertake. It is particularly important that the analyst read such reports carefully so that he is not misled into believing that the auditor is assuming here his ordinary measure of responsibility. The following are some types of special reports that the reader may encounter:

1. Reports by companies on a cash, modified cash, or tax basis of accounting.
2. Reports by regulated organizations using regulatory accounting practices.
3. Reports prepared for limited purposes. Such reports usually deal with certain aspects of the financial statements (such as computations of royalties, rentals, profit-sharing arrangements, or compliance with provisions of bond indentures, etc.).

In *FRR* No. 1 Section 304, the SEC has called for the auditor's "association" with published interim reports based on performance of a limited review.

REPORTS ON "COMPILED" AND "REVIEWED" FINANCIAL STATEMENTS

The AICPA has made available to "nonpublic entities" compilation and review services that, while falling short of a full audit, provide the reader with lower defined levels of assurance.

Compiled financial statements are accompanied by a report that indicates that a compilation has been performed and that such a service is limited to presenting, in financial statement format, information that is the representation of management or owners. The report should also state that the financial statements have not been audited or reviewed; thus no opinion or any other form of assurance is expressed on them. No reference is made to any other procedures performed before or during the compilation engagement.

Reviewed financial statements are accompanied by a report that indicates that a review was performed in accordance with AICPA standards. The report describes a review engagement, states that the information in the financial statements is the representation of management (or owners), and disclaims an opinion on the financial statements taken as a whole. The report should state that: "The accountant is not aware of any material modifications that should be made to the financial statements in order for them to be in conformity with generally accepted accounting principles, other than those modifications, if any, indicated in his report." No reference is made to any other procedures performed before or during the review engagement.

THE SEC'S IMPORTANT ROLE

The SEC has in recent years moved particularly forcefully to monitor auditor performance as well as to strengthen the hands of auditors in their dealings with managements.

Disciplinary proceedings against auditors were expanded by means of innovative remedies in consent decrees to include requirements for improvements in internal administration procedures, professional education, and a review of a firm's procedures by outside professionals, known as "peer review."

SEC *FRR* No. 1 Section 603, in moving to strengthen the auditor's position, requires increased disclosure of the relationship between auditors and their clients, particularly in cases where changes in auditors take place. Disclosure must include details of past disagreements, including those resolved to the satisfaction of the replaced auditor, as well as footnote disclosure of the effects on the financial statements of methods of accounting advocated by a former auditor but not followed by the client.

The SEC has also moved to discourage "opinion shopping," a practice under which companies canvass audit firms to gain acceptance of accounting alternatives they desire to use.

IMPLICATIONS FOR ANALYSIS

Auditing as a function and the auditor's opinion as an instrument of assurance are widely misunderstood. The responsibility for this lack of communication cannot be all laid at the auditor's door, for the profession has published a number of pamphlets in which it has endeavored to explain its function. Nor should the readers of financial statements bear the full responsibility for this state of affairs, because the accounting profession's message in this area is often couched in technical and cautious language and requires a great deal of effort and background information for a full understanding.

A useful discussion of the implications of the current state of auditing to the user of audited financial statements may be presented in two parts:

1. Implications stemming from the nature of the audit process.
2. Implications arising from the professional standards which govern the auditor's opinion.

Implications Inherent in the Audit Process

Auditing is based largely on a sampling approach to the data under audit. Statistical sampling uses a rigorous approach to this process, which lends itself to a quantification of conclusions. Nevertheless, many audit tests are based on "judgmental samples" of the data, that is, samples selected by the auditor's intuition, judgment, and evaluation of many factors. Often the size of the sample is necessarily limited by the economics of the accounting practice.

The reader must realize that the auditor does not aim at, nor can he ever achieve, complete certainty. Even a review of every single transaction—a process that would be economically unjustifiable—would not achieve a complete assurance.

Auditing is a developing art. Even its very basic theoretical underpinnings are far from fully understood or resolved. There is, for instance, no clear relationship between the auditor's evaluation of the effectiveness of the control structure and the extent of audit testing and the nature of audit procedures employed. If we add to that the fact that the qualities of judgment among auditors do vary greatly, we should not be surprised to find that the history of auditing contains many examples of significant failure. On the other hand, as is the case with the risk of accidental death in commercial aviation, the percentage of failure to the total number of audits performed is very small indeed. Thus, while the user of audited financial statements can, in general, gain some reassurance about the overall results of the audit function, he must remember that there is substantial risk in reliance on its results in specific cases. Such risks are due to many factors, including the auditor's inability and/or unwillingness to detect fraud at the highest level and the application of proper audit tests to such an end (*McKesson and Robbins* case through the *Cenco, Inc.,* case and all the way to the *Equity Funding, ESM Government Securities, ZZZ Best, Regina,* and *Lincoln Savings* cases), the auditor's inability to grasp the extent of a deteriorating situation (the *Yale Express* case), the auditor's conception of the range of his responsibilities to probe and disclose (the *Continental Vending, National Student Marketing,* and *Bank of Credit and Commerce International* cases), and the quality of the audit (*Bar Chris Construction, U.S. Financial, Whittaker Corporation,*

Mattel, McCormick Company, Saxon Paper, and the multitude of Savings and Loan Associations cases.)

Thus, while the audit function may generally justify the reliance that financial analysts place on audited financial statements, such a reliance must be a cautious and informed one. The analyst must be aware that the entire audit process is a probabilistic one subject to many risks. Even its flawless application may not necessarily result in complete assurance, and most certainly cannot ensure that the auditor has elicited all the facts, especially if there is high-level management collusion to withhold such facts. Finally, the heavy dependence of the auditing process on judgment will, of necessity, result in a wide range of quality of performance.

An insight into what can be missed, and why, in the internal and external audit of a large corporation can be obtained from a reading of the *Report of the Special Review Committee of the Board of Directors of Gulf Oil Corporation* (the McCloy report—December 1975). In searching for reasons why Gulf's internal financial controls, its internal auditors, and its external auditors failed to detect or curb the expenditure of large amounts of corporate funds through "off the books" bank accounts for unlawful purposes, the review committee concluded that internal control committees chose not to control, that the corporate comptroller did not exercise the control powers vested in him, that the internal auditing department (reporting to the comptroller rather than to an audit committee of the board) lacked independence and stature, and that while it is clear that the external auditors had some knowledge of certain unusual transactions, the extent of their knowledge could not be determined.

To provide the reader with insights into how wrong things can go in the "audit" of a major corporation, let us focus on the landmark *Equity Funding* case.[2] This case includes expected elements such as human greed and shortcomings (see also discussion in Chapter 3), and the resulting fraud and deception and audit failure. This case also includes a more unusual element in that public accountants have been charged with knowing complicity in a fraud extending over many years.

THE EQUITY FUNDING CASE.   The Equity Funding Corporation of America (EFCA) was an organization which sold mutual fund shares and used these as security against which the investor could borrow moneys for the payment of life insurance premiums on his or her behalf (the "funding" concept). From its inception as a public company in 1964, the major holders of its stock were obsessed with a desire to keep aloft the market price of its stock by fraudulently inflating reported earnings. As the fraud progressed and grew, vanity, pride, and the fear of being discovered provided added incentives to keep the fraud going.

---

[2] Most of the public documents as well as commentaries on this case are contained in L. J. Seidler, F. Andrews, and M. J. Epstein, *The Equity Funding Papers: The Anatomy of a Fraud* (New York: John Wiley & Sons, 1977).

An amazing aspect of this case is the relatively crude and unsophisticated design and execution of the fraud which relied on fictitious manual accounting entries lacking any real support.

In its early stages, the fraud consisted of recording nonexistent commission income with the charge (debit) going to a greatly inflated "Funding Loans Receivable" asset, supposedly representing borrowings by customers for life insurance premiums, and so on. Over the years, $85 million in such bogus income was recorded. As is true with most frauds, the fictitious entries involved do not, of course, create cash. Thus, to provide cash and at the same time keep the mushrooming "Funding Loans Receivable" in check, the conspirators borrowed money (on the basis of glowing earning results), and instead of booking the corresponding liabilities, credited the Funding Loans Receivable account. Other complicated shams involved foreign subsidiaries.

As the cash-hungry fraud monster grew, the expanding circle of fraud participants, now including senior as well as lower-management levels, had to invent new cash raising schemes. This led to the involvement of Equity Funding Life Insurance Company (EFLIC), a unit involved in reinsurance, that is, in the sale to others of insurance risks in force. Starting with intermediate, less crass and ambitious steps, there ultimately evolved a practice of creating totally fictitious products (insurance policies) that were sold to unsuspecting reinsurers who provided significant cash inflows. The process involved the "creation" of all needed documentation and related fictitious records. But, it also created the need for EFLIC to remit increasing amounts of cash to these reinsurers representing the premium payments which the company presumably collected from the fictitious policyholders. This created monumental documentation problems as well as severe cash flow problems (in 1972 reaching $1.7 million in cash flow deficit). These ever-growing fictions and problems that fed on themselves created a "house of cards" that would have collapsed of its own weight even without the whistle-blowing of a disgruntled dismissed employee in early 1973.

The sheer size of the deception as well as its duration should give pause to any analyst. From 1964 through 1972, at least $143 million in fictitious pre-tax income was reported in EFCA's financial statements. During the same period, the net income reported by the company amounted to about $76 million. Thus, this company whose reported success captured the imagination of Wall Street, in fact never earned a dime.

The bankruptcy proceedings and investigation which started in 1973 also revealed that:

Latecomers to the fraud benefited from and were motivated by prestigious and well-paying positions. This in turn led to a climate of dishonesty which included theft, expense account padding, and other manifestations of a breakdown of restraint and morality.

The small audit firm performed its audit during 1961–70 with such manifest incompetence that it could only be explained by a knowledge of the fraud. A larger successor audit firm that purchased the practice of the smaller firm changed practically nothing in the sloppy and uncoordinated audit approach.

The "big 8" audit firm of EFLIC failed to review internal controls and based its audit conclusions almost solely on internal records, thus omitting the crucial audit steps of independent outside verification.

The auditors had to settle for about $39 million in damages.

Rigorous financial analysis should have revealed the propensities of the defrauders if not the specific elements of the fraud. Thus, a comparison of quarterly reports in 1971 would have revealed that derived fourth-quarter income was inflated while the related expenses were understated in relation to the revenue amounts. The EFCA fraud holds many important lessons about the dynamics of a fraudulent process as well as the weak points that can be revealed to a trained and inquisitive eye.

Consider the case of ZZZ Best Company, a carpet cleaning company run by a 20-year-old. It received a clean audit opinion after booking fictitious receivables and revenues from nonexistent fire damage restoration contracts. The fraud included the renting by ZZZ Best of a building for a weekend for the sole purpose of persuading the auditors that work on a fictitious contract was in fact proceeding.

In relying on audited financial statements, the analyst must be ever aware of the risks of failure inherent in an audit; he must pay attention to the identity of the auditors and to what their record has been; and armed with a knowledge of what auditors do and how they do it, he must himself assess the areas of possible vulnerability in the financial statements. This brings us to the concept of audit risk.

Audit Risk and Its Implications

We have in Chapter 3 examined the concept of accounting risk. Audit risk, while related, is of a different dimension and represents, as a study of some of the above-mentioned cases will reveal, an equally clear and present danger to lenders and investors who rely on audited financial statements.

It is impossible for the analyst to substitute his judgment for that of the auditor. However, armed with an understanding of the audit process and its limitations, he or she can, through identification of special areas of vulnerability, make a better assessment of the degree of audit risk present in a given situation. The following are circumstances that can point to such areas vulnerability:

Glamour industry and company with need for continuing earnings growth to justify high market price or to facilitate acquisitions.

Company in difficult financial condition requiring credit urgently and frequently.

Company with high market visibility issuing frequent progress reports and earnings estimates.

Managements dominated mostly by one or a few strong-willed individuals or consisting mostly of financial people including CPAs.

Management compensation or stock options importantly dependent on reported earnings.

Managements that have displayed a propensity for earnings maximization and manipulation by various means.

Indications of personal financial difficulties by members of the senior management team.

Deterioration in operating performance.

Deterioration in liquidity or long-term solvency.

A capital structure far too complex for company's operations or size.

Problem industry displaying weaknesses in such areas as receivable collection, inventories, contract cost overruns, dependence on few products, and so forth.

Dealings with insiders or related parties, stockholder lawsuits, frequent turnover of key officers, legal counsel, or auditors.[3]

Audit conducted by a firm that has, for whatever reason, experienced a higher than normal incidence of audit failures.

While none of the above situations can be relied on to indicate situations of higher audit risk, they have been shown by experience to have appeared in a sufficient number of problem cases to warrant the analyst's close attention.

IMPLICATIONS STEMMING FROM THE STANDARDS THAT GOVERN THE AUDITOR'S OPINION

In relying on the auditor's opinion, the analyst must be aware of the limitations to which the audit process is subject, and this was the subject of the preceding discussion. Moreover, he or she must understand what the auditor's opinion means and particularly what the auditor himself thinks he conveys to the reader by means of his opinion.

Let us first consider the unqualified opinion or the so-called clean opinion. The auditor maintains that he expresses an opinion on *management's* statements. He is very insistent on this point and attaches considerable importance to it. This assertion means that normally he did not prepare the financial statements nor did he choose the accounting principles embodied in them. Instead, he reviews the financial statements presented to him by management and ascertains that they are in agreement with the books and records that he audited. He also determines that generally acceptable principles of accounting have been employed

---

[3] The SEC, in *FRR* No. 1 Section 603, required increased disclosure of relationships between registrants and their independent public accountants, including disputes, particularly in cases where changes in accountants occur.

in the preparation of the financial statements, but does not claim to represent that they are the *best* principles that could have been used. It is a well-known fact that management will often rely on the auditor, as an expert in accounting, to help them pick the principle that, while still acceptable, will come nearest to meeting their reporting objectives. Finally, the auditor will determine that the minimum standards of disclosure have been met so that all matters essential to a fair presentation of the financial statements are included in them.

One might well ask what difference it makes whether the auditor prepared the statements or not, so long as he expresses an unqualified opinion on them. The accounting profession has never clearly explained what the implications of this really are to the user of the financial statements. However, a number of such possible implications should be borne in mind by the analyst:

1. The auditor's knowledge about the financial statements is not as strong as that of the preparer who was in more intimate contact with all the factors which gave rise to the transactions. He knows only what he can discern on the basis of a sampling process and may not know all that he should know.

2. Since many items in the financial statements are not capable of exact measurement, he merely reviews such measurements for reasonableness. His are not the original determinations, and unless he can successfully prove otherwise (as, for example, in the case of estimates of useful lives of property), management's determination will prevail. Thus, the auditor's opinion contains no reference to "present exactly" or "present correctly" but rather states that the statements "present fairly."

3. While the auditor may be consulted on the use of accounting principles, he, as auditor rather than as preparer of such statements, does not select the principles to be used. Moreover, he cannot insist on the use of the *best* available principle any more than he is likely to *insist* on a degree of disclosure above the minimum considered acceptable at the time.

4. The limitations to which the auditor's ability to audit are subject have never been spelled out by the accounting profession. Knowledgeable auditors do, of course, know about them; but there seems to be a tacit agreement, of doubtful value to the profession, not to discuss them. For example, is the auditor really equipped to audit the value of complex technical work in progress? Can he competently evaluate the adequacy of insurance reserves? Can he estimate the value of problem loans? Can he second-guess the client's estimate of the percentage of completion of a large contract? While such questions are rarely raised in public, let alone answered, they cannot be unequivocally answered in the affirmative.

5. While the preparer must, under the rules of double-entry book-keeping, account for all items, large or small, the auditor is held to less exacting standards of accuracy in his work. Thus, the error tolerances are wider. He leans on the doctrine of materiality that in its basic concept simply means that the auditor need not concern himself, in either the auditing or the reporting phases of his work, with trivial or unimportant matters. What is important or significant is, of course, a matter of judgment, and so far the profession has neither defined the concept nor set limits or established criteria to govern the overall application of the concept of materiality. This has given it an unwarranted degree of reporting latitude.[4]

It is important to understand, from the point of view of accounting and audit risk, that new industries and new practices (such as novel financial instruments) spawn abuses that are not foreseen or that auditors refuse to address in the absence of specific professional guidelines. Such guidelines will generally be issued as a result of the publicity attending the next transgression or accounting or audit failure. By that time it will be too late to reverse the adverse consequences which the analyst must face.

Auditors even as a profession, in contradistinction to a business, must pay attention to the economics of their function and to the limits of the responsibilities they can assume. Thus, whether the foregoing limitations on the auditor's function and responsibility are justified or not, the analyst must recognize them as standards applied by auditors and evaluate his reliance on audited financial statements with a full understanding of them.

The auditor's reference to "generally accepted accounting principles" in his opinion should be well understood by the user of the financial statements. Such reference means that the auditor is satisfied that such principles, or standards, have authoritative support and that they have been applied "in all material respects." Aside from understanding the operation of the concept of materiality, the analyst must understand that the definition of what constitutes "generally accepted accounting principles" is often vague and subject to significant latitude in interpretation and application. For example, an *SAS* issued in 1975 states that "when criteria for selection among alternative accounting principles have not been established to relate accounting methods to circumstances (e.g., as in case of inventory and depreciation methods) the auditor may conclude that more than one accounting principle is appropriate in the circumstances."

---

[4] See Leopold A. Bernstein, "The Concept of Materiality," *The Accounting Review,* January 1967; and Sam M. Woolsey, "Approach to Solving the Materiality Problem," *Journal of Accountancy,* March 1973. The FASB has published a *Discussion Memorandum* on the subject and held public hearings on it. The FASB has no present intention to issue pronouncements on the subject beyond what is already skimpily covered in its statements.

Similarly indeterminate are present-day standards relating to disclosure. While minimum standards are increasingly established in professional and SEC pronouncements, accountants have not always adhered to them. The degree to which the lack of disclosure impairs the fair presentation of the financial statements remains subject to the auditor's judgment and discretion, and there are no definite standards that indicate at what point lack of disclosure is material enough to impair fairness of presentation thus requiring a qualification in the auditor's report.

THE AUDIT FUNCTION AS PERCEIVED BY THE AUDITOR

The auditor's misperception of his function is a major problem area for the analyst and the general user of financial statements.

Take the question of who the client is, or who the auditor is working for. Despite the 1984 decision of Chief Justice Burger, cited earlier, many auditors still consider their relationship with the companies they audit as amounting to a privileged attorney-client relationship where everything can be kept private. Some auditors even believe that they are entitled to determine when revelations of fraud or irregularities should be disclosed so as to forestall what they view as unfavorable economic or other adverse effects that could result from such disclosure.

ILLUSTRATION 1.   In 1990 the auditors gave the Bank of Credit and Commerce International a clean opinion. The auditors later admitted that at the time the opinion was issued they had knowledge of the presence of serious fraud or irregularities, the extent of which was not yet determined. The auditor's senior partner in London defended its actions by stating: "You simply can't go around qualifying the accounts of a bank without creating all sorts of problems, without the whole thing collapsing." Must users of audited financial statements now consider whether other considerations may have priority over their right to know the whole and unvarnished truth?

This confusion about auditor role and function manifests itself in other areas. Auditing, the major public franchise of the profession and the reason for its existence, often takes a back seat, sometimes as loss leader, to such tangential services as headhunting, system design, and other types of consulting.

The auditing profession did not fare well in the 1980's savings and loan debacle. In his decision re the *Lincoln Savings and Loan* vs. *Office of Thrift Supervision* case, Judge Stanley Sporkin noted that the audit partner in charge of the failed audit left his audit firm in order to assume a high-paying position with Lincoln, his former client and beneficiary of favorable reports. This, in the judge's view, certainly raised questions about the auditor's independence. In his summation of this case of substantial audit failure the judge concluded "What it is hoped the accounting profession will learn from this case is that an accountant must not blindly apply accounting conventions without . . . determining whether a transaction makes any economic sense . . . and without finding that the transaction is realistic and has economic substance. . . ."

Qualification, Disclaimers, and Adverse Opinions

When the auditor qualifies his opinion, the analyst is faced with an additional problem of interpretation, that is, what is the meaning and intent of the qualification and what effect should such qualifications have on his reliance on the financial statements? The usefulness of the qualification to the analyst depends, of course, on its clarity, its lack of equivocation, and on the degree to which supplementary information and data enable an assessment of its effect.

An additional dimension of confusion and difficulty of interpretation is introduced when the auditor includes explanatory information in his report, merely for emphasis, without a statement of conclusions or of a qualification. The analyst may in such situations be left wondering why the matter was emphasized in this way and whether the auditor is attempting to express an unstated qualification or reservation.

ILLUSTRATION 2.   In 1981, Manville Corporation stated that it had substantial defenses to legal actions. In 1982, it declared bankruptcy because of asbestos-related law suits.

Up to the first quarter of 1991, Columbia Gas failed to disclose its take-or-pay contracts to buy gas at fixed prices which proved to be far above market when gas prices declined. The subsequent sharp decline in the company's stock took many analysts by surprise.

As discussed in an earlier part of this chapter, generally when an auditor is not satisfied with the fairness of presentation of items in the financial statements, he issues an "except-for" type of qualification, and when there are uncertainties that he cannot resolve, he adds explanatory language after the opinion paragraph. At some point, the size and importance of items under qualification must result in *adverse opinions* or *disclaimers of opinion,* respectively. Where is this point? At what stage is a specific qualification no longer meaningful and an overall disclaimer of opinion necessary? Here again, the analyst won't find any explicit quantitative guidelines by turning to the auditor's own professional pronouncements or literature.

ILLUSTRATION 3.   Language of a qualification:

As more fully described in Note X to the financial statements, the Company has excluded certain lease obligations from property and debt in the accompanying balance sheets. In our opinion, generally accepted accounting principles require that such obligations be included in the balance sheets.

In our opinion, except to the effect of not capitalizing certain lease obligations as discussed in the preceding paragraph. . . .

Explanatory Language for Uncertainties.   When the auditor cannot assess the proper carrying amount of an asset or determine the extent of a possible liability or find other uncertainties or contingencies that cannot be determined or measured, he will describe such uncertainties in his report and refer the reader to the relevant notes to the financial statements. The analyst using financial statements that contain such explanatory language is, quite bluntly, faced with a situation where the auditor has passed on to him the uncertainty described and, consequently, the task of evaluating its possible impact. The analyst should recognize the situation for what it really is and not assume that he is dealing with a mere formality designed only for the auditor's self-protection. Moreover, the auditor's efforts to estimate future uncertainties cannot normally be expected to exceed those of management itself. As an *SAS* issued in 1974 put it, "The auditor's function in forming an opinion on financial statements does not include estimating the outcome of future events if management is unable to do so."

In those cases where explanatory language is inserted because of uncertainties that cannot be resolved, it is hard to blame the auditor for shifting the burden of evaluation on to the reader. At the same time, it must be remembered that as between the reader and the auditor, the latter, due to his firsthand knowledge of the company's affairs, is far better equipped to evaluate the nature of the contingencies as well as the probabilities of their occurrence. Thus, the analyst is entitled to expect, but will unfortunately not always get, a full explanation of all factors surrounding the uncertainty.

Lest the absence of explanatory language because of uncertainty in the auditor's report lull the analyst into a false sense of security, it must be borne in mind that there are many contingencies and uncertainties that do not call for explanatory language but that may nevertheless have very significant impact on the company's financial condition or results of operations. Examples of such contingencies or possibilities are:

1. Obsolescence of a major product line.
2. Loss of a significant customer.
3. Overextension of a business in terms of management capabilities.
4. Difficulty of getting large and complex production units on-stream on time.

These matters may, however, affect a company's ability to continue as a going concern. They must, moreover, be discussed by management in the SEC-mandated "Management's Discussion and Analysis of Financial Condition and Results of Operations" (see Chapter 20).

From the above discussion it should be obvious that the analyst must read with great care the auditor's opinion as well as the supplementary information to which it refers. While the analyst can place some reliance on the auditor, he must maintain an independent and open-minded attitude towards the assurances which the auditor's report convey.

QUESTIONS

1. In relying on an auditor's opinion, what should the financial analyst know about the auditor and his work?
2. What are "generally accepted auditing standards"?
3. What are auditing procedures? What are some of the basic objectives of a financial audit?
4. What does the opinion section of the auditor's report usually cover?
5. Which are the four major categories of conditions that require of the auditor explanatory language, qualifications, disclaimers, or adverse opinions?
6. What is an "except-for" type of audit report qualification?
7. What is a *(a)* disclaimer of opinion and *(b)* an adverse opinion? When are these properly rendered?
8. What is the practical effect of explanatory language because of uncertainty in an auditor's report?
9. How does the auditor report on an inconsistency in the application of GAAP?
10. What are the major disclosures required by SEC's *FRR* No. 1, Section 603, on the relationship between auditors and clients?
11. What are some of the implications to financial analysis which stem from the audit process itself?
12. The auditor does not prepare the financial statements on which he expresses an opinion but instead he samples the data and examines them in order to render a professional opinion on them. List some of the possible implications of this to those who rely on the financial statements.
13. What does the auditor's reference to "generally accepted accounting principles" mean to the analyst of financial statements?
14. Of what significance to the financial analyst is explanatory language because of uncertainty?
15. What are some of the circumstances which can point to areas of higher audit risk?

FINANCIAL STATEMENT ANALYSIS—THE MAIN AREAS OF EMPHASIS

Chapter 16

ANALYSIS OF SHORT-TERM LIQUIDITY

SIGNIFICANCE OF SHORT-TERM LIQUIDITY

The short-term liquidity of an enterprise is measured by the degree to which it can meet its short-term obligations. Liquidity implies the ready ability to convert assets into cash or to obtain cash. The short term is conventionally viewed as a time span up to a year, although it is sometimes also identified with the normal operating cycle of a business, that is, the time span encompassing the buying-producing-selling and collecting cycle of an enterprise.

The importance of short-term liquidity can best be gauged by examining the repercussions that stem from a lack of ability to meet short-term obligations.

Liquidity is a matter of degree. A lack of liquidity may mean that the enterprise is unable to avail itself of favorable discounts and is unable to take advantage of profitable business opportunities as they arise. At this stage, a lack of liquidity implies a lack of freedom of choice as well as constraints on management's freedom of action.

A more serious lack of liquidity means that the enterprise is unable to pay its current debts and obligations. This can lead to the forced sale of long-term investments and assets and, in its most severe form, to insolvency and bankruptcy.

To the owners of an enterprise, a lack of liquidity can mean reduced profitability and opportunity or it may mean loss of control and partial or total loss of the capital investment. In the case of owners with unlimited liability, the loss can extend beyond the original investment.

To creditors of the enterprise, a lack of liquidity can mean delay in collection of interest and principal due them or it can mean the partial or total loss of the amounts due them.

Customers as well as suppliers of goods and services to an enterprise can also be affected by its short-term financial condition. Such effects may take the form of inability of the enterprise to perform under contracts and the loss of supplier relationships.

From the above description of the significance of short-term liquidity it can be readily appreciated why the measures of such liquidity have been accorded great importance. For, if an enterprise cannot meet its current obligations as they become due, its continued existence becomes doubtful and that relegates all other measures of performance to secondary importance if not to irrelevance. In terms of the framework of objectives discussed in Chapter 1, the evaluation of short-term liquidity is concerned with the assessment of the unsystematic risk of the enterprise.

While accounting determinations are made, as we have seen in Chapter 3, on the assumption of indefinite continuity of the enterprise, the financial analyst must always submit the validity of such assumption to the test of the enterprise's liquidity and solvency.

One widely used measure of liquidity is working capital. In addition to its importance as a pool of liquid assets that provides a safety cushion to creditors, net working capital is also important because it provides a liquid reserve with which to meet contingencies and the ever-present uncertainty regarding an enterprise's ability to balance the outflow of cash with an adequate inflow of cash.

WORKING CAPITAL

The basic concept of working capital is relatively simple. It is the excess of current assets over current liabilities. That excess is sometimes referred to as *net working capital* because some businessmen consider current assets as working capital. A working capital deficiency exists when current liabilities exceed current assets.

The importance attached by credit grantors, investors, and others to working capital as a measure of liquidity and solvency has caused some enterprises, desiring to present their current condition in the most favorable light, to stretch to the limit the definition of what constitutes a current asset and a current liability. For this reason, the analyst must use his or her own judgment in evaluating the proper classification of items included in working capital.

Current Assets

Current assets include cash and other assets that are reasonably expected to be realized in cash or sold or consumed during the normal operating cycle of the business or within one year if the operating cycle is shorter than one year. Current liabilities include those expected to be satisfied by either the use of assets classified as current in the same balance sheet or the creation of other current liabilities, or those expected to be satisfied within a relatively short period of time, usually one year. [APB *Statement 4,* par. 198.]

The general rule about the ability to convert current assets into cash within a year is subject to important qualifications. The most important qualification relates to the operating cycle. As more fully described in Chapter 5, the operating cycle comprises the average time span intervening between the acquisition of materials and services entering the production or trading process to the final realization in cash of the proceeds from the sale of the enterprise's products. This time span can be quite extended in industries that require a long inventory holding period (e.g., tobacco, distillery, and lumber) or those that sell on the installment plan. Whenever no clearly defined operating cycle is evident, the arbitrary one-year rule prevails.

The most common categories of current assets are:

1. Cash.
2. Cash equivalents (i.e., temporary investments).
3. Accounts and notes receivable.
4. Inventories.
5. Prepaid expenses.

Cash is, of course, the ultimate measure of a current asset since current liabilities are paid off in cash. However, earmarked cash held for specific purposes, such as plant expansion, should not be considered as current. Compensating balances under bank loan agreements cannot, in most cases, be regarded as "free" cash, SEC *FRR* No. 1 Section 203 requires the disclosure of compensating balance arrangements with the lending banks as well as the segregation of such balances (see also Chapter 5).

Cash equivalents represent temporary investments of cash in excess of current requirements made for the purpose of earning a return on these funds. These investments must be short-term and of the highest quality, thus ensuring that they can be sold without loss.

The analyst must be alert to the valuation of such investments. Equity investments are now accounted for in accordance with *SFAS 12* as detailed in Chapter 5. Debt securities may still be carried above market if management views a decline as merely "temporary" in nature. Similarly, the "cash equivalent" nature of securities investments may sometimes be stretched quite far.

The mere ability to convert an asset to cash is not the sole determinant of its current nature. It is the intention and normal practice that governs. Intention is, however, not always enough. Thus, the cost of fixed assets that are intended for sale should be included in current assets only if the enterprise has a contractual commitment from a buyer to purchase the asset at a given price within the following year or the following operating cycle.

ILLUSTRATION 1.   Champion International Corporation classified "Operations held for disposition" as current assets and explained as follows:

> The company has entered into an agreement to sell three paperboard mills, its corrugated box manufacturing operations and all but one of its bag manufacturing operations to Stone Container Corporation ("Stone") for cash and Stone common stock. Upon consummation of the sale to Stone, the company expects to receive $372,900,000 in cash, subject to adjustment in certain circumstances. . . .

Attempts by managements to bend the rules of what constitutes a current asset reinforces the ever-recurring message in this text that the analyst cannot rely on adherence to rules or accepted principles of preparation of financial statements, but instead must exercise eternal vigilance in his or her use of ratios and all other analytical measures that are based on such statements. If anything, attempts by managements to stretch the rules in order to present a situation as better than it really is should serve as an added warning of potential trouble and risk.

Accounts receivable, net of provisions for uncollectible accounts, are current unless they represent receivables for sales, not in the ordinary course of business, which are due after one year. Installment receivables from customary sales usually fall within the operating cycle of the enterprise.

The analyst must, as the discussion in Chapter 5 indicates, be alert to the valuation as well as validity of receivables particularly in cases such as those where "sales" are made on consignment or subject to the right of return.

Receivables from affiliated companies or from officers and employees can be considered current only if they are collectible in the ordinary course of business within a year or, in the case of installment sales, within the operating cycle.

Inventories are considered current assets except in cases where they are in excess of current requirements. Such excess inventories, which should be shown as noncurrent, must be distinguished from inventories, such as tobacco, which require a long aging cycle. The variations in practice in this area are considerable and should be carefully scrutinized by the analyst.

ILLUSTRATION 2.   Some trucking concerns include the tires on their trucks as current assets, presumably on the theory that they will be used up during the normal operating cycle.

The analyst must pay particular attention to inventory valuation. Thus, for example, the inclusion of inventories at LIFO can result in a significant understatement of working capital.

Prepaid expenses are considered current, not because they can be converted into cash but rather because they represent advance payments for services and supplies that would otherwise require the current outlay of cash.

Current Liabilities

Current liabilities are obligations that would, generally, require the use of current assets for their discharge or, alternatively, the creation of other current liabilities. The following are current liabilities most commonly found in practice:

1. Accounts payable.
2. Notes payable.
3. Short-term bank and other loans.
4. Tax and other expense accruals.
5. Current portion of long-term debt.

The foregoing current liability categories are usually clear and do not require further elaboration. However, as is the case with current assets, the analyst cannot assume that they will always be properly classified. Thus, for example, current practice sanctions the presentation as non-current of current obligations that are expected to be refunded. The degree of assurance of the subsequent refunding is mostly an open question that in the case of adverse developments may well be resolved negatively as far as the enterprise is concerned.

SEC *FRR* No. 1 Section 203 has expanded significantly the disclosure requirements regarding short-term bank and commercial paper borrowing. *SFAS 6* established criteria for the balance sheet classification of short-term obligations that are expected to be refinanced (see Chapter 7).

The analyst must also be alert to the possibility of presentations designed to present the working capital in a better light than warranted by circumstances.

ILLUSTRATION 3.   Penn Central Company excluded the current maturities of long-term debt from the current liability category and included it in the "long-term debt" section of the balance sheet. This treatment resulted in an excess of current assets over current liabilities of $21 million, whereas the inclusion of current debt maturities among current liabilities would have resulted in a working capital *deficit* of $207 million. (The subsequent financial collapse of this enterprise is a well-known event.)

The analyst must also ascertain whether all obligations, regarding which there is a reasonably high probability that they will have to be met, have been included as current liabilities in computing an effective working capital figure. Two examples of such obligations follow:

1. The obligation of an enterprise for notes discounted with a bank where the bank has full recourse in the event the note is not paid when due is generally considered a contingent liability. However, the likelihood of the contingency materializing must be considered in the computation of working capital. The same principle applies in case of loan guarantees.

2. A contract for the construction or acquisition of long-term assets may call for substantial progress payments. Such obligations for payments are, for accounting purposes, considered as commitments rather than liabilities, and hence are not found among the latter. Nevertheless, when computing the excess of liquid assets over short-term obligations such commitments may have to be recognized.

Other Problem Areas in the Definition of Current Assets and Liabilities

Current deferred tax debits are no more true current assets than current deferred tax credits are real current liabilities. While, as discussed in Chapter 11, these are the result of present generally accepted methods of accounting for taxes, the resulting debits do not represent expected means of payment nor do the resulting credits necessarily represent obligations currently due.

Many concerns that have fixed assets as the main "working assets," such as, for example, trucking concerns and some leasing companies, carry as current prospective receipts from billings out of which their current equipment purchase obligations must be met. Such treatments, or the absence of any distinction between current and noncurrent on the balance sheet, as is the case with real estate companies, some contractors, banks, and insurance companies, are attempts by such concerns to convey to the reader their "special" financing and operating conditions that, they claim, make the current versus noncurrent distinction inapplicable and that have no parallel in the regular trading or industrial concern.

Some of these "special" circumstances may indeed be present, but they do not necessarily change the relationship existing between current obligations and the liquid funds available, or reasonably expected to become available, to meet them. It is to this relationship that the analyst, faced with the task of evaluating liquidity, must train his attention.

Working Capital as a Measure of Liquidity

The popularity of working capital as a measure of liquidity and of short-term financial health is so widespread that it hardly needs documentation. Credit grantors compute the relationship between current assets and current liabilities; financial analysts measure the size of the working capital of enterprises they analyze; government agencies compute aggregates of working capital of corporations; and most published balance sheets distinguish between current and noncurrent assets and liabilities. Moreover, loan agreements and bond indentures often contain stipulations regarding the maintenance of minimum working capital levels.

The absolute amount of working capital has significance only when related to other variables such as sales, total assets, and so forth. It is at best of limited value for comparison purposes and for judging the adequacy of working capital. This can be illustrated as follows:

	Company A	*Company B*
Current assets	$300,000	$1,200,000
Current liabilities ...	100,000	1,000,000
Working capital	$200,000	$ 200,000

While both companies have an equal amount of working capital, a cursory comparison of the relationship of current assets to current liabilities suggests that Company A's current condition is superior to that of Company B.

CURRENT RATIO

The above conclusion is based on the ratio of current assets to current liabilities. It is $3:1$ ($300,000/$100,000) for Company A and $1.2:1$ ($1,200,000/$1,000,000) for Company B. It is this ratio that is accorded substantial importance in the assessment of an enterprise's current liquidity.

Some of the basic reasons for the widespread use of the current ratio as a measure of liquidity are obvious:

1. It measures the degree to which current assets cover current liabilities. The higher the amount of current assets in relation to current liabilities, the greater the assurance that these liabilities can be paid out of such assets.
2. The excess of current assets over current liabilities provides a buffer against losses that may be incurred in the disposition or liquidation of the current assets other than cash. The more substantial such a buffer is, the better for creditors. Thus, the current ratio measures the margin of safety available to cover any possible shrinkage in the value of current assets.
3. It measures the reserve of liquid funds in excess of current obligations that is available as a margin of safety against uncertainty and the random shocks to which the flows of funds in an enterprise are subject. Random shocks, such as strikes, extraordinary losses, and other uncertainties, can temporarily and unexpectedly stop or reduce the inflow of funds.

What is not so obvious, however, is the fact that the current ratio, as a measure of liquidity and short-term solvency, is subject to serious theoretical as well as practical shortcomings and limitations. Consequently, before we embark on a discussion of the uses of the current ratio and related measures of liquidity, these limitations must be thoroughly understood.

Limitations of the Current Ratio

The first step in our examination of the current ratio as a tool of liquidity and short-term solvency analysis is to examine the components that are normally included in the ratio shown in Exhibit 16–1.

Disregarding, for purposes of this evaluation, prepaid expenses and similar unsubstantial items entering the computation of the current ratio, we are left with the above four major elements that comprise this ratio.

Now, if we define liquidity as the ability to balance required cash outflows with adequate inflows, including an allowance for unexpected interruptions of inflows or increases in outflows, we must ask: Does the relationship of these four elements at a given point in time—

1. Measure and predict the pattern of future cash flows?
2. Measure the adequacy of future cash inflows in relation to outflows?

Unfortunately, the answer to these questions is mostly negative. The current ratio is a static or "stock" concept of what cash resources are available at a given moment in time to meet the obligations at that moment. The existing reservoir of cash resources does not have a logical or causative relationship to the future cash that will flow through it. And yet it is the future flows that are the subject of our greatest interest in the assessment of liquidity. These flows depend importantly on elements *not* included in the ratio itself, such as sales, cash costs and expenses, profits, and changes in business conditions. To elaborate, let us examine more closely the four elements comprising the ratio.

Cash and cash equivalents The amount of cash held by a well-managed enterprise is in the nature of a precautionary reserve, intended to take care of short-term imbalances in cash flows. For example, in cases of a business downturn, sales may fall more rapidly than outlays for purchases and expenses. Since cash is a nonearning asset and cash equivalents are usually low-yielding securities, the investment in such assets

Exhibit 16–1

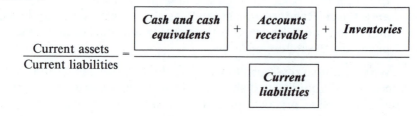

$$\frac{\text{Current assets}}{\text{Current liabilities}} = \frac{\boxed{\textit{Cash and cash equivalents}} + \boxed{\textit{Accounts receivable}} + \boxed{\textit{Inventories}}}{\boxed{\textit{Current liabilities}}}$$

is kept at a safe minimum. To conceive of this minimum balance as available for payment of current debts would require the dropping of the going-concern assumption underlying accounting statements. While the balance of cash has some relation to the existing level of activity, such a relationship is not very strong nor does it contain predictive implications regarding the future. In fact, some enterprises may use cash substitutes in the form of open lines of credit that, of course, do not enter at all into the computation of the current ratio.

The important link between cash and solvency in the minds of many is due to the well-known fact that a shortage of cash, more than any other factor, is the element that can clinch the insolvency of an enterprise.

| *Accounts receivable* | The major determinant of the level of accounts receivable is sales. The size of accounts receivable in relation to sales |

is governed by terms of trade credit policy, and collection experience. Changes in receivables will correspond to changes in sales though not necessarily on a directly proportional basis.

When we look at accounts receivable as a source of cash, we must, except in the case of liquidation, recognize the revolving nature of the asset with the collection of one account replaced by the extension of fresh credit. Thus, the level of receivables per se is not an index to future net inflows of cash.

| *Inventories* | As is the case with accounts receivable, the main determinant of the size of inventories is the level of sales, or |

expected sales, rather than the level of current liabilities. Given that the level of sales is a measure of the level of demand then, scientific methods of inventory management (economic order quantities, safe stock levels, and reorder points) generally establish that inventory increments vary not in proportion to demand but vary rather with the *square root* of demand.

The relationship of inventories to sales is further accented by the fact that it is sales that is the one essential element that starts the conversion of inventories to cash. Moreover, the determination of future cash inflows through the sale of inventories is dependent on the profit margin that can be realized because inventories are generally stated at the lower of *cost* or market. The current ratio, while including inventories, gives no recognition to the sales level or to profit margin, both of which are important elements entering into the determination of future cash inflows.

| *Current liabilities* | The level of current liabilities, the probability of satisfaction of which the current ratio is intended to measure, is also |

largely determined by the level of sales.

Current liabilities are a source of cash in the same sense that receivables and inventories tie up cash. Since purchases, which give rise to accounts payable, are a function of the level of activity (i.e., sales), these payables vary with sales. As long as sales remain constant or are rising, the payment of current liabilities is essentially a refunding operation. Here again the components of the current ratio give little, if any, recognition to these elements and their effects on the future flow of cash. Nor do the current liabilities that enter into the computation of the current ratio include prospective outlays, such as commitments under construction contracts, loans, leases, or pensions, all of which affect the future outflow of funds.

Implications of Current Ratio Limitations

There are a number of conclusions that can be reached on the basis of the foregoing discussion:

1. Liquidity depends to some extent on cash or cash equivalents balances and to a much more significant extent on prospective cash flows.
2. There is no direct or established relationship between balances of working capital items and the pattern that future cash flows are likely to assume.
3. Managerial policies directed at optimizing the levels of receivables and inventories are oriented primarily toward efficient and profitable assets utilization and only secondarily at liquidity.[1]

Given these conclusions, which obviously limit the value of the current ratio as an index of liquidity, and given the static nature of this ratio and the fact that it is composed of items that affect liquidity in different ways, we may ask why this ratio enjoys such widespread use and in what way, if any, it can be used intelligently by the analyst.

The most probable reasons for the popularity of the current ratio are evidently the simplicity of its basic concept, the ease with which it can be computed, and the readiness with which data for it can be obtained. It may also derive its popularity from the credit grantor's, and especially the banker's, propensity to view credit situations as conditions of last resort. They may ask themselves: "What if there were a complete cessation of funds inflow? Would the current assets then be adequate to pay off the current liabilities?" The assumption of such extreme conditions is, of course, not always a useful way of measuring liquidity.

To what use can the intelligent analyst put the current ratio?

---

[1] The nature of the business is also a factor. In the case of many electric utilities, current liabilities exceed current assets because the prompt payment by utility customers enables the utilities to pay off their obligations on time. In other words, utility current assets get converted into cash faster than current obligations must be met. As an added example from another field, Fair Lanes, a bowling lanes operator, obviously does not sell on credit and thus has no receivables. It also carries no inventories of any consequence. As a result, it has during most of its 50-year existence operated with a working capital deficiency. With almost all of its current assets in cash, it has no problem meeting current obligations.

Let it first be said that the analyst who wishes to measure short-term liquidity and solvency will find cash flow projections and pro forma financial statements to be the more relevant and reliable tools to use. This involves obtaining information that is not readily available in published financial statements and it also involves the need for a great deal of estimation. This area of analysis will be discussed in the next chapter.

The Current Ratio as a Valid Tool of Analysis

Should the analyst want to use the current ratio as a static measure of the ability of current assets to satisfy the current liabilities, he or she will be employing a different concept of liquidity from the one discussed above. In this context, liquidity means the readiness and speed with which current assets can be converted to cash and the degree to which such conversion will result in shrinkage in the stated value of current assets.

It is not our purpose here to discredit the current ratio as a valid tool of analysis but rather to suggest that its legitimate area of application is far less wide than popularly believed.

Defenders of this, the oldest and best known of financial ratios, may say that they are aware of the multitude of limitations and inconsistencies of concept outlined above but that they will "allow" for them in the evaluation of the ratio. A careful examination of these limitations suggests that such process of "allowing" for such limitations is well nigh impossible.

The best and most valid way to use this ratio is to recognize its limitations and to restrict its use to the analytical job it can do, that is, measuring the ability of *present* current assets to discharge *existing* current liabilities and considering the excess, if any, as a liquid surplus available to meet imbalances in the flow of funds and other contingencies. This should be done with an awareness of the fact that the test envisages a situation of enterprise liquidation,[2] whereas in the normal, going-concern situation current assets are of a revolving nature (for example, the collected receivable is replaced with a newly created one) while the current liabilities are essentially of a refunding nature (the repayment of one is followed by the creation of another).

Given the analytical function of the current ratio, as outlined above, there are two basic elements that must be measured before the current ratio can form the basis for valid conclusions:

1. The quality of the current assets and the nature of the current liabilities that enter the determination of the ratio.

---

[2] The circumstances leading to bankruptcy or liquidation will have an effect on how much the amounts realized on asset dispositions will shrink. They will, for example, be likely to shrink more severely if the liquidation is caused by overall adverse industry conditions than if caused by specific difficulties such as poor management or inadequate capitalization.

2. The rate of turnover of these assets and liabilities, that is, the average time span needed to convert receivables and inventories into cash and the amount of time that can be taken for the payment of current liabilities.

To measure the above, a number of ratios and other tools have been devised, and these can enhance the use of the current ratio as an analytic tool.

Measures That Supplement the Current Ratio

The most liquid of current assets is, of course, cash, which is the standard of liquidity itself. A close second to cash is "temporary investments" that are usually highly marketable and relatively safe temporary repositories of cash. These are, in effect, considered as "cash equivalents" and usually earn a modest return.

Cash Ratios   The proportion that cash and cash equivalents constitute of the total current assets group is a measure of the degree of liquidity of this group of assets. It is measured by the cash ratio that is computed as follows:

$$\frac{\text{Cash} + \text{Cash equivalents}}{\text{Total current assets}}$$

Evaluation   The higher the ratio, the more liquid is the current asset group. This, in turn, means that with respect to this cash and cash equivalents component there is a minimal danger of loss in value in case of liquidation and that there is practically no waiting period for conversion of these assets into usable cash.

APB Opinion 18 generally requires the carrying of investments, representing an interest of 20 percent or higher, at underlying equity. This is, of course, neither cost nor, necessarily, market value. While such substantial positions in the securities of another company are not usually considered cash equivalents, *should* they nevertheless be so considered, their market value would be the most appropriate figure to use in the computation of liquidity ratios. The equity method of accounting is discussed in Chapters 5 and 9.

As to the availability of cash, the analyst should bear in mind possible restrictions that may exist with respect to the use of cash balances. An example is compensating balances that banks extending credit expect their customers to keep. While such balances can be used, the analyst must nevertheless assess the effect on a company's credit standing and credit availability, as well as on its banking connection, of a breach of the tacit agreement not to draw on the compensating cash balance.

Two additional factors bearing on the evaluation of cash ratios should be mentioned. One is that modern computerized cash management methods have led to more efficient uses of cash by corporations and this has led to lower need for cash for ordinary operations. The other is that open lines of credit and other standby credit arrangements are effective substitutes for cash balances and should be so considered.

An additional ratio that measures cash adequacy should be mentioned. The cash to current liabilities ratio is computed as follows:

$$\frac{\text{Cash + Cash equivalents}}{\text{Current liabilities}}$$

It measures how much cash is available to pay current obligations. This is a severe test that ignores the refunding nature of current assets and liabilities. It supplements the cash ratio discussed above in that it measures cash availability from a somewhat different point of view.

To view the cash ratio as a further extension of the acid-test ratio (see page 566) would, except in extreme cases, constitute a test of short-term liquidity too severe to be meaningful. Nevertheless, the importance of cash as the ultimate form of liquidity should never be underestimated. The record of business failures provides many examples of insolvent companies, possessing sizable noncash assets, current and noncurrent, and no cash to pay debts or to operate with.

Measures of Accounts Receivable Liquidity

In most enterprises that sell on credit, accounts and notes receivable are a significant part of working capital. In assessing the quality of working capital and of the current ratio, it is important to get some measure of the quality and the liquidity of the receivables.

Both the quality[3] and liquidity of accounts receivable are affected by their rate of turnover. By quality is meant the likelihood of collection without loss. An indicator of this likelihood is the degree to which receivables are within the terms of payment set by the enterprise. Experience has shown that the longer receivables remain outstanding beyond the date on which they are due, the lower is the probability of their collection in full. Turnover is an indicator of the age of the receivables, particularly when it is compared with an expected turnover rate that is determined by credit terms granted.

The measure of liquidity is concerned with the speed with which accounts receivable will, on average, be converted into cash. Here again turnover is among the best measures to use.

---

[3] The validity of the collection claim is also one aspect of quality. Thus, the analyst must be alert to problems that can arise from "sales" on consignment or those with right of return that are more fully discussed in Chapters 5 and 10.

AVERAGE ACCOUNTS RECEIVABLE TURNOVER RATIO

The receivable turnover ratio is computed as follows:

$$\frac{\text{Net sales on credit}}{\text{Average accounts receivable}}$$

The quickest way for an external analyst to determine the average accounts receivable is to take the beginning receivables of the period, add the ending receivables, and divide the sum by two. The use of monthly or quarterly sales figures can lead to an even more accurate result. The more widely sales fluctuate, the more subject to distortion this ratio is, unless the receivables are properly averaged.

Notes receivable arising from normal sales should be included in the accounts receivable figure in computing the turnover ratio. Discounted notes receivable that are still outstanding should also be included in the accounts receivable total.

The sales figure used in computing the ratio should be that of credit sales only, because cash sales obviously do not generate receivables. Since published financial statements rarely disclose the division between cash and credit sales, the external analyst may have to compute the ratio under the assumption that cash sales are relatively insignificant. If they are not insignificant, then a degree of distortion may occur in the ratio. However, if the proportion of cash sales to total sales remains relatively constant, the year-to-year comparison of changes in the receivables turnover ratio may nevertheless be validly based.

The average receivables turnover figure indicates how many *times,* on average, the receivables revolve, that is, are generated and collected during the year.

For example, if sales are $1,200,000 and beginning receivables are $150,000 while year-end receivables are $250,000, then receivable turnover is computed as follows:

$$\frac{\$1,200,00}{(\$150,000 + \$250,000) \div 2} = \frac{\$1,200,000}{\$200,000} = 6 \text{ times}$$

While the turnover figure furnishes a sense of the speed of collections and is valuable for comparison purposes, it is not directly comparable to the terms of trade that the enterprise normally extends. Such comparison is best made by converting the turnover into days of sales tied up in receivables.

Collection Period for Accounts Receivable

This measure, also known as *days sales in accounts receivable,* measures the number of days it takes, on average, to collect accounts (and notes) receivable. The number of days can be obtained by dividing the average accounts receivable turnover ratio discussed above into 360, the approximate round number of days in the year. Thus,

$$\text{Collection period} = \frac{360}{\text{Average accounts receivable turnover}}$$

Using the figures of the preceding example, the collection period is:

$$\frac{360}{6} = 60 \text{ days}$$

An alternative computation is to first obtain the average daily sales and then divide the *ending gross* receivable balance by it.

$$\text{Accounts receivable} \div \frac{\text{Sales}}{360}$$

The result will differ from the foregoing computation because the average accounts receivable turnover figure uses *average* accounts receivable, while this computation uses *ending* accounts receivable only; it thus focuses specifically on the latest accounts receivable balances. Using the figures from our example, the computation is:

$$\text{Average daily sales} = \frac{\text{Sales}}{360} = \frac{\$1,200,000}{360} = \$3,333$$

$$\frac{\text{Accounts receivable}}{\text{Average daily sales}} = \frac{\$250,000}{\$3,333} = 75 \text{ days}$$

Note that if the collection period computation would have used ending receivables rather than *average* receivables turnover, the identical collection period, that is, 75, could have been obtained as follows:

$$\frac{\text{Sales}}{\text{Accounts receivable (ending)}} = \frac{\$1,200,000}{\$250,000} = 4.8 \text{ times}$$

$$\frac{360}{\text{Receivables turnover}} = \frac{360}{4.8} = 75 \text{ days}$$

The use of 360 days is arbitrary because while receivables are outstanding 360 days (used for computational convenience instead of 365), the sales days of the year usually number less than 300. However, consistent computation of the ratio will make for valid period-to-period comparisons.

Evaluation

Accounts receivable turnover rates or collection periods can be compared to industry averages (see Chapter 4) or to the credit terms granted by the enterprise.

When the collection period is compared with the terms of sale allowed by the enterprise, the degree to which customers are paying on time can be assessed. Thus, if the average terms of sale in the illustration used above are 40 days, then an average collection period of 75 days reflects either some or all of the following conditions:

1. A poor collection job.
2. Difficulty in obtaining prompt payment from customers in spite of diligent collection efforts.
3. Customers in financial difficulty.

The first conclusion calls for remedial managerial action, while the last two reflect particularly on both the quality and the liquidity of the accounts receivable.

An essential analytical first step is to determine whether the accounts receivable are representative of company sales activity. Significant receivables may, for example, be lodged in the captive finance company of the enterprise. In that case, the bad debt provision may also relate to receivables not on company books.

It is always possible that an *average* figure is not representative of the receivables population it represents. Thus, it is possible that the 75-day average collection period does not represent an across-the-board payment tardiness on the part of customers but is rather caused by the excessive delinquency of one or two substantial customers.

The best way to investigate further an excessive collection period is to *age* the accounts receivable in such a way that the distribution of each account by the number of days past due is clearly apparent. An aging schedule in a format such as given below will show whether the problem is widespread or concentrated:

Accounts receivable aging schedule

	Current	\[Days past due\] 0–30	31–60	61–90	Over 90
Accounts receivable					

The age distribution of the receivables will, of course, lead to better informed conclusions regarding the quality and the liquidity of the receivables as well as the kind of action that is necessary to remedy the situation. Another dimension of receivables classification is by quality ranges of credit agencies such as Dun & Bradstreet.

Notes receivable deserve the particular scrutiny of the analyst because while they are normally regarded as more negotiable than open accounts, they may be of poorer quality than regular receivables if they originated as an extension device for an unpaid account rather than at the inception of the original sale.

In assessing the quality of receivables, the analyst should remember that a significant conversion of receivables into cash. except for their use as collateral for borrowing, cannot be achieved without a cutback in sales volume. The sales policy aspect of the collection period evaluation must also be kept in mind. An enterprise may be willing to accept slow-paying customers who provide business that is, on an overall basis, profitable; that is, the profit on sales compensates for the extra use by the customer of the enterprise funds. This circumstance may modify the analyst's conclusions regarding the *quality* of the receivables but not those regarding their *liquidity.*

In addition to the consideration of profitability, an enterprise may extend more liberal credit in cases such as (1) the introduction of a new product, (2) a desire to make sales in order to utilize available excess capacity, or (3) special competitive conditions in the industry. Thus, the relationship between the level of receivables and that of sales and profits must always be borne in mind when evaluating the collection period. The trend of the collection period over time is always important in an assessment of the quality and the liquidity of the receivables.

Another trend that may be instructive to watch is that of the relationship between the provision for doubtful accounts and gross accounts receivable. The ratio is computed as follows:

$$\frac{\text{Provision for doubtful accounts}}{\text{Gross accounts receivable}}$$

An increase in this ratio over time may indicate management's conclusion that the collectibility of receivables has deteriorated. Conversely, a decrease of this ratio over time may lead to the opposite conclusion or may cause the analyst to reevaluate the adequacy of the provision for doubtful accounts.

Measures of accounts receivable turnover are, as we have seen in this section, important in the evaluation of liquidity. They are also important as measures of asset utilization, a subject that will be covered in Chapter 19.

MEASURES OF INVENTORY TURNOVER

Inventories represent in many cases a very substantial proportion of the current asset group. This is so for reasons that have little to do with an enterprise's objective of maintaining adequate levels of liquid funds. Reserves of liquid funds are seldom kept in the form of inventories. Inventories represent investments made for the purpose of obtaining a return. The return is derived from the expected profits that may result from sales. In most businesses, a certain level of inventory must be kept in order to generate an adequate level of sales. If the inventory level is inadequate, the sales volume will fall to below the level otherwise attainable. Excessive inventories, on the other hand, expose the enterprise to expenses such as storage costs, insurance, and taxes, as well as to risks of loss of value through obsolescence and physical deterioration. Moreover, excessive inventories tie up funds that can be used more profitably elsewhere.

Due to the risk involved in holding inventories as well as the fact that inventories are one step further removed from cash than receivables (they have to be sold before they are converted into receivables), inventories are normally considered the least liquid component of the current assets group. As is the case with most generalizations, this is not always true. Certain staple items, such as commodities, raw materials, and standard sizes of structural steel, enjoy broad and ready markets and can usually be sold with little effort, expense, or loss. On the other hand, fashion merchandise, specialized components, or perishable items can lose their value rapidly unless they are sold on a timely basis.

The evaluation of the current ratio, which includes inventories in its computation, must include a thorough evaluation of the quality as well as the liquidity of these assets. Here again, measures of turnover are the best overall tools available for this purpose.

Inventory Turnover Ratio

The inventory turnover ratio measures the average rate of speed with which inventories move through and out of the enterprise.

Computation   The computation of the average inventory turnover is as follows:

$$\frac{\text{Cost of goods sold}}{\text{Average inventory}}$$

Consistency of valuation requires that the cost of goods sold be used because, as is the case with inventories, it is stated principally at *cost.* Sales, on the other hand, normally include a profit. Although the cost of goods sold figure is now disclosed in most published income statements, the external analyst is still occasionally confronted with an unavailability of such a figure. In such a case, the sales figure must be substituted. While this results in a theoretically less valid turnover ratio, it can still be used for comparison and trend development purposes, especially if used consistently and when sharp changes in profit margins are not present.

The average inventory figure is most readily obtained as follows:

$$\frac{\text{Opening inventory} + \text{Closing inventory}}{2}$$

Further refinement in the averaging process can be achieved, where possible and necessary, by averaging quarterly or monthly inventory figures.

When an inventory turnover ratio is computed in order to evaluate the *level* of inventory at a certain date, such as the year-end inventory, the inventory figure in the denominator should be the figure as of that date rather than an average inventory figure.

Before a turnover ratio is computed, the analyst must carefully examine the composition of the inventory figure and make adjustments, such as those from LIFO to FIFO.

Days to Sell Inventory

Another measure of inventory turnover that is also useful in assessing purchasing policy is the required number of *days to sell inventory*. The computation that follows, that is,

$$\frac{360 \text{ days}}{\text{Average inventory turnover}}$$

measures the number of days it takes to sell the average inventory in a given year, and an alternative computation

$$\frac{\text{Ending inventory}}{\text{Cost of average day's sales}}$$

measures the number of days that are required to sell off the ending inventory, assuming the given rate of sales where the

$$\text{Cost of an average day's sales} = \frac{\text{Cost of goods sold}}{360}$$

Example of computations

Sales	$1,800,000
Cost of goods sold	1,200,000
Beginning inventory	200,000
Ending inventory	400,000

$$\text{Inventory turnover} = \frac{\$1,200,000}{(\$200,000 + \$400,000) \div 2} = \frac{\$1,200,000}{\$300,000} = 4 \text{ times}$$

$$\text{Number of days to sell average inventory} = \frac{360}{4} = 90 \text{ days}$$

Alternatively, the computation based on ending inventory is as follows:

Step 1:

$$\frac{\text{Cost of goods sold}}{360} = \frac{\$1,200,000}{360} = \$3,333 \text{ (cost of average day's sales)}$$

Step 2:

$$\frac{\text{Ending inventory}}{\text{Cost of average day's sales}} = \frac{\$400,000}{\$3,333} = 120 \text{ days}$$

Interpretation of Inventory Turnover Ratios   The current ratio computation views its current asset components as sources of funds that can, as a means of last resort, be used to pay off the current liabilities. Viewed this way, the inventory turnover ratios give us a measure of the quality as well as of the liquidity of the inventory component of the current assets.

The quality of inventory is a measure of the enterprise's ability to use it and dispose of it without loss. When this is envisaged under conditions of forced liquidation, then recovery of cost is the objective. In the normal course of business, the inventory should, of course, be sold at a profit. Viewed from this point of view, the normal profit margin realized by the enterprise assumes importance because the funds that will be obtained, and that would theoretically be available for payment of current liabilities, will include the profit in addition to the recovery of cost. In both cases, costs of selling will reduce the net proceeds.

In practice, a going concern cannot use its investment in inventory for the payment of current liabilities because any drastic reduction in normal inventory levels will surely cut into the sales volume.

A rate of turnover that is slower than that experienced historically, or that is below that normal in the industry, would lead to the preliminary conclusion that it includes items that are slow moving because they are obsolete, in weak demand, or otherwise unsalable. Such conditions do, of course, cast doubt on the feasibility of recovering the cost of such items.

Further investigation may reveal that the slowdown in inventory turnover is due to a buildup of inventory in accordance with a future contractual commitment, in anticipation of a price rise, in anticipation of a strike or shortage, or for any number of other reasons that must be probed further.

The analyst should be aware of the "just-in-time" inventory management approach which aims to keep inventory levels as low as possible by carefully integrating the ordering, producing, selling, and distributing functions. The implementation of this approach will lead to increases in inventory turnover.

A better evaluation of inventory turnover can be obtained from the computation of separate turnover rates for the major components of inventory such as (1) raw materials, (2) work in process, and (3) finished goods. Departmental or divisional turnover rates can similarly lead to more useful conclusions regarding inventory quality. One should never lose sight of the fact that the total inventory turnover ratio is an aggregate of widely varying turnover rates of individual components.

The biggest problem facing the external analyst who tries to compute inventory turnover ratios by individual product components is obtaining the necessary detailed data. This data is, at present, rarely provided in published financial statements. It can, however, be obtained from companies willing to provide such information.

The turnover ratio is, of course, also a gauge of liquidity in that it conveys a measure of the speed with which inventory can be converted into cash. In this connection, a useful additional measure is the conversion period of inventories.

Conversion Period of Inventories   This computation adds the collection period of receivables to the days needed to sell inventories in order to arrive at the time interval needed to convert inventories into cash.

Using figures developed in our examples of the respective ratios above, we get:

	Days
Days to sell inventory	90
Days to collect receivables	60
Total conversion period of inventories	150

It would thus normally take 150 days to sell inventory on credit and to collect the receivables. This is a period identical to the *operating cycle* that we discussed earlier in this chapter.

The Effect of Alternative Methods of Inventory Management

In evaluating the inventory turnover ratio, the analyst must be alert to the influence that alternative accounting principles have on the determination of the ratio's components. The basic discussion on alternative accounting principles of inventory measurement is found in Chapter 5. It is obvious that the use of the LIFO method of inventory valuation may render both the turnover ratios as well as the current ratio practically meaningless. Information is usually found in published financial statements that enable the analyst to adjust the unrealistically low LIFO inventory valuation occurring in times of rising price levels so as to render it useful for inclusion in turnover ratio or the current ratio. Even if two companies employ LIFO cost methods for their inventory valuation computation of their ratios, using such inventory figures may nevertheless not be comparable because their respective LIFO inventory pools (bases) may have been acquired in years of significantly different price levels. The inventory figure enters the numerator of the current ratio and also the denominator because the inventory method utilized affects the income tax liability.

The analyst must also bear in mind that companies using the so-called natural year may have at their year-end an unrepresentatively low inventory level and that this may increase the turnover ratio to unrealistically high levels.

Prepaid Expenses

Prepaid expenses are expenditures made for benefits that are expected to be received in the future. Since most such benefits are receivable within a year or within an enterprise's operating cycle, they will conserve the outlay of current funds.

Usually, the amounts included in this category are relatively small compared to the size of the other current assets, and consequently no extensive discussion of their treatment is needed here. However, the analyst must be aware of the tendency of managements of enterprises with weak current positions to include in prepaid expenses deferred charges and other items of dubious liquidity. Such items must consequently be excluded from the computation of working capital and of the current ratio.

CURRENT LIABILITIES

In the computation of working capital and of the current ratio, current liabilities are important for two related reasons:

1. A basic objective of measuring the excess of current assets over current liabilities is to determine whether the latter are covered by current assets and what margin of safety is provided by the excess of such assets over current liabilities.
2. Current liabilities are deducted from current assets in arriving at the net working capital position.

In the computation of the current ratio, the point of view adopted toward current liabilities is *not* one of a continuing enterprise but rather of an enterprise in liquidation. This is so because in the normal course of operations, current liabilities are not paid off but are rather of a refunding nature. As long as the sales volume remains stable, purchases will also remain at a stable level, and that in turn will cause current liabilities to remain level. Increasing sales, in turn, will generally result in an increasing level of current liabilities. Thus, generally the trend and direction of sales is a good indication of the future level of current liabilities.

In assessing the quality of the current ratio, the nature of the current liabilities must be carefully examined.

Differences in the "Nature" of Current Liabilities

Not all liabilities represent equally urgent and forceful calls for payment. At one extreme we find liabilities for taxes of all kinds that must be paid promptly regardless of current financial difficulties. The powers of collection of federal and local government authorities are as well known as they are powerful.

On the other hand, current liabilities to suppliers with whom the enterprise has a long-standing relationship and who depend on, and value, the enterprise's business are of a very different degree of urgency. Postponement and renegotiation of such debts in times of financial stringency are both possible and common.

The "nature" of current liabilities in terms of our present discussion must be judged in the light of the degree of urgency of payment that attaches to them. It should be understood that if fund inflows from current revenues are viewed as sources of funds available for the payment of current liabilities, then labor costs and other current fund-requiring costs and expenses have a first call on sales revenues and that trade bills and other liabilities can be paid only after such recurring outlays have been met. This dynamic aspect of funds flow will be examined more closely in the chapter that follows.

The analyst must also be aware of unrecorded liabilities that may have a claim to current funds. Examples of these are purchase commitments and obligations under pensions and leases. Moreover, under long-term loan acceleration clauses, a failure to meet current installments of long-term debt may render the entire debt due and payable, that is, cause it to become current.

Days Purchases in Accounts Payable Ratio

A measure of the degree to which accounts payable represent current rather than overdue obligations can be obtained by calculating the *days purchases in accounts payable ratio*. This ratio is computed as follows:

$$\frac{\text{Accounts payable}}{\text{Purchases per day*}} = \text{Days purchases in accounts payable}$$

* Computed: Purchases/360.

The difficulty that the external analyst will encounter in computing this ratio is that normally purchases are not separately disclosed in published financial statements. For retailers a rough approximation of the amount of purchases can be obtained by adjusting the cost of goods sold figure for depreciation and other noncash-requiring charges as well as for changes in inventories. Thus:

$$\text{Purchases} = \frac{\text{Adjusted cost}}{\text{of goods sold}} + \frac{\text{Ending}}{\text{inventory}} - \frac{\text{Beginning}}{\text{inventory}}$$

The cost of goods sold figure may, however, contain significant cash charges, and this may reduce the validity of a computation that contains an approximation of purchases on credit.

INTERPRETATION OF THE CURRENT RATIO

In the foregoing sections, we have examined the means by which the quality and the liquidity of the individual components of the current ratio is measured. This evaluation is, of course, essential to an overall interpretation of the current ratio as an indicator of short-term liquidity and financial strength.

The analyst must, however, exercise great care if he wants to carry the interpretation of the current ratio beyond the conclusion that it represents an excess of current resources over current obligations as of a given point in time.

Examination of Trend

An examination of the trend of the current ratio over time can be very instructive. Two tools of analysis that were discussed in Chapter 4 are useful here. One is *trend analysis,* where the components of working capital as well as the current ratio would be converted into an index to be compared over time. The other is *common-size analysis,* by means of which the *composition* of the current asset group is examined over time. A historical trend and common-size comparison over time, as well as an intra-industry comparison of such trends, can also be instructive.

Interpretation of Changes over Time

Changes in the current ratio over time must, however, be interpreted with great care. They do not automatically imply changes in liquidity or operating results. Thus, for example, in a prosperous year an increased liability for taxes may result in a lowering of the current ratio. Conversely, during a business contraction, current liabilities may be paid off while there may be a concurrent involuntary accumulation of inventories and uncollected receivables causing the ratio to rise.

In times of business expansion, which may reflect operating successes, the enterprise may suffer from an expansion in working capital requirements, otherwise known as a prosperity squeeze with a resulting contraction of the current ratio.

As can be seen from this example, a doubling of current assets, accompanied by a quadrupling of current liabilities and an unchanged amount of working capital will lead to a halving of the current ratio. This is the effect of business expansion unaccompanied by an added capital investment.

	Year 1	Year 2
Current assets	$300,000	$600,000
Current liabilities ...	100,000	400,000
Working capital	$200,000	$200,000
Current ratio	3 : 1	1.5 : 1

Inflation can have a similar effect on a business enterprise in that it will lead to a substantial increase in all current items categories.

Possibilities of Manipulation

The analyst must be aware of the possibilities of year-end manipulation of the current ratio, otherwise known as window dressing.

For example, toward the close of the fiscal year, the collection of receivables may be pressed more vigorously, advances to officers may be called in for temporary repayment, inventory may be reduced to below normal levels, and normal purchases may be delayed. Proceeds from these steps can then be used to pay off current liabilities. The effect on the current ratio of the reduction of current liabilities through the use of current assets can be seen in the following example:

	Payoff of $50,000 in liabilities	
	Before	After
Current assets	$200,000	$150,000
Current liabilities ...	100,000	50,000
Current ratio	2 : 1	3 : 1

The accounting profession, sensing the propensity of managements to offset liabilities against assets, has strengthened its prohibitions against offsets by restricting them strictly to situations where the legal right to offset exists.

To the extent possible, the analyst should go beyond year-end measures and should try to obtain as many interim readings of the current ratio as possible, not only to guard against the practice of window dressing described above but also to gauge the seasonal changes to which the ratio is exposed. The effect of a strong current ratio in December on an assessment of current financial condition may be considerably tempered if it is discovered that at its seasonal peak in July the enterprise is dangerously close to a serious credit squeeze.

The Use of "Rules of Thumb" Standards

A popular belief that has gained considerable currency is that the current ratio can be evaluated by means of *rules of thumb*. Thus, it is believed that if the current ratio is 2 : 1 (or 200 percent), it is sound and anything below that norm is bad while the higher above that figure the current ratio is, the better.

This rule of thumb may reflect the lender's, and particularly the banker's, conservatism. The fact that it is down from the norm of 2.5 : 1 prevailing at the turn of the century may mean that improved financial reporting has reduced this size of the "cushion" that the banker and other creditors would consider as the minimum protection they need.

What the 2 : 1 standard means is that there are $2 of current assets available for each dollar of current liabilities or that the value of current assets can, on liquidation, shrink by 50 percent before it will be inadequate to cover the current liabilities. Of course, a current ratio much higher than 2 : 1, while implying a superior coverage of current liabilities, may also mean a wasteful accumulation of liquid resources which do not "carry their weight" by earning an appropriate return for the enterprise.

It should be evident by now that the evaluation of the current ratio in terms of rules of thumb is a technique of dubious validity. This is so for two major reasons:

1. As we have learned in the preceding sections, the quality of the current assets, as well as the composition of the current liabilities that make up this ratio, are the most important determinants in an evaluation of the quality of the current ratio. Thus, two companies that have identical current ratios may nevertheless be in quite different current financial condition due to variations in the quality of the working capital components.
2. The need of an enterprise for working capital varies with industry conditions as well as with the length of its own particular *net trade cycle*.

The Net Trade Cycle

An enterprise's need for working capital depends importantly on the relative size of its required inventory investment as well as on the relationship between the credit terms it receives from its suppliers as against those it must extend to its customers. These relationships, known as the trade cycle, are exemplified in Illustration 4 below:

ILLUSTRATION 4.   Assume a company shows the following data at the end of year 1:

$$
\begin{array}{lr}
\text{Sales of year 1} & \$360,000 \\
\text{Receivables} & 40,000 \\
\text{Inventories*} & 50,000 \\
\text{Accounts payable}^\dagger & 20,000 \\
\text{Cost of goods sold (including} & \\
\quad\text{depreciation of \$30,000)} & 320,000 \\
\end{array}
$$

    * Beginning inventory was $100,000.
    † In this example we assume that these relate to only purchases included in cost of goods sold.

To find purchases per day:

$$
\begin{array}{lr}
\text{Ending inventory} & 50,000 \\
\text{Cost of goods sold} & \underline{320,000} \\
 & 370,000 \\
\text{Less: Beginning inventory} & \underline{(100,000)} \\
\text{Cost of goods purchased and manufactured} & 270,000 \\
\text{Less: Depreciation expense included in cost} & \\
\quad\text{of goods sold} & \underline{(30,000)} \\
\text{Purchases} & \underline{240,000} \\
\end{array}
$$

Purchases per day = 240,000 ÷ 360 = $666.67

Net trade cycle:

Number of days in:

$$\text{Accounts receivable} = \frac{40,000}{360,000 \div 360} = \underline{40.00}\ \text{days}$$

$$\text{Inventories} = \frac{50,000}{320,000 \div 360} = \underline{56.24}\ \text{days}$$

$$96.24$$

$$\text{Less: Accounts payable} = \frac{20,000}{666.67} = \underline{30.00}\ \text{days}$$

$$\text{Net trade cycle (days)} \qquad\qquad \underline{\underline{66.24}}$$

Please note that in the above computations the numerator and denominator are stated on a consistent basis. Thus accounts receivable, which are expressed in terms of sales prices, are divided by sales per day. Inventories, which are stated at cost, are divided by cost of goods sold per day. Accounts payable are divided by purchases per day.

The company has 40 days of sales tied up in receivables. It keeps 56.24 days of goods sold in inventory. On the other hand, it receives only 30 days of purchases as credit from its suppliers. Thus, while the day measures are expressed on different bases, the approximation of the net trade cycle is computed on a consistent basis. The higher the net trade cycle the larger the investment in working capital required. A reduction in the number of days sales in receivables or cost of sales in inventories will lower working capital requirements. An increase in the days of purchases credit received from suppliers will have a similar effect.

The working capital requirements of a supermarket with its high inventory turnover and low outstanding receivables are obviously lower than those of a tobacco company with its slow inventory turnover.

Valid Working Capital Standards

Comparison with industry current ratios, as well as analyses of working capital requirements such as the net trade cycle analysis described above, can lead to far more valid conclusions regarding the adequacy of an enterprise's working capital than can a mechanical comparison of its current ratio to the 2 : 1 rule of thumb standard.

The amount of working capital needed by an enterprise is importantly determined by industry conditions and practices. In recent years, the average industrial company needed about 15 cents of working capital for every dollar of sales. But averages can be misleading, and therefore it is best to focus on specific industry conditions and standards as cases for comparison.

The Importance of Sales

In an assessment of the overall liquidity of current assets, the trend of sales is an important factor. Since it takes sales to convert inventory into receivables or cash, an uptrend in sales indicates that the conversion of inventories into more liquid assets will be easier to achieve than when sales remain constant. Declining sales, on the other hand, will retard the conversion of inventories into cash.

Common-Size Analysis of Current Assets Composition

The composition of the current asset group, which can be analyzed by means of common-size statements, is another good indicator of relative working capital liquidity.

Consider, for example, the following comparative working capital composition:

	Year 1		Year 2	
Current assets:				
Cash....................	$ 30,000	30%	$ 20,000	20%
Accounts receivable	40,000	40	30,000	30
Inventories	30,000	30	50,000	50
Total current assets	$100,000	100%	$100,000	100%

The simple illustration above shows, even without the computation of common-size percentages, that the liquidity of the current asset group has deteriorated in year 2 by comparison with year 1. However, the use of common-size percentage comparisons will greatly facilitate the evaluation of comparative liquidity, regardless of the size of the dollar amounts involved.

The Liquidity Index

The measurement of the comparative liquidity of current assets can be further refined through the use of a *liquidity index*. The construction of this index (first suggested by A. H. Finney) can be illustrated as follows:

Using the working capital figures from the common-size computation above, and assuming that the conversion of inventories into accounts receivable takes 50 days on average and that the conversion of receivables into cash takes an average of 40 days, the index is computed as follows:

Year 1

	Amount	$\times$	Days removed from cash	$=$	Product dollar-days
Cash	$ 30,000		—		—
Accounts receivable	40,000		40		1,600,000
Inventories	30,000		90		2,700,000
Total	$100,000 *(a)*				4,300,000 *(b)*

$$\text{Liquidity index} = \frac{b}{a} = \frac{4,300,000}{\$100,000} = \underline{\underline{43}}$$

Year 2

	Amount	× Days removed from cash	= Product dollar-days
Cash	$ 20,000	—	—
Accounts receivable	30,000	40	1,200,000
Inventories	50,000	90	4,500,000
Total	$100,000		5,700,000

$$\text{Liquidity index} = \frac{5,700,000}{\$100,000} = \underline{57}$$

The computation of the respective liquidity indexes for the years 1 and 2 tells what we already knew instinctively in the case of this simple example, that is, that the liquidity has deteriorated in year 2 as compared to year 1.

The liquidity index must be interpreted with care. The index is in itself a figure without significance. It gains its significance only from a comparison between one index number and another as a gauge of the period-to-period change in liquidity or as a company-to-company comparison of relative liquidity. Increases in the index signify a deterioration in liquidity while decreases signify changes in the direction of improved liquidity. The index that is expressed in days is a weighing mechanism and its validity depends on the validity of the assumptions implicit in the weighing process.

An additional popular technique of current ratio interpretation is to submit it to a somewhat sterner test.

ACID-TEST RATIO

This test is the acid-test ratio, also known as the *quick ratio* because it is assumed to include the assets most quickly convertible into cash.

The acid-test ratio is computed as shown in Exhibit 16–2.

Exhibit 16–2

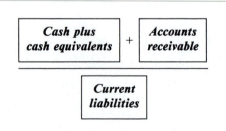

$$\frac{\boxed{\textit{Cash plus cash equivalents}} + \boxed{\textit{Accounts receivable}}}{\boxed{\textit{Current liabilities}}}$$

The omission of inventories from the acid-test ratio is based on the belief that they are the least liquid component of the current asset group. While this is generally so, we have seen in an earlier discussion in this chapter that this is not always true and that certain types of inventory can be more liquid than are slow-paying receivables. Another reason for the exclusion of inventories is the belief, quite often warranted, that the valuation of inventories normally requires a greater degree of judgment than is required for the valuation of the other current assets.

Since prepaid expenses are usually insignificant in relation to the other current assets, the acid-test ratio is sometimes computed simply by omitting the inventories from the current asset figure.

The interpretation of the acid-test ratio is subject to most of the same considerations which were discussed regarding the interpretation of the current ratio. Moreover, the acid-test ratio represents an even sterner test of an enterprise's liquidity than does the current ratio, and the analyst must judge what significance the omission of inventories has on the evaluation of liquidity.

OTHER MEASURES OF SHORT-TERM LIQUIDITY

The static nature of the current ratio that measures the relationship of current assets to current liabilities, at a given moment in time, as well as the fact that this measure of liquidity fails to accord recognition to the great importance that cash flows play in an enterprise's ability to meet its maturing obligations, has led to a search for more dynamic measures of liquidity.

Cash Flow Related Measures

Since liabilities are paid with cash, the relationship of cash provided by operations to current liabilities is significant. Chapter 13 discusses the derivation of the "cash from operations" amount.

The ratio of operating cash flow to current liabilities overcomes the weakness of the static current ratio in that its numerator represents a flow over time. Since operating cash flow encompasses a year it is appropriate for the current liabilities in the denominator to be the average for the period.

The ratio is computed:

$$\frac{\text{Cash flow from operations}}{\text{Average current liabilities}}$$

The computation for Campbell Soup for 1991 is as follows:

$$\frac{805.2 \boxed{64}}{(1,278 + 1298.1) \div 2 \boxed{45}} = 0.62$$

An empirical study[4] determined that a ratio of operating cash flow to current liabilities of 0.40 was common for healthy firms.

THE CONCEPT OF FINANCIAL FLEXIBILITY

In addition to the tools of analysis of short-term liquidity with which we have dealt here and which lend themselves to quantification, there are important qualitative considerations that also have an important bearing on the short-term liquidity of an enterprise. These can be usefully characterized as depending on the financial flexibility of an enterprise.

Financial flexibility is characterized by the ability of an enterprise to take steps to counter unexpected interruptions in the flow of funds for reasons however unexpected. It means the ability to borrow from a variety of sources, to raise equity capital, to sell and redeploy assets, and to adjust the level and the direction of operations in order to meet changing circumstances.

The capacity to borrow depends on numerous factors and is subject to rapid change. It depends on profitability, stability, relative size, industry position, asset composition, and capital structure. It depends, moreover, on such external factors as credit market conditions and trends.

The capacity to borrow is important as a source of cash in time of need for cash and is also important when an enterprise must roll over its short-term debt. Prearranged financing or open lines of credit are more reliable sources of cash in time of need than is potential financing.

Other factors that bear on the assessment of the financial flexibility of an enterprise are the ratings of its commercial paper, bonds, and preferred stock; restrictions on the sale of its assets; the degree to which expenses are of a discretionary nature as well as the ability to respond quickly to changing conditions such as strikes, shrinking demand, or the cessation of sources of supply.

Financial flexibility is also important in the assessment of long-term solvency (see Chapter 18).

MANAGEMENT'S DISCUSSION AND ANALYSIS (MD&A)

Within the framework of its Integrated Disclosure System, the SEC requires an expanded management discussion and analysis of Financial

---

[4] C. Casey and N. Bartzcak, "Cash Flow—It's Not the Bottom Line," *Harvard Business Review,* July–August 1984, pp. 61–66.

Condition and Results of Operations. The "Financial Condition" section requires a discussion of liquidity factors—including known trends, demands, commitments, or uncertainties likely to have a material impact on the enterprise's ability to generate adequate amounts of cash. If a material deficiency in liquidity is identified, management must discuss the course of action it has taken or proposes to take in order to remedy the deficiency. In addition, internal and external sources of liquidity as well as any material unused sources of liquid assets must be identified and described.

Campbell Soup Company (Chapter 4, Appendix B) presents a "Liquidity and Capital Resources" section as part of its MD&A (see item 10).

Quaker Oats (Appendix to Chapter 23) presents its "Liquidity and Capital Resources MD&A discussion in item 142

Financial analysts should benefit significantly from a careful reading and evaluation of such required management discussion and analysis (see also Chapter 20).

Projecting Changes in Conditions or Policies

It is possible and often very useful to trace through the effects of changes in conditions and/or policies on the cash resources of an enterprise.

ILLUSTRATION 5.   Assume that the Prudent Company has the following account balances at December 31, Year 1:

	Debit	Credit
Cash	$ 70,000	
Accounts receivable	150,000	
Inventory	65,000	
Accounts payable		$130,000
Notes payable		35,000
Accrued taxes		18,000
Fixed assets	200,000	
Accumulated depreciation		43,000
Capital stock		200,000

The following additional information is available for Year 1:

Sales	$750,000
Cost of sales	520,000
Purchases	350,000
Depreciation	25,000
Net income	20,000

The company anticipates a growth of 10 percent in sales for the coming year. All corresponding revenue and expense items are also expected to increase by 10 percent, except for depreciation which will remain the same. All expenses are paid in cash as they are incurred during the year. The year 2 ending inventory will be $150,000. By the end of year 2, the company expects to have a notes payable balance of $50,000 and no balance in the accrued taxes account. The company maintains a minimum cash balance of $50,000 as a managerial policy.

I. Assume that the company is considering a change in credit policy so that the ending accounts receivable balance will represent 90 days of sales. What impact will this change have on the company's cash balance? Will it have to borrow?

This can be computed as follows:

Cash, January 1, Year 2			$ 70,000
Cash collections:			
Accounts receivable, January 1, Year 2		$150,000	
Sales		825,000	
		975,000	
Less: Accounts receivable, December 31, Year 2		206,250[a]	768,750
Total cash available			838,750
Cash disbursements:			
Accounts payable, January 1, Year 2	$130,000		
Purchases	657,000[b]		
	787,000		
Accounts payable, December 31, Year 2	244,000[c]	543,000	
Notes payable, January 1, Year 2	35,000		
Notes payable, December 31, Year 2	50,000	(15,000)	
Accrued taxes		18,000	
Cash expenses[d]		203,500	749,500
			89,250
Cash balance desired			50,000
Cash excess			$ 39,250

Explanation:

(a) $825,000 \times \dfrac{90}{360} = \$206,250.$

(b) Year 2 cost of sales*: $520,000 \times 1.1 = \$572,000$

Ending inventory (given)	150,000
Goods available for sale	722,000
Beginning inventory	65,000
Purchases	$657,000

* which excludes depreciation.

(c) $\text{Purchases} \times \dfrac{\text{Old accounts payable}}{\text{Old purchases}} = \$657,000 \times \dfrac{\$130,000}{\$350,000}$

$= \$244,000$

(d)
Gross profit ($825,000 − $572,000)		$253,000
Less: Net income	$24,500*	
Depreciation	25,000	49,500
Other cash expenses		$203,500

* 110 percent of $20,000 (Year 1 N.I.) + 10 percent of $25,000 (Year 1 depreciation).

II. What would the effect be if the change, instead of as in I, is to an *average* accounts receivable turnover of 4?
    We compute this as follows:

Excess cash balance as computed above	$39,250

Change from an *ending* to an *average* accounts receivable turnover will increase year-end accounts receivable balance to:

$\dfrac{\$825,000}{4} = \$206,250 \times 2$

$= \$412,500 − \$150,000 = .. \$262,500^{(e)}$

Less: Accounts receivable balance as above (I)	206,250	(cash 56,250 decrease)
Cash required to borrow		$17,000

(e) $\dfrac{\text{Sales}}{\text{Average A/R turnover}}$ = Average A/R;

Ending A/R = [(Average A/R) × 2] − Beginning A/R

III. Assuming that in addition to the conditions prevailing in II above, suppliers require the company to pay within 60 days. What would be the effect on the cash balance?

The computation is as follows:

Cash required to borrow (from II above) . . . . $ 17,000
Ending accounts payable (I above) $244,000
Ending accounts payable under 60-day payment

$\quad$ = Purchases $\times \dfrac{60}{360}$ = $657,000 $\times \dfrac{60}{360}$ = ...   109,500

Additional disbursements required   134,500
Cash to be borrowed $151,500

QUESTIONS

1. Why is short-term liquidity so significant? Explain from the viewpoint of various parties concerned.
2. The concept of working capital is simple, that is, the excess of current assets over current liabilities. What are some of the factors that make this simple computation complicated in practice?
3. What are cash equivalents? How should an analyst value them in his or her analysis?
4. Can fixed assets be included in current assets? If so, explain the situation under which the inclusion may be allowed.
5. Some installment receivables are not collectible within one year. Why are they included in current assets?
6. Are all inventories included in current assets? Why or why not?
7. What is the theoretical justification for including prepaid expenses in current assets?
8. The company under analysis has a very small amount of current liabilities, but the long-term liabilities section shows a significant balance. In the footnote to the audited statements, it is disclosed that the company has a "revolving loan agreement" with a local bank. Does this disclosure have any significance to you?
9. Some industries are subject to peculiar financing and operating conditions that call for special consideration in drawing the distinction between what is *current* and what is *noncurrent*. How should the analyst recognize this in his evaluation of working capital?
10. Your careful computation of the working capitals of Companies A and B reveals that both have the same amount of working capital. Are you ready to conclude that the liquidity position of both is the same?
11. What is the current ratio? What does it measure? What are the reasons for its widespread use?
12. The holding of cash generally does not yield a return. Why does an enterprise hold cash at all?
13. Is there a relationship between the level of inventories and that of sales? Are inventories a function of sales? If there is a functional relationship between the two, is it proportional?
14. What are the major objectives of management in determining the size of inventory and receivables investment?

15. What are the theoretical limitations of the current ratio as a measure of liquidity?
16. If there are significant limitations attached to the current ratio as a measure of liquidity, what is the proper use of this tool?
17. What are cash ratios? What do they measure?
18. How do we measure the "quality" of various current assets?
19. What does the average accounts receivable turnover measure?
20. What is the collection period for accounts receivable? What does it measure?
21. A company's collection period is 60 days this year as compared to 40 days last year. Give three or more possible reasons for this change.
22. What is an accounts receivable aging schedule? What is its use in the analysis of financial statements?
23. What are the repercussions to an enterprise of *(a)* overinvestment or *(b)* underinvestment in inventories?
24. What problems would you expect to encounter in an analysis of a company using the LIFO inventory method in an inflationary economy? What effects do the price changes have *(a)* on the inventory turnover ratio and *(b)* on the current ratio?
25. Why does the "nature" of the current liabilities have to be analyzed in assessing the quality of the current ratio?
26. An apparently successful company shows a poor current ratio. Explain the possible reasons for this.
27. What is *window dressing?* Is there any way to find out whether the financial statements are window dressed or not?
28. What is the rule of thumb governing the expected size of the current ratio? What dangers are there in using this rule of thumb mechanically?
29. Describe the importance which the sales level plays in the overall current financial condition and liquidity of the current assets of an enterprise.
30. What is the liquidity index? What significance do the liquidity index numbers have?
31. What do cash flow ratios attempt to measure?
32. In addition to the tools of analysis of short-term liquidity that lend themselves to quantification, there are important qualitative considerations that also have an important bearing on the short-term liquidity of an enterprise. What are such considerations? And what are the SEC disclosure requirements that would help financial analysts in this regard?
33. What is the importance of projecting the effects of changes in conditions or policies on the cash resources of an enterprise?

Chapter 17

FUNDS FLOW ANALYSIS AND FINANCIAL FORECASTS

The preceding chapter examined the various measures that are derived from past financial statement data and that are useful in the assessment of short-term liquidity. The chapter that follows will focus on the use of similar data in an evaluation of longer-term solvency. The limitations to which these approaches are subject are due mainly to their static nature, that is, to their reliance on status reports, as of a given moment, of claims against an enterprise and the resources available to meet these claims.

An important and, in many cases, superior alternative to such static measures of conditions prevailing at a given point in time is the analysis and projection of more dynamic models of cash flows. Such models use the present only as a starting point, and while building on reliable patterns of past experience, utilize the best available estimates of future plans and conditions in order to forecast the future availability and disposition of cash.

The forecasting process is a difficult one and analysts must be aware of this. As Mark Twain once said: "The art of prophesy is very difficult, especially with respect to the future."

OVERVIEW OF CASH FLOW PATTERNS

Before we examine the methods by means of which cash flow projections are made, it would be useful to get a thorough understanding of the nature of cash flow. Exhibit 17–1 presents a diagram of the flow of cash through an enterprise. This diagram parallels the accounting cycle diagram presented in Chapter 2 (Exhibit 2–1).

The flow diagram focuses on cash. Cash (including cash equivalents) is the ultimate liquid asset. Almost all decisions to invest in assets or to incur costs require the immediate or eventual use of cash. This is why managements focus, from an operational point of view, on *cash* rather than on other concepts of liquid funds, such as working capital. The focus on the latter represents mainly the point of view of creditors who consider as part of the liquid assets pool other assets, such as receivables and

Exhibit 17-1   Flow of cash through an enterprise

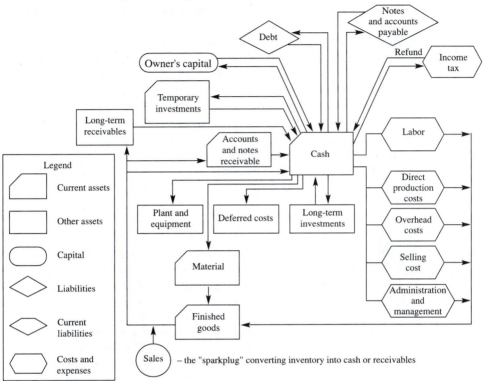

inventories, which are normally converted into cash within a relatively short time span.

Careful examination of the flows depicted in Exhibit 17–1 should contribute greatly to the reader's understanding of the importance of cash in an enterprise as well as the factors which cause it to be converted into assets and costs. The following factors and relationships are worthy of particular note:

Since the diagram focuses on cash flows only, assets, liabilities, and other items that are not directly involved, such as prepayments and accruals, as well as the income account, are not included in it. Some flows are presented in simplified fashion for an easier understanding of relationships. For example, accounts payable are presented as direct sources of cash, whereas in reality they represent a temporary postponement of cash payment for the acquisition of goods and services.

It is recognized that the holding of cash provides no return or a very low return and that in times of rising price levels, cash as a monetary asset is exposed to purchasing power loss. However, these considerations aside, the holding of this most liquid of assets represents, in a business sense, the lowest exposure to risk. Management must make the decision to invest cash in assets or costs, and such a conversion increases risk because the certainty of ultimate reconversion into cash is less than 100 percent. There are, of course, a variety of risks. Thus, the risk involved in a conversion of cash into temporary investments is lower than the risk involved in committing cash to long-term, long-payout assets such as plant, machinery, or certain inventories. Similarly, the investment of cash in a variety of assets and costs for the creation and marketing of a new product involves serious risk regarding the recovery in cash of amounts so committed. The short-term liquidity as well as the long-term solvency of an enterprise depends on the recovery and realizability of such outlays.

The inflow and outflow of cash are highly interrelated. A failure of any part of the system to circulate can affect the entire system. A cessation of sales affects the vital conversion of finished goods into receivables or cash and leads, in turn, to a drop in the cash reservoir. Inability to replenish this reservoir from sources such as owners' capital, debt, or accounts payable (upper left-hand corner of diagram) can lead to a cessation of production activities that will result in a loss of future sales. Conversely, the cutting off of expenses, such as for advertising and marketing, will slow down the conversion of finished goods into receivables and cash. Longer-term blockages in the flows may lead to insolvency.

The diagram clarifies the interrelationship between profitability, income, and cash flow. The only real source of funds from operations is sales. When finished goods, which for the sake of simplicity represent the accumulation of *all* costs and expenses in the diagram, are sold, the profit margin will enhance the inflow of liquid funds in the form of receivables and cash. The higher the profit margin, the greater the accretion of these funds.

Income, which is the difference between the cash and credit sales and the cost of goods sold, can have a wide variety of effects on cash flow. For example, the costs that flow from the utilization of plant and equipment or from deferred charges generally do not involve the use of cash. Similarly, as in the case of land sales on long-term installment terms, the creation of long-term receivables through sales reduces the impact of net income on cash flow. It can be readily seen that adding back depreciation to net income creates only a very crude measure of cash flow.

The limitation of the cash flow concept can be more clearly seen. As cash flows into its reservoir, management has a *degree* of discretion as to where to direct it. This discretion depends on the amount of cash already committed to such outlays as dividends, inventory accumulation, capital expenditures, or debt repayment. The total cash inflow also depends on management's ability to tap sources such as equity capital and debt. With respect to noncommitted cash, management has, at the point of return of the cash to the reservoir, the discretion of directing it to any purpose it deems most important. It is this noncommitted cash flow segment that is of particular interest and importance to financial analysts. This noncommitted cash is also referred to as "free cash flow."

Under present accounting conventions, certain cash outlays, such as those for training, sales promotion, or for most research and development costs, are considered as period costs and are not shown as assets. These costs can, nevertheless, be of significant future value in either the increasing of sales or in the reduction of costs.

SHORT-TERM CASH FORECASTS

In the measurement of short-term liquidity, the short-term cash forecast is one of the most thorough and reliable tools available to the analyst.

Short-term liquidity analysis is of particular interest to management in the financial operations of an enterprise and to short-term credit grantors who are interested in an enterprise's ability to repay short-term loans. The analyst will pay particular attention to the short-term cash forecast when an enterprise's ability to meet its current obligations is subject to substantial doubt.

Realistic cash forecasts can be made only for relatively short time spans. This is so because the factors influencing the inflows and outflows of cash are many and complex and cannot be reliably estimated beyond the short term.

Importance of Sales Estimates

The reliability of any cash forecast depends very importantly on the forecast of sales. In fact, a cash forecast can never reach a higher degree of reliability than the sales forecast on which it is based. Except for transactions involving the raising of money from external sources or the investment of money in long-term assets, almost all cash flows relate to, and depend on, sales.

The sales forecast involves considerations such as:

1. The past direction and trend of sales volume.
2. Enterprise share of the market.
3. Industry and general economic conditions.

4. Productive and financial capacity.
5. Competitive factors.

These factors must generally be assessed in terms of individual product lines that may be influenced by forces peculiar to their own markets.

Pro Forma Financial Statements as an Aid to Forecasting

The reasonableness and feasibility of short-term cash forecasts can be checked by means of pro forma financial statements. This is done by utilizing the assumptions underlying the cash forecast and constructing, on this basis, a pro forma statement of income covering the period of the forecast and a pro forma balance sheet as at the end of that period. The ratios and other relationships derived from the pro forma financial statements should then be checked for feasibility against historical relationships that have prevailed in the past. Such relationships must be adjusted for factors that it is estimated will affect them during the period of the cash forecast.

Techniques of Short-Term Cash Forecasting

ILLUSTRATION 1.   The Forward Corporation has recently introduced an improved product that has enjoyed excellent market acceptance. As a result, management has budgeted sales for the six months ending June 30, year 1, as follows:

	Estimated sales
January	100,000
February	125,000
March	150,000
April	175,000
May	200,000
June	250,000
Total	1,000,000

The cash balance at January 1, year 1, is $15,000, and the treasurer foresees a need for additional funds necessary to finance the sales expansion. She has obtained a commitment from an insurance company for the sale to them of long-term bonds as follows:

April	$50,000 (less $2,500 debt costs)
May	60,000

She also expects to sell real estate at cost: $8,000 in May and $50,000 in June. In addition, equipment with an original cost of $25,000 and a book value of zero was to be sold for $25,000 cash in June.

The treasurer considers that in the light of the expanded sales volume the following minimum cash balances will be desirable:

January	$20,000
February	25,000
March	27,000
April, May, and June	30,000

She knows that during the next six months she will not be able to meet her cash requirements without resort to short-term financing. Consequently, she approaches her bank and finds it ready to consider her company's needs. The loan officer suggests that in order to determine the cash needs and the sources of funds for loan repayment, the treasurer prepare a cash forecast for the six months ending June 30, year 1, and pro forma financial statements for that period.

The treasurer, recognizing the importance of such a forecast, proceeded to assemble the data necessary to prepare it.

The pattern of receivables collections based on experience was as follows:

Collections	*Percent of total receivable*
In month of sale	40
In the second month	30
In the third month	20
In the fourth month	5
Write-off bad debts	5
	100

On the basis of this pattern and the expected sales, the treasurer constructed Schedule A shown in Exhibit 17–2.

An analysis of past cost patterns resulted in the estimates of cost and expense relationships for the purpose of the cash forecast (Schedule B) shown in Exhibit 17–3.

It was estimated that all costs in Schedule B (exclusive of the $1,000 monthly depreciation charge) will be paid for in cash in the month incurred, except for material purchases that are to be paid 50 percent in the month of purchase and 50 percent in the following month. Since the product is manufactured to specific order, no finished goods inventories are expected to accumulate.

Exhibit 17–2

SCHEDULE A
Estimates of Cash Collections
For the Months January-June, Year 1

	January	February	March	April	May	June
Sales	$100,000	$125,000	$150,000	$175,000	$200,000	$250,000
Collections:						
1st month—40% .	40,000	50,000	60,000	70,000	80,000	100,000
2nd month—30%		30,000	37,500	45,000	52,500	60,000
3rd month—20% .			20,000	25,000	30,000	35,000
4th month—5% ..				5,000	6,250	7,500
Total cash						
collections ..	40,000	80,000	117,500	145,000	168,750	202,500
Write-offs—5%				5,000	6,250	7,500

Exhibit 17–3

SCHEDULE B
Cost and Expense Estimates for Six Months
Ending June 30, year 1

Materials	30% of sales
Labor	25% of sales
Manufacturing overhead:	
Variable	10% of sales
Fixed	$48,000 for six months (including $1,000 of depreciation per month)
Selling expenses	10% of sales
General and administrative expenses:	
Variable	8% of sales
Fixed	$7,000 per month

The raw materials inventory at the end of each month for the period January to June year 1 is expected to be as follows: $67,000, $67,500, $65,500, $69,000, $67,000, and $71,000, respectively. Raw materials inventory on January 1, year 1, was $57,000.

Schedule C (Exhibit 17–4) shows the pattern of payments of accounts payable (for materials).

Equipment costing $20,000 will be bought in February for notes payable that will be paid off, starting that month, at the rate of $1,000 per month. The new equipment will not be fully installed until sometime in August year 1.

Exhibit 17–5 presents the cash forecast for the six months ending June 30, year 1, based on the data given above. Exhibit 17–6 presents the pro

Exhibit 17–4

SCHEDULE C
Pro Forma Schedule of Cash Payments for Materials Purchases
For the Months January–June Year 1

	January	February	March	April	May	June
Materials purchased during month*	$40,000	$38,000	$43,000	$56,000	$58,000	$79,000
Payments:						
1st month—50% ...	20,000	19,000	21,500	28,000	29,000	39,500
2nd month—50% ..		20,000	19,000	21,500	28,000	29,000
Total payments ..	$20,000	$39,000	$40,500	$49,500	$57,000	$68,500

* These reconcile with material costs and changes in inventories.

forma income statement for the six months ending June 30, year 1. Exhibit 17–7 presents the actual balance sheet of The Forward Corporation as at January 1, year 1, and the pro forma balance sheet as of June 30, year 1.

The financial analyst should examine the pro forma statements critically and submit to feasibility tests the estimates on which the forecasts are based. The ratios and relationships revealed by the pro forma financial statements should be analyzed and compared to similar ratios of the past in order to determine whether they are reasonable and feasible of attainment. For example, the current ratio of The Forward Corporation increased from 2.6 on January 1, year 1, to 3.5 in the pro forma balance sheet as of June 30, year 1. During the six months ended June 30, year 1, a pro forma return on average equity of over 8 percent was projected. Many other significant measures of turnover, common-size statements, and trends can be computed. The reasonableness of these comparisons and results must be assessed. They can help reveal serious errors and inconsistencies in the assumptions that underlie the projections and thus help strengthen confidence in their reliability.

Differences between Short-Term and Long-Term Forecasts

The short-term cash forecast is, as we have seen, a very useful and reliable aid in projecting the state of short-term liquidity. Such a detailed approach is, however, only feasible for the short term, that is, up to about 12 months. Beyond this time horizon the uncertainties become so great as to preclude detailed and accurate cash forecasts. Instead of focusing on collections of receivables and on payments for labor and materials, the longer-term estimates focus on projections of net income and the resulting cash flow from operations as well as on other sources and uses of cash.

Exhibit 17–5

THE FORWARD CORPORATION
Cash Forecast
For the Months January–June Year 1

	January		February		March	
Cash balance—beginning	$15,000		$20,000		$ 25,750	
Add: Cash receipts:						
Collections of accounts receivable						
(Schedule A)	40,000		80,000		117,500	
Proceeds from sale of real estate						
Proceeds from additional long-						
term debt						
Proceeds from sale of						
equipment						
Total cash available		$ 55,000		$100,000		$143,250
Less: Disbursements:						
Payments for:						
Materials purchases						
(Schedule C)	20,000		39,000		40,500	
Labor	25,000		31,250		37,500	
Fixed factory overhead	7,000		7,000		7,000	
Variable factory overhead	10,000		12,500		15,000	
Selling expenses	10,000		12,500		15,000	
General and administrative ...	15,000		17,000		19,000	
Taxes						
Purchase of fixed assets			1,000		1,000	
Total disbursements		87,000		120,250		135,000
Tentative cash balance (negative) ..		(32,000)		(20,250)		8,250
Minimum cash balance required ...		20,000		25,000		27,000
Additional borrowing required ..		52,000		46,000		19,000
Repayment of bank loan						
Interest paid on balance						
outstanding at rate of ¹/₂% per						
month*						
Ending cash balance		$ 20,000		$ 25,750		$ 27,250
Loan balance		$ 52,000		$ 98,000		$117,000

* Interest is computed at the rate of ¹/₂ percent per month and paid on date of repayment which occurs at month end. Loan is taken out at beginning of month.

The projection of future statements of cash flow is best begun with an analysis of prior year cash statements. To these data can then be added all available information and estimates about the future needs for cash and the most likely sources of cash needed to cover such requirements.

April		May		June		Six-month totals	
$ 27,250		$ 30,580		$ 30,895		$ 15,000	
145,000		168,750		202,500		753,750	
		8,000		50,000		58,000	
47,500		60,000				107,500	
				25,000		25,000	
	$219,750		$267,330		$308,395		$959,250
49,500		57,000		68,500		274,500	
43,750		50,000		62,500		250,000	
7,000		7,000		7,000		42,000	
17,500		20,000		25,000		100,000	
17,500		20,000		25,000		100,000	
21,000		23,000		27,000		122,000	
				19,000		19,000	
1,000		1,000		1,000		5,000	
	157,250		178,000		235,000		912,500
	62,500		89,330		73,395		46,750
	30,000		30,000		30,000		
	—		—		—		117,000
	30,000		58,000		29,000		(117,000)
	1,920		435		145		2,500
	$ 30,580		$ 30,895		$ 44,250		$ 44,250
	$ 87,000		$ 29,000		—		—

ELECTRONIC SPREADSHEET PROGRAMS

The wide variety and sophistication of available electronic spreadsheet programs, and the ease of changing variables which they afford, can aid greatly in the preparation of pro forma statements. That ease and flexibility of use should not be confused with the fact that the quality of

Exhibit 17–6

THE FORWARD CORPORATION
Pro Forma Income Statement
For the Six Months Ending June 30, Year 1

			Source of estimate
Sales		$1,000,000	Based on sales budget (page 580)
Cost of sales:			
Materials	300,000		Schedule B
Labor	250,000		Schedule B
Overhead	148,000		Schedule B
		698,000	
Gross profit		302,000	
Selling expense	100,000		Schedule B
Bad debts expense	18,750		Schedule A
General and administrative expense	122,000		Schedule B
Total		240,750	
Operating income		61,250	
Gain on sale of equipment		25,000	
Interest expense		(2,500)	Exhibit 17–5, footnote
Income before taxes		83,750	
Income taxes		33,500	40% combined state and federal rate. Pay $19,000 in June and accrue balance.
Net income		$ 50,250	

projections is critically dependent on the validity of estimates and assumptions. The reasonableness of such assumptions is dependent on rigorous analysis and judgment rather than computer program manipulations.

ANALYSIS OF STATEMENTS OF CASH FLOWS

In Chapter 13, we examined the principles underlying the preparation of the *Statement of Cash Flows (SCF)* as well as the uses to which the statement may be put by the analyst. We shall now focus on the analysis of the SCF, paying particular attention to the value of such an analysis to a projection of future cash flows.

Exhibit 17–7

THE FORWARD CORPORATION
Balance Sheets

	Actual January 1, Year 1		Pro forma June 30, Year 1	
Assets				
Current assets:				
Cash	$ 15,000		$ 44,250	
Accounts receivable (net)	6,500		234,000	
Inventories—raw materials	57,000		71,000	
Total current assets		$ 78,500		$349,250
Real estate	58,000		—	
Fixed assets	206,400		201,400	
Accumulated depreciation	(36,400)		(17,400)	
Net fixed assets		228,000		184,000
Other assets		3,000		3,000
Deferred debt expenses				2,500
Total assets		$309,500		$538,750
Liabilities and Equity Capital				
Current liabilities:				
Accounts payable	2,000		41,500	
Notes payable	28,500		43,500	
Accrued taxes	—		14,500	
Total current liabilities		$ 30,500		$ 99,500
Long-term debt	15,000		125,000	
Common stock	168,000		168,000	
Retained earnings	96,000		146,250	
		279,000		439,250
Total liabilities and equity capital		$309,500		$538,750

In any analysis of financial statements, the most recent years are the most important because they represent the most recent experience. Since there is an inherent continuity in business events, it is this latest experience that is likely to have the greatest relevance to the projection of future results. So it is with the SCF.

It is important that the analyst obtain SCFs for as many years as possible.[1] This is particularly important in the case of an analysis of this statement since the planning and execution of plant expansions, of modernization schemes, of working capital increases as well as the financing of such activities by means of short- and long-term debt and by means

---

[1] Statements which have been presented in a different format in preceding years may have to be restated.

of equity funds is an activity that is likely to encompass many years. Thus, in order for the analyst to be able to assess management's plans and their execution, SCFs covering a number of years must be analyzed. In this way, a more comprehensive picture of management's financial habits can be obtained and an assessment of them made.

Because conditions vary so greatly from enterprise to enterprise, only a few useful generalizations regarding the thrust of such analysis are possible.

The analyst must first establish which the major sources of cash over the years were and what the major uses were to which cash was put. A common-size analysis of the SCF will aid in this year-to-year comparison. Detailed SCF often tend to obscure the major sources and uses of cash. In assessing overall trends and practices, it is best to cumulate the major sources and uses over a span of years, such as 5 or 10, because single fiscal periods are too short for purposes of reaching meaningful conclusions. Thus, for example, the financing of a major capital expansion may be accomplished years before it is in full swing.

In evaluating sources and uses of cash, the analyst should focus on questions such as these:

- Has the enterprise been able to finance fixed asset *replacements* from internally generated cash? Historical-cost as well as current-cost depreciation may be useful in this assessment. Many companies do not provide adequate information to enable the analyst to distinguish between replacement and capacity expansion.
- How have expansion and business acquisitions been financed?
- To what extent is the enterprise dependent on outside financing? How frequently is it required, and what form does it take?
- What does the company's need for cash and its access to cash suggest as implications for its dividend policy?

ILLUSTRATION OF THE ANALYSIS OF STATEMENTS OF CASH FLOWS

In this illustration, we shall analyze the statements of cash flow of Campbell Soup Company (see Exhibit 23–4), covering the six-year period ending July 28, 1991. Exhibit 23–15 presents these statements in common-size format.

During the six-year period the *major* sources of cash of Campbell Soup Company were operations $3010 million, long-term debt $854 million, and short-term debt $737 million. The major uses were plant purchases (net of sales) of $1647 million, business acquisitions (net of sales) of $718 million, and cash dividends of $649 million. During this period cash and cash equivalents increased by $24 million. Sources of cash from operations as a percentage of total sources averaged 48.5 percent and reached a low of 29 percent in 1989. Of these six years, 1991 was the most profitable, reflecting a recovery after two years of very poor results and of restructuring.

Over the six-year period, cash from operations covered handily net cash used in investing activities as well as most of dividends paid. The sharp declines in earnings in 1989 and 1990 were mitigated from a cash-flow point of view by the fact that restructuring charges of $682 million did not use cash.

An analysis of the SCF over the years is helpful as the basis of cash flow forecasts. A forecast of future SCF would have to take into consideration all above-discussed trends that the enterprise has exhibited, such as those relating to income, the elements that convert it to sources of cash from operations, fixed assets additions, and the relationship of sales to growth in operating working capital. The size of noncash adjustments, such as depreciation, depends on future depreciation policies and equipment acquisitions. The latter, as well as write-off methods to be used for tax purposes, will in turn determine the size of the deferred tax adjustments. The more we know about factors such as these the more reliable the forecast will be.

EVALUATION OF THE STATEMENT OF CASH FLOWS

The foregoing example of an analysis of the SCF illustrates the variety of information and insights that can be derived. Of course, the analysis of SCF is to be performed within the framework of an analysis of all the financial statements, and thus the conclusion reached from an analysis of one statement may be strengthened and corroborated by an analysis of the other financial statements.

There are some useful generalizations that can be made regarding the value of the analysis of the SCF to the financial analyst.

This statement enables the analyst to appraise the quality of management decisions over time, as well as their impact on the results of operations and financial condition of the enterprise. When the analysis encompasses a longer period of time, the analyst can evaluate management's response to the changing economic conditions as well as to the opportunities and the adversities which invariably present themselves.

Evaluation of the SCF analysis will indicate the purposes to which management chose to commit funds, where it reduced investment, the source from which it derived additional cash, and to what extent it reduced claims against the enterprise. Such an analysis will also show the disposition of earnings over the years, as well as how management has reinvested the internal cash inflow over which it had discretion. The analysis will also reveal the size and composition of cash from operations, as well as their pattern and degree of stability.

As depicted in Exhibit 17–1 earlier in this chapter, the circulation of cash in an enterprise involves a constant flow of cash and its periodic reinvestment. Thus, cash is invested in labor, material, and overhead costs, as well as in long-term assets, such as inventories and plant and equipment, which join the product-cost stream at a slower rate. Eventually, by the process of sales, these costs are converted back into accounts receivable and into cash. If operations are profitable, the cash recovered will exceed the amounts invested, thus augmenting the cash inflow or cash flow. Losses have, of course, the opposite effect.

What constitutes cash flow is the subject of considerable confusion. Generally, the cash provided by operations, that is, net income adjusted for items needed to convert it to a cash basis, is an index of management's ability to redirect funds away from areas of unfavorable profit opportunity into areas of greater profit potential. However, not all the cash provided by operations may be so available because of existing commitments for debt retirement, stock redemption, equipment replacement, and dividend payments. Nor is cash provided by operations the only potential cash inflow, since management can avail itself of external sources of capital in order to bolster its funds inflow. The components of the "cash from operations" figure hold important clues to the stability of that source of cash. Thus, for example, depreciation is a more stable element in the total than net income itself in that it represents a recovery by the enterprise of the investment in fixed assets out of selling prices even before a profit is earned. Cash recovered from depreciation must normally be reinvested in the productive assets used up. This is not the case with goodwill amortization. The recovery of this noncash charge does not have to be reinvested in the assets which have been amortized.

In evaluating the SCF, the analyst will judge a company's quality of earnings by the impact that changes in economic and industry conditions have on its flow of cash. The statement will also reveal noncash generating income that may have a bearing on the evaluation of earnings quality.

If in his estimates of future earnings potential the analyst foresees a need for additional capital, his analysis of the SCF will be directed toward a projection of the source from which cash will be obtained, and what dilution of earnings per share, if any, this will involve.

The analysis and evaluation of the SCF is, as the foregoing discussion suggests, an important early step in the projection of future SCFs.

PROJECTION OF STATEMENTS OF CASH FLOWS

No thorough model of an enterprise's future results is complete without a concurrent forecast of the amount of cash needed for the realization of the projections in the model as well as an assessment of the possible sources from which such cash can be derived.

If a future expansion of sales and profits is forecast, the analyst must know whether the enterprise has the "financial horsepower" to see such an expansion through, by means of internally generated cash and, if not, where the required cash is going to come from.

The projection of the SCF will start with a careful estimate of the expected changes in each individual category of assets and the cash that will be derived from or required by such changes. Some of the more important factors to be taken into consideration follow:

1. The net income expected to be generated by future results will be adjusted for noncash items, such as depreciation, depletion, deferred income taxes, and nonremitted earnings of subsidiaries and investees, in order to arrive at estimates of cash provided by operations.
2. The needs for operating working capital will be arrived at by estimating the required level of the individual working capital items such as receivables and inventories and reducing this by the expected levels of payables. Over the long term, working capital required to support a level of estimated sales can also be estimated on an aggregate or net basis. There is usually a relationship between incremental sales and the corresponding increment in required working capital amounts.
3. Sources of cash from disposals of assets, sales of investments, and the sale of stocks and bonds will be estimated.
4. Expected capital expenditures will be based on the present level of operations as compared with productive capacity, on an estimate of the future level of activity implied by the profit projections, as well as on current replacement cost data.
5. Mandatory debt retirement and desirable minimum levels of dividend payments will also be estimated.

ILLUSTRATION OF THE PROJECTION OF STATEMENTS OF CASH FLOWS

Based on the financial statements of the Campbell Soup Company (see Chapter 4, Appendix B) and on the preceding analysis we can prepare a forecast of the SCF of the Campbell Soup Company for 1992 and 1993 based on the following assumptions (all dollar amounts in millions):

1. Sales in 1992 will be $6350, and in 1993 $6800.
2. Net income 1992 will be as presented in the projected income statement for 1992 (Exhibit 23–16). For 1993, net income will be 7.9 percent of projected sales.
3. Net income for 1989 and 1990, which are used in the projecting

process, are before the net effect of divestitures, restructuring, and unusual charges of $260.8 in 1989 and $301.6 in 1990.

4. Depreciation and amortization in 1992 and 1993 will bear the same relationship to net income as the average depreciation and amortization during the 1989–91 period bore to the average net income over the same period.

5. Deferred income taxes will be in 1992 at a level that reflects the relationship of total 1990–91 deferred taxes to total 1990–91 net income. It will change in 1992 by the percentage change that 1993 estimated net income bears to 1992 estimated net income.

6. Other, net will be in 1992 at a level that reflects the relationship of total 1989–91 other, net to total 1989–91 net income. It will change in 1993 by the percentage change that 1993 estimated net income bears to 1992 estimated net income.

7. The level of operating working capital items, accounts receivable, inventory, and other current assets and liabilities (exclusive of cash and temporary investments) prevailing at fiscal year-end of 1992 and 1993 will be estimated as follows:

   a. Determine the percentage relationship between 1991 fiscal year-end operating working capital items and 1991 sales.

   b. Multiply the percentage relationship in (a) above by the estimated sales levels for 1992 and 1993, respectively.

8. The fiscal year-end level of cash and temporary investments is estimated to bear the same relationship to the estimated sales of the respective 1992 and 1993 years as does the fiscal year-end of cash and temporary investments in 1991 bear to sales in 1991.

9. All other amounts shown in the projected Statement of Cash Flows are estimated (est.) on the basis of the best available information, including situations where the moving average of the last six years is used.

Exhibit 17–8 presents the projected SCF for Campbell Soup for 1992 and 1993.

The Impact of Adversity

The projected SCF is useful not only in estimating the cash implications of future expansion and opportunity but also in assessing the impact on the enterprise of sudden adversity.

A sudden adversity will usually manifest itself in a serious interruption in the inflow of cash.

This can be brought about by such events as recessions, strikes, or the loss of a major customer or market. In this context, a projection of the

Exhibit 17–8

CAMPBELL SOUP COMPANY
Projected Statements of Cash Flows
($ millions)

	1993	1992
Cash flows from operating activities:		
Net earnings[a]	$540.0	$480.0
To reconcile net earnings to net cash provided by operating activities:		
Depreciation and amortization[b]	331.1	294.3
Deferred taxes[c]	30.0	26.7
Other, net[d]	65.5	58.3
(Increase) decrease in accounts receivable[e]	(38.2)	(12.4)
(Increase) decrease in inventories[f]	(51.2)	(16.6)
Net change in other current assets and liabilities[g]	85.9	27.9
Net cash provided by operating activities	963.1	858.2
Cash flows from investing activities:		
Purchases of plant assets[h]	(443.1)	(400.0)
Sale of plant assets (est.)[i]	31.5	28.4
Businesses acquired (est.)[i]	(85.3)	(77.0)
Sale of businesses (est.)[i]	25.5	23.0
Increase in other assets (est.)[i]	(53.9)	(48.6)
Net change in other temporary investments (est.)[i]	12.3	11.1
Net cash used in investing activities	(513.0)	(463.1)
Cash flows from financing activities:		
Long-term borrowings (est.)	132.0	142.3
Repayments of long-term borrowings[j]	(218.9)	(227.7)
Increase (decrease) in short-term borrowings[k]	(200.3)	(95.7)
Other short-term borrowings (est.)	131.2	122.9
Repayments of other short-term borrowings (est.)[l]	(140.4)	(200.0)
Dividends paid (est.)	(108.8)	(108.2)
Treasury stock purchases (est.)	(49.4)	(42.4)
Treasury stock issued (est.)	15.6	14.2
Other, net (est.)	9.1	10.4
Net cash provided (used in) financing activities	(429.9)	(384.2)
Effect of exchange rate changes on cash (est.)	(7.5)	(6.7)
Net increase (decrease) in cash and cash equivalents[m]	12.7	4.2
Cash and cash equivalents at the beginning of year[m]	183.1	178.9
Cash and cash equivalents at the end of year[m]	$195.8	$183.1

SCF would be a first step in the assessment of the defensive posture of an enterprise. The basic question to which such an analysis is directed is this: what can the enterprise do; and what resources, both internal and

(continued on page 593)

Exhibit notes:

Note: Some assumptions in the above projections may be considered as somewhat mechanical. They are presented here merely for purposes of illustration. In practice, more refined relationships may be calculated on the basis of detailed studies of past relationships.

(a) Projected net income for:

−1992 is 7.6% of projected sales.

−1993 is 7.9% of projected sales.

These projections are corroborated in the *Value Line Investment Survey* of February 21, 1992.

(b) Average percentage of depreciation and amortization to net income in 1989–91

$$\frac{\text{Total depreciation and amortization}}{\text{Total net income*}} = \frac{\$601.8}{\$981.4} = 61.32\%$$

Depreciation and amortization for 1992 = $480.0 × 0.6132 = $294.3

Depreciation and amortization for 1993 = $540.0 × 0.6132 = $331.1

(c) Average percent of deferred taxes to net income in 1990–91

$$\frac{\text{Total deferred taxes}}{\text{Total net income*}} = \frac{\$39.4 \boxed{59}}{\$707.5} = 5.57\%$$

Deferred taxes for 1992 = $480.0 × 0.0557 = $26.7

Percentage change of 1993 net income to 1992 net income =
$540.0 / $480.0 = 112.5%

Deferred taxes for 1993 = $26.7 × 1.125 = $30.0

(d) Average percent of other, net to net income in 1989–91:

$$\frac{\text{Total other, net}}{\text{Total net income*}} = \frac{\$119.1 \boxed{60}}{\$981.4} = 12.14\%$$

Other, net for 1992 = $480.0 × 0.1214 = $58.3

Percentage change of 1993 net income to 1992 net income = 112.5%

Other, net for 1993 = $58.3 × 1.125 = $65.5

(e) Percentage of year-end accounts receivable to sales in 1991:

$$\frac{\text{A/R} \boxed{33}}{\text{Sales} \boxed{13}} = \frac{527.4}{6204.1} = 8.5\%$$

Fiscal year end A/R in 1992 = 6350.0 × 0.085 = $539.8

Fiscal year end A/R in 1993 = 6800.0 × 0.085 = $578.0

Change in A/R in 1992 = $539.8 − $527.4 = $12.4 increase.

Change in A/R in 1993 = $578.0 − $539.8 = $38.2 increase.

Data in Chapter 23 indicate that over a 10-year period A/R had year-to-year increases over 9 years.

(f) Percentage of year-end inventories to sales in 1991:

$$\frac{\text{Inventories} \boxed{34}}{\text{Sales} \boxed{13}} = \frac{706.7}{6204.1} = 11.39\%$$

Fiscal year-end inventories in 1992 = 6350.0 × 0.1139 = $723.3

Fiscal year-end inventories in 1993 = 6800.0 × 0.1139 = $774.5

Change in inventories in 1992 = $723.3 − $706.7 = $16.6 increase.

Change in inventories in 1993 = $774.5 − $723.3 = $51.2 increase.

$^{(g)}$ Percentage of year-end net other current assets and liabilities (NOCACL) to sales in 1991:

$$\frac{\text{Total current liabilities } \boxed{45} - \text{Prepaid expenses } \boxed{35}}{\text{Sales } \boxed{13}} = \frac{\$1278.0 - \$92.7}{\$6204.1} = 19.11\%$$

Fiscal year-end NOCACL in 1992 = $\$6350.0 \times 0.1911 = \$1213.2$
Fiscal year-end NOCACL in 1993 = $\$6800.0 \times 0.1911 = \$1299.1$

Change in NOCACL in 1992 = $\$1213.2 - \$1185.3 = \$27.9$ increase in liabilities.
Change in NOCACL in 1993 = $\$1299.1 - \$1213.2 = \$85.9$ increase in liabilities.

$^{(h)}$ For 1992 see item $\boxed{11}$ of managements' discussion. . . .—statements of cash flows: Investing activities. For 1993: Percentage change in capital expenditures from 1991 to 1992:

$$\frac{\$400.0}{\$361.1 \ \boxed{65}} = 110.8\%$$

Projected capital expenditures = $\$400.0 \times 110.8\% = \$443.1$

$^{(i)}$ From (h) above, a percentage of 110.8% of last year balance is used also in relatively similar areas.

$^{(j)}$ See item $\boxed{172}$ and $\boxed{173}$, for maturity dates of LTD.

In 1993, $100.0 million due in 1996 at interest rate of 10.5% and redeemable in 1993, given that interest rates continue to fall which may call for refinancing.

$^{(k)}$ Net amount needed to balance the statement.

$^{(l)}$ For 1992, see item $\boxed{170}$, 13.99% Notes due 1992.

For 1993, estimated using average of 1987–1992.

$^{(m)}$ Cash and cash equivalents balance at the end of fiscal year is assumed to be related to the net sales of that year.

$$\text{For 1991} = \frac{\$178.9 \ \boxed{31}}{\$6204.1 \ \boxed{13}} = 2.88\%$$

For 1992 = $\$6350.0 \times 0.0288 = \$183.1$
For 1993 = $\$680.0 \times 0.0288 = \$195.8$

---

*	*For 1991*	*For 1990*	*For 1989*	
Total net income =	$401.5	+ (4.4 + 301.6)	+ (13.1 + 260.8)	= $981.4
For 90 and 91 =	401.5	+ (4.4 + 301.6)		= $707.5

external, can it marshal to cope with a sudden and serious reduction in the inflow of cash?

The strategies and alternatives available to an enterprise faced with such adversities are ably examined and discussed in a work by Professor Donaldson. Dr. Donaldson defines financial mobility as the capacity to redirect the use of financial resources in response to new information about the company and its environment.[2] This concept is related to that of "financial flexibility" discussed in the preceding chapter.

---

[2] Gordon Donaldson, *Strategy for Financial Mobility* (Boston: Graduate School of Business Administration, Harvard University, 1969).

The projected SCF is an important tool in the assessment of the resources available to meet such "new information" as well as in planning the changes in financial strategy that this may require.

To the prospective credit grantor such an approach represents an excellent tool in the assessment of risk. In estimating the effects of, for example, a recession, on the future flow of cash he or she can trace through not only the potential shrinkage in cash inflows from operations but also the effects of such shrinkage on the uses of cash and on the sources from which they can be derived.

Published Financial Forecasts

The subject of published and/or audited financial forecasts is considered in Chapter 22.

The Cash Flow Adequacy Ratio

The purpose of this ratio is to determine the degree to which an enterprise generated sufficient cash from operations to cover capital expenditures, net investment in inventories, and cash dividends. To remove cyclical and other erratic influences, a five-year total is used in the computation of the ratio, thus:

$$\frac{\text{Five-year sum of cash from operations}}{\substack{\text{Five-year sum of capital expenditures, inventory} \\ \text{additions, and cash dividends}}}$$

The investment in the other important working capital item, receivables, is omitted on the theory that it can be financed primarily by short-term credit (i.e., growth in payables, and so forth). Only additions to inventories are counted. In years in which inventories decline the change counts as zero.

A ratio of 1 indicates that an enterprise has covered its needs based on attained levels of growth without the need for external financing. To the degree that the ratio falls below 1, internally generated cash may be inadequate to maintain dividends and current operating growth levels. This ratio may also reflect the effect of inflation on the fund requirements of an enterprise. The reading of this, like any other ratio, can provide no definitive answers and is only a pointer to further analysis and investigation.

Based on the data available in the financial statements of Campbell Soup (Chapter 4, Appendix B), we present here a five-year computation:

$$\frac{\text{5-year sum of sources of cash from operations}}{\substack{\text{5-year sum of capital expenditures, inventory} \\ \text{additions and cash dividends}}}$$

$$\frac{\$2545.8(a)}{\$2418.5(b) + \$117.1(c) + \$544.8(d)} = 0.83$$

(a) Cash from operations—Item 64
(b) Property additions—items 65 and 67
(c) Inventories—item 62
(d) Cash dividends—item 77

This computation indicates that for the five years ending in 1991, Campbell's cash from operations fell short of covering the three items in the denominator of the ratio. A six-year computation in Chapter 23 reveals a slightly more favorable ratio.

Cash Reinvestment Ratio

This ratio is useful in measuring the percentage of the investment in assets, which represents operating cash retained and reinvested in the enterprise for the replacement of assets and for growth in operations. The formula is:

$$\frac{\text{Cash provided by operations} - \text{Dividends}}{\text{Gross plant} + \text{Investment} + \text{Other assets} + \text{Working capital}}$$

A reinvestment rate of 8 to 10 percent is considered generally to be at a satisfactory level. The ratio for Campbell Soup (Chapter 4, Appendix B) for 1991 is:

$$\frac{\$805.2(e) - \$137.5(f)}{[\$2921.9 + \$477.6](g) + \$404.6(h) + [\$1518.5 - \$1278.0](i)} = 16.5\%$$

(e) Cash from Operations—Item 64
(f) Cash dividends—item 77
(g) Gross plant assets—items 158 thru 161
   Plus: Intangibles—items 163 and 164
(h) Other assets—item 39
(i) Total current assets—item 36
   Less: Total current liabilities—item 45

CONCLUSION

In the assessment of future liquidity, the use of cash inflows and outflows forecasts for the short term, and of projected SCF for the longer term, represent some of the most useful tools available to the financial analyst. In contrast to ratio measures of liquidity, these tools involve a detailed examination of sources and uses of cash. Such examination and estimation processes can be subjected to feasibility tests by means of pro forma statements and to the discipline inherent in the double-entry accounting system.

QUESTIONS

1. What is the primary difference between funds flow analysis and ratio analysis? Which is superior and why?
2. "From an operational point of view, management focuses on cash rather than working capital." Do you agree with the statement? Why or why not?
3. What is the relationship between inflows and outflows of cash?
4. Why is the short-term cash forecast important to the financial analyst?
5. What is the first step to be taken in preparing a cash forecast, and what considerations are required in such a step?
6. What are pro forma financial statements? How are they utilized in conjunction with funds flow projections?
7. What are the limitations of short-term cash forecasts?
8. If the usefulness of a short-term cash forecast is limited, what analytical approach is available to the financial analyst who wants to analyze future cash flows?
9. What questions will the analyst focus on in evaluating sources and uses of funds?
10. What useful information do you, as a financial analyst, expect to get from the analysis of past SCF (cash statement)?
11. What would a forecast of future SCF have to take into consideration?
12. What are the differences between short-term and long-term financial forecasts?
13. What analytical function does the common-size SCF serve?
14. Why is a projected SCF necessary when you have historical data which are based on actual performance?
15. If actual operations are seriously affected by unforeseen adversities, would a projected SCF still be useful?
16. "Cash flow per share" is sometimes used in common stock analysis in the same fashion as *earnings per share.* In financial analysis, shouldn't the former be used more often than the latter? Explain. (CFA)

Chapter 18

ANALYSIS OF CAPITAL STRUCTURE AND LONG-TERM SOLVENCY

The financial strength and stability of a business entity and the probability surrounding its ability to weather random shocks and to maintain its solvency in the face of adversity are important measures of risk associated with it. This evaluation of risk is critical because, as discussed in Chapter 1, the equity investor as well as the lender require returns that are commensurate with the levels of risk that each assumes. This and the preceding two chapters deal with the evaluation of the financial strength and viability of enterprises within different time frames.

KEY ELEMENTS IN THE EVALUATION OF LONG-TERM SOLVENCY

The process of evaluation of long-term solvency of an enterprise differs markedly from that of the assessment of short-term liquidity. In the latter, the time horizon is short and it is often possible to make a reasonable projection of cash flows. It is not possible to do this for the longer term, and thus the measures used in the evaluation of longer-term solvency are less specific but more all-encompassing.

There are a number of key elements involved in the evaluation of the long-term solvency of an enterprise. The analysis of capital structure is concerned with the types of capital funds used to finance the enterprise, ranging from "patient" and permanent equity capital to short-term funds that are a temporary, and, consequently, a much more risky source. There are different degrees of risk associated with the holding of different types of assets. Moreover, assets represent secondary[1] sources of security for lenders ranging from loans secured by specific assets to assets available as general security to unsecured creditors.

On a long-term basis, earnings and earning power (which implies the recurring ability to generate cash from operations in the future) are some

---

[1] When lending to going concerns, lenders should regard the liquidation of assets for the purpose of recovery of principal and interest as a measure of last resort and as an undesirable source of funds to rely on at the time credit is granted.

of the most important and reliable indicators of financial strength available. Earnings are the most desirable and reliable sources of cash for the longer-term payment of interest and repayment of principal. As a surrogate for cash generated by operations, earnings are the yardstick against which the coverage of interest and other fixed charges is measured. Moreover, a reliable and stable trend of earnings is one of the best assurances of an enterprise's ability to borrow in times of cash shortage and its consequent ability to extricate itself from the very conditions that lead to insolvency.

In addition to general measures of financial strength and long-term solvency, lenders rely on the protection afforded by loan covenants or the pledges of specific assets as security. All loan covenants define default and the legal remedies available when it occurs in order to give the lender the right to step in at an early stage. Most are designed to alert the lender to the deterioration in such key measures of financial health as the current ratio and the debt to equity ratio, against the issuance of further debt, or to ensure against the disbursement of resources through the payments of dividends above specified levels or through acquisitions. Of course, there can be no prohibition against operating losses, a core problem attending most cases of deterioration in financial condition. Thus, the existence of protective provisions cannot substitute for alertness and a continuous monitoring of the results of operations and of the financial condition of an enterprise in which long-term funds are at risk.[2]

The vast amount of public and private debt outstanding has led to standardized approaches to its analysis and evaluation. By far the most important is the rating of debt securities by rating agencies that is discussed in Appendix 18A to this chapter. Appendix 18B examines the use of ratios as predictors of failure.

In this chapter, we shall examine in further detail the tools and the measures available for the analysis of long-term solvency.

IMPORTANCE OF CAPITAL STRUCTURE

The capital structure of an enterprise consists basically of equity funds and debt. It is measured in terms of the relative magnitude of the various sources of funds of the enterprise. The inherent financial stability of an enterprise and the risk of insolvency to which it is exposed are importantly dependent on the sources of its funds as well as on the type of

---

[2] Lenders have learned that senior positions in the debt hierarchy do not always afford in practice the security they seem to afford in theory. Thus, subordinated debt is not akin to capital stock because subordinated creditors have a voice in determining whether a debtor should be rescued or be thrown into bankruptcy. This interdependence between junior and senior lenders has led some to the belief that one might as well buy the highest yielding obligation of an enterprise since any situation serious enough to affect the value of the junior security is likely to affect the senior security as well.

assets it holds and the relative magnitude of such asset categories. Exhibit 18–1 presents an example of the distribution of assets of an enterprise and the sources of funds used to finance their acquisition. It is evident from the diagram in Exhibit 18–1 that within the framework of equality prevailing between assets and liabilities plus capital, a large variety of combinations of assets and sources of funds used to finance them is possible.

ACCOUNTING PRINCIPLES

The amounts at which liabilities and equity accounts are shown on the financial statements are governed by the application of GAAP. The principles governing the measurement of liabilities are discussed in Chapter 7, and those governing the accounting for equities are covered in Chapter 8. The analyst must keep these principles in mind when analyzing the capital structure and its effect on long-term solvency. While it can be stated, as a broad generalization, that the accounting principles governing the measurement of liabilities and equities do not affect the analysis of

Exhibit 18–1   Asset distribution and capital structure of an enterprise

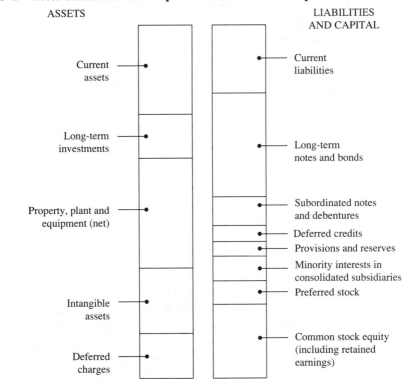

financial statements as importantly as do those governing the measurement of assets, a study of the above-mentioned chapters will reveal aspects of real importance to the analyst.

The relationship between liabilities and equity capital, the two major sources of capital in an enterprise, is always an important factor entering into the assessment of long-term solvency. Thus, an understanding of their nature is essential to the analyst. There are liabilities that are not fully reflected in the balance sheet, and there are accounts whose accounting classification as debt or equity should not be automatically accepted by the analyst. The proper decision of how to classify or deal with these depends on a thorough understanding of their nature and/or the particular conditions of issue to which they are subject. The discussion that follows supplements the important analytical considerations covered in Chapters 7 and 8.

Deferred Taxes

Most deferred credits, such as bond premiums, represent allocation accounts designed primarily to aid in the measurements of income. They do not present an important problem of analysis and are relatively insignificant in size. Deferred income items, such as subscription income received in advance, represent an obligation for future service and are, as such, clearly liabilities.

One type of deferred liability that is generally much more sizable, and consequently much more important, is *deferred income taxes*. As already pointed out in Chapters 7 and 11, this account is not a liability in the usual sense because the government does not have a definite short-term or even longer-term claim against the enterprise. Nevertheless, this account does represent in large measure the aggregate exhaustion in tax deductibility of assets and other items, over and above that recorded for book purposes, and this means that at some time in the future the deferred tax liability account (credit) will be used to reduce the higher income tax expense that corresponds to *increased* tax liabilities. Even if the likelihood of the deferred tax account "reversing" in the foreseeable future is quite good, there still remains the question of whether the time-adjusted present value of such future expected "reversals" should not be used instead of the nominal face value amount of the deferred credit. After all, most other liabilities on the balance sheet including pensions and leases are carried at present value. The higher the interest rates (cost of debt) applicable to an entity are, the more significant the impact of discounting to present value. In *SFAS 109* the board considered the issue of discounting deferred taxes and decided against discounting at the time.

To the analyst, the important question here is whether to treat the deferred tax account as a liability, as an equity item, or as part debt and part equity. The decision depends on the nature of the deferral, the past experience with the account (e.g., has it been constantly growing?), and the likelihood of future "reversal."

In making his or her judgment, the analyst must recognize that under normal circumstances, deferred tax liabilities will reverse, that is, become payable, when a firm shrinks in size. Generally, a shrinkage in size is attended by losses rather than by taxable income. In such circumstances, the drawing down of the deferred tax account is more likely to involve credits to tax loss carryforwards or carrybacks, rather than to the Cash account.

To the extent that such future "reversal" is only a remote possibility, as may be the case with timing differences due to accelerated depreciation, the deferred credit should be viewed as a source of funds of such long-term nature as to be classifiable as equity. On the other hand, if the possibility of a "drawing down" of the deferred tax account in the foreseeable future is quite strong, then the account, or a part of it, is more in the nature of a long-term liability. In classifying the deferred tax account as between debt and equity, the analyst must be guided by considerations such as the ones discussed above.

When the analyst decides to classify deferred tax credits as equity (either in whole or in part), the following *analytical* entry is appropriate:

Deferred Income Taxes—Current* X
Deferred Income Taxes—Noncurrent* . . . . Y
    Owners' Equity . . . .   Z

* As applicable.

Long-Term Leases

Under *SFAS 13,* most financing long-term noncancelable leases must be shown as debt. While *SFAS 13* has tightened the rules considerably, companies can still find ways around them by the way leases are written and by other means. If the analyst concludes that leases that are not capitalized by the reporting entity should be capitalized, he can, for analytical purposes, book them as follows:

Leasehold Assets X
    Liabilities under Long-Term Leases . . . .   Y

Chapter 7 contains a discussion of the methodology involved in the capitalization of leases.

Off-Balance-Sheet Financing

SFAS 13 has significantly curtailed one of the most significant and widely used methods of off-balance-sheet financing. However, in trying to determine the total debt to which an entity is subject, the analyst must be aware that some managements will attempt to understate debt and that new methods of doing this are constantly tried. Chapter 7 contains a discussion of recent methods in use such as "take or pay contracts," "sales" of receivables, and inventory repurchase agreements. A careful reading of footnotes and of management comments along with inquiries of management can shed light on the existence of unrecorded liabilities.

Liabilities for Pensions and for Other Postretirement Employee Benefits (OPEB)

As was discussed in Chapter 7, *SFAS 87* recognizes that if the fair value of pension assets falls short of the accumulated pension benefit obligation, a liability for pensions exists. However, this liability does not take into consideration the *projected* benefit obligation which recognizes an estimate for future pay increases when pension plans base their benefits on future pay formulas. Analysts who judge such understatement as serious and who can estimate such understatement may want to adjust the pension liability for analytical purposes.

As was similarly discussed in Chapter 7, companies can, on adoption of *SFAS 106,* recognize the unfunded OPEB obligation immediately or over as many as 20 years. Under the latter amortization option a company is, unlike under pension accounting, not required to record a minimum liability. Thus, the analyst will need to assess the present value of the unrecorded liability for OPEB.

There are distinctions between pension debt, as well as possibly OPEB liabilities, and other debt in that the former do not present as immediate a threat to force a company into bankruptcy as does the latter. Research into these differences also supports this view.[3] While the Pension Benefit Guaranty Corporation (PBGC) has the authority to take control of an underfunded plan and place a lien on company assets, for the protection of employee benefits, it has, so far, moved very cautiously in this area. The Internal Revenue Service also has established procedures under which companies in financial difficulty can obtain waivers to defer their contributions to a pension fund.

Unconsolidated Subsidiaries

As we saw in Chapter 9, the preferred method of presenting the financial statements of a parent and its subsidiary is in consolidated format. This is also the preferred method from the analyst's point of view for most analytical purposes, although separate financial statements of the consolidated entities are necessary in some cases, such as when the utilization

---

[3] W. Landsman, "An Empirical Investigation of Pension Fund Property Rights," *The Accounting Review,* October 1986, pp. 662–91.

of assets of a subsidiary (e.g., an insurance company or a bank) is not subject to the full discretion of the parent.

Information on unconsolidated subsidiaries may also be important because bondholders of such subsidiaries can look only to the latter's assets as security for their bonds. Moreover, bondholders of the parent company (particularly holding companies) may derive a significant portion of their fixed-charge coverage from the dividends of the unconsolidated subsidiaries. Yet, in the event of the subsidiary's bankruptcy, the parent bondholders may be in a junior position to the bondholders of the subsidiary.

When the financial statements of a subsidiary are not consolidated with the parent, consolidation may be undertaken as an analytical adjustment as follows:

```
Subsidiary's Assets* .................................. X
    Subsidiary's Liabilities* ...........................    Y
    Parent's Investment in Subsidiary ...................    Z
```
* Using as much detail as is needed or is available.

If the subsidiary has unrecorded lease or pension liabilities, they too may be consolidated for purposes of analysis.

Provisions, Reserves, and Contingent Liabilities

Provisions such as for guarantees and warranties represent obligations to offer future service and should be classified as such. Generally speaking, reserves created by charges to income may also be considered as liabilities. However, general contingency reserves or reserves for very indeterminate purposes (most of which are now prohibited by *SFAS 5*) should not be considered as genuine liabilities.

The analyst must make a judgment regarding the probability of commitments or contingencies becoming actual liabilities and should then treat these items accordingly. Thus, guarantees of indebtedness of subsidiaries or others that are likely to become liabilities should be treated as such.

Minority Interests

Minority interests in consolidated financial statements represent the ownership interests of minority shareholders of the subsidiaries included in the consolidated group. These are not liabilities similar in nature to debt because they have neither mandatory dividend payment nor principal repayment requirements. Capital structure measurements concentrate on the mandatory payments aspects of liabilities. From this point of view, minority interests are more in the nature of outsiders' claims to a portion of the equity or an offset representing their proportionate ownership of assets.[4]

Convertible Debt

Convertible debt is generally classified among liabilities. However, if the conversion terms are such that the only reasonable assumption that can be made is that the debt will be converted into common stock, then it may be classified as equity for purposes of capital structure analysis.

Preferred Stock

Most preferred stock entails no absolute obligation for payment of dividends or repayment of principal, possessing thus the characteristics of true equity. However, as was discussed in Chapter 7, preferred stock with a fixed maturity or subject to sinking fund requirements should, from an analytical point of view, be considered as debt.

As discussed in Chapter 7, preferred stock with mandatory redemption requirements is akin to debt and should be considered as such by the analyst. This is so even though in some cases default by the company on the redemption provisions does not carry repercussions as severe as those flowing from the nonpayment of debt.

ADJUSTMENTS TO THE BOOK VALUE OF ASSETS

Because the owners' equity of an enterprise is measured by the excess of total assets over total liabilities, any analytical revision of asset book values (i.e., amounts at which assets are shown in the financial statements) will also result in a change in the amount of the owners' equity. For this reason, in assessing capital structure, the analyst must decide whether or not the book value amounts of assets are realistically stated. The following are examples of the need for possible adjustments. Different or additional adjustments may be needed depending on circumstances.

Recognition of Market Values

In industries such as mining, petroleum, timber, or other natural resources, or in real estate, the market value of assets can exceed significantly the historical costs carried on the balance sheets. Adjustments to

---

[4] Minority interests are shown at book value. Thus, if the analyst wants to assess what the parent company would have to pay in order to acquire the minority interest, market rather than book values will be the determining factor.

market value of these assets will have a corresponding enhancing effect on equity capital. The higher values of these assets should also be reflected in increased earning power with a corresponding enhancing effect on the fixed-charge coverage ratio—an effect that is not dependent on analytical adjustments discussed here.

As will be seen below, some analysts use market values of the company's equity securities, rather than equity at book values, to adjust for the higher market values of assets. This is based on the assumption that the market is best able to reflect the value inherent in a company's total financial condition.

Inventories

Inventories carried at LIFO are generally understated in times of rising prices. The amount by which inventories computed under FIFO (which are closer to replacement cost) exceed inventories computed under LIFO is generally disclosed. Such disclosures should enable the analyst to adjust inventory amounts and the corresponding owners' equity amounts (after tax) to more realistic current costs or values.

Marketable Securities

Marketable securities are often stated at cost that may be below market value. Using parenthetical, footnote, or other information, the analyst can make an analytical adjustment increasing this asset to market value and owners' equity (after tax) by a corresponding amount.

Intangible Assets

Intangible assets and deferred items of dubious value that are included on the asset side of the balance sheet affect the computation of the total equity of an enterprise. To the extent that the analyst cannot evaluate or form an opinion on the present value or future utility of such assets, they may be excluded from consideration, thereby reducing the amount of equity capital (after tax) by the amounts at which such assets are carried. However, the arbitrary exclusion of all intangible assets from the capital base is an unjustified exercise in overconservatism.

The foregoing discussion related to the evaluation and the classification of debt and equity accounts. Let us now turn to an examination of the significance of capital structure in financial analysis.

THE SIGNIFICANCE OF CAPITAL STRUCTURE

The significance of capital structure is derived, first and foremost, from the essential difference between debt and equity.

The equity is the basic risk capital of an enterprise. Every enterprise must have some equity capital that bears the risk to which it is inevitably exposed. The outstanding characteristic of equity capital is that it has no guaranteed or mandatory return that must be paid out in any event and no definite timetable for repayment of the capital investment. Thus, capital that can be withdrawn at the contributor's option is not equity capital and has, instead, the characteristics of debt.[5] From the point of view of an enterprise's stability and exposure to the risk of insolvency, the outstanding characteristic of equity capital is that it is permanent, can be counted on to remain invested in times of adversity, and has no mandatory requirement for dividends. It is such funds that an enterprise can most confidently invest in long-term assets and expose to the greatest risks. Their loss, for whatever reason, will not necessarily jeopardize the firm's ability to pay the fixed claims against it.

Both short-term and long-term debt, in contrast to equity capital, must be repaid. The longer the term of the debt and the less onerous its repayment provisions, the easier it will be for the enterprise to service it. Nevertheless, it must be repaid at certain specified times regardless of the enterprise's financial condition; and so must interest be paid in the case of most debt instruments. Generally, the failure to pay principal or interest will result in proceedings under which the common stockholders may lose control of the enterprise as well as part or all of their investment. Should the entire equity capital of the enterprise be wiped out by losses, the creditors may also stand to lose part or all of their principal and interest due.

It can be readily appreciated that the larger the proportion of debt in the total capital structure of an enterprise, the higher the resulting fixed charges and repayment commitments and the greater the probability of a chain of events leading to an inability to pay interest and principal when due.

To the investor in the common stock of an enterprise, the existence of debt represents a risk of loss of the investment, and this is balanced by the potential of high profits arising from financial leverage. Excessive debt may also mean that management's initiative and flexibility for profitable action will be stifled and inhibited. Leverage acts to magnify managerial mistakes. It can also increase risk already present because of such factors as commodity price fluctuations or technological obsolescence.

The creditor prefers as large a capital base as possible as a cushion that will shield against losses that can result from adversity. The smaller

---

[5] For example, during the financial crisis that befell many brokerage houses in the late 1960s, it was discovered that much "equity" capital that was thought to lend strength to the enterprise and additional security to customers and creditors was in effect subject to withdrawal by owners. At the sign of real trouble, these owners withdrew their capital, thus compounding the financial problems even more.

the relative capital base, or conversely, the larger the proportionate contribution of funds by creditors, the smaller is the creditors' cushion against loss and consequently the greater the risk of loss.

While there has been a considerable debate, particularly in academic circles, over whether the *cost of capital* of an enterprise varies with different capital structures, that is, with various mixes of debt and equity, the issue seems significantly clearer from the point of view of outsiders to the enterprise, such as creditors or investors, who must make decisions on the basis of conditions as they are. In the case of otherwise identical entities, the creditor exposes himself to greater risk if he lends to the company with 60 percent of its funds provided by debt (and 40 percent by equity capital) than if he lends to a similar company that derives, say, only 20 percent of its funds from debt.

Under the Modigliani-Miller thesis, the cost of capital of an enterprise in a perfect market is, except for the tax deductibility of interest, not affected by the debt to equity relationship.[6] This is so, they assert, because each individual stockholder can inject, by use of personally created leverage, his own blend of risk into the total investment position. Thus, under this theory, the advantage of debt will be offset by a markdown in a company's price-earnings ratio.

The degree of risk in an enterprise, as judged by the outside prospective investor is, however, a given; and our point of view, as well as our task here, is to measure the degree of risk residing in the capital structure of an enterprise.

REASONS FOR EMPLOYMENT OF DEBT

In addition to serving as an inflation hedge, a primary reason for the employment of debt by an enterprise is that up to a certain point, debt is, from the point of view of the ownership, a less expensive source of funds than equity capital. This is so for two main reasons:

1. The interest cost of debt is fixed,[7] and thus, as long as it is lower than the return that can be earned on the funds supplied by creditors, this excess return accrues to the benefit of the equity.
2. Unlike dividends, which are considered a distribution of profits, interest is considered an expense and is, consequently, tax deductible.

A further discussion of these two main reasons follows.

---

[6] F. Modigliani and M. Miller, "The Cost of Capital, Corporation Finance and the Theory of Investment," *American Economic Review,* June 1958, pp. 261–97.

[7] Except for debt subject to variable interest rates.

The Concept of Financial Leverage

Financial leverage means the inclusion in the capital structure of an enterprise of debt that pays a fixed return. Since no creditor or lender would be willing to put up loan funds without the cushion and safety provided by the owners' equity capital, this borrowing process is also referred to as "trading on the equity," that is, utilizing the existence of a given amount of equity capital as a borrowing base.

In Exhibit 18–2, a comparison is made of the returns achieved by two companies having identical assets and earnings before interest expense. Company X derives 40 percent of its funds from debt while Company Y has no debt. In year 1, when the average return on total assets is 12 percent, the return on the stockholders' equity of Company X is 16 percent. This higher return is due to the fact that the stockholders benefited from the excess return on total assets over the cost of debt. For Company Y, the return on equity always equals the return on total assets. In year 2, the return on total assets of Company X was equal to the interest cost of debt and, consequently, the effects of leverage were neutralized. The results of year 3 show that leverage is a double-edged sword. Thus, when the return on total assets falls below the cost of debt, Company X's return on the equity is lower than that of debt-free Company Y.

The Effect of Tax Deductibility of Interest

The second reason given for the advantageous position of debt is the tax deductibility of interest. This can be illustrated as follows:

Assume the facts given in Exhibit 18–2 for year 2, and that the operating earnings of Company X and Company Y, $100,000 for each, are both of equal quality.[8] The results of the two companies can be summarized as follows:

	Company X	Company Y
Income before interest and taxes	$100,000	$100,000
Interest (10% of $400,000)	40,000	
Income before taxes	60,000	100,000
Taxes (40%)	24,000	40,000
Net income	36,000	60,000
Add back interest paid to bondholder	40,000	
Total return to security holders (debt and equity)	$ 76,000	$ 60,000

---

[8] The concept of the quality of earnings is discussed in Chapter 22.

Exhibit 18–2 Trading on the equity—results under different earning assumptions (dollars in thousands)

	Assets	Debt payable	Stock-holders' equity	Income before interest and taxes	10 percent debt interest	Taxes[a]	Net income	Net income + (Interest) × (1 – Tax rate)	Return on Total assets[b]	Return on Stock-holders' equity[c]
Year 1:										
Company X	$1,000,000	$400,000	$ 600,000	$200,000	$40,000	$64,000	$ 96,000	$120,000	12.0%	16.0%
Company Y	1,000,000	–	1,000,000	200,000	–	80,000	120,000	120,000	12.0	12.0
Year 2:										
Company X	1,000,000	400,000	600,000	100,000	40,000	24,000	36,000	60,000	6.0	6.0
Company Y	1,000,000	–	1,000,000	100,000	–	40,000	60,000	60,000	6.0	6.0
Year 3:										
Company X	1,000,000	400,000	600,000	50,000	40,000	4,000	6,000	30,000	3.0	1.0
Company Y	1,000,000	–	1,000,000	50,000	–	20,000	30,000	30,000	3.0	3.0

[a] Assuming a 40 percent tax rate.

[b] $\dfrac{\text{Net income + Interest (1 – 0.40)}}{\text{Total Assets}}$.

[c] $\dfrac{\text{Net income}}{\text{Stockholders' equity}}$.

Disregarding leverage effects that are neutral in the above example, even if the return on assets is equal to the interest rate, the total amount available for distribution to the bondholders and stockholders of Company X is $16,000 higher than the amount available for the stockholders of Company Y. This is due to the lower total tax liability to which the security holders of Company X are subject.

It should be borne in mind that the value of the tax deductibility of interest is dependent on the existence of sufficient earnings. However, unrecovered interest changes can be carried back and carried forward as part of tax loss carryovers permitted by law.

Other Advantages of Leverage

In addition to the advantages accruing to equity stockholders from the successful employment of financial leverage and the tax deductibility of interest expenses, a sound longer-term debt position can result in other advantages to the equity owner. A rapidly growing company can avoid earnings dilution through the issuance of debt. Moreover, if interest rates are headed higher, all other things being equal, a leveraged company paying fixed interest rates will be more profitable than its nonleveraged competitor. The reverse is, of course, also true. There is, moreover, a financial benefit from advantageously placed debt because debt capital is not always available to an enterprise and the capacity to borrow may disappear should adverse operating results occur. Finally, in times of inflation, monetary liabilities will result in price-level gains (see Chapter 14).

Measuring the Effect of Financial Leverage

The effect of leverage on operating results is positive when the return on the equity capital exceeds the return on total assets. This difference in return isolates the effect that the return on borrowed money has on the return on the owner's capital. As was seen in the example in Exhibit 18–2, leverage is positive when the return on assets is higher than the cost of debt. It is negative when the opposite conditions prevail. The terms *positive* and *negative* are not used here in the strict algebraic sense.

The effect of financial leverage can be measured by the following formula:

$$\text{Financial leverage index} = \frac{\text{Return on common equity}}{\text{Return on total assets}}$$

Using the data in Exhibit 18–2, we compute the financial leverage indexes of Company X for years 1, 2, and 3 as follows:

Financial Leverage Index

$$\text{Year 1: } \frac{16.0}{12.0} = 1.33$$

$$\text{Year 2: } \frac{6.0}{6.0} = 1$$

$$\text{Year 3: } \frac{1.0}{3.0} = 0.33$$

In year 1, when the return on equity exceeded that on total assets, the index at 1.33 was positive. In year 2, when the return on equity equaled that on total assets, the index stood at 1, reflecting a neutralization of financial leverage. In year 3, the index, at 0.33, was way below 1.0, thus indicating the very negative effect of financial leverage in that year. The subject of return on investment is discussed in Chapter 19.

ILLUSTRATION OF COMPUTATION

The computation of a variety of ratios for Campbell Soup based on data in Chapter 4, Appendix B, and on data presented in Chapter 23 will be illustrated in the latter chapter as part of a comprehensive analysis.

In this and other chapters we will also be using the financial statements of Quaker Oats Company (also referred to as QO) as the basis for various illustrations so as to enrich the database on which we draw. The financial statements of QO are found in Appendix 23 and are also annotated with reference numbers for ease of identification of the data used.

The financial leverage index for Quaker Oats for 1991 is calculated as follows:

$$\frac{\text{Return on common equity}}{\text{Return on total assets}} = \frac{21.01\%}{8.61\%} = 2.44$$

with both returns calculated as follows:

Return on common equity:

$$\frac{\text{Net income} - \text{Preferred dividends}}{\text{Average common stockholders' equity}}$$

$$= \frac{\$205.8^{(a)} - \$4.3^{(b)}}{(\$901 + \$1,017.5)^{(c)} / 2} = 21.01\%$$

Return on total assets:

$$\frac{\text{Net income} + \text{Net interest expense } (1 - \text{Tax rate})}{\text{Average total assets}}$$

$$= \frac{\$205.8^{(a)} + \$101.9^{(d)} (1 - 0.34)^{(e)}}{(\$3,016.1 + \$3,326.1)^{(f)} / 2} = 8.61\%$$

[a] Net income—item 11
[b] Preferred stock dividend—item 111
[c] Common shareholders' equity—item 91
[d] Interest expense (net)—item 156
[e] 1—marginal tax rate
[f] Total assets—item 69

THE FINANCIAL LEVERAGE RATIO

The financial leverage ratio measures the relationship between total assets and the common equity capital that finances them. It is expressed as:

$$\frac{\text{Total assets}}{\text{Common equity capital}}$$

The more assets that are financed on a given common equity capital base the higher the financial leverage ratio. As will be seen in Chapter 19 the financial leverage ratio is an element in the analytical disaggregation of the return on equity. Thus, in an enterprise that utilizes leverage profitably, a higher financial leverage ratio will enhance the return on equity. At the same time the risk inherent in a change in profitability is also greater.

The financial leverage ratio of Quaker Oats (Appendix to Chapter 23) for 1991 is computed as follows:

$$\frac{\text{Average total assets}}{\text{Average common equity}} = \frac{\boxed{69} \ (\$3,016.1 + \$3,326.1) \div 2}{\boxed{91} \ (\$901.0 + \$1,017.5) \div 2} = 3.31$$

QO's financial leverage ratio indicates that every dollar of common equity commands $3.31 in assets for the company.

MEASURING THE EFFECT OF CAPITAL STRUCTURE ON LONG-TERM SOLVENCY

From the foregoing discussion it is clear that the basic risk involved in a leveraged capital structure is the risk of running out of cash under conditions of adversity.

Debt involves a commitment to pay fixed charges in the form of interest and principal repayments. While certain fixed charges can be postponed in times of cash shortage, those associated with debt cannot be postponed without adverse repercussion to the ownership and also to the creditor groups.

Another important repercussion of excessive debt is a loss of financing flexibility (i.e., the ability to raise funds particularly in adverse capital markets).

LONG-TERM PROJECTIONS—USEFULNESS AND LIMITATIONS

If a shortage of cash required to service the debt is the most adverse possibility envisaged, then the most direct and most relevant measure of risk inherent in the leveraged capital structure of an enterprise would be a projection of future cash resources and flows that would be available to meet these cash requirements. These projections must assume the worst set of economic conditions that are likely to occur, since this is the most realistic and useful test of safety from the creditor's point of view. If only prosperous and normal times are to be assumed, then the creditor would not need his preferred position and would be better off with an equity position where the potential rewards are higher.

In Chapter 17, we concluded that detailed cash flow projections can be reliably made only for the short term. Consequently, they are useful only in the measurement of short-term liquidity.

The statement of cash flows (SCF) can be projected over a relatively longer term because such a projection is far less detailed than a projection of cash flows. However, as we saw in the discussion of such projections in the preceding chapter, this lack of detail as well as the longer time horizon reduces the reliability of such projections.

The short term is understood to encompass, generally, a period of up to one year. The longer term, however, is a much wider ranging period. Thus, it may include a solvency analysis with respect to a three-year term loan, or it may encompass the evaluation of risk associated with a 30-year bond issue. Meaningful projections covering the period over which the interest and principal of the term loan will be paid can still reasonably be made. However, a 30-year projection of funds flow covering the bond issue would be an unrealistic exercise. For this reason, longer-term debt instruments often contain sinking fund provisions that act to reduce the uncertain time horizon, and stipulations of additional security in the form of specific assets pledged as collateral. Moreover, they often contain provisions requiring the maintenance of minimum working capital levels or restrictions on the payment of dividends, all of which are designed to ensure against a deterioration in the financial ratios prevailing at the time the bonds are issued. They cannot, of course, prohibit adverse operating results—a major and severe cause of cash flow deficiencies.

Desirable as cash flow projections may be, their use for the extended longer term is severely limited. For this reason, a number of measures of long-term solvency have evolved that are more static in nature and are based on measures of capital structure as well as on asset and earnings coverage tests. These measures will be considered below.

CAPITAL STRUCTURE ANALYSIS— COMMON-SIZE STATEMENTS

A simple measure of financial risk in an enterprise is the composition of its capital structure. This can be done best by constructing a common-size statement of the liabilities and equity section of the balance sheet as shown in Exhibit 18–3.

An alternative way of analyzing capital structure with common-size percentages would be to focus only on the longer-term capital funds by excluding the current liabilities from total funds.

The advantage of a common-size analysis of capital structure is that it presents clearly the relative magnitude of the sources of funds of the enterprise, a presentation that lends itself readily to a comparison with similar data of other enterprises.

A variation of the approach of analyzing capital structure by means of common-size or component percentages is to analyze it by means of ratios.

CAPITAL STRUCTURE RATIOS

The basic ratio measurements of capital structure relate the various components of the capital structure to each other or to their total. Some of these ratios in common use are explained below.

Exhibit 18–3   Liabilities and equity section—with common-size percentages

Current liabilities	$ 428,000	19.0%
Long-term debt	500,000	22.2
Equity capital:		
Preferred stock	400,000	17.8
Common stock	800,000	35.6
Paid-in capital	20,000	0.9
Retained earnings	102,000	4.5
Total equity capital	1,322,000	58.8
Total liabilities and equity capital	$2,250,000	100.0%

TOTAL DEBT TO TOTAL CAPITAL (DEBT AND EQUITY)

The most comprehensive ratio in this area is that which measures the relationship between *total debt* (i.e., Current liabilities + Long-term debt + any other form of liability determined by the analyst to be debt, such as deferred income taxes and redeemable preferred stock) to *total capital* that in addition to total debt includes the stockholders' equity (inclusive of preferred stock). The ratio can thus be expressed as

$$\frac{\text{Total debt}}{\text{Total capital}} \text{ as defined above}$$

and can also be expressed as debt as a percentage of total capitalization (rather than the ratio of one to the other).

The 1991 debt to total capital ratio for Quaker Oats (Appendix to Chapter 23) is computed as follows:

$$\frac{\$926.9^{(a)} + \$701.2^{(b)} + \$115.5^{(c)} + \$366.7^{(d)}}{\$99.3^{(e)} + \$806.5^{(f)} + \$2,100.3^{(g)}} = \frac{\$2,110.3^{(g)}}{\$3,016.1} = 0.70$$

[a] Current liabilities—item [78]
[b] Long-term debt—item [79]
[c] Other liabilities—item [80]
[d] Deferred income taxes—item [81]
[e] Preferred stock outstanding—items [82–84]
[f] Shareholders' equity—items [91–83]
[g] Total debt (numerator)

The result can be expressed as a ratio of 0.70 or as debt being 70 percent of Quaker Oats's total capital (Debt + Equity).

Ratio of Total Debt to Total Equity Capital

An alternate measure of the relationship of debt to capital sources is the ratio of total debt (as defined above) to total equity capital only. Thus:

$$\frac{\text{Total debt}}{\text{Total stockholders' equity}}$$

This ratio for 1991 for Quaker Oats is computed as follows:

$$\frac{\$2,110.3^*}{\$99.3^* + \$806.5^*} = 2.33$$

* See above for derivation

This ratio means that QO's total debt is 2.33 times its equity capital or that the company borrowed from all sources $2.33 for every dollar of equity capital it has.

A reciprocal measure of the above is:

$$\frac{\text{Total stockholders' equity}}{\text{Total debt}}$$

For QO

$$\frac{\$905.8}{\$2,110.3} = 0.43$$

and this can be interpreted from the creditor's point of view as meaning that every dollar of debt is backed by only 43 cents of equity capital. This also clarifies the fact that the owners have a smaller stake in the enterprise than do all creditors.

Long-Term Debt/Equity Capital

This ratio measures the relationship of long-term debt to equity capital.[9] A ratio in excess of 1:1 indicates a higher long-term debt participation as compared to equity capital. This ratio is the familiar debt to equity ratio that is computed as follows:

$$\frac{\text{Long-term debt}}{\text{Equity capital}}$$

For QO, the 1991 long-term debt to stockholders' equity ratio is computed as follows:

$$\frac{\$2,110.3^{(a)} - \$926.9^{(b)}}{\$905.8^{(c)}} = 1.31$$

[a] Total debt.
[b] Total current liabilities.
[c] Stockholders' equity.
See above for derivation of amounts.

Confusion in Terminology

Analysts must be aware that in this area, as in many others, the popular name of a ratio may not convey precisely its meaning and, hence, the method of its computation. Before any measure or ratio is used, care must be taken that the method of its computation is thoroughly understood.

Short-Term Debt

The ratio of debt that matures over the short term to total debt is an important indicator of the short-run cash and financing needs of an enterprise. Short-term debt, as opposed to long-term debt or sinking fund requirements, is an indicator of enterprise reliance on short-term (mostly bank) financing. Moreover, short-term debt is subject to frequent changes in interest rates.

---

[9] The term *long-term debt* usually includes *all* liabilities that are not current.

Equity Capital at Market Value

Accounting principles in current use place primary emphasis on historical costs rather than on current values.[10] Since the shareholders' capital is the residual of assets minus liabilities, this accounting can result in equity capital book value figures that are far removed from realistic market values.

One method of correcting this flaw in the stated equity capital amounts, particularly when they enter importantly into the computation of many of the ratios that we have considered above, is to restate them by converting the assets from historical cost to current market values. This may be particularly important in the case of natural resource companies whose book values greatly understate the market value of their assets.

Although disclosure requirements affecting certain companies may provide analysts with some replacement cost data (see Chapter 14), we are still far from having complete market values available.

One way of overcoming the problem of giving recognition to market values is to compute the equity capital at current (or some kind of average) market value of the stock issues that comprise it. On the assumption that the valuation placed by the market on the equity capital recognizes the current values of assets and their earning power, this amount can then be used in the computation of the various debt to equity ratios.

A serious objection to this method is that stock prices fluctuate widely and may, particularly in times of overspeculation or market panic, not be representative of "true" values at a given moment. However, this argument can be countered with considerable evidence that the judgment of the marketplace is most of the time superior to that of other judgmental processes and that use of average market prices would solve the problem of temporary aberrations. Thus, the use of equity capital figures computed at current, or at average, market values has much to commend it. Being more realistic, they can improve the ratio measurements in which they are used and can provide a more realistic measure of the asset cushion that bondholders can count on.[11]

A persistent trend of equity at book value that is in excess of equity at market value can be interpreted as a sign of financial weakness and of restricted financial capability, affecting the ability to sell equity capital

---

[10] Starting with *SFAS 107* the FASB has moved to require the *disclosure* of the fair value of financial instruments.

[11] B. Graham, D. L. Dodd, and S. Cottle in their *Security Analysis,* 4th ed. (New York: McGraw-Hill, 1962), p. 361, suggest that the ratio of

$$\frac{\text{Market value of junior equity}}{\text{Par value of bonds}}$$

should not be less than 0.5 and can be used to corroborate earnings coverage measures. It would not be prudent to have to assume, they maintain, that the junior equity is undervalued by the market.

or even raise new debt capital. Conversely, an excess of market value of equity securities over book value is a strong protecting factor for bondholders and other creditors. It indicates an ability to raise equity capital at advantageous cost, which is an indicator of financial strength.

One important advantage of earnings-coverage ratios, as will be seen in the subsequent discussion of this subject, is that they are based on the earning power of assets rather than on the amount at which they are carried in the financial statements. Market values do, of course, give recognition to such earning power of an entity's assets. In that sense, ratio measures, such as debt to equity ratios, that use equity capital amounts at market value, are more consistent with earnings-coverage ratios than are ratios using historical book values.

Using Quaker Oats' (see Appendix to Chapter 23) average common stock market price for 1991 we can compute:

$$\frac{\text{Total debt}}{\text{Common equity at market value} + \text{Preferred equity at book value}}$$

$$\frac{\$2,110,300,000^{(a)}}{76,328,721^{(b)} \times \$53.32^{(c)} + \$4,800,000^{(d)}} = \frac{\$2,110,300,000}{\$4,074,647,400} = 0.52$$

$^{(a)}$ Total debt—item $\boxed{78}$ + $\boxed{79}$ + $\boxed{80}$ + $\boxed{81}$
$^{(b)}$ Number of common stock outstanding—item $\boxed{85}$ – $\boxed{90}$
$^{(c)}$ Average stock price for 1991—item $\boxed{137}$ (range 64.88—41.75)
$^{(d)}$ Preferred stock at book value—item $\boxed{82}$ + $\boxed{83}$ + $\boxed{84}$

Market values of the equity capital can be important because they take into consideration the earnings power of assets, market values, and so on. If we compare the 0.52 that we get when using the market value of the equity to the 2.33 that was computed above when using the book values, we see that the market value ratio is far more favorable.

PREFERRED STOCK WITHIN THE CAPITAL STRUCTURE

Within the total stockholders' equity, preferred stock holds a preferential position with a prior claim on assets ahead of the common stock. Thus, it is instructive to compute the ratio of preferred stock to total stockholders' equity which is done as follows:

$$\frac{\text{Preferred stock at stated value (or liquidating value if higher)}}{\text{Total stockholders' equity}}$$

The ratio of preferred stock to total stockholders' equity would be computed as follows for Quaker Oats:

$$\frac{(1,282,051 - 10,089)^{(a)} \times \$78^{(b)}}{\$905.8^{(c)}} = \frac{\$99.2}{\$905.8} = 10.9\%$$

$^{(a)}$ Number of shares outstanding—item $\boxed{82}$ – $\boxed{84}$
$^{(b)}$ Liquidating value—item $\boxed{82}$
$^{(c)}$ Total shareholders' equity—item $\boxed{91}$ + $\boxed{82}$ + $\boxed{83}$ + $\boxed{84}$

The analyst must always consider how to treat preferred stock subject to mandatory redemption requirements. While, as discussed in Chapter 7, such stock is akin to a liability more than to equity, it must be recognized that a failure to meet the redemption requirements may not have as dire a result on the entity's status as would a failure to meet a sinking fund requirement of debt.

THE ANALYTICALLY ADJUSTED RATIO OF LONG-TERM DEBT TO EQUITY

In our earlier discussion of the elements that enter into an entity's capital structure, we concluded that there are many types of analytical adjustments that the analyst may wish to make to the published financial data in computing debt to equity ratios. An illustration of the computation of the analytically adjusted long-term debt to equity ratio is given in Appendix C to this chapter.

INTERPRETATION OF CAPITAL STRUCTURE MEASURES

The common-size and ratio analyses of capital structure, which have been examined above, are all measures of risk inherent in the capital structure of an enterprise. The higher the proportion of debt, the larger the fixed charges of interest and debt repayment, the greater the likelihood of insolvency during protracted periods of earnings decline or other adversities.

One obvious value of these measures is that they serve as screening devices. Thus, when the ratio of debt to equity capital is relatively small, say, 10 percent or less, there is normally no need to be concerned with this aspect of an enterprise's financial condition; and the analyst may well conclude that time is better spent by directing attention to the more critical areas revealed by analysis.

Should an examination of the debt to equity ratios reveal that debt is indeed a significant factor in the total capitalization, then further analysis is necessary. Such an analysis will encompass many aspects of an enterprise's financial condition, results of operations, and future prospects.

An analysis of short-term liquidity is always important because before the analyst starts to assess long-term solvency he has to be satisfied about the short-term financial survival of the enterprise. Chapter 16 examines the analysis of short-term liquidity, and the analyst will use the tools discussed there to assess the situation and also to relate the size of working capital to the size of long-term debt. Loan and bond indenture covenants requiring the maintenance of minimum working capital ratios attest to the importance attached to current liquidity in ensuring the long-term solvency of an enterprise.

Additional analytical steps of importance will include an examination of debt maturities (as to size and spacing over time), interest costs, and other factors that have a bearing on the risk. Among those, the earnings stability of the enterprise and its industry as well as the kind of assets its resources are invested in are also important factors.

"EVENT" AND OTHER TYPES OF RISK

There are additional risks to which bondholders are exposed which are not always susceptible to measurement and which must be provided for by protective bond-indenture provisions or by other means.

One such risk is that the borrowing entity will issue significant additional numbers of bonds of equal or higher priority. This type of risk, referred to as *event risk,* has occurred recently, particularly in conjunction with leveraged buyouts, tender offers, and going-private transactions. Such transactions have resulted in serious declines in the value of outstanding bonds.

Additional risk of loss of value can impact bondholders when a borrower increases dividends to stockholders to unreasonable levels, invests in riskier assets, or jeopardizes bond security in other ways.

MEASURES OF ASSETS DISTRIBUTION

The type of assets an enterprise employs in its operations should determine to some extent the sources of funds used to finance them. Thus, for example, it is customarily held that fixed and other long-term assets should not be financed by means of short-term loans. In fact, the most appropriate source of funds for investment in such assets is equity capital, although debt also has a place in such financing especially in industries such as utilities that generally enjoy stable revenue sources. On the other hand, working capital, and particularly seasonal working capital needs, can be appropriately financed by means of short-term credit. The ratio of working capital to long-term debt should generally not fall below 1, and in most industries that are affected by the business cycle, a ratio below 1.5 to 2 may indicate weakness and vulnerability.

In judging the risk exposure of a given capital structure, the asset composition is one of the important factors to consider. This asset composition is best measured by means of common-size statements of the asset side of the balance sheet. For example, Exhibit 18–4 shows the

Exhibit 18–4   Assets section—with common-size percentages

Current assets:		
Cash	$ 376,000	16.7%
Accounts receivable (net)	425,000	18.9
Merchandise inventory	574,000	25.5
Total current assets	1,375,000	61.1
Investments	268,000	11.9
Land, property, and equipment (net)	368,000	16.4
Intangibles	239,000	10.6
Total assets	$2,250,000	100.0%

common-size asset section of the balance sheet whose liabilities and equity section was presented in Exhibit 18–3.

Judging *only* by the distribution of assets and the related capital structure, it would appear that since a relatively high proportion of assets is current (61 percent), a 41 percent debt and current liabilities position (see Exhibit 18–3) is not excessive. Other considerations and measurements may, however, change this conclusion.

Asset coverage is an important element in the evaluation of long-term solvency. Assets of value provide protection to holders of debt obligations both because of their earning power and because of their liquidation value. Additionally, they represent the bases on which an enterprise can obtain the additional financing that may be required to tie it over a period of financial stringency.

The relationship between asset groups and selected items of capital structure can also be expressed in terms of ratios.

Fixed assets to equity capital is a ratio that measures the relationship between long-term assets and equity capital. A ratio in excess of 1:1 means that some of the fixed assets are financed by means of debt.

Net tangible assets as a percentage of long-term debt is a measure of asset coverage of long-term obligations. It excludes assets of doubtful realizability or value and represents a measure of safety of debt based on liquidation of assets.

Total obligations to total net tangible assets (including net working capital) is another useful measure of the relationship between debt and the entity's investment in operating assets. An analysis of the property backing enjoyed by creditors is likely to be most useful in the case of companies, such as those in the natural resource field, where book values may be significantly understated.

If the financial structure ratios are such that they require further analysis, one of the best means for further investigation are tests that measure an enterprise's ability to service its debt requirements out of earnings. This is the area we shall turn to next.

CRITICAL IMPORTANCE OF "EARNING POWER"

One conclusion of our discussion of debt to equity ratios was that a major usefulness of these measurements lies in their function as a screening device, that is, a means of deciding whether the apparent risk inherent in the capital structure of an enterprise requires further investigation and analysis. An important limitation of the measurements of debt to equity relationships is that they do not focus on the availability of cash flows that are necessary to service the enterprise's debt. In fact, as a debt obligation is repaid, the debt to equity ratio tends to improve whereas the yearly amount of cash needed to pay interest and sinking fund requirements may remain the same or may even increase, as, for example, in the case of level payment debt loans with "balloon" repayment provisions or zero coupon bonds.

The long-term creditor must in the final analysis rely on the enterprise's earning power as the most reliable source of interest and principal repayments. While a highly profitable enterprise can in the short run be illiquid because of the composition of its assets, earning power is in the long run the major source of liquidity and of borrowing capacity.

MEASURES OF EARNINGS COVERAGE

Earnings-coverage ratios measure directly the relationship between debt-related fixed charges and the earnings available to meet these charges.[12] The concept of the basic earnings coverage of fixed-charges ratio is simple:

$$\frac{\text{Earnings available to meet fixed charges}}{\text{Fixed charges (as defined)}}$$

While the concept behind this measurement is simple and straightforward, its practical implementation is complicated by the problem of defining what should be included in "earnings" and in "fixed charges."

Earnings Available to Meet Fixed Charges

As was seen in Chapter 13, net income determined under the principles of accrual accounting is not the same thing as cash provided by operations. Specifically, certain items of income, such as undistributed earnings of subsidiaries and controlled companies or sales on extended credit terms, do not create cash. Similarly, certain expenses such as depreciation, amortization, depletion, and deferred income tax charges do not require

---

[12] Fixed-charges-coverage ratios represent important inputs in bond-rating decisions. Bond indentures often specify that minimum levels of this ratio must be maintained before additional debt can be issued.

the outlay of cash. On the other hand, it should be borne in mind that a parent company can determine the dividend policy of a controlled subsidiary.

Fixed-debt charges are paid out of cash rather than out of net income. Thus, the analyst must realize that an unadjusted net income figure may not be a correct measure of cash available to meet fixed charges.

The use of net income as an approximation of cash provided by operations may, in some instances, be warranted while in others it may significantly overstate or understate the amount actually available for the servicing of debt. Thus, the soundest approach to this problem lies not in generalizations but rather in a careful analysis of the noncash generating items included in income as well as the noncash requiring expenses charged to that income. Thus, for example, in considering depreciation as a noncash requiring expense, the analyst must realize that over the long run an enterprise must replace its plant and equipment.

The problem of determining the amount of income to be included in fixed-charges-coverage ratios requires consideration of a number of additional factors:

1. *The treatment of extraordinary gains and losses.* As pointed out in the more comprehensive discussion of this subject in Chapters 11 and 22, extraordinary gains and losses enter into the determination of longer-term average earnings power. As such they must be recognized as a factor that may, over the longer term, contribute to or reduce the cash available to pay fixed charges. Any computation of earnings-coverage ratios utilizing average earnings figures must recognize the existence of extraordinary gains and losses over the years. This is particularly true of earnings-coverage ratios where what we measure is the risk of loss of sources of cash for payment of fixed charges.

2. *Preferred dividends* need not be deducted from net income because the payment of such dividends is not mandatory. However, in consolidated financial statements, preferred dividends of a subsidiary whose income is consolidated must be deducted because they represent a charge that has priority over the distribution of earnings to the parent.

3. Earnings that are attributed to *minority interests* are usually deducted from net income available for fixed charges even though minority shareholders can rarely enforce a cash claim under normal conditions. An exception arises where the consolidated subsidiary has fixed charges. In such instances, the coverage ratio should be computed on the basis of earnings before deducting minority interests.

If a subsidiary with a minority interest has a loss, the credit in the income statement that results from the minority's share in the loss should be excluded from consolidated earnings for purposes of the coverage ratio computation. The parent would, in most cases, meet fixed-charges obligations of its subsidiary to protect its own credit standing, whether or not legally obligated to do so.

4. *The impact of income taxes* on the computation of earnings-coverage ratios should always be carefully assessed. Since interest is a tax-deductible expense, it is met out of pre-tax income. Thus, the income out of which interest payments are met is pre-tax income. On the other hand, preferred dividends or sinking fund payments are not tax deductible and must be paid out of after-tax earnings.

5. *Add-back of fixed charges.* In order to determine the amount of pre-tax earnings available to meet specific fixed charges, those fixed charges that were deducted in arriving at pre-tax earnings must be added back to pre-tax income in the numerator of the ratio.

6. *The level of income* used in the computation of earnings-coverage ratios deserves serious consideration. The most important consideration here is: what level of income will be most representative of the amount that will actually be available in the *future* for the payment of debt-related fixed charges. An average figure of earnings from continuing operations encompassing the entire range of the business cycle, and adjusted for any known factors that may change it in the future, is most likely to be the best approximation of the average source of cash from future operations that can be expected to become available for the payment of fixed charges. Moreover, if the objective of the earnings-coverage ratio is to measure the creditor's maximum exposure to risk, then the proper earnings figure to use is that achieved at the low point of the enterprise's business cycle.

Fixed Charges to Be Included

Having considered the amount of earnings that should be included in the earnings coverage, we shall now turn to an examination of the types of fixed charges that are generally includable in the computation of this ratio.

1. Interest Incurred

Interest incurred is the most direct and most obvious fixed charge that arises from the incurrence of indebtedness. Interest expense includes the amortization of deferred bond discount and premium. The bond discount and issue expenses represent the amount by which the par value of the bond indebtedness exceeded the proceeds from the bond issue. As such, the discount amortization represents an addition to the stated interest expense. The amortization of bond issue premium represents the reverse situation, and thus results in a reduction of interest expense over the period of amortization.[13]

---

[13] Bond discount and premium amortization, which are usually relatively insignificant in amount, do not, strictly speaking, require a current outlay of funds. They represent cost or income item allocations over the term of the loan.

If low coupon bonds have only a short period to run before maturity and it is likely that they will have to be refinanced with higher coupon bonds, it may be appropriate to incorporate in fixed charges the expected higher interest costs.

Interest on income bonds must be paid only as earned. Consequently, it is not a fixed charge from the point of view of the holder of fixed-interest securities. It must, however, be regarded as a fixed charge from the point of view of the income bond issuer.

When information disclosed is so vague or limited that it is impossible to determine the amount of interest incurred and interest capitalized, the amount of interest *incurred* can be approximated by referring to the mandatory disclosure of *interest paid* in the statement of cash flows. Interest incurred will differ from interest paid as disclosed due to changes in interest payable, because interest capitalized is often netted, because of interest discount and premium amortization, and possibly for other reasons. However, in the absence of other data, interest *paid* is a better approximation of interest incurred than any other amount.

2. Capitalized Interest

SFAS 34 requiring the capitalization of certain interest costs (see Chapter 11) has greatly increased the practice of interest capitalization. Care must be taken to arrive at proper amounts in both the numerator and the denominator of the fixed-charges-coverage ratio.

Let us clarify where interest can be found in the income statement and the terminology that relates to it. Interest that the enterprise pays or is obligated to pay during a period is referred to as *interest incurred.* This is the amount we focus on as being covered by earnings. Interest incurred that is not immediately expensed but rather charged to some asset account is *interest capitalized.* Interest incurred less interest capitalized equals *interest expensed.* Since interest that is expensed is that which enters into the determination of pre-tax income, it should be added back to the pre-tax income found in the numerator of the ratio in order to arrive at pre-tax preinterest income. The denominator of the ratio will, however, include as a fixed-charge interest incurred whether capitalized or not.

Interest capitalized in one period will find its way into the income statements of subsequent periods in the form of costs such as depreciation or amortization. Such amortized interest that was previously capitalized must be added back to pre-tax income.[14] In effect, failure to add back such interest results in including earnings in the numerator *after* some interest costs rather than *before* interest, with a resulting understatement of the fixed-charges-coverage ratio. Since the FASB has not required the

---

[14] SEC regulations require that different methods of computation apply to rate-regulated public utilities. In their case, the allowance for funds used during construction shall be added to gross income but not deducted from interest expense. Utilities may not add to earnings the amount of previously capitalized interest amortized during the period.

disclosure of the amount of previously capitalized interest that is amortized in a given period, analysts can obtain these amounts through voluntary disclosure by companies or they can sometimes derive them from other disclosures such as those relating to deferred taxes.

In item 156 Quaker Oats presents details of interest expense allocable to continuing operations, discontinued operations, as well as interest expense capitalized.

3. Interest Implicit in Lease Obligations

Chapter 7 on the analysis of liabilities discusses the present status of accounting recognition of leases as financing devices. *SFAS 13* requires the capitalization of most financing leases.

When a lease is capitalized, the interest portion of the lease payment is included in the interest expense on the income statement while most of the balance is usually considered as repayment of the principal obligation. A problem arises, however, when the analyst considers that certain leases that should have been capitalized are not so treated in the financial statements. The issue here actually goes beyond the pure accounting question of whether capitalization is, or is not, appropriate. It stems rather from the fact that a long-term lease represents a fixed obligation that must be given recognition in the computation of the earnings-coverage ratio. Thus, even long-term leases that, from an accounting theory point of view, need not be capitalized may be considered as including fixed charges that have to be included in the coverage-ratio computation.[15]

The problem of extracting the interest portion of long-term lease payments is not a simple one. The external analysts can possibly obtain the rate of interest implicit in the lease, from an examination of the more extensive disclosure now available on the subject. Otherwise a rough rule of thumb, such as that interest represents one third of rentals, originally suggested by Graham and Dodd, may have to be used.[16] The SEC, which had encouraged use of this rule, no longer accepts it automatically and insists on a more reliable estimate of the portion of rentals that represent interest.[17] "Delay rentals" in the extractive industries represent payment for the privilege of deferring the development of properties and, being in the nature of not regularly recurring compensation to owners, are not considered as rentals includable in the earnings-coverage ratio.

---

[15] In the discussion preceding the release of its 1982 revised regulations concerning the computation of the fixed-charges-coverage ratio, the SEC has reemphasized that "some long-term leases may narrowly miss the criteria for a capital lease but still have the characteristics of a financing transaction. The Commission does not believe that the presence of an interest factor is dependent upon the rental contract extending over any given period of time."

[16] Graham, Dodd, and Cottle, *Security Analysis,* 4th ed. (New York: McGraw-Hill, 1962), p. 344. (This rule was developed in a previous edition of this book.)

[17] SEC *Accounting Series Release 155* (now superseded), as well as discussion preceding the SEC's release of revised rules concerning the computation of the ratio in 1982.

As with the prohibition against the offsetting of interest income against interest expense, the general rule is that rental income should not be offset against rental expense when determining fixed charges. An exception is made, however, where the rental income represents a direct reduction in rental expense.

4. Preferred-Stock Dividend Requirements of Majority-Owned Subsidiaries

These are considered fixed charges because they have priority over the distribution of earnings to the parent. Items that would be or are eliminated in consolidation should not be considered fixed charges.

Income Tax Adjustment of Fixed Charges

Fixed charges that are not tax deductible must be tax adjusted. This is done by increasing them by an amount equivalent to the income tax that would be required to obtain an after-tax income sufficient to cover such fixed charges. The above preferred-stock dividend requirement is one example of such nontax-deductible fixed charges. The following adjustment is made to compute the "grossed-up" amount:

$$\frac{\text{Preferred-stock dividend requirements}}{1 - \text{Income tax rate}}$$

The tax rate to be used should be based on the relationship of the provision for income tax expense applicable to income from continuing operations to the amount of pre-tax income from continuing operations (i.e., the company's normal effective tax rate). The effective tax rate, rather than the statutory tax rate we normally use for this purpose, is used here in "grossing up," because this is the SEC's requirement.

Other Elements to be Included in Fixed Charges

The foregoing discussions concerned the determination of fixed financing charges, that is, interest and the interest portion of lease rentals. These are the most widely used measures of "fixed charges" included in conventional fixed-charges-coverage ratios such as those required by the SEC which we adopt as the standard required computation.

However, if the purpose of this ratio is to measure an enterprise's ability to meet fixed commitments that if unpaid could result in repercussions ranging all the way from financial embarrassment to insolvency, there are other fixed charges to be considered. The most important categories of such additional fixed charges that we shall consider here are principal repayment obligations such as sinking fund requirements, serial repayment provisions, and the principal repayment component of lease rentals. These items are not usually included as fixed charges, and the inclusion of some may be quite controversial. The inclusion of these fixed charges will not be illustrated here.

5. Principal Repayment Requirements

Principal repayment obligations are, from a cash-drain point of view, just as onerous as obligations to pay interest. In the case of rentals, the obligations to pay principal and interest must be met simultaneously.

A number of reasons have been advanced to indicate why the requirements for principal repayments are not given recognition in earnings-coverage ratio calculations:

1. The coverage of fixed-charges ratio is based on income. It is assumed that if the ratio is at a satisfactory level, it will be possible to refinance obligations as they become due or mature. Consequently, they may not have to be met from funds provided by earnings.
2. If the company has an acceptable debt to equity ratio it should be able to reborrow amounts equal to the debt repayments.
3. Another objection to the inclusion of sinking fund or other periodic principal repayment provisions in the calculation of the earnings-coverage ratio is that this may result in double counting, that is, the funds recovered by depreciation already provide for debt repayment. Thus, if earnings reflect a deduction for depreciation, then fixed charges should not include provisions for principal repayments.
   There is some merit to this argument if the debt was used to acquire depreciable fixed assets and if there is some correspondence between the pattern of depreciation charges and that of principal repayments. It must, moreover, be borne in mind that depreciation funds are recovered generally only out of profitable, or at least break-even, operations, and consequently this argument is valid only under an assumption of such operations.
   Our discussion of the definition of "earnings" to be included in the coverage-ratio calculations emphasized the importance of cash provided by operations as the measure of resources available to meet fixed charges. The use of this concept would, of course, eliminate the double-counting problem since nonfund-requiring charges such as depreciation would be added back to net income for the purpose of the coverage computations.

A more serious problem regarding the inclusion of debt repayment provisions among "fixed charges" arises from the fact that not all debt agreements provide for sinking fund payments or similar repayment obligations. Any arbitrary allocation of indebtedness over time would be an unrealistic theoretical exercise and would ignore the fact that to the extent that such payments are not required in earlier years, the immediate pressure on the cash resources of the enterprise is reduced. In the longer run, however, larger maturities as well as "balloon" payments will have to be met.

The most useful solution to this problem lies in a careful analysis and assessment of the yearly debt repayment requirements that will serve as the basis on which to judge the effect of these obligations on the long-term solvency of the enterprise. The assumption that debt can always be refinanced, rolled over, or otherwise paid off from current operations is not the most useful approach to the problem of risk evaluation. On the contrary, the existence of debt repayment obligations as well as the timing of their maturity must be recognized and included in an overall assessment of the long-term ability of the enterprise to meet its fixed obligations. The inclusion of sinking fund or other early repayment requirements in fixed charges is one way of recognizing the impact of such requirements on fund adequacy. Another method would, as a minimum, call for scheduling total debt repayment requirements over a period of 5 to 10 years into the future and relating these to after-tax funds expected to be available from operations.

6. Other Fixed Charges

While interest payments and debt repayment requirements are the fixed charges most directly related to the incurrence of debt, there is no logical justification to restrict the evaluation of long-term solvency only to these charges and commitments. Thus, a complete analysis of fixed charges that an enterprise is obliged to meet must include all long-term rental payment obligations[18] (not only the interest portion thereof) and particularly those rentals that must be met under any and all circumstances under noncancelable leases, otherwise known as "hell-and-high-water" leases.

The reason why short-term leases can be excluded from consideration as fixed charges is that they represent an obligation of limited duration, usually less than three years, and can consequently be discontinued in a period of severe financial stringency. Here, the analyst must, however, evaluate how essential the rented items are to the continuation of the enterprise as a going concern.

Other charges that are not directly related to debt but that may nevertheless be considered as long-term commitments of a fixed nature are long-term purchase contracts in excess of normal requirements not subject to cancellation and other similar obligations.

---

[18] Capitalized long-term leases affect income by the interest charge implicit in them as well as by the amortization of the property right. Thus, to consider the "principal" component of such leases as fixed charges (after income was reduced by amortization of the property right) may amount to double counting.

7. Guarantees to Pay Fixed Charges

Guarantees to pay fixed charges of unconsolidated subsidiaries or of unaffiliated persons (such as suppliers) should result in additions to fixed charges if the requirement to honor the guarantee appears imminent.

RATIO OF EARNINGS TO FIXED CHARGES

In its revised regulations concerning the "Ratio of Earnings to Fixed Charges," the SEC's concept of computing this ratio moved so close to our own that we present it on page 631 as the standard conventional[19] computation.

The key letters below explain items in the formula and will serve as a reference to computations as well as to the summary-amplifying notes which follow:

A Income before discontinued operations, extraordinary items, and cumulative effects of accounting changes.

B Interest incurred *less* interest capitalized.

C Is often included in interest expense.

D Since all financing leases are capitalized, the interest implicit in these is already included in interest expense—the interest portion of long-term operating leases is included on the theory that many long-term operating leases narrowly miss the criteria for a capital lease under *SFAS 13* but still have many of the characteristics of a financing transaction.

E Excluding in all cases items eliminated in consolidation. The dividend has to be increased to pre-tax earnings that would be required to cover such dividend requirements, that is:

$$\frac{\text{Preferred stock dividend requirements}}{100 \text{ percent} - \text{Income tax rate}^*}$$

* Based on relationship between applicable actual income tax provision to income *before* income taxes, extraordinary items, and cumulative effect of accounting changes.

F Applies to nonutility companies only. In most cases, disclosure of this amount is not made.

G Minority interest in income of majority-owned subsidiaries that have fixed charges may be included in income.

H Whether expensed or capitalized.

---

[19] Still in use but so simple as not to require elaboration here is the times-interest-earned ratio which considers only interest as a fixed charge to be covered, thus:

$$\frac{\text{Pretax income} + \text{Interest expense}}{\text{Interest expense}}$$

The SEC's formula for computing the ratio is:

(Numerator)

(A) Pre-tax income from continuing operations *plus* (B) Interest expensed *plus* (C) Amortization of debt expense and discount or premium *plus* (D) Interest portion of operating rental expenses *plus* (E) Tax-adjusted preferred stock dividend requirements of majority-owned subsidiaries *plus* (F) Amount of previously capitalized interest amortized during the period *minus* (G) Undistributed income of less than 50-percent-owned persons (affiliates)

(Denominator)

(H) Total interest incurred *plus* (C) Amortization of debt expense and discount or premium *plus* (D) Interest portion of operating rental expenses *plus* (E) Tax-adjusted preferred stock dividend requirements of majority-owned subsidiaries

General

To reduce the complexity of the formula, two items (provisions) were left out:

1. In computing earnings, the *full* amount of losses of majority-owned subsidiaries should be considered.
2. Losses on investments in less than 50-percent-owned companies accounted for by the equity method should not be included in earnings *unless* the company has guaranteed the debt of the affiliate.

If the ratio of earnings to fixed charges is less than one, the amount of insufficiency of earnings to cover the fixed charges should be given (rather than a ratio).

Illustration of Earnings-Coverage-Ratio Calculations

Having discussed the various considerations that enter into the decision of what factors to include in the earnings-coverage-ratio computation, we will address ourselves now to the question of how the ratio is computed. The computation of the various coverage ratios will be based on the illustration in Exhibit 18–5.

Using the data in Exhibit 18–5 and letter references to the above formula, we compute the ratio of earnings to fixed charges as follows (dollars in thousands):

$$\frac{\$2,200 \text{ (A)} + \$700 \text{ (B and C)} + \$300 \text{ (D)} + \$80 \text{ (F)} - \$600 \text{ (G)} + \$200^*}{\$840 \text{ (H)} + \$60 \text{ (C)} + \$300 \text{ (D)}} = \underline{\underline{2.4}} \text{ times}$$

* The SEC permits the inclusion in income of the minority interest in the income of majority-owned subsidiaries that have fixed charges. This amount is added in order to reverse a similar deduction from income.

Exhibit 18–5

THE LEVERED CORPORATION
Abbreviated Income Statement

Net sales		$13,400,000
Income of less than 50%-		
owned affiliates (all undistributed)		600,000
		14,000,000
Cost of goods sold	$7,400,000	
Selling, general, and administrative expenses	1,900,000	
Depreciation (excluded from above costs) (3)	800,000	
Interest expense (1)—net	700,000	
Rental expense (2)	800,000	
Share of minority interests in		
consolidated income*	200,000	11,800,000
Income before taxes		2,200,000
Income taxes:		
Current	800,000	
Deferred	300,000	1,100,000
Income before extraordinary items		1,100,000
Gain on sale of investment in land (net of $67,000		
tax)		200,000
Net income		$ 1,300,000
Dividends:		
On common stock	200,000	
On preferred stock	400,000	600,000
Earnings retained for the year		$ 700,000

* These subsidiaries have fixed charges.

Selected notes to the financial statements:

1. The interest expense is composed of the following:

Interest incurred (except items below)	$740,000
Amortization of bond discount	60,000
Interest portion of capitalized leases	100,000
Interest capitalized	(200,000)
Interest expense	$700,000

2. Interest implicit in noncapitalized leases amounts to $300,000.
3. Depreciation includes amortization of previously capitalized interest of $80,000.

Additional information (during year covered by Income Statement):

Increase in accounts receivable	$310,000
Increase in inventories	180,000
Increase in accounts payable	140,000
Decrease in accrued taxes	20,000

The ratio of earnings to fixed charges of Quaker Oats (see Appendix to Chapter 23), for 1991 can be computed as follows (letter references are to the formula above—dollars in millions):

$$\frac{(A)\ 411.5^{(a)} + (B)101.9^{(b)} + (D)14.8^{(c)}}{(H)103.8^{d} + (D)14.8^{(c)}} = 4.45$$

[a] Income from continuing operations before taxes—item [7].
[b] Interest expensed—item [156].
[c] One third of operating lease rentals or $\frac{1}{3}$ of $44.5 = $14.8. [154].
[d] Interest incurred $101.9 + 1.9 = 103.8 [156].

PRO FORMA COMPUTATIONS OF COVERAGE RATIOS

In cases where fixed charges yet to be incurred are to be recognized in the computation of the coverage ratio, as, for example, interest costs under a prospective incurrence of debt, it is quite proper to estimate the offsetting benefits that will ensue from such future inflows of cash and to include these estimated benefits in the pro forma income. Benefits to be derived from a prospective loan can be measured in terms of interest savings obtainable from a planned refunding operation, income from short-term investments in which the proceeds may be invested, or similarly reasonable estimates of future benefits.

The SEC will usually insist on the presentation of a pro forma computation of the ratio of earnings to fixed charges that reflects changes to be effected under prospective financing plans when the effect of the refinancing changes the historical ratio by 10 percent or more.

CASH FLOW COVERAGE OF FIXED CHARGES

The discussion earlier in this chapter pointed out that net income is generally not a reliable measure of cash provided by operations that is available to meet fixed charges. The reason is, of course, that fixed charges are paid with cash while net income includes items of revenue that do not generate cash as well as expense items which do not require the current use of cash. Thus, a better measure of fixed-charges coverage may be obtained by using in the numerator cash obtained by operations rather than net income. This figure can be obtained from the SCF.

Under this concept, the coverage ratio would be computed as follows:

$$\frac{\text{Pre-tax cash provided by operations} + \text{Fixed charges}}{\text{Fixed charges}}$$

Using the data in Exhibit 18–5 we compute the coverage ratio as follows:

Cash provided by operations (pre-tax):

Pre-tax income	$2,200,000
Add (deduct) adjustments to cash basis:	
Depreciation	80,000
Deferred income taxes (already added back)	—
Amortization of bond discount	60,000
Share of minority interest in income	200,000
Undistributed income of affiliates	(600,000)
Increase in receivables	(310,000)
Increase in inventories	(180,000)
Increase in accounts payable	140,000
Decrease in accrued tax	(20,000)
Cash provided by operations (CFO)	$2,290,000

The fixed charges to be added back to pre-tax cash provided by operations of

	$2,290,000
Interest expensed (less bond discount added back above)	640,000
Interest portion of operating rental expense	300,000
Amount of previously capitalized interest amortized during period*	—
Total numerator	$3,230,000

* Assumed here to be included in depreciation (already added back).

Note that the numerator does not reflect a deduction of $600,000 (undistributed income of affiliates) because that figure, being a noncash providing item, was already deducted at arriving at pre-tax cash provided by operations. Similarly, the "share of minority interests in consolidated income" has already been added back in arriving at the pre-tax cash provided by operations figure.

The fixed charges in the denominator are computed as follows:

Interest incurred	$ 900,000
Interest portion of operating rentals	300,000
	$1,200,000

Thus, the ratio of pre-tax cash provided by operations to fixed charges is:

$$\frac{\$3,230,000}{\$1,200,000} = \underline{\underline{2.69}}$$

Quaker Oats' (see Appendix to Chapter 23) cash provided by operations to fixed charges ratio is computed as follows:

Numerator	*$ millions*
Cash provided by operating activities—item 31	532.4
Add back	
Income tax expense (except deferred)[a]—item 158	161.4
Interest expensed—item 156	101.9
Amortization of previously capitalized interest (already added	
back)—presumably included in item 20	—
Total numerator	795.7

Thus the ratio is

$$\frac{\$795.7}{\$103.8^{(b)} + \$14.8^{(c)}} = \underline{\underline{6.7}}$$

[a] Deferred tax already added back in computation of CFO.
[b] Interest incurred—item 156 (101.9 + 1.9).
[c] 1/3 of operating lease rentals of $44.5 154.

STABILITY OF "FLOW OF CASH FROM OPERATIONS"

Since the relationship between the "flow of cash from operations" to the fixed charges of an enterprise is so important to an evaluation of long-term solvency, it is important to assess the stability of that flow. This is done by a careful evaluation of the elements that comprise the sources of cash from operations. For example, the depreciation add-back to net income is a more stable element than is net income itself because the recovery of the depreciation cost from selling prices precedes the earning of any net income, and has thus a higher degree of probability of happening. Even in very competitive industries selling prices must, in the long run, reflect the cost of plant and equipment used up in production.

It should be noted that the depreciation add-back assumes that the cash-flow benefits of the recovery of depreciation from sales prices will be available to meet debt service. This, however, can be true only in the short run or in an emergency. In the long run such cash recovery must be dedicated to replacement of plant and equipment. This may not be true in the case of add-backs such as amortization of goodwill, which does not have to be replaced.

The stability of the change in the "current assets and current liabilities related to operations" component of cash from operations is more difficult to assess. This component is more strongly related to sales than to pre-tax income and may thus be more stable than the latter.

EARNINGS COVERAGE OF PREFERRED DIVIDENDS

In the evaluation of preferred stock issues, it is often instructive to calculate the earnings coverage of preferred dividends, much in the same way the interest or fixed-charges coverage of debt issues is computed. The computation of the earnings coverage of preferred dividends must include as charges to be covered by earnings all fixed charges that take precedence over the payment of preferred dividends.[20] As is the case with all fixed-charges-coverage computations, the final ratio depends on a definition of "fixed charges."

Since preferred dividends are not tax deductible, after-tax income must be used to cover them. Consequently, the basic formula for computing preferred dividend coverage is:

$$\frac{\text{Income before tax} + \text{Fixed charges*}}{\text{Fixed charges*} + \text{Preferred dividends} \times \left(\dfrac{1}{1 - \text{Tax rate}}\right)}$$

* Which *are* tax deductible.

To the formula we used earlier (see page 631) to compute the ratio of earnings to fixed charges for The Levered Corporation based on data in Exhibit 18–5, we now add the tax-adjusted preferred-dividend requirement in order to derive the preferred-dividend coverage ratio as follows (dollars in thousands):

$$\frac{\$2,200 \text{ (A)} + \$700 \text{ (B and C)} + \$300 \text{ (D)} + \$80 \text{ (F)} - \$600 \text{ (G)} + \$200^*}{\$840 \text{ (H)} + \$60 \text{ (C)} + \$300 \text{ (D)} + \$400 \left(\dfrac{1}{1 - 0.50}\right)^{\dagger}} = 1.44$$

* Minority interest in income of majority-owned subsidiaries (see prior discussion).

† Tax-adjusted preferred dividend requirement.

---

[20] This is also the position of the SEC. Care must be exercised in comparing these coverage ratios because some analysts and financial services include only the preferred dividend requirements in the computation.

If there are two or more preferred issues outstanding, a by-class coverage ratio can be computed by omitting the dividend requirements of the junior issue but always including all prior fixed charges and preferred dividends.

EVALUATION OF EARNINGS-COVERAGE RATIOS

The earnings-coverage ratio test is a test of the ability of an enterprise to meet its fixed charges out of current earnings. In a classic and pioneering analysis of investor experience in bonds, Hickman[21] found the following life span default rates at offering during 1900–1943 and their relationship to the Times-Charges-Earned Ratio:

Times-Charges-Earned Ratio	Default rate	Promised yield	Realized yield	Loss rate
3.0 and over	2.1	4.0	4.9	−0.9
2.0–2.9	4.0	4.3	5.1	−0.8
1.5–1.9	17.9	4.7	5.0	−0.3
1.0–1.4	34.1	6.8	6.4	0.4
Under 1.0	35.0	6.2	6.0	0.2

The correlation of the times-charges-earned ratio and the default rate is unmistakable.

The orientation toward earnings is a logical one because the bondholder or other long-term creditor, while interested in asset coverage or what can be salvaged in times of trouble, relies even more on the ability of the enterprise to stay out of trouble by meeting its obligations currently and as a going concern. Given the limited returns obtainable from debt instruments, an increase in the interest rate can rarely compensate the creditor for a serious risk of loss of principal. Thus, if the probability of the enterprise meeting its obligations as a going concern is not strong, then a creditor relationship can hardly be advantageous.

The coverage ratio is influenced by the level of earnings and by the level of fixed charges, which in turn depend importantly on the debt to equity relationship within the capitalization.

Importance of Earnings Variability

One very important factor in the evaluation of the coverage ratio is the pattern of behavior of cash flows over time, or the behavior of its surrogate—earnings. The more stable the earnings pattern of an enterprise

---

[21] W. B. Hickman, *Corporate Bond Quality and Investor Experience* (Princeton, N.J.: Princeton University Press, 1958), also found (p. 11) that bonds with poor earnings coverage had a probability of default 17 times greater than those with good coverage.

or industry, the lower the relative earnings-coverage ratio that will be acceptable. Thus, a utility, which in times of economic downturn is likely to experience only a mild falloff in demand, can justify a lower earnings-coverage ratio than can a cyclical company, such as a machinery manufacturer, that may experience a sharp drop in sales in times of recession. Variability of earnings is, thus, an important factor in the determination of the coverage standard. In addition, the durability and the trend of earnings are important factors that must be considered apart from their variability.[22]

Importance of Method of Computation and of Underlying Assumptions

The coverage standard will also depend on the method of computation of the coverage ratio. As we saw above, varying methods of computing the coverage ratio assume different definitions of "income" and of "fixed charges." It is reasonable to expect lower standards of coverage for the ratios that employ the most demanding and stringent definitions of these terms.

The SEC formula for computing the fixed-charges-coverage ratio that we have adopted here is based on income *before* discontinued operations, extraordinary items, and cumulative effects of accounting changes. While these exclusions impart a degree of stability to the earnings, they also remove from them important elements that must be considered as part of the operating experience of the entity. These elements should always be included in computing the *average* coverage ratio over a number of years.

The standards will also vary with the kind of earnings that are utilized in the coverage computation, that is, average earnings, the earnings of the poorest year, and so on. Moreover, the quality of earnings is an important consideration (see Chapter 22).

It is not advisable to compute earnings-coverage ratios under methods that are not theoretically sound and whose only merit is that they are conservative. Thus, using after-tax income in the computation of the coverage ratio of fixed charges that are properly deductible for tax purposes is not logical and introduces conservatism in the wrong place. Any standard of coverage adequacy must, in the final analysis, be related to the willingness and ability of the lender to incur risk.

---

[22] Most factors that will affect an entity's equity securities will also affect its bonds. For example, when Consolidated Edison Company passed its dividend in 1974, its bonds plunged along with its common stock which was the security directly affected. The market, aside from taking its cue from this action, may also have concluded that the company's ability to sell equity securities as well as its overall financing flexibility had been impaired.

Appendix 18A includes references to standards of fixed-charges-coverage ratios used by rating agencies in determining the ratings of individual debt securities.

CAPITAL STRUCTURE, LEVERAGED BUYOUTS, "JUNK BONDS," AND OTHER FINANCIAL "INNOVATIONS"

The reader may find it instructive to relate some recent developments in finance to the basic characteristics of risk inherent in a company's capital structure, as discussed above.

It is possible to increase the risks (as well as the potential rewards) of equity holders by increasing the degree of leverage of an entity. The leveraged buyout of a company accomplishes this by using increased leverage and other factors favorable to buyers such as the existence of undervalued assets which can be sold off for cash. Thus, in a leveraged buyout debt is used to take a company private and to buy out equity holders. The acquirors rely on cash flow to service the increased debt and on an anticipated sale of assets to reduce it. Also working to the advantage of debt issuers is the fact that interest on debt is tax deductible while dividends paid to equity holders are not.

A massive substitution of debt for equity (also referred to as decapitalization) inevitably results in a much riskier capital structure. Thus, many bonds used to finance such leveraged buyouts are referred to as "junk bonds." A junk bond, unlike its higher quality counterpart, is part of a highly risky capital structure and its interest payments are barely covered or poorly covered by earnings. Thus, economic adversity can easily jeopardize the payment of interest and principal on them. These bonds have more of the risk of equity than the safety of debt as their real characteristics.

Financial history has, time and again, proven to those who ignore its lessons that higher risk means higher probability of loss. That a highly speculative financial era has spawned risky securities is no surprise. The surprise is that so many refused to believe that the adjective *junk* when applied to bonds, meant what it implied. Similarly, zero coupon bonds, which defer all payment of interest to maturity, have great advantages if issued by the U. S. government. When issued, however, by those with less than impeccable credit credentials the risk inherent in zero coupon instruments is greatly increased because all interest as well as principal repayment is postponed into the far-off future. PIK Securities, standing for "payment in kind," pay interest by issuing additional debt. There the assumption must surely be that a debtor, too weak to pay interest currently, will somehow be strong enough to pay it much later.

While many novel approaches to the financing of companies have been tried and new words coined which stress form over substance, the basic truths about the relationships of risk and reward inherent in a capital structure remain unchanged.

THOROUGH ANALYSIS IS ESSENTIAL

The factors contributing to risks and the available tools of analysis discussed in this and the preceding chapters point to the need for care and thoroughly grounded analysis in the extension of credit.

Reliance on credit ratings, which will be discussed below, is basically a delegation of the analysis and evaluation function. It is very risky to place exclusive reliance on a single source of analysis, no matter how reputable, without forming some degree of independent judgment regarding the merit of a credit extension.

ILLUSTRATION 1.   In June 1987, World of Wonder Inc. raised $80 million from the sale of convertible debentures by the highly reputable firm of Smith Barney Inc. Before even paying its first coupon, the company filed for protection from its creditors under Chapter 11 of the Bankruptcy Act. The bonds, which were initially sold for $1,000 each, traded for $75 after the filing.

APPENDIX 18A

THE RATING OF DEBT OBLIGATIONS

Over many years there has become established in the United States a comprehensive and sophisticated system for rating debt securities. Most ratings are performed by two highly regarded investment research firms, Moody's and Standard & Poor's (S&P).[23]

A bond credit rating is a composite expression of judgment about the creditworthiness of the bond issuer as well as the quality of the specific security being rated. A rating measures credit risk, that is, the probability of occurrence of developments adverse to the interests of the creditor.

This judgment of creditworthiness is expressed in a series of symbols that express degrees of credit risk. Thus, the top four rating grades of Standard & Poor's are:

AAA.   Bonds rated AAA are highest-grade obligations. They possess the ultimate degree of protection as to principal and interest. Marketwise they move with interest rates, and hence provide the maximum safety on all counts.

---

[23] Ratings are also performed by Duff and Phelps and by Fitch Investors Service. Many institutions also develop their own "in house" ratings.

AA.   Bonds rated AA also qualify as high-grade obligations, and in the majority of instances differ from AAA issues only in small degree. Here, too, prices move with the long-term money market.

A.   Bonds rated A are regarded as upper medium grade. They have considerable investment strength but are not entirely free from adverse effects of changes in economic and trade conditions. Interest and principal are regarded as safe. They predominantly reflect money rates in their market behavior, but to some extent, also economic conditions.

BBB.   The BBB, or medium-grade category is borderline between definitely sound obligations and those where the speculative element begins to predominate. These bonds have adequate asset coverage and normally are protected by satisfactory earnings. Their susceptibility to changing conditions, particularly to depressions, necessitates constant watching. Marketwise, the bonds are more responsive to business and trade conditions than to interest rates. This group is the lowest that qualifies for commercial bank investment.

There is a lower range of ratings ranging from BB which are lower medium grade all the way to the D category representing bonds in default.

The major reason why debt securities are widely rated while equity securities are not lies in the fact that there is a far greater uniformity of approach and homogeneity of analytical measures used in the evaluation of creditworthiness than there can be in the evaluation of the future market performance of equity securities. Thus, the wide agreement on what is being measured in credit risk analysis has resulted in a widespread acceptance of and reliance on published credit ratings.

The criteria that enter into the determination of a rating have never been precisely defined, and they involve both quantitative measures (e.g., ratio analysis) as well as qualitative factors such as market position and management quality. The major rating agencies refuse to be pinned down on what precise mix of factors enter into their rating process (which is a committee decision) because it is both art and science and also because to do so would cause endless arguments about the validity of the many judgmental factors that enter into a rating decision.

We can then see that in arriving at ratings these agencies must undertake analyses along the lines discussed throughout this book, the differences being mainly in the vast number of debt issues covered and the standardization of approaches which this entails. The following description of factors entering the rating process is based on published sources as well as on discussions with officials of the rating agencies.

THE RATING OF CORPORATE BONDS

In rating an industrial bond issue, the rating agency will focus on the issuing company's asset protection, financial resources, earning power, management, and the specific provisions of the debt security.

Also of great importance are size of firm, market share, industry position, susceptibility to cyclical influences,[24] and other broad economic factors.

Asset protection is concerned with measuring the degree to which a company's debt is covered by the value of its assets. One measure is net tangible assets to long-term debt. At S&P, an industrial needs a ratio of 5 to 1 to get an AAA rating, a ratio of over 4 to 1 to qualify for an AA rating, 3 to 3.5 to 1 for an A, and about 2.5 to 1 for a BBB rating.

Understated assets, such as those of companies in the natural resource or real estate fields, are generally accorded recognition in the rating process.

The long-term debt as a percentage of total capitalization calls for a ratio of under 25 percent for an AAA, around 30 percent for an AA, 35 percent for an A, and about 40 percent for a BBB rating.

Other factors entering the consideration of asset protection include the determination of book value, the makeup of working capital, the quality and age of property, plant, and equipment as well as questions of off-balance-sheet financing and unrecorded liabilities.

Financial resources encompass, in particular, such liquid resources as cash and other working capital items. Quality measures here include the collection period of receivables and inventory turnover. These are judged by means of industry standards. The use of debt, both short term and long term, as well as the mix between the two is also investigated.

Future earning power and the resulting cash-generating ability is a factor of great importance in the rating of debt securities because the level and the quality of future earnings determine importantly an enterprise's ability to meet its obligations. Earning power is generally a more reliable source of security than is asset protection.

A prime measure of the degree of protection afforded by earning power is the fixed-charges-coverage ratio. To qualify for consideration for an AAA rating, an industrial company's earnings should cover its interest and rental charges after taxes above five to seven times, for an AA rating above four times, for an A rating over three times, and a BBB over two times.

Another measure of debt service paying ability is cash flow (from operations) to total funded debt. It should be 65 percent or more for an AAA, 45 to 60 percent for an AA, 35 to 45 percent for an A, and 25 to 30 percent for a BBB rating.

---

[24] There are, for example, no AAA-rated companies in the steel or paper industries.

Management abilities, philosophy, depth, and experience always loom importantly in any final rating judgment. Through interviews, field trips, and other analyses, the raters probe into the depth and breadth of management, as well as into its goals, the planning process, and strategies in such areas as research and development, product promotion, new product planning, and acquisitions.

The specific provisions of the debt security are usually spelled out in the bond indenture. What is analyzed here are the specific provisions in the indenture that are designed to protect the interests of bondholders under a variety of future conditions. Included in consideration here are, among others, conditions for issuance of future debt issues, specific security provisions such as mortgaging, sinking fund and redemption provisions, and restrictive covenants.

As can be seen, debt rating is a complex process involving quantitative as well as qualitative factors, all of which culminate in the issuance of a single quality rating. The weights that may be assigned to each factor will vary among analysts, but the final conclusion will generally represent the composite judgment of several experienced raters.

THE RATING OF MUNICIPAL SECURITIES

Buyers of municipal bonds depend for their security of principal and interest on factors that are quite different from those that determine the quality of corporate debt. Hence, the processes of analysis differ.

Municipal securities, those issued by state and local governmental authorities, comprise a number of varieties. Many are general obligation bonds backed by the full faith and credit of the governmental unit that issues them. Others are special tax bonds that are limited in security to a particular tax that will be used to service and retire them. Then there are revenue bonds secured only by revenues of municipal enterprises. Other categories comprise housing authority bonds, tax anticipation notes, and so forth. Although the amount of information provided to buyers of municipal bonds is of very uneven quality there are moves to correct this, primarily by way of legislation.

Raters require a great variety of information from issuers of municipal debt. In the case of general obligation bonds, the basic security rests on the issuer's ability and willingness to repay the debt from general revenues under a variety of economic conditions.[25] The fundamental revenue source is the taxing power of the local municipality. Thus, the information

---

[25] The decision of New York State's highest court to overturn the New York City Moratorium on its notes strengthens the meaning of the concept of "full faith and credit." Said Chief Justice C. J. Breitel: "A pledge of the city's faith and credit is both a commitment to pay and a commitment of the city's revenue generating powers to produce the funds to pay . . . that is the way both words 'faith' and 'credit' are used and they are not tautological."

they require includes current population and the trend and composition of population, the largest 10 taxpayers, the current market value of taxable properties, the gross indebtedness, and the net indebtedness (i.e., after deducting self-sustaining obligations, sinking fund, etc.), recent annual reports, budgets, and estimates of capital improvement and future borrowing programs, as well as an overall description of the area's economy.

While rating techniques have the same objectives as in the case of corporate bonds, the ratios used are adapted to the specific conditions that exist with respect to municipal debt obligations. Thus, debt as a percentage of market value of real estate is an important indicator: 10 percent is considered high while 3–5 percent is on the low side. Annual debt service of 10 percent of total revenue is considered comfortable while percentages in the high teens are considered as presenting a warning sign. Per capita debt of $400 or less is considered low while debt in the $900 to $1,000 area is considered excessive and, hence, a negative factor. Tax delinquencies should generally not exceed 3–4 percent.

Other factors of interest include unfunded pension liabilities as well as the trend of indebtedness. A steady increase in indebtedness is usually a danger sign. As in all cases of debt rating, the factor of management, though largely intangible and subject to measurement only through ultimate results, is of critical importance.

LIMITATIONS OF THE RATING PROCESS

As valuable and essential as the rating process is to buyers of the thousands upon thousands of bond issues of every description, the limitations of this standardized procedure must also be understood.[26] As is true in any phase of security analysis, the analyst who can, through superior analysis, improve on what is conventionally accepted stands to benefit accordingly. As was seen in Chapter 1, this is even more true in the case of debt securities than in the case of equity securities.

Bond ratings cover a wide range of characteristics, and they consequently present opportunities for those who can identify these differences within a rating classification. Moreover, rating changes generally lag the market, and this presents additional opportunities to the analyst who with superior skill and alertness can identify important changes before they become generally recognized.

---

[26] As the huge defaults of the Washington Public Power Supply System Project 4 and 5 bonds have shown, good ratings can be withdrawn and can evaporate quickly. It appears that in this case the rating agencies paid more attention to legal obligations than to the economic underpinnings of these issues.

References

"The Rating Game." New York: The Twentieth Century Fund, 1974.

H. C. Sherwood. *How Corporate and Municipal Debt Is Rated: An Inside Look at Standard & Poor's Rating System.* New York: John Wiley & Sons, 1976.

Corporate Bond Ratings: An Overview. New York: Standard & Poor's Corporation, 1978.

D. F. Hawkins, B. A. Brown, W. J. Campbell. "Rating Industrial Bonds." Morristown, N.J.: Financial Executives Research Foundation, 1983.

"The Ratings Game," *Institutional Investor,* August 1991, p. 73.

APPENDIX 18B

RATIOS AS PREDICTORS OF BUSINESS FAILURE

The most common use to which financial statement ratios are put is to use them as pointers in the direction of further investigation and analysis. Some investigation and experimentation has been undertaken to determine to what extent ratios can be used as predictors of failure. As such they could provide valuable additional tools in the analysis of long-term solvency.

The basic idea behind bankruptcy prediction models is that through observation of the trend and behavior of certain ratios of various firms before failure, those characteristics in ratios that predominate in failing firms can be identified and used for prediction purposes. The expectation is that signs of deterioration observed in ratio behavior can be detected early enough and clearly enough so that timely action can be taken to avoid substantial risk of default and failure.

Empirical Studies

Among the earliest studies to focus on the behavior of ratios prior to the failure of firms were those of Winakor and Smith who studied a sample of 183 firms that experienced financial difficulties for as long as 10 years prior to 1931, the year when they failed.[27] Analyzing the 10-year trend of 21 ratios, they concluded that the ratio of net working capital to total assets was among the most accurate and reliable indicator of failure.

Fitzpatrick analyzed the three- to five-year trends of 13 ratios of 20 firms that had failed in the 1920–29 period.[28] By comparing them to the

---

[27] Arthur Winakor and Raymond F. Smith, *Changes in Financial Structure of Unsuccessful Firms,* Bureau of Business Research (Urbana, Ill.: University of Illinois Press, 1935).

[28] Paul J. Fitzpatrick, *Symptoms of Industrial Failures* (Washington, D.C.: Catholic University of America Press, 1931); and Paul J. Fitzpatrick, *A Comparison of the Ratios of Successful Industrial Enterprises with Those of Failed Companies* (Washington, D.C.: The Accountants Publishing Co., 1932).

experience of a control group of 19 successful firms, he concluded that all of his ratios predicted failure to some extent. However, the best predictors were found to be the return on net worth and the net worth to total debt ratio.

Merwin studied the experience of a sample of 939 firms during the 1926–36 period.[29] Analyzing an unspecified number of ratios he found that three ratios were most sensitive in predicting "discontinuance" of a firm as early as four to five years before such discontinuance. The three ratios were the current ratio, net working capital to total assets, and net worth to total debt. They all exhibited declining trends before "discontinuance" and were at all times below estimated normal ratios.

Focusing on the experience of companies that experienced defaults on debt and bank credit difficulties, Hickman studied the experience of corporate bond issues during 1900–43 and reached the conclusion that the times interest earned ratio and the net profit-to-sales ratio were useful predictors of bond issue defaults.[30]

In a study using more powerful statistical techniques than used in its predecessors, Beaver found that financial ratios proved useful in the prediction of bankruptcy and bond default at least five years prior to such failure. He determined that ratios could be used to distinguish correctly between failed and nonfailed firms to a much greater extent than would be possible by random prediction.[31]

Among his conclusions were that both in the short term and the long term, cash flow to total debt ratios were the best predictors, capital structure ratios ranked second, liquidity ratios third, while turnover ratios were the worst predictors.

In an investigation of the ability of ratios to predict bond-rating changes and bond ratings of new issues, Horrigan found that the rating changes could be correctly predicted to a much greater extent by the use of ratios than would be possible through random prediction.[32]

Altman extended Beaver's univariate analysis to allow for multiple predictors of failure.[33] Altman used multiple discriminant analysis (MDA) that attempts to develop a linear function of a number of explanatory variables to classify or predict the value of a qualitative dependent

---

[29] Charles L. Merwin, *Financing Small Corporations in Five Manufacturing Industries, 1926–36* (New York: National Bureau of Economic Research, 1942).

[30] W. Braddock Hickman, *Corporate Bond Quality and Investor Experience* (Princeton, N.J.: Princeton University Press, 1958), pp. 395–431.

[31] William H. Beaver, "Financial Ratios as Predictors of Failure," *Empirical Research in Accounting, Selected Studies, 1966,* Supplement to *Journal of Accounting Research* 4, pp. 71–127.

[32] James O. Horrigan, "The Determination of Long-Term Credit Standing with Financial Ratios," *Empirical Research in Accounting, Selected Studies, 1966,* Supplement to *Journal of Accounting Research* 4, pp. 44–62.

[33] Edward Altman, "Financial Ratios, Discriminant Analysis, and the Prediction of Corporate Bankruptcy," *Journal of Finance* 22 (September 1968), pp. 589–609.

variable; for example, bankrupt or nonbankrupt. Twenty-two financial ratios, based on data one period before bankruptcy, were examined, and Altman selected five of these to be included in his final discriminant function: working capital/total assets (liquidity), retained earnings/total assets (age of firm and cumulative profitability), earnings before interest and taxes/total assets (profitability), market value of equity/book value of debt (financial structure), and sales/total assets (capital turnover rate).

Altman used the above five ratios to construct the Z-score which is currently the best known bankruptcy prediction model:

$$
\text{Z-score} = 1.2 \left[\frac{\text{Net working capital}}{\text{Total assets}} \right] + 1.4 \left[\frac{\text{Retained earnings}}{\text{Total assets}} \right]
$$

$$
+ 3.3 \left[\frac{\text{Earnings before interest and taxes}}{\text{Total assets}} \right] + 0.6 \left[\frac{\text{Market value of equity}}{\text{Book value of liabilities}} \right]
$$

$$
+ 1.0 \left[\frac{\text{Sales}}{\text{Total assets}} \right]
$$

Experience with the Z-score model led Altman to conclude that Z-scores of less than 1.81 indicate a high probability of bankruptcy while Z-scores above 3.00 indicate a low probability of bankruptcy.

Conclusions

The above research efforts, while pointing out the significant potential that ratios have as predictors of failure, nevertheless indicate that these tools and concepts are in an early stage of development.

The studies focused on experience with failed firms *after the fact.* While they presented evidence that firms that did not fail enjoyed stronger ratios than those that ultimately failed, the ability of ratios alone to predict failure has not been conclusively proved. Another important question yet to be resolved is whether the observation of certain types of behavior by certain ratios can be accepted as a better means of the analysis of long-term solvency than is the integrated use of the various tools described throughout this work. Further research may show that the use of ratios as predictors of failure will best complement and precede, rather than replace, the rigorous financial analysis approaches suggested in this work. However, as screening,[34] monitoring, and attention-directing devices they hold considerable promise.

---

[34] Banks have for years been using credit scoring for personal loans, which gives weight to creditworthiness characteristics such as income, employment, and homeownership. But for loans above $10,000–$25,000, banks no longer rely on the mass-production techniques of credit scoring.

APPENDIX 18C

ILLUSTRATION OF THE COMPUTATION OF THE ANALYTICALLY ADJUSTED LONG-TERM DEBT TO EQUITY RATIO

The conventional long-term debt to equity ratio is expressed as

$$\frac{LTD}{OE}$$

The formula that follows incorporates other analytical adjustments which can be made:

$$\frac{LTD + NFL}{OE + NDT + FIFOA + MSA}$$

where:

LTD = Long-term debt consists of all long-term liabilities inclusive of noncurrent deferred taxes judged *likely* to reverse and other noncurrent liabilities.

NDT = Noncurrent deferred taxes—which are judged as *unlikely* to reverse in the foreseeable future.

OE = Owners' equity (including minority interests).

FIFOA = Excess of disclosed FIFO value of ending inventory over reported LIFO amount.

MSA = Excess of market value of marketable securities over cost.

NFL = Present value of noncapitalized financial leases.

Using the 1991 data of Quaker Oats (see Appendix 23) we can compute the analytically adjusted debt to equity ratio as follows:

$$\frac{701.2^{(a)} + 115.5^{(b)} + 147^{(c)}}{806.5^{(d)} + 220^{(e)} + 18.9^{(f)}} = \frac{963.7}{1045.4} = 0.92$$

[a] Long-term debt-item 79.
[b] Other liabilities—80.
[c] 40% of deferred income taxes 81 assumed liability portion.
[d] Shareholders' equity 91–83.
[e] 60% of deferred income taxes 81-assumed equity portion.
[f] Excess of mostly average cost over LIFO 143.

Not all the items in the formula described earlier were found or were disclosed in Quaker Oat's report.

QUESTIONS

1. Generally speaking, what are the key elements in the evaluation of long-term solvency?

2. How should deferred income taxes be treated in the analysis of capital structure?

3. In the analysis of capital structure how should lease obligations that have not been capitalized be treated? Under what conditions should they be considered the equivalent of debt?

4. What is off-balance-sheet financing? Name some examples.

5. What are liabilities for pensions? What factors should analysts assessing total pension obligations of the firm take into consideration?

6. When will information on unconsolidated subsidiaries be important to the analysis of long-term solvency?

7. How would you classify (i.e., equity or liability) the items that follow? State your assumptions and reasons.
   a. Minority interest in consolidated financial statement.
   b. General contingency reserve for indefinite purpose.
   c. Reserve for self-insurance.
   d. Guarantee for product performance on sale.
   e. Convertible debt.
   f. Preferred stock.

8. a. Why might the analyst need to adjust the book value of assets?
   b. Give three examples of the need for possible adjustments.

9. Why is the analysis of capital structure important?

10. What is meant by "financial leverage," and in what case(s) is such leverage most advantageous?

11. In the evaluation of long-term solvency why are long-term projections necessary in addition to a short-term analysis? What are some of the limitations of long-term projections?

12. What is the difference between common-size analysis and capital structure ratio analysis? Why is the latter useful?

13. The amount of equity capital shown on the balance sheets, which is based on historical cost, at times differs considerably from realizable market value. How should a financial analyst allow for this in the analysis of capital structure?

14. Why should the analyst compute the ratio of preferred stock to total stockholders' equity? How should preferred stock with mandatory redemption requirements be treated?

15. Why is the analysis of assets distribution necessary?

16. What does the earnings-coverage ratio measure and in what respects is it more useful than other tools of analysis?

17. For the purpose of earnings-coverage-ratio computation, what are your criteria for inclusion of an item in "fixed charges"?

18. The company under analysis has a purchase commitment of raw materials under a noncancelable contract that is substantial in amount. Under what conditions would you include the purchase commitment in the computation of fixed charges?

19. Is net income generally a reliable measure of funds available to meet fixed charges?

20. Company B is a wholly owned subsidiary of Company A. The latter is also Company B's principal customer. As potential lender to Company B,

what particular facets of this relationship would concern you most? What safeguards, if any, would you require?

21. Comment on the statement: "Debt is a supplement to, not a substitute for, equity capital."

22. A company in need of additional equity capital decides to sell convertible debt, thus postponing equity dilution and ultimately selling its shares at an effectively higher price. What are the advantages and disadvantages of such a course of action?

23. *a.* What is the basic function of restrictive covenants in long-term debt indentures (agreements)?

    b. What is the function of provisions regarding:
    (1) Maintenance of minimum working capital (or current ratio)?
    (2) Maintenance of minimum net worth?
    (3) Restrictions on the payment of dividends?
    (4) Ability of creditors to elect a majority of the board of directors of the debtor company in the event of default under the terms of the loan agreement?

24. What is your opinion on the use of ratios as predictors of failure? Your answer should recognize the empirical research that has been done recently in this area.

25. Dogwood Manufacturing, Inc., a successful and rapidly growing company, has always had a favorable difference between the rate of return on its assets and the interest rate paid on borrowed funds. Explain why the company should *not* increase its debt to the 90-percent level of total capitalization and thereby minimize any need for equity financing. (CFA)

26. Why are debt securities widely rated while equity securities are not?

27. On what aspects do the rating agencies focus in rating an industrial bond? Elaborate.

28. *a.* Municipal securities comprise a number of varieties. Discuss.

    b. What factors are considered in the rating of municipal securities?

29. Can the analyst improve on a rating judgment? Discuss.

Chapter 19

ANALYSIS OF RETURN ON INVESTMENT AND OF ASSET UTILIZATION

DIVERSE VIEWS OF PERFORMANCE

In this age of increasing social consciousness, there exist many views of what the basic objectives of business enterprises are or should be. There are those who will argue that the main objective of a business enterprise should be to make the maximum contribution to the welfare of society of which the enterprise is capable. That includes, aside from the profitable production of goods and services, consideration of such immeasurables as absence of environmental pollution and a contribution to the solution of social problems. Others, who adhere to the more traditional *laissez faire* school, maintain that the major objective of a business enterprise organized for profit is to increase the wealth of its owners and that this is possible only by delivering to society (consumers) that which it wants. Thus, the good of society will be served.

An extended discussion of these differing points of view on performance is beyond the purpose of this book. Since the analysis of financial statements is concerned with the application of analytical tools to that which can be measured, we shall concentrate here on those measures of performance that meet the objectives of financial analysis as outlined in Chapter 1. In that context, performance is the source of the rewards required to compensate investors and lenders for the risks that they are assuming.

CRITERIA OF PERFORMANCE EVALUATION

There are many criteria by which performance can be measured. Changes in sales, in profits, or in various measures of output are among the criteria frequently utilized.

No one of these measurements, standing by itself, is useful as a comprehensive measure of enterprise performance. The reasons for this are easy to grasp. Increases in sales are desirable only if they result in increased profits. The same is true of increases in volume of production. Increases in profits, on the other hand, must be related to the capital that is invested in order to attain these profits.

IMPORTANCE OF RETURN ON INVESTMENT (ROI)

The relationship between net income and the capital invested in the generation of that income is one of the most valid and most widely recognized measures of enterprise performance. In relating income to invested capital, the ROI measure allows the analyst to compare it to alternative uses of capital as well as to the return realized by enterprises subject to similar degrees of risk. The investment of capital can always yield some return. If capital is invested in government bonds, the return will be relatively low because of the small risk involved. Riskier investments require higher returns in order to make them worthwhile.[1] The ROI measure relates income (reward) to the size of the capital that was needed to generate it.

MAJOR OBJECTIVES IN THE USE OF ROI

Economic performance is the first and foremost purpose of business enterprise. It is, indeed, the reason for its existence. The effectiveness of operating performance determines the ability of the enterprise to survive financially, to attract suppliers of funds, and to reward them adequately. ROI is a prime measure of economic performance. The analyst uses it as a tool in three areas of great importance:

1. An indicator of managerial effectiveness.
2. A measure of an enterprise's ability to earn a satisfactory return on investment.
3. A method of projecting earnings.

However, the discussion later in this chapter will show that ROI is not a completely reliable measure of an enterprise's ability to reward its owners—the suppliers of its equity capital.

An Indicator of Managerial Effectiveness

The earning of an adequate or superior return on funds invested in an enterprise depends first and foremost on the resourcefulness, skill, ingenuity, and motivation of management. Thus, the longer-term ROI is of great interest and importance to the financial analyst because it offers a prime means of evaluating this indispensible criterion of business success: the quality of management.

---

[1] See Chapter 1 for an examination of the importance of the evaluation of risk and return in investing and lending decisions.

A Measure of Enterprise Ability to Earn a Satisfactory ROI

While related to managerial effectiveness, this measure is a far more reliable indicator of long-term financial health than is any measure of current financial strength based only on balance sheet relationships. For this reason, ROI is of great importance and interest to longer-term creditors as well as to equity investors.

A Method of Projecting Earnings

A third important function served by the ROI measure is that of a means of earnings projection. The advantage of this method of earnings projection is that it links the amount of earnings that it is estimated an enterprise will earn to the total invested capital. This adds discipline and realism to the projection process, which applies to the present and expected capital investment the return that is expected to be realized on it. The latter will usually be based on the historical and incremental rates of return actually earned by the enterprise and adjusted by projected changes, as well as on expected returns on new projects.

The rate of ROI method of earnings projection can be used by the analyst as either the primary method of earnings projection or as a supplementary check on estimates derived from other projection methods.

Internal Decision and Control Tool

While our focus here is on the work of the external financial analyst, mention should be made of the very important role that ROI measures play in the individual investment decisions of an enterprise as well as in the planning, budgeting, coordination, evaluation, and control of business operations and results.

It is obvious that the final return achieved in any one period on the total investment of an enterprise is composed of the returns (and losses) realized by the various segments and divisions of which it is composed. In turn, these returns are made up of the results achieved by individual product lines, projects, and so forth.

The well-managed enterprise exercises rigorous control over the returns achieved by each of its "profit centers" and rewards its managers on the basis of such results. Moreover, in evaluating the advisability of new investments of funds in assets or projects, management will compute the estimated returns it expects to achieve from them and use these estimates as a basis for its decision.[2]

---

[2] Managements' emphasis on these techniques has been challenged. In their article "Managing Our Way to Economic Decline" in the *Harvard Business Review* of July—August 1980, Professors R. Hayes and W. Abernathy argue that this preoccupation with ROI and the related discounted cash flow measures has led to an emphasis on short-term profits at the expense of long-term risk taking based on improved technology.

BASIC ELEMENTS OF ROI

The basic concept of ROI is relatively simple to understand. However, care must be used in determining the elements entering its computation because there exist a variety of views, which reflect different objectives, of how these elements should be defined.

The basic formula for computing ROI is as follows:

$$\frac{\text{Income}}{\text{Investment}}$$

We shall now examine the various definitions of *investment* and of the related *income*.

Defining the Investment Base

There is no one generally accepted measure of capital investment on which the rate of return is computed. The different concepts of investment reflect different objectives. Since the term *return on investment (ROI)* covers a multitude of concepts of investment base and income, there is need for more specific terms to describe the actual investment base used.

Total Assets   Return on total assets is perhaps the best measure of the *operating efficiency* of an enterprise. It measures the return obtained on *all* the assets entrusted to management. By removing from this computation the effect of the method used in financing the assets, the analyst can concentrate on the evaluation or projection of operating performance.

Modified Asset Bases   For a variety of reasons, some ROI computations are based not on total assets but rather on an adjusted amount.

One important category of adjustments relates to "unproductive" assets. In this category, assets omitted from the investment base include idle plant, facilities under construction, surplus plant, surplus inventories and surplus cash, intangible assets, and deferred charges. The basic idea behind these exclusions is not to hold management responsible for earning a return on assets that apparently do not earn a return. While this theory may have validity in the use of ROI as an internal management and control tool, it lacks merit when applied as a tool designed to evaluate management effectiveness on an overall basis. Management is entrusted with funds by owners and creditors, and it has discretion as to where it wants to invest them. There is no reason for management to hold on to assets that bring no return. If there are reasons for keeping funds invested in such assets, then there is no reason to exclude them from the investment base. If the long-run profitability of an enterprise is benefited by keeping funds invested in assets that have no return or a low return in the interim, then the longer-term ROI should reflect such benefits. In conclusion, it can be said that from the point of view of an enterprise evaluation by the external analyst, there is rarely any justification to omit assets from the investment base merely because they are not productively employed or do not earn a current return.

The exclusion of intangible assets from the investment base is often due to skepticism regarding their value or their contribution to the earning power of the enterprise. Under generally accepted accounting principles (GAAP), intangibles are carried at cost. However, if the cost exceeds their future utility, they must be written down or else the analyst should at least find an uncertainty reference regarding their carrying value included in the auditor's opinion. Accounting for intangible assets was discussed in Chapter 6. The exclusion of intangible assets from the asset (investment) base must be justified on more substantial evidence than a mere lack of understanding of what these assets represent or an unsupported suspicion regarding their value.

Depreciable Assets in the Investment Base   An important difference of opinion prevails with respect to the question of whether depreciable assets should be included in the investment base at original cost or at an amount net of the accumulated allowances for depreciation.

One of the most prominent advocates of the inclusion of fixed assets at gross amount in the investment base for purposes of computing the ROI was the management of E. I. du Pont de Nemours Company which pioneered the use of ROI as an internal management tool.

In a pamphlet describing the company's use of the ROI method in the appraisal of operating performance, this point of view is expressed as follows:

> *Calculation of return on investment.* Return on investment as presented in the chart series is based upon *gross* operating investment and earnings *net* of depreciation.
>
> Gross operating investment represents all the plant, tools, equipment and working capital made available to operating management for its use; no deduction is made for current or other liabilities or for the reserve for depreciation. Since plant facilities are maintained in virtually top productive order during their working life, the depreciation reserve being considered primarily to provide for obsolescence, it would be inappropriate to consider that operating management was responsible for earning a return on only the net operating investment. Furthermore, if depreciable assets were stated at net depreciated values, earnings in each succeeding period would be related to an ever-decreasing investment; even with stable earnings, Return on Investment would continually rise, so that comparative Return on Investment ratios would fail to reveal the extent of trend of management performance. Relating earnings to investment that is stable and uniformly compiled provides a sound basis for comparing the

"profitability of assets employed" as between years and between investments.

In the case of any commitment of capital—e.g., an investment in a security—it is the expectation that in addition to producing earnings while committed, the principal will eventually be recovered. Likewise, in the case of funds invested in a project, it is expected that in addition to the return earned while invested, the working capital will be recovered through liquidation at the end of the project's useful life and the plant investment will be recovered through depreciation accruals. Since earnings must allow for this recovery of plant investment, they are stated net of depreciation.[3]

It is not difficult to take issue with the above reasoning. It must, however, be borne in mind that the Du Pont system is designed for use in the internal control of separate productive units as well as for the control of operating management. Our point of view here is, however, that of evaluating the operating performance of an enterprise taken as a whole. While by an enterprise operating at a profit, the recovery of capital out of sales and revenues (via depreciation) can be disregarded in the evaluation of a *single* division or segment, it cannot be disregarded for an enterprise taken as a whole because such recovery is reinvested somewhere within that enterprise even if it is not reinvested in the particular segment that gave rise to the depreciation and that is evaluated for internal purposes. Thus, for an enterprise taken as a whole, the "net of depreciation" asset base is a more valid measure of investment on which a return is computed. This is so for the reasons given above and also because the income that is usually related to the investment base is net of the depreciation expense.

The tendency of the rate of return to rise as assets are depreciated (see also Chapter 10) is offset by the retention of capital recovered by means of depreciation, on which capital a return must also be earned. Moreover, maintenance and repair costs rise as equipment gets older, thus tending to offset the reduction, if any, in the asset base.

Among other reasons advanced in support of the use of fixed assets at their gross amount is the argument that the higher amounts are designed to compensate for the effects of inflation on assets expressed in terms of historical cost. In the discussion of the price-level problem in Chapter 14, it was pointed out that price-level adjustments can validly be made only within the framework of a complete restatement of all elements of the financial statements. Crude "adjustments," such as using the gross asset amount, are apt to be misleading and are generally worse than no adjustments at all.

Long-Term Liabilities plus Equity Capital   The use of long-term liabilities plus equity capital as the investment base differs from the "total

[3] American Management Association, *Executive Committee Control Charts*, AMA Management Bulletin No. 6, 1960, p. 22.

assets" base only in that current liabilities are excluded as suppliers of funds on which the return is computed. The focus here is on the two major suppliers of longer-term funds, that is, long-term creditors and equity shareholders. In this context, working capital required to support operations is regarded as the excess of current assets over current liabilities.

Shareholders' Equity   The computation of return on shareholders' equity measures the return accruing to the owners' capital. As was seen in the discussion of financial leverage in Chapter 18, this return reflects the effect of the employment of debt capital on the owners' return. Since preferred stock, while in the equity category, is usually nevertheless entitled only to a fixed return, it is also omitted from the calculation of the final return on equity computation.

Book versus Market Values in the Investment Base

Return on asset calculations are most commonly based on book values appearing in the financial statements rather than on market or fair values that are, in most cases, analytically more significant and relevant. Also, quite often, a return is earned by enterprises on assets that either do not appear in the financial statements or are significantly understated therein. Examples of such assets are intangibles such as patents, trademarks, expensed research and development (R&D) costs, advertising and training costs, and so forth. Other excluded assets may include leaseholds and the value of natural resources discovered.

One avenue to the use of such data is to rely on the valuation that the market places on the equity securities of the enterprise in order to approximate fair values. Thus, we can substitute the market value of equity securities and debt for the book value of total assets in computing a proper investment base.

Difference between Investor's Cost and Enterprise Investment Base

For purposes of computing the ROI, a distinction must be drawn between the investment base of an enterprise and that of an investor. The investor's investment base is, of course, the price paid for his or her equity securities. Except for those cases in which he or she acquired such securities at book value, the investment base is going to differ from that of the company in which he or she has invested. In general, the focus in ROI computations is on the return realized by the enterprise rather than the return realized on the investment cost of shareholders. Later in this chapter we will focus on the measurement of results achieved by the latter.

Averaging the Investment Base

Regardless of the method used in arriving at the investment base, the return achieved over a period of time is always associated with the investment base that was, on average, actually available to the enterprise over that period of time. Thus, unless the investment base did not change significantly during the period, it will be necessary to average it.

The most common method of averaging for the external analyst is that of adding the investment base at the beginning of the year to that at the end of the year and dividing their total by two. Care must, however, be used in employing this method of averaging. Companies in some industries choose a "natural" rather than the calendar business year. Thus, for example, in retailing, the natural business year ends when inventories are at their lowest (e.g., January 31 after the holiday selling season) and when it is easiest to count them. In such case, averaging two year-ends may yield the *lowest* rather than the average amount of assets employed.

In such or similar cases, more accurate methods of averaging, where the data are available, are to average by month-end balances, that is, adding the month-end investment bases and dividing the total by 12, or to average on a quarterly basis.

Relating Income to the Investment Base

In the computation of ROI, the definition of return (income) is dependent on the definition of the investment base.

If the investment base is defined as comprising total assets, then income *before* interest expense is used.[4] The exclusion of interest from income deductions is due to its being regarded as a payment for the use of money to the suppliers of debt capital in the same way that dividends are regarded as a reward to suppliers of equity capital. Before deductions for interest or dividends, income is used when it is related to total assets or to long-term debt plus equity capital (assuming most of the interest expense is on long-term obligations).

The income of a consolidated entity that includes a subsidiary that is partially owned by a minority interest usually reflects a deduction for the minority's share in that income. The consolidated balance sheet, however, includes all the assets of such a subsidiary, that is, those belonging to the parent as well as those belonging to the minority (see also Chapter 9). Because the investment in the denominator includes all the assets of the consolidated entity, the income (in the numerator) should include all the income (or loss), not just the parent's share. For this reason, the minority's

---

[4] Interest expense means interest incurred less interest capitalized. In theory, the amount of previously capitalized interest currently amortized and included in expenses should also be added back to income.

share of earnings (or loss) must be added back to income in computing return on total assets. When the denominator is the equity capital only, the minority share in income (or loss) need not be added back if equity capital excludes minority interest.

When the return on the equity capital is computed, net income *after* deductions for interest and preferred dividends is used. If the preferred dividends are cumulative, they are deducted in arriving at the balance of earnings accruing to the common stock, whether these dividends were declared or not.

The final ROI must always reflect all applicable costs and expenses and that includes income taxes. Some computations of ROI nevertheless omit deductions of income taxes. One reason for this practice is the desire to isolate the effects of tax management from those of operating performance. Another reason is that changes in tax rates affect comparability over the years. Moreover, companies that have tax loss carryforwards find that the deduction of taxes from income adds confusion and complications to the ROI computations.

It must, however, be borne in mind that income taxes reduce the final return and that they must be taken into consideration particularly when the return on shareholders' equity is computed. Later in this chapter we discuss the disaggregation of ROI where one element is the tax burden borne by the entity

ADJUSTING THE COMPONENTS OF THE ROI FORMULA

In computing any measure or ratio, the analyst uses the amounts in the financial statements only as starting points. As was seen in the discussion in Chapter 18 on the adjustment of the debt to equity ratios, some amounts need analytical adjustment and some amounts not found in the financial statements need to be included in the adjusted computation. Reference to the discussion in Chapter 18 will reveal that some of the items discussed therein, such as adjustment of inventory amounts, may affect the ROI computation while others, such as reclassification of deferred taxes, may not. Moreover, some adjustments, such as those relating to inventory amounts, affect both the numerator and the denominator of the formula, thus moderating the net effect on the ratio.

The computation of ROI under the various concepts of "investment base" discussed above will now be illustrated by means of the data contained in Exhibits 19–1 and 19–2. The computations are for year 9 and are based on figures rounded to the nearest million dollars.

Return on Total Assets   Applying the basic formula to the data of American Company for year 9 we get:

Exhibit 19–1

AMERICAN COMPANY
Statement of Income
For Years Ended December 31, year 8 and year 9
(in thousands)

	Year 8	Year 9
Net sales	$1,636,298	$1,723,729
Costs and expenses	1,473,293	1,579,401
Operating income......................	163,005	144,328
Other income net	2,971	1,784
	165,976	146,112
Interest expense*	16,310	20,382
Income before tax	149,666	125,730
Provision for federal and other taxes on income	71,770	61,161
Net income..........................	77,896	64,569
Less dividends:		
Preferred stock	2,908	2,908
Common stock	39,209	38,898
	42,117	41,806
Net income reinvested in the business	$ 35,779	$ 22,763

* In year 9, interest on long-term debt was $19,695.

$$
\frac{\text{Net income} + \text{Interest expense} \times (1 - \text{Tax rate}) + \text{Minority interest in earnings}}{(\text{Beginning total assets} + \text{Ending total assets}) \div 2}
$$

$$
= \frac{\$65 + \$20\,(1 - 0.40) + 0^*}{(\$1,334 + \$1,372) \div 2} = 0.057, \text{ or } 5.7 \text{ percent}
$$

* No minority interest in this case.

The tax adjustment of the interest expense recognizes that interest is a tax-deductible expense and that if the interest cost is excluded, the related tax benefit must also be excluded from income. The *tax rate* we use is the approximate *marginal* or corporate tax rate of 40 percent because the tax incidence with respect to any one item (such as interest expense) can be measured by the marginal tax rate. In computing the fixed-charges-coverage ratio (see Chapter 18), we use the *effective* tax rate because we have adopted the SEC's computation which requires its use.

The assets have been averaged by using the year-end figures for total assets. As discussed earlier, this method of computing the average may yield misleading results in some cases.

Exhibit 19–2

AMERICAN COMPANY
Statements of Financial Position
As at December 31, year 8 and year 9
(in thousands)

	Year 8	Year 9
Assets		
Current assets:		
Cash	$ 25,425	$ 25,580
Eurodollar time deposits and temporary cash		
investments	38,008	28,910
Accounts and notes receivable—net	163,870	176,911
Inventories	264,882	277,795
Total current assets	492,185	509,196
Investments in and receivables from		
nonconsolidated subsidiaries	33,728	41,652
Miscellaneous investments and receivables	5,931	6,997
Funds held by trustee for construction	6,110	
Land, buildings, equipment, and timberlands—net . .	773,361	790,774
Deferred charges to future operations	16,117	16,452
Goodwill and other intangible assets	6,550	6,550
Total assets	$1,333,982	$1,371,621
Liabilities		
Current liabilities:		
Notes payable to banks—principally Eurodollar ..	$ 7,850	$ 13,734
Accounts payable and accrued expenses	128,258	144,999
Dividends payable	10,404	10,483
Federal and other taxes on income	24,370	13,256
Long-term indebtedness payable within one year	9,853	11,606
Total current liabilities	180,735	194,078
Long-term indebtedness	350,565	335,945
Deferred taxes on income	86,781	101,143
Total liabilities	618,081	631,166
Capital		
Preferred, 7% cumulative and noncallable, par value		
$25 per share; authorized 1,760,000 shares	41,538	41,538
Common, par value $12.50 per share; authorized		
30,000,000 shares	222,245	222,796
Capital in excess of par value	19,208	20,448
Earnings reinvested in the business	436,752	459,515
Less: Common treasury stock	(3,842)	(3,842)
Total capital	715,901	740,455
Total liabilities and capital	$1,333,982	$1,371,621

Return on Modified Asset Bases   Since our discussion earlier in the chapter came to the conclusion that in normal circumstances most of the modifications in the amount of total assets are not logically warranted, no illustrations of such computation will be given.

Return on Long-Term Liabilities plus Equity Capital

$$\frac{\text{Net income} + \text{Interest expense*} \times (1 - \text{Tax rate}) + \text{Minority interest in earnings}}{\text{Average long-term liabilities} + \text{equity capital}}$$

Using the data in Exhibits 19–1 and 19–2 for year 9:

$$\frac{\$65 + \$20* (1 - 0.40) + 0}{(\$437 + \$716 + \$437 + \$740) \div 2} = 0.066, \text{ or } 6.6 \text{ percent}$$

* On long-term debt (\$19,695 rounded).

Decisions of how to classify items such as deferred taxes as between debt and equity will have to be made by the analyst using the considerations already discussed in Chapter 18. It should be noted that deferred taxes on income are included here among the long-term liabilities. In the computation of return on long-term liabilities and equity capital, the question of how to classify deferred taxes does not really present a problem because in this computation both debt and equity are aggregated anyway. The problem of classification becomes more real in computing the return on shareholders' equity. In the examples that follow, we assume circumstances where deferred taxes are considered to be more in the nature of long-term liability than equity. In many cases, the classification decision can have a significant effect on the return computation.

Return on Stockholders' Equity   The basic computation of return on the equity excludes from the investment base all but the common stockholders' equity.

$$\frac{\text{Net income} - \text{Preferred dividends}}{\text{Average common stockholders' equity}}$$

Using data in Exhibits 19–1 and 19–2 for year 9:

$$\frac{\$65 - \$3}{(\$674 + \$699) \div 2} = 9 \text{ percent}$$

The higher return on shareholders' equity as compared to the return on total assets reflects the positive workings of financial leverage.

Should it be desired, for whatever reason, to compute the return on total stockholders' equity, the investment base would include the preferred shareholders' equity, while net income would not reflect a deduction for preferred dividends. The formula[5] would then be:

$$\frac{\text{Net income}}{\text{Average total shareholders' equity (common and preferred)}}$$

Where convertible debt sells at a substantial premium above par and is clearly held by investors for its conversion feature, there is justification for treating it as the equivalent of equity capital. This is particularly true when the company can choose at any time to force conversion of the debt by calling it.

Analysis and Interpretation of ROI

Earlier in the chapter we mentioned that ROI analysis is particularly useful to the analyst in the areas of evaluation of managerial effectiveness, enterprise profitability, and as an important tool of earnings projection.

The evaluation of ROI and the projection of earnings by means of ROI analysis are complex processes requiring thorough analysis. The reason for this is that the ROI computation usually includes components of considerable complexity.

Components of the ROI Ratio   If we focus first on return on total assets, we know that the primary formula for computing this return is:

$$\frac{\text{Net income} + \text{Interest} \times (1 - \text{Tax rate})^*}{\text{Average total assets}}$$

* Omitting the add-back of minority interest in earnings in order to simplify the discussion does not impair its validity.

For purposes of our discussion and analysis, let us look at this computation in a simplified form:

$$\frac{\text{Net income}}{\text{Total assets}}$$

---

[5] The return on common stockholders' equity may also be computed thus:

$$\frac{\text{Earnings per share}}{\text{Book value per share}}$$

But the results will often not be identical because the earnings per share computation includes adjustments for common stock equivalents, etc. (see Chapter 12).

Since sales are a most important yardstick in relation to which profitability is measured and are, as well, a major index of activity, we can recast the above formula as follows:

$$\frac{\text{Net income}}{\text{Sales}} \times \frac{\text{Sales}}{\text{Total assets}}$$

The relationship of net income to sales measures operating performance and profitability. The relationship of sales to total assets is a measure of asset utilization or turnover, a means of determining how effectively (in terms of sales generation) the assets are utilized. It can be readily seen that both factors, profitability as well as asset utilization, determine the return realized on a given investment in assets.

Profitability and asset utilization are, in turn, complex ratios that normally require thorough and detailed analysis before they can be used to reach conclusions regarding the reasons for changes in the return on total assets.

Exhibit 19–3 presents the major factors that influence the final return on total assets. In the next section, we shall be concerned with the interaction of profitability (net income/sales) and of asset utilization or turnover (sales/total assets) that in Exhibit 19–3 is regarded as the first level of analysis of the return on total assets. As can be seen from Exhibit 19–3, the many important and complex factors that, in turn, determine profitability and asset utilization represent a second level of analysis of the return on total assets. Chapters 20 and 21 will take up the analysis of results of operations, and Chapter 22 will deal with the evaluation and projection of earnings. The analysis of asset utilization will be discussed in subsequent sections of this chapter.

Relationship between Profitability and Asset Turnover   The relationship between return on total assets, profitability, and capital turnover (utilization) is illustrated in Exhibit 19–4, which indicates that when we multiply profitability (expressed as a percentage) by asset utilization (expressed as a turnover) we obtain the return on total assets (expressed as a percentage relationship).

Company X realizes its 10 percent return on total assets by means of a relatively high profit margin and a low turnover of assets. The opposite is true of Company Z, while Company Y achieves its 10 percent return by means of a profit margin half that of Company X and an asset turnover rate twice that of Company X. It is obvious from Exhibit 19–4 that there are many combinations of profit margins and turnover rates that can yield a return on assets of 10 percent.

In fact, as can be seen from Exhibit 19–5, there exist an infinite variety of combinations of profit margin and asset turnover rates that yield a 10 percent return on assets. The chart in the exhibit graphically relates asset turnover (vertical axis) to profitability (horizontal axis).

Exhibit 19–3

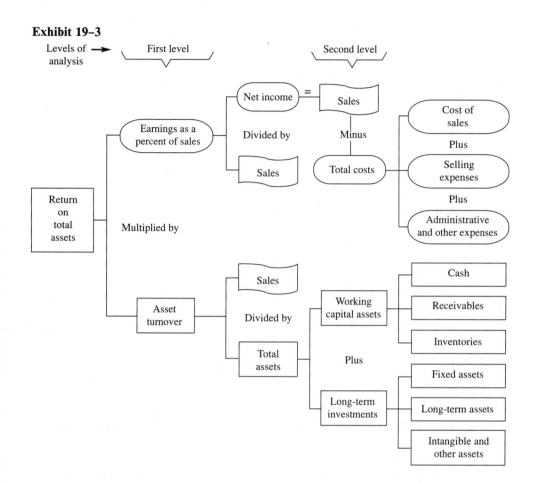

Exhibit 19–4   Analysis of return on total assets

	Company X	Company Y	Company Z
1. Sales	$5,000,000	$10,000,000	$10,000,000
2. Net income	500,000	500,000	100,000
3. Total assets	5,000,000	5,000,000	1,000,000
4. Profit as percent of sales $\left(\frac{2}{1}\right)$	10%	5%	1%
5. Asset turnover $\left(\frac{1}{3}\right)$	1	2	10
Return on total assets (4 × 5)	10%	10%	10%

The curve, sloping from the upper left area of low profit margins and high asset turnover rates, traces out the endless combinations of profitability and asset turnover rates that yield a 10 percent return on total

Exhibit 19–5

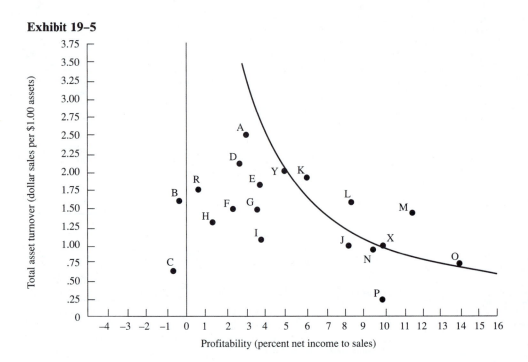

assets. The data of Companies X and Y (from Exhibit 19–4) are represented by dots on the graph, while the data of Company Z cannot be fitted on it since the full curve has not been shown. The other lettered dots represent the profit-turnover combination of other companies within a particular industry. This clustering of the results of various companies around the 10 percent return on assets slope is a useful way of comparing the return of many enterprises within an industry and the major two elements that comprise them.

The chart in Exhibit 19–5 is also useful in assessing the relative courses of action open to different enterprises that want to improve their respective returns on investments.

Companies B and C must, of course, restore profitability before the turnover rate becomes a factor of importance. Assuming that all the companies represented in Exhibit 19–5 belong to the same industry and that there is an average representative level of profitability and turnover in it, Company P will be best advised to pay first and particular attention to improvement in its turnover ratio, while Company R should pay foremost attention to the improvement of its profit margin. Other companies, such as Company I, would best concentrate on both the turnover and the profit margin aspects of ROI improvement.

While the above analysis treats profitability and turnover as two independent variables, they are, in fact, interdependent. As will be seen from the discussion of break-even analysis in Chapter 21, when fixed expenses are substantial, a higher level of activity (turnover) will tend to increase the profit margin because within a certain range of activity, costs increase proportionally less than sales. In comparing two companies within an industry, the analyst, in evaluating the one having the lower asset turnover, will make allowance for the potential increase in profitability that can be associated with a projected increase in turnover that is based primarily on an expansion of sales.

Analysis of return on total assets can reveal the weaknesses as well as the potential strengths of an enterprise. Assume that two companies in the same industry have returns on total assets as follows:

	Company A	Company B
1. Sales	$ 1,000,000	$20,000,000
2. Net income	100,000	100,000
3. Total assets	10,000,000	10,000,000
4. Profitability $\left(\dfrac{2}{1}\right)$	10%	0.5%
5. Turnover of assets $\left(\dfrac{1}{3}\right)$	0.1 times	2 times
Return on investment (4 × 5) ..	1%	1%

Both companies have poor returns on total assets. However, remedial action for them lies in different areas, and the analyst will concentrate on the evaluation of the feasibility of success of such improvement.

Company A has a 10 percent profit on sales that, let us assume, is about average for the industry. However, each dollar invested in assets supports only 10 cents in sales, whereas Company B gets $2 of sales for each dollar invested in its assets. The analyst's attention will naturally be focused on Company A's investment in assets. Why is its turnover so low? Are there excess assets that yield little or no return or are there idle assets that should be disposed of? Or, as often is the case, are the assets inefficiently or uneconomically utilized? Quite obviously, Company A can achieve more immediate and significant improvements by concentrating on improving turnover (by increasing sales, reducing investment, or both) than by striving to increase the profit margin beyond the industry average.

The opposite situation prevails with respect to Company B where attention should first be focused on the reasons for the low profit margin and to the improvement of it as the most likely avenue of success in increasing ROI. The reasons for low profitability can be many, including inefficient equipment and production methods, unprofitable product lines, excess capacity with attendant high fixed costs, excessive selling or administrative costs, and so on.

The company with the low profitability may discover that changes in tastes and in technology have resulted in an increased investment in assets being needed to finance a dollar of sales. This means that in order to maintain its return on assets, the company must increase its profit margin or else production of the product is no longer worthwhile.

There is a tendency to regard a high profit margin as a sign of high earnings quality. It is necessary to emphasize the importance of return on capital as the ultimate test of profitability. The following table compares during a given year the similar profit margins of five companies with their respective returns on capital:

	Profit margin as percent of sales	Profit as percent of capital
Whirlpool	5.3	17.1
Corn Products	5.9	12.0
Goodyear	5.5	9.6
U.S. Plywood	5.5	8.0
Distillers Seagram	5.0	6.7

It is evident that in the case of these five companies, which have similar profit margins, the rate of capital turnover made the difference in the return on capital performance, and this must be taken into account by the analyst. Thus, a supermarket chain will be content with a net profit margin of 1 percent or less because it has a high rate of turnover due to a relatively low investment in assets and a high proportion of leased assets (such as stores and fixtures). Similarly, a discount store will accept a low profit margin in order to obtain a high rate of asset turnover (primarily of inventories). On the other hand, capital-intensive industries such as steels, chemicals, and autos, which have heavy investments in assets and resulting low asset turnover rates, must achieve high net profit margins in order to offer investors a reasonable return on capital.

In most cases, the focus on single-year rates of return are apt to be misleading. The cyclical nature of many industries cause such swings in profitability that some years' profits may appear exorbitant while others barely are sufficient to justify the related investment. Such enterprises can only be validly evaluated on the basis of average returns over a number of years covering a full economic cycle.

ANALYSIS OF ASSET UTILIZATION

As is graphically illustrated in Exhibit 19–3, the return on total assets depends on (1) getting the largest profit out of each dollar of sales and (2) obtaining the highest possible amount of sales per dollar of invested capital (net assets). Throughout this work we use sales and revenues as synonymous concepts.

The intensity with which assets are utilized is measured by means of asset turnover ratios.[6] That utilization has as its ultimate measure the amount of sales generated since sales are in most enterprises the first and essential step to profits. In certain special cases, such as with enterprises in developmental stages, the meaning of turnover may have to be modified in recognition of the fact that most assets are committed to the development of future potential. Similarly, abnormal supply problems and strikes are conditions that will affect the state of capital utilization and, as such, will require separate evaluation and interpretation.

Evaluation of Individual Turnover Ratios

Changes in the basic turnover ratio that enters the determination of the ROI calculation, that is,

$$\frac{\text{Sales}}{\text{Total assets}}$$

can be evaluated meaningfully only by an analysis of changes in the turnover rates of individual asset categories and groups that comprise the total assets.

Sales to Cash   As was seen in the discussion in Chapter 16, cash and cash equivalents are held primarily for purposes of meeting the needs of day-to-day transactions as well as a liquidity reserve designed to prevent the shortages that may arise from an imbalance in cash inflows and outflows. In any type of business, there is a certain logical relationship between sales and cash level that must be maintained to support it.

Too high a rate of turnover may be due to a cash shortage that can ultimately result in a liquidity crisis if the enterprise has no other ready sources of funds available to it.

Too low a rate of turnover may be due to the holding of idle and unnecessary cash balances. Cash accumulated for specific purposes or

---

[6] P. F. Drucker in *Managing in Turbulent Times* (New York: Harper & Row, 1980) writes: "In the United States the General Electric Co., for example, does not owe its leadership position primarily to technological achievement. What sets it apart from Westinghouse, its closest competitor and the industry's number two, is above all productivity of capital. GE gets about twice as much work out of a dollar as Westinghouse does."

known contingencies may result in temporary decreases in the rate of turnover.

The basic trade-off here is between liquidity and the tying up of funds that yield no return or a very modest return.

Sales to Receivables   Any organization that sells on credit will find that the level of its receivables is a function of sales. A relatively low rate of turnover here is, among other reasons, likely to be due to an over-extension of credit, to an inability of customers to pay, or to a poor collection job.

A relatively high rate of turnover may indicate a strict credit extension policy or a reluctance or inability to extend credit. Determining the rate of turnover here is the trade-off between sales and the tying up of funds in receivables.

Sales to Inventories   The maintenance of a given level of sales generally requires a given level of inventories. This relationship will vary from industry to industry depending on the variety of types, models, colors, sizes, and other classes of varieties of items that must be kept in order to attract and keep customers. The length of the production cycle as well as the type of item (e.g., luxury versus necessity; perishable versus durable) has a bearing on the rate of turnover.

A slow rate of turnover indicates the existence of problems such as overstocking, slow-moving or obsolete inventories, overestimating of sales, or a lack of balance in the inventory. Temporary problems such as strikes at important customers may also be responsible for such a condition.

A higher than normal rate of turnover may mean an underinvestment in inventory that can result in lack of proper customer service and in loss of sales.

In this case, the trade-off is between tying up funds in inventory, on one hand, and sacrificing customer service and sales, on the other.

Sales to Fixed Assets   While the relationship between property, plant, and equipment and sales is a logical one on a long-term basis, there are many short-term and temporary factors that may upset this relationship. Among these factors are conditions of excess capacity, inefficient or obsolete equipment, multishift operations, temporary changes in demand, and interruptions in the supply of raw materials and parts.

It must also be remembered that increases in plant capacity are not gradual but occur, instead, in large increments. This too can create temporary and medium-term changes in the turnover rates. Often, leased facilities and equipment, which do not appear on the balance sheet, will distort the relationship between sales and fixed assets (see, however, Chapter 7).

The trade-off here is between investment in fixed assets with a correspondingly higher break-even point, on one hand, and efficiency, productive capacity, and sales potential, on the other.

Sales to Other Assets   In this category, we find among others, such assets as patents and deferred charges or other costs. While the direct relationship between these individual categories of assets and current sales levels may not be evident, no assets are held or should be held by an enterprise unless they contribute to sales or to the generation of income. In the case of deferred R&D costs, the investment may represent the potential of future sales. In the evaluation of rates of asset utilization, the analyst must allow for such factors.

Sales to Short-Term Liabilities   The relationship between sales and short-term trade liabilities is a predictable one. The amount of short-term credit that an enterprise is able to obtain from suppliers depends on its needs for goods and services, that is, on the level of activity (e.g., sales). Thus, the degree to which it can obtain short-term credit depends also importantly on the level of sales. This short-term credit is relatively cost-free and, in turn, reduces the investment of enterprise funds in working capital.

Use of Averages

Whenever the level of a given asset category changes significantly during the period for which the turnover is computed, it is necessary to use averages of asset levels in the computation. The computation then becomes

$$\frac{\text{Sales}}{(\text{Asset at beginning of period} + \text{Asset at end of period}) \div 2}$$

To the extent that data are available and the variation in asset levels during the period dictates it, the average can be computed on a monthly or quarterly basis.

Other Factors to Be Considered in Return on Asset Evaluation

The evaluation of the return on assets involves many factors of great complexity. As will be seen from the discussion in Chapter 22, the inclusion of extraordinary gains and losses in single-period and average net income must be evaluated. Chapter 14 has examined the effects of price-level changes on ROI calculations, and these, too, must be taken into account by the analyst.

In analyzing the trend of return on assets over the years, the effect of acquisitions accounted for as poolings of interest (see Chapter 9) must be isolated and their chance of recurrence evaluated. The effect of discontinued operations must be similarly evaluated.

The external analyst will not usually be able to obtain data on ROI by segments, product lines, or divisions of an enterprise. However, where his bargaining power or position allows him to obtain such data, they can make a significant contribution to the accuracy and reliability of the analysis.

A consistently high return on assets is the earmark of an effective management and can distinguish a growth company from one experiencing merely a cyclical or seasonal pickup in business.

An examination of the factors that comprise the return on assets will usually reveal the limitations to which their expansion is subject. Neither the profit margin nor the asset turnover rate can expand indefinitely. Thus, an expanding asset base via external financing and/or internal earnings retention will be necessary for further earnings growth.

Return on Shareholders' Equity

Up to now we have examined the factors affecting the return on total assets. However, of great interest to the owner group of an enterprise is the return on the stockholders' equity. The rate of return on total assets and that on the stockholders' equity differ because a portion of the capital with which the assets are financed is usually supplied by creditors who receive a fixed return on their capital or, in some cases, no return at all. Similarly, the preferred stock usually receives a fixed dividend. These fixed returns differ from the rate earned on the assets (funds) that they provide, and this accounts for the difference in returns on assets and those on stockholders' equity. This is the concept of financial leverage that was already discussed in Chapter 18.

ANALYSIS OF RETURN ON COMMON STOCKHOLDERS' EQUITY (ROCSE)

The ROCSE can be disaggregated into the following elements that facilitate its analysis:

$$\frac{\text{Net income} - \text{Preferred dividends}}{\text{Average common stockholders' equity}} = \frac{\text{Net income} - \text{Preferred dividends}}{\text{Sales}} \times \frac{\text{Sales}}{\text{Average total assets}} \times \frac{\text{Average total assets}}{\text{Average common stockholders' equity}}$$

Descriptively, we can express this formula as follows:

$$
\begin{array}{l}
\text{Rate of return} \\
\text{on CSE}
\end{array}
=
\begin{array}{c}
\text{Net income margin} \\
\text{after preferred} \\
\text{dividends}
\end{array}
\times
\begin{array}{c}
\text{Asset} \\
\text{turnover} \\
\text{ratio}
\end{array}
\times
\begin{array}{c}
\text{Common} \\
\text{stockholders'} \\
\text{leverage ratio}
\end{array}
$$

The net income margin represents the portion of the sales dollar that is left for the common shareholder after providing for all costs and claims (e.g., those of the preferred shareholders). The asset turnover was discussed above. The common stockholders' leverage ratio measures the extent to which total assets are financed by common stockholders. The larger this ratio is the smaller the proportion of assets financed by common stockholders and the greater the extent of leverage. Leverage can also be measured by means of the financial leverage index as was illustrated in Chapter 18.

Using the data in Exhibits 19–1 and 19–2 of the American Company, we can compute the disaggregated ROCSE for year 9 as follows (dollars in millions):

$$
\frac{\$65 - \$3}{(\$674 + \$699) \div 2} = \frac{\$65 - \$3}{\$1,724}
$$

$$
\times \frac{\$1,724}{(\$1,334 + \$1,372) \div 2} \times \frac{(\$1,334 + \$1,372) \div 2}{(\$674 + \$699) \div 2} \quad \text{or}
$$

Rate of return on CSE	Net income margin after preferred dividends		Assets turnover ratio		Common stockholders' leverage ratio
9%	=	3.6%	×	1.27 ×	1.97

There is another useful way to look at the disaggregated ROCSE of American Company. Each dollar of common equity was used as the basis for borrowing 97 cents in various ways by means of long-term debt and short-term credit and considering, for simplicity's sake, deferred taxes as interest-free debt.

This $1.97 was able to generate $2.50 in sales because assets (which equal total capital plus total debt) are turning over (i.e., generating sales) at a rate of 1.27 (i.e., $1.97 × 1.27 = $2.50).

The $2.50 in sales earned a net margin after all costs and preferred dividends of 3.6 percent thus resulting in a return on the common stockholders' investment of 9 percent ($2.50 × 3.6%).

A further refinement can be introduced into this analysis by disaggregating the net income margin into its *pre-tax* component and its tax retention component. When the *pre-tax* profit margin is multiplied by 1 – effective tax rate paid by the company (i.e., the retention rate), we get the net income profit margin. This analysis separates the pre-tax margin, a measure of operating effectiveness, from the retention rate, a measure of tax-management effectiveness. This segregates one more factor contributing to the return on equity.

In the example of American Company the net income margin of 3.6% can be disaggregated as follows:

$$\frac{\text{Pre-tax earnings less Preferred dividends}}{\text{Sales}} \times \frac{\text{Net Income} - \text{Preferred dividends}}{\text{Pre-tax earnings less Preferred dividends}}$$

$$= \frac{126 - 3}{1724} \times \frac{65 - 3}{126 - 3}$$

$$= 7.1\% \times 50.4\%^* = 3.6\%$$

* This is the retention rate, that is, the percentage of pre-tax income remaining after taxes.

ILLUSTRATION OF ANALYSIS OF RETURN ON TOTAL ASSETS AND ON EQUITY

Based on the financial statements of Campbell Soup (Appendix B to Chapter 4), we will now illustrate the analysis of various returns.

Return on Total Assets (ROTA)

$$\frac{\text{Net income } \boxed{28} + [\text{Interest expense } \boxed{18} \times (1 - \text{Tax rate})] + \text{Minority interest in income } |25}{\text{Average total assets } \boxed{39A}}$$

For 1991 (millions)

$$\frac{401.5 + 116.2 (1 - 0.34) + 7.2}{(4,149.0 + 4,115.6)/2} = \frac{485.4}{4,132.3} = 11.75\%$$

Disaggregated

$$\frac{\text{Net income } + \text{Interest} (1 - \text{Tax interest}) + \text{Minority interest}}{\text{Sales}} \times \frac{\text{Sales}}{\text{Average total assets}}$$

$$= \frac{\$485.4}{\$6,204.1} \times \frac{\$6,204.1}{\$4,132.3}$$

or

$$\underset{0.078}{\text{Profit margin}} \times \underset{1.5}{\text{Asset turnover}} = \underset{11.75\%}{\text{ROTA}}$$

Return on Common Stockholders' Equity (RCSE)

$$\frac{\text{Net income } \boxed{28} - \text{Preferred dividends}}{\text{Average common equity* } \boxed{54}\ \boxed{176}}$$

* Including 50% of deferred taxes which is assumed to be equity.

For 1991

$$\frac{401.5}{[(1,793.4 + 129.3) + (1,691.8 + 117.5)]/2} = \frac{401.5}{1,866} = 21.52\%$$

Disaggregated

$$\frac{\text{Net income} - \text{Preferred dividends}}{\text{Sales } \boxed{13}} \times \frac{\text{Sales}}{\text{Average total assets}}$$

$$\times \frac{\text{Average total assets}}{\text{Average common equity}} = \text{ROCSE}$$

For 1991

$$\frac{401.5}{6,204.1} = 6.47\% \ \frac{6,204.1}{4,132.3} = 1.50 \ \frac{4,132.3}{1,866.0} = 2.22$$

	Net income margin	Asset turnover ratio	Common stockholders' leverage ratio	ROCSE
or	6.47% ×	1.50 ×	2.22	= 21.52%

The 1991 net income margin of Campbell can be further disaggregated as follows:

$$\frac{\text{Pre-tax earnings}}{\text{Sales}} \times \frac{\text{Net earnings}}{\text{Pre-tax earnings}}$$

$$= \frac{667.4 \ \boxed{26}}{6204.1} \times \frac{401.5 \ \boxed{28}}{667.4}$$

$$= \underset{\substack{\text{margin}\\10.8\%}}{\text{Pre-tax profit}} \times \underset{\substack{\text{rate}\\60.2\%}}{\text{Tax retention}} = 6.5\%$$

For a comparative analysis of these ratios with those of preceding years please refer to the Return on Investment section of Campbell Soup's comprehensive analysis in Chapter 23.

This type of analysis over a period of time can be very instructive. If the ROCSE has declined, then it would be important to know which of these factors is most responsible for such a decline. Similarly, the areas of the most likely improvement in the ROCSE can be assessed by means of such analysis. Assuming that leverage is already high and that it would not be prudent to increase it, then the areas of improvement would be the profit margin and/or the asset turnover. The likelihood of improvements in these factors depends on industry conditions, competition, and similar influences. Is the profit margin high or low in comparison with what is achieved within the company's industry? How fast an asset turnover can be reasonably achieved in this industry? These are the considerations which the analyst will focus on in the analysis of changes in the ROCSE.

Expanded Disaggregation of ROCSE

We can introduce *interest burden* and the *tax rate* (or tax retention) into this disaggregation as follows:

EBIT = Net income \$401.5 + Interest \$116.2 + Taxes \$265.9 $\boxed{27}$
= $\underline{\underline{\$783.6}}$

(Preferred dividends would be deducted if applicable)

Revenues = same as sales
ATA = average total assets
ACE = average common equity
ETR = effective tax rate = 265.9 $\boxed{27}$ ÷ 667.4 $\boxed{226}$ = $\underline{\underline{0.398}}$

Disaggregation Formula

$$\frac{\text{EBIT}}{\text{Revenues}} \times \frac{\text{Revenues}}{\text{ATA}} - \frac{\text{Interest}}{\text{ATA}} \times \frac{\text{ATA}}{\text{ACE}}$$

$$\times (100 - \text{ETR}) = \frac{\text{NI*}}{\text{ACE}} = \text{ROCSE}$$

* Net income—by definition *after tax.*

Additional Factors Disaggregated

$\dfrac{\text{Interest}}{\text{ATA}} =$ known as *interest burden* (the higher the interest burden the lower the ROCSE)

$(100 - \text{ETR}) = $ *Tax retention* (the higher the tax retention the higher the ROCSE).

For Campbell 1991

$$\left(\frac{783.6}{6,204.1} \times \frac{6,204.1}{4,132.3} - \frac{116.2}{4,132.3}\right) \times \frac{4,132.3}{1,866.0} \times (1.000 - 0.398)$$

$$= (0.126 \times 1.50 - 0.028) = 0.161 \times 2.22 \times 0.602 = \underline{\underline{0.2149^*}}$$

* Or 21.49%—difference with preceding calculation due to rounding.

Equity Growth Rate

The equity growth rate by means of *earnings retention* can be calculated as follows:

$$\frac{\text{Net income}^* - \text{Dividend payout}}{\begin{array}{c}\text{Average common}\\\text{shareholders' equity}\end{array}}$$

= Percent increase in common equity

* Minus preferred dividend requirements.

This is the growth rate due to the retention of earnings and assumes a constant dividend payout over time. It indicates the possibilities of earnings growth without resort to external financing. These increased funds, in turn, will earn the rate of return that the enterprise can obtain on its assets and thus contribute to growth in earnings.

For the American Company (Exhibits 19–1 and 19–2), the equity growth rate can be computed for year 9 as follows:

$$\frac{\$65 - \$3 - \$39^*}{(\$674 + \$699) \div 2} = 3.4 \text{ percent}$$

* Common stock dividends.

Sustainable Growth Rate

The internal growth of a business entity depends on: (1) the earnings retained and reinvested in the entity and (2) the rate of return earned on the earnings retained. Thus, the sustainable growth rate is

$$(1 - \text{payout rate}) \times \text{ROCSE}$$

For American Company (Exhibits 19–1 and 19–2) the sustainable growth rate for year 9 is:

$$\text{Dividend payout rate} = \frac{41,806}{64,569} = 0.65$$

Earnings retention rate $\times$ ROCSE = Sustainable growth rate

$$(1 - 0.65) \times 0.09 = 0.058 \text{ or } 5.8\%$$

Due to a significant earnings drop from year 8 to year 9 with a steady dividend payout as well as a decline in the ROCSE, the sustainable growth rate declined year to year. In estimating future growth rates it is best to average the sustainable growth rates over a number of years and to consider projected changes in expected earnings retention rates as well as in projected ROCSE.

Analysis of Financial Leverage Effects

The effect that each noncommon equity capital source has on the return on the common equity can be analyzed in detail. Using the data of American Company that was included in Exhibits 19–1 and 19–2 earlier in this chapter, we can undertake such an analysis as follows:

An analysis of the American Company balance sheet as at December 31, year 9[7] discloses the following major sources of funds (in thousands):

Current liabilities (exclusive of current portion of long-term debt)		$ 182,472
Long-term debt....................	$335,945	
Current portion	11,606	347,551
Deferred taxes		101,143
Preferred stock		41,538
Common stockholders' equity		698,917
Total investment or total assets ..		$1,371,621

The income statement for year 9 includes (in thousands):

Income before taxes	$125,730
Income taxes	61,161
Net income	64,569
Preferred dividends	2,908
Income accruing to common shareholders	$ 61,661
Total interest expense	$ 20,382
Assumed interest on short-term notes (5%)	687
Balance of interest on long-term debt	$ 19,695

[7] A year-end based analysis (rather than one based on average for the year amounts) is used here in order to simplify the computations.

The return on total assets is computed as follows:

$$\frac{\text{Net income} + \text{Interest} \times (1 - \text{Tax rate})}{\text{Total assets (year-end)}}$$

$$= \frac{\$64,569 + \$20,382\,(1 - 0.40)}{\$1,371,621} = 5.6 \text{ percent}$$

The 5.56 percent return represents the average return on all assets employed by the company. To the extent that suppliers of capital other than the common stockholders get a lower reward than an average of 5.56 percent, the common equity benefits by the difference. The opposite is true when the suppliers of capital receive more than a 5.56 percent reward in year 9.

Exhibit 19–6 presents an analysis showing the relative contribution and reward of each of the major suppliers of funds and their effect on the returns earned by the common stockholders.

As can be seen from Exhibit 19–6, the $9,806,000 accruing to the common equity from use of current liabilities is largely due to its being free of interest costs. The advantage of $7,646,000 accruing from the use of long-term debt is substantially due to the tax deductibility of interest.

Exhibit 19–6   Analysis of composition of return on shareholders' equity (approximate computations in thousands of dollars)

Category of fund supplier	Fund supplied	Earnings on fund supplied at rate of 5.56 percent	Payment to suppliers of funds	Accruing to (detracting from) return on common stock
Current liabilities	$ 182,472	$10,218	$ 412[a]	$ 9,806
Long-term debt	347,551	19,463	11,817[b]	7,646
Deferred taxes	101,143	5,664	none	5,664
Preferred stock	41,538	2,326	2,908[c]	(582)
Earnings in excess of compensation to suppliers of funds				22,534
Add: Common stockholders' equity	698,917	39,139		39,139
Totals	$1,371,621	$76,810	$15,137	
Total income (return) on stockholders' equity				$61,673[d]

[a] Interest cost of $687 less 40 percent tax.
[b] Interest cost of $19,695 less 40 percent tax.
[c] Preferred dividends—not tax deductible.
[d] Slight differences with statement figures are due to rounding.

Since the preferred dividends are not tax deductible, the unimpressive return on total assets of 5.56 percent resulted in a disadvantage to the common equity of $582,000. The value of tax deferrals can be clearly seen in this case where the use of cost-free funds amounted to an annual advantage of $5,664,000.

We can now carry this analysis further (dollars in thousands).

The return on the common stockholders' equity is as follows:

$$\frac{\text{Net income less preferred dividends}}{\text{Common stockholders' equity}} = \frac{\$61,673^*}{\$698,917} = 8.8 \text{ percent}$$

* Ties in with total income accruing to common stockholders in Exhibit 19–6.

The net advantage that the common equity reaped from the working of financial leverage (Exhibit 19–6) is $22,534.

As a percentage of the common stockholders' equity, this advantage is computed as follows:

$$\frac{\text{Earnings in excess of compensation to outside suppliers of funds}}{\text{Common stockholders' equity}} = \frac{\$22,534}{\$698,917} = 3.22 \text{ percent}$$

The return on common stockholders' equity can now be viewed as being composed as follows:

Return on assets	5.60%
Leverage advantage accruing to common equity	3.22
Return on common equity	8.82%

RETURN ON EQUITY VERSUS RETURN ON SHAREHOLDER INVESTMENT

As was pointed out in the preceding discussion, return on common shareholder's equity (ROCSE) measures the relationship of new income (attributable to common shareholders) to common equity at book value. However, that measure does not indicate how shareholders have fared in terms of return on *their* investment (i.e., the price they paid for common stock).

Shareholders don't buy at book value; in fact they often pay at a multiple of book value. Consider the following assumptions (data per share):

Company net income	$ 6
Dividends	2
Earnings retained	4
Book value	$60
Ratio of market value to book value	2
Market valuation of retained earnings	$ 4

$$\text{ROCSE } \frac{6}{60} = 10\%$$

$$\text{Return on stockholder investment } \frac{\$2 + \$4}{2 \times \$60} = 5\%$$

Thus, the price paid by the investor plays a decisive role in determining *his* or *her* return on investment. A price below book value would have the opposite effect.

In this example we assume that the market accords at least *full* valuation to the earnings retained by the entity. This, as the study discussed below reveals, can hardly be taken for granted. Therefore, the additional factor to be considered is how the market values the earnings that have been retained by the entity.

If a company earns $1,000 then the shareholders will benefit (1) from the portion of earnings paid out as dividends, say $300, and (2) the value the market places on the retained earnings (RE) of $700, assumed here to be $900 over a period of time. Thus:

Shareholder enrichment =

$$\frac{\$300 \text{ (dividend)} + \$900 \text{ (change in market value associated with } \$700 \text{ increase in retained earnings)}}{\$1,000 \text{ in earnings}}$$

$$= \frac{\$1,200}{\$1,000} = 1.20$$

which means that each dollar earned by the company enriched shareholders by $1.20 (ignoring tax effects).

This concept of shareholder enrichment was used by Ben C. Ball, Jr. in a remarkable study[8] which examined the 50 largest mature companies for the 1970–84 period and came to the surprising conclusion that many companies' profits don't find their way to shareholders as either dividends or higher stock value over time.

Mr. Ball found that ROCSE does not correlate with Return on Stockholders Investment (ROSI) expressed as

$$\text{ROSI} = \frac{\text{Dividends} + \text{Market value}}{\text{Number of shares} \times \text{Share price (cost)}}$$

Using the above concept of Shareholder Enrichment he related it to Net earnings as follows:

$$\text{Measure of shareholder benefit (MSB)} = \frac{\text{Shareholder enrichment}}{\text{Net earnings}}$$

---

[8] "The Mysterious Disappearance of Retained Earnings," *Harvard Business Review,* July–August 1987.

His findings were that of the companies examined, the MSB of Schlumberger was 346 percent (i.e., its shareholders were enriched by $3.46 for each dollar the company earned) while over the same time the shareholders of General Electric and General Motors were enriched by only 54 cents and 53 cents, respectively, for each dollar earned. At the low-end extreme shareholders of Xerox lost $1.19 for each dollar the company earned.

On average, the relationship of Change in market value/Increase in retained earnings was only 84 percent. That means that an investor holding a portfolio of the stocks included in the Ball study did not benefit from 16 percent of the earnings of these companies retained during the market period under study.

It is obvious that the additional factor not considered by ROCSE, but which affects stockholders significantly, is the judgment of the market and its valuation of retained earnings. If shareholder enrichment falls below net income it means that the market's discounting of the value of earnings retained actually offsets the value of dividends.

It is also obvious that the ROCSE measure falls short in measuring shareholder return because it omits the crucial market valuation mechanism (judgment) on which shareholder returns are so importantly dependent. Thus, as was discussed earlier, the decision set concerned with the valuation of equity securities must include, in addition to financial statement analysis, considerations such as the market valuation mechanism. This mechanism is at the heart of the distinction which sophisticated analysts draw between a company and its stock. A company may be among the best-managed entities in its industry as determined by measures such as ROCSE. It may nevertheless be a bad investment at a given point in time because it is seriously overvalued by the market. Conversely, a poorly performing company may, because of its unrealistically low market valuation, be a good investment at the time.

QUESTIONS

1. Why is return on investment (ROI) one of the most valid measures of enterprise performance? How is this measure used by the financial analyst?
2. How is ROI used as an internal management tool?
3. Discuss the validity of excluding "nonproductive" assets from the asset base used in the computation of ROI. Under what circumstances is the exclusion of intangible assets from the asset base warranted?
4. Why is interest added back to net income when the ROI is computed on total assets?
5. Under what circumstances may it be proper to consider convertible debt as equity capital in the computation of ROI?
6. Why must the minority interest's share in net income be added back when ROI is computed on total assets?

7. Why must the net income figure used in the computation of ROI be adjusted to reflect the asset base (denominator) used in the computation?
8. What is the relationship between ROI and sales?
9. Company A acquired Company B because the latter had a record of profitability (net income to sales ratio) exceeding that of its industry. After the acquisition took place, a major stockholder complained that the acquisition resulted in a low ROI. Discuss the possible reasons for his complaint.
10. Company X's profitability is 2 percent of sales. Company Y has a turnover of assets of 12. Both companies have ROIs of 6 percent that are considered unsatisfactory by industry standards. What is the asset turnover of Company X and what is the profitability ratio of Company Y? What action would you advise to the managements of the respective companies?
11. What is the purpose of measuring the asset utilization of different asset categories?
12. What factors enter into the evaluation of the ROI measures?
13. How is the equity growth rate computed? What does it signify?
14. *a.* How do the rate of return on total assets and that on stockholders' equity differ?
    b. What are the components of the rate of return on common stockholders' equity and what do they represent?
15. *a.* What is *equity turnover* and how is it related to the rate of return on equity?
    b. "Growth in per share earnings generated from an increase in equity turnover probably cannot be expected to continue indefinitely." Do you agree or disagree? Explain briefly, bringing out in your answer the alternative causes of an increase in equity turnover. (CFA)

Chapter 20

ANALYSIS OF RESULTS OF OPERATIONS—I

THE SIGNIFICANCE OF INCOME STATEMENT ANALYSIS

The income statement presents in summarized fashion the results of operations of an enterprise. These results, in turn, represent the major reason for the existence of a profit-seeking entity, and they are important determinants of its value and its solvency.

As was brought out in the discussion of objectives of financial analysis in Chapter 1, some of the most important decisions in security analysis and credit evaluation are based on an evaluation of income statements. To the security analyst, income is often the single most important determinant of security values, and hence the measurement and the projection of income are among the most important analytical objectives. Similarly, to the credit grantor, income and cash provided by operations are the most natural as well as the most desirable source of interest and principal repayment. In almost all other aspects of financial analysis, the evaluation and projection of operating results assume great importance.

THE MAJOR OBJECTIVES OF INCOME ANALYSIS

In the evaluation of the income of an enterprise, the analyst is particularly interested in an answer to the following questions:

1. What is the relevant net income of the enterprise and what is its quality?
2. What elements in the income statement can be used and relied upon for purposes of earnings forecasting?
3. How stable are the major elements of income and expense and what is their trend?
4. What is the "earning power" of the enterprise?

These questions will be examined in this and in the two chapters that follow.

What Is the Relevant Net Income of the Enterprise?

Based on the simple proposition that net income is the excess of revenues over costs and expenses during an accounting period, many people, including astute professional analysts, are exasperated at the difficulties they encounter in their search for the "true earnings" or the "real earnings" of an enterprise.

Why, they ask, should it be possible for so many different "acceptable" figures of "net income" to flow out of one set of circumstances? Given the economic events that the enterprise experienced during a given period, is there not only *one* "true" result, and is it not the function of accountancy to identify and measure such result?

Those who have studied Part II of this book will know why the answer to the last question must be "no." In this chapter, dealing with the analysis of income, it is appropriate to summarize *why* this is so.

Net Income Is Not a Specific Quantity   Net income is not a specific flow awaiting the perfection of a flawless meter with which it can be precisely measured. There are a number of reasons for this:

1. The determination of income is dependent on estimates regarding the outcome of future events. This peering into the future is basically a matter of judgment involving the assessment of probabilities based on facts and estimates.

While the judgment of skilled and experienced professionals, working on the basis of identical data and information, can be expected to fall within a narrow range, it will nevertheless *vary* within such a range. The estimates involve the allocation of revenues and costs as between the present and the future. Put another way, they involve the determination of the future utility and usefulness of many categories of unexpired costs and of assets as well as the estimation of future liabilities and obligations.

2. The accounting standards governing the determination and measurement of income at any given time are the result of the cumulative experience of the accounting profession, of regulatory agencies, of businessmen, and others. They reflect a momentary equilibrium that is based partly on knowledge and experience and partly on the compromise of widely differing interests and views on methods of measurement. Chapter 10 indicates the great variety of these views. While the accounting profession has moved to narrow the range of acceptable alternative measurement principles, alternatives nevertheless remain; and their complete elimination in the near future is unlikely.

3. Beyond the problem of honest differences in estimation and other judgments, as well as of the variety of alternative acceptable principles, is also the problem arising from the diverse ways in which the judgments and principles are applied.

Theoretically, the independent professional accountant should be concerned first and foremost with the fair presentation of the financial statements. He should make accounting a "neutral" science that gives expression and effect to economic events but does not itself affect the results presented. To this end, he should choose from among alternative principles those most applicable to the circumstances and should disclose all facts, favorable and adverse, that may affect the user's decision.

In fact, the accounting profession as a whole has not yet reached such a level of independence and detachment of judgment. It is subject to the powerful pressures on the part of managements who have, or at least feel that they have, a vital interest in the way in which results of operations are presented. The auditors are most vulnerable to pressures in those areas of accounting where widely differing alternatives are equally acceptable and where accounting theory is still unsettled. Thus, they may choose the lowest level of acceptable practice rather than that which is most appropriate and fair in the circumstances. Although relatively less frequent, cases of malpractice and collusion in outright deception by independent accountants nevertheless still surface from time to time.

The analyst cannot ignore these possibilities, and must be aware of them and be ever alert to them. It calls for constant vigilance in the analysis of audited data, particularly when there is reason to suspect a lack of independence and objectivity in the application of accounting principles.

In addition to the above reasons that are inherent in the accounting process, there exists another reason why there cannot be such a thing as an absolute measure of "real earnings." It is that financial statements are general-purpose presentations designed to serve the diverse needs of many users. Consequently, a single figure of "net income" cannot be relevant to all users, and that means that the analyst must use this figure and the additional information disclosed in the financial statements and elsewhere as a starting point and adjust it so as to arrive at a "net income" figure that meets his or her particular interests and objectives.

ILLUSTRATION 1.   To the buyer of an income-producing property, the depreciation expense figure that is based on the seller's cost is not relevant. In order to estimate the net income that can be derived from such property, depreciation based on the expected purchase price of the property must be substituted.

ILLUSTRATION 2.   To the analyst who exercises independent judgment and uses knowledge of the company he is analyzing and the industry of which it is a part, the reported net income marks the start of his analysis. He adjusts the net income figure for changes in income and expense items that he judges to be warranted. These may include, for example, estimates of bad debts, of depreciation, and of research costs as well as the treatment of gains and losses that are labeled extraordinary. Comparisons with other companies may call for similar adjustments so that the data can be rendered comparable.

From the above discussion it should be clear that the determination of a figure of net income is, from the point of view of the analyst, secondary to the objective of being able to find in the income statement all the disclosures needed in order to arrive at an income figure that is relevant for the purpose at hand.

The questions regarding the quality of earnings, of what elements in the income statement can be relied on for forecasting purposes, of what the stability and the trend of the earning elements are, and finally, of what the "earning power" of the enterprise is, will all be considered in Chapter 22.

We shall now proceed to examine the specific tools that are useful in the analysis of the various components of the income statement.

ANALYSIS OF COMPONENTS OF THE INCOME STATEMENT

The analysis of the income statements of an enterprise can be conceived as being undertaken at two levels: (1) obtaining an understanding of the accounting standards used and of their implication and (2) using the appropriate tools of income statement analysis.

Accounting Standards Used and Their Implication

The analyst must have a thorough understanding of the standards of income, cost, and expense accounting and measurement employed by the enterprise. Moreover, since most assets, with the exception of cash and receivables actually collectible, represent costs deferred to the future, the analyst must have a good understanding of the standards of asset and liability measurement employed by the enterprise so that he or she can relate them to the income accounting of the enterprise as a means of checking the validity of that accounting. Finally, he or she must understand and assess the implications that the use of one accounting principle, as opposed to another, has on the measurement of the income of an enterprise and its comparison to that of other enterprises.

Most chapters in Part II of this book deal with this important phase of financial statement analysis.

Tools of Income Statement Analysis

The second level consists of applying the appropriate tools of analysis to the components of the income statement and the interpretation of the results shown by these analytical measures. The application of these tools is aimed at achieving the objectives of the analysis of results of operations mentioned earlier, such as the projection of income, the assessment of its stability and quality, and the estimation of earning power.

The remainder of this chapter will be devoted to an examination of these tools and to the interpretation of the results achieved through their use.

THE ANALYSIS OF SALES AND REVENUES

The analysis of sales and revenues is centered on answers to these basic questions:

1. What are the major sources of revenue?
2. How stable are these sources and what is their trend?
3. How is the earning of revenue determined and how is it measured?

Major Sources of Revenue

Knowledge of major sources of revenues (sales) is important in the analysis of the income statement particularly if the analysis is that of a multimarket enterprise. Each major market or product line may have its own separate and distinct growth pattern, profitability, and future potential.

The best way to analyze the composition of revenues is by means of a common-size statement that shows the percentage of each major class of revenue to the total. This information can also be portrayed graphically on an absolute dollar basis as shown in Exhibit 20–1.

Exhibit 20–1   Analysis of sales by product line over time

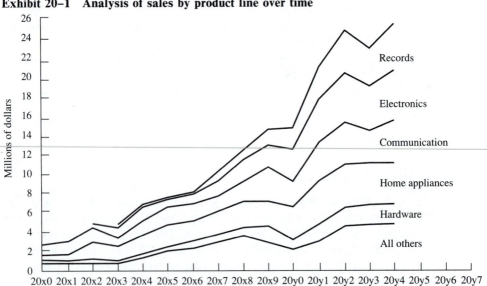

Chapter 23 contains a summary of segmental information of Campbell Soup and item 97 of its financial statements contains Geographic Area Information.

FINANCIAL REPORTING BY DIVERSIFIED ENTERPRISES

The user of the financial statements of diversified enterprises faces, in addition to the usual problems and pitfalls of financial analysis, the problem of sorting out and understanding the impact that the different individual segments of the business have on the sum total of reported results of operations and financial condition. The author of an important study in the reporting by diversified companies has defined a conglomerate company as follows:

> ... one which is so managerially decentralized, so lacks operational integration, or has such diversified markets that it may experience rates of profitability, degrees of risk, and opportunities for growth which vary within the company to such an extent that an investor requires information about these variations in order to make informed decisions.[1]

Reasons for the Need for Data by Significant Enterprise Segments

The above definition suggests some of the most significant reasons why financial analysts require as much information and detailed data as possible about the various segments of an enterprise. The analysis, evaluation, projection, and valuation of earnings requires that these be broken down into categories that share similar characteristics of variability, growth potential, and risk. Similarly, the asset structure and the financing requirements of various segments of an enterprise can vary significantly and thus require separate analysis and evaluation. Thus, the credit grantor may be interested in knowing which segments of an enterprise provide cash and which are net users of cash.

The composition of an enterprise, the relative size and profitability of its various segments, the ability of management to make profitable acquisitions, and the overall performance of management represents additional important information that the analyst seeks from its segmented data.[2] As will be seen from the discussion in Chapter 22, among the best ways

---

[1] R. K. Mautz, "Identification of the Conglomerate Company," *Financial Executive,* July 1967, p. 26.

[2] D. W. Collins in a study of 150 multisegment firms found that "SEC product-line revenue and profit disclosures together with industry sales projections published in various government sources provide significantly more accurate estimates of future total-entity sales and earnings than do those procedures that rely totally on consolidated data." *Journal of Accounting Research,* Spring 1976, pp. 163–77.

to construct an earnings forecast is to build the projections, to the extent possible, segment by segment.

The evaluation of the growth potential of earnings requires that as much information as possible be obtained about the different product lines or segments that make up the aggregate earnings. Rappaport and Lerner have illustrated the use of a segmented earnings contribution matrix that may prove useful in an assessment of earnings quality and growth potential, as well as in the valuation of aggregate earnings.[3] These are shown in Exhibits 20–2 and 20–3.

Disclosure of "Line of Business" Data

The degree of informative disclosure about the results of operations and the asset base of segments of a business can vary widely. Full disclosure would call for providing detailed income statements, statements of financial position, and statements of cash flow (SCF) for each significant segment. This is rarely found in practice because of the difficulty of obtaining such breakdowns internally, and also because of management's reluctance to divulge information that could harm the enterprise's

Exhibit 20–2   Earnings contribution and growth rates by industry segments

Industry	Earnings contributions (in thousands)	Growth rate of earnings contribution over the past three years
Leisure time:		
1. Camp equipment	$100	11%
2. Fishing equipment	50	2
3. Boats	72	15
4. Sporting goods	12	3
	234	
Agribusiness:		
1. Milk processing	85	2
2. Canning	72	8
3. Chicken farming	12	15
	169	
Education:		
1. Text publishing...........	40	3
2. Papers and supplies	17	6
	57	
Total	$460	

---

[3] A. Rappaport and E. M. Lerner, *A Framework for Financial Reporting by Diversified Companies* (New York: National Association of Accountants, 1969), pp. 18–19.

Exhibit 20–3   Segmented earnings contribution matrix

	Growth rate (in percent)			
Industry	*0–5*	*5–10*	*10–15*	*Total*
Leisure time	$ 62	$ 0	$172	$234
Agribusiness	85	72	12	169
Education	40	17	0	57
Total	$187	$89	$184	$460

competitive position. Short of the disclosure of complete financial statements by business segment, a great variety of partial detail has been suggested.

Income Statement Data

Revenues Only   In most enterprises, this should not present great difficulties.

Gross Profit   This involves complex problems of interdivisional transfer pricing as well as allocation of indirect overhead costs.

Contribution Margin   Contribution margin reporting (see also Chapter 21) is based on assigning to each segment the revenues, costs, and expenses for which that segment is solely responsible. It is a very useful concept in management accounting, but for purposes of public reporting of segment data, it presents problems because there are no generally accepted methods of cost allocation and, consequently, they can vary significantly from company to company and even within one enterprise. Disclosure of allocation methods, while helpful, will not remove all the problems facing the user of such data.

Net Income (after full cost allocation)   The further down the income statement reporting by segment occurs, the more pervasive and the more complex the allocation procedures become. Reporting segment net income would require allocating all joint expenses to each specific business activity on some rational basis, even though they may not be directly related to any particular one.

Balance Sheet Data

A breakdown by segments of assets employed is needed in an assessment of the efficiency of operations by segment, in the evaluation of segmental management, as well as in the computation of divisional return on investment.

In most companies, only certain assets, such as plant and equipment, inventories, and certain intangibles, are identified directly with a specific segment. An allocation of all assets would have to be arbitrary since in many enterprises cash, temporary investments, and even receivables are centralized at the group or corporate headquarters level.

Research Studies

Interest in the subject of reporting by diversified companies has sparked research efforts into the types of disclosures that are necessary and feasible and the problems related thereto.[4] A most extensive research effort was that undertaken by Professor R. K. Mautz,[5] and the FASB published an extensive *Discussion Memorandum* on the subject.

Statement of Financial Accounting Standards 14

In *SFAS 14* (1976), "Financial Reporting for Segments of a Business Enterprise," the Board established requirements for disclosures to be made in company financial statements concerning information about operations in different industries, foreign operations, export sales, and major customers.

The *Statement* recognizes that evaluation of risk and return is the central element of investment and lending decisions. Since an enterprise operating in various industry segments or geographic areas may have different rates of profitability, degrees and types of risk, and opportunities for growth, disaggregated information will assist analysts in analyzing the uncertainties surrounding the timing and amount of expected cash flows—and hence the risks—related to an investment in or a loan to an enterprise that operates in different industries or areas of the world.

The *Statement* requires companies to report in their annual financial statements the revenues, operating profit (revenue less operating expenses), and identifiable assets of each significant industry segment of their operations. Certain other related disclosures are required. *SFAS 14* does not prescribe methods of accounting for transfer pricing or cost allocation. However, it does require that the methods in use be disclosed.

---

[4] See Morton Backer and Walter B. McFarland, *External Reporting for Segments of a Business* (New York: National Association of Accountants, 1968). Also see Robert T. Sprouse, "Diversified Views about Diversified Companies," *Journal of Accounting Research* 7, no. 1 (Spring 1969), pp. 137–59; and A. Rappaport and E. H. Lerner, *A Framework for Financial Reporting by Diversified Companies* (New York: National Association of Accountants, 1969).

[5] R. K. Mautz, *Financial Reporting by Diversified Companies* (New York: Financial Executives Research Foundation, 1968).

A segment is regarded as significant, therefore reportable, under the *Statement* if its sales, operating profit, or identifiable assets are 10 percent or more of the related combined amounts for all of a company's industry segments.[6] To ensure that the industry segments for which a company reports information represent a substantial portion of the company's overall operations, the *Statement* requires that the combined sales of all segments for which information is reported shall be at least 75 percent of the company's total sales. The *Statement* also suggests 10 as a practical limit to the number of industry segments for which a company reports information. If that limit is exceeded it may be appropriate to combine certain segments into broader ones to meet the 75 percent test with a practical number of segments.

Under *SFAS 14,* if a company derives 10 percent or more of its revenue from sales to any single customer, that fact and the amount of revenue from each such customer also must be disclosed.

The *Statement* provides guidelines for determining a company's foreign operations and export sales and for grouping operations by geographic areas. Information similar to that required for industry segments also is required for a company's operations in different geographic areas of the world.

SEC Reporting Requirements

The SEC took an early lead in requiring disclosure of sales and profit information by lines of business. Following promulgation of *SFAS 14,* the SEC, by means of *FRR* No. 1 Section 503, conformed SEC reporting requirements to those of the *Statement.* However, the SEC reporting requirements, incorporated in Regulation S-K, differ from *SFAS 14* in that it requires that segment revenue, operating profit, and asset information be presented for three years. Moreover, an additional narrative description is called for in Regulation S-K covering the registrant's business by reportable segments including information on competition, dependence on a few customers, principal products and services, backlog, sources and availability of raw materials, patents, research and development (R&D) costs, number of employees, and the seasonality of the business.

---

[6] Specifically, an industry segment is significant if in the latest period for which statements are presented:

1. Its revenue is 10 percent or more of the *combined* revenue of all industry segments; or
2. Its operating profit (loss) is 10 percent or more of the greater of *(a)* the combined operating profit of all segments that did not incur a loss, or *(b)* the combined operating loss of all segments that did incur a loss; or
3. Its identifiable assets are 10 percent or more of the combined identifiable assets of all industry segments.

Implications for Analysis

The increasing complexity of diversified business entities and the loss of identity that acquired companies suffer in the published financial statements of conglomerates have created serious problems for the financial analyst.

The disclosure requirements of *SFAS 14* as well as those of the SEC increased the amount of segmental information available for analysis. However the analyst will have to be very careful in his assessment of the reliability of the data on which he bases his conclusions.

The more specific and detailed the information provided is, the more likely it is to be based on extensive allocations of costs and expenses. Allocation of common costs, as practiced for internal accounting purposes, is often based on such concepts as "equity," "reasonableness," and "acceptability to managers." These concepts have often little relevance to the objective of financial analysis.

Bases of allocating joint expenses are largely arbitrary and subject to differences of opinions as to their validity and precision. Some specific types of joint expenses that fall into this category are general and administrative expenses of central headquarters, R&D costs, certain selling costs, advertising, interest, pension costs, and federal and state income taxes.

There are, at present, no generally accepted principles of cost and expense allocation or any general agreement on the methods by which the costs of one segment should be transferred to another segment in the same enterprise. Moreover, the process of formulating such principles of reaching such agreement has barely begun. The analyst who uses segmented data must bear these limitations firmly in mind.

ILLUSTRATION 3.   Companies generally do not disclose internal accounting practices, which they are not obligated to disclose, unless it is in their interest to do so. The management of Murray Ohio Manufacturing Company found it to its advantage to disclose, in federal court, that its annual report did not give the true story as far as actual profit or loss by product line was concerned. Management admitted to understating losses in its bicycle division by many millions of dollars as part of an effort to fend off hostile takeover advances by a Swedish company. Murray Ohio feared that the option of closing a heavily losing bicycle division would appeal to the potential acquirer. The company simply chose not to allocate $17 million in corporate overhead to its bicycle division.

This case provides a rare glimpse into the murky area of overhead allocation and to many possibilities companies have to provide misleading segmental information if they choose to do so.

In *SFAS 14,* the Board has, in effect, recognized the above-described limitations and realities. Consequently, the disclosure of profit contribution (revenue less only those operating expenses that are directly traceable to a segment), which was proposed in the exposure draft issued for public comment, was not required in the final *Statement*. Similarly, the Board concluded that revenue from intersegment sales or transfers shall be accounted for on whatever basis is used by the enterprise to price intersegment sales or transfers. No single basis was prescribed or proscribed.

Moreover, the Board concluded that certain items of revenue and expense either do not relate to segments or cannot always be allocated to segments on the basis of objective evidence, and consequently, there is no requirement in *SFAS 14* that net income be disclosed for reportable segments. The Board also noted in the *Statement* that "determination of an enterprise's industry segments must depend to a considerable extent on the judgment of the management of the enterprise."

The implication for analysts of this lack of firmer guidelines and definitions is that segmental disclosures are and must be treated as "soft" information that is subject to manipulation and preinterpretation by managements. Consequently, such data must be treated with a healthy degree of skepticism, and conclusions can be derived from them only through the exercise of great care as well as analytical skill.

STABILITY AND TREND OF REVENUES

The relative trend of sales of various product lines or revenues from services can best be measured by means of trend percentages as illustrated in Exhibit 20–4.

Sales indexes of various product lines can be correlated and compared to composite industry figures or to product sales trends of specific competitors.

Important considerations bearing on the quality and stability of the sales and revenues trend include:

1. The sensitivity of demand for the various products to general business conditions.
2. The ability of the enterprise to anticipate trends in demand by the introduction of new products and services as a means of furthering

Exhibit 20–4   Trend percentage of sales by product line (year 1 = 100)

	Year 1	Year 2	Year 3	Year 4	Year 5
Product A	100	110	114	107	121
Product B	100	120	135	160	174
Product C	100	98	94	86	74
Service A	100	101	92	98	105

sales growth and as replacement of products for which demand is falling.
3. Degree of customer concentration (now required to be disclosed by *SFAS 14*), dependence on major customers, as well as demand stability of major customer groups.[7]
4. Degree of product concentration and dependence on a single industry.
5. Degree of dependence on relatively few star salesmen.
6. Degree of geographical diversification of markets.

ILLUSTRATION 4.   Micron Products Inc., reported sales to major customers as follows:

Sales to three major customers amounted to approximately 32 percent, 25 percent and 11 percent of the Company's net sales.
Sales to the Company's foreign customers amounted to approximately 15 percent and 13 percent of the Company's net sales.

MANAGEMENT'S DISCUSSION AND ANALYSIS OF FINANCIAL CONDITION AND RESULTS OF OPERATIONS

A significant concept of disclosure from the analyst's point of view was instituted by the SEC, further broadened in 1980, and is now codified in *FRR* No. 1 Section 501. The disclosures that are required are of an interpretative or explanatory nature that is necessary to enable investors to understand and evaluate significant period-to-period changes in the various items that report the enterprise's financial condition and results of operations. In *FRR 36* (1989) the SEC elaborated further on examples of satisfactory MDA disclosures.

Management's Discussion and Analysis of Financial Condition and Results of Operations (MDA) requirements, which are part of the SEC's integrated disclosure system, now require three years of income statements and focus on (*in addition* to results of operations) liquidity, capital resources, and the impact of inflation. These latter topics are discussed in Chapters 16, 17, 18, and 14.

In the area of results of operations, MDA must cover revenue and expense components that are needed for understanding of results by the reader, major unusual or infrequent events that materially affect reported income from continuing operations, trends or uncertainties that have affected or are likely to affect results, and impending changes in cost/revenue relationships such as increases in materials or labor costs. MDA

---

[7] *Statement on Auditing Standards (SAS) 6* (AICPA) requires disclosure of the economic dependency of a company on one or more parties with which it transacts a significant volume of business, such as a sole or major customer, supplier, franchisor, distributor, borrower, or lender.

must also include a discussion of the extent to which material increases in revenues are attributable to increases in prices or to increases in volume or amount of goods or services being sold or to the introduction of new products or services as well as a discussion of the impact of inflation and changing prices on the registrant's revenues and on income from continuing operations.

Overall, the SEC desires that MDA's emphasis be redirected from operations to financial results; that forward-looking information should, if possible, be included; and the discussion should focus on trends and implications that are not evident from an examination of the financial statements.[8]

Campbell Soup Company (Chapter 4, Appendix B) presents its MDA in items 2 to 12.

IMPLICATIONS FOR ANALYSIS

In its instructions to MDA requirements, the SEC states that the purpose of the discussion and analysis is to provide investors and others with information relevant to an assessment of the financial condition and results of operations of the registrant as determined by evaluating the amounts and the certainty of cash flows from operations and from outside sources.

Even more so than under the previous requirements, the instructions for preparation of MDA make it clear that managements have a great deal of discretion on how to communicate to the reader and what to stress in such communications. The aim is meaningful disclosure in narrative form by those in charge of operations who are really in a position to know and who can supply significant additional details not usually found in the financial statements. The results will depend on management's attitudes and objectives.

While analysts must be aware that much information included in MDA is likely to be "soft" in nature, it must be borne in mind that in reporting in accordance with SEC requirements, managements cannot risk being careless or deceptive in their statements in such financial filings.

On balance, the analyst will have here much information that is valuable, that provides added insights, and that cannot readily be obtained

---

[8] In *FRR* No. 1 Section 501, the SEC released the staff's assessment of disclosures contained in MDA sections of annual reports. Examples cited in the release cover areas such as impact on pre-tax income of closing unprofitable facilities; effect of LIFO inventory liquidation on pre-tax income; changes in revenues by segment; forward-looking information; cash flow from operations on a trend basis; available sources of liquidity; known or reasonably likely liquidity deficiencies; and impact of inflation on sales, cost of sales, assets, and liabilities. *FRR 36* (1989) covers, among others, trends, demands, commitments, events, and uncertainties as well as year-to-year changes, segment data discussion, and analysis of cash flows.

in other ways. Thus, without having to take them at face value, the analyst can nevertheless use these disclosures as valuable analytical supplements for both the information that they provide and the insights into the thinking and the attitude of managements which they afford.

METHODS OF REVENUE RECOGNITION AND MEASUREMENT

Chapter 10 contains a discussion of the variety of methods of revenue recognition and measurement that coexist in various industries. Some of these methods are more conservative than others. The analyst must understand the income recognition methods used by the enterprise and their implications as well as the methods used by companies with which the results of the enterprise under analysis are being compared. A foremost consideration is whether the revenue recognition method in use accurately reflects an entity's economic performance and earnings activities.

QUESTIONS

1. What are the major objectives of income analysis?
2. Why can "net income" not be a single specific quantity?
3. Two levels can be identified in the analysis of the income statement. Name them.
4. Why is knowledge of major sources of revenue (sales) of an enterprise important in the analysis of the income statement?
5. Why are information and detailed data about the segments of diversified enterprises important to financial analysts?
6. Disclosure of various types of information by "line of business" has been proposed. Comment on the value of such information and the feasibility of providing it in published financial statements.
7. What are the major provisions of *SFAS 14?*
8. To what limitations of public segmental data must the analyst be alert?
9. Which important considerations have a bearing on the quality and the stability of a sales and revenue trend?
10. How were the requirements for additional disclosures of an interpretive or explanatory nature in the form of Management's Discussion and Analysis of Financial Condition and Results of Operations (MDA) changed in 1980?
11. Cite some of the examples of the types of subjects that should be covered in the MDA.
12. What are the objectives of discussions required by the revised MDA?

Chapter 21

ANALYSIS OF RESULTS OF OPERATIONS—II

This chapter continues the discussion of the analysis of results of operations begun in the preceding chapter.

ANALYSIS OF COST OF SALES

In most enterprises,[1] the cost of goods or services sold is, as a percentage of sales, the single most significant cost category. As the discussion in Chapter 10 shows, the methods of determining cost of sales encompass a wide variety of alternatives. Moreover, there is, particularly in unregulated industries, no agreed-to uniform cost classification method that would result in a clear and generally accepted distinction among such basic cost and expense categories as cost of sales, administrative, general, sales, and financial expenses. This is particularly true in the classification of general and administrative expenses. Thus, in undertaking cost comparisons, the analyst must be ever alert to methods of classification and the effect they can have on the validity of comparisons within an enterprise or among enterprises.

GROSS PROFIT

The excess of sales over the cost of sales is the gross profit or gross margin. It is commonly expressed as a percentage:

Sales	$10,000,000	100%
Cost of sales	7,200,000	72
Gross profit	$ 2,800,000	28%

---

[1] Exceptions can be found, for example, in some land sales companies where selling and other costs may actually exceed the cost of land sold.

The gross profit percentage or gross margin is a very important operating ratio. In the above example, the gross profit is $2,800,000, or 28 percent of sales. From this amount, all other costs and expenses must be recovered and any net income that is earned is the balance remaining after all expenses. Unless an enterprise has an adequate gross profit, it can be neither profitable nor does it have an adequate margin with which to finance such essential future-directed discretionary expenditures as research and development and advertising. Gross profit margins vary from industry to industry depending on such factors as competition, capital investment, and the level of costs other than direct costs of sales that must be covered by the gross profit.

Factors in the Analysis of Gross Profit

In the analysis of gross profit, the analyst will pay particular attention to:

1. The factors that account for the variation in sales and costs of sales.
2. The relationship between sales and costs of sales and management's ability to control this relationship.

ANALYSIS OF CHANGES IN GROSS MARGIN[2]

A detailed analysis of changes in gross margin can usually be performed only by an internal analyst because it requires access to data such as the number of physical units sold, unit sales prices, as well as unit costs. Such data are usually not provided in published financial statements. Moreover, unless the enterprise sells a single product, this analysis requires detailed data by product line. The external analyst, unless he or she has special influence on the company analyzed, will usually not have access to the data required for the analysis of gross margin.

Despite the above limitations to which gross margin analysis is subject, it is instructive to examine its process so that the elements accounting for variations in gross margin can be more fully understood.

EXAMPLE OF ANALYSIS OF CHANGE IN GROSS MARGIN

Company A shows the following data for two years:

---

[2] In this discussion, the terms *gross profit* and *gross margin* are used interchangeably. Some writers reserve the term *gross margin* for situations where the cost of goods sold excludes overhead costs, that is, direct costing. This is not the intention here.

	Unit of measure	Year ended December 31 Year 1	Year ended December 31 Year 2	In-crease	De-crease
1. Net sales	Thousands of dollars	$657.6	$687.5	$29.9	
2. Cost of sales	Thousands of dollars	237.3	245.3	8.0	
3. Gross margin	Thousands of dollars	420.3	442.2	21.9	
4. Units of product sold	Thousands	215.6	231.5	15.9	
5. Selling price per unit (1 ÷ 4)	Dollars	$ 3.05	$ 2.97		$0.08
6. Cost per unit (2 ÷ 4)	Dollars	1.10	1.06		0.04

Based on the above data, Exhibit 21–1 presents an analysis of the changes in gross margin of $21,900 from year 1 to year 2.

This analysis is based on the principle of focusing on one element of change at a time. Thus, in Exhibit 21–1, the analysis of variation in sales involves the following steps:

Step 1: We focus on the year-to-year change in volume while *assuming* that the unit selling price remained unchanged at the former, year 1, level. Since both the volume change (15.9) and the unit selling price ($3.05) are positive, the resulting product ($48.5) is positive.

Step 2: We focus next on the change in selling price that represents a year-to-year decrease (−$0.08) and *assume* the volume (215.6) to be unchanged from the prior year level so as to single out the change due to price change. Algebraically, here the multiplication of a negative (price change) by a positive (volume) results in a negative product (−$17.2).

Step 3: We must now recognize that the *assumptions* used in steps 1 and 2 above, that is, that the volume remained unchanged while the unit price changed and vice versa, are temporary expedients used to single out major causes for change. To complete the computation, we must recognize that by making these assumptions we left out the *combined* change in volume and unit price. The change in volume of 15.9 represents an *increase* and, consequently, is *positive*. The unit selling price change represents a *decrease* (−$0.08) and hence is *negative*. As a result, the product is negative (−$1.3).

Exhibit 21–1

COMPANY A
Statements Accounting for Variation in Gross Margin
between Year 1 and Year 2 (in thousands)

I. *Analysis of variation in sales*
  1. Variation due to change in volume of products sold:
       Change in volume (15.9) × year 1 unit selling price $48.5
       ($3.05) . . . .
  2. Variation due to change in selling price:
       Change in selling price (−$0.08) × year 1 sales volume   −17.2
       (215.6) . . . .

                                                                    31.3
  3. Variation due to combined change in sales volume (15.9)   − 1.3
       and unit sales price (−$0.08) . . . .

  Increase in net sales 30.0*

II. *Analysis of variation in cost of sales*
  1. Variation due to change in volume of products sold:
       Change in volume (15.9) × year 1 cost per unit ($1.10) . . .   17.5
  2. Variation due to change in cost per unit sold:
       Change in cost per unit (−$0.04) × year 1 sales volume   − 8.6
       (215.6) . . . .

                                                                      8.9
  3. Variation due to combined change in volume (15.9) and cost   − 0.6
       per unit (−$0.04) . . . .

  Increase in cost of sales 8.3*

  Net variation in gross margin $21.7*

    * Differences are due to rounding.

Step 4: Adding up the—

         Variation due to volume change $48.5
         Variation due to price change . . . .   −17.2
         Combined change of volume and unit price . . . .   − 1.3
         We account for the causes behind the sales increase $30.0

The analysis of variation in the cost of sales follows the same principles.

Interpretation of Changes in Gross Margin

The analysis of variation in gross margin is useful in identifying major causes of change in the gross margin. These changes can consist of one or a combination of the following factors:

1. Increase in sales volume.
2. Decrease in sales volume.

3. Increase in unit sales price.
4. Decrease in unit sales price.
5. Increase in cost per unit.
6. Decrease in cost per unit.

The presence of the "combined change of volume and unit sales price" and the "combined volume and unit cost" in the analysis presents no problem in interpretation since their amount is always minor in relation to the main causative factors of change.

The interpretation of the results of the analysis of gross margin involves the identification of the major factors responsible for change in the gross margin and an evaluation of the reasons for change in the factors. Such an analysis can also focus on the most feasible areas of improvement (i.e., volume, price, or cost) and the likelihood of realizing such improvements. For example, if it is determined that the major reason for a decline in gross margin is a decline in unit sales prices and that it reflects a situation of overcapacity in the enterprise's industry with attendant price cutting, then the situation is a serious one because of the limited control management has on such a development. If, on the other hand, the deterioration in the gross margin is found to be due to an increase in unit costs, then this may be a situation over which management can exercise a larger measure of control and, given its ability to do so, an improvement is a more likely possibility.

BREAK-EVEN ANALYSIS

The second level of cost analysis is importantly concerned with the relationship between sales and the cost of sales but goes beyond that segment of the income statement. This level encompasses break-even analysis and is concerned with the relationship of sales to most costs, including, but not limited to, the cost of sales.

Concepts underlying Break-Even Analysis

The basic principle underlying break-even analysis is the behavior of costs. Some costs vary directly with sales while others remain essentially constant over a considerable range of sales. The first category of costs is classified as *variable* while the latter are known as *fixed* costs.

The distinction among costs according to their behavior can be best understood within the framework of an example. In order to focus first on the basic data involved and on the technique of break-even analysis, we shall examine it by means of a simple illustration:

An enterprising graduate student saw an opportunity to sell pocket calculators at a financial analysts' convention due to take place in her hometown. Upon inquiry, she learned that she would have to get a vendor's license from the convention organizing committee at a cost of $10 and that the rental of a room in which to sell would amount to $140. The cost of calculators was to be $3 each with the right to return any that were not sold. The student decided that $8 was the proper sales price per calculator and wondered whether the undertaking will be worthwhile. As a first step she decided to compute the number of calculators she will have to sell in order to break even.

Equation Approach

We start from the elementary proposition that:

$$\text{Sales} = \text{Variable cost} + \text{Fixed costs} + \text{Profit (or} - \text{Loss)}$$

Since at break-even there is neither gain nor loss, the equation is:

$$\text{Sales} = \text{Variable cost} + \text{Fixed costs}$$

If we designate the number of calculators that must be sold to break even as X, we have

$$\$8X = \$3X + \$150$$

where:

Sales = Unit sales price ($8) $\times$ X
Variable costs = Variable cost per unit ($3) $\times$ X
Fixed costs = License fee ($10) + Rental ($140)

These costs are fixed because they will be incurred regardless of the number of calculators sold.

Solving the equation we get:

$$\$5X = \$150$$
$$X = 30 \text{ units or calculators to be sold to break even}$$

In this example, the number of calculators to be sold is important information because the student needs to assess the likelihood of obtaining the size of demand that will make her venture profitable. This approach is, however, limited to a single product enterprise.

If, as is common in business, an enterprise sells a mix of goods, the unit sales break-even computation becomes impracticable and the focus is on dollar sales. This would be the situation if our student sold stationery and books in addition to calculators.

This more prevalent break-even computation can be illustrated with the data already given.

If we designate the dollar sales at break even as Y, we get:

$$Y = \text{Variable-cost percentage } Y + \text{Fixed costs}$$
$$= 0.375Y + \$150$$
$$0.625Y = \$150$$
$$Y = \$240 \text{ (sales at break even)}$$

In this computation, the variable-cost percentage is the ratio of variable costs ($3) to sales price ($8). This means that each dollar of sales entails an incurrence of $0.375 for variable costs, or 37.5 percent of the sales price.

Graphic Presentation

Exhibit 21–2 portrays the results attained above in graphic form. A graph drawn to scale will yield a solution approximating in accuracy that obtained by the formula method. Moreover it portrays under one set of assumptions not only the break-even point but also a whole range of profitable operations above that point as well as the losses below it.

Contribution Margin Approach

Another technique of break-even analysis that can produce additional insights into the relationship of sales, costs, and profits is the contribution margin approach. It will be illustrated here by means of the foregoing pocket calculator example.

Exhibit 21–2   Calculator illustration—break-even chart

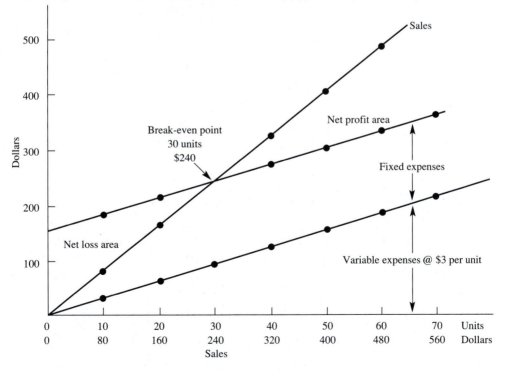

The contribution margin is what is left of the net sales price after deduction of the variable costs. It is from this margin that fixed costs must first be met and after that a profit earned.

Sales price per calculator $8
Variable costs per calculator   3
Unit contribution margin $5

Since each unit (calculator) sold contributes $5 to overhead and for profit, the break-even point in units is

$$\frac{\text{Fixed costs}}{\text{Unit contribution margin}} = \frac{\$150}{\$5} = 30 \text{ units}$$

Thus, after 30 units are sold, the fixed costs are covered and each additional unit sale yields a profit equal to the unit contribution margin, that is, $5.

If, as is more usual, the break-even point is to be expressed in dollars of sales, the formula involves use of the contribution margin ratio rather than the unit contribution margin. The contribution margin ratio is a percentage relationship computed as follows:

$$\frac{\text{Unit contribution margin}}{\text{Unit sales price}} = \frac{\$5}{\$8} = 0.625, \text{ or } 62.5 \text{ percent}$$

The calculator problem dollar break-even point can now be calculated as follows:

$$\frac{\text{Fixed costs}}{\text{Contribution margin ratio}} = \frac{\$150}{0.625} = \$240$$

The contribution margin is an important tool in break-even analysis, and its significance will be the subject of further discussion later in this section.

Pocket Calculator Problem—Additional Considerations

The break-even technique illustrated above lends itself to a variety of assumptions and requirements. The following are additional illustrations, all using the original data of our example, unless changed assumptions are introduced:

ILLUSTRATION 1.   Assume that our student decided that in order to make the venture worthwhile she requires a net profit of $400. How many calculators must be sold to achieve this objective?

$$\text{Sales} = \text{(Variable cost percent)(sales)} + \text{Fixed costs} + \text{Profit}$$
$$S = 0.375S + \$150 + \$400$$
$$0.625S = \$550$$
$$S = \$880$$
$$\frac{\$880}{\$8} = 110 \text{ units}$$

ILLUSTRATION 2.   Assume that the financial analysts' convention committee offered to provide the student with a room free of charge if she agreed to imprint on the calculators the Financial Analysts Society's seal. However, this would increase the cost of calculators from $3 to $4 per unit. Under the original assumptions, the break-even point was 30 calculators. What should it be if the student accepts the committee's proposal?

Here we have a reduction of fixed costs by $140 and an increase in variable costs of $1 per unit.

If X be the number of calculators sold at break-even point, then:

$$\text{Sales} = \text{Variables costs} + \text{Fixed costs}$$
$$\$8X = \$4X + \$10$$
$$\$4X = \$10$$
$$X = 2.5 \text{ calculators (rounded to 3)}$$

This proposal obviously involves a much lower break-even point and hence reduced risk. However, the lower contribution margin will at higher sales levels reduce total profitability. We can determine at what level of unit sales the original assumption of a $3 per unit variable cost and $150 fixed cost will equal the results of the $4 per unit variable cost and $10 fixed costs.

Let X be the number of units (calculators) sold, then:

$$\$4X + \$10 = \$3X + \$150$$
$$\$1X = \$140$$
$$X = 140 \text{ calculators}$$

Thus, if more than 140 calculators are sold, the alternative that includes the $3 variable cost will be more profitable.

Having examined the break-even analysis technique and some types of decisions for which it is useful, we will now turn to a discussion of the practical difficulties and the theoretical limitations to which the approach is subject.

Break-Even Technique—Problem Areas and Limitations

The intelligent use of the break-even technique and the drawing of reasonably valid conclusions therefrom depends on a resolution of practical difficulties and on an understanding of the limitations to which the techniques are subject.

Fixed, Variable, and Semivariable Costs   In the foregoing simple examples of break-even analysis, costs were clearly either fixed or variable. In the more complex reality found in practice, many costs are not so clearly separable into fixed and variable categories. That is, they either do not stay constant over a considerable change in sales volume or respond in exact proportion to change in sales.

We can illustrate this problem by reference to the costs of a food supermarket. As was discussed above, some costs will remain fixed within a certain range of sales. Rent, depreciation, certain forms of maintenance, utilities, and supervisory labor are examples of such fixed costs. The level of fixed costs can, of course, be increased by a simple management decision unrelated to the level of sales; for example, the grocery manager's salary may be increased.

Other costs, such as the cost of merchandise, trading stamps, supplies, and certain labor will vary closely with sales. These costs are truly variable. Certain other costs may, however, contain both fixed and variable elements in them. Examples of such *semivariable* costs are repairs, some materials, indirect labor, fuel, utilities, payroll taxes, and rents that contain a minimum payment provision and are also related to the level of sales. Break-even analysis requires that the variable component of such expenses be separated from the fixed component. This is often a difficult task for the management accountant and an almost impossible task for the outside analyst to perform without the availability of considerable internal data.

Simplifying Assumptions in Break-Even Analysis   The estimation of a variety of possible results by means of break-even calculations or charts requires the use of simplifying assumptions. In most cases, these simplifying assumptions do not destroy the validity of the conclusions reached. Nevertheless, in reaching such conclusions, the analyst must be fully aware of these assumptions and of their possible effect.

The following are some of the more important assumptions implicit in break-even computations:

1. The factors comprising the model actually behave as assumed, that is:
   a. That the costs have been reasonably subdivided into their fixed and variable components.
   b. That variable costs fluctuate proportionally with volume.
   c. That fixed costs remain fixed over the range relevant to the situation examined.
   d. That unit selling prices will remain unchanged over the range encompassed by the analysis.
2. In addition, there are certain operating and environmental assumptions that emphasize the static nature of any one break-even computation. It is assumed:

   a. That the mix of sales will remain unchanged.
   b. That efficiency of operations will remain constant.
   c. That prices of cost factors will not change.
   d. That the only factor affecting costs is volume.
   e. That beginning and end-of-period inventory levels will remain substantially unchanged.
   f. That there is no substantial change in the general price level during the period.

The formidable array of assumptions enumerated above points out the susceptibility of break-even computations to significant error. Not all the assumptions are, however, equally important, or, if not justified, will have an equal impact on the validity of conclusions. For example, the assumption that the selling price will not change with volume is contrary to economic theory and often is contrary to reality. Thus, the sales line is a curved rather than a linear function. However, the degree of error will depend on the actual degree of deviation from a strict linear relationship. Another basic assumption is that volume is *the* major, if not the only, factor affecting costs. We know, however, that strikes, political developments, legislation, and competition, to name a few other important factors, have a decided influence on costs. The analyst must, consequently, keep these simplifying assumptions firmly in mind and be aware of the dynamic factors that may require modifications in conclusions.

Break-Even Analysis—Uses and Their Implications

The break-even approach can be a useful tool of analysis if its limitations are recognized and its applications are kept in proper perspective.

The emphasis on the break-even, that is, zero profit, point is an unfortunate distortion of the objective of this type of analysis. Instead, the break-even situation represents but one point in a flexible set of projections of revenues and of the costs that will be associated with them under a given set of future conditions.

The managerial applications of break-even analysis are many. It is useful, among others, in price determination, expense control, and in the projection of profits. Along with standard cost systems it gives management a basis for pricing decisions under differing levels of activity. In conjunction with flexible budgets, it represents a powerful tool of expense control. The break-even chart is also a useful device with which to measure the impact of specific managerial decisions, such as plant expansion and new product introduction or of external influences, on the profitability of operations over various levels of activity.

To financial analysts, the function of profit projections is one of major importance. Moreover, the ability to estimate the impact of profitability of various economic conditions or managerial courses of action is also an extremely important one. Both of these are importantly aided by break-even analysis. The intelligent use of this technique and a thorough understanding of its operation are the factors that account for its importance to the external financial analyst.

Illustration of Break-Even Technique Application   Exhibit 21–3 presents the break-even chart of the Multi-Products Company at a given point in time. It is subject to the various assumptions that were discussed above including that relating to the ability to separate costs into their fixed and variable components.

At break even, a very condensed income statement of Multi-Products Company will be as follows:

Sales		$1,387,000
Costs:		
Variable	$887,000	
Fixed	500,000	1,387,000
Net income		–0–

The variable-cost percentage is $887/$1,387, or about 64 percent. The contribution margin ratio is 36 percent (100 − variable-cost percentage of 64). The variable-cost percentage means that on average, out of every

Exhibit 21–3   Multi-Products Company break-even chart—all operations

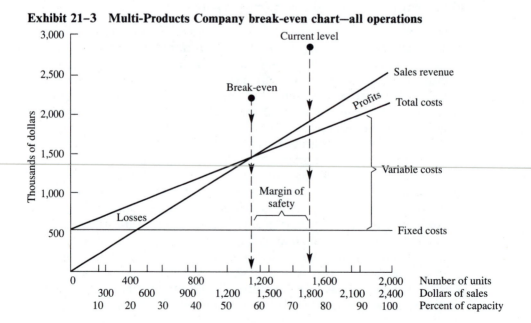

dollar of sales 64 cents go to meet variable costs, that is, costs that would not be incurred if the sale did not occur. The contribution margin ratio is basically the complement of the variable-cost percentage.

Break-even point:
Sales $1,387,000
Units   1,156,000
Average selling price per unit $1.20

This indicates that each dollar of sales generates a contribution of 36 cents toward meeting fixed expenses and the earning of a profit beyond the break-even point. The contribution margin earned on sales of $1,387,000 is just sufficient to cover the $500,000 in fixed costs. Quite obviously, the lower the fixed costs, the less sales it would take to cover them and the lower the resulting break-even point. In the most unlikely event that the Multi-Products Company would have no fixed costs, that is, all costs varied directly with sales, the company would have no break-even point, that is, it would start making a profit on the very first dollar of sales.

The break-even chart reflects the sale of a given mix of products. Since each product has different cost patterns and profit margins, any significant change in the product mix will result in a change in the break-even point and consequently in a change in the relationship between revenues, costs, and results. Although Exhibit 21–3 shows the number of units on the sales (volume) axis, this figure and the average selling price per unit are of limited significance because they represent averages prevailing as a result of a given mix of products.

The importance of a relatively stable sales mix to the successful application of break-even analysis suggests that this technique cannot be usefully employed in cases where the product mix varies greatly over the short term. Nor, for that matter, can break-even analysis be usefully applied in cases where there are sharp and frequent fluctuations in sales prices or in costs of production, such as raw materials.

Exhibit 21–3 indicates that given the existing mix of products, the present level of fixed costs of $500,000 can be expected to prevail up to a sales level of approximately $2,400,000. This is the point at which 100 percent of theoretical capacity will be reached. The break-even point is at 60 percent of capacity, while the current level of sales is at about 75 percent of capacity. This means that when the 100 percent capacity level is reached, the fixed costs may have to undergo an upward revision. If Multi-Products is reluctant to expand its capacity and thus increase its fixed costs and break-even point, assuming that variable costs do not decrease, it may have to consider other alternatives such as:

1. Forgoing an increase in sales.

2. Increasing the number of shifts, which could increase variable costs significantly.
3. Subcontracting some of its work to outsiders, thus forgoing some of the profit of increased activity.

Exhibit 21–3 also presents to the analyst at a glance the company's present position relative to the break-even point. The current level of sales of $1,800,000 is about $413,000 above the break-even point. This is also known as the *safety margin,* that is, the margin that separates the company from a no-profit condition. This concept can be expanded to indicate on the chart at what point the company will earn a desired return on investment (ROI), at what point the common dividend may be in jeopardy, and at what point the preferred dividend may no longer be covered by current earnings.

It is obvious that the data revealed by a reliably constructed break-even chart or by the application of break-even computations are valuable in profit projection, in the assessment of operating risk, as well as in an evaluation of profit levels under various assumptions regarding future conditions and managerial policies.

Analytical Implications of Break-Even Analysis

From the above discussion of a specific situation, such as that illustrated in Exhibit 21–3, we will now turn to a more general review of conclusions that can be derived from break-even analysis.

The Concept of Operating Leverage   Leverage and fixed costs go together. As we have seen in Chapter 18, financial leverage is based on fixed costs of funds for a portion of the resources used by the enterprise. Thus, earnings above that fixed cost magnify the return on the residual (or equity) funds and vice versa.

The fixed costs of a business enterprise, in the sense in which we have discussed them so far in this chapter, form the basis of the concept of operating leverage. Until an enterprise develops a volume of sales that is sufficient to cover its fixed costs, it will incur a loss. Once it has covered the fixed costs, further increments in volume will result in more than proportionate increases in profitability. The following will illustrate the nature of operating leverage:

Illustration of the Working of Operating Leverage   In a given enterprise, the cost structure is as follows:

Fixed costs = $100,000
Variable-cost percentage = 60 percent

The following tabulation presents the profit or loss at successively higher levels of sales and a comparison of relative percentage changes in sales volume and in profitability:

Sales	Variable costs	Fixed costs	Profit (loss)	Percentage increase over preceding step	
				Sales	Profit
$100,000	$ 60,000	$100,000	$(60,000)	—	—
200,000	120,000	100,000	(20,000)	100%	—
250,000	150,000	100,000	—	25	—
300,000	180,000	100,000	20,000	20	Infinite
360,000	216,000	100,000	44,000	20	120%
432,000	259,200	100,000	72,800	20	65%

The working of operating leverage is evident in the above tabulation. Starting at break even, the first 20 percent sales increase resulted in an infinite increase in profits because they started from a zero base. The next 20 percent increase in sales resulted in a 120 percent profit increase over the preceding level, while the sales increase that followed resulted in a 65 percent profit increase over the preceding level. The effects of leverage diminish as the sales increase above the break-even level because the bases to which increases in profits are compared get progressively larger.

Leverage, of course, works both ways. It will be noted that a drop in sales from $200,000 to $100,000, representing a 50 percent decrease, resulted in a tripling of the loss.

One important conclusion from this to the analyst is that enterprises operating near their break-even point will have relatively larger percentage changes of profits or losses for a given change in volume. On the upside, the volatility will, of course, be desirable. On the downside, however, it can result in adverse results that are significantly worse than those indicated by changes in sales volume alone.

Another aspect is operating *potential,* sometimes erroneously referred to as leverage, which derives from a high level of sales accompanied by very low profit margins. The potential here, of course, is the room for improvements in profit margins. Even relatively slight improvements in profit margins, applied on a large sales level, can result in dramatic changes in profits. Thus, the popular reference to a semblance of leverage for what is really a potential for improvement.

Another aspect of the same *potential* occurs when the sales volume *per share* is large. Obviously an improvement in profitability will be translated into larger earnings per share improvements.

The Significance of the Variable-Cost Percentage

The volatility of profits is also dependent on the variable-cost percentage. The low-cost enterprise will achieve higher profits for a given increment in volume once break-even operations are reached than will the high variable-cost enterprise.

ILLUSTRATION 3.   Company A has fixed costs of $700,000 and a variable cost equal to 30 percent of sales. Company B has fixed costs of $300,000 and variable costs equal to 70 percent of sales. Assume that both companies have now reached sales of $1,000,000 and are, consequently, at break even. A $100,000 increment in sales will result in a profit of $70,000 for Company A and only in a profit of $30,000 for Company B. Company A has not only greater operating leverage but can, as a result, afford to incur greater risks in going after the extra $100,000 in sales than can Company B.

From the above example it is evident that the *level* of the break-even point is not the only criterion of risk assessment but that the analyst must also pay attention to the variable-cost ratio.

The Significance of the Fixed-Cost Level

Given a certain variable-cost percentage, the higher the fixed costs, the higher the break-even point of an enterprise. In the absence of change in other factors, a given percentage change in fixed costs will result in an equal percentage change in the break-even point. This can be illustrated as follows:

First break-even situation

Sales		$100,000
Variable expenses	$60,000	
Fixed costs	40,000	100,000
Profit		–0–

Second break-even situation—20 percent increase in fixed costs

Sales (increase of 20%)		$120,000
Variable expenses (60%)	$72,000	
Fixed costs ($40,000 + 20%)	48,000	120,000
		–0–

Thus, a fixed cost increase of 20 percent, with the variable-cost ratio remaining unchanged, resulted in a 20 percent increase in the break-even point.

An increase in the break-even point of an enterprise generally increases operational risk. It means that the enterprise is dependent on a higher volume of sales in order to break even. Looked at another way, it means that the enterprise is more vulnerable to economic downturns as compared to its situation with a lower break-even point. The substantial acquisition of the large-capacity Boeing 747 aircraft by the airlines provides an example of the effects of high break-even points. While these large aircraft lowered the variable cost per passenger, they relied also on a projected increase in the number of passengers. When this failed to materialize, the airlines' profit margins deteriorated swiftly with many of them going into the red. There are other repercussions to high levels of fixed costs. For example, a higher break-even point may mean that the enterprise has less freedom of action in fields such as labor relations. A high level of fixed costs makes strikes more expensive and subjects the enterprise to added pressure to submit to higher wage demands.

Often, added fixed costs in the form of automatic machinery are incurred in order to save variable costs, such as labor, and to improve efficiency. That can be very profitable in times of reasonably good demand. In times of low demand, however, the higher level of fixed costs sets in motion the process of reverse operational leverage discussed above, with attendant rapidly shrinking profits or even growing losses. High fixed costs reduce an enterprise's ability to protect its profits in the face of shrinking sales volume.

Investments in fixed assets, particularly in sophisticated machinery, can bring about increases in fixed costs far beyond the cost of maintaining and replacing the equipment. The skills required to operate such equipment are quite specialized and require skilled personnel which the enterprise may be reluctant to dismiss for fear of not being able to replace them when business turns up again. This converts what should be variable costs into de facto fixed costs.

While fixed costs are incurred in order to increase capacity or to decrease variable costs, it is often advisable to cut fixed costs in order to reduce the risks associated with a high break-even point. Thus, a company may reduce fixed costs by switching from a salaried sales force to one compensated by commissions based on sales. It can avoid added fixed costs by adding work shifts, buying ready-made parts, subcontracting work, or discontinuing the least profitable product lines.

In evaluating profit performance, past and future, of an enterprise, the analyst must always keep in mind the effect that the level of fixed costs can have on operating results under a variety of business conditions. Moreover, in projecting future results, the analyst must bear in mind that any given level of fixed costs is valid only up to the limits of practical capacity within a range of product mixes. Beyond such a point, a profit projection must take into consideration not only the increased levels of fixed costs required but also the financial resources that an expansion will require as well as the cost and sources of the funds that will be needed.

The Importance of the Contribution Margin

The analyst must be alert to the absolute size of an enterprise's contribution margin because operating leverage is importantly dependent on it. He must, moreover, be aware of the factors that can change this margin, that is, changes in variable costs as well as changes in selling prices.

While we have focused on the individual factors that affect costs, revenues, and profitability, in practice, changes result from a combination of factors. Projected increases in sales volume will increase profits only if costs, both fixed and variable, are controlled and kept within projected limits. Break-even analysis assumes that efficiency remains constant. However, experience teaches us that cost controls are more lax in times of prosperity than they are in times of recession. Thus, the analyst cannot assume constant efficiency any more than he or she can assume a constant product mix. The latter is also an important variable that must be watched by the analyst. Questions of why an enterprise realized lower profits on a higher volume of sales can often be explained, at least in part, by reference to changes in sales mix.

In spite of its important limitations, the break-even approach is an important tool of analysis to the financial analyst.

Its ability to aid the external analyst in performance evaluation and in profit projection makes its use worthwhile to him or her in spite of the laborious work that it often entails and the fragmentary and scarce amounts of information on which, of necessity, it must be based.

ANALYSIS OF THE RELATIONSHIP BETWEEN SALES, ACCOUNTS RECEIVABLE, AND INVENTORIES

The analysis of the relationship between sales and accounts receivable and sales and inventories holds important clues to the evaluation of contemporary results of operations as well as important implications regarding future results.[3]

Accounts Receivable   We have discussed the relationship between accounts receivable and sales in Chapter 16 in the context of short-term liquidity, i.e., in the assessment of the quality (collectibility) of the receivables and their liquidity (the speed with which they are collected).

Another dimension is the relationship between sales and accounts receivable in the context of evaluating the reliability and quality of reported

---

[3] These analytical tools were developed and refined by Thornton L. O'Glove, author of the "Quality of Earnings Report," which is the source of the two illustrations that follow. For an excellent discussion of these tools as well as further examples, see Thornton L. O'Glove, *Quality of Earnings: The Investor's Guide to How Much Money a Company is Really Making* (New York: The Free Press, 1987).

earnings. If accounts receivable grow at a rate in excess of that of sales this abnormal relationship requires close investigation into its reasons. The possibility exists that present sales have been made, by means of various extraordinary incentives and/or by the extension of generous credit terms, at the expense of future sales. Such conditions may mean that present sales have borrowed from the future and a sales slowdown is possible. Such conditions can also lead to difficulties in receivable collections.

ILLUSTRATION 4.   The following table shows the relationship of sales and accounts receivable of a toy company during successive quarters:

($ in thousands)

Three months ended	3/29/x6	3/30/x5	4/29/x4	4/30/x3	5/1/x2
Net sales	$199,128	$227,449	$175,346	$197,634	$290,388
percent change		−12.4%	29.7%	−11.3%	−31.9%
Accounts receivable	$271,446	$224,952	$190,217	$276,110	$328,332
percent change		20.6%	18.2%	−31.1%	−15.9%

In the quarter ended 3/29/x6, sales declined by 12.4 percent whereas accounts receivable increased by 20.6 percent, an imbalance that contrasts with the relationships prevailing in preceding quarters. This condition warrants further exploration and analysis.

Inventories   We have discussed the relationship of inventories to cost of goods sold in Chapter 16 as part of our consideration of short-term liquidity. Inventory turnover is an important measure of inventory quality, and as seen in Chapter 19, of asset utilization. The analysis of inventory components holds important clues to future sales as well as to operating activity. Thus, for example, when an increase in the finished goods component is accompanied by a decrease in raw materials and/or work-in-process, a slowdown in production is indicated.

ILLUSTRATION 5.   The following is a tabulation of the sales and the inventory components of Burroughs Corporation for the quarters indicated.

($ in thousands)

Three months ended	3/31/x6	3/31/x5	3/31/x4	3/31/x3	3/31/x2
Net sales revenues	$ 762.7	$ 793.9	$ 689.8	$ 559.0	$ 560.0
Inventories:					
Finished equipment and supplies	$ 907.1	$ 830.6	$ 631.6	$ 677.9	$ 699.9
Work-in-process and raw materials	609.0	664.7	561.2	467.7	379.2
Total inventories	$1,516.1	$1,495.3	$1,192.8	$1,145.6	$1,079.1

This tabulation indicates that during the last two quarters finished goods inventories increased while work in process and raw materials declined, foreshadowing a possible production slowdown. An increase of inventories (especially the finished goods component) in the face of a decline in sales may also be indicative of a failure of sales to keep up with production—another reason for a future slowdown in production.

ADDITIONAL CONSIDERATIONS IN THE ANALYSIS OF COST OF SALES

Gross margin analysis focuses on changes in costs, prices, and volume. Break-even analysis, in turn, focuses on the behavior of costs in relation to sales volume and on management's ability to control costs in the face of rising and falling revenues. The effectiveness of these and other methods of cost analysis depends on the degree of data availability as well as on an understanding of the accounting principles that have been applied.

The ability of the analyst to make the rough approximations that are necessary to separate costs into fixed and variable components depends on the amount of detail available. Disclosure of major cost components such as materials, labor, and various overhead cost categories can be helpful. The more detailed the breakdowns of expense categories, the more likely is the analyst to be able to construct meaningful break-even estimates.

In the evaluation of the cost of sales and the gross margin, and particularly in its comparison with those of other enterprises, the analyst must pay close attention to distortions that may arise from the utilization of a variety of accounting principles. While this is true of all items of cost, attention must be directed particularly to inventories and to depreciation accounting. These two areas, considered in detail in Chapters 6 and 10, merit special attention not only because they represent costs that are usually substantial in amount but also because of the proliferation of alternative principles that may be employed in accounting for them.

DEPRECIATION

Depreciation is an important cost element particularly in manufacturing and service enterprises. It is mostly fixed in nature because it is computed on the basis of elapsed time. However, if its computation is based on production activity, the result is a variable cost.

Because depreciation is computed in most cases on the basis of time elapsed, the ratio of depreciation expense to income is not a particularly meaningful or instructive relationship. In the evaluation of depreciation expense, the ratio of depreciation to gross plant and equipment is more meaningful. The ratio is computed as follows:

$$\frac{\text{Depreciation expense}}{\text{Assets subject to depreciation}}$$

This ratio can, of course, be computed by major categories of assets. The basic purpose is to enable the analyst to detect changes in the composite rate of depreciation used by an enterprise as a means of evaluating its adequacy and of detecting attempts at income smoothing. The computation of average age of assets in use was covered in Chapter 6.

AMORTIZATION OF SPECIAL TOOLS AND SIMILAR COSTS

The importance of the cost of special tools, dies, jigs, patterns, and molds varies from industry to industry. It is of considerable importance, for example, in the auto industry where special tool costs are associated with frequent style and design changes. The rate of amortization of such costs can have an important effect on reported income and is important to the analyst in an assessment of that income as well as in its comparison with that of other entities within an industry. The ratios that can be used to analyze changes in the deferral and amortization policies of such costs are varied and focus on their relationship to sales and other classes of assets.

The yearly expenditure for special tools can be related to and expressed as a percentage of (1) sales and (2) net property and equipment.

The yearly amortization of special tools can be related to (1) sales, (2) unamortized special tools, and (3) net property and equipment.

A comparison of the yearly trend in these relationships can be very helpful in an analysis of the consistency of income reporting of a single enterprise. The comparison can be extended further to an evaluation of the earnings of two or more enterprises within the same industry. This approach is indicative of the type of analysis which various elements of cost lend themselves to.

MAINTENANCE AND REPAIRS COSTS

Maintenance and repairs costs vary in significance with the amount invested in plant and equipment as well as with the level of productive activity. They have an effect on the cost of goods sold as well as on other elements of cost. Since maintenance and repairs contain elements of both fixed and variable costs, they cannot vary directly with sales. Thus, the ratio of repairs and maintenance costs to sales, while instructive to compare from year to year or among enterprises, must be interpreted with care. To the extent that the analyst can determine the fixed and the variable portions of maintenance and repairs costs, the interpretation of their relationship to periodic sales will be more valid.

Repairs and maintenance are, to a significant extent, discretionary costs. That is, the level of expense can, within limits, be regulated by management for a variety of reasons including those aimed at the improvement of reported income or at the preservation of liquid resources. Certain types of repairs cannot, of course, be postponed without resulting breakdowns in productive equipment. But many types of preventive repairs and particularly maintenance can be postponed or skimped on with results whose effects lie mainly in the future. Thus, the level of repairs and maintenance costs both in relation to sales and to plant and equipment is of interest to the analyst. It has, of course, a bearing on the quality of income, a subject that we shall consider in the next chapter.

The level of repairs and maintenance costs is also important in the evaluation of depreciation expense. Useful lives of assets are estimated by the use of many assumptions including those relating to the upkeep and maintenance of the assets. If, for instance, there is a deterioration in the usual or assumed level of repairs and maintenance, the useful life of the asset will, in all probability, be shortened. That may, in turn, require an upward revision in the depreciation expense or else income will be overstated.

OTHER COSTS AND EXPENSES—GENERAL

Most, although not all, cost and expense items found in the income statement have some identifiable or measurable relationship to sales or revenues. This is so because sales are the major measure of activity in an enterprise except in instances when production and sales are significantly out of phase.

Two analytical tools whose usefulness is based, in part, on the relationship that exists between sales and most costs and expenses should be noted here:

1. The *common-size income statement* expresses each cost and expense item in terms of its percentage relationship to net sales. This relationship of costs and expenses to sales can then be traced over a number of periods or compared with the experience of other enterprises in the same industry. The analysis of Campbell Soup Company (see Chapter 23) contains an illustration of a common-size income statement covering a number of years.

2. The *index number analysis of the income statement* expresses each item in the income statement in terms of an index number related to a base year. In this manner, relative changes of income statement items over time can be traced and their significance assessed. Expense item

changes can thus be compared to changes in sales and to changes in related expense or revenue items. Moreover, by use of common-size balance sheets, percentage changes in income statement items can be related to changes in assets and liabilities. For example, a given change in sales would normally justify a commensurate change in inventories and in accounts receivable. Chapter 23 contains an illustration of an index number analysis.

Selling Expenses

The analysis of selling costs has two main objectives:

1. The evaluation over time of the relationship between sales and the costs needed to bring them about.
2. An evaluation of the trend and the productivity of future-directed selling costs.

The importance of selling costs in relation to sales varies from industry to industry and from enterprise to enterprise. In some enterprises, selling costs take the form of commissions and are, consequently, highly variable in nature, while in others, they contain important elements of fixed costs.

After allowing for the fixed and variable components of the selling expenses, the best way to analyze them is to relate them to sales. The more detailed the breakdown of the selling expense components is—the more meaningful and penetrating can such analysis be. Exhibit 21–4 presents an example of such an analysis.

Analysis of Exhibit 21–4 indicates that for the entire period selling costs have been rising faster than sales and that in year 4 they took 5.6 percent more of the sales dollar than they did in year 1. In this period, salesmen's salaries increased by 1.0 percent of sales, advertising by 3.6 percent of sales, and branch expenses by 2.2 percent of sales. The drop in delivery expense may possibly be accounted for by the offsetting increase in freight costs.

A careful analysis should be made of advertising costs in order to determine to what extent the increase is due to the promotion of new products or the development of new territories that will benefit the future.

When selling expenses as a percentage of sales show an increase, it is instructive to focus on the selling expense increase that accompanies a given increase in sales. It can be expected that beyond a certain level, greater sales resistance is encountered in effecting additional sales. That sales resistance or the development of more remote territories may involve additional cost. Thus, it is important to know what the percentage of selling expense to sales is or to new sales as opposed to old ones. This may have, of course, implications on the projection of future profitability.

Exhibit 21–4

SELLALL CORPORATION
Comparative Statement of Selling Expenses
(in thousands)

	Year 4		Year 3		Year 2		Year 1	
Sales	$1,269		$935		$833		$791	
Trend percentage ..		160.0%		118.0%		105.0%		100.0%
Selling expenses (percent are of sales):								
Advertising ...	$ 84	6.6	$ 34	3.6	$ 28	3.4	$ 24	3.0
District branch expenses* ...	80	6.3	41	4.4	38	4.6	32	4.1
Delivery expense (own trucks)	20	1.6	15	1.6	19	2.3	22	2.8
Freight-out ...	21	1.7	9	1.0	11	1.3	8	1.0
Salesmen's salary expense	111	8.7	76	8.1	68	8.1	61	7.7
Salesmen's travel expense	35	2.8	20	2.1	18	2.2	26	3.3
Miscellaneous selling expense	9	0.7	9	1.0	8	0.9	7	0.9
Total	$ 360	28.4%	$204	21.8%	$190	22.8%	$180	22.8%

* Includes rent, regional advertising, etc.

If an enterprise can make additional sales only by increasing selling expenses, its profitability may suffer. Offsetting factors, such as those related to break-even operations or to economies of scale, must also be considered.

BAD DEBT EXPENSES

These expenses are often regarded as a cost of marketing. Since the size of the expense is importantly tied to the size of "allowance for doubtful accounts," it is best evaluated in terms of the relationship between that allowance and gross accounts receivable. The following analysis of the allowance for doubtful accounts of a toy company is an example of such an evaluation:

	Fiscal year 3—quarter ending		
	Aug. 1, year 2	*May 2, year 2*	*Jan. 31, year 2*
Allowance for doubtful accounts (in thousands) ..	$ 13,500	$ 15,600	$ 19,200
Gross receivables (in thousands)	343,319	223,585	179,791
Allowance as percent of gross receivables	3.93%	6.98%	10.68%

	Fiscal year 2—quarter ending		
	Aug. 2, year 1	*May 3, year 1*	*Feb. 2, year 1*
Allowance for doubtful accounts (in thousands) ..	$ 16,600	$ 15,000	$ 12,200
Gross receivables (in thousands)	331,295	215,660	172,427
Allowance as percent of gross receivables	5.01%	6.96%	7.07%

It is noteworthy that there was a significant decline in the company's allowance for doubtful accounts in relation to gross receivables in fiscal year 3 quarters as compared to similar quarters in the preceding year. The reasons can be varied, including improvement in the collectibility of receivables or inadequate provisions that result in understated bad debt expense. This analysis certainly calls for further investigation by the analyst.

Future-Directed Marketing Costs

Certain categories of sales promotion costs, particularly advertising, result in benefits that extend beyond the period in which they were incurred. The measurement of such benefits is difficult if not impossible, but it is a reasonable assumption that there is a relationship between the level of expenditures for advertising and promotion and the sales level, present and future.

Since expenditures for advertising and other forms of promotion are discretionary in nature, the analyst must carefully follow the year-to-year trend in these expenditures. Not only does the level of such expenditures have a bearing on future sales estimates, but it also indicates whether management is attempting to "manage" reported earnings. The effect of discretionary costs on the "quality" of earnings reported will be the subject of further discussion in the chapter that follows.

GENERAL, ADMINISTRATION, FINANCIAL, AND OTHER EXPENSES

Most costs in this category tend to be fixed in nature. This is largely true of administrative costs because such costs include significant amounts of salaries and occupancy expenditures. However, there may be some "creep" or tendency for increases in this category, and this is particularly true in prosperous times. Thus, in analyzing this category of expense, the analyst should pay attention to both the trend of administrative costs as well as to the percentage of total sales that they consume.

Financial Costs

Financial costs are, except for interest on short-term indebtedness, fixed in nature. Moreover, unless replaced by equity capital, most borrowed funds are usually refinanced. This is because of the long-term nature of most interest-bearing obligations. Included in these costs are the amortization of bond premium and discount as well as of debt issue expenses. A good check on an enterprise's cost of borrowed money as well as credit standing is the calculation of the average effective interest rate paid. This rate is computed as follows:

$$\frac{\text{Total interest cost}}{\text{Average total indebtedness subject to interest}}$$

Quaker Oats (Appendix to Chapter 23) average interest rate on liabilities subject to interest can be computed as follows for 1991 (dollars in millions):

$$\frac{\text{Interest incurred}}{\text{Liabilities subject to interest}} = \frac{104^{(a)}}{815^{(b)}} = \underline{\underline{12.8\%}}$$

[a] Total interest costs (before deduction for interest capitalized)—item $\boxed{156}$

[b] Short-term debt $\boxed{147}$	$ 81
Current portion of long-term debt $\boxed{148}$	33
Long-term debt $\boxed{148}$	701
Total liabilities subject to interest ($ millions)	$815

The average effective interest rate paid can be compared over the years or compared to that of other enterprises. It is also significant in that it sheds light on the credit standing of the enterprise.

Quaker Oats has a good discussion of debt in the "Liquidity and Capital Resources" section of its MDA (item $\boxed{142}$) as well as disclosure about weighted average interest rates on various debt categories $\boxed{147}$.

A measure of sensitivity to interest changes is obtained by determining the portion of debt that is tied to the prime rate. In periods of rising interest rates, a significant amount of debt tied to the prime rate exposes an enterprise to sharply escalating interest costs. Conversely, falling interest rates are a beneficial factor to such an enterprise.

"Other" Expenses

"Other" expenses are, of course, a nondescript category. The total amount in this category should normally be rather immaterial in relation to other costs. Otherwise, it can obscure substantial costs that, if revealed, may provide significant information about the enterprise's current and future operations. Nonrecurring elements may also be included in the "other expense" category, and this may add to the significance of this category to the analyst.

The analyst must also be alert to the tendency to offset "other" expenses against "other" income. Here, too, the major problem is one of concealment of important information and data. Here it is important that details of the major items comprising the offset amount be given or determined.

OTHER INCOME

Miscellaneous income items that are small in amount are usually of no significance to the analyst. However, since "other income" may include returns from various investments, it may contain information about new ventures and data regarding investments that are not available elsewhere. Such investments may, of course, have future implications, positive or negative, that exceed by far in significance the amounts of current income that are involved.

INCOME TAXES

Income taxes represent basically a sharing of profits between an enterprise and the governmental authorities by which they are imposed. Since most enterprises with which this book is concerned are organized in corporate form, we shall focus primarily on corporate income taxes.

Income taxes are almost always significant in amount and normally can amount to a substantial portion of a corporation's income before taxes. For this reason, the analyst must pay careful attention to the impact that income taxes have on net income.

Except for a lower rate on a first modest amount of income (e.g., $100,000), corporate income is taxed at a rate determined by law (presently 34 percent). Differences in the timing of recognition of income or expense items as between taxable income and book income should not influence the effective tax rate because of the practice of interperiod income tax allocation that aims to match the tax expense with the book income regardless of when the tax is paid. Income tax allocation was discussed in Chapter 11.

The relationship between the tax accrual and the pre-tax income, otherwise known as the effective tax rate or tax ratio, will, however, be influenced by permanent tax differences.[4] The nature of and reasons for these differences were also discussed in Chapter 11.

The effective tax rate or tax ratio is computed as follows:

$$\frac{\text{Income tax expense for period}}{\text{Income before income taxes}}$$

For Quaker Oats (Appendix to Chapter 23) the effective tax rate for 1991 is best computed as follows:

$$\frac{175.7^{(a)}}{411.5^{(b)}} = 42.7\%$$

(a) Provision for income taxes—item $\boxed{8}$.
(b) Income from continuing operations before income taxes—item $\boxed{7}$.

The 42.7 percent effective tax rate corresponds to that computed by the company (item $\boxed{\text{158c}}$) and is widely used.

It should be noted, however, that the above computation uses "income from continuing operations" rather than net income.

Thus, if it is desired to compute the effective tax rate incurred by the company on all items of income and loss during the period, including discontinued operations and other items, then a different computation is required which for QO is as follows for 1991:

Income (loss)	Before tax	Related tax	After tax
Income from continuing operations before income taxes and other items	$411.5 $\boxed{7}$	$175.7 $\boxed{8}$	$235.8 $\boxed{9}$
Loss from discontinued operations— ..	(50)	(20) $\boxed{144}$*	(30) $\boxed{10}$
Net income	$361.5*	$155.7*	$205.8 $\boxed{11}$

* Derived amount.

The effective tax rate based on all items included in net income now becomes

$$\frac{\$155.7}{\$361.5} = 43 \text{ percent}$$

---

[4] This term includes differences due to state and local taxes, foreign tax rate differentials, various tax credits, untaxed income, nonallowed expenses, etc.

Quaker Oats presents an unusual case of preferred dividends [12] resulting in a tax benefit of undisclosed amount. This kind of tax effect bypassing the determination of net income (like similar tax effects relating to stock options and found in equity accounts), must be considered when reconciling all tax-related accounts as a means of understanding a company's tax picture and of reconciling the amount of taxes paid (see further discussion below).

For purposes of evaluation of the level of earnings, the trend of earnings, as well as for net income projection, the analyst must know the reasons why the effective tax rate deviated from the normal or the expected. Income taxes are such an important element of cost that even relatively small changes in the effective tax rate can result in important changes in net income. Moreover, without an understanding of the factors that cause changes in the effective tax rate of a company, the analyst is missing an important element required in forecasting future net income.

FRR No. 1 Section 204 contains rules in which the SEC expanded significantly the required analytical disclosures concerning current and deferred income taxes. Most of these disclosure requirements were adapted by *SFAS 109,* which deals with the accounting for income taxes. Chapter 11 included a description of these as well as a discussion of their significance to the analyst.

The analysis of these and other aspects of income tax disclosures are important to the analyst and will be discussed and illustrated in the section that follows.

ANALYSIS OF INCOME TAX DISCLOSURES

Objectives of the Analysis

The analysis of income tax disclosures may be undertaken with specific or specialized objectives in mind. However, the more general objectives of such an analysis are:

- To understand the tax accounting of the enterprise and its impact on income, on related assets and liabilities, as well as on the sources and uses of cash.
- To judge the adequacy of the enterprise's tax disclosure.
- To provide a basis for assessing the effect of taxes on future income and cash flows.
- To provide a basis for informed queries to be put to management in order to clear up questions arising during the analysis.
- To identify unusual gains or losses not otherwise disclosed but whose tax effect is highlighted or revealed during analysis.
- To evaluate the effectiveness of tax management by the enterprise.

Analytical Steps and Techniques

A. Establish a T-account for each tax-related account in the balance sheet and income statement.

A current tax liability and/or a current receivable for overpayment or tax refunds will almost always be found. In addition, there will be one or two deferred tax accounts (one current and one noncurrent) in the balance sheet.

Care must be taken to identify the income taxes (current and possibly deferred) that relate to each separate section of the income statement: (1) continuing operations, (2) discontinued operations, (3) extraordinary items, and (4) cumulative effect of change(s) in accounting principles. As discussed above, income tax effects can be found in items outside the income statement (e.g., QO's Preferred Dividend tax benefit [72]).

The analyst should be aware that information on income tax effects can be found in parenthetical notes to financial statements, in schedules such as those reconciling owner's equity, in sections containing management discussion, and in footnotes in general and particularly in those relating to income taxes.

B. A good next step is to attempt to reconstruct as best as is possible the summary entry by means of which the tax expense for the period was booked. It is easier to do this if the entry is divided into the current and the deferred portions of the tax expense.

C. After the opening and closing balances of all tax-related balance sheet T-accounts have been entered, the tax expense entries and income statement should be posted to the relevant tax-related accounts and data should be used to aid in as complete a reconstruction of these accounts as is possible.

The changes in the deferred tax accounts on the balance sheet should generally agree with the deferred tax expense for the period as shown in the income statement or in related footnotes. Noncash adjustments to net income and other information in the statement of cash flows (SCF) often can provide added insights. If all attempts at reconciliation fail, it is possible that a deferred tax account is buried or combined under some other caption in the balance sheet, or that the company made some undisclosed entries for purposes of correcting errors or for other reasons. In such a situation, the analyst can only identify the needed balancing amount and label it as such, realizing that the correctness of any conclusions regarding balancing (plugged) amounts in the reconciliation is subject to the validity of assumptions that have been made.

With regard to those deferred tax accounts which have not been fully reconciled, amounts needed to reconcile them should be

transferred to the Current Taxes Payable account or the Tax Refunds Receivable account.

D. After using tax law, knowledge of tax accounting, and all the disclosures in the financial statements, as well as the assumptions required in the situation, the tax T-accounts should be fully reconstructed. At this point, the amount of taxes paid during the year is
arrived at as a "plug" to the current Taxes Payable account. Conversely a credit "plug" represents a tax refund received.

It should be noted that the quality of the analysis will depend on
the quality of disclosure found in the financial statements. A lack
of good disclosure will require more analytical ingenuity such as
the combining of certain accounts (such as current tax receivable
and payable accounts). The analyst must also be aware that the
acquisition or disposition of businesses during a period may result
in related additions or deductions to balance sheet tax accounts.
Thus, for example, the acquisition of a company may result in the
assumption of its tax liabilities.

Illustration of Income Tax Analysis of Quaker Oats Company

Let us first analyze the changes in QO's 1991 income tax accounts. The
first step is to draw a T-account for each tax-related balance sheet account
and one for each income tax expense and tax effect account in the 1991
income statement. (All number references are to QO financial statements
in Appendix 23.)

In the balance sheet we find the income tax payable account and a
deferred income taxes—noncurrent account.

In the income statement we see the regular "provision for income
taxes" $\boxed{8}$ and below it all other items are shown (as they should be) net
of tax. We find the tax effect of the loss on discontinued operations $\boxed{10}$
in Note 2 $\boxed{144}$.

Neither the tax effect nor the reasons for the tax deductability of preferred dividends $\boxed{12}$ are disclosed. Assuming the marginal 34 percent tax
rate we can compute the tax effect as follows:

$$\text{Let } X = \text{preferred dividends before income tax}$$
$$X\,(1 - 34\%) = 4.3 \; \boxed{12}$$
$$X = 6.5$$

then,

$$6.5 - \text{tax effect} = 4.3$$
$$\text{Tax effect} = \$2.2$$

The *second* step is to enter the opening and ending balances in these
accounts. Tax-related accounts in the income statements do not have
opening balances and their ending balances are closed via the income

Income Tax Payable 75			
		36.3	BB
(b)	20.0	161.4	(a)
(d)	24.7	2.2	(c)
assumed paid	110.1		
		45.1	EB

Deferred Income Tax 81			
		327.7	BB
		14.3	(a)
		24.7	(d)
		366.7	EB

Income Tax Expense 8	
(a) 175.7	

Tax Effect— Discontinued Operations 144	
	20.0 (b)

Tax Effect—Preferred Dividends	
(c) 2.2	

statement to retained earnings. In the case of some analyses the opening balances may have to be derived by using changes shown in the Statement of Cash Flows.

The *third* step is to enter the tax-related activity during the year (here, 1991) into the T-accounts based on all available information and footnotes, particularly the tax footnote. This can be done through journal entries which are posted to the relevant T-accounts.

The total tax expense (including the tax effect of items shown net of tax) can be combined but it is generally easier to enter them separately as will be illustrated here:

(a) Income Tax Expense 158 .... 175.7
     Income Tax Payable 161.4 158
     Deferred Income Tax 14.3 158

(b) Income Tax Payable 20.0
     Tax Effect-Disc. Operation 20.0 144

(c) Tax Effect-Preferred Dividends 2.2*
     Income Tax Payable 2.2
  * See preceding computation.

Having entered in the T-accounts all tax-related transactions, we must now determine whether these entries have in fact fully explained the changes in all related accounts except the Tax Payable account.

In this case we find that the change in the Deferred Income Taxes account has not been fully explained and this requires an entry as follows:

(d) Income Tax Payable 24.7
         Deferred Income Tax ....   24.7 Plug

To transfer unexplained difference to the Taxes Payable account.

The best estimate of the taxes *paid* during the period can only be made after the changes in the balances of all tax-related accounts, except the Taxes Payable (or Taxes Receivable) account, have been fully accounted for. After this has been done—as in our example here—the amount of taxes paid (or received as a refund) is determined as a balancing figure (plug) in the Taxes Payable account. In our example the plug of $110.1 is on the debit side, indicating a tax payment. The amount of tax paid (or received as a refund) should be reconciled, as far as disclosure permits, to the amount of tax payments disclosed in the Statement of Cash Flows.

Quaker Oats discloses income taxes paid in 1991 of $88.7 million [159]. This is considerably less than the $110.1 million suggested by the analysis above. Complete confidence in our understanding of the company's tax accounting would require that management explain the main reasons for the discrepancy.

Explaining the Tax Rate

At another level of analysis we can explain how Quaker Oats, with a 1991 pre-tax income from continuing operations of $411.5 (all dollar amounts in millions) provided $175.7 in tax expense of which $161.4 are current federal income taxes:

		Item source	$ Millions
Expected federal income tax at 34%	$411.5 × 0.34	[7]	$140
Add: State tax net of federal benefit	$411.5 × 0.041	[158c]	16.9
			156.9
Add permanent differences [158c]			
Repatriation of foreign earnings	4.3		
Non-U.S. tax rate differential	8.2		
Miscellaneous (rounded)	6.3		18.8
			175.7
Less total deferred taxes			14.3
Total current federal, non-U.S. and state taxes		[158]	161.4

Focus on Pre-Tax Earnings

While the focus on net income and on earnings per share requires a thorough analysis of changes in the effective tax rate, it must be borne in mind that many analysts attach great importance to pre-tax earnings. This is due to the greater importance that is assigned to pre-tax operating results, which require management skills of a higher order, as compared with changes due to variations in the effective tax rate over which, it is assumed, management has comparatively more limited control.

THE OPERATING RATIO

The operating ratio is yet another intermediate measure in the analysis of the income statement. It measures the relationship between all operating costs and net sales and is computed as follows:

$$\frac{\text{Cost of goods sold} + \text{Other operating expenses}}{\text{Net sales}}$$

The ratio is designed to enable a comparison within an enterprise or with enterprises of the proportion of the sales dollar absorbed by all operating costs. Only other income and expense items as well as interest and income taxes are excluded from operating expenses.

In effect, this ratio represents but an intermediate step in the common-size analysis of the income statement. It is, in and of itself, not of great analytical significance because it is a composite of many factors that require separate analysis. These factors comprise the analysis of gross margin and of other major expense categories discussed earlier. Thus, the operating ratio cannot be properly interpreted without a thorough analysis of the reasons accounting for variations in gross margin and for changes in selling, general, administrative, and other costs.

Operating Income is generally defined as income before interest and taxes. It focuses on operating efficiency (expense control) as opposed to considerations such as optimum financing and tax management.

NET INCOME RATIO

The net income ratio is the relationship between net income and total revenues and is computed as follows:

$$\frac{\text{Net income}}{\text{Total revenues}}$$

It represents the percentage of total revenue brought down to net income. In addition to its usefulness as an index of profitability, the net income ratio represents, as was seen in Chapter 19, a main component of the computation of the return on investment (ROI).

Exhibit 21–5

CAMPBELL SOUP COMPANY
Statement Accounting for Variation in Average Net Earnings
Three-Year Period 1986–1988 (Average)
Compared to Three-Year Period 1989–1991 (Average)
(in millions)

			Percentage increase
Items tending to increase net income:			
Increase in net sales:			
Net sales (1989–1991)	$6,027.3		
Net sales (1986–1988)	4,548.7	$1,478.6	32.5%
Deduct: Increase in costs of products sold:			
Cost of products sold (1989–1991)	$4,118.4		
Cost of products sold (1986–1988)	3,218.7	$ 899.7	28.0%
Net increase in gross margin		578.9	
Increase (decrease) in interest income:			
Interest income (1989–1991)	$ 27.3		
Interest income (1986–1988)	30.0	($2.7)	(9.0)%
Total items tending to increase net income		576.2	
Items tending to decrease net income:			
Increase in marketing and sales expenses:			
Marketing and sales expenses (1989–1991)	$ 918.5		
Marketing and sales expenses (1986–1988)	634.6	$ 283.9	44.7%
Increase in administrative expenses:			
Administrative expenses (1989–1991) .	$ 283.2		
Administrative expenses (1986–1988) .	214.1	$ 69.1	32.3%
Increase in R & D expenses:			
R & D expenses (1989–1991)	$ 52.6		
R & D expenses (1986–1988)	44.6	$ 8.0	17.9%
Increase in interest expenses:			
Interest expenses (1989–1991)	$ 107.3		
Interest expenses (1986–1988)	53.9	$ 53.4	99.1%
Increase in other expenses:*			
Other expenses (1989–1991)	$ 32.2		
Other expenses (1986–1988)	5.0	$ 27.2	544.0%
Increase in income tax expenses:			
Income tax (1989–1991)	$ 178.1		
Income tax (1986–1988)	160.5	$ 17.6	11.0%
Total items tending to decrease net income		459.2	

Change in net effect of equity in earnings of affiliates and minority interests (MI):			
Equity in earnings of affiliates and MI (1989–1991)	$ 2.7		
Equity in earnings of affiliates and MI (1986–1988)	3.6	($0.9)	(25.0)%
Net increase in net income:†			
Net income (1989–1991)	$ 367.0		
Net income (1986–1988)	250.9	$ 116.1	46.3%

* Including foreign exchange losses.
† Income before both divestitures, restructuring, and unusual charges; and cumulative effect of change in accounting for income taxes.

Statement Accounting for Variation in Net Income

In the analysis of year-to-year changes in net income, it is useful to separate the elements that contributed to an increase in net income from those that contributed to a decrease. A statement that does this and also indicates the percentage increase or decrease in these factors is the "statement accounting for variations in net income." Exhibit 21–5 presents such a statement for Campbell Soup based on its income statements included in Chapter 4, Appendix B, as well as on prior-year data taken from financial reports which are summarized as part of the comprehensive analysis of Campbell Soup in Chapter 23.

QUESTIONS

1. What are the most important elements in the analysis of gross profit?
2. What is the basic principle underlying break-even analysis? What are fixed costs? Variable costs? Semivariable costs?
3. Certain assumptions that underlie break-even computations are often referred to as simplifying assumptions. Name as many of these as you can.
4. In break-even computation, what is the *variable-cost percentage?* What is its relationship to the *contribution margin ratio?*
5. What alternatives to an increase in fixed costs can an enterprise consider when it approaches 100 percent of theoretical capacity?
6. What is operating leverage? Why do leverage and fixed costs go together? What are the analytical implications of operating leverage?
7. Of what analytical significance are *(a)* the break-even point and *(b)* the variable-cost ratio?
8. What is a useful measure of the adequacy of current provisions for depreciation?
9. To what factors can maintenance and repairs costs be meaningfully related?
10. What are the main objectives of an analysis of selling expenses?

11. How can bad debt expense be evaluated most meaningfully? To what can a decline in the allowance to doubtful accounts be attributed?
12. *a.* What is the tax ratio and how is it computed?
    b. What are the objectives of an analysis of income tax disclosures?

Chapter 22

THE EVALUATION AND PROJECTION OF EARNINGS

OBJECTIVES OF EARNINGS EVALUATION

In the preceding chapters, we examined the steps that have to be taken and the understanding that must be brought to bear on the analysis of the operating performance of an enterprise. This chapter will examine the additional considerations involved in the achievement of the major objectives of income statement analysis:

The evaluation of the quality of earnings.

Evaluation of the earnings level and trend.

The estimation of earning power.

The forecasting of earnings.

Monitoring performance and results.

EVALUATION OF THE QUALITY OF EARNINGS

The discussions through Part II of this book have pointed out that much of the accounting process of income determination involves a high degree of estimation. Chapters 10 and 11 on the analysis of the income statement have explained that the income of an enterprise, as measured by the accounting process, is not a specific amount but can vary depending on the assumptions used and the various principles applied. Complicating these measurements still further is the fact that numerous accounting periods can receive benefits from a single cash outlay and that it may take a number of periods before a transaction results in the collection of all amounts due. For that reason, creditors, in particular, are greatly interested in the cash equivalent of reported earnings (see also Chapter 13).

This distinction between accrual income and the related cash flows has led some of those uninitiated in the income determination process to doubt the validity of all accounting measurements. This, however, is an extreme and unwarranted position because, as any student of accounting should know, the concept of income is the result of a series of complex assumptions and conventions, and exists only as the creation and the approximation of this system of measurement. This system is always subject to reexamination and is, despite its shortcomings, still the most widely accepted method of income determination.

In examining the level of reported income of an enterprise, the analyst must determine the effect of the various assumptions and accounting principles used on that reported income. Beyond that he or she must be aware of the "accounting risk" as well as the "audit risk" to which these determinations are subject.

Over the years, and especially since the enactment of the Securities Acts of 1933 and 1934, and with improvement in the audit function in this country, the incidence of outright fraud and deliberate misrepresentation in financial statements has diminished markedly. But they have *not* been completely eliminated and probably never will. Nor can the analyst ever rule out the possibility of spectacular failures in the audit function. While each major audit failure tends to contribute to the improvement of regulation and of auditing, they have not prevented the recurrence of such failures as the security holders of McKesson & Robbins, of Seaboard Commercial Corporation, of H. L. Green, of Miami Window, of Yale Express, of BarChris Construction Company, of Continental Vending Company, of Mill Factors Corporation, of W. T. Grant, of Equity Funding Company, of Frigitemp, of ESM Government Securities, Drysdale Securities Corporation, Crazy Eddie Inc., Regina Company, and ZZZ Best Company, well know.

The analyst must always assess the vulnerability to failure and to irregularities of the company under analysis and the character and the propensities of its management, as a means of establishing the degree of risk that it will prove to be the exception to the general rule. (The audit process is discussed in Chapter 15.)

The evaluation of the earnings level and of the earnings trend is intimately tied in with the evaluation of management. The evaluation of the management group cannot be separated from the results that they have actually achieved. Whatever other factors may have to be considered, results over a period of time are the acid test of management's ability, and that ability is perhaps the most important intangible (i.e., unquantifiable) factor in the prediction of future results. The analyst must be alert to changes in the management group and must assess its depth, stability, and possible dependence on the talents of one or a few individuals.

The Concept of Earnings Quality

The concept of earnings quality arose out of a need to provide a basis of comparison among the earnings of different entities as well as from the need to recognize such differences in "quality" for valuation purposes. There is almost no general agreement on definitions of or on assumptions underlying this concept. The elements that comprise the "quality of earnings" can be classified as follows:

a. One type of factor that affects the quality of earnings is the accounting and computational discretion of management and that of the attesting accountants in choosing from among accepted alternative accounting principles. These choices can be liberal, that is, they can assume the most optimistic view of the future, or they can be conservative. Generally, the quality of conservatively determined earnings is higher because they are less likely to prove overstated in the light of future developments than those determined in a "liberal" fashion. They also minimize the possibility of earnings overstatement and avoid retrospective changes. LIFO inventory accounting in rising markets and accelerated depreciation methods are examples of conservative accounting methods. On the other hand, unwarranted or excessive conservatism, while contributing to the temporary "quality" of earnings, actually results in a lack of reporting integrity over the long run and cannot be considered as a desirable factor. Quite apart from the impact that these accounting choices have on the financial statements, they also hold important clues to management's propensities and attitudes.

b. The second type of factor affecting the quality of earnings is related to the degree to which adequate provision has been made for the maintenance of assets and for the maintenance and enhancement of present and future earning power. In most enterprises, there exists considerable managerial discretion over the size of income streams, and particularly over the reported amounts of costs and expenses. Discretionary types of expenses, such as repairs and maintenance, advertising, and research and development (R&D) costs can be varied for the sole purpose of managing the level of reported net income (or loss) rather than for legitimate operating or business reasons. Here, too, the analyst's task is to identify the results of management practices and to judge its motivations.

c. The third major factor affecting the quality of earnings is not primarily a result of discretionary actions of managements, although skillful management can modify its effects. It is the effect of cyclical and other economic forces on earnings, on the stability of their sources, and particularly on their variability. Variability of earnings is generally an undesirable characteristic, and, consequently, the higher the variability the lower the quality of these earnings.

The fairly broad tolerances within which generally accepted accounting principles (GAAP) can be applied have been discussed throughout this book. A consideration of other aspects that affect earnings quality follows.

Evaluation of Discretionary and Future-Directed Costs   Discretionary costs are outlays that managements can vary to some extent from period to period in order to conserve resources and/or to influence reported income. For this reason, they deserve the special attention of analysts who are particularly interested in knowing whether the level of expenses is in keeping with past trends and with present and future requirements.

Maintenance and Repairs   As was already discussed in the preceding chapter, management has considerable leeway in performing maintenance work and some discretion with respect to repairs. The analyst can relate these costs to the level of activity because they do logically vary with it. Two ratios are particularly useful in comparing the repair and maintenance levels from year to year:

$$\frac{\text{Repairs and maintenance}}{\text{Sales}}$$

This ratio relates the costs of repairs and maintenance to this most available measure of activity. In the absence of sharp inventory changes, sales are a good indicator of activity. If year-to-year inventory levels change appreciably, an adjustment may be needed whereby ending inventories at approximate selling prices are added to sales, and beginning inventories, similarly adjusted, are deducted from them.

The other ratio is:

$$\frac{\text{Repairs and maintenance}}{\text{Property, plant, and equipment (exclusive of land)}}\\ \text{net of accumulated depreciation}$$

It measures repair and maintenance costs in relation to the assets for which these costs are incurred. Depending on the amount of information available to the analyst, the ratio of repair and maintenance costs to specific categories of assets can be developed. It should be noted that substandard repairs and maintenance on assets may require revisions in the assumptions of useful lives for depreciation purposes.

The absolute trend in repair and maintenance costs from year to year can be expressed in terms of index numbers and compared to those of related accounts. The basic purpose of all these measurements is to determine whether the repair and maintenance programs of the enterprise have been kept at normal and necessary levels or whether they have been changed in a way that affects the quality of income and its projection into the future.

ILLUSTRATION 1.   A review of the level of maintenance and repair expense of Campbell Soup (based on data in Appendix 4B and Chapter 23) reveals the following relationships:

	1991	1990	1989
Maintenance and repairs to net sales	2.8%	2.9%	3.1%
Maintenance and repairs to property, plant, and equipment—net*	12.2%	13.0%	13.1%

* Omitting land and construction progress.

The decline in these ratios *may* require further analysis.

Advertising   Since a significant portion of advertising outlays has effects beyond the period in which it is incurred, the relationship between advertising outlays and short-term results is a tenuous one. This also means that managements can, in certain cases, cut advertising costs with no commensurate immediate effects on sales, although it can be assumed that over the longer term sales will suffer. Here again, year-to-year variations in the level of advertising expenses must be examined by the analyst with the objective of assessing their impact on future sales and consequently on the quality of reported earnings.

There are a number of ways of assessing the trend in advertising outlays. One is to convert them into trend percentages using a "normal" year as a base. These trend percentages can then be compared to the trend of sales and of gross and net profits. An alternative measure would be the ratio of

$$\frac{\text{Advertising expenses}}{\text{Sales}}$$

which, when compared over the years, would also indicate shifts in management policy.

ILLUSTRATION 2.   Review of the relationship of advertising expense to sales of Campbell Soup (Appendix 4B and analysis in Chapter 23) reveals that the percentage of advertising expenses to sales declined from 3.5 percent in 1990 to 3.1 percent in 1991. The analyst may want to inquire into the reasons for the longer-term decline because in 1986 this relationship was 4.1 percent.

The ratio of

$$\frac{\text{Advertising}}{\text{Total selling costs}}$$

must also be examined so as to detect shifts to and from advertising to other methods of sales promotion.

An analysis of advertising to sales ratios over several years will reveal the degree of dependence of an enterprise on this promotional strategy. Comparison of this ratio with that of other companies in the industry will reveal the degree of market acceptance of products and the relative promotional efforts needed to secure it.

Research and Development Costs   The significance and the potential value of R&D costs are among the most difficult elements of the financial statements to analyze and interpret. Yet they are important, not only because of their relative size but even more so because of their significance for the projection of future results.

R&D costs have gained an aura of glowing potential in security analysis far beyond that warranted by actual experience. Mentioned most frequently are some of the undeniably spectacular and successful commercial applications of industrial research in the post-World War II era in such fields as chemistry, electronics, photography, and biology. Not mentioned are the vast sums spent for endeavors labeled *research* which are expensed or written off while benefits from these fall far short of the original costs.

The analyst must pay careful attention to R&D costs and to the absence of such costs. In many enterprises, they represent substantial costs, much of them fixed in nature, and they can represent the key to future success or failure. We must first draw a careful distinction between what can be quantified in this area and, consequently, analyzed in the sense in which we consider analysis in this book, and what cannot be quantified and must, consequently, be evaluated in qualitative terms.

In the area of R&D costs, the qualitative element looms large and important. The definition of what constitutes "research" is subject to wide-ranging interpretations as well as to outright distortion. The label *research* is placed on activities ranging from those of a first-class scientific organization engaged in sophisticated pure and applied research down to superficial and routine product-and-market-testing activities.

Among the many factors to be considered in the evaluation of the quality of the research effort are the caliber of the research staff and organization, the eminence of its leadership, as well as the commercial results of their research efforts. This qualitative evaluation must accompany any other kinds of analysis. Finally, a distinction must be drawn between government- or outsider-sponsored research and company-directed research that is most closely identified with its own objectives. From the foregoing discussion it is clear that research cannot be evaluated on the basis of the amounts spent alone. Research outlays represent an expense or an investment depending on how they are applied. Far from guaranteeing results, they represent highly speculative ventures that depend on the application of extraordinary scientific as well as managerial skills for their success. Thus, spending on research cannot guarantee results and should not be equated with them.

Having considered the all-important qualitative factors on which an evaluation of R&D outlays depends, the analyst should attempt to determine as best he can how much of the current R&D outlays that have been expensed have future utility and potential.

From the point of view of the analyst, the "future potential" of R&D costs is a most important consideration. Research cost productivity can be measured by relating R&D outlays to:

1. Sales growth.
2. New product introductions.
3. Acquisition of plant and equipment (to exploit the results of research).
4. Profitability.

Another important aspect of R&D outlays is their discretionary nature. It is true that those enterprises that have established R&D departments impart a fixed nature to a segment of these costs. Nevertheless, they can be increased or curtailed at the discretion of managements, often with no immediate adverse effects on sales. Thus, from the point of view of assessing the quality of reported income, the analyst must evaluate year-to-year changes in R&D outlays. This can be done by means of trend percentage analysis as well as by means of analysis of ratios such as the ratio of

$$\frac{\text{R\&D outlays}}{\text{Sales}}$$

A careful comparison of outlays for R&D over the years will indicate to the analyst whether the effort is a sustained one or one that varies with the ups and downs of operating results. Moreover, "one shot" research efforts lack the predictability or quality of a sustained, well-organized longer-term research program.

Other Future-Directed Costs   In addition to advertising and R&D, there are other types of future-directed outlays. An example of such outlays are the costs of training operating, sales, and managerial talent. Although these outlays for the development of human resources are usually expensed in the year in which they are incurred, they may have future utility, and the analyst may want to recognize this in his or her evaluation of current earnings and of future prospects.

Balance Sheet Analysis as a Check on the Validity and Quality of Reported Earnings

The amounts at which the assets and liabilities of an enterprise are stated hold important clues to an assessment of both the validity as well as the quality of its earnings. Thus, the analysis of the balance sheet is an important complement to the other approaches of income analysis discussed in this chapter, and elsewhere in this book.

Importance of Carrying Amounts of Assets   The importance that we attach to the amounts at which assets are carried on the balance sheet is due to the fact that, with few exceptions such as cash, some investments, and land, the cost of most assets enters ultimately the cost stream of the income statement. Thus, we can state the following as a general proposition: Whenever assets are overstated, the cumulative income[1] is overstated because it has been relieved of charges needed to bring such assets down to realizable values.

It would appear that the converse of this proposition should also hold true; that is, that to the extent to which assets are understated, cumulative income is also understated. Two accounting conventions qualify this statement importantly. One is the convention of conservatism, already discussed in Chapter 3, which calls for the recognition of gains only as they are actually realized. Although there has been some movement away from a strict interpretation of this convention, in general most assets are carried at original cost even though their current market or realizable value is far in excess of that cost.

The other qualifying convention is that governing the accounting for business combinations. As was seen in the discussions in Chapter 9, the pooling of interests concept allows an acquiring company to carry forward the old book values of the assets of the acquired company even though such values may be far less than current market values or the consideration given for them. Thus, the analyst must be aware of the fact that such an accounting will allow the recording of profits, when the values of such understated assets are realized, which represents nothing more than the surfacing of such hitherto understated assets. Since such profits have, in effect, previously been bought and paid for, they cannot be considered as representing either the earning power of the enterprise or an index of the operating performance of its management.

Importance of Provisions and Liabilities   Continuing our analysis of the effect of balance sheet amounts on the measurement of income, we can enunciate the further proposition that an understatement of provisions and liabilities will result in an overstatement of cumulative income because the latter is relieved of charges required to bring the provision or the liabilities up to their proper amounts. Thus, for example, an understatement of the provision for taxes, for product warranties, or for pensions means that cumulative income is overstated.

Conversely, an overprovision for present and future liabilities or losses results in the understatement of income or in the overstatement of losses. As was seen in the discussion in Chapter 11, provisions for future costs and losses that are excessive in amount represent attempts to shift the

---

[1] The effect on any one period cannot be the subject of generalization.

burden of costs and expenses from future income statements to that of the present.

Bearing in mind the general propositions regarding the effect on income of the amounts at which assets and liabilities are carried in the balance sheet, the critical analysis and evaluation of such amounts represents an important check on the validity of reported income.

Balance Sheet Analysis and the Quality of Earnings   There is, however, a further dimension to this kind of analysis in that it also has a bearing on an evaluation of the quality of earnings. This approach is based on the fact that various degrees of risk attach to the probability of the future realization of different types of assets.

For example, the future realization of accounts receivable has generally a higher degree of probability than has the realization of, say, inventory or unrecovered tools and dies costs. Moreover, the future realization of inventory costs can, generally, be predicted with greater certainty than can the future realization of goodwill or of deferred start-up costs. The analysis of the assets carried in the balance sheet by risk class or risk category holds clues to and is an important measure of the quality of reported income. Stated another way, if the income determination process results in the deferral of outlays and costs which carry a high degree of risk that they may not prove realizable in the future, then that income is of a lower quality than income that does not involve the recording of such high-risk assets.

Effect of Valuation of Specific Assets on the Validity and Quality of Reported Income   In order to illustrate the importance of balance sheet analysis to an evaluation of reported income, let us now examine the effect of the valuation of specific assets on the validity and quality of that income.

Accounts Receivable   The validity of the sales figure depends on the proper valuation of the accounts receivable that result from it. This valuation must recognize the risk of default in payment as well as the time value of money. On the latter score, *APB Opinion 21* provides that if the receivable does not arise from transactions with customers or suppliers in the normal course of business under terms not exceeding a year, then, except for some other stated exceptions, it must be valued using the interest rate applicable to similar debt instruments. Thus, if the receivable bears an interest rate of 8 percent while similar receivables would, at the time, be expected to bear an interest rate of 12 percent, both the receivable and the sale from which it arose would be restated at the lower discounted amount.

The relative level of accounts receivable and its relationship to sales can hold clues to income quality. If an increase in accounts receivable represents merely a shifting of inventory from the company to its distributing middlemen because of aggressive sales promotion or costly incentives, then these sales accomplish nothing more than "borrowing from the future" and thus reduce earnings quality.

Inventories   Overstated inventories lead to overstated profits. Overstatements can occur due to errors in quantities, errors in costing and pricing, or errors in the valuation of work in process. The more technical the product and the more dependent the valuation is on internally developed cost records, the more vulnerable are the cost estimates to error and misstatement. The basic problem here arises when costs that should have been written off to expense are retained in the inventory accounts.

An understatement of inventories results from a charge-off to income of costs that possess future utility and that should be inventoried. Such an understatement of inventories results in the understatement of current income and the overstatement of future income.

Deferred Charges   Deferred charges such as deferred tooling or start-up and preoperating costs must be scrutinized carefully because their value depends, perhaps more than that of other assets, on estimates of future probabilities and developments. Experience has shown that often such estimates have proven overoptimistic or that they did not contain sufficient provisions for future contingencies. Thus, the risk of failure to attain expectations is relatively higher here than in the case of other assets.

The Effect of External Factors on the Quality of Earnings   The concept of earnings quality is so broad that it encompasses many additional factors that, in the eyes of analysts, can make earnings more reliable or more desirable.

The effect of changing price levels on the measurement of earnings was examined in Chapter 14. In times of rising price levels, the inclusion of "inventory profits" or the understatement of expenses such as depreciation lowers in effect the reliability of earnings and hence their quality.

The quality of foreign earnings is affected by factors such as difficulties and uncertainties regarding the repatriation of funds, currency fluctuations, the political and social climate as well as local customs and regulation. With regard to the latter, the inability to dismiss personnel in some countries in effect converts labor costs into fixed costs.

Regulation provides another example of external factors that can affect earnings quality. The "regulatory environment" of a public utility affects the "quality" of its earnings. Thus, an unsympathetic or even hostile regulatory environment that causes serious lags in the obtaining of rate relief will detract from earnings quality because of uncertainty about the adequacy of future revenues.

The stability and reliability of earnings sources affect earnings quality. Defense-related revenues can be regarded as nonrecurring in time of war and affected by political uncertainties in peacetime.

Finally, some analysts regard complexity of operations and difficulties in their analysis (e.g., of conglomerates) as negative factors.

EVALUATION OF THE EARNINGS LEVEL AND TREND

The analyst will concentrate on identifying those elements in the income and cost streams that exhibit stability, proven relationships, and predictability, and will separate them from those elements that are random, erratic, or nonrecurring and that, consequently, do not possess the elements of stability required for a reasonably reliable forecast or for inclusion in an "earning power" computation.

The analyst must be on guard against the well-known tendency of managements to practice income smoothing, thus trying to give to the income and expense streams a semblance of stability that in reality they do not possess. This is usually done in the name of "removing distortions" from the results of operations, whereas what is really achieved is the masking of the natural and cyclical irregularities that are part of the reality of the enterprise's experience and with which reality it is the analyst's primary task to come to grips in order to assess the level of risk.

Factors Affecting the Level of Earnings

We have, so far, discussed the *qualitative* factors that may cause the analyst either to adjust the earnings number of a given period (generally, a year) or to adjust the valuation (e.g., the price-earnings multiple) accorded such earnings.

The next step in the determination of the *level* of earnings of a given period is to recast the published income statements in such a way that the stable, normal, and continuing elements in the income statement are separated and distinguished from random, erratic, unusual, or nonrecurring elements that require separate analytical treatment or consideration. Moreover, such recasting also aims at identifying those elements included in the income statement of a given period that should more properly be included in the operating results of one or more prior periods.

The Analytical Recasting and Adjustment of Income Statements

The income statement along with all other financial statements and data contained in management's report represent the logical starting point of the analysis. It is clear that reported income is but the *starting point* of analysis and that from the point of view of the intelligent analyst, the most desirable income statement is the one containing a maximum of meaningful disclosure rather than one containing built-in interpretations that channel us to specific conclusions.

Over the years, notable shifts have occurred in the thinking of the accounting profession regarding the function of the income statement. An early position was that items of gain or loss should be included or excluded from income on the basis of the accountant's interpretation of what "normal operations" are. This position has resulted in much controversy and criticism to the point where the profession has adopted the "clean surplus" approach of including *all*[2] items of gain and loss in the income of the period in which they occur and, with few exceptions, such as corrections of errors, has also taken a position against the restatement of prior period results.

Major Sources of Information   As a consequence, the analyst will find data needed for the analysis of the results of operations and for their recasting and adjustment in:

1. The income statement which is generally subdivided into the following:

    Income from continuing operations.
    Income from discontinued operations (which includes gain or loss from disposal).
    Extraordinary gains and losses.
    Cumulative effect of changes in accounting principles.

2. The other financial statements and the footnotes thereto.
3. Management's comments found throughout its published report.
4. "Management's Discussion and Analysis of Financial Condition and Results of Operations" as required by the SEC's disclosure system (see also Chapter 20).

The analyst may also find "unusual" items segregated within the income statement (generally on a pre-tax basis), but their disclosure is optional. Such disclosure may not include items that the analyst may regard as significant, noteworthy, or unusual; and, consequently, the analyst will consult all the above-mentioned sources as well as management, if possible, in order to obtain the needed facts. These will include facts that affect the comparability and the interpretation of income statements,

---

[2] It should be noted that a departure from this position occurred in *SFAS 52* where, with few exceptions, gains and losses on the translation of foreign currency financial statements of subsidiaries bypass income and are accumulated in a separate stockholders' equity account. To a more limited extent, *SFAS 12*, on accounting for marketable securities, also represented such a departure, as does *SFAS 87*, concerned with the accounting for pensions.

such as product-mix changes, production innovations, strikes, and raw material shortages that may or may not be included in management's mandatory discussion and analysis of the results of operations.

The Recasting and Adjusting Procedure

Once the analyst has secured as much information as it is possible to obtain, the income statements of a number of years (generally at least five) should be recast and adjusted in such a way as to facilitate their further analysis to evaluate the trend of earnings as well as to aid in determining the average earning power of the enterprise for the period. While this procedure can be accomplished in one statement, it is simpler and clearer to subdivide it into two distinct steps: (1) recasting and (2) adjusting.

The Recasting Process   The recasting process aims at a rearranging of the items within the income statement in such a way so as to provide the most meaningful detail and the most relevant format needed by the analyst. At this stage, the individual items in the income statement may be rearranged, subdivided, or tax effected, but the total must reconcile to the net income of each period as reported.

The analytical reclassification of items *within* a period will help in the evaluation of the earnings level. Thus, discretionary and other noteworthy expenses should be segregated. The same applies to net items such as equity in income or loss of unconsolidated subsidiaries or associated companies, which are usually shown net of tax. Items shown in the pre-tax category must be removed *together* with their tax effect if they are to be shown below normal "income from continuing operations."

Expanded tax disclosure (see Chapter 11) enables the analyst to segregate factors that reduce taxes as well as those that increase them, thus enabling an analysis of the degree to which these factors are of a recurring nature. All material permanent differences and credits should be included. The analytical procedure involves computing taxes at the statutory rate (currently 34 percent) and deducting tax benefits such as arising from a variety of tax credits, capital gains rates, tax-free income, or lower foreign tax rates, and adding factors such as additional foreign taxes, nontax-deductible expenses, and state and local taxes (net of federal tax benefit). Immaterial items may be considered in one lump sum labeled "other."

Analytically recast income statements will contain as much detail as is needed for analysis and are supplemented by explanatory footnotes. Exhibit 22–1 presents the analytically recast income statements of Campbell Soup which are annotated with key numbers for ease of reference to the financial statements found in Appendix 4B. Data preceding 1990 are taken from company reports which are summarized in Chapter 23. Chapter 23 contains a discussion of and an integration of Exhibit 22–1.

Exhibit 22–1

CAMPBELL SOUP COMPANY
Analytically Recast Income Statements
For Fiscal Years 1986 to 1991
(in millions)

Reference item		1991	1990	1989	1988	1987	1986
13	Net sales	$6,204.1	$6,205.8	$5,672.1	$4,868.9	$4,490.4	$4,286.8
19	Interest income	26.0	17.6	38.3	33.2	29.5	27.4
	Total revenue	6,230.1	6,223.4	5,710.4	4,902.1	4,519.9	4,314.2
	Costs and expenses:						
145	Cost of products sold (1)	3,727.1	3,893.5	3,651.8	3,077.8	2,897.8	2,820.5
144	Marketing and Selling expenses (2)	760.8	760.1	605.9	514.2	422.7	363.0
16	Advertising (2)	195.4	220.4	212.9	219.1	203.5	181.4
17	Repair and maintenance (1)	173.9	180.6	173.9	155.6	148.8	144.0
102	Administrative expenses	306.7	290.7	252.1	232.6	213.9	195.9
20	Research and development expenses	56.3	53.7	47.7	46.9	44.8	42.2
104	Stock price related incentive programs (3)	15.4	(0.1)	17.4	(2.7)	–	8.5
	Foreign exchange adjustment	0.8	3.3	19.3	16.6	4.8	0.7
	Other, net (3)	(3.3)	(2.0)	(1.4)	(4.7)	(0.4)	(9.0)
162A	Depreciation (1)	194.5	184.1	175.9	162.0	139.0	120.8
103	Amortization of intangible and other assets (3)	14.1	16.8	16.4	8.9	5.6	6.0
18	Interest expense	116.2	111.6	94.1	53.9	51.7	56.0
	Total costs and expenses	5,557.9	5,712.7	5,266.0	4,480.2	4,132.2	3,930.0
23	Earnings before equity in earnings of affiliates and minority interests	672.2	510.7	444.4	421.9	387.7	384.2
24	Equity in earnings of affiliates	2.4	13.5	10.4	6.3	15.1	4.3
25	Minority interests	(7.2)	(5.7)	(5.3)	(6.3)	(4.7)	(3.9)

Code							
26	Income before taxes	667.4	518.5	449.5	421.9	398.1	384.6
	Income taxes at statutory rate*	(226.9)	(176.3)	(152.8)	(143.5)	(179.1)	(176.9)
135	Income from continuing operations	440.5	342.2	296.7	278.4	219.0	207.7
	State taxes (net of federal tax benefit)	(20.0)	(6.6)	(3.8)	(11.8)	(8.6)	(8.0)
	Investment tax credit	—	—	—	—	4.4	11.6
137	Nondeductible amortization of intangibles	(4.0)	(1.6)	(1.2)	(2.6)	(1.4)	†
138	Foreign earnings not taxed or taxed at other than statutory federal rate	2.0	(2.2)	(0.2)	3.2	11.1	15.2
139	Other: Tax effects	(17.0)	(2.2)	(0.1)	(3.7)	7.5	(4.7)
22	Alaska Native Corporation transaction	—	—	—	—	4.5	—
	Divestitures, restructuring, and unusual charges	—	(339.1)	(343.0)	(40.6)	—	—
	Tax effect of divestitures, restructuring . . . etc. (4)	—	13.9	64.7	13.9	—	—
	Gain on sale of businesses (1988) and subsidiary (1987)	—	—	—	3.1	9.7	—
	Loss on sale of exercise equipment subsidiary, net of tax	—	—	—	—	(1.7)	—
	LIFO liquidation gain (1)	—	—	—	1.7	2.8	1.4
	Income before cumulative effect of accounting change	401.5	4.4	13.1	241.6	247.3	223.2
153A	Cumulative effect of accounting change for income taxes	—	—	—	32.5	—	—
28	Net income as reported	401.5	4.4	13.1	274.1	247.3	223.2
14	(1) Cost of products sold	4,095.5	4,258.2	4,001.6	3,392.8	3,180.5	3,082.8
144	Less: Repair and maintenance expenses	(173.9)	(180.6)	(173.9)	(155.6)	(148.8)	(144.0)
162A	Less: Depreciation(a)	(194.5)	(184.1)	(175.9)	(162.0)	(139.0)	(120.0)
153A	Plus: LIFO liquidation gain(b)	—	—	2.6	2.6	5.1	2.6
		3,727.1	3,893.5	3,651.8	3,077.8	2,897.8	2,821.4

		1991	1990	1989	1988	1987	1986
[15]	(2) Marketing and selling expenses	544.4	626.2	733.3	818.8	980.5	956.2
[145]	Less: Advertising	(181.4)	(203.5)	(219.1)	(212.9)	(20.4)	(195.4)
		363.0	422.7	514.2	605.9	960.1	760.8
[21]	(3) Other expenses (income)	5.5	(9.5)	(3.2)	32.4	14.7	26.2
[102]	Less: Stock price related incentive programs	(8.5)	—	2.7	(17.4)	0.1	(15.4)
[103]	Less: Amortization of intangible and other assets	(6.0)	(5.6)	(8.9)	(16.4)	(16.8)	(14.1)
	Less: Gain on sale of international businesses (1988) and sale of pet food Subsidiary (1987)	—	14.7	4.7	—	—	—
[104]	Other, net	(9.0)	(0.4)	(4.7)	(1.4)	(2.0)	(3.3)
	(4) Tax effect of divestitures, restructuring and unusual charges at the statutory rate	—	—	13.9	116.6 [a]	115.3 [c]	—
[136]	Nondeductible divestitures, . . . etc.	—	—	—	(51.9)[f]	(101.4)[e]	—
		—	—	13.9	64.7	13.9	—

	1991	1990	1989	1988	1987	1986
* Statutory federal tax rate	34%	34%	34%	34%	45%	46%

† Not disclosed for 1986

[a] Most of depreciation is assumed as to be included in cost of products sold.
[b] LIFO liquidation gain before tax. For 1988 = 1.7 / (1 − 0.34) = 2.58
[c] $339.1 [22] × 0.34 = $115.3
[d] $343.0 [22] × 0.34 = $116.6
[e] $179.4 [26] × 0.565 [136] = $101.4
[f] $106.5 [26] × 0.487 [136] = $51.9

751

The Adjustment Process   Based on data developed in the recast income statements as well as on other available information, certain items of income or loss are to be assigned by the analyst to the period to which they most properly belong.

The reassignment of extraordinary items or unusual items (net of tax) to other years must be done with care. Thus, the income tax benefit of the carryforward of operating losses should generally be moved to the year in which the loss occurred. The costs or benefits from the settlement of a lawsuit may relate to one or more preceding years. The gain or loss on disposal of discontinued operations will usually relate to the results of operations over a number of years.

If possible, all years under analysis should be placed on a comparable basis when a change in accounting principle or accounting estimate occurs. If, as is usually the case, the *new* accounting principle is the desirable one, prior years should, if possible, be restated to the new method, or a notation made regarding a lack of comparability in certain respects. This procedure will result in a redistribution of the "cumulative effect of change in accounting principle" to affected prior years. Changes in estimates can be accounted for only prospectively and GAAP prohibit prior year restatements except in specified cases (see Chapter 11). The analyst's ability to place all years on a comparable basis will depend on availability of information.

Before the trend in earnings can be evaluated it is necessary to obtain the best approximation possible of the adjusted earnings *level* of each year. All items in the income statement must be considered, and none can be excluded or "dropped by the wayside." Thus, if it is decided that an item in the income statement does not properly belong in the year in which it appears, it may be either:

1. Shifted (net of tax) to the result of another year or a number of other years, or
2. If it cannot be identified with another specific year or years, it should be included in the *average* earnings of the period under analysis. While the averaging process helps in the determination of average earning power, it is not helpful in the determination of earnings trend.

It must be realized that moving an item of gain or loss to another year or recording one's inability to assign an item to the proper year does not remedy the fact that the results of some prior year(s) have been misstated. For example, a damage award in one year for patent infringement means that prior years had suffered from lost sales or similar damage.

Exhibit 22–2 presents the analytically adjusted income statements of Campbell Soup based on data in Appendix 4B as well as data taken from earlier financial reports. A further reference to Exhibit 22–2 will be found in the comprehensive analysis of Campbell found in Chapter 23.

Exhibit 22–2

CAMPBELL SOUP COMPANY
Analytically Adjusted Income Statements 1986–1991
(in millions)

	1991	1990	1989	1988	1987	1986	Total
Net income as reported	$401.5	$ 4.4	$ 13.1	$274.1	$247.3	$223.2	$1,163.6
Divestitures, restructuring and unusual charges		339.1	343.0	40.6			
Tax effect of divestitures, restructuring, etc.		(13.9)	(64.7)	(13.9)			
Gain on sale of businesses (1988) and sale of subsidiary (1987), net of tax				(3.1)	(9.7)		
Loss on sale of exercise equipment subsidiary					1.7		
Alaska Native corporation transaction					(4.5)		
LIFO liquidation gain				(1.7)	(2.8)	(1.4)	
Cumulative effect of change in accounting for income taxes				(32.5)			
Adjusted net income for individual years	401.5	329.6	291.4	263.5	232.0	221.8	
Total net income for the period							1,163.6
Average earnings for the period							$ 193.9

753

Analysts must recognize that characterizations of income or expense items as "unusual," "nonrecurring," "infrequent," or "extraordinary" or the inclusion in equity of certain transactions (e.g., under *SFAS 12* and *52*) are all attempts to reduce earnings volatility or to explain away certain components of income. Items excluded from income by FASB direction are generally not adjusted for. However, all remaining items are part of the lifetime income of an enterprise—they do enhance or diminish the owners' wealth and they are part of the earning power of the enterprise. Thus, while it may be analytically appropriate to omit such items from any one year, they belong in any computation of *average* earning power actually achieved.

Determining the Trend of Income over the Years

Having determined the size of a company's basic earnings as well as the factors that require adjustment before those earnings can be used as a basis for forecasts, the analyst will next determine the variability of these earnings, that is, changes in their size over the business cycle and over the longer term.

Evaluation of Earnings Variability   Earnings that fluctuate up and down with the business cycle are less desirable than earnings that display a larger degree of stability over such a cycle. The basic reason for this is that fluctuating earnings cause fluctuations in market prices. Earnings that display a steady growth trend are of the most desirable type. In the evaluation of earnings, the intelligent analyst realizes the limitations to which the earnings figure of any one year is subject. Therefore, depending on his specific purposes, he will consider the following earnings figures as improvements over the single-year figure:

1. *Average earnings* over periods, such as 5 to 10 years, smooth out erratic and even extraordinary factors as well as cyclical influences, thus presenting a better and more reliable measure of "earning power" of an enterprise.
2. *Minimum earnings* are useful in decisions, such as those bearing on credit extension, which are particularly sensitive to risk factors. They indicate the worst that could happen during a complete business cycle, based on recent experience.

The Importance of Earnings Trends   In addition to the use of single, average, or minimum earnings figures, the analyst must be alert to earnings trends. These are best evaluated by means of trend statements such as those presented on page 798. The relevant earnings numbers to be included in the trend analysis will be derived from adjusted income statements as exemplified in Exhibit 22–2. The earnings trend contains important clues to the nature of the enterprise (i.e., cyclical, growth, defensive) and the quality of its management.

Distortions of Trends   Analysts must be alert to accounting distortions that affect trends. Among the most important are changes in accounting principles and the effect of business combinations, particularly purchases. These must be adjusted for.

Some of the most common and most pervasive manipulative practices in accounting are designed to affect the presentation of earnings trends. These manipulations are based on the assumptions, often true, that the trend of income is more important than its absolute size; that retroactive revisions of income already reported in prior periods have little, if any, market effect on security prices,[3] and that once a company has incurred a loss, the size of the loss is not as significant as the fact that the loss has been incurred.

These assumptions and the propensities of some managements to use accounting as a means of improving the appearance of the earnings trend has led to techniques that can be broadly described as income smoothing.

Income Smoothing and Income Distortion

A number of requirements must be met by the income-smoothing process so as to distinguish it from outright falsehoods and distortions.

The income-smoothing process is a rather sophisticated and insidious device. It does not rely on outright or patent falsehoods and distortions but rather uses the wide leeway existing in alternatively acceptable accounting principles and their interpretation in order to achieve its ends. Thus, income smoothing is performed within the framework of GAAP. It is a matter of form rather than one of substance. Consequently, it does not involve a real transaction (e.g., postponing an actual sale to another accounting period in order to shift revenue) but only a redistribution of credits or charges among periods. The general objective is to moderate income variability over the years by shifting income from good years to bad years, by shifting future income to the present (in most cases presently reported earnings are more valuable than those reported at some future date), or vice versa. Similarly, income variability can be moderated or modified by the shifting of costs, expenses, or losses from one period to another.

Income smoothing may take many forms. Hereunder are listed some forms of smoothing to which the analyst should be particularly alert:

---

[3] This was recognized by *APB Opinion 20* and later *SFAS 16,* which, with but two exceptions, forbids the retroactive restatement of prior year financial statements. For a discussion of this topic, see Chapter 11.

1. Changing accounting methods or assumptions with the objective of improving or modifying reported results. For example, to offset the effect on earnings of slumping sales and of other difficulties, Chrysler Corporation revised upward the assumed rate of return on its pension portfolio, thus increasing income significantly. Similarly, Union Carbide improved results by switching to a number of more liberal accounting alternatives.

2. Misstatements, by various methods, of inventories as a means of redistributing income among the years. The Londontown Manufacturing Company case provides a classic example of such practices.[4] Some of these practices were outside the framework allowed by GAAP.

3. The offsetting of extraordinary credits by identical or nearly identical extraordinary charges as a means of removing an unusual or sudden injection of income that may interfere with the display of a growing earnings trend. (For examples and further discussion see Chapter 11.)

4. The provision of reserves for future costs and losses as a means of increasing the adverse results of what is already a poor year and utilizing such reserves to relieve future years of charges against income that would otherwise be properly chargeable against it. (Abuses in this area are intended to be curtailed by *SFAS 5*.)

5. The substantial write-downs of operating assets (such as plant and equipment) or of intangibles (such as goodwill) in times of economic slowdown when operating results are already poor. The reason usually given for such write-downs is that carrying the properties at book value cannot be economically justified. (For example, CSX Corporation wrote off, as part of a restructuring, $533 million of marginal and unproductive assets.) Particularly unwarranted is the practice of writing down operating assets to the point at which a target return on investment (which management thinks it *should* earn) is realized.

6. Timing the inclusion of revenues and costs in periodic income in such a way as to influence the overall trend of income (or loss) over the years. (Examples are the timing of sales or other disposition of property, incurring and expensing of discretionary costs such as R&D, advertising, maintenance, etc.) This category, unlike most others, entails more than accounting choice in that it may involve the timing of actual business transactions. Thus, in recent years, Franklin Mint inflated sales and income by accelerating shipments to customers ahead of a schedule called for by customer subscription terms and booking these as sales immediately.

---

[4] Details can be found in an SEC decision issued October 31, 1963 (41 SEC 676–688).

Income Smoothing and Income Distortion—Some Implications
for Analysis

Motivation for Distortions   As was developed in the discussion at the end of Chapter 3, human nature has a most powerful and pervasive effect on measurements which affect the analysis of financial statements. This is particularly true of earnings levels and trends which enter so importantly into investing and lending decisions. As experience has repeatedly shown (some of it illustrated in this work), there is almost no limit to the degree to which beleaguered and/or greedy owners, managers, or company employees will go to manipulate or distort reported earnings in order to achieve ends which serve their objectives and interests.

Companies in financial difficulties may be motivated to engage in such practices for what they see and justify as their battle for survival. Successful companies will go to great lengths to uphold a hard-earned and well-rewarded image of earnings growth by smoothing those earnings artificially. Moreover, compensation plans or other incentives based on earnings will motivate managements to accelerate the recognition of income by anticipating revenues or deferring expenses.

The following examples are additional to those given throughout this work:

THE H. J. HEINZ COMPANY CASE.   The case of H. J. Heinz Company has shown that even second-tier divisional executives, motivated by self-interest in meeting earnings targets and in smoothing earnings, can without the knowledge of top management engage in income manipulation. In this case, "hidden reserves" were created by prepaying for services not yet received, such as advertising, and by the improper recording of sales.

THE J. W. T. GROUP, INC., CASE.   This case did not seem to involve a desire for personal gain but consisted rather in falsifying of records in order to make the syndication department look good by meeting its profit goals.

The department purchased programming from independent producers and bartered the programs to television stations in return for future commercial time that was in turn used to build "time banks" for sale to agency clients. The accounting deception involved the creation of fictitious time banks, fictitious clients, and fictitious revenues over a period of four years. So successful was the computerized deception that for a time, management invested additional capital in the division, lured by the substantial, if fictitious, returns it appeared to earn.

THE McCORMICK CO. CASE.   The SEC took this company to task for, among other things, managing its earnings by asking its advertising agency to delay mailing invoices till later periods. The company agreed not to engage in such practices in the future.

Analysts must appreciate the great variety of incentives and objectives that lead managements and, at times, second-tier management without the knowledge of top management, to engage in practices ranging from smoothing to the outright falsification of income.

The smoothing of earnings is often achieved by first understating reported earnings. Thus, Firestone Tire and Rubber Company engaged in the practice of hiding income in secret accounts for the purpose of drawing on these during leaner years.

Some reputable academicians have even suggested that smoothing is justified if it can help a company report earnings closer to its true "earning power" level. Such is not the function of financial reporting. As we have repeatedly seen in this book, the analyst will be best served by a full disclosure of periodic results and the components that comprise them. It is up to the analyst to average, smooth, or otherwise adjust reported earnings in accordance with specific analytical purposes.

As a possible case of earnings smoothing and of overprovision of costs in order to benefit future years a discussion of General Motors' accounting may be instructive:

GENERAL MOTORS' (GM) ACCOUNTING.   In 1987 GM reported that, based on a careful study, a revision of useful lives of plant and equipment resulted in a $1.2 billion reduction of depreciation and amortization charges that year. (See also Chapter 10.) The chairperson's message stated that "GM earned $3.6 billion for the year, up 21 percent from 1986 despite a 9 percent reduction in worldwide unit sales." However, without the $1.2 billion reduction in depreciation and amortization, as a result of the significant lengthening of estimated lives of assets, earnings would have *declined* rather than increased.

The 1987 accounting change came on the heels of a 1986 provision of $1.3 billion for plant closings and other restructurings. However, by the end of the decade only $0.5 billion has been charged against this provision leaving the rest to absorb costs in future years. When 1990 saw a change in leadership at GM, stockholders learned of another $2.1 billion charge to earnings to cover the costs of closing several plants, including closings which won't actually occur until years later. This sequence of accounting events left analysts puzzled about the veracity of GM's accounting and the motivation of its management. Such accounting greatly increases the difficulties in arriving at a reliable earnings trend over the years. Any reliable estimate of earning power must include in the averaging process charges and provisions of all kinds.

The accounting profession has earnestly tried to promulgate rules that discourage practices such as the smoothing of earnings. However, given the above-mentioned powerful propensities of companies and of their owners and employees to engage in such practices, analysts must realize that where there is a will to smooth or even distort earnings, ways to do so are available and will be found. Consequently, particularly in the case of companies where incentives to smooth are likely to be present, analysts should analyze and scrutinize accounting practices in order to satisfy themselves to the extent possible, regarding the integrity of the income reporting process.

Extraordinary Gains and Losses

The evaluation of current earnings levels, the determination of earnings trends as well as the projection of future earnings rely importantly on the separation of the stable elements of income and expense from those that are random, nonrecurring, and erratic in nature.

Stability and sustainability are important characteristics that enter significantly into the determination of earning power. Moreover, in making earnings projections, the forecaster relies also on repetitiveness of occurrence. Thus, in order to separate the relatively stable elements of income and expense of an enterprise from those that are random or erratic in nature, it is important, as a first step, to identify those gains and losses that are nonrecurring and unusual as well as those that are truly extraordinary.

This separation is a first step that is mostly preparatory in nature. Following it is a process of judgment and analysis that aims at determining how such nonrecurring, unusual, or truly extraordinary items should be treated in the evaluation of the level of present income and of management performance as well as in the projection of future results.

Significance of Accounting Treatment and Presentation   The value of any accounting treatment and presentation is largely dependent on its usefulness to those who make decisions on the basis of financial statements. Unfortunately, particularly in the area of the accounting for, and the presentation of, extraordinary gains and losses, the usefulness of this accounting has been impaired because of the great importance attached to it by those who report the results of operations and who are judged by them.

The accounting for, and the presentation of, extraordinary gains and losses has always been subject to controversy. Whatever the merits of the theoretical debate surrounding this issue, the fact remains that one of the basic reasons for the controversial nature of this topic is reporting management's great interest in it. Managements are almost always concerned with the amount of net results of the enterprise as well as with the manner in which these periodic results are reported. This concern is reinforced by a widespread belief that most investors and traders accept the reported net income figures, as well as the modifying explanations that accompany them, as true indexes of performance. Thus, extraordinary gains and losses often become the means by which managements attempt to modify the reported operating results and the means by which they try to explain these results. Quite often these explanations are subjective and are designed to achieve the impact and impression desired by management.

The accounting profession has tacitly, if not openly, recognized the role that the foregoing considerations play in the actual practice of reporting extraordinary gains and losses. Its last pronouncement on this subject, which was discussed in Chapter 11, has at least ensured a fuller measure of disclosure of extraordinary gains and losses and their inclusion in the income statement. This represents an improvement over prior pronouncements that, in an attempt to arrive at a "true" index of operating performance, sanctioned the exclusion of certain extraordinary gains and losses from the income statement.

Analysis and Evaluation   The basic objectives in the identification and evaluation of extraordinary items by the analyst are:

1. To determine whether a particular item is to be considered "extraordinary" for purposes of analysis, that is, whether it is so unusual, nonoperating, and nonrecurring in nature that it requires special adjustment in the evaluation of current earnings levels and of future earning possibilities.
2. To decide what form the adjustment for items that are considered as "extraordinary" in nature should take.

Determining Whether an Item of Gain or Loss Is Extraordinary   The infirmities and shortcomings of present practice as well as the considerations which motivate it, lead to the inescapable conclusion that the analyst must arrive at an independent evaluation of whether a gain or loss should be considered as extraordinary, and if so, how to adjust for it.

In arriving at this decision, it is useful to subdivide items, commonly classified as unusual or extraordinary, into three basic categories:

a. Nonrecurring operating gains or losses. By "operating" we usually identify items connected with the normal and usual operations of the business. The concept of normal operations is more widely used than understood and is far from clear and well defined. Thus, in a company operating a machine shop, operating expenses would be considered as those associated with the work of the machine shop. The proceeds from a sale above cost of marketable securities held by the company as an investment of excess cash would be considered a nonoperating gain. So would the gain (or loss) on the sale of a lathe, even if it were disposed of in order to make room for one that would increase the productivity of the shop.

The concept of recurrence is one of frequency. There are no predetermined generally accepted boundaries separating the recurring event from the nonrecurring. An event (which in this context embraces a gain or loss) occurring once a year can be definitely classified as "recurring." An event, the occurrence of which is unpredictable and which in the past has either not occurred or occurred very infrequently, may be classified as nonrecurring. On the other hand, an event that occurs infrequently but whose occurrence is predictable raises some question as to its designation. An example of the latter would be the relining of blast furnaces.

They last for many years; while their replacement is infrequent, the need for it is predictable. Some companies provide for their replacement by means of a reserve. Casualties do not, however, accrue in similar fashion.

Nonrecurring operating gains or losses are, then, gains or losses connected with or related to operations that recur infrequently and/or unpredictably.

In considering how to treat nonrecurring operating gains and losses, the analyst would do best to recognize the fact of inherent abnormality and the lack of a recurring annual pattern in business and treat them as belonging to the results of the period in which they are reported.

We must also address ourselves to the question of what should be considered as "normal operations." Thus, it is a bakery's purpose to bake bread, rolls, and cakes, but it is presumably outside its normal purpose to buy and sell marketable securities for gain or loss, or even to sell baking machinery that is to be replaced for the purpose of more efficient baking.

This narrow interpretation of the objectives of a business has undergone considerable revision in modern financial theory. Thus, rather than the "baking bread" or any other specific objective, the main objective and task of management is viewed as that of increasing the capital of the owners, or expressed differently, the enhancing of the value of the common stock. This, according to modern financial theory, can be accomplished by means of the judicious combination of an optimal financing plan and any mix of operations opportunities that may be available to achieve the desired purpose.

The analyst should not be bound by the accountant's concept of "normal operations," and thus he or she can usefully treat a much wider range of gains and losses as being derived from "operations." This approach reinforces our conclusion that from the point of view of analysis, most nonrecurring, *operating* gains and losses should be considered part of the operating results of the year in which they occur.

This approach is offered as a general guideline rather than as a mechanical rule. After examination of all attendant circumstances, the analyst may conclude that some such items require separation from the results of a single year. The relative size of an item could conceivably be a factor requiring such treatment. In this case, the best approach is to emphasize *average earnings* experience over, say, five years rather than the result of a single year. This approach of emphasizing average earnings becomes almost imperative in the case of enterprises that have widely fluctuating amounts of nonrecurring and other extraordinary items included in their results. After all, a single year is too short and too arbitrary a period on the basis of which to evaluate the earnings power of an enterprise or the prospects for future results. Moreover, we are all familiar with enterprises that defer expenses and postpone losses and come up periodically with a loss year that cancels out much of the income reported in preceding years.

ILLUSTRATION 3.   1991 was a year of particularly numerous reports of big charges to earnings for reorganization, redeployment, or regrouping. Companies taking substantial write-offs included, in billions, AT&T $2.6, Occidental Petroleum $2, Continental Airlines $1.8, Digital Equipment $1, and in millions, Columbia Gas System $765, General Dynamics $567, and Bethlehem Steel $550.

While the information supplied with such announcements seldom enables a careful analysis of years affected by such big charges there is no question but that they represent in significant measure revisions of previously reported results. Thus, in one stroke, the write-off corrects the overreporting of earnings over many years. The analyst must also be alert to indications that such charges may include "cushions" designed to relieve future results of charges properly attributable to them.

b. Recurring nonoperating gains or losses. This category includes items of a nonoperating nature that recur with some frequency. An example would be the recurring amortization of a "bargain purchase credit." Other possible examples are interest income and the rental received from employees who rent company-owned houses.

While items in this category may be classified as unusual in published financial statements, the narrow definition of *nonoperating* which they involve as well as their recurrent nature are good reasons why they should not be excluded from current results by the analyst. They are, after all, mostly the result of the conscious employment of capital by the enterprise, and their recurrence requires inclusion of these gains or losses in estimates designed to project future results.

c. Nonrecurring nonoperating gains or losses. Of the three categories, this one possesses the greatest degree of "abnormality." Not only are the events here nonrepetitive and unpredictable, but they do not fall within the sphere of normal operations. In most cases, these events are extraneous, unintended, and unplanned. However, they can rarely be said to be totally unexpected. Business is ever subject to the risk of sudden adverse events and to random shocks, be they natural or manmade. In the same manner, business transactions are also subject to unexpected windfalls. One good example in this category is the loss from damage done by the crash of an aircraft on a plant not located in the vicinity of an airport. Other, but less clear-cut, examples in this category may also include:

1. Substantial uninsured casualty losses that are not within the categories of risk to which the enterprise can reasonably be deemed to be subject.
2. The expropriation by a foreign government of an entire operation owned by the enterprise.
3. The seizure or destruction of property as a result of an act of war, insurrection, or civil disorders, in areas where this is totally unexpected.

It can be seen readily that while the above occurrences are, in most cases, of a nonrecurring nature, their relation to the operations of a business varies. All are occurrences in the regular course of business. Even the assets destroyed by acts of God were acquired for operating purposes and thus were subject to all possible risks.

Of the three categories, the third comes closest to meeting the criterion of being "extraordinary." Nevertheless, truly unique events are very rare. What looks at the time as unique may in the light of experience turn out to be the symptom of new sets of circumstances that affect and may continue to affect the earning power as well as the degree of risk to which an enterprise is subject.

The analyst must bear in mind such possibilities, but barring evidence to the contrary, items in this category can be regarded as extraordinary in nature and thus can be omitted from the results of operations of a *single* year. They are, nevertheless, part of the longer-term record of results of the enterprise.[5] Thus, they enter the computation of *average earnings,* and the propensity of the enterprise to incur such gains or losses must be considered in the projection of future average earnings.

The foregoing discussion has tried to point out that the intelligent classification of extraordinary items provides a workable solution to their treatment by the analyst. There are, however, other aspects of the evaluation of extraordinary items that must be considered here. One is the effect of extraordinary items on the resources of an enterprise; the other is their effect on the evaluation of management performance.

Effect of Extraordinary Items on Enterprise Resources   Every extraordinary gain or loss has a dual aspect. In addition to recording a gain (whether extraordinary or not), a business records an increase in resources. Similarly, a loss results in a reduction of resources. Since return on investment (ROI) measures the relationship of net income to resources, the incurrence of extraordinary gains and losses will affect this important measure of profitability. The more material the extraordinary item, the more significant that influence will be. In other words, if earnings and events are to be used to make estimates about the future, then extraordinary items convey something more than past performance. Thus, if an extraordinary loss results in the destruction of capital on which a certain return is expected, that return may be lost to the future. Conversely, an extraordinary gain will result in an addition of resources on which a future return can be expected.

This means that in projecting profitability and return on investment, the analyst must take into account the effect of recorded "extraordinary" items as well as the likelihood of the occurrence of future events that may cause extraordinary items.

---

[5] Analysts must be aware that some financial services arbitrarily exclude some gains and losses from reported earnings. Thus, *The Value Line Investment Survey* decided to "exclude most nonrecurring gains and losses from reported earnings per share."

Effect on Evaluation of Management   One implication frequently associated with the reporting of extraordinary gains and losses is that they have not resulted from a "normal" or "planned" activity of management and that, consequently, they should not be used in the evaluation of management performance. The analyst should seriously question such a conclusion.

What is "normal activity" in relation to management's deliberate actions? Whether we talk about the purchase or sale of securities, of other assets not used in operations, or of divisions and subsidiaries that definitely relate to operations, we talk about actions deliberately taken by management with specific purposes in mind. Such actions require, if anything, more consideration or deliberation than do ordinary everyday operating decisions because they are most often unusual in nature and involve substantial amounts of money. They are true tests of management ability. The results of such activities always qualify or enhance the results of "normal" operations, thus yielding the final net results.

For example, Standard Oil Co. (Ohio) took an extraordinary charge of $1.15 billion in writing down its ill-fated investment in Kennecott. It is quite likely that the loss resulted in prior years' earnings being overstated.

Similarly, management must be aware of the risk of natural or man-made disasters or impediments in the course of business. The decision to engage in foreign operations is made with the knowledge of the special risks that this involves. The decision to insure or not is a normal operating decision. Nothing can really be termed completely unexpected or unforeseeable. Management does not engage, or is at least not supposed to engage, in any activity unconsciously; hence, whatever it does is clearly within the expected activity of a business. Every type of enterprise is subject to specific risks that are inherent in it, and managements do not enter such ventures blindly.

When it comes to the assessment of results that count and results that build or destroy value, the distinction of what is normal and what is not fades almost into insignificance. Management's beliefs about the quality of its decisions are nearly always related to the normalcy, or lack thereof, of surrounding circumstances. This can be clearly seen in the management report section of many annual reports. Of course, management has to take more time to explain failure or shortcomings than to explain success. Success hardly needs an explanation, unless it involves circumstances not likely to be repeated. Failure often evokes long explanations, and more often than not, unusual or unforeseeable circumstances are blamed for it. If only normal conditions had prevailed, everything would have been much better. But in a competitive economy, normal conditions hardly ever prevail for any length of time. Management is paid to anticipate and expect the unusual. No alibis are permitted. Explanations are never a substitute for performance. In this area the letters to shareholders of Berkshire Hathaway written by its chairman, Warren Buffet, are examples of lucidity and candor.

THE CONCEPT OF EARNING POWER

The best possible estimate of the *average* earnings of an enterprise, which can be expected to be sustained and to be repeated with some degree of regularity over a *span of future years,* is referred to as its earning power. Except in specialized cases, earning power is universally recognized as the single most important factor in the valuation of an enterprise. Most valuation approaches entail in one form or another the capitalization of earning power by a factor or multiplier that takes into account the cost of capital as well as future expected risks and rewards.

The importance of "earning power" is such that most analyses of the income and related financial statements have as one of their ultimate objectives the determination of its amount. Earning power is a concept of financial analysis, not of accounting. It focuses on stable and recurring elements and thus aims to arrive at the best possible estimate of repeatable average earnings over a span of future years. Accounting, as we have seen, can supply much of the essential information for the computation of earning power. However, the process is one involving knowledge, judgment, experience, and a time horizon, as well as a specialized investing or lending point of view, such as is described in Chapter 1.

Investors and lenders look ultimately to future cash flows as sources of rewards and safety. Accrual accounting, which underlies income determination, aims to relate sacrifices and benefits to the periods in which they occur. In spite of known shortcomings, this framework represents the most reliable and relevant indicator of longer-term future probabilities of *average* cash inflows and outflows presently known.

While in its objectives, valuation is *future* oriented, we must recognize that the most sound and realistic basis for estimating future conditions and probabilities is the actual track record of the enterprise's achievement in the most recent past. Not only does such an earning record over a representative span of years, usually encompassing an entire business cycle, represent what has in fact been achieved as the actual operating experience of the enterprise, but it also represents the operating model on the basis of which we can give effect to assumptions about future conditions that we expect to differ from those prevailing in the past.

In this context, it must be realized that valuation, whether it is performed for purposes of investment, taxation, or the adjudication of disputes as to value, is of such importance to the parties at interest that estimates, if they are made, must be most soundly based. Thus, any departure from actual experience must be carefully verified and justified.

Our ability to pierce the veil of the future is limited indeed. As Bennian[6] stated it:

> It is impossible to make an economic forecast in which full confidence can be placed. No matter what refinements of techniques are employed, there still remain at least some exogenous variables. It is thus not even possible to say with certainty how likely our forecast is to be right. We must be brash enough to label a forecast as "most probable," but this implies an ability on our part to pin an approximate probability coefficient on a forecast: 1.0 if it is virtual certainty, 0.0 if it is next to an impossibility, or some other coefficient between these extremes. But, again, since we have no precise way of measuring the probability of our exogenous variables behaving as we assume them to do, there is no assurance that the estimated probability coefficient for our forecast is anything like 100 percent correct.

It is for this reason that the courts and others have been reluctant, except in the most persuasive of circumstances, to substitute guesses about the future for the experience of the past, and, for this reason, *average* past earnings enter very importantly into the determination of earning power.

Earning Power Time Horizon

It can be readily recognized that one year represents too short and too arbitrary a time period for purposes of income measurement and evaluation. Because of the length of time required to assess the ultimate workout and the results of many investments and outlays, because of the ups and downs of the business cycle, and because of the presence of numerous nonrecurring and extraordinary factors, the earning power of an enterprise is best measured by means of average earnings realized over a number of years. Thus, while gains and losses may be unusual or extraordinary with respect to any one period, they are, nevertheless, still part of the enterprise's longer-term operating experience.

The period of time over which an earnings average should be calculated will vary with the industry of which the enterprise is part and with other special circumstances. However, in general, a from 5- to 10-year earnings average will smooth out many of the distortions and the irregularities that impair the significance of a single year's results. A five-year earnings average will, in most cases, be adequate to retain an emphasis on recent experience while avoiding the inclusion of years that may no longer be representative or relevant.

Our discussion of the analysis of the income statement has shown that the analysis must focus on the level of income for each year as well as

---

[6] Edward G. Bennian, "Capital Budgeting and Game Theory," *Harvard Business Review,* November–December 1956, pp. 115–23.

on the *trend* of earnings over time. Trend is an important factor in valuation.

If the earnings are subject to a sustainable trend, the averaging process may have to be weighted so as to accord more weight to most recent earnings. Thus, in a five-year average computation, the last year may be given a weight of 5/15, the preceding year a weight of 4/15, and the first year a weight of 1/15.

The more representative the most recent enterprise experience and the nature of its operations are of what can be expected in the future, the more valid the averaging process is. Conversely, if there have been significant recent changes in the nature of the enterprise's operations, the averaging period may have to be shortened and/or greater emphasis may have to be placed on estimation of future conditions.

Adjustment of Reported Earnings per Share

In our discussion of the adjustment of earnings, we concluded that in determining the earning power of an enterprise, no item of income and expense should be excluded. Since every item of income or expense is part of the enterprise's operating experience, the question is only to what year items should be assigned or into what period of time they should be included when an average of earnings is computed.

For purposes of analysis or comparison, analysts may, however, wish to focus on an adjusted level of earnings for a short period, for example, for two years. This can be done by adding to, or removing from, reported earnings per share selected items of income or expense that were included therein. If this is to be done on a per share basis, every item must be adjusted for tax effect (by using the enterprise's effective tax rate unless the applicable tax rate is otherwise specified) and must be divided by the number of shares that are used in the basic computation of earnings per share (see Chapter 12).

The following example of such suggested analytical adjustments is adapted from a tabulation prepared by "The Quality of Earnings Report"[7] concerning the reported earnings of A. H. Robins Company.

---

[7] Published by Reporting Research Corporation, Englewood Cliffs, N.J.

Per share earnings impact

Item	year 2	year 1
Effective tax rate change	+$0.02	
Settlement of Hartz litigation	+0.07	+$0.57
Change to straight-line depreciation	+0.02	
Reserves for losses on Iranian assets	+0.02	−0.15
Loss on sale of divisions	−0.19	
Change to LIFO	−0.07	
Litigation settlements and expense	−0.09	−0.12
Foreign exchange translation	−0.03	−0.04
Above trend R&D expenditures	−0.11	
Higher percent allowance for doubtful accounts	−0.02	
± Per share earnings impact	−$0.38	+$0.26
Per share earnings as reported	*$1.01*	*$1.71*
Add back negative (−) impact to year 2	*0.38*	
Subtract positive (+) impact from year 1		*(0.26)*
Adjusted earnings per share	$1.39	$1.45

(+) Positive.
(−) Negative.

In the above tabulation, items that increased earnings are listed as positive (+) and items that diminished earnings are listed as negative (−). Thus, in order to remove them from reported earnings, positive items are deducted while negative items are added back. The validity of each adjustment is, of course, a matter for the analyst's judgment.

THE FORECASTING OF EARNINGS

A major objective of income analysis is the forecasting of income. From an analytical point of view, the evaluation of the level of earnings is closely related to their forecast. This is so because a valid forecast of earnings involves an analysis of each major component of income and a considered estimate of its probable future size. Thus, some of the considerations discussed above are also applicable to earnings forecasting.

Forecasting must be differentiated from extrapolation. The latter is based on an assumption of the continuation of an existing trend and involves, more or less, a mechanical extension of that trend into the uncharted territory of the future.

Forecasting, on the other hand, is based on a careful analysis of as many individual components of income and expense as is possible and a considered estimate of their future size taking into consideration interrelationships among the components as well as probable future conditions. Thus, forecasting requires as much detail as is possible to obtain.

In addition, the "stability" of the individual components must be assessed in terms of the likelihood of their future recurrence. This lends particular importance to the analysis of nonrecurring factors and of extraordinary items. Some of the mechanics of earnings forecasting were considered in Chapter 17 as part of the process of projecting short-term cash flows.

A financial or earnings projection differs from a forecast in that the assumptions used may not necessarily be the most probable, but rather the assumptions represent a condition that the projection desires to test.

Forecasting requires the use of an earnings record covering a number of periods. Repeated or recurring performance can be forecast with a better degree of confidence than can random events.

Forecasting also requires use of enterprise data by product line or segment wherever different segments of an enterprise are subject to different degrees of risk, possess different degrees of profitability, or have differing growth potentials.

For example, the tabulation of divisional earnings results, in the table below, indicates the degree to which the results of a component of an enterprise can be masked by the aggregate results.

Judgment on the earnings potential of the enterprise depends, of course, on the relative importance, as well as the future prospects, of segment B. The subject of product line reporting was discussed in Chapter 20.

	Earnings in millions			
	year 1	*year 2*	*year 3*	*year 4*
Segment A	$1,800	$1,700	$1,500	$1,200
Segment B	600	800	1,100	1,400
Total net income	$2,400	$2,500	$2,600	$2,600

Can Earnings be Forecast?

Statistical studies by Little,[8] and Little and Rayner[9] in England, and by Brealey[10] in the United States, documented the apparent random behavior of reported earnings. Since these studies showed that earnings growth occurs in an almost purely random fashion, the implication was drawn that earnings changes cannot be accurately forecasted. Here again we have

---

[8] I. M. D. Little, "Higgledy Piggledy Growth" (Oxford, Eng.: Oxford University Institute of Statistics, 1962).

[9] I. M. D. Little and Rayner, "Higgledy Piggledy Growth Again" (Oxford, Eng.: Basil Blackwell, 1966).

[10] Richard A. Brealey, *Introduction to Risk and Return from Commerce Stocks* (Cambridge, Mass.: MIT Press, 1983).

the problem of deriving from the behavior of large aggregates conclusions about what can or cannot be done in individual cases. Operationally, such generalized conclusions are of very limited practical use.

Serious forecasting is not done by the naive extrapolation of past growth trends of earnings. It is done by a painstaking analysis of the *components* of earnings, the revenues, and the expenses, as well as of all factors that are known or are expected to alter these in the period of the forecast. No knowledgeable forecaster would work only with the earnings figure that is merely a net residual. Thus, it was reported[11] that Days Inns, a motel chain, has been including forecasts in its annual reports for years and that their accuracy was satisfactory to many users, including bankers. Nor is it hard to envisage highly accurate forecasts in such businesses as apartment buildings or hospitals. It is equally easy to find business categories where forecasting would be very difficult and unreliable.

A paper[12] that undertook a comprehensive review of the research on earnings forecasts concluded: "We feel that both the properties of earnings forecasts and the question of their value continues to be a fertile area of research." It is equally clear that those seriously interested in the earnings forecasting function will find the study of specific tools and conditions to be of considerably more value than the statistical study of large aggregates.

SEC Disclosure Requirements—Aid to Forecasting

The "Management's Discussion and Analysis of Financial Condition and Results of Operations" disclosure requirements of the SEC (see Chapter 20) contain a wealth of information on management's views and attitudes as well as on factors that can influence enterprise operating performance. Consequently, the analyst may find much information in these analyses to aid in the forecasting process. Moreover, while not requiring it, the SEC encourages the inclusion in these discussions of forward-looking information.

Elements in Earnings Forecasts

Granted that the decision maker is interested primarily in future prospects, the approach to assessing them must be based primarily on the present as well as on the past. While expected future changes in conditions must be given recognition, the experience of the present and the past form the base to which such adjustments are applied. In doing this, the

---

[11] *Forbes,* October 26, 1981, p. 189.

[12] A. R. Abdel-Khalik and R. B. Thompson, "Research on Earnings Forecasts: The State of the Art," *The Accounting Journal,* Winter 1977–78.

analyst relies on the degree of continuity and perseverance of momentum that is the common experience of the enterprise and the industry of which it is part. Random shocks and sudden changes are always possible, but they can rarely be foreseen with any degree of accuracy.

The importance to the analyst of the underlying continuity of business affairs should not be overemphasized. One should not confuse the basis for the projection of future results, which the past record represents, with the forecast which is the end product. As a final objective, the analyst is interested in a projection of net income. Net income is the result of the offset of two big streams: (1) total revenues and (2) total costs.

Considering that net income represents most frequently but a relatively small portion of either stream, one can see how a relatively minor change in either of these large streams can cause a very significant change in net income.

A significant check on the reasonableness of an earnings projection is to test it against the return on invested capital which is implicit in the forecast. If the result is at variance with returns realized in the past and industry returns, the underlying assumptions must be thoroughly examined so that the reasons for such deviations can be pinpointed.

In terms of the framework examined in Chapter 19, the ROI depends on earnings that are a product of *management* and of *assets* that require funds for their acquisition.

1. Management. It is well known that it takes resourceful management to "breathe life" into assets by employing them profitably and causing their optimum utilization. The assumption of stability of relationships and trends implies that there has been no major change in the skill, the depth, and the continuity of the management group or a radical change in the type of business in which their skill has been proven by a record of successful performance.

2. Assets. The second essential ingredient to profitable operations is funds or resources with which the assets essential to the successful conduct of business are acquired. No management, no matter how ingenious, can expand operations and have an enterprise grow without an adequate asset base. Thus, continuity of success and the extrapolation of growth must be based on an investigation of the sources of additional funds that the enterprise will need and the effect of the method of financing on net income and earnings per share.

The financial condition of the enterprise, as was seen in Chapters 16 and 18, can have a bearing on the results of operations. A lack of liquidity may inhibit an otherwise skillful management, and a precarious or too risky capital structure may lead to limitations by others on its freedom of action.

The above factors, as well as other economic, industry, and competitive factors, must be taken into account by the analyst when forecasting the earnings of an enterprise. Ideally, in forecasting earnings, the analyst should add a lot of knowledge about the future to some knowledge of the past. Realistically the analyst must settle for a lot of knowledge about the past and present and only a limited knowledge of the future.

In evaluating earnings trends, the analyst relies also on such indicators of future conditions as capital expenditures, order backlogs, as well as demand trends in individual product lines.

It is important to realize that no degree of sophistication in the techniques used in earnings forecasting can eliminate the inevitable uncertainty to which all forecasts are subject. Even the best and most soundly based projections retain a significant probability of proving widely off the mark because of events and circumstances that cannot be foreseen.

The most effective means by which the analyst and decision maker can counter this irreducible uncertainty is to keep close and constant watch over how closely actual results conform to his forecasts. This requires a constant monitoring of results and the adjustment and updating of projections in the light of such results. The monitoring of earnings is considered later in this chapter.

Publication of Financial Forecasts

Recent years have witnessed intensified interest in publication by companies of forecasts of earnings and other financial data. The publication of forecasts in Britain in certain specialized situations as well as a belief that forecasts would be useful to investors were major factors behind this interest. This type of forecasting by insiders (i.e., management) is to be distinguished from forecasts made by financial analysts that are based on all the information that they can obtain.

Speagle, Clark, and Elgers have categorized assumptions underlying forecasted financial statements as (1) "ongoing assumptions relating to the forecast methodology, company operating characteristics, and so on; (2) standard assumptions bearing upon the continuity in accounting policy, company management, supply sources, etc.; and (3) transitory assumptions covering events in a particular year such as recapitalizations, labor settlements, new product introductions, facilities expansion, etc."[13]

The validity of any forecasted financial data depends to a high degree on the assumptions, both implicit and explicit, upon which the forecasting technique is based. The financial analyst who uses a management forecast as input to his own projections should pay first and primary attention to the assumptions on which it is based.

In early 1977, an advisory committee to the SEC recommended that the agency design procedures to encourage companies to make forecasts of their economic performance. Following this, the SEC deleted from its

---

[13] R. E. Speagle, J. J. Clark, and P. Elgers, *Publishing Financial Forecasts: Benefits, Alternatives, Risk* (Laventhol Krekstein Horwath & Horwath, 1974).

regulations a reference to predictions of "earnings" as possibly misleading in certain situations. Thus the Commission will no longer object to disclosure in filings with it of projections that are made in good faith and have a reasonable basis, provided that they are presented in appropriate form and are accompanied by information adequate for investors to make their own judgments. In 1978 the SEC issued "Guides for Disclosure of Projections of Future Economic Performance."

Following this up, in 1979 the SEC issued a rule intended to encourage companies to make public their financial forecasts by protecting them from lawsuits in case their predictions did not come true. These "safe harbor" rules against fraud charges will protect companies as long as their projections have a "reasonable basis" and are made in good faith. Because of practical legal considerations few companies have availed themselves of these "safe harbor" rules and published forecasts.

The interest in financial forecasts has resulted in a formal consideration of some of the issues by the AICPA which in 1975 issued two statements on the subject.[14]

These statements recommend, among others, that financial forecasts should be presented in a historical financial statement format and that they include regularly a comparison of the previous forecast with attained results.

Both statements recognize the primary importance that assumptions play in the reliability and creditability of a financial forecast. Consequently, those assumptions that management thinks most crucial or significant to the forecast—or are key factors upon which the financial results of the enterprise depends—should be disclosed to provide the greatest benefit to users of forecasts. There ordinarily should be some indication of the basis or rationale for these assumptions.

In 1980, the Financial Forecasts and Projections Task Force of the AICPA issued a *Guide for a Review of a Financial Forecast.* This publication set forth the scope as well as the procedures to be followed by an accountant in reviewing a financial forecast and the method of reporting on such a review.

AUDITED FINANCIAL FORECASTS AND PROJECTIONS

In 1985, the AICPA's Auditing Standards Board issued its first Statement on Standards for Accountants' Services on Prospective Financial Information, entitled "Financial Forecasts and Projections." The Statement

---

[14] "Guidelines for Systems for the Preparation of Financial Forecasts" and "Presentation and Disclosure of Financial Forecasts," AICPA, 1975. (Auditing implications are also being considered.)

establishes standards for three types of services that independent accountants can render to clients for prospective financial statements: *(a)* compilation, *(b)* examination, and *(c)* application of agreed-upon procedures.

The Statement

- Defines a financial "forecast" and "projection."

- Establishes procedures and reporting standards for a compilation service on prospective financial statements.

- Establishes procedures and reporting standards for an examination service on prospective financial statements.

- Establishes standards for service to apply agreed-upon procedures to prospective financial statements.

- Prohibits an accountant from compiling, examining, or applying agreed-upon procedures to prospective financial statements that omit a summary of significant assumptions. Also prohibits the accountant from association with a "projection" when intended for other than limited use.

A *financial forecast* consists of ". . . prospective financial statements that present, to the best of the responsible party's knowledge and belief, an entity's expected financial position, results of operations, and changes in financial position." A financial forecast, then, reflects what is expected to happen if the entity follows its existing plans and if stated assumptions regarding its business and economic environment are reasonably accurate. It may be expressed either as a single set of expected results or in terms of a range of expected results.

A *financial projection* consists of ". . . prospective financial statements that present, to the best of the responsible party's knowledge and belief, given one or more hypothetical assumptions, an entity's expected financial position." Thus, a financial projection is helpful in evaluating the effects of alternative courses of action upon expected results. It may be expressed either as a single set of expected results or in terms of a range of expected results.

MONITORING PERFORMANCE AND RESULTS

The judgments of what the proper financial forecast of an enterprise is or what its earning power is, are based on estimates that hinge on future developments that can never be fully foreseen. Consequently, the best course of action is to monitor performance closely and frequently and to compare it with earlier estimates and assumptions. In this way, one can constantly revise one's estimates and judgments and incorporate the unfolding reality into earlier judgments and conclusions. One of the best ways of monitoring performance is to follow interim reports closely.

Interim Financial Statements

The need to follow closely the results achieved by an enterprise requires frequent updating of such results. Interim financial statements, most frequently issued on a quarterly basis, are designed to fill this need. They are used by decision makers as means of updating current results as well as in the prediction of future results.

If, as we have seen, a year is a relatively short period of time in which to account for results of operations, then trying to confine the measurement of results to a three-month period involves all the more problems and imperfections. For this and other reasons the reporting of interim earnings is subject to serious limitations and distortions. The intelligent use of reported interim results requires that we have a full understanding of these possible problem areas and limitations. The following is a review of some of the basic causes of these problems and limitations, as well as their effect on the determination of reported interim results.

Year-End Adjustments   The determination of the results of operations for a year requires a great many estimates, as well as procedures, such as accruals and the determination of inventory quantities and carrying values. These procedures can be complex, time-consuming, and costly. Examples of procedures requiring a great deal of data collection and estimation include estimation of the percentage of completion of contracts, determination of cost of work in process, the allocation of under- or overabsorbed overhead for the period, and the estimation of year-end inventory levels under the LIFO method. The complex, time-consuming, and expensive nature of these procedures can mean that they are performed much more crudely during interim periods and are often based on records that are less complete than are their year-end counterparts. The result inevitably is a less accurate process of income determination which, in turn, may require year-end adjustments that can modify substantially the interim results already reported.

Seasonality   Many enterprises experience at least some degree of seasonality in their activities. Sales may be unevenly distributed over the year, and so it may be with production and other activities. This tends to distort comparisons among the quarterly results of a single year. It also presents problems in the allocation of many budgeted costs, such as advertising, R&D, and repairs and maintenance. If expenses vary with sales, they should be accrued on the basis of expected sales for the full year. Obviously, the preparer of yearly financial statements has the benefit of hindsight that the preparer of interim statements does not. There are also problems with the allocation of fixed costs among quarters.

ILLUSTRATION 4.   The following is an example of adjustments that can result from seasonal variations: "Because of a seasonal production cycle, and in accordance with practices followed by the Company in reporting interim financial statements prior to year 4, $435,000 of unabsorbed factory overhead has been deferred at July 4, year 5. Due to uncertainties as to production and sales in year 4, $487,000 of such unabsorbed overhead was expensed during the first 6 months of the year."

APB Opinion 28

In its *Opinion 28,* the APB concluded that interim reports should be prepared in accordance with GAAP used in the preparation of the latest financial statements. Adopting mostly the point of view that a quarterly report is an integral part of a full year rather than a discrete period, it calls for the accrual of revenues and for the spreading of certain costs among the quarters of a year. For example, it sanctions the accrual of such year-end adjustments as inventory shrinkages, quantity discounts, and uncollectible accounts; but it prohibits the accrual of advertising costs on the ground that benefits of such costs cannot be anticipated. Losses cannot, generally, be deferred beyond the interim period in which they occur. LIFO inventory liquidations should be considered on an annual basis. Only permanent declines in inventory values are to be recorded on an interim basis. Moreover, the *Opinion* calls for the inclusion of extraordinary items in the interim period in which they occur.[15] Income taxes should be accrued on the basis of the effective tax rate expected to apply to the full year.

SEC Interim Reporting Requirements

The SEC took a relatively early and strong interest in interim reporting and as a result brought about very significant improvements in reporting and disclosure in this area. In 1972, it required quarterly reports (on Form 10-Q) and reports on current developments (Form 8-K), disclosure of separate fourth quarter results, and details of year-end adjustments.

In 1975, the SEC issued requirements (now in codification of *FRR,* Sections 301, 303, and 304) that served to expand substantially the content and the utility of interim reports filed with the Commission. The principal requirements include:

---

[15] *SFAS 3* specifies that "if a cumulative effect type accounting change is made in other than the first interim period of an enterprise's fiscal year, no cumulative effect of the change shall be included in net income of the period of change. Instead, financial information for the pre-change interim periods of the fiscal year in which the change is made shall be restated by applying the newly adopted accounting principle to those pre-change interim periods."

Comparative quarterly and year-to-date abbreviated income statement data—this information may be labeled *unaudited* and must also be included in annual reports to shareholders. (Small companies are exempted.)

Year-to-date statements of changes of cash flow.

Comparative balance sheets.

Increased pro forma information on business combinations accounted for as purchases.

Conformity with the principles of accounting measurement as set forth in professional pronouncements on interim financial reports. Increased disclosure of accounting changes with a letter from the registrant's independent public accountant stating whether or not he or she judges the changes to be preferable.

Management's narrative analysis of the results of operations, explaining the reasons for material changes in the amount of revenue and expense items from one quarter to the next. (See discussion in Chapter 20.)

Indications as to whether a Form 8-K was filed during the quarter—reporting either unusual charges or credits to income or a change of auditors.

Signature of the registrant's chief financial officer or chief accounting officer.

In promulgating these expanded disclosure requirements, the Commission indicated that it believed that these disclosures will assist investors in understanding the pattern of corporate activities throughout a fiscal period. It maintained that presentation of such quarterly data will supply information about the trend of business operations over segments of time which are sufficiently short to reflect business turning points.

Campbell Soup (Chapter 4, Appendix B) presents quarterly data in item 184.

Implications for Analysis

While there have been some notable recent improvements in the reporting of interim results, the analyst must remain constantly aware that accuracy of estimation and the objectivity of determinations are and remain problem areas that are inherent in the measurement of results of very short periods. Moreover, the limited association of auditors with interim data, while lending some unspecified degree of assurance, cannot be equated to the degree of assurance that is associated with fully audited financial statements. SEC insistence that the professional pronouncements on interim statements (such as *APB Opinion 28*) be adhered to can offer analysts some additional comfort. However, not all principles promulgated by the APB on the subject of interim financial statements result in presentations useful to the analyst. For example, the inclusion of extraordinary items in the results of the quarter in which they occur will require careful adjustment to render them meaningful for purposes of analysis.

While the normalization of expenses is a reasonable intraperiod accounting procedure, the analyst must be aware of the fact that there are no rigorous standards or rules governing its implementation and that it is consequently subject to possible abuse. The shifting of costs between periods is generally easier than the shifting of sales; and, therefore, a close analysis of sales may yield a more realistic clue to a company's true state of affairs for an interim period.

Since the price of the common stock influences the computation of earnings per share (see Chapter 12), the analyst should in the evaluation of per share results be alert to the separation of these market effects from those related to the operating fundamentals of an enterprise.

Some problems of seasonality in interim results of operations can be overcome by considering in the analysis not merely the results of a single quarter, but also the year-to-date cumulative results which incorporate the results of the latest available quarter. This is the most effective way of monitoring the results of an enterprise and bringing to bear on its analysis the latest data on operations that are available.

QUESTIONS

1. Distinguish between income and cash flow. Why should there be a distinction between the two?
2. *a.* What is meant by *quality of earnings?* Why do analysts assess it?
   b. On what major elements does the quality of earnings depend?
3. *a.* What are discretionary costs?
   b. Of what significance are discretionary costs to an analysis of the quality of earnings?
4. *a.* Why is the evaluation of R&D costs important in the analysis and projection of income?
   b. What are some of the precautions required in analyzing R&D expenses?
5. *a.* What is the relationship between the carrying amounts of various assets and the earnings reported?
   b. What is the relationship between the amounts at which liabilities, including provisions, are carried and earnings are reported?
6. In what way is balance sheet analysis a check on the validity as well as the quality of earnings?
7. Comment on the effect which the "risk category" of an asset has on the quality of reported earnings.
8. Explain briefly the relationship between the quality of earnings and the following balance sheet items:

    a. Accounts receivable.

    b. Inventories.

    c. Deferred charges.

9. What is the effect of external factors on the quality of earnings?

10. What is the objective of recasting the income statement?

11. Where will the analyst find data needed for the analysis of the results of operations and for their recasting and adjustment?

12. What is the aim of the recasting process, and how is the recasting accomplished?

13. Describe the income statement adjustment process.

14. What is income smoothing? How can it be distinguished from outright falsehoods?

15. Name and explain three forms of income smoothing.

16. *a.* What factors and incentives motivate companies to engage in income smoothing?

    b. What are the implications for analysis?

17. Why are managements so greatly interested in the reporting of extraordinary gains and losses?

18. What are the basic objectives of the analyst in the identification and the evaluation of extraordinary items?

19. *a.* Into what categories can items which are described as unusual or extraordinary in the financial statements be usefully subdivided for purposes of analysis?

    b. Give examples of each such category.

    c. How should the analyst treat items in each category? Is such a treatment indicated under all circumstances? Explain.

20. What are the effects of extraordinary items on:

    a. Enterprise resources?

    b. The evaluation of managements?

21. Comment on the following statement:

    "Extraordinary gains or losses have not resulted from a 'normal' or 'planned' activity of management and, consequently, they should not be used in the evaluation of managerial performance."

    Do you agree?

22. What is the difference between forecasting and extrapolation of earnings?

23. How can SEC disclosure requirements aid in forecasting?

24. What are the categories of assumptions underlying forecasted financial statements? Give examples of each category. What is the importance of these assumptions to the financial analyst?

25. What is earning power? Why is it important?

26. *a.* What are interim financial statements used for?

    b. What accounting problems that are peculiar to interim statements must the analyst be aware of?

27. Interim financial reporting can be subject to serious limitations and distortions. Discuss some of the reasons for this.

28. What are the major disclosure requirements by the SEC with regard to interim reports? What are the objectives behind them?

29. What implications do interim reports hold for the financial analyst?

Chapter 23

COMPREHENSIVE ANALYSIS OF FINANCIAL STATEMENTS

THE METHODOLOGY OF FINANCIAL STATEMENT ANALYSIS

The marshaling, arrangement, and presentation of data for purposes of financial statement analysis can be standardized to some extent in the interest of consistency and organizational efficiency. However, the actual process of analysis must be left to the judgment of the analyst so that he or she may allow for the great diversity of situations and circumstances that are likely to be encountered in practice, and thus give full reign to his or her own initiative, originality, and ingenuity. Nevertheless, there are some useful generalizations and guidelines that may be stated as to a general approach to the task of financial statement analysis.

To begin with, financial statement analysis is oriented toward the achievement of definite objectives. In order that the analysis best accomplish these objectives, the first step is to define them carefully. The thinking and clarification leading up to such a definition of objectives is a very important part of the analytical process, for it ensures a clear understanding of objectives, that is, of what is pertinent and relevant and what is not, and thus also leads to avoidance of unnecessary work. This clarification of objectives is indispensable to an *effective* as well as to an *efficient* analysis; *effective,* in that, given the specifications, it focuses on the most important and most relevant elements of the financial statements; *efficient,* in that it leads to an analysis with maximum economy of time and effort.

ILLUSTRATION 1.   The bank loan officer, dealing with a request for a short-term loan to finance inventory, may define his objective as assessing the intention and the ability of the borrower to repay the loan on time. Thus, the analyst can concentrate on what is needed to achieve this objective and need not, for instance, address himself to industry conditions that can affect the borrowing entity only over the longer term.

Once the objective of the analysis has been defined, the next step is the formulation of specific questions the answers to which are needed in the achievement of such objectives.

ILLUSTRATION 2.   The loan officer in Illustration 1 now needs to define the critical criteria that will affect his decision. For instance, the question of the borrower's *willingness* to repay the short-term loan bears on his character; and financial statement analysis can reveal only the history of past loans granted it. Thus, tools other than financial statement analysis will have to be employed to get complete information on the borrower's character.

Among the other questions on which the loan officer will need information are the following:

1. What is the enterprise's short-term liquidity?
2. What will its sources and uses of cash be during the duration of the loan agreement?

Financial statement analysis can go far toward providing answers to such questions.

Having defined the objective and having translated it into specific questions and criteria that must be resolved, the analyst is ready for the third step in the analysis process. This is to decide which tools and techniques of analysis are the most appropriate, effective, and efficient ones to use in working on the particular decision problem at hand.

ILLUSTRATION 3.   Following the sequence developed in Illustrations 1 and 2, the loan officer will now decide which financial statement analysis tools are the most appropriate to use in this case. He may choose one or more of the following:

1. Short-term liquidity ratios.
2. Inventory turnover measures.
3. Cash flow projections.
4. Analyses of changes in financial position.

These analyses will have to include estimates and projections of future conditions toward which most, if not all, financial analysis is oriented.

The fourth and final step in analysis is the interpretation of the data and measures assembled as a basis for decision and action. This is the most critical and difficult of the steps, and the one requiring the application of a great deal of judgment, skill, and effort. Interpretation is a process of investigation and evaluation, and of envisaging the reality that lies behind the figures examined. There is, of course, no mechanical substitute for this process of judgment. However, the proper definition of the problem and of the critical questions that must be answered, as well as the skillful selection of the most appropriate tools of analysis available in the circumstances, will go a long way toward a meaningful interpretation of the results of analysis.

ILLUSTRATION 4.   Following the sequences of the first three examples above, the collection, by the loan officer, of the data described in Illustration 3 is, of course, not the end result of his analysis. These data must be integrated, evaluated, and interpreted for the purposes of reaching the basic decision of whether to make the loan and, if so, in what amount.

By way of analogy, the weather forecasting function provides an example of the difference between the availability of analytical data and its successful interpretation. Thus, the average listener to weather information does not know how to interpret barometric pressure, relative humidity, or wind velocity. What one needs to know is the weather forecast that results from an interpretation of these data.

The intelligent analyst and interpreter of financial statement data must always bear in mind that a financial statement is at best an abstraction of an underlying reality. Further mathematical manipulation of financial data can result in second, third, and even further levels of abstractions; and the analyst must always keep in mind the business reality behind the figures. No map of the Rocky Mountains can fully convey the grandeur of the terrain. One has to see them in order to appreciate them because maps, like financial statements, are, at best, abstractions. That is why security analysts must, at some point, leave the financial statements and visit the companies that they analyze in order to get a full understanding of the phenomena revealed by their analysis. This is particularly true because the static reality portrayed by the abstractions found in the financial statements cannot remain stable for very long. Reality is ever changing.

A recognition of the inherent limitations of financial data is needed for intelligent analysis. This does not detract from their importance because financial statements and data are the only means by which the financial realities of an enterprise can be reduced to a common denominator that is quantified and that can be mathematically manipulated and projected in a rational and disciplined way.

SIGNIFICANCE OF THE "BUILDING BLOCK" APPROACH TO FINANCIAL ANALYSIS

The six major building blocks of financial analysis that we have examined in this text are:

1. Short-term liquidity.
2. Funds flow.
3. Capital structure and long-term solvency.
4. Return on investment (ROI).
5. Asset utilization.
6. Operating performance.

The building block approach to financial statement analysis involves:

1. The determination of the major objectives that a particular financial analysis is to achieve.
2. Arriving at a judgment about which of the six major areas of analysis (i.e., our "building blocks") must be evaluated with what degree of emphasis and in what order of priority.

For example, the security analyst, in the evaluation of the investment merit of a particular issue of equity securities, may attach primary importance to the earning capacity and potential of the enterprise. Thus, the first building block of the analysis will be the evaluation of *operating performance* and the next, perhaps, *return on investment (ROI)*. A thorough analysis will, of course, require that attention be paid to the other four major areas of analysis, although with perhaps lesser degrees of emphasis; that is, depth. This attention to the other major areas of analysis is necessary in order to detect possible problem areas; that is, areas of potential risk. Thus, further analysis may reveal a liquidity problem arising from a "thin" working capital condition, or it may reveal a situation of inadequate capital funds that may stifle growth and flexibility. It is conceivable that these problem areas may reveal themselves to be so important as to overshadow the question of earning power, thus leading to a change in the relative emphasis that the analyst will accord to the main areas of his or her particular analysis.

While the subdivision of the analysis into six distinct aspects of a company's financial condition and performance is a useful approach, it must be borne in mind that these areas of analysis are highly interrelated. For example, the operating performance of an enterprise can be affected by the lack of adequate capital funds or by problems of short-term liquidity. Similarly, a credit evaluation cannot stop at the point where a satisfactory short-term liquidity position has been determined because existing or incipient problems in the "operating performance" area may result in serious drains of funds due to losses. Such drains can quickly reverse the satisfactory liquidity position that may prevail at a given point in time.

At the start of the analysis, the analyst will tentatively determine the relative importance of the areas that he or she will examine and the order in which they will be examined. This order of emphasis and priority may subsequently change in the light of the analyst's findings and as the analysis progresses.

THE EARMARKS OF GOOD FINANCIAL ANALYSIS

As we have noted, the foundation of any good analysis is a thorough understanding of the objectives to be achieved and the uses to which it is going to be put. Such understanding leads to economy of effort as well as to a useful and most relevant focus on the points that need to be clarified and the estimates and projections that are required.

In practice, rarely can all the facts surrounding a particular analysis be obtained, so that most analyses are undertaken on the basis of incomplete and inadequate facts and data. The process of financial analysis is basically one of reducing the areas of uncertainty—which can, however, never be completely eliminated.

A written analysis and report is not only a significant medium of communication to the reader but it also serves importantly to organize the thinking of the analyst as well as to allow him or her to check the flow and the logic of the presentation. The process of writing reinforces our thinking and vice versa. As we revise our words, we also refine our thoughts—and improvements in style lead, in turn, to the sharpening and improvement in the thinking process itself.

A good analysis separates clearly for the reader the interpretations and conclusions of the analysis from the facts and data upon which they are based. This not only separates fact from opinion and estimate but also enables the reader to follow the rationale of the analyst's conclusions and allows him to modify them as his judgment dictates. To this end, the analysis should contain distinct sections devoted to:

1. General background material on the enterprise analyzed, the industry of which it is a part, and the economic environment in which it operates.
2. Financial and other data used in the analysis as well as ratios, trends, and other analytical measures that have been developed from them.
3. Assumptions as to the general economic environment and as to other conditions on which estimates and projections are based.
4. A listing of positive and negative factors, quantitative and qualitative, by important areas of analysis.
5. Projections, estimates, interpretations, and conclusions based on the aforementioned data. (Some analyses list only the positive and negative factors developed by the analysis and leave further interpretations to the reader.)

A good analysis should start with a brief "Summary and Conclusion" section as well as a table of contents to help the busy reader decide how much of the report he wants to read and on which parts of it to concentrate.

The writer of an analytical report must guard against the all-too-common tendency to include irrelevant matter. For example, the reader need not know the century-old details of the humble beginnings of the enterprise under analysis nor should he be taken on a "journey" along all the fruitless byways and missteps that the analyst inevitably encountered in the process of ferreting out and separating the important from the insignificant. Irrelevant bulk or "roughage" can only serve to confuse and distract the reader of a report.

Ambiguities and equivocations that are employed to avoid responsibility or to hedge conclusions do not belong in a good analytical report. Finally, the writers of such reports must recognize that we are all judged on the basis of small details. Consequently, the presence of mistakes in grammar or of obvious errors of fact in a report can plant doubt in the reader's mind as to the competence of the author and the validity of the analysis.

SPECIAL INDUSTRY OR ENVIRONMENTAL CHARACTERISTICS

In this book, the analysis of the various segments of financial statements was treated from the point of view of the ordinary commercial or industrial enterprise. The financial analyst must, however, recognize that there are industries with distinct accounting treatments that arise either from their specialized nature or from the special conditions, such as governmental regulation, to which they are subject. The analysis of the financial statements of such enterprise requires a thorough understanding of the accounting peculiarities to which they are subject, and the analyst must, accordingly, prepare himself for his task by the study and the understanding of the specialized areas of accounting that affect his particular analysis.

Thus, for example, the analysis of a company in the oil and gas industry requires a thorough knowledge of accounting concepts peculiar to that industry such as the determination of "cost centers," prediscovery costs, discovery costs, and the disposition of capitalized costs. There are particular problems in the treatment of exploratory, development, and other expenditures as well as in amortization and depletion practices.

Life insurance accounting, to cite another example, also requires specialized knowledge that arises from the peculiarities of this industry and from the regulation to which it is subject. There are special problems in the area of recognition of premium revenues, the accounting for acquisition costs of new business, and the determination of policy reserves.

Public utility regulation has resulted in specialized accounting concepts and problems of which every utility analyst must be aware. There are tax allocation problems resulting in differences among companies that "normalize" taxes versus those which "flow" them through. Then there are problems related to the adequacy of provisions for depreciation, and problems concerning the utility's "rate base" and the method by which it is computed.

As in any field of endeavor, specialized areas of inquiry require that specialized knowledge be brought to bear upon them. Financial analysis is, of course, no exception.

ILLUSTRATION OF A COMPREHENSIVE ANALYSIS OF FINANCIAL STATEMENTS—CAMPBELL SOUP COMPANY

The following analysis of the financial statements and other data of the Campbell Soup Company (Campbell) will serve as an illustration of this process.

Introduction

Campbell Soup Company is one of the world's largest and best-known food companies which manufactures prepared convenience foods for human consumption.

The company's operations are managed by three divisions; Campbell North America, Campbell Biscuit and Bakery, and Campbell International. Within each division there are groups and business units; as an example, within the Campbell North America division the major sectors are Soups, Convenience Meals, Grocery, Condiments, and the Canadian company operations.

The company's products are primarily for home use, but various items are also manufactured for restaurants, vending machines, and institutions. The company distributes its products through direct customers, including chain stores, wholesalers, and distributors that maintain central warehouses, institutional and industrial customers, convenience stores, club stores, and certain governmental agencies. In the United States, sales solicitation activities are conducted by subsidiaries and through independent brokers and contract distributors. No material part of the business is dependent upon a single customer. Shipments are made promptly by the company after receipt and acceptance of orders; therefore, there is no significant backlog of unfilled orders.

Exhibit 23–1 shows sales contribution by division for 1986 to 91. As can be seen, Campbell North America and International are the largest contributors of sales, accounting for 68.7 percent and 19.7 percent, respectively, in 1991.

Soup is the core business of Campbell U.S.A., with about 60 percent of the overall soup market, and the more recent introductions of dry, ramen noodle, and microwavable soups. Other Campbell Soup brands include ready-to-serve soups—"Home Cooking," "Chunky," and "Healthy Request." An integral part of the soup business is Swanson's canned chicken broth. Americans purchase more than 2.5 billion cans of

Exhibit 23–1

CAMPBELL SOUP COMPANY

	1991	1990	1989	1988	1987	1986
Sales contribution by division (in millions)						
Campbell North America:						
Campbell U.S.A.	$3,911.8	$3,932.7	$3,666.9	$3,094.1	$2,881.4	$2,910.1
Campbell Canada	352.0	384.0	313.4	313.1	312.8	255.1
	4,263.8	4,316.7	3,980.3	3,407.2	3,194.2	3,165.2
Campbell Biscuit and Bakery:						
Pepperidge Farm	569.0	582.0	548.4	495.0	458.5	420.1
International Biscuit	219.4	195.3	178.0	–	–	–
	788.4	777.3	726.4	495.0	458.5	420.1
Campbell International	1,222.9	1,189.8	1,030.3	1,036.5	897.8	766.2
Interdivision	(71.0)	(78.0)	(64.9)	(69.8)	(60.1)	(64.7)
Total sales	$6,204.1	$6,205.8	$5,672.1	$4,868.9	$4,490.4	$4,286.8
Percent of sales by division						
Campbell North America:						
Campbell U.S.A.	63.0%	63.4%	64.7%	63.6%	64.2%	67.9%
Campbell Canada	5.7	6.2	5.5	6.4	6.9	5.9
	68.7	69.6	70.2	70.0	71.1	73.8
Campbell Biscuit and Bakery:						
Pepperidge Farm	9.2	9.4	9.7	10.2	10.2	9.8
International Biscuit	3.5	3.1	3.1	–	–	–
	12.7	12.5	12.8	10.2	10.2	9.8
Campbell International	19.7	19.2	18.2	21.3	20.0	17.9
Interdivision	(1.1)	(1.3)	(1.2)	(1.4)	(1.3)	(1.5)
Total sales	100.0%	100.0%	100.0%	100.0%	100.0%	100.0%

Campbell's soups each year, and on average have nine cans in their pantry at any time during the year.

Fiscal 1991 was a successful transition year for Campbell. Major divestitures were completed and significant restructuring and reorganization projects were accomplished. Corporate goals concerning earnings, returns, and cash flows were exceeded. The North America and International divisions had exceptionally strong earnings results. The company entered fiscal 1992 with a reconfigured product portfolio, positioned well to support a continued strong financial performance. The strong margin growth had given Campbell an opportunity to increase consumer advertising which fostered the introduction of new products, line extensions, and continued revitalization of flagship products.

FINANCIAL STATEMENTS

The financial statements of Campbell Soup which are included in the 1991 annual report, along with the notes and commentaries contained therein and data from Form 10-K are presented in Chapter 4, Appendix B. Exhibits 23–2, 23–3, and 23–4 present summary financial statements for the six fiscal years ending in 1991.

The auditor's opinions on the financial statements have been unqualified for the past six years.

ADDITIONAL INFORMATION

Exhibit 23–5 presents growth rates, annually compounded, for periods as described. Most impressive is the growth in net income per share over the past five years (12.93%). Growth in sales per share over the most recent five-year period has been at a rate lower than that of net income. Equity per share growth in the latest 5-year period declined compared to the 10-year period. This, plus the two cells in the exhibit which show negative growth rates, is due to the significant divestitures and restructuring implemented in 1989 and 1990.

Exhibits 23–6 through 23–9 are based on the financial statements of Campbell.

FOCUS OF ANALYSIS

Based on the foregoing data and information, we are to analyze the financial statements of Campbell Soup Company with the following alternative points of view (objectives) in mind.

1. That of a bank which has been requested to make available to the

Exhibit 23–2

CAMPBELL SOUP COMPANY
Income Statements
For Years 1986 to 1991

	1991	1990	1989	1988	1987	1986
Net sales	$6,204.1	$6,205.8	$5,672.1	$4,868.9	$4,490.4	$4,286.8
Costs and expenses:						
Cost of product sold	4,095.5	4,258.2	4,001.6	3,392.8	3,180.5	3,082.7
Marketing and selling expenses	956.2	980.5	818.8	733.3	626.2	544.4
Administrative expenses	306.7	290.7	252.1	232.6	213.9	195.9
Research and development expenses	56.3	53.7	47.7	46.9	44.8	42.2
Interest expense	116.2	111.6	94.1	53.9	51.7	56.0
Interest income	(26.0)	(17.6)	(38.3)	(33.2)	(29.5)	(27.4)
Foreign exchange losses, net	0.8	3.3	19.3	16.6	4.8	0.7
Other expense (income)	26.2	14.7	32.4	(3.2)	(9.5)	5.5
Divestitures, restructuring, and unusual charge	0.0	339.1	343.0	40.6	0.0	0.0
Total costs and expenses	5,531.9	6,034.2	5,570.7	4,480.3	4,082.9	3,900.0
Earnings before equity in earnings of affiliates and minority interests	672.2	171.6	101.4	388.6	407.5	386.8
Equity in earnings of affiliates	2.4	13.5	10.4	6.3	15.1	4.3
Minority interests	(7.2)	(5.7)	(5.3)	(6.3)	(4.7)	(3.9)
Earnings before taxes	667.4	179.4	106.5	388.6	417.9	387.2
Taxes on earnings	265.9	175.0	93.4	147.0	170.6	164.0
Earnings before cumulative effect of accounting change	401.5	4.4	13.1	241.6	247.3	223.2
Cumulative effect of change in accounting for income taxes	0	0	0	32.5	0	0
Net earnings	$401.5	$4.4	$13.1	$274.1	$247.3	$223.2
Net earnings per share	$3.16	$0.03	$0.10	$2.12*	$1.90	$1.72
Weighted average shares outstanding	127.00	126.60	129.30	129.30	129.90	129.50

* Including $0.25 per share cumulative effect of change in accounting for income taxes

Exhibit 23–3

CAMPBELL SOUP COMPANY
Balance Sheets
For Years 1986 to 1991
(in millions)

	July 28, 1991	July 29, 1990	July 30, 1989	July 31, 1988	August 2, 1987	August 3, 1986
Assets						
Current assets						
Cash and cash equivalents	$ 178.90	$ 80.70	$ 120.90	$ 85.80	$ 145.00	$ 155.10
Other temporary investments, at cost which approximates market	12.80	22.50	26.20	35.00	280.30	238.70
Accounts receivable	527.40	624.50	538.00	486.90	338.90	299.00
Inventories	706.70	819.80	816.00	664.70	623.60	610.50
Prepaid expenses	92.70	118.00	100.40	90.50	50.10	31.50
Total current assets	1,518.50	1,665.50	1,601.50	1,362.90	1,437.90	1,334.80
Plant assets, net of depreciation	1,790.40	1,717.70	1,540.60	1,508.90	1,349.00	1,168.10
Intangible assets, net of amortization	435.50	383.40	466.90	496.60	—	—
Other assets	404.60	349.00	323.10	241.20	310.50	259.90
Total assets	$4,149.00	$4,115.60	$3,932.10	$3,609.60	$3,097.40	$2,762.80
Liabilities and Shareowners' Equity						
Current liabilities						
Notes payable	$282.20	$202.30	$271.50	$138.00	$93.50	$88.90
Payable to suppliers and others	482.40	525.20	508.20	446.70	374.80	321.70
Accrued liabilities	408.70	491.90	392.60	236.90	182.10	165.90
Dividend payable	37.00	32.30	29.70	—	—	—
Accrued income taxes	67.70	46.40	30.10	41.70	43.40	49.60
Total current liabilities	1,278.00	1,298.10	1,232.10	863.30	693.80	626.10

Long-term debt	772.60	805.80	629.20	525.80	380.20	362.30
Other liabilities, principally deferred income taxes	305.00	319.90	292.50	325.50	287.30	235.50
Shareowners' equity						
Preferred stock; authorized 40,000,000 sh.; none issued	—	—	—	—	—	—
Capital stock, $0.15 par value; authorized 140,000,000 sh.; issued 135,622,676 sh.	20.30	20.30	20.30	20.30	20.30	20.30
Capital surplus	107.30	61.90	50.80	42.30	41.10	38.10
Earnings retained in the business	1,912.60	1,653.30	1,775.80	1,879.10	1,709.60	1,554.00
Capital stock in treasury, at cost	(270.40)	(107.20)	(70.70)	(75.20)	(46.80)	(48.40)
Cumulative translation adjustments	23.60	63.50	2.10	28.50	11.90	(25.10)
Total shareowners' equity	1,793.40	1,691.80	1,778.30	1,895.00	1,736.10	1,538.90
Total liabilities and shareowners' equity	$4,149.00	$4,115.60	$3,932.10	$3,609.60	$3,097.40	$2,762.80

Exhibit 23-4

CAMPBELL SOUP COMPANY
Consolidated Statements of Cash Flows
For Years 1986 to 1991
(in millions)

	1991	1990	1989	1988	1987	1986	Total
Cash flows from operating activities:							
Net earnings	$401.5	$ 4.4	$ 13.1	$274.1	$247.3	$223.2	$1,163.6
To reconcile net earnings to net cash provided by operating activities:							
Depreciation and amortization	208.6	200.9	192.3	170.9	144.6	126.8	1,044.1
Divestitures and restructuring provision	—	339.1	343.0	17.6	—	—	699.7
Deferred taxes	35.5	3.9	(67.8)	13.4	45.7	29.0	59.7
Other, net	63.2	18.6	37.3	43.0	28.0	16.6	206.7
Cumulative effect of accounting change	—	—	—	(32.5)	—	—	(32.5)
(Increase) decrease in accounts receivable	17.1	(60.4)	(46.8)	(104.3)	(36.3)	(3.6)	(234.3)
(Increase) decrease in inventories	48.7	10.7	(113.2)	54.2	(3.9)	23.1	19.6
Net change in other current assets and liabilities	30.6	(68.8)	(0.6)	30.2	42.9	48.7	83.0
Net cash provided by operating activities	805.2	448.4	357.3	466.6	468.3	463.8	3,009.6
Cash flows from investing activities:							
Purchases of plant assets	(361.1)	(387.6)	(284.1)	(245.3)	(303.7)	(235.3)	(1,817.1)
Sale of plant assets	43.2	34.9	39.8	22.6	—	29.8	170.3
Businesses acquired	(180.1)	(41.6)	(135.8)	(471.9)	(7.3)	(20.0)	(856.7)
Sale of businesses	67.4	21.7	4.9	23.5	20.8	—	138.3
Increase in other assets	(57.8)	(18.6)	(107.0)	(40.3)	(50.1)	(18.0)	(291.8)
Net change in other temporary investments	9.7	3.7	9.0	249.2	(60.7)	(144.1)	66.8
Net cash used in investing activities	(478.7)	(387.5)	(473.2)	(462.2)	(401.0)	(387.6)	(2,590.2)

Cash flows from financing activities:

Long-term borrowings	402.8	12.6	126.5	103.0	4.8	203.9	853.6
Repayments of long-term borrowings	(129.9)	(22.5)	(53.6)	(22.9)	(23.9)	(164.7)	(417.5)
Increase (decrease) in short-term borrowings*	(137.9)	(2.7)	108.2	8.4	(20.7)	4.6	(40.1)
Other short-term borrowings	117.3	153.7	227.1	77.0	89.3	72.9	737.3
Repayments of other short-term borrowings	(206.4)	(89.8)	(192.3)	(87.6)	(66.3)	(88.5)	(730.9)
Dividends paid	(137.5)	(124.3)	(86.7)	(104.6)	(91.7)	(104.6)	(649.4)
Treasury stock purchases	(175.6)	(41.1)	(8.1)	(29.3)	–	–	(254.1)
Treasury stock issued	47.7	12.4	18.5	0.9	1.6	4.0†	85.1
Other, net	(0.1)	(0.1)	23.5	2.3	18.6	17.9	62.1
Net cash provided (used in) financing activities	(219.6)	(101.8)	163.1	(52.8)	(88.3)	(54.5)	(353.9)
Effect of exchange rate change on cash	(8.7)	0.7	(12.1)	(10.8)	(7.1)	(3.7)	(41.7)
Net increase (decrease) in cash and cash equivalents	98.2	(40.2)	35.1	(59.2)	(28.1)	18.0	23.8
Cash and cash equivalents at the beginning of year	80.7	120.9	85.8	145.0	173.1	155.1	760.6
Cash and cash equivalents at the end of year	178.9	80.7	120.9	85.8	145.0	173.1	784.4

* With less than three months maturities.
† 2.8 issued for a pooling of interest.

Exhibit 23–5

CAMPBELL SOUP COMPANY

Five-year growth rates*
(annually compounded)

Per share	1986–1991	1986–1988 to 1989–1991
Sales	8.09%	5.95%
Net income	12.93	−10.53
Dividends	11.50	6.69
Equity	3.55	0.53

Ten-year growth rates*
(annually compounded)

Per share	1981–1991	1981–1983 to 1989–1991
Sales	8.51%	7.22%
Net income	12.19	−0.44
Dividends	8.18	6.62
Equity	6.22	5.13

* Growth rates (annually compounded) are computed using the compound interest method.

$$\text{Future value } (FV) = \text{Present value} \quad (PV) \times \left(1 + \frac{r}{100}\right)^n$$

For example, net sales per share during 1986–1991 grew at a rate of:

$PV = \$33.10$

$FV = \$48.85$

$n = 5$

$r = \text{rate of growth}$

$$FV = PV\left(1 + \frac{r}{100}\right)^n$$

$$48.8 = 33.1\left(1 + \frac{r}{100}\right)^5$$

$r = 8.09\%$

company a line of credit (for short-term operating purposes) of up to $60 million.

2. That of an insurance company to whom the company wants to sell privately $50 million of 25-year bonds.

3. That of an investor considering a substantial investment in the company.

These diverse and broad points of view require that we analyze all major aspects of the company's financial condition and results of operations, that is:

1. Short-term liquidity.
2. Funds flow.
3. Capital structure and long-term solvency.

Exhibit 23–6

CAMPBELL SOUP COMPANY
Common Size Income Statements
For Years 1986 to 1991

	1991	1990	1989	1988	1987	1986
Net sales	100.00%	100.00%	100.00%	100.00%	100.00%	100.00%
Costs and expenses:						
Cost of products sold	66.01%	68.62%	70.55%	69.68%	70.83%	71.91%
Marketing and selling expenses	15.41	15.80	14.44	15.06	13.95	12.70
Administrative expenses	4.94	4.68	4.44	4.78	4.76	4.57
Research and development expenses	0.91	0.87	0.84	0.96	1.00	0.98
Interest expense	1.87	1.80	1.66	1.11	1.15	1.31
Interest income	(0.42)	(0.28)	(0.68)	(0.68)	(0.66)	(0.64)
Foreign exchange losses, net	0.01	0.05	0.34	0.34	0.11	0.02
Other expense (income)	0.42	0.24	0.57	(0.07)	(0.21)	0.13
Divestitures, restructuring, and unsual charge	—	5.46	6.05	0.83	—	—
Total costs and expenses	89.17%	97.23%	98.21%	92.02%	90.93%	90.98%
Earnings before equity in earnings of affliates and minority interests	10.83%	2.77%	1.79%	7.98%	9.07%	9.02%
Equity in earnings of affiliates	0.04	0.22	0.18	0.13	0.34	0.10
Minority interests	(0.12)	(0.09)	(0.09)	(0.13)	(0.10)	(0.09)
Earnings before taxes	10.76%	2.89%	1.88%	7.98%	9.31%	9.03%
Taxes on earnings	4.29	2.82	1.65	3.02	3.80	3.83
Earnings before cumulative effect of accounting change	6.47%	0.07%	0.23%	4.96%	5.51%	5.21%
Cumulative effect of change in accounting for income taxes	—	—	—	0.67	—	—
Net earnings	6.47%	0.07%	0.23%	5.63%	5.51%	5.21%

Exhibit 23–7

CAMPBELL SOUP COMPANY
Common Size Balance Sheets
For Years 1986 to 1991

	July 28, 1991	July 29, 1990	July 30, 1989	July 31, 1988	August 2, 1987	August 3, 1986	Industry Composite
Current assets							
Cash and cash equivalents	4.31%	1.96%	3.07%	2.38%	4.69%	5.61%	3.4%
Other temporary investments, at cost which approximates market	0.31	0.55	0.67	0.97	9.05	8.64	
Accounts receivable	12.71	15.17	13.68	13.49	10.94	10.82	16.5
Inventories	17.03	19.92	20.75	18.41	20.13	22.10	38.6
Prepaid expenses	2.23	2.87	2.55	2.51	1.62	1.14	2.2
Total current assets	36.60%	40.47%	40.73%	37.76%	46.43%	48.31%	60.70%
Plant assets, net of depreciation	43.15	41.74	39.18	41.80	43.55	42.28	21.0%
Intangible assets, net of amortization	10.50	9.32	11.87	13.76	–	–	
Other assets	9.75	8.48	8.22	6.68	10.02	9.41	18.3
Total assets	100.00%	100.00%	100.00%	100.00%	100.00%	100.00%	100.00%
Current liabilities							
Notes payable	6.80%	4.92%	6.90%	3.82%	3.02%	3.22%	6.7%
Payable to suppliers and others	11.63	12.76	12.92	12.38	12.10	11.64	10.2
Accrued liabilities	9.85	11.95	9.98	6.56	5.88	6.00	15.8
Dividend payable	0.89	0.78	0.76	–	–	–	
Accrued income taxes	1.63	1.13	0.77	1.16	1.40	1.80	
Total current liabilities	30.80%	31.54%	31.33%	23.92%	22.40%	22.66%	32.70%

Long-term debt	18.62%	19.58%	16.00%	14.57%	12.27%	13.11%	19.7%
Other liabilities, principally deferred income taxes	7.35	7.77	7.44	9.02	9.28	8.52	1.5
Shareowners' equity							
Preferred stock; authorized 40,000,000 sh.; none issued	—	—	—	—	—	—	
Capital stock, $0.15 par value; authorized 140,000,000 sh.; issued 135,622,676 sh.	0.49	0.49	0.52	0.56	0.66	0.73	
Capital surplus	2.59	1.50	1.29	1.17	1.33	1.38	
Earnings retained in the business	46.10	40.17	45.16	52.06	55.19	56.25	
Capital stock in treasury, at cost	−6.52	−2.60	−1.80	−2.08	−1.51	−1.75	
Cumulative translation adjustments	0.57	1.54	0.05	0.79	0.38	−0.91	
Total shareowners' equity	43.22%	41.11%	45.23%	52.50%	56.05%	55.70%	46.10%
Total liabilities and shareowners' equity	100.00%	100.00%	100.00%	100.00%	100.00%	100.00%	100.00%

Exhibit 23–8

CAMPBELL SOUP COMPANY
Trend Index of Selected Accounts
(1986 = 100)

	1991	1990	1989	1988	1987	1986
Cash and cash equivalents	115%	52%	78%	55%	93%	$ 155.1
Accounts receivable	176	209	180	163	113	299.0
Temporary investments	5	9	11	15	117	238.7
Inventory...................	116	134	134	109	102	610.5
Total current assets	114	125	120	102	108	1,334.8
Total current liabilities	204	207	197	138	111	626.1
Working capital	34	52	52	70	105	708.7
Plant assets, net	153	147	132	129	115	1,168.1
Other assets	156	134	124	93	119	259.9
Long-term debt	213	222	174	145	105	362.3
Total liabilities	192	198	176	140	111	1,223.9
Shareowners' equity	117	110	116	123	113	1,538.9
Net sales	145	145	132	114	105	4,268.8
Cost of products sold	133	138	130	110	103	3,082.7
Administrative and research						
expenses	157	148	129	119	109	195.9
Marketing and sales expenses ...	176	180	150	135	115	544.4
Interest expense	199	191	161	104	101	58.5
Total costs and expenses.......	142	155	143	115	105	3,900.0
Earnings before taxes	172	46	28	100	108	387.2
Net income	180	2*	6*	123	111	223.2

* Excluding the net effect of divestitures, restructuring, and unusual charges, will change these amounts to: 1990—137 and 1989—123

Exhibit 23–9

CAMPBELL SOUP COMPANY
Per Share Results

	1991	1990	1989	1988	1987	1986
Sales	$48.85	$47.88	$43.87	$37.63	$34.57	$33.10
Net income	3.16	0.03	0.10	2.12	1.90	1.72
Dividends	1.12	0.98	0.90	0.81	0.71	0.65
Book value (shareowners'						
equity)	14.12	13.09	13.76	14.69	13.35	11.86
Average shares outstanding						
(in millions)	127.0	129.6	129.3	129.4	129.9	129.5

4. Return on investment (ROI).
5. Asset utilization.
6. Operating performance.

In this analysis Industry Composite figures are used for comparison purposes. These are drawn primarily from Dun & Bradstreet Industry Norms and Key Business Ratios, and are based on composite financial statements constructed from the 1991 financial statements of companies included in the SIC classification 2033.

ANALYSIS OF SHORT-TERM LIQUIDITY

Exhibit 23–10 presents some important measures of short-term liquidity over the past six years along with comparative data.

The current ratio of the company in 1991 is at its lowest level in the last six years under analysis. At 1.19 it is relatively lower than the industry composite of 1.86. This is due in part to the rate of growth in current liabilities in recent years, where we find them double what they were in 1986, while current assets in 1991 are only 114 percent of the 1986 level. A substantial amount of notes payable were reclassified as long-term debt in 1990. This contributed to improvement of the current ratio. Exhibit 23–11 reveals that the cash and cash equivalents in 1991 represent a greater proportion of current assets (11.78%) than is the case with the industry composite (5.60%).

Campbell's acid-test ratio in the last three years (0.56) is only slightly below the 1991 industry composite (0.61). Exhibit 23–7 shows the relative variation between current assets included in the acid-test ratio and current liabilities of the company and those of the industry composite. As can be seen from Exhibits 23–7 and 23–11, inventories represent a much lower proportion of total assets (17%) and total current assets (46.5%) than they do for the industry (63.6% and 22%, respectively). Also, inventory turnover for Campbell in 1991 is 5.37 times versus 2.53 for the industry average. These are strong indicators that Campbell does not tie up a great amount of funds in inventory relative to the industry average. This conclusion is strengthened by looking at Exhibit 23–8, where inventory growth is much slower than growth in sales (116% vs. 145%). Further, these improvements in inventory management may be seen to be a result of Campbell's institution of the "just-in-time" inventory system particularly at the raw materials level. Exhibit 23–12 sets forth data on Campbell's inventories. Over the years there had been a decline in the proportion of raw materials to total inventories, a trend confirming the above conclusion.

The company uses the LIFO inventory method to account for approximately 70% of consolidated inventories in 1991 and 64% in 1990

Exhibit 23–10

CAMPBELL SOUP COMPANY
Short-Term Liquidity Analysis

Units		1991	1990	1989	1988	1987	1986	Industry composite
Ratio	1. Current ratio	1.19	1.28	1.30	1.58	2.07	2.13	1.86
Ratio	2. Acid-test ratio	0.56	0.56	0.56	0.70	1.10	1.11	0.61
Times	3. Accounts receivable turnover	10.77	10.68	11.07	11.79	14.08	15.13	8.37
Times	4. Inventory turnover	5.37	5.21	5.41	5.27	5.15	5.14	2.53
Days	5. Collection period for ending A/R	30.60	36.23	34.15	36.00	27.17	25.11	43.01
Days	6. Days to sell ending inventory	62.12	69.31	73.41	70.53	70.59	71.29	142.03
Days	7. Conversion period	92.72	105.54	107.56	106.53	97.76	96.40	185.32
Percent	8. Cash to current assets	11.78%	4.84%	7.55%	6.30%	10.14%	11.62%	5.60%
Percent	9. Cash to current liabilities	14.00%	6.22%	9.81%	9.94%	20.90%	24.77%	10.40%
Days	10. Liquidity index	59.87	72.62	72.55	71.46	52.29	52.07	130.62
M$'s	11. Working capital	240.50	367.40	369.40	499.60	744.10	708.70	54.33
Days	12. Average no. of days to pay accounts payable	46.03	46.56	46.20	49.30	44.25	39.33	
Days	13. Average net trade cycle	46.69	58.98	61.36	57.23	53.51	57.07	
Percent	14. Cash provided by operations to average current liabilities	62.51%	35.44%	34.10%	60.22%	71.36%	77.34%	

Notes:
For 1991 (in millions):

(3) $\dfrac{\text{Net sales } \boxed{13}}{\text{Average accounts receivable } \boxed{33}} = \dfrac{6{,}204.1}{(527.4 + 624.5)/2} = 10.77$ times

(4) $\dfrac{\text{Cost of products sold } \boxed{14}}{\text{Average inventory } \boxed{34}} = \dfrac{4{,}095.5}{(706.7 + 819.8)/2} = 5.37$ times

(5) $\dfrac{\text{Ending accounts receivable } \boxed{33}}{\text{Sales } \boxed{13}\ /\ 360} = \dfrac{527.4}{6{,}204.1/360} = 30.6$ days

(6) $\dfrac{\text{Ending inventory } \boxed{34}}{\text{Cost of products sold } \boxed{14}\ /\ 360} = \dfrac{706.7}{4{,}095.5/360} = 62.12$ days

(7) = (5) + (6)

(10)

		Days removed from cash		Product
Cash and temporary investments $\boxed{31} + \boxed{32}$	191.7 ×	0	=	0
Accounts receivable $\boxed{33}$	527.4 ×	30.6	=	16138
Inventories $\boxed{34}$	706.7 ×	92.7	=	65511
Prepaid expenses $\boxed{35}$	92.7 ×	100*	=	9270
	1518.5			90919

* Assumed number.

Liquidity index $= \dfrac{90919}{1518.5} = 59.87$ days

(12) $\dfrac{\text{Accounts payable } \boxed{41}}{\text{Purchases per day}^{\dagger}} = \dfrac{482.4}{10.48} = 46.03$ days

† From Exhibit 23–12.

(13) Number of days' sales in:

Accounts receivable	30.60
Inventories	62.12
	92.72
Less: accounts payable	46.03
	46.69

(14) $\dfrac{\text{Cash from operation } \boxed{64}}{\text{Beginning + ending current liabilities } \boxed{45} \div 2} = \dfrac{805.2}{1{,}288} = 62.51$

Exhibit 23–11

CAMPBELL SOUP COMPANY
Common-Size Analysis of
Current Assets and Current Liabilities

	July 28, 1991	July 29, 1990	July 30, 1989	July 31, 1988	August 2, 1987	August 3, 1986	Industry composite
Current assets							
Cash and cash equivalents	11.78%	4.85%	7.55%	6.30%	10.09%	11.62%	5.60%
Other temporary investments, at cost which approximates market	0.84	1.35	1.64	2.57	19.49	17.88	—
Accounts receivable	34.73	37.50	33.59	35.72	23.57	22.40	27.18
Inventories	46.54	49.22	50.95	48.77	43.37	45.74	63.60
Prepaid expenses	6.11	7.08	6.27	6.64	3.48	2.36	3.62
Total current assets	100.00%	100.00%	100.00%	100.00%	100.00%	100.00%	100.00%
Current Liabilities							
Notes payable	22.08%	15.58%	22.04%	15.99%	13.48%	14.20%	20.49%
Payable to suppliers and others	37.75	40.46	41.25	51.74	54.02	51.38	31.19
Accrued liabilities	31.98	37.89	31.86	27.44	26.25	26.50	
Dividend payable	2.89	2.49	2.41	—	—	—	= 48.32
Accrued income taxes	5.30	3.58	2.44	4.83	6.25	7.92	
Total current liabilities	100.00%	100.00%	100.00%	100.00%	100.00%	100.00%	100.00%

Exhibit 23–12

CAMPBELL SOUP COMPANY
Inventory Data
(in millions)

	1991	1990	1989	1988	1987	1986
1. Beginning inventory	$ 819.8	$ 816.0	$ 664.7	$ 623.6	$ 610.5	$ 623.1
2. Plus: production inputs	3,982.4	4,262.0	4,152.9	3,433.9	3,193.6	3,070.1
3. Goods available for sale	4,802.2	5,078.0	4,187.6	4,057.5	3,804.1	3,693.2
4. Less: Ending inventory	706.7	819.8	816.0	664.7	623.6	610.5
5. Cost of products sold	4,095.5	4,258.2	4,001.6	3,392.8	3,180.5	3,082.7
6. Depreciation	208.6	200.9	192.3	170.9	144.6	126.8
7. (2) – (5) = Purchases	3,773.8	4,061.1	3,960.6	3,263.0	3,049.0	2,943.3
8. (6) / 360 = Purchases per day	$ 10.48	$ 11.28	$ 11.00	$ 9.06	$ 8.47	$ 8.18
Ending inventories:						
Raw materials, containers, and supplies	$ 342.3	$ 384.4	$ 385.0	$ 333.4	$ 333.6	$ 340.4
Finished products	454.0	520.0	519.0	412.5	372.4	348.1
	796.3	904.4	904.0	745.9	706.0	688.5
Less: Adjustment of inventories to LIFO	89.6	84.6	88.0	81.2	82.4	78.5
Total	$ 706.7	$ 819.8	$ 816.0	$ 664.7	$ 623.6	$ 610.5
Raw materials, containers, and supplies	43.0%	42.5%	42.6%	44.7%	47.3%	49.4%
Finished products	57.0	57.5	57.4	55.3	52.7	50.6
	100.0%	100.0%	100.0%	100.0%	100.0%	100.0%

Exhibit 23–13

CAMPBELL SOUP COMPANY
Inventory Data under FIFO
(in millions)

	1991	1990	1989	1988	1987	1986
Beginning inventory	$ 904.4	$ 904.0	$ 745.9	$ 706.0	$ 688.5	$ 707.0
Production inputs (same as under LIFO)	3,982.4	4,262.0	4,152.9	3,433.9	3,193.6	3,070.1
Goods available for sale	4,886.8	5,166.0	4,898.8	4,139.9	3,882.1	3,777.1
Less: Ending inventory	796.3	904.4	904.0	745.9	706.0	688.5
Cost of products sold (FIFO)	$4,090.5	$4,261.6	$3,994.8	$3,394.0	$3,176.1	$3,088.6
Cost of products sold (LIFO)	$4,095.5	$4,258.2	$4,001.6	$3,392.8	$3,180.5	$3,082.7
Effect of restatement to FIFO is to increase (decrease) cost of products sold by:	$ (5.0)	$ 3.4	$ (6.8)	$ 1.2	$ (4.4)	$ 5.9
Net of tax* effect of restatement to FIFO is to decrease (increase) net income by:	$ (3.3)	$ 2.2	$ (4.5)	$ 0.8	$ (2.4)	$ 3.2
* Tax rate	34.0%	34.0%	34.0%	34.0%	45.0%	46.0%

(disclosure in item 153A). Exhibit 23–13 contrasts the effect on income resulting from the company's use of the LIFO method as opposed to the FIFO method. Normally, in times of rising prices LIFO income is lower than FIFO income. However, we see here that this was true in Campbell's case only every other year, 1987, 1989, and 1991. During the other years the opposite was true. This may be due to declining costs, and possibly inventory liquidation, at least in two of the three years. There is, of course, a limit to how much income can, over the years, benefit from LIFO liquidation.

The accounts receivable turnover has declined over the past six years, but it is still above the industry level in 1991 (Exhibit 23–10). In addition, Exhibit 23–8 shows that accounts receivable grew much faster than sales, and reached a peak in 1990 (209), then declined in 1991 (176). This may indicate a more aggressive credit policy in recent years to forestall the effects of the general state of economic recession.

As can be seen from Exhibit 23–10, the collection period for A/R deteriorated between 1986–90, then started to turn around in the right direction in 1991. The same, to a lesser degree, can be said about the number of days to sell inventory. However, the conversion period in 1991 is back to 92.7 days versus 96.4 days in 1986, due primarily to an enhanced inventory turnover, which causes Campbell to compare favorably in its conversion period against the industry norms.

Campbell has managed its current liabilities with varying results. Overall, the tendency over the last three years has been for the average days to pay A/P (Exhibit 23–10) to stay relatively stable. The company's average net trade cycle has fluctuated during the last six years. However, in 1991 it is back below the 1986 level of 46.7 (vs. 57 days), which corroborates the conclusion of improving liquidity.

ANALYSIS OF CASH FLOWS

This analysis has two main objectives:

1. To analyze the statement of cash flows (SCF) in order to assess the implications on longer term flows of cash (e.g., long-term solvency) and to discern cash flow patterns over time.
2. To supplement the static measures used to assess short-term liquidity by means of a short-term cash flow forecast.

We will start with an analysis of Cash Flow from Operations (CFO), that very important subset of total cash flows. Campbell presents cash flows from operations by the indirect method and so we recast these to the analytically more significant and useful inflow-outflow format (also known as the direct method), as shown in Exhibit 23–14.

Exhibit 23–14

CAMPBELL SOUP COMPANY
Analysis of Cash from Operations
Utilizing the Inflow-Outflow Format
(in millions)

	1991	1990	1989	1988	1987	1986
Inflows:						
Net sales	$6,204.1	$6,205.8	$5,672.1	$4,868.9	$4,490.4	$4,286.8
(Increase) decrease in accounts receivable	17.1	(60.4)	(46.8)	(104.3)	(36.3)	(3.6)
Cash collections on sales	6,221.2	6,145.4	5,625.3	4,764.6	4,454.1	4,283.2
Interest income	26.0	17.6	38.3	33.2	29.5	27.4
Total cash collections from operations	6,247.2	6,163.0	5,663.6	4,797.8	4,483.6	4,310.6
Outflows:						
Cost of products sold*	3,823.7	4,038.7	3,772.0	3,178.9	3,007.9	2,939.3
Marketing and sales expenses	956.2	980.5	818.8	733.3	626.2	544.4
Administrative expenses	306.7	290.7	252.1	232.6	213.9	195.9
Foreign exchange losses	0.8	3.3	19.3	16.6	4.8	0.7
Interest expense	116.2	111.6	94.1	53.9	51.7	56.0
Adjusted by: (Increase) decrease in deferred taxes	(35.5)	(3.9)	67.8	(13.4)	(45.7)	(29.0)
Research and development expenses	56.3	53.7	47.7	46.9	44.8	42.2
Other expenses (income)	26.2	14.7	32.4	19.8	(9.5)	5.5
Increase (decrease) in inventories	(48.7)	(10.7)	113.2	(54.2)	3.9	(23.1)
Net change in other current assets and liabilities	(30.6)	68.8	0.6	(30.2)	(42.9)	(48.7)
Income tax expense	265.9	175.0	93.4	147.0	170.6	164.0
Net effect of equity in earnings of affiliates and minority interests†	4.8	(7.8)	(5.1)	0.0	(10.4)	(0.4)
Total cash outflows for operations	5,442.0	5,714.6	5,306.3	4,331.2	4,015.3	3,846.8
Cash from operations	$ 805.2	$ 448.4	$ 357.3	$ 466.6	$ 468.3	$ 463.8

* Adjusted by items which don't effect cash. For 1991:

Cost of products sold as per IS (item 14)	$4095.5
Less: Depreciation and amortization as per SCF (item 57)	208.6
Less: Other, net as per SCF (item 60)	63.2
	$3823.7

† This is aggregated for convenience. It is also correct to include dividend receipts under "inflows."

This analysis reveals that CFO represents a steady and growing source of cash for Campbell especially in 1991 ($805 million). The interruption in this trend in 1989 is due primarily to the increase in inventories (113 millions) and the negative (decrease in) deferred taxes (68 millions). The increase in inventories is due to management's objective to improve customer service. As for the deferred taxes, the large amounts of restructuring and unusual charges which were not tax deductible resulted in credits to tax expense of about $78 million, but higher *current* tax liabilities. It is noteworthy that the sharp declines in net income in 1989 and 1990 had no effect on CFO, because the declines resulted from large restructuring and divestiture charges which had no cash effects in those years.

Cash outflows maintained an increasing trend throughout 1990. In 1991 outflows declined due mainly to a decline in cost of products sold, combined with relatively lower marketing and selling expenses, and a relatively higher decrease in inventories, and less payables. Those factors were partially offset by higher taxes and other expenses.

Overall, Campbell has been able to translate, over the years, its growing sales and lately its enhanced margin into a commensurately growing stream of operating cash flows.

Exhibit 23–15, on pages 810–811, presents the common-size consolidated statements of cash flows for the six years ending with 1991 as well as the composite of that period. This exhibit affords an interesting and instructive overview of the company's cash flow patterns over the past six years. Thus, temporary or erratic changes, such as caused by the relatively high usage of cash in investing activities in 1987 (62%), can be seen in perspective and are smoothed out by the aggregate figures for the six years shown in the "total" column.

Over the years, cash provided by operations constituted about half of all cash inflows. This, in conjunction with the fact that financing activities were mostly refinancing in nature (using only 7% of cash inflows) is a fair testimony to the soundness and the strength of Campbell's financial condition and financing practices.

Cash used for acquisition of assets and businesses represented, over the six-year period, about 50 percent of cash inflows and dividends about 12%. In summary, cash inflows from operations (56%) and net cash used in financing (7%) approximate the net cash used in investing activities (48%). Therefore, the cash position throughout the six-year period tended to stay even while fluctuating somewhat. It grew by less than half of one percent (0.44%) during the period.

A summary of cash inflows and outflows by major categories of activity is analytically instructive. From Exhibit 23–4, we can extract the following tabulation of cash inflows and outflows (in millions). (See the table on the following page):

Summary of Cash Inflows and Outflows by Major Category of Activity

	1991	1990	1989	1988	1987	1986	Total
From operations	$805.2	$448.4	$357.3	$466.6	$468.3	$463.8	$3,009.6
Investing activities	(478.7)	(387.5)	(473.2)	(462.2)	(401.0)	(387.6)	(2,590.2)
Financing activities	(219.6)	(101.8)	(163.1)	(52.8)	(88.3)	(54.5)	(353.9)
Increase (decrease) in cash ...	98.2	(40.2)	35.1	(59.2)	(28.1)	18.0	23.8

The remarkable picture that emerges from an analysis of Campbell's major cash flows is that throughout the six-year period cash from operations (CFO) has supported substantial investing outlays of about $2.6 billion, financing outlays (inclusive of dividends) of about $354 million, and a slight cumulative increase in cash. In 1987, 1988, and 1990 cash balances were drawn down to support investing and financing activities. Overall, especially with 1991 included, the CFO was adequate to fund all of the company's investing and financing needs leaving excess cash of $24 million.

Having considered the pattern of cash flows over recent years we can now turn to a short-term cash flow forecast which will supplement the static measures of short-term liquidity which were covered earlier.

A first step in the projection of CFO is the projection of earnings. Exhibit 23–16, on page 812, is a projected statement of earnings for Campbell for 1992. Sales are projected to be approximately 2.35 percent higher than 1991.[1]

Net earnings in fiscal 1992 are projected at $480.0 million, which is approximately 20 percent higher than in 1991. This increase reflects more the increase in operating margin than in sales. The profit margin expansion is primarily due to an easing in manufacturing costs, where labor cost has increased very modestly, lately, and the cost of metal food containers was considerably lower in the recent past, due to increased competitive conditions and greater capacity in the aluminum industry. In addition, financing costs are expected to decrease, benefiting from the decline in short-term interest rates. Campbell is also expected to enjoy additional favorable operating leverage as a result of a major restructuring program.

Expenses are calculated based on the assumptions stated in Exhibit 23–16. Taxes on earnings are estimated on the basis of the current federal statutory tax rate of 34 percent.

Exhibit 17–9, which presents a Projected Statement of Cash Flows for fiscal 1992 and fiscal 1993, is mainly based on the presentation above, in addition to its own set of assumptions. The projected statements indicate that, based on the assumptions as stated, Campbell is expected to finance the expected level of investments in plant assets and acquisition of businesses mainly from cash from operations, and even redeem some of its high coupon long-term debts. In fact, should these projections hold, Campbell will have enough free cash for dividends and other uses.

Exhibit 23–17 presents two additional measures of Campbell's cash flows. The purpose of the cash flow adequacy ratio is to evaluate the degree to which the company generated sufficient cash from operations to cover capital expenditures, investment in inventories, and cash dividends.

---

[1] The estimate is corroborated in *The Value Line Investment Survey* of February 21, 1992.

Exhibit 23–15

CAMPBELL SOUP COMPANY
Common-Size Consolidated Statements of Cash Flows*
For Years 1986 to 1991

	1991	1990	1989	1988	1987	1986	Total
Cash flows from operating activities:							
Net earnings	26.89%	0.54%	1.15%	25.14%	38.42%	27.88%	21.54%
To reconcile net earnings to net cash provided by operating activities:							
Depreciation and amortization	13.97	24.58	16.82	15.67	22.47	15.84	19.33
Divestitures and restructuring provisions	—	41.49	30.00	1.61	—	—	12.95
Deferred taxes	2.38	0.48	(5.93)	1.23	7.10	3.62	1.11
Other, net	4.23	2.28	3.26	3.94	4.35	2.07	3.83
Cumulative effect of accounting change	—	—	—	(2.98)	—	—	(0.60)
(Increase) decrease in accounts receivable	1.15	(7.39)	(4.09)	(9.57)	(5.64)	(0.45)	(4.34)
(Increase) decrease in inventories	3.26	1.31	(9.90)	4.97	(0.61)	2.89	0.36
Net change in other current assets and liabilities	2.05	(8.42)	(0.05)	2.77	6.67	6.08	1.54
Net cash provided by operating activities	53.92	54.86	31.25	42.80	72.76	57.94	55.72
Cash flows from investing activities:							
Purchases of plant assets	(24.18)%	(47.42)%	(24.85)%	(22.50)%	(47.19)%	(29.39)%	(33.64)%
Sale of plant assets	2.89	4.27	3.48	2.07	—	3.72	3.15
Businesses acquired	(12.06)	(5.09)	(11.88)	(43.28)	(1.13)	(2.50)	(15.86)
Sale of businesses	4.51	2.66	0.43	2.16	3.23	—	2.56
Increase in other assets	(3.87)	(2.28)	(9.36)	(3.70)	(7.78)	(2.25)	(5.40)
Net change in other temporary investment	0.65	0.45	0.79	22.86	(9.43)	(18.00)	1.24
Net cash used in investing activities	(32.06)	(47.41)	(41.39)	(42.39)	(62.31)	(48.42)	(47.95)

Cash flows from financing activities:

Long-term borrowings	26.97%	1.54%	11.07%	9.45%	0.75%	25.47%	15.80%
Repayments of long-term borrowings	(8.70)	(2.75)	(4.69)	(2.10)	(3.71)	(20.57)	(7.73)
Increase (decrease) in short-term borrowings	(9.23)	(0.33)	9.46	0.77	(3.22)	0.57	(0.74)
Other short-term borrowings	7.86	18.81	19.87	7.06	13.88	9.11	13.65
Repayments of other short-term borrowings	(13.82)	(10.99)	(16.82)	(8.03)	(10.30)	(11.06)	(13.53)
Dividends paid	(9.21)	(15.21)	(7.58)	(9.59)	(14.25)	(13.07)	(12.02)
Treasury stock purchases	(11.76)	(5.03)	(0.71)	(2.69)	–	–	(4.70)
Treasury stock issued	3.19	1.52	1.62	0.08	0.25	0.50	1.58
Other, net	(0.01)	(0.01)	2.06	0.21	2.89	2.24	1.15
Net cash provided (used in) financing activities	(14.71)	(12.46)	14.27	(4.84)	(13.72)	(6.81)	(6.55)
Effect of exchange rate change on cash	(0.58)%	0.09%	(1.06)%	(0.99)%	(1.10)%	(0.46)%	(0.77)%
Net increase (decrease) in cash and cash equivalents	6.58	(4.92)	3.07	(5.43)	(4.37)	2.25	0.44

* Common-size percentages are based on total cash inflows of all kinds = 100%. For 1991 the 100% is composed of:
CFO + Sale of plant assets + Sale of bus. + Decrease in temp. invest. + LT borrowings + ST borrowings + Treas. st. issued
53.92 + 2.89 + 4.51 + 0.65 + 26.97 + 7.86 + 3.19

Exhibit 23–16

CAMPBELL SOUP COMPANY
Projected Statement of Earnings
For Year Ended August 2, 1992
(in millions)

		Percent
Net sales*	$6,350.0	100.00%
Costs and expenses:†		
Cost of products sold	4,095.8	64.50
Marketing and selling expenses	990.6	15.60
Administrative expenses	308.0	4.85
Research and development expense	57.2	0.90
Interest expense	114.3	1.80
Interest income	(31.8)	−0.50
Other expense (income), including foreign		
exchange losses	88.9	1.40
Total costs and expenses	5,623.0	88.55%
Earnings before taxes‡	727.0	11.45
Taxes on earnings§	(247.0)	−3.89
Net earnings	$ 480.0	7.56%

* Projected at approximately 2.35 % higher than 1991 sales of $6,204.1. *The Value Line Investment Survey,* Feb. 21, 1992 release.

† Based on the following assumptions:
—Cost of products sold is expected to be 64.5% of 1992 sales. It is along the lines of the 1989–91 average and recognizes the enhancement in the gross margin in recent years, which resulted from the series of divestitures and restructurings.
—Marketing and selling expenses are expected to be along the lines of the 1989–91 average with a slight increase due to increase in advertising.
—Administrative expenses are expected to increase slightly from the 1989–91 average.
—All other items are assumed to be approximately at the same relative level as 1989–91 average.

‡ Effects of equity in earnings of affiliates and minority interests are ignored as immaterial.

§ At the federal statutory rate of 34%.

Campbell's cash flow adequacy ratio for the six-year period is approximately 0.88, which means that funds generated from operations were not sufficient to cover the items in the denominator, and there was a need for external financing. However, this is an aggregate ratio and when we look at individual years, particularly 1991, we find that this problem did not show up in most years, except for 1987 and 1989.

The cash reinvestment ratio measures the percentage of the investment in assets that is being retained and reinvested in the enterprise for replacement of assets and for the growth in operations. Campbell's average reinvestment ratio is 11.8 percent for the six-year period. This reinvestment rate is at a satisfactory level. The 1991 reinvestment rate is at a

Exhibit 23–17

CAMPBELL SOUP COMPANY
Analysis of Cash Flow Ratios
(in millions)

(1) Cash flow adequacy ratio $=$ $\dfrac{\text{6-year sum of sources of cash from operations}}{\text{6-year sum of capital expenditures, inventory additions, and cash dividends}}$

$$= \frac{3,009.6}{(1817.1 + 856.7) + (113.2 + 3.9) + 649.4}$$

$$= 0.875$$

(All amounts are per SCF)

(2) Cash reinvestment ratio $= \dfrac{\text{Cash provided by operations} - \text{Dividends}}{\text{Gross PPE} + \text{Investments} + \text{Other assets} + \text{W/C}}$

1986 to 1991 =	$\dfrac{3009.6 - 649.4}{15,183.7 + 1,888.3 + 2,929.7}$	= 11.8%
1991 =	$\dfrac{805.2 - 137.5}{2921.9 + 404.6 + 240.5}$	= 18.7%
1990 =	$\dfrac{448.4 - 124.3}{2734.9 + 349.0 + 367.4}$	= 9.4%
1989 =	$\dfrac{357.3 - 86.7}{2,543.0 + 323.1 + 369.4}$	= 8.4%
1988 =	$\dfrac{466.6 - 104.6}{2539.7 + 241.2 + 499.6}$	= 11.0%
1987 =	$\dfrac{468.3 - 91.7}{2355.1 + 310.5 + 744.1}$	= 11.0%
1986 =	$\dfrac{463.8 - 104.6}{2089.1 + 259.9 + 708.7}$	= 11.7%

(Numerator amounts are per SCF and denominator amounts are per BS)

much higher level. This ratio has been at an acceptable level over the years except for 1989 and 1990 which is attributable to the decrease in cash from operations for reasons discussed earlier.

ANALYSIS OF CAPITAL STRUCTURE AND LONG-TERM SOLVENCY

Having examined the funds aspect of Campbell Soup's long-term solvency, we now turn to an examination of its capital structure and the risks inherent in it. Changes in the company's capital structure can be gauged by means of a number of measurements and comparisons.

Exhibit 23–18 details the capital structure of Campbell for the six years ended 1991. For analytical purposes half of the deferred taxes were considered as long-term liabilities and the other half as equity. Changes resulting from *SFAS 109,* "Accounting for Income Taxes," and currently applicable corporate tax rates, are likely to slow the growth in deferred taxes. Exhibit 23–19 presents a common-size analysis of the capital structure. In 1991, liabilities constituted 53 percent of total invested capital and equity the balance of 47 percent.

Exhibit 23–20 presents selected capital structure and long-term solvency ratios. The debt to equity ratios have increased markedly in the last three years of the six-year period, but remain below the industry average. The long-term debt component grew the most, which can be seen in Exhibit 23–8, where the trend index of long-term debt (213) has exceeded that of current liabilities (204), total liabilities (192), and especially shareowners' equity (117). However, Campbell's debt to equity ratios compare favorably to the industry composites, except in the case of long-term debt to equity, where in 1991, Campbell shows a ratio of 48 percent versus an industry composite of 43 percent. Furthermore, the analytically adjusted long-term debt to equity ratio does not differ significantly from its unadjusted counterpart. Generally, one can say that Campbell is moving away from the conservative capital structure it used to maintain in the past and turning to a more aggressive one. This is corroborated by a lower level of fixed charge coverage ratios measured by both earnings and cash from operations. The company's long-term debt is rated AA by the major rating agencies, down from the AAA rating the company enjoyed previously, but still a very favorable rating.

Overall, Campbell enjoys outstanding financial strength, ranking A+ according to *The Value Line Investment Survey* release of February 21, 1992. Further, according to the same source, Campbell ranks second in terms of "Safety" on a scale of 1(best) to 5(worst). The company's creditors continue to enjoy sound asset and earning power backing.

ANALYSIS OF RETURN ON INVESTMENT

Exhibit 23–21 presents selected return on investment ratios for Campbell. The return on total assets was essentially stable over the years 1986 to 1988 and declined sharply during fiscal 89 and fiscal 90. It did rebound strongly to 11.75 percent in 1991. The extremely low returns for 89 and 90 are due to substantial divestitures and restructuring charges. We must be alert to the fact that the exceptional improvement in 1991 may be due, in part, to the substantial write-offs of the previous years.

The 1991 RTA was composed of profit margin of 7.83%, and an asset turnover of 1.50. Both these components show improvement over their

Exhibit 23–18

CAMPBELL SOUP COMPANY
Analysis of Capital Structure
(in millions)

	1991	1990	1989	1988	1987	1986
Long-term liabilities:						
Notes payable	$ 757.8	$ 792.9	$ 610.3	$ 507.1	$ 358.8	$ 346.7
Capital lease obligation	14.8	12.9	18.9	18.7	21.4	15.6
Total long-term debt	772.6	805.8	629.2	525.8	380.2	362.3
Deferred income taxes*	129.3	117.6	109.0	140.3	124.0	99.6
Other long-term liabilities	23.0	28.5	19.6	15.6	15.8	16.3
Total long-term liabilities	924.9	951.9	757.8	681.7	520.0	478.2
Current liabilities†	1,278.0	1,298.1	1,232.1	863.3	693.8	626.1
Total liabilities	$2,202.9	$2,250.0	$1,989.9	$1,545.0	$1,213.8	$1,104.3
Equity capital:						
Common shareholders' equity	$1,793.4	$1,691.8	$1,778.3	$1,895.0	$1,736.1	$1,538.9
Minority interests	23.5	56.3	54.9	29.3	23.5	20.1
Deferred income taxes*	129.2	117.5	109.0	140.3	124.0	99.5
Total equity capital	1,946.1	1,865.6	1,942.2	2,064.6	1,883.6	1,658.5
Total liabilities and equity	$4,149.0	$4,115.6	$3,932.1	$3,609.6	$2,097.4	$2,762.8

* For analytical purposes 50 percent of deferred income taxes are considered debt and the balance equity.
† Including notes payable–current.

815

Exhibit 23–19

CAMPBELL SOUP COMPANY
Common-Size Analysis of Capital Structure

	1991	1990	1989	1988	1987	1986
Long-term liabilities:						
Notes payable	18.26%	19.27%	15.52%	14.05%	11.59%	12.55%
Capital lease obligation	0.36	0.31	0.48	0.52	0.69	0.56
Total long-term debt	18.62	19.58	16.00	14.57	12.28	13.11
Deferred income taxes*	3.12	2.86	2.77	3.88	4.00	3.61
Other long-term liabilities	0.55	0.69	0.50	0.43	0.51	0.59
Total long-term liabilities	22.29%	23.13%	19.27%	18.88%	16.79%	17.31%
Current liabilities†	30.80	31.54	31.34	23.92	22.40	22.66
Total liabilities	53.09%	54.67%	50.61%	42.80%	39.19%	39.97%
Equity capital:						
Common shareholders' equity	43.22	41.11	45.22	52.50	56.05	55.70
Minority interests	0.57	1.37	1.40	0.81	0.76	0.73
Deferred income taxes*	3.12	2.85	2.77	3.89	4.00	3.60
Total equity capital	46.91%	45.33%	49.39%	57.20%	60.81%	60.03%
Total liabilities and equity	100.00%	100.00%	100.00%	100.00%	100.00%	100.00%

* For analytical purposes 50 percent of deferred income taxes are considered debt and the balance equity.
† Including notes payable–current.

Exhibit 23–20

CAMPBELL SOUP COMPANY
Capital Structure and Long-Term Solvency Ratios

	1991	1990	1989	1988	1987	1986	Industry composite
1. Total debt to equity	1.13	1.21	1.02	0.75	0.64	0.67	1.17
2. Total debt to total debt plus equity	0.53	0.55	0.51	0.43	0.39	0.40	0.54
3. Long-term liabilities to equity	0.48	0.51	0.39	0.33	0.28	0.29	0.43
4. Analytically adjusted long-term liabilities to equity	0.46	0.50	0.38	0.33	0.27	0.28	
5. Total equity to total liabilities	0.88	0.83	0.98	1.34	1.56	1.50	0.86
6. Fixed assets to equity	0.92	0.92	0.79	0.73	0.72	0.70	0.46
7. Short-term liabilities to total liabilities	0.58	0.58	0.62	0.56	0.58	0.57	0.61
8. Ratio of earnings to fixed charges	5.16	2.14	1.84	6.06	6.41	6.28	
9. Cash from operations coverage of fixed charges	7.47	5.27	5.38	8.94	8.69	9.26	

Notes:

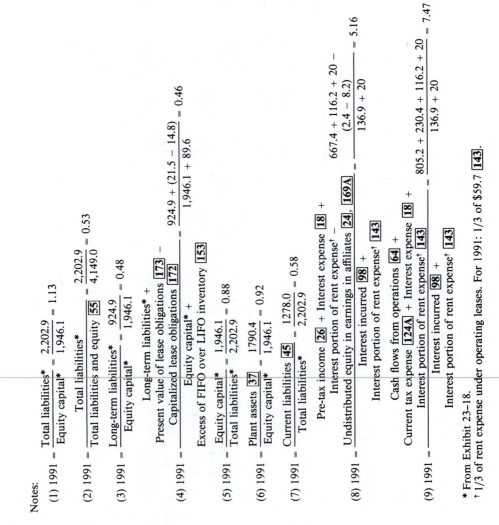

(1) 1991 = $\dfrac{\text{Total liabilities*}}{\text{Equity capital*}}$ = $\dfrac{2{,}202.9}{1{,}946.1}$ = 1.13

(2) 1991 = $\dfrac{\text{Total liabilities*}}{\text{Total liabilities and equity } [55]}$ = $\dfrac{2{,}202.9}{4{,}149.0}$ = 0.53

(3) 1991 = $\dfrac{\text{Long-term liabilities*}}{\text{Equity capital*}}$ = $\dfrac{924.9}{1{,}946.1}$ = 0.48

(4) 1991 = $\dfrac{\text{Long-term liabilities*} + \text{Present value of lease obligations } [173] - \text{Capitalized lease obligations } [172]}{\text{Equity capital*} + \text{Excess of FIFO over LIFO inventory } [153]}$
$= \dfrac{924.9 + (21.5 - 14.8)}{1{,}946.1 + 89.6}$ = 0.46

(5) 1991 = $\dfrac{\text{Equity capital*}}{\text{Total liabilities*}}$ = $\dfrac{1{,}946.1}{2{,}202.9}$ = 0.88

(6) 1991 = $\dfrac{\text{Plant assets } [37]}{\text{Equity capital*}}$ = $\dfrac{1790.4}{1{,}946.1}$ = 0.92

(7) 1991 = $\dfrac{\text{Current liabilities } [45]}{\text{Total liabilities*}}$ = $\dfrac{1278.0}{2{,}202.9}$ = 0.58

(8) 1991 = $\dfrac{\text{Pre-tax income } [26] + \text{Interest expense } [18] + \text{Interest portion of rent expense}^\dagger - \text{Undistributed equity in earnings in affiliates } [24],\,[169A]}{\text{Interest incurred } [98] + \text{Interest portion of rent expense}^\dagger\,[143]}$
$= \dfrac{667.4 + 116.2 + 20 - (2.4 - 8.2)}{136.9 + 20}$ = 5.16

(9) 1991 = $\dfrac{\text{Cash flows from operations } [64] + \text{Current tax expense } [124A] + \text{Interest expense } [18] + \text{Interest portion of rent expense}^\dagger\,[143]}{\text{Interest incurred } [98] + \text{Interest portion of rent expense}^\dagger\,[143]}$
$= \dfrac{805.2 + 230.4 + 116.2 + 20}{136.9 + 20}$ = 7.47

* From Exhibit 23–18.
† 1/3 of rent expense under operating leases. For 1991: 1/3 of $59.7 [143].

818

Exhibit 23–21

CAMPBELL SOUP COMPANY
Return on Investment Ratios

	1991	1990*	1989*	1988	1987	1986	Industry composite
1. Return on total assets (RTA)	11.75%	2.08%	2.13%	9.42%	9.57%	9.90%	9.20%
2. Return on equity**	21.52%	0.24%	0.67%	14.07%	14.14%	14.40%	19.80%
3. Return on long-term liabilities and equity	17.07%	3.04%	2.96%	12.27%	12.35%	12.90%	13.50%
4. Financial leverage index (times) (2) / (1)	1.83	0.12	0.31	1.49	1.48	1.46	2.15
5. Equity growth rate	13.85%	−6.30%	−3.67%	8.59%	8.79%	8.96%	—
** Disaggregation of return on equity:							
Net income margin	6.47%	0.07%	0.23%	5.63%	5.51%	5.10%	6.60%
	×	×	×	×	×	×	×
Assets turnover ratio	1.50	1.54	1.50	1.45	1.53	1.68	1.38
	×	×	×	×	×	×	×
Common stockholders' leverage	2.22	2.18	1.92	1.72	1.68	1.68	2.17
	21.52%	0.24%	0.67%	14.07%	14.14%	14.40%	19.80%

* Excluding the effect of divestitures, restructuring, and unusual charges, net of tax, of $301.6 million in 1990 and $260.8 million in 1989 will drastically change these ratios. For example, RTA for 1990 and 1989 will become 9.57% and 9.03%, respectively.

819

Notes:

(1) For 1991 RTA

$$= \frac{\text{Net income} + \text{Interest expense } (1 - \text{tax rate}) + \text{Minority interest (MI)}}{\text{Average total assets}}$$

$$= \frac{401.5 + 116.2 (1 - 0.34) + 7.2}{(4,149.0 + 4,115.6) / 2} = 11.75\%$$

RTA disaggrated

$$= \frac{\text{Net income} + \text{Interest expense } (1 - \text{TR}) + \text{MI}}{\text{Sales}} \times \frac{\text{Sales}}{\text{Average total assets}}$$

$$= \left[\frac{401.5 + 116.2 (1 - 0.34) + 7.2}{6,204.1} = 7.83\% \right] \times \left[\frac{6,204.1}{(4,149.0 + 4,115.6)/2} = 1.5 = 11.75\% \right]$$

$$= 6.6\% \times 1.4 = 9.24\%$$

1991 Industry composite

(2) For 1991 Return on equity

$$= \frac{\text{Net income}}{\text{Average common equity*}}$$

$$= \frac{401.5}{[(1,946.1 - 23.5) + (1,865.6 - 56.3)] / 2} = 21.52\%$$

$$= \frac{\text{Net income}}{\text{margin}} \times \frac{\text{Asset turnover}}{\text{ratio}} \times \frac{\text{Common stockholders'}}{\text{leverage ratio}}$$

Return on equity disaggregated

$$= \frac{401.5}{6,204.1} \times \frac{6,204.1}{(4,149.0 + 4,115.6)/2} \times \frac{(4,149.0 + 4,115.6)/2}{1865.95*}$$

$$= 6.47\% \times 1.50 \times 2.22 = 21.52\%$$

(3) For 1991 Return on LTD and equity

$$= \frac{\text{Net income} + \text{Interest expense } (1 - \text{tax rate}) + \text{MI}}{\text{Average long-term liabilities}^\dagger + \text{Average equity}^\dagger}$$

$$= \frac{401.5 + 116.2 (1 - .34) + 7.2}{(924.9 + 951.9)/2 + (1,946.1 + 1,865.6)/2} = 17.07\%$$

(4) For 1991 Financial leverage index

$$= \frac{\text{Return on equity capital}}{\text{Return on total assets}} = \frac{21.52\%}{11.75\%} = 1.83$$

(5) For 1991 Equity growth rate

$$= \frac{\text{Net income} - \text{Dividends paid}}{\text{Average common stockholders' equity}^\dagger} = \frac{401.5 - 137.5}{(1,946.1 + 1,865.6) / 2} = 13.85\%$$

* Including 50% of deferred taxes, which is assumed to be equity, and excluding minority interests (MI). See Exhibit 23–18.
† Including 50% of deferred taxes. See Exhibit 23–18.

counterparts in 1988 (comparison with 90 and 89 ratios is not meaningful). They compare also favorably with the industry yardsticks. The improvements in 1991 can be seen as, hopefully, early results of what Campbell's management intended to accomplish through the major restructuring, closings, and business reorganizations they undertook during 89 and 90. As a result of those restructuring programs and cost-cutting efforts, profit margins are widening. Previously, the company's returns had been held down by a number of poorly performing or ill-fitting businesses. Management has divested those lines, while streamlining and modernizing its manufacturing facilities.

Campbell's return on equity at 21.52 percent exceeds both the industry as well as the company's own recent experience. This is due to superior net income margin as well as leverage ratio. The greatly improved net income margin may have benefited from the rebound from the 1990 and 1989 depressed levels.

Referring to the disaggregation of Campbell's return on equity we notice that a major factor responsible for fluctuations in the return on equity over the years are changes in the net income margin. Over the six-year period, it recorded an extreme low of 0.07 percent in 1990 due to the substantial restructuring, and a high of 6.47 percent in 1991 possibly affected by the rebound absence of heavy charges, and *possibly* due to overprovisions in 1989 and 1990. The asset turnover declined slightly in 1987 from 1986, then stayed relatively level throughout the rest of the period but below the 1986 level. The leverage ratio improved gradually because of the company's increasingly leveraged capital structure.

Comparison of the disaggregated factors comprising Campbell's return on equity with those of the industry reveals the company's superior assets turnover and leverage ratios and a slightly inferior net income margin. Thus, the company's higher asset turnover (1.50) and higher leverage ratio (2.22) are primarily responsible for the return on equity of 21.52 percent compared to the industry's 19.8 percent. The increased leverage ratio had a cost in that it resulted in a lower credit rating for the company.

In 1991 Campbell was borrowing $1.22 on each dollar of equity. This considered 50 percent of deferred taxes as interest-free debt. The $2.22 in funds were able to generate $3.33 in sales because assets were turning over at a rate of 1.50 times. The $3.33 in sales were earning 6.47 percent in net income resulting in a return on equity of 21.52 percent.

The return on long-term liabilities and equity displays a relatively similar pattern to that of return on equity. In 1991, this ratio, at about 17 percent, compares very favorably with an industry composite of 13.5 percent.

The financial leverage index is positive and for the first three years, it was stable before declining in 89 and 90 for reasons discussed earlier. In 1991 it rebounded very strongly and showed material improvement over earlier years. This ratio confirms what we know from other evidence, that Campbell utilizes its debt profitably.

The equity growth rate has drastically improved in 1991 over earlier years, and stood at almost double the level of the first three years in the period under analysis. Because the company maintained its dividend payout while undergoing major costs of restructuring, this ratio turned negative in 1989 and 1990. The strong rebound in this ratio in 1991 bodes well for future growth in sales and earnings. A higher level of reinvestment frees the company from reliance on outside sources of capital to finance growth needs. In 1991, a net income of $401.5 million and dividends of $142.2 million was generating substantial funds for reinvestment and internally financed growth.

ANALYSIS OF ASSET UTILIZATION

As indicated in Exhibit 23–22, Campbell's total asset turnover has remained relatively stable over the years. However, this relative stability masks the significant changes of turnover within the component categories. The area of most significant fluctuation throughout the period is cash and cash equivalents. This can also be observed from Exhibit 23–8, which also shows a gradual elimination of temporary investments. In 1991, cash and cash equivalents increased by $98.2 million (Exhibit 23–4). This increase in cash is mostly from operations.

The accounts receivable turnover also showed a recent improvement over the last couple of years, due mainly to the decrease of $97.1 million in receivables in 1991. Management's desire to decrease inventories at every stage of the manufacturing process is not showing up, so far, in better overall turnover ratios.

The asset turnover ratios of Campbell do compare favorably to the industry in several key areas such as receivables, inventories, short-term liabilities, and most importantly working capital. As for cash and fixed assets it is not a favorable comparison, and with other assets the company approximates the industry. Overall, the sales to total assets ratio give the company an edge over the industry.

ANALYSIS OF OPERATING PERFORMANCE

Exhibit 23–23 indicates that Campbell's gross profit ratio is higher than that of the industry. However, the net income to sales ratio is slightly below the industry level. Still, Campbell's net income ratio has improved overall between 1986 and 1991 after the heavy costs of 1989 and 1990. Campbell's management has slimmed down overstaffed administrative ranks and unwieldy corporate divisions. Thus, in 1991 we can see early

Exhibit 23–22

CAMPBELL SOUP COMPANY
Asset Utilization Ratios

	1991	1990	1989	1988	1987	1986	Industry composite
1. Sales to cash and equivalents	34.7	76.9	46.9	56.8	31.0	27.6	40.6
2. Sales to receivables	11.8	9.9	10.5	10.0	13.2	14.3	8.4
3. Sales to inventories	8.8	7.6	7.0	7.3	7.2	7.0	3.6
4. Sales to working capital	25.8	16.9	15.4	9.8	6.0	6.1	4.9
5. Sales to fixed assets	3.5	3.6	3.7	3.2	3.3	3.7	6.6
6. Sales to other assets*	7.4	8.5	7.2	6.6	14.5	16.5	7.5
7. Sales to total assets	1.5	1.5	1.4	1.4	1.5	1.6	1.4
8. Sales to short-term liabilities	4.9	4.8	4.6	5.6	6.5	6.9	4.2

* Including intangible assets.

Exhibit 23–23

CAMPBELL SOUP COMPANY
Analysis of Profit Margin Ratios

	1991	1990	1989	1988	1987	1986	Industry composite
1. Gross profit to sales	34.00%	31.38%	29.45%	30.32%	29.17%	28.09%	29.30%
2. Operating income to net revenue	12.63%	4.69%	3.54%	9.09%	10.46%	10.34%	—
3. Net income to sales	6.47%	0.07%	0.23%	5.63%	5.51%	5.21%	6.60%

Notes:

(1) Gross profit to net sales $= \dfrac{\text{Net sales} - \text{Cost of products sold}}{\text{Net sales}}$

For 1991 $= \dfrac{6204.1 - 4{,}095.5}{6{,}204.1} = 34\%$

(2) Operating income to sales $= \dfrac{\text{Income before taxes and interest expenses}}{\text{Net sales}}$

For 1991 $= \dfrac{667.4 + 116.2}{6{,}204.1} = 12.63\%$

indications of tighter control over several areas of operating expenses. This should allow the company to continue improving the net income ratio and exceed its counterpart of the industry.

Exhibit 23–6 confirms the earlier observation about gross margin, where cost of products sold continue to decline (about 66 percent in 1991 versus 72 percent in 1986). This improvement in gross margin may continue over the coming years, but will not be easy to achieve. The key for a net income ratio that benefits from improving gross margins is ample control over administrative and marketing expenses.

The trend index analysis in Exhibit 23–8 shows that while sales in 1991 are at a level 145 percent higher than 1986, cost of products sold is at a level of 133 percent only, total costs and expenses at a level of 142, and net income at an impressive level of 180 compared to 1986. The important conclusion from all of these trends is the fact that sales, gross margin, and, in turn, net income are growing at a relatively faster rate than do costs and expenses.

Interest expense grew throughout the six-year period at a relatively lower rate than did total liabilities, except for 1991 (Exhibit 23–8). This indicates a lower cost of borrowing resulting primarily from lower interest rates even though Campbell now seems to be a more risky borrower as its debt to equity ratio is increasing.

From item $\boxed{1}$ of Campbell's 1991 annual report, included in Chapter 4, Appendix B, we can see that foreign operations contributed to 1991 operating earnings a total of $92.3 million from Campbell Canada, International Biscuit, and Campbell International. This total represents about 11.6 percent of total operating earnings. In 1990 and 1989 foreign operations contributed negatively to total earnings, as a result of the major restructuring in those years, reducing total operating earnings by 134.1 million in 1990 and by 82.3 million in 1989. These negative contributions were additional to losses from foreign currency translation of 3.8 million in 1990 and 20.0 million in 1989. This latter item in 1991 was insignificant, though positive. Overall, foreign operations continued throughout the years to represent roughly 20 percent of total operations (Exhibit 23–1). They will continue to exert a significant impact on Campbell's earnings.

Campbell's effective tax rate (item $\boxed{140}$) was 39.8 percent in 1991, 97.5 percent in 1990, and 87.7 percent in 1989. The extraordinarily high rates for 90 and 89 are mainly due to the large amounts of nondeductible divestitures, restructuring, and unusual charges, representing 56.5 and 48.7 percent of earnings before taxes, respectively (item $\boxed{135}$). Excluding the effect of these divestitures brings down the effective tax rate to about 40 percent.

The company is using substantial tax loss carryforward benefits of foreign subsidiaries and at the end of 1991 still has 77.4 million in unused tax loss carryforward benefits. About half will expire through 1996 and the rest will be available indefinitely. Most deferred taxes result from depreciation book/tax differences, pensions, and divestitures, restructuring, and unusual charges. The deferred tax due to depreciation differences stayed relatively high through 1990, then in 1991 declined to a low of $5.9 million.

Exhibit 23–24 indicates that accumulated depreciation as a percentage of gross plant assets has essentially remained fairly stable with some minor variations. The same can be said about the other two indicators in that exhibit. Thus, earnings quality seems not to have been affected in this area.

An analysis of discretionary costs, as it appears in Exhibit 23–25, shows that 1991 spending in each major category has decreased compared to most other previous years. This may possibly be evidence of more controlled spending and enhanced efficiencies.

Exhibit 21–5 analyzes the factors accounting for the variation in average net earnings over two three-year spans. This analysis is corroborative of some of the factors mentioned or discussed above. Gross margins increased, while on a relative basis, increases in marketing and selling expenses, interest expense, and other expenses outpaced the increase in sales by a big margin. However, administrative expenses and research and development expenses did not increase as much as sales. Statutory tax rates declined over the period thus holding down growth in tax expenses. Profitability increased because the increase in gross margin has, quantitatively, a much larger impact on the bottom line.

Exhibit 22–1 presents analytically recast income statements for the six fiscal periods ending in 1991 and discloses many elements already discussed above. Exhibit 22–2 presents Campbell's analytically adjusted income statements for the six fiscal periods ending in 1991. On an adjusted basis there is an increasing trend in net income from 1989 to 1990, which is in contrast to reported net income. The adjustments for divestitures, restructuring, and unusual charges do reveal a trend. However, the average earning power calculation for the six-year period must include all charges and stands at about $194 million.

SUMMARY AND CONCLUSIONS

This analysis has examined all facets of Campbell Soup Company's record of results of operations and financial position and has estimated the projected results and cash flows for one year. An analysis such as this, adjusted to fit the requirements of the specific situation and circumstances at hand, is an indispensable step in arriving at a decision. Nevertheless, essential as the data and information developed by this analysis are, it is not sufficient in most cases to arrive at a final conclusion. This is so because qualitative and other factors can have an important bearing on

Exhibit 23–24

CAMPBELL SOUP COMPANY
Analysis of Depreciation Data

	1991	1990	1989	1988	1987	1986
1. Accumulated depreciation as a percentage of gross plant assets*	44.6%	42.3%	43.1%	43.7%	46.6%	48.6%
2. Annual depreciation expenses as a percentage of gross plant assets	7.7%	7.7%	7.6%	6.9%	6.4%	6.4%
3. Annual depreciation expenses as a percentage of sales	3.1%	3.0%	3.1%	3.3%	3.1%	2.8%

Notes:

(1) For 1991 = $\dfrac{1,131.5\ \boxed{162}}{758.7\ \boxed{159} + 1,779.3\ \boxed{160}} = 44.6\%$

(2) For 1991 = $\dfrac{194.5\ \boxed{162A}}{758.7\ \boxed{159} + 1,779.3\ \boxed{160}} = 7.7\%$

(3) For 1991 = $\dfrac{194.5\ \boxed{162A}}{6,204.1\ \boxed{13}} = 3.1\%$

* Exclusive of land and projects in progress.

Exhibit 23–25

CAMPBELL SOUP COMPANY
Analysis of Discretionary Costs
(in millions)

	1991	1990	1989	1988	1987	1986
Net sales	$6,204.1	$6,205.8	$5,672.1	$4,868.9	$4,490.4	$4,286.8
Plant assets (net)*	1,406.5	1,386.9	1,322.6	1,329.1	1,152.0	974.1
Maintenance and repairs	173.9	180.6	173.9	155.6	148.8	144.0
Advertising	195.4	220.4	212.9	219.1	203.5	181.4
R & D	56.3	53.7	47.7	46.9	44.8	42.2
Percent of maintenance and repairs to sales	2.8%	2.9%	3.1%	3.2%	3.3%	3.4%
Percent of maintenance and repairs to plant . . .	12.4	13.0	13.1	11.7	12.9	14.8
Percent of advertising to sales	3.1	3.6	3.8	4.5	4.5	4.2
Percent of R & D to sales	0.9	0.9	0.8	1.0	1.0	1.0

* Exclusive of land and projects in process.

the final evaluation. Only when all the factors, those developed by the analysis as well as the others, have been assembled can a decision be reached by the application of judgment.

For example, a *bank* that may be asked to extend short-term credit must take into consideration the character of the management, past loan experience, as well as the ongoing relationship with the loan applicant.

In addition to the foregoing intangibles, the long-term lender will focus on such matters as security arrangements, provisions that safeguard the solvency of the recipient of the loan, and events risks (see also Chapter 18).

The *equity investor* is, of course, interested in earning power and in earnings per share, but many considerations and judgments must be joined with these data before an investment decision is made. Thus, for instance, what earnings are, and what they are likely to be, is the product of financial analysis. At what price-earnings ratio they should be capitalized is a question for investment judgment. Similarly, the risk inherent in an enterprise, the volatility of its earnings, and the breadth and quality of the market for its securities are factors which must also be considered. They determine whether an investment fits into the investor's portfolio and whether it is compatible with his or her investment objectives.

Since the ultimate conclusions regarding problems, such as the lending and investing decision that we consider in this case, are based on more than the data and facts brought out by financial analysis alone, it follows that the most useful way to present the results of financial analysis is to summarize them by listing the most relevant and salient points which were developed by the analysis and which the decision maker should consider. This we shall do in this case.

The following are the main points that have been developed by our analysis of Campbell Soup Company.

Short-Term Liquidity

Campbell's short-term liquidity position is a mixed one. Both current and acid-test ratios do not compare favorably with the industry, while the cash position of the company compares very favorably with the industry. Moreover, both accounts receivable and inventory turnover ratios are higher than their counterparts of the industry. The company's conversion period is much lower than that of the industry.

The cash position of Campbell is strong and may allow for some cash to be used beyond operations, especially for acquisitions.

Cash Flows

With only 1989 as an exception, because of material increases in inventories, Campbell has generated substantial and increasing cash from operations in recent years. They represent over half of all cash inflows.

Purchases and acquisitions of plant assets represent outflows totaling about 50 percent of all cash inflows. Dividends required about 12 percent of cash inflows.

A cash forecast for 1992 and 1993, based on assumptions as stated, projects that Campbell is expected to finance the expected investments in plant assets from an increasing cash flow from operations and to require only relatively small additions to debt.

The cash flow adequacy ratio confirms the earlier conclusion that the company is generating sufficient cash from operations to cover the majority of their capital expenditures, net investment in inventories, and cash dividends. Campbell's average cash reinvestment ratio was at a good level of 16.5 percent over the last six-year period.

Capital Structure and Long-term Solvency

Compared to its industry, and by any other standard, Campbell has developed in recent years a less conservative capital structure. Total debt is about 53 percent of total invested capital, and long-term debt alone is about half of equity. However, both earnings-based and cash from operations-based, fixed-charge coverage ratios are at strong levels, with the exception of coverage based on earnings in 1989 and 1990, due to restructuring. These strong ratios attest to the significant protection enjoyed by the company's creditors. Further, the company is still having ample debt capacity and the market has accorded the company a superior credit rating (AA).

Return on Investment

The company's return on total assets over the years 1986–88 was essentially stable at about 9.5 percent. During 1989 and 90 it declined to a low of about 2 percent, due in a major way to divestitures, restructuring, and unusual charges. In 1991, the ratio rebounded back to a strong 11.75 percent, composed of a profit margin of 6.47 percent and an asset turnover of 1.50. This return, overall, compares favorably to the industry average return of 9.2 percent.

At 21.52 percent the return on equity, which suffered a setback in 1989 and 90, is also above the industry average of 19.8 percent. The determining factor of this ratio, beyond RTA elements, is the common stockholder's leverage, which stands at 2.22 in 1991. This leverage is at a relatively higher level than preceding years, due mainly to a more risky capital structure which Campbell is allowing in recent years.

Campbell's equity growth rate has increased drastically in 1991 over earlier years, due in a major part to strong and healthy earnings and a higher rate of earnings retention.

Asset Utilization

While Campbell's total asset turnover has remained relatively stable over the years, the turnover of cash and cash equivalents has fluctuated from year to year. Meanwhile, accounts receivable and inventories turnovers have improved and are above their industry counterparts. These improvements are due mainly to the continuous efforts of the company to reduce working capital through lower receivables and lower inventories, among other things.

Asset turnover compares favorably to that of the industry composite, despite the relatively low cash turnover and fixed assets turnover.

Operating Performance

While Campbell's gross profit ratio has been improving in recent years and is clearly above the industry average, its net income to sales ratio is not as advantageously placed. This is due mainly to more corporate operating expenses, and the fact that Campbell's management does not have as much control over those expenses as it ought to have. Recent developments indicate that the company is going to exercise tighter control over costs.

Market Measures

Exhibit 23–26 presents some market measures of Campbell. Except for the dividend payout ratio which is a measure reflecting management discretion, these measures reflect the impact of the market's valuation of the company's equity securities. The 1989 and 1990 earnings-per-share figures are adjusted to exclude the effect of the enormous amounts of divestitures, restructuring, and unusual charges, which if unadjusted make most of the market measures meaningless for analytical purposes.

Thus, while earnings per share increased from $1.72 in 1986 to $3.16 in 1991, the earnings yield declined for the same period, because of steadily increasing price earnings ratios over the years. These are due mainly to strong equity markets. Similarly, while dividends per share increased from $0.65 in 1986 to $1.12 in 1991, the dividend yield declined from 2.5 percent to 1.74 percent over the same period.

The decline in the earnings yield and the dividend yield over this period is attributable in a major way to the steady and significant expansion in price-earnings ratios over this period of time. Price-earnings ratios reflect the appreciation and confidence with which investors view a company's performance, and as our analysis indicates, Campbell's operating performance over this period was relatively superior, despite the temporary interruption in 1989 and 90. They do, however, also reflect exceptionally euphoric market conditions.

Exhibit 23–26

CAMPBELL SOUP COMPANY
Market Measures

	1991	1990*	1989*	1988	1987	1986
1. Price-earning ratio (range) . .	27–14	26–18	29–12	16–11	19–14	20–10
2. Earnings yield (percent)	4.91	4.53	4.91	7.45	6.20	6.61
3. Dividend yield (percent) . . .	1.74	1.88	2.08	2.85	2.32	2.50
4. Dividend payout ratio (percent)	35.44	41.53	42.45	38.21	37.37	37.79

Notes:
(1) 1991: High-low for the year (84.88 / 3.16 = 27)

    $\boxed{184}$ (43.75 / 3.16 = 14)

(2) 1991: Earnings per share / Average market price

$$3.16 / [(84.88 + 43.75) / 2] = 4.91\%$$

(3) 1991: Dividend per share / Average market price

$$1.12 / 64.32 = 1.74\%$$

(4) 1991: Dividend per share / Earnings per share

$$1.12 / 3.16 = 35.44\%$$

* 1990 and 1989 results are shown for EPS before effects of divestitures, restructuring, and unusual charges of $2.33 and 2.02 per share respectively.

Higher price earnings ratios brought about by active stock markets benefit a company in many ways; for example, in being able to raise capital inexpensively and in its ability to use common stock as the coin of payment for acquisitions. However, these increasing valuations expose existing and particularly new common stockholders to increasing risks—risks that these rich valuations can be quickly downgraded and reversed. This is so because, unlike in the early stages of the bull market, prices are no longer based on fundamental factors but are based on hope for continuation of the upward price momentum. Thus the stock price includes an evergrowing "enthusiasm component" which, as experience has shown time and again, can be quickly deflated. These considerations, important and crucial as they are for the equity investor in times of euphoric markets, cannot be assessed by means of the analytical tools developed here. They involve a study of market psychology and market cycles. These factors must be given the most serious consideration by the equity investor. The difference between the return a company earns on *its* investment and that which the investors earn on investments is discussed at the end of Chapter 19.

USES OF FINANCIAL STATEMENT ANALYSIS

The foregoing analysis of the financial statements of Campbell Soup Company consists of two major parts: (1) the detailed analysis and (2) the summary and conclusions. As was mentioned earlier, in a formal analytical report the summary and conclusions section may precede the detailed analysis so that the reader is presented with material in the order of its importance to him or her.

The bank loan officer who has to decide on the short-term loan application by the company will normally give primary attention to short-term liquidity analysis and to the funds flow projection, and secondarily to capital structure and operating results.

The investment committee of the insurance company may, in taking a longer-term point of view, pay attention first to capital structure and long-term solvency and then to operating performance, ROI, asset utilizations, and short-term liquidity, and in that order of emphasis.

The potential investor in Campbell shares will, of course, be interested in all the aspects of our analysis. The emphasis may, however, be different again and take the following order of priority: results of operations, ROI capital structure, and long-term solvency and short-term liquidity.

An adequate financial statement analysis (as the Campbell Soup Company analysis illustrates) will contain, in addition to the analysis of the data, enough information and detail so as to allow the decision maker to follow the rationale behind the analyst's conclusions as well as to allow him or her to expand it into areas not covered by the analysis.

QUESTIONS

1. What kind of processes should normally precede an analysis of financial statements?
2. What are the analytical implications of the fact that financial statements are, at best, an abstraction of underlying reality?
3. Name the six major "building blocks" of financial analysis. What does the "building block" approach involve?
4. What are some of the earmarks of a good analysis? Into what distinct sections should a well-organized analysis be divided?
5. What additional knowledge and analytical skills must an analyst bring to bear upon the analysis of enterprises in specialized or regulated industries?

APPENDIX 23

This appendix presents portions from the financial sections of Quaker Oats Company's 1991 annual report which includes Form 10K data. The data in this appendix form the basis for illustrations in the text as well as for questions and problems.

Quaker is a worldwide marketer of consumer grocery products. In the geographic markets in which it competes, Quaker is a major producer of cereals, mixes, grain-based snacks, syrup, corn products, value-added rice and pasta products, chocolates, canned beans, edible oils, thirst-quenching beverages, and pet foods. At the end of fiscal 1991, the company had plant facilities in 16 states in the United States as well as in Western Europe, Canada, and Latin America. Approximately 10,900 of Quaker's 21,000 employees are located in the United States.

The auditor's opinion in the 1991 annual report was unqualified.

The Quaker Oats Company and Subsidiaries

Consolidated Statements of Income

Dollars in Millions (Except Per Share Data)

Year Ended June 30		1991	1990	1989
[1]	Net Sales	$5,491.2	$5,030.6	$4,879.4
[2]	Cost of goods sold	2,839.7	2,685.9	2,655.3
[3]	Gross profit	2,651.5	2,344.7	2,224.1
[4]	Selling, general and administrative expenses	2,121.2	1,844.1	1,779.0
[5]	Interest expense—net of $9.0, $11.0 and $12.4 interest income	86.2	101.8	56.4
[6]	Other expense—net	32.6	16.4	149.6
[7]	**Income from Continuing Operations Before Income Taxes**	411.5	382.4	239.1
[8]	Provision for income taxes	175.7	153.5	90.2
[9]	**Income from Continuing Operations**	235.8	228.9	148.9
[10]	Income (loss) from discontinued operations—net of tax	(30.0)	(59.9)	54.1
[11]	**Net Income**	205.8	169.0	203.0
[12]	Preferred dividends—net of tax	4.3	4.5	—
[13]	**Net Income Available for Common**	$ 201.5	$ 164.5	$ 203.0
	Per Common Share:			
[14]	Income from Continuing Operations	$ 3.05	$ 2.93	$ 1.88
[15]	Income (loss) from discontinued operations	(.40)	(.78)	.68
[16]	**Net Income**	$ 2.65	$ 2.15	$ 2.56
[17]	Dividends declared	$ 1.56	$ 1.40	$ 1.20
[18]	**Average Number of Common Shares Outstanding** (in 000's)	75,904	76,537	79,307

See accompanying notes to the consolidated financial statements.

Consolidated Statements of Cash Flows

Year Ended June 30	1991	1990	1989
Cash Flows from Operating Activities:			
19 Net income	$ 205.8	$ 169.0	$ 203.0
Adjustments to reconcile net income to net cash (used in) provided by operating activities:			
20 Depreciation and amortization	177.7	162.5	135.5
21 Deferred income taxes and other items	45.3	15.2	79.9
22 Provision for restructuring charges	10.0	(17.5)	124.3
Changes in operating assets and liabilities—continuing operations:			
23 Change in receivables	(97.8)	(55.9)	(77.1)
24 Change in inventories	30.7	(2.2)	(90.3)
25 Change in other current assets	(13.7)	(14.1)	(48.9)
26 Change in trade accounts payable	26.1	31.4	102.2
27 Change in other current liabilities	43.2	83.4	(53.1)
28 Other—net	9.5	0.4	(8.4)
29 Change in payable to Fisher-Price	29.6	—	—
30 Change in net current assets of discontinued operations	66.0	74.9	14.5
31 Net Cash Provided by Operating Activities	532.4	447.1	381.6
Cash Flows from Investing Activities:			
32 Additions to property, plant and equipment	(240.6)	(275.6)	(223.2)
33 Cost of acquisitions, excluding working capital	—	—	(112.9)
34 Change in other receivables and investments	(10.7)	(22.6)	(5.7)
35 Disposals of property, plant and equipment	17.9	11.9	26.7
36 Other—discontinued operations	(19.8)	(58.4)	(46.7)
37 Net Cash Used in Investing Activities	(253.2)	(344.7)	(361.8)
Cash Flows from Financing Activities:			
38 Cash dividends	(123.0)	(110.5)	(95.2)
39 Proceeds from issuance of debt for spin-off	141.1	—	—
40 Change in deferred compensation	(0.2)	3.5	(248.4)
41 Change in short-term debt	(265.6)	(7.2)	42.1
42 Proceeds from long-term debt	1.8	252.1	251.2
43 Reduction of long-term debt	(39.7)	(34.8)	(30.1)
44 Issuance of common treasury stock	25.6	12.8	10.1
45 Purchase of common stock	—	(223.2)	(68.5)
46 Issuance of preferred stock	—	—	100.0
47 Purchase of preferred stock	(0.7)	—	—
48 Net Cash Used in Financing Activities	(260.7)	(107.3)	(38.8)
49 Effect of Exchange Rate Changes on Cash and Cash Equivalents	(6.0)	1.6	(7.4)
50 Net Increase (Decrease) in Cash and Cash Equivalents	$ 12.5	$ (3.3)	$ (26.4)
51 Cash and Cash Equivalents—Beginning of Year	$ 17.7	$ 21.0	$ 47.4
52 Cash and Cash Equivalents—End of Year	$ 30.2	$ 17.7	$ 21.0

See accompanying notes to the consolidated financial statements.

The Quaker Oats Company and Subsidiaries

Consolidated Balance Sheets

Assets

June 30		1991	1990	1989
Current Assets:				
[53]	Cash and cash equivalents	$ 30.2	$ 17.7	$ 21.0
[54]	Short-term investments, at cost which approximates market	—	.6	2.7
[55]	Receivables—net of allowances	691.1	629.9	594.4
	Inventories:			
[56]	Finished goods	309.1	324.1	326.0
[57]	Grain and raw materials	86.7	110.7	114.1
[58]	Packaging materials and supplies	26.5	39.1	39.0
[59]	Total inventories	422.3	473.9	479.1
[60]	Other current assets	114.5	107.0	94.2
[61]	Net current assets of discontinued operations	—	252.2	328.5
[62]	Total current assets	1,258.1	1,481.3	1,519.9
[63]	**Other Receivables and Investments**	79.1	63.5	26.4
[64]	Property, plant and equipment	1,914.6	1,745.6	1,456.9
[65]	Less accumulated depreciation	681.9	591.5	497.3
[66]	**Properties—Net**	1,232.7	1,154.1	959.6
[67]	**Intangible Assets, Net of Amortization**	446.2	466.7	484.7
[68]	**Net Non-current Assets of Discontinued Operations**	—	160.5	135.3
[69]	**Total Assets**	$3,016.1	$3,326.1	$3,125.9

See accompanying notes to the consolidated financial statements.

Liabilities and Common Shareholders' Equity

June 30	1991	1990	1989
Current Liabilities:			
70 Short-term debt	$ 80.6	$ 343.2	$ 102.2
71 Current portion of long-term debt	32.9	32.3	30.0
72 Trade accounts payable	350.9	354.0	333.8
73 Accrued payrolls, pensions and bonuses	116.3	106.3	118.1
74 Accrued advertising and merchandising	105.7	92.6	67.1
75 Income taxes payable	45.1	36.3	8.0
76 Payable to Fisher-Price	29.6	—	—
77 Other accrued liabilities	165.8	173.8	164.9
78 Total current liabilities	926.9	1,138.5	824.1
79 **Long-term Debt**	701.2	740.3	766.8
80 **Other Liabilities**	115.5	100.3	89.5
81 **Deferred Income Taxes**	366.7	327.7	308.4
82 **Preferred Stock,** no par value, authorized 1,750,000 shares; issued 1,282,051 of $5.46 cumulative convertible shares in 1989 (liquidating preference $78 per share)	100.0	100.0	100.0
83 **Deferred Compensation**	(94.5)	(98.2)	(100.0)
84 **Treasury Preferred Stock,** at cost, 10,089 shares at June 30, 1991	(.7)	—	—
Common Shareholders' Equity:			
85 Common stock, $5 par value, authorized 200,000,000 shares; issued 83,989,396 shares	420.0	420.0	420.0
86 Additional paid-in capital	7.2	12.9	18.1
87 Reinvested earnings	1,047.5	1,164.7	1,106.2
88 Cumulative exchange adjustment	(52.9)	(29.3)	(56.6)
89 Deferred compensation	(168.0)	(164.1)	(165.8)
90 Treasury common stock, at cost, 7,660,675 shares; 8,402,871 shares; and 5,221,981 shares, respectively	(352.8)	(386.7)	(184.8)
91 Total common shareholders' equity	901.0	1,017.5	1,137.1
92 **Total Liabilities and Common Shareholders' Equity**	$3,016.1	$3,326.1	$3,125.9

The Quaker Oats Company and Subsidiaries

Consolidated Statements of Common Shareholders' Equity

		Common Stock Issued	
		Shares	Amount
93	Balance at June 30, 1988	83,989,396	$420.0
94	Net income		
95	Cash dividends declared on common stock		
96	Common stock issued for option, stock purchase and profit-sharing plans		
97	Repurchases of common stock		
98	Current year foreign currency adjustments (net of allocated income taxes of $1.2)		
99	Deferred compensation		
100	Balance at June 30, 1989	83,989,396	$420.0
101	Net income		
102	Cash dividends declared on common stock		
103	Cash dividends declared on preferred stock		
104	Common stock issued for stock purchase and incentive plans		
105	Repurchases of common stock		
106	Current year foreign currency adjustments (net of allocated income taxes of $6.4)		
107	Deferred compensation		
108	Balance at June 30, 1990	83,989,396	$420.0
109	Net income		
110	Cash dividends declared on common stock		
111	Cash dividends declared on preferred stock		
112	Distribution of equity to shareholders from spin-off of Fisher-Price		
113	Common stock issued for stock purchase and incentive plans		
114	Current year foreign currency adjustments (net of allocated income taxes of $3.0)		
115	Deferred compensation		
116	Balance at June 30, 1991	83,989,396	$420.0

See accompanying notes to the consolidated financial statements.

Dollars in Millions

Additional Paid-in Capital	Reinvested Earnings	Common Stock in Treasury		Cumulative Exchange Adjustment	Deferred Compensation	Total
		Shares	Amount			
$19.5	$ 998.4	4,593,664	$ (132.9)	$ (36.5)	$ (17.4)	$1,251.1
	203.0					203.0
	(95.2)					(95.2)
(1.4)		(601,383)	16.7			15.3
		1,229,700	(68.6)			(68.6)
				(20.1)		(20.1)
					(148.4)	(148.4)
$18.1	$1,106.2	5,221,981	$ (184.8)	$ (56.6)	$ (165.8)	$1,137.1
	169.0					169.0
	(106.9)					(106.9)
	(3.6)					(3.6)
(5.2)		(522,110)	21.3			16.1
		3,703,000	(223.2)			(223.2)
				27.3		27.3
					1.7	1.7
$12.9	$1,164.7	8,402,871	$ (386.7)	$ (29.3)	$ (164.1)	$1,017.5
	205.8					205.8
	(118.7)					(118.7)
	(4.3)					(4.3)
	(200.0)					(200.0)
(5.7)		(742,196)	33.9			28.2
				(23.6)		(23.6)
					(3.9)	(3.9)
$ 7.2	$1,047.5	7,660,675	$ (352.8)	$ (52.9)	$ (168.0)	$ 901.0

The Quaker Oats Company and Subsidiaries

Eleven-Year Selected Financial Data

Year Ended June 30	5-Year Compound Growth Rate	10-Year Compound Growth Rate	1991
[118] Operating Results (a)(b)(c)(d)			
Net sales	13.1%	10.7%	$5,491.2
Gross profit	15.3%	14.5%	2,651.5
Income from continuing operations before income taxes	10.0%	11.1%	411.5
Provision for income taxes	9.2%	10.7%	175.7
Income from continuing operations	10.6%	11.4%	235.8
Income (loss) from discontinued operations—net of tax			(30.0)
Income (loss) from the disposal of discontinued operations—net of tax			—
[119] Net income	2.8%	6.9%	$ 205.8
Per common share:			
Income from continuing operations	11.5%	12.5%	$ 3.05
Income (loss) from discontinued operations			(.40)
Income (loss) from the disposal of discontinued operations			—
[120] Net income	3.4%	7.8%	$ 2.65
[121] Dividends declared:			
Common stock	16.5%	14.0%	$ 118.7
Per common share	17.4%	14.6%	$ 1.56
Redeemable preference and preferred stock			$ 4.3
[122] Average number of common shares outstanding (000's)			75,904

(a) Excludes the operating results of businesses reported as discontinued operations (see Note 2).
(b) See Management's Discussion and Analysis for discussion of fiscal 1989 through 1991 restructuring charges and credits.

Dollars in Millions (Except Per Share Data)

	1990	1989	1988	1987	1986	1985	1984	1983	1982	1981
	$5,030.6	$4,879.4	$4,508.0	$3,823.9	$2,968.6	$2,925.6	$2,830.9	$2,172.4	$2,114.7	$1,989.8
	2,344.7	2,224.1	2,111.0	1,751.9	1,299.1	1,174.7	1,085.7	879.1	790.6	683.7
	382.4	239.1	314.6	295.9	255.8	238.8	211.3	180.1	158.9	144.1
	153.5	90.2	118.1	141.3	113.4	110.3	99.0	81.9	68.4	63.7
	228.9	148.9	196.5	154.6	142.4	128.5	112.3	98.2	90.5	80.4
	(59.9)	54.1	59.2	33.5	37.2	28.1	26.4	14.1	26.8	24.8
	—	—	—	55.8	—	—	—	(55.5)	(20.4)	—
	$ 169.0	$ 203.0	$ 255.7	$ 243.9	$ 179.6	$ 156.6	$ 138.7	$ 56.8	$ 96.9	$ 105.2
	$ 2.93	$ 1.88	$ 2.46	$ 1.96	$ 1.77	$ 1.53	$ 1.35	$ 1.19	$ 1.11	$ .94
	(.78)	.68	.74	.43	.47	.35	.32	.17	.34	.31
	—	—	—	.71	—	—	—	(.70)	(.26)	—
	$ 2.15	$ 2.56	$ 3.20	$ 3.10	$ 2.24	$ 1.88	$ 1.67	$ .66	$ 1.19	$ 1.25
	$ 106.9	$ 95.2	$ 79.9	$ 63.2	$ 55.3	$ 50.5	$ 44.4	$ 39.5	$ 35.3	$ 31.9
	$ 1.40	$ 1.20	$ 1.00	$ .80	$ .70	$ .62	$ .55	$ .50	$ .45	$ .40
	$ 3.6	—	—	—	$ 2.3	$ 3.6	$ 3.9	$ 4.1	$ 4.3	$ 4.6
	76,537	79,307	79,835	78,812	79,060	81,492	80,412	79,008	77,820	80,322

(c) Fiscal 1989 net income was decreased by $16 million (after-tax) or $.20 per share due to the adoption of the last-in, first-out ("LIFO") method of valuing inventories.
(d) Per share data reflect the November 1986 and 1984 two-for-one stock split-ups.

The Quaker Oats Company and Subsidiaries

Eleven-Year Selected Financial Data

Year Ended June 30	5-Year Compound Growth Rate	10-Year Compound Growth Rate	1991
Financial Statistics (a)(b)(c)			
[123] Current ratio			1.4
Working capital	2.2%	2.8%	$ 331.2
Working capital turnover (d)			16.3
[124] Property, plant and equipment—net	12.3%	8.4%	$1,232.7
[125] Depreciation expense	16.2%	14.3%	$ 125.2
[126] Total assets	9.2%	8.3%	$3,016.1
[127] Long-term debt			$ 701.2
[128] Preferred stock net of deferred compensation, and preference stock			$ 4.8
[129] Common shareholders' equity			$ 901.0
[130] Book value per common share			$ 11.80
[131] Return on average common shareholders' equity			24.1%
[132] Gross profit as a percentage of sales			48.3%
[133] Advertising and merchandising as a percentage of sales			25.6%
[134] Research and development as a percentage of sales			.8%
[135] Income from continuing operations as a percentage of sales			4.3%
[136] Long-term debt ratio (e)			43.6%
Total debt ratio (f)			47.4%
Common dividends as a percentage of income available for common shares			58.9%
Number of common shareholders			33,603
Number of employees worldwide			20,900
[137] Market price range of common stock—High			$ 64%
—Low			$ 41%

(a) Income-related statistics exclude the results of businesses which have been reported as discontinued operations. Balance sheets and related statistics have not been restated for discontinued operations other than Fisher-Price due to immateriality.
(b) Per share data reflect the November 1986 and 1984 two-for-one stock split-ups.
(c) During fiscal 1991, common shareholders' equity and book value per common share, as well as number of employees worldwide, were reduced by the spin-off of Fisher-Price (see Note 2).

Dollars in Millions (Except Per Share Data)

	1990	1989	1988	1987	1986	1985	1984	1983	1982	1981
	1.3	1.8	1.4	1.4	1.4	1.7	1.6	1.6	1.6	1.6
	$ 342.8	$ 695.8	$ 417.5	$ 507.9	$ 296.8	$ 400.7	$ 316.8	$ 261.9	$ 266.6	$ 252.4
	9.7	8.8	9.7	9.5	8.5	8.2	9.8	8.2	8.1	7.7
	$1,154.1	$ 959.6	$ 922.5	$ 898.6	$ 691.0	$ 616.5	$ 650.1	$ 533.0	$ 533.8	$ 552.2
	$ 103.5	$ 94.2	$ 88.3	$ 81.6	$ 59.1	$ 56.3	$ 57.4	$ 40.1	$ 35.2	$ 32.9
	$3,326.1	$3,125.9	$2,886.1	$3,136.5	$1,944.5	$1,760.3	$1,726.5	$1,391.9	$1,383.3	$1,360.3
	$ 740.3	$ 766.8	$ 299.1	$ 527.7	$ 160.9	$ 168.2	$ 200.1	$ 152.8	$ 162.1	$ 164.5
	1.8	—	—	—	—	37.9	38.5	41.3	45.4	46.7
	$1,017.5	$1,137.1	$1,251.1	$1,087.5	$ 831.7	$ 786.9	$ 720.1	$ 639.4	$ 630.5	$ 612.6
	$ 13.46	$ 14.44	$ 15.76	$ 13.68	$ 10.64	$ 9.76	$ 8.89	$ 8.02	$ 8.04	$ 7.99
	20.8%	12.5%	16.8%	16.1%	17.3%	16.6%	15.9%	14.8%	13.9%	12.7%
	46.6%	45.6%	46.8%	45.8%	43.8%	40.2%	38.4%	40.5%	37.4%	34.4%
	23.8%	23.4%	24.9%	22.9%	21.7%	19.4%	18.4%	18.6%	16.6%	15.3%
	.9%	.8%	.8%	.8%	.8%	.7%	.8%	.8%	1.0%	1.0%
	4.6%	3.1%	4.4%	4.0%	4.8%	4.4%	4.0%	4.5%	4.3%	4.0%
	42.1%	40.3%	19.3%	32.7%	16.2%	16.9%	20.9%	18.3%	19.4%	20.0%
	52.3%	44.2%	33.8%	50.2%	35.7%	28.9%	35.4%	32.9%	32.4%	35.2%
	65.1%	46.9%	31.3%	25.9%	31.2%	33.0%	32.9%	75.8%	37.8%	32.0%
	33,859	34,347	34,231	32,358	27,068	26,670	26,785	27,943	29,552	30,418
	28,200	31,700	31,300	30,800	29,500	28,700	28,400	25,200	26,000	30,900
	$ 68%	$ 66%	$ 57%	$ 57%	$ 39%	$ 26%	$ 16%	$ 12%	$ 10%	$ 9%
	$ 45%	$ 42%	31	$ 32%	$ 23%	$ 14%	$ 10%	$ 8%	$ 7%	$ 6%

(d) Net sales divided by average working capital.
(e) Long-term debt divided by long-term debt plus total equity including preferred stock net of related deferred compensation and preference stock.
(f) Total debt divided by total debt plus total equity including preferred stock net of related deferred compensation and preference stock.

Management's Discussion and Analysis

138 **Financial Review**

On June 28, 1991, the Company completed the distribution of Fisher-Price to its shareholders and Fisher-Price, Inc., an independent, free-standing company, was created (see Note 2). Fisher-Price has been presented as a discontinued operation within these financial statements for all periods shown. Also in fiscal 1991, the Company recorded a $10 million pretax restructuring charge, or 8 cents per share, to close a Golden Grain pasta manufacturing plant.

In fiscal 1990, the Company reassessed a previously announced plan to close two European pet food facilities and invest in a new pet food plant. This reassessment resulted in management's decision to upgrade existing facilities and forego building a new plant. As a result, reserves of $17.5 million, 18 cents per share, charged to fiscal 1989 earnings were reversed in fiscal 1990.

In fiscal 1989, the Company recorded a variety of restructuring charges aimed at improving productivity and lowering costs. The most significant of these related to the closure of its Marion, Ohio Pet Foods Division plant, which resulted in a $70 million pretax charge to income. Also in fiscal 1989, the Company recorded a charge of $20.7 million for the planned consolidation of European pet food facilities (referenced above). In total, these restructuring charges reduced pretax income by approximately $125 million, or $1.00 per share.

139 **Fiscal 1991 Compared with Fiscal 1990 Operations**

Fiscal 1991 consolidated sales reached a record $5.5 billion, up 9 percent over fiscal 1990, aided by a solid unit volume increase of 5 percent. U.S. and Canadian Grocery Products sales of $3.9 billion were up 7 percent on a 5 percent volume increase. Most businesses had volume increases, led by *Gatorade* thirst quencher, up over 15 percent. International Grocery Products sales of $1.6 billion were up 15 percent on a 5 percent volume increase. The sales gain was driven by the European and Mexican businesses, due to favorable currency trends and strong volume gains in *Gatorade* and pet foods.

Gross profit margin rose to 48 percent of net sales versus 47 percent in fiscal 1990 due largely to lower commodity and packaging costs in the domestic grocery business.

Selling, general and administrative expenses of $2.1 billion rose 15 percent over fiscal 1990, and were also higher as a percentage of sales versus last year. The increases in both dollar and percentage terms were due to higher planned

advertising and merchandising (A&M) expenditures in the domestic cereals and *Gatorade* businesses as well as the expansion of *Gatorade* thirst quencher in Europe.

140 Net interest expense declined 15 percent to $86.2 million due primarily to lower financing costs in Brazil due to the hyper-inflationary environment in that country in fiscal 1990.

Fiscal 1991 other expense included foreign exchange gains of $5.1 million compared to losses of $25.7 million in fiscal 1990, due largely to improvement in Brazil. Restructuring items included in other expense were a $10 million Golden Grain plant closing charge in fiscal 1991 and a $17.5 million credit in fiscal 1990.

Consolidated operating income was $533 million compared to $544.2 million last year. Excluding restructuring charges and credits in both years, operating income would have been $543 million in fiscal 1991, or 3 percent higher than the $526.7 million of a year ago. Operating income for U.S. and Canadian Grocery Products for fiscal 1991 was $429 million, up 15 percent from last year's $372.5 million. Excluding the fiscal 1991 restructuring charge of $10 million, operating income rose 18 percent for the year. International Grocery Products operating income in fiscal 1991 was $104 million, versus last year's $171.7 million. The year-to-year comparisons largely reflect the impact of a hyper-inflationary economic environment in Brazil in fiscal 1990 and a downturn in the business in fiscal 1991 because of deteriorating economic conditions in that country, as well as the fiscal 1990 restructuring credit of $17.5 million. The operating income shortfall in Brazil was largely offset by lower financing costs in that country. In addition, significant A&M expenditures were incurred to launch *Gatorade* thirst quencher into Germany, France, Spain and Mexico. A more detailed discussion of operating performance by segment is provided on pages 14 through 32 in the Operations Review section of this report.

Income from continuing operations of $235.8 million increased 3 percent over fiscal 1990. See Note 2 for a discussion of discontinued operations, which include the Company's Fisher-Price business.

In December 1987, the Financial Accounting Standards Board (FASB) issued Statement #96, "Accounting for Income Taxes," which introduces an asset-and-liability approach to financial accounting and reporting for income taxes. This statement has not yet been adopted, although adoption is required by fiscal 1993. Based on preliminary evaluations, Statement #96 is not expected to have a material impact on the Company's financial results.

In December 1990, the FASB issued Statement #106, "Employers' Accounting for Postretirement Benefits Other Than Pensions." This new standard requires that the expected cost of these benefits be charged to expense during the years that the employees render service. This is a significant change from the Company's current policy of recognizing these costs on the cash basis. The Company is required to adopt the new accounting and disclosure rules no later than fiscal 1994, although earlier implementation is permitted. See Note 11 to the consolidated financial statements for a further discussion of Statement #106.

[141] Fiscal 1990 Compared with Fiscal 1989 Operations

Fiscal 1990 sales of $5 billion rose 3 percent above fiscal 1989, driven by solid gains in International Grocery Products. U.S. and Canadian Grocery Products sales of $3.6 billion were essentially even with the prior year, although volumes declined 6 percent.

The gross profit margin increased to 47 percent of net sales versus 46 percent in fiscal 1989 due primarily to sharply higher margins from the Company's Brazilian business. This resulted from aggressive pricing during a period of dramatic inflation in that country and from lower commodity costs, especially oats, in the domestic grocery business. Partially offsetting the benefit of lower commodity costs were charges of approximately $15 million, recorded in fiscal 1990 for oat bran inventory write-downs.

Selling, general and administrative expenses increased 4 percent over fiscal 1989 to $1.8 billion but remained steady with fiscal 1989 as a percent of net sales. The dollar increase was driven by higher advertising and merchandising spending, especially for the expansion of *Gatorade* thirst quencher in Europe.

Net interest expense increased 80 percent to $101.8 million due primarily to higher financing costs in Brazil and, to a lesser extent, domestic interest expense incurred on debt used for the repurchase of the Company's common stock.

Fiscal 1989 other expense included approximately $125 million in restructuring charges.

Operating income increased 56 percent from fiscal 1989. The increase is attributable to the above-mentioned restructuring charges in fiscal 1989 and credits in fiscal 1990 as well as significantly higher operating income from the

Brazilian business. The higher Brazilian operating income was achieved in that country's hyper-inflationary environment and was largely offset by accompanying higher financing costs.

Income from continuing operations increased 54 percent over fiscal 1989 due primarily to the restructuring charges in fiscal 1989 and credits in 1990.

[142] Liquidity and Capital Resources

The ability to generate funds internally remains one of the Company's most significant financial strengths. Net cash flow from operations of $532.4, $447.1 and $381.6 million during fiscal 1991, 1990 and 1989, respectively, was well in excess of the Company's dividend and capital expenditure requirements. Capital expenditures for fiscal 1991, 1990, and 1989 were $240.6, $275.6 and $223.2 million, respectively, with no material individual commitments outstanding.

Short-term and long-term debt (total debt) decreased $301.1 million from last year, due primarily to proceeds from debt spun off with the Fisher-Price business. Total debt increased $216.8 million from June 30, 1989 to June 30, 1990, driven primarily by the common share repurchase program (see Note 7). During fiscal 1990, the Company repurchased 3.7 million shares of outstanding common stock as part of a 7 million share repurchase program announced in May 1989. No shares were repurchased in fiscal 1991, because of the impending spin-off of Fisher-Price, leaving 3.3 million shares available to repurchase under this program. The Company's debt to total capitalization ratio was 47.4 percent at June 30, 1991 compared to 52.3 percent and 44.2 percent at June 30, 1990 and June 30, 1989, respectively.

On January 31, 1990, the Company filed a shelf registration with the Securities and Exchange Commission covering $600 million of debt securities. As of June 30, 1991, no securities have been issued under this registration statement.

Commercial paper has been the Company's primary source of short-term financing. Quaker's ratings of "A1" (Standard & Poor's) and "P1" (Moody's) have been maintained throughout the year. The available levels of borrowings are adequate to meet the Company's seasonal working capital needs. The Company maintains domestic and non-U.S. bank lines of credit for future corporate general requirements. For a discussion of these lines of credit, see Note 5.

845

The Quaker Oats Company and Subsidiaries

Notes to the Consolidated Financial Statements

[143] Note 1

Summary of Significant Accounting Policies

Consolidation. The consolidated financial statements include The Quaker Oats Company and all of its subsidiaries ("the Company"). All significant intercompany transactions have been eliminated. Businesses acquired are included in the results of operations since their acquisition date. The Company's toy and juvenile products segment ("Fisher-Price") is reflected in the accompanying financial statements as a discontinued operation (see Note 2). Accordingly, unless otherwise indicated, the following notes relate to continuing operations only.

Foreign Currency Translation. Assets and liabilities of the Company's foreign affiliates, other than those located in highly inflationary countries, are translated at current exchange rates, while income and expenses are translated at average rates for the period. For entities in highly inflationary countries, a combination of current and historical rates is used to determine currency gains and losses resulting from financial statement translation and those resulting from transactions. Translation gains and losses are reported as a component of shareholders' equity, except for those associated with highly inflationary countries, which are reported directly in the Consolidated Statements of Income.

Cash and Cash Equivalents. Cash equivalents are composed of all highly liquid investments with an original maturity of three months or less. All other temporary investments are classified as short-term investments.

Inventories. Inventories are valued at the lower of cost or market, using various cost methods, and include the cost of raw materials, labor and overhead. The percentage of year-end inventories valued using each of the methods is as follows:

June 30	1991	1990	1989
Last-in, first-out (LIFO)	61%	62%	63%
Average quarterly cost	27%	27%	22%
First-in, first-out (FIFO)	12%	11%	15%

If the LIFO method of valuing certain inventories were not used, total inventories would have been $18.9 million, $27.9 million, and $31 million higher than reported at June 30, 1991, 1990 and 1989, respectively.

The Company takes positions in the commodity futures and options markets as part of its overall raw materials purchasing strategy in order to reduce the risk associated with price fluctuations of commodities used in manufacturing. The gains and losses on futures contracts and options are included as a part of product cost.

Properties and Depreciation. Property, plant and equipment are carried at cost and depreciated on a straight-line basis over their estimated useful lives. Useful lives range from 5 to 50 years for buildings and improvements and from 3 to 20 years for machinery and equipment.

Intangibles. Intangible assets consist principally of excess purchase price over net tangible assets of businesses acquired (goodwill).

Goodwill is amortized on a straight-line basis over periods not exceeding 40 years. Accumulated goodwill amortization as of June 30, 1991, 1990 and 1989 is $86.5 million, $71.2 million and $55.6 million, respectively.

Income Taxes. Deferred income taxes are provided when tax laws and financial accounting standards differ in respect to the recording of depreciation, capitalized leases and other items. Federal income taxes have been provided on $96.1 million of the $311.5 million of unremitted earnings from foreign subsidiaries. Taxes are not provided on earnings expected to be indefinitely reinvested. See page 40 for a discussion of SFAS #96, "Accounting for Income Taxes."

Interest Rate Futures, Currency Swaps, Options and Forward Contracts. The Company enters into a variety of interest rate futures, currency swaps, options and forward contracts in its management of interest rate and foreign currency exposures. Realized and unrealized gains and losses on interest rate futures and options are deferred and recognized as interest expense over the borrowing period. Realized and unrealized gains and losses on foreign currency options and forward contracts which hedge operating income are recognized currently in other income and expense. Realized and unrealized gains and losses on foreign currency options that hedge exchange rate exposure on future raw material purchases are deferred and recognized in cost of sales in the period in which purchases occur. Realized and unrealized gains and losses on foreign currency options, currency swaps, and forward contracts which are effective as net investment hedges are recognized in shareholders' equity.

Income Per Common Share. Income per common share is based on the weighted average number of common shares outstanding during the period.

Software Costs. As of July 1, 1989, the Company began deferring significant software development project costs, which had previously been expensed as incurred. Software costs of $12.2 million and $6.8 million were deferred during fiscal 1991 and 1990, respectively, pending capitalization at the projects' completion. In fiscal 1991, $3 million of the deferred costs were capitalized and are being amortized over a three-year period.

[144] **Note 2**

Discontinued Operations

In April 1990, the Company's Board of Directors approved in principle the distribution of Fisher-Price to the Company's shareholders. Accordingly, Fisher-Price has been reflected as a discontinued operation in the accompanying financial statements for all periods presented. The tax-free distribution was completed on June 28, 1991 and Fisher-Price, Inc., an independent free-standing company, was created. The distribution reduced reinvested earnings by $200 million. The $29.6 million payable to Fisher-Price at June 30, 1991 represents an estimate of the final cash settlement pursuant to the Distribution Agreement. Each holder of Quaker common stock on July 8, 1991 received one share of Fisher-Price, Inc. common stock for every five shares of Quaker common stock held as of such date. Fisher-Price, Inc. common stock is publicly traded.

The loss from discontinued operations for fiscal 1990 was $59.9 million, or 78 cents per share, including $25.5 million, or 33 cents per share, for the loss from the first nine months of fiscal 1990 and an after-tax provision of $34.4 million, or 45 cents per share, recorded in the fourth quarter. The third-quarter results included charges of $10.7 million, or 8 cents per share, for the East Aurora, New York manufacturing facility closing and $17 million, or 23 cents per share, for anticipated transaction expenses of the planned spin-off and projected operating losses (including allocated interest expense) through the expected completion date of the spin-off. The fourth-quarter provision included charges of $8.6 million, or 7 cents per share, for the pending closing of Fisher-Price's Holland, New York manufacturing facility and $4.8 million, or 4 cents per share, for costs relating to staff reductions. The fourth-quarter provision also included $25.4 million, or 21 cents per share, for inventory write-downs and the cost of maintaining related trade programs and $18.1 million, or 13 cents per share, for higher projected operating losses through the spin-off date due to lower than previously anticipated sales volumes.

During fiscal 1991, the Company recorded an additional $50 million pretax charge ($30 million after tax), or 40 cents per share to discontinued operations. The charge related primarily to receivables credit risk exposure, product recall reserves and severance costs.

The following summarizes the results of operations for discontinued operations:

Dollars in Millions	1991	1990	1989
Sales	$601.0	$702.6	$844.8
Pretax earnings (loss)	$ (50.0)	$ (96.2)	$ 89.6
Income taxes (benefit)	(20.0)	(36.3)	35.5
Income (loss) from discontinued operations	$ (30.0)	$ (59.9)	$ 54.1

Fisher-Price operating loss for fiscal 1991 was approximately $35 million.

Fisher-Price operating losses for the fourth quarter of fiscal 1990, including the Holland, New York plant closing and severance charges, were $40 million, including allocated interest expense of $1.2 million. Interest expense of $6.7 million, $7.4 million and $7.1 million was allocated to discontinued operations in fiscal 1991, 1990 and 1989, respectively.

[145] **Note 3**

Accounts Receivable Allowances

Dollars in Millions	1991	1990	1989
Balance at beginning of year	$16.5	$16.5	$18.1
Provision for doubtful accounts	5.8	3.8	2.8
Provision for discounts and allowances	15.8	6.7	7.2
Write-offs of doubtful accounts, net of recoveries	(4.6)	(2.0)	(5.3)
Discounts and allowances taken	(14.8)	(8.5)	(6.3)
Balance at end of year	$18.7	$16.5	$16.5

The Quaker Oats Company and Subsidiaries

[146] **Note 4**
Property, Plant and Equipment

Dollars in Millions

1991

	Balance at Beginning of Year	Additions	Retirements and Sales	Other Changes	Balance at End of Year
Gross property:					
Land	$ 31.0	$ .8	$ (.2)	$ (.6)	$ 31.0
Buildings and improvements	395.2	41.5	(4.4)	(5.1)	427.2
Machinery and equipment	1,319.4	198.3	(38.1)	(23.2)	1,456.4
Total	$1,745.6	$240.6	$(42.7)	$(28.9)	$1,914.6
Accumulated depreciation:					
Buildings and improvements	$ 94.1	$ 13.6	$ (1.8)	$ (1.8)	$ 104.1
Machinery and equipment	497.4	115.0	(23.0)	(11.6)	577.8
Total	$ 591.5	$128.6	$ (24.8)	$(13.4)	$ 681.9

1990

	Balance at Beginning of Year	Additions	Retirements and Sales	Other Changes	Balance at End of Year
Gross property:					
Land	$ 30.6	$ .5	$ (1.1)	$ 1.0	$ 31.0
Buildings and improvements	348.2	36.4	(1.5)	12.1	395.2
Machinery and equipment	1,078.1	238.7	(36.1)	38.7	1,319.4
Total	$1,456.9	$275.6	$(38.7)	$ 51.8	$1,745.6
Accumulated depreciation:					
Buildings and improvements	$ 80.9	$ 11.3	$ (.7)	$ 2.6	$ 94.1
Machinery and equipment	416.4	95.2	(26.2)	12.0	497.4
Total	$ 497.3	$106.5	$ (26.9)	$ 14.6	$ 591.5

1989

	Balance at Beginning of Year	Additions	Retirements and Sales	Other Changes	Balance at End of Year
Gross property:					
Land	$ 30.1	$ 3.9	$ (3.7)	$ .3	$ 30.6
Buildings and improvements	341.7	36.4	(24.3)	(5.6)	348.2
Machinery and equipment	1,031.3	208.4	(142.5)	(19.1)	1,078.1
Total	$1,403.1	$248.7	$(170.5)	$(24.4)	$1,456.9
Accumulated depreciation:					
Buildings and improvements	$ 75.0	$ 11.1	$ (3.7)	$ (1.5)	$ 80.9
Machinery and equipment	405.6	85.9	(66.2)	(8.9)	416.4
Total	$ 480.6	$ 97.0	$ (69.9)	$(10.4)	$ 497.3

The "Additions" column for fiscal 1989 includes acquisitions made by the Company during that year. Included in the "Other Changes" column for fiscal 1991, 1990 and 1989 are net increases (decreases) of $(18.1), $22.7 and $(13.2) million, respectively, reflecting the effect of translating non-U.S. property at current exchange rates as required by SFAS #52.

[147] **Note 5**
Short-term Debt and Lines of Credit

Dollars in Millions	1991	1990	1989
Notes payable—			
Non-U.S. subsidiaries	$ 67.6	$127.1	$ 49.6
Commercial paper—U.S.			
Dealer-placed on the open market	13.0	216.1	302.6
Commercial paper to be refinanced	—	—	(250.0)
	$ 80.6	$343.2	$102.2
Weighted average interest rates on debt outstanding at end of year—			
Notes payable to banks—non-U.S.	12.1%	17.4%	14.5%
Commercial paper—U.S.	5.9%	8.2%	9.4%
Weighted average interest rates on debt outstanding during the year—			
Notes payable to banks—non-U.S. (computed on month-end balances)	50.7%(a)	76%(a)	50.5%(a)
Commercial paper—U.S. (computed on daily balances)	7.2%	8.5%	8.9%
Average amount of debt outstanding during the year	$263.5	$264.6	$357.7
Maximum month-end balance during the year	$391.4	$355.7	$486.5

(a) The interest rate on debt outstanding was driven principally by periods of high real interest rates in Latin America combined with proportionately lower devaluation of local currencies resulting in high interest rates in dollar terms.

The consolidated balance sheet at June 30, 1989 reflects the reclassification of $250 million of short-term debt, reflecting the Company's intent to refinance this debt on a long-term basis. During fiscal 1990, the Company issued $250 million of medium term notes. (See Note 6).

The Company has a Revolving Credit Agreement with various banks, which supports its commercial paper borrowings and is also available for direct borrowings. The amount of available borrowings under the agreement was $500 million. The

Agreement, which expires no sooner than June 30, 1996, requires a commitment fee of one-eighth percent per annum, payable on any available and unused portion. There were no borrowings under the Agreement during fiscal 1991, 1990 or 1989. As of July 2, 1991, the amount of available borrowings under the Agreement was reduced to $300 million.

The Company's non-U.S. subsidiaries have additional unused short-term lines of credit of approximately $195 million at June 30, 1991.

Under the most restrictive terms of the various loan agreements in effect at June 30, 1991, minimum working capital of $250 million must be maintained.

148 **Note 6**
Long-term Debt

Dollars in Millions

	1991	1990	1989
Sinking Fund Debentures:			
7.7% due through 2001	$ 16.1	$ 18.5	$ 21.5
8% due through 1999	8.4	9.5	10.6
Industrial Revenue Bonds:			
6%-11.5% due through 2010, tax-exempt	39.0	46.0	46.0
4.5%-8.375% due through 2003, taxable	7.1	8.2	7.4
Non-interest bearing installment note due 2014	3.1	2.7	2.4
7.83% Senior ESOP Notes due through 2002	94.5	98.2	100.0
8.07% Senior ESOP Notes due through 2002	148.2	150.0	150.0
8.75% ESOP installment loan due through 1996	12.2	14.1	15.8
7.2%-7.9% Series A Medium-term Notes due through 2000	119.6	134.6	157.1
5.415% and 6.63% deutsche mark swaps due 1993 and 1998	25.6	27.9	23.8
8.15%-9.34% Series B Medium-term Notes due 1993 through 2020	250.0	250.0	—
Commercial paper to be refinanced	—	—	250.0
Other	10.3	12.9	12.2
	$734.1	$772.6	$796.8
Less: Current portion	32.9	32.3	30.0
Net Long-term Debt	$701.2	$740.3	$766.8

All maturity dates presented refer to fiscal years.

Aggregate required payments of maturities on long-term debt for the next five fiscal years are as follows:

Dollars in Millions

Year ended June 30	1992	1993	1994	1995	1996
Required Payments	$32.9	$45.3	$48.5	$46.1	$38.9

During fiscal 1990, the Company issued $250 million of Series B Medium-term Notes bearing interest rates ranging from 8.15 percent to 9.34 percent per annum with maturities from 3 to 30 years. The debt issuance was covered under a $250 million shelf registration filed with the Securities and Exchange Commission during March 1987. Although none of these securities were issued as of June 30, 1989, the consolidated balance sheet as of that date reflects a reclassification of $250 million of commercial paper to long-term debt due to the Company's intent to issue the medium-term notes in fiscal 1990.

During January 1990, the Company filed a shelf registration with the Securities and Exchange Commission covering $600 million worth of debt securities. No securities have been issued under the registration statement as of June 30, 1991.

The Quaker Employee Stock Ownership Plan (ESOP) was expanded during fiscal 1989 through two separate transactions:

- In January 1989, the ESOP through a trust issued $150 million Senior ESOP Notes bearing interest at a rate of 8.07 percent per annum. The proceeds from these notes were used to purchase the Company's common stock on the open market.

- In June 1989, the ESOP incurred an additional $100 million of indebtedness through the issuance via a trust of 7.83 percent Senior ESOP Notes. The proceeds from these notes were used to acquire shares of the Company's Series B ESOP Convertible Preferred Stock.

Both issues of Senior ESOP Notes are due through fiscal 2002 and are unconditionally guaranteed by the Company. See Note 8 for a further description of these transactions.

The Quaker Oats Company and Subsidiaries

In July 1987, $25 million of 8.55 and 9.2 percent medium-term notes were issued, completing the $200 million Series A Medium-term Note offering begun in January 1987. The notes mature during fiscal years 1993 and 1998. This note offering was concurrently swapped into deutsche marks at interest rates of 5.415 percent and 6.63 percent. The swap is effective as a net investment hedge.

The non-interest bearing note for $55.5 million (due fiscal 2014) has an unamortized discount of $52.4 million, $52.8 million and $53.1 million as of June 30, 1991, 1990 and 1989, respectively, based on an imputed interest rate of 13 percent.

The 7.7 percent sinking fund debenture requires annual payments of $1.8 million through fiscal 2000 and a final payment of $6.8 million due in June 2001. The 8 percent sinking fund debenture, which is an obligation of Stokely-Van Camp Inc., a subsidiary of the Company, requires annual payments of $1.3 million through October 1997 with a final payment of $5.3 million due in October 1998. Amounts held in treasury for these sinking fund requirements were as follows:

		Dollars in Millions	
June 30	**1991**	1990	1989
7.7% Sinking Fund Debenture	**$6.9**	$6.3	$5.1
8% Sinking Fund Debenture	**$5.2**	$5.2	$5.2

[149] Note 7
Capital Stock

In May 1989, the Company announced its intent to repurchase, from time to time, up to seven million shares of its outstanding common stock through open market purchases and privately negotiated transactions. As of June 30, 1991, 3,703,000 shares have been repurchased. In June 1989, the ESOP through a trust issued $100 million of Senior ESOP Notes due through fiscal 2002 and bearing interest at a rate of 7.83 percent per annum. Concurrently, the Company sold 1,282,051 shares of the newly authorized issue of Series B ESOP Convertible Preferred Stock to the ESOP. Each share of the preferred stock, of which 1,750,000 shares are authorized, is convertible into one share of the Company's common stock and pays a dividend of $5.46. The preferred stock will be issued only for the ESOP and will not trade on the open market.

In June 1989, the Company completed the repurchase of two million shares under a program announced in fiscal 1988, and in January 1988 completed a two million

share repurchase program (adjusted for the November 1986 stock split-up), announced in fiscal 1986. Repurchased shares are used for general corporate purposes including stock option and incentive plans.

The Company is authorized to issue one million shares of redeemable preference stock and an additional ten million shares of a new class of preference stock to be issued in series, whose terms will be fixed by resolution of the Board of Directors. As of June 30, 1991, none of the preference stock and 1,282,051 shares of the preferred stock have been issued.

The Dividend Reinvestment and Stock Purchase Plan exists for eligible employees and shareholders. The Plan allows for the use of open market, unissued or treasury shares. The shares used in fiscal 1991, 1990 and 1989 were open market shares.

[150] Note 8
Deferred Compensation

The Quaker Employee Stock Ownership Plan (ESOP) was expanded during fiscal 1989 through two separate transactions. In January 1989, the ESOP through a trust issued $150 million Senior ESOP Notes due through fiscal 2002 and bearing interest at a rate of 8.07 percent per annum. The proceeds from the notes, which were received by the trust, were used to purchase 2,813,152 shares of the Company's common stock on the open market. The Senior ESOP Notes are unconditionally guaranteed by the Company.

During May 1989, the Company announced that its Board of Directors authorized the ESOP to incur up to an additional $125 million of indebtedness, which would also be guaranteed by the Company. The Company announced that a new issue of up to $125 million of convertible preferred stock for the ESOP would be purchased with the proceeds of the ESOP debt. In June 1989, the ESOP through a trust issued $100 million of Senior ESOP Notes due through fiscal 2002 and bearing interest at a rate of 7.83 percent per annum. The proceeds from these notes were used to acquire 1,282,051 shares of Series B ESOP Convertible Preferred Stock.

These transactions represent an expansion of the original ESOP, which was adopted during fiscal 1986. The loans from the original and expanded ESOP programs are included as long-term debt on the Company's consolidated balance sheets. Deferred compensation of $262.5 million represents primarily the Company's payment of future compensation expense related to the original and expanded ESOP programs.

As the Company makes annual contributions to the ESOP, these contributions, along with the dividends accumulated on the Company's common and preferred stock held by the ESOP, will be used to repay the outstanding loans. As the loans are repaid, common and preferred stock is allocated to ESOP participants, and deferred compensation is reduced by the amount of the principal payment on the loans.

The following table presents the ESOP loan repayments:

Dollars in Millions

	1991	1990	1989
Principal payments	$ 7.4	$ 3.5	$1.6
Interest payments	20.9	17.4	1.5
Total ESOP payments	$28.3	$20.9	$3.1

As of June 30, 1991, 883,395 shares of common stock and 166,470 shares of preferred stock have been allocated to the accounts of ESOP participants.

[15] Note 9
Employee Stock Option and Award Plans

During fiscal 1990, Quaker shareholders approved the adoption of The Quaker Long-Term Incentive Plan of 1990 ("the Plan"). The purpose of the Plan is to promote the interests of the Company and its shareholders by providing the officers and other key employees with additional incentive and the opportunity through stock ownership to increase their proprietary interest in the Company and their personal interest in its continued success. The Plan provides for benefits to be awarded in the form of options, stock appreciation rights, restricted stock (with corresponding cash awards), performance shares, performance units, and other stock based awards. Six million shares of common stock have been authorized for grant under the Plan. Previously, stock options were issued under the 1984 Long-Term Incentive Plan, which expired by its terms on December 31, 1990. Restricted stock awards were previously issued under the 1984 Restricted Stock Plan, which was terminated during fiscal 1990. Officers and other managerial employees may be granted options for the purchase of common stock at a price not less than the fair market value at date of grant. Options are generally exercisable after one or more years and expire no later than ten years from date of grant. As of June 30, 1991, 534 persons held such options. Changes in stock options outstanding are summarized as follows:

	Shares	Options Price (Per Share)
Balance at June 30, 1988	3,226,408	$ 5.64-44.25
Granted	796,820	53.88
Exercised	(651,108)	5.64-44.25
Expired or terminated	(87,633)	10.67-53.88
Balance at June 30, 1989	3,284,487	$ 6.74-53.88
Granted	809,300	57.00
Exercised	(535,194)	6.74-53.88
Expired or terminated	(103,356)	6.74-57.00
Balance at June 30, 1990	3,455,237	$ 7.08-57.00
Granted	781,100	49.50
Exercised	(600,065)	7.08-57.00
Expired or terminated	(210,554)	28.69-57.00
Balance at June 30, 1991	3,425,718	$ 8.30-57.00

During July 1991, the number and exercise price of all options outstanding at the time of the Fisher-Price spin-off (see Note 2) were adjusted to compensate for decreases in the economic value of the options as a result of the distribution to shareholders. This adjustment increased the number of options outstanding by 293,241 and decreased the exercise price of the options outstanding by approximately 8 percent.

At June 30, 1991, options for 2,664,490 shares were exercisable. As of June 30, 1991, the average per share option price of unexercised options expiring during the period January 13, 1992 to January 9, 2001 was $43.46.

Since fiscal 1977, the stock option plans have provided for the granting of stock appreciation rights in tandem with the granting of stock options. At June 30, 1991, 42,156 stock appreciation rights were attached to outstanding options.

Restricted stock awards grant shares of the Company's common stock to key officers and employees. These shares are subject to a restriction period from the date of grant, during which they may not be sold, assigned, pledged or otherwise encumbered. The number of shares of the Company's common stock awarded were 172,700, 3,700 and 10,200 in fiscal years 1991, 1990, 1989, respectively. Restrictions on these awards lapse after a period of time designated by the Plan committee. In addition, participants may receive a cash award at the end of the restricted period not to exceed 200 percent of the current market value of the shares received as designated by the committee.

The Quaker Oats Company and Subsidiaries

[152] Note 10
Shareholder Rights Plan

The Company's Shareholder Rights Plan, adopted July 9, 1986 and amended July 12, 1989, is designed to deter coercive or unfair takeover tactics and to prevent a person or group from gaining control of the Company without offering a fair price to all shareholders.

Under the terms of the plan, all common shareholders of record on July 30, 1986 received for each share owned one "Right" entitling them to purchase from the Company one one-hundredth of a newly issued share of Series A Junior Participating Preferred Stock at an exercise price of $300.

The Rights become exercisable (1) ten days after a public announcement that a person or group has acquired shares representing 20 percent or more of the voting power of the Company's capital stock, (2) ten business days following commencement of a tender offer for more than 20 percent of such voting power, or (3) ten business days after a holder of at least 15 percent of such voting power is determined to be an adverse person by the Board of Directors. The time periods can be extended by the Company. Unless the Board of Directors has made a determination that any person is an adverse person, the Company can redeem the Rights for $.05 per Right at any time prior to their becoming exercisable. The Rights will expire on July 30, 1996 unless redeemed earlier by the Company.

If after the Rights become exercisable the Company is involved in a merger or other business combination at any time when there is a holder of 20 percent or more of Quaker's stock, the Rights will then entitle a holder, upon exercise of the Rights, to receive shares of common stock of the acquiring company with a market value equal to twice the exercise price of each Right. Alternatively, if a 20 percent holder acquires the Company by means of a reverse merger in which the Company and its stock survive, or if any person acquires 20 percent or more of the Company's voting power or acquires 15 percent of the Company's voting power and is determined by the Board to be an adverse person, each Right not owned by such 20 percent shareholder or adverse person would, upon exercise of the Right, entitle the holder to common stock of the Company (or in certain circumstances other consideration) having a market value equal to twice the exercise price of the Right. The rights described in this paragraph shall not apply to an acquisition, merger or consolidation which is determined by a majority of the Company's independent directors, after consulting one or more investment banking firms, to be fair and otherwise in the best interest of the Company and its shareholders.

[153] Note 11
Pension Plans and Other Post-Employment Benefits

The Company has various pension plans covering substantially all of its domestic and certain foreign employees. Plan benefits are based on years of service and earnings. Company policy is to make contributions to its U.S. plans within the maximum amount deductible for federal income tax purposes. Plan assets consist primarily of equity securities as well as government, corporate and other fixed-income obligations.

The components of net pension cost for defined benefit plans are detailed below:

Dollars in Millions	1991	1990	1989
Service cost (benefits earned during the year)	$28.5	$26.7	$22.7
Interest cost on projected benefit obligation	39.7	36.5	34.1
Actual return on plan assets	(70.5)	(66.7)	(51.6)
Net amortization and deferral	9.8	10.6	(3.3)
U.S. and Canadian pension cost	7.5	7.1	1.9
Multi-employer plans	.7	.8	.7
Foreign plans	3.2	.6	3.7
Net pension cost	$11.4	$ 8.5	$ 6.3

Reconciliations of the funded status of the Company's defined benefit plans to the accrued pension asset (liability) included in the consolidated balance sheets are as follows:

Dollars in Millions	Overfunded			Underfunded		
	1991	1990	1989	1991	1990	1989
Vested benefits	$363.6	$336.8	$307.7	$ 43.6	$ 42.8	$ 37.8
Non-vested benefits	8.1	12.9	10.5	.2	.6	.3
Accumulated benefit obligation	371.7	349.7	318.2	43.8	43.4	38.1
Effect of projected future salary increases	54.2	61.7	56.7	5.4	11.8	7.1
Projected benefit obligation	425.9	411.4	374.9	49.2	55.2	45.2
Plan assets at market value	588.2	543.7	499.3	28.0	26.7	25.5
Projected benefit obligation less (greater) than plan assets	162.3	132.3	124.4	(21.2)	(28.5)	(19.7)
Unrecognized net (gain)	(81.3)	(39.5)	(12.4)	(14.1)	(5.7)	(6.3)
Unrecognized prior service cost	10.4	9.1	9.5	5.6	6.3	1.6
Unrecognized net (asset) liability at transition	(83.8)	(90.8)	(109.0)	5.6	6.3	7.1
Prepaid (accrued) pension costs (in the Balance Sheet)	$ 7.6	$ 11.1	$ 12.5	$(24.1)	$(21.6)	$(17.3)
Assumptions:						
Weighted average discount rate: 9%						
Rate of future compensation increases: 6%						
Long-term rate of return on plan assets: 9%						

Foreign pension plan assets and accumulated benefit obligations are not significant in the aggregate. Therefore, SFAS #87 disclosures have not been presented for these plans.

In addition, the Company provides certain health care and life insurance benefits to its retired employees. A substantial number of the Company's domestic employees and certain employees in foreign countries become eligible for these benefits if they meet retirement age and service requirements while still working for the Company. These costs are expensed as incurred and amounted to $7.4 million, $6.9 million and $6.4 million in fiscal 1991, 1990 and 1989, respectively.

In December 1990, the Financial Accounting Standards Board issued Statement #106, "Employer's Accounting for Postretirement Benefits Other Than Pensions." This new standard requires that the expected cost of these benefits be charged to expense during the years that the employees render service. This is a significant change from the Company's current policy of recognizing these costs on the cash basis. The Company is required to adopt the new accounting and disclosure rules no later than fiscal 1994, although earlier implementation is permitted. The Company may adopt the new standard prospectively or via a cumulative catch-up adjustment.

The Company has not decided when it will adopt the new standard or if it will adopt the new accounting method prospectively or by recording a cumulative catch-up adjustment in the year of adoption. Because of the complexities of the new standard, management has not yet determined the effect that the change in accounting will have on the Company's reported financial position and results of operations. However, management expects that the annual postretirement benefit expense computed in accordance with the new standard will be significantly greater than the annual cash payments.

154 Note 12
Leases and Other Commitments

Certain equipment and operating properties are rented under non-cancellable operating leases that expire at various dates through 2002. Total rental expense under operating leases was $44.5 million, $44.3 million and $42.4 million in fiscal 1991, 1990 and 1989, respectively. Contingent rentals and subleases are not significant. Capital leases, which are included in fixed assets, and minimum lease payments under such leases are not significant.

The following is a schedule of future minimum annual rentals on non-cancellable operating leases, primarily for sales offices, warehouses and corporate headquarters in effect at June 30, 1991:

Dollars in Millions	1992	1993	1994	1995	1996	Later	Total
Total payments	$16.5	$16.5	$15.7	$15.2	$15.0	$66.8	$145.7

155 Note 13
Supplementary Expense Data

Dollars in Millions	1991	1990	1989
Advertising, media and production	$ 277.5	$ 282.8	$ 256.5
Merchandising	1,129.9	912.5	886.2
Total advertising and merchandising	$1,407.4	$1,195.3	$1,142.7
Maintenance and repairs	$ 96.1	$ 96.6	$ 93.8
Depreciation expense	$ 125.2	$ 103.5	$ 94.5
Research and development	$ 44.3	$ 43.3	$ 39.3

156 Note 14
Interest (Income) Expense

Dollars in Millions	1991	1990	1989
Interest expense on long-term debt	$ 43.3	$ 38.3	$25.7
Interest expense on short-term debt and other	60.5	84.7	52.4
Interest expense capitalized—net	(1.9)	(2.8)	(2.2)
Total interest expense	101.9	120.2	75.9
Interest income on securities	(5.5)	(7.2)	(7.3)
Interest income, other	(3.5)	(3.8)	(5.1)
Total interest income	(9.0)	(11.0)	(12.4)
Net interest allocated to discontinued operations	(6.7)	(7.4)	(7.1)
Total net interest expense	$ 86.2	$101.8	$56.4

The Quaker Oats Company and Subsidiaries

157 Note 15
Other (Income) Expense

Dollars in Millions	1991	1990	1989
Foreign exchange (gains) losses—net	$(5.1)	$25.7	$14.8
Amortization of intangibles	22.4	22.2	18.2
Losses (gains) from plant closings and operations sold or to be sold—net	8.8	(23.1)	119.4
Miscellaneous—net	6.5	(8.4)	(2.8)
Net other expense	$32.6	$16.4	$149.6

158 Note 16
Provision for Income Taxes

Provisions for income taxes applicable to continuing operations were as follows:

Dollars in Millions	1991	1990	1989
Currently payable—			
Federal	$103.0	$72.7	$12.7
Non-U.S.	36.6	44.3	26.9
State	21.8	17.9	10.0
Total currently payable	161.4	134.9	49.6
Deferred—net			
Federal	6.7	13.4	30.8
Non-U.S.	4.1	5.4	8.2
State	3.5	(.2)	1.6
Total deferred—net	14.3	18.6	40.6
Total income tax provision	$175.7	$153.5	$90.2

158A
The components of the deferred income tax provision were as follows:

Dollars in Millions	1991	1990	1989
Accelerated tax depreciation	$8.4	$14.5	$15.0
Receipt of tax benefits	(1.3)	(2.8)	(2.1)
Long-term tax liability	—	—	18.2
Tax benefits—ANC(a)	—	—	(1.7)
Other—net	7.2	6.9	11.2
Total deferred income tax provision	$14.3	$18.6	$40.6

158B
The sources of pretax income from continuing operations were as follows:

Dollars in Millions	1991	1990	1989
U.S. sources	$328.7	$265.2	$162.2
Non-U.S. sources	82.8	117.2	76.9
Total income before taxes	$411.5	$382.4	$239.1

158C
A reconciliation of the statutory federal income tax rate to the effective income tax rate follows:

	1991		1990		1989	
Dollars in Millions	Amount	% of Pretax Income	Amount	% of Pretax Income	Amount	% of Pretax Income
Tax provision based on the federal statutory rate	$139.9	34.0%	$130.0	34.0%	$81.3	34.0%
State and local income taxes, net of federal income tax benefit	16.7	4.1	11.9	3.1	7.7	3.2
ANC benefit(a)	—	—	—	—	(1.7)	(.7)
Repatriation of foreign earnings	4.3	1.0	4.8	1.3	(2.1)	(.9)
Non-U.S. tax rate differential	8.2	2.0	9.8	2.5	8.8	3.7
U.S. tax credits	(.2)	(.1)	(.1)	—	(.7)	(.3)
Miscellaneous items—net	6.8	1.6	(2.9)	(.8)	(3.1)	(1.3)
Actual tax provision	$175.7	42.7%	$153.5	40.1%	$90.2	37.7%

(a)In fiscal 1989, the Company recognized $1.7 million of tax benefits in its provision for income taxes related to Alaskan Native Corporation (ANC) agreements. The ANC agreements granted the Company the right to utilize net operating losses of the ANC's for tax purposes during fiscal 1987 and 1988. At June 30, 1991, $67.8 million relating to these agreements are included in deferred taxes.

[159] **Note 17**
Supplemental Cash Flow Information

Dollars in Millions	**1991**	1990	1989
Interest paid	**$101.7**	$96.8	$ 73.8
Income taxes paid	**$ 88.7**	$90.7	$140.0

Interest paid and income taxes paid include amounts related to Fisher-Price. The Company assumed liabilities in conjunction with acquisitions in fiscal 1989 of $13.6 million.

[160] **Note 18**
Financial Instruments

Foreign Currency Forward Contracts. At June 30, 1991, the Company had forward contracts for the purchase and sale of European and Canadian currencies to hedge foreign exchange operating income and balance sheet exposure, purchases totaling $47.2 million and sales totaling $148.9 million. While the contracts generally mature in less than 12 months, the total sales include obligations to sell $8.2 million in British pounds in fiscal 1998 and $7.6 million in Canadian dollars in fiscal 1994.

Deutsche Mark Swap. During fiscal 1988, the Company swapped $25 million for deutsche marks in two separate transactions. The Company is committed to re-exchange 18.5 million deutsche marks for $10 million in August 1992 and 27.9 million deutsche marks for $15 million in August 1997. The Company is also committed to make semi-annual interest payments of 1.4 million deutsche marks through August 1992 and, thereafter, 0.9 million deutsche marks through August 1997.

[161] **Note 19**
Litigation

On December 18, 1990 Judge Prentice H. Marshall of the United States District Court for the Northern District of Illinois issued a memorandum opinion stating that the Court would enter judgment against the Company in favor of Sands, Taylor & Wood Co. The Court found that the use of the words "thirst aid" in advertising *Gatorade* thirst quencher infringed the Plaintiff's rights in the trademark THIRST-AID. On July 9, 1991 Judge Marshall entered a judgment of $42.6 million, composed of $31.4 million in principal, plus prejudgment interest of $10.6 million, and fees, expenses and costs of $0.6 million. The order enjoins use of the phrase "THIRST-AID" in connection with the advertising or sale of *Gatorade* thirst quencher in the United States. The Company and its subsidiary, Stokely-Van Camp, Inc., ceased use of the words "thirst aid" in December 1990. The Company on the advice of inside and outside counsel, strongly believes that it will prevail in an appeal of the judgment. Therefore, no provision for loss has been made in the accompanying financial statements.

The Company is not a party to any other pending legal proceedings which it believes will have a material adverse effect on its financial position or results of operations.

[162]
Note 20
Quarterly Financial Data (Unaudited)

Year Ended June 30				*Dollars in Millions (Except Per Share Data)*
1991	First Quarter	Second Quarter(*a*)	Third Quarter	Fourth Quarter(b)
Net sales	$1,326.5	$1,293.8	$1,334.6	$1,536.3
Cost of goods sold	685.2	689.0	682.3	783.2
Gross profit	$ 641.3	$ 604.8	$ 652.3	$ 753.1
Income from continuing operations	$ 33.2	$ 33.1	$ 63.1	$ 106.4
(Loss) from discontinued operations, net of tax	—	(30.0)	—	—
Net income	$ 33.2	$ 3.1	$ 63.1	$ 106.4
Per common share:				
Income from continuing operations	$ 0.42	$ 0.43	$ 0.82	$ 1.38
(Loss) from discontinued operations	—	(0.40)	—	—
Net income	$ 0.42	$ 0.03	$ 0.82	$ 1.38
Cash dividends declared	$ 0.39	$ 0.39	$ 0.39	$ 0.39
Market price range:				
High	$ 50⅛	$ 53	$ 60¼	$ 64⅞
Low	$ 41¼	$ 42⅞	$ 47¼	$ 55⅛

(a) Includes a provision for discontinued operations of $30 million after-tax ($.40 per share) for Fisher-Price receivables credit risk exposure, product recall reserves, and severance costs.
(b) Includes a charge of $6.6 million after-tax ($.08 per share) for the closing of a Golden Grain pasta manufacturing facility. Also includes a $4.2 million after-tax ($.05 per share) credit for favorable LIFO price variances that were not projected in the prior fiscal 1991 quarters.

Problems

Chapter 3

3–1. Many astute observers have likened the accounting standards-setting process to a political process. C.T. Horngren has expressed his view as follows:

"My hypothesis is that the setting of accounting standards is as much a product of political action as of flawless logic or empirical findings. Why? Because the setting of standards is a social decision. Standards place restrictions on behavior; therefore, they must be accepted by the affected parties. Acceptance may be forced or voluntary or some of both. In a democratic society, getting acceptance is an exceedingly complicated process that requires skillful marketing in a political arena."

Many parties affected by proposed standards intervene to protect their own interests while disguising their motivations as altruistic or theoretical. It has often been said, "if you like the answer, you will love the theory."

To some, the influence of those who are regulated by the standard-setting process, that influence is excessive.

Arthur R. Wyatt stated "The business community has much greater influence than it's ever had over standard setting. I think it's unhealthy. It is the preparer community that is really being regulated in this process, and if we have those being regulated having a dominant role in the regulatory process, that's asking for major trouble."

These and other concerns have led to Mr. Wyatt's resignation from the FASB.

Required:

Is the nature of the accounting standards-setting process relevant to the analyst of financial statements? Discuss.

3–2. David Solomons has likened financial reporting to cartography, as follows:

"Information cannot be neutral—it cannot therefore be reliable—if it is selected or presented for the purpose of producing some chosen effect on human behavior. It is this quality of neutrality which makes a map reliable; and the essential nature

---

Note: Chapters 1 and 2 have no problems.

of accounting, I believe, is cartographic. Accounting is financial mapmaking. The better the map, the more completely it represents the complex phenomena that are being mapped. We do not judge a map by the behavioral effects it produces. The distribution of natural wealth or rainfall shown on a map may lead to population shifts or changes in industrial location, which the government may like or dislike. That should be no concern of the cartographer. We judge his map by how well it represents the facts. People can then react to it as they will."

Required:
1. Why is neutrality such a cardinal quality of financial statements?
2. What are some examples of a lack of neutrality in accounting presentations?

3–3.   In his review of the first edition of this work, the editor of the *Financial Analysts Journal* wrote:

"Broadly speaking, accounting numbers are of two types: those that can be measured and those that have to be estimated. Investors who feel that accounting values are more real than market values should remember that, although the estimated numbers in accounting statements often have a greater impact, singly or together, than the measured numbers, accountants' estimates are rarely based on any serious attempt by accountants at business or economic judgment.

"Accountants are understandably nervous about this; Professor Bernstein provingly cites the following language from *Accounting Research Study No. 1:* "The function of accounting is (1) to measure the resources held by specific entities . . ." By "resources" presumably is meant inventory, bricks and mortar, machines. The accountant cannot "measure" such "resources"; he can only estimate their value. The main reason accountants shy away from precise statements of principle for the determination of asset values is that neither they nor anyone else has yet come up with principles that will consistently give values plausible enough that, if accounting statements were based on these principles, users would take them seriously."

Required:
a. What do we mean by measurement in accounting?
b. According to the editor, what kind of measurements do analysts want?
c. Can these aims of measurement be reconciled?

3–4.   Part A.   The following quotation was included in an article discussing corporate profits:

"One of the real problems with profits is that you never really know what they are," Alan Greenspan says. "The only way you can find out is to liquidate a corporation and reduce everything to cash. Then you can subtract what went into the company from what came out and the result is profits.

"Until then, profits are only a product of the accountants."

Required:
    Is there a practical solution to the "problem with profits" to which Mr. Greenspan alludes?

Part B. Russell J. Morrison, a well-known analyst, wrote:

"There are *reported earnings* and then there are *earnings*. There are balance sheets as produced by accountants and then there are "true" balance sheets. Accountants are concerned with accounting. After all, accountants do accounting.

Required:

What kind of earnings, do you think, does Mr. Morrison refer to as compared to *reported* earnings? Who would produce such earnings and by what means? What would be a likely source of the "true" balance sheet to which the writer is referring?

3–5. FASB member David Moso expressed the following view:

"Are we going to set accounting standards in the private sector or not? . . . Part of the answer depends on how the business community views accounting standards. Are they *rules of conduct,* designed to restrain unsocial behavior and arbitrate conflicts of economic interest? Or are they *rules of measurement,* designed to generalize and communicate as accurately as possible the complex results of economic events? . . . Rules of conduct call for a political process. . . . Rules of measurement, on the other hand, call for a research process of observation and experimentation. . . . Intellectually, the case is compelling for viewing accounting as a measurement process. . . . But the history of accounting standard setting has been dominated by the other view—that accounting standards are rules of conduct. The FASB was created out of the ashes of predecessors burned up in the fires of the resulting political process."

Required:
a. How do you view the difference between "rules of conduct" and "rules of measurement"?
b. In what way is the standard-setting process a political process? What would be arguments for and against considering it as such?

3–6. The purpose of *Statement of Financial Accounting Concepts No. 2,* "Qualitative Characteristics of Accounting Information," is to examine the characteristics that make accounting information useful. The characteristics or qualities of information discussed in *Concepts No. 2* are the ingredients that make information useful and are the qualities to be sought when accounting choices are made.

Required:
A. Identify and discuss the benefits which can be expected to be derived from the FASB's conceptual framework study.
B. What is the most important quality for accounting information as identified in *Statement of Financial Accounting Concepts No. 2* and explain why it is the most important.

C. *Statement of Financial Accounting Concepts No. 2* describes a number of
    key characteristics or qualities for accounting information. Briefly discuss
    the importance of any three of these qualities for financial reporting
    purposes.

3–7.   Russell J. Morrison wrote in the *Financial Analysts Journal:*

"Strictly speaking, the objectives of financial reporting are the objectives of
society and not of accountants and auditors, as such. Similarly, society has objective law and medicine—namely, justice and health for the people—which are
not necessarily the objectives of lawyers and doctors, as such, in the conduct of
their respective 'business.'

"In a variety of ways, society exerts pressure on a profession to act more nearly
as if it actively shared the objectives of society. Society's pressure is to be measured by the degree of accommodation on the part of the profession under pressure, and by the degree of counter-pressure applied by the profession. For example,
doctors accommodate society by getting better educations than otherwise and
reducing incompetence in their ranks. They apply counter-pressure and gain protection by forming medical associations."

Required:
a.   In what way has society brought pressure on accountants to serve it better?
b.   How has the accounting profession responded to these pressures? Are there
     better responses?

3–8.   "Despite its intrinsic intellectual appeal, complete uniform accounting
seems unworkable in a complex industrial society that relies, at least in part, on
economic market forces."

Required:
a.   Discuss briefly at least three disadvantages of national or international
     accounting uniformity.
b.   Does uniformity in accounting necessarily mean comparability? Explain.
                                                                                                     (CFA)*

3–9   A professor of finance wrote:

"An accountant's job is to conceal, not to reveal. An accountant is not asked
to give outsiders an accurate picture of what's going on in a company. He is asked
to transform the figures on a company's operations in such a way that it will be
impossible to recreate the original figures.

"An income statement for a toy company doesn't tell how many toys of various
kinds the company sold, or who the company's best customers are. The balance
sheet doesn't tell how many of each kind of toy the company has in inventory,
or how much is owed by each customer who is late in paying his bills.

---

* Reprinted, with permission, from *CFA Examinations.* Association for Investment Management and Research, Charlottesville, Virginia.

"In general, anything that a manager uses to do his job will be of interest to some stockholders, customers, creditors, or government agencies. Managerial accounting differs from financial accounting only because the accountant has to hide some of the facts and figures managers find useful. The accountant simply has to throw out most of the facts and some of the figures that the managers use when he creates the financial statements for outsiders."

The rules of accounting reflect this tension. Even if the accountant thought of himself as working only for the good of society, he would conceal certain facts in the reports he helps write. Since the accountant is actually working for the company, or even for the management of the company, he conceals many facts that outsiders would like to have revealed.

Required:

a. Comment on the professor's view of the accountant's job.

b. What type of omitted information is the writer referring to?

3–10. There are two permissible ways that companies account for the cost of drilling for oil. Under the *full-cost method,* a drilling company capitalizes costs both for successful wells and dry holes; in other words, it classifies those costs as assets on its balance sheet. Those costs are then charged against revenues as the oil is extracted and sold. Under the *successful-effort method,* the costs of dry holes are taken as expenses as they are incurred, resulting in immediate charges against earnings. The costs of successful wells are capitalized.

Most small and midsized drilling companies use the full-cost method and as a result have millions of dollars of drilling costs appearing as assets on their balance sheets.

The SEC imposed a limit to full-cost accounting. Costs capitalized under this method could not exceed a ceiling defined as the present value of company reserves. Capitalized costs above the ceiling would have to be expensed.

Oil companies, primarily smaller ones, have been successful in the past in prevailing on the SEC to keep the full-cost accounting method as an alternative even though the accounting profession took a position in favor of the successful-efforts method as the only one to be permitted. Because the imposition of the "ceiling" rule occurred during a time of relatively high oil prices the companies accepted it, confident that it would have no practical effect on them.

With the collapse of petroleum prices in 1986 many of the companies found that the sharply lower "ceilings" were exceeded by drilling costs carried as assets on their balance sheets. Thus they were faced with serious write-offs.

Oil companies, concerned about the effect that big write-downs would have on their ability to conduct business, had begun a fierce lobbying effort to try to win a change in the commission's accounting rules so as to avoid sizable write-downs which threatened to lower their earnings as well as their equity capital. The SEC staff supported a suspension of the rules because, they maintained, oil prices could soon turn up and because companies would still be required to disclose the difference between the market value and book value of their oil reserves. The staff proposal would have temporarily relaxed the rules pending the results of a study by the Office of the Chief Accountant on whether the ceiling test should be changed or rescinded. The proposal would have suspended the requirement to use current prices when computing the ceiling amount in determining whether a write-down of reserves is required.

The Commission unanimously rejected the staff proposal that would have enabled 250 of the nation's oil and gas producing companies to postpone write-downs on the declining values of their oil and gas reserves while acknowledging that the impact of the decision could trigger defaults on bank loans. Commission Chairman Shad said "the rules are not stretchable at a time of stress."

Tenneco Co. found a way to cope with the SEC's refusal to sanction postponement of the write-offs. In April 1986 it announced a switch to successful-efforts accounting and that it will take $988 million in charges against prior years' earnings. In effect, Tenneco will take the unamortized dry-hole drilling costs currently on its balance sheet and begin applying them against prior years' revenues. Thus, these costs would affect prior year results only and would not show up as write-offs against currently reported income.

Required:
1. What conclusions can an analyst derive from the evolution of the accounting for oil and gas?
2. What effect would Tenneco's proposed change in accounting method have on the reporting of its operating results over the years?

Chapter 4

4–1.   Having just been hired by the Eager National Bank as a junior analyst, your supervisor hands you the financial statements of Campbell Soup (Appendix 4B), and the list of ratios for 1991 (found on pages 89–92). "Please compute the identical ratios for 1990" said she, and added, "Although it amounts to only a two-year comparison, please comment on whether each ratio change was favorable or adverse and why."

(Hint: Using skills you will learn in Chapter 13, you determine that the 1989 year-end inventory is $830.5 million. Total assets and total equity for 1990 are disclosed elsewhere in Campbell's financial statements. For market measures use average of last quarter price.)

Required:
Please comply with the supervisor's request.

4–2.   Please refer to the financial statements of Quaker Oats (Appendix to Chapter 23).

Required:
(a) Please compute following ratios for Quaker Oats for the years 1991 and 1990.
   Short-term liquidity ratios:
      Current ratio.
      Acid-test ratio.
      Days sales in year-end receivables (collection period).

Inventory turnover.
Capital structure and long-term solvency ratios:
    Total debt to total capital.
    Long-term debt to equity capital.
    Times interest earned[a][b] (simplified version).

[a] Use interest incurred in denominator = interest expensed + interest capitalized.
[b] Use income from continuing operations.

Return on investment ratios:
    Return on total assets.
    Return on common equity capital.
Operating performance ratios:
    Gross margin ratio.
    Operating profits to sales.
    Pretax income[a] to sales.
    Net income to sales.

[a] From continuing operations.

Asset-utilization ratios:
    Sales to cash.
    Sales to accounts receivables.
    Sales to inventories.
    Sales to working capital.
    Sales to fixed assets.
    Sales to total assets.
Market measures:
    Price-earning ratio (use average market price for year).
    Earnings yield.
    Dividend yield.
    Dividend payout ratio.

(b) Although it amounts to only a two-year comparison, please comment on the significance of the year-to-year changes.

4–3. Complete the following comparative operating statement of Toro Corporation.

TORO CORPORATION
Operating Statement
For Years Ending on December 31
(in thousands)

	Year 6	Year 5	Year 4	Cumulative amount	Annual average amount
Net sales		3,490	2,860		
Cost of goods sold	3,210				2,610
Gross profit	3,670	680	1,050		1,800
Total operating expenses					
Income before taxes	2,740	215	105		
Net income	1,485	145	58		

4–4. Compute the increases (decreases) from the preceding year in percentage and fill in the blanks in the following table:

| | Year 7 | | Year 6 | | Year 5 |
	Index no.	Change in percent	Index no.	Change in percent	Index no.
Net sales		29	100		90
Cost of goods sold	139		100		85
Gross profit	126		100		80
Total operating expenses		20	100		65
Income before tax		14	100		70
Net income	129		100		75

4–5. You are currently employed as a management consultant in the Mesco Company. The following data are the only accounting records available to you in relation to your financial analysis assignment. From the data given below construct the 12/31/year 5 balance sheet necessary for your analysis. All data are for or as of December 31, year 5 unless otherwise indicated.

Retained earnings 12/31/year 4	$ 98,000
Gross profit	25%
Acid-test ratio	2.5:1
Noncurrent assets	$280,000
Inventory turnover (based on ending inventory)	8
Days sales in receivables	18 days
Common stock $15 par—	
10,000 shares issued and outstanding sold at $21 per share	
Net worth to total debt	4:1
Sales for the year (all on credit)	$920,000

Expenses excluding taxes incurred in the year were $180,000 in addition to cost of goods sold. Assume a 40 percent tax rate. Use a 360-day year in your computation. No dividends were paid in year 4 and year 5. Current assets consist of cash, accounts receivable, and inventories.

4–6. You are a management consultant to the Fox Company. The following data are the only records available in relation to your financial analysis assignment.

Current ratio	2
Accounts receivable turnover ratio	16
Beginning accounts receivable	$ 50,000
Return on equity	20%
Sales for the year (all on credit)	$1,000,000
Inventory turnover (based on ending inventory)	10
Gross profit on sales	50%
Expenses (excluding cost of goods sold)	450,000
Debt to equity ratio	1
Noncurrent assets	$ 300,000

Required:
Construct the December 31, year 2 balance sheet necessary for your analysis. All data are for or as of December 31, year 2, unless otherwise indicated. Current asset consists of cash, accounts receivable, and inventory. Balance sheet includes cash, accounts receivable, inventory, noncurrent assets, current assets, current and noncurrent liabilities, and equity.

4–7. Flam Bay Inc. recently had a fire which partially destroyed the company's financial records. You are hired as a management consultant to construct the December 31, year 3 balance sheet with the available information. All data are as of 12/31/year 3. All assets are current. Total assets = cash, accounts receivable, inventory, land, and building.

Cash	90
Gross profit on sales	50%
Expenses (excluding cost of goods sold)	540
Current liabilities (total debt)	300
Debt to equity	1:1
Return on equity	20%
Ending inventory turnover	10
Current ratio	2:1
Acid-test ratio	0.6
Total assets	600
Retained earnings	120

Carrying amount of land = 2/3 building

4–8. It is Sunday and you have just opened your briefcase in order to work with Vague Company's December 31, year 6, balance sheet. To your dismay you discover that the computer printouts that your assistant stuffed into your briefcase contained only the following sketchy information:

1. Accounts receivable and inventory were the same at the end of the year as at the beginning.
2. Net income, $1,300.
3. Times interest earned is 5 times (ignore income taxes). The company has outstanding 5 percent bonds issued at par.

4. Net income to sales, 10 percent. Gross margin ratio, 30 percent. Inventory turnover, 5.
5. Accounts receivable turnover, 5.
6. Sales to working capital, 4. Current ratio, 1.5.
7. Acid-test ratio, 1.0 (exclude prepaid expenses).
8. Plant and equipment is one-third depreciated.
9. Dividends paid on 8 percent nonparticipating preferred stock were $40. There was no change in common shares outstanding during year 6. The preferred shares were issued two years ago at par.
10. Earnings per common share, $3.75.
11. Common stock has a $5 par value and was issued at par.
12. Retained earnings at January 1, year 6 were $350.

Required:
Given the information available, complete the balance sheet as of December 31, year 6. Also, determine the amount of dividends paid on the common stock in year 6.

Cash	_____
Accounts receivable	_____
Inventory	_____
Prepaid expenses	_____
Plant and equipment (net)	$6,000
Total assets	_____
Current liabilities	_____
Bonds payable	_____
Stockholders' equity	_____
Total liabilities and equity	_____

4–9. The following balance sheet and income statement are for Chicago Refrigerator Inc.

CHICAGO REFRIGERATOR INC.
Balance Sheet
As of December 31
($ thousands)

	Year 4	Year 5
Assets		
Current assets		
Cash	$ 683	$ 325
Accounts receivable	1,490	3,599
Inventories	1,415	2,423
Prepaid expenses	15	13
Total current assets	$3,603	$6,360
Property, plant, equipment, net	1,066	1,541
Other	123	157
Total assets	$4,792	$8,058

Liabilities

Current liabilities		
Notes payable to bank	$ —	$ 875
Current portion of long-term debt	38	116
Accounts payable	485	933
Estimated income tax	588	472
Accrued expenses	576	586
Customer advance payments	34	963
Total current liabilities	$1,721	$3,945
Long-term debt	122	179
Other liabilities	81	131
Total liabilities	$1,924	$4,255

Shareholders' Equity

Common stock, $1.00 par value; 1,000,000 shares authorized; 550,000 and 829,000 outstanding, respectively	$ 550	$ 829
Preferred stock, Series A 10%; $25 par value; 25,000 authorized; 20,000 and 18,000 outstanding, respectively	500	450
Additional paid-in capital	450	575
Retained earnings	1,368	1,949
Total shareholders' equity	$2,868	$3,803
Total liabilities and shareholders' equity	$4,792	$8,058

CHICAGO REFRIGERATOR INC.
Income Statement
Years Ending December 31
($ thousands)

	Year 4	Year 5
Net sales	$7,570	$12,065
Other income, net	261	345
Total revenues	$7,831	$12,410
Cost of goods sold	$4,850	$ 8,048
General administrative and marketing expense	1,531	2,025
Interest expense	22	78
Total costs and expenses	$6,403	$10,151
Net income before tax	$1,428	$ 2,259
Income tax	628	994
Net income	$ 800	$ 1,265

Required:
Please compute the following for Year 5:

(1) The quick ratio.
(2) The return on assets.

(3) The return on common equity.
(4) Earnings per share.
(5) Profit margin ratio (before interest).
(6) Times interest charges earned.
(7) Average number of days of inventory on hand.
(8) Long-term debt to equity ratio.
(9) The leverage ratio.
(10) Working capital turnover.
    Note: Use a 40 percent tax rate.

(CFA adapted)

4–10. As a consultant to FRY Company you are informed that the company is planning to acquire the Low Corporation and requests that you prepare certain financial statistics for year 5 and year 4 from the following statements of Low Corporation.

LOW CORPORATION
Balance Sheet
December 31, year 5 and year 4

	Year 5	Year 4
Assets		
Current assets:		
Cash	$ 1,610,000	$ 1,387,000
Marketable securities, at cost (market value $550,000)	510,000	
Accounts receivable, less allowance for bad debts:		
Year 5, $125,000; year 4, $110,000	4,075,000	3,669,000
Inventories, at lower of cost or market	7,250,000	7,050,000
Prepaid expenses	125,000	218,000
Total current assets	13,570,000	12,324,000
Plant and equipment, at cost:		
Land and buildings	13,500,000	13,500,000
Machinery and equipment	9,250,000	8,520,000
Total plant and equipment	22,750,000	22,020,000
Less allowances for depreciation	13,470,000	12,549,000
Total plant and equipment—net	9,280,000	9,471,000
Long term receivables	250,000	250,000
Deferred charges	25,000	75,000
Total assets	$23,125,000	$22,120,000
Liabilities and Shareholders Equity		
Current liabilities:		
Accounts payable	$ 2,950,000	$ 3,426,000
Accrued expenses	1,575,000	1,644,000
Federal taxes payable	875,000	750,000
Current maturities on long-term debt	500,000	500,000
Total current liabilities	5,900,000	6,320,000

Other liabilities:

5% sinking fund debentures, due January 1, year 6 ($500,000 redeemable annually)	5,000,000	5,500,000
Deferred taxes on income, related to depreciation	350,000	210,000
Total other liabilities	5,350,000	5,710,000

Shareholders' equity:
Capital stock:

Preferred stock, $1 cumulative, $20 par, preference on liquidation $100 per share (authorized: 100,000 shares; issued and outstanding: 50,000 shares)	1,000,000	1,000,000
Common stock, $1 par (authorized: 900,000 shares; issued and outstanding: year 5, 550,000 shares; year 4, 500,000 shares)	550,000	500,000
Capital in excess of par value of common stock	3,075,000	625,000
Retained earnings	7,250,000	7,965,000
Total shareholders' equity	11,875,000	10,090,000
Total liabilities and stockholders' equity	$23,125,000	$22,120,000

LOW CORPORATION
Statement of Income and Retained Earnings
For the Years Ended December 31, year 5 and year 4

	Year 5	Year 4
Income:		
Net sales	$48,400,000	$41,700,000
Royalties	70,000	25,000
Interest	30,000	
Total	48,500,000	41,725,000
Costs and expenses:		
Cost of sales	31,460,000	29,190,000
Selling, general and administrative	12,090,000	8,785,000
Interest on 5% sinking fund debentures	275,000	300,000
Provision for Federal income taxes	2,315,000	1,695,000
Total	46,140,000	39,970,000
Net income	2,360,000	1,755,000
Retained earnings, beginning of year	7,965,000	6,760,000
Total	10,325,000	8,515,000
Dividends paid:		
Preferred stock, $1.00 per share in cash	50,000	50,000
Common stock:		
Cash—$1.00 per share	525,000	500,000
Stock—(10%)—50,000 shares at market value of $50 per share	2,500,000	
Total	3,075,000	550,000
Retained earnings, end of year	$ 7,250,000	$ 7,965,000

Additional information:

1. The inventory at January 1, year 4 was $6,850,000.

2. The market prices of the common stock at December 31, year 5 and year 4 were $73.50 and $47.75, respectively.

3. The cash dividends for both preferred and common stock were declared and paid in June and December of each year. The stock dividend on common stock was declared and distributed in August, year 5.

4. Plant and equipment sales and retirements during year 5 and year 4 were $375,000 and $425,000, respectively. The related depreciation allowances were $215,000 in year 5 and $335,000 in year 4. At December 31, year 3 the plant and equipment asset balance was $21,470,000 and the related depreciation allowances were $11,650,000.

Required:

Prepare a schedule computing the following selected statistics for year 5 and year 4.

At December 31:
1. Current ratio.
2. Acid-test (quick) ratio.
3. Book value per common share.

Year ended December 31:
4. Gross margin rate.
5. Inventory turnover rate.
6. Times interest earned (before taxes).
7. Common stock price-earnings ratio (end of year value).
8. Gross capital expenditures.

4–11. Comparative financial position and operating statements are commonly used tools of analysis and interpretation.

Required:

a. Discuss the inherent limitations of single-year statements for purposes of analysis and interpretation. Include in your discussion the extent to which these limitations are overcome by the use of comparative statements.

b. Comparative balance sheets and comparative income statements that show a firm's financial history for each of the last 10 years may be misleading. Discuss the factors or conditions that might contribute to misinterpretations. Include a discussion of the additional information and supplementary data that might be included in or provided with the statements to prevent misinterpretations.

Chapter 5

5–1. Please refer to the financial statements of Campbell Soup in Appendix 4B and Chapter 23.

Required:

Compute the 1990 Cost of Goods Sold under the FIFO method. (Note: On July 30, 1989, the excess of FIFO inventory over LIFO inventory was 88 million.)

5–2. Please refer to the financial statements of Quaker Oats in Appendix 23.

Required:

I. Quaker Oats uses mostly the LIFO cost assumption in determining its cost of goods sold and beginning and ending inventory amounts for the majority of inventory items. Determine the gross profit of Quaker Oats if average cost had been used for all items of inventory. (See Note 1 and use a 84 percent tax rate.)
   (1) For 1991.
   (2) For 1890.
II. Compute the effect on net income of using LIFO rather than average cost and comment on the differences.
III. Give the journal entry needed to restate the financial statements from a LIFO to an average cost basis for the year 1991.

5–3. Although cash generally is regarded as the simplest of all assets to account for, certain complexities can arise for both domestic and multinational companies.

Required:

a. What are the normal components of cash?
b. Under what circumstances, if any, do valuation problems arise in connection with cash?

5–4. Part A. On July 1, year 1, Carme Company, a calendar-year company, sold special-order merchandise on credit and received in return an interest-bearing note receivable from the customer. Carme Company will receive interest at the prevailing rate for a note of this type. Both the principal and interest are due in one lump sum on June 30, year 2.

Required:

1. When should Carme Company report interest income from the note receivable? Discuss the rationale for your answer.
2. Assume that the note receivable was discounted without recourse at a bank on December 31, year 1. How would Carme Company determine the amount of the discount and what is the appropriate accounting for the discounting transaction?

Part B. On December 31, year 1, Carme Company had significant amounts of accounts receivable as a result of credit sales to its customers. Carme Company uses the allowance method based on credit sales to estimate bad debts. Based on past experience, 1 percent of credit sales normally will not be collected. This pattern is expected to continue.

Required:
1. Discuss the rationale for using the allowance method based on credit sales to estimate bad debts. Contrast this method with the allowance method based on the balance in the trade receivables accounts.
2. How should Carme Company report the allowance for bad debts account on its balance sheet at December 31, year 1? Also, describe the alternatives, if any, for presentation of bad debt expense in Carme Company's year 1 income statement.

(AICPA adapted)

5–5. **Please refer to problem 18–8.** Dean is aware that the use of certain accounting methods can distort reported operating results.

Required:
Discuss how ABEX's use of the FIFO method of accounting for its petrochemical inventories affected that division's operating margin during *each* of the following *two* periods.

Part A. Use the data in Tables 1 through 4.
    (i)   1985 through 1987
    (ii) 1987 through 1989
Part B. ABEX is considering adopting the LIFO method of accounting for its petrochemical inventories in either 1990 or 1991.

Required:
Recommend an adoption date for LIFO, and justify your choice.

(CFA adapted)

5–6. Steel Company, a wholesaler that has been in business for two years, purchases its inventories from various suppliers. During the two years, each purchase has been at a lower price than the previous purchase.

Steel uses the lower of FIFO cost or market method to value inventories. The original cost of the inventories is above replacement cost and below the net realizable value. The net realizable value less the normal profit margin is below the replacement cost.

Required:
a. In general, what criteria should be used to determine which costs should be included in inventory?
b. In general, why is the lower of cost or market rule used to report inventory?
c. At what amount should Steel's inventories be reported on the balance sheet? Explain the application of the lower of cost or market rule in this situation.

d. What would have been the effect on ending inventories and net income for the second year had Steel used the lower of average cost or market inventory method instead of the lower of FIFO cost or market inventory method? Why?

(AICPA)

5-7. Use the following data in answering questions I and II.

Zeta Corporation uses LIFO inventory accounting. The footnotes to the 1989 financial statements contain the following:

	1988	1989
Inventories		
Raw materials	$392,675	$369,725
Finished products	401,342	377,104
	$794,017	$746,829
Less adjustments to LIFO basis	(46,000)	(50,000)
	$748,017	$696,829

Zeta Corporation has a marginal tax rate of 35 percent.

I. Under FIFO, the 1989 retained earnings of Zeta would have been different by:
   a. $ (4,000)
   b. $ 4,000
   c. $ 17,500
   d. $ 32,500

II. If FIFO had been used for both years, the 1989 net income would have changed by:
   a. $(2,600)
   b. $ 1,400
   c. $ 2,600
   d. $ 4,000

III. The Hanks Company began operations on January 1, 1989, and on December 31, 1989, had the following investment portfolios of marketable equity securities:

	Short-term marketable securities	Long-term marketable securities
Aggregate cost	$200,000	$275,000
Aggregate market value	$150,000	$200,000
Net unrealized loss	$ 50,000	$ 75,000

All of the declines are judged to be temporary. The valuation allowance accounts at December 31, 1989, should reflect a charge against:

	Income	*Stockholders' Equity*
a.	$ –0–	$125,000
b.	$125,000	$ –0–
c.	$ 50,000	$ 75,000
d.	$ 75,000	$ 50,000

(CFA adapted)

5–8.   Cost for inventory purposes should be determined by the inventory cost flow method most clearly reflecting periodic income.

Required:
1. Describe the fundamental cost flow assumptions of the average cost, FIFO, and LIFO inventory cost flow methods.
2. Discuss the reasons for using LIFO in an inflationary economy.
3. Where there is evidence that the utility of goods, in their disposal in the ordinary course of business, will be less than cost, what is the proper accounting treatment and under what concept is that treatment justified?

(AICPA)

5–9.   The financial statements of Columbia Pictures Industries, Inc., included the following footnote:

"**Inventories.** The costs of feature films and television programs, including production advances to independent producers, interest on production loans and distribution advances to film licensors, are amortized on bases designed to write off costs in proportion to the expected flow of income.

"The cost of general release feature productions is divided between theatrical exhibition and television exhibition, based on the proportion of net revenues expected to be derived from each source. The portion of the cost of feature productions allocated to theatrical exhibition is amortized generally by the application of tables which write off approximately 62 percent in 26 weeks, 85 percent in 52 weeks, and 100 percent in 104 weeks after release. Costs of two theatrical productions first released on a reserved-seat basis are amortized in the proportion that rentals earned bear to the estimated final theatrical and television rentals.

"Because of the depressed market for the licensing of feature films to television and poor acceptance by the public of a number of theatrical films released late in the year, the company made a special provision in year 1 for additional amortization of recent releases and those not yet licensed for television to reduce such films to their currently estimated net realizable values."

Required:
a. What are the main determinants in the valuation of feature films, television programs, and general release feature productions by Columbia?
b. Do the bases of valuation appear reasonable?
c. What additional information on inventory valuation would an unsecured lender to Columbia want to obtain?

5–10. The Falcon Store purchases its merchandise, a standard item, at the current market price and resells the same product at a price 20 cents higher. The purchase price remains the same throughout the year. Data on number of units in inventory at the beginning of year, unit purchases, and unit sales are shown as follows:

> No. units in inventory—
> beginning of year ($1 cost) 1,000
> No. units purchased in year @ $1.50 .. 1,000
> No. units sold in year @ $1.70 1,000

Required:
a. Calculate the after-tax profit for the Falcon Store under the (1) FIFO and (2) LIFO methods of inventory valuation if the company has no expenses other than cost of goods sold but pays income taxes at the rate of 50 percent. Taxes are accrued currently and paid the following year.
   The beginning-of-year balance sheet for Falcon Store is as follows:

> *Inventory*   *Net worth*
> ($1,000 units @ $1) = $1,000 $1,000

b. If all sales and purchases are for cash, construct the balance sheets as of the end of the year using both methods of inventory valuation.
c. What is the significance of each of these methods of inventory valuation upon profit determination and financial position in a period of increasing prices?
d. What problem does the LIFO method pose in constructing interim financial statements?

(CFA)

Chapter 6

6–1. Please refer to the financial statements of Campbell Soup in Appendix 4B.

Required:
By means of T-account analysis explain the changes in Property, Plant, and Equipment accounts for 1991. Provide as much detail as the disclosure enables you to supply. (Hint: utilize information disclosed on Form 10-K schedules.)

6–2. Please refer to the financial statements of Quaker Oats in Appendix 23.

Required:
By means of a T-account analysis explain the changes in Property, Plant, and Equipment accounts for 1990 and 1991. Provide as much detail as the disclosure enables you to supply.

6–3. The balance sheet, which is intended to present fairly the financial position of a company, is frequently criticized for not reflecting many corporate liabilities. Similarly, the balance sheet is also faulted for not reflecting many corporate assets. Two examples are the excess of replacement value of plant and equipment over cost, and the LIFO inventory reserve.

Required:

List *five* other examples of *assets* that are not presently included on corporate balance sheets.

(CFA)

6–4. **Part A.** *SFAS 12* was issued to clarify accounting methods and procedures with respect to certain marketable securities. An important part of the Statement concerns the distinction between noncurrent and current classification of marketable securities.

Required:

(1) Why does a company maintain an investment portfolio of current and noncurrent securities?
(2) What factors should be considered in determining whether investments in marketable equity securities should be classified as current or noncurrent, and how do these factors affect the accounting treatment for unrealized losses?

Part B. Presented below are four *unrelated* situations involving marketable equity securities:

Situation I. A noncurrent portfolio with an aggregate market value in excess of cost includes one particular security whose market value has declined to less than one half of the original cost. The decline in value is considered to be other than temporary.

Situation II. The statement of financial position of a company does not classify assets and liabilities as current and noncurrent. The portfolio of marketable equity securities includes securities normally considered current that have a net cost in excess of market value of $2,000. The remainder of the portfolio has a net market value in excess of cost of $5,000.

Situation III. A marketable equity security, whose market value is currently less than cost, is classified as noncurrent but is to be reclassified as current.

Situation IV. A company's noncurrent portfolio of marketable equity securities consists of the common stock of one company. At the end of the prior year, the market value of the security was 50 percent of original cost, and this effect was properly reflected in a valuation allowance account. However, at the end of the current year, the market value of the security had appreciated to twice the original cost. The security is still considered noncurrent at year-end.

Required:

What is the effect upon classification, carrying value, and earnings for each of the above situations? Complete your response to each situation before proceeding to the next situation.

6-5. Among the principal topics related to the accounting for the property, plant, and equipment of a company are acquisition and retirement.

Required:

a. What expenditures should be capitalized when equipment is acquired for cash?

b. Assume that the market value of equipment acquired is not determinable by reference to a similar purchase for cash. Describe how the acquiring company should determine the capitalizable cost of equipment purchased by exchanging it for each of the following:

(1) Bonds having an established market price.

(2) Common stock not having an established market price.

(3) Similar equipment having a determinable market value.

c. Describe the factors that determine whether expenditures relating to property, plant, and equipment already in use should be capitalized.

d. Describe how to account for the gain or loss on the sale of property, plant, and equipment for cash.

6-6. Jay Manufacturing, Inc., began operations five years ago producing probos, a new type of instrument it hoped to sell to doctors, dentists, and hospitals. The demand for probos far exceeded initial expectations, and the company was unable to produce enough probos to meet demand.

The company was manufacturing its product on equipment that it built at the start of its operations. To meet demand, more efficient equipment was needed. The company decided to design and build the equipment since that currently available on the market was unsuitable for producing probos.

In year 8, a section of the plant was devoted to development of the new equipment and a special staff of personnel was hired. Within six months, a machine was developed at a cost of $170,000 which successfully increased production and reduced labor costs substantially. Sparked by the success of the new machine, the company built three more machines of the same type at a cost of $80,000 each.

Required:

a. In addition to satisfying a need that outsiders cannot meet within the desired time, why might a firm construct fixed assets for its own use?

b. In general, what costs should be capitalized for a self-constructed fixed asset?

c. Discuss the propriety of including in the capitalized cost of self-constructed assets:

(1) The increase in overhead caused by the self-construction of fixed assets.

(2) A proportionate share of overhead on the same basis as that applied to goods manufactured for sale.

d. Discuss the proper accounting treatment of the $90,000 ($170,000 – $80,000) by which the cost of the first machine exceeded the cost of the subsequent machines.

(AICPA)

6–7.   The following is a news item:

"The greatest nonevent in the annals of the sea occurred last Thursday in Japan, when the world's biggest oil tanker, the 484,377-ton Nissei Maru, was completed—and went straight into lay-up. Between the time the keel of the monster vessel was laid and its delivery, its hypothetical market value plunged 90 percent. Moreover, it will cost a small fortune to maintain it in lay-up. Then there is the delicate problem of accepting a ship without putting it through its sea trials. What will be the validity of the shipyard's guarantees if it is put through its paces for the first time two or three years hence?"

Required:
a.   What determines the value of assets?
b.   Do present-day accounting principles give prompt recognition to changes in economic values? Discuss.

6–8.   On June 30, year 1, your client, The Vandiver Corporation, was granted two patents covering plastic cartons that it has been producing and marketing profitably for the past three years. One patent covers the manufacturing process, and the other covers the related products.

Vandiver executives tell you that these patents represent the most significant breakthrough in the industry in the past 30 years. The products have been marketed under the registered trademarks Safetainer, Duratainer, and Sealrite. Licenses under the patents have already been granted by your client to other manufacturers in the United States and abroad and are producing substantial royalties.

On July 1, Vandiver commenced patent infringement actions against several companies whose names you recognize as those of substantial and prominent competitors. Vandiver's management is optimistic that these suits will result in a permanent injunction against the manufacture and sale of the infringing products and collection of damages for loss of profits caused by the alleged infringement.

The financial vice president has suggested that the patents be recorded at the discounted value of expected net royalty receipts.

Required:
a.   What is an intangible asset? Explain.
b.   (1)   What is the meaning of "discounted value of expected net receipts"? Explain.
      (2)   How would such a value be calculated for net royalty receipts?
c.   What basis of valuation for Vandiver's patents would be generally accepted in accounting? Give supporting reasons for this basis.
d.   (1)   Assuming no practical problems of implementation and ignoring generally accepted accounting principles, what is the preferable basis of evaluation for patents? Explain.

(2) What would be the preferable theoretical basis of amortization? Explain.

e. What recognition, if any, should be made of the infringement litigation in the financial statements for the year ending September 30, year 1? Discuss.

(AICPA)

6–9. Which of the following can be classified as assets on a balance sheet?

a. Depreciation.
b. President's salary.
c. Cash.
d. Deferred income taxes.
e. Installment receivable (to be collected in three years).
f. Capital withdrawal.
g. Inventories.
h. Prepaid expenses.
i. Deferred charges.
j. Work in process.
k. Allowance for depreciation.
l. Allowance for bad debt.
m. Loan to officers.
n. Loan from officers.
o. A fully trained sales force.
p. Common stock of a subsidiary.
q. Trade name purchased.
r. Company developed goodwill.
s. Valuable franchise agreements obtained at no cost.

Chapter 7

7–1. Please refer to the financial statements of Campbell Soup in Appendix 4B.

I. Campbell has zero coupon notes payable outstanding. [170]
  (a) What is the amount that will be due to noteholders on the maturity date of these notes?
  (b) The liability for these notes is lower than its maturity value. How will this liability be shown in future years? Without amounts show the yearly journal entry that Campbell will make to record the liability for accrued interest.

II. (a) The footnote on leases gives future minimum lease payments under capital leases as $28.0 million [173] and the present value of such payments as $21.5 million. Which amount will actually be paid over future years?
  (b) Where in the financial statements is the payment obligation concerning operating leases of $71.9 [143] million reflected?

7–2. Please refer to the financial statements of Quaker Oats. (See Appendix 23.)

Required:
I. How much long-term debt was paid during 1991?
II. In fiscal 1990 total debt increased by $217 million. What was the major reason for this increase in debt?

7–3. On January 1, 1988, Von Company entered into two noncancellable leases for new machines to be used in its manufacturing operations. The first lease does not contain a bargain purchase option; the lease term is equal to 80 percent of the estimated economic life of the machine. The second lease contains a bargain purchase option; the lease term is equal to 50 percent of the estimated economic life of the machine.

Required:
a. What is the theoretical basis for requiring lessees to capitalize certain long-term leases? Do not discuss the specific criteria for classifying a lease as a capital lease.
b. How should a lessee account for a capital lease at its inception?
c. How should a lessee record each minimum lease payment for a capital lease?
d. How should Von classify each of the two leases? Why?

(AICPA)

7–4. On December 29, year 7, Mother Prewitt's Handmade Cookies Corporation acquired a numerically controlled chocolate chip milling machine. Due to differences in tax and financial accounting, depreciation for tax purposes was $150,000 more than indicated in the financial statements, adding $60,000 to deferred taxes. At the same time, Mother Prewitt's sold $200,000 worth of cookies on an installment contract, and recognized the resulting $100,000 profit immediately. For tax purposes, however, $80,000 of the profit will be recognized in the next accounting year, so that an additional $32,000 was added to deferred taxes.

Required:
The deferred tax items described above do not have the same economic impact. Briefly explain how they are different.

(CFA)

7–5. On January 1, year 1, Burton Company leased equipment from Nelson Company at an annual lease rental of $10,000. The lease term was five years, and the lessor's interest rate implicit in the lease was 8 percent. The lessee's incremental borrowing rate was 8¼ percent.

The useful life of the equipment was five years, and it is estimated that its residual value will be equal to its removal cost.

The annuity tables indicate that the present value of annual rental of $1 (at 8 percent rate) is $3.993. The fair value of the leased equipment equals the present value of rentals.

Required:
Assuming that the lease is capitalized:

a. Show entries required in Burton Company's books for year 1.
b. Show the effect on the income statement for the year ended December 31, year 1, and on the balance sheet as at December 31, year 1.
c. Construct a table to show payments of interest and of principal to be made every year for the five-year term of the lease.
d. Construct a table to show expenses to be charged to the income statement for five-year term of the lease (show a column for amortization, a column for interest and a third column for total) if the equipment is purchased.

7–6.   On January 1, Borman Company, a lessee, entered into three noncancelable leases for brand new equipment, Lease J. Lease K, and Lease L. None of the three leases transfers ownership of the equipment to Borman at the end of the lease term. For each of the three leases, the present value at the beginning of the lease term of the minimum lease payments, excluding that portion of the payments representing executory costs such as insurance, maintenance, and taxes to be paid by the lessor, including any profit thereon, is 75% of the excess of the fair value of the equipment to the lessor at the inception of the lease over any related investment tax credit retained by the lessor and expected to be realized by the lessor.

The following information is peculiar to each lease:

- Lease J does not contain a bargain purchase option; the lease term is equal to 80 percent of the estimated economic life of the equipment.
- Lease K contains a bargain purchase option; the lease term is equal to 50 percent of the estimated economic life of the equipment.
- Lease L does not contain a bargain purchase option; the lease term is equal to 50 percent of the estimated economic life of the equipment.

Required:
a. How should Borman Company classify each of the three leases above, and why? Discuss the rationale for your answer.
b. What amount, if any, should Borman record as a liability at the inception of the lease for each of the three leases above?
c. Assuming that the minimum lease payments are made on a straight-line basis, how should Borman record each minimum lease payment for each of the three leases above?

(AICPA)

7–7.   **Part A.** Capital leases and operating leases are the two classifications of leases described in FASB pronouncements, from the standpoint of the *lessee*.

Required:
1. Describe how a capital lease would be accounted for by the lessee both at the inception of the lease and during the first year of the lease, assuming the lease transfers ownership of the property to the lessee by the end of the lease.

2. Describe how an operating lease would be accounted for by the lessee both at the inception of the lease and during the first year of the lease, assuming equal monthly payments are made by the lessee at the beginning of each month of the lease. Describe the change in accounting, if any, when rental payments are not made on a straight-line basis.

Do *not* discuss the criteria for distinguishing between capital leases and operating leases.

Part B. Sales-type leases and direct financing leases are two of the classifications of leases described in FASB pronouncements, from the standpoint of the *lessor.*

Required:
Compare and contrast a sales-type lease with a direct financing lease as follows:

1. Gross investment in the lease.
2. Amortization of unearned interest income.
3. Manufacturer's or dealer's profit.

Do *not* discuss the criteria for distinguishing between the leases described above and operating leases.

7–8.   Financial publications frequently carry articles similar to the one from *Forbes,* from which excerpts are quoted below:

"The Supersolvent—No longer is it a mark of a fuddy-duddy to be free of debt. There are lots of advantages to it. One is that you always have plenty of collateral to borrow against if you do get into a jam. Another is that if a business investment goes bad, you don't have to pay interest on your mistake.

"Debt-free, you don't have to worry about what happens if the prime rate goes to 12 percent again. You might even welcome it. You could lend out your own surplus cash at those rates."

The article then went on to list 92 companies that reported on their balance sheets no more than 5 percent of total capitalization in noncurrent debt.

Required:
Give examples and explain why so-called debt-free companies in the sense used by this article may actually have long-term debt or other long-term liabilities.
(CFA)

7–9.   One way for a corporation to accomplish long-term financing is through the issuance of long-term debt instruments in the form of bonds.

Required:
a. Describe how to account for the proceeds from bonds issued with detachable stock purchase warrants.
b. Contrast a serial bond with a term (straight) bond.

    c. For a five-year term bond issued at a premium, why would the amortization in the first year of the life of the bond differ using the interest method of amortization instead of the straight-line method? Include in your discussion whether the amount of amortization in the first year of the life of the bond would be higher or lower using the interest method instead of the straight-line method.

    d. When a bond issue is sold between interest dates at a discount, what journal entry is made and how is the subsequent amortization of bond discount affected? Include in your discussion an explanation of how the amounts of each debit and credit are determined.

    e. Describe how to account for and classify the gain or loss from the reacquisition of a long-term bond prior to its maturity.

7–10. On November 1, year 5, Abbott Company sold its 5-year, $1,000 face value, 11 percent term bonds dated October 1, year 5, at a discount resulting in an effective annual interest rate (yield) of 12 percent. Interest is payable semiannually, and the first interest payment date is April 1, year 6. Abbott uses an acceptable method of amortizing bond discount. Bond issue costs were incurred in preparing and selling the bond issue.

    On December 1, year 5, Abbott sold its 6-year, $1,000 face value, 9 percent nonconvertible bonds with detachable stock warrants for an amount exceeding the sum of the face value of the bonds and the fair value of the warrants.

Required:

    a. What facts above determined that the 11 percent term bonds were sold at a discount? Why?

    b. How would all the items related to the 11 percent term bonds, except cash, be presented in a balance sheet prepared immediately after the term bond issue was sold, and in a balance sheet prepared at December 31, year 5?

    c. (1) Over what period of time would the bond discount be amortized?

        (2) Compare the straight-line and the interest methods of amortization.

        (3) Which of the two methods is preferable? Why?

    d. How should Abbott account for the proceeds from the sale of the 9 percent nonconvertible bonds with detachable stock purchase warrants? Why?

                                                      (AICPA)

7–11. Loss contingencies may exist for companies.

Required:

1. What conditions should be met for an estimated loss from a loss contingency to be accrued by a charge to income?

2. When is disclosure required, and what disclosure should be made for an estimated loss from a loss contingency that need not be accrued by a charge to income?

Chapter 8

    8–1. Please refer to the financial statements of Campbell Soup in Appendix 4B.

Required:

I.   What caused the $101.6 million increase in shareowners' equity during 1991 and the $86.5 million decrease in 1990?

II. Compute the July 28, 1991, book value of the common stock.

8-2.   Please refer to the financial statements of Quaker Oats (see Appendix 23).

Required:

I.   What caused the $116.5 million decrease in stockholders' equity during 1991 and the $119.6 million decrease during 1990?

II. Compute the June 30, 1991 book value of the common stock and the preferred stock.

8-3.   Mother Prewitt's Handmade Cookie Corporation (MPH), relying on forecasts of increasing cookie consumption by aging baby boomers, constructed a highly sophisticated manufacturing facility in the early 1980s. Unfortunately for MPH, recent medical findings have encouraged a swing in consumer preferences toward high-fiber bran products and resulted in lower cookie consumption. Following several years of losses, the company is being offered for sale. You have been instructed to consider the purchase of MPH.

The current balance sheet of the firm is as follows:

Assets

Current assets	$14,000,000
Plant & equipment (net)	14,000,000
Total assets	$28,000,000

Stockholders' Equity

Preferred stock–authorized 200,000 shares, issued 100,000, par value $150, 5% cumulative, nonparticipating, liquidation value of $160, callable at $165	$15,000,000
Common stock-authorized 300,000 shares, issued 200,000 shares, par value $75	15,000,000
Capital contributed in excess of par value	100,000
Retained earnings (deficit)	(2,100,000)
Total stockholders' equity	$28,000,000

Note: Preferred dividends are two years in arrears.

Required:

A.   Calculate the book value per share of MPH common stock. Show all calculations.

B. Briefly describe the adjustments you might make to the book value in order to arrive at an estimate of the fair market value of MPH common stock.

(CFA)

8-4.   **(1)** It has been said that the use of the LIFO inventory method during an extended period of rising prices and the expensing of all human resource costs are among the accepted accounting practices which help create "secret reserves."

Required:
a. What is a "secret reserve"? How can "secret reserves" be created or enlarged?
b. What is the basis for saying that the two specific practices cited above tend to create "secret reserves"?
c. Is it possible to create a "secret reserve" in connection with accounting for a liability? If so, explain or give an example.
d. What are the objections to the creation of "secret reserves"?

(2) It has also been said that "watered stock" is the opposite of a "secret reserve."

Required:
a. What is "watered stock"?
b. Describe the general circumstances in which "watered stock" can arise.
c. What steps can be taken to eliminate "water" from a capital structure?

(AICPA)

8-5.   The ownership interest in a corporation is customarily reported in the balance sheet as stockholders' equity.

Required:
a. List the principal transactions or items that reduce the amount of retained earnings. (Do not include appropriations of retained earnings.)
b. In the stockholders' equity section of the balance sheet, a distinction is made between contributed capital and earned capital. Why is this distinction made? Discuss.
c. There is frequently a difference between the purchase price and sale price of treasury stock, but accounting authorities agree that the purchase or sale of its own stock by a corporation cannot result in a profit or loss to the corporation. Why isn't the difference recognized as a profit or loss to the corporation? Discuss.

8-6.   **Part A.** Capital stock is an important area of a corporation's equity section. Generally the term *capital stock* embraces common and preferred stock issued by a corporation.

Required:
(1) What are the basic rights inherent in ownership of common stock, and how are they exercised?
(2) What is preferred stock? Discuss the various preferences afforded preferred stock.

Part B. In dealing with the various equity securities of a corporate entity, it is important to understand certain terminology related thereto.

Required:
Define the following terms:
(1) Treasury stock.
(2) Legal capital.
(3) Stock right.
(4) Stock warrant.

8–7.   I. Fox Corporation was organized on January 1, year 1, with the following capital structure:

> 10% cumulative preferred stock, par and
>   liquidation value $100; authorized,
>   issued, and outstanding 1,000 shares $100,000
> Common stock, par value $5; authorized
>   20,000 shares; issued and outstanding
>   10,000 shares   50,000

Fox's net income for the year ended December 31, year 1, was $450,000, but no dividends were declared. How much was Fox's book value per common share at December 31, year 1?

II. Grey, Inc., was organized on January 2, year 4, with the following capital structure:

> 10% cumulative preferred stock, par value
> $100 and liquidation value $105;
>   authorized, issued and outstanding 1,000
>   shares $100,000
> Common stock, par value $25; authorized
>   100,000 shares; issued and outstanding
>   10,000 shares $250,000

Grey's net income for the year ended December 31, year 4, was $450,000, but no dividends were declared.

Required:
a. How much was Grey's book value per preferred share at December 31, year 4?

   b. How much was Grey's book value per common share at December 31, year 4?

8–8. On a given day, the stock of Superior Oil Corporation sold on the N.Y. Stock Exchange for $1,492, while Getty Oil Company was selling for $64.

Required:
a. How can you account for the fact that Superior Oil was selling for a much greater price? What can you conclude about the relative profitability of the two companies?
b. On the previous day, Superior Oil stock had sold for $1,471, while Getty Oil sold for $62. Which stock had the greater price rise?
c. If you had purchased Getty Oil at $62 and sold it the next day for $64, what effect would this have on the accounting records of the company?

Chapter 9

9–1. Please refer to the financial statements of Campbell Soup in Appendix 4B.

  I. As of July 28, 1991, Campbell owned 33 percent of Arnott's Limited. Where are the amounts representing this investment shown?
  II. Item 169A contains disclosure of the market value of the company's investment in Arnotts' Limited. Is this market value reflected in Campbell's financial statements beyond the disclosure referred to?
  III. In July 1991, Campbell acquired the remaining shares of Campbell Canada. That is in addition to one other acquisition during 1991. What does the relationship of the purchase price paid for these acquisitions to the fair market value of net assets acquired tell us?
  IV. Please give a composite journal entry recording the total 1991 acquisitions.
  V. Explain what you consider the likely causes of the changes in the cumulative translation adjustment accounts for (1) Europe and (2) Australia.

9–2. Please refer to the financial statements of Quaker Oats in Appendix 23.

  I. The financial statements of fiscal years 1990 and earlier reflected the company's decision to discontinue (divest) the operations of Fisher-Price. Where, in the financial statements, are the assets and liabilities of Fisher-Price reflected in 1990?
  II. The company reports no acquisitions in 1990 and 1991. However, goodwill amortization, which the company discloses to be on a straight-line basis, increased in both years. How can this be reconciled?
  III. *a.* The company had forward contracts to purchase and sell currencies in order to hedge balance sheet exposure. Where would gains or losses on these contracts be reflected?
     b. The company reports on hyper-inflationary conditions in Brazil. Where, on the financial statements, would gains and losses on the translation of Brazilian subsidiaries be reflected?

9–3. The diagram below portrays Company X (the parent or investor company), its two subsidiaries C1 and C2, and its "50 percent or less owned" affiliate C3.

Each of the companies has only one type of stock outstanding, and there are no other significant stockholders in either Corporation C2 or Corporation C3. All four companies are engaged in commercial and industrial activities.

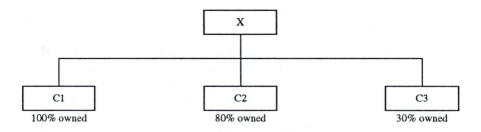

Required:

The following questions require short answers.

1. Will each of the above companies maintain separate accounting records?
2. What type of financial statements will each company present for public reporting purposes?
3. Assuming that the analyst has the ability to enforce his requests, what type of financial statements and other information of these companies, separate or consolidating, can he request?
4. What will Company X show in its assets for C1 Corporation?
5. If C1 Corporation were legally dissolved into Company X, how would Company X's balance sheet be changed?
6. If C1 Corporation were legally dissolved into Company X, how would the consolidated balance sheet be changed?
7. In the consolidated balance sheet, how is the 20 percent of C2 Corporation not owned by Company X shown?
8. What transaction would be required before C3 Corporation could be included line by line in the consolidated statements?
9. If "combined" statements were presented for C1 Corporation and C2 Corporation, would there be any elimination entries?
10. Suppose that Company X sold its entire investment in C2 Corporation to C1 Corporation (C2 Corporation would be 80 percent owned by C1 Corporation). How would the consolidated balance sheet be changed?
11. If C1 Corporation sold additional common stock to Company X for cash, how would the consolidated balance sheet be changed?

9–4. The following data are derived from the annual report of San Francisco Company, a manufacturer of cardboard boxes:

	1986	1987	1988
Sales	$25,000	$30,000	$35,000
Net income	2,000	2,200	2,500
Dividends paid	1,000	1,200	1,500
Book value per share (year-end)	$ 11.00	$ 12.00	$ 13.00

San Francisco had 1,000 common shares outstanding during the entire period. There is no public market for San Francisco shares.

Potter Company, a manufacturer of glassware, made the following acquisitions of San Francisco common shares:

January 1, 1986 ...... 10 shares at $10 per share

January 1, 1987 ...... 290 shares at $11 per share, increasing ownership to 300 shares

January 1, 1988 ...... 700 shares at $15 per share, resulting in 100% ownership of San Francisco

In answering the following questions, ignore income tax effects and the effect of lost income on funds used to make these investments.

Required:
A. Calculate the effect of these investments on Potter's reported sales, net income, and cash flow for *each* of the years 1986 and 1987.
B. Calculate the carrying value of Potter's investment in San Francisco as of December 31, 1986 and December 31, 1987.
C. Briefly discuss how Potter would account for its investment in San Francisco during 1988. State the additional information needed to calculate the impact of the acquisition on Potter's financial statements for 1988.

(CFA)

9–5.   Spellman Company will acquire 90 percent of Moore Company in a business combination. The total consideration has been agreed upon. The nature of Spellman's payment has not been fully agreed upon. Therefore, it is possible that this business combination might be accounted for as either a purchase or a pooling of interests. It is expected that at the date the business combination is to be consummated, the fair value will exceed the book value of Moore's assets minus liabilities. Spellman desires to prepare consolidated financial statements which will include the financial statements of Moore.

Required:
a. (1) Would the method of accounting for the business combination (purchase versus pooling of interests) affect whether or not goodwill is reported?
   (2) If goodwill is reported, explain how the amount of goodwill is determined.

   (3) Would the method of accounting for the business combination (purchase versus pooling of interests) affect whether or not minority
interest is reported? If the amount reported differs, explain why.
b. (1) From a theoretical standpoint, why should consolidated financial
statements be prepared?
   (2) From a theoretical standpoint, what is the usual first necessary condition to be met before consolidated financial statements can be
prepared?
   (3) From a theoretical standpoint, does the method of accounting for the
business combination (purchase versus pooling of interests) affect
the decision to prepare consolidated financial statements? Why?

9–6. You have been asked by your supervisor to analyze a potential purchase
of the Drew Company by your firm, Pierson, Inc. You are given the following
information:

($ Millions)

	Pierson, Inc. historical cost	Drew Company Historical cost	Drew Company Fair value	Pro forma combined (pooling method)
Current assets	$ 70	$ 60	$ 65	$130
Land	60	10	10	70
Building	80	40	50	120
Equipment	90	20	40	110
Total assets	$300	$130	$165	$430
Current liabilities	$120	$ 20	$ 20	$140
Shareholders' equity	180	110		290
Total liability/equity	$300	$130		$430

Required:
A. Prepare a pro forma combined balance sheet under the purchase method
of accounting, assuming Pierson pays $180 million in cash for Drew, to be
obtained by issuing long-term debt.
B. Discuss how the differences between the pooling and purchase methods of
accounting for acquisitions would affect the future reported earnings of
the Pierson/Drew combination.

(CFA)

9–7. Burry Corporation acquired 80 percent of The Bowman Company for
$40 million on January 1, 1986. At the time of the acquisition, Bowman had
total net assets with a fair value of $25 million.
   For the years ended December 31, 1986 and December 31, 1987, Bowman
reported earnings and paid dividends as shown in the table below:

	Net income (loss)	Dividends paid
1986	$2,000,000	$1,000,000
1987	$ (600,000)	$ 800,000

Assume that the excess of the acquisition price over net assets at fair value is amortized over 40 years.

Table A

BURRY CORPORATION
(dollar amounts in thousands)

	Cost Method		Equity Method	
	Investment	Income	Investment	Income
Cost of Bowman aquisition	$40,000		$40,000	
Dividends for 1986		$800 (1)		
Earnings pickup for 1986		800		*
Dividends for 1987		640 (2)		
Earnings (loss) pickup 1987		640		*
Investment as of December 31, 1987	40,000		*	

(1) 80 percent of 1,000.
(2) 80 percent of 800.

Required:
A. Table A presents the accounting treatment for Burry's investment in Bowman under the cost method. Following the format in Table A, calculate the value of Burry's investment in Bowman as of December 31, 1987 under the *equity method,* including the *earnings pickup* for the years 1986 and 1987. Show all calculations.
B. Based on your answer in Part A, discuss the advantages of the equity method over the cost method.

(CFA)

9–8. Your firm is considering investing in the equity securities of companies in several different countries. After a preliminary review of financial statements, you realize there is a range of international accounting practices that can materially affect net income and other financial data relevant for equity valuation purposes.

Required:
A. Briefly discuss *two* plausible approaches to comparing companies from different countries that use different accounting principles.
B. Briefly discuss how international variations in *each* of the following three accounting principles affect reported net income:
   • Revaluation of fixed assets.

- Treatment of acquired goodwill.
- Discretionary reserves.

9–9.   Axel Company acquired 100 percent of the stock of Wheal Company on December 31, year 4. The following information pertains to Wheal Company on that date:

	Book value	Fair value
Cash	$ 40,000	$ 40,000
Accounts receivable	60,000	55,000
Inventory	50,000	75,000
Property, plant, and equipment (net)	100,000	200,000
Secret formula		30,000
	$250,000	$400,000
Accounts payable	30,000	30,000
Accrued employee pensions	20,000	22,000
Long-term debt	40,000	38,000
Capital stock	100,000	—
Other contributed capital	25,000	—
Retained earnings	35,000	—
	$250,000	$ 90,000

Axel Company issued $110,000 par value (market value on December 31, year 4—$350,000) of its own stock to the stockholders of Wheal to consummate the transaction, and Wheal became a wholly owned, consolidated subsidiary of Axel Company.

Required:
a.   Entries to record the acquisition of Wheal Company stock.
b.   Entries to eliminate in working papers the investment in Wheal Company stock for a consolidated balance sheet at December 31, year 4.
c.   A calculation of consolidated retained earnings at December 31, year 4— Axel's retained earnings at that date are $150,000—if:
  (1)   Axel uses the pooling of interests method for the business combination.
  (2)   Axel uses the purchase method for acquisition of Wheal.

9–10.   The *Financial Accounting Standards Board's Statement No. 52 (FASB 52)* deals with foreign currency translation. It is intended to apply to foreign currency transactions and financial statements of foreign branches, subsidiaries, partnerships, and joint ventures which are consolidated, combined, or reported under the equity method in financial statements prepared in accordance with generally accepted accounting principles.

Required:
A. Describe the following key concepts of *FASB 52:*
   (1) Functional currency.
   (2) Translation.
   (3) Remeasurement.
B. Describe the effect of *FASB 52* on a multinational company located in a high inflationary country.

9–11. An accounting controversy concerns the widespread use of pooling in mergers. Opponents of the use of pooling believe that the surviving company often uses pooling (rather than purchase) to hide the "true" effects of the merger.

Required:
   What may be "hidden" and how is the analysis of a company's securities affected by pooling practices?

(CFA)

9–12. On December 31, 1988, U.S. Dental Supplies (USDS) created a wholly owned foreign subsidiary, Funimuni, Inc. (FI), located in the country of Lumbaria. The balance sheet of FI as of December 31, 1988, stated in local currency (the pont), was as follows:

FUNIMUNI, INC.
Balance Sheet
December 31, 1988

	Ponts (millions)
Cash	180
Fixed assets	420
Total assets	600
Capital stock	600

FI initially had adopted the U.S. dollar as its functional currency and had translated its 1989 balance sheet and income statement in accordance with *FASB Statement No. 52* (shown in Exhibits 1 and 2). USDS subsequently has instructed FI to change its functional currency to the pont.
   Assume the following exchange rates (Ponts/U.S. Dollars):

- January 1, 1989   3.0
- 1989 average   3.5
- December 31, 1989   4.0

Required:

A. Prepare a pro forma balance sheet as of December 31, 1989, *and* a 1989 income statement for FI, both in U.S. dollars, using the pont as the functional currency for FI.

B. Describe the impact of the change in FI's functional currency to the pont on FI's:
   (i) U.S. dollar balance sheet as of December 31, 1990.
   (ii) U.S. dollar 1990 income statement.
   (iii) U.S. dollar financial ratios for 1990.

Exhibit 1

FUNIMUNI, INC.
Balance Sheet
December 31, 1989

	Ponts (millions)	Exchange rate (ponts/U.S.$)	U.S.$ (millions)
Cash	$ 82	4.0	$ 20.5
Accounts receivable	700	4.0	175.0
Inventory	455	3.5	130.0
Fixed assets (net)	360	3.0	120.0
Total assets	$1,597		$445.5
Accounts payable	$ 532	4.0	$133.0
Capital stock	600	3.0	200.0
Retained earnings	465		112.5
Total liabilities and shareholders' equity	$1,597		$445.5

Exhibit 2

FUNIMUNI, INC.
Income Statement
Year Ended December 31, 1989

	Ponts (millions)	Exchange rate (ponts/U.S.$)	U.S.$ (millions)
Sales	$3,500	3.5	$1,000.0
Cost of sales	(2,345)	3.5	(670.0)
Depreciation expense	(60)	3.0	(20.0)
Selling expense	(630)	3.5	(180.0)
Translation gain (loss)	—		(17.5)
Net income	$ 465		$ 112.5
			(CFA)

9–13. Bethel Company uses the U.S. dollar as its functional currency worldwide. Star Company uses the local currency for each country in which it operates as its functional currency.

Required:
Explain how the choice of the functional currency affects *each* of the following:

- Reported sales.
- Computation of translation gains and losses.
- Reporting of translation gains and losses.

(CFA)

9–14. The trial balance of Swisco Corporation, a Swiss corporation at December 31, year 8, is shown below (in Swiss francs).

	Debit	*Credit*
Cash	50,000	
Accounts receivable	100,000	
Property, plant, and equipment, net	800,000	
Depreciation expense	100,000	
Other expenses (including taxes)	200,000	
Inventory, January 1, year 8	150,000	
Sales		2,000,000
Allowance for doubtful accounts		10,000
Accounts payable		80,000
Notes payable		20,000
Capital stock		100,000
Retained earnings, January 1, year 8		190,000
Purchases	1,000,000	
	2,400,000	2,400,000

Additional information:
1. Swisco uses the periodical inventory system as well as the FIFO method for measuring inventory and cost of goods sold. On December 31, year 8, inventory on hand was SFr120,000. It is carried at cost.
2. The capital stock was issued six years ago when the company was established, at which time the exchange rate was SFr1 = 30 cents. Plant and equipment were purchased five years ago when the exchange rate was SFr1 = 35 cents; the note payable was made out to a local bank at the same time.
3. Revenue and expense items were realized or incurred uniformly throughout year 8. However, inventory on hand on December 31, year 8, was purchased throughout the second half of year 8.
4. The retained earnings balance in the December 31, year 7, balance sheets (in U.S. dollars) of Swisco Corporation was $61,000, and the inventory balance was $47,000.
5. The spot rates for SFr in year 8 were as follows:

January 1, year 8	32 cents
Average for year 8	37
Average for second half of year 8	36
December 31, year 8	38

6. Management determined that the functional currency of Swisco is the Swiss franc.

Required:
a. Prepare a trial balance in dollars for Swisco Corporation at December 31, year 8.
b. Prepare the income statement for the year ending December 31, year 8, and the balance sheet at that date (in dollars) for Swisco Corporation.
c. Assuming that Unisco Corporation, a U.S. firm, purchased a 75 percent ownership interest in Swisco Corporation at book value on January 1, year 8, prepare the entry that Unisco would make at December 31, year 8, to record its equity in Swisco's year 8 earnings (Unisco uses the complete equity method to account for its investments in Swisco).

Chapter 10

10–1.   Please refer to the financial statements of Quaker Oats in Appendix 23.

Required:
I. For analytical measures of plant age derive the following:
  (1) The average total life span of plant and equipment.
  (2) The average age of plant and equipment.
  (3) The average remaining life of plant and equipment.
II. Discuss the importance of such ratios.

10–2.
I. In preparing its 1989 adjusting entries, the Singapore Co. neglected to adjust rental fees received in advance for the amount of rental fees earned during 1989. What is the effect of this error?
  a. Net income is understated, retained earnings are understated, and liabilities are overstated.
  b. Net income is overstated, retained earnings are overstated, and liabilities are unaffected.
  c. Net income, retained earnings, and liabilities all are understated.
  d. None of the above.
II. The Sutton Construction Company entered into a contract in early 1988 to build a tunnel for a city at a cost of $11 million. The company estimated that the total cost of the project would be $10 million and would take three years to complete. Actual costs incurred (on budget) and billings to the city were as follows:

	Costs incurred	Billings to city
1988	$2,500,000	$2,000,000
1989	$4,000,000	$3,500,000
1990	$3,500,000	$5,500,000

Using the percentage-of-completion method for revenue recognition, what would Sutton Construction Company have reported for revenues and profits for 1989?

	Revenues	*Profits*
a.	$4,000,000	$300,000
b.	$4,400,000	$400,000
c.	$3,850,000	$350,000
d.	$3,500,000	$500,000

III. Using the percentage-of completion method in accounting for long-term projects, a firm can increase reported earnings by:
 a. Accelerating recognition of project expenditures.
 b. Delaying recognition of project expenditures.
 c. Switching to completed-contract accounting.
 d. Overestimating the total cost of the project.
IV. Revenue may be recognized at the time of:
 a. Production.
 b. Sale.
 c. Collection.
 d. All of the above.
 V. In October, a company shipped a new product to retailers. Which *one* of the following conditions would block the immediate recognition of revenue?
 a. The terms of the sale require the company to provide extensive promotional material to the retailers before December 1.
 b. The retailers are not obligated to pay the purchase price until February, after their Christmas sales have been collected.
 c. On the basis of past performance, reliable estimates are that 20 percent of the product will be returned.
 d. The company is unable to enforce agreements concerning discounting of the retail sales of the product.

(CFA)

10–3.
 I. In accounting for long-term contracts, how does the percentage-of-completion method of revenue recognition differ from the completed contract method?
 I. The present value of income tax payments is minimized.
 II. Revenue during each period of the contract reflects more closely the results of construction activity during the period.
 III. The current status of uncompleted contracts will be reported more accurately.
 IV. The percentage-of-completion method relies less on estimates as to the degree of completion and the extent of future costs to be incurred.
 a. I and II

      b. I and III
      c. II and III
      d. II and IV

II. The James Construction Company entered into a contract in early 1985 to build a tunnel for a city at a cost of $11,000,000. The company estimated that the total cost of the project would be $10,000,000 and would take three years to complete. Actual costs incurred (which came in on budget) and billings to the city were as follows:

	Cost incurred	*Billings to city*
1985	$2,500,000	$2,000,000
1986	$4,000,000	$3,500,000
1987	$3,500,000	$5,500,000

Using the percentage-of-completion method for revenue recognition, what would James have reported for revenues and profits for 1986?

	Revenues	*Profits*
a.	$3,850,000	$350,000
b.	$4,000,000	$363,636
c.	$4,400,000	$400,000
d.	None of the above	

III. Lot Corporation, which began business on January 1, year 7, appropriately uses the installment sales method of accounting. The following data are available for December 31, year 7 and year 8.

	Year 7	*Year 8*
Balance of deferred gross profit on sales account:		
year 7	$300,000	$120,000
year 8	—	$440,000
Gross profit on sales	30%	40%

The installment accounts receivable balance at December 31, year 8 is
    a. $1,000,000
    b. $1,100,000
    c. $1,400,000
    d. $1,500,000

                                                                   (CFA)

10–4.   Company S, a profitable organization, has built and equipped a $2,000,000 plant which was brought into operation early in year 1. Earnings of the company before depreciation on the new plant and before income taxes have been projected as follows:

	Year
1	$1,500,000
2	2,000,000
3	2,500,000
4	3,000,000
5	3,500,000

The company may use the straight-line, double-declining balance, or sum-or-the-years'-digits methods of depreciation for the new plant.

Required:
Calculate the effect that each of these methods of depreciation would have on—
a. Federal income taxes.
b. Net income.
c. Cash flow.

Assume income tax rate of 50 percent, and that the useful life of the plant is 10 years. (No salvage value)

(CFA adapted)

10–5.   Toro Manufacturing Company was organized January 1, year 5. During year 5 it has used in its reports to management the straight-line method of depreciating its plant assets.

On November 8 you are having a conference with Toro's officers to discuss the depreciation method to be used for income tax and stockholder reporting. The president of Toro has suggested the use of a new method, which he feels is more suitable than the straight-line method for the needs of the company during the period of rapid expansion of production and capacity that he foresees. Following is an example in which the proposed method is applied to a fixed asset with an original cost of $32,000, an estimated useful life of 5 years, and a scrap value of approximately $2,000.

Year	Years of life used	Fraction rate	Depreciation expense	Accumulated depreciation at end of year	Book value at end of year
1	1	1/15	$ 2,000	$ 2,000	$30,000
2	2	2/15	4,000	6,000	26,000
3	3	3/15	6,000	12,000	20,000
4	4	4/15	8,000	20,000	12,000
5	5	5/15	10,000	30,000	2,000

The president favors the new method because he has heard that—

1. It will increase the funds recovered during the years near the end of the assets' useful lives when maintenance and replacement disbursements will be high.
2. It will result in increased write-offs in later years and thereby reduce taxes.

Required:
a. What is the purpose and, hence, the nature of accounting for depreciation?
b. Is the president's proposal within the scope of generally accepted accounting principles? In making your decision discuss the circumstances, if any, under which the method would be reasonable and those, if any, under which it would not be reasonable.
c. The president wants your advice.
   (1) Do depreciation charges recover or create cash? Explain.
   (2) Assume that the Internal Revenue Service will accept the proposed depreciation method in this particular case. If the proposed method were used for stockholder and tax reporting purposes, how would it affect the availability of cash, generated by operations?

10–6. Revenue is usually recognized at the point of sale. Under special circumstances, however, bases other than the point of sale are used for the timing of revenue recognition.

Required:
a. Why is the point of sale usually used as the basis for the timing of revenue recognition?
b. Disregarding the special circumstances when bases other than the point of sale are used, discuss the merits of each of the following objections to the sale basis of revenue recognition:
   (1) It is too conservative because revenue is earned throughout the entire process of production.
   (2) It is not conservative enough because accounts receivable do not represent disposable funds, sales returns and allowances may be made, and collection and bad debt expenses may be incurred in a later period.
c. Revenue may also be recognized (1) during production and (2) when cash is received. For each of these two bases of timing revenue recognition, give an example of the circumstances in which it is properly used and discuss the accounting merits of its use in lieu of the sales basis.

(AICPA)

10–7. The Michael Company is accounting for a long-term construction contract using the percentage-of-completion method. It is a four-year contract that is presently in its second year. The latest estimates of total contract costs indicate that the contract will be completed at a profit to Michael Company.

Required:

a. What theoretical justification is there for Michael Company's use of the percentage-of-completion method?
b. How would progress billings be accounted for? Include in your discussion the classification of progress billings in the Michael Company financial statements.
c. How would the income recognized in the second year of the four-year contract be determined using the cost-to-cost method of determining percentage of completion?
d. What would be the effect on earnings per share in the second year of the four-year contract of using the percentage-of-completion method instead of the completed-contract method? Discuss.

(AICPA)

10–8.   Trinket Company started with $3,000 cash in a business to produce trinkets using a simple assembly process. During the first month of business, the company signed sales contracts for 1,300 units (sales price of $9 per unit), produced 1,200 units (production cost of $7 per unit), shipped 1,100 units, and collected in full for 900 units.

Production costs are paid at the time of production. The company has only two other costs: *(a)* sales commissions of 10 percent of sales price are paid at the same time that the company collects from the customer and *(b)* shipping costs of $0.20 per unit are paid at time of shipment.

The sales price and all costs have been constant per unit and are likely to remain the same.

Required:

A. Prepare comparative (side-by-side) balance sheets and income statements for the first month of Trinket Company for *each* of the following *three* alternatives:
   (a) Profit is recognized at the time of shipment.
   (b) Profit is recognized at the time of collection.
   (c) Profit is recognized at the time of production.
   Note: Net income for each of the three alternatives should be *(a)* $990, *(b)* $810, and *(c)* $1,080, respectively.
B. (a) The method whereby profit is recognized only at time of collection, known as the "installment method" is acceptable for financial reporting only in rare and specialized cases. Why would Trinket Company be likely to prefer this method for tax purposes?
   (b) Comment on the usefulness of the "installment method" to a credit analyst.

10–9.   Crime Control Company accounts for a substantial part of its alarm systems sales under the sales-type (capitalized) leases method. Simply stated, under this method, the company computes the present value of the total receipts it expects to get (over periods as long as eight years) from a lease and takes that present value amount into sales in the first year of the lease. Justification for this accounting is that the 8-year lease represents more than 75 percent of the 10-year useful life of the equipment.

While the above accounting is done for book purposes, for tax purposes the company reports revenues only as they are received. Since first-year expenses of a lease are particularly heavy, the company reports substantial tax losses on these leases.

Required:

a.   Critics maintain that this accounting "front loads" income and that the reported earnings may not be received in cash for years. Comment on this criticism.
b.   Will the company's tax accounting benefit reported income?
c.   The company asserts that it could achieve earnings results similar to those achieved by its present sales-type lease accounting by selling the lease receivables to third-party lessors or financial institutions. Comment on this assertion.

10–10.   An analyst must be familiar with the concepts involved in determining earnings of a business entity. The amount of earnings reported for a business entity is dependent on the proper recognition, in general, of revenue and expense for a given time period. In some situations, costs are recognized as expenses at the time of product sale; in other situations, guidelines have been developed for recognizing costs as expenses or losses by other criteria.

Required:

a.   Explain the rationale for recognizing costs as expenses at the time of product sale.
b.   What is the rationale underlying the appropriateness of treating costs as expenses of a period instead of assigning the costs to an asset? Explain.
c.   In what general circumstances would it be appropriate to treat a cost as an asset instead of as an expense? Explain.
d.   Some expenses are assigned to specific accounting periods on the basis of systematic and rational allocation of asset cost. Explain the underlying rationale for recognizing expenses on the basis of systematic and rational allocation of asset cost.
e.   Identify the necessary conditions in which it would be appropriate to treat a cost as a loss.

(AICPA adapted)

Chapter 11

11–1.   Please refer to the financial statements of Campbell Soup in Appendix 4B.

The footnote "Pension Plans and Retirement Benefits" (item 110) describes the computation of pension expense, projected benefit obligation, and other elements of the pension plan (all amounts in millions).

Required:

a. What is the service cost of $22.1 for fiscal 1991?

b. What discount rate did the company assume for 1991? What is the effect of the change from the discount rate used in 1990?

c. How is the "interest on projected benefit obligation" computed?

d. The actual return on assets is shown as $73.4. Does this item enter in its entirety as a component of pension cost? Why or why not?

e. Campbell shows an accumulated benefit obligation (ABO) of $714.4. What is this obligation?

f. What is the projected benefit obligation (PBO) and what accounts for the difference between it and the accumulated benefit obligation?

g. Has Campbell funded its pension expense at the end of fiscal 1991?

11–2. Please refer to the financial statements of Campbell Soup in Appendix 4B.

Required:

a. Estimate the amount of depreciation expense shown on Campbell's 1991, 1990, and 1989 tax returns. Use a tax rate of 34 percent.

b. Identify the amount for 1991, 1990, and 1989 of following (combine federal, foreign, and state taxes) and show your source.

1. Earnings before income taxes.
2. Expected income tax at 34 percent.
3. Total income tax expense.
4. Total income tax due to governments.
5. Total income tax due and not yet paid at end of fiscal 1991, 1990, and 1989.

c. Why does the effective tax rate for 1991, 1990, and 1989 differ from 34 percent of income before taxes? Compute the dollar amounts of the permanent differences.

d. There is a very small tax benefit derived from the divestiture and restructuring charges in 1990. What are possible reasons? Can you estimate the cash outlays for these charges in 1990?

11–3. Please refer to the financial statements of Quaker Oats (see Appendix 23).

Required:

a. Estimate the amount of depreciation expense shown on Quaker Oats 1991, 1990, and 1989 tax returns. Use a tax rate of 34 percent.

b. Identify the amount for 1991, 1990, and 1989 of the following (combine federal, foreign, and state taxes) and show your source.

(1) Earnings before income taxes.
(2) Expected income tax at 34 percent.
(3) Total income tax expense.
(4) Total income tax due to governments.

(5) Total income tax due and not yet paid at June 30, 1991, 1990, and 1989.

c. (1) Why does the effective tax rate for 1991, 1990, 1989, differ from 34 percent of income before taxes?
   (2) Is it likely that the effective tax rate will continue to be high in the future?

d. Was the company's effective tax rate in 1991 different from that in 1990? And if it was what were the main reasons?

e. (1) What was the increase or decrease in deferred tax (current) during 1991, 1990 and 1989?
   (2) What was the increase or decrease in deferred tax (noncurrent) during 1991, 1990, and 1989?

11–4. Please refer to the financial statements of Quaker Oats (see Appendix 23).

In Note 2 "Discontinued Operations," various transactions are discussed concerning the operations and disposal of certain lines of business.

Required:
a. What is the best estimate of the summary journal entry recording the disposal of discontinued operations in 1991?
b. What were the expenses of discontinued operations in 1990?

11–5. The Primrose Company appropriately uses the deferred method for interperiod income tax allocation.

Primrose reports depreciation expense for certain machinery purchased this year using the accelerated cost recovery system (ACRS) for income tax purposes and the straight-line basis for accounting purposes. The tax deduction is the larger amount this year.

Primrose received rent revenues in advance this year. These revenues are included in this year's taxable income. However, for accounting purposes, these revenues are reported as unearned revenues, a current liability.

Required:
a. What is the theoretical basis for deferred income taxes?
b. How would Primrose determine and account for the income tax effect for the depreciation and rent? Why?
c. How should Primrose classify the income tax effect of the depreciation and rent on its balance sheet and income statement? Why?

11–6. Big Deal Construction Company specializes in building dams. During the years 3, 4, and 5, three dams were completed. The first dam was started in year 1 and completed in year 3 at a profit before income taxes of $120,000. The second and third dams were started in year 2. The second dam was completed in year 4 at a profit before income taxes of $126,000, and the third dam was completed in year 5 at a profit before income taxes of $150,000.

The company uses the percentage-of-completion method of accounting in its books and the completed-contract method of accounting for income tax purposes.

Data relating to the progress toward completion of work on each dam as reported by the company's engineers are set forth below:

Dam	year 1	year 2	year 3	year 4	year 5
1.............	20%	60%	20%		
2............		30	60	10%	
3............		10	30	50	10%

Required:

Assuming that the applicable income tax rate is 50 percent, for each of the five years 1 through 5 show *(a)* the book income, *(b)* the taxable income, and *(c)* the change in deferred income taxes.

11-7. Steady Corporation was formed in year 4 to take over the operations of a small business. This business proved to be very stable for Steady as can be seen below (dollars in thousands):

	year 5	year 5	year 6
Sales	$10,000	$10,000	$10,000
Expenses (except income tax)	9,000	9,000	9,000
Income before taxes	1,000	1,000	1,000

In addition, Steady expended $1,400,000 on preoperating costs for a new product during year 4. These costs were deferred for financial reporting purposes but were deducted in calculating year 4 taxable income. During year 5, the new product line was delayed; and in year 6, Steady abandoned the new product and charged the deferred cost of $1,400,000 to the year 6 income statement.

Required (assume 50 percent tax rate):
a. Prepare comparative income statements in good form for the three years. Be certain to identify all tax amounts as either "current" or "deferred."
b. List each tax item on the balance sheets at the end of each year (assume all tax payments and refunds occur in the year following the reporting year).

11-8. Playgrounds Inc. was granted a distribution franchise by Shady Products in year 1. Operations were profitable until year 4 when certain of the company's inventories were confiscated and large legal expenses were incurred. Playgrounds' tax rate was 50 percent each year (assume the year 4 expenses to be deductible; in thousands).

	year 1	year 2	year 3	year 4	year 5	year 6	year 7	year 8
Sales	$50	$80	$120	$100	$200	$400	$500	$600
Cost of sales	20	30	50	300	50	120	200	250
General and administrative	10	35	20	100	20	30	40	50
Net before tax	20	35	50	(300)	130	250	260	300

Required:

Prepare journal entries to record tax expense for each of these years and present the comparative income statements.

11–9. General Company adopted *SFAS No. 87.* Net periodic pension expense was reported as:

	Year ended December 31, 1986 ($ thousands)
Service cost	$586
Interest cost	129
Actual return on plan assets	(196)
Deferred loss	(48)
Amortization of transition asset	(19)
Net periodic pension expense	$452

The weighted average discount rate used in determining the actuarial present value of the Projected Benefit Obligation was 8.5 percent, and the assumed rate of increase in future compensation was 7.5 percent. The expected long-term rate of return on plan assets was 11.5 percent. The Projected Benefit Obligation at the end of 1986 was $2,212,000, and the Accumulated Benefit Obligation was $479,000. Fair value of assets was $3,238,000, and a transition asset of $581,000 remained.

Required:

Calculate your forecast of General Company's 1987 net periodic pension expense, given a 10 percent growth in service cost, amortization of deferred loss over 30 years, and no change in the other assumed rates. Show all calculations.

(CFA)

11–10. Carson Company sponsors a single-employer defined benefit pension plan. The plan provides that pension benefits are determined by age, years of service, and compensation. Among the components that should be included in the net pension cost recognized for a period are service cost, interest cost, and actual return on plan assets.

Required:
a. What two accounting problems result from the nature of the defined benefit pension plan? Why do these problems arise?
b. How should Carson determine the service cost component of the net pension cost?
c. How should Carson determine the interest cost component of the net pension cost?
d. How should Carson determine the actual return on plan assets component of the net pension cost?

(AICPA)

11–11. In 1990, the FASB issued *Statement 106 (FAS 106)*, which altered the accounting treatment of post-retirement benefits other than pensions in the United States. This statement requires that companies offering such benefits adopt accrual accounting (similar to the requirements of *FAS 87* for pension plans), rather than the pay-as-you-go accounting which had been widely used.

You are considering an investment in one of two U.S. firms subject to the change and are concerned about the relative impact of the new accounting procedure. The two firms are of roughly equal size and have identical retiree medical plans. *Firm X* is more labor-intensive, has a greater ratio of retirees to workers, and an older, more strongly unionized work force than *Firm Y*.

Required:
A. Compare the relative impact of adopting *FAS 106* on:
  i. The size of the post-retirement benefit obligation recognized by *each* of the two firms.
  ii. The size of the post-retirement benefit cost reported by *each* of the two firms.
B. For *each* of the three forms of the Efficient Market Hypothesis, explain the effect that adoption of the new standard will have on the per share price of a firm. Comment on the applicability of the implications to actual markets.

(CFA)

11–12. The preliminary condensed income statements of Disposo Corporation is shown below.

	Year 8	Year 7
Sales	$1,100	$900
Costs and expenses	990	860
Loss on asset disposal	10	—
Income before taxes	100	40
Tax expense	50	20
Net income	$ 50	$ 20

Note: On August 15, year 8, the company decided to discontinue its Metals Division. The business was sold on December 31, year 8, at book value except for a factory building with a book value of $25 which was sold for $15.

Operations of the Metals Division were:

	Sales	Income (loss)
Year 7	$300	$ 8
Jan. 1 to Aug. 15, year 8	250	(3)
Aug. 16 to Dec. 31, year 8	75	(1)

Required:

a. Correct the statements to reflect the proper presentation of the discontinued operations.

11–13.   The following quotation from an article written by Leopold Bernstein highlights the issue concerning the use of reserves to recognize future costs and losses—are they valid or merely a means of further clouding reports?

"The growing use of reserves for future costs and losses impairs the significance of periodically reported income and should be viewed with skepticism by the analyst of financial statements. That is especially true when the reserves are established in years of heavy losses, when they are established in an arbitrary amount designed to offset an extraordinary gain, or when they otherwise appear to have as their main purpose the relieving of future income of expenses properly chargeable to it.

"The basic justification in accounting for the recognition of future losses stems from the doctrine of conservatism which, according to one popular application, means that one should anticipate no gains, but take all the losses one can clearly see as already incurred."

Required:

a. Discuss the merits of Bernstein's arguments and apprehensions.
b. Explain how such information may be factored into your review of past trends, the estimates of future earnings, and valuation of the common stock.

(CFA)

11–14.   There are various types of accounting changes, each of which is required to be reported differently.

Required:

a. What type of accounting change is a change from the sum-of-the-years'-digits method of depreciation to the straight-line method for previously recorded assets? Under what circumstances does this type of accounting change occur?

b. What type of accounting change is a change in the expected service life of an asset arising because of more experience with the asset? Under what circumstances does this type of accounting change occur?

c. With respect to a change in accounting principle,
   1. How should a company calculate the effect?
   2. How should a company report the effect?

Do not discuss earnings per share requirements.

d. 1. Why are accounting principles, once adopted, normally continued?
   2. What is the rationale for disclosure of a change from one accounting principle to another accounting principle?

(AICPA)

Chapter 12

12-1.   Public enterprises are required to present earnings per share data on the face of the income statement.

Required:

Compare and contrast primary earnings per share with fully diluted earnings per share for each of the following:
1. The effect of common stock equivalents on the number of shares used in the computation of earnings per share data.
2. The effect of convertible securities that are not common stock equivalents on the number of shares used in the computation of earnings per share data.
3. The effect of antidilutive securities.

(CPA adapted)

12-2.   Generally accepted accounting principles require the presentation of corporate earnings per share data on the face of the income statement.

Required:

(1) Explain the meaning of "primary earnings per share."
(2) Explain how "fully diluted earnings per share" differs from primary earnings per share."

(CFA)

12-3.   Champion Lion Tamers had 2 million shares outstanding on December 31, 1987. On March 31, 1988, Champion paid a 10% stock dividend. On June 30, Champion sold $10 million of 5% convertible debentures, convertible into common shares at $5 per share. The AA Bond rate on the issue date was 10%.

Part 1.   Primary earnings per share for 1988 will be computed on the following number of shares:
   a.   2,050,000
   b.   2,200,000
   c.   3,200,000
   d.   4,200,000

Part 2.   Assume that Champion also has outstanding warrants to purchase 1
          million shares at $5 per share. Assume that the price of Champion
          common shares is $8 per share at December 31, 1988, and that the
          average share price for 1988 is $4. For the computation of primary
          earnings per share, how many *additional* shares must be assumed to
          be outstanding because of the warrants?
          a.   None
          b.   375,000
          c.   625,000
          d.   1,000,000

Part 3.   Given the same facts as in Part 2, how many *additional* shares must
          be assumed to be outstanding because of the warrants when comput-
          ing *fully diluted* earnings per share?
          a.   None
          b.   375,000
          c.   625,000
          d.   1,000,000

                                                                              (CFA)

12–4.

THE WRESTLING FEDERATION OF AMERICA, INC.
Capital Structure and Earnings for the Year 1987

Number of common shares outstanding on December 31, 1987	2,700,000
Number of common shares outstanding during 1987 (weighted average)	2,500,000
Market price per common share on December 31, 1987	$25
Weighted average market price per common share during 1987	$20
Options outstanding during 1987:	
Number of shares issuable on exercise of options	200,000
Exercise price	$15
Convertible bonds outstanding (December 1983 issue):	
Number	10,000
Shares of common issuable on conversion (per bond)	10
Coupon rate	5.0%
Proceeds per bond at issue (= par value)	$1,000
Average Aa corporate bond yield at time of issue	8.5%
Net income for 1987	$6,500,000
Tax rate for 1987	40.0%

Required:

A.   Primary earnings per share for 1987 were:
     a. $2.45.
     b. $2.57.
     c. $2.62.

    d. none of the above.
B. Fully diluted earnings per share for 1987 were:
    a. $2.43.
    b. $2.48.
    c. $2.54.
    d. none of the above.

(CFA)

12–5. FAN, Inc., showed the following for year 6:

Income before extraordinary item	$800,000
Extraordinary item—casualty loss (net after taxes)	200,000
Net income for period	$600,000

At January 1, year 6 there were 200,000 shares of common stock outstanding. On October 1, year 6, an additional 60,000 shares were sold for cash.

In year 4, 6 percent bonds were issued at par, $1,000,000. These are convertible into 20,000 shares of common stock. None have been converted. At date of issue, the AA bond rate was 8 percent.

In year 2, 25,000 shares of $3 cumulative preferred stock were issued at $90 per share. Each preferred share is convertible into two shares of common stock. None have been converted. At date of issue, the AA bond rate was 9 percent.

In year 3, 50,000 options were granted to purchase common stock (one option for each share) at $45 per share. None have been exercised. During year 6, the average market price per share of common stock was $50 and on December 31, year 6, the market price was $60. Assume an income tax rate of 40 percent.

Required:
a. Calculate primary earnings per share.
b. Calculate fully diluted earnings per share.

12–6. Company A has a net income for the year of $4 million and the number of common shares outstanding is 3 million (there was no change during the year). The company also has options and warrants outstanding to purchase 1 million common shares at $15 per share.

Required:
a. If the average market value of the common share was $20, the year-end price was $25, interest rate on borrowings is 6 percent, and the tax rate is 50 percent, compute the primary and the fully diluted EPS.
b. Do the same requirement as in *(a)* above, assuming that net income for the year was only $3 million and average market value per common share was $18 and year-end price was $20 per share.

12–7. The officers of Environmental Protection, Inc., had considered themselves fortunate when the company had been able to sell a $9,000,000 subordinated convertible debenture issue on June 30, year 1 with only a 6 percent coupon.

They had had the alternative of refunding and enlarging the outstanding term loan, but the interest cost would have been one half a point above the AA bond rate. The latter had been as high as 8½ percent until March 29, year 1 when it was lowered to 8 percent, the rate that prevailed until September 21, year 1 when it was lowered again to 7½ percent.

Environmental Protection, Inc., had the following capital structure at December 31, year 1:

7% term loan* $3,000,000
6% convertible subordinated debentures year 6† 9,000,000
Common stock, $1 par, authorized 2,000,000 shares, issued and
  outstanding 900,000   900,000
900,000 warrants, expiring July 1, year 6‡
Capital surplus 1,800,000
Retained earnings 4,500,000

  * The term loan (originally $5,000,000) is repayable in semiannual installments of $500,000.
  † The convertible subordinated debentures, sold June 30, year 1 are convertible at any time at $18 until maturity. Sinking fund of $300,000 per year to start in year 6.
  ‡ Warrants entitle holder to purchase one share for $10 to expiration on July 1, year 6.

Additional data for year 1:

Interest expense .... $ 500,000
Net income 1,500,000
Dividends paid   135,000
Earnings retained   900,000
Market prices December 31, year 1
  (which are also the averages for year 1)
    Convertible debentures 6% 75   107
    Common 13.00
    Warrants 4.50
    Treasury bills interest rate at 12/31/year 1 ....   6%

Required:

a. Calculate (show your computations) the earnings per share figures for the common stock as they would be required to be shown in the year 1 annual report.

b. What would be the times interest earned before tax on the 6 percent convertible subordinated debentures (assume a 50 percent federal income tax rate for the company) for year 2 assuming net earnings before interest and taxes were the same as in year 1?

(CFA adapted)

12–8.   Part A. Information concerning the capital structure of the Dole Corporation is as follows:

	December 31	
	Year 5	Year 6
Common stock	90,000 shares	90,000 shares
Convertible preferred stock	10,000 shares	10,000 shares
8% convertible bonds	$1,000,000	$1,000,000

During year 6, Dole paid dividends of $1 per share on its common stock and $2.40 per share on its preferred stock. The preferred stock is convertible into 20,000 shares of common stock; but is not considered a common stock equivalent. The 8 percent convertible bonds are convertible into 30,000 shares of common stock and are considered common stock equivalents. The net income for the year ended December 31, year 6 was $285,000. Assume that the income tax rate was 50 percent.

Required:
1. What are the primary earnings per share for the year ended December 31, year 6, rounded to the nearest penny?
2. What are the fully diluted earnings per share for the year ended December 31, year 6, rounded to the nearest penny?

Part B. The Lot Company's net income for the year ended December 31, year 6, was $10,000. During year 6, Lot declared and paid $1,000 cash dividends on preferred stock and $1,750 cash dividends on common stock.

At December 31, year 6, 12,000 shares of common stock were issued and outstanding, 10,000 of which had been issued and outstanding throughout the year and 2,000 of which were issued on July 1, year 6. There were *no* other common stock transactions during the year, and there is *no* potential dilution of earnings per share. What should be the year 6 earnings per common share of Lot, rounded to the nearest penny?

12–9. On October 1, year 5, the management of the Allen Corporation decided to merge the Simon and Duke Corporations. Following is some additional information (the merger was accounted for as a pooling):

	Simon Corporation	Duke Corporation	Allen Corporation
Net income from 1/1 to 9/30/year 5	$100,000	$150,000	$250,000
Common shares outstanding on 10/1/year 5................................	50,000	40,000	
Shares issued on 7/1/year 5	25,000	—	150,000
Shares issued on 9/1/year 5		10,000	—
Net income from 10/1 to 12/31/year 5 ...			$250,000
Number of shares issued for acquisition of:			
Simon Corporation (2 for 1)			100,000
Duke Corporation (5 for 1)			200,000

Required:

Compute earnings per share for the Consolidated Company on December 31, year 5.

12–10.   On October 1, year 5 the management of the Morning Corporation decided to merge with the Afternoon and Evening Corporations. Following is some additional information (assume pooling accounting):

	Afternoon Corporation	Evening Corporation	Morning Corporation
Net income from 1/1 to 9/30/year 5	$200,000	$300,000	$100,000
Common shares outstanding on 10/1/year 5	100,000	80,000	300,000
Shares issued on 7/1/year 5	50,000		
Shares issued on 9/1/year 5		20,000	
Net income from 10/1 to 12/31/year 5 ...			$400,000
Number of shares issued for acquisition of:			
Afternoon Corp. (2 for 1)			200,000
Evening Corp. (5 for 1)			400,000

Required:

Compute earnings per share for the Consolidated Company on December 31, year 5.

Chapter 13

13–1.

I. *SFAS 95* "Statement of Cash Flows" (SCF) requires the classification of cash inflows and outflows into three categories—please describe them.

II. Which noncash activities must be reported in conjunction with the SCF and how must these be reported?

III. First Corporation has retained you to advise with the preparation of the SCF on an indirect basis for the year ended December 31, year 8. Advise how the following will affect items in the SCF and how they would be shown on the statement:

1. The amount of net income for the fiscal year was $950,000, which included an extraordinary gain of $60,000.

2. Depreciation expense of $80,000 was included in the earnings statement.

3. Uncollectible accounts receivable of $50,000 were written off against the allowance for uncollectible accounts. Also, $24,000 of bad debts expense was included in determining earnings for the fiscal year, and the same amount was added to the allowance for uncollectible accounts.

4. Accounts receivable have increased by $140,000 during the fiscal year and inventories declined by $60,000.

5. Taxes paid to governments amounted to $380,000.
6. A gain of $5,000 was realized on the sale of a machine; it originally cost $75,000 of which $25,000 was undepreciated on the date of sale.
7. On June 5, year 8 building and land were purchased for $600,000; First gave in payment $100,000 cash, $200,000 market value of its unissued common stock, and a $300,000 purchase-money mortgage.
8. On August 8, year 8, $700,000 face value of First's 6 percent convertible debentures was converted into $140,000 par value of its common stock. The bonds were originally issued at face value.
9. The board of directors declared a $320,000 cash dividend on October 30, year 8, payable on January 15, year 9, to stockholders of record on November 15, year 8.
10. On December 15, year 8, First declared a 2-for-1 stock split payable on December 25, year 8.

13–2.   Part A. The following data were taken from accounting records of Saro Corporation and subsidiaries for year 1:

Net income	$10,000
Depreciation, depletion, amortization	8,000
Major disposals of property, plant, and equipment (book value) for cash	1,000
Deferred income taxes for year 1 (noncurrent)	400
Undistributed earnings of unconsolidated affiliates	200
Amortization of discount on bonds payable	50
Amortization of premium on bonds payable	60
Decrease in noncurrent assets	1,500
Cash proceeds from exercise of stock options	300
Increase in accounts receivable	900
Increase in accounts payable	1,200
Decrease in inventories	850
Increase in dividends payable	300
Decrease in notes payable to banks	400

Required:
Determine the amount of cash provided by operations in year 1.

Part B. Regarding the following items (I) Explain their nature and (II) whether they need to be considered in adjusting net income in order to arrive at cash from operations.

1. Issuance of treasury stock as employee compensation.
2. Capitalization of interest incurred.
3. Amount charged to pension expense that differs from the amount funded.

13–3. Presented below are the balance sheets of Barrier Corporation as of December 31, year 2 and year 1 and statement of income and retained earnings for the year ended December 31, year 2.

BARRIER CORPORATION
Balance Sheets
As of December 31, year 2 and year 1

	Year 2	Year 1	Increase (decrease)
Assets			
Cash	$ 275,000	$ 180,000	$ 95,000
Accounts receivable	295,000	305,000	(10,000)
Inventories	549,000	431,000	118,000
Investment in Ort. Inc., at equity	73,000	60,000	13,000
Land	350,000	200,000	150,000
Plant and equipment	624,000	606,000	18,000
Less: accumulated depreciation	(139,000)	(107,000)	(32,000)
Goodwill	16,000	20,000	(4,000)
Total assets	$2,043,000	$1,695,000	$348,000
Liabilities and Stockholders' Equity			
Accounts payable	$ 604,000	$ 563,000	$ 41,000
Accrued expenses	150,000	–	150,000
Bonds payable	160,000	210,000	(50,000)
Deferred income taxes	41,000	30,000	11,000
Common stock, par $10	430,000	400,000	30,000
Additional paid-in capital	226,000	175,000	51,000
Retained earnings	432,000	334,000	98,000
Treasury stock, at cost	–	(17,000)	17,000
	$2,043,000	$1,695,000	$348,000

BARRIER CORPORATION
Statement of Income and Retained Earnings
For the Year Ended December 31, year 2

Net sales		$1,937,000
Undistributed income from Ort. Inc.		13,000
		1,950,000
Cost of sales		1,150,000
		800,000
Depreciation expense	32,000	
Amortization of goodwill	4,000	
Other expenses (including income taxes)	623,000	659,000
Net income		141,000
Retained earnings, January 1, year 2		334,000
		475,000
Cash dividends paid		43,000
Retained earnings, December 31, year 2		432,000

1. Capital stock was sold to provide additional cash.
2. All accounts receivable and payable relate to operations.
3. Accounts payable relate only to items included in cost of sales.
4. There were no noncash transactions.

Required:
1. Determine: cash collected from sales during year 2.
2. Determine: cash payments on accounts payable during year 2.
3. Determine: cash receipts during year 2 which were not provided by operations.
4. Determine: cash payments for noncurrent assets purchased during the year.

13–4. A fellow analyst who became aware of your understanding of financial statements asks for your help in understanding the variety of flows of Zett Company in which she is interested. The following data are provided:

Balance Sheet
At December 31

	Year 1	Year 2
Cash	$ 34,000	$ 34,500
Accounts receivable (net)	12,000	17,000
Inventory	16,000	14,000
Investments (long-term)	6,000	
Fixed assets	80,000	93,000
Treasury stock		11,500
	$148,000	$170,000
Accumulated depreciation	$ 48,000	$ 39,000
Accounts payable	19,000	12,000
Bonds payable	10,000	30,000
Common stock................	50,000	61,000
Retained earnings	21,000	28,000
	$148,000	$170,000

Additional data for the period January 1, year 2, through December 31, year 2:

a) Sales on account, $70,000.
b) Purchases on account, $40,000.
c) Depreciation, $5,000.
d) Expenses paid in cash, $18,000.*
e) Decrease in inventory, $2,000.
f) Sold fixed assets for $6,000 cash; cost $21,000 and two-thirds depreciated (loss or gain is included in income).
g) Purchased fixed assets for cash, $4,000.
h) Fixed assets were exchanged for bonds payable of $30,000.
i) Sold the investments for $9,000 cash.

j) Purchased treasury stock for cash, $11,500.
k) Retired bonds payable by issuing common stock, $10,000.
l) Collections on accounts receivable, $65,000.
m) Sold unissued common stock for cash, $1,000.
  * Including $4,000 of interest and $6,000 in taxes.

Required:
  I. Prepare a statement of cash flows using the T-account method for the
     year ending 12/31/year 2.
 II. Prepare a side-by-side comparative statement comparing two bases of
     reporting *(a)* income and *(b)* cash from operations.
III. The fellow analyst asks which of the two statements reflect profitability
     better. Please comment.

13–5.   Dax Corporation's genetically engineered coronary artery clot dissolver
has suddenly gained market acceptance and shipments to customers have increased dramatically. The company also had to gear up for significant increases
in production. Management has noted that despite increasing profits the cash
balance has declined and it had to double debt in the past year.
    You have been asked to advise management as to the specific causes of the
cash stringency and how to remedy the situation. You have been given the following balance sheets of Dax Corporation for year 1 and year 2 ($ thousands):

		Year 2		Year 1
Cash		500		640
Accounts receivable (net)		860		550
Inventories		935		790
Prepaid expenses		25		—
Total current assets		2,320		1,980
Patents	140			
Amortization	10	130		—
Plant and equipment	2,650		1,950	
Accumulated depreciation	600		510	
		2,050		1,440
Other assets	200		175	
Accumulated depreciation	30	170	25	150
Total noncurrent assets		2,350		1,590
Total assets		4,670		3,570
Accounts payable		630		600
Deferred income tax		57		45
Other current liabilities		85		78
Total current liabilities		772		723
Long-term debt		1,650		850
Common stock, $1 par		2,000		1,800
Retained earnings		248		197
Total long-term debt and equity		3,898		2,847
Total liabilities and equity		4,670		3,570

In addition, the following information is available:

1. Net income for year 2 was $160,000 and for year 1 was $130,000.
2. Cash dividends paid during year 2 were $109,000 and during year 1 were $100,000.
3. Depreciation expense charged to income during year 2 was $95,000, and provision for bad debt (expense) was $40,000. Expenses include cash payments of $28,000 in interest costs and $70,000 in income taxes.
4. During year 2 the company purchased patents for $140,000 in cash. Amortization of patents during the year amounted to $10,000.
5. Deferred income tax for year 2 amounted to $12,000 and for year 1 amounted to $15,000.

Required:
a. Prepare a statement of cash flows for year 2 using the T-account method.
b. Explain the significant discrepancy between net income and "cash from operations." What are the major reasons? Describe the options available to management given the present situation.

13–6. Using the data in Tables I and II, prepare a Statement of Cash Flows for the Niagara Company for the year ended December 31, year 9, in accordance with *SFAS No. 95* on the direct, or inflow-outflow basis.

Table I

NIAGARA COMPANY
Income Statement
Year Ended December 31, year 9

Sales	$1,000
Cost of goods sold	(650)
Depreciation expense	(100)
Sales and general expense	(100)
Interest expense	(50)
Income tax expense	(40)
Net income	$ 60

Table II

NIAGARA COMPANY
Balance Sheets As of December 31

	Year 8	Year 9
Assets		
Cash	$ 50	$ 60
Accounts receivable	500	520
Inventory	750	770
Current assets	$1,300	$1,350
Fixed assets	500	550
Total assets	$1,800	$1,900
Liabilities & Capital		
Notes payable to banks	$ 100	$ 75
Accounts payable	590	615
Interest payable	10	20
Current liabilities	$ 700	$ 710
Long-term debt	300	350
Deferred income tax	300	310
Capital stock	400	400
Retained earnings	100	130
Total liabilities & capital	$1,800	$1,900

(CFA adapted)

13–7. Indicate if the following transaction is a source or a use of cash, or an adjustment leading to a source or use of cash and the category: operations (O), financing (F), investing (I), noncash-significant (NCS), noncash-nonsignificant (NCN), no effect (NE).

Transaction	Source	Use	Category
Example: Cash dividend received	X		O

1. Increase in accounts receivable
2. Paid bank note
3. Issued common stock
4. Sold marketable securities
5. Retired bonds
6. Declared stock dividend
7. Purchased equipment
8. Converted bonds to preferred stock
9. Paid dividend
10. Increase in accounts payable

13–8. Indicate if the following transaction is a source or a use of cash, or an adjustment leading to a source or use of cash and the category: operations (O), financing (F), investing (I), noncash-significant (NCS), noncash-nonsignificant (NCN), no effect (NE).

Transaction	Source	Use	Category
Example: Sold bonds for cash	X		F

1. Decrease in inventory
2. Paid current portion long-term debt
3. Retired treasury stock
4. Bought marketable securities (noncurrent)
5. Issued bonds for property
6. Declared stock dividend
7. Sold equipment for cash
8. Converted bonds to preferred stock
9. Purchase inventory on credit
10. Decrease in accounts payable by return of merchandise.

13–9. The ability to visualize quickly the effect of a given transaction on the cash resources of an enterprise is a valuable analytical skill. Such visualization requires an understanding of the reality behind the transaction as well as how it is accounted for. Expressing such accounting in journal entry form is the most helpful approach.

Required:

A simplified schematic Statement of Cash Flows of the company for the year is shown below. The company closes its books once each year, on December 31.

The titles of the lines in the schematic shown below are given labels (letters). For each of the activities listed identify which of these lines is affected and by *how much*. Each activity is separate and unrelated to other activities. Do not consider subsequent activities. Use the labels (letters) shown below. Do not indicate the effect on any line not given a label. If a transaction has no effect, write *none*. In indicating effect for lines *Y* and *C,* use a + to indicate an increase and a − to indicate a decrease. Be sure to show the amount!

Note: *Every activity, with an effect, affects at least two lines* (equal debits and credits). A journal entry is helpful in arriving at a solution.

Schematic Statement of Cash Flows of the Company for the Year.

Sources of cash:

(Y)	Net income	_____(Y)
(YA)	Additions or addbacks for expenses, losses, etc., not using cash.....................................	_____(YA)
(YS)	Subtractions for revenues, gains, etc., not generating cash	_____(YS)
	Changes in current assets and current liabilities related to operations	
(CC)	Add credit changes	_____(CC)
(DC)	Deduct debit changes	_____(DC)
(NC)	Add (deduct) changes in noncurrent accounts related to operations	_____(NC)
	Cash flow from operations Y + YA − YS + CC − DC + or − NC	_____
(DE)	Proceeds of debt and equity issues	_____(DE)
(IL)	Increase in nonoperating current liabilities	_____(IL)
(AD)	Proceeds of long-term assets dispositions	_____(AD)
(OS)	Other sources of cash	_____(OS)
	Total sources of cash	_____

Uses of cash:

(ID)	Income distributions	_____(ID)
(R)	Retirements of debt and equity	_____(R)
(DL)	Decreases in nonoperating current liabilities	_____(DL)
(AA)	Long-term assets acquisitions	_____(AA)
(OU)	Other uses of cash	_____(OU)
	Total uses of cash	_____
(C)	Increase (decrease) in cash	_____(C)

Schedule of Noncash Investing and Financing Activities

NDE	Issue of debt or equity.........................	_____(NDE)
NCR	Other noncash generating credits	_____(NCR)
NAA	Acquisitions of assets	_____(NAA)
NDR	Other noncash requiring debits...................	_____(NDR)

Illustration:

0. Sales of $10,000 are made on account.
00. Dividends of $4,000 are paid.
000. Entered into long-term capital lease obligation (present value $60,000).

Answers:

0.	DC	10,000 + Y 10,000
00.	ID	4,000 − C 4,000
000.	NAA	60,000 NDE 60,000

Activities:

1. Provision for bad debt of $11,000 for the year was included in selling expenses.
2. Depreciation of $16,000 was charged to cost of goods sold.
3. A building was acquired by issuance of a long-term mortgage note for $100,000.
4. Treasury stock with a cost of $7,000 is retired and canceled.
5. The company has outstanding 50,000 shares of common stock with par value of $1. The company declared a 20 percent stock dividend at the end of the year when the stock was selling for $16 a share.
6. Inventory costing $12,000 has been destroyed by fire. The insurance company paid only $10,000 for that loss, although the market value of the inventory was $15,000.
7. Inventories that originally cost $25,000 have been used by production departments in producing finished goods that have been sold for $35,000 in cash and $5,000 in accounts receivable.
8. Accounts receivable of $8,000 are written off. There was an allowance for doubtful accounts balance of $5,000 only.
9. The company acquired a long-lived asset for $100,000 in cash on January 1. The company decided to depreciate $20,000 each year.
10. A machine that cost $15,000 and had an accumulated depreciation of $6,000 is sold for $8,000 in cash.

13–10   Please satisfy the requirements of problem 13–9 using the activities listed below:

A. 1. The annual installment of $100,000 due on the long-term debt was paid on its due date.
  2. Equipment that originally cost $12,000 and has $7,000 of accumulated depreciation is sold for $4,000 cash.
  3. Obsolete inventory that cost $75,000 is written down to zero.
  4. Treasury stock that cost $30,000 is sold for $28,000 cash.
  5. A plant is acquired by the issuance of a $300,000 mortgage payable due in equal installments over 6 years.
  6. The Company's 30 percent-owned unconsolidated company earned $100,000 and paid total dividends of $20,000. The Company recorded its 30 percent share of these items using the cost plus equity method.
  7. A product was sold for $40,000, to be paid $10,000 down plus $10,000 each year for three years. Also, interest at 10 percent of the outstanding balance is due. Consider only the effect at the time of sale (the Company's normal operating cycle is *less* than one year).
  8. The Company uses a periodic inventory method. Certain inventory was valued at $1,000. This was a mistake. It should have been valued at $10,000. Show the effect of correcting the error.
  9. Cash of $400,000 is given to acquire 100 percent of ZXY Manufacturing Company. At date of acquisition, ZXY had current assets of $300,000 (including $40,000 in cash); plant and equipment, $600,000; goodwill, $70,000; current liabilities, $160,000; and long-term debt, $410,000.

10. A provision for bad debt expense of $60,000 is made (calculated as a percentage of sales for the period).

B.   *a.* Investment of $120,000 cash in 30 percent-owned company.

    b. The 30 percent-owned company earned $25,000 (in total) and paid no dividends.

    c. Assume instead that the 30 percent-owned company earned $30,000 (in total) and paid dividends of $10,000 (in total).

    d. Equipment with an original cost of $15,000 and accumulated depreciation of $12,000 was sold for $4,000 cash.

    e. The Company borrowed $60,000 from its banks on November 30 payable on June 30 of next year.

    f. Convertible bonds with a face value of $9,000 are converted into 1,000 shares of common stock with a par value of $2 per share.

    g. Treasury stock with a cost of $4,000 is sold for $6,000 cash.

    h. Common stock (par value $2) with a fair market value of $100,000 plus $100,000 cash are given to acquire 100 percent of ZYX Mfg. Co. At date of acquisition ZYX had: current assets of $120,000 (including $40,000 cash); plant and equipment of $150,000; goodwill of $30,000; current liabilities of $60,000; and long-term debt of $40,000.

      (1) Effect on *parent's* statement.

      (2) Effect on *consolidated* statement.

    i. The minority's share of income was $4,000.

    j. Inventory with a cost of $80,000 was written down to its market value of $30,000.

    k. The accounts receivable of Worman for $1,200 is written off. The company uses an allowance for doubtful accounts.

    l. A noncancelable lease of equipment for 10 years with a present value of $120,000 is capitalized.

    m. A 15 percent stock dividend is declared. The 60,000 shares of common stock issued as the dividend have a par value of $2 per share and a fair market value of $3 per share.

    n. A provision of $27,000 for uncollectible accounts is made (calculated as a percentage of sales for the period).

    o. Dividends of $40,000 are declared on December 20 and are payable on January 20 of *next* year. (Consider only the effect for this year.)

13–11.   While on an urgent assignment you discover to your dismay that you have left behind the balance sheet of Bird Corporation as of January 1, year 1. You realize that you do have the following data on that company:

BIRD CORPORATION
Postclosing Trial Balance
December 31, Year 1

Debit balances:

Cash	$ 100,000
Accounts receivable	120,000
Inventory	130,000
Property, plant, and equipment	550,000
Other noncurrent investments	200,000
	$1,100,000

Credit balances:

Accounts payable	$ 100,000
Current portion of long-term debt	80,000
Accumulated depreciation	270,000
Long-term debt	200,000
Common stock	300,000
Retained earnings	150,000
	$1,100,000

BIRD CORPORATION
Statement of Cash Flows
For the Year Ended December 31, Year 1

Cash from operations:			
Net income			150,000
Add (deduct) adjustments to cash basis:			
Depreciation		85,000	
Loss on sale of equipment		5,000	
Gain on sale of noncurrent investments		(50,000)	
Increase in accounts receivable		(30,000)	
Increase in inventories		(20,000)	
Increase in accounts payable		40,000	30,000
Cash from operations			180,000
Investing activities:			
Additions to property and equipment ...		(150,000)	
Sale of equipment		10,000	
Sale of investments		95,000	
Cash used for investing activities			(45,000)
Financing activities:			
Issuance of common stock		10,000	
Additions to long-term debt	15,000		
Decrease in current portion of LTD	(30,000)	(15,000)	
Cash dividends		(80,000)	
Cash used for financing activities ...			(85,000)
Increase in cash			50,000

Additional information:
a. The equipment which has been sold had accumulated depreciation of $50,000.

Required:
Reconstruct the T-accounts of Bird Corporation by use of the above data and information. Use the T-accounts to prepare the balance sheet of Bird Corporation as of January 1, year 1, which you so urgently need.

13–12.   During a stormy meeting of the management committee of the Weak Corporation a number of proposals were made to alleviate a weak cash position as well as an inadequate level of income. Evaluate and comment on the immediate effect of the following suggested steps on the measures indicated, as well as possible other longer-term effects. Indicate increase (+) decrease (−) or no effect (NE).

	Effect on		
	Net income	*Cash from operations*	*Cash position*
1. Substitute stock dividends for cash dividends.			
2. Delay needed capital expenditures.			
3. Reduce repair and maintenance outlays.			

4. Increase the provision for depreciation:
   a. For books only.
   b. For tax only.
   c. For both books and tax.			

5. Require quicker payments from customers.			
6. Stretch out payments to suppliers and pass up cash discounts.			
7. Borrow money short term.			
8. Switch from sum-of-the-years' digits to straight-line depreciation for books only.			
9. Pressure dealers to buy more.			

13–13.   Indicate whether the following independent transactions increase (+), decrease (−) or do not affect (0) the current ratio, the amount of working capital, cash from operations and by how much. The company presently has a current ratio of 2 to 1 and current liabilities of $160,000.

	Cur-rent ratio	Working Capital		Cash from operations	
		Effect	$	Effect	$
a. Paid accrued wages of $1,000.					
b. Purchased $20,000 worth of material on account.					
c. Received judgment notice from the court that the company has to pay $70,000 as damages for patent infringement within six months.					
d. Company collected $8,000 of accounts receivable.					
e. Purchased land for factory building for $100,000 cash.					
f. Repaid currently due bank note payable of $10,000.					
g. Received currently due note receivable of $15,000 from customer as consideration for a sale of land.					
h. Received cash of $90,000 from stockholders as donated capital.					
i. Purchased machine costing $50,000; $15,000 down and the balance to be paid in 7 equal annual installments.					
j. Retired the company's bond maturing five years hence for par of $50,000. Bond has unamortized premium of $2,000.					
k. The company declared dividends of $10,000 payable after year-end.					
l. The company paid the above dividends in cash.					
m. The company declared a 5% stock dividend.					
n. The company paid the above stock dividend.					
o. The company signed a long-term purchase contract of $100,000 to commence a year from now.					

(concluded)

	Cur-rent ratio	Working Capital		Cash from operations	
		Effect	$	Effect	$
p. The company borrowed $40,000 cash for one year.					
q. The company pays accounts payable of $20,000.					
r. The company purchases a patent for $20,000.					
s. The company writes off $15,000 of current marketable securities which became worthless.					
t. $8,500 of organization expenses were written off.					
u. Depreciation expense of $70,000 is recorded.					
v. Sold $28,000 of merchandise on account.					
w. A building was sold for $90,000. It has a book value of $45,000.					
x. A machine was sold at cost for $5,000; $2,500 down and the balance receivable in six months.					
y. Income tax expense was booked as $80,000, half of which was deferred (long-term).					

13–14.   Your banker friend confides to you that after looking at a number of financial statements she is confused about the difference between two operating flow concepts (i.e., net income and cash from operations).

Required:
a. Clarify the purpose and significance of these two operating flow concepts.
b. Several financial events are listed below. For each event, indicate whether it resulted in an increase (+), decrease (−), or no change (NC) for each of the two concepts. If you have any difficulty, try illustrating the appropriate T-account "in words" to help.

| | Effect of the financial event upon | |
	Net income	Cash from operations
1. Sale of marketable securities for cash at more than their original cost.		
2. Sale of merchandise to be paid during the following two years (one half within one year and one half after one year).		
3. Movement of noncurrent receivable to current receivables.		
4. Payment of current portion of long-term debt.		
5. Collection of an account receivable.		
6. Recording the cost of goods sold.		
7. Purchase of inventories on account (credit terms).		
8. Accrual of sales commissions (to be paid at a later date).		
9. Payment of accounts payable (which resulted from purchase of inventory).		
10. Provision for depreciation on a sales office.		
11. Borrowing cash from a bank on a 90-day note payable.		
12. Accrual of interest on the bank loan.		
13. Sale of partially depreciated equipment for cash at less than its book value.		
14. Flood damage to merchandise inventories (no insurance coverage).		
15. Declaration and payment of a cash dividend on preferred stock.		
16. Sale of merchandise on 90-day credit terms.		
17. Provision for uncollectible accounts receivable.		

(concluded)

| | Effect of the financial event upon | |
	Net income	Cash from operations
18. Write-off of the uncollectible receivable from Zoro, Inc.		
19. Provision for income tax expense (to be paid the following month).		
20. Provision for deferred income taxes (set up because depreciation for tax reporting exceeded depreciation for financial reporting).		
21. Purchase of a machine (fixed asset) for cash.		
22. Payment of accrued salary expense to employees.		

13–15.   A well-known text on economics contained the following statement: "For the business firm there are, typically, three major sources of funds. Two of these, depreciation reserves and retained earnings, are internal. The third is external, consisting of funds obtained either by borrowing, or by the sale of new equities."

Required:
a.   Is depreciation a source of cash? (Exclude all considerations pertaining to depreciation expense tax-book differences.)
b.   If not, what has led to the widespread belief that depreciation *is* a source of cash?
c.   If yes, in what sense is depreciation a source of cash?

13–16.   The managers of Wyatt Corporation had become frustrated in recent years because its corporate parent, Snow Corporation, repeatedly rejected Wyatt's capital spending requests. These perennial refusals led the managers to conclude that the operations of Wyatt played no role in the parent's longer-range plans. Acting on that suspicion, the managers of Wyatt approached a merchant banking firm about the possibility of organizing a leveraged buyout of their subsidiary. In the proposal, the managers stressed the stable, predictable cash flows from Wyatt's operations as more than adequate to service the debt needed to finance the proposed leveraged buyout.

As a partner in the merchant banking firm, you have begun to investigate the feasibility of the managers' proposal. You have received the "Statement of Financial Position" and "Supplementary Information" of the Wyatt Corporation shown below. The managers of Wyatt further disclose that following the purchase of Wyatt they intend to purchase machinery costing $325,000 in each of the next three years to overcome the very low level of capital spending while a subsidiary of Snow Corporation. Such spending is needed to meet intense competition.

Required:

a. Using the information in the tables below, prepare a Statement of Cash Flows for the year ended December 31, 1990.
b. Using the statement prepared in your answer to *(a)* and assuming that debt service will be $300,000 per year after the leveraged buyout, evaluate the feasibility of the transaction.

WYATT CORPORATION
Statement of Financial Position
As of December 31

	1989	*1990*
Assets		
Current assets:		
Cash	$ 175,000	$ 192,000
Accounts receivable	248,000	359,000
Inventory	465,000	683,000
Total current assets	$ 888,000	$1,234,000
Noncurrent assets:		
Land	$ 126,000	$ 138,000
Buildings and machinery	3,746,000	3,885,000
Less accumulated depreciation	(916,000)	(1,131,000)
Total noncurrent assets	$2,956,000	$2,892,000
Total assets	$3,844,000	$4,126,000
Liabilities and Shareholders' Equity		
Current liabilities:		
Accounts payable	156,000	259,000
Taxes payable	149,000	124,000
Other short-term payables	325,000	417,000
Total current liabilities	$ 630,000	$ 800,000
Bonds payable	842,000	825,000
Total liabilities	$1,472,000	$1,625,000
Shareholders' Equity:		
Common stock	$ 846,000	$ 863,000
Retained earnings	1,526,000	1,638,000
Total shareholders' equity	$2,372,000	$2,501,000
Total liabilities and shareholders' equity	$3,844,000	$4,126,000

Supplementary Information:
1. Dividends declared and paid in 1990 were $74,000.
2. Depreciation expense for 1990 was $246,000.
3. Machinery originally costing $61,000 was sold for $34,000 in 1990.

(CFA adapted)

13–17. The management of Dover considers the shares of the company to be severely undervalued by the market. They propose to take it private by means of a leveraged buyout. Their plan contains the following changes:
1. The leveraged buyout will result in additional after-tax annual interest costs of $200,000.
2. Making the company competitive will require
   a. Annual investments in equipment of $180,000
   b. Annual buildup of inventory of $60,000.
3. No financing beyond that referred to in (1) above is contemplated and subsequently management will look to cash generated by operations as the primary financing source.

Management has asked you to analyze the feasibility of their plans. They give you the data below to assist you in your work.

	December 31		
	Year 8	*Year 7*	*Net change*
Assets			
Cash	$ 471,000	$ 307,000	$ 164,000
Marketable equity securities, at cost	150,000	250,000	(100,000)
Allowance to reduce marketable equity securities to market	(10,000)	(25,000)	15,000
Accounts receivable, net	550,000	515,000	35,000
Inventories	810,000	890,000	(80,000)
Investment in Top Corp., at equity	420,000	390,000	30,000
Property, plant, and equipment ...	1,145,000	1,070,000	75,000
Accumulated depreciation	(345,000)	(280,000)	(65,000)
Patent, net	109,000	118,000	(9,000)
Total assets	$3,300,000	$3,235,000	$65,000
Liabilities and Stockholders' Equity			
Accounts payable and accrued liabilities	$ 845,000	$ 960,000	$ (115,000)
Note payable, long-term	600,000	900,000	(300,000)
Deferred income taxes	190,000	190,000	—
Common stock, $10 par value	850,000	650,000	200,000
Additional paid-in capital	230,000	170,000	60,000
Retained earnings	585,000	365,000	220,000
Total liabilities and stockholders' equity	$3,300,000	$3,235,000	$ 65,000

Additional Information:
- On January 2, year 8, Dover sold equipment costing $45,000, with a carrying amount of $28,000, for $18,000 cash.
- On March 31, year 8, Dover sold one of its marketable equity holdings for $119,000 cash. There were no other transactions involving marketable equity securities.
- On April 15, year 8, Dover issued 20,000 shares of its common stock for cash at $13 per share.
- On July 1, year 8, Dover purchased equipment for $120,000 cash.
- Dover's net income for year 8 is $305,000. Dover paid a cash dividend of $85,000 on October 26, year 8.
- Dover acquired a 20% interest in Tops Corporation's common stock during year 5. There was no goodwill attributable to the investment which is appropriately accounted for by the equity method. Tops reported net income of $150,000 for the year ended December 31, year 8. No dividend was paid on Tops' common stock during year 8.

Required:
Prepare an analysis evaluating the financial feasibility of management's plans. (Hint: Prepare a statement of cash flows by use of T-accounts or another method, as a basis for applying the adjustments which the analysis requires.)

13-18. Following the completion of the acquisition of Kraft, Philip Morris released its 1988 year-end financial statements.

The portfolio managers of O'Hara's firm, Green Securities, have complained in the past that "sources and uses of funds" statements are inadequate as indicators of a company's true cash flow. O'Hara is aware that *Statement of Financial Accounting Standards (SFAS) 95*, that became effective in 1988, requires companies to prepare a Statement of Cash Flows showing cash flows from operating, investing, and financing activities.

Required:
A. Using *only* the actual 1988 financial data contained in Tables 1 through 3, prepare a Statement of Cash Flows for Philip Morris Companies based on the format utilized in *SFAS 95*.

   (*Important Note:* The acquisition of Kraft requires that you remove the assets acquired and liabilities incurred as a result of that acquisition from the balance sheet changes used to prepare the Statement of Cash Flows. Philip Morris paid $11.383 billion for Kraft, net of cash acquired. A breakdown of the purchase of the purchase price is contained in Table 3.)
B. Based on your answer to Part A, compute Philip Morris' free cash flow for 1988, and discuss how free cash flow may impact the Company's future earnings and financial condition.

Table 1

PHILIP MORRIS COMPANIES, INC.
Balance Sheets
As of December 31
($ millions)

	1988	1987
Assets		
Cash and cash equivalents	$ 168	$ 90
Accounts receivable	2,222	2,065
Inventories	5,384	4,154
Current assets	$ 7,774	$ 6,309
Property, plant, & equipment (net)	8,648	6,582
Goodwill (net)	15,071	4,052
Investments	3,260	3,665
Total assets	$34,753	$20,608
Liabilities & Stockholders' Equity		
Short-term debt	$ 1,259	$ 1,440
Accounts payable	1,777	791
Accrued liabilities	3,848	2,277
Income taxes payable	1,089	727
Dividends payable	260	213
Current liabilities	$ 8,233	$ 5,448
Long-term debt	17,122	6,293
Deferred income taxes	1,719	2,044
Stockholders' equity	7,679	6,823
Total liabilities & stockholders' equity	$34,753	$20,608

Table 2

PHILIP MORRIS COMPANIES, INC.
Income Statement
For the Year Ending December 31, 1988
($ millions)

Sales	$31,742
Cost of goods sold	(12,156)
Selling and administrative expenses	(14,410)
Depreciation expense	(654)
Goodwill amortization	(125)
Interest expense	(670)
Pre-tax income	$ 3,727
Income tax expense	(1,390)
Net income	$ 2,337

Dividends declared $941 million

Table 3

PHILIP MORRIS PURCHASE OF KRAFT
Allocation of Purchase Price
($ millions)

Accounts receivable	$ 758
Inventories	1,232
Property, plant, and equipment	1,740
Goodwill	10,361
Short-term debt	(700)
Accounts payable	(578)
Accrued liabilities	(530)
Long-term debt	(900)
Purchase price (net of cash acquired)	$11,383

(CFA adapted)

13–19. Please refer to the financial statements of ZETA Corporation in Problem 23–5.

Required:
a. Prepare a worksheet to compute cash from operations on an inflow-outflow basis. Include revenues and expenses of discontinued operations. Include a list of important *assumptions* and *weaknesses* as a footnote to your cash statement. Support all amounts shown. (Hint: Discontinued operations cannot be separated from continuing operations, but unadjusted income and expense of discontinued operations can be segregated.)
b. ZETA's statement of cash flows discloses income taxes paid in year 6 of $2,600. Verify this amount independently.
c. Reconcile the change in "accounts payable and accruals" shown in the SCF with that which can be derived from the balance sheet. Explain clearly the reason for any difference. (Hint: refer to Notes 3 and 4.)

13–20. Please refer to the financial statements of Campbell Soup in Appendix 4B.

Required:
   In general, how is it possible for this company to have a net income of $401.5 million, but generate $805.2 million in cash from operations in 1991? Explain this in language which can be understood by a non-accountant. Illustrate your explanation by using only the major reconciling items.

13–21. Recast Campbell Soup's published statement of cash flows for 1991, so as to show cash from operations on an inflow-outflow basis. For the purposes of this assignment *only* assume the following:

a. The "Net change in other current assets and liabilities" ⬚63 of $30.6 is composed of the following assumed details:

Decrease in prepaid expenses	(25.3)
Decrease in accounts payable	42.8
Increase in taxes payable	(21.3)
Increase in accruals and payrolls	(26.8)
	($30.6)

b. Campbell disposed of a division in 1991 which had revenues of $7.5 million and an after-tax loss of $5.3 million. The loss is included in expenses. The CFO presentation should include revenues and expenses of discontinued operations in 1991.

13–22. Recast Campbell Soup's published statement of cash flows for 1990 so as to show:

I. Cash from operations on an inflow-outflow basis.
II. An adjusted analytical statement of cash flows subdivided into three major areas of activities.

For purposes of this assignment *only* assume that Campbell disposed of a division in 1990 which had revenues of $7.5 million and an after-tax loss of $5.3 million. The loss is included in expenses. The CFO presentation should include revenues and expenses of discontinued operations in 1990.

13–23. Please refer to the financial statements of Campbell Soup in Appendix 4B and in Chapter 23.

Required:
Prove that the changes in the company's balance sheets (beginning to end of fiscal 1990) are explained in the 1990 statement of cash flows.

Draw T-accounts for the balance sheet items showing the beginning and ending balances and one T-account for cash and temporary investments subdivided appropriately. Post all items shown in the 1990 SCF to these T-accounts in the order in which they appear there. "Key" each amount to an explanation using key references already provided. Use an "unexplained differences" T-account to accumulate all unexplained amounts and differences requiring further analysis. Analyze carefully all differences (hint: refer to footnotes and Form 10-K data and provide the best possible explanation for them, use format illustrated in text).

13–24. Please refer to the financial statements of Campbell Soup in Appendix 4B.

Required:
I. How much cash was collected from customers during 1990? (Hint: Use SCF to derive beginning balance of receivables.)

II. How much was *paid* in cash dividends on common stock during 1991?

III. How much was the total cost of goods and services produced and otherwise generated in 1991? Consider *all* inventories.

IV. How much was the deferred tax provision for 1991? What effect did it have on current liabilities?

V. What effect did the 1991 depreciation expense have on cash from operations?

VI. Why is the "Divestitures & restructuring" provisions in the SCF in 1990 added back to net income in arriving at cash from operations?

VII. What does the adjustment "effect of exchange rate changes on cash" represent?

VIII. Item 96 discusses the accounting for disposal of property. Where is the required adjustment of gain or loss found in the SCF?

13–25. Please refer to the financial statements of Quaker Oats (see Appendix 23).—Dollars in millions.

Required:

I. How much cash was collected from customers during 1990?

II. How much was paid in cash dividends on common stock during 1991?

III. How much was the cost of goods and services produced and otherwise generated in 1991? (Consider all inventories.)

IV. If the company had acquired property by issuing common stock, where in the SCF would this appear?

V. How much was the deferred tax provision for 1991? What effect did it have on current liabilities?

VI. What effect did the 1991 depreciation expense have on cash from operations? Discuss as fully as you can.

VII. (a) What does the ($97.8) adjustment for receivables in the 1991 SCF mean?

(b) What is the objective of the ($55.9) adjustment for changes in receivables in the 1990 SCF?

VIII. Does the CFO amount of $532.4 reported in 1991 include discontinued operations?

13–26. Please refer to the financial statements of Quaker Oats in Appendix 23.

Required:

Determine cash from operation for 1991, 1990, and 1989 under inflow-outflow approach. Use a worksheet to compute cash flow from operation and include income and expenses of discontinued operations.

13–27.   Please refer to the financial statements of Quaker Oats (Appendix 23).

Required:
  I.   In general, how it is possible for this company to have in 1991 a net
       income of $205.8 million but generate $532.4 million cash from opera-
       tions? (Describe in general using selected figures—do not merely repeat
       the calculation shown in the financial statements.)
  II. Where is the provision for uncollectible accounts probably included?
       How can this affect the presentation of the SCF?
  III. Of the $532.4 million reported in 1991 as cash generated by operations
       what is the best estimate of cash provided by continuing operations?

13–28.   Please refer to the financial statements of Quaker Oats in Appendix
23.

Required:
   Prove that the changes in the company's balance sheets (beginning to end of
fiscal 1991) are explained in the 1991 statement of cash flows.
   Draw T-accounts for the balance sheet items showing the beginning and ending
balances and one T-account for cash and temporary investments subdivided appropriately. Post all items shown in the 1991 SCF to these T-accounts in the
order in which they appear there. "Key" each amount to an explanation using
key references already provided. Use an "unexplained differences" T-account to
accumulate all unexplained amounts and differences requiring further analysis.
Analyze carefully all differences (hint: refer to footnotes, MDA, etc. and provide
the best possible explanation for them).

Chapter 14

14–1.   Financial reporting should provide information to help investors, creditors, and other users of financial statements.

Required:
 a. Describe the historical-cost/constant dollar (HC/CD) method of accounting.
     Include in your discussion how historical-cost amounts are used to make
     HC/CD measurements.
 b. Describe the principal advantage of the HC/CD method of accounting
     over the historical-cost method of accounting.
 c. Describe the current cost method of accounting.
 d. Why would depreciation expense for a given year differ using the current
     cost method of accounting instead of the historical-cost method of ac-
     counting? Include in your discussion whether depreciation expense is likely
     to be higher or lower using the current cost method of accounting instead
     of the historical-cost method of accounting in a period of rising prices, and
     why.

14–2.   You have deposited $20,000 in a savings account at a local bank on
January 2, year 1. The balance on December 31, year 1, is $21,200. You made

no withdrawals during the year. The general price-level index on January 1, year 1, was 110, but it increased to 121 by December 31, year 1. Inflation progressed evenly throughout the year.

Required:
a. Compute the interest rate and amount of interest earned.
b. Compute the loss due to inflation on principal, if any.
c. Compute the net increase or decrease in your wealth caused by the savings account, inclusive of interest earned.

14–3. On January 1, year 2, Trek Company, sole proprietorship, was formed. Mr. Trek contributed $200,000 cash. On the same day, land and a building were purchased for $50,000 and $200,000, respectively, paid for by $150,000 cash and $100,000 mortgage. No payments were made on the mortgage, and no other transactions occurred during the year. The consumer price index was 150 on January 1, year 2, and 165 on December 31, year 2. Depreciation is computed at 4 percent, straight line (no salvage value).

Required:
Prepare the balance sheet, restated for general price-level changes, at December 31, year 2, and any necessary schedules to accompany it.

14–4. Following are the conventional financial statements of Eddy Company for year 2:

EDDY COMPANY
Income Statement
For the Year Ended December 31, Year 2
(in thousands)

Sales		$400,000
Cost of goods sold:		
Beginning inventory	$ 35,000	
Purchases	135,000	
	170,000	
Less: Ending inventory	65,000	
Cost of goods sold		105,000
Gross profit		295,000
Selling and administrative expenses	50,000	
Depreciation expense	25,000	
Interest expense	25,000	100,000
Pretax income		195,000
Income tax expense		42,000
Net income		153,000

EDDY COMPANY
Comparative Balance Sheets
As of December 31, year 2, and year 1
(in thousands)

	Year 2	Year 1
Assets		
Current assets:		
Cash	$ 5,000	$ 10,000
Accounts receivable	30,000	25,000
Inventories	65,000	35,000
Total current assets	100,000	70,000
Property, plant, and equipment	270,000	270,000
Less: Accumulated depreciation	(75,000)	(50,000)
Total assets	$295,000	$290,000
Liabilities and Equity		
Liabilities:		
Current liabilities	$ 47,000	$ 46,000
Long-term debt	60,000	60,000
Deferred income taxes	3,000	8,000
Total liabilities	110,000	114,000
Equity:		
Capital stock	165,000	165,000
Retained earnings	20,000	11,000
Total equity	185,000	176,000
Total liabilities and equity	$295,000	$290,000

Additional information:

(1) The following are current cost estimates provided by management at December 31:

	Year 2	Year 1
Inventories	$ 75,000	$ 41,000
Property, plant, and equipment	300,000	290,000
Accumulated depreciation	(84,000)	(55,000)
For year ending December 31:		
Cost of goods sold at dates of sale	150,000	
Depreciation expense	30,000	

(2) Sales, purchases, expenses (except depreciation), taxes, and dividends are assumed to have occurred evenly throughout the year.

Required:
Develop a worksheet to prepare CC/ND financial statements for Eddy Company for year 2.

14–5.   Some companies and industries show comparatively small differences between earnings per share, as reported in their annual reports, and "current cost earnings."

Required:
List and briefly explain *seven* financial characteristics of companies that would tend to *reduce* the differences between earnings per share, as reported in their annual reports, and "current cost earnings."

(CFA adapted)

14–6.   Financial policies that are advantageous in an extended inflationary period can lead to liquidity problems for a corporation in a business slowdown.

Required:
a.   Illustrate this point by discussing appropriate balance sheet items.
b.   How can inflation result in overstating net income?
c.   How can inflation result in overstating a company's return on net worth?

(CFA)

Chapter 16

16–1.   The questions that follow are based on the financial statements of Quaker Oats (Appendix 23):

I. *(a)*   Construct a table containing the following short-term liquidity ratios for the three-year period 1989–1991
Current ratio.
Acid-test ratio.
Cash and cash equivalents to total current assets.
Average accounts receivable turnover.
Average collection period.
Average inventory turnover.
Average number of days to sell inventory.
Average number of days to pay accounts payable.
Average conversion period
Net trade cycle.
Liquidity index.
Cash provided by operations to current liabilities.
(b)   Based on your table in *(a)* above, present your best possible analysis and evaluation of short-term liquidity of the company.

II. Management projects for 1992 a 15 percent growth in sales, purchases, and expenses. The average inventory turnover for 1992 is expected to be 6.5. To achieve these operating goals, management will set the receivable collection period to 40 days, based on year-end accounts receivable. Ending accounts payable for 1992 will be $380 and accounts payable turnover will be 8. $40 million in notes are to be paid off. Management desires to maintain a minimum cash balance of $70 million. Effective income tax rate for 1992 is expected to be 45 percent and 10 percent of tax expense is expected to be deferred. Dividends on preferred stock will be $4.3 million and on common stock will be $128 million.

Required:

Will the company have to borrow in 1992? (Hint: Prepare a projected income statement and cash flow statement for 1992.)

16–2.   Please refer to the financial statements of Campbell Soup in Appendix 4B.

Required:
I. Compute the following for 1990:
    1. Current ratio
    2. Acid-test ratio
    3. Accounts receivable turnover*
    4. Inventory turnover†
    5. Average collection period of ending accounts receivable
    6. Days to sell ending inventory
    7. Conversion period
    8. Cash‡ to current assets
    9. Cash‡ to current liabilities
    10. Liquidity index (assume prepaid expenses last for 100 days)
    11. Number of days to pay ending accounts payable
    12. Net trade cycle
    13. Cash provided by operations to current liabilities
II. Compute for 1990 ratios 1, 4, 5, 6, and 7 above using inventories valued on a FIFO basis (the 7/89 FIFO inventory was $904).
III. *a.* What are the limitations of the current ratio as a measure of short-term liquidity?
     b. How can the analysis of other, related, measures enhance the usefulness of the current ratio?

* Accounts Receivable ending fiscal 1989 were $538.0.
† Ending Inventory for fiscal 1989 was $816.0.
‡ Plus cost equivalent.

16–3.   The Lux company had the following unrelated transactions during year 1.

(The present current ratio is 2:1 and quick ratio is 1.2:1.)

1. Determined that $5,000 of accounts receivable were uncollectible.

2. The bank notified the company that a customer's check for $411 had been returned marked "insufficient funds." The customer went bankrupt.
3. The owners of the company made an additional cash investment of $7,500.
4. Inventory which had cost of $600 was considered obsolete when the physical inventory was taken.
5. Declared a $5,000 cash dividend to be paid during the first week of the next accounting period.
6. The company purchased a long-term investment for cash, $10,000.
7. Accounts payable of $9,000 were paid in cash.
8. The company borrowed $1,200 from the bank and gave a 90-day, 6 percent promissory note.
9. Sold a vacant lot that had been used in the business for cash, $20,000.
10. Purchased a three-year insurance policy for $1,500.

Required:
Considering the above transactions separately, and only the immediate effect, how would each affect the company's:

a. Current ratio
b. Quick ratio (acid-test ratio)
c. Working capital

16–4. State the effect of the events or transactions that follow on the following ratios. Consider each transaction or event independently.
A. Accounts receivable turnover ratio. (3 before the event)
B. Collection period.
C. Inventory turnover ratio. (3 before the event)

The three columns to the right of the transactions that follow are identified as (A), (B), and (C) and correspond to the three measures above. For each transaction or event, indicate the effect in each of the three columns as follows: I for increase, D for decrease, and N for no effect.

	A	B	C
1. Beginning inventory understatement of $500 is now being corrected.	____	____	____
2. Sales on account were under-recorded by $10,000.	____	____	____
3. $10,000 of accounts receivable were written off by charge to the allowance for doubtful accounts.	____	____	____
4. $10,000 accounts receivable were written off using the direct write-off method.	____	____	____

5. Under the lower-of-cost-or-market
   method, inventory was reduced
   to market by $1,000.   _____ _____ _____
6. Beginning inventory overstatement
   of $500 is now being corrected.   _____ _____ _____

16–5.   State the effect of the events or transactions that follow on the following
ratios. Consider each transaction or event independently.
A.   Accounts receivable turnover ratio. (4 before the event)
B.   Collection period.
C.   Inventory turnover ratio. (4 before the event)

The three columns to the right of the transactions that follow are identified
as (A), (B), and (C) and correspond to the three measures above. For each transaction or event, indicate the effect in each of the three columns as follows: I for
increase, D for decrease, and N for no effect.

		A	*B*	*C*
1.	$5,000 of accounts receivable were written off by charge to the allowance for doubtful accounts.	_____	_____	_____
2.	Beginning inventory understatement of $1,000 is now being corrected.	_____	_____	_____
3.	Under the lower-of-cost-or-market method, inventory was reduced to market by $2,000.	_____	_____	_____
4.	Obsolete inventory of $3,000 was found and written off.	_____	_____	_____
5.	Beginning inventory overstatement of $2,000 is now being corrected.	_____	_____	_____
6.	Sales on account were overstated by $10,000 and are now being corrected.	_____	_____	_____

16–6.   Forward Company presents the following balances on 12/31 Year 1

	Debit	Credit
Cash	$ 42,000	
Accounts receivable	90,000	
Inventory	39,000	
Fixed assets	120,000	
Notes payable		$ 21,000
Accrued taxes		10,800
Accumulated depreciation		25,800
Capital stock		120,000
Accounts payable		78,000

The following additional information is available for year 1:

Sales	450,000
Cost of goods sold (excluding depreciation)	312,000
Purchases	210,000
Depreciation	15,000
Net income	12,000

For year 2 the company anticipates a growth of 5 percent in sales. To counter-balance this low growth rate, the company has implemented cost-cutting strategies which are expected to reduce cost of goods sold by 2 percent from the year 1 level. All other expenses are expected to increase by 5 percent. Expected net income for year 2 is $20,000. The ending year 2 inventory is estimated to be $90,000 and there will be no balance in accrued taxes. The company needs $175,000 to buy new equipment. The minimum desired cash balance is $30,000. The company offers a discount of 2 percent if payment is received in 10 days. It is expected that 10 percent of the sales will be collected with this discount. The remaining 90 percent will be collected on average in 60 days.

Required:
Prepare a cash forecast for year 2. Will Forward Company have to borrow?

16–7. Fax Corporation presents the following income statement and balance sheet for the year ended December 31, Year 1:

FAX CORPORATION
Income Statement
For the Year Ended December 31, year 1

Net sales		960,000
Cost of goods sold (excluding depreciation)		550,000
Gross margin		410,000
Depreciation	30,000	
Selling and administrative expenses	160,000	190,000
Income before taxes		220,000
Income taxes (state and federal)		105,600
Net income		114,400

FAX CORPORATION
Balance Sheet
As of December 31, year 1

Assets

Current assets:

Cash	$ 30,000	
Marketable securities	5,500	
Accounts receivable	52,000	
Inventory	112,500	
Total current assets		$200,000
Plant and equipment	630,000	
Less: Accumulated depreciation	130,000	500,000
Total assets		$700,000

Liabilities and Equity

Current liabilities:

Accounts payable	60,000	
Notes Payable	50,000	
Total current liabilities		$110,000 .
Long-term debt		150,000
Equity:		
Capital stock	250,000	
Retained earnings	190,000	440,000
Total liabilities and equity		$700,000

Additional information:
1. Purchases in year 1 were $480,000.
2. In year 2, management expects 15 percent growth in sales and a 10 percent increase in all expenses except for depreciation which will increase by only 5 percent.
3. Management expects an average inventory turnover ratio of 5.5 for year 2.
4. A receivable collection period of 90 days, based on year-end accounts receivable, is planned for year 2.
5. Income taxes at the same rate on pre-tax income as in year 1 will be paid in cash.
6. The ending balance of notes payable on 12/31/year 2 will be $30,000.
7. Long-term debt of $25,000 will be paid in cash in year 2.
8. Fax desires a minimum cash balance of $20,000 in year 2.
9. The ratio of accounts payable to purchases will remain the same in year 2 as it was in year 1.
10. All selling and administration expenses will be paid in cash in year 2.
11. In year 2, the ending balance of marketable securities and equity accounts will remain the same as they were in year 1.

Required:

a. Prepare a statement of expected cash inflows and outflows for year ending 12/31/year 2.

b. Will Fax Corporation have to borrow in year 2?

16–8.   Below are some of the accounts of RAM Corporation as of December 31, year 1:

	Debit	Credit
Cash	$ 80,000	
Accounts receivable	150,000	
Inventory	65,000	
Accounts payable		$130,000
Notes payable		35,000
Accrued taxes		20,000
Fixed assets	200,000	
Accumulated depreciation		45,000
Capital stock		200,000

The following additional information is available for year 1:

Sales	$800,000
Cost of sales	520,000
Purchases	350,000
Depreciation	25,000
Net income	20,000

The company anticipates a growth of 10 percent in sales for the coming year. All corresponding revenue and expense items will also increase by 10 percent, except for depreciation which will remain the same. All expenses are paid in cash as they are incurred during the year. Year 2 ending inventory will be $150,000. By the end of year 2 the company expects to have a notes payable balance of $50,000 and no balance in the accrued taxes account. The company maintains a minimum cash balance of $50,000 as a managerial policy.

Required:

Consider each of the following circumstances separately and independently of each other and focus only on changes described.

I.   Assume the company is considering to change its credit policy so that the ending accounts receivable represent 90 days of sales. What would be the impact of this policy on the company's current financial position? Will the company have to borrow?

II.   Assume the change is to a 120-day collection period based on ending accounts receivable. What will the effect be?

III. Assume that the suppliers change their policy of extending credit to RAM so that payment on purchases must be made within 60 days, and there is no change in the collection period.

(Suggested approach: Determine first what the cash forecast for year 2 is. Then proceed to calculate the effect of each of the three alternative scenarios.)

16-9. Kopp Corporation presents the following income statement and balance sheet for the year end December 31, year 1:

KOPP CORPORATION
Income Statement
For the Year Ended December 31, year 1

Net sales		960,000
Cost of goods sold		550,000
Gross margin		410,000
Depreciation	30,000	
Selling and administrative expenses	160,000	190,000
Income before taxes		220,000
Income taxes (48%)		57,600
Net income		162,400

KOPP CORPORATION
Balance Sheet
As of December 31, year 1

Assets

Current assets:		
Cash	$ 30,000	
Marketable securities	6,000	
Accounts receivable	52,000	
Inventory	112,000	
Total current assets		$200,000
Plant and equipment	630,000	
Less: Accumulated depreciation	130,000	500,000
Total assets		$700,000

Liabilities and Equity

Current liabilities:		
Accounts payable	$ 60,000	
Notes payable	50,000	
Total current liabilities		$110,000
Long-term debt		150,000
Equity:		
Capital stock	250,000	
Retained earnings	190,000	440,000
Total liabilities and equity		$700,000

Additional information:
1. Purchases in year 1 were $450,000.
2. In year 2, management expects 15 percent growth in sales and a 10 percent increase in all expenses except for depreciation which will increase by only 5 percent.
3. Average inventory turnover for year 1 was 5, and management expects an average inventory turnover ratio of 6 for year 2.
4. A receivable collection period of 90 days, based on year-end accounts receivable, is planned for year 2.
5. Income taxes at the same rate on pre-tax income as in year 1 will be paid in cash.
6. Notes payable of $20,000 will be paid during year 2.
7. Long-term debt of $25,000 will be repaid in cash in year 2.
8. Yankee desires a minimum cash balance of $20,000 in year 2.
9. The ratio of accounts payable to purchases will remain the same in year 2 as it was in year 1.

Required:
a. Prepare a statement of expected cash inflows and outflows.
b. Will Kopp Corporation have to borrow in year 2?

16–10. Given below are some balances at the end of year 5 and some estimated balances at the end of year 6 for Top Corporation:

	Year 5	Year 6
Cash	35,000	?
Accounts receivable	75,000	?
Inventory	32,000	75,000
Accounts payable	65,000	122,000
Notes payable	17,500	15,000
Accrued taxes	9,000	0
Fixed assets	100,000	100,000
Accumulated depreciation	21,500	25,000
Capital stock	100,000	100,000

You are also given the following information for year 6:

1. Estimated sales   412,500
2. Cost of sales   70%
3. Net income   10,000
4. Ending accounts receivable is 90 days of sales.

Required:
Assuming that all expenses are paid in cash when incurred, and that cost of sales is exclusive of depreciation, estimate the ending cash balance for year 6. If the company desires to maintain a minimum cash balance of $50,000, will it be required to borrow?

16–11. The Ian Manufacturing Company was organized five years ago and manufactures toys. Its most recent three years' balance sheets and income statements are presented below.

IAN MANUFACTURING COMPANY
Comparative Condensed Balance Sheets
As of June 30, year 5, year 4, and year 3

	Year 5	Year 4	Year 3
Assets			
Cash	$ 12,000	$ 15,000	$ 16,000
Accounts receivable, net	183,000	80,000	60,000
Inventory	142,000	97,000	52,000
Other current assets	5,000	6,000	4,000
Plant and equipment (net)	160,000	110,000	70,000
Total assets	$ 502,000	$ 308,000	$ 202,000
Liabilities and Equity			
Accounts payable.................	$ 147,800	$ 50,400	$ 22,000
Federal income tax payable	30,000	14,400	28,000
Long-term liabilities	120,000	73,000	22,400
Common stock, $5 par value	110,000	110,000	80,000
Retained earnings	94,200	60,200	49,600
Total liabilities and equity	$ 502,000	$ 308,000	$ 202,000

IAN MANUFACTURING COMPANY
Condensed Income Statements
For the Years Ended June 30, year 5, year 4, and year 3

	Year 5	Year 4	Year 3
Net sales	$1,684,000	$1,250,000	$1,050,000
Cost of goods sold	927,000	810,000	512,000
Gross margin on sales	757,000	440,000	538,000
Marketing and administrative costs ..	670,000	396,700	467,760
Operating income	87,000	43,300	70,240
Interest cost	12,000	7,300	2,240
Income before federal income tax ...	75,000	36,000	68,000
Income tax	30,000	14,400	28,000
Net income	$ 45,000	$ 21,600	$ 40,000

A reconciliation of its retained earnings for the years ended June 30, year 4, and June 30, year 5, is as follows:

IAN MANUFACTURING COMPANY
Statement of Retained Earnings
For the Years Ended June 30, year 5, and year 4

	Year 5	Year 4
Balance, beginning	$ 60,200	$49,600
Add: Net income	45,000	21,600
Subtotal	105,200	71,200
Deduct: Dividends paid	11,000	11,000
Balance, ending	$ 94,200	$60,200

Additional information:
1. All sales are on account.
2. Long-term liabilities are owed to the firm's bank.
3. The firm's terms of sale are net 30 days.

Required:
a. Compute the following for year 4 and year 5:
   (1) Working capital.
   (2) Current ratio.
   (3) Acid-test ratio.
   (4) Accounts receivable turnover.
   (5) Collection period of receivables.
   (6) Inventory-turnover ratio.
   (7) Days to sell inventory.
   (8) Debt to equity ratio.
   (9) Times interest earned.
b. Using year 3 as the base year, compute an index-number trend series for:
   (1) Sales.
   (2) Cost of goods sold.
   (3) Gross margin.
   (4) Marketing and administrative costs.
   (5) Net income.
c. Based on your above analyses, would you advise the bank to grant a loan? Write a brief report giving the reasons for your recommendation.

16–12. L. G. Sprout is an investment analyst at Valley Insurance. Bob Jollie, a CFA and Sprout's superior, recently requested that Sprout prepare a report on Giant Corporation's solvency. Giant Corporation is a manufacturer of heavy equipment for the agricultural, forestry, and mining industries. Most of its plant capacity is located in the United States and a majority of its sales are exported to foreign markets. Giant Corporation's investment bankers are offering Valley Insurance a participation in a private placement debenture issue.

In addition to traditional ratio analysis, Sprout's memo to Jollie highlighted the following points:

- The company has a 2 to 1 current ratio.
- During the last fiscal year, working capital increased by a substantial amount.
- Although earnings are not at record levels, rigorous cost control has resulted in an acceptable level of profitability, thus providing the basis for continued corporate solvency.

Jollie, upon reading Sprout's memo, dismissed it as being "totally inadequate," *not* because it did not include a quantitative analysis of financial ratios, but because it did not effectively address the matter of corporate solvency.

He then went on to lecture Sprout with respect to the nature and significance of corporate solvency:

"... Solvency is a cash phenomenon. Solvency analysis is a process of evaluating the risk of whether a company can pay its debts as they come due. The vagaries and inconsistencies of working capital definitions do not adequately address this issue. Further, 'funds' as defined as working capital simply account for the change in a company's working capital position, and therefore add little to the assessment of solvency."

Required:
a. List *five* key items of information which may directly impact Giant's solvency that Sprout should attempt to derive from the company's financial statements and management interviews.
b. Identify *five* qualitative financial and economic assessments specific to Giant and its industry that Sprout should consider in further analyzing Giant's solvency.

(CFA)

16–13.   The management of Fast Corporation wants to improve the appearance of their current position, that is, current and quick ratios, on their financial statements.

Required:
a. List and briefly describe four ways in which they might accomplish this goal.
b. For each, state the procedures, if any, that an analyst can use to detect these window-dressing devices.

(CFA)

16–14.   As a lending officer for the Prudent Bank you were handed the financial statements of Zeta Corporation (see Problem 23–5), which has applied for a loan. Your superior wants you to evaluate Zeta's short-term liquidity based on the limited two-year information supplied. (All dollar amounts in thousands.)

The following additional information applies to this problem only:

Inventory at January 1, year 5	$32,000
Accruals:	
Year 5	3,000
Year 6	4,000

Required:
I. Compute the following for year 5 and year 6:
   (a) Current ratio.
   (b) Collection period (use ending accounts receivable).
   (c) Inventory turnover.
   (d) Days to sell inventory (use ending inventory).
   (e) Days' purchases in accounts payable (simplifying assumption: all cost of sales items are purchased).
   (f) Funds provided by operations to current liabilities.
   (g) The liquidity index (base number of days to sell inventory on cost of goods sold; assume prepaid expenses are 90 days removed from cash).
II. Comment on the significance of the year-to-year change.

Chapter 17

17-1. The questions that follow are based on the financial statements of Quaker Oats (Appendix 23).

Required:
Prepare a projected income statement for 1992 given the following assumptions (dollars in millions.)

a. It is estimated that revenues will be $6,000 in 1992.
b. Cost of sales is estimated to be at a level representing the average percentage of cost of sales to sales as prevailed in the four-year period ending June 30, 1991.
c. Selling, general, and administrative expense in 1992 are expected to increase by the same percentage as these expenses increased from 1990 to 1991.
d. Other expenses are expected to be 8 percent higher in 1992 than in 1991.
e. There will be a $2 million loss net of taxes from the disposal of net assets from discontinued operations in 1992.
f. Interest expense net of interest capitalized and interest income will increase by 6 percent due to increased financial needs.
g. The effective tax rate in 1992 will equal that of 1991.

17-2. Please refer to the financial statements of Quaker Oats (Appendix 23).

Required:

I. Based on the financial statements of Quaker Oats and your analytical skills, please prepare a forecast of the Projected Statement of Cash for Quaker Oats for 1992 based on the following assumptions:

Forecast
(in millions)

		1992
Sources of cash:		
Assets retirements	$	20
Uses of cash:		
Repayment of long-term debt		45
Capital expenditures:		
PP&E		300
Cash dividends on capital stock		135
Other changes		30
Other projections:		
Revenues		6000

Assumptions:

The remaining sources and uses of cash will be estimated based on the following assumptions:

a. Income from continuing operations in 1992 will be at a level representing the average percentage of income from continuing operations to sales as prevailed in the three-year period ended June 30, 1991.

b. Depreciation and amortization in 1992 will bear the same relationship to net income as has the average depreciation and amortization borne to income from continuing operations over the period 1989–91. This was determined to be 82.33 percent.

c. Deferred income taxes (noncurrent portion) and other items will be in 1992 at a level that reflects the past three years' relationship of deferred taxes (noncurrent) and other items to total income from continuing operations.

d. Assume the provision for restructuring charges will be zero in 1992.

e. Assume 42-day-collection period for 1992; therefore, A/R turnover = 8.5.

f. Assume inventory turnover is 6.5 and percentage of cost of sales to sales is 0.51 and that these rates will prevail in 1992.

g. Change in the other current assets is the same as the average increase/decrease over the past 3 years.

h. Assume A/P turnover to be 8 for 1991 and 1992 and that purchases will increase in 1992 12 percent over 1991.

i. The change in other current liabilities is the same as the average increase/decrease over the past 3 years.

j. There will be no more changes related to Fisher-Price and assume no change in net current assets of discontinued operations.

k. Decrease in the short-term debt is estimated at 40 million each year.

l. Assume there will be no cash inflows from issuance of debt for spin-off and no cash effect on purchase and issuance of common and preferred stock.

m. The assumed year-end cash needs will be at a level that is measured by the ratio of cash to revenues reflecting the cash to revenue ratio that prevailed in 1991.

n. Addition to long-term debt in 1992 will be at the level needed to meet the needed year-end cash balance.

17–3. Please refer to the financial statements of Quaker Oats (Appendix 23).

Required:

I. By means of common size statements (total sources = 100%) analyze the statements of cash flows of Quaker Oats, covering the three-year period ending June 30, 1991. Discuss the major sources and major uses of cash.

17–4. Please refer to the financial statements of Quaker Oats. (Appendix 23).

Required:

I. Please compute cash flow adequacy ratio of Quaker Oats for 1991. To remove cyclical and other erratic influences, a three-year total should be used in the computation of the ratio.

II. Discuss the importance and significance of the cash flow adequacy ratio.

III. Please compute Cash from Operations Reinvestment ratio of Quaker Oats for 1991 and 1990.

IV. Discuss the importance and significance of the Cash from Operations Reinvestment ratio.

17–5. The Lion Corporation is a merchandising concern. The following data have been gathered for the month of July. Prepare a cash budget for the month (amounts are in thousands).

Cash on hand, July 1, year 6	$ 20
Accounts receivable, July 1, year 6	20
Sales for July (forecast)	150
Expected accounts receivable, July 31, year 6	21
Gross profit, 20 percent of cost of goods sold	
Inventory, July 1, year 6	25
Desired inventory, July 31, year 6	15
Depreciation on expense	4
Miscellaneous outlays	11
Minimum cash balance desired	30
Accounts payable, July 1, year 6	18

Other information:
(1) All inventory is bought on the first day of the month and received the following week.
(2) Lion Corporation ordinarily pays 75 percent within the month of purchase and the balance in the following month.
(3) All other expenses are paid in cash.

17–6.   Toro Corporation, a newly formed corporation, will begin its operations on January 1, year 3. The following information is available for the development of its six months' estimated performance covering the period January 1 to June 30, year 2.

1.	Expected monthly sales	$250,000
2.	Monthly operating expenses (all paid in cash except as indicated)	
	a. Manufacturing labor	30,500
	b. Rent for building	10,000
	c. Overhead costs	22,500
	d. Depreciation	35,000
	e. Amortization of patents	500
	f. Selling and administrative expenses	47,500
	g. Purchase of materials	125,000
3.	Other information:	
	a. terms of sale	n/30
	b. collection period expected to be	45 days
	c. purchase terms	n/30
	d. ending finished goods inventory (no goods in process)	100,000
	e. ending raw material inventory	35,000
	f. accrued taxes (50% effective rate)	as incurred
	g. beginning cash balance was $60,000 and minimum cash balance required is $40,000	
	h. prepaid expenses on June 30, year 2 are expected to be $7,000	

Required
    Develop a pro forma operating statement and balance sheet in order to portray the expected financial position of Toro at the end of the six-month period. Assume
(1) No inventory in process on June 30, year 2.
(2) Sales are made evenly.
(3) All expenses are paid in cash.
(4) Balance sheet on January 1, year 2:

Cash	60,000
Equipment	1,200,000
Patents	40,000
Equity	1,300,000

17–7. Miller Company is planning to construct a two-unit facility for the loading of iron ore into ships. On or before January 1, year 2, the stockholders will invest $100,000 in the company's capital stock to provide its initial working capital. To finance the construction program (the total planned cost of which is $1,800,000), the company will obtain a commitment from a lending organization for a loan of $1,800,000. This loan is to be secured by a 10-year mortgage note bearing interest at 5 percent per year on the unpaid balance. The principal amount of the loan is to be repaid in equal semiannual installments of $100,000 beginning June 30, year 3.

Inasmuch as the proceeds of the loan will only be required as construction work progresses, the company has agreed to pay a commitment fee beginning January 1, year 2 equal to 1 percent per year on the unused portion of the loan commitment. This fee is payable at the time amounts are "drawn down," except at the time of the first "draw-down."

Work on the construction of the facility will commence in the fall of year 1. The first payment to the contractors will be due on January 1, year 2, at which time the commitment and loan agreement will become effective and the company will make its first "draw-down," for payment to the contractors, in the amount of $800,000. As construction progresses, additional payments will be made to the contractors by "drawing down" the remaining loan proceeds as follows (it is assumed that payment to the contractors will be made on the same dates as the loan proceeds are "drawn down"):

April 1, year 2	$500,000
July 1, year 2	300,000
December 31, year 2	100,000
April 1, year 3	100,000

Because of weather conditions, the facility can operate only from April 1 through November 30 of each year. The construction program will permit the completion of the first of the two plant units (capable of handling 5,000,000 tons) in time for its use during the year 2 shipping season. The second unit (capable of handling an additional 3,000,000 tons) will be completed in time for the year 3 season. It is expected that 5,000,000 tons will be handled by the facility during the year 2 season; thereafter, the tonnage handled is expected to increase in each subsequent year by 300,000 tons until a level of 6,500,000 tons is reached.

The company's revenues will be derived by charging the consignees of the ore for its services at a fixed rate per ton loaded. Billing terms will be net, 10 days. Based upon past experience with similar facilities elsewhere, it is expected that Miller Company's operating profit should average $0.04 per ton before charges for interest, finance charges, and depreciation totaling $0.03 per ton.

Required:
A cash forecast for each of three calendar years starting with year 2 to demonstrate the sufficiency of cash, to be obtained from (1) the sale of capital stock, (2) "draw-downs" on the loan, and (3) the amount to be produced by the operating facility, to cover payments to the contractor and on the debt principal and interest.

17–8. Royal Manufacturing Co. has incurred substantial losses for several years, and has become insolvent. On March 31, year 5, Royal petitioned the court for protection from creditors, and submitted the following statement of financial position:

ROYAL MANUFACTURING CO.
Statement of Financial Position
March 31, year 5

	Book value	Liquidation value
Assets:		
Accounts receivable	$100,000	$ 50,000
Inventories	90,000	40,000
Plant and equipment	150,000	160,000
Totals	$340,000	$250,000
Liabilities and Stockholders' Equity:		
Accounts payable—general creditors	$600,000	
Common stock outstanding	60,000	
Deficit	(320,000)	
Total	$340,000	

Royal's management informed the court that the company has developed a new product, and that a prospective customer is willing to sign a contract for the purchase of 10,000 units of this product during the year ending March 31, year 6, 12,000 units of this product during the year ending March 31, year 7, and 15,000 units of this product during the year ending March 31, year 8, at a price of $90 per unit. This product can be manufactured using Royal's present facilities. Monthly production with immediate delivery is expected to be uniform within each year. Receivables are expected to be collected during the calendar month following sales.

Unit production costs of the new product are expected to be as follows:

Direct materials	$20
Direct labor	30
Variable overhead	10

Fixed costs (excluding depreciation) will amount to $130,000 per year.

Purchases of direct materials will be paid during the calendar month following purchase. Fixed costs, direct labor, and variable overhead will be paid as incurred. Inventory of direct materials will be equal to 60 days' usage. After the first month of operations, 30 days' usage of direct materials will be ordered each month.

The general creditors have agreed to reduce their total claims to 60 percent of their March 31, year 5 balances, under the following conditions:

- Existing accounts receivable and inventories are to be liquidated immediately, with the proceeds turned over to the general creditors.
- The balance of reduced accounts payable is to be paid as cash is generated from future operations, but in no event later than March 31, year 7. No interest will be paid on these obligations.

Under this proposed plan, the general creditors would receive $110,000 more than the current liquidation value of Royal's assets. The court has engaged you to determine the feasibility of this plan.

Required:
Ignoring any need to borrow and repay short-term funds for working capital purposes, prepare a cash budget for the years ending March 31, year 6 and year 7 showing the cash expected to be available to pay the claims of the general creditors, payments to general creditors, and the cash remaining after payment of claims.

(AICPA adapted)

17–9. The senior loan officer of your employer, The Pacific Bank, hands you the following data and information supplied by the Union Corporation, which has applied for a loan.

Current assets:	
Cash on deposit	$ 12,000
Inventory	63,600
Accounts receivable	10,000
Plant and equipment—net	100,000
Current liabilities	–0–
Recent and anticipated sales:	
September year 6	40,000
October year 6	48,000
November year 6	60,000
December year 6	80,000
January year 7	36,000

Sales are 75 percent for cash and 25 percent on account. Receivables are collected in full in the month following the month in which the sales occur. Thus the accounts receivable balance of $10,000 as of 30 September year 6 are the result of sales on account during September.

Gross profit averages 30 percent of sales before considering purchase discounts. Thus the gross invoice cost of goods sold is 70 percent of sales.

Salaries and wages average 15 percent of sales, rent average 5 percent of sales, and all other expenses except depreciation average 4 percent of sales; these expenses involve cash disbursements in the same month in which they are incurred. Depreciation expense is $750 per month, computed on a straight-line basis.

The basic inventory is $30,000. Union Corporation follows the policy of purchasing each month additional inventory sufficient to provide for the anticipated sales of the following month. Purchase terms are 2/10, n/30. Since purchases are made in the early portion of the month and all discounts are taken, payments are invariably made in the month of purchase.

Plant and equipment expenditures are budgeted as $600 in October and $400 in November; depreciation thereon will not be recorded until year 7.

A minimum cash balance of $8,000 is to be maintained. Any borrowings are made at the beginning of the month and any repayments are made at the end of the month of repayment, both in multiples of $1,000 (excluding interest). Interest is paid only at the time principal is repaid, at the rate of 6 percent per year.

Required:

(I) On the basis of the data given above, the loan officer requests that you prepare schedules for the months of October, November, December, and the quarter of:
  A. Estimated cash receipts.
  B. Estimated cash disbursements for purchases. (Note that purchases are 70 percent of sales of the following month.)
  C. Estimated cash disbursements for operating expenses.
  D. Estimated total cash disbursements.
  E. Estimated cash receipts and disbursements.
  F. Financing required.

(II) Prepare for the fourth quarter of year 6:
  a. A forecasted income statement.
  b. A forecasted balance sheet.

Chapter 18

18–1.   Please refer to the financial statements of Quaker Oats (Appendix 23).

Required:

I. Compute the following ratios for 1989–1991. Use the statutory income tax rate in all ratios except the fixed charge coverage ratios for which you are to use the effective tax rate. Consider all deferred taxes as liabilities. Assume fixed charges include interest portion of operating rental expense, which is ¹/₃ of the operating lease expense.
  A. Financial leverage index.
  B. Total long-term debt to equity capital.
  C. Total liabilities to total liabilities and equity capital.
  D. Total liabilities to equity capital.
  E. Preferred stock to total owners' equity (use stated value of preferred stock for all years).
  F. The analytically adjusted ratio of long-term debt to equity—1990 only. (Consider 50 percent of deferred income taxes as debt for this part only).
  G. Earnings coverage of fixed charges.
  H. Cash flow coverage of fixed charges.
  I. Cash from operations to total debt.

    J. Earnings coverage of preferred dividends.
    K. Equity capital to net fixed assets.
  II. Comment on the significance of the level as well as the trend of the above measures and ratios.

18–2.   Please refer to the financial statements of Quaker Oats (Appendix 23).

Required:
  I. Using Quaker Oats' average common stock market price for 1991 (item 13) compute the ratio of total liabilities to common equity at market value.
  II. Discuss the importance and significance of ratios based on the equity capital at market value.

18–3.   Please refer to the financial statements of Campbell Soup in Appendix 4B.
    Assume that 50 percent of deferred income taxes will reverse in the foreseeable future. (The balance should be considered as equity.)

Required:
  I. Compute the following for 1990.
      1. Total debt to equity capital.
      2. Total debt to total capital.
      3. Long-term liabilities to equity capital.
      4. Analytically adjusted long-term debt to equity ratio.
      5. Total equity capital to total liabilities.
      6. Fixed assets to total equity.
      7. Short-term liabilities to total debt.
      8. Ratio of earnings to fixed charges.
      9. Cash from operations coverage of fixed charges.
     10. Working capital to total debt.
  II. Under "Balance Sheets" in its "Management's Discussion and Analysis ..." section, Campbell is referring to the ratio of total debt to capitalization. Check the company's computation for 1990.

18–4.   The following information is available for Companies A, B, and C.

	A	B	C
Total assets	$1,000,000	$2,000,000	$3,000,000
Total liabilities..................	300,000	—	1,200,000
Interest rate on liabilities	10%	—	5%
Operating income	80,000	210,000	300,000
Percentage of operating income to			
total assets	8%	10.5%	10%

Required:
    Compute the financial leverage indexes for Companies A, B, and C. Assume a tax rate of 40 percent. What do the respective levels of the leverage indexes for these companies mean?

18–5. Please state the effect of the transaction below on the following ratios. Each transaction should be considered independently—consider only the immediate effect.

A. Total debt to equity capital.
B. Long-term debt to equity capital.
C. Earnings coverage of fixed charges.
D. Cash from operations coverage of fixed charges.

Selected company data	($000)
Short-term liabilities	500
Long-term liabilities	800
Equity capital	1,200
Cash from operations	300
Pretax income	200
Interest expense	40

Indicate I for Increase, D for Decrease, 0 for No Effect.

                                   A   B   C   D

1. Tax rates increase.
2. Retired bonds—paid in cash.
3. Financed expansion by issue of bonds.
4. Financed expansion by issue of preferred stock.
5. Depreciation expense increased.
6. Collected accounts receivable.
7. Refinanced debt resulting in higher interest cost.
8. Capitalized higher proportion of interest expense due to self-constructed assets.
9. Converted convertible debt into common stock.
10. Acquired inventory on credit.

18–6. Following is the income statement of Kim Corporation for the year ended December 31, year 1:

KIM CORPORATION
Consolidated Income Statement
For the Year Ended December 31, Year 1
(in thousands)

Sales		$14,000
Undistributed income of less than 50%-owned affiliates .		300
		14,300
Cost of goods sold	$6,000	
Selling and administrative expenses	2,000	
Depreciation	600	
Rental expense	500	
Share of minority interest in consolidated income	200	
Interest expense	400	9,700
Pre-tax income		4,600
Income taxes		
Current	900	
Deferred	400	1,300
Net income		3,300
Dividends:		
Common stock	300	
Preferred stock	400	700
Earnings retained for the year		$ 2,600

Additional information:
    The following are changes in current accounts:

	Increase (decrease)
Accounts receivable	$900
Inventories	(800)
Dividend payable	(100)
Notes payable to bank	(200)
Accounts payable	700

1. The effective tax rate is 40%.
2. Shares of minority interests in consolidated income do not have fixed charges.
3. Interest expense includes:

Interest incurred (except items below)	$600
Amortization of bond premium	(300)
Interest on capitalized leases	140
Interest incurred	440
Less—interest capitalized	40
= interest expense	400

4. Amortization of previously capitalized interest
   (included in depreciation) .... $ 60
5. Interest implicit in operating lease rental payment
   (included in rental expense) $120

Required:
a. Compute ratio of earnings to fixed charges.
b. Compute cash from operations coverage of fixed charges.
c. Compute coverage of preferred dividends.

18–7. Following is the income statement of Lot Corporation for the year ended December 31, year 1:

LOT CORPORATION
Income Statement
For the Year Ended December 31, year 1
(in thousands)

Sales		$27,400
Undistributed income of less than 50%-owned affiliates .		400
		$27,800
Less: Cost of goods sold		14,000
Gross profit		13,800
Selling and administrative expenses	$3,600	
Depreciation (a)	1,200	
Rental expense (b)	1,400	
Share of minority interest in consolidated income (c)	600	
Interest expense (d)	1,200	8,000
Pre-tax income		$ 5,800
Income taxes		
Current	$2,000	
Deferred	1,000	3,000
Net income		2,800
Dividends:		
Preferred stock	$ 400	
Common stock	1,000	1,400
Earnings retained for the year		$ 1,400

    (a) Represents depreciation excluded from all other expense categories and includes $100 of amortization of previously capitalized interest.
    (b) Includes $400 of interest implicit in operating lease rental payments that should be considered as having financial characteristics.
    (c) These subsidiaries have fixed charges.
    (d) Interest expense includes:

Interest incurred (except items below)	880
Amortization of bond discount	100
Interest portion of capitalized leases	340
Interest capitalized	(120)
	$1,200

Additional Information:

The following are changes in current accounts:

	Increase (Decrease)
Accounts receivable	$(1,600)
Inventories	2,000
Dividends payable	240
Notes payable	(400)
Accounts payable	2,000

Use a 40% tax rate.

Required:

Compute the following coverage ratios.

  I. Ratio of earnings to fixed charges.
 II. Cash from operations coverage of fixed charges.
III. Earnings coverage of preferred dividends.

18–8.   Use the following information for Questions I and II

Austin Corporation's year 8 financial statement footnotes include the following information:

- Austin has recently entered into operating leases with total future payments of $40 million and a discounted present value of $20 million.
- Included in long-term assets are marketable securities carried at their original cost of $10 million. Fair market value of these securities is $20 million.
- Austin has guaranteed a $5 million bond issue, due in 1993, issued by Healey, a nonconsolidated 30%-owned affiliate.

Mr. Morgan, CFA, decides to adjust Austin's balance sheet by giving recognition to each of these three items.

  I. The effect of these adjustments on the interest coverage ratio (times interest earned) will be that:
  a. Lease capitalization will increase the ratio.
  b. Lease capitalization will decrease the ratio.
  c. Recognition of debt guarantee will decrease the ratio.
  d. Marketable securities adjustment will increase the ratio.
 II. The effect of these adjustments on the long-term debt to equity ratio will be that:
  a. Only the marketable securities adjustment will decrease the ratio.
  b. Only lease capitalization will decrease the ratio.
  c. All three adjustments will decrease the ratio.
  d. All three adjustments will increase the ratio.

III. All other things being equal, what effect will the payment of a cash dividend have on the following ratios?

	Times interest earned	*Debt/equity ratio*
a.	Increase	Increase
b.	No effect	Increase
c.	No effect	No effect
d.	Decrease	Decrease

IV. All other things being equal, what effect will the sale of inventory at a profit have on the following ratios?

	Times interest earned	*Debt/equity ratio*
a.	Increase	Increase
b.	Increase	Decrease
c.	Decrease	Increase
d.	Decrease	Decrease

V. The effect of significant uncapitalized operating leases is to:
   a. Overstate the coverage ratio.
   b. Overstate fixed charges.
   c. Overstate working capital.
   d. Understate the debt ratio.

(CFA)

18–9. Ms. J.T. Mixon, your supervisor, has been contemplating taking a position in the bonds and preferred shares of ARC Corporation. She hands you the following income statement of the corporation expressing concern about how well fixed charges are covered.

ARC CORPORATION
Consolidated Income Statement
For the Year Ended December 31, Year 5

Sales		$27,400
Income of less than 50%-owned affiliates (Note 1)		800
		28,200
Cost of goods sold		14,000
		14,200
Sales and administrative expenses	$3,600	
Depreciation (Note 2)	1,200	
Rental expenses (Note 3)	1,400	
Share of minority interests in consolidated income (Note 4).....................................	600	
Interest expense (Note 5)	1,200	8,000
		6,200
Income taxes:		
Current	2,000	
Deferred	1,000	3,000
		3,200
Net income:		
Preferred stock dividends	400	
Common stock dividends	1,000	1,400
Increase in retained earnings		$ 1,800

Notes:
1. Of this income $600 is undistributed.
2. Includes $80 of amortization of previously capitalized interest.
3. Includes $400 of interest implicit in operating lease rental payments.
4. These subsidiaries do not have fixed charges.
5. Includes:

a.	Interest incurred (except items below)	$ 880
b.	Amortization of bond discount	100
c.	Interest portion of capitalized leases	340
d.	Interest capitalized	(120)
		$1,200

6. The following are changes in some balance sheet accounts— increase or (decrease):

a.	Accounts receivable	(600)
b.	Inventories	160
c.	Payables and accruals	120
d.	Dividends payable	(80)
e.	Current portion of long-term debt	(100)

7. Use 40 percent tax rate.

Required:
1. Compute ratio of earnings to fixed charges.
2. Compute cash from operations coverage of fixed charges.
3. Compute coverage of preferred dividends.

18–10. Based on the data on Fox Industries Limited in Exhibits I and II, answer the following questions:
1. Compute the earnings coverage ratio for year 7, and the average annual earnings coverage ratio for the five-year period year 3–year 7 inclusive, on the first mortgage bonds and on the sinking fund debentures outstanding as of December 31, year 7.
2. Compute the debt to equity ratio as of December 31, year 7 and state what proportion of the company's equity is represented by shares senior to the common shares.
3. Assuming a 50 percent income tax rate, compute the earnings coverage on the $1.10 cumulative redeemable preferred shares for the fiscal year ended in year 7.
4. Assuming a 50 percent income tax rate and full conversion of the Class A shares, calculate earnings per common share for the fiscal year ended in year 7.

Exhibit I

FOX INDUSTRIES LIMITED
Condensed Earnings Statement
(in thousands)

	Fiscal year ended				
	Year 7	Year 6	Year 5	Year 4	Year 3
Earnings before depreciation, interest on long-term debt and taxes on income	$8,750	$8,250	$8,000	$7,750	$7,250
Less: Depreciation	4,000	3,750	3,500	3,500	3,250
Earnings after depreciation but before interest on long-term debt and taxes on income . .	$4,750	$4,500	$4,500	$4,250	$4,000

Exhibit II

FOX INDUSTRIES LIMITED
Capitalization as of December 31, year 7
(in thousands)

Long-term debt:
First mortgage bonds:

5.00% serial bonds due x8-y0	$ 7,500
6.00% sinking fund bonds due y5 (Note 1)	17,500

Debentures:

6.50% sinking fund debentures due y6 (Note 1)	10,000
Total long-term debt	$35,000

Capital stock:

$1.10 cumulative redeemable preferred, stated value $5.00 per share (redeemable at $20.00 share)	$ 1,500
400,000 Class A shares, no-par value (Note 2)	14,000
1,000,000 common shares, no par value	6,000
Total capital stock	$21,500
Paid-in capital	7,000
Retained earnings	18,500
Total long-term debt, capital stock, paid-in capital, and retained earnings	$82,000

Note 1: Combined annual sinking fund payments $500,000
Note 2: Subject to the rights of the preferred shares, the Class A shares are entitled to fixed cumulative dividends at the rate of $2.50 per share per annum, and are convertible at the holder's option, at any time, into common shares on the basis of two common shares for one Class A share.

(CFA adapted)

18–11. The Top Company is planning to invest $20,000,000 in an expansion program that is expected to increase earnings before interest and taxes by $4,000,000. The company currently is earning $5 per share on 1,000,000 shares of common stock outstanding. The capital structure prior to the investment is:

Debt	$20,000,000
Equity	50,000,000
	$70,000,000

The expansion can be financed by sale of 400,000 shares at $50 each, or by issuing long-term debt at a 6 percent interest cost. The firm's recent income statement was as follows:

Sales	$100,000,000
Variable cost	60,000,000
Fixed cost	20,000,000
Total costs	80,000,000
Earnings before interest and taxes	20,000,000
Interest	1,000,000
Earnings before taxes	19,000,000
Taxes (40%)	7,600,000
Earnings after taxes	$ 11,400,000

Required:

a. Assuming the firm maintains its current earnings and achieves the antici-pated earnings from the expansion, what will be the earnings per share
   (1) if expansion is financed by debt
   (2) if expansion is financed by equity?

b. At what level of earnings before interest and taxes will the earnings per share under either alternative be the same amount?

18–12.   Rogan Development Company, a real estate developer, had only one project under development in 1987, an office building in Charlottesville, Virginia. The account "building under construction" had an average balance of $10,000,000. Rogan had the following long-term debt outstanding during the year:

	Average balance	Weighted interest rate
Development loan	$ 6,000,000	11%
Mortgage debt	10,000,000	9
Senior debentures (secured)	40,000,000	10

Required:

a. Calculate the interest incurred, capitalized interest, and interest expense for 1987. Show all calculations.

b. As a bond analyst, list and justify what adjustments you would make to the "times interest charges earned ratio" for companies, such as Rogan, which report significant amounts of capitalized interest.

(CFA adapted)

18–13.   Byron Smart, CFA, a senior portfolio manager with Reilly Investment Management, reviewed the biweekly printout of the equity value screens prepared by one of the leading brokerage firms. One of the screens used to determine relative value is a "low long-term debt/total long-term capital ratio." Smart noticed that the printout indicated that this ratio for Lubbock Corporation was 23.9 percent. Smart, a practitioner of value investing, felt that Lubbock may be a potential takeover target, and proceeded to analyze the Lubbock balance sheet that appears below.

A. Explain how the information contained in *each* footnote would be used to adjust relevant items on Lubbock's balance sheet, and calculate an adjusted long-term debt/total long-term capitalization ratio. Ignore potential income tax effects.

B. As a potential investor, Smart should consider other accounting considerations in evaluating the balance sheet of Lubbock, such as:

    I.   The valuation of marketable securities.

    II. Treatment of deferred taxes.

Briefly discuss how *each* of these *two* accounting considerations might impact a company's long-term debt/total long-term capital ratio.

LUBBOCK CORPORATION
Condensed Balance Sheet
December 31, 1987
($ millions)

Cash and notes	$ 100
Receivables	350
Marketable securities	150
Inventory	800
Other	400
Total current assets	$1,800
Net plant and equipment	1,800
Total assets	$3,600
Note payable	$ 125
Accounts payable	175
Taxes payable	150
Other	75
Total current liabilities	$ 525
Long-term debt	$ 675
Deferred taxes (noncurrent)	175
Other liabilities	75
Minority interest	100
Common stock	400
Retained earnings	1,650
Total liabilities and shareholders' equity	$3,600

Upon reading Lubbock's annual report, Smart finds the following footnotes:

- "... a subsidiary, Lubbock Property Corp., holds, as joint venture partner, a 50 percent interest in its head office building in Chicago, and 10 regional shopping centers in the United States. The parent company has guaranteed the indebtedness of these properties, which totalled $250,000,000 at December 31, 1987."

- "... the LIFO cost basis was used in the valuation of inventories at December 31, 1987. If the FIFO method of inventory was used in place of LIFO, inventories would have exceeded reported amounts by $200,000,000."
- "... the company leases most of its facilities under long-term contracts. These leases are categorized as operating leases for accounting purposes. The following table summarizes future minimum rental payments as of December 31, 1987. These leases carry an implicit interest rate factor of 10 percent, which translates to a present value of approximately $750,000,000."

1988	$90,000,000
1989	90,000,000
1990	90,000,000
1991	90,000,000
1992	90,000,000
1993–2007	90,000,000 per year

(CFA)

18–14. Philip Morris Companies is one of the world's largest cigarette manufacturers as well as a major producer and distributor of a broad line of food and beverage products. As a leading producer of cigarettes, Philip Morris has compiled a steady record of growth in sales, earnings, and cash flow, offering such brands as Marlboro (the world's best selling cigarette), Marlboro Lights, Virginia Slims, and Benson & Hedges. Philip Morris recently diversified into beer and food with the acquisitions of Miller Brewing and General Foods.

In October 1988, Philip Morris announced an unsolicited cash tender offer for all the 124 million outstanding shares of Kraft at $90 per share. Kraft subsequently accepted a $106 per share all-cash offer from Philip Morris.

Kraft is about the same size as General Foods in terms of revenues. Major products include cheese, edible oils, non-fluid dairy products, and frozen foods.

Shortly after the cash tender offer, L. B. O'Hara, an analyst with Green Securities, was asked by her department head to review the acquisition of Kraft and assess its impact on the credit standing of Philip Morris. With this in mind, O'Hara assembled relevant information using projected 1988 and 1989 data that are contained in Tables 1 and 2.

A. O'Hara decided that she would visit management. Based on the information provided, identify and discuss *five* major *industry considerations* that O'Hara should pursue when questioning management.

B. Table 2 shows the median values according to bond rating category for the following *three* financial ratios:
   - Pre-tax interest coverage.
   - Long-term debt as a percent of total capitalization.
   - Cash flow as a percent of total debt (for the purpose of calculating this ratio, Standard & Poor's defines "Cash Flow" as net income plus depreciation, amortization, and deferred taxes, less equity in undistributed earnings of unconsolidated subsidiaries).

Using the information provided in Tables 1 and 2:

Table 1

PHILIP MORRIS COMPANIES, INC.
Projected Financial Data
($ millions)

	1988 estimate excluding Kraft	1989 estimate			
		Before Kraft	Kraft only	Adjustments	Consolidated
Selected Income Statement Data					
Sales					
Domestic tobacco	$ 8,300	$ 8,930			$ 8,930
Int'l. tobacco	8,000	8,800			8,800
General Foods	10,750	11,600			11,600
Kraft			$11,610		11,610
Beer	3,400	3,750			3,750
Total sales	$30,450	$33,080	$11,610		$44,690
Operating income					
Domestic tobacco	$ 3,080	$ 3,520		$ 35	$ 3,555
Int'l. tobacco	800	940			940
General Foods	810	870			870
Kraft			$1,050	50	1,100
Beer	190	205			205
Other	105	125			125
Goodwill amortization	(110)	(110)		(295)	(405)
Total operating income	$ 4,875	$ 5,550	$ 1,050	$ (210)	$ 6,390
Percent of sales	16.0%	16.8%	9.0%		14.3%
Interest expense	(575)	(500)	(75)	(1,025)	(1,600)
Corporate expense	(200)	(225)	(100)	(40)	(365)
Other expense	(5)	(5)			(5)
Pre-tax income	$ 4,095	$ 4,820	$ 875	$ (1,275)	$ 4,420
Percent of sales	13.4%	14.6%	7.5%		9.9%

Table 1 (*continued*)

PHILIP MORRIS COMPANIES, INC.
Projected Financial Data
($ millions)

	1988 estimate excluding Kraft	1989 estimate			
		Before Kraft	*Kraft only*	*Adjustments*	*Consolidated*
Income taxes	(1,740)	(2,000)	(349)	493	(1,856)
Tax rate	42.5%	41.5%	40.0%		42.0%
Net income	$ 2,355	$ 2,820	$ 526	$ (782)	$ 2,564
Selected balance sheet data as of year-end 1988					
Short-term debt	$ 1,125	$ 1,100	$ 683		$ 1,783
Long-term debt	4,757	3,883	895	$11,000	15,778
Stockholders' equity	8,141	9,931	2,150	(2,406)	9,675
Other selected financial data					
Depreciation and amortization	720	750	190	295	1,235
Deferred taxes	100	100	10	280	390
Equity in undistributed earnings of unconsolidated subsidiaries	110	125			125

Table 2   Median Ratios according to Bond Rating Category

Ratio	AAA	AA	A	BBB	BB	B	CCC
Pre-tax interest coverage	14.10x	9.67x	5.40x	3.63x	2.25x	1.58x	(0.42x)
Long-term debt as a percent of capitalization	11.5%	18.7%	28.3%	34.3%	48.4%	57.2%	73.2%
Cash flow* as a percent of total debt	111.8%	86.0%	50.9%	34.2%	22.8%	14.1%	6.2%

* For the purpose of calculating this ratio, Standard & Poor's defines "Cash Flow" as net income plus depreciation, amortization, and deferred taxes, less equity in undistributed earnings of unconsolidated subsidiaries.

Source: Standard & Poor's.

(1) Calculate these ratios for Philip Morris for 1989, *first* using the figures *before* taking into account the Kraft acquisition, and *second* using the consolidated figures *after* the acquisition.

(2) Relate these *two* sets of ratios to the medians for *each* rating category.

(3) Formulate and support an opinion as to the appropriate rating category for the new Philip Morris (after the Kraft acquisition).

(CFA adapted)

18–15.   Please refer to the material that follows:

Dean was asked by the firm's fixed income portfolio manager to investigate whether the credit quality of ABEX's debt has changed during the period 1987 through 1989.

A. Dean first needs to examine certain financial ratios for ABEX, focusing on the areas of asset protection, short-term liquidity, and earning power in relation to the debt burden. Identify *five* ratios from Table 3 that adequately cover these *three* general areas, and discuss the trends in these ratios from 1987 through 1989.

B. In deciding whether ABEX's credit quality has changed, compare the pipeline and petrochemical divisions in terms of *three* qualitative characteristics.

C. Based on your answers to Parts A and B above, briefly discuss whether ABEX's credit quality has changed.

James Dean, CFA, is a pipeline and utility analyst at a large brokerage firm. One of the companies he follows is ABEX Chemicals, Inc. (ABEX) that historically has been a pure pipeline company but is now also a major producer of petrochemicals (principally polyethylene).

About six months ago Dean became uneasy as more and more companies in the petrochemical business announced expansions, and his firm's economist began to express concern about the possibility of a recession in the next year or two. At that time, he compiled a summary of the relevant industry statistics included in Table 4 on page 980, and concluded that the price of petrochemicals produced by ABEX would likely decline over the ensuing 12 to 18 months. For this reason, he had issued a "sell" opinion for the ABEX common stock.

The price of ABEX common stock subsequently declined from $15 to $9. As a result of this price decline, Dean is now not sure his sell recommendation is still correct for the longer term and feels another detailed analysis of the company is warranted.

Dean conducts his analysis by focusing on the external environment, company fundamentals, and stock price evaluation. A discussion of his observations follows.

External environment. Even though there is controversy about the overall direction of the economy for 1990, Dean concludes that the key issue for the petrochemical industry is not demand, but overcapacity. As shown by the data in Table 4 on page 980, he expects polyethylene production to remain essentially flat in 1990 and capacity to increase, thereby causing operating rates to fall significantly. The combined impact would result in increased competition and lower product prices. Longer term he expects the use of polyethylene to continue to grow by 4% per annum and prices to rise by 5% per annum, beginning in 1992.

Company fundamentals. ABEX's operating earnings are dependent primarily on two businesses: pipeline distribution of natural gas (gas transmission) and petrochemical production. The gas transmission business has been declining because of lower gas production and pricing constraints, but Dean's outlook is for modest increases in volume and transmission rates. The summary of key statistics for pipeline operations is shown in Table 4.

The more volatile component of ABEX's operating income is the petrochemical operation. Operating earnings from petrochemicals are very sensitive to the selling price, the production costs, and the volume of polyethylene sales. The key to estimating operating profits is successful estimation of future prices and costs, and ABEX's market share. ABEX's management is confident that their lower cost structure will allow them to be price competitive and achieve a higher capacity operating rate than their competitors. The summary of key statistics for polyethylene operations is shown in Table 4.

Stock evaluation. Dean has traditionally valued companies on the basis of discounted cash flows, but he is now placing more emphasis on the quality of cash flow, earnings momentum, yield, book value, and the components of income. As a first step in this process, he gathered all the required data to make a full evaluation. These data are included in Tables 1 through 4.

As part of Dean's research team, you are asked to assist in the analysis of ABEX.

Table 1

ABEX CHEMICALS, INC.
Consolidated Statements of Earnings
($ millions)

	1985	1986	1987	1988	1989
Revenues					
Petrochemicals	$ 757	$ 725	$1,021	$2,472	$2,575
Pipelines	1,328	1,235	1,156	1,106	1,123
Total revenues	2,085	1,960	2,177	3,578	3,698
Operating costs*					
Petrochemicals	(622)	(607)	(818)	(1,691)	(1,970)
Pipelines	(988)	(899)	(840)	(820)	(822)
Total operating costs	(1,610)	(1,506)	(1,658)	(2,511)	(2,792)
Operating income					
Petrochemicals	135	118	203	781	605
Pipelines	340	336	316	286	301
Total operating income	475	454	519	1,067	906
Interest on long-term debt					
Petrochemicals	(60)	(84)	(78)	(211)	(266)
Pipelines	(169)	(166)	(166)	(172)	(178)
Total interest	(229)	(250)	(244)	(383)	(444)
Administrative expenses	(22)	(24)	(23)	(28)	(40)
Rental expenses	(15)	(17)	(17)	(20)	(22)
Income from investments	25	8	4	7	4
Earnings before taxes	234	171	239	643	405
Income taxes					
Current	(78)	(30)	(45)	(40)	(44)
Deferred	(23)	(35)	(67)	(201)	(136)
Total taxes	(101)	(65)	(112)	(241)	(180)
Net income	133	106	127	402	225
Preferred dividends	(77)	(74)	(26)	(17)	(17)
Net available for common	$ 56	$ 32	$ 101	$ 385	$ 208
Average shares outstanding†					
(millions).................	128	135	185	231	253
Earnings per common share	$0.44	$0.24	$0.54	$1.67	$0.82
Common dividends per share ...	0.40	0.40	0.40	0.40	0.50
Cash flow per common share ...	2.52	2.44	2.26	3.85	2.85

* Operating costs are costs of goods sold including depreciation as follows:

Depreciation					
Petrochemicals	$ 48	$ 60	$ 62	$135	$233
Pipelines	96	95	97	98	102
Total depreciation	$144	$155	$159	$233	$335

† 1990 estimate = 305 million shares outstanding.

Table 2

ABEX CHEMICALS, INC.
Combined Balance Sheets
($ millions)

	1985	1986	1987	1988	1989
Assets					
Current assets					
Cash & short-term investments .	$ 45	$ 48	$ 74	$ 102	$ 133
Accounts receivable	279	300	414	868	923
Inventories	125	121	128	501	535
Total current assets	$ 449	$ 469	$ 616	$1,471	$1,591
Investments & other assets	631	380	167	252	400
Goodwill	35	90	105	330	560
Property, plant, & equipment					
Petrochemicals	1,184	1,245	1,323	2,670	3,275
Pipelines	2,282	2,484	2,547	2,540	2,530
Total assets	$4,581	$4,668	$4,758	$7,263	$8,356
Liabilities					
Current liabilities					
Bank indebtedness	$ 226	$ 77	$ 72	$ 215	$ 245
Accounts payable & accrued					
liabilities	333	312	377	768	787
Current portion of long-term					
debt	99	70	76	86	136
Other payables	35	33	32	34	54
Total current liabilities	$ 693	$ 492	$ 557	$1,103	$1,222
Long-term debt					
Petrochemicals	553	743	721	2,017	2,176
Pipelines	1,686	1,648	1,638	1,702	1,725
Advances-gas contracts	115	135	186	290	210
Deferred income taxes	125	160	227	428	564
Total liabilities	$3,172	$3,178	$3,329	$5,540	$5,897
Shareholders' Equity					
Preferred shares	$ 861	$ 826	$ 329	$ 216	$ 216
Common shares & retained					
earnings	548	664	1,100	1,507	2,243
Total shareholders' equity	$1,409	$1,490	$1,429	$1,723	$2,459
Total liabilities & shareholders'					
equity	$4,581	$4,668	$4,758	$7,263	$8,356
Average shares outstanding					
(millions)*	128	135	185	231	253

* 1990 estimate = 305 million shares outstanding.

Table 3

ABEX CHEMICALS, INC.
Selected Financial Ratios

	1985	1986	1987	1988	1989
Petrochemicals operating margin	17.8%	16.3%	19.9%	31.6%	23.5%
Pipeline operating margin	25.6%	27.2%	27.3%	25.9%	26.8%
Return on assets (EBIT/total assets)	10.1%	9.0%	10.2%	14.1%	10.2%
Pre-tax profit margin	11.2%	8.7%	11.0%	18.0%	10.9%
Tax rate	43.0%	38.0%	46.9%	37.5%	44.4%
Petrochemicals asset turnover (sales/fixed assets)	0.64X	0.58X	0.77X	0.93X	0.79X
Pipelines asset turnover (sales/ fixed assets)	0.58X	0.50X	0.45X	0.44X	0.44X
Turnover (sales/total assets)	0.46X	0.42X	0.46X	0.49X	0.44X
Debt to common equity	4.30X	3.80X	2.31X	2.66X	1.83X
Net tangible assets to long-term debt	58.4%	55.4%	52.0%	34.7%	46.2%
Long-term debt to total capitalization	62.6%	62.9%	64.0%	70.0%	62.6%
Total assets to total shareholders' equity	3.25X	3.13X	3.33X	4.22X	3.40X
Pre-tax interest coverage	1.63X	1.46X	1.80X	2.54X	1.84X
Operating cash flow to total funded debt	20.2%	18.0%	20.4%	26.6%	22.1%
Collection period	48 days	55 days	68 days	87 days	90 days
Inventory turnover	11.0X	11.0X	12.0X	7.2X	4.7X
Percent short-term debt to total debt	12.1%	5.5%	5.8%	7.5%	9.3%
Petrochemicals average cost of long-term debt	10.9%	11.3%	10.8%	10.5%	12.2%
Pipeline average cost of long-term debt	10.0%	10.1%	10.1%	10.1%	10.3%
Average cost of preferreds	8.9%	9.0%	7.9%	7.9%	7.9%

Table 4

ABEX CHEMICALS, INC.
Selected Key Statistics

	1985	1986	1987	1988	1989	1990E
Polyethylene operations						
Production (millions of pounds)	1,840	1,975	2,870	4,835	5,000	4,950
Approximate capacity (millions of pounds)	1,900	2,100	2,950	5,000	5,500	5,500
Capacity operating rate	97%	94%	97%	97%	91%	90%
Average price received	$0.411	$0.367	$0.356	$0.511	$0.515	$0.470
Average cost/pound produced	$0.338	$0.307	$0.285	$0.350	$0.394	$0.370
Pipeline transportation operations						
$/1,000 cubic feet (price)	$0.286	$0.253	$0.248	$0.221	$0.192	$0.187
Gas transported (trillion cubic feet)	4.64	4.88	4.67	5.00	5.85	6.29
Operating profit margin	25.6%	27.2%	27.3%	25.9%	26.8%	27.0%

Total U.S. Polyethylene Capacity, Production and Prices

	1985	1986	1987	1988	1989	1990E	1991E	Compound annual growth
Total production (millions of pounds)	15,600	16,100	17,600	18,900	19,700	19,700	19,800	
Growth rate	7.6%	3.2%	9.3%	7.4%	4.2%	0.0%	0.5%	4.5%
Total capacity (millions of pounds)	17,600	17,700	18,600	20,100	21,200	23,400	24,300	
Growth rate	2.9%	0.6%	5.1%	8.1%	5.5%	10.4%	3.8%	5.2%
Capacity operating rate	88.6%	91.0%	94.6%	94.0%	92.9%	84.2%	81.5%	
Average price per pound	$0.41	$0.37	$0.36	$0.51	$0.52	$0.47	$0.57	
Percent change	-9.8%	-10.8%	-2.7%	24.4%	2.0%	-9.6%	21.3%	1.2%

(CFA adapted)

18–16. You are considering the bonds of ZETA Company (see Problem 23–5) for long-term investment. Incident to your decision-making process, you decide to compute pertinent ratios for years 5 and 6.

The following are additional data and information to be considered *only* for purposes of this problem (in thousands):

		Year 6	Year 7
a.	Interest is composed of:		
	Interest incurred (except items below)	$ 9,200	$5,000
	Amortization of bond discount	2,500	2,000
	Interest portion of capitalized leases	80	—
	Interest capitalized	(1,780)	(1,000)
		$10,000	$6,000

b. Depreciation includes amortization of previously capitalized interest of $1,200 for year 6 and $1,000 for year 5.
c. Interest portion of operating rental expense that should be considered a fixed charge: $20 in year 6 and $16 in year 5.
d. The associated company is less than 50 percent owned.
e. You have concluded that deferred taxes constitute a long-term liability.
f. Present value of noncapitalized financing leases is $200 for both years.
g. The excess of the projected pension benefit obligation over the accumulated pension benefit obligation is $2,800 for both years.
h. Year-end, year 4 total assets and equity capital are $94,500 and $42,000, respectively.
i. Average market price for year 6 and year 5 per share of ZETA's common stock was $40 and $45, respectively.

Required:
 I. Compute for year 6 and year 5:
   A. Financial leverage index.
   B. Total liabilities to total liabilities and equity capital.
   C. Total liabilities to total liabilities and equity capital (based on market value of common equity).
   D. Total liabilities to equity capital.
   E. Long-term debt to equity capital.
   F. Ratio of earnings to fixed charges.
   G. Cash flow coverage of fixed charges.
 II. Comment on the level as well as on the year-to-year trend of these measures.
III. Compute the analytically adjusted long-term debt to long-term debt and equity ratio for year 6 and year 5 and comment on the conclusion one can derive from it. (For purposes of *this* ratio assume that only 60% of deferred taxes constitute a long-term liability.)

Chapter 19

19–1.   Please refer to the financial statements of Quaker Oats (Appendix 23).

Required:
I.   Compute the following return on investment ratios for Quaker Oats for 1991 and 1990:
Return on total assets
Disaggregated return on total assets.
Return on long-term liabilities plus equity.
Return on common equity.
Return on total equity.
Equity growth rate.
Disaggregated return on common stockholders' equity.
II.   Compute following assets utilization ratios for Quaker Oats for 1991 and 1990.
Revenues to cash.
Revenues to receivables.
Revenues to inventories.
Revenues to PP&E.
Revenues to other current assets.
Revenues to total assets.
III.   Based on your answers to I and II above, analyze and evaluate the return on investment and asset utilization of Quaker Oats for 1991 and 1990.
IV.   Analyze the composition of the return on common stockholders' equity for Quaker Oats for 1991. Hint: Construct a table showing the net amounts accruing to [or detracting from] return on common equity from various sources of financing including current liabilities and then comment on the table. List any assumption that you make and use averages for fund suppliers.
V.   Compute return on investment for 1991 under the following investment bases:
   (a)   Gross productive assets, assuming that 20 percent of other current assets are not productive.
   (b)   Market value of common stock assuming that the market value to be used is equal to the average price for 1991.

19–2.   In its 1991 annual report the management of Quaker Oats made the following observations:

Financial Objectives: Provide total shareholder returns (dividends plus share price appreciation) that exceed both the cost of equity and the S&P 500 stock index over time.

Quaker's total return to shareholders for fiscal 1991 was 34 percent. That compares quite favorably to our cost of equity for the year, which was about 12 percent, and to the total return of the S&P 500 stock index, which was 7 percent. Driving this strong performance, real earnings from continuing operations grew 7.4 percent over the last five years, return on equity rose to 24.1 percent . . . (Note Quaker Oats approximate prices on 7/1/90 was 48 and on 6/30/91 was $62).

The Benchmark for Investment

We use our cost of capital as a benchmark, or hurdle rate, to ensure that all projects undertaken promise a suitable rate of return. The cost of capital is used as the discount rate in determining whether a project will provide an economic return on its investment. We estimate a project's potential cash flows and discount these cash flows back to present value. This amount is compared with the initial investment costs to determine whether incremental value is created. Our cost of capital is calculated using the approximate market value weightings of debt and equity used to finance the Company.

$$\text{Cost of equity} + \text{Cost of debt} = \text{Cost of capital}$$

When Quaker is consistently able to generate and reinvest cash flows in projects whose returns exceed our cost of capital, economic value is created. As the stock market evaluates the Company's ability to generate value, this value is reflected in stock price appreciation.

The cost of equity.   The cost of equity is a measure of the minimum return Quaker must earn to properly compensate investors for the risk of ownership of our stock. This cost is a combination of a "risk-free" rate and an "equity risk premium." The risk-free rate (the U.S. Treasury Bond rate) is the sum of the expected rate of inflation and a "real" return of 2 to 3 percent. For fiscal 1991, the risk-free rate was approximately 8.4 percent. Investors in Quaker stock expect the return of a risk-free security plus a "risk premium" of about 3.6 percent to compensate them for assuming the risks in Quaker stock. The risk in holding Quaker stock is inherent in the fact that returns depend on the future profitability of the Company. In fiscal 1991, Quaker's cost of equity was approximately 12 percent.

The cost of debt.   The cost of debt is simply our after-tax, long-term debt rate, which was around 6.4 percent.

Required:
A. Quaker calculates the return to shareholders for 1991 to be 34%.
    1. How was this computed?
    2. How does this return differ from return on equity?
    3. Compare the company's concept of return to shareholder to the concept of Return on Stockholder's Investment discussed in the chapter.
    4. Can you verify the company's computation of return on equity?
B. 1. How does Quaker arrive at a 3.6% "risk premium" needed by common shareholders as compensation for assuming the risks in Quaker stock?
    2. How was the 6.4% "cost of debt" arrived at?

19–3.   Please refer to the financial statements of Campbell Soup in Appendix 4B and Exhibit 5 in Chapter 23.

Required:
(Assume that half of deferred income taxes should be considered equity).

A. Compute the following for 1990:
    1. Return on total assets.

2. Return on equity.
3. Return on long-term liabilities and equity.
4. Financial leverage index.
5. Equity growth rate.

B. Disaggregate the return on common stockholders' equity and comment on the results.

C. Compute 1990 asset utilization ratios for major asset categories (based on year-end assets).

D. You want to invest some of your funds in Campbell's common stock. There is another investment of equal quality and risk that has a 12.7 percent return on common equity. Which investment would you prefer? Is other information needed to make this decision?

19–4.   Roll Corporation earns 10 percent on total assets. Its total assets ($10 million) are financed entirely by common equity. The management is considering using bonds to finance expansion of $6 million. Return on total assets is expected to remain unchanged. There are two alternatives to be followed:

1. Financing expansion by issuing $2 million bonds with 5 percent coupon, and $4 million common equity.
2. Financing expansion by issuing bonds of $6 million with 6 percent coupon.

Required:
1. If tax rate is 40 percent, what is the current operating income?*
2. Determine operating income under each of the two financing alternatives (tax rate 40 percent).
3. What is return on equity under each alternative?
4. Explain the difference in results in (3).
    * Note: Operating Income = Income before interest & taxes

19–5.   Fit Corporation earns 10 percent return on total assets. Its total assets ($4 million) are financed entirely by common equity. The management is considering using bonds to finance an expansion of $2 million. Return on total assets is expected to remain unchanged. There are two alternatives to be followed:

1. Financing expansion by issuing $1 million bonds with 12 percent coupon, and $1 million common equity.
2. Financing expansion by issuing bonds of $2 million with 12 percent coupon.

Required:
1. Determine operating income (= income before interest and taxes) under each of the two financing alternatives (tax rate 40 percent).
2. What is return on equity under each alternative?
3. What is the financial leverage index under each alternative?
4. Explain the level of the financial leverage index under each above alternative.

19–6.   Please refer to data in Problem 18–15. Focusing on the company as a whole, Dean feels it is important to differentiate between operating success and financing decisions.

Required:
A. Explain the differences between ABEX's overall profitability in 1985 and in 1989. (Your analysis should include *calculation* and *discussion* of the impact of the components that determine *ROE.*)
B. Explain why ABEX's EPS almost doubled between 1985 and 1989 despite the decline in its ROE.

(CFA adapted)

19–7.   The following is some information about Rolf Corporation:

1. Total asset turnover (using end of period assets)   2
2. Return on sales 5%
3. Total assets to total equity 1.786
4. Sales $5,000,000
5. Capital structure is composed of $100,000 minority interests, 10 percent current liabilities (average interest cost is 5 percent for one-half of current liabilities), 30 percent long-term debt (average interest cost of 6 percent), and common equity.
6. Tax rate is 40 percent.
7. Minority interest in earnings $1,000

Required:
1. Compute return on equity using the three major components into which it can be disaggregated.
2. Compute return on total assets.
3. Analyze the composition of return on common equity. What is the leverage advantage (in percent return) accruing to common stockholders?

19–8.   Rose Corporation supplied you with the following condensed balance sheet for year 2:

Assets

Current assets	$ 250,000
Noncurrent assets	1,750,000
Total assets	2,000,000

Liabilities and Equity

Current liabilities	$ 200,000
Noncurrent liabilities (8% bonds)	675,000
Stockholders' equity	1,125,000
Total liabilities and equity	2,000,000

Additional information:
1. Net income for the year is $157,500.
2. Income tax rate is 50 percent.

Required:
a. Based on the above information, determine whether financial leverage (long-term debt) benefits Rose's stockholders.
b. If Rose Corporation achieved a 20 percent return on total assets, determine what its return on equity would be and the level of the financial leverage index.
c. What can you conclude from the level of its financial leverage index that you have computed in *(b)* above?

19-9.   The following is some information about ADAM Corporation:

1. Total assets turnover (using end of period assets which
    approximate average total assets)   3
2. Net income to sales 7%
3. Financial leverage ratio (i.e., total assets to total
    equity)....................................... 1.667
4. Sales $12,000,000
5. Capital structure is composed of $200,000 minority
    interests, 15 percent current liabilities (average interest
    cost is 4 percent for one-third of current liabilities),
    20 percent long-term debt (average interest cost 5
    percent), and 60 percent common equity.
6. Tax rate is 50 percent.
7. Minority interest in earnings $2,000

Required:
1. Compute return on equity using the three major components into which it can be disaggregated.
2. Compute return on total assets.
3. Present an analysis of the composition of return on shareholders' equity indicating the advantage accruing to common equity from the use of leverage.

19-10
I. Which one of the following *best* explains a ratio of "net sales to average net fixed assets" that *exceeds* the industry average?
    a. The firm expanded its plant and equipment in the past few years.
    b. The firm makes less efficient use of its assets than other firms.
    c. The firm has a lot of old plant and equipment.
    d. The firm uses straight-line depreciation.
II. The rate of return on assets is equivalent to:
       I. Profit margin ratio × Total asset turnover ratio

II. Profit margin ratio × Total asset turnover ratio × Leverage ratio/Interest expense

III. Net income + Interest expense net of income tax + Minority interest in earnings

Average total assets

IV. Net income + minority interest in earnings

Average total assets

a. I only
b. I and III
c. II only
d. II and IV

III. A measure of asset utilization is:
a. Sales divided by working capital.
b. Return on total assets.
c. Return on equity capital.
d. Operating profit divided by sales.

IV. Return on total assets is a function of:
a. Interest rates and pre-tax profits.
b. The debt-equity ratio.
c. The after-tax profit margin and the asset turnover ratio.
d. Sales and fixed assets.

V. The rate of return on assets is equivalent to:

I. Profit margin ratio × Total asset turnover ratio

II. Profit margin ratio × Total asset turnover ratio × Leverage ratio/interest expense

III. Net income + Interest expense net of income tax + Minority interest in earnings

Average total assets

IV. Net income + Minority interest in earnings

Average total assets

a. I only
b. I and III
c. II only
d. II and IV

19–11.   Zear Manufacturing Company is a major producer of faucets that it sells on a wholesale basis to the plumbing trade at $10 per unit. In its year 8 fiscal year, just ended, it sold 500,000 units. Fixed costs last year totaled $1,500,000 which included interest charges on its 7½ percent debentures. Variable costs are $4 per unit for materials. There are 100 hourly paid plant employees each earning $7,000 in year 8.

Labor negotiations are now underway, with the union demanding substantial increases in the hourly rated plant workers. Zear Manufacturing is budgeting for a 6 percent increase in overall fixed costs and foresees no change in unit price or unit costs for materials. A 10 percent growth in sales volume is forecast for the current year, and to obtain the necessary increase in production 10 more hourly rated plant employees have been hired.

A condensed balance sheet for Zear Manufacturing at the end of fiscal year 8 is shown as follows:

Current assets:			
Cash	$ 700,000	Current liabilities	$2,000,000
Receivables	1,000,000	Long-term debt 7½%	
Other	800,000	debenture	2,000,000
		6% preferred stock	
Total current		10,000 shares, $100	
assets........	2,500,000	par value	1,000,000
Fixed assets (net of		Common stock and	
depreciation)	5,500,000	retained earnings	3,000,000
	$8,000,000		$8,000,000

Required:

a. Assuming an income tax rate of 50 percent, calculate the percentage return for year 8 on (1) total invested capital and (2) common equity.
b. Calculate the maximum annual wage increase Zear Manufacturing can afford to pay each plant employee and show a 10 percent return on total invested capital. (Total invested capital can be based on that shown at the end of the year 8 fiscal year.)

(CFA adapted)

19–12.   The duPont formula defines the net return on shareholders' equity as a function of the following components:
- Operating margin
- Asset turnover
- Interest burden
- Financial leverage
- Income tax rate

Using *only* the data in Table A shown below:
A. Calculate *each* of the *five* components listed above for 1985 *and* 1989, and calculate the return on equity (ROE) for 1985 *and* 1989, using all of the *five* components. Show calculations.
B. Briefly discuss the impact of the changes in asset turnover *and* financial leverage on the change in ROE from 1985 to 1989.

Table A

	1985	1989
Income statement data		
Revenues	$542	$979
Operating income	38	76
Depreciation and amortization	3	9
Interest expense	3	0
Pre-tax income	32	67
Income taxes	13	37
Net income after tax	19	30
Balance sheet data		
Fixed assets	$ 41	$ 70
Total assets	245	291
Working capital	123	157
Total debt	16	0
Total shareholders' equity	159	220

19-13. The value of the components affecting the ROE of Merck & Co., Inc. for 1985 are indicated in Table 1 below. Selected 1990 income statement and balance sheet information for Merck can be found in Table 2 below.
A. Calculate *each* of the *five* ROE components for Merck in 1990. Using the *five* components, calculate ROE for Merck in 1990. Show all calculations.
B. Based on your calculations, describe how *each* ROE component contributed to the change in Merck's ROE between 1985 and 1990. Identify the major underlying reasons for the change in Merck's ROE.

Table 1

MERCK & COMPANY, INC.
1985 ROE Components

Tax burden (net income/pre-tax income)	0.628
Interest burden (pre-tax income/EBIT)	0.989
Operating (or profit) margin	0.245
Asset turnover	0.724
Financial leverage	1.877

Table 2

MERCK & COMPANY, INC.
1990 Selected Financial Data
($ millions)

Income statement data

Sales revenue	$7,120
Depreciation	230
Interest expense	10
Pre-tax income	2,550
Income taxes	900
Net income	1,650

Balance sheet data

Current assets	$4,850
Net fixed assets	2,400
Total assets	7,250
Current liabilities	3,290
Long-term debt	100
Shareholders' equity	3,860
Total liabilities & shareholders' equity	7,250

19–14. Susan Smith, the senior portfolio manager at Investment Counsellor, Inc., has made a decision to increase exposure to communication stocks in the managed funds. As the in-house analyst, you are assigned the task of recommending one stock to meet this objective.

You have diligently analyzed and evaluated all the communication stocks, and have now narrowed the stock purchase decision to two newspaper publishing companies, Thomson Newspapers, Ltd. and Southam, Inc.

> Thomson Newspapers, Ltd., one of the largest pure newspaper companies in North America, owns and publishes predominantly small city daily newspapers. Within individual markets, Thomson is usually the dominant newspaper advertising vehicle. A very successful record of acquisitions has assured future growth opportunities, without jeopardizing current earnings.
>
> Southam, Inc. is a diversified communications company, deriving 70% of income from newspaper publishing, with the remainder from commercial printing, book retailing, and information services in Canada and the United States. Southam is Canada's largest daily newspaper company with publishing operations primarily in large competitive markets. While Southam has diversified into the higher growth segments of communications to augment growth, its more cyclical large city newspapers continue to dominate earnings performance.

Smith wants you to discuss the internal sources of earnings growth for each company. In the past, you have successfully used the duPont formula to analyze the internal growth rate components for a company to explain the trend in the important variable, return on equity. You have identified five key return on equity components:

- Operating profit margin
- Interest burden
- Income taxes
- Asset utilization
- Financial leverage

Using only the data in Table A

(1) Calculate the return on equity for 1988 for both Thomson and Southam using the ratios in Table A that correspond to the five components of the duPont formula listed above. Show calculations.

(2) Discuss how the ten-year trend in *each* of the *five* components has affected the return on equity for *each* company.

Table A   Thomson Newspapers, Ltd.

Year	Total assets/ common equity	Profit margin	Income tax rate	Revenues/ total assets	EBIT*/ revenues	Interest/ total assets	Return on average equity
1988E	1.53	21.2%	28.0%	0.61	32.2%	1.9%	❑
1987	1.31	21.0	38.1	0.77	33.5	0.5	20.5%
1986	1.32	19.5	43.8	0.86	35.4	0.6	22.1
1985	1.41	19.0	41.6	0.80	34.2	1.5	21.2
1984	1.41	18.9	43.0	0.84	34.4	1.0	22.3
1983	1.45	17.9	44.3	0.86	33.2	1.0	22.2
1982	1.60	14.9	42.9	0.98	28.4	2.2	23.5
1981	1.67	15.0	45.7	0.91	30.8	3.2	22.6
1980	1.48	14.5	48.5	0.95	30.9	3.0	20.0
1979	1.37	19.4	46.9	0.81	38.1	1.3	21.4
1978	1.34	18.5	48.0	0.81	37.0	1.4	19.9

Southam, Inc.

Year	Total assets/ common equity	Profit margin	Income tax rate	Revenues/ total assets	EBIT*/ revenues	Interest/ total assets	Return on average equity
1988E	2.39	4.6%	43.0%	1.29	7.3%	2.7%	❑
1987	2.22	5.4	44.7	1.38	8.9	3.1	11.3%
1986	2.20	5.6	42.7	1.37	9.4	3.1	12.4
1985	2.47	4.2	42.7	1.46	8.9	3.6	13.3
1984	2.82	4.1	46.4	1.61	9.9	4.3	17.6
1983	2.70	4.5	46.7	1.57	10.2	3.3	18.2
1982	2.65	2.3	46.0	1.54	7.9	5.8	9.1
1981	2.73	5.4	46.1	1.62	13.5	6.2	23.2
1980	2.39	6.1	45.9	1.54	12.9	4.1	20.4
1979	2.03	7.0	44.3	1.62	13.0	2.5	21.1
1978	1.85	8.2	41.1	1.64	12.2	1.1	20.6

* Earnings before interest and taxes.
E = Estimated.

19–15.   As a financial analyst at a debt-rating agency you were asked to analyze the return on investment and the asset utilization measures of Zeta Corporation based on the limited information contained in its two-year financial statements (see Problem 23–5).

The additional information that follows pertains to this problem *only:*

Balances at December 31, year 4 (in thousands):

Total assets	$94,500
Long-term debt	11,200
Deferred income taxes (assume to be long-term liability)	1,000
Minority interest	800
Stockholders' equity	42,000

Interest expense on long-term debt is $4,000 for year 6 and $3,000 for year 5. Use a 50 percent tax rate.

Required:
I.   Compute the following for year 5 and year 6:
(a)   Return on total assets.
(b)   Return on long-term liabilities plus equity capital.
(c)   Return on common stockholders' equity (ROCSE).
(d)   Disaggregate the ratio in (c) above and comment on the usefulness of such disaggregation.
(e)   Equity growth rate.
(f)   Analyze the composition of return on stockholders' equity for year 6 only.
II.   Comment on the year-to-year changes in the above measures. What is the significance of the analysis in I (f) above?

Chapter 20

20–1.   The following data are available for Kemp Corporation.

KEMP CORPORATION
Product-Line Information
(in thousands)

	Year 1	Year 2	Year 3	Year 4
Data communications equipment:				
Net sales	$4,616	$ 5,630	$ 4,847	$ 6,890
Income contribution	570	876	996	1,510
Inventory	2,615	2,469	2,103	1,897
Time recording devices:				
Net sales	3,394	4,200	4,376	4,100
Income contribution	441	311	34	412
Inventory	1,193	2,234	2,574	2,728
Hardware for electronics industry:				
Net sales	...	...	1,564	1,850
Income contribution	...	...	771	919
Inventory	...	...	331	287
Home sewing products:				
Net sales	1,505	1,436	1,408	1,265
Income contribution	291	289	276	342
Inventory	398	534	449	526
Corporate totals:				
Net sales	9,515	11,266	12,195	14,105
Income contribution	1,302	1,476	2,077	3,183
Inventory	4,206	5,237	5,437	5,438

Required:
a.   List the products in the order of variability of income contribution trend.
b.   For year 4, list the products in the order of amount of dollars invested in ending inventory to generate a dollar of sales and a dollar of income contribution.
c.   (1)   List products in the order of relatively consistent contribution to the growth of corporate total income contribution.
     (2)   Compute the percentage of product lines' income contribution to the total for each year.
d.   Assume that you can invest in one product line only. Comment on the desirability of investment in each product line.

20–2.   The comparative income statements of the Spyres Manufacturing Company for year 9 and year 8 are as follows:

	Year 9	Year 8
Net sales	$600,000	$500,000
Cost of goods sold	490,000	430,000
Gross margin on sales	110,000	70,000
Operating expenses	101,000	51,000
Income before taxes	9,000	19,000
Federal income taxes	2,400	5,000
Net income after taxes	$ 6,600	$ 14,000

Required:

a. Prepare common-size statements that show the percentage of each item to sales for the two years. Include a column for percent of increase or decrease of year 9 amounts from year 8. Round to the nearest tenth of 1 percent.

b. Is a good trend indicated by your percentage calculations? What areas should be a matter of managerial concern?

20–3. The most recently published statement of consolidated income of Standard Industries, Inc., appears as follows:

STANDARD INDUSTRIES, INC.
Statement of Consolidated Income
For the Year Ended March 31, year 8

Revenue:	
Net sales	$38,040,000
Other revenue	408,600
Total revenue	38,448,600
Cost and expenses:	
Cost of products sold	27,173,300
Selling and administrative expenses	8,687,500
Interest expense	296,900
Total cost and expenses	36,157,700
Income before income taxes	2,290,900
Provision for income taxes	1,005,000
Net income	$ 1,285,900

Charles Norton, a representative of a firm of security analysts, visited the central headquarters of Standard Industries for the purpose of obtaining more information about the company's operations.

In the annual report, Standard's president stated that Standard was engaged in the pharmaceutical, food processing, toy manufacturing, and metal-working industries. Mr. Norton complained that the published income statement was of limited utility in his analysis of the firm's operations. He said Standard should have disclosed separately the profit earned in each of its component industries.

Further, he maintained that several items appearing on the statement of consolidated retained earnings should have been included on the income statement, namely, a gain of $633,400 on the sale of the furniture division in early March of the current year and an assessment of additional income taxes of $164,900 resulting from an examination of the returns covering the years ended March 31, year 5 and year 6.

Required:

a. Explain what is meant by the term *conglomerate* company.

b. (1) Discuss the accounting problems involved in measuring net profit by industry segments within a company.

   (2) With reference to Standard Industries' statement of consolidated income, identify the specific items where difficulty might be encountered in measuring profit by each of its industry segments and explain the nature of the difficulty.

c. (1) What criteria should be applied in determining whether a gain or loss should be excluded from the determination of net income?

   (2) What criteria should be applied in determining whether a gain or loss that is properly includable in the determination of net income should be included in the results of ordinary operations or shown separately as an extraordinary item after all other items of revenue and expense?

   (3) How should the gain on the sale of the furniture division and the assessment of additional taxes each be presented in Standard's financial statements?

(AICPA adapted)

20–4. Super Corporation is a diversified company that discloses supplemental financial information as to industry segments of its business. Summary information for its segments is as follows:

	Segment		
	A	B	C
Information for segments:			
Sales to unaffiliated customers	$12,200	$ 800	$300
Sales to affiliated customers	200	500	200
Operating profit	700	(50)	30
Identifiable assets	11,500	1,360	420
Depreciation and depletion	1,200	140	110
Capital expenditures	1,600	80	230
Other information:			
Total operating profit			$680
Less:			
General expenses		$ 20	
Interest expense		35	
Minority interest income		15	
Income taxes		300	370
Net income			$310

Required:
a. Which of the Super Corporation segments are reportable segments? (Support your answer computationally.)
b. Is the A segment a dominant segment?

20–5. The following is a summary of Petersen Corporation's revenue and income (contribution):

Line of business	Year 1	Year 2	Year 3	Year 4
Revenue:				
Manufactured and engineered products:				
Engineered equipment	$ 30,341	$ 29,807	$ 32,702	$ 43,870
Other equipment	5,906	5,996	6,824	7,424
Parts, supplies, and services ...	29,801	29,878	33,623	44,223
Total	66,048	65,681	73,149	95,517
Engineering and erection services	—	—	12,261	36,758
Total environmental systems group	66,048	65,681	85,410	132,275
Frye Copysystems	25,597	28,099	31,214	39,270
Sinclair & Valentine	—	53,763	57,288	60,973
A. L. Garber	16,615	15,223	20,445	24,808
Total graphics group	42,212	97,085	108,947	125,051
Total consolidated revenue	$108,260	$162,766	$194,357	$257,326
Income:				
Manufactured and engineered products	$ 3,785	$ 3,943	$ 9,209	$ 10,762
Engineering and erection services	—	--	1,224	3,189
International operations	2,265	2,269	2,030	2,323
Total environmental systems group	6,050	6,212	12,463	16,274
Frye Copysystems	1,459	2,011	2,799	3,597
Sinclair & Valentine	—	3,723	4,628	5,142
A. L. Garber	(295)	926	1,304	1,457
Total graphics group	1,164	6,660	8,731	10,196
Total divisional income	7,214	12,872	21,194	26,470
Unallocated expenses and taxes	(5,047)	(8,146)	(13,179)	(16,449)
Total income from continuing operations	$ 2,167	$ 4,726	$ 8,015	$ 10,021

Required:
A. Analyze by means of common-size statements each division's (1) contribution to total consolidated revenue and (2) contribution to total divisional income. Also compute each division's ratio of income to revenue.
B. Comment on the trends revealed by your computations.

Chapter 21

21–1. PLease refer to the financial statements of Quaker Oats (Appendix 23).

Required:
Reconstruct all entries related to income taxes for 1990. Post these to all T-accounts that are affected by taxes and reconstruct them to the best of your ability. State clearly any assumption you make. Determine the amount of income taxes paid and compare it with that disclosed by the company.

21–2. Please refer to the financial statements of Quaker Oats (Appendix 23).

Required:
I. Compute the following for 1991 and 1990:
   A. Ratio of depreciation expense to assets subject to depreciation.
   B. Effective interest rate on liabilities subject to interest.
   C. Ratio of tax expense to income before tax (effective tax rate).
   D. Ratio of cost of goods sold plus other operating expenses to net sales.
   E. Ratio of net income to total revenues.
II. Comment on the trend of the ratios in (I) above from 1990 to 1991.

21–3. Please refer to the financial statements of Quaker Oats (Appendix 23).

Required:
Please prepare a Statement Accounting for Variations in Net Income of Quaker Oats comparing the years ended June 30, 1991 and June 30, 1990.

21–4. Please refer to the financial statements of Campbell Soup Co. in Appendix 4B (all figures in millions).

Required:
1. Reconstruct all entries related to income taxes for 1991. Post these to all T-accounts that are affected by taxes and reconstruct them to the best of your ability. State clearly any assumptions you made. Determine the amount of income taxes paid in 1991 and compare it to that disclosed by the company.
2. Explain how Campbell with income before tax of $667.4 in 1991 reports $185.8 of current federal income tax while the statutory tax rate is 34%.

21–5.   Please refer to the financial statements of Campbell Soup Co. in Appendix 4B.

Required:

Compute the following for 1990:

1. Accumulated depreciation as a percentage of gross plant assets subject to depreciation.
2. Depreciation expense as a percentage of gross plant assets subject to depreciation.
3. Depreciation expense as a percentage of sales.

21–6.   Please refer to the financial statements of Campbell Soup Co. in Appendix 4B.

Required:

Prepare a Statement Accounting for Variations in Net Income comparing fiscal years ending 7/28/91 and 7/29/90.

21–7.   The Jackson Corporation sells two products, A and B. Its gross-margin components for the past two years were as follows:

	Year 7	*Year 6*
Sales revenue:		
Product A	$60,000	$35,000
Product B	30,000	45,000
Total	$90,000	$80,000
Deduct cost of goods sold:		
Product A	$50,000	$28,000
Product B	19,500	27,000
Total	$69,500	$55,000
Gross margin	$20,500	$25,000

In year 6 the selling price of A was $5 a unit, while in year 7 it was $6. Product B sold for $50 a unit in each year. Management was shocked to see that a 12.5 percent increase in sales resulted in a $4,500 decrease in gross margin.

Required:

Prepare a detailed explanation of the causes of the decline in gross margin, showing effect of changes in quantities, prices, costs, and product mix.

21–8.   The LUX Corporation manufactures basketballs. The business has been in existence for a number of years.

Because the business has its ups and downs, the corporation has retained you to analyze its cost structure and develop certain cost/price relationships.

The following data apply:

1. Fixed costs are $100,000 per year.
2. Variable costs per unit are $1.50.
3. The selling price per unit is $3.50.

Required:
a. Determine the volume break-even point.
b. Assuming present sales are 120,000 units, determine the increase (decrease) in profits resulting from—
   (1) Fifteen percent increase in volume.
   (2) Fifteen percent decrease in volume.
c. Assuming present sales are 150,000 units, determine the change in operating results resulting from—
   (1) A 10 percent drop in selling price.
   (2) A 20 percent decrease in variable costs.
   (3) A 20 percent increase in volume.
   (4) Combined effect.

Consider each case independently.

21–9. The Better Publishing Company has provided you with the following data related to one of the company's new publications:

Variable costs per copy:	
Printing, binding, and paper	$1.30
Bookstore discounts	2.00
Authors' royalties	1.30
Commissions	0.40
General and administrative expenses	1.00
Total variable costs per copy:	$6.00
Fixed costs:	
Editorial costs	$ 6,000.00
Illustrations	12,000.00
Typesetting	22,000.00
Total fixed costs:	$40,000.00
List price per copy	$10.00

Recognizing that break-even analysis can be an important analytical tool to study the relationships among costs, revenues, and profits, compute the number of copies that would be produced at the break-even point and prepare and correctly label a basic break-even chart to illustrate the various components of this analysis.

21–10. The All Seasons Company produces three products A, B, and C. The revenue and variable costs of these products are as follows:

	A	B	C
Sales price per unit	$2.00	$3.00	$5.00
Variable costs	1.50	2.00	2.50
Contribution margin	$0.50	$1.00	$2.50

Fixed common costs for the firm total $13,000.

Required:
Assume a sales mix of 1 : 2 : 3 for the products A, B, and C, respectively. Compute the number of units of each product that needs to be sold to reach the break-even point.

21–11.   The following are the cost structures of Companies A and B:

	Company A	Company B
Fixed costs	$12,000	$10,000
Variable costs (% of sales)	40%	60%

Required:
a. What are the break-even points in sales dollars for Companies A and B?
b. What will be the net income at sales of $18,000?
c. What will be the net income at sales of $27,000?
d. (1) Assume that sales can be increased to $30,000. What percentage of accounts receivable does each company have to collect to break even? (All sales are made on credit.)
    (2) How much additional cost outlays beyond the break-even point are required by each company to increase sales to $30,000? (Assume all sales on credit are fully collectible.)
    (3) What is the rate of incremental profits on additional cost outlays at a sales level of $30,000 in (1) above?
e. (1) Past experience has been that bad debts amounted to 10 percent of accounts receivable. What are the sales required if the company wants to net a profit of $10,000?
    (2) Assume that the present sales are $30,000 and that a maximum sales level of $40,000 can be achieved with an additional incurrence in fixed costs of $4,000 while variable costs per unit remain the same. The bad debt ratio is 10 percent. What is the net income for each company?
f. (1) Is a lower fixed cost always advantageous?
    (2) Which company is in a better position to take marginal risk in Requirement e (2) above?

21–12.   Seco Corporation, a wholesale supply company, engages independent sales agents to market the company's lines. These agents currently receive a commission of 20% of sales, but they are demanding an increase to 25% of sales made during the year ending December 31, 1989. Seco had already prepared its 1989 budget before learning of the agents' demand for an increase in commissions. The following pro forma income statement is based on this budget:

SECO CORPORATION
Pro Forma Income Statement
For the Year Ending December 31, 1989

Sales		$10,000,000
Cost of sales		6,000,000
Gross margin		4,000,000
Selling and administrative costs		
Commissions	$2,000,000	
All other costs (fixed)	100,000	2,100,000
Income before income tax		1,900,000
Income tax (30%)		570,000
Net income		$ 1,330,000

Seco is considering the possibility of employing its own salespersons. Three individuals would be required, at an estimated annual salary of $30,000 each, plus commissions of 5% of sales. In addition, a sales manager would be employed at a fixed annual salary of $160,000. All other fixed costs, as well as the variable cost percentages, would remain the same as the estimates in the 1989 pro forma income statement.

Required:
a. Compute Seco's estimated break-even point in sales dollars for the year ending December 31, 1989 based on the pro forma income statement prepared by the company.
b. Compute Seco's estimated break-even point in sales dollars for the year ending December 31, 1989 if the company employs its own salespersons.
c. Compute the estimated volume in sales dollars that would be required for the year ending December 31, 1989 to yield the same net income as projected in the pro forma income statement, if Seco continues to use the independent sales agents and agrees to their demand for a 25% sales commission.
d. Compute the estimated volume in sales dollars that would generate an identical net income for the year ending December 31, 1989, regardless of whether Seco employs its own salespersons or continues to use the independent sales agents and pays them a 25% commission.

(AICPA)

21–13. A press report carried the following news item: "General Motors, Ford, and Chrysler are expected to post losses on fourth-quarter operations despite sales gains. Auto makers' revenues are based on factory output rather than retail sales by dealers, and last quarter's sales increases were from the bulging inventories at the end of the third quarter, rather than from models produced in the fourth quarter."

Required:

Describe the most likely specific reason for the auto makers' fourth-quarter losses.

21-14. The following portions of financial statements are excerpts from the year 6 annual report of the Gotham Tire Co.

Income Statements
(in millions)

	Year 6	Year 5
Income (loss) from continuing operations before income taxes	$37	$(73)
Income taxes	34	(46)
Income (loss) from continuing operations	3	(27)
Discontinued operations	16	21
Income (loss) before extraordinary credits and cumulative effect of accounting change	19	(6)
Extraordinary credits	—	9
Cumulative effect of change in pension reversion accounting	66	—
Net income	$85	$ 3

Statement of Cash Flows
(in millions)

	Year 6	Year 5
Cash from operations		
Add (deduct) items not using (providing) cash:		
Deferred income taxes	($22)	($94)

Balance Sheets
(in millions)

	Year 6	Year 5
Current assets:		
Recoverable income taxes	56	33
Current liabilities:		
Taxes payable	122	114
Long-term liabilities:		
Deferred income taxes	49	—

Income Taxes
(in millions)

Income (loss) from continuing operations before income taxes segregated as to U.S. or foreign source is as follows:

	Years ended October 31	
	Year 6	Year 5
U.S. source	$(22)	$(124)
Foreign source	59	51
Total income (loss) from continuing operations before income taxes	$ 37	$ (73)

A summary of income tax expense is as follows:

	Years ended October 31	
	Year 6	Year 5
Currently payable:		
Federal	$13	$ 8
Foreign	43	51
State and local.................................	7	13
Adjustment of estimated income tax liabilities	—	(16)
Deferred:		
Federal	37	(89)
Foreign	1	(1)
State and local.................................	4	(5)
Charge equivalent to tax effects for:		
Use of foreign loss carryforwards....................	—	2
Use of foreign tax credit carryforwards	—	7
Taxes related to:		
Discontinued operations...........................	(12)	(16)
Extraordinary gains on debt repurchases and early retirements	—	—
Cumulative effect of change in pension revision accounting .	(59)	—
Total income taxes attributable to continuing operations ...	$34	$(46)

Extraordinary credits consist of the following:

	Years ended October 31	
	Year 6	*Year 5*
Foreign loss and tax credit carryforwards	$ —	$9
Gains on debt repurchases and early retirements (21 cents a share)	—	—
Total extraordinary credits	$ —	$9

Required:

By means of T-account analysis reconcile as best you can the year 6 tax-related accounts of Gotham Tire Co., and determine the amount of income taxes paid in year 6.

21–15.   The following portions of financial statements are excerpts from the 1991 annual report of The Mead Corporation and Subsidiaries.

Consolidated Statements of Earnings
(in millions)

	1991	1990
Earnings from continuing operations before income taxes	$148.0	$147.0
Income taxes (Note M)	54.3	52.3
Earnings from continuing operations before equity in net earnings (loss) of jointly-owned companies	93.7	94.7
Equity in net earnings (loss) of jointly-owned companies (Note C)	(18.1)	11.7
Earnings from continuing operations	75.6	106.4
Loss from discontinued operation (Note N)	(10.0)	(74.8)
Earnings before extraordinary item and cumulative effect of change in accounting principle	65.6	31.6
Extraordinary item, gain on retirement of debt		6.9
Cumulative effect of change in accounting principle (Note P)	(58.7)	
Net earnings	$ 6.9	$ 38.5

Consolidated Balance Sheets
(in millions)

	1991	1990
Current liabilities:		
Taxes, other than income	$ 57.4	$ 52.8
Other current liabilities	196.4	152.3
Noncurrent Liabilities:		
Deferred items:		
Income taxes	248.8	294.5

Note M—Income taxes (in millions)

Year ended December 31	1991	1990
Currently payable:		
Federal	$29.3	$43.0
Federal alternative minimum tax	29.6	12.3
State and local	5.3	(0.8)
Foreign	3.2	5.2
	67.4	59.7
Deffered:		
Excess tax depreciation	26.1	33.9
Alternative minimum tax carryforward	(29.6)	(12.3)
Pension income	7.7	7.5
Employee benefits		(8.6)
Other expenses	(10.3)	(25.6)
Miscellaneous	(7.0)	(2.3)
	(13.1)	(7.4)
	$54.3	$52.3

Principal reasons for the variations between the statutory federal rate and the effective rate are:

Year ended December 31	1991	1990
Federal income tax rate	34.0%	34.0%
State and local income taxes, net of federal benefit	(1.1)	(1.2)
Other	3.8	2.8
Effective tax rate	36.7%	35.6%

Note N—Discontinued operations (in millions)

1991

Insurance operations:
  Provision for loss during runoff of insurance operations, net of
    income tax benefit of $6.0 .... $(10.0)
Loss from discontinued operations .... $(10.0)

Note P—Postretirement benefits other than pensions.

In 1991, the company adopted *Statement of Financial Accounting Standards No. 106,* "Employers' Accounting for Postretirement Benefits Other than Pensions." The company elected to immediately recognize the cumulative effect of the change in accounting for postretirement benefits of $93.5 million ($58.7 million net of income tax benefit) which represents the accumulated postretirement benefit obligation (APBO) existing at January 1, 1991, of $107.9 million, less $14.4 million recorded in prior years.

Note S—Additional information on cash flows (in millions)

Year ended December 31	*1991*	*1990*
Cash paid during the year for:		
Interest (net of amount capitalized)	$112.5	$93.2
Income taxes	$ 41.9	$43.3

Required:

The Mead Corporation does not present Income Taxes Payable as a separate line item in its balance sheets. We assume that the Income Taxes Payable are included in "Other current liabilities."

We also assume that the beginning balance of the Income Taxes Payable account as of January 1, 1991 was $50 million. After posting all the income-tax-related transactions, determine the ending balance of the Income Taxes Payable account as of December 31, 1991.

21–16. The following portions of financial statements are excerpts from the 1990 annual report of Armstrong World Industries, Inc. and subsidiaries.

Consolidated Statement of Earnings
(millions)

	1990	*1989*
Earnings from continuing business before income taxes ..	$218.5	$239.4
Income taxes	75.3	84.5
Earnings from continuing business	$143.2	$154.9
Discontinued business:		
Earnings (losses), net of income tax benefit of $0.7 in 1990 and tax expense of $7.6 in 1989	(1.1)	11.0
Provision for (loss) gain on disposition of discontinued business, net of income tax benefit of $3.8 in 1990 and tax expense of $8.0 in 1989	(9.1)	21.7
Cumulative effect of change in accounting for income taxes	8.0	—
Net earnings	$141.0	$187.6

Consolidated Balance Sheets
(millions)

	1990	*1989*
Current liabilities:		
Income taxes	$ 18.6	$ 20.3
Noncurrent liabilities:		
Deferred income taxes	167.5	167.7

Consolidated Statement of Cash Flows
(millions)

	1990	*1989*
Supplemental cash flow information:		
Interest paid	$ 37.7	$ 42.9
Income taxes paid	$ 67.7	$ 87.6

Shareholders' equity changes for 1990, 1989 (millions):

	1990	*1989*
Foreign currency translation:		
Balance at beginning of year	$ 21.9	$ 24.1
Translation adjustments and hedging activities	21.2	(2.9)
Allocated income taxes	5.2	0.7
Balance at end of year	$ 48.3	$ 21.9

Details of taxes (millions):

	1990	1989
Income taxes:		
Payable:		
Federal	$ 24.6	$ 54.4
Foreign	32.5	30.0
State	1.5	9.2
	$ 58.6	$ 93.6
Deferred:		
Federal	$ 10.5	($ 9.3)
Federal	1.3	0.8
State	4.9	(0.6)
	$ 16.7	($ 9.1)
Total income taxes	$ 75.3	$ 84.5

Reconciliation to statutory U.S. federal income tax rates is as follows:

	1990	1989
Effective tax rate	34.4%	35.3%
State income taxes	(2.0)	(2.4)
Benefit on ESOP dividend	3.0	1.4
Taxes on foreign income	(1.9)	(0.9)
Other items	0.5	0.6
Statutory tax rate	34.0%	34.0%

Required:
By means of T-account analysis reconcile as best you can the 1990 tax-related accounts of Armstrong World Industries, Inc. and subsidiaries and determine the amount of income taxes paid in 1990. Compare your estimate to the amount of tax paid disclosed by the company.

21–17.   The following are financial statement captions and footnotes relating to income taxes taken from the 1991 annual report of Abbott Laboratories and Subsidiaries.

Consolidated Statement of Earnings
(in thousands)

	1991	1990
Earnings before taxes	$1,544,222	$1,350,733
Taxes on earnings	455,545	384,959
Earnings before extraordinary gain and accounting change	$1,088,677	$ 965,774
Extraordinary gain, net of tax $74,068	128,182	—
Cumulative effect of accounting change, net of tax $78,151	$(128,114)	—
Net earnings	$1,088,745	$ 965,774

Consolidated Balance Sheets
(in thousands)

	1991	1990
Assets:		
Prepaid income taxes	$ 425,442	$ 296,861
Current liabilities:		
Income taxes payable	194,255	234,338
Other liabilities and deferrals:		
Deferred income taxes	347,245	409,090

Consolidated Statement of Cash Flows
(in thousands)

	1991	1990
Supplemental cash flow information:		
Interest paid	$ 59,915	$ 94,204
Income taxes paid	$ 651,442	$ 353,623

Consolidated Statement of Shareholders' Investment
(in thousands)

	1991	1990
Common shares		
Issued at beginning of year	$297,522	$241,576
Issued under incentive stock programs	49,423	49,266
Tax benefit from sale of option shares	19,000	16,683
Retired	(4,937)	(10,003)
Issued at end of year	$361,008	$297,522
Cumulative translation adjustments		
Balance at beginning of year	$ 74,328	$ 18,289
Translation adjustments	(36,750)	59,787
Allocated income taxes	43	(3,748)
Balance at end of year	$ 37,621	$ 74,328

Notes to the financial statement:
Note 2—Taxes on Earnings
The related provisions for taxes on earnings are as follows:

	1991	1990
Taxes on earnings (in thousands)		
Current:		
U.S. federal and possessions	$316,377	$266,454
State	50,758	41,903
Foreign	140,559	109,129
Total current	$507,694	$417,486
Deferred:		
Domestic	($ 49,998)	($ 34,582)
Foreign	(2,151)	2,055
Total deferred	($ 52,149)	($ 32,527)
Total	$455,545	$384,959

Required:
By means of T-account analysis reconcile as best you can the 1991 tax-related accounts of Abbott Laboratories and Subsidiaries and determine the amount of income taxes paid in 1991. Compare your derived amount to the amount of taxes paid as disclosed by the company.

21–18.   At a meeting of your institution's Investment Policy Committee, at which Zeta Corporation (see Problem 23–5) was considered for investment, a member wondered about which were the major factors that accounted for the year 5 to year 6 change in the net income of that company.

Required:
Prepare a statement accounting for the variation in Zeta's net income for the period in question.

21–19.   Please refer to the financial statements of Zeta Corporation in Problem 23–5.

Required:
A.   Reconstruct all entries and T-accounts related to income taxes for year 6 and show the amount of income tax paid.
B.   Estimate the amount of depreciation expense shown for *tax return* reporting.

Chapter 22

22–1.   Please refer to the financial statements of Quaker Oats (Appendix to Chapter 23).

Required:

Please recast analytically the income statements for the three years ended June 30, 1991 (Hint: Use item 155, 156 and 157 to find discretionary expenses. Use federal tax at the statutory rate of 34 percent.) Comment on the trends revealed by the restatement.

22-2.   Please refer to the financial statements of Quaker Oats (Appendix 23).

Required:

Construct a table in which maintenance and repair expense is shown as a percentage of revenues and as a percentage of property, plant, and equipment— net for 1989, 1990 the average of 1989 and 1990 and for 1991.

How does the level of spending on maintenance and repairs in 1991 compare with the average level of spending in 1989 and 1990?

22-3.   Please refer to the financial statements of Campbell Soup (Appendix 4B). Present an analytically recast income statement for the three years 1991, 1990 and 1989 showing as much significant detail as disclosure permits. Comment on trends revealed by the restatement.

22-4.   Hereunder are the income statements of Ferro Corporation and Note 7 on income taxes:

**Consolidated Statements of Income and Earnings Retained in the Business
Years Ended December 31, year 6, and year 5
(in thousands)**

	Year 6	Year 5
Net sales	$376,485	$328,005
Cost of sales	266,846	237,333
Selling and administrative expenses	58,216	54,140
Research and development	9,972	8,205
	335,034	299,678
Operating income	41,451	28,327
Other income:		
Equity in net earnings of affiliated companies	1,394	504
Royalties	710	854
Interest earned	1,346	1,086
Miscellaneous	1,490	1,761
	4,940	4,205
Other charges:		
Interest expense	4,055	4,474
Unrealized foreign currency translation loss	4,037	1,851
Miscellaneous	1,480	1,448
	9,572	7,773
Income before taxes	36,819	24,759
United States and foreign income taxes, including deferred taxes of $493,000 in year 6 and $64,000 in year 5 (Note 7)	16,765	11,133
Net income	$ 20,054	$ 13,626

Notes to the financial statements:

7. Income Tax Expense: Income tax expense is comprised of the following components (dollars in thousands):

	United States federal	Foreign	Total
Year 6:			
Current	$5,147	11,125	16,272
Deferred	353	140	493
Total	$5,500	11,265	16,765
Year 5:			
Current	$2,974	8,095	11,069
Deferred	180	(116)	64
Total	$3,154	7,979	11,133

Deferred income taxes were mainly the result of using accelerated depreciation for income tax purposes and straight-line depreciation in the consolidated financial statements.

State and local income taxes totaling approximately $750,000 and $698,000 in year 6 and year 5, respectively, are included in other expense categories.

A reconciliation between the United States federal income tax rate and the effective tax rate for year 6 and year 5 follows:

	Year 6	Year 5
United States federal income tax rate	48.0%	48.0%
Earnings of consolidated subsidiaries taxed at rates less than the United States federal income tax rate	(5.3)	(5.3)
Equity in after-tax earnings of affiliated companies	(1.4)	(0.8)
Unrealized foreign exchange translation loss	5.3	3.6
Additional U.S. taxes on dividends from subsidiaries and affiliates ..	0.8	1.0
Investment tax credit	(1.5)	(0.9)
Miscellaneous	(0.4)	(0.6)
Effective tax rate	45.5%	45.0%

In addition, you were able to obtain the following information from Form 10-K filed with the SEC:

1. Cost of sales includes the following items (in thousands):

	Year 6	Year 5
Repairs and maintenance	$15,000	$20,000
Loss on disposal of chemicals division	—	7,000

2. Selling and administrative expenses include (in thousands):

	Year 6	Year 5
Advertising	$ 6,000	$ 7,000
Employee training program	4,000	5,000

Required:
I. Identify erratic and unstable factors, as well as the factors that caused income tax expense to differ from 48 percent of pre-tax income, and present analytically recast income statements for year 5 and year 6.
II. What significant changes, if any, do you notice in the company's operational policies in year 6? (Limit your analysis to outlays for repairs and maintenance, advertising, and employee training program expense.)

22–5.   On January 2, year 2 you purchase all the outstanding shares of the Finex Co. for $700,000. The following are the financial statements of the company:

FINEX COMPANY
Balance Sheet
As of December 31, year 1

Cash	$ 55,000
U.S. government bonds	25,000
Accounts receivable (net)	150,000
Merchandise inventory	230,000
Land	40,000
Buildings (net) [a]	360,000
Equipment (net) [b]	130,000
Total assets	$990,000
Accounts payable	$170,000
Notes payable (current)	50,000
Bonds payable (due year 12) [c]	200,000
Preferred stock (6%, $100 par)	100,000
Common stock ($100 par)	400,000
Paid-in surplus	43,000
Retained earnings [d]	27,000
Liabilities and Capital	$990,000

Condensed Income Statement
For Year Ended December 31, year1

Net sales	$860,000
Cost of goods sold	546,000
Gross profit	$314,000
Selling and administrative expenses	240,000
Net operating income	$ 74,000
Provision for income tax	34,000
Net income	$ 40,000

[a] Accumulated depreciation on buildings, $35,000. Depreciation expense in year 1, $7,900.
[b] Accumulated depreciation on equipment, $20,000. Depreciation expense in year 1, $9,000.
[c] Bonds were sold at par.
[d] Dividends paid in year 1: preferred, $6,000; common, $20,000.

You want to adjust the net income figure in order to estimate the net income realizable under your ownership after the purchase. The company uses the FIFO method of inventory valuation and all inventories can be sold without loss. With the change in ownership you expect that about 5% of the accounts receivable will become uncollectible. Assume that sales as well as all percentage relationships remain constant except as changed by the required adjustments.

Required:
A. What cost should be assigned to Land, Buildings, and Equipment, respectively? (Allocate the amount paid for the three assets in proportion to their respective book values on the 12/31/year 1 balance sheet.)
B. Prepare a balance sheet of the Finex Co. immediately after the purchase.
C. How much do you expect will Finex Co.'s net operating income be in year 2 under the new ownership? (Use same ratio of depreciation expense to assets; 1/3 of depreciation expense is charged to cost of goods sold.)
D. If your minimum required ratio of net operating income to net sales were 8.0%, would you purchase the company?

22–6.   Aspero Inc. is a small company of $500,000 sales a year. The company was in need of a short-term loan of $100,000 to finance its working capital requirements. Two banks were ready to give the required loan to the company but each bank required certain conditions to be satisfied. Bank A expects at least a 25 percent gross margin on sales and Bank B requires a 2:1 current ratio.
   The following information is available:

1. Sales returns and allowances—10 percent of sales.
2. Purchases returns and allowances—2 percent of purchases.
3. Sales discount—2 percent of sales.
4. Purchase discount—1 percent of purchases.
5. Ending inventory—$138,000.
6. Cash is 10 percent of accounts receivable.

7. Credit terms that the company gives to its customers are 45 days, while credit terms that the company gets from its suppliers are 90 days.
8. Purchases for the year were $400,000.
9. The percentage increase in ending inventory over beginning inventory was 38 percent.
10. Accounts payable is the only item of current liabilities.

Required:
From which, if any, bank can the company get a loan?

22–7. Cupola Brothers, Inc., produces large steel castings and metal fabrications for sale to manufacturers of heavy construction machinery and agricultural equipment. Early in year 3 the company's president sent the following memorandum to his financial vice president:

TO: Bob
FROM: Jack
SUBJECT: Accounting and Financial Policies

As you know, fiscal year 2 was a tough year, and the recession seems likely to continue to affect us in year 3. My thought is that, although the whole industry is suffering, we may be hurting our performance unnecessarily with accounting and business policies which are no longer appropriate.

Specifically:

(1) We depreciate most fixed assets (foundry equipment) over their estimated useful lives on the "tonnage-of-production" method. Accelerated methods and shorter lives are used for income tax purposes. It seems a switch to the "straight-line method" for book purposes could: *(a)* eliminate the deferred tax liability on our balance sheet, and *(b)* leverage our profits if business picks up in year 4.

(2) Ten years ago, you convinced me to change from the FIFO to the LIFO inventory method. Well, inflation is now down to a 4 percent year-over-year rate, and balance sheet strength seems important in this economic environment. I estimate we could increase shareholders' equity by about $2.0 million, working capital by $4.0 million, and year 3 earnings by $0.5 million if we return to FIFO in year 3. This adjustment is real . . . these profits were earned by our company over the last 9 years and should be recognized.

(3) If we make the inventory change, the stock repurchase program can be continued this year. The same shareholder who sold us 50,000 shares last year at $100 per share would like to sell another 20,000 shares at the same price. However, to obtain additional bank financing, we must maintain the current ratio at 3:1 or better. It seems prudent to decrease our capitalization if return on assets is unsatisfactory and our industry is declining. Moreover, interest rates have fallen (11 percent prime), and we could save $60,000 after taxes annually once our $3.00 per share dividend is resumed.

These actions would have a favorable effect on our profitability and liquidity ratios as shown in the pro forma income and balance sheet data for year 3:

	(In millions)		
	Year 1	*Year 2*	*Year 3E*
Net sales	$ 50.6	$ 42.3	$ 29.0
Net income (loss)	2.0	(5.7)	0.1
Percent margin	4.0%	—	0.3%
Dividends	$ 0.7	$ 0.6	$ 0.0
Return on investment	7.2%	—	0.4%
Return on equity	11.3%	—	0.9%
Current assets	$ 17.6	$ 14.8	$ 14.5
Current liabilities	6.6	4.9	4.5
Long-term debt	2.0	6.1	8.1
Shareholders' equity	17.7	11.4	11.5
Shares outstanding (000)	226.8	170.5	150.5
Per common share:			
Shareholder's equity	$ 78.05	$ 66.70	$ 76.41
Market price range	$42–34	$65–45	$62–55*

* Year to date

"Bob, give me your reaction by the end of next week."

Assuming that you are Bob, the financial vice president, appraise the rationale for each of the president's proposals, with particular emphasis on how each accounting or business decision might affect the quality of earnings. Support your reply with ratio analysis.

(CFA)

22–8   Robert G. Wingerter, president, Libbey-Owens-Ford Company, said, among others, in an address to analysts:

"While on the subject of management attitudes, I would like to comment that LOF has resisted joining a seemingly increasing number of companies who along with earnings announcements also make extraordinary or non-recurring loss announcements. Many of these situations read like regular operating problems when you get into the detail. When we closed plants and the like, we have charged earnings for the costs involved or reserved as we approached the event. Such costs in my judgment are quite usually a normal operating expense and something that good management should expect or anticipate. That, of course, brings up the question as to what earnings figure should be regarded by your profession in assigning a P/E ratio and what is the quality of the reported earnings figure."

Required:

a. Comment on Mr. Wingerter's statement.

b. What factors determine whether an item of gain or loss is extraordinary or not?

c. Which of the following would you classify as extraordinary and why? All amounts are material.

    (1) Loss suffered by foreign subsidiaries because of a change in the foreign exchange rate.

    (2) Write-down of inventory from cost to market.

    (3) Loss attributable to the appearance of improved product developed by a competitor.

    (4) Decrease in net profit as a result of higher tax rates.

    (5) Increase in net profit as a result of the liquidation of low-cost LIFO inventories because of long strikes.

    (6) Expenses incurred in relocating plant.

    (7) Expenses incurred in liquidating unprofitable product lines.

    (8) Research and development costs written off as a result of product failure (nonmarketed).

    (9) Software costs written off because demand for a product proved to be weaker than anticipated.

  (10) Failure of a major customer resulting in a substantial bad debt provision.

  (11) Loss on the sale of rental cars by a car rental company.

  (12) Gains on sales of fixed assets.

  (13) Rentals received from employees who rented company-owned houses.

  (14) Uninsured casualty losses.

  (15) The expropriation by a foreign government of an entire operation owned by the enterprise.

  (16) The seizure or destruction of property as a result of an act of war.

22–9.   A prominent financial analyst stated:

"For my part I think we should drop the word extraordinary and leave it to each reader to decide whether a strike will recur next year or not, to decide whether a lease abandonment will recur or not. In other words, an all-inclusive statement, with no category of 'extraordinary.' Let the reader use that statement for predictive purposes by eliminating those items which will not recur next year. But let the record show all the events which had an impact, with no 'below the line' items, no adjustments which 'really don't count.'

"The 'current operating performance' philosophy really has no point, I am arguing. Everything is to be included; it is all part of the collapse or success this year. By omitting items from 'current operating performance' we are relegating them to a lesser role. I do not believe that is conceptually correct. Thus, (1) we include everything in order to judge the performance of management and (2) we are also trying to guess at next year's results.

"For this purpose the reader may well decide that there will not be a big inventory write-off, and that no plant will be sold or abandoned. Both items deserve to adversely affect income because they are measuring management performance. Both items may be excluded by the reader in predicting the next year.

"Finally, the existing system has resulted in abuses. An earthquake is part of the picture. A defalcation in Basel is part of banking. A lease abandonment recurs in the oil industry. No man is wise enough to cut the Gordian knot on this issue by picking and choosing what is extraordinary, recurring, typical, different from typical or customary."

Required:

Evaluate this statement and present clearly and concisely your views of—

a. How "extraordinary items" should be presented.
b. How the analyst should evaluate such items.

22–10. Interim financial reporting is an important topic in accounting. There has been considerable discussion as to the proper method of reflecting results of operations at interim dates. *APB Opinion No. 28* clarifies some aspects of interim financial reporting.

Required
a. Discuss generally how revenue should be recognized at interim dates and specifically how revenue should be recognized for industries subject to large seasonal fluctuations in revenue and for long-term contracts using the percentage-of-completion method at annual reporting dates.
b. Discuss generally how product and period costs should be recognized at interim dates. Also discuss how inventory and cost of goods sold may be afforded special accounting treatment at interim dates.
c. Discuss how the provision for income taxes is computed and reflected in interim financial statements.

(AICPA adapted)

22–11. What factors *(a)* within the company and *(b)* within the economy have and are likely to affect the degree of variability in the earnings per share, dividends per share, and market price per share, of common stock?

(CFA)

Chapter 23

23–1. Below are condensed financial statements constructed on a percentage basis. Total sales revenues are shown as 100 percent and all other numbers are divided by sales revenue for the year. The nine companies identified by numbers belong to the following industries.
a. Utility company.
b. Drug company.
c. Brewery.
d. Public opinion survey firm.
e. Grocery store chain.
f. Manufacturer of tobacco products.
g. Computer equipment and software.
h. Hospital and health care company.
i. Mutual fund and investment adviser.

Balance Sheet at Year-End

	(1)	(2)	(3)	(4)	(5)	(6)	(7)	(8)	(9)
Current receivables	9.77%	19.20%	3.35%	25.96%	0.55%	8.10%	26.34%	17.38%	15.33%
Inventories	6.22	14.87	5.18	0.00	7.91	20.11	31.69	0.00	0.00
Net plant and equipment	224.39	28.20	51.20	24.52	6.94	26.25	31.36	88.97	3.19
All other assets	46.56	29.15	5.48	26.65	3.71	18.50	16.91	24.35	219.59
Total assets	286.94%	91.42%	65.21%	77.13%	19.11%	72.96%	106.30%	130.70%	238.11%
Cost of P&E (gross)	279.83%	39.06%	70.33%	35.78%	9.64%	39.31%	45.91%	106.64%	6.29%
Current liabilities	18.78%	22.70%	11.19%	29.92%	7.31%	13.31%	19.30%	19.33%	76.89%
Long-term liabilities	158.69	9.22	26.65	10.19	6.06	16.40	4.11	73.32	72.18
Owners' equity	109.47	59.50	27.37	37.02	5.74	43.25	82.89	38.05	89.04
Total equities	286.94%	91.42%	65.21%	77.13%	19.11%	72.96%	106.30%	130.70%	238.11%

Income Statement at Year-End

	(1)	(2)	(3)	(4)	(5)	(6)	(7)	(8)	(9)
Revenues	100.00%	100.00%	100.00%	100.00%	100.00%	100.00%	100.00%	100.00%	100.00%
CGS (excluding depreciation or operating expenses)	49.50	31.11	67.48	63.29%*	77.20	68.16	56.24	81.06%*	16.55%*
Depreciation	8.36	2.26	2.47	3.51	1.14	3.50	4.76	4.33	0.81
Interest expense	8.81	1.14	2.03	0.47	0.59	1.26	0.31	4.04	10.75
Advertising expense	0.00	2.39	4.82	0.12	3.89	6.97	3.86	0.00	6.24
R&D expense	0.76	7.95	0.24	0.00	0.00	0.00	11.06	0.00	0.00
Income taxes	11.47	8.11	2.44	6.80	0.77	4.71	2.98	4.44	33.01
All other items (net)	6.63	29.08	15.59	18.54	15.50	8.89	14.15	(0.46)	0.73
Total expenses	85.53%	82.04%	95.07%	92.73%	99.09%	93.49%	93.36%	93.41%	68.09%
Net income	14.47%	17.96%	4.93%	7.27%	0.91%	6.51%	6.64%	6.59%	31.91%

Required:

By examining the percentage relationships in the financial statements match the numbered companies with the nine industry categories listed above. You may want to consult industry ratios for the above industries in your library. Appendix 4A contains a list of sources of industry ratios.

23–2. Discuss the factors which would determine the relative P/E ratios to be applied to each of these two makers of industrial machinery for which the following financial data are available:

	A	B
Capital structure:		
5% 20-year notes	$10,000,000	$ None
Common and surplus	20,000,000	30,000,000
Number of common shares	500,000	750,000
Earnings per share:		
Year 6	$ 4.25	$ 3.00
Year 5	3.50	2.50
Year 4	2.25	1.67
Year 3	2.75	2.00
Year 2	1.70	1.95
Sales (year 6)	30,000,000	30,000,000
Net income	2,125,000	2,250,000
Balance sheet data at 12/31/year 6:		
Cash	3,000,000	5,850,000
Receivables	5,000,000	3,750,000
Inventories	12,000,000	10,000,000
Total current assets	$20,000,000	$19,600,000
Accounts payable	4,000,000	3,500,000
Accruals	2,000,000	2,000,000
Taxes	1,000,000	1,100,000
Total current liabilities	$ 7,000,000	$ 6,600,000
Net plant	13,000,000	15,900,000
Patents, etc.	4,000,000	100,000

(CFA adapted)

23–3.   Select a company from a nonregulated industry for which you can obtain adequately informative financial statements for at least six years.

Required:

Based on the financial statements, background information on the company and its industry, as well as financial measures of other companies in the industry, prepare a *comprehensive analysis and report* covering the following specific points:

a. General (brief) description of the company and its industry.
b. An evaluation of the following areas:
  (1) Short-term liquidity (current debt-paying ability).
  (2) Capital structure and long-term solvency.
  (3) Return on investment (including capital utilization).
  (4) Operating performance.
c. Comment on the degree of informative disclosure, useful to the analyst, which was found in the financial statements examined.
d. In what way did alternative principles of accounting used in the financial statements affect the analytical measures used in this report?

You are expected to use a broad variety of financial analysis tools in your analysis and evaluation leading to a conclusion regarding the four areas detailed above.

23–4.   Please refer to data in Problem 18–15
A. Estimate ABEX's total operating income for 1990, using the data in Tables 1 through 4.
B. Identify the additional information needed to complete a reasonable estimate for earnings per share (EPS) in 1990, and identify *five* primary sources from which you can obtain this information. (You should identify *primary* sources and *not* external sources for the data needed.)
C. Estimate and discuss the incremental changes in ABEX's EPS based on *each* of the following *two* potential scenarios for the petrochemical division *only*.
  (i) The price of polyethylene in 1990 is 8% higher than shown in Table 4 and everything else is the same.
  (ii) The volume of production and sales of polyethylene is 8% higher than shown in Table 4 and everything else is the same.

(CFA adapted)

23–5.   REVIEW PROBLEM

The following are the financial statements of ZETA Corporation:

ZETA CORPORATION
Consolidated Balance Sheets
as of December 31, Year 6, and Year 5
(in thousands)

	Year 6	Year 5
Assets		
Currents assets:		
Cash	$ 2,000	$ 2,000
Receivables	25,000	20,000
Inventories (Notes 1 and 2)	56,000	38,000
Prepaid expenses	1,000	1,000
Total current assets	84,000	61,000
Investment in associated company	14,000	11,000
Property, plant, and equipment	61,000	52,000
Less: Accumulated depreciation	23,000	19,000
Net property, plant, and equipment	38,000	33,000
Goodwill	2,000	—
Total assets	$138,000	$105,000
Liabilities and Stockholders' Equity		
Current liabilities:		
Notes payable to banks	$ 16,000	$ 14,000
Accounts payable and accruals	29,000	23,000
Income taxes payable	7,000	2,000
Current portion of long-term debt (Note 6)	2,000	1,000
Total current liabilities	54,000	40,000
Long-term debt due after one year (Note 6)	25,000	15,200
Deferred income taxes (Note 5)	3,600	2,000
Minority interest	1,400	800
Stockholders' equity (Note 7):		
Common stock, $5 par value	5,500	5,000
Paid-in capital	24,500	15,000
Retained earnings	24,000	27,000
Total stockholders' equity	54,000	47,000
Total liabilities and stockholders' equity	$138,000	$105,000

ZETA CORPORATION
Consolidated Statement of Income
For the Years Ended December 31, year 6 and year 5
(in thousands)

	Year 6	Year 5
Net sales	$186,000	$155,000
Equity in income (loss of associated companies)	2,000	(1,000)
Expenses:		
Cost of sales	120,000	99,000
Selling and administration	37,000	33,000
Interest expense	10,000	6,000
Total expenses	167,000	138,000
	21,000	16,000
Income tax expense (Note 5)	10,000	7,800
	11,000	8,200
Minority interest	200	–
Income from continuing operations	10,800	8,200
Discontinued operations (Note 4):		
Operations, net of tax	(1,100)	(1,200)
Loss on disposal, net of tax	(700)	–
Total	(1,800)	(1,200)
	9,000	7,000
Cumulative effect of change in accounting, net of tax (Note 1)	1,000	–
Net income	$ 10,000	$ 7,000
Pro forma income (assuming the effect of change in accounting is applied retroactively):		
Income from continuing operations	$ 10,800	$ 8,500
Discontinued operations	(1,800)	(1,200)
Total	$ 9,000	$ 7,300

Earnings per share (information omitted)

ZETA CORPORATION
Consolidated Statement of Cash Flows
For the Years Ended December 31, year 6 and year 5
(in thousands)

	Year 6	Year 5
Cash provided from (used for) operations:		
Net income	$10,000	$7,000
Add (deduct) adjustments to cash basis:		
Depreciation	6,000	4,000
Deferred income taxes	1,600	1,000
Minority interest	200	—
Undistributed income of associated companies	(1,400)	1,300
Loss on discontinued operations	700	—
Increase in accounts receivable (5,000 − 2,000†)	(3,000)	(2,400)
Increase in inventories (18,000 + 100* − 2,200†)	(15,900)	(6,000)
Increase in prepaid expenses	—	(200)
Increase in accounts payable and accruals (6,000 − 300* − 3,200†)	2,500	2,000
Increase in income taxes payable (5,000 + 700)*	5,700	1,000
Net cash provided from (used for) operations	6,400	7,700
Cash provided from (used for) investing activities:		
Additions to property, plant, and equipment	(6,500)	(5,800)
Acquisition of TRO Company (excluding cash of $4,200)		
Property, plant, and equipment	(6,000)	—
Goodwill	(2,000)	—
Long-term debt	4,800	—
Minority interest	400	—
Current assets (A/R In'v)	(4,200)	—
Current liabilities	3,200 (3,800)	—
Investment in associated companies	(1,600)	—
Proceeds from disposal of equipment	500	—
Net cash used for investing activities	(11,400)	(5,800)

Cash provided from (used for) financing:

Issuance of long-term debt	7,500	5,000
Reduction in long-term debt	(1,500)	(1,000)
Dividends paid	(3,000)	(2,000)
Increase (decrease) in notes payable to bank	2,000	(3,500)
Net cash provided from (used for) financing activities	5,000	(1,500)
Net increase (decrease) in cash	0	400

* Adjustments of noncash transactions arising from discontinued operations (see Note 4).

† Adjustments relating to acquisition of TRO Co (Note 3).

Supplemental disclosures of cash flow information:

Cash paid during the year for interest	10,000	6,000
Cash paid during the year for income taxes	2,600	4,800

Schedule of Noncash Activities:
Capital lease of $1,000 incurred on the lease of equipment

ZETA CORPORATION
Notes to Consolidated Financial Statements
For the Years Ended December 31, year 6, and year 5
(all amounts in thousands)

Note 1: Change in accounting principle

During year 6, the company broadened its definition of overhead costs to be included in the determination of inventories to more properly match costs with revenues. The effect of the change in year 6 was to increase income from continuing operations by $400. The adjustment of $1,000 (after reduction for income taxes of $1,000) for the cumulative effect for prior years is shown in the net income for year 6.

The pro forma amounts show the effect of retroactive application of the revised inventory costing assuming that the new method had been in effect for all prior years.

Note 2: Inventories

Inventories are priced at cost (principally last-in, first-out [LIFO] method of determination) not in excess of replacement market. If the first-in, first-out (FIFO) method of inventory accounting had been used, inventories would have been $6,000 and $4,500 higher than reported at December 31, year 6, and December 31, year 5, respectively.

Note 3: Acquisition of TRO Company

Effective December 31, year 6, the company purchased most of the outstanding common stock of TRO Company for $8,000 in cash. The excess of the acquisition cost over fair value of the net assets acquired, $2,000, will be amortized on a straight-line basis over a 40-year period.

The following unaudited supplemental pro forma information shows the condensed results of operations as though TRO Company had been acquired as of January 1, year 5.

	Year 6	Year 5
Revenues	$205,000	$172,000
Net income	10,700	7,400

Details of acquisition (data not usually provided):

Cash	4,200	
Accounts Receivable	2,000	
Inventories....................	2,200	
Property, Plant, & Equipment	6,000	
Long Term Debt		4,800
A/P & Accruals		3,200

Note 4: Discontinued operations

As of October 31, year 6, the board of directors adopted a plan authorizing the disposition of the assets and business of its wholly owned subsidiary, Shortlife Corporation. The "Loss on Disposal" is $700 (net of income tax credits of $700) and is based upon the estimated realizable value of the assets to be sold plus a provision for costs of $300 for operating the business until its expected disposition in early year 7.

Property, plant, and equipment has been reduced by $1,000 and inventories were reduced by $100 to net realizable value. The provision for costs of $300 was included in "Accounts payable and accruals" and has been reduced to $200 at year-end.

Net sales of the operations to be discontinued were $18,000 in year 6 and $23,000 in year 5.

Note 5: Income taxes

The income tax expense consists of the following:

	Year 6	Year 5
Current	$ 8,400	$6,800
Deferred	1,600	1,000
Total	$10,000	$7,800

The effective tax rates of 47.6 percent and 48.8 percent for year 6 and year 5, respectively, differ from the statutory federal income tax rate of 50 percent* due to research and development tax credits of $500 in year 6 and $200 in year 6.

* A 50 percent tax rate has been used throughout these financial statements for calculation convenience—the actual statutory rate was lower.

Deferred taxes result from the use of accelerated depreciation methods for income tax reporting and the straight-line method for financial reporting.

Note 6: Long-term debt

	Year 6	Year 5
10% promissory notes to institutional investors payable in annual installments of $900 through 1990	$13,000	$13,900
Unsecured notes to banks—interest 1% over prime	4,000	—
Capitalized lease obligations—payable to year 9 with an average interest rate of 8%	1,000	—
11% subordinated note payable in annual installments of $500 from year 7 through year 6	5,000	—
Other mortgages, notes, etc.	4,000	2,300
	27,000	16,200
Less current maturities	2,000	1,000
Total	$25,000	$15,200

The various loan agreements place certain restrictions on the corporation including the payment of cash dividends on common stock and require the maintenance of working capital, as defined, of not less than $18,000. Approximately $10,000 of retained earnings was available for payment of cash dividends on common stock at December 31, year 6.

The corporation entered into several long-term noncancelable leases of equipment during year 6 which have been capitalized for financial reporting. There are no other significant lease arrangements.

Note 7: Stockholders' equity

The corporation has 5 million shares of authorized common stock, par value $5. There were 1 million shares outstanding at December 31, year 5, and this was increased by a 10 percent dividend payable in common stock during year 6.

The changes in retained earnings are as follows:

	Year 6	Year 5
Beginning balance	$27,000	$22,000
Add net income	10,000	7,000
Less cash dividends	(3,000)	(2,000)
Less 10% stock dividend	(10,000)	—
Ending balance	$24,000	$27,000

Required (in thousands):
Support all conclusions! Identify specific accounts and amounts!
A. What caused the $7,000 increase during year 6 in stockholders' equity?
B. Note 6 shows "capitalized lease obligations" of $1,000. What journal entry was made in year 6 to record these leases *and* how are these leases reflected in the statement of cash flows?
C. How much long-term debt was paid during year 6?
D. Note 1 describes a change in accounting principle.
    (1) What effect did this change in accounting have on the December 31, year 6, balance sheet *and* the year 6 income statement?
    (2) Describe how the year 5 balance sheet *and* year 5 income statement should be changed for *analytical* purposes to make year 5 comparable to year 6.

(3) How would the $1,000 "cumulative effect" for year 6 be shown in a statement of cash flows with an "inflow-outflow" explanation of cash from operations? Your description must be clear enough that someone else could prepare a cash statement using your description. (You will need to show some figures.) *Hint:* Remember to start by reconstructing the journal entry to record the $1,000.

E. Note 3 describes the acquisition of TRO Company.
  (1) Is TRO a separate legal entity at December 31, year 6, or has it been dissolved into ZETA Corporation?
  (2) What effect did the acquisition of TRO Company have at December 31, year 6 (date of acquisition) on:
    (i) ZETA Corporation balance sheet?
    (ii) Consolidated balance sheet?
  (3) What were TRO's revenues for year 6?

F. For the asset "investment in associated company":
  (1) Explain all changes during year 6.
  (2) Identify all effects in the cash statement which relate to this investment.
  (3) How much cash dividends were received by ZETA during year 6 from the associated company?

G. For the minority interest shown on the balance sheet:
  (1) Explain all changes during year 6.
  (2) Show how this account relates to the asset "investment in associated company."

H. If the FIFO method of inventory valuation had been used (instead of LIFO), how much would year 6 net income have been increased or decreased?

I. Note 4 describes "discontinued operations":
  (1) What journal entries were made on October 31, year 6, to record the loss on disposal?
  (2) What effect did the loss on disposal of $700 have on the statement of cash flows? (Identify specific items and amounts.)
  (3) How should the discontinued operation and $(1,100) loss be shown in a statement of cash flows with CFO shown in an "inflow-outflow" format if we desire to include these operations in the inflows and outflows?

J. How will "goodwill" be reflected in the year 7 (*next year*) SCF?

K. Explain all changes during year 6 in the *net* property, plant, and equipment account.

Note: For additional problems based on the financial statements of ZETA, see Problems 13–19, 16–11, 18–11, 19–13, 21–14, 21–18 and 21–19.

23–6 The Policy Committee of your firm has decided to shift investment strategies. This shift entails an increase in exposure to the stocks of large companies producing consumer products dominated by leading brands. The Committee has decided that the soft drink industry, specifically Coca-Cola Company (KO) and Coca-Cola Enterprises (CCE), qualify as potential purchases for the firm's portfolios. As the firm's beverage industry expert, you must prepare an extensive financial analysis of these two soft drink producers.

KO owns the brands included in its broad product line. Its marketing efforts center on worldwide advertising promoting these soft drinks. KO manufactures primarily soft drink extract. The production process requires only low-cost raw materials and relatively limited fixed asset investment. Extract is inexpensive to ship and requires only 44 production facilities throughout the world. KO's position as a leading soft drink extract producer is protected by the technical nature of its manufacturing process, the secret formula for the product, and strong brand names established in over a century of operations. Competition is limited almost entirely to one other firm, PepsiCo, Inc. KO plays almost no direct role in the domestic manufacturing and distribution beyond the output of soft drink extract.

The business of CCE is also dominated by soft drinks. CCE, however, purchases extract from KO and transforms it into completed products sold in a wide variety of retail outlets throughout the United States. This costly, complex production and distribution system requires approximately 300 plants and warehouses, and approximately 18,000 vehicles. Marketing efforts emphasize local promotion. Competition consists of a large number of other highly automated, similarly organized firms also manufacturing soft drinks from extract.

Required:

Use *only* the financial information shown in Tables I through IV, in answering Parts A, B and C.

A.   Your comparative analysis of these two soft drink companies required calculations of various ratios shown in Table IV. You have identified four key areas of comparison:
   (1)   Short-term liquidity.
   (2)   Capital structure and long-term solvency.
   (3)   Asset utilization.
   (4)   Operating profitability.
   Discuss the differences between KO and CCE in these *four* areas based on all the ratios presented in Table IV, and the financial statements in Tables I and II.
B.   Using the information in Tables I, II and III, identify a *total* of *five* adjustments to the financial statements that you feel will enhance their comparability and usefulness for financial analysis.
C.   For *each* of the *five* adjustments identified in Part B, discuss the effects of these adjustments on your answer to Part A.

(CFA)

Table I

Consolidated Balance Sheets
December 31, 1988
($ millions)

	Coca-Cola Company (KO)	Coca-Cola Enterprise (CCE)
Assets		
Current assets		
Cash & equivalents	$1,231	$ —
Trade accounts receivable	627	294
Inventories	779	125
Other current assets	608	69
Total current assets	$3,245	$ 488
Other investments		
Investments in affiliates		$
	$1,912	—
Other	478	66
Total other investments	$2,390	$ 66
Fixed assets		
Land	$ 117	$ 135
Plant and equipment	2,500	1,561
Other	293	42
Total fixed assets	$2,910	$1,738
Less: accumulated depreciation	(1,150)	(558)
Total net fixed assets	$1,760	$1,180
Goodwill	$ 57	$2,935
Total assets	$7,451	$4,669
Liabilities & shareholders' equity		
Current liabilities		
Short-term debt	$1,363	$ 148
Accounts payable	1,081	402
Other	425	—
Total current liabilities	$2,869	$ 550
Long-term debt	761	2,062
Deferred income taxes	270	222
Other long-term liabilities	206	27
Shareholders' equity		
Preferred stock	$ 300	$ 250
Common stock	3,045	1,558
Total shareholders' equity	$3,345	$1,808
Total liabilities & shareholders' equity ..	$7,451	$4,669

Table II

1988 Consolidated Statements of Income
($ millions except per share data)

	Coca-Cola Company (KO)	Coca-Cola Enterprise (CCE)
Revenue	$8,338	$3,874
Cost of goods sold	(3,702)	(2,268)
Gross profit	$4,636	$1,606
Selling, general, & administrative expenses	(3,038)	(1,225)
Provision for restructuring............	—	(27)
Operating profit	$1,598	$ 354
Interest expense	(231)	(211)
Gain on sale of operations	—	104
Equity in income of affiliates	48	—
Other income	167	21
Pre-tax income	$1,582	$ 268
Income taxes	(538)	(115)
Net income	$1,044	$ 153
Preferred dividends	(6)	(10)
Income available for common	$1,038	$ 143
Earnings per share	$ 2.85	$ 1.03

Table III

Data Extracted from Financial Statement Footnotes

Coca-Cola Company (KO)

(1) Certain soft drink and citrus inventories are valued on the last-in-first-out (LIFO) method. The excess of current costs over LIFO stated values amounted to approximately $30 million at December 31, 1988.
(2) The market value of the company's investments in publicly-traded equity investees exceeded the company's carrying value at December 31, 1988 by approximately $291 million.
(3) The company is contingently liable for guarantees of indebtedness owed by some of its licensees and others, totaling approximately $133 million at December 31, 1988.
(4) Pension plan assets total $496 million. The projected benefit obligation for all plans totals $413 million.

Coca-Cola Enterprises (CCE)

(1) Inventory cost is computed principally on the last-in-first-out (LIFO) method. At December 31, 1988 the LIFO reserve was $2,077,000.
(2) In December 1988 the company repurchased for cash various outstanding bond issues. These transactions resulted in a pre-tax gain of approximately $8.5 million.

(3) The company leases office and warehouse space, and machinery and equipment under lease agreements. At December 31, 1988 future minimum lease payments under noncancellable operating leases were as follows:

($ thousands)

1989	$11,749
1990	8,436
1991	6,881
1992	4,972
1993	3,485
Later years	11,181
Total	$46,704

(4) Pension plan assets total $197 million. Total projected benefit obligation for all plans is $151 million.

Table IV

Selected Financial Ratios*
As of Year-End 1988
($ millions)

	Coca-Cola Company (KO)	Coca-Cola Enterprises (CCE)
Return on total assets	0.16	0.06
Total debt to total capital	0.55	0.61
Net income to sales	0.13	0.04
Receivable turnover	13.30x	13.18x
Property, plant, & equipment turnover . .	4.74x	3.28x
Return on common equity	0.34	0.09
Current ratio	1.13	0.89
Inventory turnover	4.75x	18.14x
Long-term debt to equity	0.23	1.14
Gross profit to sales	0.56	0.41
Acid-test ratio	0.65	0.53
Asset turnover	1.12x	0.83x
Times interest earned	7.85x	2.27x

* For simplicity, ratios have been computed on year-end data rather than on 1988 average data.

23–7. Colleen Lee is the portfolio manager of a high-yield bond portfolio at Sunrise Advisers. She is concerned about the financial stability of Florida Gypsum Corporation (FGC) whose bonds represent one of the holdings in her portfolio. The bonds she holds, the 13.25% senior subordinated debentures due 7/15/2000, were issued at par in July 1989 and are currently priced in her portfolio at 53. However, her high-yield bond salesmen are not optimistic that they can even develop a bid at that level.

FGC is a large producer of gypsum products, accounting for approximately one third of total gypsum sales in the United States. The company also manufactures ceiling tile, caulks, sealants, floor and wall adhesives, and other specialty building products. In addition, FGC operates 137 distribution centers, through which it markets many of its building products, particularly gypsum wallboard.

In 1989, the company did a leveraged recapitalization of its balance sheet. This involved the payment of a large dividend to common shareholders financed with several new subordinated debt financings, including the 13.25% debentures that Lee holds. The company's primary competitor, American Gypsum, is also highly leveraged, following its acquisition by a large Canadian concern.

As a result of a downturn in residential and commercial construction activity that began in 1988, demand for gypsum wallboard had fallen off significantly by mid-1990. However, capacity has continued to expand at a rate of almost 2% per year. As a result, capacity utilization has declined to 85% currently, from 87% in 1988 and a peak of 95% in 1985–86. The price of 1/2-inch wallboard, that peaked in 1986 at about $121 per 1,000 square feet, has declined to about $83 currently.

To help in her analysis of FGC's prospects, Lee assembled the data shown in Tables 1, 2, and 3.

The director of fixed income research at Sunrise Advisers suggested that Lee look carefully at ratios of short-term liquidity and operating performance, specifically the quick ratio, the accounts receivable turnover ratio, the inventory turnover ratio, and the operating profit margin. Lee prepared the data shown on the following page and went to the director's office to discuss what the firm should do with FGC.

FLORIDA GYPSUM CORPORATION
Selected Liquidity and Operating Performance Ratios

	Year ended		Six months ended
	9/30/88	9/30/89	3/31/90
Quick ratio	0.73X	0.78X	0.77X
Accounts receivable turnover	8.9X	8.1X	7.4X
Inventory turnover	11.4X	12.4X	13.3X
Operating margin	16.6%	13.3%	14.9%

A. The director of fixed income research noted that the four ratios calculated above do not reveal significant changes in the financial condition of FGC. Discuss the limitations of these ratios in assessing the liquidity needs and operating performance of a company like FGC.

B. Lee suggested that there are better measures of short-term liquidity and operating performance for FGC. Identify *two* better measures and discuss their trend over the period September 30, 1988, through March 31, 1990. Explain why these measures more fairly reflect FGC's financial condition.

C. Based on the analysis performed in Part B *and* on the background information provided previously, recommend and justify whether Lee should attempt to sell the FGC bonds, retain her position, or buy more FGC bonds.

(CFA)

Table 1

FLORIDA GYPSUM CORPORATION
Balance Sheets
($ millions)

	As of 9/30/88	As of 9/30/89	As of 3/31/90
Assets			
Current assets			
Cash & cash equivalents	$ 31.3	$ 250.0	$ 95.6
Accounts receivable	274.1	278.3	320.4
Inventories	144.1	124.6	128.4
Net assets of discontinued operations	415.1	20.4	—
Total current assets	$ 864.6	$ 673.3	$ 544.4
Property, plant & equipment	909.0	906.4	878.4
Purchased goodwill	148.9	146.5	144.5
Other assets	35.0	95.0	90.0
Total assets	$1,957.5	$1,821.2	$1,657.3
Liabilities and shareholders' equity			
Current liabilities			
Commercial paper & notes payable	$ 38.3	$ 1.3	$ 1.6
Accounts payable	141.6	125.4	125.2
Accrued expenses	188.2	256.9	244.0
Other current liabilities	14.8	38.7	13.7
Current portion of long-term debt	33.0	259.3	154.5
Total current liabilities	$ 415.9	$ 681.6	$ 539.0
Long-term debt	724.9	2,384.3	2,344.0
Deferred income taxes	194.1	206.2	212.6
Minority interest	12.8	20.0	22.0
Shareholders' equity	609.8	(1,470.9)	(1,460.3)
Total liabilities and shareholders' equity	$1,957.5	$1,821.2	$1,657.3

Table 2

FLORIDA GYPSUM CORPORATION
Income Statements
($ millions)

	Year ended		6 months ended
	9/30/88	*9/30/89*	*3/31/90*
Net sales	$2,254.4	$2,248.0	$1,107.7
Cost of goods sold	(1,598.6)	(1,671.9)	(841.4)
Gross profit	$ 655.8	$ 576.1	$ 266.3
Selling and administrative expenses	(268.7)	(253.7)	(122.9)
Interest expense	(69.2)	(178.3)	(148.9)
Interest income	5.3	12.7	4.8
Recapitalization & restructuring expenses	(53.4)	(20.0)	—
Other expenses, net	34.3	(15.9)	17.0
Pre-tax earnings from continuing operations	$ 304.1	$ 120.9	$ 16.3
Income taxes	(130.9)	(48.2)	(5.9)
Earnings from continuing operations	$ 173.2	$ 72.7	$ 10.4

Table 3

FLORIDA GYPSUM CORPORATION
Selected Cash Flow Data
($ millions)

	Year ended		6 months ended
	9/30/88	9/30/89	3/31/90
Cash flow from operations			
Earnings from continuing operations	$173.2	$ 72.7	$ 10.4
Depreciation, depletion & amortization ...	76.6	83.0	42.5
Non-cash interest expense	—	19.1	22.3
Minority interest	13.2	9.1	4.0
Deferred income taxes	1.5	12.6	6.4
Other non-cash items relating to operations	15.2	(6.1)	(11.7)
(Increase)/decrease in working capital			
(excluding cash)	43.8	91.8	(84.1)
Other cash flows from operations	(24.0)	(62.0)	3.9
Total net cash flow from operations	$299.5	$220.2	$ (6.3)
Net liquid balance			
Cash and cash equivalents	$ 31.3	$250.0	$ 95.6
Less notes payable	(38.3)	(1.3)	(1.6)
Less current portion of long-term debt	(33.0)	(259.3)	(154.5)
Net Liquid Balance	$ (40.0)	$ (10.6)	$ (60.5)
Net Liquid Balance as % of Total Assets ...	(2.0)%	(0.6)%	(3.7)%

33–8
A. Using the financial ratios contained in Table A, analyze the relative credit
   position of:
   I.   The brewing industry compared with the S&P 400.
   II. Anheuser-Busch compared with the brewing industry.
   III. Anheuser-Busch compared with the S&P 400.
B. Using Table A and your analysis from Part A, describe the current position
   of Anheuser-Busch, and discuss whether you feel that there has been a
   change in the credit quality of Anheuser-Busch based upon the recent
   trend in the financial ratios.

Table A   Selected financial ratios for the S&P 400, the brewing industry, and Anheuser-Busch Companies, Inc. (BUD) (1982–1986)

	1982			1983			1984			1985			1986		
	S&P 400	Brewing Industry	BUD	S&P 400	Brewing Industry	BUD	S&P 400	Brewing Industry	BUD	S&P 400	Brewing Industry	BUD	S&P 400	Brewing Industry	BUD
Current ratio	1.5	1.3	1.1	1.5	1.4	1.2	1.5	1.3	1.1	1.4	1.5	1.2	1.4	1.4	1.0
Quick ratio	0.9	0.7	0.4	0.9	0.8	0.7	0.8	0.7	0.5	0.8	1.0	0.6	0.7	0.8	0.4
Long-term debt/Total assets (%)	24	21	25	23	18	22	25	15	18	26	15	17	27	17	19
Total debt*/Total assets (%)	43	37	41	42	36	39	44	31	34	48	32	33	48	34	37
Times interest earned	4.0	7.2	12.2	4.6	7.5	12.7	4.8	7.6	13.3	4.2	10.1	14.9	3.6	11.0	9.8
Cash flow/Long-term debt (%)	54	52	43	61	70	55	65	84	71	57	88	79	51	80	73
Cash flow/Total debt* (%)	23	29	26	25	35	32	25	39	38	20	40	40	20	38	38
Total asset turnover	1.2	1.2	1.2	1.2	1.4	1.4	1.2	1.5	1.6	1.2	1.3	1.5	1.1	1.3	1.4
Net profit margin (%)	3.95	5.36	6.3	4.42	5.58	5.8	4.77	5.12	6.0	3.84	5.73	6.3	3.75	6.16	6.17
Return on total assets (%)	4.64	6.46	7.4	5.10	7.98	8.0	5.80	7.47	8.7	4.41	7.66	8.7	3.97	7.90	8.89

* Total Debt is defined as Long-Term Debt plus Current Liabilities.

Appendix

COMPOUND-INTEREST TABLES

Table 1: Future Value of 1, $f = (1 + i)^n$

Periods	2%	2½%	3%	4%	5%	6%	7%	8%	9%	10%
1	1.02000	1.02500	1.03000	1.04000	1.05000	1.06000	1.07000	1.08000	1.09000	1.10000
2	1.04040	1.05063	1.06090	1.08160	1.10250	1.12360	1.14490	1.16640	1.18810	1.21000
3	1.06121	1.07689	1.09273	1.12486	1.15763	1.19102	1.22504	1.25971	1.29503	1.33100
4	1.08243	1.10381	1.12551	1.16986	1.21551	1.26248	1.31080	1.36049	1.41158	1.46410
5	1.10408	1.13141	1.15927	1.21665	1.27628	1.33823	1.40255	1.46933	1.53862	1.61051
6	1.12616	1.15969	1.19405	1.26532	1.34010	1.41852	1.50073	1.58687	1.67710	1.77156
7	1.14869	1.18869	1.22987	1.31593	1.40710	1.50363	1.60578	1.71382	1.82804	1.94872
8	1.17166	1.21840	1.26677	1.36857	1.47746	1.59385	1.71819	1.85093	1.99256	2.14359
9	1.19509	1.24886	1.30477	1.42331	1.55133	1.68948	1.83846	1.99900	2.17189	2.35795
10	1.21899	1.28008	1.34392	1.48024	1.62889	1.79085	1.96715	2.15892	2.36736	2.59374
11	1.24337	1.31209	1.38423	1.53945	1.71034	1.89830	2.10485	2.33164	2.58043	2.85312
12	1.26824	1.34489	1.42576	1.60103	1.79586	2.01220	2.25219	2.51817	2.81266	3.13843
13	1.29361	1.37851	1.46853	1.66507	1.88565	2.13293	2.40985	2.71962	3.06580	3.45227
14	1.31948	1.41297	1.51259	1.73168	1.97993	2.26090	2.57853	2.93719	3.34173	3.79750
15	1.34587	1.44830	1.55797	1.80094	2.07893	2.39656	2.75903	3.17217	3.64248	4.17725
16	1.37279	1.48451	1.60471	1.87298	2.18287	2.54035	2.95216	3.42594	3.97031	4.59497
17	1.40024	1.52162	1.65285	1.94790	2.29202	2.69277	3.15882	3.70002	4.32763	5.05447
18	1.42825	1.55966	1.70243	2.02582	2.40662	2.85434	3.37993	3.99602	4.71712	5.55992
19	1.45681	1.59865	1.75351	2.10685	2.52695	3.02560	3.61653	4.31570	5.14166	6.11591
20	1.48595	1.63862	1.80611	2.19112	2.65330	3.20714	3.86968	4.66096	5.60441	6.72750
21	1.51567	1.67958	1.86029	2.27877	2.78596	3.39956	4.14056	5.03383	6.10881	7.40025
22	1.54598	1.72157	1.91610	2.36992	2.92526	3.60354	4.43040	5.43654	6.65860	8.14027
23	1.57690	1.76461	1.97359	2.46472	3.07152	3.81975	4.74053	5.87146	7.25787	8.95430
24	1.60844	1.80873	2.03279	2.56330	3.22510	4.04893	5.07237	6.34118	7.91108	9.84973
25	1.64061	1.85394	2.09378	2.66584	3.38635	4.29187	5.42743	6.84848	8.62308	10.83471

Periods	11%	12%	14%	15%	16%	18%	20%	22%	24%	25%
1	1.11000	1.12000	1.14000	1.15000	1.16000	1.18000	1.20000	1.22000	1.24000	1.25000
2	1.23210	1.25440	1.29960	1.32250	1.34560	1.39240	1.44000	1.48840	1.53760	1.56250
3	1.36763	1.40493	1.48154	1.52088	1.56090	1.64303	1.72800	1.81585	1.90662	1.95313
4	1.51807	1.57352	1.68896	1.74901	1.81064	1.93878	2.07360	2.21533	2.36421	2.44141
5	1.68506	1.76234	1.92541	2.01136	2.10034	2.28776	2.48832	2.70271	2.93163	3.05176
6	1.87041	1.97382	2.19497	2.31306	2.43640	2.69955	2.98598	3.29730	3.63522	3.81470
7	2.07616	2.21068	2.50227	2.66002	2.82622	3.18547	3.58318	4.02271	4.50767	4.76837
8	2.30454	2.47596	2.85259	3.05902	3.27841	3.75886	4.29982	4.90771	5.58951	5.96046
9	2.55804	2.77308	3.25195	3.51788	3.80296	4.43545	5.15978	5.98740	6.93099	7.45058
10	2.83942	3.10585	3.70722	4.04556	4.41144	5.23384	6.19174	7.30463	8.59443	9.31323
11	3.15176	3.47855	4.22623	4.65239	5.11726	6.17593	7.43008	8.91165	10.65709	11.64153
12	3.49845	3.89598	4.81790	5.35025	5.93603	7.28759	8.91610	10.87221	13.21479	14.55192
13	3.88328	4.36349	5.49241	6.15279	6.88579	8.59936	10.69932	13.26410	16.38634	18.18989
14	4.31044	4.88711	6.26135	7.07571	7.98752	10.14724	12.83918	16.18220	20.31906	22.73737
15	4.78459	5.47357	7.13794	8.13706	9.26552	11.97375	15.40702	19.74229	25.19563	28.42171
16	5.31089	6.13039	8.13725	9.35762	10.74800	14.12902	18.48843	24.08559	31.24259	35.52714
17	5.89509	6.86604	9.27646	10.76126	12.46768	16.67225	22.18611	29.38442	38.74081	44.40892
18	6.54355	7.68997	10.57517	12.37545	14.46251	19.67325	26.62333	35.84899	48.03860	55.51115
19	7.26334	8.61276	12.05569	14.23177	16.77652	23.21444	31.94800	43.73577	59.56786	69.38894
20	8.06231	9.64629	13.74349	16.36654	19.46076	27.39303	38.33760	53.35764	73.86417	86.73617
21	8.94917	10.80385	15.66758	18.82152	22.57448	32.32378	46.00512	65.09632	91.59155	108.42022
22	9.93357	12.10031	17.86104	21.64475	26.18640	38.14206	55.20614	79.41751	113.57352	135.52527
23	11.02627	13.55235	20.36158	24.89146	30.37622	45.00763	66.24737	96.88936	140.83116	169.40659
24	12.23916	15.17863	23.21221	28.62518	35.23642	53.10901	79.49685	118.20502	174.63064	211.75824
25	13.58546	17.00006	26.46192	32.91895	40.87424	62.66863	95.39622	144.21013	216.54199	264.69780

Table 2:   Present Value of 1, $p = \dfrac{1}{(1 + i)^n}$

Periods	2%	2½%	3%	4%	5%	6%	7%	8%	9%	10%
1	.98039	.97561	.97087	.96154	.95238	.94340	.93458	.92593	.91743	.90909
2	.96117	.95181	.94260	.92456	.90703	.89000	.87344	.85734	.84168	.82645
3	.94232	.92860	.91514	.88900	.86384	.83962	.81630	.79383	.77218	.75131
4	.92385	.90595	.88849	.85480	.82270	.79209	.76290	.73503	.70843	.68301
5	.90573	.88385	.86261	.82193	.78353	.74726	.71299	.68058	.64993	.62092
6	.88797	.86230	.83748	.79031	.74622	.70496	.66634	.63017	.59627	.56447
7	.87056	.84127	.81309	.75992	.71068	.66506	.62275	.58349	.54703	.51316
8	.85349	.82075	.78941	.73069	.67684	.62741	.58201	.54027	.50187	.46651
9	.83676	.80073	.76642	.70259	.64461	.59190	.54393	.50025	.46043	.42410
10	.82035	.78120	.74409	.67556	.61391	.55839	.50835	.46319	.42241	.38554
11	.80426	.76214	.72242	.64958	.58468	.52679	.47509	.42888	.38753	.35049
12	.78849	.74356	.70138	.62460	.55684	.49697	.44401	.39711	.35553	.31863
13	.77303	.72542	.68095	.60057	.53032	.46884	.41496	.36770	.32618	.28966
14	.75788	.70773	.66112	.57748	.50507	.44230	.38782	.34046	.29925	.26333
15	.74301	.69047	.64186	.55526	.48102	.41727	.36245	.31524	.27454	.23939
16	.72845	.67362	.62317	.53391	.45811	.39365	.33873	.29189	.25187	.21763
17	.71416	.65720	.60502	.51337	.43630	.37136	.31657	.27027	.23107	.19784
18	.70016	.64117	.58739	.49363	.41552	.35034	.29586	.25025	.21199	.17986
19	.68643	.62553	.57029	.47464	.39573	.33051	.27651	.23171	.19449	.16351
20	.67297	.61027	.55368	.45639	.37689	.31180	.25842	.21455	.17843	.14864
21	.65978	.59539	.53755	.43883	.35894	.29416	.24151	.19866	.16370	.13513
22	.64684	.58086	.52189	.42196	.34185	.27751	.22571	.18394	.15018	.12285
23	.63416	.56670	.50669	.40573	.32557	.26180	.21095	.17032	.13778	.11168
24	.62172	.55288	.49193	.39012	.31007	.24698	.19715	.15770	.12640	.10153
25	.60953	.53939	.47761	.37512	.29530	.23300	.18425	.14602	.11597	.09230

Periods	11%	12%	14%	15%	16%	18%	20%	22%	24%	25%
1	.90090	.89286	.87719	.86957	.86207	.84746	.83333	.81967	.80645	.80000
2	.81162	.79719	.76947	.75614	.74316	.71818	.69444	.67186	.65036	.64000
3	.73119	.71178	.67497	.65752	.64066	.60863	.57870	.55071	.52449	.51200
4	.65873	.63552	.59208	.57175	.55229	.51579	.48225	.45140	.42297	.40960
5	.59345	.56743	.51937	.49718	.47611	.43711	.40188	.37000	.34111	.32768
6	.53464	.50663	.45559	.43233	.41044	.37043	.33490	.30328	.27509	.26214
7	.48166	.45235	.39964	.37594	.35383	.31393	.27908	.24859	.22184	.20972
8	.43393	.40388	.35056	.32690	.30503	.26604	.23257	.20376	.17891	.16777
9	.39092	.36061	.30751	.28426	.26295	.22546	.19381	.16702	.14428	.13422
10	.35218	.32197	.26974	.24718	.22668	.19106	.16151	.13690	.11635	.10737
11	.31728	.28748	.23662	.21494	.19542	.16192	.13459	.11221	.09383	.08590
12	.28584	.25668	.20756	.18691	.16846	.13722	.11216	.09198	.07567	.06872
13	.25751	.22917	.18207	.16253	.14523	.11629	.09346	.07539	.06103	.05498
14	.23199	.20462	.15971	.14133	.12520	.09855	.07789	.06180	.04921	.04398
15	.20900	.18270	.14010	.12289	.10793	.08352	.06491	.05065	.03969	.03518
16	.18829	.16312	.12289	.10686	.09304	.07078	.05409	.04152	.03201	.02815
17	.16963	.14564	.10780	.09293	.08021	.05998	.04507	.03403	.02581	.02252
18	.15282	.13004	.09456	.08081	.06914	.05083	.03756	.02789	.02082	.01801
19	.13768	.11611	.08295	.07027	.05961	.04308	.03130	.02286	.01679	.01441
20	.12403	.10367	.07276	.06110	.05139	.03651	.02608	.01874	.01354	.01153
21	.11174	.09256	.06383	.05313	.04430	.03094	.02174	.01536	.01092	.00922
22	.10067	.08264	.05599	.04620	.03819	.02622	.01811	.01259	.00880	.00738
23	.09069	.07379	.04911	.04017	.03292	.02222	.01509	.01032	.00710	.00590
24	.08170	.06588	.04308	.03493	.02838	.01883	.01258	.00846	.00573	.00472
25	.07361	.05882	.03779	.03038	.02447	.01596	.01048	.00693	.00462	.00378

Table 3: Future Value of Annuity of n Rents of 1 Each (ordinary), $F_0 = \dfrac{(1 + i)^n - 1}{i}$

Periodic rents (n)	2%	2½%	3%	4%	5%	6%	7%	8%	9%	10%
1	1.00000	1.00000	1.00000	1.00000	1.00000	1.00000	1.00000	1.00000	1.00000	1.00000
2	2.02000	2.02500	2.03000	2.04000	2.05000	2.06000	2.07000	2.08000	2.09000	2.10000
3	3.06040	3.07563	3.09090	3.12160	3.15250	3.18360	3.21490	3.24640	3.27810	3.31000
4	4.12161	4.15252	4.18363	4.24646	4.31013	4.37462	4.43994	4.50611	4.57313	4.64100
5	5.20404	5.25633	5.30914	5.41632	5.52563	5.63709	5.75074	5.86660	5.98471	6.10510
6	6.30812	6.38774	6.46841	6.63298	6.80191	6.97532	7.15329	7.33593	7.52333	7.71561
7	7.43428	7.54753	7.66246	7.89829	8.14201	8.39384	8.65402	8.92280	9.20043	9.48717
8	8.58297	8.73612	8.89234	9.21423	9.54911	9.89747	10.25980	10.63663	11.02847	11.43589
9	9.75463	9.95452	10.15911	10.58280	11.02656	11.49132	11.97799	12.48756	13.02104	13.57948
10	10.94972	11.20338	11.46388	12.00611	12.57789	13.18079	13.81645	14.48656	15.19293	15.93742
11	12.16872	12.48347	12.80780	13.48635	14.20679	14.97164	15.78360	16.64549	17.56029	18.53117
12	13.41209	13.79555	14.19203	15.02581	15.91713	16.86994	17.88845	18.97713	20.14072	21.38428
13	14.68033	15.14044	15.61779	16.62684	17.71298	18.88214	20.14064	21.49530	22.95338	24.52271
14	15.97394	16.51895	17.08632	18.29191	19.59863	21.01507	22.55049	24.21492	26.01919	27.97498
15	17.29342	17.93193	18.59891	20.02359	21.57856	23.27597	25.12902	27.15211	29.36092	31.77248
16	18.63929	19.38022	20.15688	21.82453	23.65749	25.67253	27.88805	30.32428	33.00340	35.94973
17	20.01207	20.86473	21.76159	23.69751	25.84037	28.21288	30.84022	33.75023	36.97370	40.54470
18	21.41231	22.38635	23.41444	25.64541	28.13238	30.90565	33.99903	37.45024	41.30134	45.59917
19	22.84056	23.94601	25.11687	27.67123	30.53900	33.75999	37.37896	41.44626	46.01846	51.15909
20	24.29737	25.54466	26.87037	29.77808	33.06595	36.78559	40.99549	45.76196	51.16012	57.27500
21	25.78332	27.18327	28.67649	31.96920	35.71925	39.99273	44.86518	50.42292	56.76453	64.00250
22	27.29898	28.86286	30.53678	34.24797	38.50521	43.39229	49.00574	55.45676	62.87334	71.40275
23	28.84496	30.58443	32.45288	36.61789	41.43048	46.99583	53.43614	60.89330	69.53194	79.54302
24	30.42186	32.34904	34.42647	39.08260	44.50200	50.81558	58.17667	66.76476	76.78981	88.49733
25	32.03030	34.15776	36.45926	41.64591	47.72710	54.86451	63.24904	73.10594	84.70090	98.34706

Periodic rents (n)	11%	12%	14%	15%	16%	18%	20%	22%	24%	25%
1	1.00000	1.00000	1.00000	1.00000	1.00000	1.00000	1.00000	1.00000	1.00000	1.00000
2	2.11000	2.12000	2.14000	2.15000	2.16000	2.18000	2.20000	2.22000	2.24000	2.25000
3	3.34210	3.37440	3.43960	3.47250	3.50560	3.57240	3.64000	3.70840	3.77760	3.81250
4	4.70973	4.77933	4.92114	4.99338	5.06650	5.21543	5.36800	5.52425	5.68422	5.76563
5	6.22780	6.35285	6.61010	6.74238	6.87714	7.15421	7.44160	7.73958	8.04844	8.20703
6	7.91286	8.11519	8.53552	8.75374	8.97748	9.44197	9.92992	10.44229	10.98006	11.25879
7	9.78327	10.08901	10.73049	11.06680	11.41387	12.14152	12.91590	13.73959	14.61528	15.07349
8	11.85943	12.29969	13.23276	13.72682	14.24009	15.32700	16.49908	17.76231	19.12294	19.84186
9	14.16397	14.77566	16.08535	16.78584	17.51851	19.08585	20.79890	22.67001	24.71245	25.80232
10	16.72201	17.54874	19.33730	20.30372	21.32147	23.52131	25.95868	28.65742	31.64344	33.25290
11	19.56143	20.65458	23.04452	24.34928	25.73290	28.75514	32.15042	35.96205	40.23787	42.56613
12	22.71319	24.13313	27.27075	29.00167	30.85017	34.93107	39.58050	44.87370	50.89495	54.20766
13	26.21164	28.02911	32.08865	34.35192	36.78620	42.21866	48.49660	55.74591	64.10974	68.75958
14	30.09492	32.39260	37.58107	40.50471	43.67199	50.81802	59.19592	69.01001	80.49608	86.94947
15	34.40536	37.27971	43.84241	47.58041	51.65951	60.96527	72.03511	85.19221	100.81514	109.68684
16	39.18995	42.75328	50.98035	55.71747	60.92503	72.93901	87.44213	104.93450	126.01077	138.10855
17	44.50084	48.88367	59.11760	65.07509	71.67303	87.06804	105.93056	129.02009	157.25336	173.63568
18	50.39594	55.74971	68.39407	75.83636	84.14072	103.74028	128.11667	158.40451	195.99416	218.04460
19	56.93949	63.43968	78.96923	88.21181	98.60323	123.41353	154.74000	194.25350	244.03276	273.55576
20	64.20283	72.05244	91.02493	102.44358	115.37975	146.62797	186.68800	237.98927	303.60062	342.94470
21	72.26514	81.69874	104.76842	118.81012	134.84051	174.02100	225.02560	291.34691	377.46477	429.68087
22	81.21431	92.50258	120.43600	137.63164	157.41499	206.34479	271.03072	356.44323	469.05632	538.10109
23	91.14788	104.60289	138.29704	159.27638	183.60138	244.48685	326.23686	435.86075	582.62984	673.62636
24	102.17415	118.15524	158.65862	184.16784	213.97761	289.49448	392.48424	532.75011	723.46100	843.03295
25	114.41331	133.33387	181.87083	212.79302	249.21402	342.60349	471.98108	650.95513	898.09164	1054.79118

Table 4: Present Value of Annuity of n Rents of 1 Each (ordinary), $P_0 = \dfrac{1 - \dfrac{1}{(1+i)^n}}{i}$

Periodic rents (n)	2%	2½%	3%	4%	5%	6%	7%	8%	9%	10%
1	.98039	.97561	.97087	.96154	.95238	.94340	.93458	.92593	.91743	.90909
2	1.94156	1.92742	1.91347	1.88609	1.85941	1.83339	1.80802	1.78326	1.75911	1.73554
3	2.88388	2.85602	2.82861	2.77509	2.72325	2.67301	2.62432	2.57710	2.53129	2.48685
4	3.80773	3.76197	3.71710	3.62990	3.54595	3.46511	3.38721	3.31213	3.23972	3.16987
5	4.71346	4.64583	4.57971	4.45182	4.32948	4.21236	4.10020	3.99271	3.88965	3.79079
6	5.60143	5.50813	5.41719	5.24214	5.07569	4.91732	4.76654	4.62288	4.48592	4.35526
7	6.47199	6.34939	6.23028	6.00205	5.78637	5.58238	5.38929	5.20637	5.03295	4.86842
8	7.32548	7.17014	7.01969	6.73274	6.46321	6.20979	5.97130	5.74664	5.53482	5.33493
9	8.16224	7.97087	7.78611	7.43533	7.10782	6.80169	6.51523	6.24689	5.99525	5.75902
10	8.98259	8.75206	8.53020	8.11090	7.72173	7.36009	7.02358	6.71008	6.41766	6.14457
11	9.78685	9.51421	9.25262	8.76048	8.30641	7.88687	7.49867	7.13896	6.80519	6.49506
12	10.57534	10.25776	9.95400	9.38507	8.86325	8.38384	7.94269	7.53608	7.16073	6.81369
13	11.34837	10.98318	10.63496	9.98565	9.39357	8.85268	8.35765	7.90378	7.48690	7.10336
14	12.10625	11.69091	11.29607	10.56312	9.89864	9.29498	8.74547	8.24424	7.78615	7.36669
15	12.84926	12.38138	11.93794	11.11839	10.37966	9.71225	9.10791	8.55948	8.06069	7.60608
16	13.57771	13.05500	12.56110	11.65230	10.83777	10.10590	9.44665	8.85137	8.31256	7.82371
17	14.29187	13.71220	13.16612	12.16567	11.27407	10.47726	9.76322	9.12164	8.54363	8.02155
18	14.99203	14.35336	13.75351	12.65930	11.68959	10.82760	10.05909	9.37189	8.75563	8.20141
19	15.67846	14.97889	14.32380	13.13394	12.08532	11.15812	10.33560	9.60360	8.95011	8.36492
20	16.35143	15.58916	14.87747	13.59033	12.46221	11.46992	10.59401	9.81815	9.12855	8.51356
21	17.01121	16.18455	15.41502	14.02916	12.82115	11.76408	10.83553	10.01680	9.29224	8.64869
22	17.65805	16.76541	15.93692	14.45112	13.16300	12.04158	11.06124	10.20074	9.44243	8.77154
23	18.29220	17.33211	16.44361	14.85684	13.48857	12.30338	11.27219	10.37106	9.58021	8.88322
24	18.91393	17.88499	16.93554	15.24696	13.79864	12.55036	11.46933	10.52876	9.70661	8.98474
25	19.52346	18.42438	17.41315	15.62208	14.09394	12.78336	11.65358	10.67478	9.82258	9.07704

Periodic rents (n)	11%	12%	14%	15%	16%	18%	20%	22%	24%	25%
1	.90090	.89286	.87719	.86957	.86207	.84746	.83333	.81967	.80645	.80000
2	1.71252	1.69005	1.64666	1.62571	1.60523	1.56564	1.52778	1.49153	1.45682	1.44000
3	2.44371	2.40183	2.32163	2.28323	2.24589	2.17427	2.10648	2.04224	1.98130	1.95200
4	3.10245	3.03735	2.91371	2.85498	2.79818	2.69006	2.58873	2.49364	2.40428	2.36160
5	3.69590	3.60478	3.43308	3.35216	3.27429	3.12717	2.99061	2.86364	2.74538	2.68928
6	4.23054	4.11141	3.88867	3.78448	3.68474	3.49760	3.32551	3.16692	3.02047	2.95142
7	4.71220	4.56376	4.28830	4.16042	4.03857	3.81153	3.60459	3.41551	3.24232	3.16114
8	5.14612	4.96764	4.63886	4.48732	4.34359	4.07757	3.83716	3.61927	3.42122	3.32891
9	5.53705	5.32825	4.94637	4.77158	4.60654	4.30302	4.03097	3.78628	3.56550	3.46313
10	5.88923	5.65022	5.21612	5.01877	4.83323	4.49409	4.19247	3.92318	3.68186	3.57050
11	6.20652	5.93770	5.45273	5.23371	5.02864	4.65601	4.32706	4.03540	3.77569	3.65640
12	6.49236	6.19437	5.66029	5.42062	5.19711	4.79322	4.43922	4.12737	3.85136	3.72512
13	6.74987	6.42355	5.84236	5.58315	5.34233	4.90951	4.53268	4.20277	3.91239	3.78010
14	6.98187	6.62817	6.00207	5.72448	5.46753	5.00806	4.61057	4.26456	3.96160	3.82408
15	7.19087	6.81086	6.14217	5.84737	5.57546	5.09158	4.67547	4.31522	4.00129	3.85926
16	7.37916	6.97399	6.26506	5.95423	5.66850	5.16235	4.72956	4.35673	4.03330	3.88741
17	7.54879	7.11963	6.37286	6.04716	5.74870	5.22233	4.77463	4.39077	4.05911	3.90993
18	7.70162	7.24967	6.46742	6.12797	5.81785	5.27316	4.81219	4.41866	4.07993	3.92794
19	7.83929	7.36578	6.55037	6.19823	5.87746	5.31624	4.84350	4.44152	4.09672	3.94235
20	7.96333	7.46944	6.62313	6.25933	5.92884	5.35275	4.86958	4.46027	4.11026	3.95388
21	8.07507	7.56200	6.68696	6.31246	5.97314	5.38368	4.89132	4.47563	4.12117	3.96311
22	8.17574	7.64465	6.74294	6.35866	6.01133	5.40990	4.90943	4.48822	4.12998	3.97049
23	8.26643	7.71843	6.79206	6.39884	6.04425	5.43212	4.92453	4.49854	4.13708	3.97639
24	8.34814	7.78432	6.83514	6.43377	6.07263	5.45095	4.93710	4.50700	4.14281	3.98111
25	8.42174	7.84314	6.87293	6.46415	6.09709	5.46691	4.94759	4.51393	4.14742	3.98489

Index